Letters And Papers, Foreign And Domestic, Of The Reign Of Henry Viii

LETTERS AND PAPERS,

FOREIGN AND DOMESTIC,

OF THE REIGN OF

HENRY VIII

LETTERS AND PAPERS,

FOREIGN AND DOMESTIC,

OF THE REIGN OF

HENRY VIII.

PRESERVED IN THE PUBLIC RECORD OFFICE, THE BRITISH MUSEUM,
AND ELSEWHERE IN ENGLAND.

ARRANGED AND CATALOGUED

BY

J. S. BREWER, M.A.,

UNDER THE DIRECTION OF THE MASTER OF THE ROLLS, AND WITH THE SANCTION OF
HER MAJESTY'S SECRETARIES OF STATE.

VOL. I.
nos. 4075 - END

LONDON:
LONGMAN, GREEN, LONGMAN, & ROBERTS.
1862.

CONTENTS OF THIS VOLUME.

	Page
PREFACE - - - - - - - - - - vii
CORRESPONDENCE - - - - - - - - 1
GENERAL INDEX - - - - - - - - - 979
ERRATA - - - - - - - - - - 1177

1513.
16 May. **4075.** Ric. [Fox] Bp. of Winchester to Wolsey.
R. O.

This afternoon Fitzwilliam came to the court; says the Admiral will be here with the next wind. What with him and Sir Charles, the business will succeed. Fitzwilliam will tell him the news. A truce has been taken for one year between the Kings of France and Arragon and their adherents. Hears the Emperor will dance the same dance. As Wolsey is so much occupied, hopes he will make Brian Tuke write soon. The Admiral wants 100 seamen—there are none to be had ;—also bows, serpentines, &c. "If this journey be intended as great as is spoken, it will not be finished shortly." At Hampton, this Whitsun-Monday.

Hol., p. 1. Addressed: "To my brother the King's almoner." *Seal, a pelican.*

Calig. D. vi. 102.**4076.** Lord Thomas Howard to Wolsey.
B. M.

Windbound in the Peter at Katt Water, which prevents him from following the King's pleasure. The Sovereign and others are at St. Nicholas' Island. Intends to go to Asshe Water, and send the victuallers to Hampton with Anthony Poynes, Wisman, and Draper. Desires a letter on his arrival at Southampton enjoining no captain or seaman to go [ashore]. Has made a pair of gallows at the waterside, where some will "towter" to-morrow. Sends a writing in Spanish given him by a merchant of Bristol. The King shall speed better if he trust his own. Is informed by Fabyan that Brest Castle was won by Mons. de Rohan in consequence of his threatening the Bretons in the castle with destruction of their lands. Hopes, when he and Sir Charles come to Hampton, to find there my Lord of Winchester to debate with him. Trusts to "ryte" him well in every cause ; "for when I am not occupied," he says, " it is my most business to be instructed of them that can skill." "I had rather the posts to be payne in sporring their horsis then I shuld be fownd to slow in writing or working when time shall require." On Tuesday night the victuallers will be at Hampton. In the Mary Rose at 1 in the afternoon. *Signed.*

P.S.—Appointed ships here for . . . . . . Broke and Sir Piers Egecome, &c.

Addressed : To Master Almoner, with the King's grace. "Delivered at Plymouth this Whitsuntide, before 2 at afternoon." *Pp. 2.*

16 May. **4077.** Sir Ric. Wingfield to Wolsey.
R. O.

Received his letter on Friday last. Thanks Wolsey for his good offices. Will require a good purse to occupy the honorable room intended for him in the absence of his cousin Sir Charles. Will repair with all diligence to the King, though after taking the musters the King will soon come over. Will leave his bedfellow "to make quarell," if he can be spared only one night at home, "as sche hathe cawse ; the wyche I thynke sche wylle not faylle to do and her hartte schalle serve here accordynglye to here wyll." Thinks it would be advisable, as Marshal of Calais, to be attended with the horsemen of that town to wait upon the King in this voyage, and for the conveying of such sums of money as shall be paid to the Emperor, or the town of Graveling. Will send Byschoppe to consult Wolsey what foot he should employ in executing his office. Thos. Spinelly is glad that his services have satisfied Wolsey.

o o

Wrote to Jerome Friscobald on Saturday. Sends his answer.
Master Comptroller (Wiltshire) has leave to return. Brussels,
16 May.

Hol., pp. 4. *Addressed:* " To the right honorable Mr. Almoner
with the King's grace."

17 May. 4078.   SIR ROB. WINGFIELD to HEN. VIII.

Vitell. B. xviii. 45.
B. M.

Had [lately] written a long letter to his highness, and now only
desired to advertize him that the Emperor sent for him at 7 o'clock
" . . . . of one Hedyug, which is one of my Lady
of [Savoy's household.]   He showed me these things that
follow, [willing] me to advertise your grace of the same."
He first " showed that he had received letters from [Andre] de
Bourge that is now with the Duke of Milan . . . . from a
secretary of his, called Anthony de Rorariis " . . . . know
well, and also from the Duke of Milan."   By the former of these
letters the Emperor was informed that the Duke of Milan had sent
the said Andre to the King of Arragon, desiring to learn his mind,
who advised De Bourge to return to the kingdom of Naples, and
leave the Duke to provide for himself, as Milan was lost.   By the
letter from Anthony Rorarij, who is with the Viceroy, the Emperor
was advertised that he had communed with the Viceroy, and moved
him to tarry till he had advertised the Pope and the Emperor,
and known their mind ; to which the Viceroy answered that
neither Pope nor Emperor should cause him to vary from his
master's commandment ; that he would keep Brescia as long as
he could ; and with regard to the artillery there belonging to the
Emperor, he would write to the Count of Cariate, the Venetian
ambassador, to speak to the seignory of Venice that it might be
restored to the Emperor, from which the Emperor thought that the
Viceroy had sold Brescia to the Venetians, and " his master and he
together betrayed not only all Italy, but him and you also."   The
Emperor desired Wingfield to write these things to " your grace,"
showing that if he had been advertised of these news before making
his oath he would not have sworn, for he felt [that it was as im]pos-
sible for him to send an army into France as he had become bound,
as for one that had promised [to run] a furlong to do so if he
broke his leg by the way ; and that such shift as he shall be able
to make would be little enough " to save Verona and his county of
. . . . . . of Milan, clearly lost for this time ;" and that, though
he might not run out the furlong as he had promised, he should do
what lay in his power by running out the remnant with a stilt.

" And for the first tw[o payments] of yowr money, if they might
be set forward qwy[ckly he would] find the means that 6,000
Swiss and 2,000 horse, [with a] sufficient band of artillery, should
be set forth . . . . as I wrote in my former letter that
he had pourv[eyed] . . for the payment of 4,000 Swiss, he must
employ th[e money] . . . . . that he can make beside ; " wherefore
he desires to know your mind as soon as possible.   For [having
found] the King of Arragon so unstable, he is in great [fear] that
the Swiss will hold foot with the Pope, " and him . . . . . .
thereto found some mean to entertain them sho . . . ."   Wingfield said he would advertise " his master of the premises; notwithstanding the Emperor would find that the matter should go all
. . . . . . and he was of his former opinion that " the Viceroy
intended not [to keep] Lombardy, or to do as is suspected ;" to
which, with sharper words and countenance than usual, the Emperor

1513.

bade him farewell. The French are so subtle they can blind and corrupt the whole world, but it is Wingfield's opinion, that if the English army cross the sea they will make but a small attempt on Italy, especially if it be sure the Emperor will unite with England. Augsburgh, 17 May 1513.

Pp. 4. Mutilated.

17 May. **4079.** SIR GILBERT TALBOT to WOLSEY.
R. O.

They are carrying victuals into Turwayne. Men of war have advanced to the frontiers here and at Whitsand. Calais, 17 May. *Signed.*

P. 1. Addressed: "To the Right Hon. Master Almoner with the King's grace."

17 May. **4080.** SIR GILBERT TALBOT to WOLSEY.
R. O.

The letter enclosed came to him so shortly, he has no time to write more. The matter must be well looked to. Calais, 17 May. *Signed.*

In Wriothesley's (?) hand, p. 1. Addressed.

R. O. **4081.** 2. THOS. MEDELMORE and THOS. PERPOYNT, deputies of the MERCHANT ADVENTURERS, to SIR GILB. TALBOT, Lieut. of Calais.

Have heard by Will. Hughe that 6 men of war, out of Dieppe, are on the coast of Flanders betwixt Newport and Sluce. After plundering him they demanded whether the hoys were departed to England. They are lying in wait for the King's artillery from Antwerp. The merchants dare not start. Will. Chamberlain of London has brought up fish in Holland to be sent to Calais. A remedy must be provided in this behalf, or great loss will ensue. Middleburg, 14 May 1513.

P. 1. Addressed. Endorsed.

17 May. **4082.** TRANSPORTS.

For William Lord Mountjoy, William Atclyff, and Miles Gerard to provide transports for the army. Knoll, 17 May.

Fr. 5 Hen. VIII. m. 6.

17 May. **4083.** For SIR EDW. PONYNGES, constable of Dover.
Rym. XIII. 369.

To make proclamation, when required by Will. Lord Mountjoy, Will. Atclyff, and Miles Gerard, that they have been appointed to oversee the shipment of the King's forces at the Cinque Ports. Knoll, 17 May.

Fr. 5 Hen. VIII. m. 12.

17 May. **4084.** For MARINUS GARET, native of Normandy, the King's
P. S. cutler, resident in London.

Licence to employ native or foreign apprentices. Greenwich, 8 May 5 Hen. VIII. *Del.* Otford, 17 May.

Pat. 5 Hen. VIII. p. 1, m. 13.

o o 2

1513.
May.   4085.   HENRY VIII. to [PONYNGES].

Vitell. B. xviii. 34.
B. M.

Understands how he had [persuaded] the Duchess of Savoy to write to the Emperor [respecting] the truce between the Venetians and him ; and also how discreetly [he had acted respecting] the certificate made by the ambassador of Spain, resident in England ; "which to advance, our said cousin was by him informed, we were agreeable . . . . . . condescended to conclude the said confederation according to the articles last reformed for the 100,000 g. cr. by him demanded." Understands also that as yet he had made no overture of the . . . . [of] the personal going of the Emperor in the war against France. Thanks him for his diligence in the foregoing, and desires that during his abode at [Brussels] he would "solicit our said cousin" to be a mediator [for] peace or truce betwixt him and the Venetians. Desires him to make up the articles for conclusion of the confederation between the Emperor and himself (Hen. VIII). The King and his council are desirous that the 25,000 crowns be used to induce the Emperor to insert an article in the said confederation binding himself to proceed in person to the war against the common enemy. He is also to persuade "the Duchess to conclude the confederation under that form, for the Emperor's person[al going] without hy . . . . . . of the other treaty, whereunto the Emperor is now agreed," albeit it were necessary to conclude the other confedsration first ". . . . . [consid]ering of your proposal for the treaty . . . . King of Arragon in the same, and also for the abbreviation . . . . for the place where the 100,000 crowns shall be paid which they desire . . . ."

And for as much as Almighty God hath called the late Pope to [his mercy, who] would have been well pleased to have been com prised in the first article of the said confederation, the King desires a place should be reserved at the end of the treaty for the Pope elect to enter the confederation. On the conclusion of the treaty it is to be sent to the English ambassador at Rome [for learning] the Pope's mind in that behalf ; all the King's endeavours having been for the defence of the church, as might appear by the inclosed letters lately received from the [Cardinal] of York. The King of Arragon having approved of the articles, may be permitted to stand therein. Thinks it not necessary that the time for the last payment should be shortened, for the longer the payments continue the longer the Emperor will ontinue in the wars.

Draft, in Ruthal's hand, pp. 2. Mutilated.

May.   4086.   HENRY VIII. to PONYNGS, &c.

Galba, B. iii. 56.
B. M.

Since their letters containing the articles delivered by the Duchess of Savoy, for the retaining of the Swiss, a credence has been received from the Emperor, enclosed, offering to lead the war in person, which is a greater inducement to the King to advance him money. If they can obtain a resolute answer in the points touching the confederation contained in the King's former letters, they are not to make overtures of the credence for the present. If they cannot, except upon the advance to the Emperor of 125,000 crowns, they are then to proceed point by point :—1. That the King is well content to retain the Swiss in his pay, but has already expended large sums of money in his army royal to cross the sea, and therefore has less need of them 2. That the King has substantially provided artillery. 3. That the King accepts with pleasure

1513.

the Emperor's proposal to join in his own person, and looks upon it as an infallible argument of his friendship ; and they are to urge the Duchess to confirm him in his purpose, and obtain an article to this effect to be inserted in the confederation ; and that in so doing the King will advance him 125,000 crowns, specifying the time and manner in which the money shall be paid ; that the King will then cross the sea with 30,000 men ; but if the Emperor will not bind himself, it must be considered that he does not intend to do anything. 4. The King will negotiate with the Venetians to make peace with the Emperor. 5. It is the Emperor's object to induce the King of England to retain the Swiss at his own cost, which he cannot do for reasons contained in his last letter. His own army is sufficient without them.

Draft corr. by Ruthal, pp. 13. *Mutilated.*

4087. For JOHN MILLET, one of the King's Secretaries.

S. B.

Commission to pay in the city of Gravelyn, in Flanders, two instalments of 100,000 g. cr., sc. 35,000 to the Emperor Maximilian or the Lady Margaret one month after the declaration of war by the said Emperor against the King of France ; sc. 35,000 crowns of gold on commencement of the war. 30,000 to be paid three months afterwards. According to a treaty made by Sir Edward Ponynges K.G., John Yong, Sir Thomas Boleyn, and Sir Richard Wyngfield, with Archduchess Margaret.

Fr. 5 Hen. VIII. m. 15.

18 May. **4088.** For HENRY STRETE.

P. S.

To be serjeant-at-arms, with 12*d.* a day. Greenwich, 16 May 5 Hen. VIII. *Del.* Knoll, 18 May.

Pat. 5 Hen. VIII. p. 1, *m.* 8.

18 May. **4089.** For WILLIAM COMPTON.

S. B.

Letters patent to the tenants, and others, of the King's lands, the lands of any monasteries of which William Compton is steward, and of the lands belonging to the said William, authorising him to retain able persons for the war. *Del.* Westm., 18 May 5 Hen. VIII.

Pat. 5 Hen. VIII. p. 1, *m.* 10*d.*

18 May. **4090.** MARGARET OF SAVOY to HENRY VIII.

Galba, B. III. 78a.
B. M.

Has received his letters of the 29th April ; is glad of the good news. Encloses him a copy of the Emperor's letters. Brussels, 18 May 1513. *Signed.*

Fr., p. 1, *mutilated. Add.*

18 May. **4091.** SPINELLY to [HENRY VIII.]

Galba, B. III. 105.
B. M.

Wrote last on the 15th. Encloses a letter from Lewis Maraton, whom he recommends to the King. This morning Madame shewed the ambassadors the Emperor's letters. She told them that one of her council had persuaded the French ambassador on his return home to have letters sent to the Prince of Castile, that if he suffered his subjects to serve against France the counties of Flanders and Artois should be confiscated, "because of the sovereignty of the crown of France." Maraton states that the Emperor has retained 6,000 Swiss, the Duke of Wirtemburg and Frederick Count Palatine

1513.

a younger brother. Lewis de Marlion, physician to the Prince of Castile, is coming from the Duke of Milan on an embassy to the Emperor, thence to England. It is thought that Don Pedro D'Orea, ambassador of Arragon, has left the Emperor's court for Brussels, and will pass by England to go to Spain. Some say a brother-in-law of the Bishop of Gurck is with him; others say Symon de Farrett. Gurck has desired the Emperor's leave to go and give "the obeisance unto the Pope's holiness." Madame would rather he were in Jerusalem than Rome. They are in good hopes of concluding a league with the Duke of Gueldres without mention of Arragon or France; Spinelly thinks it unlikely. The army of the Venetians is not more than 500 men at arms, 1,200 light horse, and 6,000 foot; it lies as before. News has come from Bruges, by certain merchants that left Lyons on the 2nd, that no French men of war have crossed the mountains, "and that they be nothing so hot in their going forward as they have published." Madame has the ratification of the treaty for England, and will ask to be advanced the first two payments of 100,000 crowns. She delays going into Flanders for a few days. Berghes will be here to-morrow. Sends a paper of news reported by Bonnet at his coming from France. She urges the King to take into his service 4,000 Almayns; she says if the French be beaten at first they lose their courage. Begs he may have his half yearly salary of 50*l*. Brussels, 18 May 1513.

Pp. 4. *Signed.*

19 May. **4092.**   SIR GILBERT TALBOT to WOLSEY.
Vesp. F. XIII. 106 b.
B. M.
His wine is ready bought, and shall surely be laid in against his coming. Sends by the bearer his gown cloth that he wrote for.
P. 1. *Signed.*
To the Right Honble. Mr. Almoner with the King's Grace.

19 May. **4093.**   DAWTREY to WOLSEY.
R. O.
Has received his letter desiring to know whether he can pay Sir Chas. Brandon's and my Lord Admiral's army. Has no such warrant. Had only expected to provide victuals, payments for the beerhouses at Portsmouth, the Sowchyvers, &c. Hampton, 19 May.
Hol., p. 1. *Addressed as before.*

19 May. **4094.**   RICHARD [FOX] BP. OF WINCHESTER to WOLSEY.
R. O.
Received this day his letter dated London, 17 May, by which Wolsey will perceive the speed of the posts. Has written to the King. None of the army victuallers, or my Lord Admiral, have arrived at Portsmouth or here. Hears they are windbound in the harbour of Plymouth. None of the victuallers have come out of the Thames or from Sandwich. Will learn from John Dawtrey's letter the state of the navy. Hopes that ships will be sent at once to scour the narrow seas, and waft the hoys to Calais. Must not venture the artillery till then. Thinks he might man some of the Spaniards at Sandwich for this purpose. Sir Charles [Brandon] has not come, nor any save Bruges. Has provided lodgings for the companies two days' journey in the country. Thinks the King of Arragon will keep his bond if the French King be not in fault; "and as for the Emperor, I think his will be good, but powder will fail him." He will have enough to do with the Venetians confederated with France; "and they have at Mylayn again;" so the French power will be divided. The Pope, the Emperor, the King of Arragon, will have too much to do to help England. The

1513.

Emperor and Arr gon might, however, prevent a French army going into Italy. The King has written to the Duke of Buckingham to keep the middle ward, and be ready to take ship 15 June, as one of the King's company. Hampton,. 19 May, about noon.

Hol., pp. 2. Addressed : To my brother the King's almoner.

19 May. **4095.** RICHARD [FOX] BP. OF WINCHESTER to HENRY VIII.

R. O.

Has received a letter from the Almoner, stating the King's desire that the Admiral should come to Portsmouth, and wait there for Sir Charles Brandon. If he reaches there before this Thursday, Fox is to advertise the King by post from England, that the King may visit Portsmouth secretly. The admiral is not yet come, as he is wind-bound. Advises the King to come to Hampton, not to Portsmouth. There is no shipping fit for Sir Charles Brandon, except two Spaniards. The despatching the same will require time. John Dawtrey has made provision for the admiral and his company. Lacks only empty pipes. Hampton, this Thursday, 19 May.

Hol., pp. 2. Addressed : To the King's grace at Windsor.

Endorsed.

19 May. **4096.** PETER MARTYR to LUD. FURTADO, son of TENDILLA.

Pet. Mart. Epist.
No. 521.

They say that San Severin and Carvael are at Florence, hoping to be reconciled to the Pope, as Leo is of a more kindly nature. This Pope finds his nest better feathered than any of his predecessors.—John Hastil (Stile), the English ambassador, tells him that his King will cross over to Calais about the middle or the end of May. Trivulcio, Martyr's fellow citizen, who loves his country, as the beaver loves its children by eating their heads off, commands the French forces in the duchy of Milan, and is trying to seduce the Swiss. They say the Swiss will sell Duke Maximilian, as it is thought they sold his father to the French at Novara. There is some murmur at court at the sudden and secret departure of Pedro Quintana ; it is thought he has been sent by Ferdinand to make peace with France. That is a game John Hastil does not approve of, though Almaçan openly denies it. The Rhodians are in daily fear of the Turks. Valladolid, 19 May 1513.

John Hastil (Stile), the English ambassador, told him that a band of robbers had attacked the King's wagons carrying money for the wars, who afterwards took Sanctuary ; that the King caught 80 of them before they could escape, and hanged them all. The Swiss have imposed upon Vercelli a tribute of 15,000 ducats, and plundered San Germano. They have also laid a fine on Turin. Valladolid, 5 July 1513.

Lat.

19 May. **4097.** For ANTONY CAVALLARI, merchant of Lucca.

S. B.

Licence to export kerseys, leather, lead, and other merchandize, not belonging to the staple of Calais, to the sum of 150*l.* customs dues. 19 May.

S. B.

2. Similar licence to the sum of 100*l.* customs dues. 19 May.

Fr. 5 Hen. VIII. m. 5. Knoll, 19 May 5 Hen. VIII.

20 May. **4098.** JOHN EARL OF ARUNDEL to WOLSEY.

Vesp. F. xiii. 82.
B. M.

Thanks him for his kindness at all times. Desires to hear of the prosperous success of the King and Queen. Sends a present

1513.,

of venison. The weather has been so dry there is little pasture, even now so far from Midsummer. Douneley, 20 May. *Signed.*

End., p. 1.

Add.: — " My very good and entirely well-beloved friend Mr. Almoner."

20 May.   **4099.**   WILL. HATTECLYFF to WOLSEY.
R. O.

Requests him to get his bill of pardon signed by the King. Hopes the King will be good lord to him, remembering his life has been spent in the King's service and that of his ancestors, "as father and grandfather, whom God assoil." The bearer is appointed to deliver the victuals commanded to John Dawtrey of Hampton. As he needs to be with Miles Gerard at the seaside, hopes he may be excused waiting upon Wolsey. Begs the King's letters may pass through Dawtrey to Heron. "In haste, the 20th day of May, at my departing."

Hol., p. 1. Addressed: "To the Right Hon. and mine especial good master, Master Dr. Wolsey, aumosner to the King's grace." *Endorsed.*

20 May.   **4100.**   SIR GILBERT TALBOT to WOLSEY.
R. O.

Sends the news received by one of his spies. Calais, 20 May. Will send him word if it be true that the French King is coming downwards.

20 May.   **4101**   JOHN DE VERE EARL OF OXFORD.
R. O.

"Inventarium omnium et singulorum bonorum debitorum catallorum ac summarum pecuniarum nobilis ac præpotentis viri domini Johannis de Veere Comitis Oxoniæ, Magni Camerarii ac Admiralli Angliæ, Vicecomitis Bulbck, et Domini de Scalis, factum et appreciatum per me, Thomam Mercer, apparitorem generalem Reverendissimi Domini Willielmi Cant. Archiepiscopi, 20° die Maii A.D. 1513."

At Coolne within the priory ; in the White Chamber, p. 55 ; in Mr. Veere's chamber, 60 ; in the armoury house, 61 ; in Mr. Voyell's chamber, 62 ; in Mr. Veer's servants' chamber, ib.; in Mr. Burton's chamber, ib. ; in the clerk of the kitchen's chamber, 63 ; in the armoury chamber, ib. ; in the parlour, 64 ; in the ewery, 65 ; in my lord's great chamber, ib. ; in the inner chamber of my ladies, 66 ; in the gentlewomen's chamber, 67 ; in the revestry within the priory of Coolne, ib. ; in the parlour under Mr. Veere's chamber, 68 ; in Mr. Walgrave is chamber, ib.; in the chamber over the porch, 69 ; stuff given to my young lord of Oxenford, ib. ; horses and geldings, 71 ; in the kitchen, ib. ; in wine, ib. ; stuff at Henyngham, ib. ; plate and jewels in a great standard within the college of Sudbery as hereafter followeth, 72 (*large quantities of church plate in the list*) ; plate and jewels in another strong coffer, all of iron, with six locks upon the same, 78, and in another standard bound with bars of iron, 81 ; plate in another coffer of wood, 89 ; plate at Coolne in divers offices, 94 ; ready money at the hour of his death (2,100*l.*), 95 ; in another standard, chapel stuff at Sudbury, ib. (*in the list* " a chest full of French and English books ;") my lord's apparel, 105 ; wardrobe stuff at Sudbury in the Friers, 107 ; stuff at Colchester within St. John is abbey, 115 ; debts owing to the testator at the hour of his death (1,333*l.* 6*s.* 8*d.*), 119.

1513.

20 May. **4102.** For HENRY LONG, of Draycote, Wilts.

Protection ; going to the war. Westm., 20 May.
Fr. 5 Hen. VIII. m. 10.

21 May. **4103.** RICH. [FOX] BP. OF WINCHESTER to WOLSEY.

R. O.

No ships have come from the Admiral, Sandwich, or London.
Hopes they will come, as the 15th day of June is at hand, when he
must be at Dovor. Thinks the King's ward will not have com-
pletely passed till the 30th of that month. He may possibly be
among the last. Wishes Wolsey's opinion. Desires Brian Tuke
may write, as Wolsey is so much occupied. My Lord of Devonshire has been with his mother since before Mid Lent. She
wishes to know whether he should remain with her, or be sent to
the King to Calais, and go with the ordnance to the Prince of
Castile. The Captain of the Isle of Wight desires Wolsey's favor
in the matter now before him. Some of my Lord Lisle's captains
desire wages for their folks that shall attend on their carracks to
Calais. John Dawtrey will tell him the rest. Wants empty pipes
for the beer. "I fear that the pursers will deserve hanging for
this matter. I pray God send us with speed, and soon deliver
you of your outrageous charge and labor ; and else ye shall have
a cold stomach, little sleep, pale visage, and a thin belly, cum pari
egestione." Hampton, 21 May.

Hol., pp. 2. *Addressed :* "To my brother the King's almoner."

21 May. **4104.** JOHN DAWTREY to WOLSEY.

R. O.

This day Belknap came for wages for my Lord Lisle's retinue.
Lacks money ; it goes away very fast here many ways. A purser of
the *John Baptist* has promised him some empty pipes. Complains
of the outrageous lack on the part of the pursers. A great part
of the foists had been burned. Master Wylshier would not suffer
any hoys to come over for the pipes and the fish. Hampton,
21 May.

Hol., p. 1. *Addressed as before.*

21 May. **4105.** THOMAS LORD DARCY to WOLSEY.

R. O.

Has written to the King of all occurrents on the marches. If
some ships lay at Dovor, and some upon the North Seas, thinks
they would win honour. Begs he may have knowledge, by
Mr. Lister, if the King delay his passage over sea beyond the
15 June. Will find it expensive if his company lies long about
London. "Written at Tempilnewsum your cabin," 21 May.

Hol., p. 1.

" To the right worshipful Mr. Amsner unto the Kyng is grace."

21 May. **4106.** For HENRY HILL.

P. S.

To be sergeant-at-arms, with 12*d.* a day. Greenwich, 19 May
5 Hen. VIII. *Del.* Knoll, 21 May.

Pat. 5 Hen. VIII. p. 1, *m.* 8.

21 May. **4107.** For THOMAS COMPTON, page of the Chamber.

[S. B.

To be keeper and paler, during pleasure, of the new park of
Wakefield, Yorkshire, in the King's hands by death of William
Snayth ; with fees out of the issues of the lordship of Wakefield.
Also reversion of the farm granted to Richard Pek and Thomas

1513.

Grice by patent 9 Nov. 16 Hen. VII. for 20 years :—viz., farm of the town of Wakefield, the office of bailiff there, and the bakehouse and fishery of the said town, with the profits, called Wilbyght, Depford, and Erlesyng, parcel of the lordship of Wakefield, the mills of Wakefield and Horbery, and a certain mill called "Le Newe Mille uppon the Damme," with fishery of the same;—to hold to the said Compton for twenty years after expiration of the said term. *Del.* Knoll, 21 May 5 Hen. VIII.
Pat. 5 Hen. VIII. p. 1, m. 12.

22 May.   **4108.**   For NICHOLAS JAKSON.
P. S.

To be sergeant-at-arms, with 12*d.* a day.   Greenwich, 18 May 5 Hen. VIII.   *Del.* Westm., 22 May.
Pat. 5 Hen. VIII. p. 1, m. 7.

22 May.   **4109.**   For WILLIAM KEBY.
P. S.

To be sergeant-at-arms, with 12*d.* a day.   Greenwich, 18 May 5 Hen. VIII.   *Del.* Westm., 22 May.
Pat. 5 Hen. VIII. p. 1, m. 7.

23 May.   **4110.**   PONYNGES and WINGFIELD.
R. O.

Accounts of Sir Edward Ponynges and Sir Richard Wingfield, for the pay of mercenaries. 23 May 5 Hen. VIII.

23 May.   **4111.**   For RICHARD PARKER, an officer of the Butlery.
S. B.

Annuity of 4*l.* out of the issues of the lordship of Denbigh ; *vice* Humphrey Wynyngton, deceased. *Del.* Otford, 23 May 5 Hen. VIII.
Pat. 5 Hen. VIII. p. 1, m. 12. See 25 May.

24 May.   **4112.**   JAMES IV. to HENRY VIII.
Calig. B. vi. 77.
B. M.
Ellis. 1 S. i. 76.

Sends by "our herald the bearer," a copy of the truce between France and Spain made on the 1 April, wherein the Emperor and England for the King of Arragon, the Duke of Gueldres and James IV. for France, are comprehended if they desire it. France has written to him to enter if England does. Wishes to be informed without delay of Henry's mind, that he may treat for further amity and instruct the Bp. of Murray beyond sea to "do his uter besines the forsaid treuxis pendant, for universale peax and expedicioun agains the Infidelis." Surely Henry's late Admiral, "quha decessit to his grete honour," was a greater loss to him than the winning of all the French galleys would have been an advantage. The valiant Knights, who will perish on both sides if war continue, had better be engaged against the enemies of Christ. Begs Henry to take this in good part, for verily he is sorry for this loss, "throu acquentance we had of his fader, that noble knitht, wha convoyt oure derrest fallow the Qwene unto ws." Given under our signet at our palace of Edinburgh," 24 May. *Signed.*
Add. P. 1.

24 May.   **4113.**   For RICHARD EARL of KENT.
P. S.

Protection for Robert Barboure of Cotton near Northampton, glover, going to serve the King in the Earl's retinue. 24 May 5 Hen. VIII. [*Del.*] Westm., 24 May. *Signed.*

1513.

24 May.   4114.   For RAPHAEL MARUFF.
S. B.   *See* 4 May.

24 May.   4115.   For ROBERT PHILIPSON, chaplain.
P. S.   Presentation to the perpetual vicarage of Broughing, London
dioc., void by death, at the King's disposal when the temporalities
of the monastery of Holy Trinity, Aldgate, were lately in the King's
hands. Greenwich, 23 May 5 Hen. VIII. *Del.* Westm., 24 May.
Pat. 5 Hen. VIII. p. 1, *m.* 12.

24 May.   4116.   For EDWARD BELLEKANAPP.
P. S.   Pardon and release as late overseer of the prerogative of Hen. VII.;
—release of indentures dated 1 July 23 Hen. VII., between Sir
Thomas Lovell, Sir Richard Emson, Edmund Dudley and Henry
Wyat, on the King's part, and the said Edward ;—release of his
recognisance of 1,000 marks, made 4 July 23 Hen. VII., by the name
of Edward Belknapp of Weston, Warw., to Sir Richard Emson
and Edmund Dudley (attainted 1 Hen. VIII.), Sir Thomas Lovell
and Henry Wyat. Greenwich, 16 May 5 Hen. VIII. *Del.* Westm.,
24 May.
Pat. 5 Hen. VIII. p. 1, *m.* 12.

24 May.   4117.   For JOHN WODHALL, clk.
P. S.   Next vacancy in the chapel of Gresmer, archdeaconry of
Richmond, York dioc.   Greenwich, 21 Feb. 3 Hen. VIII.   *Del.*
24 May 5 Hen. VIII.

24 May.   4118.   COMMISSION OF THE PEACE.
              Gloucestershire. —W. Bp. of Lincoln, E. (*sic*, qu. R.) Bp. of
Hereford, Edw. Duke of Buckingham, Thos. Earl of Arundel, Hen.
Abbot of Tewksbury, John Abbot of Gloucester, John Abbot of
Cirencester, Robt. Brudenell, Chas. Bothe, clk , Sir Gilb. Talbot,
Sir Thos. Inglefeld, Sir Maurice Barkeley, Sir Wm. Uvedale,
Sir Robt. Poyntz, Sir Alex. Baynham, John Hungerford, Peter
Newton, John Broke, Geo. Bromeley, Thos. Lynom, Wm. Rudhale,
Giles Grevyle, Thos. Poyntz, John Whitington, Thos. Godman,
Edm. Tame, Edm. Wykys, Wm. Denys, Edw. Wadham, Rich.
Barkeley, Rich. Pole, John Butler, Robt. Wye, Wm. Lyngeston (*sic*),
John Pauncefote, Christopher Baynham, Wm. Freme, John Pakyng-
ton, Wm. Tracy, Hen. Knyght, Thos. Matston, and Roger Porter.
Westm., 24 May.
Pat. 5 Hen. VIII. p. 1, *m.* 3d.

25 May.   4119.   LADY MARGARET POLE.
Titus, B. IV. 109.   Form of acknowledgment by Thomas Wolcy, the King's Almoner,
B. M.   of the receipt by Thomas Hall his servant, from Lady Margaret
Pole, sister of Edward late Earl of Warwick, of 1,000*l.* for the first
payment of 5,000 marks granted of her benevolence towards the
King's wars "for his high and great goodness as restoring her
to the inheritance of her said brother." 25 May 5 Hen. VIII.
P. 1.

25 May.   4120.   For WILLIAM EDWARDS, clk.
P. S.   Pension which the newly elected Abbot of St. Edmund's Bury is
bound to give unto a clerk of the King's nomination till he be pro-

1513.

moted to a competent benefice by the said Abbot.   Greenwich,
23 May 5 Hen. VIII.   *Del.* Westm., 25 May.

25 May.   **4121.**   For JOHN WARTON.
P. S.   Licence to export kerseys and other merchandise for six years.
Greenwich, 24 May 5 Hen. VIII.   *Del.* Westm., 25 May.
Fr. 5 Hen. VIII. m. 5.

25 May.   **4122.**   For HENRY EARL OF NORTHUMBERLAND.
Protection ; going to the war.   Westm., 25 May.
Fr. 5 Hen. VIII. m. 14.

25 May.   **4123.**   For JOHN GYVOR, clk., of Scotland.
S. B.   Denization.   *Del.* Westm., 25 May 5 Hen. VIII.
Pat. 5 Hen. VIII. p. 1, m. 12.

25 May.   **4124.**   For RIC. PARKER, one of the officers of the Butlery.
Annuity of 4*l.* out of the issues of the lordship of Dynbigh, *vice*
Humph. Wynyngton, deceased.   Otford, 25 May.
Pat. 5 Hen. VIII. p. 2, m. 10.   See 23 May.

26 May.   **4125.**   For SIR HENRY WYAT, the King's councillor.
S. B.   To be treasurer of the King's jewels ; with annuity of 50*l.*, and
appointment of two yeomen and one page.   *Del.* Westm., 26 May
5 Hen. VIII.
Pat. 5 Hen. VIII. p. 1, m. 12.

26 May.   **4126.**   For CHARLES VISCOUNT LISLE, K.G.
S. B.   To be marshal of the King's army.   Westm., 26 May 5 Hen. VIII.

Rym. XIII. 367.   ii. For GEORGE EARL OF SHREWSBURY, steward of the
Household, K.G.
To be lieutenant-general of the King's army.   Westm., [12] May
5 Hen. VIII.
Fr. 4 Hen. VIII. m. 13.

iii. For JOHN HOPTON, gentleman usher of the Chamber.
Rym. ib. 368.   To be captain of the fleet to carry the King's army to Calais.
Westm., 13 May 5 Hen. VIII.
Fr. 5 Hen. VIII. m. 13.

iv. To the CHAMBERLAIN of NORTH WALES.
To see order kept in the marches, as the King intends to cross
the sea. . . . . . 12 May 5 Hen. VIII.

v. For WILLIAM LORD·MOUNTJOY, WILLIAM ATTCLYFF,
Rym. ib.   and MILES GERRARD.
To be overseers of the shipment of the King's army.   Knoll,
17 May 5 Hen. VIII.
Fr. 5 Hen. VIII. m. 6.

vi. For SIR EDWARD PONYNGES.
See 17 May.
Defaced.

1513.

26 May. **4127.** SIR RALPH LANGFORD, deceased.

Derby.—Commission to John Port, German Pole, Roger Meynours, Anth. Babyngton. Roger Ayre, and Christ. Medeley, escheator, to make inquisitions as to the possessions and heir of Sir Ralph Langford, deceased. Westm., 26 May.

Notts.—Similar commission to Sir Wm. Meryng, Wm. Hastynges, John Dunham, Rob. Nevell, Anth. Babyngton, Henry Perpount, and Christ. Medelay, escheator. *No date.*

Pat. 5 Hen. VIII. p. 1, m. 7d.

26 May. **4128.** For GONSALVO FERDINAND, clk., the King's chaplain,
S. B.   native of Spain.

Release. of the fourth part of his benefices, the last convocation in St. Paul's having granted to the King the fourth part of the benefices of all foreign clergy in England. *Del.* Westm., 26 May 5 Hen. VIII.

Pat. 5 Hen. VIII. p. 1, m. 16.

27 May. **4129.** ANTH. COUNT FAULCONBERG.
R. O.

Acknowledgment by Anthony Count Fauquenberghue Lord De Lygne, of 3,000 crowns received from the King of England by the hands of Sir Gilbert Talbot, Deputy of Calais, in order to raise a force for the taking of the castle of Bothan. Bellocile in Hainault, 27 May 1513.

Vell. Signed and sealed.

28 May. **4130.** HENRY VIII.
R. O.

Commission for Anthony de Ligne Count De Faucomberge to levy troops in the dominions of the Emperor against the French. Greenwich, 28 May 1513.

Fr.

R. O.   ii. Modern copy.

28 May. **4131.** HARNESS for FOOT SOLDIERS.
Campbell Chart.
VIII. 20.   Receipt by Guido Portenary, merchant of Florence, to John
B. M.   Daunce, for 1,600*l.* paid for 2,000 harness for footmen, supplied according to an indenture, and delivered to John Blewbery in the King's armory. 28 May 5 Hen. VIII. *Signed.*

28 May. **4132.** For SIR HENRY GULDEFORD.
S. B.

To be standard-bearer, with 40*l.* a year, *vice* Sir Edward Howard. *Del.* Westm., 28 May 5 Hen. VIII.

Pat. 5 Hen. VIII. p. 1, m. 12.

28 May. **4133.** For WILLIAM STANDON, yeoman of the Chamber.
P. S.

Fee of the Crown, being 6*d.* a day, lately held by Nicholas Jakson. Greenwich, 23 May 5 Hen. VIII. *Del.* Westm., 28 May.

Pat. 5 Hen. VIII. p. 1, m. 16.

29 May. **4134.** For THOMAS STAPILTON.
S. B.

Licence for 6 years to export kerseys, tin, lead, corn, and other commodities (wools and hides excepted). *Del.* Westm., 29 May 5 Hen. VIII.

1513.

30 May.　**4135.**　For CHRISTOPHER ROCHESTRE, page of the Chamber, and
S. B.　　　　　　　WILLIAM HOGSON, yeoman of the Butlery.

Grant, in survivorship, of an annuity of 10*l.* out of the issues
of the lordship of Denbigh, from Mich. 4 Hen. VIII., *vice* Hugh
Egerton, deceased. *Del.* Westm., 30 May 5 Hen. VIII.
Pat. 5 Hen. VIII. p. 1, *m.* 16.

30 May.　**4136.**　For WILLIAM HOGGESON, yeoman of the Butlery, and
S. B.　　　　　　　JOHN BRENT, page for the King's mouth in the cellar.

Grant, in survivorship, of an annual rent of 4*l.* 10*s.* and 40*s.* of
increase, paid by Nicholas Warde, for two messuages in the parish
of St. Michael, Cornhill, (between a tenement of the prioress of
St. Helen's on the east side and a lane called Fenkislane on the
west,) and for one messuage and eight cottages in the said lane,
for five years from Easter last. *Del.* Westm., 30 May 5 Hen. VIII.
Pat. 5 Hen. VIII. p. 1, *m.* 16.

30 May.　**4137.**　For HUGH AP ROBERT AP MEREDITH, chaplain.
P. S.

Presentation to the church of St. George of Kegedog, Asaph
dioc., void by resignation of Edward ap Tudor. Greenwich,
25 May 5 Hen. VIII. *Del.* Westm., 30 May.

31 May.　**4138.**　PAPAL LEAGUE WITH THE SWISS.
Vitell. B. II. 59.
. B. M.

" Articuli inter S. D. N., Leonem X. pontificem [. . . ad] magni-
ficos dominos confœderatos Alemanniæ Altæ percutienam (*sic*)
confœderationem ;" being propositions made by the Pope for a
league with the Swiss, to last 5 years, with liberty to renew it.
Lat., pp. 4. *In the Cardinal of Sion's hand* (?).

R. O.　**4139.**　[WOLSEY] to the LORD ADMIRAL.

Has received his loving letters, dated Plymouth, the 21st of this
month, stating that he trusted shortly to be at the Wyt (Isle of
Wight), which the King will rejoice to hear, who doubtless will
not fail to be with him soon. Cannot give him his desired supply
of victuals for six weeks, if foysts be not more plenteously brought
from the navy to Hampton, instead of being wastefully burnt and
broken. Some ships, ten weeks ago, received 756 pipes, and have
re-delivered scarce 80 foysts of them ; this appears to have been
done "by some lewd persons that would not have the King's navy
continue any longer on the sea." Orders should be taken that the
offenders be punished, otherwise it will lead to the failure of the
enterprise, and the Admiral will be blamed.
P. 1. *The commencement in Wolsey's hand, the rest in Tuke's.*
Endorsed : "Minutes of Letters."

1 June.　**4140.**　For WILLIAM GONSON.
P. S.

Licence to export 100 sacks of wool. Greenwich, 16 April
5 Hen. VIII. *Del.* Westm., 1 June.
Fr. 5 Hen. VIII. m. 11.

1 June.　**4141.**　For JOHN LORD AUDELEY.
P. S .b.

Protection for Simon Byrte, retained by the said Lord to serve
in the war. London, 1 June 5 Hen. VIII. *Signed.*
See Fr. 5 Hen. VIII. m. 10.

1513.

1 June. **4142.** For RICHARD BP. OF WINCHESTER.
P. S. b. Protection for John Gyle his servant, going in the King's wars to wait upon the Bishop. 1 June 5 Hen. VIII. *Signed.*

1 June. **4143.** For RICHARD BP. OF WINCHESTER.
P. S. b. Protection for John Studde, retained to serve in the war. 1 June 5 Hen. VIII. *Signed.*

1 June. **4144.** For THOMAS STEYNTON, of London, draper.
Protection; going to the war. Westm., 1 June.
Fr. 5 Hen. VIII. m. 1.

1 June. **4145.** For JOHN SHARP.
P. S. Licence to him and Anthony de Vivaldis, merchant of Genoa, to export kerseys and Malvesey wine. Also pardon and release to the said John and Lawrence Bonvixi, merchant of Lucca, of all unlawful entries and valuations of 2,000 kerseys and 440 butts of Malvesey. Greenwich, 24 May 5 Hen. VIII. *Del.* Westm., 1 June.
Pat. 5 Hen. VIII. p. 2, *m.* 10.; *and Fr. 5 Hen. VIII. m.* 13.

1 June. **4146.** For WILLIAM BENE, grocer of London.
P. S. Protection; going in the suite of Sir Gilbert Talbot, Deputy of Calais. Greenwich, 10 May 5 Hen. VIII. *Del.* Westm., 1 June.

1 June. **4147.** For ANTHONY DE VIVALDIS, native of Italy.
P. S. Denization. Greenwich, 26 May 5 Hen VIII. *Del.* Westm., 1 June.

1 June. **4148.** GAOL DELIVERY.
Midland Circuit.—Commission to Humph. Conyngesby, Guy Palmes and John Jenour. Westm., 1 June.
Pat. 5 Hen. VIII. p. 1, *m.* 8*d.*

1 June. **4149.** For WM. ATKYNSON, yeoman purveyor of calves to the Household.
Commission for six months to provide calves, porkers, boars, and young pigs for the Household. Westm., 1 June.
Pat. 5 Hen. VIII. p. 2, *m.* 8.

2 June. **4150.** SIR THOMAS LUCY.
R. O. Receipt by Thomas Leson, receiver of Master Compton, to Sir Thomas Lucee, for 10*l.* sterling, a half year's fee due to Compton at Lady Day last. 2 June 5 Hen. VIII. *Signed.*

2 June. **4151.** For LORD RICHARD GREY.
P. S. b. Protection for Henry Butteler, going with the said Lord in the King's wars. 30 May 5 Hen. VIII. *Del.* Westm., 2 June. *Signed.*

1513.

3 June. **4152.** LEWIS XII. to the LIEUTENANT OF MONTFERRAT.

Calig. E, I. 140.
B. M.

Anthony Spinolle is to reside at Montferrat. He is to present himself to the Lieutenant every day,—to write no letter, and send no message, without its being overlooked. Blois, 3 June.

Fr., mutilated, p. 1. Endorsed: "[Copie] dune lettre que le Roy a fait [et e]script au Lieutenant de Montferrat [qu]ant Authoine Spinolle fut [env]oye prisonnier pardela."

4153. HENRY BOHER to the LIEUT. OF MONTFERRAT.

R. O.

The King writes to him by this bearer, sending to Montferrat Antony [Spinelly], a Genoese (*Gennevoys*), who has lived in England, and whom the King suspects of sending news thither. The King gives orders that Spinelly present himself once a day before the Lieutenant, and that he be not allowed to write unless he show his letters. The Lieutenant is to lodge Lovell in a house of which the host shall be in the King's interest.

Fr., copy, p. 1. Endorsed: "Le double d'unes lettres que Monsr. le Général de Languedoc a rescript à Monsr. le Lieutenant de Montferrant, durent que Anthoine Spinolle estoit prisonnier en Auvergne."

3 June. **4154.** MARGARET OF SAVOY to HENRY VIII.

Galba, B. III. 79.
B. M.

For restitution to be made to Andrew de la Coste, a merchant of Bruges and officer of Prince Charles, who has been deprived of 1,685 balls of alum, (*balles d'all* . . . .,) by the servants of Mr. Conton, of the King's Household, according to the decree made by the council in London, for their restitution. Brussels, 3 June 1513. *Signed.*

Fr., mutilated, pp. 2.

3 June. **4155.** MARGARET to the PRIVY COUNCIL IN ENGLAND.

Galba, B. III. 81.
B. M.

On behalf of Andrew de la Coste. Brussels, 3 June 1513. *Signed.*

Fr., p. 1., mutilated. Add.

3 June. **4156.** For HARRY HOWARD, master of the new ship Henry Grace de Dieu.

P. S. b.

Protection for Thomas Deynys, Thomas Bettys, and William Smyth of Great Yarmouth, Norf., retained to serve in the said ship during the war. 3 June 5 Hen. VIII. *Signed.*

3 June. **4157.** For C. SOMERSET [LORD HERBERT].

P. S. b.

Discharge of fines for Sir Richard Wentworth, going over sea in the Earl's company, London, 3 June 5 Hen. VIII. *Signed and sealed.*

3 June. **4158.** For JOHN PAKYNGTON.

Grant, for 20 years, of land in Sandherst, Glouc. (formerly held by Ralph Avenell), and a messuage and land in Lanford, Glouc., lately belonging to Thos. Inglys, attainted on Thursday after the feast of St. Mary, 3 Hen. IV., being the 16 Aug., subject to the annual rent of 15s. 8d., and 2s. 4d. increase ;—Thos. Taylowe and Rob. Milton, of Glouc., being his bail. Westm., 3 June.

Pat. 5 Hen. VIII. p. 1, m. 8.

1513.
3 June. **4159.** Commission of the Peace.

Hants.—W. Abp. of Canterbury, R. Bp. of Winchester, T. Bp. of Bangor, Thos. Earl of Arundel, Wm. Blount Lord Mountjoy, Wm. Lord Mautravers, John Tuchet of Audley, Thos. West Lord De la Warre, Ric. Elyott, Lewis Pollerd, Sir Wm. Uvedale, Sir And. Wyndesore, Sir Nic. Wadham, Sir John Lisle, Guy Palmes, John Neuporte, Arthur Plantagenet, John Dale, Wm. Froste, John Dautrey, Ralph Pexsall, Thos. More, and Ric. Norton. Westm., 3 June.
Pat. 5 Hen. VIII. p. 1, m. 3d.

3 June. **4160.** For Robert Baron Curson, captain for the wars.
P. S. b.

Protection for John Herteley of Cambridge, retained in the Baron's company. London, 1 June 5 Hen. VIII. [*Del.*] 3 June. *Signed.*
See Fr. 5 Hen. VIII. m. 10.

3 June. **4161.** ⁒ For John Lord Audeley.
P. S. b.

Protection for John Benger, serving in the said Lord's company. London, 3 June 5 Hen. VIII. *Signed and sealed.*

4 June. **4162.** Anthoine Brusset to Ponynges.
Galba, B. iii. 81b.
B. M.

Begs he will recommend him to the King of England, according to his promise made at Gravelinghes. Is ready to serve him with certain troops against the French under De Walham. His people have taken a Frenchman of consequence at Therouane, named Maquelu, and sent him to the castle at Calais. Does not intend to deliver him until the King shall have spoken with him, and discovered the secrets of the King of France and Mons. De Piennes. The French are so angry with him they have sworn to burn his houses in Artois, and do him all the harm they can. Begs the King will give him the house and seignory of Cauchie in the Boullenois, belonging to a French captain, and grant him his letters patent accordingly. Gravelinghes, 4 June 1513. *Signed.*
Fr., p. 1.
" Mons. de Ponynghes, Chevalier de la Garetiere de l'ordre du noble et puissant Roy d'Engleterre."

4 June. **4163.** Sir Ric. Wingfield to Henry VIII.
R. O.

Wrote his last on the 31 May. This evening took leave of my Lady, and presented to her the sergeant of the poultry with the letters and presents. Thos. Spinelly's letter will inform him of the news from the Emperor and from Italy. Leaves for Antwerp to-morrow to prepare a passage for the Almains to Calais. Will proceed with all diligence in the musters. Brussells, 4 June. *Signed.*
P. 1. Add.

4 June. **4164.** Sir Rich. Wingfield to Wolsey.
Galba, B. iii. 80.
B. M.

Dares not write to the King in his rude hand, as he thinks it would not be understood. Has had no letters from the King or Council what orders to take for advancing the troops towards Calais. Wolsey will see by his letters that he has obeyed the orders of the Lady Margaret.—Leaves tomorrow homewards. Has spoken to the sergeant of the poultry, who shewed him that Wolsey desires to

P P

1513.

have two drumslads (?) Brussells, 4 June. *Add.:* "To the R. H. Mr. Almoner, with the King's Grace."
Hol., p. 1, *mutilated.*

4 June. **4165.**   [PONYNGES and others to HENRY VIIL]
Galba B. III. 27.   Have not disclosed their mission to the Emperor, who rode on
B. M.   the 29th to Our Lady of Hawes, to give the French audience, as
stated in their last, and had not yet returned to Brussels. The two
days have been prolonged to six. They have been asked by him
whether the ships have yet been despatched from Hampton, and
finding they were still remaining there the 22d. ult., knew not what
to answer. A letter has been sent to the commander of Spain
resident in the imperial court, that the promised levy at Hampton,
of 10,000 men. is only 8,000 ; so their information and the etter do
not agree, nor yet the number promised fo· Guienne in the late
treaty between England and Arragon. Brussels, 4 June.
Mutilated, pp. 2. *From a letter book.*

4 June. **4166.**   For CLEMENT HARLESTON.
P. S.   Livery of lands as kinsman and heir of Alice, widow of Robert
Harleston, and late wife of John Hevyngham, deceased. Green-
wich, 9 May 5 Hen. VIII. *Del.* Westm., 4 June.
Pat. 5 *Hen. VIII. p.* 1, *m.* 19.

4 June. **4167.**   For GEORGE NEVYLE LORD BERGEVENNY.
P. S. b.   Writs of recovery for Thomas Darcy, appointed to serve in the
wars. London, 4 June 5 Hen. VIII. *Signed.*

5 June. **4168.**   MARGARET OF SAVOY to HENRY VIII.
Galba, B. III. 82.   Has received his letters by Estienne Cope of the Buttery, with his
B. M.   beautiful presents. Needed no such testimony of his liberality—
was glad to be employed in promoting the alliance between him and
the Emperor. Brussels, 5 June 1513.
P. S. Yesterday the marshal of Calais left. *Signed.*
Fr., pp. 2., *mutilated.*

5 June. **4169.**   THOMAS LORD HOWARD to WOLSEY.
R. O.   Has found him so kind, he can do no less than write to him from
Ellis, 3 S. I. 157.   time to time, as never poor gentleman was in greater fear to take
rebuke than he. His late brother was exposed to calumny, "many
men putting fear what he durst do, which opinions the day of his
death he well proved untrue." On his last interview with the
King, it was proposed he should enter Brest, and destroy the havens
or burn the ships. Since his departure the Lords Winchester and
Lisle have, in the King's name, countermanded the order. Thinks
the French will not come abroad unless they are joined by the
Scots and Danes. If they will not, the army had better be discharged. The Spaniards would fain be home, since they heard of
the truce. Begs his friendly advice from time to time. Hampton,
5 June.
" To Mr. Almoner, with the King's grace."

5 June. **4170.**   For RICHARD BISHOP OF WINCHESTER.
P. S. b.   Protection for Andrew Chesham, of London, tailor, retained to
serve in the wars. Southampton, 5 June 5 Hen. VIII. *Signed.*

1513.

6 June. **4171.** [WOLSEY] to my LORD ADMIRAL.

R. O.

As the Council are now writing, and his hands are full, forbears writing for the present. Is to take such habiliments for war as were appointed for Lord Lisle, leaving the rest with Ric. Palshyde. It is not possible to convey anchors or cables by land. Has shipped them by four hoys four days ago. Begs he will be sparing of the victuals. Written at my poor house at Bridewell, the 6th day of June.

Draft, in Tuke's hand, p. 1.

6 June. **4172.** GEORGE DE GADDIS, ducal secretary, to BANNISIUS.

Addit. 21, 382.
f. 49.
B. M.

The French camp was broken up this morning, by the Swiss alone, without the Spaniards. Will write the particulars as the news arrives. Como, 6 June 1513.

On a slip attached to the letter : Triulcius and Tremouille are said to be prisoners.

In Spinelly's hand.

6 June. **4173.** EMMANUEL KING OF PORTUGAL to the POPE.

Nero, B. 1. 70.
B. M.

Thinks it proper to write to him, as the head of Christendom, of his successes in India. After many obstinate battles and much bloodshed, his general, Alfonso de Albecherque, to repair the losses of previous years, sailed to the Aurea Chersonesus, called by the natives Malacha, between the Sinus Magnus and the Ganges' estuary, a town of immense size, supposed to contain 25,000 houses, and abounding in spices, gold, pearls, and precious stones. After two engagements, and considerable slaughter of the Moors, the place was captured, sacked, and burned. The King, who fought upon an elephant, was badly wounded and fled; many were taken, and much spoil carried off, including seven war elephants, with towers and harness of silk and gold, and 2,000 brass guns of the finest workmanship. Albuquerque caused a fortress to be built at the mouth of the river which flows through the city, with walls 15 feet thick, of stones taken from the ruins of the mosques. There were then at Malacca foreign merchants, from Sumatra, Pegu, Java? (*Ja'aes*), Gores, and from the extreme east of China, who, being allowed by Alfonso liberty to trade, removed their habitations near the citadel, and promised obedience to Portugal, and to take its currency. The Malachese subscribed for 1,000 *catholici* of gold money and 100,000 for silver (*auream catholicos mille scilicet nummorum argenteam centum valore Malachenses inscripsere.* On hearing this the King of Ansiam (Siam), the most powerful King of the East, from whom Malacca had been usurped by the Moors, sent a golden cup, with a carbuncle and a sword inlaid with gold, as a pledge of amity. Hereupon Alfonso sent him some of his cleverest men, with gifts, to explore the country, which will doubtless augment the Catholic faith.—Returning to India, he found Goa, which he had formerly won with great bloodshed, besieged by the Moors, and another strong citadel raised beside it ; "unde Ruminum Turcorum quæ sex milia nostros continue infestabant." He attacked and took it, found a great booty, punished the Christian renegades serving in the ranks of the Moors, sailed to Dabuli, received an embassy from Prester John, who requested him to cross the Red Sea, and unite with himself in war against the Infidels. He has sent home to the King a large fragment of the wood of the true cross, and asks to have some

P P 2

1513.

clever workmen, in order that he may divert the Nile from the country of the Sultan. There was with him at the time the ambassador of the Pagan King of Narsigua, who has 1,500 elephants of war, 40,000 horse, as much foot as he wishes, and so much territory as can scarce be traversed in six months. There was also with him an ambassador from the King of Cambaye, from Sabay, formerly Lord of Goa and King Grosapa, with presents and offers of alliance. In the last fleet that appeared was an ambassador from the King of Ormuz (*Armusii*), with a present of pearls and jewellery. Alfonso had taken this King, and made tributary the chief town of Ormuz, in which he found 15,000 *seraphini*=gold ducats. Many nations in India have embraced Christianity. It may therefore be expected that God's favor will attend Albuquerque in his attempts upon the Red Sea, when he will shut the door on the commerce of the Saracens. He will effect a union with Prester John, and, raising the standard of the Cross, inflict a blow upon Mahometanism. Lisbon, viii id. June 1513.

Lat. Copy, pp. 4.

6 June.   **4174.**   RONSAR[D] to SIR RICE AP THOMAS.
[Calig. E. I. II.?]
B. M.

Had written to him a letter for the deliverance of his kinsmen Gilles de Sanglier and Francoyas, in exchange for David de Pouel ap Thomas's servant. Has since heard from the Deputy of Calais that Thomas intends to allow only one in exchange, contrary to the written engagement he had sent by Guisnes herald to Corbye, where the French King then was. Expects he will adhere to his written promise. Blois, 6 . . . .

Hol., Fr., mutilated, pp. 2. *Addressed* : "A Mons. Mysire Riz ap Thomas chevalier de l'ordre d'Angleterre."

6 June.   **4175.**   For RICHARD EDSAWE, tailor of London.
P. S.

Protection for one year ; going in the suite of Sir Gilbert Talbot, Deputy of Calais. Greenwich, 31 May 5 Hen. VIII. *Del.* Westm., 6 June.

6 June.   **4176.**   For HENRY BOURCHIER EARL OF ESSEX, captain of the
P. S. b.   King's spears.

Protections for Thomas Clyfford of Aspesden, Herts, William Bradbury of Claveryng, Thomas Burneby late of Berkyng, Thomas Kynwolmershe of Moche Dunmowe, and William Kynwolmershe of Brokestede, Essex, in the Earl's retinue. 6 June 5 Hen. VIII. *Signed.*

6 June.   **4177.**   For CHARLES EARL OF SOMERSET.
P. S. b.

Writs of recovery for Arthur Hopton to serve in the war in the Earl's retinue. 6 June 5 Hen. VIII. *Signed.*

6 June.   **4178.**   For WILLIAM COURTENAY.
P. S. b.

Protection for Edward Creswell, yeoman of the Crown, and captain of a ship called "The Mighell Ratt," of Plymouth, in the said William's company. 6 June 5 Hen. VIII. *Signed.*

1513.

S. B. **4179.** For KATHARINE, QUEEN CONSORT.

To be Regent and Governess of England, Wales, and Ireland, during the King's absence in his expedition against France, for the preservation of the Catholic religion, and recovery of his rights;—with power to issue commissions of muster and array;—to grant congés d'élire to the chapters of conventual churches, not being cathedrals ;—to give assent to the elections thereupon made ;—to present to vacant churches, in the King's gift, rated between 20 and 40 marks; and to issue warrants under her sign manual to John Heron, treasurer of the King's chamber, for payment of such sums as she may require.

Pat. 5 Hen. VIII. p. 1, m. 9.

6 June. **4180.** For CHARLES BRANDON VISCOUNT LISLE and GERRARD DANETT, squire of the Body.

Grant, in survivorship, of the office of steward of the possessions late belonging to Thomas Higford in the counties of Warwick, Gloucester, Worcester, and Oxford, in the King's hands, by reason of a feoffment made to the said Thomas and others by Richard late Earl of Warwick, as part of the possessions of the said Earl ; with annuity of 6*l.* 13*s.* 4*d.*, as held by Sir Edward Ralegh. *Del.* Westm., 6 June 5 Hen. VIII.

Pat. 5 Hen. VIII. p. 1, m. 13.

6 June. **4181.** For JOHN LONGLAND, D.D.

P.S. Presentation to the church of Lyffton, Exeter dioc., void by death. Greenwich, 6 June 5 Hen. VIII. *Del.* Westm., 6 June.

Pat. 5 Hen. VIII. p. 1, m. 10.

7 June. **4182.** [PONYNGES to HENRY VIII.*]

Galba, B. iii. 28.   * * " to the consiliable he made none answer. To the third

B. M.   he said that [he] was content, at the request of my Lady, specially for the love that he hath to your grace, to make a new league and confederacion between h[is] Majesty, your grace, and the Prince of Castile, leaving place for the Pope's holiness and for the King of Arragon."—For greater expedition he referred them to my Lady, whom they are to see this evening. He said he had sent a letter to England telling the King that he had detained for his service 2,000 Almains under Rob. De la Marche ; on which Wingfield said he had already written, and that the King was content to entertain these troops for three months in lieu of the aid he had promised the Prince of Castile, on receiving a bond of the Emperor for repayment. " The Emperor and my Lady went eftsoons apart, and with them my Lord Berges, and anon my said Lady returned unto us giving right good hearty thanks unto us for your kind offer, praying us to write unto your grace that the wages of the said 1,000 Almains might be advanced by your highness the space of one month more." The Emperor is very poor, which my Lady knows well. She asked therefore whether they had brought with them the wages of these Almains, begging it might be sent speedily to Antwerp. Till the money comes they can expect nothing but the usual delays. The Emperor told them that in eight days he would declare himself

---

* First leaf lost.

1513.

against the French. Thos. Spinelly will write of the news from
Italy. Brussels, 7 June.
Mutilated, pp. 2. From a letter book.

7 June.   **4183.**   For EDWARD DUKE OF BUCKINGHAM.
P. S. b.
Protection for Christopher Hillyarde, one of the King's spears,
and to Edward Noury and Walter Redmere, his servants, serving
beyond sea. 7 June 5 Hen. VIII. *Signed.*

7 June.   **4184.**   For EDWARD HIGGYNS, clk., the King's chaplain.
Grant of the deanery of the college of St. Mary, Shrewsbury,
Lichfield dioc., *vice* Adam Grafton, resigned ; a pension of 6 marks
being reserved for the said Adam out of the issues of the deanery.
Westm., 7 June.
Pat. 5 Hen. VIII. p. 2, m. 15.

7 June.   **4185.**   For EDW. CRESWELL, yeoman of the Crown.
Protection ; setting out in a ship called *The Michell Ratt* of
Plymouth. Westm., 7 May.
Fr. 5 Hen. VIII. m. 14.

7 June.   **4186.**   For ROBERT GRYSLEY of London, leather-seller, alias
P. S.   poyntmaker.
Protection ; going in the suite of Sir Gilbert Talbot, Deputy of
Calais. Greenwich, 26 May 5 Hen. VIII. *Del.* Westm., 7 June.

8 June.   **4187.**   For THOMAS STANLEY [EARL OF DERBY.]
P. S. b.
Protection for George Hyne to serve in the war in the Earl's com-
pany. 22 May 5 Hen. VIII. [*Del.*] 8 June. *Signed.*
Fr. 5 Hen. VIII. m. 14.

8 June.   **4188.**   For JOHN CAMPUCI, merchant of Lucca.
P. S.
Licence to export wools to the value of 2,000 marks for six
years. Greenwich, 29 May 5 Hen. VIII. *Del.* Westm., 8 June.
Fr. 5 Hen. VIII. m. 11.

8 June.   **4189.**   For JOHN JAKSON, yeoman of the Guard.
P. S.
Fee of the crown, being 6*d.* a day, on promotion of John Almer,
to be sergeant-at-arms. Greenwich, 7 June 5 Hen. VIII. *Del.*
Westm., 8 June.
Pat. 5 Hen. VIII. p. 2, m. 13.

8 June.   **4190.**   For REYNOLD POLE, student in the University of
P. S.   Oxford.
Pension which the newly elected prior of St. Frideswide is bound
to give to a clerk of the King's nomination until he be promoted
to a competent benefice by the said prior. Greenwich, 26 April
5 Hen. VIII. *Del.* Westm., 8 June.

8 June.   **4191.**   For JOHN ALMER, yeoman usher of the Chamber.
S. B.
To be bailiff, during pleasure, of the lordship of Welington-under-
Wreykyn, Salop ; with fees from 1 Hen. VIII. *Del.* Westm.,
8 June 5 Hen. VIII.

1513.

8 June.   **4192.**   FOR HARRY MARNY.
P. S. b.

Writs of recovery for John Cheyny, squire of the Body, of certain manors in Kent and Berks, at the suit of Sir Thomas Inglefeld, Sir Thomas Fetiplace, and others, against the said John Cheyny, who has been appointed one of the petty captains of the King's guard to attend the wars. 8 June 5 Hen. VIII. *Signed.*

9 June.   **4193.**   MARGARET OF SAVOY to HENRY VIII.
R. O.

Has received good news from Italy ; he will see the prosperous state of affairs there. Brussels, 9 June 1513. *Signed.*
Fr., p. 1.

9 June.   **4194.**   FOR JOHN CHAMBER.
P. S.

To be serjeant-at arms, with 12*d.* a day.   Greenwich, 6 June 5 Hen. VIII.   *Del.* Westm., 9 June.
Pat. 5 *Hen. VIII. p.* 1, *m.* 8.

9 June.   **4195.**   FOR JAMES REVET.
P. S.

To be serjeant-at-arms, with 12*d.* a day.   Greenwich, 6 June 5 Hen. VIII.   *Del.* Westm., 9 June.
Pat. 5 *Hen. VIII. p.* 1, *m.* 9.

10 June.   **4196.**   CARDINAL BAINBRIDGE to [HENRY VIII.]
Vitell. B. II. 42.
B. M.
Fiddes' Wol. C. 8.

This day, at 22 of the clock, the Pope had news of a cruel battle fought at Neware upon Sunday last, where the Duke of Milan was with 5,500 Swiss. The town was assaulted by 8,000 French, who beat down 50 yards of the walls. The Swiss issued out, took possession of the French artillery, on perceiving the arrival of 7,000 of their countrymen. Mons. De la Tremouille and his two sons, John Jacobo Tryulcio and his son Camillo, and all the French captains, were slain, with the exception of Baron de Ba . . . who is besieged in a castle with a small company. The Swiss have lost 5,000. As the Viceroy of Naples was crossing the Po to help the Swiss, the Duke of Milan sent him word to turn his arms against the Venetians, and gave order to the Emperor's captains of Verona to stop the passage of the Venetians. The Pope on hearing the news has more declared himself against the French, and has shot a peal of guns from St. Angelo. They expect to hear daily that the English have exterminated the French. Rome, 10 June 1513, "at 3 of the clock after that the sun was set." *Signed.*
Mutilated, pp. 2.

10 June.   **4197.**   FOR THOMAS STRANGWISHE.
P. S.

To be master porter of Berwick ; with fee of 20*l.* a year, 20 men of the old retinue in wages, and 20 of the "new crew." Greenwich. 10 June 5 Hen. VIII. *Del.* Westm., 10 June.
Pat. 5 *Hen. VIII. p.* 1, *m.* 8.

10 June.   **4198.**   COMMISSION OF THE PEACE.
S. B.

Marches of Wales.—G. Bp. of Coventry and Lichfield, Charles Bothe, clk., Sir William Uvedale, Sir Griffith Rice, Peter Newton, George Bromeley, and Thomas Lynom, to make inquisition of treason and other offences in N. and S. Wales, in the counties of Salop, Hereford, Gloucester, Worcester, Chester, and Flint. Westminster, 10 June 5 Hen. VIII.
Pat. 5 *Hen. VIII. p.* 1, *m.* 9*d.*

1513.

11 June. 4199.   For JOHN SHARPE, groom of the Chamber, and HUGH
S. B.   EDWARDIS, sewer.

Grant, in survivorship, of the offices of constable of the castle of
Maxey, Northt., with 3*d*. a day out of the issues of the lordship of
Maxey ;—bailiff of the said lordship, and keeper of the park of
Bourne, Linc., with the usual fees out of the issues of the lordships
of Bourne and Maxey ;—and keeper of the swans in the counties
of Northampton and Lincoln ;—now in the King's hands by death
of Margaret Countess of Richmond. *Del.* Westm., 11 June
5 Hen. VIII.

Pat. 5 Hen. VIII. p. 2, m. 8.

11 June. 4200.   For LAWRENCE ECCLESFELD, yeoman usher of the
S. B.   Chamber.

To be bailiff of the lordship of Sherifhoton, keeper and paler of
the park ; on surrender of patent granting the same to Thomas
Barkeley. *Del.* Westm., 11 June 5 Hen. VIII.

Pat. 5 Hen. VIII. p. 1, m. 16.

11 June. 4201.   For JOHN CAVALARI.
S. B.

To be master of the Hospital of St. Mary, Bethlehem, London.
Del. Westm., 11 June 5 Hen. VIII.

Pat. 5 Hen. VIII. p. 1, m. 16.

11 June. 4202.   KATHARINE the QUEEN.
S. B.
Rym. XIII. 370.   Mandate to John Heron, Treasurer of the Chamber, to pay any
sums of money ordered by the Queen, by letters under her sign
manual, to whatever persons she may appoint, for defence of the
kingdom, during the King's absence. *Del.* Westm., 11 June
5 Hen. VIII.

Pat. 5 Hen. VIII. p. 1, m. 9d.

11 June. 4203.   For JOHN and LEWIS HARPYSFELDE, mercers of London.
S. B.   Protection for one year. *Del.* Westm., 11 June 5 Hen. VIII.

Pat. 5 Hen. VIII. p. 1, m. 16.

11 June. 4204.   For THOMAS SOUNDE, yeoman of the Guard.
S. B.   Annuity of 5 marks out of the issues of the lordship of Denbigh,
from Mic. 4 Hen. VIII. *Del.* Westm., 11 June 5 Hen. VIII.

Pat. 5 Hen. VIII. p. 1, m. 16.

11 June. 4205.   For SIR HENRY MARNY, SIR EDWARD PONYNGES, SIR
S. B.   EDWARD STANLEY, SIR WILLIAM SANDIS, SIR JOHN
PECCHY, SIR THOMAS PARRE, JOHN CARRE, WILLIAM
PASTON, and EDWARD GERNYGAN.

Grant, during the life of Margaret, widow of Edmund De la
Pole, of the castle and lordship of Eye, Suffolk, and of the manors
of Neding and Virleys, Suffolk, Ewelme, Turnours, and Hokenorton,
Oxfordshire, and Westcompton, Philbertis, and Buklande, Berks,
forfeited by the said Edmund. *Del.* Westm., 11 June 5 Hen. VIII.

Pat. 5 Hen. VIII. p. 2, m. 9.

1513.

11 June. **4206.** For HUMPHREY CONYNGESBY, Justice of the King's
S. B.   Bench.

Licence to found a perpetual chantry for one chaplain, to be called the chantry of St. Mary the Virgin and St. George the Martyr, in the chapel of St. Mary and St. George, founded by him at Copthorn Hill in the parish of Aldenham, Hertfordshire, two miles from the parish church ;—with mortmain licence to acquire lands to the annual value of 8*l*. *Del.* Westm., 11 June 5 Hen. VIII.

Pat. 5 Hen. VIII. p. 1, m. 14.

11 June. **4207.** For JOHN VULVESTON of Ely, Camb.

Protection ; going to the war. Westm., 11 June.

Fr. 5 Hen. VIII. m. 10.·

11 June. **4208.** For HUMPHREY CONYNGESBY, Justice of the King's
S. B.   Bench.

Licence to found a perpetual chantry of one chaplain in the chapel of St. Mary the Virgin and St. George the Martyr in the church of St. Peter de Rok, in the diocese of Hereford ; and mortmain licence to acquire lands to the annual value of 6*l*. *Del.* Westm., 11 June 5 Hen VIII.

Pat. 5 Hen. VIII. p. 1, m. 13.

11 June. **4209.** JOHN YOTTON late DEAN OF LICHFIELD.
P. S.

Licence to Richard Salter, Richard Delves, Richard Strete, and Thomas Langworth, clerks, executors of John Yotton late Dean of the cathedral church of Lichfield, to found a chantry there for one chaplain to pray for the late and present Kings and Queens ; with mortmain licence to acquire lands to the annual value of 12*l*. Greenwich, 6 June 5 Hen. VIII. *Del.* Westm., 11 June.

Pat. 5 Hen. VIII. p. 1, m. 7.

12 June. **4210.** AND. DE BURGO to MARGARET OF SAVOY.
Vitell. B. 11. 146.

B. M.   "Extract of a letter from the secretar[y of] Andrew de Bourgo, dated at Milan, the x[ij(?) day] of June, directed unto my Lady of Savoy."

1. De Burgo entered Milan on the 7th, and was received with great triumph for his victory over the French ;—2, on news of which the previous day the people "took the Erbes," and attacked the palace, where were the Lord of Concersault (Concressault) with 500 Frenchmen, Lord Antony Marq. Palvesyne, the 2 brothers . . . Sieur Sacramor, &c., who with difficulty escaped into the castle from the stones that the women and children cast at them. 3. De Burgo went next day to an interview with the Viceroy at Placenza, whom he induced to pursue the French to Alexandria and send Prosper Colonna to stop their passage across the Po at Turin and Susa. 4. It was supposed that the Viceroy had done this to restore the Duke of Genoa. 5. De Burgo went with the Viceroy to Vercelli, where the Duke of Milan was with the Swiss ; concluded for a sum of 10,000 gold gilders that they should go to Turin and attack the French. The General of Savoy with the Duke has lent him 6,000 ducats. The Swiss are enraged at the Duke of Savoy for favoring the French.

Pp. 3, mutilated. In the hand of Spinelly's clerk.

1513.

12 June. **4211.** For LORD WYLLUGHBY.
P. S. b.
Protection for John Rawlyns, serving in the war. 12 June
5 Hen. VIII. *Signed and sealed.*

12 June. **4212.** For JOHN SIGEWYKE, page of the Wardrobe of Beds.
P. S.
Corrody in the monastery of Kyllingworth, void by death of
Matthew Baker. Greenwich, 8 June 5 Hen. VIII. *Del.* Westm.,
12 June.

12 June. **4213.** For the DEAN and CANONS of ST. GEORGE'S, WINDSOR.
S. B.
Mortmain licence to purchase lands to the annual value of
1,000*l. Del.* Westm., 12 June 5 Hen. VIII.
Pat. 5 Hen.VIII. p. 1, *m.* 9.

12 June. **4214.** For JOHN TUCHETT LORD AUDELEY. ·
P. S. b.
Protection for Morgan Coudrey late of Langton, Dorset, re-
tained to serve in the war. Dover, 12 June 1513. *Signed.*

12 June. **4215.** GAOL DELIVERY.
Oxford Circuit.—Commission to Robt. Brudenell, sen., John
Neuport, and Robert Brudenell, jun. Westm., 12 June.
Pat. 5 Hen.VIII. p. 1, *m.* 8*d.*

13 June. **4216.** SIR ROBT. WINGFIELD to HENRY VIII.
Galba, B. III. 83.
B. M.
Ellis, 2 S. I. 210.
Wrote last on the 12th from Estlynge—spends money in sending
letters to the Emperor's postmaster to prevent delay, as he is
seldom in a place where news is. His knowledge is in manner a day
after the fair. Lewis Maraton never fails to write to my Lady
of Savoy, and thence to your grace. Thomas Spinelly also makes
the posts run.—News has come this morning that the Duke of
Milan with the Swiss have surprised the French army—slain the
Almayns, and taken the Lords of T[renou] and John James of
[Trevulcio,] with many others. Sagramour the Viscount, who had
entered the city, was killed. Hopes to hear of similar success on
the part of the Emperor and the Viceroy against the Venetians,
and that the Swiss have passed the mountains to Dolphynye. The
King will have all the advantages he had last year, and more,
"though it was thought by many expert folks that the said advantages had been hard to have been recovered. But such is God, and
better, which only is the head of your enterprise and hath given
the noble courage and hardiness to elect of yourself the cost,
travell, and jeopardy to attain the honor and glory that must
needs follow." Bruxssels (Brucksal), in Swabia, 13 June 1513.
Hol., pp. 3, *mutilated. Add.*
P.S.—Sends a letter he has received from the Swiss.

13 June. **4217.** For SIR THOS. LOVELL, K.G.
Commission to act as steward and marshal of the Household in
the absence of George Earl of Shrewsbury. Westm., 13 June.
Pat. 5 Hen.VIII. p. 1, *m.* 16*d.*

13 June. **4218.** For ROGER LUPTON, clk., and JOHN HERON, treasurer
S. B.   of the Chamber.
Grant, in survivorship, of the office of clerk of the hanaper,
with usual fees, as held by William Smyth, clk.; with an annual rent

1513.

of 40*l.* out of the issues of the hanaper, and 18*d.* a day for expenses, when attending with the Chancellor. *Del.* Westm., 13 June 5 Hen. VIII.
Pat. 5 Hen. VIII. p. 1, *m.* 17.

13 June.　**4219.**　For WILLIAM LAMBERT, lancer of Calais.

S. B.

Annuity of 10*l.*, parcel of 20 marks payable at the exchequer of Calais, portion of an annuity of 100 marks, lately held by Sir Richard Lovelas, deceased, of Henry VII. *Del.* Westm., 13 June 5 Hen. VIII.
Pat. 5 Hen. VIII. p. 1, *m.* 18.

13 June.　**4220.**　For JAMES WORSELEY, groom of the Robes.

S. B.

Reversion of the constableship of the castle of Caresbroke. *Del.* Westm., 13 June 5 Hen. VIII.
Pat. 5 Hen. VIII. p. 1, *m.* 11.

13 June.　**4221.**　For GEORGE SEYNTLEGER.

P. S. b.

Protection for John Cracheroode, serving in the war. 6 June 5 Hen. VIII. [*Del.*] 13 June. *Signed and sealed.*
Fr. 5 Hen. VIII. m. 10.

13 June.　**4222.**　For WILLIAM COMPTON.

P. S. b.

Writs under the Great Seal, for Francis Acton, serving in the war. London, 13 June 5 Hen. VIII. *Signed.*

13 June.　**4223.**　For JOHN TURNER and GEORGE QUARLES.

P. S.

To be auditors, in survivorship, of Warwyke's, Salysbury's, and Spencer's lands, *vice* John Clerk and Edward Sharp. Greenwich, 11 June 5 Hen. VIII. *Del.* Westm., 13 June.
Pat. 5 Hen. VIII. p. 2, *m.* 8.

13 June.　**4224.**　For HUMPHREY BARYNGTON.

P. S.

To be sergeant-at-arms, with 12*d.* a day. Greenwich, 9 June 5 Hen. VIII. *Del.* Westm., 13 June.
Pat. 5 Hen. VIII. p. 1, *m.* 10.

13 June.　**4225.**　For JOHN WARDE of North Dighton, York.

P. S.

Protection while serving in the war. Greenwich, 31 May 5 Hen. VIII. *Del.* Westm., 13 June.
Fr. 5 Hen. VIII. m. 10.

13 June.　**4226.**　For RICHARD CORNEWALL, squire of the Body.

P. S.

To be steward of the lordships of Clyfford, Glasbery, and Wynsorton in the marches of Wales ; constable of the Castle of Clyfford, as Ralph Hackulnet held the same. Greenwich, 22 May 5 Hen. VIII. *Del.* Westm., 13 June.
Pat. 5 Hen. VIII. p. 2, *m.* 15.

13 June.　**4227.**　For GODFREY FOLJAMB.

P. S. b.
Rym. XIII. 371.

Protection for James Langley, serving in the war. 13 June 5 Hen. VIII. *Signed.*
See Fr. 8 Hen. VIII. m. 7.

14 June.　**4228.**　For EDWARD DUKE OF BUCKINGHAM.

P. S. b.

Protection for Richard Hartewell, mercer of London, victualler in the war. London, 14 June. *Signed.*

1513.

14 June. **4229.** For JOHN GYLE, late of Chertsey in Surrey.

Rym. xiii. 371. Protection ; going to the war in the train of Richard Bp. of Winchester. Westm., 14 June.

ii. For LEWIS WYNGFELD of Southwerk, Surrey.

Similar protection in train of the Bp. of Winchester. Same date.

Fr. 5 Hen.VIII. m. 13.

14 June. **4230.** For ROGER RADCLYFF.

S. B. Licence to alienate the manor of Whythcoke, granted him, with a piece of land called Seway Whythcoke, by patent 19 Nov. 2 Hen. VIII. *Del.* Westm., 14 June 5 Hen. VIII.

Pat. 5 *Hen.VIII. p.* 1, *m.* 14.

14 June. **4231.** For SIR HENRY MARNY, knight of the Body.

S. B. Grant of all the goods late belonging to Edmund Dudley, in the house of the said Edmund in Canwyk Strete, in the city of London. *Del.* Westm., 14 June 5 Hen. VIII.

Pat. 5 *Hen.VIII. p.* 2, *m.* 21.

15 June. **4232.** TENTS FOR THE ARMY.

R. O. Various sums paid to laborers from Friday 9th to Wednesday 15th June, 5 Hen. VIII., " then entering into wages of war;" sc. 100 pavillioners, 19 carpenters, 18 laborers, 4 wheelers, and 2 smiths, all at 6*d.* a day,—p. 96.

ii. Account of Cordage, p. 97 :—Small and great ropes at 2*d.* per pound, bought 1 July, for repairing tackling broken in the tempest on St. Peter's night.—5th July, " of the roper of Saint Umbris, 30 double knots of spelcyng lyen " at 12*d.* a knot.—6th July, of the roper of Mark, 3 cwt. of " weighted " ropes at 16*s.* 8*d.* the cwt., to repair damage done by tempest 4 July.—9th of July, of the Serjeant of Fynis, tackle of divers sorts.—14th Sept., ropes at Turney, the first day of the King's coming before that town, &c.

iii. Account of Thread, at 11*d.* per lb., p. 99 :—Grey thread, at 11*d.* per lb.—6th Aug., 4 lbs. of pack thread " to sew the mat for the King's lodging " at 4*d.* per lb.—6th Aug., 10 dozen threaden " poymtys " (points), for " lopys " (loops) for the King's lodgings and for the tent of cloth of gold at 2*d.* a dozen.—1 Sept., 8 lbs. of " Cordeneres " thread at 5*d.* per lb.;—also " rossen " for shoemakers' wax for their thread ; and grey thread at 16*d.* per lb.

iv. Account of Canvas, p. 101 :—13 July, 600 " Awndes " of canvas for tents, bought of a merchant stranger at 43*s.* 4*d.* the hundred.—29th August, 300 aundes of canvas at 5½*d.* the aunde.

v. " Naylles and yeran worke " (ironwork), p. 102,—10th June, wheeler's " tolys " (tools) of Richd. Harteshorne ; sc. an axe, a spokeshave, a squier (square), 5 augers, 4*s.* 5*d.*—Bought of William Tyrrell an axe, a " wrybytt " and auger, 8*d.* — Bought of Thos. Rychards an axe, " 2 holon Bruses," a spokeshave, " a naddes " (an adze), 5*s.*—Bought of Robt. Chapman, amongst other things, " 3 cornbrusys."—29th June, 4,000 nails for repairing carts 2*s.* 6*d.* per 1,000.—7th July, 4 " botteres," 4 " harers," and 4 pincers for shoeing horses, bought of a Dutchman in the market, spikes for nailing standards 6*s.* per 100.—13th July, 2,000 tin nails at 3*s.* 4*d.* a 1,000.—Carpenters' tools delivered to Thomas Wyllyamson the 28th inst.—18 Aug., 3,000 nails at 3*d.* Flem. per 100,

1513.

and 20d. sterling per 1,000 ; also at 4d. Fl.=2s. 2½d.; also 2,000 tin unets for lattés at 6d. per 1,000 ; a spade 20d.—Nov. 21, 30 staples to hang the tents and halys upon to dry 2s. 6d., also 100 spikes 2s. 6d. ; at Guingate, 6 Sept., on the King's removing, 12 triangles and 24 iron pins 13s. 4d.—18 Aug., at Ayre, 100lbs. of iron to make pins and " gogyns."

vi. Account for carriage, p. 106 :—18 Nov., Paid to divers persons for the carriage of the King's tents, pavilions, &c. from Blackfriars to the ship at 4d. a cart, whips 1d. each, grease 1d. per lb.—place they are kept in at Calais ; sc. hire of a house and meadow at Antwerp for the tents 5s., wharfage 4d.

vii. Timber and timber work, p. 112: – Sums paid to Thos. Rychardes—to the wardens of St. Mary Church at Calais for 6 poles of " vyr " (fir), on the 27th June, " that were broken in the tempest"—James Yerfforde, merchant of the staple"—"to the Goodman of iij Kinges without Lanthorne gate at Calais"—to Adryan Fyssher and others. Poplar boards for the King's house ; a hamper for the hangings, 12d.—7 Aug., 2,000 stakes on the night of the Emperor's coming ; boards for stools ; one for the King 12s.

viii. For leather, p. 115, to protect the hangings, and cover the Emperor's house in the fields.

ix. Rewards to labourers, p. 116, viz.: for sanding the pavement at Tournay against the guests, 13s. 4d. To Cornelius Cookes, for hire of his ground at " Armew" to spread the tents abroad.

P. 125, hoyes and other crayers retained and freighted with the King's ordnance to Calais at 3s. 8d. a ton a month, from 1 March 5 Hen. VIII.

---

15 June. **4233.**   For WILLIAM BLOUNT LORD MOUNTJOY, SIR ROBERT
S. B.   POYNTZ, and SIR RICHARD CHOMLEY.

Collation of the next vacant prebend in St. Stephen's chapel, Westminster, or the collegiate church of St. George, Windsor. *Del.* Westm., 15 June 5 Hen. VIII.

Pat. 5 Hen. VIII. p. 2, m. 15.

---

15 June. **4234.**   CHARLES VISCOUNT LISLE.
P. S. b.

Certificate that he has retained Lewis Orell to serve in the King's wars. 15 June 1513. *Signed.*

---

15 June. **4235.**   For ROBERT BRIGHT, LL.D., the King's chaplain.
P. S.

Grant of the chantry of Argaston, Oxon., void by death. Greenwich, 12 June 5 Hen. VIII. *Del.* Westm., 15 June.

Pat. 5 Hen. VIII. p. 1, m. 10.

---

15 June. **4236.**   For RIC. TEMPEST, squire of the Body.

Protection ; going to the war. Westm., 15 June.

Fr. 5 Hen. VIII. m. 14.

---

16 June. **4237.**   THE KING'S ARMY.
Talbot Pap. I. 1.

The Vanguard.—The King's harbingers, Sir Richard Carewe, • the Lord Lisle lord marshal, Sir Nicholas Vaux, the Lord Willoughby, Sir Thomas Parr, Sir Thomas Boleyn, Mr. Belkenap, Sir John Seymour, Sir Edward Hungerford, Mr. Egerton, standardbearer.

The Lord Abergavenny, the Lord Awbeney, Sir Henry Wyatt, Andrew Windsor's company, Edward Ferrers, John Vere, Sir Morris Berkeley, Sir William Sands, Edward Nevill with his retinue of the King's guard, the Almains, the Lord D'Arcy, Fitzwilliam with his retinue of the King's guard, Askew and Hansard, the Duke's company, the Marquis's company, Mr. Compton's company, Mr. Dalby's men, Sir Thomas Bury, John Nevill.

The Mid Ward.—The banner of Household, the captains of the Bishops of Winchester and Durham and Mr. Almoner, and their retinues, the Duke and the Lord Ross, Mr. Poynings, Sir Henry Guildford.

The Rear Ward.—Sir Henry Marney, the Lord Berners, with the footmen of the spears and his own retinue, the servants of the petty captains of the King's guard, Sir John Raynesford, Godfrey Folgeham, Sir Anthony Owtred, captain for the time, with all the residue of men of arms, ditto lances, and archers on horseback, to scour and conduct the said ordnance and rereward, my Lord of Essex, Sir John Peachy.

Endorsed : " Order of the army."

16 June. **4238.**   ORDNANCE FOR THE KING'S ARMY.

Talb. Pap. i. 3.

Bows, &c. delivered by Sir Sampson Norton to Lord D'Arcy to William Kingston, to Sir Henry Marney, to Thomas Hart ; gunpowder to John Jeffron, to the Earl of Kildare ; bows, &c. to Richard Falconer, gunpowder, &c. to William Pawn, to Richard Peper of Calais; saltpetre, &c. to Richard Ockam ; various to Sir John Peachy, to Humphrey Walker, to William Dawtry*, to Henry Creme, to Christopher Clapham of Berwick, to Richard Falcon, to Sir Edward Howard, and Sir Edward Poynings.

Endorsed : Ordnance and artillery delivered by Sir Sampson Norton, by virtue of the King's warrants."

16 June. **4239.**   To WILLIAM ABP. OF CANTERBURY, Chancellor.

S. B.

To make letters patent, granting wardships, subscribed by Sir Thomas Lovell, knight of the Body and treasurer of the Household, as the said Sir Thomas has been appointed ruler of the King's wards. *Del.* Baynard's Castle, 16 June 5 Hen. VIII.

16 June. **4240.**   For JOHN and LEWIS HARPESFELDE, mercers of London.

S. B.

Protection for one year ; going in the retinue of Sir Gilbert Talbot, Deputy of Calais. *Del.* Westm., 16 June 5 Hen. VIII. *Pat. 5 Hen. VIII. p.* 1, *m.* 16.

16 June. **4241.**   For CHARLES VISCOUNT LISLE.

P. S. b.

Protection and writs of recovery for John and Lewis Harpesfelde, appointed to serve in the war under the said Viscount. 12 June 5 Hen. VIII. [*Del.*] 16 June. *Signed.*

16 June. **4242.**   For WILLIAM WILCOK and JOHN SALESBURY, sewer of

S. B.   the Chamber.

Grant, in survivorship, of the office of keeper of the park of Gorssnodeok, in the lordship of Denbigh, in the marches of Wales,

* Dawby in the text.

1513.

with 2d. a day ; on surrender of patent granting the same to Wilcok. *Del.* Westm., 16 June 5 Hen. VIII.
Pat. 5 Hen. VIII. p. 2, m. 20.

16 June.   **4243.**   For NICHOLAS BONDE, clk.
S. B.

Presentation to the church of Northlewe, Exeter dioc., void by resignation of John Maltby. *Del.* Westm., 16 June 5 Hen. VIII.
Pat. 5 Hen. VIII. p. 1, m. 16.

16 June.   **4244.**   For FRANCIS, son of AMBROXIUS SALVAGE, native of
S. B.   Italy.

Denization. *Del.* Westm., 16 June 5 Hen. VIII.
Pat. 5 Hen. VIII. p. 1, m. 15.

16 June.   **4245.**   For JOHN VAN FOUNTAINE MYLMAN, glasier of the
P. S.   King's harness.

Annuity of 10*l.* during pleasure, from Mic. 4 Hen. VIII. Greenwich, 12 June 5 Hen. VIII. *Del.* Westm., 16 June.

16 June.   **4246.**   For DOMINIC LOMELIN, LORENZO DE MARINIS and
P. S.   PANTALEO DE SPINULIS, natives of Italy.

Denization. Greenwich, 24 (?) May 5 Hen. VIII. *Del.* Westm., 16 June.
Mem. that the above was sealed on 16 June.
Pat. 5 Hen. VIII. p. 2, m. 10.

16 June.   **4247.**   For WILLIAM PORTER.
P. S.

To be sergeant-at-arms, with 12*d.* a day.   Greenwich, 14 June 5 Hen. VIII. *Del.* Westm., 16 June.
Pat. 5 Hen. VIII. p. 2, m. 10.

16 June.   **4248.**   For RICHARD BISHOP OF WINCHESTER.
P. S.

Wardship of Thomas, as son and heir of William Bruyn, kinsman and heir of William Bruyn, son of Katharine, d. and heir of William Rengebourn.   Greenwich, 14 June 5 Hen. VIII.   *Del.* Westm., 16 June.
Pat. 5 Hen. VIII. p. 2, m. 10.

16 June.   **4249.**   For JOHN FORTESCU, squire of the Body.
P. S. b.

Protection for John Gough of Hertford, retained to serve under the said John in the war.   16 June 5 Hen. VIII. *Signed.*

16 June.   **4250.**   For FABIAN JUSTYNIAN and MICHAEL DEMONELIA,
P. S.   merchants of Genoa, and FRANCIS BACHO, Milanese.

Licence to import kerseys, tin, &c., and export merchandize, in a ship of the said Francis called *St. Mary*, for 12 months. Greenwich, 13 June 5 Hen. VIII. *Del.* Westm., 16 June.

16 June.   **4251.**   For SIR JOHN AUDELEY, captain in the wars.
P. S. b.

Protection for John Vyncent, Thomas Holt, John Godehale, and Thomas Payne, appointed to serve in the war.   16 June 5 Hen. VIII. *Signed.*
Fr. 5 Hen. VIII. m. 10.

1513.
16 June. **4252.**   JUSTICES OF ASSIZE.

Northern Circuit.—Rob. Henrison and Thos. Strey, with Wm. Fairfax and ... Erneley. Westm., 16 June.

Pat. 5 Hen. VIII. p. 1, m. 7d.

16 June. **4253.**   THE BADGES OF THE CAPTAINS IN THE KING'S ARMY.
Cleop. C. v. 59.
B. M.

" Hereafter foloyn the names of the captayns and pety captayns, wyth the bagges in ther standerts of the aremy and vantgard of the Kyngis lefftenant, enteryng yn to Fraunce the 16th day of Jun, in the 5th yere of the reign of King Henry the VIIIth."

Geo. Earl of Shrouesbury, lieutenant of the vanguard;—standard, gules, sables, &c. Thos. Earl of Derby, Lord St. John's, Lord Fitzwater, Lord Hastings, Lord Cobham, gold eagle, &c.,* Sir Rice ap Thomas and Sir John Oghan in his retinue. *Shropshire banneret,* Sir Thos. Cornwell† Baron of Burford, and Robt. Pole his petty captain. *Stafford banneret,* Sir John Aston†, and Thos. Kynersley, his petty captain. *Nottingham banneret,* Sir Will. Pierrepoynt†, and Roger Pierrepoynt his petty captain. *Derby banneret,* Sir Henry Saucheverell† and John Bradburn his petty captain. *Shropshire banneret,* Sir Thos. Leighton.† *Shropshire banneret,* Sir Thos. Blount†, and Edw. Blount his son and petty captain.‡ *Leicester,* Sir John Dygbe, marshal of the vanguard. *Middlesex,* Sir Sampson Norton, master of the ordnance. *Leicester,* Sir Ric. Saucheverell, treasurer of the vanguard. *Stafford,* Sir John Draycott, and Ric. Draycott his brother and petty captain. *Stafford,* Sir Lewes Bagott, and Robt. Cawrdyn his petty captain. *Nottingham,* Sir Thos. Sutton, and Roland Revell his petty captain. *Nottingham,* Sir John Dunham, and Charles Barnbe his petty captain. · *Shropshire,* John Dod, and John Maynwaryng his petty captain. *Notts,* Ric. Savage, and Thos. Leyke baylle of Chesterfield, his petty captain. *Notts,* Sir Ric. Bassett§, and John Wykersley his petty captain. *Derby,* Robt. Barley, and John Parker his petty captain. *Derby,* Nich. Fitherberd, and John Irton his petty captain. *Stafford,* Ric. Astley, and John Chetwen his petty captain. *Derby,* Sir John Leyk§, and Thos. Leyk his brother and petty captain. *Worcester,* Humphrey Rydyng, and Andrew Bykley his petty captain. *Cheshire,* John Pessall, and Will. Egerton his petty captain. *Shropshire,* John Cottes, and Ric. Cresset his petty captain. *Shropshire,* Will. Chorltou, and Will. Chorlton his petty captain. *Shropshire,* Sir John Maynwaryng§ of Eghtfeld, and Rondell Maynwaryng his petty captain. *Shropshire,* John Blount, and Ric. Laycon his petty captain. *Derby,* Sir Thos. Cokyn§, and Robt. Cokayn§ his petty captain. *Derby,* Sir Will. Gresley, and John Gresley his petty captain. *[Derby ?],* Sir Gilbert Talbot the younger§, and Humphrey Butler his petty captain. *Derby,* Robt. Lynaker, and Geo. Palmer his petty captain. *Derby,* Thos. Twyford, and Roger Rolleston his petty captain. *Derby,* Sir John Sowch of Codnour§, and Dave Sowch his brother petty captain. *Derby,* Arthur Eyr, and Thos. Eyr his brother petty captain. *Cambridge,* John More, and Edmund Everyngham his petty captain. *Derby,* Ralph Leych and Ric. Leych his petty captain. *Stafford,* Ric. Myners and John Wyscott, jointly

1513.

bearing Sir John Aston's standard as above. *Stafford,* Will. Chetwen, and Philip Chetwen his brother and petty captain. *Stafford,* Edw. Lyttylton, and Edmund Acton his petty captain. *Walsh,* Meredith ap Matheu, and his son petty captain. *Notts,* Sir Ric. Bossom*, and Robt. Knyston baylle of Ashburn, his petty captain. *Derby,* John Cursson of Croksall, and Edw. Cumburford his petty captain. *Cheshire,* Thos. Bulkley, and Rondyll More his petty captain. *Hereford,* Sir Edw. Croft*, and Thos. ap Guylham his petty captain. *Shropshire,* Humphrey Kynaston and Thos. Trentham, without standard. *Stafford,* Francis Cradok, and Thos. Bromley his petty captain. Will. Vernon, with banner of St. George. John Leych, with lieutenant's arms. Thos. Rolleston, bearing the talbot.

In the middle ward of the King's army, Lord Herbert, lord Chamberlain, the King's Lieutenant, and in his company the Earl of Northumberland, the Earl of Wiltshire, the Earl of Kent, Lord Audley, Lord Broke, Sir Robt. Dimmok, treasurer, Sir Randell Brurton, marshal, Baron Carew, master of the ordnance, the Baron Cursson, and others.

" The progress of the vauntgard into Fraunce, anno 5° Hen. VIII." —On 13 June, from Calais to Neunham Bridge. On the 15th entered Picardy, all the above standards displayed, and lodged at Lullingham, thence to Margysson. thence to Lysk, from which to Dornham ; from Dornham to Cordes, from Cordes to Tirwyn, where they remained from 27 June till 6 Sept., when the King and the whole army removed. Mons. Pont-Remy was captain of Tirwyn, and left the town with 4,000 soldiers (468 of whom were men at arms on horseback), on which the walls were cast down. On 6 Sept. the army removed nigh to the castle of Cotteney, and so to Losenmarle ; from thence to Lanuce near to Betten (Bethune), a walled town, and so to Pont Avaudyn, leaving St. Omer, Ayryth, and Bethune 2 miles on the left hand. From Pont Avandyn to Seclyng, thence to Pont Abovyn, leaving Lille 2 miles on the left hand ; from Pont Abovyn to Hardyn, and so to Aree 1½ mile from Tournay, 6 days before the town was entered, which was on 23 Sept., where the King and his armies rested till 13 Oct. At the jousts before the Archduke and Duchess of Savoy, and others of Flanders, the King broke 15 spears the same day ; when the Archduke and Lady Margaret were present. On 13 Oct. the vanguard left Tournay, and lodged at Hardyn, from which to Cauwey, thence to Yper. From Ypern to Dykesmeu, thence to Fourn, from Fourn by Dunkirk, and so to Gravelines and Calais on 23 Oct. The Emperor Maximilian continued with the King throughout this journey, and left him at Tournay. There were also the Lords Wallen, Leny, Emere, and Isylsteyn.

" The names of the French prisoners taken beside Tirwyn, 16 Aug. in the 5th year of the reign of King Henry the VIIIth:"— The Duke of Longueville. The steward to the French King. The Lord Claremont, vice-admiral of France, lieutenant of the Dauphin's company. The Dauphin's standard-bearer. The Lord Fayette, lieutenant of the Duke of Alençon's company. The Captain Bayart. The standard-bearer of Robynet Framgelly's company. The standard-bearer of the Grand Ecuyer of France. The Lord Brye. The Lord Robert of St. Severin ; and others.

" The names of part of them that were slain :"—The Lord Bushy, The Great Bastard of Vendôme, and others.

---

* Made knight at Lille.

1513.

"The standards that were taken the same time :" — The Dauphin's, The Duke of Alençon's, The Grand Ecuyer of France, The Seneschal of Armaygant [Armagnac], Robynet Framgelles, The Lord Busshey, and of Sir Robt. De la March.

Pp. 12.

17 June. **4254.** EDMUND LATE EARL OF SUFFOLK'S LANDS.

Suffolk.—Commission to John Goldyngham, Humph. Everton, Wm. Latymer, Th. Ayer, and Wm. Bagard to make inquisition as to statements in the petition of Sir Rob. Drury, Sir John Heydon, and Edm. Gelgett, that Edmund late Earl of Suffolk, by his indenture tripartite dated at Claxton 10 Oct. 12 Hen. VII., granted, in fee, to the petitioners, and to John Lord Scrope, Sir John Wyndham, Sir Hen. Heydon, John Yaxlee, serjeant-at-law, Simon Wyseman, and Th. Wyndham, the honor of Eye, and the manors of Westrop, Wyverston, Huntyngfeld, Thorndon, Virleys, Moundevyles, Swannes, Nedyng, Beuhale and Haughlee, Suff., to the use of Margaret the Earl's wife. Afterwards, by deed dated 10 Dec. 13 Hen. VII., the said Lord Scrope, Sir John Wyseman, and Th. Wyndham, quitclaimed to the petitioners and to Hen. Heydon and John Yaxle (who died not long after), all their interest in the premises.—But on the Earl's attainder, 19 Hen. VII., the petitioners were by certain inquisitions (stated) unjustly disseized ; and by patent 20 Dec. 22 Hen. VII., the manor of Wyverston was granted to Th. Marquis of Dorset, in tail male ; by patent 15 Nov. 23 Hen. VII. the park of Beuhale was granted to William Lord Willoughby and Erysby ; by patent 21 Feb. 23 Hen. VII. the manor of Swannes was granted to George Nevyll Lord Burgevenny, in tail male ; by patent 7 Oct. 2 Hen. VIII. the offices of bailiff of the lordship of Haweley, and keeper of the park there, were granted to Th. Bell, yeoman for the King's mouth in the cellar ; by patent 22 Nov. 2 Hen. VIII., the offices of steward and overseer of all possessions in Norfolk and Suffolk of the said Earl and John De la Pole late Earl of Lincoln, were granted to Sir Robert Southwell ; by patent 13 Jan. 2 Hen. VIII., the manors of Thorndon and Wattesfeld, Suff., etc., were granted to Sir Rob. Brandon, knight of the Body, in tail male, with remainder to Charles Brandon, squire of the Body, and further remainder to the King ; by patent 10 Feb. 2 Hen. VIII., an annuity of 100 marks out of the honor of Eye, granted to Sir Rob. Wyngfeld, knight of the Body ; by patent 20 March 3 Hen. VIII. the manor of Westhorp was granted to Rob. Wasshynton, serjeant-at-arms, and Anne his wife, in survivorship ; and by patent 10 July 4 Hen. VIII., the manors of Moundevyles, Segeford, and Ryngeston, Norf. and Suff., were granted to Ric. Fermoure.—The petitioners also state that they were not attainted by the act of attainder ; that the said Earl Edmund died at London, 4 May 5 Hen. VIII. ; and that the said Margaret still lives at Lullyng[ston], Kent. Westm., 17 June.

Pat. 5 Hen. VIII. p. 1, *m.* 11 *and* 12*d.*

ii. *Oxon.*—Similar commission to Simon Harcourte of Staunton Harcourte, Th. Denton of Caresfeld, Th. Langston of Stowe, and Wm. Cottesmore of Brightwell, to make inquisition as to the petition of the above-named persons respecting the manors of Carsyngton and Swerford, Oxon., granted and quitclaimed as aforesaid. After the Earl's attainder the manor of Carsyngton was granted to John Whytyng by patent 15 April 20 Hen. VII. ; and the manor of

1513.

Swarford, with appurtenances in Swarford, Southorp, Southend, and Hokenorton, were granted to Ralph Verney, by patent 6 Nov. 1 Hen. VIII. Westm., 17 June.

Pat. 5 *Hen. VIII. p.* 1, *m.* 13d.

iii. *Norfolk.*—Similar commission to Hen. Inglus of Attilburgh, Wm. Spilman, Hen. Warner, Wm. Ramesbury, and Wm. Drury, to make inquisition as to the petition of the above-named persons respecting the manors of Caweston, Cardeston, Saxlyngham, Burgh near Aylesham, and Segeford, Norf., granted and quitclaimed as aforesaid. After the Earl's attainder the manor of Cawston was granted in tail male to Jerard Fitz-Jerard Earl of Kildare, and Elizabeth Souche his wife, by patent 12 Dec. 20 Hen. VII.; the manor of Cardeston was granted by patent 5 June 22 Hen. VII. to Sir John Peche; the office of steward of the possessions of the said Earl and of John late Earl of Lincoln, in cos. Norf. and Suff., was granted by patent 22 Nov. 2 Hen. VIII. to Sir Rob. Southwell; the manor of Saxlyngham was granted to Edw. Wadham and Th. Fogge by patent 7 May 2 Hen. VIII.; the manor of Borough near Aylesham was granted to Wm. Botry by patent 9 Oct. 3 Hen. VIII.; and the manor of Segeford (by name of the manors of Moundevyles, Segeford, and Ryngeston, Norf. and Suff.) was granted by patent 10 July 4 Hen. VIII. to Ric. Fermour. On the death of the said Th. Fogge, s. p. m., the moiety of the manor of Saxlyngham was granted by patent 12 April 4 Hen. VIII. to Christ. Garneys. Westm., 17 June.

Pat. 5 *Hen. VIII. p.* 1, *m.* 14 *and* 15d.

---

17 June. **4255.** For CHARLES BRANDON VISCOUNT LISLE.

S. B.

Pardon and release as executor of Sir Edward Howard, knight of the Body, late admiral and captain-general of the king's fleet against the French, and of Alice Lady Morley, widow of the said Edward. *Del.* Westm., 17 June 5 Hen. VIII.

Pat. 5 *Hen. VIII. p.* 1, *m.* 16.

---

17 June. **4256.** For THOMAS LESON, clk.

P. S.

Presentation to the church of Newelme, Linc. dioc., void by death. Greenwich, 13 June 5 Hen. VIII. *Del.* Westm., 17 June.

Pat. 5 *Hen. VIII. p.* 1, *m.* 16; *and p.* 2, *m.* 8.

---

17 June. **4257.** To JOHN SHURLEY, cofferer of the Household, and keeper

P. S. of the Wardrobe.

To deliver to Edward Weldon all tails, bills, &c. appointed for the expenses of the Queen's household, during his absence with the King. Greenwich, 14 June 5 Hen. VIII. *Del.* Westm., 17 June 5 Hen. VIII.

Pat. 5 *Hen. VIII. p.* 1, *m.* 16d.

---

17 June. **4258.** For HENRY LONGE.

P. S. b.

Protection for Robert Coweley, John Bonde, and William Richardes, appointed to serve in the war. 17 June 5 Hen. VIII. *Signed.*

1513.
17 June.   **4259.**   For [SIR] HARRY MARNY.
P. S. b.   Protection and writs of recoveries in Oxon., Sutht., and Wilts, for
                          William Barantyne, squire of the Body, appointed to serve in the
                          war. 12 June 5 Hen. VIII. [*Del.*] 17 June. *Signed.*

17 June.   **4260.**   For LAURENCE BONVIXI, merchant of Lucca, and WIL-
P. S.   LIAM BULLA, mercer of London.
                          Licence to export kerseys and other merchandise not belonging to
                          the staple of Calais, and to import cloths of silk and gold, wine called
                          Malveseys, &c. ;—the customs not to exceed 180*l.* Greenwich,
                          15 June 5 Heu. VIII. *Del.* Westm., 17 June.

17 June.   **4261.**   For LAURENCE BONVIXI, merchant of Lucca, and JOHN
P. S.   SHARP, groom of the Chamber.
                          Licence to export kerseys and other merchandise not belonging to
                          the staple of Calais, and to import cloths of silk and gold, wine, &c.;
                          —the customs not to exceed 120 marks. Greenwich, 15 June
                          5 Hen. VIII. *Del.* Westm., 17 June.

17 June.   **4262.**   For SIR RICHARD FITZLOWIS, knight of the Body.
P. S.   Grant, in tail male, of the manor of Virlays, Suff., forfeited by
                          Edmund Earl of Suffolk ; with the issues from Mic. 17 Hen. VII.
                          Greenwich, 15 June 5 Hen. VIII. *Del.* Westm., 17 June.
                          Pat. 5 Hen. VIII. p. 2, m. 7. m. 9.

17 June.   **4263.**   For SIR THOMAS LOVELL, treasurer of the Household.
P. S.   To be master of the King's wards as long as they remain in the
                          King's hands ; with appointment, during pleasure, of feodaries and
                          receivers of their lands. Greenwich, 14 June 5 Hen. VIII. *Del.*
                          Westm., 17 June.
                          Pat. 5 Hen. VIII. p. 1, m. 7.

17 June.   **4264.**   For JOHN BOURCHIER LORD BARNES.
                          Protection ; going to the war. Westm., 17 June.
                          Fr. 5 Hen. VIII. m. 10.

17 June.   **4265.**   For WILLIAM BARENTYNE, squire of the Body.
                          The same. Same date.
                          Fr. ib.

17 June.   **4266.**   For WILLIAM HERTEWELL, mercer of London.
                          Protection; going in the suite of Edw. Duke of Buckingham.
                          Westm., 17 June.
                          Fr. 5 Hen. VIII. m. 13.

17 June.   **4267.**   KNIGHT and STILE to HENRY VIII. (In cipher.)
Vesp. C. I. 40.   We (the most humyl servantys to yowr grace, Doctur Wyllyam
B. M.   Knyghte and John Style,) certefy un to yowr hyzghnys that on the
                          tenth day of thys present monyth of June cam hether yowr subjecte
                          Rychard Prows, the berer here of, (servant to me John Style,) by
                          whom we receveyed yowr royal letter of the date of elevynyth day
                          of May, and also wyth the same yowr royal conmyssyon and the
                          copys of the nw treaty and of the actys upon the sâme don on Sant
                          Markys day that last past; upon the whych, acordeyng to the hyzghe

1513.
17 June.

Stile's cipher.
Ferdinand de-
clines entering
on a new league
with England.

conmandament of yowr grace, yn medyatly and dyvers tymys syth, we have had conmunycacyon wythe the Kyng yowr good fader of Aragon, and also, by hys conmandament, wythe hys secretary Almasan, we yowr servantys by al the ways and resons that hath byn to us yn al goodly maner possybyl have sulucyteyd to the Kyng yowr sayd fader that hys Majesty schuld confyrme the late treaty that hys ambassatur hath made wyth yowr hyzghnys and wyth themperor on Sant Markys day ; to the whyche, and yt plese yowr grace, the answer of yowr sayd fader was in lyke maner as that yt hath byn to us byforetyme syth the recepte of yowr other royal letters of the dates of the ayzghte and twenty and last day of Apryel, acordeyngly as that we by fore thys by our other sundry letters and sent by dyvers messengers we have certefyed un to yowr grace, how that yowr sayd fader ys gretely dyspleseyd wyth hys ambassatwr for that he granteyd to the sayd treaty, sayeyng that hys sayd ambassatwr had non suche atoryte nor canmandament from hym for to make any suche nw lyage or treaty wyth yowr hyzghnys, other than the first treaty conserneyng the enterpryse of Ghyan, whych was begon the last yere. And now hys sayeyng ys that the sayd treaty and holy lyage ys and standyth voyde by the reson of the returneyng of yowr armey from hens, and also for that the late Pope Julyo and the Ytalyans kepeyd no promyse wyth hym, and that therefore he hath takeyn a trwys wyth the Frensche Kyng for oon yere from the furst day of Apryl last past, the whych hys Majesty sayth that he wyl yn no wyse breke, on les that the Frensche men do contrary to the sayd trwys ; and sayeyng also that for as muche as that the ryzghte and enterpryse of Ghyayn be longyth to yowr grace, and not to hym, that hyt standyth not wyth reson nor consyens that he schwld make war yn that behalf unto the Frensche Kyng at his aune proper costys and chargys, the whych hys Majesty sayth that he ys not abyl for to do, and schawyng hym self to be yn grete extreme nescessyte of tresore, for the whych he sayth that he yn no wyse may folow the sayd warrys ; sayeyng also that yt ys gretely to be mervelyd that yowr grace wythdrawyth the thyngys and offers to hym made by the copy of a nw treaty to hym sent by the conmendador Musschyka for the foloynge of thenterpryse of Ghyayn, so that now by the treaty made on Sant Markys day yt ys syngnyfyeyd that he schul, al alone, and at hys proper costys and chargys, make war to the Frensch Kyng on thys partys ; the whych he sayth playnly that he wyl not so do, but that furst a nwe treaty and apoyntament must for the same be made by twyxt yowr hyzghnys and hym, so that he wyl be sure of the ayde that yowr grace wyl geve to hym for the same.

Denies that he
gave his ambas-
sador authority
to renew the
league.

Wyth oute the ayde some what of yowr grace, we fere us that yowr sayd good fader wyl do any thynge yn affecte a yenyste the Frensche Kyng, on les that he schalbe drevyn there unto for the safgard of hys aun causys. And where, and yt plese yowr grace, that the sayeyng of yowr good fader to us had byn dyverse tymys that hys ambassatur had of hym no conmyssyon nor atoryte for to conclude any other treaty wyth yowr hyzghnys then the furst holy lyage ; whereupon, sythe the recepte of yowr royal letter and yowr other wryteyngys by yowr subjecte Rychard Prows, the berer hereof, we have comunyd wythe the Kyng yowr good fader of that mater. For as yt apereyth by the sayd wryteyngys that yn the monyth of July that last past, he sent a nw suffycyant power and atoryte unto hys sayd ambassatur for to make and conclude any nw lyage wyth yowr hyzghnys, and wyth the Pope and other that the sayd hys ambas- satur schuld thynke convenyent and nescessary for to be don, or

1513.
17 June.

Stile's cipher.

wyth any oonly. To the whych then, and yt plese yowr grace, the sayeyng of yowr sayd fader was, that trawyth yt was that at the sayd tyme he had geveyn a conmyssyon and atoryte to hys sayd ambassatur for to make and conclude a nw lyage generral wyth the Pope and wythe yowr hyzghnys and wythe themperor and other joyntly, and not oonly specyal wyth yowr grace and themperowr as yt is nowe don. Aud we yowr servantys, acordeyng to the tenurys of the copy of hys atoryte in that be half gevyn to hys ambassatur, resonyd largely with yowr sayd fader ; upon the whych hys Majesty determynyd that hys secretary Almasan schulde comune wyth us farther of that and all other causeys, sayeyug that he wold do al that he may in any wyse for yowr grace, how be that yn no wyse he wold not breke the tryws that he hath made wyth France on les that yt be yn thayre aun defaute.

Interview with
Almaçan.

And so, and yt plese yowr grace, the second day after thys conmunycacyou we had also conmunycacyon wythe the secretary Almasan, the whych at lengyth wyth myche argumentys granteyd that the sayd conmyssyon granted to the sayd ambassatur was suffyuschyeant and good for to conclude a nw lyage wyth yowr hyzghnys ; how be that the sayeyng of the sayd secretary ys that or then that any such nw lyage was made the Kyng hys lord had wreteyn ayen unto hys ambassatur, conmandeyng hym that ynno wyse he schuld not make any nw lyage wyth yowr grace, uuto such tyme that he schuld have other conmyssyon and conmandment, for as much as that yowr sayd fader had taken trwys wythe the Frensche Kyng for oon yere. Of the whych, and yt plese yowr grace, the sayd secretarys sayeyng ys that yowr hyzghnys had the knowlyche by the sayd ambassatur and other wyse by fore the makeyng of the nw lyage made on Sant Markys day, and yn a maner schwyd and sayed that the sayd thayr ambassatur hath wretyn that he confessythe that he dyd contrary to the Kyng hys lordys conmyssyon for fere, and for to fulfyl the plesure of yowr graoe. And that notwythstandeyng, the sayd secretary sayed that the King yowr good fader hys lord wol do al that he may ayenyst the Frenchmen yn the favor of yowr grace, so that he may not breke the trwys taken and sworn by hym wyth the Frensch Kyng, and that the Kyng hys lord for that consydoracyon by polyce when that he toke the trwys wyth the Frensche Kyng lefte owte of the sayd trws the late Kyng of Navar and the cwntray of Byern; for that he knowyth verrely that yn case that at any tyme that he wyl or do make warrys yn and to the partys of Byerne that yt schalbe no les dysplesure to the Frensche Kyng then that he made war to and yn the partys of Ghyayn, the whyche ho sayed that the Kyng yowr good fader entendyth for to do and make war yn Byerne. And then yn case so be, that the Frensshemen in anywyse do take the late Kyng of Navarrys parte for the defence of the cuntray of Byerne, thay so doyng, the trwys schalbe brokyn by thayr defaulte, whereby the Kyng yowr good fader schalbe dyschargeyd of hys othe and promyse, and schalbe at lyberty for to make war to France by any other parte that he thynke schalbe most advantage. But by fore the afore sayd occasyons inno wyse he wyl not breke nor proclayme war wyth France after thys.

Ferdinand intends making
war in Bearne.

And yt plese yowr grace we spake wyth the Kyng yowr sayd fader, the whych hath confyrmeyd by hys royal word ys the sayeyngys of hys aforesayd secretary Almasan, and that he entendeyth for to begyn schortely for to make some warrys by the partys of Byerne, and that for that entente, and for the farther foloyng of the same

1513.
17 June.

Stile's cipher.

wyth the ayde of yowr grace, hys Majesty doth send unto yowr hyzghnys a jantylman whych ys brother to the conmendador Don John de Nosa, whych conmendador was of late yn yowr royal corte, and ys now ambassatur yn the corte of yowr good brother the Prynce of Castyl. And thys man that now from hens ys sent unto yowr grace hath, as we be ynformed, conmyssyon for to conmune wyth yowr hyzghnys for the warrys to be made yn Byerne now and for the next yere further ; whych by that we can persayve, Soverayn Lord, schalbe no grete warrys nor of no grete poysance wyth owte the ayde of yowr grace, but pastymys, on les that as we have byfore wretyn, that they of nescessyte for thayr aun safgard be drevyn therunto.

Reduction of
fortresses in
Navarre.

And yt plese yowr grace, now of late the Markes de Comarys, whych ys the Kyng yowr good faders deputy yn the ream of Navar, assemblyd fowr thowsand men, lytel more or les, for to subdu thre forturesys that be yn the ream of Navar belongyng to Monsyr de Egramownt and to Monsyr de Lusa. And al the contray of Byern and Bayon, and al the contray there abowte, fereyd that the sayd Markes wold have procedeyd farther on the partys of Ghyayn or Byerne ; for that the castyl of Bedasen ys belongyng to Monsyr de Egramownt, mayre of Bayon, and the sayd castyl standyth but thre legys from Bayon on the ryver that comeyth from Af, and al the cheyf vytualys that comeyth to Bayon by water must cum yn the danger of the sayd castyl, and the sayd castyl standythe yn the ream of Navar. For the whych Monsyr de Egramownt, seying non other remedy on les that he schuld have by the causer of the brekeyng of the trwys by twyxt the Kyng of Arragon and the Frensch Kyng, for the whych he consentyd that the cundstabyl of the said castyl, and al thoys there beyng dwelyng under the same, be sworne to the obbedyence of yowr sayd good fader ; and in lyke wyse be thay of the other placys belongyng to Monsyr de Lusa, so that al that ys in the ream of Navar now ys under the abaysance of the Kyng yowr said fader. And the late Kyng of Navar ys yn the town of Salvaterra in Bierne, and hath no power of men wyth hym; for the whych, and yt plese yowr grace, in case that the Kyng yowr good fader of Arragon wyl make warrys now un to Byerne or Ghyayn, he hathe many grete advantajys, and may do yt wyth oute inportabyl chargys, whych chargys hys Majesty gretely alygeythe, now there ys no power yn Ghyayn nor Byerne for [to] make anny assystance ayenyst hym ; for al the Almaynys that were in Bayon, and there abowte, and al other men of war be departeyd from thoys partys towardys Pycardy and Bretayn, for to make resystance ayenyst yowr grace, and another grete power of France be departeyd yn to Ytaly ; and yowr good fader whych now hath the hole ream of Navar at hys conmandament, and hys artelary al redy at San John Pe del Pwerto, whych ys ajoynant to Ghyayn and Byern : and the sayd artelary ys al redy pasyd the mowntaynys, and al evyl ways, whych ys a grete advantage, the whych such lyke advantagys yowr sayd fader peraventure schal not fynd hereafter. How be that of a swerty, Soverayn Lord, for dyvers causys thys warrys cannot be parfytely foloyed by the Kyng yowr sayd fader. Oon ys that hys sawldyers and men of war be not wel payeyd at anny tyme ; another ys that he putyth the ream of Castyl to the greteyst costys and chargys for the makeyng of the sayd warrys, and that thyngys that he conquereyth and geteyth, he anyxyth yt to the crown of Arragon rather then to the crown of Castyl ; and the Castyllyans, nor other that be under the ream of Castyl, be not there wyth pleseyd, nor welwylyng for to make any

1513.
17 June.

Stile's cipher.

warrys whych twrnyth thaym to no profyte ; and the thyrd ys that the Kyng yowr sayd fader hath fue other cownsolorys aboute hym but Aragonesys and covetuys pepyl, and not nobyl, but such as that set nother by thayr onurys nor wordys, and so yt apereyth by thayr dedys.

And yt plese yowr grace, the verry tydeyngys that ys here, that the Frenchmen have taken Jeyn and Myllan, and that the Duke of Myllan ys fled, and that the Lumbardys wold not be agreabyl that the Vysorey of Napolys capytayn of yowr good faders armey schuld helpe for to defend theym ayenyst the Frenschemen ; and that therefore the sayd Vysorey ys returnyd bacward towardys Bonany, and wyl to Napolys yn case that the Ytalyans do not send for hym ayen, for to have hys ayde. Tydeyngys from Rome here hath cum nou thys monythe past or more, the whych ys thowzghte a grete armey of Jeyn was departeyd from thens by the ze for to have encowntryd the French army by fore the takeyng of the city of Jeyn. The sayd armeys met not, and the Duke or Govornur of Jeyn ys fled to the sayd armey. Dyverse of yowr subjectys of late beyng on hys cost of Byskay by the ze have taken of yowr ennymys of France and Bretayn, the whych be redelyverd ayen, and put at thayr lybertys by the conmandament of the Kyng yowr good fader for the kepeyng of hys trwys wyth France. And as the farther nwys schal folow from tyme to tyme we schal certefy the same unto yowr hyzghnys by the grace of the Holy Gost, who perserve yowr royalyst asstate long for to endure. Wretyn yn Valadalyd and corte of yowr fader of Aragon, on the sevyntyn day of Juny, the fyvyth yere of yowr nobylyst reygne, by the most hwmyl servantys to yowr grace, Wylyam Knyzghte and John Style.

[The following is in Stile's ordinary hand :]
And yt plese yor grace, by the berer hereof, my servant Richard Prows, y do send unto yor hizghnys of the commodites of thys contrey a litell whyte wyne of San Martyns, whereof yor grace so beynge pleseyd maye have more ; and also by my said servant y do send xij. pair of glovys for yor grace, humylly besecheynge yor hizghnys to pardon of yor grace for my unkunynge writeynge.

The Kynge yor good faders ambassatur nor themperors ambassatur be not yet come hether from thempero^r.

William Knyghte. (*Stile's monogram.*)

Vesp. C. i. 88.
B. M.

2. Decipher of the above with a few omisions.

S. B.   **4268.**   For WILLIAM KNIGHT and JOHN STYLE.

To receive the oath of Ferdinand King of Arragon for observance of the treaty concluded at London, 18 April 1513.

18 June.   **4269.**   For ANTHONY UGHTREDE.
P. S.

Wardship of Joan, kinswoman and heir of Edward Redemayn, of Harwode, York ; viz., d. and heir of Henry, s. and h. of the said Edward Redemayn. Greenwich, 17 Jan. 4 Hen. VIII. *Del.* Westm., 18 June 5 Hen. VIII.

Pat. 5 Hen. VIII. p. 1, m. 16 ; and Pat. 4 Hen. VIII. p. 2, m. 12.

18 June.   **4270.**   For JOHN YONG.
P. S. b.

Protection for Martyn Pollarde, of Bristol, merchant, bound to serve in the army, and carry victuals to the said John. London, 18 June 5 Hen. VIII. *Signed and sealed.*

1513.
18 June. **4271.** FOR JOHN GOUGH.

Protection ; going in the suite of John Fortescue. Westm.,
18 June.

Fr. 5 Hen. VIII. m. 14.

19 June. **4272.** SIR ROB. WINGFIELD to HENRY VIII.

Vitell. B. xviii. 47.
B. M.

Wrote his last letter of this month from the town of Bruxellis in
Swabia; the [same] day had written to the council in answer
to their letter from . . . . . . Castell the 3rd of the same. Also,
" with the same letter [came one] from your grace to the Emperor,
and one to the Dw[chess, with] the copies of the same, and also
the copy of a [letter from] your highness to the Pope." The same
17th day the Emperor [came] to Spires, and was advertised
. . . : . . . . . . from your grace, whereupon he appointed next
day at 12 o'clock [to meet] Wingfield at a town mid-way between
Spires and Worms, when the letters were delivered and read to
him, with the contents of which he seemed pleased, and also
with those your grace had sent to the Venetians. "And showed
that the . . . . was now changed far from the state
. . . . I should send your said . . . .
must needs serve to good purpose, and especially [for] them to
know their folly, and showed me that I [was] to send the said
letters by his posts to Augsburg." The Emperor also was pleased
with the copy of the letter to the Pope, and showed the copy of a
similar letter to the Pope written 15 days before. The Emperor's
ambassadors were to be ready to go with those from England whenever it should be convenient to send them. The Emperor asked if
an answer had been returned respecting " your second payment,"
and seemed to marvel that no advices had been received respecting
it, saying he was afraid " delay will do harm to us both," and that
any machinations seducing Hen. VIII. from his interests would do
more damage than the suspicions that arose between the Emperor
and the King of England's father. He also shewed that he had
ordained the Lord . . . . . . to meet at Calais with Henry VIII.,
for whom he expressed sentiments of good will. Wingfield answered
that there should be little likelyhood of any suspicions, especially
concerning such things as the King of England was bound to perform.
The Emperor shewed that the principal " huswyffe " of his county
of Tirol was dead, and also his vice-chancellor, who were two of the
most necessary of his councillors, especially in this time of war with
the Venetians, so that the rest of the council ceased not [to urge]
" him to return towards those parts." Wingfield dissuaded some
and confirmed others of the many things said by the Emperor;
[especially agreeing with him] that if there be not tidings shortly
that the Viceroy has made some exploit against [the Venetians] who
were in an inevitable trap, the Viceroy should be esteemed the
most unfortunate and most cowardly gentleman that ever leapt
on horseback; " and over that the Emperor is . . . .
divers places that the Viceroy and Jerome Wyk . . . . and
the Count de Carryate, that is at Venice, hath . . . . of the
Venetians in large manner, which must . . . . shortly."
Having been with the Emperor more than an hour [he desired
Wingfield] to ride before him to Worms, as he wished to meet
Magnus by the way, and then took leave of him, saying that in two
or three days he would send letters to the King of England in

answer to those received from him, wherein Wingfield trusts he
will inform "your grace" what he will do concerning his army.
Worms, 19 June 1513.

Pp. 6, mutilated.

20 June. **4273.**　　SPINELLY to HENRY VIII.

Galba, B. III. 107.
B. M.

Wrote last on the xv[ij.]—Went on the 18th to Mr. . . . .
to send gunners to Calais, and other officers of the Prince of Castile
to conduct the King's ordnance, as Sir Richard Wingfield desired.
My Lady has received letters from the Duke of Savoy, dated Tunon
on the Lake of Geneva, the 9th inst., with a copy of a letter from
the Governor of Vercelli of the defeat of the French in Novara.
The Baron of Saxes named in it is pensionary, and the Emperor's
friend.—Sends letters written to Chevres and Rewex, from the
Emperor, containing the news of the conflict, and the succour of
the Duke of Milan by the Swiss.—The Prince of Semay has heard
a report of the departure of the French King from Paris to Blois
on receipt of the news.—It is a token that he will not " have any
field with your grace." France is much discouraged. At the discussion with the ambassadors of Gueldres they declined the
proposition that each party should remain in statu quo. They
now declare that their master intends to have " the land of Kessell
and Koke a this sid the river of Mosa and abought Graves." Does
not think it probable the terms will be agreed to. Spinelly
thinks that Gueldres will follow the French. Has heard from the
Hubbartz of Seeryssey that ten days since two ships arrived at
Camfera from Scotland. They say the King of Scots will make
no war — that three French men of war were in Scotland—the
greatest not 60 tons—that they intend to return on the back side
of Scotland, and not between Dover and Calais—that one of them
was taken and sent to Rouen—that Lord Pyennes, when asked to
deliver it, said, " the King our master hath not enemies enow, but
ye must seek to find him more "—that all the ships of Normandy
had discharged their ordnance at Amflower. Symon Differret and
Pawle Armestoft leave to-morrow for England with the Emperor's
ratification—they have with them the license for the men of war.
As soon as my Lady hears of the King's arrival this side the sea
she will send my Lord Berges. To-morrow, Baptiste de Taxis
goes to Gravelyn for the two payments for the Emperor. Brussells,
20 June 1513.

Pp. 5, mutilated. Signed. Add.

2i June. **4274.**　　SIR ROB. WINGFIELD to HEN. VIII.

Vitell. B. xviii 50.
B. M.

Had on the . . . . . . of this present month written his last ;
this morning received [those] dated 31 May, with them one
sent from Rome to the . . . . . ambassador resident in England.
The letters from England had been sent to Augsburg, and had
come very opportunely, for [the Emperor] took it very strangely
[that there should have been any delay] in the second payment ;
suspicions having arisen that the craft proceeded from the King of
[Arragon], who thereby, it was thought, desired that [the Empe-
ror], being out of credit with the Swiss for lack of the payment he
had agreed to give them, would cause the Swiss to join with the
French, and " condescend to let the duchy of Milan in peace." As
soon as Wingfield had received these letters he went to the
Emperor, [who expressed satisfaction] on learning that they con-

1513.

tained favorable news, saying he had slept ill a night or two. The Emperor then said that the Swiss had sent a messenger from Novara showing how the battle was fought, with the losses of the French and the artillery that had been taken. Then Wingfield communicated the King's letter of 31 May, which had gone out of the way, containing, in the first place, "the King's determination not only to observe all bounden engagements; but also, for the advancement of the common affair, to send the second payment with all convenient speed. Secondly, that your grace had no suspicion of the King of [Arragon]. Thirdly, that if it should happen that the King of Arragon "would have [so little] regard to his honor as to leave his friends and allies to their mortal enemies [the French, then the King] and your grace, with the help of such other friends [as would be] glad to join with you, might order so that he should be brought in such [peril and] danger, that the peril should not be only in [the kingdoms] of Naples and Navarre, but also in all the rest that [the said King is] governor of at this day."

To the first part the Emperor expressed his thanks, and his determination to do his best for the common cause. "To the third part he showed that [he hoped there would be none] occasion to his brother the King of Arragon, which [should] force him and his friends to press him with such loss [and heavy] displeasure;" yet if he saw no other remedy, he would cause him to know that deceitful dealing among friends is worthy of great penance. Touching another article in the letter concerning the schismatic cardinals, the Emperor had not yet written in their favor; nevertheless, at some future communication he will tell the Emperor Henry's mind in that matter. Has received the Emperor's confirmation under the Great Seal, and signed with his hand. My Lady of Savoy has written many sharp letters for the recovery of the Emperor's licence for men of war of the Low Countries to serve "your grace;" saying, that if the same and the Emperor's confirmation were not sent shortly, there could no money be paid to the Emperor. Wherefore the Emperor caused another confirmation to be made, and sent to her with the licence for the men of war, in consideration of which Wingfield kept the copy in his hands, believing that "my Lady" [would give] the copy she had to "your grace." "Sire, with these I send unto your [grace] . . . . . . which hath been delayed by mean . . . . . never-theless by mean of the said D . . . . adventures as hath chanced, his letters . . . . . . be more ample and fruitful than . . . . dispatched or this." Sends also with these, tidings of the duchy of Milan, and such offers as are made by [the French] King to the Pope, and to his brother Julian. If Wingfield continues in his office he must have money, without which he cannot properly serve the King. Those that convey despatches in this court think the small gratuities he has given them during the past three years to be of [little account] in such great matters. Worms, 21 June 1513.

Pp. 6, much mutilated.

21 June. **4275.** For MORGAN COWDRAY of Langton Guylden, Dorset. Protection; going to the war. Westm., 21 June.

Fr. 5 Hen. VIII. m. 10.

1513.

22 June. **4276.**   SIR ROB. WINGFIELD to HENRY VIII.

Vitell. B. xviii. 53.
B. M.

Informed the King in his last that the Emperor had received a letter from his secretary resident with the Viceroy, affirming the [capture] of Milan, and also a letter from a captain of the Spaniards . . . . . . captains of Verona, both of which letters stated that Jacques de Trevulci was taken ; and one of these letters stated that Lord Tremoyle was slain, while the other asserted that he was taken. Both letters agreed that the Viceroy was determined to pros . . . . The Venetians had repassed the river Athi . . The letter from Rorarii stated that the V[iceroy] ordained that Fabricius Colonna with 4,000 spears [should] join with the Swiss to pass the mountains. Worms, [22 June] 1513. With a postscript.

Pp. 2, *mutilated.*

22 June. **4277.**   For WILLIAM TYLER.

P. S.

Wardship of Anne, daughter of John, the son and heir of Robert Tempest. Greenwich, 26 April 5 Hen. VIII. *Del.* Westm., 22 June.

Pat. 5 *Hen. VIII. p.* 2, *m.* 18.

22 June. **4278.**   For THOMAS VAULTER, a native of Normandy.

P. S.

Denization. Greenwich, 15 June 5 Hen. VIII. *Del.* Westm., 22 June.

22 June. **4279.**   GAOL DELIVERY.

Western Circuit.—Commission to Ric. Eliot, Lewis Pollard, and Thos. Eliot. Westm., 22 June.
Home Circuit. — Commission to John Boteler, John More, and Simon Fitz. Same date.
Northern Circuit. — Commission to William Fairefax, John Erneley, Robt. Henryson, and Thos. Stray. Same date.
Pat. 5 *Hen. VIII. p.* 1, *m.* 8*d.*

23 June. **4280.**   SPINELLY to HENRY VIII.

Galba, B. iii. 110.
B. M.

Wrote last the [20th] inst. Has received a letter from Sir Robt. Wingfield for the King, which he encloses. On the 3rd inst. sent a packet of letters to the King's ambassador. On the 17th it had not reached him, as he had left Awsburg, and a servant there put it in the wrong budget ; consequently it has come back again. Since the defeat at Novara it is said that Latrymoll and Sir John Jacques have fled. Sends a letter written by the Swiss to the Emperor, showing their dislike of the French. On the 5th the French, being at the siege of Novara, had beaten down the wall 30 fathoms—but hearing that succour was coming, removed their siege two English miles. These succours were 8,000 Swiss that entered Novara the same day, held a council, and resolved to attack the French at daybreak. The French with 4[00] lanceknights they had with them, made such obstinate resistance they were in doubt who should have the victory—they took many prisoners, much ordnance, and all the pavilions. A French captain, Monsr. de la Clee . . . . . ., was slain in Milan.—The Swiss have raised 15,000 more men. Barth. Dalbian has succoured the castle of Cremona, and slain Galleas Palavesyne, who had received

1513.

the city for the French. The troops of the Viceroy of Naples have killed 80 Venetian horse in a skirmish. The Addornes have entered Genoa for the French, and the Fregosys fled to the Isle of Corsica.—My Lady is very anxious for peace between the Emperor and the Venetians. Brussels, 23 June 1513. *Signed.*

Pp. 5, mutilated. Add.

23 June. **4281.** For WILLIAM SMYTH.

Protection ; going to the war. Westm., 23 June.

Fr. 5 Hen.VIII. m. 14.

25 June. **4282.** SIR ROB. WINGFIELD to HEN. VIII.

Vitell. B. xviii. 54.
B.M.

Wrote last . . . of this month [from] this city. Yesterday received a letter from Thomas Spynelly, " wherein appeared, where you . . . . lodged beside Bologne, and that your grace [would be] at Calais before the feast of St. John, and [that upon the] arrival of John Millett, one of the clerks of you[r grace's council] at Calais, with your twain payme[nts] . . . . Baptist de Taxsis should depart the 21st day of . . . . toward Gravelines, to receive the same." [Went] to show the Emperor the said tidings, as to . . . . of the King of Arragon ; about 8 o'clock, found means to speak with him. Enquired if the Emperor had any tidings [out] of Italy, "and he showed that as for the Viceroy he [had] nought ; for whereas he had the Venetians in [destruction] inevitable, he had let them go, so that the[y had made] a bridge over the Athis (Adige), and have done much [injury to the] cornys of Verona. And then somewhat he . . . . in speaking of the King of Arragon [saying that he was] surely advertised that he goeth a . . . . and that within three or . . . . answer continuing mine former opinion . . . . se, I modified the same according to the tenor [of your grace's] last letters to me, in the third part ; with which [he she]wid to be well pleased, and much beholden to your grace that ye had so friendly advertised him of your mind ; [and] in conclusion showed that he doubted not, but either the King of Arragon should change purpose, and reduce his mind and order to yours, or else he should may repent as other hath done, that hath refused their friends and joined with their enemies."

" Then he showed me that the Duke of Saxe should be here shortly, so that he trusted the Princes of the Empire would condescend to some good aid in these necessary affairs, and desired me that I should speak with all the Princes and move them to the same; which I showed to do with good will ; and so I departed from him at that time. This day, in the morning at 4 o'clock, the Emperor departed hence, of which no man was ware yestereven when it was late, and all his carriage is departed, so that it seemeth he will not return hither." He is to rest this night [fi]ve Duche miles hence, and tomorrow at Frankfort, where it is thought the Duke of Saxe will meet him, "and [if he] . . . find the said Duke favorable to his desire, he will [cause a diet] of the Princes to come thither or else to Colleyn . . . . will pass straight from thence to Brabant, and though so be he find . . . . that he assemble the said Duke with the p[rinces] . . . . . . he cause them to assemble in some . . . . as I can perceive himself intendeth . . . . his way to Bra-

1513.

bant."—"As for news from Italy they be confirmed of . . . .
. . . of pietons, howbeit the lands of Tremoyle and Trevo . . . . .
of the horsemen be fled into Alessandria, never . . . .
particularity worthy writing, is not yet kn[own]." Worms, June
1513.

Pp. 3. *Addressed.* *Endorsed:* "Sir Rob." *Much mutilated.*

25 June. **4283.**   CARDINAL BAINBRIDGE to HENRY VIII.

Vitell. B. II. 43.
B. M.

Wrote on the 11th (dated 10th) of the overthrow of the French
at Noware. Tremouille and Trivulce are not dead, as then stated.
The Swiss have imposed a fine upon Milan of 50,000 ducats, on
Pavia 40,000, on Lodi 30,000 for their rebellion against the Duke.
The Duke and the Swiss have entered Savoy and burned San Germano. They will cripple the Power of Savoy. The Duke has now
in his company Prosper Colonna. When Lewis first heard of the
rebellion of Genoa, and of the exclusion of the Duke put in by Pope
Julius, he boasted he would attack the English. Now all things
are contrary to his hopes. Genoa has returned to the Fregoses ;
their Duke has pursued the French. All who assisted the French
in Alexandria are slain or punished. Thinks the King should make
some confederation with the Swiss, who are anxious to join him in
his attack upon France, and that letters of thanks be sent to the
Cardinals St. George, Sinogalen, St. Vitall, and Sion, for their good
minds shown in the restitution of the schismatics Saint Cross and
St. Severin. The Pope sends the King two briefs confirming the
grants made to him by Pope Julius against the enemies of the
Church, and will keep the promise to the King, but he cannot yet
openly invade the French King, as he is bound by an oath to promote the peace of Christendom. He has written to the Scotch King,
threatening him, if he does not desist, to grant Henry a still harder
bull against Scotland. He has confirmed the interdict against that
realm. *Sends a copy of the proceedings against the schismatic
Cardinals, read on the x[vii.] of this month, in the 7th session of the
Lateran council. They shall be restored, but not without disgrace.
The Pope will never do anything for the absolution of France from
the interdict without consent of his confederates. Cardinal Hadrian falsely presumes on his services against the schismatics. The
Arragonese ambassador has informed him that Hadrian did divul-
gate amongst the cardinals things to his dishonor, 1. that the King
had crossed the sea, not to invade the enemies of the Church, but to
make peace ; 2. that no one had true tidings from England, except himself, by reason of his factor there, " named Polydorus, who, he said,
was body and soul to my Lord of Winchester." The Cardinal denies it, though it can be proved before his face. The Emperor's
army who kept the city of Verona against the Venetians, have
abandoned it for lack of pay. The Pope has promised the Viceroy
money to attack the Venetians. He and others have demanded of the
Pope that nothing should be done in the restitution of the schismatic
Cardinals without the consent of the confederates. Advises the
King not to receive the papal Legate that is to be sent to treat
for peace. It is only a show. All here have regard only to their
own honor and profit, " wherefore, I doubt not but that your grace
will do the same." The Bishop of Worcester is very active. Rome,
25 June 1513. *Signed.*

Mutilated, pp. 5. Add.

---

* The remainder of this letter is printed in Fiddes' Wol. C. 5.

1513.
25 June. **4284.**
Cleopat. C. v. 64.
B. M.

DIARY of JOHN TAYLOR, clerk of the Parliament.

i. Dedication to John Yong, master of the rolls.—Proposes to give a brief outline of events from the day of his arrival at Calais, 25 June 1513.

ii. On the 26th June was brought to Calais the body of Lord Carewe, killed by a gun-shot before Terouenne, and buried in the chapel of the Resurrection in the church of St. Nicholas.—On the 27th, 100 wagons with victuals and a garrison of 500 soldiers sent to the siege of Terouenne, were intercepted by the French near Ardes and the provisions carried off to Boulogne.—On the 28th, news came that 200 Englishmen were slain in the encounter, that the French had carried off their dead, whose number could not be ascertained, had stripped the bodies, and so mutilated their faces that it was difficult to tell which were English or which French; nevertheless 20 fine horses of the French were found dead on the field. Has seen some that were taken by the English in the fight in the market place of Calais, while the English did not lose a single horse.—On the 29th, St. Peter's day, strong wind and continued rain towards evening; all the ships driven into Calais harbour by a north wind. Northumberland and Darcy set out for Terouenne.—30th, saw from the walls of Calais the King coming with his fleet (such as Neptune never saw before); saluted with such firing of guns from the ships and from the towers, you would have thought the world was coming to an end;—conducted by a procession of the clergy to the church of St. Nicholas,—thence to his lodging by the nobles. Ambassadors arrive from the Emperor.

July. 1 July, the King heard mass in the church of St. Nicholas, and spent the afternoon with his councillors.—3rd July, the King ratified certified articles, in the presence of the Imperial ambassadors, at the high altar in St. Mary's church. Great pageantry. —4th July, the town of Whitsand betwixt Calais and Boulogne was almost entirely destroyed by fire, having submitted to the English on the first coming of the King's lieutenant, and afterwards plundered an English vessel driven upon their shores, and sent the crew prisoners to Boulogne. Just as was the punishment, every one was ashamed of the victory. Thinks the Almighty did not approve of it, for that night a terrible storm wrecked five vessels before their eyes, the crews of which perished after long struggling with the waves.—8th July, St. Thomas' day, came three ambassadors; viz, the chief officers of Ghent and Bruges, with a man of letters from Lord Fynys, Governor of Flanders, to the King, who was practising archery in a garden with the archers of his guard. He cleft the mark in the middle, and surpassed them all, as he surpasses them in stature and personal graces. The ambassadors remained ten days.—16th, Lords Lisle, Darcy, Willoughby, Essex, Sir Wm. Sandes, Sir Maurice Berkeley, and 7,000 horse and foot, left Calais to prepare the way for the King.—On the 17th arrived ambassadors from the Duke of Brunswick, more I think to do themselves good than us.—On the 21st, the King left Calais with a magnificent army increased by 8,000 German mercenaries. Sir Henry Marney's leg was broken by the kick of a horse. Pitched their camp that night at Frodon near Calkwell, a place well fortified by nature with an impassable marsh on their left, and their artillery on the right. Such heavy rains fell in the afternoon and night, that the tents could scarcely protect them. The King did not put off his clothes, but rode round at 3 in the

1513.
25 June.

Taylor's Diary.

morning comforting the watch—saying " Well, comrades, now that
we have suffered in the beginning, fortune promises us better things,
God willing." Came on the 23rd to Hamswel.—On the 25th, pitched
their camp in the enemy's land near Ardes ; that night the town
was nearly consumed by fire. At day-break an alarm was raised
that the French were at hand, for that day some citadels were
mischievously burned by the Germans, who did not respect the
churches. The King had 3 of them hanged that night. The King
had 12 guns of unusual magnitude — each cast with the image
of an apostle. One of them got upset in a pond ; 100 workmen
were sent to get it out, but, owing to their negligence in not
setting a guard, they were attacked by the French, who killed
or wounded most of them. Pitched their camp that night near
Dornham. Had the French preoccupied it, might have sustained
considerable injury.—Next morning were called to arms. The fog
was so dense they could scarce see each other. The King drew up
his army in person, and arranged the places for the artillery,
awaiting an attack from the French, who were said to be near ;
heard their spy had been slain, and the French decamped. Marched
3 miles, get sight of French, when a Frenchmen challenged an
Englishman to single combat. Encounters on all sides :—a pleasant sight, if a man's skin had not been in hazard. The French fled
before Sir Rice ap Thomas. In the skirmishes that day fell one
Englishman and 20 French ; the army much fatigued with
the long march and the heat. News that provisions sent from
Calais had been intercepted.—On the 29th the Earl of Essex and
Sir Rice ap Thomas with 300 Burgundian horse, a body of German
foot, and some archers, were sent to recover the guns, for the
French had taken another of the apostles.—Account of the engagement. The French never expose themselves.

Aug.

1st August, pitched the camp at the first mile stone before Therouenne — heavy rain in the night, which lasted day and night
following, with violent wind ; the soldiers up to their knees in
mud. Some of the besieged made a sally and escaped,—there never
passed a day but they did some damage to the English. The
French cut off the stragglers, and are always on the alert.—4th
August, joined the besieging army.—5th, important secrets revealed
by a deserter.—On the 8th called to arms. A stradiot brought in
prisoner. The French did considerable injury from a powerful
rampart covered with turf, called the green rampart.—On the 9th,
two horsemen were taken by Lord Darcy ; being brought before
the King, they said a large force of French were fighting with the
Burgundians 2 miles off ;—a body of light horse were sent thither,
before whose arrival the French had slain the Sieur Barret ; pre-
sently they decamped. Sir Rice ap Thomas made 3 prisoners, but
lost 2 men. Heavy rains the whole night and the day following,
which injured a tent woven of gold and purple for the reception
of the Emperor Maximilian. Same day the King met the Emperor
at Are, had but a short interview on account of the badness of
the weather. On the following night a Herald from the King
of Scots exposed the perfidy of his master, declaring he would
invade England unless the King desisted from the invasion of
France. After a patient hearing, the King said he could not
easily believe that his brother of Scotland would break his solemn
oath, but if such were his intention, he doubted not he should
repent it. This day the Bp. of Winchester was much hurt by the
kick of his mule ; for some days he could neither sit nor stand.—
12th August, the weather improved ; the Emperor visited the

1513.
25 June.

Taylor's Diary.

trenches, and returned the next morning to Are. He is of middle height, with open and manly countenance ; pallid complexion ; has a snub nose, and a grey beard. Is affable, frugal, an enemy to pomp. His attendants are in black silk or woollen. — On Assumption day a fray took place between the Germans and the English, in which many were killed on both sides. The same evening their Majesties determined to advance the camp beyond the stream. Next day at dawn, as soon as the camp had been moved, an alarm was given that the French were at hand ; they· were seen from the top of a hill. Description of the battle of Bomy (*Spurs*). Prisoners taken : Duke of Longueville, Louis Marquis of Rotelyn, Lord Cleremount vice-admiral of France, Lord Bayar lieut. of the Duke of Lorraine (*a page left blank for the other names*). A quarrel arose between the English and Burgundians about the prisoners.—On Sunday, 21st August, moved the camp from the east to the west side of Therouenne. A report spread that the French had sent victuals to the besieged—part of the prisoners sent to Are for safe custody. Afterwards the more important of them to England.— 22nd, Lord Mountremy (Pont-dormy), chief captain of the besieged, sent a messenger to demand a parley, and terms were agreed upon for the surrender of the town. Lord Talbot appointed captain. Next day, St. Bartholomew's eve, the garrison left the town, and passed through the King's camp in sight of the two generals to the number of 4,000— such soldiers as any prince would wish to have. On St. Bartholomew's day their Majesties entered Therouenne with great pomp. There is nothing worth mention in Therouenne, except the Cathedral. Description of it and situation of the town. One so fortified with ramparts and mines no age ever saw before. It was determined to demolish them.—On the 27th, the demolition commenced ; a violent storm in the night—many of the tents injured. The 29th, four English-men went to Are, raised some disturbance in the town, two of them, being brothers, were hanged, the other two, also brothers, were sent back to the tents.

Sept.

About this time news arrived from England that the Scotch had besieged Norham, and invaded England, not without great damage to themselves. Having blown up the fortifications of Therouenne, by gunpowder, the camp removed on the 6th September. As the city belonged to the House of Burgundy, Lord Talbot promised it to the Emperor, whose soldiers cruelly destroyed it by fire. Slept that night at a place called Malenous, where news came that the King of Scots had taken Norham, and wasted the country. Next night, at Ferthyng in the dominion of Sieur de Bruere—next night at Verkamen—the next at old Vendome near the bridge, a place well fortified by nature with an impassable marsh divided by a narrow causeway a quarter of a mile long, with room for one carriage only. —The next march was over six miles of equally difficult ground. Came on the 12th of September to Lille, a place having much the appearance of an island in the middle of a marsh, which the King entered with as much pomp as ever he did at Westminster with his crown on, to visit Lady Margaret of Savoy. The people crowded out of the town to meet him in such numbers you would have thought none had been left behind ; girls offered crowns, sceptres, and garlands ; outlaws and malefactors with white rods (*virgubas*) in their hands besought pardon. Between the gate of the town and the palace the way was lined with burning torches, altho' it was bright day, and there was scarce room for the riders to pass.—Tapestries were hung from the houses, a tent erected at frequent intervals, where

R R

histories of the Old and New Testament and of the poets were acted. The Emperor sent the King a great bull as a present. Taylor saw nothing worth notice in it except its unwieldy size. At this time Lord Lynye, captain of Burgundians, submitted to the King, and received the Castle of Morteyn—which was next day taken from him by some Germans under Lord Walayn ; the case was referred to the council.—On the 15th September pitched the camp near the walls of Tournay in a street (*in vico*) called Ork. That day Ponynges, Yong, and Sir Rob. Wingfield had an interview with the men of Tournay. A suspension of hostilities agreed to ; nothing came of it. Lord Talbot prepared to lay siege to the city.—Letters from the Queen of the defeat of the Scots.—The 17th, mass celebrated in a pavilion of gold and purple for the victory, and Te Deum sung : Bp. of St. Asaph preached.—The 21st, confirmation of the news of the defeat of James IV., by a messenger, who brought the Scotch King's plaid (*paludiamentum seu tunicam*) with the royal arms upon it. Reflexions on his fall.

To batter down the iron gates and stone towers of Tournay, guns came from Lille of immense magnitude, enough to conquer by the very sight of them. On the 21st, before they were tried, the city submitted, and next day handed over the keys. Lord Lysle, chief marshal of the army, was made Governor.—On the 24th, the King entered it, met by the chief men of the city—their horses and mules having the English ensigns painted on paper before them. At the first gate the King passed under a canopy of gold and silk prepared by the citizens, and carried by six of the principal burgesses —others attending bearing wax torches conducted him to the Cathedral, where after service the King made several knights. After dinner in the market place a deputy chosen by the citizens offered the city, its inhabitants, and their goods, to Henry, on which the people shouted *Vive le Roi.* That day appeared in the sky a clear sun, a pale moon, and a bright star, which Taylor rose from dinner to look at. Next night the Emperor, Lady Margaret, and a splendid suite of ladies in chariots, with gentlemen on horseback, entered the city by torchlight.

Refrain from describing this magnificent city of Tournay, with its river Schalde, which Cæsar mentions by the same name ; its bridges, water-mills, and splendid buildings ; no one can conceive its beauty who has not seen it. On the 4th October news arrived that the only child of the King of Scots had been crowned King. On the 5th, Ponynges was appointed Lieutenant of Tournay. On the 10th the Prince of Castile, a boy of great promise, was received into the city with great pomp. Next day tournaments were held in the public place, but injured by the rains. The King and Lord Lisle challenged all comers—the King excelled every one as much in agility and in breaking spears, as in nobleness of stature. The 13th, after knighting several persons, left Tournay, where they were contracting great expenses, and the soldiers had remained too long inactive. That night came to Lille with the Archduke and Lady Margaret, and staid there three days.—Left on the 17th. On the preceding night was a new kind of tournament. "In quodam enim amplo et oblongo triclinio per multos gradus a terrâ elevato ac quadrato lapide nigro marmori simillimo strato equites egregie armati lanceis concurrerunt. Quorum equi ne pede laberentur vel nimio sonitu colliso pavimento perstreperent loco ferri thomate vel feltro armabantur. Effractis lanceis ensibus præacutis digladiabatur." — The following night the King came to Ypres and rested at the monastery of St. Benedict. Thence to Bergues, the

1513.
25 June.

Taylor's Diary.

roads being excessively heavy. Here is a monastery founded in honor of St. Gwinocus, son of a certain King of England, in which is buried the body of St. Oswald the King. That day a French prisoner named Ruyaulx escaped. On the 19th came to Calais, where they lost much time, as no vessels were ready. Were attended thither by the Marquis of Banborogh (Brandenburg), Counts Nassau and Isylstyne, Lord Wallayne, and the Bastard Aymery.— On the 21st the King embarked for England, leaving a council to govern the borders.—The day he came to Calais the French burned a church named Pitta.

During this whole journey the Emperor shewed the greatest condescension, declaring publicly that he came to be of use to the King of England, and calling the King at one time his son, at another his King, and at another his brother. When they entered Therouenne together the King of England alone carried a flag of triumph before him—and in the Cathedral the Emperor yielded to him the place of honor, returning afterwards to Are like a private person. He also put off for some days his entry into Tournay, that he might not detract from the King of England's glory. The army was very fortunate in having fine weather on marching days, although at night, and when the camp stood still, there were great storms, which spoiled the tournaments at Tournay and the day of St. Luke. One thing must be noted to be guarded against in future : English money, which greatly excels foreign coinage in value, was recklessly thrown away, thus occasioning a great loss.

Lat., pp. 64, small quarto. Corrected by Taylor.

25 June.
S. B.

4285. For THOMAS ARCHER, late of Theydon, alias of [W]rittyll, Essex.

Protection for one year ; going in the retinue of Sir Gilbert Talbot, Deputy of Calais. *Del.* 25 June 5 Hen. VIII.
Fr. 5 Hen. VIII. m. 15.

25 June.
Harl. 6,064, f. 67.
B. M.

4286. TEROUENNE.

The summons of the city of Terevan, "made the 25 day of June," 5 Hen. VIII., by Bluemantle pursuivant.
Modern copy.

27 June.
Vitell. B. II. 47.
B. M.

4287. HADRIAN CARDINAL ST. CHRISOGON to HENRY VIII.

Had already written of the preparations of the French for war ;— of their defeat by the Swiss ;—of the Spaniards in Lombardy ;—of the attempts of the Venetians against the city . . . . ;—of the siege of Verona, and the efforts of the Pope to restore order. In the last sessions of the Lateran, a note was read from two cardinals (*patres*) at Florence, professing their adherence to the Council. They started a few days after from Florence ; entered Rome without the insignia of the Cardinalate ; passed the night in the same chamber, and were next day brought to the Consistory, without rochet and hat. Like private persons they approached the Pope through a great crowd, with three genuflexions, confessed their error, asked for pardon, and, abjuring the schism, were absolved by the Pope, who restored to them the red hat, rochet, cape, and pileus, admitting them to kiss his feet. Rome, 27 June 1513.
Signed.
Lat., pp. 3. Add.

1513.

27 June.
R. O.
4288. **LEO X.** to **HENRY VIII.**

On this day, the 27 June, restored to their rank as Cardinals Bernard Carvajal and Frederic de Sancto Severino, on acknowledgment of their errors. Is glad to have restored to the bosom of the Church two such principal members. They had subscribed and read a schedule in the Lateran Council in testimony of their adherence, and a few days after, in the Consistory at Rome, confessed their errors and asked pardon. Sends a copy of their absolution and restitution. Rome, 27 June 1513, 1 pont.

Lat., p. 1. *Add.*

27 June.
P. S.
4289. For **JOHN VEYRERI,** "Nemausen. ex regione linguæ Auxitanæ," chief surgeon of the Body.

Denization for him and his heirs male. Greenwich, 31 May 5 Hen. VIII. *Del.* Westm., 27 June.

Pat. 5 Hen. VIII. p. 1, *m.* 17.

27 June.
4290. For **THOS. CROSSE** of London, grocer.

Protection; going in the suite of Sir Gilbert Talbot, Deputy of Calais. Westm., 27 May.

Pat. 5 Hen. VIII. p. 1, *m.* 10.

28 June.
S. B.
4291. To **JOHN YONG,** Master of the Rolls, or his deputy.

To cancel two recognizances of 240 marks, dated 10 July 23 Hen. VII.; 1st, made by John Foggis of Asshetford, Kent, Sir Mathew Brown of Becheworthe, Surrey, and John Norton of Norwode, Kent; 2d, by the said John Foggis, Rauf Seyntleger of Ulcombe, and Richard Lee of Maydeston, Kent. Castle of Dover, 28 June 5 Hen. VIII.

28 June.
4292. For **RIC. BEAUMOUNT** of Whitley, Yorkshire.

Protection; setting out to the war. Westm., 28 June.

Fr. 5 Hen. VIII. m. 12.

28 June.
P. S.
4293. For **JOHN HANSTEDE,** wax-chandler of London.

Protection for one year; going in the suite of Sir Gilbert Talbot, Deputy of Calais. Dover Castle, 28 June 5 Hen. VIII.

28 June.
4294. For the **DEAN AND CANONS OF ST. GEORGE'S COLLEGE WINDSOR CASTLE.**

Custody of the manors of Knapton, Norf., Cillysworthe, Suff., and Benfeldbury, Essex, during the minority of John Veer, kinsman and heir of John Earl of Oxford. Westm., 28 June.

Pat. 5 Hen. VIII. p. 1, *m.* 16.

29 June.
S. B.
4295. For **RICHARD** the **PRIOR,** and the **CONVENT OF ST. JOHN, PONTEFRACT.**

Charter to hold a fair for three days every year, beginning on the eighth day after the feast of the Purification, in the town of Barnesley, Yorkshire. *Del.* Westm., 29 June 5 Hen. VIII.

1513.

29 June. **4296.** SPINELLY to [HENRY VIII.]

Galba, B.iii. 115.
B. M.

Wrote last on the 25th. Has received a packet from Germany, and a letter from Sir Robt. Wingfield, with sundry news. If the Swiss enter Dauphiny the French King will not be able to withdraw his troops. The Emperor will pay 48,000 gold florins to the Swiss under Lord Bergy. Hears from Jakys de Banisius that 600 spears of the Pope and Florentines have entered Pleasaunce. The former have sent 22,000 ducats to the Viceroy of Naples. The French King has promised the Pope's brother his kinswoman in marriage, with a rent of 30,000 ducats to procure the Pope's amity, to abolish the council, and renounce the prematica. Sends a minute of the communications between Madame and the ambassadors of Arragon. She shewed Spinelly a paper, saying " that the King of Arragon is a great wise Prince, and . . . . and that in his subtle understanding is comprised many profound matters which cannot be enpace unto any . . . . but that his intent and mind is good." Spinelly answered, he thought so, but that the King of England ought to be made privy to it, when the King of Arragon practised with his enemies. The letter for the King is sent to Armostorf and Symon de Ferret, with two from Milan from Andrew de Berges.—Sends a copy of one, and an abstract of the other, in English.—She still urges the accommodation with the Venetians ; and desires the King would retain 1,000 foot and 200 horse of the Duke of Brunswick, now at liberty. Nothing has been said of the carrack, as Tousaynt Dor is not arrived. The Lord of Nassaw is at Bumbill. The Lord Reux speaks highly of the King's army. Pyenys and Delapalys have sent to Eden that they should deal lovingly with my Lord Prince's subjects. The Emperor is expected shortly. Brussells, 29 June 1513. *Signed.*

ii. " News [sent] by my Lady of Savoy un[to Thomas] Spinelly, which she hath understood of the [ambassador] of Arragon." A courier has come by France from the King his master with letters dated Vagladolyt, 12th of [June], on which the Arragonese envoy left the French court. The French state that my Lady would not allow the King of England to have any aid out of her country ; at which he is surprised, and exhorts her to assist England. Begs her to urge the King of England, for whom he has great affection, to use his (King of Arragon's) counsel. Much disliked the prosperity of the French in Italy, expecting they would send the second son of King Frederick into the realm of Naples. Is ready to attack Berne, whenever the King's army sets forth. Assents to the alliance between the Princess Mary and the Prince of Castile, and whatever will advance the amity of England.

Pp. 7, mutilated.

29 June. **4297.** For THOS. SENAWGH.

To be controller of the customs in the port of Breggewater ;— the office to be performed in person. Westm., 29 June.

Pat. 5 Hen. VIII. p. 2, m. 18.

30 June. **4298.** For MILES GERARDE.

S. B.

Licence to export 100 sacks of wool. *Del.* Westm., 30 June 5 Hen. VIII.

Fr. 5 Hen. VIII. m. 7.

30 June. **4299.** For THOMAS VAUGHAN, late bailiff of Dover.

S. B.

Pardon. *Del.* Westm., 30 June 5 Hen. VIII.

Pat. 5 Hen. VIII. p. 1, m. 17.

1513.
30 June.   **4300.**   For ROBERT ROBYNSON, barber, alias sherman, of London,
S. B.   alias of Estham, Essex.

      ' Exemption from serving on juries, being made collector, assessor, justice of the peace, or other commissioner ; &c. *Del.* Westm., 30 June 5 Hen. VIII.

30 June.   **4301.**   For WILLIAM COMPTON.
S. B.

      To be keeper of the park of Hastley, Warw., with all fees, as held by Rowland Stafford ; keeper of Grome Park, and bailiff of Budbroke, alias Hampton-on-the-Hyll, with annuity of 3*l.* out of the issues of the same ; keeper of Berkeswell park; bailiff of the manor of Berkeswell, as held by Edward Gryffyth ; to hold 18 acres of meadow in Bereford, in the lordship of Warwick, 11 in Brodham and Oxlease, and 18 acres of meadow adjoining, at a yearly rent of 5*l.* ; also a pasture in the said lordship called "le Felde," subject to an annual rent of 10*l.* ;—to be keeper of Hendley park, Surrey, as held by William Coop, at a stipend of 6*d.* a day, with herbage, &c. ; also grant of the manor of Cleygate, subject to an annual rent of 11*l.* 1*s.* 4*d.* ; of the manor of Worplesdon, subject to an annual rent of 17*l.* 12*s.*;—and to be keeper of the manor of Wokyng, Surrey, with 2*d.* a day ; with a meadow called "Puremede," in Wokyng, subject to an annual rent of 3*l.* *Del.* Westm., 30 June 5 Hen. VIII.

      Pat. 5 *Hen. VIII. p.* 1, *m.* 15. Partly vacated 8 Feb. 8 Hen. VIII.

30 June.   **4302.**   For WILLIAM COMPTON.
S. B.

      Reversion in fee of the manors of Tottenham, Penbrokes, Bruses, Dawbeneyes, and Mokkynges in Tottenham, Middlesex, and of all other lands and tenements in Tottenham, Edelmeton, and Enfeld, Middlesex, formerly belonging to Richard Turnant, afterwards to Sir John Rysley, or Thomasina his wife, d. and heir of the said Richard; granted to the said William by act of parliament, 4 Feb. 3 Hen. VIII. *Del.* Westm., 30 June 5 Hen. VIII.

      Pat. 5 *Hen. VIII. p.* 1, *m.* 21.

30 June.   **4303.**   For WILLIAM FITZWILLIAM, and MABEL CLYFFORD his
S. B.   intended wife.

      Grant of the manor and advowson of Yoxhall, Staff., a pasture called "le Carres, Newclose, and Tenacurre," a water-mill in the town, and a pasture called Halorchard adjoining the said mill, parcel of the manor of Yoxhall, lately belonging to Francis Viscount Lovel, and attainted and granted by Hen VII. to Thomas Wolton, deceased, in tail male ; on whose death without such issue they came again into Hen. VII.'s hands ;—to hold the same to the said William and Mabel in tail male ;—also grant of an annual rent of 44*l.*, payable by Robert Ordern, for the above premises, granted him on lease for 21 years by patent 24 Sept. 23 Hen. VII.; to have the same for the remainder of the said term ;—and grant, in survivorship, of annuity of 100*l.*, payable at the receipt of the hanaper. *Del.* Westm., 30 June 5 Hen. VIII.

      Pat. 5 *Hen. VIII. p.* 2, *m.* 7.

30 June.   **4304.**   LEWIS MAROTON to the MAITRE DES POSTES.
R. O.

      The Tyrolese pay 5,000 foot soldiers and 40,000 florins d'or, and have started against the Venetians. Begs he will advertise the Sieur de Berghes of the same. Frankfort, 30 June '13.

      Hol., Fr., p. 1. *Add.*

1513.

30 June. **4305**. LEWIS MAROTON to FRANCIS DE TAXIS, master of the
R. O. Posts.

Begs him to hand this letter (*ceste lettre*) to De Berghes.
Thinks De Taxis has heard the news from his brother. The
Emperor is come to Frankfort to speak with the elector of Hesse.
Thinks that the "journée imperiale" will be successful. Begs he
will tell Spinelly that the money has been delivered. The Swiss
went into France 10 days since. The Emperor is informed that
the Viceroy "veult faire à la part aux porterons (poltrons ?) de
Venesse ;" if he do he will soon be destroyed. Frankfort, 30 June
n° 13.

Begs to be recommended to his nephew Baptiste.

Hol., Fr., p. 1. Add.

30 June. **4306**. WAR IN FRANCE.

Lansd. 818. f. 2 b. "The King's ward passing out of Calais, anno 1513, the last day
B. M. June."

1. Main body of the ordnance.—The Almains 1,500, Sir Maur.
Berkeley 100, Sir W. Sands 100, Sir Ric. Carew 100, Sir Edw. Ferrers 100, Geoffrey Goghe and Thos. ap Glinn (?) 120, Ralph Egerton
and the King's standard 100, the Lord Burgevenny 400, the Duke
of Buckingham 400, Mr. Almoner 200, the Bp. of Durham 100,
the Bp. of Winchester 100, the Trinity banner with the King's
household 300, the King's majesty and his banner with the guard
600, Sir Hen. Gilford 100, Sir Edw. Poynings 100, Will. Compton
200, Sir Andrew Windsor 100, pikes of the Lord Lisle 900, pikes
of the Duke of Buckingham 100, pikes of the Lord Burgany 100.
"All along the baggage meddled (mixed) with the ordnance."

2. Left wing—horse. "This wing of the Lord Darcy 1,500
men. Three ranks of archers, 200. Three ranks of bills, 200.
Three ranks of archers every rank, 200."

3. The same on the right wing under Lord Marney.

ii. The order the King shall keep dislodging from Calais towards
Terouenne and Tourney. N.B. The fore ward was passed before
under the conduct of the Viscount Lisle.

The middle ward. With the number of men, the King's chapel
and priests and his household, list of ordnance and guard, attendants.

The rear ward.—The Lord Chamberlain (Worcester) 1,067, the
Earl of Northumberland 500, the Earl of Wiltshire 519, the Earl
of Kent 508 ; the Lords Maltravers 100, Audeley 126, Zouche's
son 102, Dudley's son 200, La Warre's son 51, Dacres of the
South 120 ; Sirs John Hussey 340, Hen. Willoughby 123, John
Worbleton 201, Randolph Brereton 204, John Savage 204, Edw.
Carewe slain at Terouenne 102, Richd. Wentworth 104, David
Owen 103, Alex. Baynham 103, Rob. Dymok 54 ; Messieurs
Morgan 103, Edw. Bray 102, Arthur Hopton 103 ; the Baron
Curson 113, George St. Leger 100, Thos. Phelips 100, the Almain
foot 500, the horsemen strangers 1,000, the ordnance 900.

iii. An account of the King's march day by day from the
30 June 1513 to the entry into Lisle 11 Sept., containing "the
proclamation in the army," the summons of Tournay, a chanson of
5 stanzas beginning—

> "Que ne vous rendrez
> Povres Theourneoys ?"

1513.

the safe-conduct given to the deputies of Tournay, the surrender of the city, "the names of the prisoners sent from the King's field unto Ayre, and committed to the governance of Sir John Peche, accompanied by Garter and Mr. Iden, clerk of the council."
Pp. 14.　*Copy.**

June.　**4307.**　The KING'S RETINUE.

Faustina, E. vii. 6.
B. M.

A list of nobleman [who went over with the King to Calais] with the numbers [of their retinues]. Headed "The King's ward."

The Viscount Lisle 900 — The Lord Darcy 400—The Marquis [Dorset] 300—Sir Wm. Sandes 100—Sir Maurice Berkeley 100—Sir Richd. Carew 100—Sir Nicholas Vaus 100 — Sir Tho. Aparre 100—Edwd. Ferers 100—Egerton with the King's standard 100—The Lord Daubeney 100—The Lord Burgeveny 500 —The Duke † of Buckingham 500—Sir Henry Guldeford 100— The Banner of the Household, with the company assigned thereto, 800—The King with his guard 600—Sir Edwd. Ponynges 500— The Lord Willughby 200—Willm. Compton 400—Edwd. Belknap 200—Sir Henry Wyot 100— Sir Tho. Boleyn 100—Sir John Seymour 100—Edward Hungerford 100—Sir Andrew Wyndesore 100 —Maynwaring 100—Askue and Hansard 100—Sir Tho. Lucy 66— John Nevell 30—Spearsmen 1,000—. . . . Pole 100—Sir Adrian Fortescue 50—Sir John Reynesford 100—Godfrey Fuljambe 100— John Vere 100—Sir Henry Marney's son 800— ‡the Earl of Essex 400, *struck out*—John Fortescue 50—Harcourt 6—Smythe 50— Baryngton 12—Barantyne 12—Leynham (?) 7—Walleden (?) 13— Sir Harry Clifford 60—Total, 9,466 men, besides the Lord Barners with the gunners, and pioneers, and Almaynes, and the spears on horseback, &c.‡

Two notes in the margin—one in English the other in Latin— but so mutilated as to be unintelligible.
P. 1, *mutilated.*

June.　**4308.**　The SPANISH AMBASSADOR to MADAME.

Galba, B. iii. 118b.
B. M.

Begs her to write to the King of England on the subjects proposed.
Sp., p. 1.
This is probably the letter referred to in Spinelly's letter of the 29th June.

June.　**4309.**　ARMY.

Rot. Reg.
14 B. xli.
B. M.

" An estimate of all man[ner . . . .] of an army royal by land to pass over the sea with the King's most royal [person, with] retinues of horsemen to be retained in the parties of Flanders to serve his highness [and the Emperor against his] most ancient enemy the French King."

Coats and conduct money, outward and homeward, for 26,000 English foot, including 260 captains, etc. (every coat 40d.) ; their wages and diets ;—wages of Almains ;—of horsemen to be retained in Flanders ; wagons for victuals ; transports.

Total, 292,689l. 6s. 4d.

---

* At p. 27 of this volume occurs this note in the same hand :—" 15th Dec. 1584, taken out of the book that I borrowed of Mr. Stowe, which he had of Clarenceux, which book was Thomas Wrythesley's alias Garter."
† " of Buckingham," in Wolsey's hand.　　‡ Added in Wolsey's hand.

1513.

2. Charges of a garrison of 980 men for the defence of Calais for 6 months, 4,620*l.*

3. Charges for defence against Scotland, 47,460*l.*

4. Coats and conduct outward of the army by sea, 1,461*l.* 2*s.*

5. Wages, victuals, &c.

Grand total, 372,404*l.* 18*s.* 8*d.*

A paper roll.

On the dorse : " Memorandum to move the Lady Margaret for bearing of the charges, during the King's wars beyond sea, of— Almains, 3,000 ; horsemen, 3,000."

June.

Rot. Reg.
14 B. xii.
B. M.

4310. ARMY.

" Wages appointed by the King and his council for the master of the ordnance, and all other officers, artificers, gunners, and laborers of the King's rear-ward :"

Master of the ordnance, my Lord Carson ; wages by day ——— (*blank*) ; with 4 councillors and 4 clerks at his nomination ; treasurer of the ordnance, appointed by the King's council, 2*s.* per day; controller, provost, purveyor, &c. — The master trenchermaker's wages " as it was by Sir Robert Dymmokk's book."

June.

R. O.

4311. WOLSEY'S MEMORANDA.

Headed : " For the King's shipping at Hampton and the charges thereof."

1. The tondage of 50 ships to come from Spain, and victuals for 3 months, 8,000*l.*—2. As many transports of like portage for the King, and 10,000 men, 8,000*l.*—3. 132 ships of from 60 to 100 tons, for conveying victuals from the Thames to Hampton for 3 months, 3,500*l.*—4. Victuals for the King and 10,000 men for 2 months, 8,600*l.*—5. Conduct money to Hampton, and thence to Dover, 1,200*l.*—6. The retinue to be divided—the horse to go to Dover, the foot to Hampton.—7. The loss of time in taking shipping for lack of wind.—8. The like danger on the King's return.—9. " To remember the sickness that now is in Brest."— 9. All these expences uncertain. — 10. " To know the King's resolute answer in the p[remises]."

ii. *On the back :* " To write to Coplond for the sending of the satin for the King's " (*sic.*)—2. To make a letter to my Lord Cardinal [Bainbridge] for the Bp. of Worcester." — 3. " Item another to my said Lord."

In Wolsey's hand, pp. 2. *Endd.*

June.

4312. ABP. WARHAM to HENRY VIII.

Stating that in a convocation of his province held at St. Paul's, 6 Feb. to the 17 Dec. 1511 following, for the extirpation of heresy &c., the clergy had granted the King 4 dismes,—the first to be paid on the Feast of St. Martin 1513; the second in 1514, &c. With certain provisoes. . . . June 1513.

Part illegible.

June.

R. O.

4313. WOLSEY to [SIR ROB.] DYMMOKE.

Has bargained with the bearer, John Van Esyll of Acon, for the carrying of the King's two great culverins with 28 mares, at 10*d.* a day for each mare.

Signed : "Thomas Wulcy."

Below, in another hand : "Notandum, that this warrant serroffes for the 4*l.* 13*s.* 4*d.* that John Van Essell had for 4 days wages for 28 mares at 10*d.* by the day for every mare."

1513.
June.
R. O.

4314. "THE MYDDLEWARDE."

"The names, with the retinue, of the lords, knights, and other noblemen now mustered." The King, with his horsemen, attendants, pages, and custodes. The King Spears with furniture and retinues; the King's guard, with yeomen gunners; the King's chapel, 115; the King's secretary of Latin, 5; the clerk of the King's Council; the King's wardrobe; grooms and pages of the Privy Chamber; the wardrobe of the King's beds; the clerks of the signet, with their retinues; the master of the posts, with the messengers, 14; the clerk of the Privy Seal, with his retinue; the auditor, with his servants; serjeants of arms, with their servants; the chamber, with knights and squires of the Body, gentlemen ushers, sewers, grooms, and pages, with Petre de Brecia [Carmelianus, luter; the King's henxemen; the King's trumpeter; the King's minstrels and players, 10; the King's toyle setters; artificers of the King's armoury; the King's household; the stables; petty captains of the guard, with their retinue; kings of arms, heralds and pursyvaunts; the King's bower and fletcher, with their retinues; the King's physician and surgeons, with their retinues, 31; the devisor of the King's artillery; the ordnance, with their retinue of the same.

John Nevyll; William Ascugh and William Hanserde; Sir Thomas Bolayne; Rauff Eggerton; Sir Thomas A. Parre; Sir Thomas Lucye; William Pole; Sir Adryan Fortescue; the Lord Marquis; the Lord Roosse; Godfrey Folyambe; Sir Henry Wyott; the Lord Barnes; William Compton; Sir Andrew Wyndesore; Arthur Plantagenett; Edward Ferrers; John Bere; Sir John Raynesforde; the Lorde Burgevenny; the Lord Lysle; the retinue of the serjeants of the King's tents; Richard Tempast; the Lord Darcie; the Bishop of Wynchestre; John Maynewaryng; the Bishop of Duresme; George Seyntleger; Sir Henry Marney; Master Almosyner; the Lorde Dawbeney; the Lord of Essex; Sir Edward Ponyngs.

"As yet not mustered nor paid in Daunce's Book."

The Duke of Buckingham; the Lord Willoughby; Sir John Saymere; Sir William Sandys; Sir Maurice Barkeley; Sir Nicholas Vaux; Sir Richard Carowe; M. Dalbye.

Total of the Middlewarde as afore specified, 14,032.

Roll. The numbers of all the items are given severally.

1 July.
P. S.

4315. For WILLIAM CORTENEY, squire of the Body.

To be lieutenant of the forest of Racche and keeper of the park of North Petherton, with the forest and chace adjoining, lately held by Sir Edmund Carrewe, deceased, formerly by Giles late Lord Dawbeney. Dover Castle, 28 June 5 Hen. VIII. *Del.* Westm., 1 July.

Pat. 5 Hen. VIII. p. 2, m. 17.

P. S.

2. Duplicate of the above. A fragment.

1 July.
S. B.

4316. For EDWARD GREGSON late of Fladeburg, Worc., alias late of Kirton, Devon, clk., and JAMES GREGSON late of Kirton.

Pardon for all trespasses against vert and venison; and of the judgments obtained against them in the Common Pleas by Hugh Bp. of Exeter.

Pat. 5 Hen. VIII. p. 2, m. 17. Westm., 1 July.

1513.

1 July. **4317.** GAOL DELIVERY.

Norfolk Circuit.—Commission to Sir John Fyneux, Sir Rob. Reed, and Wm. Mordaunt. Westm., 1 July.

Pat. 5 Hen. VIII. p. 1, m. 8d.

1 July. **4318.** GEORGE EARL OF SHREWSBURY to HENRY VIII.
R. O.

Received his letters dated Canterbury, 21 June, complaining of his having taken certain munition, &c. for the vanguard which had been appointed for the rereward, and blaming Sir Sampson Norton for permitting it. Is ordered to restore them to Lord Herbert. Sends enclosed a list of artillery now before Terouenne. The Lord Walleyn has six of the serpentines. Obliged to make their field strong with carts. Has sent the horses and traces of one mount to Calais. Had seen no other book of provision, except Morland's. Anthy. Nele, the bearer, will explain. Tyrwyn, 1 July.

Pp. 2. Add. End.: " My Lord Stuard's letters."

3 July. **4319.** THOMAS SPINELLY to HENRY VIII.
R. O.

Wrote last on the 29th June. Received his letters of the same date on the 1st. Presented his despatches to my Lady, who has sent a gentleman, named Azne, who left yesterday, to the Duke of Brunswick, persuading him to enter the King's service. The Duke has compounded for his service in Flanders at 36,000 gold guilders. It is supposed the Emperor will retain him as commander of the Swiss. The Count of Nassau retains 104 score of the Duke's horsemen for 8 gold guilders a month each. Lord Walham has been disappointed in a similar arrangement. The Duke's foot are gone to the Bp. of Luke to arrange with the French commissioners. Will make no arrangement till they hear from England. My Lady would be very glad if the Duke were retained in the English service, as he is a most expert, wise, and hardy prince. She thinks that the importance of the enterprise is above the consideration of expense. The Duke of Gueldres has sent for a safe conduct. It is thought he will assent to the truce. My Lady and my Lord Bergis advise the King of England to retain the Lord d'Issilsteyne for provision of 1,000 horse. They are glad of the favorable letters from England to the Venetians for the peace between the Emperor and the latter. Yesterday received a letter of the King's arrival at Calais. My Lady has written to the Emperor of it, and shown the news to my lord Prince. She sent for the ambassador of Arragon to advertise his master of it, and enjoin the performance of the enterprise of Berne. Spinelly is to advertise Cardinal York of the news. Received from her a letter of the Lord Royse, governor of Eden, concerning the damages done by the English to the Prince of Castile's subjects near St. Thomas. Begs notification may be sent to all captains not to make enemies of their friends. She has heard out of Burgundy the Lord Verge has a band of horse. Another in Ferrett is raised for the Emperor. Brussels, 3 July 1513. *Signed.*

Pp. 6. The two portions found apart. Addressed.

4 July. **4320.** ORDER IN COUNCIL.
Rym. XIII. 372. from Claus. 5 H. VIII. 2d.

As the King on Thursday, June 30, took passage at Dover, and arrived at Calais 7 o'clock of the evening the same day, during his

1513.

absence the teste of all patents &c. shall run, *Teste Katherina Angliæ Regina,* &c. 4 July.

4 July.
P. S.

4321. For JOHN TURNOR and ROBERT BROWNE.

To be bailiffs and receivers in survivorship of the lordship and manor of Ailewarton and Pensaunce, Cornw., parcel of the lands and possessions of Alianora late Countess of Somerset, now in the King's hands ; in as ample manner as the said John held the offices temp. Hen. VIII.;—to be keepers of the mansion or hospice called Warwike's Inne, in the city of London, and receivers general of the possessions of the said Alianora called Coopercionarslandes ;—to hold the said offices from the first day of the reign. Greenwich, 15 June 5 Hen. VIII. *Del.* Westm., 4 July.

Pat. 5 Hen. VIII. p. 1, m. 18, and p. 2, m. 30. Teste Regina.

5 July.
Galba, B. III. 119.
B. M.

4322. SPINELLY to HENRY VIII.

Wrote last on the 3rd. The messenger sent to the Duke of Brunswick found he had left Antwerp, and would not follow him to Maestrich for fear of the Gueldrois.—Thinks as he has got so far he will not be willing to return. Ambassadors from Gueldres are daily expected. The Emperor is at Frankfort ; this will delay Berghis coming. The Duke of Brunswick's foot are negotiating with the French commissioners in Luke.—Differret and Armystorf have written of their kind reception in England. The governor of Betton has written to the governor of Bresse, that the English " being before Torraana make but easy their skultwacchis, and also that the Welchmen have done great hurt thereabouts to my Lord Prince's subjects." She has ordered Lord Fenys to advertise the King of all news from France. Encloses two letters from Loys Moraton, and an extract of one written by himself to the Cardinal of York. Brussels, 5 July 1513. *Signed.*

Pp. 3, mutilated. Add.

July.
Galba, B.VI. 160.
B. M.

4323. SPINELLY to the CARDINAL OF YORK [BAINBRIDGE.]

Is glad he has recovered from his illness. Trusts the Pope will continue to favor Henry's enterprise against the enemies of the Church, though my Lady of Savoy is informed that the French are endeavouring to win him over to a general peace, with view of attacking the infidels ; they are making use of the Florentines in France for that purpose. Jacomo Salviati, the Pope's brother-in-law, who is their ambassador at Florence, has agents at Lyons. Bainbridge knows the Cardinal of Volterra is inclined to the French. Thinks he will not openly favor them, on account of the opposition between his house and that of the Medici. Considering what injuries they have done to that house, cannot believe the Pope will have any intelligence with the French. As already stated, two things are to be chiefly insisted upon ; 1st, that the Swiss shall invade Dauphiny; and 2ndly, that the Pope shall make peace between the Venetians and the Emperor. The Bishop of Luke has been all along leaning to the French, and is doing his best to get them men. The King landed at Calais on Thursday last with his army royal.

Copy, pp. 3, mutilated. Headed: "An . . . . Spinelly to my Lord Cardinal of York."

1513.

5 July. **4324.** PETER MARTYR to LUDIVICO FURTATO.

Pet. Mart. Epist.
No. 524.

He will remember, Peter Martyr wrote to him on a previous occasion that when Henry the late King of England had the Archduke Philip in his power he exacted a promise from him. There was a certain duke of Suffolk named Emond de la Pulla (Edmund De la Pole) of the great nobility in England, sprung of the fourth daughter of King Edward. He was shut up in the tower; was much in debt; fled into Burgundy, returned, resumed his old habits, and fled a second time to Gueldres; came into the hands of Philip on the conquest of that duke; and was delivered by him to Henry VII., but on condition confirmed by oath that his life should be spared. Henry his successor, has ordered him to be put to death because he held correspondence with Richard De la Pole his brother, an exile in France, and commander of the French fleet, for a rising in England.

5 July. **4325.** For HENRY POLE, son and heir of Sir Richard Pole.

P. S.

Livery of lands : viz. the manors of Ellesborough and Medmynham, Bucks, and elsewhere. Greenwich, 14 June 5 Hen. VIII. *Del.* Westm., 5 July.

Pat. 5 Hen. VIII. p. 1, m. 19. Teste Regina.

6 July. **4326.** SPINELLY to HENRY VIII.

Galba, B. III. 121.
B. M.

Wrote last yesterday. Letters have come from my Lord of York to the master of the posts, which Spinelly forwards. News has come from Verona of the 28th, that the Viceroy of Naples had arrived there. He had received from Genoa 60,000 ducats, and put in the Fregosys. Cremona had paid him 50,000—Bergamo 30,000—Bresse 15,000, and all on the Lake of Garda 15,000. The Viceroy had proposed on the 30th of June to march towards the Venetians to recover Lynago (Lugano) and attack Padua. Considering the loss of the Venetians, thinks they will condescend to a truce. The Emperor will shortly enter Burgundy. Anthony de Lusy, who left Lyons ten days ago, saw Latrymolle enter it with about 20 horses; he says the French lost all their horse in the battle. Many had no armor. The French will not fight with England, but put their troops in garrison.—My Lady says, that the siege of Terouenne is not carried on so actively as it should be. The Swiss have taken Mountferrate, and are at Salucio. The Duke of Milan was at Haste on the 22nd of June. Brussels, 6 July 1513. *Signed.*

Pp. 3, mutilated. Add.

7 July. **4327.** CHR. [BAINBRIDGE] CARDINAL OF YORK to [RUTHAL]
R O. BP. OF DURHAM.

As he writes at length to the King, will not cumber him with his scribbling. Hopes the King of Spain will, for his own interest in Naples and Navarre, concur with England against the French, *præter opinionem meam* "though it be with some slowness like to my Lord of Arundel." The Pope proceeds marvellously well; instead of sending legates to the Emperor, England, Arragon, and France, according to the chapters of the conclave, he has been induced by Bainbridge to send four prelates. Adrian [de Corneto] wished to have been sent as legate to Henry and the Emperor. He "is as parciall a Francheman as I hame a Ynglisman. I pray God geve hymme evyll triste." Commends himself to my lord steward, chamberlain, and Bregavenny. Rome, 7 July.

Hol., pp. 2.

1513.
9 July.　**4328.**　SPINELLY to [HENRY VIII.]
Galba, B. III.113.
B. M.

Wrote last on the . . . . inst. Received the King's of the said date, stating the King's wish to retain the Duke of Bru[ns-wick] in his service. My Lady has as yet received no answer. A councillor of the Duke thinks he will serve the King on these conditions. He will bring 2,000 horsemen, at 2,000 gold florins a month, have money for transports, and 10 gold florins a month as the price of the horsemen. As these requests were so far out of the way, Spinelly went no further. By letters from the Emperor at Covelence on the 5th, my Lady is commanded to send the Duke to the Emperor at Treves. Has had no correspondence with Dissilsteyne, as he will ask the same terms as the Duke. Berghis will consider the interest only of his son the Lord Walham. Various horsemen, if the truce take effect, will be glad to serve the King at 8 florins a month. My Lady thinks it prudent that one month's wages should be sent by the King at once for 1,000 horse ; if they cannot be got elsewhere, she will procure them from the Emperor, "and such a covert way shall be founden by means of the Emperor, that if they shall have 10 florins a month it shall not be prejudicial to your grace for the others." She is anxious that they shall be commanded by an Almayn. Sends a copy of a letter to her from the Emperor, showing his anxiety for some arrangement with the Venetians.

Mr. Richard Barrados, secretary to the Prince of Castile, has returned from France. The French King told him that my Lady and Lord Berghis had assisted England against the opinion of others, "and he keepeth for them a pensee." The French Queen said the same. He heard a Frenchman call the King of Arragon traitor, which shows they are not content with him. The city of Luke is at variance with the Bishop, de-manding restitution of the impositions, and defying the French. Has begged my Lady to obtain an inhibition, and prevent those of Julyers and Cleves from serving the French. The eldest son of Robert de la Marche was slain at the battle in Italy. The Governor of the Duke of Sax at Antwerp stated to the Almayns that the French horse abandoned the foot at that battle. The herald that was to go to the King of Scots has not yet been dispatched. A Spaniard, Dego Decastre, once a merchant in England, secretary in the Spanish tongue with the Prince of Castile, who went into France, has been arrested on suspicion, and confessed that, by the credence of Don John de Manuell and con-sent of certain Lords in this country, he had practised for a nego-tiation between France and the Emperor, and to break the treaty of marriage between the Prince of Castile and "my Lady your sister." My Lady has commanded he shall "be put in tourne-ment." The Emperor's ambassadors in England have written to say that the ratification is not correctly drawn. Sends a memorial of the things declared by the Frenchman taken at Eden. Brussels, 9 July, began the 8th, 1513. *Signed.*

Pp. 8, *mutilated. Noted by Ruthal.*

B. O.

2. A memorandum of divers things declared by the Frenchman taken at Eden to the Secretary Marnyx, in the presence of Thomas Spynelly. 1. A priest born in Normandy, near Argentan, of brown visage, having his left brow higher than the other, has been divers times within a year out of England with the French King, and lately about Easter, when he was rewarded with 120 crowns.

1513.

He is kinsman to Mr. John Demyneres, advocate of the council of Roan.—A French merchant, called Bonsons, married in London, writes daily by Audewarp to his brother at Rouen. — Denys Lecharon, gunner of Lord Penys, was to set fire to the gunpowder.—The priest carried letters to Edmund De la Pole's kinsmen.

"The said Frenchman is a poor fellow, and ill-arrayed, with a sharp tongue; and considering the subtilty and craft of the Frenchmen, my Lady and others suppose rather that he is sent for to put suspicion and division than otherwise." Spinelly does not believe the rumors.

P. 1.

Addit. 21, 382. **4329.** HECTOR DE VICQUEMARE to MADAME [MARGARET OF
f. 47.   SAVOY].
B. M.

Relates what he has seen himself and learned from a relative with the Chancellor of the state of the King [of France]. Has been both at the King's assembly at Blois, and in Normanby where the naval force was getting ready, and seen nothing which can do her much harm. Has done his best for her, remembering that he has been long supported in her territories, and that she gave him money at Antwerp for giving her warning of a man of De Piennes,—as also at Cambray at the meetings (*aux appointements*). Requested the officers of Hedine to allow him to go to her at Malines; but they detained him, doubting whether he had formerly spoken to her and the governor of Brescia and her treasurer Don Diego. The King has beyond the mountains 1,380 men of arms and 14,000 foot, among whom are De Trenou, Jean Jacques, and De la Trymouille; and here, for his army against England, 800 men of arms only, with the gentlemen of his household and archers, which are a considerable band. He has 10,000 or 12,000 Swiss now at Rains, for whose pay Graville, Admiral of France, has lent him 80,000 livres, 14,000 lanzknechts at St. Espert (?) de Ruee, who will be at Montreuil in 2 days; 3,000 Picards, and 3,000 Normans. He has recalled De la Marche from beyond the mountains with his 4,000 lanzknechts. He has made and brought from Paris and Bloys great pieces of artillery, and there are 12 pieces made at Rouen since Easter, among the largest ever seen, which he is likewise bringing hither. He has also prepared 1,200 hacquebuttes to break the English ranks. His naval force is poor and ill-manned. If he can beat the English he will attack Hainault and Flanders. The embassies he now sends to her are only a blind. The writer saw at Blois a Norman priest of the territory of the Duke of Alençon, who has come several times from England. The King has paid him to reside in the English court as a spy. He has brought letters to those of the family of Suffolk, and gained over one of the King of England's secretaries. Has seen a gunner named Denis le Charon, who has engaged to blow up the English magazines and destroy all the mills in the county of Guisnes. They are carrying all the victuals to the camp at Boulogne. 400 men will be at Montreuil in 2 days, where De Piennes means to remain. The King is at Paris, "bien mal disposé; il n'a que la langue et ung petit de coeur." Is ready to go either to France or England at Madame's bidding, with a recommendation to some of her captains (?), as he knows nothing of England or Calais.

Hol. Fr., pp. 4.

1513.

4330. FRENCH NAVY.

Calig. D. vi. f. 88.
B. M.

A paper addressed to the King, entitled "Rapport de Joes Pierdux;" containing an account of his survey of the men of war and warlike preparations at Abbeville, Poitiers, Heu in Normandy, Dieppe, Hondfleur, Stocques, St. Sauveur, Brest, and Harfleur, at which last place he met with Robert Barton, and had communications with him respecting a new boat built by him. He left Vere 1 March 1512. At Dieppe he was taken prisoner, but released after a time.

Fr., mutilated, pp. 4.

9 July.
Lettres de
Louis XII.
t. IV. 175.

4331. HENRY VIII. to the SIEUR DE FIENNES, Governor General of Flanders.

Has received his letters by François de Mastaing, his lieutenant, grand bailly of Ghent, Jean de Praet, bailly of Bruges, and Jean Caulier, master of requests of the Prince of Castile, whom he sent to England. They have declared their charge touching (1) the carriage of victuals to the English army, (2) depredations committed by the English on the subjects of the Prince of Castile, and (3) the neutrality of the lordship of Fiennes; on which subjects some of his Council have spoken with them. Understands by the bearers that proclamation has been made, to avoid the displeasure of France, allowing the English to purchase provisions in the Prince's countries, but forbidding his subjects to carry provisions to the army. This is contrary to the treaties made with the Emperor and the Prince, and the licence given by the former to serve the English against France. Hopes he will not allow such proclamation to be made, as it would be against the will of the Emperor and the Duchess of Savoy. As to the depredations, means to do justice to the Prince's subjects. Calais, 9 July 1513.

Fr. Add.

9 July.
P. S.

4332. For CHRISTOPHER URSWIK, clk., and ROBERT CRESSY.

Next presentation to a prebend and canonry in the collegiate chapel of St. Stephen, Westminster. Greenwich, 15 June 5 Hen. VIII. *Del.* Westm., 9 July.

Pat. 5 Hen. VIII. p. 1, m. 20. Teste Regina.

10 July.
R. O.

4333. SIR ROB. WINGFIELD to HENRY VIII.

In his letters of the 9th, stated that the Emperor expected news from the Swiss. Dined the next day with the Emperor, who has heard there is a mutiny in Switzerland. The cantons that have lost men in Italy have attacked Berne and Basle, which adhere to the French. He has written this morning to the Swiss to hasten their proceedings, and has been at great charge in keeping ambassadors among them all this year, who have written to say they are in good hopes the Swiss will now attack France. Wingfield told him his master would not like to have paid such large sums of money to his Majesty with such little result. He answered quickly, if his advice had been followed, the Swiss would have been in France before the English, Milan out of danger, the Venetians colder in their enterprise against him. This said, he would listen to no answer. "Covalence," 10 July 1513.

Hol., pp. 3. Add.

1513.

10 July. **4334.** For the PRIOR and CONVENT of the church of ST. MARY
P. S.   and ST. NICHOLAS, LEDES, Kent.

Mortmain licence to acquire lands to the annual value of 20*l.*
Dover Castle, 28 June 5 Hen. VIII. *Del.* Westm., 10 July.

Pat. 5 Hen. VIII. p. 2, m. 6.

10 July. **4335.** For the PRIORY of MERTON.
P. S.

Mortmain licence for John Norton, John Baker, clk., Bartholomew Stable, clk., Richard Otterburne, Thomas Weresdale, Thomas Launne, Nicholas Maland, and Thomas Gammyll, to alienate 24 acres of meadow and 116 acres of pasture in Cornburgh, to the prior and convent of St Mary Marton. Greenwich, 15 June 5 Hen. VIII. *Del.* Westm., 10 July.

Pat. 5 Hen. VIII. p. 2, m. 14.

11 July. **4336.** ERASMUS to COLET.
Eras. Ep. XII. 21.

Colet makes too serious an answer to a letter written in jest; ought not, perhaps, to have ventured on a joke with so great a patron. Colet writes to say that Erasmus is his debtor, whether he likes it or not; there is no one to whom Erasmus would sooner be under obligations, and he would be most ungrateful not to acknowledge it. Is sorry for Colet's hard circumstances; his own are worse; and how unwilling he is to trouble him may appear by the long interval elapsed before he claimed Colet's promise. Reminds him that some time since, when they were walking in Colet's garden, and talking about the *De Copia*, he had told Colet that he proposed to dedicate some little work (*puerile opus*) to the Prince, then a boy,—that Colet begged him to dedicate it to his school;—that Erasmus replied his school was too poor, and he must have something in hand:—that on mentioning the terms Colet demurred, but agreed at last to give 15 angels—on which the bargain was struck. Friends tell him that Colet is something hard and scrupulous in parting with his money; not from niggardliness, but because he is too modest in refusing the importunate. If Colet will not refuse to make good the rest of his promise, Erasmus, as matters now stand, will thankfully receive it as a favor, and make due return. Was sorry to find, from the close of his letter, that Colet was troubled with business. Would be glad if such talents as his could bo devoted exclusively to the service of Christ. Advises him to oppose a sound conscience to the gabble (*blateramentis*) of the malevolent.

Camb., 5 id. Jul.

P.S.—Has finished collating the New Testament;—is attacking St. Jerome; and on its completion will visit Colet. Speaks highly of the service Thos. Lupset renders him in these collations.

1511.

11 July. **4337.** For GEORGE THROGMORTON, the King's spear.
P. S.

To be keeper of the park of Claredon, Warw., as held by John Whyting. Dover Castle, 29 June 5 Hen. VIII. *Del.* Westm., 11 July.

Pat. 5 Hen. VIII. p. 1, m. 9.

1513.

11 July. **4338.** For THOMAS CHAMBRE, grocer, London.
P. S.
Protection for one year ; going in the suite of Sir Gilbert Talbot,
Deputy of Calais. Greenwich, 5 June 5 Hen. VIII. *Del.* Westm.,
11 July.
Pat. 5 Hen.VIII. p. 1, *m.* 17.

11 July. **4339.** JUSTICES OF ASSIZE
Norfolk Circuit. — Wm. Mordaunt with Sir John Fyneux and
Sir Rob. Rede. Westm., 11 July.
Western Circuit.—Thos. Elyott and Thos. Fitzhugh with Ric.
Elyott and Lewis Pollard. Same date.
Midland Circuit.—John Jenour and Ric. Heigham with Hum-
phrey Conyng[esby] and Guy Palmes. Same date.
Home Circuit.—Simon Fitz with John Butteler and John
More. Same date.
Pat. 5 Hen.VIII. p. 1, *m.* 7*d.*

12 July. **4340.** For BARTHOLOMEW WESTBY, second baron of the
P. S.   Exchequer.
Annuity of 40 marks during pleasure, out of the petty customs
of London, with arrears from 22 April 1 Hen. VIII. Greenwich,
14 June 5 Hen. VIII. *Del.* Westm., 12 July.
Pat. 5 Hen.VIII. p. 1, *m.* 17.

12 July. **4341.** COMMISSION OF THE PEACE.
[*Berks.*]— Thos. Abbot of Abingdon, Rob. Brudenell, John
Neuport, Sir Thos. Lovell, Sir Thos. Inglefeld, Sir Andr. Wynde-
sore, Sir Edw. Darell, Sir Geo. Foster, Sir Thomas Fetiplace, Guy
Palmes, Ric. Weston, Will. Beselles, Wm. Essex, Jas. Strang-
ways, John Fetiplace, Hen. Brigges, Thos. Unton, Wm. Swayne,
Christ. Belyngeham, Ric. Harecourte, John Man, Geo. Wodeward,
Wm. Yong, and John Tate. Westm., 12 July.
Pat. 5 Hen.VIII. p. 1, *m.* 3*d.*

12 July. **4342.** For WALTER HARPER, yeoman of the Male, and WIL-
S. B.   LIAM HOLME, page of the Cellar.
Grant, in survivorship, of the manor of Frutewell, Oxon., and
lands in Frutewell, lately held for life by Sir Robert Spencer, on
surrender of patent 28 June 3 Hen. VIII., granting the said Walter
two tenements in Frutewell. *Del.* Westm., 12 July 5 Hen. VIII.
Pat. 5 Hen.VIII. p. 2, *m.* 19.

12 July. **4343.** SPINELLY to [HENRY VIII.]
Galba, B. III. 125.
B. M.
Wrote last on the 9th. Encloses letters from the Duke of Bruns-
wick to my Lady, who advises the King to conclude with him. She
considers the truce with Gueldres concluded. Brussells, 12 July
1513. *Signed.*
Pp. 2, *mutilated.*

13 July. **4344.** For JOHN CAVALLARI, merchant of Lucca.
S. B.
Denization. *Del.* Westm., 13 July 5 Hen. VIII.
Pat. 5 Hen.VIII. p. 1, *m.* 15.

1513.
13 July.   **4345.**   WYGESTON'S HOSPITAL, Leicester.

P. S.

Licence for William Wygeston, of Leicester, junr., merchant of the staple of Calais, Thomas Wygeston, clk., Roger Wygeston and William Fissher, clk., to found a hospital for two chaplains and twelve poor men in the town of Leicester, to be called the hospital of William Wygeston ; with mortmain licence to acquire lands, &c. to the annual value of 40 marks.   Calais, 3 July 5 Hen. VIII. *Del.* Mortlake, 13 July.
Pat. 5 *Hen.VIII. p.* 1, *m.* 17.

13 July.   **4346.**   For THOS. SENEAWGH.

To be searcher in the port of Breggewater, performing the office in person ; with moiety of the forfeitures of prohibited goods. Westm., 13 July.
Pat. 5 *Hen.VIII. p.* 2, *m.* 18.

14 July.   **4347.**   For JOHN GROS.

P. S.

To be receiver general, during pleasure, of all the King's farms ; viz., arrears of the lands of the late Lord Fitzwater, Simon Mounford, Humphrey Stafford Killingworth, Fenwik, of William Kendale and afterwards of John Trefry in Gloucester, and Botryngon ; the fee farms of the city of York, of Rochestre, of Aylesbury ; the farm of the office of sheriff of Northumberland ; the farm of the swans in the Thames, Yoxhale, Grymston Shawe (?), Werke, Plenymellor, Norstede, and Cleygate, the ulnage in York, and Charleton in Craven, with the members of Penrith ; the herbage of the forests of Galtres, Chebsey, and Southwold, with the temporalities, as well of bishoprics as of abbeys and priories ; annuities of the Lord de Roos, Earl of Devon, Francis Cheyny, Catisby, Skelton, Baten, Denghby, and William De la Pole ; of the manors of Stillingflete, Ryngehouses, Bryansaham and Upton ; of 6s. 8d. on every butt of Malvesey wine imported, and all fines of the crown lands, demised by Sir Robert Southwell, and Bartholomew Westby, the King's overseers ; with an annuity of 20 marks.   Dover Castle, 28 June 1513.   *Del.* Westm., 14 July.

14 July.   **4348.**   For SIR ROB. SOUTHWELL and BARTH. WESTBY, baron of

P. S.   the Exchequer.

Warrant to let for 40 years such crown lands as are specified in patent 7 May 5 Hen. VIII.   Greenwich, 12.June 5 Hen. VIII. *Del.* Westm., 14 July.

15–17 July. **4349.**   FOX BISHOP OF WINCHESTER to [   ].

Vitell. B. xviii. 89.   " . . . . . the Emperor's advice is, that the King . . . .
B. M.   wik folks, and appoint with them in . . . . which the
Emperor would should be appointed by . . . ."

15 July.

"That the Emperor was not content with the truce of Gueldres, specially . . . . the ransoming of Monsr. de Wafner, albeit . . . . have patience because he thought thereby to bry . . . Base contre to the war and to give sufficient assistance.   Item that the Emperor thought by such knowledge as he had out [of . . .] that if the French King may be sure that the King of . . . . will keep the truce betwixt them he would give . . . . the King of England.   And he thinketh that consi[dering] the fame of

1513.

the Swiss and that within 2 days [they] be personally within
6 days' journeys of Paris the [Emperor] will withdraw part of his
power to those . . . . Item that the Emperor marvelleth
that the King would not a[dvertise him] . . . . . what way he
would take after his descent and [thinketh that] the King wasteth
both money and time in [laying] siege to Tirwayne for lack of
expert folks. An[d if the] King intend to have his assistance in
body, that from henceforth he will ask his advice [which shall]
procede of long experience and true meaning. Item that he hath
sent to the Switzers the Mares[chal of Bur]goyne with 500 horsemen, 300 horse of the Du[ke of . . berges, 100 horse of the
Marquis of Branden[burgh . . . .] the Counte of Somme and
200 [* * * * *some lines lost*] to the King to have . . . . . King's
matters to his comfort ; for he hath a [notion] that the King's
matters should go well, and he [calleth] him the King's soldier,
because he hath [rece]ived his money, and after the making of
his oath [hath] shewed always that he intended in his own person
to enter into France and to speak with you, and that he marvelled
that he had never knowledge by Sir Robert Wingfield that it
should be the King's desire that he should so do." As he is coming
nearer, will think it strange if he be not advertised of the premises. When he enters Luxembourg expects to know how the
affairs of France go.

17th July.

When Sir Robert Wingfield requested the licence the Emperor
readily consented to it. The Emperor says he wrote to the King,
on the 15th of July, of his intended entry into France, and that
he had urged the Swiss to haste. Wingfield says he does not appear
to meditate an enterprise against Burgundy unless the Prince's
subjects consent. "And that he was cause the Swissers to . . . .
. . . . through his country of Ferrat and so to pass into Champayne
. . . . that he may come in betwixt both armies,
and that [he did not kno]w whether the French King will give
the King battle . . . . one of puissance
out of such quarters as it . . . . thereof 15 days'
warning, and if he . . . . with the King, and if the
battle be . . . .
Very badly mutilated, pp. 2.

15 July.　**4350.**　To JOHN YONG, Master of the Rolls.
S. B.

To cancel two recognizances, each of 500*l*.,—made by Domynyk
Lomylyn, Lawrence de Marinis, and Bartholomew Lomelyn, merchants of Jeane (Genoa), 30 October 23 Hen. VII. Richmond,
18 July 3 Hen. VIII. Delivered 15 July 5 Hen. VIII. to J. T. by
Lomelyn, to be cancelled.

16 July.　**4351.**　JAMES IV. to HENRY VIII.
Calig. B. VI. 57.
B. M.

Letter of defiance, as printed in Hall, with some verbal differences,
of which the most important are the following : " Raff harald" in
Hall is here more correctly "Rosse harald ;" "xv^th day of October"
is here " xxv^th day of October."
Contemporary, pp. 4.
R. O.　　2. Another copy.

18 July.　**4352.**　LEONARD FRISCOBALD.
R. O.

Money due to him for victualling his ship *The Annunciation* of
300 tons, and another called *The Mary of Bilboa*, at the rate of 5*s*.

1513.

per man per month. Mariner's wages 7s. 1d. a month, gromett's 4s. 9d., page's 2s. 5d.

A paper roll.

19 July. **4353.** The SIEUR DE GRUTUSE to the VICONTE DE GAND.

R. O.

Has received a notice from the lieutenant of the bailly of Amiens of four or five thieves who had set upon three French merchants, and whom the officers of Arras had refused to deliver. If they are not delivered the people of Arras must be considered as the King's enemies. Abbeville, 19 July.

Fr., Copy, p. 1. *Endorsed by Spinelly:* "Copye des lettres que le Sieur de la Greythuyse a escryptes à le gouverneur d'Arras touchant les Franchoys que furent pryns par Sampson Norton."

19 July. **4354.** The CONCLAVE to HENRY VIII.

Vitell. B. 11. 46b.
B. M.
Rym. xiii. 373.

Notifying the death of Julius II. on the 21 Feb., and the election of Leo. X. the 11 March. Rome, 19 July.

Lat., mutilated, p. 1. *Add.*

19 July. **4355.** SPINELLY to [HENRY VIII.]

Galba, B. 111. 126.
B. M.

Wrote last on the 17th. Delivered his letters to Lady Margaret. She will use her influence with Dissilsteyne to serve the King. Details the terms of his service. By letters that came yesternight from the Emperor he is at Treves; by letters from Verona, the 10th, the Viceroy of Naples was at Montagnana. Barth. Dalbiano has fled to Padua and Treviso. The Bp. of Gource started for Verona on the 8th. Has offered 4,000 g. guilders to compound the matter of the carrack. My Lady recommends Loys Moraton. Lord Berghis told him that one of the chief causes of his being sent to the King was to persuade him to go to Rens in Champagne, where the Emperor would meet him, and see him crowned. The ratification had not come from Gueldres. Sends a letter from Sir Robt. Wingfield to the King. Brussells, 19 July 1513. *Signed.*

Pp. 4, *mutilated.* *Noted by Fox.*

20 July. **4356.** For SIR WILLIAM SYDNEY.

P. S.

Annuity of 50 marks. Calais, 13 July 5 Hen. VIII. *Del.* Westm., 20 July.

Pat. 5 Hen. VIII. p. 1, *m.* 24.

20 July. **4357.** For EDMUND HORDE, "juris canonice inceptor."

P. S.

Canonry or prebend of Yerdington, in the collegiate church of St. Mary Magdalene, Bridgenorth, void by death of Master Esterfeld. Calais, 13 July 5 Hen. VIII. *Del.* Westm., 20 July.

Pat. 5 Hen. VIII. p. 1, *m.* 18. *Teste Regina.*

20 July. **4358.** COMMISSION OF THE PEACE.

Lincolnshire (Lindsey).—W. Bp. of Lincoln, Wm. Lord Willoughby, Robt. Brudenell, Humph. Conyngesby, Guy Palmes, Sir Robt. Sheffeld, Sir John Husee, Sir Wm. Tirwhyt, Sir John Skippewith, Sir Robt. Waterton, Robt. son of Robt. Sheffeld, Christ. Willoughby, Thos. Burgh, jun., Wm. Askewe, Geo. Fitzwilliam, Christ. Broun, Lionel Dymmok, Christ. Askogh, John Topclyffe, Robt. Sutton, Robt. Sheffeld, Thos. Missenden, John Mounson, Robt. Belwode, Nicholas Upton, John Fulnetby, John Hennege, Thos. Burgh, John Seyntpoll, Edw. Forman, Wm. Han-

1513.

shard, Thos. Tocoste, Andrew Byllesby, and Ric. Clerke. Westm.,
xx .. July.
Pat. 5 Hen. VIII. p. 1, m. 3d.

22 July.   **4359.**   SPINELLY to HENRY VIII.
Galba, B.III. 128.
B. M.

Wrote his last on 20th. The same day the Emperor arrived at
Namur ; he is expected at Mechlin on Sunday next. Dissilsteyne
is gone to Grave to get ready. The Lord of Shmurzemborg will
join him with 150 horse. They will send their contingents to-
morrow morning. The Swiss have passed by Geneva. The Lords
Vargy and Varembon have left Burgundy to join them. The
French have burnt the suburbs of Lyons in dread of their approach.
My Lady has sent to the Emperor to have the Viceroy of Naples
joined in commission with the Bp. of Gource, who she suspects is
not well affected to the treaty between the Emperor and the
Venetians. Delaroche urges her to do justice to the patron of the
carrack, and grant him letters of reprisal. Brussells, 22 July 1513.
Signed.
Pp. 3, mutilated. Add.

22 July.   **4360.**   For WILLIAM POLE of Pole, Cheshire, alias of London,
S. B.   serjeant-at-arms.

Pardon to him and Richard Dawne of Utkynton, Cheshire,
Thomas Massy of Podyngton, John Whitmore of Thursteston,
Richard Bunbury of Staney, Henry Gleyve of Carnesdale,
Hamlet Treves, John Aldersey, Peter Motton, Peter Mynchull,
John Radley, John Wilde, Ranulph Hough, Richard Hunt,
Richard Birkhed, and Richard Hale, late of London ; and release
to the said William Pole and Margaret his wife, late wife of Sir
William Troutbek, of all fines due to the King for marrying with-
out licence ; and of all reliefs in respect of the lands of the said
Sir William. *Del.* Westm., 22 July 5 Hen. VIII.
Pat. 5 Hen. VIII. p. 2, m. 11.

23 July.   **4361.**   SIR ROB. WINGFIELD to HENRY VIII.
R. O.

Wrote last on the 21st, stating the Emperor had asked him
whether he had heard from England. Yesterday Sir Symond de
Ferrette came to him from the Emperor with Mr. Hans Reynner,
demanding whether he had yet received news from England, as
Ferrette had shown him that the King was glad the Emperor
had come into these parts, and had advertised Ferrette to that
effect. Wingfield replied, that though the King was pleased with
the Emperor's arrival, there must be some misunderstanding as
to his words ; that whenever a place for a meeting is appointed,
Wingfield will be advertised thereof. They said the Emperor was
willing to go over to Henry, and trust him as his own son.
Thinks there is some mystery in it, and there are "some sherewis
that would your words should be taken to the worst sense." Some
persons have been setting the Emperor against the King's enterprise in France. Brussells, 23 July 1513.
Hol., pp. 3. Add.

23 July.   **4362.**   NEWS FROM GERMANY.
R. O.

" Coppie des lettres que le maistre d'hostel (Jehan Bourdot) de
Monsieur le mareschal de Bourgoyne, estant devers lempereur, a
escript a ung gentil homme nomme Bellegarde, qui est a la court

1513.

de Monsieur larchiduc avec le filz de mondit seigneur le mareschal, et luy a rescript affin que Madame fut advertye du voulloir et emprinses des Suiches desquelles la tenur sensuit."—Arrived this evening at Cologne, and has spoken to the Emperor touching the affair of the Swiss, who wish to go by Burgundy, and sent to Mons. le Marechal requiring horse and artillery. The marshal is waiting the determination of the Emperor. The writer, hearing he had started for Cologne, had taken his way thither. The marshal will send the news and copies of the correspondence. Cologne, 23 July.

Endorsed by Spinelly.

Fr., p. 1.

23 July. **4363.** For WM. BYSLEY of Longe Assheton, Somerset.

Protection ; going to the war. Westm., 23 July.

Fr. 5 Hen. VIII. m. 10.

26 July. **4364.** SPINELLY to HENRY VIII.

R. O.

Wrote last on the 25th. The Emperor had arrived at the castle of Voura with Lord Berghes only. The ambassadors of Gueldres have brought the ratification of the truce. The Lady Margaret proposes that England should retain all the 1,500 foot that served in Gueldres. She will give orders that the horse in the retinue of Dissilstain be sent to the English army. The governor of the merchants adventurers departs tomorrow. Lord Fenys has written that the English will be successful at Terouenne. The captains there do not very well agree. Sir Rob. Wingfield will transmit the news from Rome sent by the Emperor. The Arragonese ambassador has come hither from the Emperor. Marnyx tells him they are urgent that Lewis Morton (Maroton) should be sent to England. Sends a letter he has received from the man at Camfere, and a copy of one written by the Count de Carpe to the Emperor for the restitution of the two schismatic cardinals. Trusts my Lord Cardinal of York (Bainbridge) has sent the other writings to the King comprised in the same some days ago. Wishes him victory over his enemies. Brussells, 26 July 1513.

Has just learned that the Emperor has sent Simon de Ferrett to the King, for what intent neither Spinelly nor my Lady knows.

Signed.

Pp. 3. *Add.*

26 July. **4365.** KATHARINE OF ARRAGON to WOLSEY (Almoner).

Calig. D. vi. 92.
B. M.
Ellis, 1 S. i. 79.

As she is not likely to hear from the King since his departure from Calais, "for the great business in his journey that every day he shall have "—sends her servant to bring her word, and begs that Wolsey will write by her messengers successively of the King's health. As he draws near the enemy, she will never be at rest till she often have letters from Wolsey.—Was glad to see the brief sent by the Pope to the King ;—will be more so, if he make an honorable peace for the King, or "help on his part as much as he can, knowing that all the business that the King hath was first the cause of the Church."—Trusts he will come home shortly, with as great a victory as ever prince had. "Mr. Almoner, touching Frauncesse de Cassery's matter, I thank you for your labor therein ; true it is she was my woman before she was married, but now since she cast herself away, I have no more charge of her. For very pity to see her lost I prayed you in Canterbury to find the means to send her home into her country. Now ye think that with my letter of

1513.

recommendation to the Duchess of Savoy, she shall be content to take her into her service. This, Mr. Almoner, is not meet for her, for she is so perillous a woman that it shall be dangerous to put her in a strange house. And ye will do so much for me, to make her go home by the way with the ambassador of the King my father, it should be to me a great pleasure, and with that ye shall bind me to you more than ever I was." Would be glad if he will ask the King to write and thank the Council for their diligence. R[ichmond] 26 July.

The Lord Admiral has sent [a prisoner] taken with his ship, and brought to him as the said . . . . from Depe towards Flanders. *Add.* : To Master Almoner.

26 July.	**4366.**	SIR ROBT. WINGFIELD to HEN. VIII.

Galba, B. III. 85.
B. M.

Wrote last on the 23rd from Brussells. Yesterday the Emperor sent James de Bannisfis to him, stating he had received letters from Count de Carpi, his ambassador at Rome. After long solicitation the Pope declines to join the league, which he considers to be made "so straightly betwixt the Emperor and you against the French King"—he is, however, ready to join a league betwixt the Emperor, England, Arragon, Duke of Milan, and the Swiss generally, without naming the French. Hereupon the Card. of England, Jerome Vyke, and the ambassador of Milan, proceeded to execute their authority, and Carpi sent to the Emperor for instructions. Wingfield brought to the notice of Bannisius that article in the treaty specifying it should remain, though both the Pope and the King of Arragon should refuse to join—and that the mandate should be sent at once to Carpi. My Lady continues friendly to England, and trusts the King of Arragon will join. Yesternight visited the ambassador of Spain and Don John de la Newce, who came lately to England from the King of Arragon.—To-night the Emperor will be at Brussells.—Brussells, 26 July 1513.
Hol., pp. 3, mutilated. Add.

26 July.	**4367.**	For SIR JOHN RAYNESFORD jun., late of East Greenwich,
P. S.	alias of Danbury, Essex, alias of London.

Pardon to him and to Edmund Vale, Thomas Cokke, John Bourne alias Borne, all late of Danbury, Maurice Walsaheman alias Griffith, John Gettyng, Thomas Hyggyns, John Owen, Robert Cuthbert, Robert Butler, Richard Cornewell, and William Courtnay, all of East Greenwich, for all felonies committed before the 29th April last. Calais, 18 July 5 Hen. VIII. *Del.* Westm., 26 July.
Pat. 5 Hen. VIII. p. 1, m. 18. Teste Regina.

S. B.	2. To the same effect.

26 July.	**4368.**	For JOHN DE BERNI, merchant of Toulouse, BAR-
S. B.	THOLOMEW PANSATICHI and MICHAEL BANCHI, merchants of Florence.

Licence to import 1,000 tons of Toulouse woad. *Del.* Mortlake, 26 July 5 Hen. VIII.

26 July.	**4369.**	For ROBERT WARCOPP.
P. S.

Wardship of Thomas s. and h. of Richard Goldsborogh ; on surrender of patent 22 July 1 Hen. VIII., found to be invalid. Canterbury, 23 June 5 Hen. VIII. *Del.* Westm., 26 July.
Pat. 5 Hen. VIII. p. 1, m. 14. Teste Regina.

1513.

26 July. **4370.** For RIC. CORNEWELL of Greenwich.

Pardon of all murders and felonies committed before the 29th April 5 Hen. VIII. Westm., 26 July.

Pat. 5 Hen. VIII. p. 1, *m.* 10.

27 July. **4371.** PETER MARTYR to LUDOVICO FURTADO.

Pet. Mart. Epist. No. 525.

Pescara has gone to Genoa, which has surrendered. D'Alviano after laying siege to Verona has joined Pescara and Prosper Colonna. Leo has received the revolted Cardinals, who made their submission in a very humble manner. The English and Swiss Cardinals condemned Leo, and would not be present at the ceremony ; they said it was opening the door to similar offences, and left Rome in anger. The King of England has besieged Terouenne. The French endure the disgrace and dare not attack them. The English have lost some of their wagons sent to fill up the foss at Terouenne, on a sally from the French, as they had advanced too far and were not supported. Valladolid, vi. kal. Aug.

29 July. **4372.** For EDWARD STANBANKE.

P. S.

To be bailiff of Hollesworthy, Devon, in the King's gift by death of his grandmother. Richmond, 26 July 5 Hen. VIII. *Del.* Mortlake, 29 July.

Pat. 5 Hen. VIII. p. 1, *m.* 18. *Teste Regina.*

30 July. **4373.** For RICHARD PYNSON, native of Normandy.

P. S.

Denization. Richmond, 26 July 5 Hen. VIII. *Del.* Westm., 30 July.

Pat. 5 Hen. VIII. p. 1, *m.* 18. *Teste Regina.*

31 July. **4374.** WAR WITH FRANCE.

R. O.

Receipt indented 31 July 5 Hen. VIII. by Henry Earl of Northumberland, grand captain of his own retinue, to Sir Rob. Dymok, treasurer of the King's rearward, for 489*l.* 9*s.* 8*d.*, being a month's wages for himself and his retinue. *Signed.*

4375. WAR WITH SCOTLAND.

R. O.

Account of Edward Bensted, late treasurer of the wars in the King's army in the North, under Thomas Earl of Surrey, Treasurer and Marshal of England, Lord Lieutenant and Captain-General of the said army,—by virtue of the King's letter missive directed to the said Edward, dated 4 Aug. 4 Hen. VIII., of monies received and paid by him for the expenses of the army, for 84 days, from 4 August to 27 October 4 Hen. VIII.

Received of Master William Lychefeld, one of the King's chaplains, by virtue of two warrants dated 9th and 14th August 4 Hen. VIII.; of Edmund Abbot of St. Mary's Abbey, York, and Master Thomas Magnus, one of the King's chaplains, by virtue of a warrant dated 12 Oct. 4 Hen. VIII. 2,127*l.* 2*s.* 8*d.*

Paid for wages, coats, and conduct money for the retinue of the Earl of Surrey, for one month, beginning 20 Aug. 4 Henry VIII.; viz., for 500 coats of white and green at 4*s.* each ; to Lord Surrey, for himself 5*l.* a day ; to Lord Barnes, Marshal of the army, 6*s.* 8*d.* a day ; 10 petty captains 2*s.* each a day ; 22 demi-lances, 9*d.* each a day ; one spear 18*d.* a day ; 462 archers 8*d.* each a day ; 2 surgeons 8*d.* each a day ; 1 trumpet 16*d.* a day.—Wages, &c. for the treasurer of the wars and 15 men of his retinue ; viz., a coat of white and green for the treasurer, 4s.; wages of the treasurer at 6s. 8d. a day, for 42 days from 5 August to 17 Sept. ; a coat of white and green for Thomas Warton, clerk of the wars, 4s. ; his wages at 2s. a day for 40 days ; for coats of white and green, for 13 soldiers at 4s. a coat ; their wages at 8d. a day.—To Wm. Butteler, sergeant-of-arms, for coats of white and green for himself and 2 soldiers ; his wages at 2s. a day ; his 2 soldiers at 8d. a day.—Coats and wages to John Millett, comptroller of the wars, and his 6 soldiers at the same rate as above. —Wages to Master Clarencieux 6s. a day, and Rougecrosse 2s. a day.—To John Mortymer, King's messenger, for conveyance of King's letters from Bishop's Waltham to the Lords of divers shires in the North during 28 days, 1s. a day ; to Willm. Grene of Pomfret for riding 56 miles for Sir John Constable and others at 2d. a mile ; for 2 carriages of the Earl of Surrey from Lambeth to Pomfret, 96 miles, at 2d. a mile for each carriage ; same for the carriages of the marshal and the treasurer ; for bags to hold the King's money, 20d. ; for 2 coffers and a casket for the same, 28s. 4d.; for ink and writing paper 12d.

Wages at Pomfret for one month, beginning 17 Sept. 4 Hen. VIII. —To Willm. Grene of Pomfret for riding 41 miles to the Earl of Northumberland and others ; to Ralph Purser of Pomfret for riding 72 miles to Lord Derby and others ; for the hire of a horse standing at "harde mete," for 28 days, 9s. 4d.—Conduct money for the retinue of the Earl of Surrey homewards for 13 days, beginning 15 Oct. 4 Hen. VIII., viz.; to Lord Surrey 5l. a day ; to Avery Berwick, a spear ; to Edw. Bellingeham, a demy-lance.—To 14 archers of Sussex ; to 29 archers of do. ; to Edmund Walsingham a demilance, and his 3 archers ; to John Byrley do., and his 3 archers ; to Tho. Stydolff do., and his 30 archers ; to Mighell Denys do., and his 6 archers ; to Willm. Westbroke do., and his 9 archers ; to Edward Gorge, a petty captain ; to Tho. Newton. a demi-lance, and their 18 archers.

Charges for the King's ordnance in the Tower of London conveyed northwards, viz., to Willm. Blaknall, clerk of the ordnance, for his wages at 2s. a day from the 9th to the 22 Aug. 4 Hen. VIII. ; to 4 carpenters at 8d. each a day ; to 4 wheelwrights at 8d. each a day ; to 4 smiths at 8d. each a day ; to 4 purveyors at 12d. each a day ; to 4 yeomen carters at 8d. each a day ; to 2 horse harness makers at 8d. each a day ; to 114 men labouring in the Tower of London, loading the ordnance and attending the same, at 8d. each a day.—To Willm. Pawne, master of the ordnance, 6s. 8d. a day ; to 4 soldiers at 8d. a day.—To Raynkyn Hegster, captain of the gunners, 12s. a day ; 4 quartermasters gunners at 8d. each a day ; 55 gunners at 6d. a day.— Sum total of the payments 2,166l. 11s., " and so the said Edward Bensted is in a surplusage of 39l. 8s. 4d., which John Heron, treasurer of the King's chamber, paid him by virtue of a warrant dated . July 5 Hen. VIII.

Pp. 13. *Signed at the end of the account by the King.*

July.   **4376.**   ACCOUNTS OF THE NAVY.

R. O.

A file of warrants from the Earl of Surrey to Sir Thos. Wyndham, for wages and expenses connected with the following and other ships :—*The Leonard* of Dartmouth, Ric. Mercer, capt.; *The Trinity* of Hampton ; *The Sovereign*; *The Mary Katharine* of London, Walter Loveday, capt. ; *The Michael* of Plymouth. Pursers at 8d.

1513.

a day. *The Nicholas* of Hampton, with the bills appended, of which the following are most noticeable :—a carpenter working at gunstocks 8*d.* a day ; ordinary 6*d.* A spritsail yard 9*s.* ; 100 feet of oak plant 6*s.* ; a kettle 4*s.* ; 1 cwt. of small ropes 11*s.* 4*d.* ; 2 cwt. tallow 13*s.* 4*d.* ; elm stock for a gun 7*s.* ; a boat hook 4*d.* ; a compass 2*s.* ; a foreyard 14*s.*; 2 gallons of vinegar to make fine powder for handguns, 8*d* ; 100 tenpenny nails 10*d.* ; 100 clench nails 16*d.* ; sail twine 6*d.* per lb. ; 100 feet of elm board 2*s.* 6*d.* ; horse-hire from London to Hampton 3*s.* 4*d.*; a mizzen mast for *The Sweepstake* 10*s.*, anchor for ditto 20*s.* ; 100 sail needles 12*d.* With memoranda by Wolsey in some places. Various dates in 5 Hen. VIII.

July. **4377.** NAVY.

R. O.

[Sum] of the captains, soldiers, masters, gunners, and mariners appointed to be in the . . . . sea this year . . . . . [Lord] Ferrers, capt. ; Marny; . . . . one of Gloucetour; . . . . Clerk. master.— *The Gabriell Royal*, 1,000 tons ; Sir William Trevelian captain ; Sir Edward Pomerey; John Byron ; Hervy master, crew 602.— *Maria de Loreta*, 800 t. ; Courteney and Cornewall ; the Countess of Devon ; the city of Exeter ; Sir Amys Pollet, Rutter master, 604.—*The Kateryn Fortileza*, 700 t.; Flemyng captain ; Bishop of Lincoln ; Bishop of Chester ; Lord Sturton ; Broghton master ; the Abbot of Westmynster ; Freman master, 542.—*The Mary Rose*, 600 t.; Sir Edward Haward captain ; William Fitzwilliam ; Thomas Spert master, 402.— *The Peter*, 450 t. ; Sir Weston Browne, captain ; the Bishop of Canterbury ; John Clogge master, 302.—*The Nycholas Reede*, 400 t. ; Sir William Pirton captain ; Thomas Forgon master, 302.—*The John Hopton*, 400 t. ; Sir Thomas Wyndham; captain ; Sir John Cutte ; Sir Rich. Lewis* John Kemp master, 302.—*The Mary George*, 300 t. ; Barcley, captain ; Spodell master, 252.—*The Mary James*, 300 t. ; Eldircar captain ; Sir Robert Scheffielde master, 252.—*The Christe*, 300 t.; Thomas Cheyny captain ; the Abbot of Peturburowe ; the Abbot of Saint Albons ; Mycholl master, 252.—*The Great Barke*, 200 t. ; Schurborne and Sidney captains ; Sir Charles [Brandon] ; Browne master, 253.—*The Lesse Barke*, 240 t. ; Sir Stevyn Bull captain ; the Abbot of Gloweetor ; Henry Modall ; Spert master, 202.— *The Nicholas of Hampton*, 200 t.; Mr. Arthure captain; the town of Worcester ; Thomas Coll master, 162.—*The ship of Bristow*, 160 t. ; Anthony Poyntes captain ; Fuller master, 162.—*The Christopher Davy*, 160 t. ; Wiseman captain ; the Abbot of Bury ; the town of Bury ; the city of Norwch ; John Gofton master, 162.—*Sancho de Gara*, 320 t. ; Walop captain; Sir Thomas Lovell ; Sir John Saynt John ; the city of London ; Sanchio master, 293.— *The Erasmus Sebestian*, 160 t. ; Frances Pygot captain ; Sir Robert Peyton ; Herasmus master.—*The Anthony Montrigo*, 240 t. ; Jamys Delabere captain ; the city of London ; Sir John Lyngen ; John Erneley ; John Bastiriacho master, 202. — *The Mathew Cradok*, 240 t.; Mariswell captain; —— master, 200.—*Sancta Maria de Lakeyton*, 200 t. ; John Baker captain ; Sir Robert Cotton ; the Abbot of Habyndon ; the town of Oxford ; Urtino de Chariago master, 142.—*The Barbara of Grenewich*, 160 t.; Yeldirton captain; Sir Thomas Benyngfeld ; Roger Townesende ; Sir Edward Haward ; Wirall master, 162.—*The Lezarde*, 120 t. ; Coo captain ; Sir Robert Southwell; Sir Robert Clerc, —— master, 102.—*The Germyn*, 100 t.; my Lord of Arundell's servant, capt.; —— master, 92.—*The Sabyne*,

* Added by Wolsey.

120 t.; Sabyne captain; —— master, 102. — *The Jenet,* 70 t.; Gournay captain; John Richards master, 62. — *The Nicholas Draper,* 160 t.; Draper captain; Robert Sutton; Thomas Reede master, 162.—*The Erasmus of London,* 160 t.; Ric. Mercer captain; the town of Salisbury; Sir Richard Fouler; Robt. Silverton master, 62. — *Gibbes' ship,* 140 t.; Gibbes captain; —— master, 122.—*The Margaret of Topsam,* 140 t.; Jamys Knyvet captain; Stukeley; Sir Roger Lewkenor; —— master, 103.—*The Anne Galonte,* 140 t.; Loveday captain; Sir Robt. Clifton; Robt. Nele master, 132.—*The Baptist of Calais,* 120 t.; Charles Clifford captain; Harry Hunte master, 102.—*The Mary of Walsyngham,* 120 t.; Barnard captain; Sir John Henyngham; Sir Ph. Bothe; Sir Thomas Fenes; Sir John Devenyshe; Thomas Germyn master, 102.—*The Mary of Brixam,* 120 t.; Calthrop captain; Sir John Heydon; Sir Jamys Hobarde; Vincent Turpyne master, 101.— *The Jamys of Dartmouth,* 120 t.; Goldyngham captain; Sir Edward Hawarde; Coope; Sir John Speke; —— master, 107.—*The Margaret Bone Aventure,* 120 t.; Richard Bardisley captain; John Johnson master, 102. — *The Christopher of Dartmouth,* 124 t.; Vowell captain; the Bishop of London; the city of London; —— master, 102.—*The Julian of Dartmouth,* 100t.; George Wytwombe; Sir Edmund Lucy; Robt. Jonys; Sir John Hungreford; —— master, 104.—*The Thomas of Hull,* 80 t.; William Eldircar captain; Sir Mylis Bush; Oxynbruge; —— master, 76.—*The Elizabeth of New Castill,* 120 t.; Lewis captain; Mr. Crocker; John Arnalde master, 122.—*The Great New Spanyard,* 300 t.; Throgmerton captain; Knyghtley; —— master; the town of Grauntham, 301.—*The second new Spanyard,* 250 t.; Ichyngham captain; Coventry; Sir Thomas Greynfeld; —— master, 198.—*Henry of Hampton,* 160 t.; West captain; Sir John Trevenyan; Sir Edward Haward; Sir William Filoll; Mr. Chichester of Devon; Sir George Forster; John Harrison master, 135.—*The Swipestake,* 80 t.; Toley captain; Richard Godart master, 72.—*The Baptiste of Hariche,* 70 t.; Harper captain;—— master, 62.—*The Swalow,* 80 t.; Cooke captain; John Peryn master, 72.—*The bark to the Trinite;* —— captain; —— master, 128.—*The bark to the Kateryn;* —— captain; and —— master.—*The bark to the Mary Rose;* Sir Edward H. captain; Davison master, 68.—Leonard Friscaballis ship, 300 t.; Alexander captain; the Earl of Arundel; Sir Hugh Luttrell; Richard Eliotts master, 252.—Other ships that be not yet coming, which yet above the said ships, shall join with King's army. *The Peter of Foya,* and two other ships of Bristowe.
Roll.

4378.   The WAR IN FRANCE.

R. O.   "A proportion made of the King's ordinance, artillery, and other habillements necessary for the rerewarde, with draught and carriage for the same :"—

Flanders mares for draught. English horses for draughts of smaller guns carted. Carriage for guns and for frames, as of, potguns; frames to shoot them; hagbuzshes in chests, handguns in chests, carriage of shot and powder; shot for bombard and curtowes; shot for other guns. All this powder and shot serveth the battrie of eight days and nights.—A great staple of shot and powder to remain at Calais. Carriage of artillery, viz., whole speres; demi lances, &c. Carriage of tools for labourers and carters, viz., felling axes, hedging bills, &c. Carriage of divers necessaries for the ordnance, viz., smyths' forges and tools, iron, seacoals, crows of iron, screws, and ropes, &c. &c. Carts of tools

1513.

for artificers, viz., carpenter tools, seasoned timber, hoops for cooper of all sorts, &c. For the master of the ordinance, and the treasurer of the same, one pavilion each, " a hale for gunpowder," and " a hale for bowyers and fletchers." Sum of the Flanders mares, 260. Sum of the English horses for draught, 230. Sum of waggon for carriage of shot, 30. Sum of " fan " carts, 250. Sum of horses for the " fan " carts, 1,540. Sum of English carters for the whole ordnance of the rearward, 6.
Roll.

July. **4379.** ORDNANCE.
R. O.
" Ordnances particularly set out needful for furnishing the army royal pretended to be set to the sea in this the 5th year of the reign of our sovereign Lord King Hen. VIII."
Pp. 5, large paper.

1 Aug. **4380.** KATHARINE OF ARRAGON to MARGARET OF SAVOY.*
Lord Londes-
borough.
Requests her to send a physician to attend upon the King her husband. Windsor, 1 Aug.

1 Aug. **4381** For the MAYOR, CONSTABLES, and MERCHANTS of the
S. B.
STAPLE OF CALAIS.
Mortmain licence to acquire lands to the yearly value of 300*l.*
Del. Mortlake, 1 Aug. 5 Hen. VIII.
Pat. 5 *Hen. VIII. p.* 1, *m.* 14. *Teste Regina.*

1 Aug. **4382.** For WILLIAM GOWER, page of the Chamber.
P. S.
To be ranger of the forests of Shottore, Stowodde, and Barne-wode, Oxon., on surrender by Hamet Clegge of patent 5 Feb. 3 Hen. VII. Greenwich, 11 April 5 Hen. VIII *Del.* Westm., 1 Aug.
Pat. 5 *Hen. VIII. p.* 2, *m.* 1.

1 Aug. **4383.** For JOHN MORGAN, clk., B.D.
P. S.
Presentation to the church of St. Iltuti de Neth, Llandaff dioc., void by death of Morgan ap Hopkyn. Richmond, 29 July 5 Hen. VIII. *Del.* Mortlake, 1 Aug.
Pat. 5 *Hen. VIII. p.* 1, *m.* 18. *Teste Regina.*

1 Aug. **4384.** For WILLIAM GOWRE, groom of the Chamber.
P. S.
Corrody, in reversion, in the priory of Worcester, now held by William Reton. Calais, 20 July 5 Hen. VIII. *Del.* Westm., 1 Aug.

2 Aug. **4385.** For WILLIAM STUDDON, yeoman of the guard.
P. S.
Annuity of 10*l.* out of the customs of Exeter and Dartmouth ; on surrender of patent of 25 Nov. 3 Hen. VIII., granting him the like annuity out of the customs of Exmouth, during pleasure, *vice* Robert Simmonds, of Barnstable, deceased. Greenwich, 14 June 5 Hen. VIII. *Del.* Mortlake, 2 Aug.
Pat. 5 *Hen. VIII. p.* 1, *m.* 22. *Teste Regina.*

2 Aug. **4386.** PHILIPPE DE BREGILLES to MARGARET OF SAVOY.
Lett.de LouisXII.
t. iv. 189.
Has received her letters of the 30th ult., and executed her commission in such wise that the King has written to Messire

---
* From Moore's sale-catalogue.

1513.

Thomas [Spinelly] to come to him, as she commanded. The King showed him her letters, apparently to let him see that she did not trust him. Could only reply that she had not dared to trust the posts on such an important matter.—The King came on the first, within five or six bowshots of Terouenne. To-day he will be in the camp. They are determined to do something good ere long. Yesterday letters were intercepted from young De Crequy to his father, saying that the enemy had fought hard since Friday, but if they were fools enough to give the assault they should be well received. A cipher also was found, which no one has been able to read. Sends it in the letter of Messire to see if Marnix can decipher it. From the camp, 2 Aug. *Signed.*

On a separate paper :—The English are in bad order notwithing their high spirits ; " et tiens les Français bien mechans qui ne nous font autres venues." Thinks the King very anxious for the Emperor's coming to create order. Doubts if, when he has done so, they will believe it ; for there are two obstinate men, who govern everything, the grand esquire [Brandon] and the almoner. The King has just received him joyfully. Begs she will not forget to bring Moricande.* He will give her a dress, presented to him by the King, if she will wear it.
Fr.

3 Aug.   **4387.**   ACCOUNTS of JOHN HOPTON.
R. O.

For wages, &c., 25 June to 3 Aug. Wages of laborers who kept themselves, 5*d.* and 6*d.* 100 of Flemish fish, 28*s.* 8*d.* ; 8 bushels of salt, 3*s.* 4*d.* ; 2 bushels of oatmeal, 20*d.* ; 4 bushels of same, 4*s.* 8*d.* ; 17 gallons of oil, 10*d.* a gallon, &c.

4 Aug.   **4388.**   T. [RUTHAL] BP. OF DURHAM to WOLSEY.
R. O.

Thanks him for his letter, which he received 20 miles out of London, on his journey towards Wolsey, for the more speedy conveyance of the King's letters to the King of Scots and the Lord Dacre. Has returned to London, spoken with my Lord Treasurer (Surrey), ordered such things as are necessary for the defence of Norham. Hears it is in good case. Sent to his constable there 200 sheaf of arrows and 100 bows. Will take his journey to-morrow to Wolsey. Thanks him for the directions taken for the defence of the realm against Scotland. Hears that a servant of my Lord Marquis is coming to the court with news. Encloses a letter from my Lord Treasurer. London, 4 Aug.
Hol., p.1. Addressed : "[To] Master Almoner this be [del]ivered at Portismouthe with the King's grace.

6 Aug.   **4389.**   SIR ROB. WINGFIELD to HENRY VIII.
Vitell. B.xviii. 56.
B. M.

" I wrote my last letters to your high[ness . . . .] the double of the same unto you which I . . . . unto your gracious hands.—And where in the same I advertised your grace that [the Emperor intended] to be nigh unto you as upon Tuesday next com[ing, and at] that time I doubted partly, because [he] intended to by[d his] daughter farewell ; but, blessed be God, h[ath been such] good diligence on both sides, that the Emperor she . . . . even, and it pleased them to have me at supper, and t[o show me that he] is comyn this night to this

----
* Note by the Ed. of the Lettres :—" C'etoit, comme on croit, sa fille."

1513.

village of Deysne, 6 l[eagues from] you, so that without fail shall keep his point[ment. The Emperor] hath spoken with the Earl of Nassau, and appointed with him . . . . . . to be with him within 15 days, and hath written to the [said Earl] to make haste, with many other good and necessary things [which I] have no leisure to write, and many good things; as . . . . follow by the Emperor's coming to you, for all such as . . . . with him, as well the Swissers as others. When t[hat it pleaseth] his Majesty to be personally in France they shall . . . . make better diligence, and your grace may te[ll him that] the French shall have but small trust in such . . . . be with them, when they shall hear the Emperor [has come] into your company, for out of doubt the . . . . Almain in France that hath any wit . . . . that dare adventure to be against him . . . . . . [Thomas Spinelly hath written to] me this day that he will send you [your artillery] which shall be at Calais by water within 8 days [if] the wind serve, with your courtawdes, that shall come from [Mal]yns."— My Lady of Savoy will not return to Malines, but will proceed by easy journeys to St. Omer, accompanied by all the great men of those parts, "and many of them be right ille aferde." It is supposed this country will be forced to enter into the war, "which and [it] may be brought about, on the Emperor's part your grace shall be well and justly served, for the Swiss concluded on Sunday last by what way they will enter into France, and set forward strey[ghts]." The Emperor expects to hear of them to-night or to-morrow. "As far as I can perceive the Emperor intendeth to come to you as your familiar friend, without looking for any ceremonies, but, after salutations made, to talk of such things as shall be necessary for your enterprise, and especially for ordering your artillery." Thinks that on Wednesday the two sovereigns may be together. Deysne, 6 Aug. 1513.

Hol., pp. 2.

6 Aug.
P. S.
Rym. xiii. 374.

4390. For MARCELLUS DE LA MORE, the King's principal surgeon.

To be sergeant of the King's surgeons, with wages, and precedence as customary since the reign of Edw. IV. Calais, 18 July 5 Hen. VIII. *Del.* Westm., 6 Aug.

Pat. 5 *Hen.VIII. p.* 1, *m.* 4. *Teste Regina.*

6 Aug.
P. S.

4391. For SIR RICHARD WYNGFELD, knight of the Body, and SIR ROBERT WYNGFELD.

Grant, in survivorship, of the office of marshal of the town and marches of Calais from the 6th Oct. last, with the same number of soldiers under them and allowances as Sir William Meryng, or any other marshal there. Calais, 14 July 5 Hen. VIII. *Del.* Westm., 6 Aug.

Pat. 5 *Hen.VIII. p.* 1, *m.* 21. *Teste Regina.*

6 Aug.
P. S.

4392. For SIR GILBERT TALBOT, and SIR RICHARD WYNFELD, knight of the Body.

Grant, in survivorship, of the office of Deputy of Calais, from the 6th Oct. next, with an annuity of 100*l.* out of the issues of the lordship of Marc and Oye, and another annuity of 104*l.* out

1513.

of the same issues called " spyall money ;"—the said Gilbert and
Richard to have under them 31 soldiers for the defence of the
town, viz., one spear, two riders called archers, and 28 soldiers,
with the same wages as in the time of the said Gilbert, now
Deputy, or of Richard Nanfan, Deputy in the time of Hen. VII. :
the said Gilbert and Richard to take at pleasure 10 soldiers besides
the said 31, out of the King's retinue or that of the treasurer of
war for Calais. Also granting them the nomination and removal
of all soldiers and officers of the town not belonging to the retinue
of the lieutenant of the castle, marshal, treasurer, comptroller,
doorward or sub-marshal ; and power to grant safe-conducts, and,
in case of need, to lay disobedient and rebel parishes under tribute.
If this patent be not valid, it shall be renewed on being shown to
the Chancellor. Calais, 13 July 5 Hen. VIII. *Del.* Westm., 6 Aug.
Pat. 5 Hen. VIII. p. 1, m. 22.   Teste Regina.

---

7 Aug.   **4393.**   MARGARET OF SAVOY to HENRY VIII.

Galba, B. III. 86a.   In behalf of Thomas Spinelly, going to Henry, for whom she
B. M.   begs credence. Oudenarde, 7 Aug. 1513. *Signed.*
            Fr., p. 1. Add.

---

7 Aug.   **4394.**   COMMISSION OF THE PEACE.

         Salop.—G. Bp. of Coventry and Lichfield, R. Bp. of Hereford,
T. Bp. of Bangor, Edw. Duke of Buckingham, Thos. Earl of
Arundel, Geo. Earl of Shrewsbury, Rob. Brudenell, Humph.
Conyngesby, Chas. Bothe, clk., Sir Gilb. Talbott, Sir Wm. Uve-
dale, Sir Griffin Rice, Sir Hen. Vernon, Sir Thos. Cornewall,
Sir Thos. Blount, Sir Thos. Leyghton, Sir John Maynwaryng, Sir
Peter Newton, Wm. Rudhall, Rich. Litelton, Thos. Scryven, Thos.
Lacon, John Salter, Geo. Bromeley, Rich. Horde, Geo. Hare-
browne, Thos. Lynom, Ric. Forster, and Ric. Shelman. Croydon,
7 A[ug.]
         Pat. 5 Hen. VIII. p. 1, m. 6d.

---

8 Aug.   **4395.**   MONS. DE WALHAM.

Calig. E. I. 127.   Disbursements of Mons. de Walham [in England] . . 18 July
B. M.   1513 to the 8th Aug., for payment of 100 pioneers.
            Fr., mutilated, p. 1.

---

11 Aug.   **4396.**   MARGARET OF SAVOY to HENRY VIII.

Galba, B. III. 89b.   Has received his letters of the 8th, speaking of the Sieur de
B. M.   Castre, and the other respecting money (*du fait des monneyes*).
            Has sent his letters to the Emperor, to whom these affairs belong.
            Begs the King will write to him about it, and that he will send
            Thomas Spinelly as soon as he can to communicate the news.
            Oudenarde, 11 Aug. 1513. *Signed.*
            Fr., p. 1, mutilated. Add.

---

12 Aug.   **4397.**   HENRY VIII. to JAMES IV.

Calig. B. VI. 49.   "The copie of thaunswere made to the Kinges of Scottes letter."
B. M.   With slight verbal differences from that printed in Hall and in
Rym. XIII. 312.   Rymer. Among other variations, James's defiance is mentioned as
from   of date 16 July instead of 26.
Harl. 787, f. 58.   *Contemporary copy, pp. 2.*

R. O.   2. Another copy.

1513.

13 Aug. **4398.** KATHARINE OF ARRAGON to WOLSEY.

Calig. D. vi. 93.
B. M.
Ellis, 1 S. i. 82.

Received both his letters by Copynger and John Glyn. Was glad to hear the King passes so well "his dangerous passage," and trusts he will always have the best of his enemies. Was troubled to hear the King was so near the siege of Terouenne until Wolsey's letter assured her of the heed he takes to avoid all manner of dangers. With his health and life nothing can come amiss to him ; without them, "I can see no manner good thing shall fall after it." Begs Wolsey to write frequently, remembering she is without any other comfort. They are not so busy with war in Terouenne as she is encumbered with it in England ;—they are all there very glad "to be busy with the Scots, for they take it for a pastime. My heart is very good to it, and I am horribly busy with making standards, banners, and badges." Wishes to know if he received her letters with those she sent of her father Ferdinand, and what answer Wolsey gave. Richmond, 13 Aug.

"Master Almoner."

15 Aug. **4399.** PAUL ARMESTORFF to MARGARET OF SAVOY.

Lett. de Louis XII.
t. iv. 192.

The Emperor and the King of England dined together yesterday before Therouenne, and showed such cordiality that one might suppose them father and son rather than brothers. The Swiss have written to the Emperor that they will have 16,000 men in his service at Besançon on the 27th, with banners displayed. They have also written to the King of England on the same subject. The King of Scots has sent a defiance to the King of England, who, however, was prepared before his departure. Though the Emperor, experienced in war, makes many difficulties about assaulting Therouenne, the King of England desires to head the attack, promising to make sufficient breaches in three days. It is hard to keep them back. The French frequently show themselves and retire. Before Therouenne, 15 Aug.

Fr.

15 Aug. **4400.** For WILLIAM BROWN, clk

P. S.

Presentation to the church of Wenvo, Llandaff, dioc., void by death. Richmond, 14 Aug. 5 Hen. VIII. *Del.* Mortlake, 15 Aug.

16 Aug. **4401.** BAPTISTE DE TASSIS, MASTER OF THE POSTS TO MARGARET OF SAVOY.

Lett. de Louis XII.
t. iv. 195.

Early in the day the Emperor and the King of England encountered 8,000 French horse ; the Emperor, with 2,000 only, kept them at bay until four in the afternoon, when they were put to flight. A hundred men of arms were left upon the field, and more than a hundred taken prisoners, of the best men in France ; as the Sieur de Piennes, the Marquis de Rotelin, &c. Aire, the 16th, 7 o'clock.

Fr.

4402. LIST [OF PRISONERS AT THE BATTLE OF SPURS].

Add. 21,382. f. 52.
B. M.

Duke of Longueville, Marquis of Ruthelin, Count Dunois, René de Cleremont, vice-admiral of France, Capt. Bayart, Ramon de Lisle, archer of the guard, John de Lalu, Willm. de la Calege, John Bourne, bastard, and one named Quiery, John de la Ryne, gunner, George Beule and Willm. Dorvey, gunners, Pierre de la Rocque,

T T

1513.

René de Cely, standard bearer in Duke d'Alençon's company, Wodirt Perison, Jean Gramato, Estienne Shaw, gentlemen of the Duke of Longueville.

17 Aug.   **4403.**   DACRE to RUTHAL.
Calig. B. III. 3.
B. M.
> Thanks him for his kindly writings and news of the appointment of Surrey as lieutenant-general of the North. On receipt of the King's letters at F[or]de, sent a servant to the King of Scots with Henry's letters. Has sent his answer by post, testifying a desire for peace. Dacre thinks it would be politic to overdrive the time, that "the corn might be . . . . . and housed, and the stubble eten bare with the cattle, and then it should be hard to the Scots to make [any] enterprise within this realme," as he has written to the King. Desires that the writings may be delivered according to a minute enclosed sent by the secretary of Scotland, and that he may have answer by next post. The treasurer of Scotland suggested to his servant that Henry might arrange matters by sending 4 or 5,000 angels to the King his master. He and the Bp. of Glasgow are good and discreet men, by whom Dacre gets much intelligence. Perceives James is much displeased at the Queen's being deprived of her legacy. Submits that it were honorable to pay it, the sum is so small. Sent to the assize at Newcastle divers misdoers, who have been executed. His brother, Philip Dacre, arrested Gawin Ogle there, and delivered him to the sheriff; but he escaped when the justices left the town. Will answer for it this shall be remedied. Carlisle, 17 Aug. *Signed.*
> *Addressed:* "To my Lord of Durham."
> *P. 1.*

17 Aug.   **4404.**   To the ABP. OF CANTERBURY, Chancellor.
S. B.
> For letters patent to Lord Ferres, appointing him one of the King's commissioners and of the King's council in the marches of Wales. Dated at the field on the north-east side of Tiroan, 10 Aug. *Del.* Mortlake, 17 Aug. 5 Hen. VIII.

17 Aug.   **4405.**   PHILIPPE DE BREGILLES to MARGARET OF SAVOY.
Lett. de Louis XII.
t. IV. 196.
> The King is writing to her, with the names of the prisoners taken on Tuesday, among whom was the Duke of Longueville, " un tres honneste jeune prince," whom he would pity if he were not a Frenchman ; must pity himself that he had not left the camp for five weeks, fearing to miss the sight of the action, and when it took place he had gone to St. Omer to procure arms, because the King had told him that he would give the assault in two days. The King urges the Emperor to hasten Margaret's coming. The Grand Ecuyer, Lord Lisle, offers her his services ; she is aware he is a second king, and it would be well to write him a kind letter, for it is he who does and undoes. Before Therouenne, Wednesday. *Fr.*

18 Aug.   **4406.**   For JOHN HERON alias HEYRON of Crawley, Northumberland, alias of Harebotell, bastard.
S. B.
> Pardon. *Del.* Westm., 18 Aug. 5 Hen. VIII.
> *Pat. 5 Hen. VIII. p.* 1, *m.* 18. *Teste Regina.*

1513.

.19 Aug. 4407. MARGARET OF SAVOY to HENRY VIII.

Galba, B. iii. 87.
B. M.

Has received his letters dated from the camp at Terouenne, announcing the victory he had gained. No one can be more delighted. The Emperor will be as willing to support him as if he were his father, and will not spare his own person. Hopes that both will be preserved from danger. Lisle, 19 Aug. 1513. *Signed.*
Fr. pp. 2. Mutilated.

19 Aug. 4408. For HENRY STOKES of Calais, merchant.

P. S.

Protection for two years. Calais, 18 July 5 Hen. VIII. *Del.* Mortlake, 19 Aug.
Pat. 5 Hen. VIII. p. 1, m. 21. Teste Regina.

20 Aug. 4409. MAXIMILIAN [SFORZA] DUKE [OF MILAN] to HENRY VIII.

Vitell. B. ii. 47.
B. M.

If he had known that the Emperor was to have had an interview with Hen. VIII. would never have allowed his secretary to approach him without a special commission. Has sent him certain credentials. Milan, 20 Aug. 1513. *Signed.*
Lat., mutilated, p. 1. Add.

22 Aug. 4410. "THE APPOINTMENT OF TYRWENNE."

Lansdowne 858,
f. 21.
B. M.

Anthoine de Crequy Sieur de Pont Remy and François de Thylyny sieur de Lyerville and seneschal of Rouarque agree to deliver Therouenne to Henry VIII., to morrow at 9 o'clock a.m., on condition ; (1.) That they shall go out with bag and baggage, colours flying (estandars ployes), their helmets on their heads and their lances on their thighs &c.—(2.) That they shall have safe conduct to their own party.—(3.) That the pioneers and victuallers shall be at liberty to leave the town, and those who remain shall be treated as the King's subjects. The above articles have been agreed between the Earl of Shrewsbury and the said captains, 22 Aug. 1513.
Fr., pp. 2.

22 Aug. 4411. TEROUENNE.

Aug. I. vol. ii.
No. 72.
B. M.

A plan of Terrouene and of the camps and works of a besieging army.

4412. TEROUENNE.

R. O.

List of broken guns at Terouenne, sold by Sir Sampson Norton ; part of the metal delivered to Hans Popenruyter to be new cast ; with the distribution of gunpowder, and purposes for which it was used.
A roll of paper.

4413. TEROUENNE.

Add. 11,321. f. 97.
B. M.

The King's halls and tents, with measurements, at the siege of Terouenne and Tournay.
Pp. 5.

23 Aug. 4414. FEODARIES OF CROWN LANDS.

S. B.

Oxford and Berks ; Appointment of William Yonge as receiver-general of the possessions of the crown in the above counties, with authority in the King's name to take the persons of heirs under age,

1513.

and deliver them to Sir Thomas Lovell, treasurer of the King's household.

Similar appointments as under; in—

Somerset and Dorset; Christopher Power.
Wilts and Glouc.; Gregory Morgan.
Hants; John Dawtrey.
Worc.; Thomas Walssh.
Staff. and Salop; John Wellys.
London and Middlesex; Richard Hawkis.
Essex and Herts; William Goche.
Norfolk and Suffolk; John Hacon.
Camb. and Hunts; Hugh Danyell.
Northt.; Robert Chauntrell.
Warw. and Leic.; John a Lee.
Surrey and Sussex; Thomas Polsted.
Notts; William Wymbeswold.
Linc.; John Mounson.
Derb.; Christopher Metheley.
Heref. and Marches of Wales; John Rudhale.
Cornwall and Devon; John Walsshe.
Westmoreland and Cumberland; Robert Warcop.
Del. Westm., 23 Aug. 5 Hen. VIII. *Signed:* Thomas Lovell.
Pat. 5 Hen. VIII. *p.* 1, *m.* 22d.

24 Aug. 4415. LAUR. DE GORREVOD to MARGARET OF SAVOY.

Addit. 21,382.
f. 50.
B. M.

Has received her letters stating that his secretary ought to have written to Marnix. Vindicates himself from the accusation of his secretary, that he had paid his respects to the King of England in the camp of Terouenne, before seeing the Emperor. The King of England was not in his tent at the time, but in his wooden house, and was not even ready to hear mass. Hopes soon to return with Varax, Candie, and other gentlemen who were with him at the time. At the abbey of St. John, where the Emperor lodges, before Therouenne, Wednesday 24 Aug.

All the English are anxious to see her, and tell her the story of the victory. *Signed.*

Fr., pp. 3. *Add.:* "A Madame."

24 Aug. 4416. For JOHN DE SERFFE, native of Flanders.

P. S.
Rym. XIII. 374.

Annuity of 20*l.* from Mich. next, till the marriage of the King's sister, Mary Princess of Castile, with Charles Prince of Castile. The King's camp near Turwyn, 8 Aug. 1513. *Del.* Westm., 24 Aug.

Pat. 5 Hen. VIII. *p.* 1, *m.* 7. *Teste Regina.*

25 Aug. 4417. KATHARINE OF ARRAGON to WOLSEY.

Calig. D. VI. 94.
B. M.
Ellis, 1 S. I. 84.

Rejoices at his tidings. The victory hath been such she thinks nothing like it was ever seen before. Trusts all things shall follow as they have begun. Thanks him for his letters, begs he will continue them. Hopes the King will adhere to his resolution. "I think with the company of the Emperor, and with his good counsel, his grace shall not adventure himself so much as I was afeard of before." Thinks the meeting very honorable to the King. "The Emperor hath done everything like himself. I trust to God he shall be thereby known for one of the excellentist princes in the world, and taken for another man than he was before thought."

1513

With the King's consent would like to be remembered to the Emperor. "Almighty God helps here our part as well as there." Thinks it is owing to the King's piety. Richmond, 25 Aug.

P. 1. "*Master Almoner.*"

25 Aug. **4418.** THOMAS SPINELLY to HENRY VIII.

Galba, B. III. 88, B. M.

Wrote last on the 20 ... Since then my Lady was commanded by the Emperor to stop the wagons laden with harness from going into France—which she did. To morrow she sends the Lord Berges to the Emperor to know when she shall have leave to visit the King. It is thought that some of the Emperor's servants will not be very glad of her coming, as they can rule him better in her absence. Is told that the ambassador of Arragon has made urgent requests to her "to find some way wherewith your grace to have the Duke of Longevile for to recover Peter of Navarre, captain of the King of Arragon, being prisoner in France, and this in recompense of the 6,000 footmen that the said King asketh of your grace for to make war into France, which manner of doing me seemeth very subtle and full of cawtele."—Lasschaw is here—good French and a crafty fellow.—My Lady would be glad if he were sent into Burgundy—he does no good here. Lord Berges will visit the King—and he advises that no more money be given to Dissilstain, as he did not keep his former covenant. Understands that the Lord Walham has a great person a prisoner, whom he hath not disclosed to the King, but keeps him to pledge the Lord Wassenaw, prisoner in Gueldres. Begs this information may not be disclosed. Lysle, 25 Aug. 1513.

Hol., pp. 3, *mutilated. Add.*

25 Aug. **4419.** For JOHN STUDDE, of London, alias of Egham, Surr.

P. S.

Pardon. Greenwich, 14 June 5 Hen. VIII. *Del.* Westm., 25 Aug.

Pat. 5 Hen. VIII. p. 2, *m.* 28.

25 Aug. **4420.** For JOHN WARE and JOHN SHIPMAN of Bristol, merchants.

P. S.

Licence to import 100 tuns of Gascon wine, and 60 tons of Tolouse woad. Richmond, 23 Aug. 5 Hen. VIII. *Del.* Otford, 25 Aug.

Fr. 5 Hen. VIII. m. 9.

27 Aug. **4421.** THE WAR WITH FRANCE.

R. O.

Indenture made .... 5 Hen. VIII. between ...... ward on the one part, and Sir [Robert Willoughby] Lord Broke on the other, acknowledging the receipt by the latter of a month's wages from [31 July] to the 27 [Aug.] for himself at 6s. 8d. a day, 3 captains at 4s., 3 petty captains at 2s., 300 soldiers at 6d., and 10 men assigned for his carriages and horses, 6d.

Signed: "Wylughby." *Mutilated.*

Receipt, indented by Will. Morgan, to Sir Robert Dymoke, treasurer of the King's rearward, for 79l. 2s., being a month's wages of the said William and his retinue from the 31 July to the 27 Aug. *Signed.*

The same, by Sir Alex. Beynam, for 81l. 18s. for the same period. *Signed.*

1513.

The same, by John Savage, for 156*l.* 16*s.* for the same period. *Signed.*

The same, by Thos. Philippes, for 79*l.* 16*s.* for the same period. *Signed.*

27 Aug.   **4422.**   SCOTCHMEN IN ENGLAND.
R. O.

An article to be added to a commission for inquiring after aliens, enjoining that in consequence of the war between England, France, and Scotland, all Scotchmen living in England should be deemed enemies ; but that all Scotchmen that have married English women and have children may remain, on forfeiture of half their goods and security for the other half ; the same to be estimated by the sheriff and the King's commissioners.   All others to have their goods seized and their persons banished, under penalty of their lives.

Draft, corrected by Ruthal, pp. 3.

27 Aug.   **4423.**   SCOTCHMEN IN ENGLAND.
S. B.

Blank commission to seize and sell the lands and goods of all born subjects of the King of Scots in the county of Oxford ; and to make correct inventories of the same and the value thereof, between them and the said Scotch subjects ; any disputes that may arise to be determined by other commissioners.   Westm., 27 Aug. 5 Hen. VIII.   *Teste Regina.*

Signed : " Katherine the Qwene."

2. Similar commissions, with the names, ordered for other counties.

Pat. 5 Hen. VIII. p. 1, m. 22d.

4424.   MARGARET QUEEN OF SCOTS to [Q. KATHARINE].
Vesp. F. xiii. 74.
B. M.

" My good Lady, I pray you remember a pon me in your good prayers.   Your loving friend, Margaret the Queen of Scots."

Hol., p. 1.

28 Aug.   **4425.**   NAVY.
R. O.

Covenant between Thomas Earl of Surrey, treasurer, and Edw. Madison, owner of the *Mawdelen* of Hull, with 3 score men of war, for conducting a wool fleet from Hull to Calais for 55*l.* 28 Aug. 5 Hen. VIII.   *Signed.*

4426.   MARGARET OF SAVOY to HENRY VIII.
R. O.

Requests he will commission Thomas Spinelly to be the bearer of a special message from her to the King.

Hol., Fr., p. 1.   *Addressed :* " Au Roy mon tres honore frere et cousin, en sa main."

1 Sept.   **4427.**   ERASMUS to AMMONIUS.
Er. Ep. viii. 19.

Supposes Ammonius has received his letter.   Was pleased to find that he had thought of him so kindly in his letter to John. His ὑγιεινὰ παραγγέλματα, dedicated to the Master of the Rolls, has been lately reprinted at London.   John promised to send Ammonius a copy.   Begs his compliments to the Master of the Rolls, and that Ammonius will show him the book if he is in camp.   The sickness is as fierce in London as war there ;—keeps therefore at Cambridge ready to flit.   The University still retains in its hands

1513.

the 30 nobles Erasmus expects at Michaelmas. Sixtinus is gone to Brabant. Is greatly bent on correcting St. Jerome. Has already done most part of it at incredible expense. Laughed heartily at the quaint description of life in the camp in his letter to John. Begs him, whatever he does, to fight where he will take no harm; —may slay with his pen as many thousands as he likes. If he visits St. Omer, Erasmus begs his compliments to the Abt. S. Bertin, to Ant. Lutzenburg his steward, and Guibert his physician. Begs him to ask what has become of Maurice. Knows he need not ask Ammonius to promote John's interests. Sends his compliments to Baptista ;—expects nothing less than a Greek letter from him. London, kl. Sept. 1511.

1 Sept.   **4428.**   [UNIVERSITY OF CAMBRIDGE] to LORD MOUNTJOY.

R. O.

Requesting his assistance towards the payment of the huge stipend (*immensum stipendium*) for their Greek professor, [Erasmus] whom they must otherwise lose.

Lat., p. 1.

1 Sept.   **4429.**   SPINELLY to HENRY VIII.

R.O.
St. P. vi. 23.

Wrote last on the 27th. The Emperor has since reported to the Archduchess the good and wise communications he has had with Mr. Almoner (Wolsey). If Berghes has not in her absence brought matters to a good resolution, she is ready to join her father and Henry at some convenient place. Letters from Burgundy of the 20 Aug. mention that 28,000 Swiss, besides the horsemen, had arrived within six leagues of the duchy. My Lady sends the originals to Lord Berghes. She considers this highly favourable to Henry's enterprise. Great part of the duchy is believed to have gone over to the Swiss, for the Emperor. It is very necessary for Henry to set forth and follow up the good beginning, as winter is so near. The Burgundians in Henry's service care not how long the war lasts, as they have no other living. Some of Lord Ligne's men have been here with passports. "Unto whom I spare not to speak ; and whatsoever the said Lord Ligne said unto your grace, I can believe none other but he or his lieftenaunt is condiscend to it.' They will find plenty of excuses. Lord Isselstein and his company have gone towards the King. Most of them are Low Almains, retained at eight gildyrns. Henry should not engage them at a higher price ; if more be demanded Isselstein should be told that Henry promised no more, and that my Lady must make up the deficiency, according to the bargain. As he has not kept his day there must be a new arrangement for the beginning of his term. Vadencort, a gentleman of Ligne's company, has brought hither some French prisoners, of whom one named Mons. Darpaggion is kinsman to the Master of Rhodes, and spends 500 or 600 marks a year. Lisle, 1 Sept. 1513.

The Governor of Brescia arrived last night.

Signed.

Pp. 3.   *Add.*

1 Sept.   **4430.**   For RALPH RYVELEY and ROBERT BELL late of Doding-

P. S.

ton, Northumb., alias of Norham in the liberty of the Bishopric of Durham.

Pardon. Camp near Terouenne, 1 Sept. 5 Hen. VIII.   *Del.* Westm., 1 Sept.

1513.
2 Sept.
Archæol. xxvi. 475.
Appendix.
MS. *apud* Sir
John Trevelyan.

4431. GILES AP. . . . . . to the EARL OF DEVON.

The King had a goodly passage from Dover to Calais, where he remained three weeks. On the 20 July marched with his army into France, and on St. Anne's day, as he was coming towards St. Omer's, was informed of a great company of Frenchmen, who fled, although they were five to one. The King then went to the south side of St. Omer's, where he continued three days, and then to the east side. Sir Rice ap Thomas with some spears went back for one of the King's great guns, which he recovered, though it had been captured by the French. The Emperor came to the King on the east side of the town, and was entertained in "a goodly tent with a gallery all of cloth of gold set up with a cobbord in the richest manner, and so continued unto the 16th day of August," when the King removed his field to Gyngat, a mile from thence. On the morning before setting forth, having heard that a large army of Frenchmen were coming to victual Tyroan, he advanced and followed them from morning till night to a place called Bomye, more than six miles from his "leger," and there attacked them. Although the odds were six to one on their side, they fled. At that time the emperor was under the King's standard, and when required to spread his standard refused to do so, [saying] he would that day be the servant of the King and St. George.

There were taken,—the Duke of Longville, Marquis of Ruthelyn, and Earl of Dunoys, Mons. de Cleremont vice-admiral of France, the Lord Ymbercourt captain of 100 spears, the Duke of Longvill's steward, the steward of the French king's house, the lieutenant of the Lord Nyon, captain Bayard, captain of 100 spears, one called Mount Clere, one of the 200 gentlemen of the French king's house, one Gardif, a man of arms of the said house, Jenyn Fraunces, Fraunces de Sarran, Jenan de la Peyon, three of the gentlemen of the French King's house, six standards and their bearers, and three other standards unknown. My Lord Steward and Sir Rice have four standards. There were also taken 21 persons in cloth of gold and velvet, men-at-arms, archers on horseback, and others. It is said that above 3,000 Frenchmen were slain, and that the King has not lost above three men. "The chase of the same bickering endured four miles and above; and so, that done, being very near night, the King's highness with his said army returned again unto Gyngate, where he continued until the 20th day of August, and so removed unto the south side of the city of Tyroan."

On the 21st the captains of the city entreated the Lord Steward to move the King to allow them to depart with their lives, and on the 22nd the King, with the Emperor's consent, rode unto the walls and gave them mercy. The captains left the town on the 23rd, the soldiers in three guards. One guard had written in gold letters on their breasts, *Heilly*; the second, *Sarcuz*; the third, *Picarde*. The next day the King, with a goodly company of estates, men-at-arms, hynschemen, &c., all richly apparelled, rode into Tyroan, where the Emperor met him, bringing with him six hynshemen, dressed (like himself) in black velvet. The gates were opened by the Earl of Shrewsbury, who delivered the keys to the King, who kept them "a certain while," and returned them to the Lord Steward. The King entered the city, where the people met him in the streets, and cried in French, "Welcome, most merciful King." He rode to the cathedral, and entered it with the Emperor. In the King's chapel they had an anthem of our Lady and another of St. George. The King then departed to his field, and the Emperor to St. Omer's.

1513.

On the 26th the King again removed his field to Gyngate, where he yet remains "according to law of arms, for in case any man would bid battle for the besieging and getting of any city or town, then the winner to give battle, and to abide for the same certain days." The King has and does set daily 800 or 900 laborers and miners to destroy the walls of Tyroan, so it is almost level, and all the towers are down. "Verily, my lord, it was a stronghold; the ditches on the outside were so deep that a man walking and looking into them feared for falling down to come nigh the banks, gaily wooded upon the banks and bushed with quick set every corner, and wide walls and other, full of great bulwarks, and besides the walls on the inside mightily fortified with great trenches, many bulwarks made with timber and earth, and in certain places of the said trenches sundry deep pits for to have made fumigations, to the intent that men upon the assaulting of the same should have been poisoned and stopped; and as for the houses within forth very sore beaten with guns, and such importunate and continual shot made with guns into the same, that no person might stir in the streets. And thus the King's highness and the Emperor be together, and have every others' counsel, with the most amiable and loving wise that can be thought." Gingate, 3 Sept. *Signed.*
Add.

2 Sept.   **4432.**   QUEEN KATHARINE to WOLSEY.

R. O.

Ellis, 3 S. I. 152.

Received his letter by post informing her of the coming hither of the Duke (Longueville), and that he is to be in her household. Has advised with the council. There is none fit to attend upon him except Lord Mountjoy, who is now going over to Calais. Advises he should be sent to the Tower, "specially the Scots being so busy as they now be, and I looking for my departing every hour." Begs to have an answer from the King. Excuses herself, that being so bound to Wolsey, she had sent him no letter. Had written to him two days before by Copynger. Her greatest comfort now is to hear from Wolsey of the King's health and all the news. "And so I pray you, Mr. Almoner, to continue as hitherto ye have done; for I promise you that from henceforth ye shall lack none of mine, and before this ye should have had many mo, but I think that your business scantly giveth you leisure to read my letters." Pray God "to send us as good luck against the Scots as the King hath there." Richmond, 2 Sept.

Signed: "Katherine the Qwene."

"[To] Master Almoner." *Endorsed.*

P. 1.

3 Sept.   **4433.**   SPINELLY to HENRY VIII.

R. O.

St. P. vi. 25.

Wrote last on the 1st inst. Berghes has since written that matters have gone on well, and that the King's army will remove on Monday next. The Archduchess is very glad, and expects to-night or to-morrow to know the Emperor's pleasure where she shall meet the King. No more news from Burgundy. The pensionary of Antwerp arrived this morning. The Duke of Gueldres has assembled 3,000 foot in the land of Kessyll, on the borders of Brabant, for the service of France. Louis Moreton (Maraton) complains that Henry has rewarded others of the Emperor's service, and neglected him. My Lady says he deserves better than any other, for he had often run in posts himself. The French prisoner, "which the Lord Walham hath not discovered," is Mons. de

1513.

Busshy, nephew of the late Cardinal of Rouen, "and he is counted the best that was taken next the Duke of Longevile." The governor of Bresse has reported to my Lady the arguments used by the lords of Henry's council in justification of the ambassador of Arragon's complaints. My Lady is satisfied "that all the default lieth in them, but she is always of opinion that your grace should dissemble, and cherish them, if any other way cannot be found." Lisle, 3 Sept. *Signed.*
Add.   Pp. 2.

3 Sept.   **4434.**   KATHARINE THE QUEEN.
S. B.
Rym. XIII. 374.
i. Commission of array for Sir Thomas Lovell, K.G., in the counties of Nottingham, Derby, Warwick, Leicester, Stafford, Rutland, Northampton, and Lincoln, and the neighbouring counties, if convenient (subject to the commands of Queen Katharine, Regent) against the Scots. Teste Katharina. Westm., 3 Sept. 5 Hen. VIII.

ii. Warrant to Sir Thomas Lovell, K.G., to punish all who obstruct the above. Teste Katharina. Westm., 4 Sept. 5 Hen. VIII.

Rym. ib. 375.
iii. Commission to Sir Thomas Lovell, K.G., to hear and determine as to all treasons, murders, &c., in the absence of Thomas Earl of Surrey, marshal of England, captain-general against the Scots. Teste Katharina.   Westm., 7 Sept. 5 Hen. VIII.
Signed : "Katherine the Qwene."   *Countersigned :* T. Englefild, Robert Southwell, R. Becansaw, John Cutte.
Pat. 5 Hen. VIII. p. 1, m. 22d.

4 Sept.   **4435.**   MAXIMILIAN.
R. O.
Acknowledgment of his having received from Henry VIII. 100,000 crowns of gold in conformity with the treaty lately concluded between them. Aire, 4 Sept. 1513.
Vellum.   Signed.

4 Sept.   **4436.**   For SIR JOHN FENEUX, chief justice of the King's
S. B.
Bench, ROBERT REDE, chief justice of the Common Pleas, ROBERT BRUDNELL, justice of the King's Bench. CHRISTOPHER URSWIK, clk., SIR THOMAS LOVELL, SIR THOMAS ENGLEFELD, SIR ROBERT SOUTHWELL, SIR JOHN CUTT, and JOHN HERON.

Grant of the manors of Billing, alias Billing-Magna, Chappell Brampton, and Eyton, Northt., Enderby, Leic., Tidburst and Kendall, Herts, Meydecroft, Beds, Wrashyngworth, Camb., Lanmershe and Colneywake, in Essex, Billingburgh, Linc., Milbourneporte, Somerset, Escoyd and Gunyonneth, Cardigan in South Wales, and all other lands, &c., lately belonging to Margaret Countess of Richmond ;—with mortmain licence to alienate the premises to the Dean and Canons of St. George, Windsor Castle.   *Del.* Richmond, 4 Sept. 5 Hen. VIII.
Pat. 5 Hen. VIII. p. 1, m. 21. Teste Regina.

5 Sept.   **4437.**   HENRY VIII. to MARGARET OF SAVOY.
Fr. Moore's sale,
lot 511.
Has received her ambassador De Berghes, who is about to return, having acquitted himself entirely to Henry's satisfaction. Commends his fidelity. Camp beside Therouenne, 5 Sept. 1513.
Fr., p. 1.   Signed.

1513.

5 Sept.
S. B.

4438.   For THOMAS RUTHAL BP. OF DURHAM.

Wardship of Anne, daughter and heir of Thomas Middelton.
Del. Westm., 5 Sept. 5 Hen. VIII.
Pat. 5 Hen.VIII. p. 2, m. 30.

7 Sept.
R. O.
Ellis, 1 S. I. 86.
from
Calig. B. VI. 73.
B. M.

4439.   THOMAS EARL OF SURREY to JAMES IV.

Lately sent Rougecross to announce that he was come to repress the invasion of the Scots, and offer battle Friday next "on this half." Though James expressed himself by Islay as right joyous of the news, and ready to abide Surrey's coming, he had since withdrawn himself to a ground more like a fortress. Begs James will wait for him to morrow on the Scotch side of the plain of Milfield, where Surrey will be ready to give battle between 12 o'clock and 3 in the afternoon, upon sufficient warning had from James by 8 or 9 o'clock in the morning. Begs James and his nobles will subscribe this engagement, as Surrey has done, and those with him. Written in the field in Wollerhaughe, 7 September, 5 o'clock in the afternoon.
Signed: Thomas Surrey.
Thomas Haward, Thom. Dacre, Clifford, Henerie [Scrope]* Ralphe Scroope, Rich. Latimer, William Conyers, J. Lomley, R. Ogle, W. Percye, [E. Stanley, William Molynex]*, Marmaduke Constable, W. Gascoigne, W. Griffith, [George Darcy,]* W. Bulmer, Thom. Strangwayes.
Contemporaneous copy, p. 1.

7 Sept.
R. T. 137.
R. O.

4440.   THE WAR WITH FRANCE.

Commission for Louis de Bresze, the French King's lieutenant in Normandy, for arming three ships stationed at Dieppe, to form part of the fleet of Honfleur against the English. Honefleur, 7 Sept. 1513.   *Signed.*
Fr.

9 Sept.
R. O.
St. P. IV. 1.

4441.   ACCOUNT OF THE BATTLE OF FLODDEN.

When the two armies were within three miles of each other Surrey challenged the King of Scots to battle, by Rugecross ; who answered he would wait for him till Friday at noon. At eleven on 9 Sept. Howard passed the bridge of Twyssell with the vanguard and artillery, Surrey following with the rear. The army was divided into two battles, each with two wings. The Scotch army was divided into five battles, each a bowshot distant from the other, and all "in grete plumpes, part of them quadrant," and some equally distant from the English, likewise, and were on the top of the hill, being "a quarter of a mile from the foot thereof." Howard caused the van to scale in a little valley till the rear joined one of the wings of his battle ; then both advanced in line against the Scots, who came down the hill, and met them "in good order, after the Almayns manner, without speking a word." Earls of Huntley, Eroll, and Crawford met Howard with 6,000 men, but were soon put to flight, and most of them slain. The King of Scots with a great power attacked Surrey, who had Lord Darcy's son on his left. These two bore the brunt of the battle. James was slain within a spear's length of Surrey ; many noblemen with him : no prisoners taken. At the same time, Lennox and Argyle joined battle with Sir Edward Stanley, and were put to flight. Edmund Howard was

---

* Supplied from modern copy in Calig. B. VI.

on the right wing of Lord Howard with 1,000 Cheshire and 500 Lancashire men, who were defeated by the Lord Chamberlain of Scotland (Alex. Lord Hume). Mr. Gray and Sir Hump. Lyle are taken prisoners, Sir Wynchard Harbottle and Maurice Barkley slain ; Edm. Howard was thrice "feled," when Dacre came to his relief and routed the Scots. The battle began between 4 and 5 in the afternoon, and the chase was continued three miles with great slaughter ; 10,000 more would have been slain if the English had been horsed. The Scots were 80,000, of whom 10,000 were killed ; the English lost only 400.* The English and Scotch ordnance has been conveyed by the help of Dacre to Etall Castle. The King of Scots' body is brought to Berwick. No great man of Scotland has returned, except the Chamberlain.

Pp. 2.

9 Sept. **4442.**   FLODDEN.

R. O.

Memorandum of certain armour delivered to Will. Gur by Sir Thos. Lovell and Sir Jo. Cutt, and part sold at the Scottish field, part left with Harry Coste, sheriff of Nottingham, as appears by indentures.

P. 1.

9 Sept. **4443.**   BATTLE OF FLODDEN.

Salisbury MSS.

"Invocatio de inclyta invictissimi Regis nostri Henrici VIII. in Gallos et Scotos victoria, per Bernardum Andrée poetam regium, cum præfatione ejusdem," 4.

"Ad sereniss. potentissimumque Angliæ et Franciæ Regem, Henricum Octavum, propter suam felicem ut sic dicam octavitatem, qua Octaviano Imperatore, ob res tam bello quam pace feliciter gestas, non est inferior, aliquot Senarii Iambici."

10 Sept. **4444.**   LEO X. to HENRY VIII.

R. O.

Begs credence for Raphael de Medici, Florentine merchant in England, his kinsman. Rome, 10 Sept. 1513, 1 pont.

Lat., p. 1. *Addressed.*

11 Sept. **4445.**   CARRIAGE OF ARTILLERY.

Calig. D. vi. 330.
B. M.

Paper headed: " Sensicult le declaration de la despence faicte par Bauduin Caudron, bailly de la Basterre, en ensuivant le commandement et ordonnance à lui faicte par Mons. le Gouverneur de Bethune pour avoir chargié sur six navire l'artillerie du Roy d'Engleterre, et icelle amené et conduit jusques au rivage de Lille, et icelle artillerie desquerquiés desdictes navires et le mené en la Halle seant sur le marchié de la ville de Lille par les personnes ainsy que cy apres sera declairé ; que se fait à mony Artois.

i. " Et premiers le xe jour de Septembre 1513, depences faicte à Bethune." Parties paid : Jehan le Rouge, Bihalle, and Collin Jorgue, Jehan de le Rache, Collin Garin, Druet le Josne, Robinet du Boult, Mayart Semoult, Vincent Quaresmel, Petitian Ressignol, Fierin de Vielle Ville, Willemme de Hemen, Simon Sacquespee, Mahier Bacheller, Pasquièr Viti, Estiene le Josne, Henri Fiemeux, Massin Haye, Bettremen Franchois, Haquin le Roy, Baudechen

---

* The following passage scored out, is not printed in St. P. " The Borders not only stale away as they lost 4 or 5,000 horses, but also they took away the oxen that drew the ordnance, and came to the pavilions and took away all the stuff therein, and killed many that kept the same."

1513.

Barbet, Licnin de Pont, Jacotin Cleret, Jehan Pounillon, Pierre Mayeur, Mullin Sanate, Pierre Caillan, Hennam Valonain, Denis Floury, Petit Roy, Simon Mayeur, Tisse Venduffle, Moran Sauvaige, Ameux Destraielles, Anthoine Derviller, Jerome Suel, Jehan Lausart, Pierre de Huby, Pierckin Grette, Simon Fruville, Andrieu Le Misre, Bertran Masengarbe, Jehan Hanegrave Willemene Obri, Jacot de Rocqueur, Jehan Desgardins, Bertoul Mallet, Collin Marchant, Jacquet de Sam, Collin Bocquet, Charlot Ricquier, Pierre Capelier, Jacquet de Bailleul, Jacquenet le Grant Jerommet, Walleric Senatele, Petitian Torrelet, Marcus du Quesne Jacquemart de Grarier (?), Bil Alle, navigateur, David Chanetier, Estienne Samyer, the master of the works of Bethune, Pierre Linceux, Pierre de le Place, Collin Hallebi, &c.

ii. "Pour pluiseurs despens soustenus et fais par les iiij^{es} varletz et aultres compaignons serviters dudict Roy, qui estoient et conduissoient la dicte artillerie le xj^e jour Septembre audict an 1513, à le Gorghe au soupper en la maison dudict Bauduin en ce comprins mouton et demi-pain, bure, biere et aultres vivres que furent mis esdicts navires pour mengier; leauwe, 13*l.* 10*s.*"

Parties paid: Collin George, Josse de la Croix, Bihalle and Vitte, Jehan le Baugon, Noel Reveleux, Haquin le Raye, Jacquet Picart, Martin, Jehan Tesur, Haquin Grisel, Collin Bosquet, Hayne Liegne, Pierchon Lefrere, Piere Van Brenghe, Braquemart, Jehan Mahieu, Raunbau du Bantus, Jacquet Heselin, Jason Carton, Franchois, Jehan de Tourchelles, &c.

*** Most of the payments are at the rate of 4 sous per diem ; one or two are at 8 sous.

The last entry is : "A ung clercq pour son sallaire d'aver fait ce present compte et le mis en double, 18*s.*"

12 Sept. **4446.** CARDINAL BAINBRIDGE to [HENRY VIII.]

Vitell. B. II. 49.
B. M.
Rym. XIII. 376.

The Pope was advertised on the 5th, by the Florentine ambassador resident at the French court, of Henry's victories over the enemies of the Church. Went next day to Cardinal Sinegal, and demanded the brief; who refused to deliver it until he received order in writing from your Majesty, for so he was commanded by Pope Julie. The present Pope has confirmed all the indulgences in the said brief. Thinks that the King might demand it in more ample manner under lead. Encloses a letter from Sinegal. Thinks he ought to be recompensed. As the Emperor is now with the King, the Venetian ambassador prays him to negotiate peace between him and the signory. Doubts not the Venetians will address him on the premises. Though Cardinal Hadrain has anticipated him in this news, hopes he may not be thought wanting in diligence. The Cardinal bribed the secretary for a copy, that he might show his pretended diligence. He was much more active in bringing about the reconciliation of the schismastics. Rome, 12 Sept. 1513. *Signed.*
Mutilated, pp. 2.

13 Sept. **4447.** ERASMUS to COLET.

Eras. Ep. x. 17.

Sends Colet what he had asked for,—*Officium Chrysostomi,*— and the letter, of which Colet, who despises rhetoric, will not entirely approve ; but Erasmus thinks it not undesirable in a teacher. Begs him not to distrust Linacre, as he knows him to be very friendly ; and not be too much concerned about the rejected grammar (*de rejecta grammatica*) ; he will get over it in time. Has not yet been

1513.

able to find a suitable under-master for Colet's school. Had a brush with the Scotists and Thomists in Colet's defence. — Has begun translating Basil on Isaiah. — Will send a specimen to the Bp. of Rochester (Fisher), and see if he will recompense his labours. Colet will smile at his importunity. Camb., id. Sep.

If Colet has any money in hand, begs him to send a few nobles to Richard Croke, Grocin's former pupil, now staying at Paris. Paris,* 1513.

Sept.   **4448.**   COLET to ERASMUS.

Eras. Ep. App. 4.

Has read his letter with great delight, and wishes boys could be taught in conformity with its directions. How much he wished to have Erasmus for a master in his school ; but when he leaves Cambridge, hopes to have his aid in training his masters. Will do in Linacre's matter as Erasmus advises. Wishes him to look out an under-master for him. Encourages him in the translation of St. Basil, and advises him to imitate Diogenes in despising money. Fortune follows those who fly from her ; though Erasmus does not admire such paradoxes. Has no money of others to help Croke ; has some of his own for Erasmus if he begs humbly. London, 1513.

14 Sept.   **4449.**   PETER MARTYR to LUDOVICO FURTADO.

Pet. Mart. Ep.
No. 526.

The Russians and Tartars have attacked Poland, who has asked for aid from the Pope. Maximilian is ill of a fever at Hasta. Miseries of Italy and dread of the Swiss, as they act like the Goths. The King of England has undermined Terouenne, which has only been saved by the incessant rain. The Emperor was in the camp, then on the north side, and open to the enemy ; but its site has been changed by advice of the Emperor. Lewis, though ill, was brought from Paris in a carriage, made his appearance, and sent the flower of his troops to the siege. A small body of Germans and English drove back the numerous forces of the French, and took many prisoners. Valladolid, 14 Sept. 1513.

14 Sept.   **4450.**   ———— to HEN. VIII.

Calig., D. vi.
B. M.

Excusing himself, that at the request of the captain of Mortaigne some of his followers had entered the town in the King's name. He is daily subjected to grievous insults in the Tournesis and Haynault. Marchienne, 14 Sept 1513. *Signature destroyed.*
P. 1. Add. Fr.

16 Sept.   **4451.**   KATHARINE OF ARRAGON to HENRY VIII.

Vesp. F. iii. 15.
B. M.
Burnet, Ref. P. iii.
B. i. § 2.
Ellis, 1 S. i. 88.

"My Lord Howard hath sent me a letter open to your grace, within one of mine, by the which ye shall see at length the great victory that our Lord hath sent your subjects in your absence."— Thinks the victory the greatest honor that could be. The King will not forget to thank God for it. Could not, for haste, send by Rouge Cross "the piece of the King of Scots coat which John Glyn now bringeth. In this your grace shall see how I can keep my promys, sending you for your banners a King's coat. I thought to send himself unto you, but our Englishmen's hearts would not suffer it. It should have been better for him to have been in peace than have this reward. All that God sendeth is for the best." Surrey wishes to know the King's pleasure as to

* A blunder.

1513.

burying the King of Scots' body. Prays for his return, and for the same is going to our Lady at Walsingham, "that I promised so long ago to see." Woborne, 16 Sept.

Sends a bill found in a Scotchman's purse of the instigation used by France to induce James to war with England. Begs he will send Matthew.

16 Sept. **4452.** KATHARINE OF ARRAGON to WOLSEY.

Calig. B. vi. 35.
B. M.
Ellis, 1 S. i. 89.

Did not write to him by the last messenger, as she had not sure tidings of the battle with the Scots. Since then a post has come with news from Lord Howard, which she sends the King. Thinks its God's doing that his subjects should gain such a victory in his absence.—When the King was at Calais "a great while ago" he sent her a letter touching "the matter betwixt my Lord of Canterbury and my Lord of Winchester."—She showed it to Canterbury before Sir Thomas Lovell and Mr. Englefeld, but could never get an answer from him until now, which she sends. Begs he will continue writing, as it is a great comfort to her. Woborne, 16 Sept.

P. S. Cannot send the Archbishop's letter by this post, as the coffer in which it is, is gone to her lodgings.

17 Sept. **4453.** LOUIS XII.

R. T. 137.
R. O.

Patent appointing Louis de Rouville, grand veneur de France, as lieutenant general of the united fleet of France and Scotland against the English. Cordie, 17 Sept. 1513, 16 Louis XII.

Fr. p. 1.

17 Sept. **4454.** CARDINAL BAINBRIDGE to WOLSEY.

Vitell. B. ii. 51.
B. M.
Fiddes' Wol. c. 2.

The glory of the King for this victory is deemed immortal. Wishes he could be of their company in this their journey. Hears that the benefice of Cottyngham is vacant by the Bp. of Murray's promotion to Bourges. Would have been glad to have favored Wolsey in this matter. Would have opposed the Bishop, hoping his preferment would have fallen into Wolsey's hands. If the King succeeds, Murray will have but hard neighbourhood in his new promotion, "condign for his demerits." Rome, 17 Sept. 1513. *Signed.*

P. 1. *Add.:* "To my right entirely loved brother in Christ, Master Thomas Wulsey, the King's almoner, and dean of my church of York."

17 Sept. **4455.** CHR. [BAINBRIDGE], CARDINAL OF ENGLAND, and SIL-
Vitell. B. ii. 50.   VESTER BP. of WORCESTER, to HENRY VIII.
B. M.

On the 13th received his letters from Terouenne dated 31 Aug., and one for the Pope, giving an account of the victory. The French ambassador told the Pope that the Scotch king had entered England with 100,000 chosen men, leaving 100,000 at home; had taken the Lord Treasurer (Surrey) prisoner, with 15 other lords of coat armour, and slain 30,000 Englishmen. This was divulged and believed. The French and Scots at Rome were sought greatly; but when the King's letter came all their joy was turned into shame. On the 15th the writers, with Cardinal Surrentinus and the ambassadors of the Emperor and of Arragon, were secretly with the Pope, desiring him to fulminate a new bull against the Scotch king for this

brench. To avoid the displeasure of the French cardinals his Holiness has arranged that Bainbridge should present in the consistory to-morrow a bill of remembrance for the same, promising to remit the same unto three cardinals, who would give it in the King's favor. Meantime St. Severin presented letters in the French King's name, praying the Pope to pass no censures on the Scots, as they were his allies. Bainbridge and Surrentinus spoke for England, Cardinal Hadrian kept silence. Many of the cardinals favor France. The Pope has promised that before Michaelmas he will send a resident to England, who shall bring with him the required censures under lead. Thinks that the Bps. of Durham and Carlisle, by force of Pope Julio's bull, have already fulminated the censures against the Scots. The Pope hopes the King will keep silence till the bull arrives. The writers know not why the temporal powers have not been sent from Italy, unless it be owing to Cardinal Gurk and the Emperor. The Bp. of Murray's bulls have been long expedited. Wished to stop them and the benefice of Cottyngham. "The Pope's holiness is not only singularly well contented with the contents of your grace's letters in the Latin tongue, but also doth very greatly praise the form and order of your secretary in the same. There cometh no letters from any other prince unto his Holiness to be exhibited in the Consistory that be judged more elegantly written than they be." Rome, 17 Sept. *Signed.*
Mutilated, pp. 3. Add.

17 Sept. 4456. GEORGE VAN CUTSEGHEM.

R. O.   Certificate by the burgomaster and eschevins of the town of Muda (Muyden) et Juris Aquarum in Flanders, in behalf of George van Cutseghem of the town of Sluyse, who on the 16 March sued George Nichol, an Englishman, for the sum of 15*l.* 3*s.* 3*d.* due to him for nine weeks' service with his ship in supplying provisions and warlike weapons, which he delivered to the said George Nichol as a servant of the English admiral, but was unable to recover the money, owing to the liberty granted by Philip King of Castile to the port of Muda. 17 Sept. 1513.
Lat.

18 Sept. 4457. T. [RUTHAL] BP. OF DURHAM to WOLSEY.

R. O.   Was afraid to be the first to write of the lamentable chances that have occurred. Understands Wolsey is informed of them both by his friends and his enemies. Heard at Calais of the King's glorious victory against the French, and sent news of it to the Queen. Four days afterwards lost 50 of his horses on the sea. On coming to the Queen, learned how valiantly Sir Wm. Bulmer, his sheriff, had discomfited the Scots, as Wolsey has doubtless heard. The King of Scots had stormed Norham Castle, "which news touched me so near with inward sorrow that I had lever to have been out of the world than in it," especially as he had been assured of its security by Will. Pawne and others. He shall never forget it or recover from grief. Will trust, however, within five years, to set 10,000 marks upon it, though he take penance and live a more moderate life. "I never felt the hand of God so sore touching me as in this, whereof I most humbly thank Him, and, after the inward search of conscience to know the cause of the provocation of God's displeasure against me, I shall reform it, if it

1513.

lie in my power, and regard Him more than the world hereafter."
Durham, 18 Sept.* _Signed._

_Pp._ 2.

Added in his own hand: "This letter was written before the battle, which I reserved in hope of better tidings, which God hath now sent."

Headed in his own hand: "This letter is sorrowful, and the other comfortable.—Recedant vetera, nova sint omnia."

_Pp._ 2.

20 Sept. **4458.**   LEO X. to HENRY VIII.

R. O.   Begs credence and safe conduct for Balthazar, the notary, sent with the concurrence of Cardinal Bambridge to James King of Scotland, to arrange a peace, and the preliminaries of an expedition against the Turks. Rome, 20 Sept. 1513, 1 pont. _Add._

Vellum.

20 Sept. **4459.**   [SPINELLY], Ambassador with the Lady MARGARET, to
Harl. 3462, f. 32b.   CARDINAL BAINBRIDGE.

B. M.   Wrote last on the 17th of the great victory gained by the
Ellis, 3 S. I. 163.   Earl of Surrey over the Scots. Yesterday the King was informed by the Earl, that the King of Scots fell in the engagement, not a spear's breadth from him. The corpse was taken to Berwick, and the King has received the Scotch King's plaid (_paludamentum_). 12,000 Scots were slain; all their artillery, tents, and baggage taken. On the English side less than 500 fell. The most part of the Scotch chieftains were slain. None but the Treasurer returned into Scotland. Lord Sauarde (Howard) led the English van, the Earl of Surrey the rear.—Lord Lisle at the siege of Tournay has obtained possession of one of the gates of the city, and carried off two images. The city is so much battered it has sent to the King to beg mercy, and will have an audience today.—Of the Frenchmen who served in the Scotch army, some fell in the engagement, others were cut to pieces by the Scots, who reproached the French with being the cause of their destruction. Lisle, 20 Sept.

_Lat. Contemporaneous copy, in an Italian hand, p._1.

20 Sept. **4460.**   T. [RUTHAL] BP. OF DURHAM to WOLSEY.

R. O.   Thinks that the King should advance my Lord Treasurer to the honor of Duke, for his victory against the Scots, and that letters of thanks should be sent to him and other knights and lords who were at this happy day. "And if ye made 20 for lords with their styles, and the residue with trusty and well beloved, it would do very much good." The Lord Treasurer, Lords Howard and Dacre, Sir Will. Bulmer, and Sir Edw. Stanley must have special clauses. Is glad to hear of the King's victory. Written "as above" [20 Sept.]

The Scotch ordnance was not carried to Berwick, but is at Etall. It is the finest that has been seen. Will send him further information of Norham in three days. The dungeon stands.

---

* "Newark, 8 Sept.," as it originally stood, has been altered to "Durham, 18 Sept."

1513.

The walls, gates, and ordnance taken away, and the lodgings destroyed.

Hol. p. 1. *Addressed :* " [To the r]yght honourable and [my lovi]ng brother, maister Thomas [Wul]cy, the Kynges almoner." *Enclosing—*

4461. Ruthal to Wolsey.

R. O.

Is in great sorrow. His castle of Norham has been razed to the ground. Will study how to renew it. The dungeon stands, and part of the wall. On the 9 Sept. the King of Scots was defeated and slain. Surrey, and my Lord Howard the admiral, his son, behaved nobly. The Scots had a large army, and much ordnance, and plenty of victuals. Would not have believed that their beer was so good, had it not been tasted and viewed " by our folks who viewed their great refreshing," who had nothing to drink but water for three days. They were in much danger, having to climb steep hills to give battle. The wind and the ground were in favor of the Scots. 10,000 Scots are slain, and a great number of noblemen. They were so cased in armour the arrows did them no harm, and were such large and strong men, they would not fall when four or five bills struck one of them. The bills disappointed the Scots of their long spears, on which they relied. Lord Howard led the van, followed by St. Cuthbert's banner and the men of the bishopric. The banner men won great honor, and gained the King of Scots' banner, which now stands beside the shrine. The King fell near his banner. Their ordnance is taken. The English did not trouble themselves with prisoners, but slew and stripped King, bishop, lords, and nobles, and left them naked on the field. There might be seen a number of goodly men, well fed and fat, amongst which number was the King of Scots' body found, having many wounds and naked. Whilst engaged in battle the English tents were plundered by the Borderers.

Copy, with corrections in Ruthal's hand, p. 2.

20 Sept. ### 4462. Ruthal to Wolsey.

R. O.

This victory has been the most happy that can be remembered. All believe it has been wrought by the intercession of St. Cuthbert, who never suffered injury to be done to his Church unrequited. Has spoken to Sir Will. Scot, who is with Sir Will. Bulmer, and others. They say, that after the King had attacked Norham, 20,000 of his men left him, foreboding mischief. The attack proceeded of his own sensual mind, by the instigation of the Bp. of Murray, against the wish of the nobles. There is no wisdom or virtue in that prelate. Is contented to bear the pains of the injury done to Norham, considering what has ensued. The Scots might have done much more injury if they had not attacked St. Cuthbert. There was nothing to oppose them ; they lacked no ordnance ; they had made provision for seven years. Trusts they will never be able to do the same while Scotland stands. My Lord Treasurer (Surrey) has taken the body of the King to York,—would not be persuaded to leave it at Durham : " my folks under St. Cuthbert's banner brought whom (home) his banner, his sword, and his gwyschys, that is to say, the harness for his thighs." After Surrey and Lord Howard no man did better than Sir. Will. Bulmer ; with 700 or 800 men he attacked the chamberlain of Scotland [Hume] with 10,000 and took 400 or 500 prisoners, Sir Edw. Stanley behaved well. Some shrank, of whom Howard will tell him. His lordship has written an account of the battle to the King. Overtures have been made

1513.

for a truce, by the chamberlain, to Lord Dacre, who has written to the Queen about it. Fears they must assent; the weather is so foul, and their victuals deficient. The Borderers are not to be trusted. They have done much harm. They never lighted from their horses till the battle joined, and then they plundered both sides. The English have lost 1,000 men, but one only of eminence, Sir Jo. Bothe of Lancashire. Sends a list of the Lords of Scotland that were slain in the field. Begs him to show this letter to my Lord Privy Seal, to whom he has written. Wishes Wolsey and the King the same success where they are. Durham, 20 Sept.

Hol., pp. 2. (*On the same paper with the above.*)

21 Sept. **4463.** WOLSEY to the LORD CHAMBERLAIN [WORCESTER].
R. O.

The King desires him to pay the pioneers sent by the Emperor at the rate of 6d. a day, "as long as they shall be with you." St. Matthew's day.

Signed : Thomas Wulcy.

P. 1. *Add.*

23 Sept. **4464.** PETER MARTYR to LUD. FURTATO.
Pet. Mart. Ep.
No. 527.

Longueville, Rothelin, with 100 noblemen, Laclete, Bayard, have been taken prisoners at Terouenne. Palice, who commanded at Pampeluna, was wounded and taken, but let go on parole. Terouenne has surrendered. The army of England consists of 15,000 Germans, 34,000 English, besides artillery. The King and the Emperor sent letters to Ferdinand 23 Aug. The Swiss are preparing to attack Dijon. The Florentine ambassador now in Spain has received information that all France is in consternation. It is said the King of Scots has invaded England, after warning Henry he should do so if he did not desist from his enterprise against France. "Let him do it, in God's name," said Henry, for he should not desist from the enterprise. Queen Katharine, in imitation of her mother Isabella, who had been left regent in the King's absence, made a splendid oration to the English captains, told them to be ready to defend their territory, that the Lord smiled upon those who stood in defence of their own, and they should remember that English courage excelled that of all other nations. Fired by these words, the nobles marched against the Scots, who were then wasting the Borders, and defeated them. Their King is supposed to be among the slain. Valladolid, 23 Sept. 1513.

23 Sept. **4465.** LOUIS XII.
R. T. 137.
R. O.

Order for the receiver general of Normandy, Jean Lalemant, to place at the disposal of the Count De Meaulevriez, Lieutenant of Normandy, and Louis de Vigars, Sieur De la Londe, the sums necessary for the equipment of the Scotch, Breton, and Norman vessels. Amiens, 23 Sept. 1513, 16 Louis XII.

Fr.

23 Sept. **4466.** TOURNAY.
R. T. 137.
R. O.

Submission to Henry VIII. by Charles de Crequy the dean, John abbot of St. Martin, Philip abbot of St. Nicholas des Pretz, according to the conditions specified in the King's letter recited. Dated at the camp, 23 Sept. 1513.*

Fr.

---

* A copy of the same letter is preserved in R. T. 144.

1513.

25 Sept. **4467.**   TOURNAY.

Archæol. xxvii.
258.*

"De l'entrée du Roi Henri comme Roi de France et d'Angleterre," into the town of Tournay, Sunday, 25 September 1513.

On the surrender, the council of the town waited on the King
to know when he would make his entry. He said, between
8 and 9 o'clock a.m. on Sunday. As the time was short, preparations were hastened for his reception. The council met the King
at "la porte Sainte Fontaine." The keys had been given up the
day preceding by command of the chief councillor. Having met
the chief of the town at the said gate, the King passed along the
great street Saint Jaques, "par le Saingle sur le Marchie," and
through the street of Our Lady, to the great church, where he
saluted God and St. Mary, and then went to his lodging in the
house of a canon named Simon Huland. As he returned through
the same streets (which were hung with tapestry), all the bells
were rung, and the officers of the said town, holding flam-
beaux in their hands, conducted him (with his princes and nobles on
horseback before him, and his guard, with a great number following,)
to his lodgings. After dinner the chief of the law and the
council presented to the King "six breues de vin de Beaune," and
the King confirmed the privileges of the town as he had promised,
released the prisoners, &c.

Fr.

25 Sept. **4468.**   TOURNAY.

Harl. 6069. f. 112.
B. M.

"Knights made at Tourayne (Tournay) in the church after the
King came from mass, under his banner in the church, 25 Dec.,†
5th year of his reign"; viz., The Lord Awdeley, The Lord Cob-
ham, The Lord Ric. Graye, The Lord Edw. Graye, Sir Henry
Poole, Sir Anthony Wingfelde, Sir Tho. Tirrell, Sir Tho. Bourough,
Sir Tho. Tyrrell of Heron, Sir Tho. Fairefax, Sir Tho. Lovell, Sir
John Veer, Sir John Marney, Sir John Markham, Sir John Savage,
Sir John Raglande, Sir John Nevill, Sir John Sharppe, Sir John
Maynwaring, Sir Edw. Guylforde, Sir Edw. Belknapp, Sir Edw.
Hungerforde, Sir Edw. Stradling, Sir Edw. Nevile, Sir Edw.
Doon, Sir Edw. Ferrers, Sir Wm. Compton, Sir Wm. Evers, Sir
Wm. Husse, Sir Wm. Fitzwilliam, Sir Wm. Brerton, Sir Wm.
Essex, Sir Wm. Gryffyth, Sir Wm. a Parre, Sir Wm. Tyler, Sir
Rauf Chamberlayn, Sir Ric. Sacheverell, Sir Ric. Tempest, Sir
Ric. Jernyngham, Sir Robt. Tyrwhyt, Sir Rauf Egerton, Sir Gyles
Capell, Sir Geoffrey Gates, Sir Christopher Willoughby, Sir
Christopher Garneys, Sir Owen Perrot, Sir Henry Owen, Sir
James Fremlingham, and Sir Lewis Orell.

Copy, not contemporaneous, p. 1.

26 Sept. **4469.**   For ROGER DEELE.

P. S.

Licence to import 50 tuns of Gascon wine. Huchyn, 17 Sept.
5 Hen. VIII. *Del.* Mortlake, 26 Sept.

Pat. 5 Hen. VIII. p. 1, m. 21; and Fr. 5 Hen. VIII. m. 7.

28 Sept. **4470.**   HENRY VIII. to LEO X.

Vat. Trans.
Add. MSS.
15,387, f. 1.
B. M.

Received with due reverence letters of his Holiness announcing
his assumption of the Pontifical dignity. Though he has already

---

* From the register "Cuir oir,' amongst the archives of Tournay.
† So in MS.

1513.

written to congratulate him cannot express his joy at the hopes he conceives from his timely elevation. Will send ambassadors to express his devotion. Nothing would be more agreable to him than the expedition proposed by Leo against the Infidels if affairs were once settled in Christendom. Tournay, 28 September 1513.

Lat. Copy, pp. 5.

---

30 Sept.   **4471.**   [JULIUS] CARDINAL DE MEDICIS to HENRY VIII.

Vitell. B. II. 35.   On his exaltation with three others to the cardinalate. Offers his
B. M.   services. Rome, 30 Sept. 1513. *Sig. burnt away.*

Rym. XIII. 378.   *Hol., Lat., p. 1. Add. Endorsed:* "Cardinalis de Medicis."

---

30 Sept.   **4472.**   TOURNAY.

R. T. 144.   Proclamation by Henry VIII. of his having accepted the sub-
R. O.   mission of the town. Tournay, 30 Sept. 1513, 5 Hen. VIII.
     Fr.

Sept.   **4473.**   ARTILLERY.

Calig. D. VI. 336.   "S'ensuit la declaration des sallaires desservis et fais par Jehan
B. M.   Bournage navie', du Duch Charles, d'avoir mené sur six navires l'artillerie du Roy d'Engleterre depuis Bethune jusques à Lille; et se font les somes de deniers cy apres decla[rées] à mony Artois, en la maniere qui s'ensuit."

Fr. At the end, in a different hand: "For bote hyre and costs of maryners from Bethon de Lyle as it apperith by the . . . ."
Pp. 2, mutilated.

4474.   NAVY.

R. O.   "The names of such ships as be appointed to come into the Thames straight from Hampton, viz. :—*The Sovereign.—The Mary Rose.—The Petre Pomegranate.— Hopton's ship.—The Nicholas Red.—The Barbara.*—These be victualled to the 14th day of October, wherewith they shall hold them contented.

The names of the ships that shall be discharged and delivered to their owners at Hampton :—*The Charite. — The Magdalene.— The Saraguse.—The Petre* of Fowaye.—*The George* of Felmouth. —*The Gabriell* of Topsam . . . . . . hath the[ir] full victual and . . . . . pon. . . . . . yng their soldiers and ma[ri]ners . . . . money after the rate . . . . forth over the . . . . . *The Mary and John.—The Mary George.—The Anne* of Fowaye.— *The Christopher Davy.—The Nicholas Draper.— The New Barke.—The Jenet.— The Henry.—The Margaret* of Topsam. — *The Sabyn.—The Lyzard* . . . .—*The Dragon.*—The two rowbarges.—*The Elizabeth* of Newcastle.—*Pemberton's ship.* —*The Nicholas* of Hampton.

These be the ships that be appointed to keep the sea [this] winter . . . . The ship of Walter Campion ; portage 160 ; Loveday capt.—*The Nicholas* of Hampton ; portage 140 ; John Flemyng capt.—*The Elizabeth* of Newcastle ; portage 130 ; Lewis capt.—*The Sabyn* ; portage 140 ; Sabyn capt.—*The Jenyt;* portage 80; Gournaye capt.

The vice-admiral shall victual the whole army and receive money for the same and for their wages. They shall victual at Sand-wich from 2 months to 2 months during 4 months. And all this

1513.

shall be shewed to the said vice-admiral, and he to shew his mind upon the same.

The division of such ships as be appointed to keep the sea this winter. [W]estward. (*Some lines are here wanting*).

Northward, *The Great Barke;* portage 300 ; Sir Weston Browne capt.—*Draper's* ship ; portage 160 ; Keby and Draper capts.—*The Lezard;* portage 120 ; Ichyngham capt.—*The Elizabeth* of Newcastle; portage 130 ; Lewis capt.

Dover and Calais.—*The Less Barke;* portage 200 ; Young Courtenay capt.—*The Christopher Davy;* portage 140 ; Wiseman capt.—*The Sabyn;* portage 140 ; Sabyn capt.—*The Jenet* of Perwyne (?) ; Gournay capt.

Mutilated, pp. 4.

Sept.
R. O.

4475.   NAVY.

Payments made by John Dawtreye at Portsmouth to the King's ships, by command of the Bp. of Winchester, the Lord Bergeveny, Sir Harry Marney, and Sir Edw. Poynyngs ;—to Thomas Bascatt captain of *The Ragesey* for one month ending 1 Oct. 4 Hen. VIII., and to John Rogers, for the victualler. To Sir Nicholas Waddam, owner of *The Trinity* victualler to the Sovereign ; after 12d. per ton, the month ; and Sir Charles Brandon for conduct money ; in all 15l. To Anthony Ughtrede capt. of *The Mary James* for conduct money. To Maurice Berkeley capt. of *The Charity*, his wages 18d. per diem ; soldiers 5s. per month. To Harry Hayward for tonnage ; to Robt. Byrde, owner of *The Mary Bryde* vict. 5l. To Roger Bowterworthe, owner of *The James* of London vict. 9l. 10s. To Will. Keby and Robt. Draper, capts. of *The Nicholas Nevill,* 7l. 14s. 6d. To Ralph Ellerkar, captain of *The Mary James,* 6l. To Sir Chas. Brandon and Sir Harry Gyldeforde, capts. of *The Sovereign,* wages each 5s. a day, and for soldiers 159l. 12l. 6d. To Sir Steph. Bulle and Tho. Harte, capts. of the King's new bark, 6l. 6s. 0d. and to Sir John Carrowe. To Rich. Cornewalle, capt. of *The Gabriel* of Topsham, 18d. To Tho. Munjoye owner of *The Gabriel.* The King's reward to 60 seamen hurt in his service, 20l. Total 101l. 8s. 2d.

Pp. 3.

4476.   CALAIS.

R. O.

An order from [Fox] Bp. of Winchester, and Wolsey, to Mr. Conway, to advance the wages of the undernamed spears and archers "of this town of Calais," &c.

Spears.—Thos. Thwayttes, John Midilton, John Lisle, John Tremayle, John Cokson, Willm. Vernon, Ric. Wetehill, Arthur Somerset, Hugh Talbot, Will. Pelham, Guy Ormeston, John Russel, Ric. Hodchowse, Geo. Grey, Humph. Banestir, Will. Palin'zon, Roger Cheny, and Rob. Sidney.

Archers Achevall.—Hen. Walter, Will. Bromewiche, Rob. Pynketh, Rob. Elvys, John Colpyn, Roger Frodesam, Edw. Techet, Pers Gruffith, Nich. Mihelton, Rob. Jurden, Hen. Wodford, And. Baret, John Lynden, Geo. Hasel, Tho. Lloid, John Stobill, Will. Massy, and Hen. Massy.

Signed: Ri Wynton—Thomas Wulcy.
P. 1.

4477.   THE WAR IN FRANCE.

R. O.

Muster roll of the King's army, with names of the captains, and numbers of petty captains, archers, bills, and marispikes under each.

1513.

Captains' names .... Lord Curson, retinue 113 ; Lord Herbert, chief captain of the rearward, 1,063 ; Sir Henry Willoughby, 123 ; Sir Randolf Brereton, 204 ; Lord Duddeley, 200 ; the Earl of Wilteshyre, 619 ; Sir David Owen, 103 ; Lord Zouche, 102 ; Sir Robert Dymmoke, treasurer, 54 ; Lord Audeley, 126 ; the Earl of Kent, 108 ; Sir John Husey, 320 ; William Morgan, 102; Edmund Bray, 102 ; the Baron of Carowe, 104 ; Arthur Hopton, 103 ; Thomas Phylyppes, 104 ; Sir Th. West, 54 ; Lord Dakers, 124 ; Earl of Northumberland, 514 ; John Skarlett, Wyndesore Harold, 2, (himself and trumpeter); George Seyntleger, 101 ; Lord Broke, 308 ; Sir John Arundell, 204 ; Sir Piers Eggecombe, 101; Edward Grevile, 102 ; ordnance, 800 ; strangers horsemen, 800. Total of the retinue, 7,372.

Pp. 3.   Very much mutilated and defaced by damp.

4478.   EXPENCES OF THE WAR.

R. O.

Declaration made by Sir. Edw. Ponynges, controller of the Household, and Sir Ric. Wynkfeld, joint commissioners in Flanders of the monies received by them from Sir Gilbert Talbot, Deputy of Calais, and of payment of the same for soldiers employed in the King's army against France. The account commences from 28 March 4 Hen. VIII.

Pp. 2.

4479..   ORDNANCE.

R. O.

Account headed—1. " These be the parcels of ordnance shipped from Lisle to Antwerp, and from Antwerp to Calais, by me William Loyal at the commandment of my Lord Barnes, as it appeareth by bills of receipt at Calais." 2. Ditto, by Peter at Tournay, in boats of Ghent, to Antwerp. 3. Ditto, shipped at Tournay by Rich. Sidenham to Antwerp, and from thence to Calais, by the commandment of Sir Sampson Norton, master] of the ordnance. 4. " Ditto, shipped by Edw. Hart, clk., to my Lord H. Corson, at Tournay, in boats of Ghent, and from Antwerp to Calais." 5. "Parcels of ordnance left at St Thomas, and from thence brought to Calais by water." 6. "Parcels of ordnance sent to Calais from Antwerp by Will. . . . . . . the which was never . . . ."

Pp. 7.

4480.   EXPENCES OF THE WAR.

R. O.

An account of conduct money and wages for three months, commencing 1 July, for the army starting from Portsmouth to Brittany.

Memorandum on the back, of money paid to Mr. Fitzherbert, Thos. Altherton, and to the serjeant of the catrye, and of 12*l.* received by John Coope.

Pp. 2.

4481.   MONEY FOR THE WAR.

R. O.

The King's money received by the hands of Thomas Parderyche of Master Deputy of Calais," viz. 8,360 crowns of the sun valued at 4*s.* 3*d.*=17,176*l.* 10*s.* ; royals to the value of 741*l.* 10*d.* ; half royals=247*l.* 10*s.* ; quarter royals=33*l.* 7*s.* 6*d.* ; ducats 8,286 at 4*s.* 7*d.*=1,898*l.* 17*s.* 6*d.* ; nobles and half nobles=181*l.* 3*s.* 4*d.* ; old crowns 229, at 4*s.* 2*d.* ; golden guylders 1,734 at 3*s.* 4*d.* ; also

1513.

Utryche gyldens, Ghuelmus gyldens, old nobles of England, Scut-
kyns, Salmytts, Lewys, Andreas gyldens, Phillippus gyldens, Ry-
ders, and Toyzons, amounting in all to 1,784*l.* 7*s.* 6*d.*

ii. The valuation in Flanders of such money as hereafter followeth ; viz. crowns of the sun at 6*s.* 1*d.* Fl. ; royals of England at
14*s.* 2*d.* Fl. ; ducats at 6*s.* 6*d.* Fl.; ducats de Camera at 6*s.* 3*d.* Fl.;
nobles of England at 9*s.* 5*d.* Fl. ; old crowns at 5*s.* 11*d.* Fl. ; golden
gyldens at 4*s.* 8*d.* Fl. ; Utryche gyldens at 4*s.* Fl ; Ghuelmus gyldens at 4*s.* 10*d.* Fl.; old nobles at 12*s.* 6*d.* Fl., &c.

Pp. 4. *Addressed :* [To] the King's most noble grace. *Endorsed :* Money received by Thomas Partridge.—Divers other
things concerning the war and payments of money.

4482.　Thos. Lord Dacre to [Ruthal Bp. of Durham]. *

R. O.

Is averse to show his mind to any but his lordship, as my Lord
Howard, in his letter to him and Dacre, is displeased at their
writing to the council for the coming up of Sir Jo. Forman, brother
to the Bp. of Murray, " which was devised for a good intent, and
specially for the displeasure of the said Bishop, who was the chief
provoker of this business. Hears that he is slandered by lords and
gentlemen who were on the field, because the Lord Treasurer and
my Lord Howard took him into council in preference to others.
Has exposed himself to strangers whom he cannot trust, notwithstanding Sir Will. Gascoigne and others were commanded, the day
after the field, by my Lord Treasurer, to help the writer in securing
and conveying the guns. All went home with seven days' wages
in their purses. *Signed.*

P. 1.

4483.　Instructions for Lord Dacre.

R. O.

. . . . " King's grace, or at the least wise the Queen of Scots being
ordered by the King's highness may the rather cause the said young
King to be also ordered and ruled by the King's grace, and his
grace to set such protectors and rulers as he shall think good."—Is
to endeavour what he can to have the young King of Scots placed
in the hands of the King of England, who is his natural guardian.
The Scots have no reason to remove the young King into any out-
isles or other part. Is to inform the Lord Chamberlain that the
Queen of England, for the love she bears to the Queen of Scots,
would gladly send her a servant. Is to advertise the Queen of all
occurrents.

P. 1.　*First leaf lost.*

Sept.

R. T. 137.
R. O.

4484.　Scots in France.

Letters of naturalization granted to them by Lewis XII. Amiens,
Sept. 1513, 16 Lewis XII.

Fr., pp. 2.

1 Oct.

R. T. 144.
R. O.

4485.　Tournay.

Letters patent of Henry VIII., declaring, at the request of the
provost and jurats of Tournay, that the general pardon recently
granted to persons banished from the city is not intended to include
murderers, traitors, violators, incendiaries, ravishers, &c. Tournay,
1 Oct. 1513, 5 Hen. VIII.

Fr.

* Headed by Ruthal, " The third."

1513.

1 Oct. **4486.** TOURNAY.
R. T. 144.
R. O.
    Exceptions from the general pardon and licence to return, of certain offenders guilty of murder and other crimes, granted at the request of the provost and others of the town of Tournay.
    Fr.

3 Oct. **4487.** SUDBURY.
R. O.
    Certificate of a transfer of a house called the Cheker, in Sudbury, by Edw. Stracey of Sudbury, to John Oxburgh. 3 Oct. 5 Hen. VIII.

4 Oct. **4488.** For WILLIAM FERRYS, felmonger of London, alias merchant adventurer.
    Protection, going to the war; granted by Queen Katharine. Westm., 4 Oct.
    Fr. 5 Hen. VIII. m. 10.

4 Oct. **4489.** ¦ For RICHARD ATCOK, clk.
P. S.
    Presentation to the church of Brynkeley, Ely dioc., void by resignation of William Cadiov. Walsingham, 23 Sept. 5 Hen. VIII. *Del.* Westm., 4 Oct.
    Pat. 5 Hen. VIII. p. 1, m. 23.

6 Oct. **4490.** TOURNAY.
R. T. 144.
R. O.
    General pardon to offenders, and licence to return to the city. Tournay, 6 Oct. 1513.
    Fr., pp. 2.

Ib.
    2. Proclamation that whereas the inhabitants were allowed 20 days to make their oath to Henry VIII., they shall be at liberty after taking that oath to settle where they please, except in countries hostile to England.
    Fr., p. 1.

7 Oct. **4491.** JULIAN DE MEDICIS to HENRY VIII.
R. O.
    Credence for Balthazar Stuerd. Rome, 7 Oct. 1513. *Signed. Lat., p. 1. Addressed. Endorsed.*

7 Oct. **4492.** To the ABP. OF CANTERBURY, Chancellor.
S. B.
    For writs to the Cinque Ports to be in readiness with their ships at Calais, by the 15th instant, for the transporting of the King and his army to the towns of Dover and Sandwich. Tournay, 7 Oct. *Del.* Heron, 7 Oct. 5 Hen. VIII.

7 Oct. **4493.** For WILLIAM APPREIS of London, draper.
    Protection, going to the war; granted by Queen Katharine. Westm., 7 Oct.
    Fr. 5 Hen. VIII. m. 10.

8 Oct. **4494.** MAXIMILIAN I. and CHARLES PRINCE OF SPAIN.
R. T. 144.
R. O.
    Letters patent allowing the inhabitants of Tournay to trade in their dominions. Tournay, 8 Oct. 1513, 28 Max. and 24th of Hungary.
    Fr., pp. 2.

1513.

8 Oct.   **4495.**   GAOL DELIVERY.

Canterbury.—John Broker, mayor, John Roper, Thos. Wode, John Hales, Hen. Eastbourne, Wm. Crumpe, and Thos. Wainflett. Westm., 8 Oct.

Pat. 5 Hen. VIII. p. 2. m. 4d.

8 Oct.   **4496.**   For JOHN MERBURY, clk.

P. S.

Presentation to the church of Alscote, Linc. dioc., void by death. Heron, 6 Oct. 5 Hen. VIII. *Del.* Heron, 8 Oct. 5 Hen. VIII.

Pat. 5 Hen. VIII. p. 1, m. 23.

9 Oct.   **4497.**   DACRE to [RUTHAL] BP. OF DURHAM.*

Calig. B. III. 235.
B. M.

Has received his letter dated Awkland the 17th. At the meeting of the Chamberlain and himself on Saturday last the weather was so grievous, and he was " so sore chafed and encumbered with the Scots," whom he found extreme in the ransoming of English prisoners, that he forgot to ask the Chamberlain of the charge committed to Ross herald. Intended this last Tuesday to have made a great raid into Scotland, but was prevented by the waters. If they continue, will have to wait for the next moon. Thinks it desirable for the article contained in his letter to the Queen for the manning of Etall and Ford to be remembered, as there is no abstinence at this time. Has seen the Bishop's plan for rebuilding Norham. Carlisle, 9 Oct. *Signed.*

Pp. 2. Addressed: [To m]y Lord' of Duresme. *Endorsed:* Letters of the Lord Dacre to my Lord of Duresme.

10 Oct.   **4498.**   For WILLIAM HATTCLYFF.

S. B.

Pardon and release as clerk of accounts of the King's household, and one of Henry VII.'s commissioners in the Western Counties for trying and making compositions with the adherents of Michael Joseph and Peter Warbek. Also grant of the issues of his messuage and 40 acres of land in Leuesham, Kent, from the time that they were distrained into the hands of King Henry VII. *Del.* Mortlake, 10 Oct. 5 Hen. VIII.

Pat. 5 Hen. VIII. p. 1, m. 23.

11 Oct.   **4499.**   [MAX. SFORZA DUKE OF MILAN] to [HENRY VIII.]

Vitell. B .II. 52.
B. M.

Received his letters announcing his victory over the French and Scots, which was to be expected from so brave an army, and so experienced a leader. Begs to hear from him again. After the defeat of the French at Novara many have surrendered; others have been defeated, among whom are Barnabas Marquis Malaspina and Alexandrinus, who have suffered death. Has no fear of the Venetians any longer, who had set a garrison in Crema, and have been defeated at Ulmo near Vicenza. Bartholomew Alvianus fled; the rest saved themselves in Padua. The hopes of the French are ruined in Italy. Milan, 11 Oct. 1513.

P.S. in his own hand. It only remains for Henry to finish the war. It will be much to his credit to have rescued Italy from the foul yoke of the French. [*Signature lost.*]

Lat., mutilated, pp. 2.

⁎⁎ *The wrapper of a letter, add. in the same hand to Hen. VIII., and endorsed,* " the 15th of October 1513," *occurs at f.* 56 *b.*

---

* Headed by Ruthal, " The first."

1513.

11 Oct. **4500.** SILVESTER [DE GIGLIS] BP. OF WORCESTER to HENRY
R. O. VIII.

After he and Cardinal Bainbridge had written their letter in common, the Pope told De Giglis privately that he was strongly urged
by the Cardinal to send legates to the different Christian Princes,
according to the decisions of the Lateran council, for a general union
against the Turks ; and as Lewis, the schismatic King of France, is
in so low a condition that he cannot refuse, he hopes that England
will agree to the proposition. He is anxious, however, first to
know Henry's decision, and trusts that the messenger sent with this
letter may go and return within 22 days. Rome 11 Oct. 1513.
Signed.

Lat., pp. 2. Addressed and sealed. Endorsed.

11 Oct. **4501.** TOURNAY.
R. T. 143. Notarial copy of the town's submission to Henry VIII. on the
R. O. 23 Sept. Dated 11 Oct. 1513.

12 Oct. **4502.** HENRY VIII. to LEO X.
Vat. Trans. That he may not be deceived by false rumors, writes briefly of
Addit.MSS. the great success which God has continuously vouchsafed to him.
15,387, f. 4. Has already informed him of the late victory gained by the Earl of
B. M. Surrey, with small loss, over 13,000 Scots. Has sent the particulars,
as related to him in numerous letters, to the Cardinal of York and
the Bp. of Worcester to show to his Holiness, that he may be able
to prove that God is fighting in behalf of the Holy Alliance. Notwithstanding his affinity to the King of Scots, and repeated promises
of amity received from him, had been always as much prepared for
war as for peace. James was seduced by France, from whom he received a large sum of gold, and a great number of men and guns, to
invade England in Henry's absence, by which he has inflicted a
heavy blow upon his own kingdom. Henry will not fail to follow up
his advantage, although one of the Scotch nobles, who alone escaped,
having saved himself by flight, has submissively desired a truce. And
now this great and wealthy city of Tournay has surrendered to him
after eight days' siege, along with other neighbouring castles. Had
intended to pursue the French, who were said to have retreated to
Cambray, but they fled so rapidly that he despaired of overtaking
them. He accordingly remained at Tournay to consult with the
Emperor and the Lady Margaret for the consummation of the marriage of the Prince of Castile. The Prince himself arrived on the
10th. Is much delighted with his conversation. Must return to
England, now that winter is close at hand, and the Scotch affairs
are urgent, to meet his parliament, which is summoned for the 1st
of Nov. Will return as soon as possible, with a larger army, and
prosecute the war with all possible vigor. Will leave to-morrow.
—Begs he will revoke certain concessions made to the King of Scots
which are injurious to England. The archbishoprick of St. Andrew's used always to be subject to the see of York, and the last
archbishop was slain in the battle. Begs he will recall the grant of
metropolitan honors to that see, and reduce it to the dignity of a
bishopric, and also restore the priory of Coldingham, which had
been given *in commendam* to the late Archbp. of St. Andrew's, to
the see of Durham. As the affairs of Scotland concern him nearly,

1513.

begs he will not dispose of any of the Scotch bishoprics, rendered vacant by the slaughter of the prelates who were in the battle, armed and without sacerdotal habit, until Henry has expressed his wishes with regard to them. Requests that he will write to the Bp. of London to allow the body of the King of Scots, who died under ex communication, to be carried to London, and buried with royal honors at St. Paul's. Tournay, 12 Oct. 1513.

Lat. copy, pp. 17.

12 Oct.   **4503.**   THO. STEYNTON of London, draper.

Revocation of protection granted 1 June 5 Hen. VIII. to the said Thomas while serving in the war; being still in London, as certified by John Dawn? and John Brugge, sheriffs of London. Teste Regina, Westm. 12 Oct.

Pat. 5 Hen. VIII. p. 1, *m.* 21d.

12 Oct.   **4504.**   For SIR JOHN RAYNESFORD.
S. B.

To have the custody and stewardship of the forest of Essex, which John Earl of Oxford, deceased, held in fee, with the appointment of officers, in as ample a manner as the said Earl and his ancestors; viz. :— "a riding forster," and three "yeomen forsters," in the three bailiwicks of Heynold, Onger and Wodefarde of the said forest, and another forester under the nomination of the Abbot of Waltham Holy Cross; during the minority of John now Earl of Oxford, son of George brother of the said late Earl.— Also annuity of 9l. 2s., during pleasure, out of the issues of the manor and lordship of Ralegh, Essex, which was granted to the said late Earl by patent 2 Dec. 5 Hen. VII. *Del.* Westm., 12 Oct. 5 Hen. VIII.

Pat. 5 Hen. VIII. p. 1, *m.* 12.

13 Oct.   **4505.**   For SIR EDWARD GREY.
P. S. b.

Protection to Manuell (Mauncell ?) Rise, retained to serve in the war in France. Tournay, 13 Oct. 5 Hen. VIII. *Signed :* Sir Edward Grey, broder to my Lord Marquis.

14 Oct.   **4506.**   M. BP. OF PALESTRINA [CARDINAL SENEGALENSIS] to
Vitell. B. II. 53.   HENRY VIII.
B. M.
Rym. XIII. 379.

Has received his letters by the Cardinal of York, promising a reward for his service. Was keeping his narrow chamber with a fit of rheumatism. Gave up his deposit, which the Cardinal took with him. Sorry that owing to illness he cannot assist in the confirmation required by Henry. Will do so as soon as he recovers. Rome, 14 Oct. 151[3]. *Signed.*

Lat., mutilated, p. 1. *Add.*

14 Oct.   **4507.**   For MARGARET POLE, sister of EDWARD late EARL OF
S. B.   WARWICK AND SALISBURY.

Grant, in fee, of the possessions of Richard late Earl of Salisbury, her grandfather, son and heir of Alice Countess of Salisbury, and husband of Anne Countess of Warwick, which came into Henry VII.'s hands by attainder of the said Edward ;—this grant not to extend to any possessions held by the said Earl Richard in

1513.

right of his wife, the said Countess Anne, which descended to her on the death of Henry Duke of Warwick, her father. *Del.* Mortlake, 14 Oct. 5 Hen. VIII.

Pat. 5 Hen. VIII. p. 1, m. 24.

---

15 Oct.   **4508.**   MARRIAGE OF PRINCE CHARLES AND MARY.

Galba, B. III. 90.
B. M.
Rym. XIII. 379.

Articles of agreement between England and the Emperor against France, and for the marriage of Prince Charles with the Princess Mary. Lisle, 15 Oct. 5 Hen. VIII.

Lat., pp. 6, mutilated.

R. O.

2. The oath of Will. de Croy Lord Shierve (*sic*), lieutenant of the King of Castile, Thos. de Playne, chancellor of the same King, Mich. de Croy Lord of Sempi, and Hieronynmus Lauwerirum (?) Lord de Watrevliet, treasurer of the same King, John de Sauvage Lord de Schaubeke, president of Flanders, taken before John Yong, LL.D., ambassador of England, to the matrimonial treaty between England and Castile. *Signed.*

P. 1.

         4509.   MAXIMILIAN to MARGARET.

Addit. 21,382.
f. 56.
B. M.

Is satisfied with her arrangements for the household of the Princess Mary in the appointment of the wife of Charles Ourssin, Margaret's controller, as her *femme de chambre*, and John Glennet, nephew of de Sallans, treasurer of Burgundy, as controller.

Fr., p. 1. Copy.

---

16 Oct.   **4510.**   HENRY VIII. and MAXIMILIAN.

R. O.

Treaty concluded by Margaret of Savoy with Henry VIII. in the name of the Emperor, allowing him to return into England after leaving a sufficient garrison in Tournay, on condition of contributing 200,000 cr. of gold for the Emperor's expences in supporting 4,000 horse and 6,000 foot in Artois, Hainault, &c. Lisle, 16 Oct. 1513.

Lat. Signed and sealed.

---

17 Oct.   **4511.**   HENRY VIII., MAXIMILIAN, and FERDINAND OF AR-

Vesp. C. I. 91.
B. M.

RAGON, against FRANCE.

Treaty concluded by Don Pedro de Urrea, ambassador with the Emperor, Don Lewis Carroz, ambassador in England, Johannes de la Nuza, ambassador of Arragon, with the Prince of Castile, on the part of Ferdinand ; John Lord de Bergis, Gerard de Pleine Lord De la Roche, on the part of the Emperor; Richard Bishop of Winchester, Privy Seal, Lord Thomas Grey, Marquis of Dorset, on the part of England. It is agreed that Ferdinand shall invade Guienne or Aquitaine with 15,000 foot, 1,500 heavy-armed horse, and 1,500 light-armed horse, and 25 pieces of artillery, 12 large and 13 small, and shall give up his conquests to England. Henry is to contribute 20,000 cr. of gold, equal to 4*s.* sterling each, to the expenses of Arragon from the time Ferdinand commences the war in Guienne. England to invade Picardy or Normandy before June, and each power to send a fleet to sea before the end of April. The Pope and Charles of Castile to be at liberty to enter the league. Lisle, 17 Oct. 1513.

Signed by the Spanish plenipotentiaries.

Vellum.

R. O.

2. Confirmation of the treaty concluded at Lisle, 17 Oct. 1513.

1513.

17 Oct.   **4512.**   [HENRY VIII. to his AMBASSADORS.]

Galba, B. v. 392 b.
B. M.

Touching the convention and interview to be had between the King, Queen, the Prince of Castile, the Archduchess, and the Lady Mary, "Princess of Castile," for solemnisation of the marriage to be made in Calais in May next ; for the due preparation of which much discussion is required.

*Draft in Ruthal's hand, mutilated, p.*1.

17 Oct.   **4513.**   PETER MARTYR to LUD. FURTATO.

Pet. Mart. Ep.
No. 528.

Miseries of Italy. The Venetians have collected all their forces at Padua against the Spaniards. Every turret and pinnacle is bristling with guns. The Venetians have cleared away every tree, to give free scope to their projectiles. The Swiss are besieging Dijon. To gain time La Palisse demanded an opportunity of consulting Lewis, on their proposals, and fortified Dijon in the interval. Terouenne has been taken and destroyed by the English. Tournay has surrendered, and promised Henry 40,000 ducats, who has moved towards Amiens, where Lewis is with 30,000 men. Francis Duke of Angouleme has been wounded in the skirmish. The King of Hungary has cut to pieces 4,000 Turkish cavalry. Valladolid, 17 Oct. 1513.

18 Oct.   **4514.**   For WALTER AP RICE of London, draper alias vintner.

P. S.

Protection ; going in the suite of Sir Gilbert Talbot, Deputy of Calais. Tournay, 6 Oct. 5 Hen. VIII. *Del.* Westm., 18 Oct.

19 Oct.   **4515.**   For ROBERT WHITE, merchant.

P. S.

Licence to import 40 tuns of Gascon wine. Windsor Castle, 18 Oct. 5 Hen. VIII. *Del.* Westm., 19 Oct.

20 Oct.   **4516.**   TOURNAY.

R. T. 144.
R. O.

Letters patent of Henry VIII. in favor of Guillaume Espanault, Guillaume de Bruges, Jehan Huart l'aisné, and others, inhabitants of Tournay, who could not conveniently return to the city within the 40 days allowed by the act. Calais, 20 Oct. 1513, 5 Hen. VIII.

Fr., p. 1.

20 Oct.   **4517.**   HENRY VIII.

Calig. D. vi. 98.
B. M.

Annuity of 200 flor. of gold to John de Lusy, out of the revenues of Tournay. Calais, 20 Oct. 1513. Also appointment of Allart Bentinck, as receiver of Tournay.

Pp. 3.

20 Oct.   **4518.**   DACRE to RUTHAL.*

Calig. B. iii. 12.
B. M.

Has received the King's letter and his ; has returned an answer to the King. The Duke of Gloucester late warden of the West Marches, the Earl of Northumberland of the East and Middle, thought it a great enterprise to make a raid into Tevydale with all their friends and adherents. Though a man of much less substance.

---

* Headed by Ruthal, "The second."

1513.

Dacre will attempt it on the West at the King's desire. Cannot attempt the East March at present. My Lord of Norfolk, in the last war, with my Lords of Winchester, Conyers, Sir William Bulmer and others, and 1,000 soldiers, supported by Berwick and Norham, found it as much as they could do to make a raid in Tevydale. Little help from Northumberland, it being so poor and wasted. Carlisle, 20 Oct. *Signed.*
Addressed: To my Lord of Duresme.
Pp. 2.

21 Oct.   **4519.**   SIR EDWARD PONYNGES, lieutenant of Tournay.
P. S. b.

Appointment of Lawrence Nicholles of London. merchant, to pass and repass with victuals for the said Sir Edward and the King's garrison in Tournay, for one year. 21 Oct. 5 Hen. VIII.
Signed.

22 Oct.   **4520.**   DACRES to HENRY VIII.
Calig. B. vi. 41.
B. M.

Has received his letters dated at Tournay, 30th Sept., commanding him to make two raids into Scotland, the one upon the West, and the other upon the Middle Marches ; assigning him 1,000 marks for this service and intimating that Lord Darcy is to make a third raid upon the East Marches. The King's other letters of the 10th, commanding him (Dacres) to make the third raid with the help of the people of the bishopric of Durham, and assigning him another 1,000 marks, arrived this morning. Will endeavour to execute the first orders as soon as the moon and weather will serve ; meantime making such small raids as shall be no less annoying to the Scots. It will be difficult to gather the people for the third raid, in consequence of the distance from the far side of the West Marches, viz. the castle of Millom belonging to John Huddilston in Cumberland, to Berwick, 105 miles and more. From the nearest part of the West Marches it is 60 miles. Thinks Darcy had better perform it, as he has taken in at Berwick a new crew of 250 soldiers, besides the 500 he had before, and as he is the King's officer for the shire of Bamborough and lordship of Dunstanborough, having command of the men there. If the writer were to bring the men of the West Marches, whom he needs for his own security, to the third raid, the country would be very weak, and the Scots would certainly know it before they could pass the Middle Marches. The friends he had left behind him in these parts when he departed to "this victorious field" were very much molested. At the battle, his men not being strong enough to be a wing to my Lord Treasurer, he assigned him Bamboroughshire and Tynemouth, but they fled at the first shot of the Scottish guns, as my Lord Admiral can report. Thinks they will serve Darcy better. The late King of Scots' ordnance in Etall Castle, which the King commanded to be sent to Newcastle, has been conveyed to Berwick in safety by William Bawne and the men of Bamboroughshire and Elandshire. As to the King's orders for not ransoming prisoners, he never took any. Those that were taken were ransomed without his knowledge before the King's orders were known. Has given warning, as commanded, as to those remaining, or "latten to suertie upon entre again," and my Lord Treasurer has made proclamation that no man should let his prisoner depart till the King's pleasure were known. Carlisle Castle, 22 October. *Signed.*
Addressed: To the King's grace.
Pp. 4.

1513.

22 Oct.   **4521.**   For WILLIAM COMPTON, RICHARD DYCONS and JOHN
S. B.   CHAMBER.

Next presentation to the church of Myvot, in St. Asaph's dioc.
Del. Mortlake, 22 Oct. 5 Hen. VIII.
Pat. 5 Hen. VIII. p. 1, m. 23.

23 Oct.   **4522.**   DACRE to RUTHAL.*
Calig. B. III. 1.
B. M.   Received by post, at 2 o'clock this morning, his right discreet
letter, advising him to undertake raids into Teviotdale, which he
will accomplish, besides the other raid upon the West March. Since
meeting the Chamberlain on Saturday se'nnight made four raids in
Tevidale ; one to the tower of Howbaslot, which he burnt, carrying off 28 score sheep within sight ; one to Carlangrick, which he
burnt ;—a great raid made by the inhabitants of Tyndale, who
burnt Ancrom, and took 60 prisoners ;—and three raids on the West
Marches in Annandale. Intends Tevidale shall be kept waking. The
marsh in the East Marches is beyond his power to deal with, being
an angle betwixt Tevidale and the sea, fronting Berwick and Norham,
and as far as York. Has no intelligence, as reported, with the Lord
Chamberlain of Scotland, or any other Scot, but for the advancement
of the King's objects, and will spare neither him nor his lands.
Thanks him for his good mind towards him in this matter, and
desires advice how to conduct himself so as to void misconstruction.
Carlisle, 23 Oct. *Signed.*
Addressed: To my Lord of Durham.
Pp. 2.

24 Oct.   **4523.**   RUTHAL to WOLSEY.
Calig. B. VI. 40.
B. M.   Thanks him for his loving letters, the more comfortable to him
from the obloquies of his enemies. Ascertains by them the King's
great victories, the more joyous as the responsibility of that expedition was attributed to him and Wolsey. Received a letter from
the King at the same time. Had advised, after the victory, the
appointing of some captain in these parts, which was not well
taken, but, if adopted, had led to good effect. Has, in compliance
with the King's wish, sent to Lord Dacres to learn what men and
aid he will require in the "raids and winter wars against the
Scots." Has not yet had his answer ; he has, however, like a
wise captain, made large musters, and done much injury to the
Scots, as will be seen by his letters, which the Bishop encloses.
Ruthal will urge him to attack the East Marches. Is not surprised
at his disliking to do so, as already many reports have been circulated to his dishonor. Advises that a letter should be sent from the
King to Dacres for his encouragement. The Scotch herald passed
him without his knowledge. His mission is kept secret ; it is probably known to Wolsey by this time. Friar Langley, sent by the
Queen's grace to the Queen of Scotland, goes by Carlisle, and therefore Ruthal will not see him to give him advice.
As for Norham castle, "thanked be God and St. Cuthbert,"
it is not as he supposed. The dungeon and inner ward will
shortly be renewed, and, if not hindered by the Scots, hopes
they will be in better case than ever by Whitsuntide. His
smiths are working on the iron gates and doors, his carpenters
upon roofs, and his masons in rebuilding the said dungeon and
inner ward. He intends applying to the King for commissions

----

* Headed by Ruthal, " The fourth."

1513.

to take workmen " ayenst the time of year for reëdifying of the castle ;" on which he will spare no money, but make all his friends assist, and " live a poor life" till it be finished. " But, Maister Almosner, the hospitalitie of this countray agrethe not with the buyldyng so greate a worke ; for that I spend here wold make many towris and refreshe my ruynous howses, the lyke whereof I trow never Cristenman lokyd on, onlesse thay had be pullyd down by men of warre." Had he not " refreshed" them from year to year, before his coming, he might as well have lodged in the open field as in them. Should be better able to build the castle, if he were removed from " this chargeful country." Till it be finished " I purpose not to keep any great sail, but get me to a corner and live upon you, emendis suffragiis, as my Lord of York did when he was Bishop here. For the love of God, Maister Almosner, remembre this matter, and kepe it secrete, using policy."

Will arrange in his absence that Sir William Bulmer shall be always ready to do the King service. After he has seen the King, will return hither, " if the wars continue here, and that it be his pleasure," though he spend all and more too. Has written about this to the King. Brought with him eight tuns of wine, " and, our Lord be thankyd, I have not two tunne left at this howre. And this is fayre utterance in two monethys. And schame it is to say how many befis and motons have been spent in my hows sens my cummyng, besides other fresh acats, whete, malt, fysche, and suche baggages. On my faith ye wold marvayle." Had not his fortunes been " somewhat stored befcre," he would have been much behind ; " for 300 persons some day is a small number," and sometimes 60 or 80 beggars at the gate. " And this is the way to keep a poor man in state." Akland, 24 Oct. *Signed.*

Addressed : [To my] worshipful [Master Almoner to t]he King's grace.

Endorsed : My Lord of Duresme and the Lord Dacre's lettres. *Ip.* 3.

---

24 Oct.
P. S.

4524. FOR THOMAS LEGH, M.A., the King's chaplain.

To have the canonry or prebend of Underton in the collegiate church of Brigenorth, void by death of Henry Narbon. Windsor Castle, 12 Oct. 5 Hen. VIII. *Del.* Mortlake, 24 Oct.

Pat. 5 *Hen. VIII. p.* 1, *m.* 23.

---

25 Oct.
Pet. Mart. Ep.
No. 529.

4525. PETER MARTYR to LUD. FURTATO.

Fortune smiles upon England, but scowls upon France. The King of Scotland had built for aid of Lewis a large ship with five others, which the English have taken and scuttled, and, besides, a large Danish ship which was sailing to join them. The Scots have been defeated and their King slain. To complete his good fortune John Astil says that the rebel Prince of Ireland has submitted to Henry. Leo has created four Cardinals, much to the dislike of the order, who voted for him on condition or the number being reduced. Ferdinand is in the abbey of Valbona, hunting the stag. He does not look well. Three things keep him from perfect recovery ; old age, for he is now 62, a wife that never leaves him, and hunting and living in the woods. Valladolid, 25 Oct. 1513.

---

29 Oct.
R. O.

4526. EXPENSES OF THE KING'S VOYAGE.

" The book of payments of wagons and other charges in the King's voyage, a-war beyond the sea, by Roger More, clerk of the King's Larder, anno quinto Regis Henrici Octavi."

X X

i. Receipts from Mr. Dauncy by John Ketilby, sergeant of the Chandlery,—from Allen King, one of the purveyors of wine, and Will. Brown, junr.,—from Rich. Gibson, yeoman of the tents, by Roger More,—and from John Morley : at Turreyn, 18th Aug. and 16th Sept., and at Calais. Total, 2,126*l.*

ii. Payments to 28 wagoners (named) of Bruges, Mechlin, Brussels, Ghent, Peperyng, Ostend, Calais, Gravelyng, and Wandom, for the carriage of the King's tents, toyle and standards belonging to the Guard; at 3*s.* 4*d.* a day each wagon, for 4 months. Total, 451*l.* 12*s.* 8*d.* for 31 wagons. 4*l.* 1*s.* 8*d.* for jackets; 31*s.* for messengers.

iii. Payments for wagons that serve the King's household. To 61 waggoners of Spur, Mechlin, Antwerp, Cologne, Sukyrke, Castyll besides St. Homer's, London, Dunkirk, Brunarde, Bavynco, Heryngham, Dowey, Poperyng, Lovere, Namur, &c. for the same period. Wages per month 4*l.* 13*s.* 4*d.*

iv. Wages of 2 carters at 6*d.* a day : John Ketilby, sergeant of the chandlery, at 2*s.* a day ; Thos. Jakes and Edw. Chamberlain, carters of the bath, at 6*d.* a day ; John Sharpe, Roger More, John Tirrell, Henry Acres, Robt. Dyker, and John Gough, for wagons for the King's removal from Calais at 3*s.* 4*d.* each ; and to 31 carters for the second and third months (of 28 days), commencing 6th Aug. and 3rd Sept.

v. Special payments to Valentine Haryson, Will. Pole, &c., *Mutilated and illegible.*

vi. Four months wages to the above carters, beginning 1 Oct. *Pp.* 54.

4527. ORDNANCE.

Receipts by John Dawtrey temp. Henry VII. and VIII.[*]

Of Elys Hylton, 11 May 4 Hen. VIII., 2,538 old and new bows, left by the Marquis of Dorset in the West, 7,219 sheaves of arrows; 11 June, 7,300 bowstrings, 1,900 stakes. Of Sir Sampson Norton, 28 July, 120 half-barrels of gunpowder, 100 gross of bowstrings, 2,000 iron and lead shot, 100 ditto, 500 marespikes, (at different times) 3,691 ditto, 1,000 bills. Of Thos. Hart, 5 May, 21 lasts 6 barrels of gunpowder. Of Lord Lisley, by John Gelston, 10 June 5 Hen. VIII., 51 sheaves, 668 bills. From the customer of Pole, by order of the Bp. of Winchester, 3 brass guns, 1 iron gun. From Will. Bussheler, 4 April, 170 pair of harness and 12 cables. From John Hode, 12 April, 340 harness, 32 cables. Of John Blewbery, 9 Aug., coats of white and green cloth 638, white and green chamlet 13, white and green satin 13, damask 1, 10 ulronds, 5 fardels of Veteri canvas. Of George Harward, 6 Sept. 5 Hen. VIII., 200 ulronds. Of Will. Twedy, 1 Aug. 5 Hen. VIII., 13 anchors, 5 lasts of tar, 11 barrels not full, 8 lasts of pitch, 1 barrel not full, 6 run out. Of John Gowthe, master of *The Mary and Jessey,* 6 Sept. 5 Hen. VIII., 56 cables. Of Richard Dyat, master of *The George Wyndesore,* 6 Sept. 5 Hen. VIII., 29 cables. Of Thos. Wryght, master of *The Mary Grase* of London, 28 Oct. 5 Hen. VIII. 14 great cables. Of Frescobald, 11 March 4 Hen. VIII., 16 cables from Italy bought by the King. 49 cables brought from London.

Here follow accounts of the deliveries of bows, gunpowder, salt-

---

[*] The particulars for Henry VII. are not here specified.

1513.

peter, brimstone, coal powder, arrows, bowstrings, white and green coats, pitch and tar, &c., sold to various persons temp. Hen. VII. and VIII.

ii. Costs for the ordnance, house rent for ditto. *Pp.* 40.

29 Oct. **4528.** ERASMUS to COLET.

Eras. Ep. x. 18.

Is busy in completing his work *De Copia ; " in media Copia, in summa versatur inopia."* This is the reason he did not answer Colet's before. Avoids the Scotists that he may not waste time. Has cooled in the translation of St. Basil, because the Bp. of Rochester, to whom he sent a specimen, did not rise to the bait, and had written to say that he wished a translation of St. Basil should come out under his auspices at Cambridge (*ex illius Academia*). Erasmus has been told that the Bishop thought the specimen sent was not genuine ; only an old translation vamped up. Had written to him about Croke, not because he thought Colet had other men's money, but because he thought he would rather show his liberality to an Englishman. Thanks him for his offer, but does not like his phrase, " *si humiliter mendicaveris ;* "—remonstrates with Colet for using this and other expressions. It is discreditable that he should be obliged to beg after spending so much time in England. Has had so much from the Archbishop (Warham) it would be a shame to accept more if he offered it. Has asked N., and been refused. Even Linacre, who knew he was leaving London with no more than six angels, and his health indifferent, urged him not to apply to the Archbishop or Mountjoy, but habituate himself to poverty. Could do this when health was strong—must beg now to save his life. Will not refuse Colet's bounty.

P. S. When he broached the subject of an under-master among certain Masters of Arts, one said, " Who would be a schoolmaster that could live in any other way ? " When Erasmus urged that this was a Christian work above all others, his interlocutor replied, " If a man wishes to serve Christ let him enter a monastery." When Erasmus rejoined that to do good to others was charity, he was answered, perfection consisted in leaving all things.

Cambridge, postrid. Simonis & Judæ.

29 Oct. **4529.** DACRE to RUTHAL.

Calig. B. III. 11. B. M.

Has received by post his letters dated at Akeland the 22d, 25th, and 26th. Thanks him for his news of the King's coming home to Richmond. The council of Scotland has assembled this week in St. John's town. Sent 60 of his tenants to Eskdale Moor, and burnt seven houses, on Tuesday last ; on Wednesday his brother Sir Christopher made a raid into Scotland,—on Thursday burnt the Stakehugh, the manor place of Irewyn, and the hamlets down Irewyn burn, the Chamberlain of Scotland's own lands, and continued burning from break of day till 1 in the afternoon ;—two men slain. The weather very contagious—the floods and rains out. Kirkoswald, 29 Oct. *Signed. Addressed :* To my Lord of Duresme.

P. 1.

29 Oct. **4530.** For SIR WILLIAM COMPTON.

S. B.

To be keeper of the manor and park, bailiff of the lordship, minister of the hospital, and steward of the manor of Donyngton, Berks. *Del.* Mortlake, 29 Oct. 5 Hen. VIII.

Pat. 5 *Hen. VIII. p.* 2, *m.* 5.

X X 2

1513.
29 Oct.   **4531.**   For RALPH RYVELEY and ROBERT BELL.

Pardon, as of Dodyngton, alias of Eland, alias of Norham, Northumb., in the liberty of the bishopric of Durham. Westm. 29 Oct.

Pat. 5 Hen. VIII. p. 1, *m.* 24.

31 Oct.   **4532.**   For RANULPH CHALNAR.
S. B.

Wardship of William, son and heir of Nicholas Aiston ; granted by patent 13 Nov. 3 Hen. VIII. to Robert Moreton, who forfeited it by waste. *Del.* Mortlake, 31 Oct. 5 Hen. VIII.

Pat. 5 Hen. VIII. p. 1, *m.* 23.

31 Oct.   **4533.**   EXPENCES OF THE WAR.
R. O.

Declaration by Sir Rob. Southwell of money received for the King's wars against France, according to the King's letters missive dated 23 Oct. 5 Hen. VIII. according to bills signed by Sir Edw. Howard, late admiral ; beginning 15 March 4 Hen. VIII., ending 31 Oct. following.

i. *For the King's own ships.* To the late admiral and the present, 10s. a day ; to the treasurer of the wars, 3s. 4d ; captains 18d., clerks 8d., soldiers and others, 5s. per month, with deedshares and rewards ; master gunners 5s., masters 2s. 6d., gunners 20d. Total 1,486l. 11s. 10d.

2. Indicts and rewards, 1,605l. 9s. 4d.

3. For another month ending July, 1,631l. 6s. 4d.

4. For another month ending 28 Aug., 1,437l. 5s. 2d.

5. For half a month, 952l. 9s. 1d.

ii. *For English ships retained,* 6,259l. 3s. 5d.

iii. *For Spanish ships.* Captains at 18d. a day, &c., 2,975l. 13s. 1½d.

iv. *English victuallers.* Mariners 5s. a month ; deedshares, at 5s. a month, &c., 1,503l. 12s. For *The Nicholas Beulay,* 48l. 10s.

v. *Spanish victuallers.* Master and pilot, 30s. a month each ; mariners, 7s. 1d. ; grooms, 4s. 9d. ; pages, 2s. 5d. ; deedshares, at 6s. the share, 127l. 17s 1¾d.

vi. *Hoys.* 226l. 0s. 12d. *The James* of Antwerp, at 3s. 8d. the ton, 40l. 4s. 2d.

vii. Wages for my Lord Ferrers, captain of *The Trinity Sovereign,* himself 5s. 2d. a day ; residue at 6s. 8d. a day given him by the King over 18d. by the day. Under captains 12d. a day ; petty captains 8d. 56l. 5s. 4d.

viii. Accounts of John Daryllio, Peter Leman, Sharante. (*Struck out.*)

ix. Surgeons' wages. Master surgeon 13s. 4d. a month ; others, at 10s ; total 88l. 6s. 8d. Clerks and officers of war, 1s. a day, 16l. 10s. Pilots, 50l. 19s. 4d. Rewards miscellaneous, 892l. 8s. 11¼d.

x. Beer for the fleet tarrying in the Downs for the Scotch fleet, when the victuallers could not come out 86l. 9s. 3d.

xi. My Lord Ferrers in reward, 40l.

xii. Repairs, 291l. 17s. 9½d.

xiii. For conveyance of prisoners, &c., 9l. 19s. 2d.

1513.

xiv. For tackle bought, 55l. 6s. 8d.

xv. Pursers' costs, 38l. 17s. 4d.

xvi. Trumpeters at 16d. a day, 24l. 8s.

xvii. Conduct money, 1,175l. 9s. 2d.

xviii. Various, 13l. 6s. 8d.

Oct.

R. O.

4534. EXPENCES OF THE WAR.

258 documents and receipts for payment of wages in the war with France, commencing with June and ending in Oct. ; signed by C. Somerset (Lord Herbert), Sir Edmund Carewe, master of the ordnance, J. de Lusy lieutenant of the Prince of Castile, (for the wages of Hen. le Grand and others), Sir Rob. Corson called Lord Curson, master of the rearward, Sir Ric. and Sir Randolph Brereton knight marshal, George Seyntleger, John Dudley, Alex. Baynham, Sir Thos. West, Will. Morgan, John Huse, Ric. Earl of Kent, Thos. Philipps, John Savage, Sir John Werburton, Sir Henry Willoughby, Sir Richard Wentworth, John Tychet Lord Audeley, John Ralye, John Zouche, Arthur Hopton, Sir David Owen, Henry Stafford Earl of Wiltshire, Sir Piers Edgecomb, Thomas Fynes Lord Dacre, Sir Rob. Willoughby Lord Broke, Edw. Grevylle, Sir John Arundell, Hen. Earl of Northumberland grand captain of his own retinue, Noel de Wasteby, Authoine de Ligne Count Faulquemberghe, Edmund Bray, Nich. Marland, Gerard de Fromont, provost to John de Lusy, and John Lord Berners.

Two warrants addressed to Sir Rob. Dymmoke, treasurer of the King's rearward ; — indentures with Thos. Prout, Sir Edw. Ponynges, controller of the Household, and Sir Ric. Wingfield, marshal of Calais; for chaplains, foreign soldiers, ordnance, pioneers, carters of Lincolnshire, Huntingdonshire, Burgundians, at 8d. a day, wheelers, and lists of persons paid by Thos. Proud mayor of Calais, &c.

4535. EXPENCES OF THE WAR.

R. O.

Account of Miles Gerrard, commanded by the King's council to pay wages, victuals, and other charges to divers ships of war lately being northwards, and also to such ships and other charges as my Lord Admiral shall command ; also to pay his costs and charges northwards, and the carriage of artillery to the North field. Wages to passengers over with the King's grace into England, and conduct money to the soldiers and mariners of the ships of war, discharged this winter time.

Received of John Heron, treasurer of the King's Chamber, for the premises, by the Queen's warrant and the Council, 1,500l.

"Payments as well as wages for divers ships of war of the King's army royal, and other charges and prests of money to passengers of the King's belonging to the same, as for carriage of artillery northwards, and expenses there and other places, by commandment of the King's council, as hereafter particularly doth appear. To Sir Henry Shirborne, captain of the King's *Great Bark*, for a month's wages for the said ship, beginning 26 Sept. 5 Hen. VIII. reckoning 28 days to the month, as follows : To the said Henry, wages at 18d. a day ; wages of 140 soldiers and 101 mariners for a month, at 5s. each ; of a pilot to convey the said ship northward, 20s. ; 21 deedshares allowed to the master and other mariners, at 5s. a deedshare ; 1 master gunner, at 10s. a month, 4 quarter-masters at 7s. 6d. each, and 7 gunners at 6s. 8d. a month ;

1513.

total expenses of the ship 70l. 19s. 2d.—A month's wages to the captain, sailors, and soldiers of *The Mary George*, from 26 Sept. to 28 Oct., as follows : To John Rey, capt., 18d. a day ; 100 soldiers and 84 mariners 5s. a man ; 15 deedshares allowed to the master and mariners, at 5s. a deedshare ; reward to 6 gunners as they used to be paid before, with 5s. each as wages ; 6 master gunners 10s., 2 quarter masters 15s. 3d., other gunners 20s. ; —total expenses of the ship, 55l. 4s. 6d. For *The Barbara* of Greenwich, Rich. Hert purser, 34 mariners, at the same rate; total, 20l. 0s. 10d. The King's *Less Bark*, Sir Stephen Bull capt., 54 soldiers, gunners, at the same rate ; total, 46l. 5s. 4d. *The Mary and John*, Edw. Bray capt., 40 soldiers and gunners ; total, 43l. 6s. 2d. 100 mariners at 5s. a man ; deedshares allowed to master and mariners as usual at 5s. a share ; rewards to the gunners in deedshares 1l. 6s. 8d ; total expenses of the ship, 43l. 6s. 2d.— A month's wages to *The Julyan* of Dertmouth, George Witwang capt. ; 55 soldiers, mariners, and gunners ; rewards to 4 gunners, 10s. 10d. ; tonnage of the same ship, 100 tons at 12d. the ton ; —total, 25l. 15s. 4d. — A month's wages to *The Mary Rose*, Thomas Pert master ; 101 mariners ; 6 gunners ; 27 deedshares allowed to the master and mariners, at 5s. a deedshare ;—total, 34l. 2s. 2d.—A month's wages to the *Second Spaniard*, ending 24 October, Sir Edward Ychyngham capt., John Furnando master, a Spaniard, 60s. ; 40 Spanish mariners ; 16 mariners gromettis at 4s. 9d. each a month ; 4 pages mariners at 2s. 5d. ; deedshares to the same ; Spaniards for a month, 60s. ; tonnage, the ship being of 280 tons, at 1s. 3¾d. a ton ; 40 English mariners and soldiers at 5s. a man ; deedshares to 7 English mariners at 5s. a share ; 6 gunners at 5s.; rewards to the same, 14s. 2d. ;—total expense, 58l. 8s. 10¾d.—A month's wages to *The Mary George*, Sir Henry Shirborne capt., from 25 Oct. 5 Hen. VIII. ; 101 mariners; 100 soldiers ; 12 gunners; rewards to the gunners, 27s. 6d. : 19 deedshares to the master and mariners, 5s. a share; victuals for the captain, 214 soldiers and gunners at 1s. 6d. each a week ; wages to a pilot for conveying the ship out of danger from Harwich to the Downs, 20s. ;—total, 124l. 14s.—A month's wages to *The Barbara* of Greenwich, Bartholomew Wyrrall master, beginning 25 Oct. 5 Hen. VIII. ; 40 mariners ; 19 deedshares at 5s. a share ; reward for 3 gunners 7s. 6d., and to the said Wyrrall for victuals for the said mariners and gunners 10l. ; total, 25l. 5s.

ii. The account is continued for the King's *Less Bark*, *The Mary and John*, and the King's row-barge, John Ravon purser ; at the same rates.

iii. Payments ordered by the Council by a letter of 7 Oct. 5 Hen. VIII., for 189l. 10s., for ships to be in readiness to bring the King and his army home.

For conveying the King's money to Yarmouth, a man and his horse, 16d. a day. To John Holond, my Lord Admiral's servant, for carrying 100l. to Ipswich, 2s. For conduct money to different commanders. For charges of Miles Gerrard, treasurer in the war against the Scots, &c. (*Apparently imperfect.*)
Pp. 16.

1 Nov.   **4536.**   For the DEAN AND CANONS OF ST. GEORGE'S COLLEGE,
S. B.   WINDSOR.

Custody of the lordships of Knapton, Norfolk, Cillysworthe, Suffolk, and Benfeldbury, Essex, during the minority of John Veer,

1513.

kinsman and heir of John Earl of Oxford. The premises were sold by Elizabeth Veer Countess of Oxford, mother of John Earl of Oxford, to Richard Duke of Gloucester, late King of England, of whom they were purchased for 1,000l., as Thomas Earl of Arundel can vouch, by Edward IV., to the use of the aforesaid college ; after which the said Earl of Oxford wrongfully obtained possession thereof by suit to Henry VII. under color of restitution of his possessions which had come to the hands of Edw. IV. and Hen. VII. by his attainder ; and just before his death, the Earl appointed his counsel and that of the College to communicate as to his title to the premises. *Del.* Mortlake, 1 Nov. 5 Hen. VIII. *Pat. 5 Hen.VIII. p.* 1, *m.* 24.

| 3 Nov. | **4537.** | For THOMAS BARKER, prior of NEWBURY, York. |

R. O.
Rym. xiii. 383.

Letters patent enabling him to obtain bulls from Rome for himself and his successors to hold the church of Exworth, Lincolnshire, in commendam. Westm., 3 Nov.
Per breve de p. sigillo. Not found.
Pat. 5 Hen. VIII. p. 2, *m.* 28.

| 4 Nov. | **4538.** | For JOHN PILLESTON, sewer of the Chamber. |

P. S.

To be sergeant-at-arms, with 12d. a day, *vice* John Roydon, deceased. Tournay, 23 Sept. 5 Hen. VIII. *Del.* Westm., 4 Nov. *Pat. 5 Hen.VIII. p.* 1, *m.* 24.

| 5 Nov. | **4539.** | COMMISSION OF THE PEACE. |

Devon. — H. Bp. of Exeter, Hen. Earl of Wiltshire, Rob. Willoughby Lord Broke, John Bourghchier Lord Fitzwaren, Hen. Lord Daubney, Ric. Elyott, Lewis Pollerd, Edw. Willoughby, Sir Peter Eggecombe, Sir Edw. Pomerey, Sir Edm. Carewe, Sir Amyas Paulett, Sir John Basset, Sir John Kirkeham, Sir Thos. Greynfeld, John Souche, Wm. Courteney, Jas. Chudlegh, John Rowe, Rob. Yoo, Rob. Bouryng, John Gilbert, Thos. Stukeley, Ric. Reigne, John Crokker, Andr. Hillarsdon, Ric. Coffyn, Edm. Larder, John Asshe, Rob. Shilston, John Cole of Slade and John Kailwey. Westm., 5 Nov.
Pat. 5 Hen.VIII. p. 1, *m.* 3d.

| 6 Nov. | **4540.** | For JOHN BYNG of Wolverhampton, Staff., laborer, |

P. S.

alias capper, alias mercer.
Pardon. Windsor Castle, 6 Nov. 5 Hen. VIII. *Del.* Mortlake, 6 Nov.
Pat. 5 Hen.VIII. p. 1, *m.* 24.

| 6 Nov. | **4541.** | For WILLIAM COMPTON. |

S. B.

To be bailiff of Burley, Hants, with the fees enjoyed by Maurice Barkeley. *Del.* Mortlake, 6 Nov. 5 Hen. VIII.
Pat. 5 Hen.VIII. p. 2, *m.* 2.

| 6 Nov. | **4542.** | For SIR WILLIAM COMPTON. |

S. B.

To be Chancellor of Ireland. *Del.* Mortlake, 6 Nov. 5 Hen. VIII.
Pat. 5 Hen.VIII. p. 2, *m.* 2.

| 6 Nov. | **4543.** | For LEWIS CLIFFORD. |

S. B.

Exemption from serving on juries, &c. *Del.* Westm., 6 Nov. 5 Hen. VIII.
Pat. 5 Hen.VIII. p. 2, *m.* 2.

1513.
7 Nov.   **4544.**   SHERIFF ROLL.
S. B.
Cumb.—John Lamplewe; *Edm. Sampforde; Sir Edward Musgrave.

Northumb.—*Chr. Clapham ; Wm. Swynbourne ; Robt. Colyngwode, " hæres . . . . "

York.—Sir Wm. Bulmer ; *Sir Wm. Percy ; Sir Wm. Gascoyne, sen.

Notts and Derby. — Humph. Hercy ; Hen. Bosom ; * Roger Mynore.

Linc.—*Sir Marmaduke Constable, jun.; Th. Barneston ; Andr. Billesby.

Warw. and Leic.—*Sir Edward Ferrers ; Sir Edward Grevile ; John Spenser.

Salop.—Th. Lakyn ; *Wm. Otley ; Francis Yong .

Staff.—Sir John Draycot; Ric. Astley ; *Sir John Aston.

Heref.—Sir John Lyngeyn ; Ralph Haklet ; *Edward Crofte.

Glouc.—*Wm. Tracy ; Wm. Denys ; Edm. Tame.

Oxon. and Berks. — * Walter Rodney ; Th. Denton ; John Osbaston.

Northt.—Robt. Mathewe ; Th. Lovet ; *John Catesby.

Camb. and Hunts.—*Th. Thoresby ; Robt. Frevile ; Wm. Tanfelde.

Beds and Bucks. — Wm. Bulstrode ; Michael Fissher ; *Wm. Gascoigne.

Norf. and Suff.—Sir John Heydon ; Th. Gebon ; *Sir Anth. Wyngfelde.

Essex and Herts. — *John Seyntclere ; Wm. Fitzwilliam ; Th. Clyfford.

Kent.—Sir John Fogge ; John Crips ; *Sir John Norton.

Surrey and Sussex. -- Wm. Assheburneham ; *Ric. Shirley ; Roger Copley.

Hants. — *Sir Arthur Plantagenet ; Ric. Norton ; John Caylwey.

Wilts.—*Sir John Danvers ; Sir John Scrope ; John Ludlowe.

Somers. and Dors.— *Sir Wm. Compton, Sir Th. Lyme, Edward Gorge.

Devon. — * Wm. Carewe ; Edward Willoughby ; Sir Edward Pomerey.   *

Cornw.—John Chaworth ; Peter Bovill ; *John Carmynowe.

Rutland.—John Calcot ; Th. Brokesby ; *Everard Digby.

Del. Westm., . . Nov. 5 Hen. VIII.

The names with asterisks prefixed are those marked by the King to be sheriffs.

7 Nov.   **4545.**   EDWARD EARL OF WARWICK.
R. O.
Reversal of the attainder of Edward Earl of Warwick in favour of Margaret Countess of Salisbury ; with a pedigree of descent from John Lord Warwick and Joan his wife, temp. Hen. VI.

8 Nov.   **4546.**   To the ABP. OF CANTERBURY, Chancellor.
S B.
Safe conduct, at the request of Margaret of Savoy, for Andrew Scarella of Savona, for 12 months ensuing, to solicit and procure restitution of his ship called *la Karrake de Savona,* and of the goods which were in the ship at the time of its capture, or the true value of the same. Windsor Castle, 6 Nov. 5 Hen. VIII. *Del.* Westm., 8 Nov.

Rym. XIII. 384.   2. Letters patent to the same effect. Westm., 8 Nov.
Fr. 5 Hen. VIII. m. 11.

1513.
8 Nov.
P. S.

4547. For THOMAS LORD DARCY and GEORGE DARCY his son.

Grant, in survivorship, of the custody of the water of Fosse, near York, and the fishery of the same, as held by Richard Borowe of Henry VII. and Richard Newton of Henry VIII. Tournay, 25 Sept. 5 Hen. VIII. *L'el.* Westm., 8 Nov.

Pat. 5 Hen. VIII. p. 2, m. 3.

10 Nov.
Vat. Trans.
Addit. MSS.
15,387, f. 13.
B. M.

4548. HENRY VIII. to LEO X.

In behalf of Sir Tho. Cheyny, whom he sends to Italy. Windsor, 10 Nov. 1513.

Lat. Copy, pp. 3.

11 Nov.
R. O.

4549. MARGARET QUEEN OF SCOTS to KATHARINE OF ARRAGON.

Received on 6th of this month her letters, dated Windsor, 18 Oct. Thanks her for her sympathy in the misfortune fallen upon her, signified by Bonaventure, provincial of the Friars Observant. Hopes she will keep her brother in remembrance of her, that his kindness may be known in this realm, as she has explained to Bonaventure. Perth, 11 Nov. *Signed.*

P. 1. Add.

11 Nov.

4550. For SIR WILLIAM GASCOIGNE.

Inspeximus and exemplification of the following documents :—

i. Writ of *certiorari*, dated 23 Nov. 4 Hen. VIII., directing the Treasurer and Barons of the Exchequer to send into Chancery an inquisition taken 29 Oct. last, at Doncaster, before Hugh Serlbye, eschentor, on death of Edw. Redeman.

ii. The above-mentioned inquisition, by which it was found that the said Edward was seized in his demesne as of fee of moiety of the manor of Harwod, York ; lands in Otley Pole Holynghall, York ; and lands in Harwod ;—that the manor of Harwod is held of the King, the manor of Holynghall is held of the heir of John Whates, and the tenement of Pole is held of the heir of Ric. Goldesburgh ; and that Joan Redeman is kinswoman and heir of the said Edward, viz., daughter of Henry, son of the said Edward, and is upwards of three years old ;—and that he died 27 Sept. 2 Hen. VIII. Westm., 11 Nov.

Pat. 5 Hen. VIII. p. 2, m. 22.

11 Nov.
S. B.

4551. THOMAS GIBBON.

Writ to the Chancellor, for Thomas Gybbon to be sheriff of Norfolk and Suffolk, *vice* Sir Anthony Wyngfyld, discharged. Windsor Castle, 11 Nov. 5 Hen. VIII.

S. B.

ii. For Thomas Guybon to be sheriff of Norfolk and Suffolk during pleasure.

11 Nov.
P. S.

4552. For THOMAS TYRELL, master of the horse to the Queen.

Licence to import from Flanders 100 tuns of Gascon wine in one year. Calais. 23 Oct. 5 Hen. VIII. *Del.* Westm., 11 Nov.

Fr. 5 Hen. VIII. m. 7.

11 Nov.

4553. GAOL DELIVERY.

London, Newgate Gaol. — Wm. Broun, mayor of Norwich (London), Sir John Fyneux, Sir Rob. Rede, Sir Wm. Hody, Rob. Brudenell, Humph. Conyngasby, John Butteler, Wm. Fayrefax, and Ric. Broke. Westm., 11 Nov.

Pat. 5 Hen. VIII. p. 2, m. 4d.

1513.

11 Nov.   **4554.**   For THOMAS AP OWEN, " one of the graünde capitaynes
P. S.   with Sir Ryse ap Thomas."

Protection for William Horton, chapman, to serve in the war in
his retinue. 9 Nov. 5 Hen. VIII. *Del.* 11 Nov. by Th. ap Owen.

12 Nov.   **4555.**   For JOHN ALMER.
S. B.

To be serjeant-at-arms, with 12*d.* a day from Easter last. *Del.*
Mortlake, 12 Nov. 5 Hen. VIII.
Pat. 5 Hen. VIII. p. 1, *m.* 24.

13 Nov.   **4556.**   DACRE to HENRY VIII.
Calig. B. vi. 37.
B. M.

Ellis, 1 S. 1. 93.

Has received the King's letter of thanks, to his singular comfort;—he perceives by it that the King gives no credence to the
sinister reports surmised against him. On Thursday last assembled
1,000 Northumberland horse, and rode in at Gallespeth, and so to
the water of Kale, two miles within Scotland. His brother Philip.
with 300 men, destroyed the town of Rowcastell with all the corn—
Sir Roger Fenwike did the same with Langton. Came with a
stale to a place called the Dungyon, a mile from Jedworth—so to the
Sclater Ford ; was pursued by the Scots, assisted by David Kerr of
Fernehirst, the Laird of Boudgedworth, and the sheriff of Teviotdale; the Laird of Walghope and Mark Trumbill are hurt.—His brother, Sir Christopher, entered by Ledesdale "to the Rugheswyre,"
and sent out two forays ; one under Sir John Ratclif, with 500 men,
who burnt the town of Dyker, both roof and floor ; and after, the
towns of Sowdon and Lurchestrother. Nic. Haryngton, Nic. Rydley,
Thos. Medilton, and George Skelton burnt Hyndhalghehede, floor
and roof ; W. Sawsyde and E. Sawsyde.—Forming a union with
his brother, they saw the Chamberlain with 2,000 men, on which the
Dacres retired, " and rode no faster than nowt shepe, and swyne
that we had won would drive, which was of no great substance, for
the country was warned of our coming, and the beacons burned
from midnight forward."—The gentlemen of the country are backward, as Lord Ogle and the Constable of Alnwick.—Has thus
fulfilled the King's command, with the loss of one man only.—
Cannot see how an inroad is to be made on the west marches, as he
cannot leave for fear the Scots should burn the country in his
absence. Will, however, do so " the next light." Begs the King
will send orders to the Lords Clifford and Northumberland for
their tenants to attend the warders, as usual.

John Barton, who passed into France with the navy of Scotland,
landed at Kirkobrighe, and there fell sick and died.—A great
council has been held at St. Johnstone, when it was resolved
the Bp. of Aberdeen shall be Abp. of St. Andrews, the Bp. of
Caithness Bp. of Aberdeen, a brother of the Earl of Adthill Bp. of
Caithness. The abbey of Arbroath is given to George Douglas,
s. of the Earl of Angus ; the abbey of Dunfermline to James
Hebburne; the priory of Coldingham to the Lord Chamberlain's
brother. A brother of Dand Kerr's, of Farnehirst, has forced his
way into the abbey of Kelso. — The castle of Stirling is to be
victualled and fortified, the Lord Bothwick to be captain, and have
the young King in his keeping. They have not yet been able to determine which of the Lords shall have the rule of the realm.—The
Earl of Aren, Admiral of Scotland, is come home with the ships ; and
a French knight with him has brought letters from the French King
and from Albany. Three of the greatest ships have been left in

1513.

France to assist the French navy. The great ship run aground.—
The Scotch soldiers speak ill of their entertainment by France.
Harbotill, 13 Nov.
Add. Pp. 5.

13 Nov.   **4557.**   For JOHN VAGHAN, groom of the Chamber.
P. S.
Licence to import 500 tuns of foreign wine.   Windsor Castle,
12 Nov. 5 Hen. VIII.   *Del.* Mortlake, 13 Nov.
Fr. 5 Hen. VIII. m. 7.

13 Nov.   **4558.**   GAOL DELIVERY.
Norwich.—John Ryghtwys, mayor, Sir Jas. Hobart, Ric. Burgh,
Geo. Clerk, Th. Aldrych, Ric. Aylmer, Fras. Mounford, and John
Spylman.   Westm., 13 Nov.
Pat. 5 Hen. VIII. p. 2, m. 4d.

14 Nov.   **4559.**   COMMISSION OF THE PEACE.
Oxon.—W. Bp. of Lincoln, M. Bp. of Landaff, Sir Thos. Lovell,
Rich. Elyott, Sir Rich. Fouler, Sir Wm. Rede, Sir Edw. Grevyle,
Sir Adrian Fortescu, Wm. Weste, Wm. Fermar, Ralph Massy,
Edw. Chamberleyn, Simon Harecourte, Walter Bulstrode, Thos.
Unton, John Horne, Christopher Belyngeham, John Osbaldeston,
Ralph Vyne, George Stanley, Thos. Haydok, Thos. Denton, John
Bulsterd and Wm. Councer.   Westm., 14 Nov.
Pat. 5 Hen. VIII. p. 1, m. 3d.

15 Nov.   **4560.**   MAXIMILIAN.
R. O.
Confirmation of a treaty between the Lady Margaret and
Henry VIII., for carrying on the war against France.
1—4. The Emperor to provide and support 4,000 horse and 6,000
foot in Artois and Hainault.   The King of England to invade
Aquitain, Picardy, or Normandy before June ; the Emperor to
invade France whenever he can injure Lewis most effectually, and
not enter into any treaty without consent of the other parties.
5. Before 15 May next, the Emperor, Charles Prince of Castile,
Henry, Katharine, and Mary, to assemble at Calais, and celebrate
the marriage of Charles and Mary.   Lisle, 16 Oct. 1513.
The confirmation dated at Augsburg, 15 Nov. 1513.
Lat.

15 Nov.   **4561.**   SPINELLY to [HENRY VIII.]
Galba, B. III. 130.
B. M.
Wrote last on the . . . . inst.   The Emperor has gone towards
Newrenberge, and has ordered the ambassadors to meet him at
Guesseling, three leagues from Ulme.   My Lady thinks he has done
so to be nearer Italy and the Swiss.   Encloses an extract of the news
from the Emperor to my Lady, and a copy of an article written by
himself to the Deputy of Calais respecting the coming of the French
to repair Terouenne.   Artois the herald departs for England ; my
Lady sends him the dispatch from the Emperor, drawn according
to the resolution taken by the Bp. of Winchester and Mr. Almoner.
By the news brought to Zeland by the two ships from Scotland it
appears the lords there are not pleased that the Queen should have
the rule, as they fear she will comply too much with England.
They are in constant intercourse with France, and their ships pass
by the back of Ireland.   " Charles de Sempol, of your grace's
acquaintance, at my Lady's departure from Lisle, by her licence

went unto the Lord Dangulem to bear him a falcon that was taken in this country having the French arms, of the which I understand your grace hath knowledge ; where he was well received, and gave him a gown of crimson velvet, and a jacket of cloth of gold and white satin." He said England had gained nothing by the death of the King of Scots, as the Duke of Albany would shortly go into Scotland, and there receive . . . . King, who with his experience, and the entire affection he has for France, will acquit himself better than did his predecessor. The French say that Margaret of Savoy was the sole cause of the aid given by the Emperor to England, but as soon as the Prince comes to the age of fifteen,' and is out of his minority, " if here been not taken other way and better council in the matter, they shall compel him by force to do it ;" that the alliance of marriage between the Prince and my Lady Mary is *contre le bien publique*; that he shall have no other than the second daughter of the French King, or they will give her to Don Fernando his brother, and trouble the succession.—The nobles and people of France are dissatisfied with their King, for his avarice and obstinacy ; they distrust the Swiss.—Encloses a letter respecting Tournay received from a friend, and another he has written to my lord captain there. My Lady has sent to him touching the musters. Gaunt, 15 Nov. 1513. *Signed.*

Pp. 4. Mutilated.

15 Nov. **4562.** The LIEUTENANT and COUNCIL of RHODES to
Otho, C. IX. 11.   HENRY VIII.
B. M.

By virtue of their obedience Thos. Newport, "bajulus aquilæ," and Thos. Scefild, preceptor of our pre[ceptory] of Synghai, and treasurer of the order in [England], have arrived at Rhodes. Learn from the same that the King wishes to retain with him Thos. Docray, their prior. Request that he may be sent as soon as the King can spare him. Will retain Newport and Scefield. Rhodes, 15 Nov. 1513.

Lat., mutilated, pp. 2.

16 Nov. **4563.** SIR ROB. WINGFIELD to HENRY VIII.
Vitell. B. XVIII. 57.
B. M.

Wrote in his last of this month " that the Emperor [would see] me again within a day or two. This day . . . . before 8 o'clock he sent for me, and tarried [with me in] his chamber till it was 10 o'clock, in which [after his] accustomed manner, he had many devices and demands." He showed Wingfield that audience had been given the Pope's legate, who said that the Pope desired an union of Christian princes, so that some good expedition might be made [against] the infidels ; " and that where all the weight of war th[at was] in Christendom was betwixt his Majesty and the Venetians, and betwixt your grace and the French King, in both which his Holiness judged his Majesty to have great gree . . . remedy, for the war with Venetians was his own par[t but as for] that with France, he thought that your grace would [be] advised and counselled by him, and so the rather that wa . . . nevertheless if so be that the Venetians would not c[ome to] an honorable peace with him, he would not fail to p[roceed] to their utter ruin ; and furthermore, if it might not . . . and your grace with other Christian princes that the . . . . till France were ' corecte, his Holiness w[ould condescend to] your desires. And where there is . . . . hath but gev . . . . perfect conclusion and effect."

To which the Emperor made answer that he would gladly see peace established between himself and the Venetians, and between England and France; but that as for himself he had always accepted every reasonable offer of peace, which had been broken by the Venetians; nevertheless he could be better contented to make an honorable peace with them, than to procure peace between Henry VIII. and France, because he believed there would be no steadfast peace and concord in Christendom till France be corrected; and he was in great doubt that if it be not brought to order now France would become more petulant than in time past. Wherefore he thought it best that peace should be made between himself and the Venetians, and that the Pope and the other powers of Italy should enter into a league with the Emperor, Henry, and the King of Arragon, against the French, "which as they would do effectually . . . . all things should be reformed . . . . grace and the King of . . . . by one assent will purvey . . . . that other list not lay hand to help . . . ."

The Emperor then showed "that where at the castle of Anthoyne beside . . . . . . he [advertized] me that by a secret ambassador from the Pope he was [informed] that his Holiness would undertake that the Venetians [should] condescend to give him 1,000,000 ducats, so that he w[ould consent] to part with the cities of Verona and Vincenza, and so make [firm] peace with him, and that he would in no wise condescend [to surrender] Verona, but he would deliver them the city of Cremona [which would] be as profitable to them, and under that manner at the p[resent] he was content to conclude peace with them, and with that a[nswer the] said Pope's ambassador was despatched. And where since the conflict and battle hath been between hi[s Majesty and the] Venetians, and the Venetians' army utterly destroyed, and t[he Viceroy] of Naples, with his army, hath and intended to have proceeded . . . . Frioul, and wasted and destroyed; yestereven he wa[s informed] that the Pope hath written to the Viceroy [to proceed] no farther in damaging that co[untry but to] make a peace, to which . . . . showed that where the Cardinal of Gurce . . . . . . Rome and such other as be in commission with him, have [an in]tent to conclude with the Venetians after the manner and [for]m before written, as well because of the change made by the [fo]resaid victory, as that the Emperor is informed that the Venetians are unable from poverty to pay the said sum of 1,000,000 ducats, he is content to conclude a peace with them after the form that Pope Julius and the King of Arragon ordained; and if they will not so, yet he will be content to be ordered either in peace or truce as the Pope and the King of Arragon shall order. Upon this point the Emperor desired Wingfield's advice whether he should leave the whole authority to the Pope to conclude the peace, or to him and the King of Arragon together.

To which Wingfield answered that as the case was changed by the Emperor's victory, and the report respecting the poverty of the Venetians, he thought it was well done to assemble the Pope and the King of Arragon together. The Emperor then showed Wingfield five principal reasons for his coming into these parts, and by the way; 1st, the variance existing between the Archbishop of Cologne and the county of Westphalia; 2nd, between the Archbishop of Mayence [and the Duke of Saxe; 3rd, between the county of [Swa]ve and that of Franconia; 4th, an universal dissension between the cities and towns of Almain, of the people against the

1513.

government ; and, 5th, "for his own business . . . . all the estates of all his countries to have . . . . . . in his wars with the Venetians." "And he shewed me that he was in good hope to have . . . . . the empire, all which and all other aids that may . . . . prince's countries, he would employ it in your g . ; . . the French King, and also that of his own countries, y[f they] disturb him not." The Emperor also asked if Henry were much hindered by the Scots ? To which Wingfield answered that he could not say till he had received information, but thought rather nay than yea. "It seemeth his Majesty hath been advertised that the French [intend] to send folks into Scotland, and so empesche you there, th . . . not may keep your appointment of returning in. . . " The Emperor also wished Wingfield to request [Henry] "to write a letter of credence to the ambassadors of Venice, [and to] have it ready, if any embassy shall be sent to him, as [he hopes] there shall," and to send Wingfield instructions on the same.

The Count Palatine Frederick recommends himself to Henry, and hopes soon to "depart hence towards . . . . . . his authority for the Emperor about the . . . . things that be . . . . Pope's orator that is here, that an [ambassador] from the Pope is passing to your grace, and as [far as I can] perceive he is passed through the Switzers' country. [He is] a Neapolitan born and Bishop of Chieti of the house of [C]arrapha." All nations resort to this court, and Wingfield judges that no Christian prince before Henry had so diligent an officer of arms as the Emperor, who celebrates his name and good fortune to those that come to him from strange countries ; and all Henry's actions on this side the sea to the Emperor's departure from him, and those against the Scots, are spread all over Germany. . . . Nov. 1513.

Hol., pp. 6.

16 Nov.   **4564.**   For ROBERT FAIREFAX and ROBERT BYTHESEE.
P. S.
    Annuity of 9l. 2s. 6d. in survivorship, viz., 7l. 18s. 5d. out of the farm of Colemere, Hants, by the hands of the Prior of South-wike, and 24s. 1d. from the issues of Hants ; on surrender of patent 22 June 1 Hen. VIII. granting the same to Fayrefax, gentleman of the King's chapel. Lisle, 15 Oct. 5 Hen. VIII. *Del.* Mortlake, 16 Nov.
    Pat. 5 Hen.VIII. p. 2, m. 2.

16 Nov.   **4565.**   For ROBERT THORNEY, yeoman porter of the King's
P. S.   gates.
    Annuity of 5l. out of the lordship of Dynbigh, N. Wales., which Charles Manwaryng, deceased, lately had. Windsor Castle, 14 Nov. 5 Hen. VIII. *Del.* Mortlake, 16 Nov.
    Pat. 5 Hen.VIII. p. 2, m. 2.

16 Nov.   **4566.**   For WILLIAM FYTTON, yeoman of the Butlery.
    Grant, during pleasure, of all lands in Mapilthorp late of Edmund Dudley, attainted. Mortlake, 16 Nov.
    Pat. 5 Hen.VIII. p. 2, m. 2.

1513.

18 Nov.
S. B.
4567. For WILLIAM COUSYN, the King's chaplain, Dean of Wells.

Licence to obtain bulls from Rome, licensing him to be absent from his benefice six months in the year. *Del.* Westm., 18 Nov. 5 Hen. VIII.

Pat. 5 Hen. VIII. p. 2, m. 4.

18 Nov.
4568. GAOL DELIVERY.

Surrey Gaol, Southwark. — John Boteler, Sir Thos. Lovell, John More, serjeant-at-law, Sir Hen. Wyat, Sir Ric. Cholmeley, Sir John Leigh, John Erneley, and John Scott. Westm., 18 Nov.

Pat. 5 Hen. VIII. p. 2, m. 4d.

19 Nov.
S. B.
4569. For RALPH FULSEHURST.

Wardship of George, kinsman and heir of Sir Edward Rawley, viz., son of Edward, son of the said Sir Edward. *Del.* Westm., 19 Nov. 5 Hen. VIII.

Pat. 5 Hen. VIII. p. 2, m. 4.

20 Nov.
S. B.
4570. For SIR RICHARD CAREWE, knight of the Body, and NICHOLAS his son.

To be lieutenants, in survivorship, of the castle of Calais, with power to nominate the constable, soldiers and archers there, with 2s. a day, and 20l. a year ;—as held by Sir John Donne and Sir Anthony Broun. *Del.* Westm., 20 Nov. 5 Hen. VIII.

Pat. 5 Hen. VIII. p. 2, m. 2.

20 Nov.
R. O.
4571. MAX. [SFORZA] DUKE OF MILAN to HENRY VIII.

Had heard the news of his joint victory with the Emperor ; confirmed by the King's letters of 24 Sept., stating that the King of Scots had been slain and his army defeated. The wresting of the cities of Terouenne and Tournay will bridle the power of this enemy of the Church ; without it he could have found no security in Italy. The French have restored Milan this day, which he had garrisoned, and promised the restoration of Cremona. "Ex arce portæ Jovis Mediolani," 20 Nov. 1513. *Signed.*

Lat., pp. 2. Add. End.

29 Oct.*
R. O.
4572. THE EARL OF ANGUS to [HENRY VIII.]

Has received his message by Edw. Cuyk, which he had already intended to execute. Is glad to find the King trusts to him. Sends his servant David Menzeys to explain further, whose credence he binds himself to fulfil by this writing. Edinburgh, 29 Oct.

Signed by himself, and sealed with his arms.

23 Nov.
R. O.
4573. THOS. LORD DACRE to WOLSEY.

Encloses a letter received from his brother Sir Christopher through the salmon carriers of Carlisle. His brother could make no raid into Scotland. The Earl of Angus is dead at St. Ninian's

---

* The date is quite uncertain. Probably addressed Henry VII. But see Thorpe's Calendar, Scot. Ser. I. p. 1.

1513.

in Galloway.* The inhabitants of Teviotdale in Scotland are great thieves. Waltham, 23 Nov.

P.S. in his own hand : I arttly thank yow of your gud sches and comfortabell declaration of the message schud me att the coupburds in your schamber. *Signed and sealed.*

P. 1. Addressed : To Maister Wulcy, almoigner to the Kinges grace. *Endorsed.*

23 Nov. **4574.** PETER MARTYR to LUD. FURTATO.

Pet. Mart. Fp.
No. 533.

Henry has made terms with France, and returned to England to settle the matters in Scotland. Lewis sends humble messages to Spain, but they are not to be trusted. The Pope has given a Cardinal's hat to Gurk. The Venetians say, if they do not receive aid from France they must make terms with the Emperor. Thus the whole of Italy will be shut against France. By the advice of Gurk, the Emperor presses the Venetians and exacts from them too severe conditions, which will probably his purpose. The Swiss have stripped Duke Maximilian to the skin. Nothing will satisfy their cruelty or their cupidity. Valladolid, ix. kal. Dec.

25 Nov. **4575.** For JAMES MERYKE of Wentfordton.

P. S.

Grant of the demesne lands of the lordship of Wentfordton, in the earldom of March. Tournay, 23 Sept. 5 Hen. VIII. *Del.* Knoll, 25 Nov.

Pat. 5 Hen. VIII. p. 2, m. 2.

26 Nov. **4576.** ERASMUS to AMMONIUS.

Eras. Ep. VIII.21.

Is expecting his wonderful strategy and its results (*magnifica illa stratagemata tum quantum in zonis sit allatum*). Wrote to him in the camp divers times by John of Lorraine. Has had no less a battle with the blunders of Seneca and St. Jerome than Ammonius with the French; and though he was not in the camp, has had from the spoils ten crowns by the Bp. of Durham. Waits for Ammonius' military epistle. Camb., 6 kl. Dec.

Begs Ammonius' good words for his affairs. Will in a few months throw out his sheet anchor ;—if he succeeds, will consider this as his native country, which he has preferred to Rome, and where age has overtaken him. If not, he will have to die elsewhere. Protests his own good faith ;—had *he* made such magnificent promises, would have certainly kept them. Regrets his bad fortune. 1511.

26 Nov. **4577.** SPINELLY to HENRY VIII.

R. O.
St. P. vi. 27.

Wrote last this morning. A post has since come from Rome and Almaine with a lettter from Wingfield, which he sends. The Emperor has informed the Archduchess that the Viceroy of Naples, in answer to the Pope's brief desiring him to desist from invading the Venetians, as they would submit to the arbitration of his Holiness, replied that he could not do so without express orders from Ferdinand, the Emperor, or the Bp. of Gurk, his Lieutenant-General in Italy. Considering the subtlety of the Venetians in times past, the Emperor has ordered the Viceroy to prosecute the enterprise with all celerity, intimating at the same time to the Pope that he was ready to submit to the arbitration of his Holiness and Arragon, if the Venetians would make truce for a year or two.

---

* According to Douglas' Peerage of Scotland he withdrew to Whithorn in Galloway after the battle of Flodden, and died there in 1514. The address of this letter, however, must be 1513 at the latest.

1513.

The Swiss are dissatisfied with the Duke of Milan, who refuses to deliver the castle into their hands. Thinks if they persist he will be obliged to please them or to break. The Adorni of Genoa were in treaty for a band of Swiss to go to Genoa against the Fregosi ; if they obtain it, it may produce a new revolution in Milan. Bourbon and John Jacques de Trowis have sent into Dauphiné to prepare quarters for their army, which is reported to number 1,800 spears, and 15,000 foot. Cannot understand the superiority of these Frenchmen ; they are not wiser, braver, or richer than others, only more diligent and resolute ;—summer and winter are alike to them. If they set forward it must be with consent of the Swiss. My Lady had news last night from Hainault, that 800 Almaines who had served Henry were returning from the French for lack of entertainment.

Has just received Henry's letter, dated Windsor, 6 Nov., which had been long on the road. Will not fail to execute his injunctions. Termonde, 26 Nov. 1513.

This letter was begun yesternight.

Pp. 3. *Signed.*

---

26 Nov.
B. M.
Vesp. C. xii. 231.

4578.   FERDINAND OF ARRAGON to HENRY VIII.

Requests the restoration of two ships laden with woad and alum, belonging to Gregory of Bejar and the Marquis of Cabaravias, merchants of Burgos, taken by English subjects three months ago. Madrid, 26 Nov. 1513.

Spanish, p. 1.

---

27 Nov.
R. O.

4579.   MAXIMILIAN [SFORZA] DUKE OF MILAN to HENRY VIII.

The King will remember that his intimation of the surrender of Tournay, 12 Oct., might have been augmented by the victory of Flodden, about the same time. But for the flight of the enemy, would have had another cause to congratulate him. Wishes him joy on the marriage of his sister with the King. Milan, 27 Nov. 1513. *Signed.*

Lat., p. 1. *Add.*

---

27 Nov.
P. S.

4580.   For THOMAS STOTEVYLE.

Licence to import 500 tuns of Gascon or French wine. Windsor Castle, 23 Nov. 5 Hen. VIII. *Del.* Knoll, 27 Nov.

Fr. 5 Hen. VIII. m. 8.

---

28 Nov.
R. O.

4581.   SCOTCHMEN IN ENGLAND.

Certificate of Roger Acheley, Geo. Monoux, Thos. Myrfyn, John Bruges, and John Milborne, commissioners appointed 27 Aug. 5 Hen. VIII. to seize and sell the goods of Scotchmen in London, touching the goods of Jas. Wilson, saddler, born in Scotland. 28 Nov. 5 Hen. VIII.

---

29 Nov.
Vitell. B. ii. 54.
B. M.
Rym. xiii. 395.

4582.   LEO X. to HENRY VIII.

Authorizes the body of James IV. to be carried to London, and buried in St. Paul's, notwithstanding that he had incurred the sentence of excommunication at first signing the treaty with Henry VII., and secondly, after his marriage, with Henry VIII. Though he had commissioned the Cardinal St. Praxedis [Bainbridge] to execute the sentence, yet, as it is to be presumed the King gave some signs of repentance in his extremities, the Pope

Y Y

1513.

allows him to be buried with funeral honors, trusting the oversight thereof to Richard Bp. of London, or some prelate chosen by the King. Rome, 29 Nov. 1513.

Vellum. Add. Mutilated.

29 Nov.   **4583.**   COMMISSION OF THE PEACE.

Wilts.—R. Bp. of Winchester, E. Bp. of Salisbury, Henry Earl of Wiltshire, Rich. abbot of Malmesbury, Robt. Willoughby Lord Broke, Wm. Lord Mautravers, Wm. Lord Stourton, Rich. Eliott, Lewis Pollerd, Sir Walter Hungerford, Sir Edw. Darell, Sir John Seymour, Sir John Scrope, Henry Longe, Sir Maurice Barowe, Sir Edw. Hungerford, John Neuport, Philip Baynard, John Skilling, John Gawen, John Yorke, Henry Pauncefote, Anth. Stilman, John West, Robt. Keilwey and Geo. Morgan. Knoll, 29 Nov.

Pat. 5 Hen. VIII. p. 1, m. 3d.

30 Nov.   **4584.**   G[EORGE TALBOT] EARL OF SHREWSBURY to HEN. VIII.
R. O.

A fellow, known to the treasurer and upper marshal of Calais, has arrived from Blois. Has made him write down his news, which he sends. Has re-despatched him to the same place, with promises of favor. Calais, 30 Nov. *Signed.*

P. 1. Add.

30 Nov.   **4585.**   TOURNAY.
Calig. D. VI. 98b.
B. M.

Letters patent of Edward Thwayte Lord Destyere, councillor to the King of France and of England, keeper of the Seal Royal of Tournay, reciting the grant made by Edward Lord Ponynges, K.G., the King's lieutenant of Tournay, to Allart Bent[inck], steward of the Household with the Archduchess of Austria, of the receivorship of 6,000 francs, to be paid by the town ; which grant is attested by John le Clement and Oliver le Calonne, notaries. Recites also the letters patent (dated 15 Oct. 1513) directed to Ponynges, to instal Bentinck in that office, previously held by Hymbert Gernyer. 30 Nov. 1513.

Copy, pp. 4.

Nov.   **4586.**   EXPENCES OF THE WAR.
R. O.

Account of monies paid for harness, &c., from July to November, at Lisle, Tournay, and elsewhere.

Pp. 13. Much mutilated.

Nov.   **4587.**   For RIC. KNYGHTLEY, EDM. KNYGHTLEY, THOS. ISHAM and EDW. WARNER.

Commission to make inquisition in respect of the possessions, &c. held by [Edward] late Earl of Wiltshire, Elizabeth late wife of Sir Thos. Cheyne, Constance late wife of John [Eure ?] and Alice late wife of Humph. [Beamond] ;—the said Earl, Elizabeth, Constance and Alice being all deceased. ......, .. Nov. *Much defaced.*

Pat. 5 Hen. VIII. p. 1, m. 24d.

1 Dec.   **4588.**   i. For WILLIAM ATWATER, Dean of the King's chapel,
S. B.   and JOHN YOUNGE, Master of the Rolls.

Licence to import 100 tuns of Gascon wine. Windsor Castle, 3 Nov. 5 Hen. VIII. *Del.* Knoll, 1 Dec. 5 Hen. VIII.

Fr. 5 Hen. VIII. m. 8.

1513.
2 Dec.
P. S.

ii. For PATRICK BERMYNGEHAM.

To be Chief Justice of the King's Bench in Ireland, during pleasure, with fees out of the great and small customs, tonnage and poundage, in the ports of Dublin and Drogheda. Windsor Castle, 26 Nov. 5 Hen. VIII. *Del.* Knoll, 2 Dec.
Pat. 5 Hen. VIII. p. 2, m. 4.

2 Dec.
P. S.

iii. For GERALD FITZ GERALD, EARL OF KILDARE.

To be Deputy of Ireland, during pleasure, with power to appoint all officers, except the Chancellor and Chief Justice of the King's Bench, &c., in as ample manner as Sir Edward Ponynges held the office ; with grant of all possessions he shall recover from rebels in Ireland. Windsor Castle, 26 Nov. 5 Hen. VIII. *Del.* Knoll, 2 Dec.
Pat. 5 Hen. VIII. p. 2, m. 4.

2 Dec.
P. S.

iv. For GERALD EARL OF KILDARE, Justiciary, and the Lords and Council of Ireland.

Licence to import into Ireland, by Robert Cowley, victuals and merchandize in six ships, not exceeding 120 tons burthen, at Dublin, Drogheda, Dundalk, or any other Irish ports, for relief of the King's subjects in Ireland. Castle of Windsor, 26 Nov. 5 Hen. VIII. *Del.* Knoll, 2 Dec.
Fr. 5 Hen. VIII. m. 8.

2 Dec.
P. S. b.

4589. For SIR GEORGE SEYNTLEGER.

Protection to John Gibbons of London, mercer, retained by him to serve in the war. 2 Dec. 5 Hen. VIII. *Signed and sealed.*

3 Dec.
P. S.

4590. For JOHN LOK of London, mercer.

Protection ; going in the suite of Sir Richard Wyngfylde, knight of the Body, Deputy of Calais. Windsor Castle, 2 Dec. 5 Hen. VIII. *Del.* Knoll, 3 Dec.
Fr. 5 Hen. VIII. m. 9.

4 Dec.
P. S.

4591. For CHRISTOPHER MORES, gunner.

To be gunner in the Tower of London, with 12*d.* a day from Mic. last, *vice* Roger Anglesse, deceased. Windsor Castle, 4 Nov. 5 Hen. VIII. *Del.* Knoll, 4 Dec.
Pat. 5 Hen. VIII. p. 2, m. 3.

4 Dec.
P. S.

4592. For WALTER WALSSH.

Annuity of 4*l.* (at the request of Richard Blount) out of the lands called Haloweys in Compton, in the lordship of Kynfare, Staff. The annuity was forfeited by Francis Viscount Lovel, and lately held by Humphrey Blount, deceased, of Henry VII. Windsor Castle, 11 Nov. 5 Hen. VIII. *Del.* Knoll, 4 Dec.
Pat. 5 Hen. VIII. p. 2, m. 3.

5 Dec.

4593. COMMISSION OF THE PEACE.

Lincolnshire.—Wm. Bp. of Lincoln, Wm. Lord Willoughby, Rob. Brudenell, Humphrey Conyngesby, Guy Palmes, Sir Rob.

Sheffeld, Sir John Huse, Sir Wm. Tirwytt, Sir John Skipwyth, Sir Rob. Tirwytt, Sir Rob. Waterton, Sir Wm. Askewe, Sir Wm. Hansard, Sir Andrew Billesby, Sir Christ. Ascoghe, Rob. son of Sir Rob. Sheffeld, Christ. Willoughby, Th. Burgh, jun., Geo. Fitz-william, Christ. Broun, Lionel Dynmok, John Topclyff, Rob. Sutton, Th. Barnardeston, Rob. Sheffeld, Th. Missenden, John Mounson, Rob. Belwode, Nich. Upton, John Fulnetby, John Hen-nege, Th. Burgh, John Seyntpoll, Edw. Forman, Th. Tocoste, and Ric. Clerke. Knoll, 5 Dec.

Pat. 5 Hen. VIII. p. 1, *m.* 3*d.*

---

5 Dec.   **4594.**   For RICHARD CORNEWAYLL, squire of the Body.

P. S.

Grant of the manors of Cundour, Doryngton and Ryton, Salop, late of Francis Viscount Lovel, attainted temp. Hen. VII. Windsor Castle, 28 Nov. 5 Hen. VIII. *Del.* Knoll, 5 Dec.

Pat. 5 Hen. VIII. p. 2, *m.* 4.

---

5 Dec.   **4595.**   For RICHARD OWEN and THOMAS ROBERTZ.

P. S.

To be auditors, in survivorship, of South Wales; on surrender of patent 14 June 17 Hen. VII. granting the office to the said Richard. Dover Castle, 28 June 5 Hen. VIII. *Del.* Knoll, 5 Dec.

Pat. 5 Hen. VIII. p. 2, *m.* 3.

---

5 Dec.   **4596.**   For RICHARD OWEN and JOHN PERYENT.

P. S.

To be clerks, in survivorship, at the little and great sessions in South Wales. Dover Castle, 28 June 5 Hen. VIII. *Del.* Knoll, 5 Dec.

Pat. 5 Hen. VIII. p. 2, *m.* 3.

---

6 Dec.   **4597.**   For DAVID CICILE.

P. S.

To be King's sergeant-at-arms, with 12*d.* a day. Windsor Castle, 17 Nov. 5 Hen. VIII. *Del.* Knoll, 6 Dec.

         4598.   [Fox and another] to the BP. OF WORCESTER.

Vitell. B. iv.104.
B. M.

Thank him for kindness in times past. Have seen by the Pope's briefs sent to divers prelates in England his desire for a universal peace, and his request to have an answer from the King of England, of which Master Andreas hereby sends a copy. The King is desirous to oblige the Pope in all things. Worcester is to negociate the business, which will sooner come to good effect than if it were treated by great persons, "with their morose gravities, great pomps, ceremonies, and solemnities." The Cardinal of York, who has been so long the King's ambassador at that court, cannot be sent as legate *à latere*, either to the Emperor or to England, without suspicion ; nor is the King willing to admit a legate into England or Calais, and therefore the Pope must provide, that in case he be sent as legate into Germany, he be not allowed to exercise that authority in all places where the Emperor may chance to be. For the Cardinal of York writes that the King and the Emperor are to meet at Calais in May, and he shall be there with the Emperor as legate. More-over, as the Bp. of Feltri is the papal ambassador with the Emperor and the Bp. of Civita in England, the Pope can employ them in ne-

1513.

gociating the peace ; nor does the petition of the Lateran council, "qua petitur ut mittantur legati et nuncii," prevent this arrangement. If the Emperor agrees, the King of France may be persuaded to send an ambassador to England, for the same purpose ; or both powers may send to Calais or some neutral spot ; but it is expedient that peace first of all be concluded between the Emperor and the Venetians. The King has sent them an admonition by Sir Rob. Wingfield, his ambassador with the Emperor, of which Andreas forwards a copy.

Copy, pp. 6. Mutilated.

8 Dec.
S. B.

4599. For JOHN WYLDE of Henham, Essex, husbandman.

Pardon. *Del.* Knoll, 3 Dec. 5 Hen. VIII.
Pat. 5 Hen. VIII. p. 2, m. 5.

11 Dec.
S. B.

4600. For THOMAS THORNTON, priest.

Presentation to the perpetual chantry at the altar of St. John the Baptist, in the chapel over the charnel house adjoining the church of St. Mary Aldermarichurch, London, on the nomination of the rector of the said church, and of Richard Shepard, John Gunne and Peter Middelton, churchwardens. *Del.* Knoll, 11 Dec. 5 Hen. VIII.
Pat. 5 Hen. VIII. p. 2, m. 10.

12 Dec.
S. B.

4601. For HUGH VAUGHAN and JOHN HUNTELEY, grooms of the Chamber.

Licence to import 600 tons of wine and woad. *Del.* Knoll, 12 Dec. 5 Hen. VIII.

14 Dec.
P. S.

4602. For WILLIAM SYMONDES, groom of the Chamber.

To be bailiff of Yaresthorp and Appulton in the lordship of Shiriffhoton, York, with 6d. a day, and clerk of the courts in the said lordship, with 4d. a day. Calais, 2 July 5 Hen. VIII. *Del.* Knoll, 14 Dec.
Pat. 5 Hen. VIII. p. 2, m. 21.

15 Dec.
P. S.

4603. For JOHN HARDEN, clk.

Presentation to the church of Lovel Upton, Salisb. dioc., void by death. Windsor Castle, 6 Dec. 5 Hen. VIII. *Del.* Otford, 15 Dec.
Pat. 5 Hen. VIII. p. 2, m. 24.

16 Dec.
Otho, C. ix. 12.
B. M.

4604. FABRICIUS DE CARETO to HENRY VIII.

On the death of Guido de Blanchefort, had been elected master. Will detain Sheffield and Newport for their services against the Turk. Rhodes, 16 Dec. 1513.
Lat., mutilated, p. 1. Add. End.

17 Dec.
Vitell. B. ii. 56.
B. M.
Rym. xiii. 386.

4605. LEO X. to HENRY VIII.

Understands by the letters he has received, and those to Cardinal Bainbridge, the disclination of the King to admit the Legate on a mission of peace, and to enter into any arrangements, without consent of the confederates. Does not wish him to abandon them, but, eliminating all hatred, to sow among them the seeds of peace. Is

1513.

bound to this by his promise made to the Lateran Council, and his obligation to promote the unity of Christendom. As the holy purpose for which the King took up arms has been secured, hopes he will listen to the proposals of an honorable peace. Rome, [1]7 Dec. 1513.

Much mutilated. Add. Vellum.

18 Dec.   **4606.**   PRINCE CHARLES to the PRINCESS MARY.

Galba, B.xiii. 93.
B. M.

Has charged the Sr. de Berges to inform her of his person and affairs, and to learn the state of her health, which is the best news he can hear. Malines, 18 Dec.

Signed in his own hand: V're bon mary, Charles. *Add. Fr., p. 1, mutilated.*

18 Dec.   **4607.**   To RICHARD BP. OF WINCHESTER, Keeper of the Privy
S. B.   Seal.

To issue congé d'élire to the prior and convent of the monastery of Evesham, on the death of Thomas Newbold, late abbot. Windsor Castle, 18 Dec. 5 Hen. VIII.

19 Dec.   **4608.**   LEO X. to HENRY VIII.

R. O.
St. P. vi. 28.

Is much gratified by the King's letters to himself, the Cardinal of St. Praxedis, and the Bp. of Worcester, expressing the King's fidelity towards his confederates. Would not have sent a legate to England, if it could have been avoided. But as this was resolved by the conclave at the last session of the Council, the Pope will be obliged to fulfil his duties as pastor. Begs the King will admit the Cardinal of York to enter England, as he prefers him to any other. Has requested the said Cardinal, though much against his will, to undertake the mission, that he may communicate to the King the Pope's secret intentions in the matter of war and peace. Understands the King wrote to Julius II. to have the said Cardinal as Legate. Rome, 19 Dec. 1513, 1 pont.

Add. Vellum.

19 Dec.   **4609.**   JACQUES PIERIN to HENRY VIII.

Galba, B. vi. 121.
B. M.

A long rambling letter, speaking of the writer being in the service of "iij. ax.,"—of his having received a packet at Strasbourg, "*au logis de St. Pierre,*" which he kept with great diligence,—of the difficulty of keeping the secret any longer ;—and of his having written that the Christian faith might no longer be kept in subjection by those who practised diabolical arts. 19 Dec.

This letter is followed by four postscripts, in one of which the writer begs the King to write to Madame of Scotland, stating that he would send her a letter, and prays God will assist the faith, and avert the danger of Hungary. Speaks, in another, of his being engaged in discovering treason, and of his having heard a sermon preached by a Cordelier, at which he would have made a riot had it not been for the respect he owes to Mons. St. Bertin (Ant. Berghes), but has written about it to Madame. "*Si elle ne est bien fondeie que elle men faiche avertenche au logis du poste au Gand.*" Speaks of the devil having appeared to a clerk at Rome, and their conversation.

Hol., Fr., pp. 4.

1513.

20 Dec. **4610.** M. Bp. OF PRENESTE CARDINAL SENEGALENSIS to
Vitell. B. II. 57*. HENRY VIII.

B. M.
Rym. XIII. 387.
After the storming of Terouenne the Cardinal of York urgently requested him to send the *depositum*. He is willing to do so on receiving a letter or message from the King. Has had no answer to his previous letters. Rome, 20 Dec. 1513. *Signed.*
Lat., p. 1. Add.

20 Dec. **4611.** For BEDE OLYVER, master carpenter of the Vanguard.
P. S.
To be master carpenter of Calais. The King's field beside Terouenne, 28 Aug. 5 Hen. VIII. *Del.* Knoll, 20 Dec.
Pat. 5 Hen. VIII. p. 2, m. 5.

21 Dec. **4612.** For THOMAS EYTON.
S. B.
Pardon, as of Eyton-on-Wildemore, Salop, alias of Westminster, alias of Guysnes in the marches of Calais, alias of the manor of Shriefhales, Salop. *Del.* Knoll, 21 Dec. 5 Hen. VIII.
Pat. 5 Hen. VIII. p. 2, m. 11.

21 Dec. **4613.** For WILLIAM ARCHBISHOP OF CANTERBURY, SIR ROBERT
S. B. POYNTZ and SIR WILLIAM COMPTON.
Next presentation to the deanery of St. Stephens', Westminster.
Del. Knoll, 21 Dec. 5 Hen. VIII.
Pat. 5 Hen. VIII. p. 2, m. 4.

22 Dec. **4614.** For the PRIOR and CONVENT of EVESHAM.
P. S.
Congé d'élire on death of Thomas Newbold, late abbot. Windsor Castle, 17 Dec. 5 Hen. VIII. *Del.* Knoll, 22 Dec.
Pat. 5 Hen. VIII. p. 2, m. 4.

ii. Petition for the above ;—sent by John Wyche and Hugh Bromysgrave. 8 Dec. 1513.

26 Dec. **4615.** MAXIMILIAN I. to HENRY VIII.
R. O.
In favor of Baldasar Stuerdus, papal prothonotary, sent by the Pope into Scotland, who is ordered to take in his way the Emperor and the King of England. Augsburg, 26 Dec. 1513, 28 Max.
Lat., p. 1. Add.

28 Dec. **4616.** To JOHN YONG, Master of the Rolls.
P. S.
To cancel five recognizances of 60l. each, made 12 Sept. 24 Hen. VII., of Sir George Tailboys of Kyme, Sir William Turwhite of Ketilby, John Henege of Hynton, and William Blesby of Blesby, Linc., for 60l. ; two recognizances of Tailboys with Sir John Skipwith of Southornesby, Thomas Burght of Stowe, and Robert Turwhite of Barton, Linc. ; and two recognizances of Tailboys, Sir William Askewith of Stalyngburgh, John Fulneby of Fulneby, and John Monson of Kelsey, Linc. Windsor Castle, 28 Dec. 5 Hen. VIII.

28 Dec. **4617.** To JOHN YONG, Master of the Rolls.
S. B.
To cancel a recognizance of 550l. made by William Botry, John Best, Philip Meredith, Robert Bolte, Thomas Hynde and James Gentyll, of London, mercers, made 5 Oct. 23 Hen. VII. Windsor Castle, 28 Dec. 5 Hen. VIII.

1513.

28 Dec.   **4618.**   For STEPHEN TOSSO, one of the King's footmen, and
S. B.   tumbler.

Annuity of 12*l.* from 1 April 4 Hen. VIII.   *Del.* Knoll, 28 Dec.
5 Hen. VIII.

Pat. 5 Hen. VIII. p. 2, m. 12.

30 Dec.   **4619.**   To the ABP. OF CANTERBURY, Chancellor.
S. B.

For safe-conduct for 4 months, leaving a blank for names of such
Scotchmen as shall be appointed by the Queen of Scots to repair to
the King's presence.   Windsor Castle, 22 Dec. 5 Hen. VIII.   *Del.*
Knoll, 30 Dec.   *Sealed.*

30 Dec.   **4620.**   For JOAN, widow of HENRY SMYTH of Sherford, Warw.,
S. B.   senior.

Wardship of Walter, son and heir of the said Henry ; and, if the
said Walter die a minor, of Henry his brother.   *Del.* Knoll, 30 Dec.
5 Hen. VIII.   *Signed :* Thomas Lovell.

Pat. 5 Hen. VIII. p. 2, m. 5.

31 Dec.   **4621.**   SYLVESTER [DE GIGLIS] BISHOP OF WORCESTER to
R. O.   HENRY VIII.

Has written, in conjunction with the Cardinal of York (Bainbridge), of the state of affairs here.   The usual benediction of the
sword and cap took place on Christmas Eve ; the Pope, at the
writer's instance, has conferred them on Henry.   On St. John's
day, in the presence of the cardinals, ambassadors, &c., the Pope
put them into his hands with much ceremony, and caused them to
be carried in procession with trumpets to his house, which has
not been the custom hitherto.   Leonard Spinelly, brother of
Thomas, will convey the gift to England, though he will not set
out immediately, on account of the severity of the winter.   The
Pope is better pleased, as Henry has written in Spinelly's commendation.   Is writing to [Fox] Bishop of Winchester, to whom
he refers the King for further information.   Rome, 31 Dec. 1513.
Signed.

Lat., pp. 2.   Add.   End.

Dec.   **4622.**   MARGARET OF SAVOY to HENRY VIII.
Lett. de Louis XII.
t. IV. 217.

Sir Thos. Spinelly has informed her of Henry's complaint that
the money left by him has not been applied to the support of the
troops, and that the diminution of the charges ought to be in proportion to the expences which the Emperor and Henry were bound
to sustain by the treaty.   It is not easy to carry on the war with the
French, especially in the Emperor's absence.   Their whole strength
has been on the borders of Picardy, till a few years ago, when they
sent a detachment into Burgundy, seeing that the frontier towns
were so well provided.   As to active operations, the French could
have wasted the Prince's countries much more than her troops could
have wasted theirs.   Wishing to spare Henry as much expence as
possible, she has retained 3,500 horse at eight philips a month, and
so put an end to the devastations of the Stradiots, and discon-

1513.

certed the French, who have held several councils for the recovery of Tournay and Therouenne. It was necessary to keep the gens-d'armes, for many men of these countries have sold their patrimony to serve Henry and would have been obliged to sell their horses under value, which would have been disposed of in Liege, France, and elsewhere. As to the foot, as they were costly and insubordinate, and Tournay appears to ·be safe, has only kept 1,200, who have been paid for one month with Henry's money, and shall be as long as needful.—Sends an account of them. Thinks the expence per month will not be 25,000 crowns. Has done all for Henry's good, as Spinelly will explain. Has herself paid 1,300 or 1,400 gens-d'armes during the past month, of whom she has dismissed some. The foot in Henry's service have eaten up the poor people of the Prince's territory, declaring that she had detained their payment. Fears they will have to be expelled by force. They say they ought to have 15 days' notice before they are disbanded. Has no answer from Jehan Caulier, whom she sent to the French King to get back Jo. de Habart, captain of Aire, and recover the 70 ships taken in Brouwaigne, some of which may be useful in war and also in commerce, for neither one nor other sort comes from France. Henry should send some one to the Venetians, threatening them with his enmity if they do not come to terms with the Emperor. Has just received news of the delivery of the castle of Milan to the Duke. Malignes, . . Dec. 1513.

R. MS.
‡13 B. II. f. 81.
Ep. R. Scot. I. 183.

4623. JAMES V. to LEO X.

Recommending Gawin Douglas for the Benedictine Abbacy of St. Thomas Aberbrothock, in St. Andrew's diocese.
No. 217.

R. MS.
13 B. II. f. 81.
B. M.

4624. SAME to the SAME.

Recommending Alexander Stewart for the Augustinian Abbey of Incheffray, diocese of Dunblane, void by death of Abbot Laurence.
Lat. p. 1. *No.* 218.

R. MS.
13 B. II. f. 81.
B. M.

4625. SAME to the SAME.

Recommending James Hepburne for the Benedictine Abbey of Dunfermline, void by the death of Alexander Abp. of St. Andrews, who held it *in commendam.*
Lat. p. 1. *No.* 219.

R. MS.
13 B. II. f. 81 b.
B. M.

4626. SAME to the SAME.

Recommending David Bp. of Lismore for the Cistercian Abbey of Glenluce, Galloway dioc., void by death of Cuthbert, last commendatory.
Lat. p. 1. *No.* 220.

R. MS.
13 B II. f. 81 b.
B. M.

4627. SAME to the SAME.

Recommending David Hume for the Benedictine Priory of Goldinghame, void by death of Alexander Archbp. of St. Andrews.
Lat. p. 1. *No.* 221.

1513.
R. MS.
13 B. II. f. 81b.
B. M.

R. O.

4628.   SAME to the SAME.

Recommending John Chesholme for the Deanery of Dunblane
void by death of Walter Drummond. Edinburgh.
Lat. p. 1.   *No.* 222.

4629.   TENTS, HALLS, PAVILIONS, &c.

Declaration, by Richard Gybson, of the stuff provided and
brought—" as of the King's own store, received of Sir Edward
Gylfforth, by virtue of the King's warrant to him in this behalf
directed, and delivered by the hands of Robard Dobbys at sundry
times, and also of Peter Corse, merchant, of Florans, as by indenture
thereof made," — "for making and repairing of the King's tents,
halls, pavilions, houses of timber, chimnies, iron chariots, carts, chariot
harness and cart harness, and all other necessaries belonging to
the same, and, furthermore, for the reparations done in his army
royal by the way travelling"—viz. :—

i. Canvas 30,019 ells, 1 quarter, for making the following tents:—
The Powndgarnast — The Flowerdelyce — The Whytehart — The
Harpr—The Goldestoke—The Castell—The Crowne—The Grey-
hounde—The Esteregeffether—The Gardevyaunce—The Mown—
The Mownten—The Mownde—The Goldehynde—The Brasser—The
Lessard—The Septer—The Goldeyoke—The Sonnebennd — The
Reederoose—The Reederoose and the Whyte—The Lebardes hede—
The Scheff of Arrowes—The Fawoon and the Feterlocke— The
Draggon—The Two Crownes—The Lyon—The Goldecrosse—The
Thre Flower Delyces—The Cuppe of Golde—The Poorte Colyus—
The Whett Scheffe—The Reede Schylde—The Blewe Schylde—The
Brekett—The Green Schylde—The Fyreyerun—The Maunche of
Golde —The Hewett—The Goldschylde — The Whyte Schylde
—The Blakeschylde— The Trenite—The Maree — The Myhell—
The Garland—The Annewe of Golde—The Whyte Staffe— The
Reede Sworde — The Inflamed House —The Whetere — The
Gauntle — The Flagon— The Yellow Face —The Egyll — The
F . . . .— The Lelypott — The Tombe — The Beeys — The
Challes —The Founten —The Swallowe — The Marleun — The
Hammer — The King's ow[n] lodging—The Kechyn made at
Gingatt for the King — The Knight Harbinger's hall—The Pro-
vost Marshall's hall—The King's Master-cook's hall for stoore for
the Kynges mowthe.

ii. Received of Sir Edward Gylforth, by the hands of Peter
Corse, merchant of Florens, 235 pieces of blue buckram, for garnishing the tents – also "whytted Normandy whitted clothe" 1705
ells—also "brewselles saye," red saye and green saye, for "the
crosses of the halls of the guard, and red roses barbys budd's and
synes—ropes &c. 30 knots of "sandwyche lyen" (line) "lyne" of
St. Umbers and "fyshers lyne," "wombys of netes leather—thread
and "crewell"—fringes and ribbons—"gyrthewebbe"— stakes—
buttons of timber—bolles of timber—pottes of timber—"fanes"—
carts—herdelles—barhides for chariots—leather buckets for the
stables—"a matt of fyggeffrayles"—"penselles" for wagons.—The
King's tents, halls, and pavilions, as well of the old store as of the
new; viz.,—10 halls, 12 ft. wide and 24 ft. long, The Poungarnart—
The Flowredelyce, &c.,—9 halls, 15 ft. wide and 30 ft. long, The
Moone, The Mownton, The Mownde, &c.—6 halls, 45 ft. long and
15 ft. wide, The Reede Roose, The Reede Roose and The Whyte, &c.
—7 halls, 15 ft. wide and 60 ft. long, The Two Crownes, The Lyon,

1513.

The Golde Crosse, &c.—10 halls 20 ft. wide and 50 ft. long, The Rede Schylde, The Blewe Schylde, The Brekett, The Grene Schylde, The Fyreyerun, The Maunche of Golde, The Hewett, The Goldeschylde, The Whyte Schylde, and the Blakeschylde.—4 halls, 22 ft. wide and 52 ft. long, The Trenite, The Mare, The Michell, and The Garland. —The Annewe of Golde, for the treasurer of the King's wars ; comprising, a hall 15 ft. wide and 30 ft. long, a "Tresans" 18 ft. long and 7 ft. wide, and a pavilion, joined to the hall, 20 ft. wide ; all double, with a stole place.—The Whitestaffe, for the Lord Chamberlain, similar to the above.—The Reede Sworde, for the captain of the King's guard, similar to the above, but larger.—The Inflamed House, a lodging for one of the King's Council.—The Whett Ere, a lodging for the master of the King's horses.—The Gauntlett, a lodging for the office and master of the armory.—The Flagon, for the jewel house.—The Yellow Face, a lodging for strange ambassadors.—The Egyll, a lodging for the Marshal of the King's vangnard.—The Fysche, a lodging for the Marshal of the King's ward.—The Lelypott, a lodging for the Marshall of the King's rearward.—The Combe, the pavilioners' hall. —The beds, for the surgeons to dress men.—The Challes, a hall for the chaplains to sing mass in openly.—The Fownten, the first kechyn 20 ft. wide and 46 ft. long.—The Swallow, a hall for the banarar, all white.—The Merlyon, a pavilion for the Treasurer of the King's van-guard.—The Hamner (sic), the hall for the carpenters.—The King's lodging, containing a porch 10 ft. wide and 15 ft. long, double.—A pavilion 18 ft. wide, double.—A Tresans 10 ft. wide and 30 ft. long, double.—A hall called the Frst Chamber 16 ft: wide and 40 ft. long, double.—A Tresans, between the King's great chamber and the first hall, 10 ft. wide and 34 ft. long, double.—The King's great chamber 15 ft. wide and 50 ft. long, double.—A Tresans, from this hall to the King's house of timber, 11 ft. wide and 41 ft. long, double.—Two cross tresans, leading into two pavilions, each 30 ft. long and 10 wide, all double.—Two great pavilions on either side of the King's lodging, double.—A hall, new made at Gyngatt in the felde, for the King's kitchen.—A hall for the knight harbingers.—A hall for the Provost Marshall and his prisoners.—A pavilion for the use of the King's master-cook.

Pp. 22, slightly mutilated.

R. O. **4630.** EXPENCES OF THE WAR.

"[Account of moneys in t]he hands of divers accountants upon the end [. . . . . t]aken and declared afore Sir Robert Southwell, [comptroller of] the King's wars," that is to say, [John] Shurley [officer of] the King's [household]; . . . ikelow, Thomas . . . . and Brian Roch . . . . Sir Ric. Sacheverell, late treasurer of war in the King's vanguard, Sir Tho. Wyndham, late treasurer of war of the King's army by the sea—William Keby, Will. Burwell, Henry Cales, Anthony Carleton, lately appointed, for taking and pressing of ships for the conveyance of ordnance, victuals, &c.—Henry Smyth, clerk of the King's works for provision of timber board, &c. for the brewhouses at Calais.—Walter Foster, clerk comptroller of the King's . . . . appointed for provi-sion of . . . . . kettles and other necessaries for the . . . . . . and brewhouses at Calais.—William Andrewe, late commissioner in divers shires for taking horses and presting carters.—John Ward, late commissioner in Yorkshire for taking horses and pressing carters for the carriage of victuals.— William Jekill, late com-

1513.

missioner for like taking of horses and pressing of carters for the said voyage.—John Ricroft, late appointed to provide malt and oats for the King's army in France.— . . . .
Pp. 3, *mutilated.*

R. O.   **4631.**   NAVY.

Memorandum that Sir John Wyltshyre, commissioner to provide ships for the army in France, owes the King 247*l.* 16*s.* 7*d.*

R. O.   **4632.**   ORDNANCE.

Specification of certain ordnance, viz. bows, arrows, strings, barrels of powder, bills and hakbusshes, delivered, on 24 May, to captains at Southampton, by Nich. Marlond, and not brought in again, by warrants of Lord Howard, Lord Willoughby, Sir Will. Sandes, Edw. Nevell, John Melton, Sir Gyot [de Heulle], Mr. Hatclyff, George Sybsey and Sir Mores Barcley.

ii. Names of the captains who received them :—Lord Brooke, Lord Anth. Gray, Sir Mores Barcley, Sir Gryffith ap Ryce, Sir Thos. Cornewall, Thos. Twyford, Will. Gryffyth, Jas. Strangwyshe and Thos. Thurland.

iii. Names of the captains who received ordnance, of whom some returned part and some none : Sir John Audeley, Edw. Drover, Will. Skevyngton, Edw. Chamberlayn, Mr. Fythwilliam, Mr. Kyngston, Edmund Wynkefeld, George Fastall, Everard Dygby, John Dabscort, Nich. Purley, Humph. Floyd, John Wallop, Lord Ferrys, Lord John Grey, Edmund Howard, Will. Gorge, Edw. Bray, Will. Rowse and Sir Hen. Willoughby, Master of the Ordnance. (*The whole of this last list is scored out.*)
Pp. 10.

R O.   **4633.**   ORDNANCE.

Directions and appointments for the ordnance.
Every apostle shoots of iron 20 lb., powder 20 lb.,—may be shot 30 times a day ; every curtow 60 lb., powder 40 lb.,—40 times a day ; every culverin 20 lb., powder 22 lb.,—36 times a day ; every Novemburgh 20 lb., powder 20 lb.,—30 times a day ; every lizard 12 lb., powder 14 lb., — 37 times a day ; every bombard 260 lb., powder 80 lb.,—5 times ; every minion 8 lb., powder 8 lb.; potguns 8 lb., powder 40 lb.

R. O.   **4634.**   ORDNANCE.

Costs paid by Will. Symons, captain of *The Mare Crystofer* of Bristol, for carriage of ordnance and fish to the Crane at Hampton. Part received by my Lord Lisle's servant.

    4635.   FEES DUE TO THE RETINUE OF CALAIS.

Faustina, E.vii.1.
B. M.

i. The great retinue : —The lord lieutenant at 6*s.* 8*d.* a day, and " regard" at the rate of 400 marks a year, 388*l.*, with 104*l.* 14*s.* 8*d.* for spial money; 12 mounted bowmen at 8*d.* a day, 20 mounted men at arms at 12*d.* a day, and 20 marks a year in reward; 41 lances at 8*d.*, and 5 (viz., 4 day watches and 1 crier) at 3*d.*—Sir Ric. Wingfeld, deputy, at 2*s.* a day and 20 marks a year reward, with 3 mounted men at arms at 18*d.* a day, 19 on foot at 8*d.*, and 19 others at 6*d.*—Sir Rob. Wingfeld, high marshal, at 2*s.* a day and 20 marks a year, with 5 men at arms on foot at 8*d.*, and 11 at 6*d.*—

1513.

Sir Humph. Banaster, 2s. a day and 20 m. a year.—Sir John Wilshire, controller, at 18d. a day, with 13 lances and 4 archers, 221l. 8s. 8d. —Sir Rob. Wotton, porter of the keys (altus claviger), 12d. a day and 20 m. a year, with 6 lances at 8d. and 6 archers at 6d.— Nic. Marland, sub-marshal, at 18d. a day, with 1 lance and 2 archers. —Arth. Somersett, at 18d., with 3 lances and 2 archers.—John Cokson, at 18d., with 1 lance and 2 archers.—Will. Pelham, at 18d., with 1 lance and 1 archer.—Thos. Thwaytes, at 18d., with 2 archers. —Ric. Wodehouse, at 18d., with 2 archers—Guy Armeston, Tho. Proud, Rob. Sydney, Roger Cheyny, John Middelton, Hugh Talbot, and Will. Fisher, at 18d., with 1 archer each.—Geo. Gaysford and Barth. Tate at 18d.—Ralph Broke at 12d. and 20 marks.—Rob. Jorden and Will. Gardiner at 18d.—Ric. Longe and Will. Pyrton at 12d.—Thos. Tate, John Raulyns, at 12d. and 20 marks.—16 mounted bowmen, 12 porters, and 6 serjeants, at 8d.; 4 day watches and crier at 5d. ; 17 constables at 8d. ; 70 lances at 8d. and 41 at 6d. ; 12 vintners and 12 companions at 6d. ; and 117 archers at 6d.— Total, 6,087l. 1s. 4d. Total of men, 460.

ii. The treasurer's retinue :—5 mounted men at arms at 12d. a day and 20s. a year; 5 mounted archers at 8d.; 5 lances at 8d.; 5 archers at 6d.; 18 arbalisters at 10d. ; 15 masons, 20 carpenters, 1 plumber, 1 tiler, 1 purveyor, and 1 gunner, at 8d. ; 1 mason, 1 master carpenter, and 1 master smith, at 12d. ; 1 master gunner at 12d., and a yeoman at 6d.—To the Carmelite Friars, 13l. 6s. 8d. per ann.

iii. The castle.—Sir Ric. Carewe, lieut. of the castle, 2s. a day, and 20l. reward ; 29 lances at 8d. ; and 20 archers at 6d.

iv. Tower of Ruisbank.—Sir John Peeche, lieut. of the tower, and a mounted man-at-arms, at 12d. a day, and 20 m. each ; 16 men-at-arms at 8d. and 2s. a day reward.

v. Hampnes castle.—Lord Mountjoy, lieut. of the castle, 12d.; 1 archer and 17 lances at 8d. ; and 22 archers at 6d.

vi. Guysnes castle.—Sir Nic. Vaux, lieut. of the castle, at 2s. a day, and 26l. 8s. 4d. a year; 49 lances at 8d., 50 at 6d. ; and spy money, 33l. 6s. 8d. per ann.

Total, 10,222l. 4s. 8d.

Deductions, including sums paid to Sir Andrew Winsor, master of the Great Wardrobe, and to the guild of Jesus and St. George in Calais.

1514.

A.D. 1514.

2 Jan.	**4636.**	For SIR RALPH EGERTON.
P. S.		To be standard bearer, with 100l. a year, as held by Sir Thomas
Rym. XIII. 387.		Knyvet or Sir John Cheyne. Windsor Castle, 26 Dec. 5 Hen. VIII.

Del. Knoll, 2 Jan.

Pat. 5 Hen. VIII. p. 2.

2 Jan.   **4637.**   For WILLIAM PENYNGTON.

P. S.

Reversion of the office of bailiff of the lordship of Chesthunte, Herts., and keeper of the park there ;—now held by William Bedell. Windsor Castle, 29 Dec. 5 Hen. VIII. *Del.* Knoll, 2 Jan.

Pat. 5 Hen. VIII. p. 2, m. 5.

1514.
4 Jan.　　**4638.**　　For DAVID BEDOO, clk.
P. S.
Presentation to the church of Way alias Wayhill, Winchester dioc., void by resignation. Windsor Castle, 7 Dec. 5 Hen. VIII. *Del.* Knoll, 4 Jan.
Pat. 5 Hen. VIII. p. 2, m. 10.

4 Jan.　　**4639.**　　To the ABP. OF CANTERBURY, Chancellor.
S. B.
To make out safe conduct to the bearer, in Latin, according to the tenor of a safe conduct in English subscribed by the council and inclosed. Windsor Castle, 31 Dec. 5 Hen. VIII. *Del.* Knoll, 4 Jan.

4 Jan.　　**4640.**　　For RIC. BASTARD of Bishop's Lynn, merchant.
P. S.
Protection ; going in the retinue of Sir Ric. Wingefyld, Deputy of Calais. Windsor Castle, 25 Nov. 5 Hen. VIII. *Del.* Otford, 4 Jan.
Fr. 5 Hen. VIII. m. 9.

5 Jan.　　**4641.**　　FABRICIUS DE CARETO to HENRY VIII.
Otho, C. ix. 13.
B. M.
Received his letter dated Westminster, 10 March, recommending Richard Nevel to a preceptory. Had already enrolled the said Nevel among his chamber novices (*camerariorum*). As soon as a vacancy falls, will promote him to a preceptory, but is restricted by an oath to comply with certain restrictions in the disposal of his benefices. Rhodes, 5 Jan. 1514. *Signed.*
Lat., mutilated, pp. 2.

6 Jan.　　**4642.**　　[ACCOUNTS OF RIC. GYBSON, Master of the Revels.]
R. O.
" In the 5th year of our sovereign lord the King and . . . . . . wars, by the commandment of our said Sovereign [Lord] . . . . . . made and provided for his own person and oth[er] . . . . . of the siege before Turwyn, as in the town . . . . . . city of Tournay as hereafter shall ensue."
Expences of green velvet and cloth of silver spent on six coats of rivet delivered by the King's command to Wm. a Par, Edward Nevil, Wm. Phewylliam (Fitz William), Master Garnyngam, Hen. Guilford, and Nich. Carew. For cloth of silver damask and white satin received of Ric. Smith in the King's field at Turwyn, employed in coats and covering bards for the King and Lord Lysle. Crimson satin for crosses in the King's " kette border." Costs done at Tournay at the great banquet ; for white satin, white and yellow damask, &c. " Stuff and garments delivered and worn and used in the city of Tournay at a banquet there, [of] the King with many nobles, the Prince of Castile, the Duchess of Savoy ; and after the banquet and mummery the said garments were given to divers strangers whose names I cannot rehearse." Garments, provided for an interlude devised by Sir Harry Guilford, master of the revels, for Christmas, containing a moresque of six persons and two ladies, of white and green of Breges, black, crimson, white, and yellow sarcenet, fine syperys (ciprus), copper spangs, Milan bells— used at Richmond. Payments to Ric. Rownanger, painter, and to the tailor. Boat hire to Richmond the day of the disguising, on Twelfth night.
Among the items : " 12 yards of yellow damask, the yards English, 6s. sterling, spent for 4 minstrels' garments." 4 jackets of yellow damask for the minstrels, 10s. 4 pr. of hosen for the 4 maskellors, 5s. the piece. 12 visors at 2s. each. 12 red felts, 1s. each. White

1514.

satin of Bruges, 2s. 6d. the yard, of which 6 jackets for gentlemen each 6 yards, with sleeves pendent. Black sarcenet gowns for the same, "to kever the garments," each 5 yards. For "kevering 6 bonnets," ½ yd. each. 6 pairs of slop hosen for kevering of their belts ; 6 girdles, ¾ yd. For 4 yds. of yellow sarcenet employed for a fool's coat ; and for minstrels and young gentlemen, of the same color. For "Venus'" garment, in surcoat and mantle. Crimson sarcenet employed in garnishing the fool's coat ; and in bonnets for the gentlemen, in girdles, bands for the bonnets, stomachers for the ladies, and coifs for the minstrels. Minstrels' coats, half of white sarcenet, and bonnet garded with the same. "Hover parts" of hosen and yellow damask for the young gentlemen. Expences of sypers for the lady called "Beauty," and the lady called "Venus." Spangs of Flanders 4d. per 1,000, of latin 6d. 1,000 ; for jackets broidered by Wm. Mortemer, 24 doz. bells, at 12d. the doz. To Rownanger for making a surcoat and a mantle of yellow sarcenet, with hearts and wings of silver, for the lady who played "Venus," 10s. For making, bonnets at 6d. each, jackets at 20d., lady's garment at 4s., gowns at 12d., fool's coat at 3s. 4d., and a minstrel's at 12d.
Pp. 6. *Large paper.*

7 Jan.
P. S.

4643. For JOHN PATE, groom of the Wardrobe, and GEORGE DUKEWORTHE, groom for the King's mouth in the Cellar.

Grant, in survivorship, of a tenement in "le Chepe," London, called "le Sterr," inhabited by Anthony Malyard ; another in "le Chepe," inhabited by John Adamson, tiler ; two in St. Laurence Lane, inhabited by John Sare, girdler, and Robert Hertegood, gold-beater ; a quit rent of 6s. a year from a tenement of John Sygar, fishmonger, in the parish of St. Michael, Queenhithe ; one of 3s. 6d. a year from a tenement held by Thomas Browne, salter, in the same parish ; one of 20s. a year from a tenement late of William Sowcote in the parish of St. Swithin's, Candlewick St. ; one of 3s. 4d. a year from a tenement belonging to the church of All Saints, London Wall, in the same parish ; one of 20s. a year from a tenement be-longing to the church of St. James in Garlikhythe, in the same parish ; one of 12d. a year from a tenement of William Weten-hale in the parish of St. Mary-le-Bow ; one of 4s. a year from a brewery called "le Swan," near the great conduit in "lee Chepe," belonging to the church of St. Mary-le-Bow ; one of 6s. 8d. a year from a tenement of Thomas Portaleyn in Watling Street, in the parish of All Saints in Bread Street ; one of 4l. a year from a tene-ment or waste land belonging to the masters of London Bridge in the parish of All Saints, Honey Lane ; one of 20s. a year from a tenement called "lee Crowne" in the parish of St. Peter, West Chepe, late of Thomas Gloucester ; one of 4s. a year from a tene-ment of William Pomfret in Whitecross Street in the parish of St. Giles without Cripplegate ; and one of 4s. from a tenement called "lee Panyer," in Paternoster Row ;—all formerly belonging to Sir Richard Charleton, attainted. Windsor Castle, 2 Dec. 5 Hen. VIII.
Del. Croydon, 7 Jan.
Pat. 5 *Hen. VIII. p.* 2, *m.* 5.

7 Jan.
P. S.

4644. For HUGH STERKEYE, sewer of the Chamber.

Lease, for 41 years, of the manor of Frodesham, Cheshire, from Mic. 4 Hen. VIII., at an annual rent of 48l. Windsor Castle. 27 Nov. 5 Hen. VIII. *Del.* Croydon, 7 Jan.
Pat. 5 *Hen. VIII. p.* 2, *m.* 5.

1514.

10 Jan.   **4645.**   For CHAS. BRANDON VISCOUNT LISLE.

Wardship of Roger s. and h. of Sir Rob. Corbett. Westm., 10 Jan.
Pat. 5 Hen. VIII. p. 2, m. 6.
See 30 Jan.

10 Jan.   **4646.**   For ROGER ALEXANDER of Caldon, Staff.

Reversal of outlawry ; indicted for trespass before Ric. Litelton and Th. Blount, justices of peace for co. Staff. Westm., 10 Jan.
Pat. 5 Hen. VIII. p. 2, m. 17.

12 Jan.   **4647.**   For GEORGE ASSHEBY, clerk of the Signet.
P. S.

Annuity of 20*l.* out of the issues of the manor of Flampstede, Herts. Windsor Castle, 14 Dec. 5 Hen. VIII. *Del.* Westm., 12 Jan.
Pat. 5 Hen. VIII. p. 2, m. 10.

12 Jan.   **4648.**   For JOHN HOPTON, gentleman usher of the Chamber.
P. S.

To be keeper of the King's new storehouses at Erith and Deptford, for supplying the King's ships. Windsor Castle, 21 Dec. 5 Hen. VIII. *Del.* Westm., 12 Jan.
Pat. 5 Hen. VIII. p. 2, m. 10.

12 Jan.   **4649.**   For NICHOLAS SMYTH, native of Scotland.
S. B.

Protection as ample as any English subject, he having dwelt in the county of Cambridge and elsewhere in England for 50 years, without recess. *Del.* Westm., 12 Jan. 5 Hen. VIII.
Pat. 5 Hen. VIII. p. 2, m. 10.

12 Jan.   **4650.**   For ROBERT ATKYNSON, clk., late of Scarborowe, alias of
S. B.   Strode, Kent, native of Scotland.

Denization. *Del.* Westm., 12 Jan. 5 Hen. VIII.
Pat. 5 Hen. VIII. p. 2, m. 10.

14 Jan.   **4651.**   For THOMAS WULCY, the King's Almoner, SIR WILLIAM
S. B.   COMPTON, JOHN HALLE, THOMAS SPEGHT, and WIL-
                     LIAM PORTER.

Collation to the next prebend that shall be void by death or resignation in St. Stephen's Chapel, Westminster, or in the collegiate church of St. George, Windsor. *Del.* Westm., 14 Jan. 5 Hen. VIII.
Pat. 5 Hen. VIII. p. 1, m. 20 ; and p. 2, m. 10.

15 Jan.   **4652.**   THOMAS LORD DARCY to WOLSEY.
R. O.

Recommends himself after the old manner. Wishes to know with what number he shall serve the King over the sea next summer. Weak as he is, has recovered from his sickness. Has a good appetite, "and eats fast of such poor viands as the country serves." Has had no warning yet to prepare himself. Thinks Wolsey would do well to take into his own hands the travers in the church of York between Mr. Archdeacon of Richmond, Mr. Dalby, Mr. Dr. Machell, commissary, and others. Encloses a bill in answer to his and the Council's letter to the Deputy of Berwick of the annoyances done by them on the Border. Since the field of Branxton so much has not been done. About 30 towns in the East Marches "be pattished with the Scottish warden, and lets not so

1514.

to say." This was formerly considered treason, and will grow to worse effect " than three reasonable crews lying upon the Marches would have drawn unto." They say they are compelled to this for want of defence. Hopes he will not be left behind if the King proceeds against the French. " Sir, when I was in my chief room and office within the court, ye and I were bedfellows, and each of us brake our minds to other in all our affrays, and every of us was determined and promised to do other pleasure if it should lie in either of us at any time. Sir, loving to God, now it lieth in your power to help and avaunce such of your friends as ye favor. . . . . At your late being beyond sea nigh the King's return, of your goodness it list you to say to me, that if ye had known so much as ye did I should have occupied the office of marshal, and ye had liever than great sums it had been so."—Begs he will obtain from the King a discharge of the remanet of his obligation for 1,000 marks, amounting to 266l. 13s. 4d. On account of his poverty, of which he spoke to him at Dover, he asks this favor. " Spain and France, and the occasion of those two journeys," cost him 4,000l. in three years and a half. Is about to shift his poor plate. " Was never more meet for any business, and in my life my purse never so weak." " Sir, every man will now seek to be your friend, and to be in favor with you ; but yet in no wise forget not to cherish such as were your lovers and friends, and desired and was content with your favor and company, for your own sake only, when they reckoned nothing to have you to do for them." " At Templehirst your cabin," 15 Jan. *Signed.*

Pp. 3. *Add.:* The Right Worshipful Mr. [Wolse]y, Amoner unto the King's grace.

15 Jan. **4653.** CHARLES [BRANDON] VISCOUNT LISLE to SIR JOHN
Faustina,E.vii. 4. DANCY.
R. M.

Prays that his friend Belknapp's account may be admitted ; the auditor has refused to allow it on the ground that Belknap had no commission to pay the wages of Lisle's retinue at Southampton. He has paid at Lisle's command many sums, not only to Lisle's retinue, but to Lord Howard's and Sir W. Parr's, over and above the appointment taken with John Dautrey ; to which sums Lisle has attached his signature. 15 Jan. *Signed:* Charlys Lysley.

P. 1. *Addressed :* To my loving friend Sir John Dancy, knt.

Ib.

ii. Declaration made by Sir Edward Belknapp, knight . . . . . . ayenst the sum of 5,263l. 11s. by him had and received of the King o[ur Sovereign Lord by the hands of] one of the customers of the port of Southampton for and upon the wages of sundry lords, knig[hts, ...] and soldiers underwritten, lately retained in the King's army and voyage royal ayenst the enemies of the church of Rome in the parties of France in the 5th year of the most noble reign of our said Sovereign Lord King Henry the VIII." ; so.:—

I. Lord Lisle's retinue.—To Sir Charles Viscount Lisle, 40s. a day for 49 days, 19 May–6 July 5 Hen. VIII.—To Sir Ric. Candishe, himself at 4s., his petty captains 2s., and 100 foot soldiers 6d. a day.—To Sir John Brugges, Sir Roger Pylston, Sir Will. Gryffith, Humph. Griffith, John Pylston the eldest, John his son and heir, and John Pylston the youngest, constable, Owen ap Merek, Griffith ap John, Sir Will. Essex and Sir Lewis Orwell, Will. Edwards, Sir John Shelston, Sir Edw. Chamberlain, Sir Thos.

Lovel, Sir Jas. Fremyngham, Glemham, Will. Fissher, Ric. Coke, Sir Oliver Pole, and —— *Herrys, with similar allowances for captains and followers ; to Mr. Medicus, Spaniard, surgeon, at 2s., and 5 other surgeons at 8d. a day ; 2 "dromslawes" and 2 fifers at 12d., and 2 chaplains, Blynd Dyk, and 3 other minstrels, at 6d. a day. Total, 2,635l. 15s. 10d. *Signed:* Charlys Lysley.

ii. *Captains* at Hampton (Southampton) :—Barons, Sir Rob. Wylloughby Baron of Broke, for himself 6s. 8d., with 8 captains, 3 petty captains, and 300 soldiers at the above rates ; and Sir William Willoughby, baron, for himself 6s. 8d., with 2 captains, 2 petty captains, and 195 soldiers.—Bannerets: Sir Mores Barkeley and Sir Will. Sands, with like wages for captains, &c.—Sir John Arundell, Sir Piers Eggecombe, Sir John Seymer, Sir Hen. Guldeford, Sir Griffith Donne, Sir Edw. Grevile, Sir Edw. Hungerford. —Gunners: John Gylston and John Westowe, master gunners, at 16d.; 18 others at 8d. a day.—Herald: Richmond, at 4s.—Trumpet: Francis Knyff alias Franklyn Trumpett, at 16d.—Purveyors and carters : John Morley, purveyor of horses, 12d. ; his servant and 20 carters 6d., and 20 other carters from the 9th June.—Sundries: meat for 100 horses at Winchester, standing at hardmeat, and carrying by the way to Sandwich, 4d. a horse by day.—To Sir Edw. Belknapp as paymaster, 420l. 3s. 6d.Total, 5,218l. 6s. 6d.

Further allowance prayed for the wages of Jas. Danyell, Sir Will. Apparr, with followers, &c., to the extent of 102l. 18s. 10d.

Total, payments and petitions, 5,321l. 5s. 4d. Found correct by Thomas Tamworth at Belknapp's desire. Total of men, 3,840.

15 Jan. **4654.** For JOHN HUSE.

P. S. b.　　　To have protection for Philip Conwey, appointed to serve in the war. 15 Jan. 5 Hen. VIII. *Signed.*

18 Jan. **4655.** PARLIAMENT.

S. B.　　　Prorogation of Parliament from 20 to 23 Jan. *Del.* Westm., 18 Jan. 5 Hen. VIII.

Pat. 5 Hen. VIII. p. 1, m. 24d.

19 Jan. **4656.** For WILLIAM TANFELD.

P. S.　　　Pardon and release (as kinsman and heir of Robert Tanfeld, sc. son of Robert, son of the said Robert ; and kinsman and heir of Elizabeth Tanfeld, sc. son of Robert, son of the said Elizabeth,) of all alienations of, and entries into, the manor of Gayton, Northt., the possessions of Margaret late wife of Sir John Trussell in Gayton, Northampton, Cortenhale, Myddelton, Colyntree, Blysseworth and Creton, and the manor of Horpole ;—of which the said William is seised. Windsor Castle, 22 Dec. 5 Hen. VIII. *Del.* Westm., 19 Jan.

Pat. 5 Hen. VIII. p. 2, m. 29.

19 Jan. **4657.** For SIR RALPH EGGERTON.

S. B.　　　To be steward of the manor of Loudondale, Chester, in the King's hands by attainder of Francis Viscount Lovel ; with annuity of 5l. out of the said manor. *Del.* Westm., 19 Jan. 5 Hen. VIII.

Pat. 5 Hen. VIII. p. 2, m. 10.

* Blank in MS.

1514.
20 Jan. **4658.** ORDNANCE.
R. O.
Wages to gunners employed in the ordnance, 20 Jan. 6 Hen. VIII.
Master gunner, 13d. a day ; others 6d. ; laborers 5d.
A fragment, mutilated.

20 Jan. **4659.** For JOHN COLET, D.D., Dean of St. Paul's, London.
Mortmain licence—in pursuance of patent licensing Colet to
found a chantry near his school in St. Paul's churchyard—to grant
to the wardens and company of mercers, London, the manor of Barton, Camb., and lands in Barton ; messuages and close in Colchester,
Essex ; land, with fishing wears, near Colchester ; possessions late
of Sir Th. Coke, father of Philip Coke, late of Essex ; manor
of Berewyk near Berkway, Herts ; possessions late of Thomas
Earl of Arundel ; messuages in Barton, Camb., on the west of
Colet's barn in his manor of Vaches in Barton ; land in Barton,
Whetewell and Haselyngefeld, Camb. ; lands which descend by
inheritance to Nich. Faune by death of his father Rob. Faune, in
Barton or elsewhere ;—which possessions are of the annual value
of 20l. 6s. 8d., as appears by four inquisitions before Th. Thures-
bury, late escheator in co. Camb., and Hen. Colvyle, late escheator
in Essex and Herts. Westm., 20 Jan.
Pat. 5 Hen. VIII. p. 2, m. 20.

20 Jan. **4660.** For BARON MONTJOYE, the King's first chamberlain,
S. B.   Lieutenant of Tournay.
Rym. XIII. 373.
To be bailiff of the said town, with emoluments, as held by Sir
Edward Ponyngues. Eltham, 20 Jan. 5 Hen. VIII. *French.*
Fr. 5 Hen. VIII. m. 6,

20 Jan. **4661.** For THOMAS DEACON, clk.
P. S.
To have the pension which the next elected Abbot of Evesham
is bound to give to a clerk of the King's nomination. Windsor
Castle, 19 Dec. 5 Hen. VIII. *Del.* Westm., 20 Jan.

20 Jan. **4662.** For JOHN HERON, mercer.
Protection ; going to the war. Westm., 20 Jan.
Fr. 5 Hen. VIII. m. 1.

21 Jan. **4663.** COMMISSIONS OF THE PEACE.
Kent.—Wm. Abp. of Canterbury, Edw. Duke of Buckingham,
Henry Earl of Wiltshire, Geo. Nevell Lord Bergevenny, John
Lord Clinton, Sir John Fyneux, Sir Rob. Rede, Sir Wm. Hody,
John Botteler, John More, Sir Edw. Ponynges, Sir John Pecche,
Rob. Blagge, Sir Christ. Garneys, Sir Ric. Cholmeley, Sir Wm.
Scotte, Sir John Wyltes, Sir Wm. Crowemer, Thos. Nevell, Edw.
Guldeford, Thos. Isley, Lewis Clyfford, Ralph Seyntleger, Walter
Roberth, John Rooper, Wm. Fyneux, Alex. Culpeper, Reginald
Pekham, Hen. Fane, John Engeham. Thos. Wode, Wm. Whetnall,
Edw. Culpeper, Ric. Lee, John Moven (?), John Hales, and John
Petyt. Westm., 21 Jan.
Pat. 5 Hen. VIII. p. 1, m. 4d.

Middlesex.—Wm. Abp. of Canterbury, John Abbot of St. Peter's
Westminster, Thos. Prior of St. John's, Sir John Fyneux, Humph.

1514.

Conyngesby, John Botteler, John More, John Neudegate, Sir Thos. Lovell, Ric. Cholmeley, Sir Andrew Wyndesore, Barth. Westby, Rob. Blagge, Sir Hen. Wyat, Sir Hen. Vaghan, Thos. Nevell, Thos. Jakes, John Moreton, John Mewtys, and Ric. Elryngton. Westm., 21 Jan.

Pat. 5 Hen. VIII. p. 1, m. 2d.

---

21 Jan.
S. B.

4664. For ROGER DARLEY, clk.

Presentation to the church of Westborough, Lincoln dioc., void by death. *Del.* Westm., 21 Jan. 5 Hen. VIII.

Pat. 5 Hen. VIII. p. 2, m. 10.

---

23 Jan.
R. O.

4665. SIR RIC. WINGFIELD and SIR JOHN WILSHER to HENRY VIII.

Have received his command for recovering certain anchors lost near Calais by the carack of Savoyne. Sent the water bailiff on Sunday last into St. John's road, who found that the buoys had been taken away. Have ordered search to be made for the anchors. Thos. Bote, receiver of Marke and Oye, has in charge to search for the anchor left by the carack at Wale. Calais, 23 Jan. *Signed.*

P. 1. Add.

---

23 Jan.
P. Martyr.
Epist. 535.

4666. PETER MARTYR to LUD. FURTADO.

The Pope has received an embassy from the Duke of Milan, to the bitter exasperation of the French ambassador; who has left fierce as a lion. The Scotch have refused to allow Henry to interfere with the government, have banished the Queen, and taken away her infant son. He is making great preparations against France. On the 8th of this month of January came a nuncio from the Pope to Ferdinand, named Goleaz Butrigario. It is said the Queen of France is dead; by her mediation peace was frequently secured between the two kingdoms. Valladolid, x. kl. Jan. (*sic*) 1514.

---

23 Jan.
R. T. 144.
R. O.

4667. ABBEY of ST. MARTIN, TOURNAY.

Notification by John de Preys, lieutenant-general of Mons. le Bailly, that on 23 Jan. 1513, Jehan du Bos abbot, and the fraternity of St. Martin's, exhibited to him an act dated 22 Jan. the same year, agreeing to pay for themselves and their church 3,000 cr. of gold as their part of the 50,000 cr. to be paid to Henry VIII. by the town of Tournay ; " pour icelle somme tourner et convertir en rente heritable sur ladite ville au rachat du denier seize."

Fr.

---

23 Jan.
S. B.

4668. ABBEY of TAVISTOCK.

The King, for the love he bears to the Virgin Mary and St. Rumon, grants to Richard Banham, abbot of Tavistock, Devon, that he and his successors shall be spiritual lords of parliament. In consideration of distance the King allows the abbot to be absent from parliament on payment of 5 marks. *Del.* Westm., 23 Jan. 5 Hen. VIII.

Pat. 5 Hen. VIII. p. 2, m. 9.

1514.
23 Jan. **4669.** For THOMAS the PRIOR, and the MONASTERY of ST.
S. B. MARY, SOUTHWYKE, Hants.

Licence to hold a fair for three days, on the feast of St. Philip and St. James and the two following days ; instead of a fair for two days on the eve and day of the Assumption of the Virgin, granted by Henry III., which is said to injure the neighbouring fairs. *Del.* Westm., 23 Jan. 5 Hen. VIII.
Pat. 5 Hen. VIII. p. 2, m. 1.

23 Jan. **4670.** For ROBERT STANSHAWE, groom of the Chamber.
P. S.

Grant, in tail male, at an annual rent of one red rose, of the farm lands of Kedington, with appurtenances, in the lordship of Streteley, Berks, and a close called Bromewode, in the King's gift by attainder of the late Earl of Lincoln ;—now occupied by John Stanshawe, father of the said Robert. Richmond, 16 Jan. 5 Hen. VIII. *Del.* Westm., 23 Jan.
Pat. 5 Hen. VIII. p. 2, m. 17.

24 Jan. **4671.** For SIR EDWARD GUILDEFORD, master of the Armoury.
P. S. b.

Protection for Thomas Broke, retained by the said Edward to serve the King as purveyor of leather for the armory. 24 Jan. 5 Hen. VIII. *Signed.*

24 Jan. **4672.** For JOHN BYGLAND.
P. S. b.

Certificate of the absence of John Bygland, citizen of London, deputed for management of the King's victuals remaining at Calais, at such time as the King returneth into his realm, who received monthly the King's wages by the hands of Anthony Nele. 24 Jan. 5 Hen. VIII. *Signed:* John Myklowe ; Thomas Byrkes.

24 Jan. **4673.** For ELEANOR KNYVET, widow.
P. S.

Annuity of 10*l.* Greenwich, 3 June 5 Hen. VIII. *Del.* Westm., 24 June.
Pat. 5 Hen. VIII. p. 2, m. 7.

24 Jan. **4674.** ·For JOHN FALLEY.
S. B.

To be gunner in the Tower of London, in consideration of services under the Duke of Norfolk against the King of Scots, with 6*d.* a day, *vice* Robert Scorer, deceased. *Del.* Westm., 24 Jan. 5 Hen. VIII.
Pat. 5 Hen. VIII. p. 2, m. 28.

24 Jan. **4675.** For WILLIAM BOTRY, mercer of London.
S. B.

Reversion, in fee simple, of the lordship of Borough, near Alesham, Norf., part of the forfeiture of Edmund De la Pole, granted to him and his heirs male, by patent 9 Oct. 3 Hen. VIII. *Del.* Westm., 24 Jan. 5 Hen. VIII.
Pat. 5 Hen. VIII. p. 2, m. 20.

24 Jan. **4676.** COMMISSION OF THE PEACE.

Hants.—W. Abp. of Canterbury, R. Bp. of Winchester, T. Bp. of Bangor, Thos. Earl of Arundel, Wm. Blount Lord Mountjoy, Wm. Lord Mautravers, John Tuchet Lord Audley, Thos. West Lord De la Warr, Ric. Elyott, Lewis Pollard, Sir Wm. Uvedale, Sir Andrew Wyndesore, Sir Wm. Sandys, Sir Nic. Wadham, Sir John Lysley,

1514.

Guy Palmes, John Neuport, Arthur Plantaganet, Wm. Paulet, jun., John Dale, Wm. Froste, John Dautrey, Ralph Pexsall, Thos. More, and Ric. Norton. Westm., 24 Jan.
Pat. 5 Hen. VIII. p. 1, m. 2d.

24 Jan.   **4677.**   GAOL DELIVERY.

Dunwich.—Sir Jas. Hobart, Sir Edmund Jenny, Humph. Wyngfeld, Rob. Suthtwell, jun., Lionel Talmage, Christ. Jenny, Peter Moriss, John Gentilman and Wm. Rabett. Westm., 24 Jan.
Pat. 5 Hen. VIII. p. 2, m. 6d.

25 Jan.   **4678.**   SIMON DE PRUSSIA, commissary of the vicar-general of
Vitell. B. II. 63.   the FRIARS OBSERVANTS in England and Scotland, to
B. M.   NICH. WEST, Dean of Windsor.

Admitting him to the full participation, in life and in death, of the works, prayers and suffrages of the order, on account of the services he has rendered them. Dated at our convent of Southampton, 25 Jan. 1514, Indiction 2.
Lat., p. 1.

25 Jan.   **4679.**   For ELIZABETH RUNSERY, of Brittany.
S. B.

Denization. *Del.* Westm., 25 Jan. 5 Hen. VIII.
• *Pat. 5 Hen. VIII. p. 2, m. 9.*

25 Jan.   **4680.**   For ANDREW SULYARD and EDMUND RUKWODE.
P. S.

Grant, in survivorship, of the custody of Edmund Reed, merchant, late of Norwich, and of all his lands in East Tuddenham, Bykkerston, Barnhambrowne, Colton, Rakheyth, and Sproxston, Norf., and elsewhere in Norfolk and Suffolk, during his lunacy; with the issues from 21 March 2 Hen. VIII. Westm., 4 Nov. 5 Hen. VIII. *Del.* Westm., 25 Jan.
Pat. 5 Hen. VIII. p. 2, m. 6.

26 Jan.   **4681.**   For WILLIAM JONES, of London, grocer.
S. B.

Protection; going in the suite of Sir Edward Ponyngys, Lieutenant of Tournay. Richmond, 20 Jan. 5 Hen. VIII. *Del.* Westm., 26 Jan.
Fr. 5 Hen. VIII. m. 12.

27 Jan.   **4682.**   DACRE, MAGNUS, and WILLIAMSON to the PRIVY COUNCIL.
Calig. B. I. 15.
B. M.

On the 25th received letters from the Queen of Scots, which they transmit, that the King may perceive her answer to the overtures made her through her secretary Sir James Einglisshe. They opened two addressed to the King. Have written to induce her to accept the King's offers, perceiving by her letters, and those of Gowan Douglas, "Appostelate of Arbrooth," and Einglisshe, that they are already inclined to them. Enclose copy of the letter. "The apostelate is quick in calling for his own advancement;" but makes answer with fair words far from the point. If they find by the Queen's answer that she agrees to their offer, they will follow it up as they can; if they learn anything to the contrary, they will cease writing to her, and, if the Council think fit, Magnus and Williamson will return southwards. As the King's ships of war under William Sabyn are ordered to the Firth, they have "assigned an honest, sad, and secret person, called Thomas Beverlay, to lie at Holy Eland," to convey instructions to him. The ships have

1514.

not been heard of for three weeks passed, when Sabyn was at Hull for victuals, and Magnus sent him the King's commands by William Pawne. As the Queen makes no request for the sending of them to the Firth, desire to know whether they shall be countermanded, allowed to go, or ordered to keep the North Sea. Ships have gone that way lately into Scotland, and brought news of the promotion of the Bp. of Murray to St. Andrew's. Another ship, bound for Scotland, brought a letter from the Lord Fleming in France, whereby it appears that the French Council had determined to deliver the Scotch ships. Transmit a packet of letters from Margaret, which she desired to be sent into Flanders for the apostelate's promotion. Enclose copies of letters sent into Scotland " these two several seasons," by Adam Williamson. — Since writing, have received a letter from Beverlay (enclosed), announcing that Sabyn is upon the coast of Scotland, " and furthwith woll to the Fyrth." Kirkoswald, 27 Jan.

Pp. 3. *Addressed:* U[nto th]e lordes of the K[ing]es mooste honorable C[oun]seill.

2. T. BEVERLEY to DACRE.

Calig. B. l. 23.
B. M.

Gives an account of his departure from Holyheland towards Tynemouth to inquire for the King's ships. Found Sabyan at Dunstanburgh, to whom he delivered his credence. Has arranged to lie at Bamborough. Bamborough, 24 Jan. (" this Wednesday, in the morning.")

P. 1. *Add.:* To my Lord of Dacres.

27 Jan. **4683.** For JOHN OXENBREGGE, clk.
P. S.

Licence to found a chantry for one chaplain in the church of Shitlyngton, Beds., to be called the chantry of John Oxenbrigge; with mortmain licence for the chaplain to acquire lands to the annual value of 10*l.* Windsor Castle, 2 Jan. 5 Hen. VIII. *Del.* Westm., 27 Jan.

Pat. 5 *Hen. VIII. p.* 2, *m.* 11.

28 Jan. **4684.** For THOMAS BOWDON and WILLIAM HOGESON, yeoman
S. B. of the Buttery.

Grant, in survivorship, of a corrody in the monastery of Hurley, Berks, *vice* William Babam, deceased. *Del.* Westm., 28 Jan. 5 Hen. VIII.

28 Jan. **4685.** For GEORGE LORD BERGEVENNY.
P. S. b.

Protection for William Braynewode, retained to serve in the wars beyond the sea. 25 Jan. 5 Hen. VIII. *Del.* Westm., 28 Jan. *Signed.*

Fr. 5 *Hen. VIII. m.* 10.

29 Jan. **4686.** For JOHN AYSKYRKE and RALPH CATERALL.
P. S.

Grant, in survivorship, of a corrody in the monastery of St. Eadburga of Parshor, Worc., on surrender of Ayskyrke, yeoman of the Wardrobe of Beds. Windsor Castle, 9 Dec. 5 Hen. VIII. *Del.* Westm., 29 Jan.

30 Jan. **4687.** For CHARLES BRANDON VISCOUNT LISLE.
P. S.

Wardship of Roger, son and heir of Sir Robert Corbett. Richmond, 10 Jan. 5 Hen. VIII. *Del.* Westm., 30 Jan.

See 10 *Jan.*

1514.

30 Jan.   **4688.**   For HUGH VAUGHAN and JOHN HUNTELEY, grooms of the Chamber.

Licence to import wine and woad. Westm., 30 Jan.
Fr. 5 Hen. VIII. m. 12.

30 Jan.   **4689.**   For WILLIAM DIXWELL, clk
P. S.

Presentation to the church of St. Andrew, near Baynard's Castle, London, void by death, in the King's presentation by the minority of Elizabeth Viscountess Lisle, d. and h. of John Gray late Viscount Lisle. Richmond, 25 Jan. 5 Hen. VIII. *Del.* Westm., 30 Jan.

30 Jan.   **4690.**   For PETER VAN ACCON, of Holland.
S. B.

Denization. *Del.* Westm., 30 Jan. 5 Hen. VIII.

31 Jan.   **4691.**   CHR. [BAINBRIDGE] CARDINAL OF YORK to [HENRY VIII.]
Vitell. B. II. 33.
B. M.

At the request of the King's servant Johane, had taken into his service Roger Pantter, Will. Foster, who was spoiled by the French of all he had at the battle of Ravenna, and Ranalde Chamber, a spear at Calais, who had been in the service of Henry VII. On 20 Jan. Foster informed him that Chamber proposed their going over to France to Ric. De la Pole or Sir Geo. Neville. Has committed them both to prison. Will have them further examined and send the result. Rome, 31 Jan. 1513. *Signed.*
Mutilated, p. 1.

4692.   NEWS FROM FRANCE.
Calig. D. VI. 347.
B. M.

. "News brought out of France by Yselstain poursuivant, which was sent unto the French King by those of Flanders, for the recovercraunce of their ships and goods taken by the Frenchmen."

Left Bloys, 21 Jan. The Frenchmen are resolved to keep the said goods as confiscate, "because of the viduans (voidance) which the *greffier* of Bruges made upon the King's letters patents, wherein he called his grace, King of France and of England." That he left the French King sick in bed with the gout. Saw at Blois Pregeant and other captains, who had come thither for money, wishing to go with the Duke of Albany into Scotland. That the Duke was there, and it was reported he should shortly set out for Scotland with a band of Almains. Thee French are in great fear of the Spaniards. The commons are so depressed by exactions by their own men of war that they are grown desperate, and not only desire to be in subjection to England, but rather in the Turk's, than be so treated. The Lord of Angoulesme is gone into Guienne. At Honflete on the 26th, he saw three galleys and ten . . . ships making ready to accompany the Duke of Albany. The French Queen's death "is underly lamented." On his return was taken at Abbeville and St. Quentin, and searched for letters. There are few men of war in those towns.

ii. "Other newys out of France which h[ath] been reported unto my Lady th'Arch[duchess.]"

The Lord of Angoulesme has gone to set the garrisons upon the frontiers of Spain. He is go to Britany, and thence to Blois again. The Lord of Roham had come to the French court. The Lord de la Pallyce and the principal president of Paris are in Britanny. The French Queen was buried at S. Denis with King Charles her first husband.
Mutilated, pp. 2.

1514.

Jan. **4693.** COMMISSION OF THE PEACE.

[*Surrey* ?]—W. Abp. of Canterbury, R. Bp. of Winchester, Edw. Duke of Buckingham, Thos. Duke of Norfolk, Chas. Duke of Suffolk, Thos. Earl of Arundel, Geo. Nevell Lord Bergevenny, John Bourchier Lord Berners, Sir Edm. Howard, Sir John Fyneux, Sir Robt. Rede, John Butteler, John More, Sir Thos. Lovell, Sir Rich. Carewe, Sir John Legh, Sir Hen. Wyatt, Sir Matthew Broun, Sir John Iwarby, Thos. Morton, Thos. Nevell, Edm. Bray, John Scott, Ralph Pexsall, Robt. Wyntershull, John Gaynsford of Crowherst, John Bigge, John Westbrok, John Kyrton, John Skynner, Hen. Saunder, Roger Legh, Gilbert Stoughton and Hen. Tyngilden. Westm., . . Jan.
Pat. 5 Hen. VIII. p. 1, *m.* 2*d.*

1 Feb. **4694.** For THOMAS EARL OF SURREY, Treasurer of England.

[S. B.]

Creation as Duke of Norfolk, in tail male; with annuity of 40*l.* out of the counties of Norfolk and Suffolk, and all usual privileges —and grant, in tail male, of an addition to his coat of arms (in commemoration of his victory over James King of Scots, at Brankston), viz., on a bend on the shield of Howard a demi-lion gules, pierced in the mouth with an arrow, and colored according to the arms of Scotland, as borne by the said King of Scots.—Also, grant of the manors of Acton Burnell, Holgote, Abbeton, Millenchop, Longdon, Chatwell, Smythcote, Wolstanton, Uppyngton, and Russhebury, Salop ; Sullihull, Warw.; Wolverhampton, Staff. ; Birdhurst and Updon Lovell, Wilts ; Erdescote, Berks ; Honnesdon, Estwike, Barley and Hide, Herts ; Kentcote and Herdwike, Oxon. ; Estwikham, Kent ; the castles of Bollesover Horsly and Horston, Derby ; and the manors of Clippeston, Lymby, Mancefeld Maner, Mancefeld Wodhous, and Sutton in Asshefeld, Notts. *Del.* Westm., 1 Feb. 5 Hen. VIII.
Pat. 5 Hen. VIII. p. 2, *m.* 13.

1 Feb. **4695.** For THOMAS LORD HOWARD, Admiral of England.

S. B.

Creation as Earl of Surrey for life, with annuity of 20*l.* out of the counties of Surrey and Sussex ;—and grant of the castles and manors of Folkyngham and Cathorp ; of the manors of Westburght, Stupton, Dodyngton, Ryskyngton, Dygby, Heykington, Asselakby, Welborn, Saperton, Wynterton, Burthorp, Lynwood, Beamount and Bayons, Linc. ; of the manors of Hungate and Beamount, and the rents called "Beamountes rent," in the city of Lincoln ;—in consideration of the assistance he rendered his father, Thomas, late Earl of Surrey, now Duke of Norfolk, at the battle of Branxton, 9 Sept. last.

This creation is made on surrender by the said Duke (by deed dated 1 Feb. 5 Hen. VIII.) of the title of Earl of Surrey, for the life of his son, and of the annuity of 20*l.*, granted to him in tail male, by patent 28 June 1 Ric. III. *Del.* Westm., 1 Feb. 5 Hen. VIII.
Pat. 5 Hen. VIII. p. 2, *m.* 20.

1 Feb. **4696.** For CHARLES SOMERSET LORD HERBERT, the King's Chamberlain.

S. B.

Creation as Earl of Worcester, in tail male ; with annuity of 20*l.* out of the county of Worcester.

Vacated as to the annuity, which is to be had out of the port of Bristol. *Del.* Westm., 1 Feb. 5 Hen. VIII.
Pat. 5 Hen. VIII. p. 2, *m.* 18.

1514.

S. B.

ii. Warrant to the Lord Chancellor to alter the above patent, as the said 20*l.* cannot be levied out of the county of Worcester without injury to the said Earl.

1 Feb.   **4697.**   For CHARLES SOMERSET LORD HERBERT, the King's
S. B.   Chamberlain.

To be chamberlain, in as ample a form as he has held the office from the first day of the reign. *Del.* Westm., 1 Feb. 5 Hen. VIII. *Pat. 5 Hen. VIII. p.* 2, *m.* 1.

1 Feb.   **4698.**   For CHARLES BRANDON VISCOUNT LISLE.
S. B.
Rym. XIII. 389.

Creation as Duke of Suffolk, in tail male, with grant of the castle, park, and manor of Donyngton, Berks, and annuity of 40*l.* out of the counties of Norfolk, Suffolk, and Cambridge. *Del.* Westm., 1 Feb. 5 Hen. VIII. *Pat. 5 Hen. VIII. p.* 2, *m.* 28.

1 Feb.   **4699.**   For WM. BROUN and HEN. KEBILL, aldermen of London, ROB. BLAGGE, one of the barons of the Exchequer, JOHN WEST, mercer, RIC. FERMOUR, grocer, NICH. LEVESON, mercer, of London, MORGAN WILLIAMS, SIR RIC. FOULER and JULIANA his wife.

Pardon for the alienation of the manor of Halton, with all lands &c., except the advowson of the church of Halton, which by a fine levied on the octaves of St. John the Baptist, 5 Hen. VIII., were conveyed by the said Sir Ric. Fouler and Juliana to the said Wm. Brown and the others, to hold to them and to the heirs of the said William. Westm., 1 Feb. *Defaced.* *Pat. 5 Hen. VIII. p.* 2, *m.* 30.

1 Feb.   **4700.**   COMMISSION OF THE PEACE.

Bedfordshire.—Ric. Earl of Kent, Thos. Prior of St. John's, Sir John Fyneux, Sir Robt. Rede, Hen. Grey, Sir John Seynt John, Edm. Bray, John Mordaunt, Walter Luke, Michael Fyssher, Wm. Marshall and Simon Fitz. Westm., 1 Feb. *Pat. 5 Hen. VIII. p.* 1, *m.* 5d.

1 Feb.   **4701.**   COMMISSION OF SEWERS.

Thames. — Thos. prior of St. John's, Sir John Leygh, John More, Ric. Broke, John Roper, John Hales, James Yerford, Ja[mes] Walsyngham, John Skott, Thos. More, Thos. Draper, Roger Leygh, and John Kyrton, for the district extending along the Thames between East Greenwich and Lambeth, according to the laws and customs of England and the marsh of Romney. Westm., 1 Feb. *Pat. 5 Hen. VIII. p.* 2, *m.* 21d.

1 Feb.   **4702.**   GAOL DELIVERY.

Home Circuit. Commission to John Botteler, John More, and Simon Fitz. Westm., 1 Feb.

Oxford Circuit. — Commission to Robt. Brudenell sen., John Neuport, and Rob. Brudenell jun. Westm., 1 Feb. *Pat. 5 Hen. VIII. p.* 1, *m.* 8d.

1514.

1 Feb.
P. S. b.

4703. For Sir Geoffrey Gate.

Protection for Nicholas Elveden, retained in the said Geoffrey's retinue to serve in the wars. 1 Feb. 5 Hen. VIII. *Signed.*

2 Feb.
P. S. b.

4704. For John Lord Berners.

Protection for Nicholas Elveden, retained to serve in the wars. 2 Feb. 5 Hen. VIII. *Signed.*

2 Feb.
P. S.

4705. For Lionel Talmage, of Elmyngham, alias of Bentley, Suff.

Pardon and release, as late sheriff of Norfolk and Suffolk;— and release to John Goldingham of Belstede, and Robert Talmage of Otteley, Suff., of their recognizance of 100 marks, made 15 Nov. 4 Hen. VIII. Richmond, 27 Jan. 5 Hen. VIII. *Del.* Westm., 2 Feb.

Pat. 5 Hen. VIII. p. 2, m. 11.

3 Feb.

4706. Commission of the Peace.

Leicestershire.—Thomas Marquis of Dorset, George Earl of Shrewsbury, George Lord Hastings, John Grey, Rob. Brudenell, Humph. Conyngesby, Guy Palmes, Sir Wm. Compton, Sir John Digby, Sir Thos. Neuport, Sir Ralph Sherley, Sir Everard Feldyng, Thos. Jakes, Ralph Sacheverell, Everard Digby, Thos. Pultenay, Wm. Skevyngton, Anth. Fitzherbert, Wm. Brokesby, Wm. Assheby, Christ. Nele, Ralph Swyllyngton, Thos. Entwissell, Thos. Brokesby, Thos. Hasilrygge, Wm. Wystowe and Roger Ratcliff. Westm., 3 Feb.

Pat. 5 Hen. VIII. p. 1, m. 2d.

3 Feb.
P. S. b.

4707. For Thomas Earl of Derby.

Protection for John Nokes alias Okys, brewer of London, to serve in the war in the Earl's retinue. 26 Jan. 5 Hen. VIII. *Del.* Westm., 3 Feb. *Signed.*

Fr. 5 Hen. VIII. m. 1.

3 Feb.
P. S. b.

4708. For Charles Duke of Suffolk.

Protection for Sir Robert Brandon, captain under the Duke, to serve in the war. Southwark, 3 Feb. 5 Hen. VIII. *Signed.*

3 Feb.
P. S. b.

4709. For Thomas Docwra.

Protection for William Warde, retained to serve in the wars. 3 Feb. 5 Hen. VIII. *Del.* Westm., 8 Feb. *Signed.*

Fr. 5 Hen. VIII. m. 1.

R. O.

4710. [Sir Ric. Wingfield] to Wolsey.

Understands by Langvylle, the herald, that he wishes much to speak with the King, Wolsey, and my Lord Lisle. He does not wish any of the officers of arms to know it.—Thinks he can communicate secrets of importance, and that the Duke's chaplain should come to him "against this Lent, and also Clerymond's servant, for I understand that he hath none of his own folks with him." Has received no notice of the letters which he sent to Wolsey from the Lord Doryere.

Hol. Pp. 2.

Add.: Master Almoner with the King's most noble grace.

1514.
3 Feb.   **4711.**   FEODARIES of CROWN LANDS.
S. B.

Appointment of Benedict Davy to be feodary of all the possessions held of the King in *Bucks and Beds*, with authority to take into the King's hands the persons of heirs within age, and deliver them to Sir Thomas Lovell, Treasurer of the Household ;—and to take possessions into the King's hands after inquisitions post mortem.
Similar appointments of—
     Richard Woodward, for *Kent*;
     John Baxster, for *Yorkshire*; and
     John Walshe, for *Cornwall and Devon*.
Del. Westm., 3 Feb. 5 Hen. VIII.

3 Feb.   **4712.**   For Sir WILLIAM COMPTON, knight of the Body.
S. B.

To be steward of the lordships of Stoke-under-Hampden Cormalet (*sic*), Somerset and Dorset, held by William late Earl of Huntingdon. *Del.* Westm., 3 Feb. 5 Hen. VIII.
Pat. 5 *Hen. VIII. p.* 2, *m.* 9.

4 Feb.   **4713.**   COMMISSIONS OF THE PEACE.

Dorset.— Henry Earl of Wiltshire, Wm. Lord Maltravers, Wm. Lord Stourton, Ric. Eliott, Lewis Pollard, Sir Thos. Lynde, Sir Thos. Trenchard, Sir Wm. Fyloll, Edw. Stourton, Wm. Hoby, John Marney, Giles Strangwais, John Rogers, Henry Uvedale, Jas. Frampton, Thos. Strangwais, Wm. Wadham, Roger Cheverell, Robt. More, Wm. Lovell, John Morton, John Strode and Robt. Turges. Westm., 4 Feb.

Somerset.—R. Bp. of Winchester, Edw. Duke of Buckingham, Henry Earl of Wiltshire, Wm. Lord Maltravers, John Bourchier Lord Fitzwarren, Wm. Lord Stourton, Henry Lord Daubney, Sir Wm. Hody, Ric. Eliot, Lewis Pollard, Wm. Cousyn, clk., Sir John Speke, Sir John Redney, Sir Walter Hungerford, Sir Hugh Loterell, Sir Thos. Lynde, Sir John Trevylyan, Sir Ric. Warr, Sir Nich. Wadham, Giles Strangways, John Broke, John Fitzjames, Edw. Gorge, John Sidnam of Bruton, Edm. Mille, Robt. More, Wm. Corrant, John Horsey, Baldwin Malet, Ric. Blewett, John Porter, John Brent and Thos. Jubbes. Westm., 4 Feb.
Pat. 5 *Hen. VIII. p.* 1, *m.* 4d.

Suffolk.—R. Bp. of Norwich, Thos. Duke of Norfolk, Chas. Duke of Suffolk, Thos. Earl of Surrey, Rob. Radclyff Lord Fitzwalter, Wm. Lord Willoughby, Sir John Fyneux, Sir Robt. Rede, Sir Rob. Suthwell, Sir Rob. Brandon, Sir James Hobart, Sir Rob. Drury, Sir Ric. Wentworth, Sir Thos. Boleyn, Sir Wm. Walgrave, Sir Wm. Clopton, Sir Edm. Genney, Sir Phil. Tylney, Sir Phil. Bothe, John Veer, Thos. Lucas, Wm. Ayloff, Humph. Wyngfeld, Lionel Talmage, Rob. Suthwell jun., John Wyseman, Henry Noon, John Sulyard, Wm. Playter, Edm. Lee, John Goldyngham jun., Ric. Candysshe and John Gleman. Westm., 4 Feb.
Pat. 5 *Hen. VIII. p.* 1, *m.* 5d.

4 Feb.   **4714.**   To JOHN YONG, Master of the Rolls.
S. B.

Discharge of Thomas Quadryng of Humbe, and Thomas Gyldon of Estkyrby, Linc., bail for John Uncle (bound to keep the peace towards Wm. Lyster) before Lionel Dymmoke, justice of the peace in Lyndesey, Linc. 4 Feb. 5 Hen. VIII.

1514.

4 Feb.
S. B.

4715. For SIR JOHN SHILSTON.

To be keeper of Dertyngton park, Devon, master of the hunt, bailiff of the manor, keeper of the chief mansion, &c. *Del.* Westm., 4 Feb. 5 Hen. VIII.

Pat. 5 Hen. VIII. p. 2, m. 12.

4 Feb.
P. S.

4716. For the ABBEY OF EVESHAM.

Restitution of temporalities on the election of Clement Lychefeild, B. D., *vice* Thomas Newbolde, abbot, deceased. Richmond, 8 Jan. 5 Hen. VIII. *Del.* Westm., 4 Feb. 5 Hen. VIII.

Pat. 5 Hen. VIII. p. 2, m. 30.

ii. Petition of the convent for the above. 2 Jan. 1513.

4 Feb.
P. S.

4717. For ROGER LLOYD alias THLOYD, of Hereford, alias of Pole in the Marches of Wales, mercer.

Pardon of all offences before 20 Jan. 3 Hen. VIII. Richmond, 19 Jan. 5 Hen. VIII. *Del.* Westm., 4 Feb. 5 Hen. VIII.

Pat. 5 Hen. VIII. p. 1, m. 13.

6 Feb.
Vitell. B. II. 65.
B. M.

4718. COMMENDAMS.

Decree of Pope Leo X. touching commendams. Authorizes Raphael Bp. of Ostia, his chamberlain, to see it strictly observed. Rome, 6 Feb. 1514, pont. 1.

Lat., p. 1.

6 Feb.

4719. COMMISSION OF THE PEACE.

York, East Riding.—Edw. Duke of Buckingham, Hen. Earl of Northumberland, Geo. Earl of Shrewsbury, Thos. Lord Darcy, Ric. Nevell Lord Latimer, Humph. Conyngesby, Wm. Fairfax, John Erneley, Sir John Gower, Brian Palmes, Sir Ralph Eure, Sir Ralph Elerker, Sir Ralph Bygot, Sir Walter Gryffyth, Sir Rob. Constable, Sir Thos. Metham, Sir Rob. Aske, Sir John Norton, Sir John Normanvile, Sir Wm. Constable of Carethorp, Sir Marmaduke] Constable of Everyngham, John Hothom, Thos. Fairfax, Wm. Eleson, John Rosse, John Haitfeld, Ralph Rokeby and Ric. Rokeby. Westm., 6 Feb.

Pat. 5 Hen. VIII. p. 1, m. 2d.

6 Feb.
P. S.

4720. For the ABBEY OF WHITBY.

Congé d'élire to the Prior and Convent of Whitby, on the death of John Benstede, abbot. Lambeth, 31 Jan. 5 Hen. VIII. *Del.* Westm., 6 Feb. 5 Hen. VIII.

Pat. 5 Hen. VIII. p. 2, m. 13.

ii. Petition for the above, sent by Wm. Clarkson and Thomas Kyldayll. 13 Jan. 1513.

6 Feb.
P. S. b.

4721. For JOHN BAKER, captain of the Julian Pirwyn.

Protection for Clays Evelyn, retained as gunner in the said ship, to serve in the war. 6 Feb. 5 Hen. VIII. *Signed.*

6 Feb.
R. O.
Rym. XIII. 390.

R. O.
Rym. ib.

4722. WOLSEY.

1. Bull *de absolvendo* for Wolsey's promotion to the see of Lincoln. Rome, viii. id. Feb. 1513, 1 pont.

2. Bull promoting Wolsey to the see of Lincoln on the death of William Smith. Same date.

1514.

R. O.   3. Bull to the clergy of Lincoln for their canonical obedience to
Rym. xiii. 392.   the new Bishop. Same date.
R. O.   4 and 5. To the chapter and vassals of the church of Lincoln.
                           Same date.
R. O.   6. To the city and diocese. Same date.
                           The last three to the same effect as § 3.

7 Feb.   **4723.**   WOLSEY.
B. O.   Bull for consecration, enclosing the form of the oath. Rome,
Rym. xiii. 392.   vii. id. Feb. 1513.

7 Feb.   **4724.**   LEO X. to HENRY VIII.
R. O.   According to the King's great desire has conceded a plenary
St. P. vi. 29.   indulgence to the see of Durham, of which he has commanded the
                           Bp. of Worcester to inform his Majesty. In reference to the King's
                           requests, to admit Thomas, the King's almoner, to the see of Lin-
                           coln, and remit part of the taxation usually paid for expediting the
                           same, is sorry he cannot comply with the latter, as it has been
                           rejected by the College of Cardinals as detrimental to the Holy See.
                           Rome, 7 Feb. 1514, 1 pont.
                               Add.

7 Feb.   **4725.**   SPINELLY to HENRY VIII.
Galba, B. iii. 148.   Wrote last on . . January. Received the King's 26th of the
B. M.   same month ; and as touching the re[covery] of the sealed brief,
                           my Lady Archduchess [has taken] after my mind a good way.
                           Has heard no news, however, out of Friesland, in consequence of
                           the great frost. Has represented to my Lady Margaret, the Go-
                           vernor of Bresse, and others, that they have in no point observed
                           the treaty concluded with England,—have allowed the enemies on
                           the frontiers,—have not diminished the charges, nor cashiered the
                           foot. It would be very difficult, she said, as they have now entered
                           on a new month ; to cashier them would encourage the enemy,—
                           nor are 10,000 crowns of much consequence. Spinelly answered,
                           that as the whole expence rested upon England, and nothing was
                           done against the King's enemies, it was but reasonable she should
                           moderate the charge. Has arranged that six courtaulx belonging to
                           England shall be brought to Antwerp, and delivered to Will.
                           Copland's servant. No conclusion has yet been taken between the
                           Emperor and the Venetians,—and till this be done the Emperor
                           will give no effectual aid, for all that he has is spent in Italy. "As
                           for the ransom of the Vice-admiral [of France] your mind by my
                           Lady known therein sh[all . . . . .] answer unto her Lady mistress
                           that . . . in France."
                           My Lady is very glad of the arrangement made of the marriage
                           of the Prince of Castile with the Lady Mary. Has delivered her the
                           safe conduct, and desired a proclamation to be made " of the valua-
                           tion and course of your money." The bowstaves shall be delivered
                           to Copland.—Balthazar Tuerd, born under the Duke of Savoy, the
                           Pope's secretary and ambassador unto your grace and Scotland,
                           left yesterday for Calais. A Secretary of Cardinal Cybo, the Pope's
                           nephew is with him, going to take possession, in his master's name,
                           of the archbishopric of St. Andrews, "having in charge, in case
                           of refuse, to interdict the land."—Thinks the ambassador a subtle
                           and quick fellow, who can full well say one thing and think another.
                           He says that he is going into Scotland to make peace with England.

1514.

Supposes the Pope has some design in it, especially as the ambassador passed by the coast of the Duke of Savoy, where they are all good Frenchmen, and far out of his way.—John Colla, the Emperor's ambassador [in France], told Spinelly that Balthazar was in great favor [in France], and he took him for a Frenchman. —Encloses a copy of an article that a friend of his wrote to him from Bruges out of Scotland, and a memorial of others from France.

Has heard nothing from the compagnon [Hubert]. — Has received two letters from Sir Robt. Wingfield yesternight, out of Almayn, and one from the Emperor to the King.—Loys Mauraton states, that Don Pedro Dorea and Quyntana have been in communication with the Emperor. Quyntana has now departed towards his master ;—it is not known for what purpose ;—he came by Perpignan and Languedoc, "under what manner I cannot tell." It is said that the Commander Gilbert came in post to the ambassador of Arragon here. In consequence of the solicitude of the Emperor, my Lady has been compelled to deliver her bond for 30,000 crowns of gold, according to the tenor of the King's letter, though the money should serve for the Swiss, as they say she is not very well content. Her letters from Burgundy state that the Swiss will set forth against the French. The French have taken in their [hands] from my Lady Charoloys, Chignon, &c., in recompense for the places [taken] by the Emperor from the Marquis of Ruttelyn.—Don John Manuelle is still prisoner . . . . Villeford, and no mention made of . . . . . . Don Pedro. Velis de Gyvara is departed [from] Bruges, and gone to England. He has spoken ill of the King of Arragon. Brussells, 7 [Feb.] *Signed. Add. Endd.:* 7th February.

Pp. 7, *mutilated.*

ii. "Translated out of a letter written in Italian, dated at Bruges the last day of January."—Has no news from Scotland ; the ships which came aground cast their letters into the [sea].—The man that was sent to the Duke of Albany has passed into France, and is anxiously looked for in Scotland. They are obstinate against England.

P. 1, *mutilated.*

7 Feb.   **4726.**   MARGARET OF SAVOY to WOLSEY.

R. O.   Is sorry to hear of the illness of the King. Has sent her maître d'hotel to Bregilles to visit him, and learn the state of his health. Begs he will send her the news. Brussels, 7 Feb. 1513. *Signed.*
P. 1. *Add.*: Bp. of Lincoln, grand almoner, &c.

     4727.   ERASMUS to GONELL.

Eras. Ep. vii. 37.   When in London paid his respects to his two patrons, the Archbishop and Mountjoy. Intended to have made a present to the King's almoner, now Bishop of Lincoln ; but being disgusted with London, and deeming it unsafe to stay there in consequence of the plague, he put it off to another time. Whilst Erasmus was in London the King was sick at Richmond last week (*proximo sabbato*), but the physician said he had escaped all danger. The Bishop of Chiatti (*Theatinus*), the papal nuncio, is now in London to negotiate for peace. Next May the King crosses the sea to marry his sister Mary to Prince Charles (*principi nostro*). Has sent back the horse. Compliments to Gray. 1515.

1514.

7 Feb. **4728.** For ELIZABETH, widow and executrix of SIR EDWARD
P. S. STANHOPE, late sheriff of Nottingham and Derby.

Pardon and release of all matters relating to the said office;—
grant of the profits of the manor of Houghton, Notts, late belonging to the said Edward, taken into the King's hands by William
Souche, late sheriff of Notts, Mich. 3 Hen. VIII.;—also release to
the said Elizabeth, and to Edmund Talbot of Bakshalf, York, John
Villiers of Brokesby, Leicester, Thomas Samon of Hansley Wodhous, and John Maperley of Bullwell, Notts, bail for the said
Edward. Lambeth, 31 Jan. 5 Hen. VIII. *Del.* Westm., 7 Feb.
Pat. 5 Hen. VIII. p. 2, m. 13.

7 Feb. **4729.** For JOHN BRUGGES of London, merchant.
P. S.

Licence to export 300 sacks of wool. Greenwich, 14 June.
5 Hen. VIII. *Del.* Westm., 7 Feb.
Fr. 5 Hen. VIII. m. 10.

7 Feb. **4730.** For SIMON GILFORD.
P. S.

To be ranger of the forest of Westebery alias Kingesbury,
Hants. Richmond, 21 Jan. 5 Hen. VIII. *Del.* Westm., 7 Jan.*
Pat. 5 Hen. VIII. p. 2, m. 10.

7 Feb. **4731.** For RALPH BROKE, lancer of Calais.
S. B.

Annuity of 20 marks, with present of 60*l.*, out of the issues of
Calais. *Del.* Westm., 7 Feb. 5 Hen. VIII.
Pat. 5 Hen. VIII. p. 2, m. 6.

7 Feb. **4732.** To JOHN YONG, Master of the Rolls.
S. B.

To cancel an obligation for 6,000 marks made 4 Dec. 4 Hen. VIII.
by Richard Fermor, William Brown the younger, and George Medley, merchants of the staple of Calais;—and an indenture, made
the same day, between the King and the said Richard, William, and
George, for delivery of wheat and flour. Lambeth, 7 Feb.
5 Hen. VIII.

7 Feb. **4733.** For SIR ROGER NEUBURGH, JAMES FRAMPTON, and
LAURENCE WADHAM.

Pardon for having acquired messuages, lands, &c. in Combe
alias Southcombe and Stoke, Dorset, from Sir Wm. Filoll and
Dorothy his wife, by fine levied on the morrow of All Souls last.
Westm., 7 Feb.
Pat. 5 Hen. VIII. p. 1, m. 14.

7 Feb. **4734.** COMMISSION OF THE PEACE.

Surrey.—W. Abp. of Canterbury, R. Bp. of Winchester, Edw.
Duke of Buckingham. Thos. Duke of Norfolk, Chas. Duke of
Suffolk, Thos. Earl of Arundel, Geo. Nevile Lord Bergevenny,
John Bourchier Lord Barnes, Sir John Fyneux, Sir Robt. Rede,
John Butteler, John More, Sir Thos. Lovell, Edw. Howard, Sir
Ric. Carewe, Sir John Legh, Sir Hen. Wyott, Sir Matthew Broun,
Sir John Iwarby, Thos. Morton, Thos. Nevell, Edm. Bray, John
Scott, Ralph Pexhall, Robt. Wyntershull, John Gaynsford of Crowe-
herst, John Bigge, John Westbroke, John Kirton, John Skynner,

---

* 7 Feb. on the Patent Roll, which is the correct date.

1514.

Hen. Saunder, Gilbert Stoughton, and Hen. Tyngilden. . . . . .
7 Feb.
Pat. 5 Hen.VIII. p. 1, *m.* 4*d.*

8 Feb. **4735.** JULIUS CARDINAL DE MEDICIS to HENRY VIII.
Vitell. B. II. 64.
B. M.
Thanks him for his letters, and the expression of esteem conveyed
to him by the Bp. of Worcester. Would rather have his good
opinion than the good services of others. Will do his best to serve
him. Is rejoiced to hear of Wolsey's advancement to the see of
Lincoln, and would have mentioned it in the college, had not that
office been assigned by the King to the Cardinal of York, from whom
the King will learn more as to the indulgence requested by him for
repairing the castle [Norham] destroyed by the Scots. Nothing
of consequence has happened since his last letters of the 4th. If
anything important occurs, will let the King know. Rome, 8 Feb.
1514. *Signed.*
Lat., pp. 2. *Add.*

8 Feb. **4736.** For CHARLES DUKE OF SUFFOLK.
S. B.
To repair to the dominions of the Emperor and the King of
Castile, to levy men-at-arms for the King. Westm., 8 Feb.
5 Hen. VIII.
Fr.

8 Feb. **4737.** For JOHN JOLY, groom porter at the Gate.
P. S.
To be constable of the castle of Brydgenorth, Salop, *vice* Richard
Haughton, deceased. Lambeth, 28 Jan. 5 Hen.VIII. *Del.* Westm.,
8 Feb.
Pat. 5 Hen.VIII. p. 2, *m.* 9.

8 Feb. **4738.** For PHILIP JANKYN, clk.
P. S.
Presentation to the church of Tredunnok, parcel of the earldom
of March, Llandaff dioc., void by death. Lambeth, 4 Feb.
5 Hen. VIII. *Del.* Westm., 8 Feb.
Pat. 5 Hen.VIII. p. 2, *m.* 19.

8 Feb. **4739.** For ANTONY UTRYGHT.
S. B.
To be steward of the manor of Lantyan, and constable of the
castle of Tyntagell, Cornw., from 20 Aug. 4 Hen.VIII., as Sir John
Carewe held the same. *Del.* Westm., 8 Feb. 5 Hen. VIII.
Pat. 5 Hen.VIII. p. 1, *m.* 12.

8 Feb. **4740.** For JOHN WADE.
To be chaplain in the church of Mighelstowe, Exeter dioc.
Westm., 8 Feb.
Pat. 5 Hen.VIII. p. 2, *m.* 11.

9 Feb. **4741.** For THOMAS THWAYTES, one of the spears of Calais.
P. S.
Annuity of 10 marks out of the issues of Calais, *vice* George Gray,
deceased. Lambeth, 7 Feb. 5 Hen. VIII. *Del.* Westm., 9 Feb.
Pat. 5 Hen.VIII. p. 2, *m.* 9.

3 A

1514.

9 Feb. **4742.** GAOL DELIVERY.

> *St. Alban's.* — Sir Thos. Lovell, Humph. Conyngesby, Barth. Westby, John More, John Neudegate, John Fortescu, Wm. Lytton, Rob. Turbervile, Edw. Bensted, Hen. Frowik, Wm. Panor, John Pursse and Ric. Gowdyer. Westm., 9 Feb.
> *Leicester.*—Ric. Raynold, mayor, Rob. Brudenell, Ralph Swyllyngton, Wm. Wyggeston, jun. and Ric. Eyllott. Same date.
> *Pat. 5 Hen. VIII. p. 2, m. 6d.*

10 Feb. **4743.** SIR RIC. WINGFIELD to WOLSEY.

Calig. E. II. 118.
B. M.

> Has had information from Will. Dawson, a Scot, sent by the "said Allayne" and the merchant adventurers, who has matter of importance to communicate, which he will prove on his life. He says there is a ship at Kamfer, laden with ammunition for Scotland. Has advertised Sir Thos. Spinelly to the intent he may learn Lady [Margaret's] pleasure touching its destination. Dawson says he can serve the King better at Kamfer than in England, by gaining information of the intrigues of the French and the Scots ; he had been so put on board the barge that no one knew it, as the said Allayne can show more at length. Sends his servant Byschope.— Has written divers times of the little service done by sea, and the need of some amendment. The French lately did great displeasure at Dover without hindrance. The King's ships were at anchor, their crews ashore. "As for the rowbarge, and I h[ave her] not that sche may be in the Kyngis waagis, s[che] schall schortlye make me a bare pursse." She has been constantly employed, and has brought home a boat laden with herrings. Offers to send Wolsey some. Has shipped him a piece of Gascon wine. Calais, 10 Feb.
> P.S. Yesterday the wife of Newgatt, a soldier, left for England, to complain before the council of Wingfield's having stopped her husband's pay. The character of the suitor is known to the council [here] ; besides, for very safety, the retinue should be diminished.
> *Hol., mutilated, pp. 4. Addressed :* To the Right Hon. my Lord elect of Lincoln.

10 Feb. **4744.** For the HEIRS OF JOHN TREGARTHEN.

S. B.

> Livery of lands to John Kayleway and Joan his wife, and Margaret Tregarthen, daughters of John Tregarthen, son and heir of Thomas Tregarthen and Margaret his wife, d. and heir of Richard Hendour. *Del.* Westm., 10 Feb. 5 Hen. VIII.
> *Pat. 5 Hen. VIII. p. 2, m. 1.*

10 Feb. **4745.** For WILLIAM WEST, captain of the King's ship called

P. S. b.

> "The Barbara of Brykelsey."
> Protection for Lewys Lyance of Bristowe, smith, retained to serve in the war upon the sea. 10 Feb. 5 Hen. VIII. *Signed and sealed.*

10 Feb. **4746.** For GILES TALBOT, groom of the Chamber, and JAMES

S. B.

> ASKEWE, groom of the Pantry for the King's mouth.
> Licence to import 400 tons of wine and woad. *Del.* Westm., 10 Feb. 5 Hen. VIII.
> *Fr. 5 Hen. VIII. m. 12.*

1514.
11 Feb. **4747.** SILVESTER [DE GIGLIS] BP. OF WORCESTER to WOLSEY.

Vitell. B. II. 66.
B. M.

Has received his letters of Jan. last. Congratulates him on his promotion. Received others to the Pope, to Cardinals York and Hadrian, for diminution of the annates. The Consistory would not listen to the application, saying that that church was very rich, and had always paid the usual tax. The Pope, whose portion amounts to 1,7[00] ducats, asserts that he has nothing except annates for his support, as he receives nothing from . . . . (*de exo* . . .) as his predecessors did, and is much in debt for his coronation, and his intolerable daily expenses.—He will endeavour to make it up to Wolsey in some other way, being greatly indebted to Wolsey and the Bp. of Winchester, as by their intercession his . . . . . . was admitted into the order of the garter, and his nephew obtained *protectoria*. The Pope will forego the annates for the deanery of St. Stephen. On the 10th of this month the Cardinal of York propounded in the Consistory Wolsey's promotion. Has seen the account for expediting the last bulls drawn up by Laur. Bonvix, much the same as this. The expenses daily increase. Highly commends Andreas Ammonius, who renders great service. Has expedited the bulls, which he will receive with this. The expenses amount to 6,821 ducats, 10 cat. The officials are angry with him for having brought it down so low. Of the 7,000 ducats sent him, 179 remain, for which he will make his cousin, John Campucio, responsible. Will not repeat what he has written to the Bp. of Winchester. Will be glad of a small benefice of 10 marks a year for one of his servants. Rome, 11 Feb. 1514. *Signed.*

Lat., pp. 3. *Add.:* Tho. electo Lincolniensi. *Mutilated.*

11 Feb. **4748.** For RALPH EGGERTON.

S. B.

Grant, in tail male, of the manor of Ridley, with windmill in Farnedon, lands, &c. in Bekerton, Chorley, Northwick, Frodesham, Waverton, Upton-near-Bache, Rowton, and Lawton, Chesh., messuage in the city of Chester, and land in Huredyke, Flynt, N. Wales; forfeited by Sir William Stanley, attainted temp. Hen. VII. *Del.* Westm., 11 Feb. 5 Hen. VIII.

Pat. 5 *Hen. VIII. p.* 2, *m.* 12.

11 Feb. **4749.** For SIR RICHARD JERNEGAN.

S. B.

Grant, in tail male, of the manor of Abingworth, Surrey, lately belonging to Humphrey Stafford, deceased, attainted ;—with the profits from Mic. 1 Hen. VIII. *Del.* Westm., 11 Feb. 5 Hen. VIII.

Pat. 5 *Hen. VIII. p.* 2, *m.* 12.

11 Feb. **4750.** For SIR RICHARD JERNYNGHAM.

S. B.

Annuity of 50 marks from Mich. last. *Del.* Westm., 11 Feb. 5 Hen. VIII.

Pat. 5 *Hen. VIII. p.* 2, *m.* 12.

11 Feb. **4751.** For SIR EDWARD GULDEFORD, master of the Armory.

P. S. b.

Protection for Robert Shetford, appointed to serve in the war. 8 Feb. 5 Hen. VIII. [*Del.*] 11 Feb. *Signed and sealed.*

11 Feb. **4752.** For HENRY EARL OF ESSEX, chief captain of the King's

P. S. b.   forces.

Protection for Sir Christopher Willoughby, appointed one of the King's spears, and to be attendant on his voyage beyond sea. 11 Feb. 5 Hen. VIII. *Signed.*

3 A 2

1514.

11 Feb. 4753. For JOHN MYSERY of Conysbury, Somerset, chaplain.

> Pardon for killing William a Beyton in self-defence, as certified by Ric. Elyot and Lewis Pollard, justices of gaol delivery for Ilchester. Westm., 11 Feb.
> *Pat. 5 Hen.VIII. p. 2, m. 17.*

11 Feb. 4754. COMMISSION OF THE PEACE.

> *Cornwall.*—H. Bp. of Exeter, Hen. Earl of Wiltshire, Rob. Willoughby Lord Broke, Sir Hen. Marney, Ric. Eliott, Lewis Pollard, Edw. Willoughby, Sir John Arundell de la Hern, Sir Peter Eggecombe, Sir Wm. Trevanyon, Roger Graynfelde, John Skewes, John Arundell of Talverne, Ric. Vyvyan, Peter Bevyle, John Chamond, Rob. Tredenek, Rob. Vyvyan, Ric. Penros, Wm. Lowre, Hen. Trecarell and Wm. Carnsewe. Westm., 11 Feb.
> *Pat. 5 Hen.VIII. p. 1, m. 2d.*

11 Feb. 4755. For SIR HENRY WYAT.

S. B.

> Licence to export 50 sacks of wool, of the growth of co. Norfolk, in two years. *Del.* Westm., 11 Feb. 5 Hen. VIII.
> *Fr. 5 Hen.VIII. m. 9.*

S. B.

> ii. Letters patent to John Yong, clerk, Master of the Rolls, ordering him to erase the words *ad partes Flandriæ,* "and thies wordes, *ad partes transmarinas quascumque,* to be putte in the stede of theym" in the above. Greenwich, 10 Dec. 6 Hen. VIII. *Del.* 1 Feb. by Hen. Wyat.

12 Feb. 4756. PETRUS GRYPHUS BP. OF FORLI to HENRY VIII.

Vitell. B. II. 67*.
B. M.

> Has been absent for some months, despatched on a mission by the Pope. There is no news abroad. All the talk is of peace. The Emperor and the Venetians have offered terms for that purpose, and referred them to the Pope. There is some difficulty about Cardinal Gurk, who demands an income of 100,000 ducats. It is proposed that Brescia, Bergamo and Crema be placed in the hands of the Pope for 18 months, till what is right be decided. The Spaniards and Venetians have fought at Vicenza. Fabricius del Caretto, brother of Cardinal de Finario, is made grand master of Rhodes. There is a great talk of some monsters and portents in Italy, and that the Kings of France and Arragon have made a truce for 18 months. Rome, 12 Feb. 1514.
> *Hol., Lat., p. 1. Add.*

12 Feb. 4757. For JOHN STRATTON, yeoman purveyor of carriage for the Household stuff.

> Commission to purvey conveyance for the same. Westm., 12 Feb.
> *Pat. 5 Hen.VIII. p. 1, m. 10d.*

13 Feb. 4758. For OLIVER POLE, clk., late of London, alias of Lambeth.

P. S.

> Pardon and release. Richmond, 25 Jan. 5 Hen. VIII. *Del.* Westm., 13 Feb.
> *Pat. 5 Hen.VIII. p. 2, m. 6.*

13 Feb. 4759. For PETER WARTON and JOHN DYNGLEY, page of the Chamber.

P. S.

> Grant, in survivorship, of the office of bailiff of the manor of Chelismore, Coventry, with custody of the manor and park of Che-

1514.

lismore; also of five messuages in Coventry ;—as held by Sir Henry Ferrers or Robert Haddley ;—on surrender of patent 22 Sept. 1 Hen. VII., granting the same to Warton. Greenwich, 1 May 5 Hen. VIII. *Del.* Westm., 13 Feb.
 Pat. 5 *Hen.VIII. p.* 2, *m.* 17.

ii. Original grant to Warton. Westm., 22 Sept. 1 Hen. VII. Surrendered 13 Feb. 5 Hen. VIII.

13 Feb.
P. S.
4760. For WILLIAM DE LEMAGIS, native of Normandy.
 Denization. Bishop's Waltham, 14 Aug. 4 Hen. VIII. *Del.* Westm., 13 Feb. 5 Hen. VIII.
 Pat. 5 *Hen.VIII. p.* 1, *m.* 13.

13 Feb.
P. S.
4761. For SIR WILLIAM TYLER.
 Annuity of 100*s.* paid to the abbot of Fougères in France by the church of Westkington in the archdeaconry of Wilts, from Mic. 3 Hen. VIII. Lambeth, 12 Feb. 5 Hen. VIII. *Del.* Westm., 13 Feb.
 Pat. 5 *Hen.VIII. p.* 2, *m.* 1.

13 Feb.
P. S.
4762. For ROGER RADCLIF, gentleman usher of the Queen's Chamber.

To be yeoman and groom keeper of the land of Benefeld in the forest of Rokyngham, and keeper of the outwood called Thornehawa and Woodhawe, as held by Edmund Huntwade; with usual fees by the hands of the ranger of the said forest, out of the money yearly coming to his hands out of the abbey of Peterborough, for castle ward. Lambeth, 6 Feb. Hen. VIII. *Del.* Westm., 13 Feb.

13 Feb.
S. B.
4763. For NICHOLAS GENTILE, FRANCIS PANSANO, JOHN and LUKE DE SPYNULYS, merchants of Genoa.
 Protection for five years, in trading with England. *Del.* Westm., 13 Feb. 5 Hen. VIII.
 Endorsed: Apud Greenwich, ultimo die Aprilis, anno 4to r. R. H. VIII.—Tuke.
 Fr. 5 *Hen.VIII. m.* 12.

13 Feb.
4764. COMMISSION OF THE PEACE.
 Gloucestershire.—G. Bp. Coventry and Lichfield, R. Bp. of Hereford, Edw. Duke of Buckingham, Thos. Earl of Arundel, Henry Abbot of Tewksbury, John Abbot of Gloucester, John Abbot of Cirencester, Wm. Abbot of Pershore, Robt. Brudenell, John Neuport, Chas. Bothe, clk., Sir Gilb. Talbot, Sir Thos. Inglefeld, Sir Maurice Barkeley, Sir Wm. Uvedale, Sir Robt. Poynes, Sir Griffin Rice, Sir Alex. Baynham, Sir John Hungerford, Sir Anth. Hungerford, John Broke, Peter Neuton, Geo. Bromeley, John Butler, Wm. Denys, Thos. Poyntz, Edm. Tame, John Whityngton, Wm. Rudhall, Giles Grevyll, Edw. Wadham, Thos. Goodman, Ric. Pole, Wm. Kyngeston, John Pauncefote, Christ. Baynham, Hen. Knyght, Thos. Matston, Robt. Wye, Ric. Wye, Roger Porter, John Pakyngton, and Wm. Freme. Westm., 13 Feb.
 Pat. 5 *Hen.VIII. p.* 1, *m.* 4d.

13 Feb.
4765. JUSTICES OF ASSIZE.
 Western Circuit.—Thos. Elyot and Thos. Fitzhugh, with Ric. Elyott and Lewis Pollard. Westm., 13 Feb.

1514.

Norfolk Circuit.—Wm. Mordaunt and Edw. Slade, with John
Fyneux and Sir Rob. Rede. Westm., 13 Feb.
Pat. 5 Hen. VIII. p. 2, m. 17d.

14 Feb.
R. O.

4766. JOHN EARL OF OXFORD to the ABBOT of TOWER HILL.

Requiring him to appear at his castle of Hedingham, Easter next,
to do homage and pay 100s. for lands in Meseden, in co. Herts.
Hedingham Castle, 14 Feb. *Signed.*
P. 1. Addressed.

14 Feb.
S. B.

4767. To JOHN YONG, Master of the Rolls.

To cancel four recognizances of 200l. each, and one of 100l..
made 24 July 16 Hen. VII., by Thomas Myddelton of Bethom, Sir
Thomas Parre (then Thomas Parre, Esq.), of Kendall, and Walter
Strykland, late of Cisar. Lambeth, 14 Feb. 5 Hen. VIII.
Signed : Ri. Wynton—Ric. London—T. Duresme—Jo. Roff—
T. Norfolk—J. Fyneux—R. Rede.

14 Feb.
S. B.

4768. For THOMAS GOODWYN, prior elect of St. Peter's, Ipswich.

Restitution of temporalities, with grant of the issues of the manor
of Bornehall in Whorsted, Suff., from 16 March 12 Hen. VII.,
when the priory became void by the death of John York, who held
the said manor in right of the church aforesaid, as appeared by an
inquisition then taken. *Del.* Westm., 14 Feb. 5 Hen. VIII.
Pat. 5 Hen. VIII. p. 2, m. 29.

14 Feb.
P. S.

4769. For JOHN ELYOT of Pembroke, South Wales.

Protection ; going in the suite of Sir Richard Wingfeld,
Deputy of Calais. Lambeth, 12 Feb. 5 Hen. VIII. *Del.* Westm.,
14 Feb.

14 Feb.

4770. COMMISSIONS OF THE PEACE.

Cambridge Town.—John Bp. of Rochester, John Hacomplayn,
clk., Wm, Buknam, clk., Wm. Barbour the mayor, John Parys,
John Woode, Wm. Colyn, John Hynde, Hugh Chapman, John
Bury, John Eflyth, and Hen. Halhed. Westm., 14 Feb.
Pat. 5 Hen. VIII. p. 1, m. 6d.

Worcestershire.—G. Bp. of Coventry and Lichfield, R. Bp. of
Hereford, Thos. Earl of Arundel, Geo. Earl of Shrewsbury, Edw.
Sutton Lord Dudley, John Abbot of Parshore, Clement Abbot of
Evesham, Humph. Conyngesby, Rob. Brudenell, Chas. Bothe, clk.
Sir Gilb. Talbot, Sir Thos. Inglefeld, Sir Wm. Uvedale, Sir Griffin
Ryce, Sir Wm. Compton, John Ardern, Gilb. Talbot, jun., Peter
Neuton, Geo. Bromeley, Thos. Lynom, Thos. Nevyll, Wm. Rudhall,
John Pauncefote, John Ketylby, Giles Grevell, Rob. Vampage,
Wm. Brugge, Roland Morton, Nich. Folyett, John Wasshebourne,
Thos. Litelton, Roger Wynter, Wm. Dyngley and Robt. Hunkys.
Westm., 14 Feb.
Pat. 5 Hen. VIII. p. 1, m. 2d.

14 Feb.

4771. JUSTICES OF ASSIZE.

Midland Circuit.—John Jenour and Ric. Heigham, with Humph.
Conyngesby and Guy Palmes. Westm., 14 Feb.
Northern Circuit.—Rob. Henryson and Tho. Strey, with Wm.
Fairfax and John Ernley. Same date.
Pat. 5 Hen. VIII. p. 2, m. 6d.

1514.
15 Feb. **4772.**   For JOHN CLAYMOND, President, and the Scholars of
P. S.   ST. MARY MAGDALENE COLLEGE, OXFORD.

Mortmain licence, at the request of Thomas Wolsey, Bishop elect of Lincoln, to acquire lands to the annual value of 34*l.*, and the advowson of churches and chapels to the annual value of 6*l.* ; with exemption from tenths, taxes, &c., and licence to cut wood in Shotover forest in the limits marked out in the said forest by stones ; viz. from the oak looking towards *le Hek de Conell* to the oak near the *Seggy lake,* the largest part of which oak stood in the wood belonging to the house of Litelmore, from the said oak to that near Northeslade, to the oak of *Limele Gerneing,* and from Sondywey under Whitleston to Hedendon pasture, thence out of the covert to the opposite side of *le Hek.* Lambeth, 13 Feb. 5 Hen. VIII. *Del.* Westm. 15 Feb.
Pat. 5 *Hen.VIII. p.* 2, *m.* 14.

15 Feb. **4773.**   For THOMAS TYRELL.
P. S. b.   Protection for John Crosswell of Odyam, Hants, retained to serve in the war. 15 Feb. 5 Hen. VIII. *Signed.*

15 Feb. **4774.**   For CORNELIUS JOHNSON.
P. S.   To be master smith of the King's iron works in the Tower of London, with 8*d.* a day, *vice* Christopher Wodland, deceased. Lambeth, 10 Feb. 5 Hen. VIII. *Del.* Westm., 15 Feb.

15 Feb. **4775.**   For JOHN TURNOUR.

Constat and exemplification, at the request of John Turnour (who swears the original is lost), of patent 4 Feb. 22 Hen.VII., granting the said John the office of auditor of the duchy of Cornwall, *vice* Thos. Hobson. Westm., 15 Feb.
Pat. 5 *Hen.VIII. p.* 2, *m.* 6.

15 Feb. **4776.**   COMMISSION OF THE PEACE.

Notts.—Wm. Bp. of Lincoln, Geo. Earl of Shrewsbury, Humph. Conyngesby, Guy Palmes, Sir Thos. Lovell, Sir Rob. Sheffeld, Sir Hen. Willoughby, Sir Wm. Perpoynt, Sir Wm. Meryng, Sir Thos. Sutton, John Willoughby, Simon Dygby, Wm. Clerkson, Robt. Clyfton (or Clyston), Humph. Hersey, Ric. Savage, Ric. Stanhop, John Byron, Thos. Meryng, Wm. Wymondsold, Hen. Bosom, Rob. Nevell, and Anth. Babyngton. Westm., 15 Feb.
Pat. 5 *Hen.VIII. p.* 1, *m.* 2d.

16 Feb. **4777.**   For SIR HENRY WIAT.
P. S. b.   Protection for Thomas Bekett, retained to serve in the wars. 14 Feb. 5 Hen. VIII. [*Del.*] Westm., 16 Feb. *Signed and sealed.*

16 Feb. **4778.**   For JOHN HOOPER of Morton, Devon.
Protection ; going to the war. Westm., 16 Feb.
Fr. 5 *Hen.VIII. m.* 12.

16 Feb. **4779.**   For JOHN DROSSWELL of Odyam, Hants.
Protection ; going to the war. Westm., 16 Feb.
Fr. 5 *Hen.VIII. m.* 15.

1514.

16 Feb. **4780.**   For THOMAS GRENEWAY, yeoman of the Chamber.

P. 8.

Confirmation of patent 27 May 14 Hen. VII., granting him premises in Church Alley in the parish of St. Nicholas Shambles in the ward of Farringdon, and in West Smithfield in the parish of St. Sepulchre, and in the parish of St. Andrew Holborn, London, previously held by Ralph Newnham, and Allan Messenger a Scotchman; with further grant thereof to the said Thomas and the heirs male of his body, at an annual rent of one red rose. Lambeth, 11 Feb. 5 Hen. VIII. *Del.* Westm., 16 Feb.

Pat. 5 Hen. VIII. p. 2, m. 2.

16 Feb. **4781.**   For SIR THOMAS COKEYN.

S. B.

Licence to enclose 500 acres of his demesne lands and woods in Herthyll, Stanton, and Clyfton, Derby, and make a park and warren. *Del.* Westm., 16 Feb. 5 Hen. VIII.

Pat. 5 Hen. VIII. p. 2, m. 28.

16 Feb. **4782.**   CORN.

Commissions to Rob. Birle and Hen. Parkyns to purvey corn for the army about to go to foreign parts, during the next six months. Westm., 16 Feb.

Pat. 5 Hen. VIII. p. 2, m. 19d.

16 Feb. **4783.**   COMMISSIONS OF THE PEACE.

Devon.—H. Bp. of Exeter, Henry Earl of Wiltshire, Robt. Willoughby Lord Broke, John Bourchier Lord Fitzwarren, Hen. Lord Daubney, Rich. Eliott, Lewis Pollard, Edw. Willoughby, Sir Peter Egecombe, Sir Edw. Pomery, Sir Amias Paulett, Sir John Bassett, Sir John Kyrkham, Sir Thos. Greynfeld, John Souche, Wm. Courteney, Thos. Denys, Jas. Chudleygh, John Rowe, Robt. Yoo, Robt. Bouryng, John Gilbert, Thos. Stukeley, Ric. Reigne, John Crokker, Andrew Hillarsedon, John Caleway, Rich. Coffen, Edm. Larder, John Asshe, Robt. Shilston, and John Cole of Slade. Westm., 16 Feb.

Leicestershire.—Thos. Marquis of Dorset, Geo. Earl of Shrewsbury, Geo. Lord Hastynges, John Grey, Robt. Brudenell, Humph. Conyngesby, Guy Palmes, Sir Wm. Compton, Sir John Dygby, Sir Thos. Neuport, Sir Ralph Sherley, Sir Everard Feldyng, Thos. Jakes, Rich. Saucheverell, Everard Digby, Thos. Pultney, Wm. Skevyngton, Anthony Fitzherbert, Wm. Turpyn, John Fitzherbert, Wm. Brokesby, John Villers, Wm. Assheby, Christ. Nele, Ralph Swyllyngton, Thos. Entwissell, Thos. Brokesby, Thos. Hasilrigge, Wm. Wistowe, and Roger Rattclyff. Westm., 16 Feb.

Pat. 5 Hen. VIII. p. 1, m. 5d.

16 Feb. **4784.**   For the MASTERS AND CHAPLAINS OF ALL SAINTS

S. B.   COLLEGE, MAIDSTONE.

Mortmain licence to acquire lands to the annual value of 10*l.* *Del.* Westm., 16 Feb. 5 Hen. VIII.

Pat. 5 Hen. VIII. p. 2, m. 30.

1514.
17 Feb.   **4785.**   For HUMPHREY BANASTER.
S. B.

Grant, in fee, at the annual rent of one red rose, of socage service and the annual rent of 15*l.* 0*s.* 11*d.*, due to the King from William Fermour, his heirs and assigns, by patent 12 Jan. 3 Hen. VIII., which granted them the moiety of the manor of Somerton, Oxon., and the moiety of the advowson, with court leet, view of frank pledge, &c., and the fishery of the Charwell in the said manor ; forfeited by Francis Viscount Lovel, attainted 1 Hen. VII. *Del.* Westm., 17 Feb. 5 Hen. VIII.
Pat. 5 Hen. VIII. p. 2, m. 19.

18 Feb.   **4786.**   JULIUS CARDINAL DE MEDICIS to HENRY VIII.
R. O.

Wrote lately in gratitude to his Majesty. Greater thanks still are due for his letters received to-day, constituting the writer the King's protector for England. Will endeavour to justify Henry's confidence. Has already written what has been done on the representations of the King and my Lord Almoner touching the bishopric of Lincoln, which the Cardinal of York (Bainbridge) has reported at the Pope's desire. Rome, 18 Feb. 1514.
Lat., p. 1. *Add. Endd.*

18 Feb.   **4787.**   To JOHN YONG, Master of the Rolls.
S. B.

To cancel three recognizances of 100 marks each, made by William Godfrey of Gillyngham, William Tylman of Boughton, and Robert Pery of Gyllyngham, Kent, 4 Feb. 23 Hen. VII. Lambeth, 18 Feb. 5 Hen. VIII.

18 Feb.   **4788.**   For JOHN VAZACRELY alias BRENT, and WILLIAM
P. S.   WYNSBURY, yeomen of the Guard.

Grant, in survivorship, of an annuity of 10*l.* out of the lordship of Denbigh, *vice* Christopher Savage, deceased. Lambeth, 14 Feb. 5 Hen. VIII. *Del.* Westm., 18 Feb.
Pat. 5 Hen. VIII. p. 2, m. 12.

18 Feb.   **4789.**   SPINELLY to [HENRY VIII.]
Galba, B. III. 152.
B. M.

Wrote last on the 12th. Yesterday received a letter out of Germany from Sir Rob. Wingfield, enclosed. On Wednesday last Sir Edw. Ponynges arrived, had an audience with the Prince and the Archduchess, and left on Friday after the jousts. The Emperor expresses great dissatisfaction with Chievres, and will have nothing done without my Lady's consent. He has ordered Don Diego to be stopped, and the souverayne of Flaunderyen (Savage) to be sent to England instead. The Pope does not wish to be comprised in the league with the Swiss. People about the Prince do not care much for the Emperor, and the less now he has renounced his tutelage. They expect information of the treaty with France, " putting no doubt in the deliverance at this time of the French daughter into their hands." They are in hopes, after the marriage is accomplished, the French will surrender Burgundy. People who do not like it are told there is no other way to live in peace, " and that before the perfect age of the said daughter the Prince shall be of better experience, and able to command and rule himself."—Though the Emperor and the King of Arragon dislike it, thinks it will take effect. It is reported that the English ambassadors in France circulate ill news of the Emperor. " The said Na . . . . and other his fellows " believe that they shall have

1514.

good deeds of the French, and others good words." Busshy (Boissi) has arranged with Berghes for his ransom at 20,000 philips of gold. If Johanle tarry longer he is come for other causes. Chievres told him, till he hears from the Constable in England, " he shall take a way prejudicial to no man;" but if England make a particular treaty with France, Arragon and the Emperor must strengthen their alliance with that kingdom. Has not yet seen the articles for the great league. They are much against France. Antwerp, 18 Feb. *Signed.*
Pp. 4, *mutilated.*

18 Feb.   **4790.**   For ROBERT TAWLEY, chaplain.
S. B.

Grant of the free chapel of St. George in the castle of Southampton, with 10*l.* a year out of the port of Southampton ; from Easter, 3 •Hen. VIII., as he has officiated in the said chapel, with no wages since that time. The said chapel was granted by patent 2 Aug. 1 Hen. VIII. to Thomas Vasse, chaplain, but it has been since discovered that he was born in France, and that he was a spy in this kingdom for Louis King of France, after the war with that King. *Del.* Westm., 18 Feb. 5 Hen. VIII.
Pat. 5 *Hen. VIII. p.* 2, *m.* 19.

18 Feb   **4791.**   For SIR JOHN MUSGRAVE, knight of the Body, and
P. S.   THOMAS his son.

Grant, in survivorship, of the offices of constable of the castle of Bewcastell, and chief forester of Nicholforeste, Cumb. ; with grant, for repairs of the said castle, of lands in Bewcastell Dale lately belonging to Sir John Middelton ; and the park of Plompton in the forest of Inglewood, and common of pasture there ;—with annual rent of 40*l.,* half payable from the issues of the manor aforesaid (of Sowerby ?*), and half from the manors of Randollington Arthureth and Lyddell in Nicholforest. Lambeth, 14 Feb. 5 Hen. VIII. *Del.* Westm., 18 Feb.
Pat. 5 *Hen. VIII. p.* 2, *m.* 14.

18 Feb.   **4792.**   VICTUALLING.

Essex and Sussex.—Commission to John Skern to purvey corn for the army about to go to foreign parts, during the next six months. Westm., 18 Feb.
Pat. 5 *Hen. VIII. p.* 2, *m.* 19*d.*

19 Feb.   **4793.**   PONYNGES to WOLSEY.
R. O.

Anthoine de Croy, brother of Chimay, desires to serve the King next May. Hans Rytlyng, Hans Metz, Jacob Raynart, Martin Meute, and other captains of the Almains who served the King in Spain last summer, also desire to retain service. Rytlyng advises to defer recovery of the *scelebref* till summer. The canons have met to make their election, at which he and others were present. Tournay, 19 Feb.

The day after the date hereof, being Monday, the officers whom they had chosen were sworn in his presence,—all ancient men, and probably of good condition. Recommends the provost, who has exerted himself much in the King's behalf since the King's de-

---

* See Pat. 7 Hen. VIII. p. 2. m. 21 ; 28 Oct.

1514.

parture, and John Morgan the bearer, who is going to his country to prepare himself against the King's coming over. *Signed.*
P. 1. Addressed : [To] my Lord of Lyncolne is good lordship.

19 Feb. **4794.** RECRUITS in GERMANY and FLANDERS.
S. B.
Commission to Sir Richard Wingefelde, knight of the Body, Deputy of Calais, Will. Knyght, LL.D., Prothonotary of the See Apostolic, and Sir Thomas Spinelly, to levy men for the King's army in the dominions of the Emperor and the Prince Castile, the King's allies. Westm., 19 Feb. 1513, 5 Hen. VIII.

20 Feb. **4795.** LUCAS DE RENAL[DI]* to . . . . . .†
Calig. D. vi. 87b.
B. M.
Informs him that the Bishop of Gurk would be with the Emperor within seven days with the Spanish ambassador Urreas, and when he has sanctioned a truce with the Venetians until the ides of March. . . . . He has made the Viceroy of Naples the Emperor's lieutenant, and has left in his hands Verona and the other states, subject to the Emperor. The Venetians have sent 15,000 ducats to promote the truce, and are sending all their horse to Friuli, to what end the writer cannot understand, nor why they buy so dearly a short delay, unless they have great expectations. Milan, Genoa, and Cremona are garrisoned by the French. Landas, 20 Feb. 1513.
Lat., p. 1.

21 Feb. **4796.** SPINELLY to [HENRY VIII.]
Galba, B. iii.154.
B. M.
[Wrote last] on the 18th. Two messengers have been sent from Arragon to France. One of them found his fellow at Amiens, where he had been detained. Yesterday had an audience with my Lady. She told Spinelly that the King of Arragon doubted of any accommodation between the Emperor and the Venetians ; the former was obstinate, the latter would bring in the Turks, and therefore he had made overture of peace. France is to give his second daughter to Don Ferdinand, and resign to her all the right he claims in Milan. My Lady will oppose his intentions as unreasonable and contrary to the treaty made with England, and, if he persist, will break with him. The ambassador told her that at the departure of Quintana his master was not aware the business was in so good a train between the Emperor and the Venetians. If the Emperor and England continue united, she thinks that Arragon will not dare to abandon them. The practices of the Pope are to be attributed to the unreasonable desire of the King of Arragon touching the duchy of Milan. She wishes the King to speak with the Arragonese ambassador from England. She says that the Lord of Nassau has sent Molembeys to England to know the King's mind in the war against France. Brussels, 21 Feb. *Signed.*
Pp. 4., mutilated.

21 Feb. **4797.** For JOHN HOLAND and WILLIAM WALESSE, yeomen of
S. B.
the Guard.
Licence to import 600 tons of Gascon wine or Toulouse woad. *Del.* Westm., 21 Feb. 5 Hen. VIII.
Fr. 5 Hen.VIII. m. 16.

---

* Latter part of the name burnt.
† Addresses him as " Magnifice ac generose Domine."

1514.
21 Feb.   **4798.**   For SIR RICHARD SACHEVERELL alias SAUNCHEVERELL
P. S.   of Stoke Pogys, Bucks, alias of Kerby, Leic.

Pardon and release as late treasurer of war, in the suite of
George Earl of Shrewsbury, late chief captain of the forces in
Flanders, Picardy, and France. Lambeth, 18 Feb. 5 Hen. VIII.
Del. Westm., 21 Feb.
Pat. 5 Hen. VIII. p. 2, m. 19.

21 Feb.   **4799.**   For WM. CRANE.

To be controller, during pleasure, of the tonnage and poundage
of the small customs in the port of London, *vice* Simon Dygby ;
he performing the office in person. Westm., 21 Feb.
Pat. 5 Hen. VIII. p. 2, m. 18.

22 Feb.   **4800.**   For SIR HENRY WIAT, captain of the King's wars.
P. S. b.   Protection for John Parker, retained to serve in the war. 20 Feb.
5 Hen. VIII. [*Del.*] 22 [Feb.] *Signed and sealed.*

23 Feb.   **4801.**   CHARLES   DE   CROY   [PRINCE   OF   CHIMAY]   to
Galba, B. III. 137.   HENRY VIII.
B. M.   Requests indemnification for the injuries done him by the King's
men of war. Has written before, but had no answer. Malines,
23 Feb. *Signed.*
Fr., mutilated, p. 1.   Add. and endd.

23 Feb.   **4802.**   AMMUNITION.
R. O.   Bill of Hans Wolff and others for ammunition, 23 Feb.
5 Hen. VIII.

23 Feb.   **4803.**   For JOHN SAMPER of London, "shierman."
S. B.   Protection ; going in the retinue of Sir Richard Wyngfeld,
Deputy of Calais. *Del.* Westm., 23 Feb. 5 Hen. VIII.
Fr. 5 Hen. VIII. m. 16.

23 Feb.   **4804.**   COMMISSION OF THE PEACE.

Sussex.—Wm. Abp. of Canterbury, R. Bp. of Winchester, Thos.
Duke of Norfolk, Thos. Earl of Arundel, Hen. Earl of Northum-
berland, Geo. Nevell Lord Bergevenny, Wm. Lord Maltravers,
Thos. West Lord De la War, Thos. Fenys Lord Dacre, Sir Robt.
Rede, John Butler, John More, Sir Thos. West, Sir David Owen,
Sir Thos. Fenys, Sir Godard Oxenbrigge, Sir John Devenysshe,
John Carell, John Erneley, John Dawtrey, Ric. Sakvyle, Thos.
Nevell, Wm. Asshebournham, Vincent Fynche, Thos. Theccher,
Edw. Palmer, Rich. Covert, John Goryng, John Theccher, Wm.
Shelley, Robt. Morley, John Stanney, Wm. Skardevyle and John
Rote. Westm., 23 Feb.
Pat. 5 Hen. VIII. p. 1, m. 6d.

23 Feb.   **4805.**   For SIR JOHN SHARP, groom of the Privy Chamber, and
S B.   GUTHLAC OVERTON.

Grant, in survivorship, of the tribulage in the hundreds of Pen-
with and Kerr, Cornw., and in the stannary there, from Mic. 24
Hen. VII. *Del.* Westm., 23 Feb. 5 Hen. VIII.
Pat. 5 Hen. VIII. p. 2, m. 12.

1514.

24 Feb. **4806.** For THOMAS PAYNE of Salisbury, mercer.

S. B.

Protection ; going in the retinue of Sir Richard Wyngfyld, knight of the Body, Deputy of Calais. *Del.* Westm, 24 Feb. 5 Hen. VIII.

Fr. 5 Hen. VIII. m. 16.

24 Feb. **4807.** For SIR WILLIAM VAMPAGE, harbinger and sewer, and SIR WILLIAM KYNGESTON.

S. B.

Grant, in survivorship, of the offices of sewer and harbinger with 50 marks a year for the former office and 20 for the latter ; on surrender of patent 17 Nov. 1 Hen. VIII., exemplifying patent 8 Jan. 1 Hen. VII. (which was lost), granting the said office of sewer to Vampage. *Del.* Westm., 24 Feb. 5 Hen. VIII.

Pat. 5 Hen. VIII. p. 2, *m.* 23.

R. O.

2. Draft of a warrant to the treasurer and chamberlains of the Exchequer, for payment to Sir Will. Vampage and Sir Will. Kyngeston, of their salary as the King's sewers : no mention having been made in their patent of the feast days on which the payments should be made.

24 Feb. **4808.** INQUIRY INTO WASTE.

Surrey.—Commission to Sir John Legh, Edm. Howard, John Scot, Thos. Morton, and Hen. Saunder to make inquisition concerning the waste, sale, and destruction said to be made by Ranulph Chalner and Ranulph Spurstowe, in the possessions of Nicholas Ayston alias Assheton, the custody of which (during the minority of William, son and heir of the said Nicholas) was granted by patent 13 Nov. 3 Hen. VIII. to Robt. Morton, and by him to the said Chalner and Spurstowe. Canterbury, 24 Feb.

Pat. 5 Hen. VIII. p. 1, *m.* 16d.

24 Feb. **4809.** COMMISSION OF THE PEACE.

Oxon.—M. Bp. of Landaff, Sir Thos. Lovell, Ric. Ellyott, Sir Ric. Fowler, Sir Wm. Rede, Sir Ric. Sacheverell, Sir Walter Stoner, Sir Edw. Grevyle, Sir Adrian Fortescu, Wm. West, Wm. Farmer, Ralph Massy, Edw. Chamberlayn, Simon Harecourt, Walter Bulstrode, Thos. Unton, John Horne, Christ. Belyngeham, John Osbaldeston, Ralph Vyne, Geo. Stanley, Thos. Haydock, Edm. Bury, Thos. Denton, John Busterd, and Wm. Councer. W[estm.], 24 Feb.

Pat. 5 Hen. VIII. p. 1, *m.* 6d.

25 Feb. **4810.** SPINELLY to HENRY VIII.

Galba, B. v. 98.

B. M.

Wrote last on the 21st from Brussels. Incloses a copy of it in case of any accident to the original. Hears this morning from Rome of the treaty concluded between the Emperor and the Venetians. The estates of Brabant have revoked their grant of 100,000 crowns to the Emperor till the Prince shall be put in possession of his lands. Has letters of the 12th from Sir Robt. Wingfield, who had had no audience with the Emperor on the subject of Henry's last letters. Mechlin, 25 Feb.

P.S.—Sends a letter to the King from the Cardinal of York (Bainbridge). *Signed.*

Mutilated, p. 1. *Add.*

1514.

25 Feb. **4811.** SIR RICHARD WINGFIELD to WOLSEY.

Calig. E. II. 112.
B. M.

[Body of the letter wanting.]

P.S.—Has heard that a treaty has been concluded between
. . . . the Emperor, and the Venetians. A gentleman belonging
to the Earl of Nasso is going over to England to offer the King
the services of the Earl and the Marquis of Brandenburgh.

Hol., mutilated, p. 1. Addressed; "To the right honorable,
&c., my lord elect of Lincoln."

25 Feb. **4812.** COMMISSION OF THE PEACE.

Leicestershire.—Thos. Marquis of Dorset, Geo. Earl of Shrews-
bury, Geo. Lord Hastings, John Grey, Robt. Brudenell, Humph.
Conyngesby, Guy Palmes, Sir Will. Compton, Sir John Dygby,
Sir Thos. Neuport, Sir Ralph Sherley, Sir Everard Feldyng, Thos.
Jakes, Sir Ric. Sacheverell, Everard Dygby, Th. Pulteney, Will.
Skevyngton, Anth. Fitzherbert, Will. Turpyn, John Fitzherbert,
Will. Brokesby, John Villers, Will. Assheby, Christ. Nele, Ralph
Swyllyngton, Thos. Entwisell, Thos. Brokesby, Thos. Hasilrigge,
Will. Wistowe, Roger Rattcliff, Will. Raynoldis, Will. Turvile,
and Walter Kebell. Westm., 25 Feb.

Pat. 5 Hen. VIII. p. 1, m. 5d.

25 Feb. **4813.** For GRIFFITH AP MEREDETH VAGHAN.

P. S.

Grant of the herbage and pannage of Radnour park, with a
meadow called "Castell medowe" belonging thereto, not exceeding the yearly value of 5 marks. Lambeth, 18 Feb. 5 Hen. VIII.
Del. Westm., 25 Feb.

Pat. 5 Hen. VIII. p. 2, m. 6.

25 Feb. **4814.** For EDWARD AP DAVID AP MEREDETH.

P. S.

Grant of the toll of the town of Rayadour, in the lordship of
Melenneth, marches of Wales, to the annual value of 5 marks,
vice Rice Vaughan ap Richard ap Rice. Lambeth, 19 Feb.
5 Hen. VIII. *Del.* Westm., 25 Feb.

Pat. 5 Hen. VIII. p. 2, m. 7.

25 Feb. **4815.** For MEREDETH AP RICE.

P. S.

Grant of the rents and issues of the town of Coydesoyth, in
the lordship of Mylleneth, to the annual value of 50s. Lambeth,
20 Feb. 5 Hen. VIII. *Del.* Westm., 25 Feb.

Pat. 5 Hen. VIII. p. 2, m. 7.

25 Feb. **4816.** For JAMES AP RICE.

P. S.

Grant of the herbage and pannage of Pillith forests in the lordship of Milleneth, to the annual value of 40s., *vice* David Gough.
Lambeth, 19 Feb. 5 Hen. VIII. *Del.* Westm., 25 Feb.

Pat. 5 Hen. VIII. p. 2, m. 7.

25 Feb. **4817.** For EDWARD HAWTE, mercer of London.

P. S.

Licence to import 1,600 tons of Toulouse woad. Lambeth, 22 Feb.
5 Hen. VIII. *Del.* Westm., 25 Feb.

Fr. 5 Hen. VIII. m. 1.

25 Feb. **4818.** TRUCE WITH FRANCE.

R. O.

Truce between Maximilian, Henry VIII., Ferdinand of Arragon,
Prince Charles of Spain, on the one part, and Lewis of France,

1514.

James of Scotland, and Charles Duke of Gueldres on the other, for the defence of the Church, and to avoid the effusion of Christian blood. Ratified by Odet de Foix Sieur de Lautrec for France, at Blois, 8 Feb. 1513; and by Jaques de Conichillo, Bp. of Catania, Chancellor of the King Catholic in Navarre, at Medina, 25 Feb. 1513.
Fr. P. 2, imperfect. Endd.

26 Feb. **4819.** HENRY VIII. to LEO X.

Vat. Transcripts,
Addit. MSS.
15,387, f. 15.
B. M.

In commendation of Polydore Virgil, Archdeacon of Wells, Sub-collector of the Apostolic Chamber, who, having been 12 years in England, now wishes to revisit his own country, and kiss the Pope's feet. Westm., 26 Feb. 1513.
Lat. Copy, p. 1.

26 Feb. **4820.** TOURNAY.

S. B.

Appointment of five notable personages as clerks, to hear and determine causes in the towns and cities of Tournay and Terouenne. Westm., 26 Feb. 1513, 5 Hen. VIII.
Fr.

R. T. 144.
R. O.

2. Letters patent of the above.

26 Feb. **4821.** TOURNAY.

S. B.

Proclamation for the administration of justice in Tournay. Westm., 26 Feb. 1513, 5 Hen. VIII.
Fr.

R. T. 144.
R. O.

2. Letters patent of the above.

26 Feb. **4822.** TOURNAY.

S. B.

Licence to the commonalty of Tournay to take a sixth part of the corn brought into the said town by the river, called *le mis sus,* for holding a staple, as formerly. Westm., 26 Feb. 5 Hen. VIII.
Fr.

26 Feb. **4823.** COOPERS.

Commission to John Eston, the King's cooper, to provide coopers and materials for the army about to go to foreign parts, during the next six months. Westm., 26 Feb.

ii. Similar commission to John Alane. Westm., 26 Feb.
Pat. 5 Hen. VIII. p. 2, m. 19d.

27 Feb. **4824.** ————— to —————.

Calig. E. I. 117.
B. M.

Had written to him on the . . . . . "jour des Roys" last. Has found three or four good places for the despatch of his merchandise. If the woman by whom he sends this will not serve, he must find some one else. The mourning for the Queen is very great. She is to be buried on Friday at St. Denis. All the nobility of France and Britanny will be there. The Bretons will not receive the dauphin till the marriage be accomplished between him and . . . . . A Scotch ambassador is at the court.—Albany will be sent into Scotland with 10,000 men.—The King is levying a vast number of troops for Guienne. He is assembling a fleet with victuals; God knows they will be well victualled. He is in great fear of the English, and has left all his [troops] beyond the mountains. The people are oppressed by the taxes and the pillaging of the soldiers.

1514.

He has sent 10,000 hogs to Picardy and 5,000 or 6,000 beeves,
The King and the Venetians have raised a great army against the
Turk, " affin de rompre les arm . . . . . . et Angloys, mais ilz se
entendent bien, car le . . . . consentant pour rompre sesdites
guerres de pard[e .] . . . peullent." Reminds him of the marriage
of which he spoke. 15 Feb.

Thinks he had better go to Guienne. No place so good for
traffic as Normandy.

Fr., mutilated, pp. 2. Endorsed in the same hand ; Copy
of the letter written by the compaignon being in France, whereof
the original is herewith. *In another hand :* T. Spynelly, xxvij
Februarii.

27 Feb.   **4825.**   WILL. and CHR. DACRE to LORD DACRE.
R. O.

His small friends of Northumberland have come home, demanding redress for Waistland, Tindale, or Redesdale, since Branxton
field. Sir Will. Heron can make reparation for Redesdale. Tindale
would not appear before them or Sir Ralph Fenwick. They have
combined at the suggestion of Sir John Heron of Chipchase. Criste
Milburne, Jame Dodd, Thos. Charlton of Carroteth, have secreted
their goods. They refuse to come in, and cannot be enticed by
policy. They are afraid of being sent to London. They sent
their answer by Edw. and Will. Charlton, enclosed. Arrested
the former and sent him to the Tower, Thursday 16 Feb.,
and on Sunday after Thos. Erington, called Thos. Peepe, John
Erington, the Angel, his son, and Gib. Erington of Greneriche.
On Tuesday last the Tynedale men would have broken into the
Tower, but for the precautions of the writer. Has sent to his
brother, Sir Philip, to make sure of the prisoners at Morpeth.
" In the light of this moon " will make raids on those of Tynedale
and the Waistland, who refuse to appear according to his letter
by Chr. Legh. Encloses a bill of the prisoners. Jak Musgrave
took Jame Nowble, called Yellow Hare, and kept him in Bewcastell two days, and let him go at the desire of Clement Nixon.
The Waistlands are summoned to appear at Askerton on Thursday
next. Rinion of Erington is gone as a servant of my Lord of
Northumberland to London, where Dacre can have him. Gares is
not yet come from Edinburgh, where he went with letters from the
King, ·14 days since, to Master Magnus. The Queen and the
lords are not yet agreed. When he returns will send Gibson.
Carlisle, " Monday the penult day of February." *Signed.*

Pp. 2. Add.

27 Feb.   **4826.**   For SIR EDWARD GREVYLLE.
P. S. b.

Protection for Robert Morley, retained to serve in the war in
the said Edward's retinue. 27 Feb. 5 Hen. VIII. *Signed.*

28 Feb.   **4827.**   COMMISSION OF THE PEACE.

Salop.—Ric. Bp. of Hereford, G. Bp. of Coventry and Lich-
field, Thos. Bp. of Bangor, Edw. Duke of Buckingham, Thos. Earl
of Arundel, Geo. Earl of Shrewsbury, Robt. Brudenell, Humph.
Conyngesby, Chas. Both, clk., Sir Gilbert Talbot, Sir Thos. Ingle-
feld, Sir Wm. Uvedale, Sir Griffin Rice, Sir Thos. Cornwall,
Sir Thos. Blount, Sir Thos. Leyghton, John Maynwaryng, Wm.
Ruddall, Ric. Litilton, Thos. Scryven, Thos. Lacon, John Salton,
Geo. Bromley, Geo. Harebroun, Thos. Lynom, Ric. Foster, Ric.
Selman and Ric. Hord. Westm., 28 Feb.

Pat. 5 Hen. VIII. p. 1, m. 1d.

1514.
28 Feb. **4828.** For WILLIAM TOFT, clk., minister of the King's chapel.
S. B. Presentation to the church of Fulbeke, Lincoln dioc., void by death. *Del.* Westm., 28 Feb. 5 Hen. VIII.
Pat. 5 Hen. VIII. p. 2, m. 22.

27 Feb. **4829.** HENRY VIII. to [SPINELLY.]
Lett. de Louis XII. Fears the King of Arragon desires to evade fulfilment of the
t. IV. p. 253. treaty last made at Lisle, by which he is bound to make actual war against France this summer, on condition of Henry's subsidising 6,000 men. Perceives by letters from John Stile that he wishes Henry to send him 6,000 Germans before the 1st June, which is impossible within so short a space. It would seem by the answer made to [Spinelly] by the Archduchess, on the overtures of Ferdinand's ambassadors, at the coming of two Spanish messengers through France (of which [Spinelly] has done well to give notice) that Ferdinand tries every means to make peace with France this year, as he did the last. Quintana his secretary has passed through France to the Emperor, and returned the same way; but the Emperor has not informed Henry of his charge, nor said anything of it to Wingfield, who has made frequent inquiries about it. Has heard of these secret practices in three channels. Is to urge the Archduchess to keep the Emperor in mind of his obligations, and desire him to write to the King of Arragon to keep the treaty. He may remind Margaret that at the conclusion of the treaty she undertook to answer for the King of Arragon, and that it was openly declared that England should not be obliged to provide Germans or other soldiers, but only to furnish the money. Is to request delivery of the King's six courtaulx, which are in the Prince's countries, that Sir Sampson Norton and Sir Edward Belknap may convey them to Calais. Lambeth, 27 Feb. 1513.

Feb. **4830.** —— to Secretary [MARNIX ?]
Galba, B. III. 146a. . . . . One was directed to a bailey, which the writer wished to
B. M. be shown to my Lord : That Flanders is in great danger from the French ;—that if he had been believed, affairs would not have been so bad ;—that the writer has given advertisements all through these wars. It appears "by the other copy" that the writer is a Frenchman living in England, that the originals are in the French King's hands. It states that Lovell the treasurer had arrived in England the day before, that the captain of Guisnes would be glad to be discharged of his post, "for he had never a writing from the King since the course made before Guisnes by Pont de Remy ;" that a treaty was concluded between France and England,—that no mention was made of confederates except the Scotch,—that the King shall easily pay henceforth the garrisons of Guisnes and Tournay,—that the embassy from England to the Swiss, was to declare the treaty and no more,—that the Swiss "*comme non entamez demourcrons encores orguilleuxl*,"—that the Deputy of Calais and Sir Robt. Wingfield are only waiting for their despatches.
P. 1, mutilated. In Spinelly's hand, probably inclosed in his letter of 7 Feb. 1514.

Feb. **4831.** INSTRUCTIONS to [SPINELLY].
Lett. de Louis XII. 1. The King is apprised of the good counsel taken by Madame for
t. IV. 257. the recovery of the sealed brief from the hands of the German foot.
2. As the King understands there is neutrality on both sides, contrary to the treaty and promise of the Emperor, and that the

3 B

1514.

French have no force to invade, Madame ought to discharge the remaining foot and a good part of the horse, retaining the principal men, by means of whom the force can be reconstituted to be of service to the King at his coming. 3. Madame ought also to discharge a number of gentlemen, who are at home, the most part of the time, as appeared by the musters, on which subject Thomas [Spinelly] is charged to speak plainly to Madame. 4. Is to demand that the six courtaulx lent for the war of Gueldres be brought to Antwerp, and delivered to William Copelande's servant. 5. To declare that the King has again written to the Pope and the Venetians of the advancement of the treaty between the Emperor and them. 6. To deliver the safe-conduct for the subjects " de par delà." 7. To tell her that for her sake the King has appointed some of his council to treat for the ransom of the Vice-Admiral of France [René de Clermont]. 8. To thank her for her secret advertisements, and request her to continue them. 9. That the King is making preparations for the performance of all promises touching the continuance of war, and the celebration of the marringe at Calais, and hopes she will do the like. 10. To know her mind, upon which point he will send to her the Lord Lysley. 11. To request that English money shall be current in the Low Countries at the rate of 30 sous Fl. to the pound sterling, otherwise the King will have to delay payment of the garrisons out of Tournay. 12. That the King has been lately visited by a malady named the smallpox, but is now recovered and out of danger.

Fr.

Feb.   **4832.**   TOURNAY.

R. O.

Notarial instrument, dated . . Feb. 1513, Indict. 1, 10 Julius II. stating that Peter Steenhone, a layman of the diocese of Tournay, has undertaken the publication of the papal excommunication against the Germans deserting to the King of France.

Lat. Badly mutilated.

Feb.   **4833.**   MARGARET OF SAVOY to HENRY VIII.

Lett. de Louis XII.
t. IV. p. 239.

Hopes he has not forgotten his promise made to the Emperor at Lisle, to obtain the consent of Parliament regulating the succession to the Crown, in favor of his sister the Princess of Castile, in default of heirs of Henry's body. Desires to know what steps he has taken.

1 March.   **4834.**   For WATKYN and JOHN VAUGHAN, grooms of the
S. B.   Chamber.

Licence to bring to England every year for four years, one ship, of 120 tons burden, laden with Gascon wine and woad (reckoning 8 bales to the ton) ; and to export to France any commodities of England. *Del.* Westm., 1 March 5 Hen. VIII. *Mutilated.*

Fr. 5 *Hen. VIII. m.* 16.

1 March.   **4835.**   LEO X. to HENRY VIII.

Vitell. B. II. 69.
B. M.
Rym. XIII. 393.

Sends him, by Leonard de Spinellis, a sword and cap (*pileus*), not so valuable for the matter as for the mystery. Rome, 1 March 1514, pont. 1.

Add. Lat. Vellum.

1514.

2 March. **4836.**   For HUMPHREY and DIONISIUS LOWE of Denby, and their
P. S.   sureties THOMAS TOWNESENDE of Stoneton, and JOHN
             BADECOK of Denby, Derby.

    Release of their recognizances entered into before John Fitz-
herbert, justice of the peace in co. Derby, 22 Jan. 4 Hen. VIII.
Lambeth, 23 Feb. 5 Hen. VIII. *Del.* Westm, 1 March.

2 March. **4837.**   For RICHARD CORNEWALL, squire of the Body, and
S. B.   RALPH HACKULNET.

    To be stewards, in survivorship, of the lordships of Clyfford,
Glasbery, and Wynsorton, in the marches of Wales, and constables
of Clyfford Castle. *Del.* Westm. 2 March 5 Hen. VIII.
Pat. 5 Hen. VIII. p. 2, m. 22.

2 March. **4838.**   For THOMAS DUKE OF NORFOLK.
S. B.

    To be treasurer of the exchequer during pleasure, with power to
appoint officers ; as held by Ralph late Lord Cromwell, Ralph late
Lord Sudeley, John Tiptofte late Earl of Worcester, Henry late
Earl of Essex, and John Lord Dynham. *Del.* Westm., 2 March
5 Hen. VIII.

    Surrendered 3 Dec. 14 Hen. VIII. by the Duke at his manor of
Horsham, Sussex.
Pat. 5 Hen. VIII. p. 2, m. 22.

2 March. **4839.**   For HENRY SMYTH, clerk of the King's works.
P. S.

    Acquittance for 600 pounds of silver, received by him (500*l.*
through Sir John Daunce, and 100*l.* through Sir John Cutte,) for
providing timber, &c., used in building the King's breweries and
bakeries at Calais, and for the carriage thereof ; and for the conduct
money of certain pioneers who were with the King abroad. Lambeth, 24 Feb. 5 Hen. VIII. *Del.* Westm., 2 March.
Pat. 5 Hen. VIII. p. 2, m. 14.

2 March. **4840.**   For SIR WALTER RODNEY, the King's lancer.
P. S.

    Grant of the manor of Saint Jermayns, in the isle of Jersey.
Lambeth, 25 Feb. 5 Hen. VIII. *Del.* Westm., 2 March.
Pat. 5 Hen. VIII. p. 2, m. 22.

2 March. **4841.**   For WILLIAM ATWATER, D.D., dean of the Chapel Royal,
P. S.   EDMUND GRUFF, GEOFFREY LLOYD, and WILLIAM
             MARKE, chaplains.

    Next presentation to the rectory of Bradnyche, in the duchy of
Cornwall. Lambeth, 25 Feb. 5 Hen. VIII. *Del.* Westm., 2 March.
Pat. 5 Hen. VIII. p. 2, m. 23.

2 March. **4842.**   For JOHN A DENE.

    Protection ; going to the war. Westm., 2 March.

3 March. **4843.**   ——— to WOLSEY.
Calig. D. vi. 90.
B. M.

    An account of the examination, taken Friday, 3 March 1513, by
order of the Deputy of Calais, of Baudec Puchier, aged 18, native
of Bethune in Artois, as he says. Answers to the effect, that he left
Bethune three years ago to pursue his trade of *tonnelier* at Dieppe
in Normandy, where he has since dwelt continually. Last year
it was commonly reported that the French King had got ready
300 ships, which he meant to send into England, besides six galleys

3 B 2

1514.

that the deponent had seen a year ago at Dieppe, and [were now?], as he had heard, at Hounefleur ;—they are making more ships of war at Dieppe, to the number of 20, as was intended, which are all nearly ready (*quasi toutes prestes*), only requiring to be victualled. He had left Dieppe eight days ago alone, because . . . . . and gone by Abbeville, intending to visit at Calais a brother of his who went to dwell there eight years ago, but he could hear no news of him ; says there are in harbour at Dieppe 14 or 15 ships of war well armed, of which the [chief] were Scotch, and the rest Breton. In passing hither by Abbeville he had heard that Monseigneur d'Angoulesme was dead in Britanny, which others contradicted.

Fr., pp. 2. Much burnt about the edges.

Addressed in Sir Richard Wingfield's hand : "[To] my syngwlar good Lord my Lord elect of Lyncolne."

3 March. **4844.** SPINELLY to HENRY VIII.

Galba, B. III.156.
B. M.

Wrote on the 27th. Sends an extract written by the rentmaster of Zealand to the Archduchess of the ship that departed from Camfer, to Scotland, and a memorial of men coming in a hulk from Scotland. The Scotch herald Unicorn, sent here by the Lord Fyennys, was not allowed to come abroad. She has opened all the packets, found several Scotch letters, only touching benefices.— The pensioner of Hampsterden tells him it is reported from Denmark that the King there will not help the Scots, as much for lack of inclination as of power.—The Easterlings are well treated in France.—The two Hobertys have been here, and have offered to freight a vessel of 40 tons, with onions and apples, to Scotland, with some shrewd fellows to make inquiry there. They ask 100 gold crowns for coming and going. John Merzen is master of the vessel.—A messenger is come from Spain, and another has been sent to England ; but since Quintana's interview with the Emperor things have been changed. The King of Arragon wrote to the Emperor on 6 Feb.—Bregylles, now in England, is to inform the King of Quintana's charge ; an answer has been promised the Emperor within 40 days.—The ambassadors here are in great perplexity. Lord Berges thinks that the King should write to his ambassador Sir Rob. Wingfield, and offer the Swiss the money he was bound to give to the King of Arragon, binding them to invade France on one side, while the Emperor invaded the other ; but it must be done at once, as the variance between the French and Swiss had begun. If God would save the French, which is hard to believe, there is no chance of peace unless their country be invaded. The Emperor has bound Arragon to make no truce without England, but acts suspiciously in negotiating with Quintana without the presence of the English ambassador. Some think [Arragon] will do all he can to promote the match between Don Ferdinand and the second daughter of France; but if England and the Emperor are firm, they will bring him to reason. He is not in favor with the Pope. The Emperor has the advantage in the treaty with the Venetians. Has written to the ambassadors at Rome to get the Pope to help the expedition on this side the mountains, as he does not favor the Emperor. Sends letters from the Compaignon France and the canon of Lisle, by which it appears the other writings have been lost. Has despatched the Canon with money into Brittany and Normandy to obtain information. Aubert Oberton, a Scot, with a ship containing 300 men and an ambassador going to the French King being driven by a storm into the haven of Groyngue

1514.

in Gallicia, were arrested and sent to the King of Arragon.—By letters of the 19th the Emperor had [left] Rotynbourgh for Lynse. He had no knowledge of the Venetian affair. It is thought one of the Emperor's captains, Count Christoforo Francapan, who has done great deeds against the Venetians, might do Henry service with 1,000 good horsemen. The Scotch herald brought letters to the Prince and my Lady, and is to show his credence tomorrow, Will send full particulars of his charges by next budget. As he was closing, Peter Wyldancke brought a letter concerning the retinue of certain gunners. Went immediately to my Lady, who conceded all he asked. Cannot find the copy of the rent master's letter, but will send it by his next. It was to the effect that no harness was found in the little ship of Camfer, and only some letters stating that certain Scots were gone to Dieppe to take shipping for Scotland. Is told the Scottish herald landed at Dieppe, and was at the court of France before coming here. Mechlin, 3 March. *Signed.*
Pp. 8, *mutilated.*

3 March. **4845.** PETER MARTYR to LUD. F. MENDOZA.
Epist. 537.
Lady Margaret has thrown John Emmanuel into prison ; it is supposed for speaking against Ferdinand. Henry of England has had a fever ; the physicians were afraid it would turn to the smallpox. He is now well again, and rises from his bed, fierce as ever against France. Martyr thinks it will be of no use, as Ferdinand is too old and crazy to endure war. A truce has been made for a year by Peter Quintana, of whom he had spoken before. Maximilian and the Pope have consented. Ferdinand alleges that he cannot allow himself to be abandoned by his friends as he was by England, when she left him to confront the whole power of France, alone and unprepared. The King of England bites his lips, and will not admit the validity of the excuse ; but cannot help himself. Will go to John Stilo and hear what he says about it. Valladolid, 5 non. Martii 1514.

3 March. **4846.** For JOHN TURNOUR and ROBERT BROWNE.
S. B.
To be bailiffs and receivers, in survivorship, of the lordships of Ailewarton and Pensaunce, Cornw. Also, grant of the hospice called Werwykes in the city of London, with the office of keeper of the same. Also, to be receivers general of all the possessions belonging to Eleanor late Countess of Somerset. *Del.* Westm., 3 March, 5 Hen. VIII.
Pat. 5 *Hen. VIII. p.* 2, *m.* 30.

3 March. **4847.** COMMISSION OF THE PEACE.
Kent.—W. Abp. of Canterbury, Edw. Duke of Buckingham, Hen. Earl of Wiltshire, Geo. Nevyle Lord Bergevenny, John Lord Clinton, Sir John Feneux, Sir Rob. Rede, Sir Will. Hody, John Butteler, John More, Sir Edw. Ponynges, Sir John Pechy, Sir Christ. Garneys, Rob. Blagge, Sir Ric. Cholmeley, Sir Will. Scote, Sir John Wiltes, Sir Will. Crowmer, Sir John Fogge, Sir Edw. Guldeford, Th. Nevyll, Th. Willoughby, Th. Isley, Ralph Seyntleger, Walter Roberth, John Rooper, Will. Fyneux, Nich. Boughton, Alex. Culpeper, Reginald Pekham, Hen. Fane, John Engeham. Th. Woode, Will. Whetnall, Edw. Culpeper, Ric. Lee, John Monen (?), John Hales, and John Petyt. Westm., 3 March.
Pat. 5 *Hen. VIII. p.* 1, *m.* 5*d.*

1514.

4 March. **4848.**   PARLIAMENT.

Parl. R.
5 Hen. VIII.
R. O.

Prorogued to Monday, 7 Nov. 5 Hen. VIII. Prorogued, by commission issued to the Chancellor and others, to the 20 Jan. following, at Blackfriars, London; then to the 23 Jan., Westminster, and so held till Saturday, 4 March.

1. Creation of the Duke of Norfolk. [c. 9.]
2. Creation of the Duke of Suffolk. [c. 10.]
3. Creation of the Earl of Surrey. [c. 11.]
4. Restitution of the Countess of Salisbury. [c. 12.]
5. Restitution of Humphrey Stafford. [c. 13.]
6. For the dowry of Eliz. Countess of Oxford. [c. 14.]
7. Restitution of John Audeley, second son of John Lord Audeley, brother of James Tuchet of Audeley. [c. 15.]
8. Ratification of patent granted to the city of London by Edward IV. [c. 16.]
9. Subsidy for 160,000l.; with names of the commissioners annexed. [c. 17.]
10. For the administration of justice in Tournay. [c. 1.]
11. For Sir Edw. Ponynges, lieutenant of Tournay. [c. 18.]
12. For true making of white cloths in Devonshire. [c. 2.]
13. That white cloths under 5 marks may be exported unshorn. [c. 3.]
14. For true making of worsteds. [c. 4.]
15. For the impanelling of juries in London. [c. 5.]
16. For discharging surgeons from being constables, or any office requiring the bearing of arms, they being unharnessed in the field according to the law of arms. [c. 6.]
17. Against strangers buying leather except in the open market. [c. 7.]
18. For the surveyorship of the port of London. [c. 19.]
19. Grant of the King's general pardon. [c. 8.]

Signed: John Tayler, clericus parliamentorum.

4 March. **4849.**   [SPEECH IN PARLIAMENT.]

Harl. 6464.
B. M.

" *Oratio ad excitandos contra Galliam Britannos, incerto authore.*"—After insisting on topics common on such an occasion, the speaker proceeds to show that Ferdinand the King of Spain will not fail to assist his son-in-law; Maximilian will join, " *alter nostri temporis Mavors,*" who had been a soldier from his cradle. He refers to the battles of Ravenna and Novara, and the increasing infirmities of the French King; whereas Henry is like the rising sun, that grows brighter and stronger every day.

Lat., pp. 18. *Probably by Tayler.*

4 March. **4850.**   HENRY VIII. to MAXIMILIAN.

Lett. de Louis XII.
t. IV. p. 274.

Is much displeased to hear that there is a common report that the Archduchess of Austria is to be married to the Duke of Suffolk; will make enquiry if it originated in England, that the authors may be punished. Requests the Emperor to do the like. Cannot doubt it has been caused by " *mauvais esprits* " who wished to create a difference between the King and the Emperor. Westm., 4 March 1513.

Fr.

1514.
Titus, B. 1. 142.
B. M.
Chron. Calais, 71.

4851. [CHARLES BRANDON and MARGARET OF SAVOY.]

" My Lady began this writing before the coming of Morroton, who came to Louvain on Sunday last."

" My Lord the Ambassador,—Since that I see that I may not have tidings from the Emperor so soon, it seemeth me that I should do well no longer for to tarry to dispatch this gentleman." Dares not write to the King and Duke " of this business," for fear her letters may be intercepted. Writes to him at length, in order that he may advertise them of her intent.

After she had been at Tournay, and witnessed the King's great love " to the personage which is no need to name ;" also " the virtue and grace of his person,—the which me seemed that I have not much seen [any] gentleman to approach it,"—and the desire he showed to do her service, she constrained herself to do to him honor and pleasure, in order to please the King. But when Henry asked her " whether this good will would stretch as far as marriage, seeing that it was the fashion of the ladies of England, and that it was not there holden for evil ?" she had replied, that it was impossible, and would bring upon her the evil grace of her father and all that country ; "that it was not here the custom, and that I should be dishonored, and holden for a fool and light." But, not to grieve the King, she further said, " that if now I had well the will so for to do, that yet I ne would nor durst think [of it]," as his return was so nigh. He said, when they departed, he knew well the ladies would forget them, that she would be pressed to marry, for she was too young to abide thus, and the ladies of his country did re-marry at fifty and three-score. She said she had been unhappy in husbands. Twice after, in the presence of the personage that ye know [Suffolk], the King returned to the charge, saying, " I know well, madame, and am sure, that my fellow shall be to you a true servant, and that he is altogether yours ; but we fear that ye shall not do in like wise, for one shall force you to be again married, and that she shall not be found out of this country at my return." He then made her promise that she would not marry at least until his return, or the end of the year, — " the which I did willingly, for I think not to again never to put me where I have had so much unhap and infortune,"—and afterwards made his fellow do the semblable, who said he would not marry without her consent.

These words were said at Tournay in her chamber one night after supper, well late. The other time was at Lylle, the day before they departed, when he and Suffolk spoke to her long at the head of a cupboard, " which was not without great displeasure well great of all persons ;" and after many promises he made Margaret re-confirm in his hand, and the same of Suffolk, her promise aforesaid ; " and the said personage, in my hand, without that I required him, made me the semblable." Nothing passed since, except some gracious letters, the which have been enough evil kept.

As to Suffolk having shown a diamond ring she gave him,— " which I cannot believe, for I esteem much a man of virtue and wise,"—the truth is, that " one night at Tournay, being at the banquet, after the banquet he put himself upon his knees before me, and in speaking and him playing, he drew from my finger the ring, and put it upon his, and since shewed it me ; and I took to laugh, and to him said that he was a thief, and that I thought not that the King had with him led thieves out of his country. This word *laron* he could not understand ; wherefore I was constrained to ask how one said in Flemish *laron*. And afterwards I said to him in Flemish *dieffe*, and I prayed him many times to give it me again, for that it was too much known. But he understood me not well, and kept it on unto the next day that I spake to the King, him requiring to make him to give it me, because it was too much known —I promising him one of my bracelets the which I wore, the which I gave him. And then he gave me the said ring ; the which one other tyme at Lylle, being set nigh to my Lady of Hornes, and he before, upon his knees, it took again from my finger. I spake to the King to have it again ; but it was not possible, for he said unto me that he would give me others better, and that I should leave him that. I said unto him, that it was not for the value but for that it was too much known. He would not understand it, and departed from me. The morrow after he brought me one fair point of diamond, and one table of ruby, and shewed me that it was for the other ring ; wherefore I durst no more speak of it, if not to beseech him that it should not be shewed to any person ; the which hath not all been to me done."

" Thus signed, M."

" The second writing."

" My Lord the Ambassador." Margaret feels much abashed at " the unhappy bruit" spread through Germany and all other countries, and even amongst merchant strangers. By advice of her servants, and Lord Bergues and others, has made inquiry, and found it proceeded from England ; " whereof I have had on marvellous sorrow." Has letters of an English merchant, " the which hath been the first that hath made the wagers, as Bresylle knoweth well." The King, at the request of Bresylle and " the personage" (Suffolk), has done many things to remedy this misfortune, " but yet I see that the bruit is so imprinted in the fantasies of the people, and fear, if that it continues long, that all that which is done is not enough, for I continue alway in fear. And also I know that I may not shew towards the personage the weal and honor which I desire to do, as before." Dares not write to him, nor even to speak of him, and she is constrained to treat him as a stranger, " which doth me so much displeasure that I cannot write it, seeing that I take him so much for my good friend and servant, and that I am constrained so to do ; and also I see that to this gentleman only which is here I dare not speak or look to him ; whereof I am so much displeasant that nothing more. He himself apperceiveth well that every one beholdeth him of the other side."

The descent of the King is what she desires " as much as his coming, and the same of my Lady Mary." Does not like to dissemble, and feels she " shall not dare speak or shew good semblant to the said personage ; whereas I would make to him much honor and good cheer, I shall not dare behold him with a good eye, what displeasure shall be the same to him and to me." Knows no remedy but that which Bresylle will shew him.* " I would not constrain him to it against his will, but, and he desire ever that I do him honor or pleasure, it is force that it be so, not for that I have not the good will towards him, such as ever I have had, but for that I am for mine honor constrained so to do."

* *In margin :* " Bresylle said there was no way to avoid the bruit but that my Lord should marry the Lady Lylle, as more at length I have written unto my said Lord."

1514.

Prays him to make the King and "the personage" understand this, "that I may do to him better service, and to his fellow pleasure. I pray you to do of this as of the other. Like wise assigned, M."
Pp. 5. Indorsed: Secret matters of the Duke of Suffolk.

4 March. 4852. For SIR JOHN CARRE.

S. B.

Grant, in fee, of the manors of Carleton, Bradley, Utley, and Lodirsdane, with appurtenances, in Crawvyn, York ;—a yearly rent of 16*l.*, payable by Sir John Husee, knight of the Body, and his heirs, for the manor of Braunston, the barony of Blaunkeney, and for lands in Braunston, Blaunkeney, Hanworth, Nocton, Dunston, Medryngham, Scopey, Thorp, Thymberland, Marten, Kyrkby, Grene and Walcote, Linc., granted to Husee and his heirs, by patent 2 July 4 Hen. VIII., in as ample a manner as Francis Viscount Lovell held the same. *Del.* Westm., 4 March 5 Hen. VIII.
Pat. 5 Hen. VIII. p. 2, *m.* 23.

4 March. 4853. For SIR JOHN SHARP and GUTHLAC OVERTON.

S. B.

Grant, in survivorship, of the tribulage in the hundreds and stannary of Penwith and Kerr, Cornw., viz., of every cart 2*d.*, from 24 April 1 Hen. VIII. *Del.* Westm., 4 March 5 Hen. VIII.
Pat. 5 Hen. VIII. p. 2, *m.* 23.

4 March. 4854. WOLSEY.

P. S.
Rym. XIII. 394.

Restitution of the temporalities of the see of Lincoln to Thomas Wulcy, the King's almoner. Lambeth, 3 March 5 Hen. VIII. *Del.* Westm., 4 March.
Pat. 5 Hen. VIII. p. 1, *m.* 9.

ii. Bull for his appointment, dated 6 Feb. ; *q. v.*

4 March. 4855. For the CITY OF TOURNAY.

S. B.

Inspeximus and confirmation of the act of 5 Hen. VIII. for administration of justice in Tournay. Westm., 4 March 5 Hen. VIII.
Fr.

R. T. 144.

Letters patent for the above.

4 March. 4856. For JAMES MALET, D.D.

P. S.

Grant of the canonry and prebend in St. George's Windsor, void by preferment of Thomas Wulcy. Lambeth, 2 March 5 Hen. VIII. *Del.* Westm., 4 March.
Pat. 5 Hen. VIII. p. 2, *m.* 22.

4 March. 4857. For ROBERT PIERSON, native of Scotland.

S. B.

Denization from the first day of the King's reign. *Del.* Westm., 4 March 5 Hen. VIII.
Pat. 5 Hen. VIII. p. 2, *m.* 23.

4 March. 4858. For JOHN DYNGLEY and RICHARD BRERETON.

P. S.

Annuity, in survivorship, of 10 marks, out of the lordship of Denbygh, from Mich. last. Lambeth, 14 Feb. 5 Hen. VIII. *Del.* Westm., 4 March.

1514.

4 March.   **4859.**   For RICHARD BASTARD of Bishop's Lynn, merchant.

P. S.   Protection; going in the suite of Sir Richard Wyngfeld, Deputy of Calais.   Windsor Castle, 25 Nov. 5 Hen. VIII. *Del.* Westm., 4 March.

5 March.   **4860.**   COMMISSIONS OF THE PEACE.

               Lincoln (Lindsey). — Wm. Lord Willoughby, Rob. Brudenell, Humph. Conyngesby, Guy Palmes, Sir Rob. Sheffeld, Sir John Husee, Sir Wm. Tirwhit, Sir John Skipwith, Sir Rob. Tirwhit, Sir Rob. Waterton, Sir Wm. Askewe, Sir Wm. Hansard, Sir Andrew Billesby, Sir Christ. Ascogh, Sir John Thymelby, Rob. son of Sir Rob. Sheffeld, Christ. Willoughby, Thos. Burgh jun., Geo. Fitzwilliam, Christ. Broun, Lionel Dymmok, John Topclyff, Rob. Sutton, Thos. Barnardeston, Rob. Sheffeld, Thos. Missenden, John Mounson, Rob. Belwoode, Nich. Upton, John Fulnetby, John Hennege, Thos. Burgh, John Sayntpoll, Edw. Forman, Thos. Tocoste, and Ric. Clarke.   Westm., 5 March.

               Lincoln (Holand). — Wm. Lord Willoughby, Rob. Brudenell, Humph. Conyngesby, Guy Palmes, Sir John Huse, Christ. Willoughby, Wm. Husee, John Merese, Ric. Bolles, John Markham, Geoffrey Paynell, Thos. Robertson, Fras. Broun, Wm. Gooderyk, John Robynson, Thos. Holand, John Littelbury, and Ric. Gordyng Westm., 5 March.

               Pat. 5 Hen. VIII. p. 1, m. 6d.

7 March.   **4861.**   For THOMAS WYNDAM.

P. S. b.   Protection for William Wilkynson of London, draper, retained to serve in the war.   7 March 5 Hen. VIII. [*Del.*] 7 March. *Signed.*

7 March.   **4862.**   For HENRY HERYNG.

P. S.   To be bailiff of the town of Malmeshill Lacy, Herefordshire, parcel of the earldom of March, void by death of Simon father of the said Henry.   Lambeth, 14 Feb. 5 Hen. VIII. *Del.* Westm., 7 March.

               Pat. 5 Hen. VIII. p. 2, m. 30.

7 March.   **4863.**   For MARY FRAUNCIS, widow of HENRY UVEDALE,

S. B.   deceased, alias of Flanders.

           Protection for three years against her creditors, to whom she owes 200*l.* for goods, which Bartholomew Cesson, merchant of London, and others, conveyed from Salisbury fair to that of Oxford, [and robbed her of?]   *Del.* Westm., 7 March 5 Hen. VIII.   *Defaced.*

               Pat. 5 Hen. VIII. p. 2, m. 19.

8 March.   **4864.**   PETER MARTYR to LUD. F. MENDOZA.

Ep. 538.   Three days since visited Stile, who told him Henry was very bitter against Ferdinand; swore he was betrayed; and lamented such an opportunity had been lost for crippling the pride of France. He says, " that Ferdinand induced him to enter on the war, and had

1514.

urged the Pope to use his influence with Henry for that purpose ; that he had been at great expense ; assisted Maximilian ; had taken Tournay ; and had reduced France to extremities : and now, when his enemy is at his feet, Ferdinand talks of truce. He will never trust any one." Ferdinand remains unmoved. He thinks France will be grateful for his good offices, and he is afraid of the overgrowing power of England, especially in its relations with Prince Charles. Valladolid. 8 idus Martii 1513 [1514].

| 8 March. | **4865.** | For SIR THOMAS TYRRELL. |

P. S.

Protection, under the great seal, for Reynold Love, serving in the war. 8 March 5 Hen. VIII. *Signed and sealed.*

| 9 March. | **4866.** | For SIR JOHN EVERYNGHAM. |

P. S.

Pardon and release as late sheriff of Yorkshire ; and release to John Nevill of Leversege, Richard Beamount of Whitley, Edward Knight of Southdufeld, Alfred Elys of Berwyk in Elme, York, Edward Sole of St. Mary Colchurch, London, grocer, and William Clerc of St. Ethelburga, London, armorer, of their recognizance of 100 marks made 15 Nov. 4 Hen. VIII. Greenwich, 7 March 5 Hen. VIII. *Del.* Westm., 9 March.

Pat. 5 Hen. VIII. p. 2, m. 22.

| 10 March. | **4867.** | ROSE BURDON. |

Titus, B. I. 67.
B. M.

Sign manual to John Heron, treasurer of the Chamber, for the payment of 500 marks to Rose Burdon, widow. Greenwich, 10 March 5 Hen. VIII.

Add.

| 10 March. | **4868.** | HENRY VIII. to LORD DARCY. |

Calig. B. VI. 75.
B. M.

By his letters of the 7th learns the news of the preparation made by the Scots against Berwick, and the desire of the town for aid. It shall be sent instantly. Complains of great default in the defence. The soldiers are not resident, or the number of gunners (that should be 50) complete. Is to take with him Sir Rauf Evers, who acquitted himself there substantially of late, and appoint him as deputy, in his room of captain of Berwick, before he attends the King in his voyage to France this summer with 500 men. Sir Rauf has been written to. Darcy's son can do better elsewhere, as he did at the "late voyage against the said Scots." Wages and great ordnance, as specified in his bill, shall be provided. William Pawne and George Lawson shall resort to the said town to procure gunpowder, lead, arrows, &c. Meantime certain stores at Newcastle are to be transported to Berwick. Letters have been sent to Strangewishe, the porter of Berwick, who had employed in merchandize the 500*l.* sent him for victualling the town, to see it furnished, or answer at his peril. 1,000 quarters of wheat, and as many of malt, have been provided. Greenwich, 10 March. *Signed at the top.*

Addressed : To our right trusty &c. the Lord Darcy, captain of our town of Berwick.

Pp. 3.

| 10 March. | **4869.** | DACRE to HENRY VIII. |

Calig. B. VI. 48.
B. M.

On 26th Feb. received at Carlisle the King's letters dated Lambyth the 17th, commanding him to bring by land to Newcastle in all haste the ordnance taken at the last field against the Scots, to

1514.

avoid the danger of sea-passage from Berwick. Immediately sent some of his servants into Northumberland, who provided a hundred horses with oxen obtained by the sheriff, and conveyed the King's commands to the deputy and council of Berwick. They refused to allow the ordnance to be carried over Berwick bridge without special command from the King, saying that my Lord of Norfolk had so ordered, because certain jewels "were sore accra[zed] in the bringing of it to your said town." If the King is resolved upon it he should direct "ferefull" letters of command to the persons named in a cedule. Had written to the priors of Durham and Tynemouth, and to the mayor of Newcastle, for horses and gear for the carriage of the ordnance, and is under obligation to re-deliver and pay for them. Loveday has written to him that he has arrived with his ship at Newcastle to receive it by command of the Admiral. Has bid him remain till the ordnance come. Since parting with the King he has written seldom, because the council of Scotland have been very undecided in their purposes, the young lords always thwarting the purposes of the others. His spies are still in Scotland, and have told him they agree to begin the Parliament on the 20th of this month. Understands that if they get any assurance of Albany's coming speedily, they will send an embassy to hinder it. If not, they will despatch ambassadors after Easter. Kirkoswald, 10 March. *Signed.*

Addressed : [To th]e King's highness.

Pp. 2.

12 March. **4870.** THOMAS LORD DACRE to the COUNCIL.

R. O.

On Thursday night last Sir Roger Fenwick died, who had the wardship and lands of Henry Fenwick, an idiot, granted him by Henry VIII., " for the holding of him and his kinsmen together, being a good band of men to do him service upon the middle marches."—Requests to have the wardship, during this time of war, to distribute the profits among the surname and allies of the Fenwicks. Desires no advantage for himself. My Lord of Winchester knows the value of the lands, and the men's services, by the letter which Dacre has written to the King. As the matter touches himself will pay the posts for this occasion, and has written to Bryan Tuke accordingly. At Kirkoswald, 12 March, at noon. *Signed and sealed.*

Add. : To my Lord of Norfolk's grace, my Lord Winchester, Lord Duresme, my Lord elect to Lincoln, and other my Lords of the King's most honorable council.

R. O.

2. To the same effect. The lands were let by Henry VII. for 40*l.* Kirkoswald, 12 March. *Signed.*

P. 1. *Add.*

12 March. **4871.** HENRY VIII. to LEO X.

Vat. Tran. xxxvii.
Addit. 15,387. f.17.
B. M.
Ellis, 3 S. 1. 165.

Desires his favor for the Observant Friars, who are troubled about certain convents in Cologne, &c. united to their order by Julius II. Cannot sufficiently express his admiration for their strict adherence to poverty, their sincerity, their charity, their devotion. No order battles against vice more assiduously ; none are more active in keeping Christ's fold. His ambassador, the Bishop of Worcester, will state the King's wishes more explicitly. Greenwich, 12 March 1513. *Lat. Add.*

1514.

12 March. **4872.** For ROBERT WHASHYNGTON, serjeant-at-arms, and AMY
S. B.   his wife.

Reversion of the manor of Westhorp, with the advowson and lands belonging, at the annual rent of one red rose. Edmund de la Poole late Earl of Suffolk held the same, but they are now held to the use of Margaret de la Poole, late wife of the said Edmund, by Sir Robert Drurye, Sir John Heydon, and Sir Edmund Gelget. *Del.* Otford, 12 March 5 Hen. VIII.

Pat. 5 Hen. VIII. p. 2, m. 23.

12 March. **4873.** For JOHN LYNDESEY, yeoman doorward of the King's
P. S.   gate.

Annuity of 10 marks out of the lordship of Denbigh, lately held by William ap David. Lambeth, 3 March 5 Hen. VIII. *Del.* Westm., 12 March.

Pat. 5 Hen. VIII. p. 2, m. 28.

14 March. **4874.** For JOHN SHURLEY, cofferer of the Household.
P. S.

Release of 2,126 pounds of silver, received from Sir John Daunce and John Morley, for providing and carrying the pavilions, tents, and other articles of the Household, and for other expenses, while the King was in foreign parts. Greenwich, 8 March 5 Hen. VIII. *Del.* Westm., 14 March.

Pat. 5 Hen. VIII. p. 2, m. 28.

14 March. **4875.** LOUIS XII.
Calig. D. vi. 111.
B. M.   Ratification of the truce for one year, made by Francis D. of
Rym. xiii. 395. Valois in behalf of France and Scotland, with Pet. de Quintane on the behalf of Ferdinand of Arragon, the Emperor Maximilian, Henry VIII., and Prince Charles, 13 March 1513. Orleans, 14 March 1513.

Pp. 7.

15 March. **4876.** CONVOCATION.
S. B.

Writ to William Abp. of Canterbury, Primate, Legate, and Chancellor, to summon a convocation of his diocese in St. Paul's, London. 15 March.

S. B.   2. Same to Christopher Abp. of York or his deputy. Convocation to meet in St. Peter's, York. 15 March.

15 March. **4877.** For THOMAS [WOLSEY] BP. OF LINCOLN.
P. S.

Grant of the sum, amounting nearly to 1,000*l.* a year, which the dean and chapter of Lincoln pay for custody of the temporalities of the bishopric of Lincoln, from 2 Jan. last, on which day William the late Bishop died, to the 4th inst., when the said Thomas obtained the restitution of the temporalities of the bishopric. Also grant of the knight's fees, wards, presentations, &c., belonging to the said bishopric. Greenwich, 10 March 5 Hen. VIII. *Del.* Westm. 15 March.

1514.
15 March. **4878.**   TREASURER'S ACCOUNTS.

R. O.

"Here ensueth the receipts of all such sums of money, obligations, and specialties as John Daunce, our servant, to our use and behoof hath received, from the 1st of July, the 3rd year of our reign, forward ;—as of all manner payments by the said John Daunce, by virtue of our warrants, commandment, or otherwise paid from the said first day of July forward, like as in two books thereupon made (one of them signed with our hand, and to the said John Daunce for his discharge in the premises delivered ; the other written and subscribed with the hand of the said John Daunce in our own custody, for our more perfect remembrance in that behalf remaining,) more at large is expressed and declared, as hereafter ensueth."

Received of John Heron, treasurer of the King's chamber, by virtue of a warrant under the King's signet, dated Windsor Castle, 25 Sept. the 3rd year of our reign, 1,000l. By warrant under sign manual, dated Richemounte, 25 Oct. 3 Hen. VIII., 1,000l. By warrant dated Greenwich, 24 Dec. 3 Hen. VIII., 1,000l. By warrant dated Westm., 2 Feb. 3 Hen. VIII. 2,000l.—Received of Thomas Balle and John Charles 200l. for the freight of *The Mary and John* on her voyage from London to Estland and back, 10 Feb.—Received of John Heron, treasurer, by warrant dated Greenwich, 22 April 4 Hen. VIII., 2,000l. And by warrant dated Greenwich, 25 July 4 Hen. VIII., 2,000l.—Received of Will. Roche, and other, upon an obligation 2 March, 100l. And of the same, 15 March 5 Hen. VIII., 100l.

Signed by the King.

15 March. **4879.**   For JOHN SAUNDERS, clk., native of Scotland.

S. B.

Denization. *Del.* Westm., 15 March 5 Hen. VIII.
Pat. 5 Hen. VIII. p. 2, m. 18.

15 March. **4880.**   For RICHARD EARL OF KENT.

P. S. b.

Protection for William Norton, retained to serve in the war. 28 Feb. 5 Hen. VIII. [*Del.*] Westm. 15 March. ' *Signed and sealed.*

15 March. **4881.**   For HUGH DEE, yeoman of the Crown.

P. S.

Grant, for 40 years, of the ulnage of woollen cloth of the town of Prestayne, Marches of Wales, *vice* Richard Weston. Greenwich, 7 March 5 Hen. VIII. *Del.* Westm., 15 March.
Pat. 5 Hen. VIII. p. 2, m. 1.

15 March. **4882.**   For CHARLES DUKE OF SUFFOLK.

P. S. b.

Protection for Mary Frauncys, of Antwerp in Brabant, widow, victualler in his retinue, attending the King in the war beyond the sea. 13 March 5 Hen. VIII. *Del.* Westm., 15 March. *Signed.*
Fr. 5 Hen. VIII. m. 1.

16 March. **4883.**   LOYS D'ORLEANS and THOMAS BOHIER to WOLSEY.

Calig. D. vi. 117.
B. M.
Rym. xiii. 399.

Have received between Sittingbourne and Canterbury a packet from France. Have despatched to M. Le President the letter addressed to him. He will inform Wolsey of the good feelings of Louis for Henry. Canterbury, 16 March. *Signed.*
Fr., p. 1. Add.: A Mons. Mons. de Lincone.

1514.

16 March. **4884.** For ROBERT LAWARD alias LORD, goldsmith of London,
S. B. clerk of Sir John Daunce.

Licence to import 2,000 tuns of Gascon wine, and 4,000 tons of
Toulouse woad. *Del.* Westm., 16 March 5 Hen. VIII.
Fr. 5 Hen. VIII. m. 17.

16 March. **4885.** TOURNAY.
S. B.

Licence to the inhabitants of Tournay to trade with England
as others of the King's subjects. Greenwich, 16 March 1513.
5 Hen. VIII.
Fr.

R. T. 144. 2. Letters patent for the above.
R. O.

16 March. **4886.** For SIR RICHARD HASTYNGES.
S. B. Protection. Westm., 22 Feb. 5 Hen. VIII. *Del.* Westm., 16 March.
Fr. 5 Hen. VIII. m. 17.

17 March. **4887.** FRANCIS MARQUIS OF MANTUA, Gonfalonier, to CHRIS-
R. O. TOPHER [BAINBRIDGE] CARDINAL OF YORK.

Thanks him for this further obligation in procuring him the
King's favor ; is very anxious to show his gratitude, and has requested the King's equerry (*scudier*) Thomas to take as many horses
as he pleased. Has shown him over the stables, requesting him to
take what he liked, which he declined. Wishes to present the
King with a pair or more of the best horses he has, which he will
send with one of his servants, and asks the Cardinal to represent
it to the King as coming from one of his most devoted servants.
He and Frederic are equally obliged to the Cardinal. Mantua,
17 March 1514.
Hol., Ital., p. 1. *Sealed. Add.:* "Domino patri honoratissimo,
Domino Christofero Ebor. . . . S^d Petri et . . . presbitero Car^{li}."

17 March. **4888.** For JOHN GRANTHAM, mercer of London.
P. S. Protection ; going in the retinue of Sir Richard Wyngfeld,
Deputy of Calais. Lambeth, 8 March 5 Hen. VIII. *Del.* Westm.,
17 March 6 Hen. VIII.
Fr. 5 Hen. VIII. m. 16.

17 March. **4889.** ENGLAND and DENMARK.
S. B. Ratification of a treaty of peace between Hen. VII. and John
King of Denmark, Norway, and Sweden, concluded 22 (?)* Aug.
1489, 4 Hen. VII. Westm., 17 March 1513, 5 Hen. VIII.

17 March. **4890.** GAOL DELIVERY.
Cambridge Gaol.—Commission to Wm. Barbour, mayor, John
Parys, John Woode, Wm. Colyn, John Hynde, Hugh Chapma[n],
John Bury, and John Erlyche. Westm., 17 Ma[rch].
Pat. 5 Hen. VIII. p. 2, *m.* 16*d.*

* Or 30 ?

1514.

18 March. **4891.** For RICHARD FITZ-JAMES BISHOP OF LONDON, and
S. B.   JOHN ISLYPPE ABBOT OF ST. PETER'S, WESTMINSTER.

Next collation to the prebend in the chapel of St. Stephen,
Westminster.

Pat. 5 Hen. VIII. p. 2, m. 18. Westm., 18 March.

18 March. **4892.** For JOHN MIKLOWE, THOMAS BYRKES, and BRIAN
P. S.   ROCHE.

Release of 20,910*l.* 16*s.* 10*d.*, received by them through Sir
John Daunce, for purveying provisions for the army abroad;
—and of 392*l.* 15*s.*, received by sale of a part of the said provisions; and of various quantities of flour, malt, beer, flitches of
bacon, &c. received by them from William Browne, jun., Richard
Fermour and George Medley, merchants of the staple of Calais,
John Ricrofte and John Heron, surveyor of customs, &c. in the
port of London. Greenwich, 9 March 5 Hen. VIII. *Del.* Westm.,
18 March.

Pat. 5 Hen. VIII. p. 2, m. 25.

18 March. **4893.** For THOMAS GOLDSMYTH and THOMAS his son, grocers
P. S.   of London.

Protection; going in the suite of Sir Richard Wyngefeld,
Deputy of Calais. Greenwich, 12 March 5 Hen. VIII. *Del.*
Westm., 18 March.

Fr. 5 Hen. VIII. m. 16.

18 March. **4894.** OXEN AND SHEEP.

Commission to Nicholas Carter, yeoman purveyor of the Household, to provide oxen and sheep for the household, and for victualling the land forces about to go to foreign parts, during the next
six months. Westm., 18 March.

ii. Similar commission to Philip Taillour, yeoman purveyor of
the Household. Westm., 18 March.

iii. Commission to Ric. Wodeward to provide oxen and sheep,
with forage and carriage for the same, for the land forces going
abroad, for the next six months. Westm., 18 March.

Pat. 5 Hen. VIII. p. 2, m. 16d.

18 March. **4895.** For HUGH STANFELD.

Protection; going to the war. Westm., 18 March.

Fr. 5 Hen. VIII. m. 10.

19 March. **4896.** TOURNAY.
S. B.

Grant to the town of Tournay of all debts and pensions due
from it to persons residing in hostile countries. Greenwich,
19 March 1513, 5 Hen. VIII.

Fr.

R. T. 144.   Letters patent of the above.
R. O.

1514.

19 March. **4897.** For AMBROSE BRADMAN.
S. B.
To be serjeant-at-arms, with 12d. a day. *Del.* Westm., 19 March 5 Hen. VIII.
Pat. 5 Hen. VIII. p. 2, m. 23.

19 March. **4898.** For the MAYOR and CORPORATION of NORTHAMPTON.
P. S.
Release of the yearly sum of 22l., out of their fee farm of 120l. a year. Greenwich, 18 March 5 Hen. VIII. *Del.* Westm., 19 March.
Pat. 5 Hen. VIII. p. 2, m. 27.

19 March. **4899.** For ROBERT LORD CURSON, master of the ordnance in
P. S. b.
the Rearward.
Protection for Hugh Stanfeld, retained to serve in the war. 19 March 5 Hen. VIII. *Signed and sealed.*

20 March. **4900.** For JOHN FELDE of London, cook.
S. B.
Protection, whether native of England or Scotland, as he has resided in London 40 years. *Del.* Westm., [20 March] 5 Hen. VIII. *Mutilated.*
Pat. 5 Hen. VIII. p. 2, m. 28.

20 March. **4901.** For JOHN TREGYAN.
S. B.
Licence to export ox and cow hides, commonly called salt-hides, of the county of Cornwall. All others are prohibited from carrying any such hides out of the said county during the life of the said John. *Del.* Westm., 20 March 5 Hen. VIII.
Pat. 5 Hen. VIII. p. 2, m. 19.

20 March. **4902.** THOMAS LORD DARCY to HENRY VIII.
Calig. B. II. 323.
B. M.
Has received his two letters, the first dated Greenwich, 7 March demanding his answer to a bill enclosed to my Lady of Savoy by the friends of Adrian Baiellvelle, one of his prisoners. Encloses his answer. In the second, of the 10th March, the King declares his pleasure for fortifying Berwick Castle. There is no lack of ordinary soldiers except such as are absent on furlough. All is in accordance with his indentures of the last 18 years. As to the complaint that the King pays for 50 gunners, and there are not more than six, Darcy acknowledges there are not more than 20, but Wm. Pawne is master of the ordnance, and has in his retinue 54 gunners, and cannot obtain more, as all have gone to the wars; but he has offered to instruct such soldiers in the garrison "as were lusty to learn," with the King's assent. To save powder, Darcy would not allow them to shoot. Hopes, whatever gunners are allowed, they will be Englishmen and not strangers. Trusts that reports against him be not easily credited, considering how well he served the King's father. There is no truth in the statement made by the mayor and corporation of the town. When a siege was expected they ran away. He has had great difficulty "to make them take sad order and accord amongst themselves." My Lord of Winchester knows them and their acts full well. In consequence of their discord, "every of

3 c

them improwde upon other his ferme of fishing." They pay
60*l.* per year more rent to the King than when Darcy was first
captain of Berwick, and are too impoverished to find provisions for
soldiers.

On Friday, 10th March, the Scotch burnt five towns in the East
Marches. On Saturday they came within two miles of Berwick.
They were seen lying fore against "foorthes," when my Lord
Dacres sent a chaplain of his to the council of Berwick, desiring
[the] Scots' ordnance to be conveyed to Belford. If he had
complied, it would have fallen into their hands. The Scots are
ready to lay siege to Berwick, and only wait for Albany's coming
with the French and the Danes, as he has written before. It is
impossible for him to comply with the King's demand to furnish
Berwick with 500 men, and in company with his cousin Sir Ralph
Eure attend the King in his journey over sea, not leaving his son
deputy in his absence. His son shall leave in all convenient haste.
In the short time he has been there he has done more to annoy the
Scots than has been done on all the three Marches.

Sir Ralph Eure has received the King's letter to take the
deputyship at Berwick, and begs to decline, as he cannot have his
health there because of the cold weather and the sea air. He would
gladly serve the King in any other part of the world. His son
desires to attend the King over sea. "I have no moo but him and
his brother and myself; and for God is sake, sir, spare none of us
all, for I am sure, as I shewed your grace, of the best heir in England and all three fail, and that is your noble grace." Had not
written before, waiting news from Scotland. It would be better if
he was at liberty in Yorkshire than shut up in the town. At his
intercession all the nobles and commons have shown themselves
most zealous to serve. Sir Thos. Burgh, Sir Ralph Ellerker the
father, and the son Sir Wm. Eure, or Sir Richard Mauliverer are
willing to be his deputies. The Pope's secretary has been there.
Templehurst, 20 March. *Signed.*

Pp. 5. *Addressed:* To the King's, &c., grace.
Endorsed: The Lord Darcy's letter.

20 March. **4903.** For SIR WILLIAM BULMER.
P. S.

Wardship of Anne and Elizabeth Aske, kinswomen and heirs
of William Aske, viz., daughters of Roger, son of the said William. Greenwich, 20 March 5 Hen. VIII. *Del.* Westm., 20 March.

Pat. 5 *Hen.VIII. p.* 2, *m.* 27.

21 March. **4904.** For SIR WILLIAM COMPTON.
S. B.

Grant, in fee, of the manor of Aldewyncle, Northt., called
Holandes Maner; a wood there called Bareshanke; and lands in
Brantsy and Swyllingholne in Aldewyncle; granted by patent
22 March 2 Hen. VII. to Margaret Countess of Richmond, and
afterwards to Sir John Risley, by patent 11 March 3 Hen. VII.,
after the attainder of Francis Viscount Lovel. Risley died without
heirs male. *Del.* Westm., 21 March 5 Hen. VIII.

21 March. **4905.** For JOHN DAVY of Southampton.

Protection; going to the war. Westm., 21 March.

Fr. 5 *Hen.VIII. m.* 10.

1514.

22 March. **4906.** For WILLIAM IVEE, deputy of Sir Sampson Norton,
P. S. b.   master of the King's ordnance in the vanguard beyond
           the sea.

Protection for Sir John Rickard, chaplain, alias Sir John Richardi
Clivensis in Almayne, clk., in the said Sir Sampson's retinue.
17 March 5 Hen. VIII. [*Del.*] Waltham, 22 March. *Ivee's
mark.*

22 March. **4907.** For SIR WILLIAM COMPTON and SIR WISTAN BROWNE.
S. B.   Grant, in survivorship, of the offices of steward, chancellor, and
          surveyor of the manors of Haverford West and Rowse, in the
          Marches of Wales; and keeper of the "magnus canolus" called "le
          Toyle," alias "le Pale of Canvas;"—with an annuity of 100 marks.
          Del. Waltham, 22 March 5 Hen. VIII.
          Pat. 5 Hen. VIII. p. 2, m. 24.

22 March. **4908.** For ROBT. [LORD CURSON.]
P. S. b. Writ to be issued to the sheriff of London, commanding him to
          release Roger . . . . . ., servant of the said Robert, arrested for
          debt by John Morres of London, baker, contrary to law, the said
          Roger having been retained to serve in the war as an overseer of
          the ordnance about to pass over to Calais. Morres had refused to
          discharge his action at the instance of John Bryges, sheriff of
          London.* *Signed:* Robar[t Corson.] *Sealed.*

23 March. **4909.** For SIR WILLIAM SYDNEY.
P. S.   Grant, in tail male, of the lordship of Kyngeston-upon-Hull, and
          the manor of Myton, forfeited by Edmund De la Pole, attainted.
          Tournay, 3 Oct. 5 Hen. VIII. *Del.* Westm., 23 (?) March.
          Pat. 5 Hen. VIII. p. 2, m. 2.

24 March. **4910.** JAMES WILLINGER to MARGARET OF SAVOY.
Lett. de Louis XII. Peace was concluded at Rome on the 11th, between the Emperor
t. IV. 290. and the Venetians. Has received a letter from Phintzing, men-
          tioning her answer about the delay of the delivery of the 30,000
          crowns from England. It is but a small sum for the Emperor, but
          will be a great hindrance. Leaves in four days to go to the Emperor.
          Augsburg, 24 March, '13.
          Fr.

24 March. **4911.** For KATHARINE SEMAR, late of Cheping Walden, widow,
P. S.   THOMAS STRACHY, JAMES BODLEY, WILLIAM BIRR
          and NICHOLAS RUTLAND, all of Walden aforesaid.

Licence to found a guild in honor of the Trinity, in the church
of St. Mary, Walden, to consist of one treasurer, two chamberlains,
brethen and sisters, of the parishioners of Walden; with mortmain
licence to acquire lands to the annual value of 20 marks, for a
chaplain to pray daily for the King and Queen Katharine, for
Katharine Semar, Thomas Wulcy, late almoner to the King, Joan
Bradbury, widow, John Leche, vicar of the said church, the said
Thomas [Strachy] and Joan his wife, James Bodley and Joan his
wife, William Bird and Anabella his wife, and Nicholas Rutland

---

* John Bryges was sheriff of London from Mich. 5 to Mich. 6 Hen. VIII.

1514.

and Clemence his wife ; and for the souls of Thomas Bodley, William Lawnselyn and Alice his wife, Walter Cook and Katharine his wife, Roger Pyrk and Joan his wife, Thomas Semar and Margery his wife, Nicholas, Thomas and Katharine, children of the said Katharine Semar, George Thoorne and Florence his wife, John Strachy and Alice his wife, Thomas Thoorne and Joan his wife, and Richard Mynott. . . . . 5 Hen. VIII.   *Del.* Westm., 24 March.

Pat. 5 Hen. VIII. p. 2, m. 24.

24 March. **4912.**   For WILLIAM SAUNDERS.
S. B.

Wardship of George, son and heir of John Belgrave, late of Blaby, Leic.   *Del.* Westm., 24 March 5 Hen. VIII.   *Signed:* Thomas Lovell.

Pat. 5 Hen. VIII. p. 1, m. 7.

24 March. **4913.**   For WILLIAM BROWNE.
S. B.

Commission to provide wagons for conveying the furniture of the King's army into France.   Greenwich, 24 March 5 Hen. VIII.
Fr.

24 March. **4914.**   For THOMAS PROWDE.
S. B.

Commission to provide wagons for conveying the artillery and other furniture of the King's army.   Greenwich, 24 March 5 Hen. VIII.
Fr.

26 March. **4915.**   SIR ROB. WINGFIELD to HENRY VIII.
R. O.

Wrote last on the 24th. The Emperor desires him to write in favor of the bearer, Michael de Clerfayi, who was brought up with King Philip, has served the Emperor in Italy, and been with the late Lord Walleyn, can bring 100 horses, and will act as lieutenant under Wingfield. Hopes the King will find ambassadors who can serve better than he. The office of Marshal of Calais is more suited to a man of war. Trusts that De Clerfayi will receive a favorable answer. "Lynce in Ostryke," 26 March 1514.
Hol., pp. 2. Add. Endd.

26 March. **4916.**   MATTHEW CARDINAL SION to CHR. [BAINBRIDGE] CAR-
R. O.   DINAL OF ENGLAND.

Has used his utmost diligence to dissuade the Swiss from abandoning the league, and making alliance with the French. Petrus Magni will tell him more. A rumor has been circulated that side means (*a latere*) have been used in settling a peace between the Emperor, France, and England. Is reluctant to go to Switzerland. Does not believe it. It would be an unmeet return to the Swiss. They cannot support a war with the French, the enemies of the Church, through poverty, as he has seen "*ante Duvionem.*" "Ex Viglo, vii. kl. April 1514." *Signed* at Dijon.
Lat., pp. 2. Addressed: "Rmo. etc. Chro. S. R. E. Presbytero Car^ll Anglico."

27 March. **4917.**   ASSAY OF ENGLISH AND FLEMISH COIN.
R. O.

i. Instructions by my Lady the Archduchess of Austria, for Thomas Grammay general of the mint, and John Dewsbrocke assayer at Burges, in answer to a letter received from Henry VIII. 25 Feb., requesting that the English pound sterling shall be current

1514.

for 35s. gross Flanders money, as before the King's landing at Calais. States the reasons why she declines to accede. Brussels, Feb. 20, 1513.

Modern copy, pp. 6.

R. O.

2. A report, addressed to the Lords of the council, of " the assayes of gold and of silver made in London at the Goldsmiths Hall, the 27th day of March, the 5th year of the reign of our said Sovereign Lord King Henry VIII, before his officers of the mint of the Tower of London; that is to say, William Stafford, warden of the mint, Rob. Amadas, deputy for the Lord Mountjoy, mint master, and Tho. Aunsham, deputy comptroller for Sir Hen. Wyott, knt.; and being there present, Rob. Fenrother of London, alderman and goldsmith, Nich. Warley, Rob. Preston, and Garrard Hewys, wardens of the occupation of goldsmith[s] in the said city of London, and John Jonys, commyn assayer of the same, and Hugh Say, servant to the said Lord Mountjoy, maker of this reckoning; and also in the presence of Tho. Grammay, general of the mint in Flanders, and John David Wosbroke, particular assayer of the said mint, sent unto our said Sovereign Lord from the Lady Margaret Archduchess of Austriche &c.; for the evaluation of the moneys of our Sovereign Lord foresaid, to have course in the countries of the Archduke, and for to know and make proof of the differences of fineness between them and the toisan of gold of Flanders, and toysan of silver with also the double stever of silver, as by articles of the same more at large doth appear."

Pp. 5. Endorsed: " Assayes of golde and silver betwixte the coyne of the realme of England and the toysan of Flaunders." *Also in a modern hand:* " Copied this for Mr. Newton, master of the mint, 1701."

3. Copy of the two preceding documents in an early 17th century hand; the last dated London, 14 April 1513, before Easter.

---

27 March. **4918.**
S. B.

For THOMAS REDE, clk., D.D., rector of Bekles church and WILLIAM REDE, of Bekles, Suff., merchant.

Licence to found a chantry for one chaplain, to the honor of St. Mary and St. Michael in the said church; and mortmain licence to acquire lands to the annual value of 10l. *Del.* Westm., 27 March 5 Hen. VIII.

Pat. 5 *Hen. VIII. p.* 2, *m.* 25.

---

27 March. **4919.**
P. S.

For WILLIAM STEPHYNSON, native of Scotland.

Denization. Greenwich, 22 March 5 Hen. VIII. *Del.* Otford, 27 March.

Pat. 5 *Hen. VIII. p.* 2, *m.* 25.

---

28 March. **4920.**
Vitell. B. II. 75.
B. M.
Rym. XIII. 399.

The MARQUIS OF MANTUA to HENRY VIII.

Has often requested from the Cardinal of York at Rome some opportunity of expressing his desire to serve the King. By the Cardinal's suggestion has received a visit from Thomas P . ., the King's messenger returning to England; and hearing of the King's delight in good horses, had opened his stables, and allowed him to choose what he liked for the King's use. As the messenger in modesty declined, has chosen four of his best horses, and sent them to the King by his servant Giovanni Ratti. His wife and children send their compliments. Mantua, 28 March 1514. *Signed.*

P. 1. *Address at f.* 68b. *Endorsed.*

1514.

29 March. **4921.** [The DUKE OF MILAN to HENRY VIII.]

Vitell. B. II. 74.
B. M.

Will never forget that he has been restored to his dukedom by the efforts of Henry and his confederates. Is glad to hear that Henry has recovered from his severe illness. France and the King Catholic made a truce on the 13th March at Orleans, and have confirmed it by betrothing the second daughter of France to Don Ferdinand. Can scarcely believe it, as he was bound to fulfil his promise to England. The writer's honor and interest are equally concerned. Does not write this from any doubt of Henry's intentions, but only to show his own constancy.

Added in his own hand: Earnestly begs the King will support him. Wishes for nothing more than to show his gratitude. Milan, 29 March 1514. *Signed.*

Lat., pp. 2, mutilated.

30 March. **4922.** LEO X. to HENRY VIII.

Vitell. B. II. 70.
B. M.
Rym. XIII. 400.

Requesting alms for redemption from captivity of Lancelot, father of Gonsalvo Pinto, taken prisoner with others by the Infidels at the storming of Arquila in Africa. Rome, 30 March 1514.

Add. Lat. Vellum.

30 March. **4923.** For THOMAS BENET, of Stretford, Suff., clothier.

P. S.

Protection; going in the retinue of Sir Richard Wyngfed, Deputy of Calais. Greenwich, 26 March 5 Hen. VIII. *Del.* Otford, 30 March.

Fr. 5 Hen. VIII. m. 16.

31 March. **4924.** TREATY between the KING OF FRANCE and the PRINCE

Calig. E. I. 136.
B. M.

OF CASTILE.

Notification by the commissioners for France, Anthoine du Prat, chancellor of France, Je[han] Conte de Rethel, Sieur Dorval, chevalier de l'ordre du Roy, Sieur de Lautrec, lieutenant of Guienne, René [Duke of] Savoy, Count de Villars and d'Etende, and Ymbert de Bateru . . . Boucharge, also chevalier de l'ordre, of the confederates to be included : sc. on the part of the Prince of Castile, the Pope, Emperor, Kings of Arragon, England, Hungary, Denmark, Portugal; Dukes George of Saxony, Lorraine, Savoy, Cleves, Juliers ; the Bishops, Dukes, &c. of Cambray, Liege, and Utrecht ; the Count Hornes, the Swiss, the cities of . . . . the Count of Meurs (?), the adherents of Gueldres, &c. On the part of the French, in addition to some already mentioned, the Kings of Scotland and Navarre, the Dukes of Savoy, Gueldres, and Lorraine, the Doge of Venice, the Seigneurie of Florence, the Duke of Ferrara, the Marquises of Mantua, Montferrat, Salusses, the Sieur de Montfort, the estates of the Low Countries, and the Sieur de Sedan. Paris, 31 March 15 . ., avant Pasques.

Signed: Du Pra[t], Dalebret, Odet de Foix, the Bastard of Savoy, Ymbert de Ba . . . .

Fr. Copy, pp. 3, mutilated. *Endorsed.*

31 March. **4925.** For EDWARD MATTHEW.

P. S.

Licence to import 100 tuns of Gascon wine. Town of Huchyn, 17 Sept. 5 Hen. VIII. *Del.* Otford, 31 March.

Fr. 5 Hen. VIII. m. 17.

1514.
31 March. **4926.** LEO X. to HENRY VIII.

R. O.
Had written to the King last month for release of the woad belonging to the Florentine merchants, detained in the port of Dover. Requests an indemnity for the sureties in order to its immediate delivery. Rome, 31 March 1514, 2 pont.

Lat., p. 1. *Add.*

March. **4927.** COMMISSION OF THE PEACE.

Kent.—W. Abp. of Canterbury, Edw. Duke of Buckingham, Hen. Earl of Wiltshire, Geo. Nevell Lord Bergevenny, John Lord Clinton, Sir John Fyneux, Sir Rob. Rede, Sir Wm. Hody, John Butler, John More, Sir Edw. Ponynges, Sir John Pecche, Sir Christ. Garneys, Rob. Blagge, Sir Ric. Cholmeley, Sir Wm. Scott, Sir John Wiltes, Sir Wm. Crowmer, Sir John Fogge, Sir Edw. Guldeford, Thos. Nevell, Thos. Willoughby, Thos. Isley, Ralph Sentleger, Walter Roberth, John Roper, Wm. Fyneux, Nich. Boughton, Alex. Culpeper, Thos. Turbervyle, Reginald Pekham, Hen. Fane, John Engeham, Thos. Woode, Wm. Whetnall, Edw. Culpeper, Ric. Lee, John Monen, John Halys, and John Petyt. Westm., . . March.

Pat. 5 Hen. VIII. p. 1, *m.* 6*d.*

1 April. **4928.** SPINELLY'S CREDENCE for ROB. BARON to the LORDS of R. O. the COUNCIL.

1. To ask for letters; 2, their favor for Cotingham; 3, to explain the great charges ; 4, to recover 50*l.* due to him for the half year ended Christmas last.

1 April. **4929.** SPINELLY to WOLSEY.

R. O.
Wrote last on the 28th. Heard from the master of the posts that Wolsey is discontented with him for spreading certain reports against him, which he denies. It would have been "very grete uterquydaunce" to have done so. Will do whatever Wolsey directs. Begs his servant Baron may return with money ; if he is dead, that it may be delivered to Rob. Bishop, servant of Master Deputy of Calais. Has sent money to the compaignon retained in the King's wages in France, at 4*l.* a month. The Emperor is displeased with my Lady. Cannot understand his "confusse dealing." Thinks he must declare his mind soon. Mechlin, 1 April 1513.

Signed.

Pp. 2. *Addressed :* [To the] Right Hon., &c. my Lord of Lincoln.

1 April. **4930.** SIR RIC. WINGFIELD to WOLSEY.

R. O.
Has sent his servant Bishop. Sir Thos. Spinelly. understands from Brian Tuke that Wolsey is much offended. Assures Wolsey of Spinelly's fidelity. Would not have written in his behalf, had he not full trust in his honesty. Malyns, 1 April.

Hol., p. 1. *Addressed :* [T]o my syngwlar good [L]ord my Lord of Lyncollne.

2 April. **4931.** ST. MARY'S BISHOPSGATE.

R. O.
Receipt by Richard Cressall, prior of the new hospital of Our Lady Bishopsgate Without, for 20 marks had of Sir John Cutte, undertreasurer, for the rent of a house near the said hospital, for making gunpowder. 2 April 6 Hen. VIII. *Sealed.*

1514.
3 April.
Galba, B. III. 143.
B. M.

4932. KNIGHT to [WOLSEY].

Begs he will not be surprised that he has not written oftener. They send the news daily to the King. Those about the Prince of Castile would gladly hinder his marriage with the Lady Mary, saying, he is a child, and she a woman full grown. Unless the King, when the marriage is solemnized, have these officers discharged, my Lady Mary will be in great hazard. Had a meeting this day with the Marquis of Brandenburg, De Chievres, and the Prince of Simaye, brother to the late King of Navarre. Paid his duty in the King's behalf to the Count Palatine,—who was of the company,—but "had no communication with him touching his entertainment at this time." Writes in behalf of John Newington, mercer of London, a factor for the writer and others, who is in great credit, "and did commit great charges by way of brokerage unto Richard Thyrkill," a broker, who has suddenly departed, to the great injury of Newington, the writer's kinsman. He is kept by the influence of this man, who distributes goods to the "young gentlemen now being in garrison at Tournay," from seeing the Governor and obtaining justice. He not only defrauds but defames his superiors, "as Copland hath said [to me that] the said Thyrkill hath right undiscreetly abusing his tongue against your Lordship." Sends him the "patrone of her that is mediatrix of us all." Begs for money for his diet. Has heard that he is displeased with Thomas Spinelly, because "it is persuaded that he should diminish the good opinion that my Lady Margaret hath of your lordship." Defends him from the charge. As many will be desirous to creep into his favor, they will not spare detraction. Mechline, 3 April.

Hol. pp. 4, mutilated.

3 April.
P. S.

4933. For SIR JOHN TREMAYLE.

Annuity of 20 marks out of the lordship of Marke and Oye, Calais. Greenwich, 10 March 5 Hen. VIII. *Del.* Otford, 3 April. *Pat. 5 Hen. VIII. p. 2, m. 25.*

3 April.

4934. For ELIZABETH OSBOURNE, lady of the manor of Wytte feld.

Inspeximus and exemplification of patent 12 Feb. 21 Hen. VI., inspecting and exemplifying at request of John Scotusbury, lord of the said manor, patent 30 April 16 Edw. III., inspecting and exemplifying at request of Gilbert de Imworth, then lord of the said manor, an inquisition taken before Roger Extraneus (le Strange), Peter de Lench, and John son of Nigel, justices-in-eyre of the forest in co. Northt., 15 Edw. I., wherein John de Finchewyk, forester of Wyttlewod, and other officers, question whether Peter de Montibus should have estovers and other liberties in the wood of Haselberwe and manor of Wittefeld. It was decided that he should. Otford, 3 April 1514.

Pat. 5 Hen. VIII. p. 2, m. 24.

4 April.
R. O.

4935. SIR RIC. WINGFIELD, WILL. KNYGHTE and THOS. SPINELLY to NORFOLK, FOX, and WOLSEY.

Have advertised the King by this post of the news sent by the Archduchess touching the Swiss and the discontent in Brittanny. The latter is confirmed by the Bastard of Cleves. Advise that the Lord of Roham be written to. If he place in the King's hands

1514.

the castle of Brest, it will afford great facilities for landing an army. Since the conquest of Brittany the French have left the country undefended. Mechlin, 4 April 1514. *Signed.*

Addressed : To the Right Honorables, &c. my Lords, the Duke of Norfolk, Winchester, and Lincoln.

Hol., p. 1.

4 April. **4936.** SILVESTER BP. OF WORCESTER to WOLSEY.

Vitell. B. II. 71.
B. M.

Has done the utmost he could to expedite his faculty for holding benefices of 2,000*l.* (*obtinendi beneficia pro duobus mil[libus] libris*). To have obtained it *de integro* would have cost 1,000*l.* Was rejoiced to hear of his promotion to Lincoln, and when ordered to execute his commission, and obtain a diminution of the annates, had done it with as much economy as if it had been his own affair. Is disappointed to find that Wolsey is dissatisfied, and complains that De Giglis has spent 1,000 ducats more than usual. He calls God to witness that he has expedited the matter faithfully, and spent more than 50 ducats out of his own purse. Begs he will not credit his maligners. If the account be not correct, will forfeit his head. Hopes to receive some letter to console him. Herewith Wolsey will receive a brief from the Pope. Has written fully to Andreas Ammonius, who will show his letters to Wolsey and Fox. Rome, [4] April 1514. *Signed.*

Lat., pp. 3. *Add. :* T. electo Lincolniensi.

4 April. **4937.** For JOHN WYTEWODE, clerk of the Chapel Royal.

S. B.

Presentation to the church of Bockard, Guysnes, void by death. *Del.* Otford, 4 April 5 Hen. VIII.

Pat. 5 *Hen. VIII. p.* 2, *m.* 24.

4 April. **4938.** For THOS. FRENDE.

Protection ; going to the war. Westm., 4 April.

Fr. 5 *Hen. VIII. m.* 10.

4 April. **4939.** ARRAY.

S. B.

Commission of array to the Earl of Shrewsbury, steward of the Household, in the counties of Derby, Stafford, and Salop, for the army about to cross the sea. The Earl to command the men raised in those counties. *Del.* Otford, 4 April, 5 Hen. VIII.

Pat. 5 *Hen. VIII. p.* 2, *m.* 22d.

4 April. **4940.** To JOHN YONG, Master of the Rolls.

S. B.

To cancel recognizance of 800*l.* made by Sir William Pierpount of Holme, Notts, Sir Henry Clifford of Craven, York, Sir Robert Throkmerton of Coghton, Warw., John Diron (*sic*) of Colwyk, Notts, Thomas Clyfford of Aspeden, Herts., Robert Warcop of Warcop, Westmorl., John Constable of Fleynburgh, York, William Pole of Pole, Derby, and Thomas Emson of London, 18 Dec. 4 Hen. VIII. Greenwich, 4 April 5 Hen. VIII. *Del.* Otford, 4 April 5 Hen. VIII.

1514.

4 April.
S. B.

4941. For ROLAND PHYLYPPYS, clk., the King's chaplain.

Presentation to the church of Craford, Kent, dioc. Canterbury, void by death of William Fitzherbard. The advowson and next presentation to the church were granted by Thomas Kyngeston, by deed, 8 Feb. 17 Hen. VII., to Richard Emson, but came into the King's hands by his attainder. *Del.* Otford, 4 April 5 Hen. VIII.

4 April.
S. B.

4942. For RALPH LUPTON, clk., M.A.

Presentation to the church of Toryngton, Exeter dioc., at the King's disposal, by promotion of Thomas Bp. of Lincoln (Wolsey). *Del.* Otford, 4 April 5 Hen. VIII.

Pat. 5 *Hen. VIII. p.* 2, *m.* 24.

5 April.
S. B.

4943. For WILLIAM BLAKE, yeoman of the Crown.

Lease, for 20 years, of a parcel of land called " Scorby feldes," part of the lordship of Shirefhotton, York ; woods and underwoods reserved. *Del.* Croydon, 5 April 5 Hen. VIII.

Pat. 5 *Hen. VIII. p.* 2, *m.* 26.

5 April.
P. S.

4944. For JOHN COMPTON of Copeland, in the parish of Irton, Cumb., weaver.

Pardon. Greenwich, 23 March 5 Hen. VIII. *Del.* Croydon, 5 April.

Pat. 5 *Hen. VIII. p.* 2, *m.* 25.

7 April.
P S. b.

4945. For RICHARD EARL OF KENT.

Protection for John Sampier, of Shrewsbury, alias of London, petty captain in the Earl's retinue. London, 7 April. *Signed.*

Fr. 5 *Hen. VIII. m.* 10.

8 April.
S. B.

4946. For SIR WILLIAM COMPTON.

To be steward of the possessions of Eleanor late Duchess of Somerset, called " Cooperceners landes " ; and of the manors of Tomworth, Astonthynk, Stonydelf, Wilmecote, and Pollcsworth ; as Sir Robert Southwell, late steward, held the same. *Del.* Croydon, 8 April 5 Hen. VIII.

Pat. 5 *Hen. VIII. p.* 2, *m.* 27.

8 April.
S. B.

4947. For BARTHOLOMEW TATE, lancer of Calais.

Annuity of 20*l.*, and 60*l.* as a mark of the King's regard, out of the issues of the said town. *Del.* Croydon, 8 April 5 Hen. VIII.

Pat. 5 *Hen. VIII. p.* 2, *m.* 24.

. 8 April.
P. S.

4948. For CHRISTOPHER COO.

To be bailiff of the manors of Saham Tony, Panworth Halle, and Little Cressingham, Norf., and of the hundreds of Wayland and Grymeshawe, Norf. ; and keeper of Saham Tony park. Greenwich, 4 April 5 Hen. VIII. *Del.* Croydon, 8 April.

Pat. 5 *Hen. VIII. p.* 2, *m.* 24.

1514.

8 April. **4949.** For CHRISTOPHER ROCHESTRE, groom of the chamber.

P. S.   Corrody in Glastonbury monastery, as held by Wm. Lynche. Lambeth, 3 March 5 Hen. VIII. *Del.* Westm., 8 April.

8 April. **4950.** For ST. PETER'S, GLOUCESTER.

P. S.   Congé d'élire to the prior and convent of the monastery of St. Peter, Gloucester, on the death of John Newton, D.D., abbot. Greenwich, 4 April 5 Hen. VIII. *Del.* Croydon, 8 April.

   Pat. 5 Hen. VIII. p. 2, m. 24.

   ii. Petition of John Chedworth the prior, and the convent, for the above. 31 March 5 Hen. VIII.

8 April. **4951.** DACRE to HENRY VIII.

Calig. B. III. 26.   Promised in his last, sent by post on the 18th March, to let the

B. M.   King know the answer of the gentlemen of the East Marches as to the formation of garrisons for defence of the Borders. It was, however, so small in substance, that he waited for news from Scotland. They wish the King to bear the expence. Sends the book by post. On the breaking up of the Council of Scotland on the 5th, the parliament was continued to the 15th May. They have enacted, (1,) that all fortresses in Scotland shall be delivered to the keeping of the three estates; (2,) that the Earl of Crawford shall be chief justice beyond Forth, and the Lord Chamberlain on this side. The bill for the Duke of Albany's restitution was read, but is not yet determined. A herald will be sent to England to demand safe-conduct for ambassadors, on the pretence that some of those mentioned in the last are sick ; really to prolong the time till they know if Albany is coming, in which case they will send none. They have despatched Islay herald by the West coast, to invite him to come secretly and be their protector. Wallace, a servant of Albany's, arrived at Leith on Sunday last in a little bark, and was despatched again on Wednesday last " by the narrow see." The Prothonotary sent to Scotland did not pass Coldingham till they knew his message, when he was conveyed to the Chancellor and Bp. of Aberdeen. He will be detained till the 15th May to be answered by parliament. The Queen has taken her chamber in Stirling Castle. If the French King please to marry her he can have her. Carlisle Castle, 8 April. *Signed.*

   Pp. 2. Addressed: To the King's grace. *Endd.*

8 April. **4952.** MAXIMILIAN to MARGARET OF SAVOY.

R. O.   Has received her letters stating that the King of Arragon's ambassador had advertised her that Quintana had arranged a year's truce between the Emperor, Arragon, England, and Charles on the one part, and the King of France on the other. The truth is, he had come and proposed certain articles to the Emperor, which were not satisfactory. The ambassador of the King of Arragon had told him that Quintana had concluded a truce between the Emperor and the King of France for a year. Certain propositions had been made by Ureas for a peace ; sc., that the King of England should be satisfied with the government of Scotland ; that France should assist in the total destruction of the Venetians, the recovery of Gueldres, and give his daughter Renée to Don Fernando ; that he should disavow all claim to Naples, and assist Arragon in his claim on Navarre. The Pope has promised to make peace between the Emperor and the Venetians, which is only a pretext for a confederation between France, the Swiss, and the states of Italy to obtain from France a renunciation of the claim upon Naples in behalf of Julian, the Pope's brother. For this purpose he is plotting to obtain 10,000 soldiers from the Swiss,—has sent a body of troops to Ancona, and 20,000 soldiers, under the pretext of repelling the Turks. For this reason the King of Arragon has concluded a treaty without prejudicing the affairs of the Emperor against the Venetians. Lins, 8 April 1513, avant Pasques.

Fr., pp. 3. Addressed.

9 April.   **4953.**   ————— to [MARGARET OF SAVOY.]

Addit. 21,382. f. 53.
B. M.

" Madame, sy vous lesses se biliet ouvert,• Mons. trouvera que bien humblemant me recommande a sa bonne grase." This last Sunday of Lent (*Cerremme antrant*) has seen the Princess (**Mary**) dressed in Italian fashion ; and I think never man saw a more beautiful creature, nor one having so much grace and sweetness, in public or private. As for what has been said to my said Lord and to you, Madame, the said Princess was " tant crute et an . . rnye. Je vous oze bien dire que se se netoit que toute fames sont ases fortes, que Monsieur viendra bien au bout de sete sy, car y net riens sy mennuet ne sy douset quelle est ; et vous prommes que le tour de se pays la fet pres de trois dois plus grande quelle net." Is sure that when Mons. shall have spoken with her a little privately " que liquerque tornera le rot, au sort qui sera tou brule."

Fr. p. 1.

10 April.   **4954.**   THE GREAT HARRY.

R. O.

i. " The parcels hereafter following made by me, John Brown, the Kings peyntor, for the King's royal ship called the Henry Grace a Dieu, the 10th of April, the fifth year of the reign of our Lord King Henry the VIII."

A large streamer for the main mast, 51 yards long, and the breadth according, fringed with Cadow fringe ; for shaping, sewing and workmanship, 3*l.*—Ten banners of " tewke" beaten gold and silver fringed with silk, each 5½ yards long, 40*s.* a piece.—The parcels following, made and delivered to Tho. Spert, master of the Henry Grace a Dieu by the King's commandment, for the King's great boat . . . . a streamer 30 yards long, workmanship, 20*s.*—Two flags with crosses of St. George ; for shaping, sewing, and fringe, price 10*d.* a piece.—Eight flags with crosses of St. George, 10*d.* each.

ii. The parcels here following made and delivered 5th April 5 Henry VIII. by commandment of my Lord Admiral, for the Gabriel Royal : Sc. 18 banners of " tewke," wrought with gold and silver and fringed with silk, 3 yards long, price 40*s.* apiece. —A streamer for the mainmast, 40 yards long ; for shaping, sewing, workmanship and fringe, 40*s.*—A streamer for the foremast, 36 yards long ; for shaping, sewing and workmanship 26*s.* 8*d.*— Another for the mizen mast, 28 yards long ; for shaping, sewing, fringe and workmanship, 21*s.* 8*d.*

iii. Made and delivered 7th April 5 Hen. VIII. to master Gonston, 7 banners of buckram, 2¼ yards long, with divers arms, for shaping, sewing, fringe, staff and workmanship, 8*s.* a piece.—60

1514.

staves made by Will. Heywood, joiner, for the King's great ship, price 16d. a piece. For painting the said staves in the King's colours in oil, 6d. a piece.

Copy. Ex orig. penes T. Astle.

iv. Streamers and banners which Vincent Vulp*, painter, by the King's command hath painted and made for his new ship *The Henry Grace de Dieu.* — A streamer with a dragon, 45 yards long ; for fringe and workmanship, 3l.—A streamer with a dragon, 42 yards long ; for fringe and workmanship 40s.—A steamer with a lion, 36 yards long ; for fringe and workmanship 26s. 8d.—A streamer with a greyhound, 18 yards long; for fringe and workmanship 15s.—Two little streamers with cross of St. George, one 20 and the other 12 yards long ; for fringe and workmanship 18s. —100 pencils at 12d. each.—50 banners of tuke wrought with gold and silver, 40s. each.—Received, 2 June 6 Hen.VIII., 112l. 19s. 8d. sterling.†

Pp. 3.

10 April. **4955.**　SPINELLY and others to the KING'S AMBASSADORS at
Galba, B. III. 181.　　ROME.

B. M.

The King has been informed of the practices of the King of Arragon made at the French King's request, and warns the Pope of the danger. Similar overtures were made to the Emperor, and rejected, as will appear by a letter written by him to the Archduchess. To extinguish the phantasies of the King of Arragon, they think the Pope should write to the Emperor, justifying himself, that he never intended to invade Naples or injure the confederates of the Church, and that he should exhort the Venetians to an arrangement with the Emperor, and the Swiss to continue in their ill opinions of the French. All the old enmities between the Kings of France and Arragon are put in oblivion by the subtle wit of the King of Arragon ; but if the Pope will follow the King's advice, he may frustrate the designs of Arragon on Italy. The Pope should not grudge the prosperity of the King of England, as he has always been an obedient son to the See Apostolic. Requests them to keep secret from all except the Pope, and especially from Cardinal Gurcke, the letter to the Archduchess. The post will be with them in 11 days. Are making great provision of troops. Mechlin, 10 April 1514.

Signed : Richard Wyngfield, William Knight, Thomas Spinelly.
Superscribed : Reverendissimo, &c. Christofero Cardinali Angliæ et Sil. Wigorniensi Episcopo Christianissimi Regis Angliæ oratoribus.

Endorsed by Spinelly's clerk : "Copy of the letter written to Rome to the King's ambassadors there by those being with the Lady Archduchess."

Pp. 3. *Mutilated.*

10 April. **4956.**　CHARLES DE CROY (PRINCE OF CHIMAY) to HENRY VIII.
R. O.

Has written by the ambassadors here, who have been with Henry, of the great loss he has suffered by Henry's invasion of France. Thanks the King for his favorable answer. Has

---

* Calls himself Fox elsewhere.
† Inclosed is an acknowledgment by John Bolt of London of 1,040l. st. received from Sir John Daunce for 1,300 harness, at 16s. the piece, and a list by Corn. Johnson, of ordnance ; taken from the originals in Astle's possession.

1514.

desired Monsr. de Mares to put him in mind of it again, and repeats his petition for recompense, which he hopes he may obtain in consideration of his services to the King and his father. Malines, 10 April. *Signed.*

Fr., p. 1. Addressed: " Au Roy."

11 April.   **4957.**   For JERONIMO FRISCHOBALDI, LEONARD FRISCHOBALDI of
S. B.   Florence, NICHOLAS formerly PAUL BONVIXI, ANTHONY
                           BONVIXI, and ANTHONY CAVALLARI, of Lucca, mer-
                           chants.

Pardon. *Del.* Croydon, 11 April 5 Hen. VIII.
Pat. 5 Hen. VIII. p. 2, m. 26.

11 April.   **4958.**   For MARTIN DUPYNE, OLIVER LE MARCER, and VEN-
S. B.   TURO VENTURI, merchants.

Licence to import any merchandise, except Gascon wine, for five years. *Del.* Croydon, 11 April 5 Hen. VIII.
Fr. 5 Hen. VIII. m. 18.

11 April.   **4959.**   For FRANCIS DE BARD, merchant of Florence.
P. S.

Licence to export 400 sacks of wool. Greenwich, 31 March 5 Hen. VIII. *Del.* Westm., 11 April.
Fr. 5 Hen. VIII. m. 17.

12 April.   **4960.**   SPINELLLY to WOLSEY.
R. O.

Wrote last on the 5th ; is now writing to the King. Hopes an answer touching his own affairs, without longer delay. The Bishop of Tournay is at Bruges ;—his officers say they will soon have full possession of the bishopric. Bruges, 12 April 1514. *Signed.*
P. 1. Addressed: Rᵐᵒ, &c. Tho. Arch. Ebor.

12 April.   **4961.**   NAVY.
R. O.

Costs of the *Mary Jane,* taken at Hull, from 26 Sept. 5 Hen. VIII. to 12 April following, by James Cokerell, D.D., vicar of Hessill and of Hull, John Talbot, customer, and John Cokett, searcher. *Signed.*

ii. Charges for unrigging the same.
Paper roll.

12 April.   **4962.**   For ROGER HAMERTON.

Protection ; going to the war. Croydon, 12 April.
Fr. 5 Hen. VIII. m. 10.

12 April.   **4963.**   For ANDREAS AMMONIUS, alias DE ARENA, clk., the
P. S.   King's Latin secretary.

Rym. XIII. 400.   Denization. Greenwich, 3 April 5 Hen. VIII. *Del.* Croydon, April.
Pat. 5 Hen. VIII. p. 2, m. 4.

12 April.   **4964.**   For NICHOLAS GRAY and MARCY his wife.
P. S.

Grant, in survivorship, of a tenement situated in Richmond, Surrey, near the King's manor, called the " tymber hawe," with a close on the south side, and two gardens on the north, where a messuage has been built by the said Nicholas. Lambeth, 10 Feb. 5 Hen. VIII. *Del.* Croydon, 12 April.
Pat. 5 Hen. VIII. p. 2, m. 25.

1514.

12 April. **4965.** For THOMAS EARL OF SURREY, Earl Marshal.
P. S. b.
Protection for Roger Hamerton, in the Earl's company. 10 April 5 Hen. VIII. *Del.* Westm., 12 April. *Signed.*

12 April. **4966.** For BURY ST. EDMUND'S.
P. S.
Grant to the abbot and convent of Bury St. Edmund's of the goods and chattels of their tenants who are outlawed, &c. in the hundreds of Babbergh, Cosford, Thinghowe, Thedwardstrete, Blakborn, Lakeford, and Risshebrigge, Suff., and in other lands of the said abbot and convent, with all deodands and treasure trove in the said hundreds. Greenwich, 11 April 5 Hen. VIII. *Del.* Croydon, 12 April.
Pat. 5 Hen. VIII. p. 2, m. 25.

12 April. **4967.** For THOS. FERROUR, yeoman of the Crown.
To be doorward of the chamber called the Prince's Council Chamber, at Westminster, with 10*l.* a year out of the issues of the duchy of Cornwall; *vice* Thos. Stokes, who held the office by gift of Sir Rob. Southwell, deceased. Croydon, 12 April.
Pat. 5 Hen. VIII. p. 2, m. 26.

13 April. **4968.** THE GREAT HARRY.
R. O.
"Here followeth all such parcels that I, William Childeley, the King's tourner, hath delivered to Mr. Bond, paymaster of the *Harry Grace a Dew*, from the 13th day of April 5 Hen. VIII."

ii. "The receipt of the ordnance received by me, William Bony-than, purser of *Herre Grasadeu*, of Cornellys Johnson, the King's iron gunmaker."

iii. Apparel pertaining to the foremast, mainmast, foretop, &c.
Pp. 16.

13 April. **4969.** For SIR HENRY WIOTT.
S. B.
Licence to export 100 sacks of wool of Norfolk and Kent, for four years. *Del.* Croydon, 13 April 5 Hen. VIII.
Fr. 5 Hen. VIII. m. 17.

13 April. **4970.** THE AMBASSADORS OF [THE SWISS CANTONS] to
R. O.   HENRY VIII.
Credence for their ambassadors, Maurice Hierns of Zurich and John Stoltz of Basle, whom they despatch to England to know what assistance Henry will give them against France. Basle, 13 April 1514.
Lat., p. 1. *Addressed. Endorsed by Tuke* (?) Literæ Helvetiorum ad illustrissimum Regem nostrum, the 13th of April 1524.

13 April. **4971.** To the ABP. OF CANTERBURY, Chancellor.
S. B.
For writs of *dedimus potestatem* to the Abbot of St. Mary, York, and Sir Ralph Bygot, to take the fealty of Thomas Bednell, newly elected Abbot of Whytbye. Greenwich, 13 April 5 Hen. VIII.

1514.

14 April.   **4972.**   For HENRY KEMYS.
S. B.
Pardon as late escheater of Gloucestershire and the Marches of Wales, for marriage of any widows married without the King's licence, &c. ;—also release of a recognizance for 40*l.*, made by John Champnes of Cheltenham, and William Huntley of Ree, Glouces-ter, 26 Nov. 3 Hen. VIII. *Del.* Croydon, 14 April 5 Hen. VIII.
Pat. 5 *Hen. VIII. p.* 2, *m.* 25.

14 April.   **4973.**   PETER WILDANCK.
R. O.
Account of Peter Wildanck in March and April 6 Hen. VIII. for wages, journeys, convoys, &c., in Antwerp and elsewhere.
He was employed by the Duchess and Thomas Spinelly.
Pp. 10.

17 April.   **4974.**   For JOHN YERDELEY.
S. B.
To be serjeant-at-arms, with 12*d.* a day, on surrender of patent granting the same to William More, temp. Hen. VII. *Del.* Westm., 17 April 5 Hen. VIII.

17 April.   **4975.**   For EDWARD BECKE of Manchester, merchant.
P. S.
Licence to pass and repass with merchandize into Ireland. Greenwich, 18 March 5 Hen. VIII. *Del.* Croydon, 17 April.
Pat. 5 *Hen. VIII. m.* 17.

17 April.   **4976.**   FOX BP. OF WINCHESTER to [WOLSEY].
Galba, B. III. 145.
B. M.
" . . . . my departing . . . .
. . . . that mused for the instruc[tions . . . .]
shewed the charge (if it so come to p[ass] . . . . upon
the matter that the same instruc[tions . . . . s]oon, I pray
you look upon them and a[ct upon them] as ye shall see cause.
But shew them yet . . . . for it is yet no season, and
some folks peradven[ture who should] see them would say that we
were much busier [than we ought to be] and if none effect come
thereof they might . . . . . . of mockery. Nevertheless, if the
King's grace [would take] the labor to see them at a good leisure,
I thy[nk it may] do good, for little make we but by his . . . .
is some amends. And to make the matter the [surer] it should not
be amiss if there were a commiss[ion with] glass windows, *ad trac-
tandum et concludendum*, [and like]wise a safe conduct with glass
windows had forthwith, this . . . . . because the time is very
short. And much I m[arvel] that there came no news from
Mr. Ponynges of . . . . that were sent to him by Thomas Pawlet.
Me seemeth [there] myghte some thing have be do upon them by
th[is]. Also it is not to be liked that my Lady of Savoy maketh
none answer for the marriage appointed f[or to] be at Calais. And
in case she make none answer, [or] that she will put it over to some
other time and place, t[his] is a plain matter wherewith to prove
their entents [as to] the said marriage, and whether they will perform it [as] conclud]ed upon that treaty . . . . one
article containing . . . . oratorem vel procuratores suos ad
. . . . . . [quart]um decimum ætatis suæ annum sufficienter
auct[orisatos] res postquam dictam ætatem xiiij annorum im-
[pleverit] . . . . . sequente ad dominam Mariam in regnum
Angl[iæ] . . . . . et duobus apostolica et imperiali auctoritate
notariis, et . . . . . specialiter vocatis et rogatis, cum eadem

1514.

domina Ma[ria m]atrimonium per verba de presenti ad hoc apta rea[liter] contrahet et cum effectu. This article is not derogate by the treaty made at Lysle, as may appear in the end of [the sa]me. Also the said 40 days be past, as may appear [by] account making from St. Matthew's day last past hither. And for as much as they have not observed this article it shall in my mind be right expedient if they will not perform the matter of Calais, or make none answer, but drive the time, then forthwith require [my] Lady to perform the said article ; and if she refuse so [to] do, it is plain matter that they intend no marriage, or else that they will protract it uncertainly, &c.—Much [I] muse of the word that the Governor of Bresse said, scilt. that within two months it should be seen, &c. should do harm. And thus myn own good lord," &c.

" At Esher, this Monday in Easter week ; with the hand of your loving brother, Ri. Wynton."

Hol., pp. 2, badly mutilated.

17 April. **4977.**   ORDNANCE AND STORES.
R. O.

Account of gunpowder, "corn powder," demi-lances, marespykes, bows, arrows, bowstrings, stacks for archers, fighting bills, felling axes, hedging bills, mattocks, spades, scowpes, sickles and scythes, nails, horseshoes, iron crows, cart clowts, brass boxes for gun wheels, gun wheels, axletrees with bars of iron, screws, mantells for bumbards, draughts for fore-carts, horse-harness, horse-collars, cart-saddles, trees for cart-saddles, thylbells, bits for horses, buckles and rings, headstalls without rings and bits, " hides of leather hungry," tanned hides, white leather hides, linch pins, cressets, leather buckets, "lates stakes," "lates caltroppes," ropes, " fare carts," shipped from the Tower to Calais, on 28 March.

ii. "Ordnance remaining in Flanders the 8th day of April the 5th year of the reign of our sovereign lord King Henry VIII." viz., 4 bumbards with Hans Pope Reyder gunfounder of Mechlin, one of which was given to the King by the Emperor, the others being of Hans' manufacture ; 6 curtowes with the same Hans ; 6 curtowes delivered to the Duchess of Savoy for the King's use ; 3 portguns to be recast from a broken gun ; gunpowder, and iron shot.

iii. Ordnance in the Tower of London and Hunsdyche, 17 April 5 Hen. VIII., sc. bumbardes of Herbert's making, double curtowes, serpentines, fawcons, culverines of Humph. Walker's making, demiculverins, minion pieces, serpentines, fawcons, hakbusshes, handguns, culverines of Symond's making, vice-pieces, curtowes, potguns, gunpowder, shot of iron, spears, marespykes, bows, &c.

Pp. 6, large paper. Mutilated.

18 April. **4978.**   KNIGHT and others to HENRY VIII.
Galba, B.III. 183.
B. M.

The enclosed letters were delivered to them the . . of this month. Hear from the Archduchess that the Emperor is resolved not to ratify the [peace] if the King will prosecute the enterprise, but will be glad if the King will consent to it. They said if that was the case they wondered at his "recule" to Lynche. She said she did not know the reason, but from the manner which was peculiar "to her father, to her, and to all their house," there was something he would have, which he would not press, and that the Emperor was not satisfied that the 30,000 crowns promised him at Tournay were not paid. Great offers were made him by the Kings of Arragon and France, and if the King be liberal the Emperor will be

3 D

1514.

tractable. In this she agrees with Lord Berges. She said this was
the manner of her house, "that in case their fortune had been to
a descended of humble and low stock, her father and she should a
perished rather for hunger than their courage would a served them
to ask for God's sake."—On her demand the King of Arragon said
that the governance of Scotland should be delivered to England for
a recompense, she promised that John Don Emmanuel should
depart this week for the Emperor, notwithstanding that the ambassador of Arragon hath importuned her to the contrary, and she
said she had " learned of his master to tender her singular profit
and [interest and] regard none other." Mechlin, 18 April.
Signed: R. Wyngfield—W. Knyght—T. Spinelly.
Add. p. 3, *mutilated.*

18 April. **4979.**   ARRAY.
S. B.   Commission to Nicholas Wadham, Sir William Sandes, Sir
Ralph Egerton, Sir John Lysley, William Paulet, John Dautrey,
William Pownde and John Newporte to survey ·the muster and
array, at Portsmouth, of Sir Thomas Wyndham, deputy lieutenant
and vice admiral to Thomas Earl of Surrey, High Admiral of
England, and certify us to the same. *Del.* Westm., 18 April
5 Hen. VIII.
Pat. 5 Hen. VIII. p. 2, *m.* 22d.

18 April. **4980.**   For THOMAS SALTER, sewer.
S. B.   Grant of the manor of Glyndovirdoy, in the commote of Edernyon,
Merioneth, N. Wales, at the yearly rent of one red rose.   *Del.*
Otford, 18 April 5 Hen. VIII.
Pat. 5 Hen. VIII. p. 2, *m.* 26.

18 April. **4981.**   For the ABBEY OF WHITBY.
P. S.   Assent to the election of Thomas Bednell, monk of Whitby, as
abbot, *vice* John Benstede, deceased.   Greenwich, 6 April
5 Hen. VIII.   *Del.* Croydon, 18 April.
Pat. 5 Hen. VIII. p. 2, *m.* 24.

ii. Petition of John Burn, sub-prior, and the convent, for the
above. 26 March 1514.—

19 April. **4982.**   SPINELLY to WOLSEY.
R. O.   Wrote his last on the 13th. Is writing to the King. Encloses
a packet from Dr. Sampson. Bruges, 19 April 1514.
P. S. in Latin, in his own hand: There is a great talk of the
rumor sprung up in France by the King's subjects in Tournay.
The auditors (?) (*auldientes*) have no reason to think any good of
it. *Signed.*
P. 1. *Addressed:* Rmo., etc. Tho. Arch. Ebor. *Endorsed by
Tuke.*

19 April. **4983.**   SAMPSON to [WOLSEY.]
Calig. E. II. 136.   "Please it your grace, yesterday [I received your letters] from
B. M.   M[aster] Toneys, whereby I was ascertained of yowr graces pleasure
[touching] such money as I have here received." Has accordingly
delivered to master deputy 350 marks. Has written frequently to

1514.

Wolsey in his behalf, "n[ot] only after it was thought that John de Sellier should not [recover from] his sickness, and this young man his son . . . . " more st. . . . . be his successor in his goods. States that he had "bound Phillip [lc] Sellier the son, by sureties for the assurance of your grace," because his own father thought him "light and of small credence." Considered it best to deliver the money "here to the King's [use], because it was in pence and gold at the high price .c[ur]rant here in Tournay." Wolsey is to receive it in English money from those appointed to go to Tournay. Toneys reports the tapestry sent to Wolsey "non inelegans, meo judicio t . . . . illud divi Georgii velut statua perornatum" [was satisfactory]. Begs Wolsey will accept it as a present. Tournay, 19 April.

Hol., mutilated, pp. 2. The writing on the first page much decayed.

19 April. **4984.** For HENRY PAGE, yeoman of the bottles.
S. B.

Grant of all those tenements in St. Michael's Busyngshawe, London, which John Knolles, serjeant of the bakehouse, or Sir Edmund Hampden, deceased, held by grant of Henry VII., on attainder of Sir Richard Charleton. *Del.* Otford, 19 April 5 Hen. VIII.

Pat. 5 Hen. VIII. p. 2, m. 27.

20 April. **4985.** FERDINAND OF ARRAGON to EMMANUEL KING OF POR-
R. T. 153. TUGAL.
R. O.

Congratulates him on his victories in India. Had procured a truce to be made for one year between the Emperor, the Queen of Castile, England, the Prince of Castile on the one side, and France and Scotland on the other, and that at his solicitation the Pope had made peace between the Emperor and the Venetians. Madrid, 20 April 1514. *Signed.*

Sp. Copy, pp. 4.

20 April. **4986.** TOURNAY.
R. T. 144.
R. O.

Patent of Edward Ponynges, captain of Tournay, reciting letters patent of Henry VIII., dated Tournay, 25 Sept. 1513, permitting the town to sell rents *à rachat*, and to impose new assizes, in aid of the 50,000 crowns which they have promised the King. 20 April 1514, après Pasques.

Fr. pp. 3.

20 April. **4987.** TOURNAY.
R. T. 144.
R. O.

Patent of Edward Ponynges, captain of Tournay, authenticating letters patent of Hen. VIII., dated 26 Feb. 1513, 5 Hen. VIII., confirming the old privilege of *le mis sus* exercised by the town of Tournay; viz., of taking and selling, when they think right, a sixth part of the grain passing the Escault, for the purpose of holding a staple, and returning the price to the merchants. 20 April 1514, après Pasques.

Fr., pp. 2.

20 April. **4988.** For RICHARD CORYTON alias CODRYNGTON, of Newton,
P. S. in the parish of Melam, Cornw.

Pardon. Greenwich, 17 April 5 Hen. VIII. *Del.* Otford, 20 April.

Pat. 5 Hen. VIII. p. 2, m. 26.

1514.
20 April. **4989.** . For WILLIAM COURTENEY of Ylton, Devon.
P. S. b.   Protection for Roger Gyffarde, to serve in the war in the said
               William's retinue.   20 April 5 Hen. VIII. *Signed.*

P. S. b. **4990.** For SIR EDWARD NEVILE.
               Protection for William Awdeven of London, fishmonger, to serve
               in the war in the said Edward's retinue. *Signed.*

       4991. TOURNAY.
S. B.   Confirmation of the privileges of the town of Tournay; reciting
               patent 26 Feb. last, granting *le mis sus;* patent, of same date,
               appointing five persons to hear and determine appeals; patent
               of 19 March last, granting confiscation of certain rents and pensions;
               patent of 16 March last, granting the inhabitants of Tournay the
               same privileges as English subjects; and acts of the English
               parliament of 24 Jan. last, appointing in the said cities two royal
               notaries.
               Fr.

       4992. For WILLIAM KNYVET of London, alias of Westminster.
S. B.   Pardon.
               Pat. 5 Hen. VIII. p. 1, m. 15.

       4993. For the PARISHIONERS of ST. MARY AXE, LONDON.
S. B.   Licence to gather alms in England, for repairing their church,
               in the names of John Snethe and John Scryven parishioners.
               They state that their church was built in remembrance of St.
               Ursula, daughter of a King of England, one of the 11,000 virgins
               "that tenderly shed their blood for our Christian faith and belief;"
               and that "the said poor church is edified and honored by keeping
               of a holy relic, an axe, one of the three that the 11,000 virgins were
               beheaded withal."

       4994. For JOHN ISSELYP, Abbot of Westminster, and JOHN
S. B.   BAPMANSON, D.D.
               Collation of the first vacant prebend in St. Stephen's, Westminster,
               or St. George's, Windsor.
               Pat. 5 Hen. VIII. p. 1, m. 22.

       4995. For HUGH VAUGHAN and JOHN HUNTELEY, grooms of
S. B.   the Chamber.
               Licence to import 600 tons of wine and woad.

       4996. THE SUBSIDY.
S. B.   Commission to the Lord Chancellor, to issue warrants for
               levying the subsidy in the Cinque Ports, to the following persons :—
               Sir Edward Ponynges, constable of the castle of Dover, and
               keeper of the Cinque Ports, Sir John Norton, John Copuldike.
               Hastynges.—Robert Hall, John Levet, Henry Benevere.
               Wynchelse.—John Assheburnham, Robert Sparcoke.
               Rye.—Nicholas Sutton, Clement Adam.

1514.

Romene.—Clement Baker, George Cobbe.
Hythe.—John Honywode, Clement Holwey.
Dovor.—Richard Feneux, John Waren, John Broke.
Sandwich.—John Langley, John Westclyve, John Wewe.
Feversham.—William Norton, Robert Meycote.
Lyde.—James Skan, John Pulbon.
Tenterden.—Edward Philipp, John Hoygges.
Fordwiche.—William See (or Soe), George Robertes.
Folkeston.—John Tong, Thomas Eden (or Uden).
Pevensey.—Edward Chauncy.
William Buntyng, James Swanne.

4997. SCOTLAND.

S. B.
Safe conduct for six months to Patrick Lord Lindesaye of the Byris, William Lord Borthuike, John Lord Drummond, William Lord Ruthven, Sir Robert Lawder, Sir William Kath, Patrick Covingtre, dean of Lastalrig, David Abircrumby, dean of the Chapel Royal, Adam Culquhone, canon of Glasgow, David Seyton and Alexander Symson, canons of Aberdyne ; granted at the request of the Queen of Scots, to the intent that they may repair to the King's presence, to commune with the King upon certain great matters concerning the weal of the two kingdoms.

At the foot of the above is the following : "Md. that in this saufconduyt suche provisions bee made as bee comprehended at thende of the saufconduyt whiche was last sent with voyde spaces therein."

Signed : T. Norfolk—T. Duresme—Thomas Wulcy.

4998
S. B.
For WM. SMYTH, mercer of London, alias of Estgrenewiche, Kent.

Protection ; going in the retinue of Sir Ric. Wingefeld, Deputy of Calais.

4999.
S. B.
For REGINALD LOVE, draper of London.

Protection ; going in the retinue of Sir Ric. Wingfeld, Deputy of Calais.

5000.
S. B.
For THOS. ROCHE, merchant tailor of London.

Protection ; going in the retinue of Sir Ric. Wyngefeld, Deputy of Calais.

5001. REVERSALS OF OUTLAWRY.

Kent.—Reversal of outlawry for John Atwell of Westerham, Kent, sen. Westm., 27 . . . .

London.—Reversal of outlawry for John Troughton, "de Monte Sancti Johannis," Yorkshire, sued for debt by Sir Wm. Capell. Westm., 3 May.

Pat. 5 Hen. VIII. p. 1, *m.* 3.

5002. For HEN. HERYNG.

To be bailiff of the town of Malmeshill Lucy, Heref., parcel of the earldom of March, *vice* Simon Heryng his father, deceased.

Pat. 5 Hen. VIII. p. 2, *m.* 30.

1514.

5003.   For WM. KNYVET of London.

S. B.   Pardon.
                  Pat. 5 Hen. VIII. p. 1, *m.* 15.

22 April.   **5004.**   For WALTHAM HOLY CROSS.
P. S.   Congé d'élire to the prior and convent on resignation of John
                  Shernbroke, abbot. Greenwich, 20 April 5 Hen. VIII. *Del.*
                  Otford, 22 April.
                  Pat. 5 *Hen. VIII. p.* 2, *m.* 23.
                  ii. Petition of the prior and convent for the above. 15 April 1514.

23 April.   **5005.**   HENRY VIII. to SIR JOHN DAUNCE.
R. O.   Ordering him to pay Leonard Friscobald, who has delivered to
                  Richard Fawkener and Hans Welf, gunpowder maker, 46,218 lb. of
                  saltpeter at 6*d.* per lb. Greenwich, 23 April 6 Hen. VIII.
                  Pp. 1.

24 April.   **5006.**   SPINELLY to [HENRY VIII].
Galba, B.III.160.   Wrote last on the [.. of this] month. They are preparing
B. M   an honorable reception for the French ambassador, expected on
                  Sunday next. Many ill rumors are spread against England; some
                  of them come out of France. The principal say the King will not be
                  able to keep Tournay three months. When the ambassador of Arragon
                  is informed of the same, "I promise yo[ur] grace he spareth not
                  to answer as yowr faithful servant ; what they mean thereby G[od]
                  knoweth."—Yesterday when the Prince should have kept the feast
                  of the Order of the Garter, according to the ancient custom and
                  oath, it was not observed in any point, any more than if he did not
                  belong to it. The Archduchess is sorry, but cannot oppose it, as the
                  authority of France increases. She would have changed her mind
                  but for the ambassador of Arragon. Unless the King looks to it all
                  these countries will be ruled by the French. Can see no remedy for
                  it, except a thorough understanding be shown to exist between the
                  Emperor, England, and Arragon, and the safety of Tournay made
                  manifest ; this will discourage all his enemies. Lord Chievres has
                  sent money to the Emperor in diminution of the 100,000 g. gilders;
                  he hopes thereby to make his peace with him, and, but for the Arch-
                  duchess and the ambassadors of Arragon, would rule him.
                      The Emperor has sent by Genoa Master Lewis Maræton to the
                  King of Arragon, to the dislike of Chievres. "Moreover it shall
                  please your grace to understand that, having untruly the Prince's
                  ambassadors written out of France that . . . . . [cha]pelayn of
                  th . . . . [Arra]gonnys wa[s for no other] cause saving to treat
                  a marriage betwixt . . . . [and] the daughter of France, the
                  ambassador of Arragon . . . . him thereof, and upon such know-
                  ledge the said ch[aplain] before his departing took with him
                  Hans Reyner brother . . . by the Emperor with a certain dissim-
                  mulate color had been sent . . . . and went together to the Lord
                  Nassaw, Sempy, and others, . . . that for his justification of their
                  false report he . . . in their presence before the French King and
                  his Council, to say [that] he had no charge nor never spoken of
                  such matter, where[upon] many words been grown between the
                  ambassador here and [the] Prince's council."
                      The Bishop of Tournay and his officers have used ill language to
                  Dr. Sampson. As the Bishop's father is in great authority in France,
                  his threats must not be disregarded. Spinelly has written to the

1514.

Lieutenant of Tournay to put him on his guard. Has obtained information through a friend from Thomas Nodry archdeacon of Moray, nephew of the Secretary of Scotland, who has long been at Rome, and has seen a papal brief of safe conduct "for all Princes, calling him *nuncius apostolicus.*"—The Duke of Albany has taken his leave of the French King, and is gone into Britanny to cross to Scotland. It is thought he has already arrived there on the west, and that he will soon be weary of his enterprise, owing to the divisions there, and his long residence in France. The Bishop of Moray is in the French court. He does not like the French, and had his charge thither from the late King of Scotland against his will. He has been anxious to exchange his bishopric. The French have compelled him to renounce Arbroath. He was brought up by the Earl of Angus's father, and assisted to deliver him from prison. He is anxious for peace between England and Scotland, and will do all that he can to promote it, "save to put into your highness' hands the two children."—He requires nothing at present except a safe conduct to Scotland, where he might have further communications with such persons as the King may appoint.—Spinelly's informant would not say why the Bishop did not go with the Duke, but said perhaps they did not agree together.—Though these things which he has said of the Bishop are unfavorable to his brother's interest, would not forbear mentioning them.—The Scottish herald has gone into Zeland. Bruges, 24 April 1514. *Signed.*

Pp. 6, mutilated.

24 April. **5007.** For THOMAS EARL OF SURREY, K.G.

S. B.
Rym. xiii. 402.

To be admiral and commander-in-chief of the fleet and forces going in aid of the Holy See, at the request of the Pope and the King of Arragon. *Del.* Westm., 24 April 6 Hen. VIII.

Pat. 6 Hen. VIII. p. 2, m. 1d.

24 April. **5008.** For WILLIAM STRYNGER.

P. S.

To search in all places in England for woollen cloths, and prevent their export, unless they are barbed and shorn according to act of parliament 3 Hen. VIII. Windsor Castle, 8 Nov. 5 Hen. VIII. *Del.* Croydon, 24 April 6 Hen. VIII.

26 April. **5009.** For RALPH FENWIKE.

S. B.

Wardship of Henry, an idiot, son and heir of John Fenwike. *Del.* Croydon, 26 April 5 Hen. VIII.

Pat. 6 Hen. VIII. p. 2, m. 1.

26 April. **5010.** For SIR EDWARD RADCLIF, knight of the Body, and

S. B.

RALPH FENWYK, squire of the Body, lieutenants of the Middle Marches towards Scotland.

Grant, during pleasure, (in consideration of their great expences in the King's affairs on the said marches,) of the fee farm of 10*l.* a year out of the lordship and port of Newbigging, near Wodhorne; lands and tenements of the annual value of *l*0s., formerly belonging to Thomas Sawles, in "Ley Hewghe," near Stanforthdame, forfeited by the said Thomas; 31*s.* of free rent in Ulston, near Hawkwell; the hamlet of Ryplington, near Whalton, of the annual value of 30*s.*; the fee-farm or cornage of the towns of Creswell and Ellington, of the annual value of 3*l.*; the fee-farm of the lordships of Halton and Whittington, of the annual value of 4*l.*; fee-farm of the barony of Morpeth, of the annual value of 4*l.*; fee-farm of

1514

the lordship of Edlingcham, of the annual value of 30s. ; rent from the lands called Schirlandes, near Tropton, of the annual value of 20s. ; rent of the town or lordship of Toggesden, of the annual value of 20s. ; rent from the town of Dennom, of the annual value of 10s. ; rent from the lordship of Colwell, of the annual value of 40s. ; fee-farm of the towns called the Three Middiltons, of the annual value of 30s. ; fee-farm of the barony of Bottell, of the annual value of 30s. ; rent from the barony of Bywell, of the annual value of 4l. ; rent from the barony of Dalevale, of the annual value of 26s. 8d. ; fee-farm of the barony of Mitford, to the annual value of 5l. 0s. 4d. ; fee-farm of two towns called Bustons, of the annual value of 40s. ; fee-farm of the barony of Heppell, of the annual value of 23s. ; fee-farm or socage of the lordship of Alnewyk, to the annual value of 3l. 18s. 4d. ; fee-farm of Stamforth and Emyldon, of the annual value of 9s. ; fee-farm of the towns of Branxston and Bowlsden, of the annual value of 40s. ; parcel of land called Kudges* Medowe, of the annual value of 40s. ; fee farm of the towns of Belsoo and Trewyk, of the annual value of 13s. 8d. ; fee-farm of the barony of Boltby alias Langle, of the annual value of 5l.; fee-farm of Schawden, of the annual value of 10s.; and the fee-farm of the towns of Calole and Yetlington, of the annual value of 30s. All these places are in Northumberland. *Del.* Croydon, 26 April 6 Hen. VIII.
Pat. 6 Hen. VIII. p. 2, m. 1.

---

26 April.   **5011.**   For WILLIAM DODWELL, M.A.
P. S.

Presentation to the church of Gayton in Lemershe, Linc. dioc., void by resignation. Greenwich, 21 April 5 Hen. VIII. *Del.* Westm., 26 April.
Pat. 5 (sic) Hen. VIII. p. 1, m. 11.

---

26 April.   **5012.**   For RICHARD BEDOO, M.A.
P. S.

Presentation to the church of Glawdster, St. David's dioc., *vice* John ap Rice, resigned. Greenwich, 23 April 6 Hen. VIII. *Del.* Croydon, 26 April.
Pat. 6 Hen. VIII. p. 2, m. 1.

---

26 April.   **5013.**   For BERNARD HALDEN, clk.
P. S.

Denization. Greenwich, 25 April 6 Hen. VIII. *Del.* Croydon, 26 April.
Pat. 6 Hen. VIII. p. 2, m. 1.

---

27 April.   **5014.**   For THOMAS ACTON.
S. B.

Wardship of Thomas, son and heir of Thomas Salwey. *Del.* Westm., 27 April 6 Hen. VIII. *Signed :* Thomas Lovell.

---

27 April.   **5015.**   For GEORGE EARL OF SHREWSBURY.
S. B.

Wardship of Humphrey, son and heir of Sir John Ferrers. *Del.* Croydon, 27 April 6 Hen. VIII. *Signed :* Thomas Lovell.
Pat. 6 Hen. VIII. p. 2, m. 1.

---

* Mistake for Kinges.

1514.

27 April. **5016.** FOR NICHOLAS CARUE.

S. B.
Reversion of the manors of Plompton, Bercombe, Fletching, Pedinghoo, Buskegage, and Birling, Sussex, the advowson of Plompton church, &c., which came to Hen. VII. on the death of William Viscount Beaumont, Lord Bardolf, by attainder of Francis Lord Lovel, and were subsequently granted 6 Sept. 1 Hen. VIII. to John late Earl of Oxford, deceased, and Elizabeth his wife (still living), widow of the said Lord Beaumont. *Del.* Croydon, 27 April 6 Hen. VIII.

Pat. 6 Hen. VIII. p. 2, m 1.

28 April. **5017.** NAVY.

R. O.
Costs of the *Mary Katharine* of London, by Walter Loveday, beginning 14 Jan. 5 Hen. VIII.

Captain's wages 18d. per day; victuals each man, 18d. a week ; wages of soldiers and gunners 5s. a month.

Signed with a mark, 28 April 6 Hen. VIII.

Pp. 6.

28 April. **5018.** MARGARET OF SAVOY to MAXIMILIAN.

Lett.de Louis XII.
Since she wrote of the dissatisfaction of England, and of Henry's answer to Maximilian's ambassadors, those ambassadors have returned. Encloses an extract of their letters touching the proposal lately made to the King of England by the Spanish ambassador. Could not, even with the aid of her cousin Count Felix of Wertemberg, persuade them to agree to a delay of the marriage of Mary, or an alteration of the place. Begs, therefore, to know his final answer, which cannot well be put off longer. She is already losing her credit by these delays.—As matters stand, knows not what to do on the frontiers until the Emperor decides whether to confirm the truce or not. The term of the garrison supported by the English will expire within a month. Has always told the ambassadors that the Emperor would not confirm the peace without the consent of England. Desires to know what is to be done about Gueldres. It is very necessary that the Emperor should come and settle everything. Had supposed he had given Count Felix some charge touching the truce, and commissioned him to go to England; is much perplexed that it was not so, as it is so important that the three powers should remain united. Sees well that the Emperor cannot satisfy the King of England unless the latter will assist him considerably; but if he will do so, desires him to notify it openly, to him or to her, and then it will be seen who is in fault. It is true she has received three or four letters from the Emperor about this business, but she has not been able to understand his intentions. The Pope is endeavouring to make a league with all Italy, the Swiss, and the French, in which he proposes to include England. The Emperor knows at whose expence this will be (*vous entendez, Mons*, *à la barbe de cuy cecy se feroit*). Has spoken to the treasurer Casius about the 30,000 crowns ; the latter will answer the Emperor. Every thing is ready for the departure of Mary [of Hungary], who will leave on the 2nd of May. Some say, when Charles is married he will be out of tutelage. Malines, 28 April 1514.

29 April. **5019.** For SIR JOHN MARNEY, son and heir apparent of Sir

S. B. Henry Marny, knight of the Body.

To be bailiff, in reversion, of the hundred of Rocheforde, Essex, steward of Raylegh, and keeper of the parks of Raylegh and Thun-

1514.

dersley, Essex ; on death or surrender of the said Sir Henry
Marney, to whom the said offices were granted in reversion, by
patent 26 June 1 Hen. VIII., after John Earl of Oxford, now
deceased, who held them by patent 16 May 1 Hen. VIII. *Del.*
Westm., 29 April 6 Hen. VIII.
Pat. 6 Hen. VIII. p. 2, m. 21.

29 April. **5020.** For THOMAS HENNAGE.

S. B.

Wardship of Gerard, son of Gerard Sotehill, late of Redbourn,
Linc. This grant not to extend to the reversion of manors, &c.
which will come into the King's hands on the death of Joan Sotehill, widow of the said Gerard the father. *Del.* Westm., 29 April
6 Hen. VIII. *Signed:* Thomas Lovell.
Pat. 6 Hen. VIII. p. 1, m. 18.

30 April. **5021.** SIR JOHN WILSHER to WOLSEY.

R. O.

On the 28th April received his letter dated London, the 24th.
Had sent the letters as directed, and at the same time to the Lord
Lieutenant of Tournay, Master Poynings, "evyn conteenently," with
all diligence to the post at Newport. Will see that the posts are
diligent. His son-in-law, Master Deputy, has written to the
council at Calais to send to Wolsey Sir Peter, a French priest who
was accused of treason, who had refused to go in procession, as all
other priests and clerks had done, for the winning of Terouenne
and the field of Scots. "I cann nott blame hym ; a ded lyck a
trew Frencheman. We have noo nede inn thys towne at thys
tyme, consedryng the warres with Fraunce, of anie Freche prests."
The priest has a chantry at Calais founded by Richard II. Thinks
it should be in the hands of an honest man. "And let the said Sir
Peter go into France to his natural country, and be a bishop there,
if he can." Calais, 30 April.

P.S.—The Frenchmen are forward, "and say they will look upon
us at Guisnes." They assemble 800 horse and 4,000 foot. A
pursuivant left Dieppe on Tuesday, and says that Pré Jon (Prégent) is ready to leave Dieppe with nine galleys ;—would have done
so on St. George's even but for the storm. "Pre Jon a sayd a wold
com to Cales with hys gales, and bourne ouer shepps in the haven."
It is said the French King will send 20,000 lanzknechts into
Scotland.

Hol., pp. 3. *Addressed:* To mine especial, &c. my lord of
Lincoln.

30 April. **5022.** For RALPH PUDSEY.

P. S.

Corrody in the monastery of Glastonbury on the next vacancy.
Greenwich, 20 Jan. 5 Hen. VIII. *Del.* Westm., 30 April
6 Hen. VIII.

30 April. **5023.** For RALPH ASKUE.

P. S. b.

Protection for William Scarlet of London, barber, to serve in
the war in the said Ralph's company. 30 April 6 Hen. VIII.
Signed.
Fr. 6 Hen. VIII. p. 2, m. 14.

April. **5024.** ORDNANCE.

R. O.

Three bundles of receipts for repairs of the ordnance, for bowstrings, &c. Feb. to April 5 and 6 Hen. VIII.

1514.

1 May.   **5025.**   MAXIMILIAN [SFORZA] DUKE OF MILAN to HENRY VIII.

R. O.   Wishes Baldesar Stuerdus apostolical prothonotary, to explain his intentions to the King. Is glad that the King is satisfied with him, and makes him such fair offers. Had not replied to the offers received from the King on the 3rd March, as they had first been taken to Rome. All Italy is expecting what the King and the Emperor will do, now that the *jus armorum* has been suspended by a truce concluded in Spain with the King Catholic. Berre- guardi, 1 May 1514. *Signed.*

Lat., p. 1. *Addressed.*

1 May.   **5026.**   For MAURICE BERKELEY.

P. S. b.   Protection for John Staunton of Kyngesweston, Glouc., and Thomas Tyson of Bristowe, mariner, retained to serve in the war. Hambroke, 1 May 6 Hen. VIII. *Signed.*

1 May.   **5027.**   For MAURICE BERKELEY.

P. S. b.   Protection for Harry Esterfeld of Bristowe, and Thomas Asshe- hurst of the same town, mariner, retained to serve in the war. Hambroke, 1 May 6 Hen. VIII. *Signed.*

1 May.   **5028.**   For ROGER GYFFORD of London.

Protection ; going in the retinue of Will. Courteney.   Westm., 1 May.

_ *Fr.* 6 *Hen. VIII. p.* 2, *m.* 14.

2 May.   **5029.**   KNIGHT to WOLSEY.

Galba, B. III. 13.   It is clear the Emperor does not intend to keep his promise, but
B. M.   desires the marriage should be performed, by which he and the King of Arragon think they make amends for all injuries. Advises they should not be satisfied. The Prince is young, and surrounded by a young council who are well inclined to France. He has spoken suspicious words, as Knight has written before. The Em- peror is not to be trusted, and has written to the Archduchess to defer the marriage, fearful of the Prince's health, and being disap- pointed of issue. The excuse was forged at Mechlin. The King of Arragon proposes the Prince's eldest sister should marry into the house of France, paying no regard to Henry's honor, or the charges they have brought upon him. And notwithstanding the marriage of the Queen of England, the King of Arragon has done as Wolsey knows. Dissuades therefore the marriage of my Lady Mary with the Prince, as prejudicial to England. Lord Berghez thinks the King should insist that suspected persons be removed from the Prince. Advises, as matters stand, that peace be taken with France to counteract the Emperor and the King of Arragon. Begs, if the King intend to use craft towards the King of Arragon, Knight may have the commission. Mechlin, 2 May.

Hol., pp. 3. *Addressed :* My Lord of Lincoln.

2 May.   **5030.**   KNIGHT and others to HENRY VIII.

Galba, B. III. 185.   Wrote last on 29 April, enclosing a letter from Sir Robert
B. M.   Wingfield. The Archduchess says she has received no news from the Emperor touching the charges of Count Felix, of which they had written before. The Emperor wishes the solemnization of the marriage to be deferred to the end of May, as he wished to be

1514.

present at 'it. She denies that Felix had anything to do with the change of place. The Emperor wished it to be at Antwerp or Mechlin, and that the Prince's two sisters should be present. Lord Berges thinks she is influenced in this by the Prince's council, who are afraid of their authority being diminished. Count Felix has denied that he received any charge from the Emperor, as the ambassador of Arragon asserted, to proclaim the truce and persuade England to the same. She thinks he may have received such an order, but it was countermanded when the Emperor heard of the taking of Arnheim. Berges believes that he had, and advises the King not to bring over his army, or enter into any further expense, unless the Emperor is personally with him. Believe that the Archduchess knows this, especially as they make no instance to bring the King over. When they urged the Archduchess, from the confidence that England had in her, to be more explicit, she said that the King would know the truth from the Emperor's letters. She advises the King to write a letter to the Emperor in his own hand. She desires justice to be done to John Cavelcanti, Gualterotti's factor in London. Send news from Bruges. Mechlin, 2 May.

Signed : R. Wyngffield—W. Knight—T. Spinelly.
Pp. 3, mutilated. Add. Endd.

3 May.   **5031.**   For EDWARD GULDEFFORD.
P. S. b.

Protection for Simon Cussheman of Cranbroke, Kent, weaver, retained to serve in the war. 3 May 6 Hen. VIII. *Signed.*

4 May.   **5032.**   JAN FAUCQUET to [WILTSHIRE,] controller of Calais.
Galba, B. III. 75.
B. M.

Has received his of 1 May. Sends him the news, as becomes a true and loyal servant. The French are in great numbers to succour Pont de Remy and Du Piennes, in Artois and Boulogne, and overrun Guisnes and the English. They are raising great forces by sea and land, and especially to destroy the English convoys before Calais. They intend to raze entirely Guisnes and Hammes. Has been certified by Hacquinet Dandefort and Willequin Craissier that they have heard that all the colleges of Paris are at the command of the King. They propose to come and prevent the landing of the English. He thinks that they intend to rob the town of St. Omer, which would do great hurt to the English. Many of the towns and the country thereabouts are not as good as they ought to be ; in St. Omer there are as many Mammelukes as good Frenchmen. Haquinet complains that certain persons of Guisnes have taken from him what the controller ordered for him. Recommends the bearer, who is a poor man. 4 May 1514.

Hol., Fr., p. 1. Add.

4 May.   **5033.**   SIR THOMAS WYNDHAM to DAWTRE.
R. O.

Statement of the wages due to *The Peter* of Lee. 4 May 6 Hen. VIII. *Signed.*

ii. Money due for the wages and victuals of *The Mighell Yong* of Dover, for the month beginning 22 April.
Mutilated, pp. 2.

4 May.   **5034.**   For ROBERT HOGAN, merchant tailor of London.
S. B.

Licence to export 1,000 sacks of wool. *Del.* Westm., 4 May 6 Hen. VIII.
Fr. 6 Hen. VIII. p. 2, m. 4.

1514.

5 May. **5035.** HENRY VIII. to COUNT FAUCOMBERG.

Calig. D. vi. 118.
B. M.
Rym. xiii. 403.

Informing him that the French, to the number of 8,000, with artillery, were going to lay siege to Guisnes castle, that by Tuesday [next, 20,000] of his subjects would be embarked to raise the siege, and that he had besides a large army which would cross suddenly after the first. Has requested the Archduchess of Austria would allow the Count and other captains who had been in his (Henry's) pay since his departure, to draw towards Calais and lodge about Gravelinges and the marches thereabouts. Eltham, 5 [May 1514]. *Signed.*

Addressed: A nostre, &c. le Conte de Faucomberge Baron de Ligne.

Modern Endorsement: 1514, 5 May, Eltham, Hen. 8. rex.

P. 1. Mutilated.

5 May. **5036.** For SIR JOHN SHARPE.

S. B.

To be steward of the honor and keeper of the park of Wormegey, Norf. *Del.* Westm., 5 May 6 Hen. VIII.

5 May. **5037.** For BARTHOLOMEW WESTBY, baron of the Exchequer.

S. B.

To be one of the "almesse knyghtes" in the college of St. George's, Windsor Castle, with 12d. a day. *Del.* Westm., 5 May 6 Hen. VIII.

Pat. 6 Hen. VIII. p. 2, m. 5.

5 May. **5038.** For HENRY KEMYS, and ELIZABETH formerly wife of

S. B. WILLIAM CASSY, deceased.

Pardon for marrying without the King's licence. *Del.* Westm., 5 May 6 Hen. VIII.

5 May. **5039.** For MARGARET COPULDYKE, widow, and RICHARD CLERK

S. B. of Hornecastell, Linc., tanner.

Licence to found a guild to the honor of St. Katharine, in the church of St. Mary, Hornecastell ; and mortmain licence to acquire lands to the annual value of 25 marks. *Del.* Westm., 5 May 6 Hen. VIII.

5 May. **5040.** MATTHEW CARDINAL SION to HENRY VIII.

R. O.

The Swiss have been most active in expelling the French and heretics from Italy. They despise all French alliances. Thinks their friendship should not be refused. As one born among them, knows their fidelity, and will undertake that they will cut their way through the midst of Gaul to the King's camp. Ex Viglo, iii. non. Maii 1514. *Signed.*

Lat., p. 1.

5 May. **5041.** HENRY VIII. to MARGARET OF SAVOY.

Lett. de
Louis XII.
t. iv. 312.

Has received her letters, dated Malignes, 25 April, touching the matters declared to her by his ambassadors, and a proposition made by the ambassador of Arragon, which did not agree with the Emperor's honor. Before the receipt of her letter, had been informed by Sir Rob. Wingfeld that the King of Arragon had made a truce with the French King, in which the Emperor intended to join, to avoid certain dangers which might arise, and which he thought England would do well to accept for the same reason. Has sent

1514.

a duplicate of Wingfeld's letter to the ambassador to show to Margaret. Considering the manner and condition of the truce, and that he was never consulted about it, Henry cannot agree to it. Even if he wished to gratify the Emperor, could not take part in it, unless he sued for it himself. Doubts not that, though the Emperor has accepted the truce, he will continue to aid England with men and victuals, as he did last year. As to the suspicion mentioned in her letter, the King never doubted her.

Is much surprised at the objections and alterations made touching the marriage of the King's sister at Calais. Desires to know her intentions by his ambassadors, who will speak to her on the subject. Eltham, 5 May 1514, après Pasques. *Signed.*

P.S.—Has just heard that the French have come, to the number of 8,000, to lay siege to Guisnes. Requests she will order all the captains, who have remained in the King's pay, to put themselves at the head of their companies, and repair to Calais, where they will receive their wages. By Tuesday next he will have 20,000 men embarked to raise the siege. Requests she will also give leave to all other soldiers in her countries to serve England.

Fr.

---

6 May.   **5042.**   PRESTS.
R. O.

"A book of prests paid and advanced by Sir John Daunce."
6 May 6 Hen. VIII.
Pp. 18. *Much obliterated by damp.*

---

6 May.   **5043.**   To the WARDENS of the new bridge, ROCHESTER.
S. B.

Warrant to build a temporary wooden bridge over the river Medway, to remain till the new bridge of stonework be completed, and to take toll for persons and vehicles ; the money thus received to be employed toward building and finishing the same stone bridge. 28 Feb. 5 Hen. VIII. *Del.* Westm., 6 May 6 Hen. VIII.

---

6 May.   **5044.**   For BARNARD FLOWRE, native of Almaine.
S. B.

Denization. *Del.* Westm., 6 May 6 Hen. VIII.
Pat. 6 *Hen. VIII. p.* 1, *m.* 14.

---

6 May.   **5045.**   For CHARLES EARL OF WORCESTER, and HENRY SOMER-
S. B.   SET LORD HERBERT, his son and heir.

Grant, in survivorship, of the offices of steward of the lordships of Uske, Kaerlyon, and Trillek, Wales, and of constable of the castle of Uske, on death or surrender of Sir William Morgan. *Del.* Westm., 6 May 6 Hen. VIII.

---

6 May.   **5046.**   For THOMAS HERLE.
P. S.

Livery of lands as brother and heir of George Herle, in the counties of Oxford, Berks, and Hereford, and as son and heir of John Herle. Richmond, 18 Jan. 5 Hen. VIII. *Del.* Westm., 6 May 6 Hen. VIII.
Pat. 6 *Hen. VIII. p.* 1, *m.* 10.

---

6 May.   **5047.**   For JAMES KNYVET.
P. S. b.

Protection for William Marret, late of Chertsey, Surrey, retained to serve in the war. 6 May 6 Hen. VIII. *Signed.*

1514.
7 May. **5048.** HENRY VIII. to LEO X.

Vat. Transcripts.
Addit. MSS.
1357, f. 21.
M S.

Was indignant on learning from the Bishop of Chieti (Theatinus) the Pope's ambassador, and John Baptista, procurator of Cardinal Cibo the Pope's nephew, that, in contempt of his Holiness, not only Baptista himself, a skilful and circumspect man, but also the Pope's ambassador Baltassar, were forbidden to enter Scotland, and the latter at last admitted under degrading conditions. The Scots, amid all their affliction, fear nothing, and trusting only to their misery dare things that no other Christian nation would do. This crime was not committed by the rude and uncivilized people, but by the bishops themselves. His Holiness may judge of the spirit of the nation at large. Though Leo will be informed of it by Baptista and the ambassadors themselves, Henry could not refrain from expressing how he felt it. If the Pope will commission him to do so, he will avenge the indignity, and act towards Scotland as he has acted towards France. Greenwich, 7 May 1514.
Lat. Copy, pp. 8.

8 May. **5049.** For WILLIAM WENTWORTH.
S. B.

To be serjeant-at-arms, with 12*d.* a day. *Del.* Westm., 8 May 6 Hen. VIII.
Pat. 6 Hen. VIII. p. 2, m. 3.

8 May. **5050.** For JOHN TURNOUR and GUTHLAC OVERTON.
S. B.

Grant, in survivorship, of the offices of auditors of the duchy of Cornwall, from Mich. last, with the usual fees out of the said duchy, and arrears from Mich. 22 Hen. VII. *Del.* Westm., 8 May 6 Hen. VIII.
Pat. 6 Hen. VIII. p. 1, m. 14.

8 May. **5051.** For SIR CHRISTOPHER BAYNHAM.
P. S.

Pardon and release as sheriff of Gloucestershire; and release to Sir Alexander Baynham of Wesbury, Stephen Cotton of Tewkesbury, William Huntley of London, and Mary, widow and executrix of Christopher Throkmerton of Trilley, of their recognizance of 40*l.*, made 10 Nov. 3 Hen. VIII. Greenwich, 15 March 5 Hen. VIII. *Del.* Westm., 8 May 6 Hen. VIII.
Pat. 6 Hen. VIII. p. 1, m. 10.

8 May. **5052.** For REGINALD GAYER.

Inspeximus and confirmation of patent 4 Feb. 22 Hen. VII., granting him the offices of clerk of the peace and clerk of the crown in Cornwall. Westm., 8 May.
Pat. 6 Hen. VIII. p. 1, m. 14.

8 May. **5053.** For RICHARD CAREW.
P. S. b.

Protection for John Goderyk, retained to serve in the war. 8 May 6 Hen. VIII. *Signed.*

9 May. **5054.** J. CARDINAL DE MEDICIS to HENRY VIII.
Vitell. B. II. 75.*
B. M.

Has received the King's letter written in reply to the report of Baltasar Tuerdus (Stewart). Has told what took place in the ninth session of the Lateran, to the Bishop of Worcester, whose letters will fully inform his Majesty. Rome, 9 May 1514. *Signed.*
Lat., p. 1. Add.

1514.
9 May.   **5055.**   SIR ROBERT WINGFIELD to [HENRY VIII.]

Vitell. B. xviii. 82.
B. M.

Wrote last from Lynce, from whence he came here in a " boott
without sayle ;"—this is the fairest city ever seen, " notwithstanding the inh[abitants] be as groosse as a pasty of veell." Carts go in
24 hours to the principal town in Hungary, and if Henry were now
as far to the east as he is to the north-west, Wingfield would have a
better chance of seeing him.   The Emperor is going through
Styreremark and Carynthe into [Italy] to meet the Viceroy, who
will lay siege to Treviso, having sent Urreas to spur him on.
Looks hourly for intelligence of Henry's pleasure.   Eight days ago
the Emperor intended sending Louis Marroton in post to my Lady.
Does not know that he has yet dispatched him,—if not, the dispatch
would probably go by Fume.—The Turks and Hungarians are
likely to go to war, the former claiming tribute, and the latter
certain castles that the Turk holds.   Vienna, 9 May 1514.
Hol., pp. 2, mutitated.

9 May.   **5056.**   For SIR JOHN SHARPE.

S. B.

Grant, in fee, of the manor of Brokedisshchalle alias Brokdissh in
Burston, Norf., granted by Henry VII. to James Braybroke, and
on his death to John Sharp, during pleasure, by patent 3 Nov.
1 Hen. VIII., at the annual rent of one red rose.   *Del.* Westm.,
9 May 6 Hen. VIII.
Pat. 6 *Hen. VIII. p.* 1, *m.* 14.

10 May.   **5057.**   MAXIMILIAN to MARGARET OF SAVOY.

R. O.

Is sending to Henry VIII. Gerard de Playne, Lord De la Roche,
and John Colla.   Vienna, 10 May 1514, 29 Max.   *Signed.*
P. 1.   *Addressed* "Mary," for " Margaret."

10 May.   **5058.**   MAXIMILIAN to HENRY VIII.

R. O.

Credence in behalf of Gerard de Playna, Sieur De la Roche,
president of the council, and John Colla.   Vienna, 10 May 1514,
29 Max.
Lat., p. 1.   *Addressed.*
2. The same to Queen Katharine.   To the same effect.
Lat., p. 1.   *Addressed.*

10 May.   **5059.**   KNIGHT and others to HENRY VIII.

Galba, B. iii. 167.
B. M.

[Received] two letters, dated the last of April and the 5th of this;
also a letter to the Archduchess, and another [from] Wingfield, with
copies of them both, and also the do[uble] that the said Sir Robert
lately sent unto your grace.   Found not in the packet the answer
to the Emperor's letter.   Delivered their letters to the Archduchess.
Desired of her leave to retain the troops of those parts, as the
King would continue his enterprise, and though the Emperor
had joined the truce, yet, as he was the confederate of England,
he would doubtless consent.   She excused herself, saying that any
leave she could grant would not satisfy the troops engaged by the
King unless he could get the promise of the Emperor, whose
resolution she expected by the next post, and as the Duke of
Gueldres might be troublesome, she would want the troops herself ;
to which they answered he had already accepted the truce.   She
refused to give any further answer touching the marriage.   They
said they marvelled she did not make some plainer overture, as the

1514.

King had consented to the marriage being solemnized at Calais. She said she waited for the next post ;—that she thought the Emperor would be glad to make the King's resolution for not going on with the enterprise an excuse for not joining the truce. She will comply with the King's wish, and command the captains to repair to their garrisons to be ready when called upon. The President told them that the great difficulty arose from the Emperor not having received the 30,000 crowns of gold, especially as he knew of the 20,000 given monthly unto the King of Arragon, who is a rich and mighty prince ; and he thought that " your grace might depart with like sum of money unto the Emperor, being poor." They told him of the King's bounty to the Emperor, and that the enterprise was for his good as much as for the King's. Advise a settlement with the troops that they have no claim after the 20th. Received his letters this morning by John Clyfford. Mechlin, 10 [May]. *Signed :* R. Wyngfield—W. Knyght—T. Spinelly.
Pp. 5, mutilated. Add.

10 May. **5060.** For SIR JOHN LYSLE, NICHOLAS SHELTON, alderman of
S. B. London, and ROBERT COUSYN.

Collation to the next vacant canonry and prebend in St. Stephen's Westminster, or St. George's Windsor. *Del.* Westm, 10 May, 6 Hen. VIII.
Pat. 6 Hen. VIII. p. 2, m. 5 and 15.

10 May. **5061.** To the ABP. OF CANTERBURY, Chancellor.
S. B.

For writs of *dedimus potestatem* to the Abbot of Wynchecombe and Edmund Tanne, to take the fealty of William Malvern, late elected abbot of Gloucester. Eltham, 10 May 6 Hen. VIII.

10 May. **5062.** For JOHN CONSTABLE, LL.D.
P. S.

Presentation to the church of Fulbeke, Linc. dioc., void by resignation. Eltham, 10 May 6 Hen. VIII. *Del.* Westm., 10 May.

10 May. **5063.** For GILES STRANGWAYS.
P. S.

To have writs of entry in the post, for recovery of certain lands in Somerset and Dorset, he having been appointed to wait on the King in the war. 10 May 6 Hen. VIII. *Signed.*

11 May. **5064.** For WALTER DEVEREUX LORD FERRERS.
P. S.

Wardship of Ralph, son and heir of Nicholas, kinsman and heir of Sir Ralph Langford. Eltham, 4 May 6 Hen. VIII. *Del.* Westm., 11 May.
Pat. 6 Hen. VIII. p. 2, m. 14 and 15.

11 May. **5065.** For the ABBEY of WALTHAM HOLY CROSS.
P. S.

Assent to the election of John Malyn, canon and prior of Waltham Holy Cross, as abbot, *vice* John Sherneboke, resigned. Eltham, 7 May 6 Hen. VIII. *Del.* Westm., 11 May.

ii. Petition of Robert Wodeleff canon and sub-prior, and the convent, for the above. 2 May 1514, 6 Hen. VIII.

12 May. **5066.** For THOMAS BENOLT NORROY.
R. O.

Patent appointing him Clarencieux King of Arms. 12 May 6 Hen. VIII.
Copy, p. 1.

3 E

1514.
12 May. **5067.** For THOMAS BASTON, husbandman.

Protection ; going to the war. Westm, 12 May.
Fr. 6 Hen. VIII. p. 2, m. 14.

12 May. **5068.** SILVESTER [DE GIGLIS] BP. OF WORCESTER to WOLSEY.
R. O.

Recommends Jo. Baptista and Guido de Portinariis, brothers, of
a noble family in Florence. Jo. Baptista is the rector of St. Mary
Aldercher in Wolsey's diocese. Rome, 12 May 1514.
Lat., p. 1. Addressed: Reverendo, &c. Tho. electo Lincolniensi.

12 May. **5069.** For SIR JOHN SHARP.
S. B.

Grant, in fee, of the manor of Kyrtelyng, with appurtenances in
Kyrtelyng and Long Staunton, Camb. ; — to hold at a fee-farm
rent of 33*l.* 6*s.* 8*d.* from Mic. 5 Hen. VIII. Deduction to be made
if any part of the manor be taken away. *Del.* Westm., 12 May
6 Hen. VIII.
Pat. 6 Hen. VIII. p. 1, m. 14.

12 May. **5070.** For NICHOLAS RYNG.
S. B.

To be gunner of the royal ordnance, with 12*d.* a day. *Del.*
Westm., 12 May 6 Hen. VIII.
Pat. 6 Hen. VIII. p. 2, m. 25.

12 May. **5071.** For HELIER CARTERET.
S. B.

To be bailiff of the Isle of Jersey. *Del.* Westm., 12 May
6 Hen. VIII.
Fr. 6 Hen. VIII. p. 2, m. 4.

12 May. **5072.** For SIR RICHARD TEMPEST.
P. S.

Lease for forty years of the farm of the town of Wakefeld, York,
with the office of bailiff there, the bakehouse and fishery therein, all
meadows called Wilbigh, Dibford and Erlesing, parcel of the lordship of Wakefeld, the mills of Wakefeld and Horbury, "le Newe
Milne super le dam," and the fisheries there, with timber for repairs
from the old and new park, at an annual rent of 89*l.* 16*s.* 7½*d.*,
on surrender by Richard Peke, since the death of Thomas Grice,
of patent 9 Nov. 16 Hen. VII. by which the said premises were
leased to Peke and Grice for 20 years. Lambeth, 14 Feb.
5 Hen. VIII. *Del.* Westm., 12 May 6 Hen. VIII.
Pat. 6 Hen. VIII. p. 2, m. 14.

12 May. **5073.** For SIR THOMAS WYNDHAM, alias WYMONDHAM, knight
P. S.   of the Body, of Felbrigge, Norf., alias of Danbury,
                   Essex.

Pardon and release as late treasurer of war in the retinue of
Thomas Earl of Surrey. Greenwich, 23 April 6 Hen. VIII.
Del. Westm., 12 May 6 Hen. VIII.
Pat. 6 Hen. VIII. p. 1, m. 18.

1514.

12 May. **5074.** For PHILIP BARNARD of Akenham, and THOMAS
P. S. SHELDRAKE of Berugham, Suff.

Release of bail entered 5 Dec. 5 Hen. VIII. before Sir Philip
Bothe and Robert Southwell, jun., justices of the peace in co.
Suffolk, for the appearance of Robert Hervey and Edmund Hervy,
tailor, both of Stratbroke. Eltham, 4 May 6 Hen. VIII. *Del.*
Westm., 12 May.

Pat. 6 *Hen. VIII. p.* 1, *m.* 17.

12 May. **5075.** For ST. PETER'S, GLOUCESTER.
P. S.

Assent to the election of William Malverne, B.D., of the monastery of St. Peter, Gloucester, as abbot, *vice* John Newton, D.D.,
deceased. Eltham, 8 May 6 Hen. VIII. *Del.* Westm., 12 May.

Pat. 6 *Hen. VIII. p.* 2, *m.* 25.

ii. Petition of John Chedworth, prior, and the convent, for the
above. 5 May 1514.

15 May. **5076.** WINGFIELD and SPINELLY to [HENRY VIII.]
Galba, B. III. 190.
B. M.

Have received a letter from Sir Robt. Wingfield, which they
enclose. My Lady is surprised she has received no message from
the Emperor,—complains that many reports are made of her to
him—that the surmises of the King of Arragon are known and
hated—" that lately an Arragonese being here, having the room of
the tenes playe[d] with the Prince of Castill, fell at a variance
of certain words with a Castilian upon the deliverance of Don John
de Manuell, saying unto him, amongst other things, that if the said
Lord Prince will not be obeissant unto the King of Arragon, or go
into Spain against his will, that he might be poisoned, as his father
King Philip was." — Sir Thomas Cheyny arrived this day at
Brussells with horses, three coursers and a light horse of his own
breed, as goodly beasts as may be seen, from the King for the
Marquis of Mantua.—25 sail of French and Scotch were lately on
the coast of Flanders. — Will. Copland has staid the departure
of the ordnance. Mechlin, 15 May. *Signed :* R. Wyngfield—
T. Spinelly.

Pp. 2, *mutilated.*

15 May. **5077.** For THOMAS TRACE, JOHN BALL, &c.
S. B.

Pardon for them and eight others, mariners of Hull, for the murder
of Godfrey Darold. *Del.* Westm., 15 May 6 Hen. VIII.

Pat. 6 *Hen. VIII. p.* 1, *m.* 17.

15 May. **5078.** For JOHN BAPTISTE PORTYNARY, clk., of the diocese of
S. B. Tournay.

Denization. *Del.* Westm, 15 May 6 Hen. VIII.

Pat. 6 *Hen. VIII. p.* 1, *m.* 10.

15 May. **5079.** For CHARLES DUKE OF SUFFOLK, marshal of the King's
S. B. court, alias marshal of the Marshalsea.

Pardon. *Del.* Westm., 15 May 6 Hen. VIII.

Pat. 6 *Hen. VIII. p.* 1, *m.* 15.

15 May. **5080.** For MARIAN (MARINUS) GARET, native of Normandy.
S. B.

Denization. *Del.* . . . . ., 15 May 6 Hen. VIII.

3 E 2

1514.

15 May.   **5081.**   For RALPH LANE.
S. B.
Exemption from serving on juries, or being made knight, sheriff, &c. *Del.* Westm., 15 May 6 Hen. VIII.
Pat. 6 *Hen. VIII. p.* 1, *m.* 14.

15 May.   **5082.**   For SIR THOMAS BERKELEY.
P. S.
To be constable of Berkeley castle; keeper of "le castell parke" there, with "le Worthy" inclosed; keeper of the woods of Hynton, called Cheslaunder and Redwode; keeper of the deer; and master of the hunt;—*vice* James Berkeley;—with fees out of the lordship of Berkeley, and the herbage and pannage of the said park and woods, and the fishery of Smethmore and "le Gale" in the Severn. Eltham, 12 May 6 Hen. VIII. *Del.* Westm., 15 May.
Pat. 6 *Hen. VIII. p.* 1, *m.* 11.

15 May.   **5083.**   For RICHARD SCORER, gunstone-maker.
P. S.
To be gunstone-maker, with 6*d.* a day.   Eltham, 13 May 6 Hen. VIII. *Del.* Westm., 15 May 6 Hen. VIII.
Pat. 6 *Hen. VIII. p.* 2, *m.* 3.

15 May.   **5084.**   For JOHN PORTE, the King's solicitor.
P. S.
Custody of a third part of the possessions of Sir John Montgomery, deceased, during the minority of Ellen, one of his daughters and heirs, with wardship and marriage of the said Ellen. Eltham, 14 May 6 Hen. VIII. *Del.* Westm., 15 May.
Pat. 6 *Hen. VIII. p.* 2, *m.* 15.

15 May.   **5085.**   For SIR THOMAS WEST.
P. S. b.
Protection for William Wynnall, of Winchester, carrier, retained to serve in the war.   Halnaker, Sussex, 15 May 6 Hen. VIII. *Signed.*

16 May.   **5086.**   For SIR JOHN DIGBY, knight of the Body.
S. B.
Confirmation of patent of Henry VII., granting him, in tail male, the lordship of Bedale, York; to hold by service of one knight's fee and one red rose at the feast of St. John the Baptist. The lordship came to Henry VII. by forfeiture of Francis Viscount Lovel. Further grant, in tail male, of all possessions of the said Viscount in Bedale, Aiscough, Littill Lemyng and Northlees, from 23 April 1 Hen. VIII. *Del.* Westm., 16 May 6 Hen. VIII.
Pat. 6 *Hen. VIII. p.* 2, *m.* 3.

16 May.   **5087.**   For THOMAS TAMWORTH.
S. B.
Wardship of John, son and heir of John Tamworth, of Leek, Linc. *Del.* Westm., 16 May 6 Hen. VIII. *Signed:* Thomas Lovell.
Pat. 6 *Hen. VIII. p.* 1, *m.* 17.

16 May.   **5088.**   For MARCELLUS DE LA MORE, serjeant of the surgeons.
P. S. b.
Protection for Henry Brownyng, appointed to serve in the war. 16 May 6 Hen. VIII. *Signed.*

1514.
17 May. **5089.** For Sir Richard Cholmondley, knight of the Body.

S. B.

To be steward of the manor of Cotyngham Langton on "le Olde," York, part of the duchy of Somerset, (which office was held by him with a fee of 40s. by grant of Margaret late Countess of Richmond); with annual fee of 40s. out of the same manor. Also grant to him and Nicholas Thelwell, of the office of bailiff of the said manor, and keeper of the park, with annual fee of 4l. 13s. 4d.; to hold the same during the minority of Edward, son and heir of John Grey Lord Powes, as long as the said manor remains in the King's hands. The said Richard to have 40s. for having executed the said office of steward from the death of the said Lord. *Del.* Westm., 17 May 6 Hen. VIII.

Pat. 6 Hen. VIII. p. 1, *m.* 17.

17 May. **5090.** Dacre to Norfolk and others.

Calig. B. II. 190.
B. M.
Pinkerton's App.*

Desires them to have in remembrance " that at Greenwich in the month of December was two years whereas the King of Scots, of his malicious and untrue purpose, was aboutward to have stolen the town of Berwick," when Dacre accepted the wardenship of the East and Middle Marches, refused by Lord Darcy, on condition that no report should be believed to his discredit till he could make his answer. It is misreported that he does not keep proper watch, and holds communication with the Chamberlain of Scotland.—Since he was last with the King at Windsor, in December, has never met the Chamberlain, except at Coklawe for redress. Certified the King's grace of it by a letter from Morpeth, in March. Sends a copy by Dr. Conyers, the bearer.—Has no familiarity with the Chamberlain. At the field of Brankston he and his company encountered the Earl of Huntley and the Chamberlain. Sir John Home, Sir Will. Cokburne of Langton, Cuthbert Home of Fastcastle, the son and heir of Sir John Home, Sir Will. Cokburne Sir David Home the Laird of Blacater, Will. Carr, and three brothers, Bromfelds, friends of the Chamberlain, were slain by Dacre and his folks, and his brother, Philip Dacre, taken prisoner.— The Scots love him worse than any man in England, " by reason that I found the body of the King of Scots slain in the field, and thereof advertised my Lord of Norfolk by my writing; and thereupon I brought the corpse to Berwick, and delivered it to my said Lord; at which time, as I was entreated in my said Lord's presence by one Langton of Berwick, I report me to his Lordship, and as yet it is not punished."

It is not true he has been remiss in making espial in Scotland. The Scotch council are so inconstant there is no trusting them, except at time of parliament or of a general council. Would have been sorry to pester the King and Norfolk with trifles and flying tales, as he supposes others have done. Without help it is impossible for him, a poor Baron, to keep the East, Middle, and West Marches securely, which even the Duke of Glo'ster and the Earl of Northumberland could not do. My Lords of Norfolk and Winchester, who lay upon the East borders in the last war, know the difficulty. Had informed them before, but he is badly supported. Berwick, Bamboroughshire, and Dunstanborough, with Sir Roger Grey's power, are in Lord Darcy's hands; Alnwick and Warkworth belong to the Earl of Northumberland; Elandshire, Norhamshire, and the Grey's lands, to the Bp. of

* Partly printed in Pinkerton.

Durham and William 'Heron of Furde, who will not do service with him. Since last being with the King there have not been more than 80 cottages burnt in these Marches, in value not 40*l.* at the utmost. At which time it was promised Lord Darcy, or some one else, should be sent down to the East Marches to defend them. Has kept in good order the West and Middle Marches, being 50 miles of dry borders, from Bowness to Hanging Stane, where every one may ride at his pleasure. There have not been burnt 20 houses in them. For one ox taken by the Scots he has taken 100, and for one sheep 200 ; and for the townships in his rule from the beginning of the war to this day, " as well when as the late King of Scots lay in the same East Marches, as at all other times," he has burnt and destroyed six times more in Scotland. Gives an account of the devastations. Land for 630 ploughs, and upwards of 42 miles, " lies all, and every of them, waste now, and no corn sown upon none of the said grounds." This is over and above the great raid he made in the Middle March on Martinmas day last, the particulars of which he wrote to the King. On the West Marches he has destroyed 34 townships ; " where, as there was in all times passed, 400 ploughs and above, which are now clearly wasted, and no man dwelling in any of them," except in three. So he will continue his service and diligence from time to time.

On the death of Roger Fenwick, nominated his brother Philip Dacre to succeed, according to his indentures. Complains that the council have admitted Ralph Fenwick his son, but as it is the King's pleasure has discharged his brother. If Fenwick is to continue in office, hopes he will find sufficient bond to discharge him of all responsibility, so that if anything be done amiss Fenwick and Sir Edw. Radcliffe shall answer for it. Desires that his brother Philip Dacre may continue to have the wardship of John De la Vale, notwithstanding a placard obtained from Mr Lovel this last month of April by Sir Cuthbert Ogle, priest, and Guy De la Vale, giving them the profits of the lands. The wardship of Geo. De la Vale deceased, son and heir of Ann De la Vale, widow, also deceased, and brother of John aforesaid, was granted by patent 18 July 19 Hen. VII. (which the bearer will show) to his mother, who was married to the said Philip Dacre. Kirkoswald, 17 May. *Signed.*

Addressed : To my singular good Lords, my Lord of Norfolk, my Lord of Winchester, my Lord of Durham, my Lord of Lincoln, my Lord of Surrey, and other my Lords of the King's most honorable council.

Pp. 6.

17 May. **5091.** For Sir Richard Cholmeley, knight of the Body.
S. B.

Licence to export English wools and import wines, &c. notwithstanding the act 20 Hen. VI., by which the officers of customs are prohibited from possessing ships, he being comptroller of the customs in the port of Hull by patent 8 Oct. 1 Hen. VIII. *Del.* Westm., 17 May 6 Hen. VIII.
Pat. 6 *Hen. VIII. p.* 2, *m.* 14.

17 May. **5092.** For James De la Noa and John de Cicilia, the King's
P. S. trumpeters.

Licence to import 400 butts of Malvesyes. Eltham, 15 May 6 Hen. VIII. *Del.* Westm., 17 May.
Fr. 6 *Hen. VIII. p.* 2, *m.* 3.

1514.
17 May.
P. S. b.

5093. For JOHN SHARP.

To have writs of covenant and entry in the post against Humphrey Stafford, at the suit of Richard Broke, serjeant-at-law, John Turnour, and others, *in re* the manor of Codreth, Herts, as he is appointed to serve in the war. 17 May 6 Hen. VIII. *Signed.*

18 May.
R. O.

5094. SIR ROBT. WINGFIELD to HENRY VIII.

Wrote his last from this city on the 9th, advertising him that Loys Marroton "looked every hour for his despatch from the Emperor to my Lady his daughter." He left on the 13th. Has received instructions by Marroton that De la Roche and another have charge of the Embassy in the form he has already advertised the King. The Emperor desires the Venetians may have no commerce with England. He left eight days since for Gratz. Has heard from Bannisius that letters of the 4th state the Pope is no better inclined to the Emperor. Cardinal Gource was to leave on the 6th for the Emperor receiving the Pope's resolution on the 5th. Till the Pope and Emperor are friends their enemies will be dangerous. Vienna, 18 May 1514.

Hol., pp. 2. Addressed.

18 May.

5095. For NICH. WAPLOT of Barnby, York.

Pardon for killing Oliver Hanson, in self defence. Westm., 18 May.

Pat. 6 Hen. VIII. p. 2, m. 15.

18 May.

5096. For SIR JOHN SHARP.

Licence to alienate the manor or lordship of Brokedissehehalle alias Brokdissh in Burston, Norf., to Sir Wm. Tyler, John Turnour, Hugh Edwardis, Geo. Quarles, Ric. Drewell, Guthlac Overton, John Higham, Robt. Broune of Walcote, sen., Rob. Broune, jun., his brother, John Broune, Edw. Broune, John Father, David Edwardis, John Edwardis, Francis Quarles, and John Everton, their heirs and assigns, for uses to be declared by the said John Sharp. Westm., 18 May.

Pat. 6 Hen. VIII. p. 1, m. 15.

18 May.
S. B.

5097. For JOHN BOURGHCHIER LORD BERNERS.

Reversion of the office of Chancellor of the Exchequer on death or surrender of Thomas Lovell, to whom it was granted by patent 12 Oct. 1 Hen. VII. *Del.* Westm., 18 May 6 Hen. VIII.

Pat. 6 Hen. VIII. p. 2, m. 6.

18 May.
S. B.

5098. To JOHN YONG, Master of the Rolls.

To cancel a recognizance of 200*l.*, made 26 July 16 Hen. VII. by Sir John Turbervyle of Freermayn, Dorset, Thomas Turbervyle of Mote, Kent, and Roger Cheverell of Stoke, Dorset. Greenwich, 18 May 6 Hen. VIII.

18 May.
R. O.

5099. LEO X. to HENRY VIII.

Complains of the confiscation, at the instance of the Duke of Suffolk, of a cargo of alum consigned by the Apostolic Chamber to John de Cavalcanti. As all the dues demanded at London have been paid, and the said John is a freeman of London, begs the cargo, or its value, may be restored. In villa Manlianæ, 18 May 1514, 2 pont.

Lat., p. 1. Addressed.

19 May. **5100.** FACOMBE.

Exemption for the men of the manor of Facombe, Hants, which is of the ancient demesne of the Crown, from toll or contribution to the expenses of knights sent to Parliament, according to custom. Westm., 19 May.
Pat. 6 *Hen. VIII. p.* 1, *m.* 18.

19 May. **5101.** For the MASTER and WARDENS of the Guild of ST. COR-
S. B. NELIUS THE MARTYR, in the Church of ST. MARGARET, in the Sanctuary, WESTMINSTER.

Incorporation of the same guild, and licence to found a chantry, with one chaplain, to pray for the King and Queen. *Del.* Westm., 19 May 6 Hen. VIII.
Pat. 6 *Hen. VIII. p.* 1, *m.* 28.

19 May. **5102.** For THOMAS, son of ROGER NORMAN, deceased.
P. S. Pardon and release of all alienations, &c., made by him without licence, of the lands held by him in the manor of Corton, Somerset. Eltham, 15 May 6 Hen. VIII. *Del.* Westm., 19 May.
Pat. 6 *Hen. VIII. p.* 2, *m.* 7.

19 May. **5103.** For GEORGE WARNER, rector of Pylton, Northt., alias
P. S. of Staunford, Linc., alias of London, clk.

Pardon. Eltham, 16 May 6 Hen. VIII. *Del.* Westm., 19 May.
Pat. 6 *Hen. VIII. p.* 1, *m.* 11.

20 May. **5104.** SIR RICHARD WINGFIELD to SUFFOLK.
Galba, B. III. 191.
B. M. . . . . . . "fro my cousin I have sent . . . . to Mr. Controlle . . . . in a packet addressed to my servant . . . to be delivered by him to your hand." My Lady has as yet received no answer from the Emperor. All the wise men hereabouts are abused with his long delay, as the time is passed, and no conclusion taken. The term of ratification expired on the 12th inst., so within a few days it must be known what he has done. Urges the marriage should be perfected with all diligence. All the Prince's council, except Hormistorffe, are inclined to delay it ; and, as he is the only person who upholds my Lady Mary's cause, they seek to undo him. Has told Hormistorffe that neither the King nor my Lady Mary will forget him. Thinks he should recommend him to the King. Hormistorffe told him that the Prince, in answer to those about him who urged his being in love with a damsel of the court, said, " on his faith that it was not so, nor never would be of her or any other only my Lady Mary." Hopes the marriage may soon be concluded. Malines, 20 May.

P.S. His cousin Sidney has been a little crazed with the ague.
Hol., pp. 8, *mutilated. Add.*

20 May. **5105.** SIR ROBERT WINGFIELD to HENRY VIII.
Vitell. B. XVIII. 83.
B. M. Wrote last on the . . of this month, stating that the Emperor would depart next day, but the long absence of the Emperor [would occasion] so many matters of redress that the time of his departure is uncertain. This day received two letters from the King in one cover, dated at Eltham the . . of last month, and the 5th of this ; the latter containing instructions how to answer the matters mentioned in Wingfield's of the 5th April. Is not surprised at the Emperor consenting to the " detestable

1514.

truce," when the King of Arragon justifies it, as Henry will probably have learnt by Wingfield's former letters and Marroton's to my Lady. Henry, by his letter of the 5th May, praises Wingfield for his conduct of affairs mentioned in his letter of 19th April. Wingfield thanks the King for his good opinion of him ; will not fail to inform the Emperor of the matters contained in Henry's of the 5th May. Hopes to be able to give the Emperor a satisfactory answer upon the subject of the Roman crown and the vicariate of the empire, should he touch upon those matters. Knows the Emperor to be well disposed towards Henry. Wingfield intends to follow the Emperor tomorrow, and hopes to get an audience, and will advertise Henry of the result. Vienna in Ostryk, 20 May.

P.S. Wingfield wishes to be discharged of secretary's [duties]. Sends Henry a letter from the Duke of Milan.

Hol. pp. 3, mutilated. Addressed : The King's Grace.

20 May. **5106.**

Vitell. B. II. 77.
B. M.
Ellis, 1 S. II. 226.

CHR. [BAINBRIDGE], Cardinal, to HENRY VIII.

Has written to the King of those who failed in their duty. The s[ervant] of the Bp. of Worcester was met coming in the dark night with a torch behind him, from the French ambassador's house, the Bp. of Marseilles, and instead of coming the straight way, "by my gates," struck down a secret back lane. That bishop (Marseilles) is a great enemy to England. Worcester was frequently with the Protector of France in the city, and in "vynes and garthynges" without the city, and nothing is more odious to him than to hear of the prosperity of England. His secretaries made use of these words, "Latt th[ose] barbarous people of France and Englande every oon kill odre, what shuld [we] care therefore, soo we have their money to make merry withal here." He is universally called here "the falsarie orator of Engl[and]." He will be accused of saying this from malice, as heretofore ;—but he had brought Worcester to Rome in Pope Julie's days ;—got him appointed orator, and subscribed letters with him.—Cannot say he loves him, partly for his untrue dealing towards himself in obtaining favors and writing clandestine letters, partly for his untruth to the King. Pope Julius warned him that Worcester would treat the King and Bainbridge as he had treated his Holiness. So long as he found Worcester true and diligent, used his services ;—now never allows him to subscribe his letters, and never will. For these reasons would not take Worcester with him when he showed the Pope the letter from the English ambassador. Is surprised he has had no answer to his letter, wherein he advertised the King of the Pope's willingness to send the brief "*super nomine Christianissimi Regis.*" Worcester always disliked that brief. Thinks he is the cause of this silence. Encloses a letter of Cardinal Sion. Learns from him that the Swiss remain firm. Rome, 20 May 1514.

P. S. in his own hand : Doubts not he will see the love borne to his affairs by all strangers there, from the highest to the lowest. *Signed.*

Mutilated, pp. 3. Add.

20 May. **5107.**

Vitell. B. II. 78.*
B. M.

SILVESTER BP. OF WORCESTER to HENRY VIII.

Will learn all the news by other letters sent this day ; among others that the Pope had secretly sent the Bp. of Tricarico to discover the disposition of the French King for a truce, that if England were willing to yield to the Pope's wishes on certain

1514.

conditions he might not be deceived. He has this minute sent a messenger to him to proceed from the French court to England. Rome, 20 May 1514. *Signed.*

Lat., p. 1. Add.

20 May.   **5108.**   For the SAILORS OF ENGLAND.

R. O.

Licence to found anew a guild of themselves and other persons, both men and women,[*] in the church of Depford Stronde, Kent, to be called the Guild of the Holy Trinity and St. Clement ; the brethren of the said guild to appoint one master, four wardens, and eight assistants annually, all of whom shall be removable at pleasure. Also mortmain licence to acquire lands to the annual value of 20 marks, for a chaplain. 20 May 6 Hen. VIII.

Pat. 6 Hen.VIII. p. 1, m. 10.

20 May.   **5109.**   For RIC. SCOTT of Doncaster, York.

Pardon for having killed Wm. Gibson in self defence. Westm., 20 May.

Pat. 6 Hen.VIII. p. 1, m. 15.

21 May.   **5110.**   POL[YDORE VERGIL] to [WOLSEY].

Vitell, B. II. 76.
B. M.

On his return to the city informed the Cardinal of Bath how much Wolsey had befriended him. Seeing the Cardinal anxious to show his gratitude, broke to him this business (*negotium nostrum*) of the cardinalate,—(will speak more plainly hereafter),—and asked him to use his efforts for that purpose. On his doing so the Pope thought it would be expedient, if Wolsey had great authority with the King, to make him a cardinal. Bath will write to Wolsey when the matter is near its accomplishment, to gain the royal assent. Not a word is to be said. Thinks he should write to Bath, and the matter be so managed that he shall understand from Polydore that it will be agreeable to Wolsey, and let it be generally understood that it was the spontaneous offering of the Pope, " sicut D. V. reverenda ita faciendum esse me admonuit." If he is too busy to write he may communicate with the writer's brother, Jerome. Begs Wolsey will protect him that he be not more burthened in convocation, as he is a naturalised Englishman. The Pope desires peace, but all depends on the event of a war between England and France. Gurk has left for Germany without making peace with the Venetians. [Rome], 21 May 1514.

Lat., pp. 2.

21 May.   **5111.**   LEONARD SPINELLY to HENRY VIII.

Lansd. 818, f. 12b.
B. M.

Speech on delivering to the King the cap and sword. 21 May 1514.

Copy, p. 1.

ii. Account of the entry of Spinelly, and the ceremony of presenting the cap and sword. Was met at the sea-side by the bishops, at Blackheath by the Duke of Suffolk, the Marquis of Dorset, the Bp. of Lincoln, the Earl of Essex, and all the spears. Proceeded to London with the Duke on the right hand, the Marquis on the left, with the Bp. of Lincoln, the mayor, aldermen, and city companies standing in the streets. Was met at the west door of St. Paul's by the Archbishop, the Bps. of Winchester, Durham, and Exeter, *in pontificalibus.* Proceeded with the choir to the high altar, where he deposited the cap and sword, and thence to the Austin Friars. On

1514.

Sunday the King and all the ambassadors, and the Duke of Longueville, then prisoner, the Duke of Norfolk, William Browne, the
Lord Mayor of London, proceeded from the bishop's palace to the
choir of St. Paul's, where, under a travers near the high altar,
Spinelly was introduced, delivered to the King the Pope's letters,
and was answered by Dr. Tunstall. "After the King went a procession, and both the sword that the Pope had sent, and the King's
sword. The Pope's orator bare the sword that he brought. The
procession done, began the mass suug by the Archbishop, the Bp. of
London, gospeller, the Bp. of Exeter, epistoler. The cap was put
on the King's head, and the sword girt about him by the Archbishop
of Canterbury, after the order of the book. And after mass, when
the King returned, the sword that the Pope sent was born alone by
the Duke of Suffolk, and by him in the King's chamber delivered
to the Vice Chamberlain in lieu of the Lord Chamberlain. The
strangers were" * * (*The account here breaks off abruptly.*)
P. 1. Headed: 19 May.—In same hand as the preceding.

22 May. **5112.**   EXPENCES OF THE WAR.

R. O.

"Paymentis of mony for the Kingis Riall Armye by see for
oon moneth bygynnyng the **xxv** daye of Apryll anno vj^{to} R.
Henr. viij^{ri}, which shall eende the **xxij** daye of Maye then next
after, the first and the last dayes includyd, accomptyng **xxviij** dayes
for the moneth."

The Trinyte Sovereigne.—To Sir Thomas Wyndham, vice-
admiral, 10s. a day ; Sir Arthur Plantagenet, captain, 18d. a
day ; 299 soldiers, 260 mariners and 40 gunners, at 5s. a man
per month. Rewards to the master gunner, 5s. a month,
his mate and 4 quartermasters 2s. 6d. a month, and 34 other
gunners 20d. a piece ; 2 clerks to the admiral at 8d. a day.
Total, 178l. 14s.

The Gabriell Riall.—To Sir William Travanyon, cap., 40d. a
day ; 255 soldiers, 270 mariners, 30 gunners. Tot. 153l. 3s. 4d.

The Kateryn Forteleza. — Anthony Poyntis, cap.* ; 160 sol.
200 m., 20 g. Tot. 103l. 18s. 4d.

The Mary Rose.—Sir Henry Sherburn, cap. ; 185 sol., 200 m.,
20 g. Tot. 110l. 3s. 4d.

The Peter Pomegarnet.—Sir Edward Ichyngham, cap., for his
wages, 42s. ; 143 sol., 160 m., 20 g. Tot. 90l. 0s. 4d.

The John Baptist.—Sir Rauf Ellercar* ; 140 sol., 150 m., 15 g.
Tot. 83l.

The Gret Nicholas.—John Flemyng, cap., 42s. ; 130 sol., 150 m.,
15 g. Tot. 82l. 12s.

The Gret Barke.—Sir William Pyrton, cap.; 100 sol., 120 m.,
10 g. Tot. 63l. 16s. 8d.

The Gret Barbara.—John Wallop, cap.*; 150 sol., 160 m., 20 g.
Tot. 99l. 13s. 4d.

The Mary George.—Edmund Wiscman* ; 70 sol., 120 m., 13 g.
Tot. 57l. 6s. 8d.

The Mary Jamys.—William Ellercar, cap., 42s. ; 70 sol. 120 m.,
10 g. Tot. 58l. 0s. 4d.

The Cryst.—Thomas Vowell, cap., 42s.; 61 sol., 90 m., 10 g.
Tot. 48l. 5s. 4d. "Item, more for 8 soldiers, 40s."

The Mary and John.—William Mygenall, cap., 42s. ; 70 sol.
80 m., 10 g. Tot. 48l. 0s. 4d.

---

* The wages of these captains are set down as " nil."

The Lesse Barke.—Sir Stephen Bulle, cap., 42*s.*; 71 sol., 80 m., 10 g. Tot. 48*l.* 8*s.* 8*d.*

The Barbara.—William West, cap., 42*s.*; 45 sol, 70 m., 10 g. Tot. 39*l.* 5*s.* 4*d.*

The Anne Gallant.—Thomas Denys, cap., 42*s.*; 50 sol., 75 m., 8 g. Tot. 40*l.* 17*s.*

The Lezard.—Christopher Coo, 42*s.*; 40 sol., 45 m., 7 g. Tot. 30*l.* 5*s.* 4*d.*

The Jennet Purwyn.—Laurence Fartley, cap., 42*s.*; 25 sol., 30 m., 5 g. Tot. 22*l.* 2*s.*

The Swepestake.—William Cooke, cap., 42*s.*; 25 sol, 30 m., 5 g. Tot. 25*l.* 17*s.*

The Swallowe.—Robert Mountency, cap., 42*s.*; 25 sol., 30 m., 5 g. Tot. 21*l.* 17*s.*

The Blak Barke.—Christopher Thwaytis, cap., 42*s.* ; 25 sol., 30 m., 5 g. Tot. 21*l.* 17*s.*

The Roose Gallie.—John Watkyn, master* ; 60 m., 5 g. Tot. 19*l.* 15*s.*

The Kateryn Gallye.—William Kenwode, master* ; 55 m., 5 g. Tot. 19*l.* 15*s.*

The Henry Grace a Dieu.—Sir Thomas Wyndam, vice-admiral and captain. Sir Edw. Dunne, captain, 18*d.* a day* ; 4 petty captains ; 500 sol., 500 m., 60 g. Tot. ————.

The Gret Elizabeth.—Sir Wistan Browne, cap., 18*d.* a day*; 200 sol., 260 m., 30 g. Tot. 133*l.* 20*d.*

ii.—Hyred ships in the said armye.

The Christofer Davy.—John Iseham, cap., 42*s.*; 52 sol., 75 m., 5 g. Tot. 48*l.* 2*s.*

The Mawdlyn of Poole.—William Symons, cap., 42*s.*; 35 sol., 45 m., 5 g. Tot. 33*l.* 2*s.*

The Mary of Berkyng.—William Bonham, cap., 42*s.*; 30 sol., 45 m., 5 g. Tot. 32*l.* 17*s.*

The Margret of Dertmouth.—John Forescwe, cap., 42*s.*; 45 sol., 55 m., 5 g. Tot. 40*l.* 2*s.*

The Mary Jamys of Dertmouth.—Henry Denys, cap., 42*s.*; 40 sol., 47 m., 3 g. Tot. 35*l.* 3*s.* 8*d.*

The Nicholas Draper.—Robert Draper, cap., 42*s.*; 40 sol., 65 m., 5 g. Tot. 45*l.* 2*s.*

The Mary Cradok.—Josselyn, cap., 42*s.*; 67 sol., 220 m., 10 g. Tot. 66*l.* 15*s.* 4*d.*

The Mary of Falmouth.—George Whytwombe, cap., 42*s*; 32 sol., 45 m., 5 g. Tot. 32*l.* 7*s.*

The Charyte.— Thomas Wodale, cap., 42*s.* ; 102 sol., 120 m., 10 g. Tot. 81*l.* 4*d.*

The Mary Howard.—William Gonson, cap., 42*s.* ; 61 sol., 83 m., 10 g. Tot. 58*l.* 8*s.* 8*d.*

Gonson's Berk.—The said William Gonson, owner and cap., 42*s.*; 16 sol., 30 m. 4 g. Tot. 23*l.* 5*s.* 4*d.*

The Margret of Dertmouth.—Richard Courteney, cap., 42*s.*; 30 sol., 37 m., 3 g. Tot. 29*l.* 3*s.* 8*d.*

The Baptist of Harwich.—William Harpour, cap., 42*s.*; 16 sol., 30 m., 4 g. Tot. 22*l.* 15*s.* 4*d.*

The Lyon.—John Hopton, cap., 42*s.*; 48 sol., 70 m., 8 g. Tot. 47*l.* 5*s.* 4*d.*

The Barbara Gybbes.—William Gybbes, cap., 42*s.*; 36 sol., 40 m., 8 g. Tot. 34*l.* 2*s.*

---

* The wages of these captains are set down as " *nil.*"

1514.

The Sabyn.—William Sabyn, cap., 42s. ; 40 sol., 55 m., 5 g. Tot. 38l. 12s.

The Elizabeth of Newcastill.—Lewis Southern, cap., 42s.; 40 sol., 55 m., 5 g. Tot. 38l. 12s.

The Gabriell of Toppesham. — William Fyssher, cap., 42s.; 40 sol., 55 m., 5 g. Tot. 37l. 17s.

The Fortune of Dover.—Thomas Vaughan, cap., 42s.; 30 sol., 45 m., 5 g. Tot. 32l. 17s.

The Peter of Lee.—Adrian Dunkan, cap., 42s.; 13 sol., 35 m. 2 g. Tot. 22l. 12s.

The Michell Yonge.—Peter Yong, cap., 42s.; 8 sol., 30 m. 2 g. Tot. 19l. 2s.

" Sum total with the Henry Grace a Dieu, viijml vjc xlij."

> *Note.*—48 of the 80 soldiers of John Hopton are in *The Lyon,* " and the rest be in a heyne of his owne till his gallyon comme, for which he loketh every daye."

iii.—" Paymentis of wagis to vittellers appoynted to serve the said army duryng the viage hyred to the same intent for oon moneth bygynnyng the xxv daye of Aprill the yere aforsaid, by vertu of Sir Thomas Wyndam is warraunte."

The Jamys of Salt Assh.—To John Barret, purser, for wages of 19 mariners, 4l. 15s. Tot. 10l. 15s.

The George of Hampton.—John Favour, owner ; 24 m., 6l. Tot. 12l.

The Trinyte of Hampton.—Nicholas Cowart, owner; 34 m., 8l. 10s. Tot. 18l. 7s. 6d.

The Elizabeth of Bristoll.—John Elsye; 26 m., 6l. 10s. Tot.——

The Leonard of Torre.—Gilbert Walsh; 24 m., 6l. Tot. 13l. 10s.

The Margret of Lemyngton.—John Rogers ; 12 m., 60s. Tot. 6l. 10s.

The Trinyte of Dertmouth.—Richard Predise; 24 m., 6l. Tot. 12l.

The Margret of Bristowe.—John Crokk, master ; 22 m., 110s. Tot. 11l. 10s.

The Christofer of Dertmouth.—John Tamworth, owner ; 20 m., 100s. Tot. 11l.

The Maynardis Ship.—The purser ; 24 m., 6l. Tot. 13l.

The Mawdlyn of Hamyll.—The master; 24 m., 6l. Tot. 13l. 10s.

iv.—" The Kingis ships."
" Vitellers."

The Henry of Hampton.—John Herryson, master ; 30 m. ; 7l. 10s. Tot. 10l.

The Mary Imperiall.—John Blake, master ; 23 m., 115s. Tot. 8l. 5s.

The Dragon.—Robert Sylverton, master ; 24 m., 6l. Tot. 8l. 10s.

The Antony of Brykilsey.—John Puke, master. Tot. 45s.

Pp. 21.

22 May. **5113.** For JOHN SKEWYS.

S. B.

Exemption from serving on juries, &c.; with the privilege of keeping his hat on in the presence of the King. *Del.* Westm., 22 May 6 Hen. VIII.

Pat. 6 *Hen. VIII. p.* 1, *m.* 15.

1514.

22 May.   **5114.**   FOR THOMAS SPENKE, clk.
S. B.
    Presentation to the chantry in the chapel of St. Mary the Virgin,
Wakefelde Bridge, dioc. York, void by death of Richard Coke (or
Cyke). *Del.* Westm., 22 May 6 Hen. VIII.
   Pat. 6 *Hen. VIII. p.* 2, *m.* 2, ¦3, *and* 6.

S. B.
    ii. Letters patent to the Cardinal of York for his admission.
Del. as above.

22 May.   **5115.**   FOR SIR THOMAS BOLEYN.
S. B.
    Grant of the manors of Saham Tony, Nekton, Panworth Hall
and Cressingham Parva; of the hundreds of Waylond and
Grymmeshowe, Norf., at an annual rent of 71*l.* 6*s.* 8*d. Del.*
Westm., 22 May 6 Hen. VIII.
   Pat. 6 *Hen. VIII. p.* 2, *m.* 29.

22 May.   **5116.**   TO JOHN YONG, Master of the Rolls.
S. B.
    To cancel, on payment of the sums due, &c., any of the following
recognizances of 400*l.*, made by Sir John Arundell of Lanheron,
Cornwall, and Elizabeth Lady Fitzwaren, late of Steveneth, Middlesex, widow to Sir Robert Scuthwell, and Bartholomew Westby of
the Exchequer, or by John Arundell and Ode Goefr of St. Co-
lombe, Cornwall, or John Skewys, late of "Lyncolnes In, yn
Channsler Lane," for payment of 500 marks every successive year
until Michaelmas 1518. Greenwich, 26 Jan. 4 Hen. VIII. *Del.*
22 May 6 Hen. VIII.
    ii. Receipts for the above, dated 1 Sept. 5 Hen. VIII., 1 Sept.
6 Hen. VIII., 15 Nov. 7 Hen. VIII., and 7 Sept. 9 Hen. VIII. All
signed by John Heron; the first has a note in the margin by John
Arundell, that it is a copy shown to the Master of the Rolls.

23 May.   **5117.**   SIR RICH. WINGFIELD to [WOLSEY.]
Galba, B. III. 193.
B. M.
    . . . . Received divers writings . . . . which
I perceive that your Lordship [marvelleth] greatly of such delay as
she made. Had urged my Lady to satisfy him as she had received
letters from the Emperor, and in such a way as some certain conclusion might be had. She said she would dispatch his cousin
Sidney, now at Lovaine, and write by him to the King and you.
As Wingfield was afraid her credence by Sidney would not satisfy
the King he told her blank he begged her to send the same in
writing—from which she excused herself, as her former letters had
not been kept secret—as Lord Berge and the governor of Bresse
had offered to prove. He denied it, and said it was only their
malice. She answered that the ambassador of Arragon was acquainted with them. Thinks there has been default somewhere—
whether the King has received such letters or no. She will write
to Wingfield, however, who will keep her letters secret.—She is
greatly delighted at the letters she has received from the Emperor.
Thinks he must not be lavish in the unfurnishing of his garner.
Will send further news by his cousin Sidney. Malines, 23 May.
   Hol., pp. 4, *mutilated.*

23 May.   **5118.**   FOR ROBERT BLAGGE.
S. B.
    For Barnaby Blagge, his son, to be remembrancer of the Ex-
chequer, on death or surrender of the said Robert, to whom the
office was granted by patent 6 Dec. 18 Hen. VII. [*Del.*] Westm.,
23 May 6 Hen. VIII.

1514.

23 May. **5119.** For THOMAS MARQUIS OF DORSET.

P. S. b.

Protection for John Hertwell of Preston, Northt., retained as captain to serve in the wars. London, 17 May 6 Hen. VIII. [*Del.*] 23 May. *Signed.*

23 May. **5120.** For ROBERT BULKELEY and his heirs.

Inspeximus and confirmation of a charter of Hen. II., dated at Canterbury, granting to Manass[erus] Byset, his sewer, certain possessions in cos. Worc., Wilts, Glouc., &c. Westm., 23 May.
Pat. 6 Hen. VIII. p. 2, m. 28.

24 May. **5121.** JOHN FAWNE [VICE-CHANCELLOR] and the UNIVERSITY

MS. Cole, 5783.   OF CAMBRIDGE to WOLSEY BISHOP OF LINCOLN.

B. M.

Ellis, 3 S. I. 168.

Offering him the chancellorship of their university. Cantab. 9 kl. Jun. 1514.
Lat.

MS. Cole ib.

B. M.

Ellis, 3 S. I. 170.

2. WOLSEY BP. OF LINCOLN to the UNIVERSITY OF CAMBRIDGE.

Thanks them for the undeserved honor they have paid him, and will do his utmost to serve them. Had determined to write at greater length, but is much occupied with affairs of state. Refers them to the bearers. London, 2 June 1514.
Lat.

24 May. **5122.** For WILLIAM CLYSTON, chaplain.

Presentation to the church of Newton Tracy, Exeter dioc., *vice* Thos. Alen, chaplain, resigned. Westm., 24 May.
Pat. 6 Hen. VIII. p. 2, m. 2.

24 May. **5123.** For WILLIAM STAFFERTON, grocer of London.

P. S.

Protection ; going in the retinue of Sir Richard Wyngfeild, Deputy of Calais. Eltham, 15 May 6 Hen. VIII. *Del.* Westm., 24 May.

24 May. **5124.** For JOHN DOWMAN, LL.D.

P. S.

Licence to found a guild in honor of St. Mary and St. Nicholas the Bishop, in the church of Poklyngton, York, for a master, two wardens, brethren and sisters. Also mortmain licence to acquire lands to the annual value of 20 marks. Eltham, 22 May 6 Hen. VIII. *Del.* Westm., 24 May.

25 May. **5125.** KATHARINE THE QUEEN.

Vesp. C. vi. 390.

B. M.

Admission to all the spiritual benefits of the monastery of St. Mary of Guadalupe, granted by Friar Luys of Toledo to Katharine of England. Sent by John Stile. 25 May 1514. *Signed. On vellum, illuminated.*

26 May. **5126.** SIR ROBERT WINGFIELD to HENRY VIII.

Vitell. B. xviii. 85.

B. M.

"Wrote last from Vienna on the [20th] of the present month, which were but [in answer to your] letters of the last of April and of the 5th [of this month.]"—Left next day, as he intended to follow the Emperor ; arrived here this day at 10 o'clock. Would have arrived here sooner ; but owing to the unusual heat of the weather, the badness of the road, and an accident which befel his wagon and sumpter-horse, he was delayed. Although the Emperor was at dinner when Wingfield arrived, he at once gave him audience. Wingfield informed him that he had letters in answer to his . . . ., and to those of the 19th ;—that Henry considered the declaration of Urreas "to be full of ficte and colored matter," and but for his confidence in Maximilian would have thought even he had not declared the pith of the matter to Wingfield ;—that the ambassador of Arragon in England had explained why his master had made a truce with the French King, and that he had made an overture for a marriage between that King and the Lady Eleanor the Emperor's niece [*i.e.* granddaughter].—The Emperor took in good part Wingfield's declaration of the matters mentioned in Henry's letters of the 5th. Was glad Henry perceived his danger and "importable charges." Notwithstanding the ambassador of Arragon's statement, doubted not Ferdinand knew too well to make such an offer. As to the marriage between his nephew [i.e. grandson Charles] and Henry's sister [Mary], as he has explained to my Lady his daughter, and as Henry will learn by the ambassadors sent, things cannot have the very course that . . . . of. As to the horsemen and hoys to be had from the Prince's countries, he made Wingfield no di[rect answer,] having explained his mind to his daughter ; thinks he will grant Henry "a new license . . . . to be a mover of war aga[inst] . . . . will revoke the license he granted unto you . . . . . which is sufficient enough." He agreed with Henry that England was bound to continue the war till the French King sued for peace both from him and Arragon,—wondered that Ferdinand was not more fervent in Henry's behalf,—and doubted only the good will of Henry's subjects. At Henry's meeting with the Emperor last year, nothing else was wanting to a great exploit. Wingfield was then dismissed, and Hans Reynner being ordered to tell him the news from Italy, informed him " the Cardinal of Gource . . . . [the] Emperor showing that the Pope is right well disposed towards his Majesty . . . . upon him to ratify the lawde . . . . that the' said Cardinal had taken h . . . . of this month and should depart the . . . . than to write any further, showing that . . . . his journey, he should have both more liberty an[d be able to] advertise his Majesty more amply." The matter is so confused " the Emperor wottyth neere ho . . . . it, and the rather because that sith he hath had . . . . . from the said Cardinal." A secretary of the Emperor resident with the [Viceroy] writes that he thinks the ratification [by the] Pope is but for three months. If this be so there is as much uncertainty of peace as ever. The Viceroy's army is reinforced with lance-knights and artillery to lay siege to Treviso ; but, owing to the uncertainty of the new ratification, he delays ; both time and money will be lost. " A new army out of these quarters to give s[uccour to a town] called Marrane, which is besieged b . . . . so be that they within have . . . . the Venetions at divers assaults, yet they [desp]eyre for lack of victuals, for they have begun [to eat th]eyre horses already." The Emperor has sent the Master of the Horse and other noblemen to their rescue. Wingfield is afraid they will arrive too late. Affairs here will be very confused until tidings are received from the Pope.—Although 20 days ago the Emperor ordered Urreas to go to the Victory to spur him forward, Urreas has lain still, hoping by that means to compel the Emperor to accept the truce before the 12th of this month, " which was the extreme day limited of the accepting the truce by the Emperor ;" " but his Majesty showeth himself at many times not easy to be led, and much worse to be driven, and therefore, Sire, for the love of God, have good consideration how ye do handle this old practised. Prince, which hath been but easily known in time past, because

1514.

many have sought to defame him, and few to declare and shew what manner of man he is."—Wingfield has never received the book, enclosed in Henry's letter of the last day of April, detailing the preparations made by Henry for carrying on the war; has not mentioned the matter to the Emperor. The Emperor has gone three Dutch miles from here; it is uncertain whether he returns. Wingfield complains of being in want of money. Grattz in Styremark, . . . May 1514.

Hol., pp. 7, mutilated. Addressed: The King's Grace.

26 May. **5127.** For SIR WILLIAM COMPTON.
S. B.

Pardon and release as late sheriff of Hants; and release of recognizance for 40*l.* made by Robert Turges of Turges Melcombe, Dorset, Thomas Unton of Waddeley, Berks, and Humphrey Browne and William Hawles of London, 10 Nov. 4 Hen. VIII. *Del.* Westm., 26 May 6 Hen. VIII.

Pat. 6 Hen. VIII. p. 2, m. 5.

26 May. **5128.** For SIR WILLIAM FITZWILLIAM and JOHN BYGGE.
S. B.

Grant, in survivorship, of the office of bailiff of Surrey, alias "Bagshotes Bayles," in Windsor Forest, with 6*d.* a day, on surrender by Bigge of patent 18 June 19 Hen. VII. granting the same office, in survivorship, to John Wyllyams, deceased, and Bygge. *Del.* Westm., 26 May 6 Hen. VIII.

Pat. 6 Hen. VIII. p. 2, m. 5.

26 May. **5129.** For JOHN PETER DE BRESSA, foreigner.

Licence to import and export merchandise, and to retain the customs in his hands for four years. Otford, 26 May.

Fr. 6 Hen. VIII. p. 2, m. 7.

27 May. **5130.** THOMAS EARL OF SURREY to the PRIVY COUNCIL.
Calig. D. vi. 106.
B. M.

Came yesterday to Sandwich, hoping to have found the ships in the Downs, but they were not there, and by 7 o'clock he came to Dover. The vice-admiral had sent over Sir Henry Sherborne and Sir Stephen Bole, with ten sail of small men, and the row barge, galleys, and others, well manned, in as good order, to his mind, as possible. The wind was N.N.E.; the haze great. Came to St. John's Road, and sent forward Sir Stephen Boole, Thomas Vaughan, and others. "Prior John" rode at the point of St. John's Road, towards Calais, five miles from Boleyne. The French fled with sails and oars, and got beyond reach. "My cousin Wyndam in like . . . . . . 20 sails with him; and at this hour I see him with them coming again unto us." Has sent Sir Henry Sherborne with 10 sail, and Wiseman and Wallop with other 10 sail, to get between Boleyn and the French galleys. He wished he had 2,000 or 3,000 soldiers, such as are now shipped at Calais. Has ordered Sir Thomas West to stay at Sandwich till the King's further pleasure. Written in the M[ary Rose] in Dover Road, 27 May, at 7 at night. *Signed.*

Pp. 2.

27 May. **5131.** For SIR JOHN SHARPE and HUGH EDWARDIS, sewer of
S. B. the Chamber.

Custody of the castle or manor of Burne, Linc., with all profits within the outer part of the moat, and the herbage of the trenches near the said castle, called "knyghtesfees." *Del.* Westm., 27 May 6 Hen. VIII.

Pat. 6 Hen. VIII. p. 2, m. 2.

3 F

1514.

27 May.
P. S. b.

5132.   For WILLIAM COMPTON.

Michael Verney, his servant, to be discharged of all fines, &c., as he is going to the war. 27 May 6 Hen. VIII. *Signed.*

28 May.

5133.   COMMISSIONS OF THE PEACE.

Suffolk.—R. Bp. of Norwich, Thos. Duke of Norfolk, Chas. Duke of Suffolk, Rob. Radcliff Lord Fitzwalter, Wm. Lord Willoughby, Sir John Fyneux, Sir Rob. Rede, Sir Rob. Brandon, Sir Jas. Hobart, Sir Rob. Drury, Sir Ric. Wentworth, Sir Thos. Boleyn, Sir Wm. Walgrave, Sir Wm. Clopton, Sir Edm. Genny, Sir Philip Tylney, Sir Anthony Wyngfeld, Sir Jas. Fremlyngham, Sir Philip Bothe, Sir John Glemam, John Veer, Thos. Lucas, Wm. Ayloff, Humph. Wyngfeld, Lionel Talmage, Rob. Suthwell, jun., John Wiseman, Hen. Noon, John Sulyard, Wm. Playter, Edm. Lee, John Goldyngham, jun. and Ric. Candisshe. Westm., 28 May.

28 May.

Norfolk.—R. Bp. of Norwich, Thos. Duke of Norfolk, Chas. Duke of Suffolk, Thos. Earl of Surrey, Rob. Radclyff Lord Fitzwalter, Wm. Lord Willoughby, Sir John Fyneux, Sir Rob. Rede, Sir Thos. Lovell, Sir Thos. Boleyn, Sir Wm. Knyvet, Sir Rob. Brandon, Sir Jas. Hobart, Sir Thos. Wyndham, Sir Philip Tylney, Sir Rob. Clere, Sir Rob. Lovell, Sir John Audeley, Sir John Heydon, Sir Jas. Fremlyngham, Sir John Glemam, Sir John Shelton, Sir Ric. Candissh, Nich. Appulyard, Jas. Boleyn, Walter Hobart, John Straunge, Andr. Sulyard, John Spelman, Francis Calebut, Hen. Noon, Hen. Hunston, Wm. Elys, Wm. Conyngesby, Walter Stubbes, Wm. Wotton and Francis Moundeford. Westm., 28 May.

Pat. 6 Hen. VIII. p. 1, m. 2d.

29 May.
S. B.

5134.   For LEWIS POLLARD.

To be a justice of the Common Pleas, during pleasure. *Del.* Westm., 29 May 6 Hen. VIII.

Pat. 6 Hen. VIII. p. 1, m. 16.

29 May.
S. B.

5135.   For LEONARD FRISCHOBALD and ANTHONY CAVALLARY.

Grant, in survivorship, of the office of purveyor of cloths of gold and silver, "tynsen saten, velvet saten," damask, and other cloths for the King's great wardrobe of robes, with 20*l.* a year. Also mandate to Sir Andrew Wyndesor, keeper of the Great Wardrobe, and Richard Smyth, yeoman of the same, to purvey the said articles by means of the said Leonard and Anthony. *Del.* Westm., 29 May 6 Hen. VIII.

Pat. 6 Hen. VIII. p. 2, m. 4.

29 May.
S. B.

5136.   For THOMAS DUKE OF NORFOLK.

Wardship of John Veer, kinsman and heir of John Veer late Earl of Oxford, viz., son of Sir George, brother of the said late Earl; with reversion of that portion of the possessions of the said late Earl which Elizabeth his widow holds in dower. Also, during Veer's minority, the offices of Great Chamberlain of England, steward of Essex or Waltham forest, and constable of the castle of Colchester. *Del.* Westm., 29 May 6 Hen. VIII.

Pat. 6 Hen. VIII. p. 2, m. 2.

1514.
29 May. **5137.** For ELIZABETH SOUTHWELL, widow.
S. B.

Pardon and release as executrix of Sir Robert Southwell, late chief butler of England, surveyor and approver of castles, lordships, &c. in England, Wales, and Calais, general auditor, receiver of the honors of Clare and Gloucester, in Norf., Suff., Camb., Hunts, Essex, and Herts, receiver of the duchy of York, in the said counties, farmer of Disse and Hempnale, Norf., and receiver of lands of the late Lord Fitzwalter, in Norf., Suff., and Essex ; also pardon and release for Christopher Urswik, archdeacon of Oxford, Robert Southwell and William Wutton, coëxecutors with the said Elizabeth. *Del.* Westm., 29 May 6 Hen. VIII.
Pat. 6 *Hen. VIII. p.* 2, *m.* 3.

30 May. **5138.** For MAURO DE MASSAGROSA, merchant of Lucca.
S. B.

Licence to export 300 sacks of wool. *Del.* Westm., 30 May 6 Hen. VIII.
Fr. 6 *Hen. VIII. p.* 2, *m.* 3.

May. **5139.** INSTRUCTIONS for the AMBASSADORS with the LADY
Galba, B. v. 10. MARGARET.
B. M.

Are to learn what personages will attend upon her and the Prince of Castile upon their coming to Calais, in order that suitable provision may be made. Last year, when the King was at Calais with his army, not only the corn and hay but the grass on the ground was consumed and destroyed, so that, at the King's returning thither, there was no provision, especially of hay, for the horse ; and though oats can be brought out of England, it cannot be done in any plenty ; and though hay may be had in these parts on the solemnization of the marriage, as the King will have to be there at the same time with his army, yet provision shall be made better if the number of horse coming with her and the Emperor be known. They shall obtain the number in writing with their names ; they shall inquire also whether it be usual in that case to bring their apparel to their lodgings. The King will provide in all things for the Emperor, the Prince, and my Lady, except beds, " which it is thought they will for their better ease bring with them." They are to learn what day the company will be at Calais, how long the marriage will be deferred after their arrival, whether the solemnization is to take place in a private chapel or a parish church, who shall be present, and who is to stay after the marriage, as the King must go straight to the wars. As the King wishes the Princess to be dressed in the fashion of those parts, he has provided cloth of every sort to be made up after the fashion shewn her " by the said A.B., praying her [my Lady] to devise for the making thereof after such manner as shall best please her ;" all things to be queenly and honorable. The said A.B. shall submit to my Lady a book containing a provision for the Princess's apparel, her chamber, her offices, her stables, and take my Lady's advice on the same, and what servants shall attend upon her. Also A.B., taking with him C.D., shall require of my Lady a commission for such provision of hoys as shall be necessary for the King's army for retaining the Count Palatine, Nassaw, De Lignye, Dissislstyne, nephew to Lord Burghhes, Emery Penes, to the number of 6,000 horse to serve the King this or the next year. with other necessary forces, and especially to retain the Sovereign of Flanders, &c.

Draft in the hand of Fox. Pp. 6, *mutilated.*

3 F 2

1514.
May.   **5140.**   PHILIPPE DE BREGILLES to MARGARET OF SAVOY.

Lett. de Louis XII.
t. IV. 308.

Doubts not what she desires most to know is the King's mind on the subject of the writer's charge. He is so well disposed, that immediately Bregilles entered, he asked what he could do for her. 1. He demanded that Suffolk should on no account visit her; to which the King agreed, though he said such preparations had been made for his departure that all the kingdom would be much surprised. He would, however, send the Deputy of Calais [Wingfeld] instead. 2. In regard to the merchant, the King has had him examined by Suffolk and the Bishop of Lincoln, almoner, in the writer's presence. He acknowledges having given money on security of a letter, written by another English merchant from Flanders, when the King was there. They propose both merchants shall be imprisoned; but Brigelles stated that Margaret did not desire they should be put to death. 3. As to the marriage; they find this the most serious question; the King said it was not reasonable to change it; that if Suffolk had done it, he would have been bound to her; and if the lady had been of age, she would have been at liberty to say what she pleased.* Knowing that the King and Suffolk would make objection to Margaret's demand, the writer said it could do no harm except to anticipate the time (*elle luy put porter nul prejudice si non anticiper le temps*), with which they were satisfied.

The King had been informed, two or three days before, that the Admiral of France had spoken of a marriage between the French King and Margaret. The King replied, before the whole council, he was certain of Margaret, and "he would not believe it if all the world said so ;" and he shows this, as do the Queen and Princess, by the honorable manner in which they treat the writer, "*tant que j'en suis tout honteux*" The Bishop of Lincoln has complained that the secretary of the King Catholic has passed through France on his way to the Emperor, and repassed the same way. Suffolk has spoken to him of his little daughter, (*sa petite fille*,) whom he saved from death, hoping she might not be the cause of augmenting the scandal. He also wished the English gentleman *par dela* recalled. The writer replied there was no cause for regret in that, for both one and the other were there before the rumor arose, and that Madame would not diminish her favor to either on that account. Suffolk is anxious to do all he can to remedy the mischief. London, Saturday.
Fr.

1 June.   **5141.**   For JOHN CARYLL, serjeant-at-law.
S. B.   To be the King's serjeant-at-law. *Del.* Otford, 1 June 6 Hen. VIII. *Pat.* 6 *Hen. VIII. p.* 2, *m.* 4.

1 June.   **5142.**   For GEORGE, son and heir of THOMAS PONTESBURY.
S. B.   Livery of lands. *Del.* Otford, 1 June 6 Hen. VIII. *Pat.* 6 *Hen. VIII. p.* 2, *m.* 4.

---

* " Quant au tiers point, qui est du mariage, c'est celuy lequel ils ont trouvé le plus grief, et le roy pour le premier me dit incontinent que ce point n'estoit raisonable à changer, que si Monsr. de Sufort l'eut fait, que luy eut esté lié, et que quand la fille eut esté en aage, elle se fut trouvée en liberté de dire ce que bon luy eut semblé.

1514.
1 June. **5143.** GAOL DELIVERY.

Midland Circuit.—Humph. Conyngesby, Guy Palmes, John Jenour and Ric. Higham. Westm., 1 June.

Pat. 6 *Hen. VIII. p.* 1, *m.* 17*d.*

---

1 June. **5144.** For ROBERT HERDE of London, haberdasher.
P. S.

Licence to import French, Milanese and other caps. Eltham, 22 May 6 Hen. VIII. *Del.* Otford, 1 June.

Fr. 6 *Hen. VIII. p.* 2, *m.* 4.

---

2 June. **5145.** For MAURICE CLONNE, yeoman of the Crown.
S. B.

Custody of New Radnor park, and "le Goore Mede," near the town of New Radnor, Marches of Wales;—and grant of a wood called Coyde Soweytht in "le Merewode" of Soweyth Nythian in Myleneyth. *Del.* Otford, 2 June 6 Hen. VIII.

Pat. 6 *Hen. VIII. p.* 2, *m.* 4.

---

2 June. **5146.** For RICHARD BLOUNT.
S. B.

Annual farm of 40 marks, for 31 years from Mic. 24 Hen. VII., payable to the King by Giles Grevell, and his heirs, according to patent 4 Dec. 23 Hen. VII., which granted him the manors of Upton, Snodysbury and Wykeburnell, Worc., with lands in Upton, Snodnesbury, Wyke-Burnell, Bright-Hampton, Browghton, Pepulton and Parshore—forfeited by Francis Lord Lovel,—at the rent of 40 marks. *Del.* Otford, 2 June 6 Hen. VIII.

Pat. 6 *Hen. VIII. p.* 2, *m.* 4.

---

3 June. **5147.** For GEORGE LORD BERGEVENNY.
P. S. b.

Discharge of all fines, &c. for Sir Richard Fitzlewys, who is going in the King's service. 3 June 6 Hen. VIII. *Signed.*

---

4 June. **5148.** HENRY VIII. to MARGARET OF SAVOY.
Lett. de Louis XII.
t. IV. p. 318.

Has received her letters dated Malignes 23 May, reporting the answer she made to Count Felix de Wirtemburgh about the going of the Princess of Castile to Calais, whereby it appears that she wishes the time prolonged, and the place altered. Regrets that the ceremony cannot take place in the manner agreed upon, and refers her to his ambassadors. Eltham, 4 June 1514.

---

5 June. **5149.** For NICHOLAS HURLETON.
S. B.

Lease, for 30 years, of a corn mill and fulling mill on the Dee, with a fishery called the Kingespole, at a rent of 85*l.* (*sic*) a year ; sc. 50*l.* for the corn mill, 11*l.* for the fulling mill, and 4*l.* for the fishery. Hurleton to make all necessary repairs. *Del.* Otford, 5 June 6 Hen. VIII.

---

5 June. **5150.** For WILLIAM LORD MAUTRAVERS (son and heir of THOMAS
S. B. EARL OF ARUNDELL) and ANNE his wife, sister of Henry Earl of Northumberland. .

Grant, in tail male, of the manors of Stowe, Bardolff, Cantelowe, Strumpshaugh and Scroteby, Norf. *Del.* Otford, 5 June 6 Hen. VIII.

Pat. 6 *Hen. VIII. p.* 1, *m.* 9.

1514.

5 June.   **5151.**   SIR THOMAS LOVELL to the BPS. OF WINCHESTER (FOX)
R. O.   and LINCOLN (WOLSEY).

A servant arrived from the general of Normandy, on Sunday
night, and left this Monday. The captains are not most glad at
the order of the Council to forbear excursions. Mr. Wettell and
others have taken certain horsemen licensed by Mons. Pontderemy
to plunder the English. Heard from the Admiral that he
intended a landing in these parts yesterday in revenge of the
burning of Brighthenstone. The Duke of Albany and Richard
De la Pole are making preparations to go into Scotland. Has
written at divers times to the captain of Boulogne for the redemption of the prisoners. Encloses a part copy of one in French.
Calais, 5 June. *Signed.*

Pp. 2. Addressed.

8 June.   **5152.**   PET. MARTYR to LUD. FURTADO.
Epist. 539.

Almazan, the only confidant of Ferdinand, died on 14 April, and
is succeeded by Pedro Quintana, educated under his rod. The
King is alarmed at the advance of the Moors, is very ill, and
suffering from asthma. Bastida, a friend of the Viceroy, has arrived.
He states the Venetians will not make any peace with the confederates, unless Verona, Brescia, and Bergamo be restored. The
sister of the King of England was betrothed to Prince Charles on condition that he should marry her when he passed the age of fourteen.
Henry is urgent to have the marriage completed, as the Prince was
of the age required on the 24 Feb. last. Maximilian and Ferdinand
require its postponement, as Charles is naturally of a feeble consti-
tution. Henry is exceedingly angry, and threatens to make terms
with France. Valladolid, vi. non. Jun. 1514.

Lat.

9 June.   **5153.**   TOURNAY.
R. T. 144.
R. O.   Sir Rob. Dymok ; acknowledgement on the King's behalf of the
receipt of 50,000 crowns from the city of Tournay. 9 June 1514.

9 June.   **5154.**   ROBERT FOULER to [WOLSEY] BP. OF LINCOLN.
R. O.

Has delivered to Sir Rob. Dymmok, at Tournay, 10,000l. in gold.
Dymmok will be contented for the future to take crowns at 4s. 2d.,
current at Calais at 4s. 3d. Anth. Nele does his duty. Begs that
when any more money is sent to Tournay Mr. Dymmok will send
one of his clerks for it at Calais. Has received, the day before
his departure to Tournay, 1,000l. of Richard Carewe. The worst
pence in England are good money at Tournay. At Calais.

Has received the King's letter directing him to repair again to
Tournay with the other 10,000l. Will do accordingly when he
knows of the coming of horsemen to Newport from Tournay.

P. 1. Add.

10 June.   **5155.**   SIR RICH. WINGFIELD and SIR THO. SPINELLY to
Galba, B. III. 198.   [HENRY VIII.]
B. M.

Wrote last on the . . . inst. Have not since heard from his
Highness. Send a letter of Sir Robt. Wingfield, which arrived
here yesterday by post. Think the Emperor will wait for knowledge from his ambassadors " upon such charges as they received

from your grace." Maroton will return to the Emperor as soon as an answer arrives from the King touching the 30,000 crowns, which, it is thought, will cause him to come down or to return to Italy. The three Danish ambassadors had audience two days ago : their master was ready to serve the Emperor and the Prince of Castile. Tomorrow the King of Denmark and the Lady Ysabeau will be ' made handfast. News from Rome of the 30th May states that the mission of the General of Normandy to England is for a peace. Nassaw is in Hainault with a large body of horse to resist the French. Brussels, 10 June 1514. *Signed.*

Pp. 2, *mutilated.*

Ib. f. 196.   Modern copy of the same before the fire.

---

10 June. **5156.**   LEO X. to HENRY VIII.
R. O.

Is informed by Hadrian Cardinal St. Chrysogon, collector, that one George Ardizono, a Genoese merchant, appointed to exact a penny from every ducat exported out of England, by way of exchange, has demanded the payment of this amount from the monies of the Apostolical collector. Richard [Fox] Bp. of Winchester, who for 10 years previously held the same office, never made the like demand, which is altogether contrary to custom. Rome, 10 June 1514, pont. 2.

Add. Vellum.

---

10 June. **5157.**   For JOHN PYLGRYME, late of Hengham, Norf., jun.,
S. B.   butcher.

Pardon. *Del.* Otford, 10 June 6 Hen. VIII.
Pat. 6 *Hen. VIII. p.* 2, *m.* 4.

· 12 June. **5158.**   HENRY VIII. to MARGARET OF SAVOY.
Lett. de Louis XII.
IV. 320.

Has received letters written by her own hand, reminding him that he had promised Felinger to lend the Emperor 30,000 gold crowns on her bond ; stating also that she had received letters from the Emperor written in his own hand, urging her to send him that sum if she desired his coming into these parts ; and that she is put to considerable inconvenience, as none of the states, except Brabant, have yet granted any money. Henry would have been very glad to have served her had things remained in the same state, but inasmuch as after the sudden departure of the Emperor he had expected the changes which have since taken place, he was not minded to lend the money, and only at the instance of his council had he agreed that certain sums should be received at Tournay by the hands of his treasurer of war, out of the money left there for the pay of the garrisons, to be repaid at a time named ; and as it was not asked for then, it cannot now be paid at Tourney, as that money is spent. If the Emperor had kept his agreements, and paid the sum he promised for the the garrisons, there would have been more of it in hand. As he refused the offer when made, it cannot be repeated. When the Emperor made show of offering Henry the imperial crown, and Henry made no reply, because he was ill, and wished to have the advice of his council, the Emperor told the English ambassador that a "golden coffer offered as a present, if not accepted in time, might be revoked by the donor." Henry is

1514.

therefore as free with regard to his offer as the Emperor to his coffer. Eltham, 12 June 1514.

Fr.

12 June. **5159.** KNIGHT and PONYNGES to [HENRY VIII.]

Galba, B. III. 197.   . . . . . "your highness . . . . after this . . . . directed with
B. M.   this which is of the date of the 9th of" . . The Chancellor had advertised them that a longer term of intercourse had been granted by the Prince, until the 1st of Oct. They desired until the 1st of Nov., which has been refused, after which all goods of Englishmen found in Flanders will be confiscated. Enclose a letter to that effect. Have received no answer as yet to their intimation of the effect of the article of comprehension; enclose letters about it. Have labored in the matter of Semar of Dartmouth. They are met with the treatment shewn to a Gascone named Bertram de Furen. This day the Prince leaves the Hague; will return in eight days to receive the French ambassador now at Antwerp. At the Hay in Holland, 12 June.

Signed: E. Ponynges—W. Knyght.

Pp. 2, mutilated.

12 June. **5160.** For HENRY HOLTESWELLER, native of Barg, under the
8. B.   obedience of the Duke of "Golike," the King's goldsmith.

Denization. *Del.* Otford, 12 June 6 Hen. VIII.

Pat. 6 *Hen. VIII. p.* 2, *m.* 3.

12 June. **5161.** For RALPH BATY, usher of the Hall.
P. S.

To have the serjeanty of Wygmoresland, Salop, *vice* John Mathewes, with 40s. a year, payable at the receipt of the exchequer of Wygmore. Eltham, 27 May 6 Hen. VIII. *Del.* Knoll, 12 June.

Pat. 6 *Hen. VIII. p.* 2, *m.* 5.

12 June. **5162.** For THOMAS TYRELL.
P. S. b.

Protection for Robert Dey of How Carleton, Norf., retained to serve in the war. 12 June 6 Hen. VIII. *Signed.*

13 June. **5163.** SOLDIERS' WAGES.
R. O.

31 May 6 Hen. VIII.

Paid to the "Countie of Nassou," by Pasquier Vierlyng, his secretary, for the wages of 24 halberdiers, for the latter 15 days of April last, "at 40 pays by the month, 4 ph's. for a pay," sterling 11l. 2s. 2d.;—also the wages of 50 Spaniards for the same time, 60 pays, 16l. 13s. 4d.

Signed: P. Vierling.

1 June.

Paid, by command of the Lady Margaret Duchess of Savoy, notified by her letters dated Louvan, 24 May, addressed to Monsr. Symond de Ferrot, 200 petty florins for wages during the month of April last, by Frederick Rysther, his servant=22l. 4s. 6d.— Also, by command of the Lady Margaret, to Monsr. Tho. Foxe, for

1514.

a month's wages, by the said Frederick, at 50 ph's. a month = 6l. 18s. 10d.

Signed: P. Vierling and Frederick (Rüscer), per manus proprias.

9 June.

Paid to Monsr. Dysselston, captain of the garrison at St. Thomas', 600 petty florins, as wages for April last = 66l. 13s. 4d.—Also the wages of 700 horsemen for the same period, 8 ph's. a month each man = 777l. 15s. 6d.

Signed: Florys.

9 June.

Paid to Monsr. Desessyngbard, captain of the garrison at Betton, 600 petty florins for wages, as above.—Also wages of 700 horsemen, at the same rate as above.

To Monsr. Claudy Bouton, by the King's command, and my Lady of Fayssey's letters, 100 gold florins for wages for the month of April last = 15l. 11s. 1d.

Signed: K. Bouton.

10 June.

Paid to John Desrosieres and John Braure, bringers of a quittance from Monsr. Charles de Luxonbroght captain, "unto Deffyens of the garrison at Eyrey," the wages of 178 horsemen, at 8 ph's. for April last = 197l. 15s. 6d.

Signed: Jehan des Roziers, Jehan Braure.

13 June.

Paid to Arnold Percyvall, bearer of a quittance from Monsr. de Lency Count de Fawconberge, 600 petty florins, the said Count's wages for April last=66l. 13s. 4d.—Also the wages of 700 horsemen, at 8 ph's. a month, including 12 halberdiers at 9 pays = 777l. 15s. 6d.

Signed: Ernoul Percheal.

13 June.

Paid Loys de Daymeryes by Piere Vauchier and Jaum de Merlans, his servants, 200 petty florins, his wages for April last=22l. 4s. 5d. —Also the wages of 200 horsemen, at 8 ph's. a month=222l. 4s. 5d. —Also the wages of 40 pietons (footmen) at 4 ph's. a month = 22l. 4s. 5d.

Signed: Demeries—P. Vaulchier—De Merlant.

Similar entries and receipts for the month of May, the only addition being the following:—

13 June 1514.

Paid, by command of the Lady Margaret Duchess of Savoy, by her letter dated Loven, 3 May, and by command of the Lord Lieutenant, to Bertrand de Morbage, of the garrison of the Countie of Nessou, the wages of 40 pietons, " new admitted in the garrison at Arras," at 4 ph's. each a month = 22l. 4s. 5d.

Signed: Bertram de Marba.

. **15 June. 5164.** [   ] to COLART.* ·

Calig. E. II. 181.
B. M.

Has had news touching the marriage of Angoulesme, which took place on 18 May. Bourbon is in [command] of a number

---

* *In margin:* "[Col]art is the [name] off me Sir Edward [. . . . .] Purrart du . . . . Messire Anthony . . . . . tin, wham I made a counsail [in the] affaire and the . . . . ys the said . . . . s"; *in a different hand.*

1514.

of troops within one day's march of the frontier. Has heard of
a plot for surprising Tournay in August. It is proposed to send
a number of horse and foot by night to the *"ars de Tournay"*
and by arrangement with certain persons in the place put boats
within them, by which the soldiers may descend and gain an
entrance ; the horse to raise an alarm in another quarter. The
plan has been made known to St. Genois, who will communicate it
to Colart. The Dukes of [Albany ?] and Sufforth, with their lanzknechts, have not yet left Normandy for Scotland. The King of
France is using every effort to secure peace, and has sent to England proposing a marriage with the King's sister. The Pope's
ambassador on 8 June left France for England. The *gens d'armes*
guzzle and waste as usual. Paris, 15 June.

P.S.—Angoulesme leaves on the 17th for your quarter. It is
said the Swiss side with England.

Fr., p. 1.

15 June. **5165.**   CHARLES DE CROY [PRINCE OF CHIMAY] to HENRY VIII.
Galba, B. vi. 53.   Writes again touching the losses he sustained in Henry's
B. M.   invasion of France, both at the siege of Terouenne and that of
Tournay, of which he has already written by Du Roeulx and the
Provost of Aire when they were in embassy. Notwithstanding
that Henry has given him little encouragement to persevere, has
commissioned the Provost of Cassell to make renewed application on
his behalf. Ghent, 15 June. *Signed.*

Fr., p. 1. *Add.*

16 June. **5166.**   COMMISSIONS OF THE PEACE.

York, West Riding.—Hen. Earl of Northumberland, Geo. Earl
of Shrewsbury, Thos. Lord Darcy, Hen. Lord Clifford, Ric. Nevell
Lord Latimer, Sir Edw. Stanley, John Erneley, Sir Wm. Gascoigne,
Sir Thos. Fairfax, Sir Thos. Wortley, Sir Geo. Darcy, Sir John
Norton, Sir Ralph Ryther, Sir John Rouclyff, Sir Wm. Scargyll, Ric.
Tempest, Brian Palmes, John Topclyff, Thos. Fairfax, John
Hamerton, Brian Stapleton, Thos. Meryng, Wm. Elson, John
Norton, Rob. Cliston, John Vavasour, Wm. Grene of Branby,
Thos. Stray, John Baxter, Roger Wombwell, John Bylby, Thos.
Grice, Walter Bradford and Thos. Beverley. Westm., 16 June.

Pat. 6 *Hen. VIII. p.* 1, *m.* 2*d.*

Berks.—Th. abbot of Abyngdon, Rob. Brudenell, Ric. Eliott,
John Newport, Sir Th. Lovell, Sir And. Wyndesore, Sir Edw.
Darell, Sir Geo. Foster, Sir Th. Fetyplace, Guy Palmes, Ric.
Weston, Th. Inglefeld, Wm. Besellys, Wm. Essex, Jas. Strang-
ways, John Fetiplace, Wm. Fetiplace, Th. Unton (or Vuton), Wm.
Swayne, Christ. Belyngeham, Ric. Harecourt, John Man, Geo.
Wodewarde, Wm. Yongo and John Tate. Westm., 16 June.

Pat. 6 *Hen. VIII. p.* 1, *m.* 9*d.*

16 June. **5167.**   For HENRY WHYTE, late of the parish of Ryngewold,
S. B.   alias of Owre, Kent.

Pardon. *Del.* Otford, 16 June 6 Hen. VIII.

Pat. 6 *Hen. VIII. p.* 2, *m.* 4.

---

* *In the margin :* " . . . . . bee the . . . . the ryver [of Tourn]ay joignyng
[the wa]lles off the [town] ;" *in the same hand.*

1514.
17 June. **5168.** SILVESTER BP. OF WORCESTER to [WOLSEY].

Vitell. B. II. 79.
B. M.

The Pope has written to the King to give Worcester some richer benefice, as he is much in debt, and has to pay certain fees upon his bishopric, so that he cannot well support the dignity of his station. Begs Wolsey's favor, as success in this matter depends entirely upon him. Has received Wolsey's and the King's letters on matters of his diocese, to which he will attend, but will not delay the present messenger, who carries the brief of the business of Tournay. Rome, 17 June [1514].

Lat., mutilated, p. 1. Add.

18 June. **5169.** CHR. [BAINBRIDGE] CARD. ABP. OF YORK to HENRY VIII.

R. O.

Has written before in defence of his servants, troubled by Master Dalby. Fears his letters have not been received. Is grieved, considering the service he has rendered the King since his coming to this court, that his complaints of the breaking of his jurisdiction and defects of his rents had not been attended to. Begs that his servants' causes may be determined, and they returned to their rooms without further vexation from his adversaries. Rome, 18 June 1514. *Signed.*

P. 1. Addressed. Endorsed.

18 June. **5170.** THE GREAT HARRY.

R. O.

Indenture between William Bond, clerk of the poultry, and Sir John Daunce, of sums received by the former for victualling the *Henry Grace a Dieu*, viz.; 18 Sept. 5 Hen. VIII., 500*l.* ; 10 March, 500*l.* ; 5 April, 500*l.* ; 8 May 6 Hen. VIII., 400*l.* ; 18 June, 300*l.*

18 June. **5171.** SIR RIC. WINGFIELD and SPINELLY to HENRY VIII.

Galba, B. III. 200.
B. M.

Wrote last on the [16th] inst. Received this morning Henry's letters of the 12th to the Archduchess, which they delivered.—She admitted that Henry had shewn much to justify the refusal of the 30,000 crowns, yet she had always been anxious to spare the King's money, and had bidden Spinelly to write to the Lieut. of Tournay not to be over hasty in paying it. When the bishops of Winchester and Lincoln were with her in communication with Berges, Hans Reynner, and Sir Symon Ferrette, touching the sum that Henry should leave for the defence of this country, she demanded "until the sum of 200,000 crowns,"—of which Henry granted one half,—in order that the Emperor might come down, whom Cardinal Gurck was endeavouring to keep away, and she offered her own bonds for repayment.—She said the Emperor was impoverished by his war with the Venetians, and she herself had given him 10,000 florins. She had received the confirmation of the truce by the French King, and directed the ambassadors to notify it to Henry. The Prince of Castile has fallen sick of a little ague ; yesterday it was thought serious, but having taken a little purgation, last night he had good rest. Enclose extract of news obtained by Spinelly from the master of the posts. My Lady believes the Emperor is at Inspruck, where Gurck was awaiting him. Request that the master of the posts here be paid for the double posts according to promise. Brussels, 18 June. *Signed.*

Pp. 3, mutilated. Add. Endd.

1514.

ii. **Extract** of news from Italy addressed to the master of the posts at Brussels . . .

June.—1. By letters of the 10th June from Verona, the Emperor was near Lubiana with 3,000 men and 1,500 horse.—2. The Spaniards and Almayns were attempting to close in upon the Venetians on either side.—3. By letters of the 6th from Milan, the Dukes of Milan and Barry had gone to besiege Crema ; no ambassadors had arrived from the Swiss, and at all events they would attempt the castles of Milan, Cremona, and Novara.—4. They only waited an answer from England to make war upon the French.—5. Demand that the Pope shall restore Parma and Placentia.—6. French forces have arrived in Dauphiny.—7. By letters from Verona of the 9th, the Venetians are more obstinate than ever, refusing to hear of peace.—8. The Viceroy offered to send a fleet into the straits of the sea of Venice against the Venetians.—9. Barth. de la Vienne has raised new forces in Romagna and Ferarra.—10. The Venetians have given him power to fight whenever he will.

Pp. 2, mutilated.

19 June. 5172.   TENTS AT CALAIS.
R. O.

Account by Richard Gybson, of money received of Sir John Daunce, 19 June 6 Hen. VIII., and spent upon " alderpolas, spears, malls to drive the stakes of tents, wainscots for timber houses, tables and trestylls for the same, planks for houses for workmen upon the said tents," 900 " awndes" of canvas, 19*l.* 17*s.*; blue buckram, Brussels say, red say of St. Umbres, green say, ropes and cord, wombs of neat's leather for oiletts, leathers for tents, and various other articles enumerated. Wages of Gibson, 12*d.* a day. Payments for painting wagons, carriage of timber houses from the Tower of London to the Black Friars, and thence across sea. Reward to the prior of Black Friars for the hire of his house and grounds, and the fields where the said tents were pitched, 23*s.* 4*d.* Total, 863*l.* 16*s.* 6*d.*

A roll of paper.

19 June. 5173.   GERARD DE PLEINE and JOHN COLLA to MAXIMILIAN.
Lett. de Louis XII.
t. IV. 328.

Went with all diligence to the King. Found him on Tuesday in his new great ship of 1,500 tons, which was that day dedicated with great triumph. Met the Queen, the Princess Mary, the Pope's ambassadors, several bishops, and a large number of nobles. Were most honorably received, and conducted by the King through the ship, which has no equal in bulk, and has an incredible array of guns, with a scuttle on the top of the mainmast, 80 serpentines, and hackbuts. The ship contains seven tiers, one above another. On the ambassadors leaving the ship, a salute was fired from all the guns. Came on Saturday (*die Sacramenti,* qu. *Sabbati?*) to Eltham, a castle situated between two parks, where the King gave them audience, and read the Emperor's letters. Find by various evidences that he was not pleased with their contents. When they told him the Swiss were intriguing against the Emperor and the Catholic King, and demanded money from France, in accordance with an agreement made before Dijon, offering to league with France in consequence of the practices of the Pope, he replied that the Emperor had no such grounds for making a truce, because the Swiss were in league with England against the French, and that the Pope had no other object except a defensive league, for fear of the Spaniards, and does not favor the French, but gives all possible

1514.

support to the Duke of Milan. Whenever he needs peace he will not have to send out of his kingdom for it. Finally, he referred them to his council.

On Friday, accordingly, at Baynard's Castle, met the Duke of Norfolk, the Bishops of Winchester, Durham, and Lincoln, the Prior of St. John's, the Lord Chamberlain and the Master of the Rolls. The Council expressed much surprise at the King of Arragon making this truce without giving notice to Henry, who had entered into war on his account to preserve for him Naples and Navarre, and said they would not have believed that the Emperor would have made answer to Quintana without giving notice to England. They thought their Sovereign should not have been treated like a boy, and can never expect him to accept a truce, the articles of which have not been transmitted to him either by the Emperor or Arragon. Request, therefore, that they may be transmitted. De Pleine wrote to the Emperor, from Louvain, of this difficulty. The English ambassador in Spain has written that he was present when the truce was proclaimed at the court of the King Catholic between the Emperor and the King Catholic, when the latter undertook to be security for the King of England's adherence.—The general of Normandy is still here. They told the Council he was well known to the Emperor as one accustomed to handle more difficult matters than the ransom of the Duke of Longueville. On their saying they hoped the King would not make peace without consulting the Emperor, were assured the general had not spoken on that subject. —Have made special visits to the Bishop of Winchester, Duke of Norfolk and the Bishop of Lincoln, to counteract the designs of the General and Count Louis de Canosse, who has been sent through France by the Pope. Find them all much alarmed, and very distrustful of the Emperor, though the writers have somewhat appeased them. Have learned more from the Bishop of Lincoln than the others. He says plainly, that the King might, if he would, make peace with France, but it would be ruinous to the Emperor and the Prince's countries ; he hopes, however, the King will do nothing to their prejudice. Thinks the General of Normandy has declared all that the Emperor and the Catholic King have endeavoured to bring about with France with the view of separating the King of England from them. Wolsey spoke about the marriage of Lady Eleanor, the duchy of Burgundy, Gueldres, the marriage of Renee, the sending of Bontemps with letters of ratification, &c. He said, besides, the King would cross the sea in 24 days to besiege Boulogne, which he could do more easily without horses and provisions from the Low Countries, as the transport from England was shorter, and the Swiss were more bound to the King than they ever were to the Emperor ; — that they were willing to enter France ;—but the King and his Council thought better the King and the Swiss should do so simultaneously ;—that the King will never make peace. He is very angry that the Emperor had not declared his intentions before they had gone to expence for solemnizing the marriage at Calais. The King, however, will have regard to the burthens borne by the Emperor, provided he acts friendly, and lets the King know his intentions decidedly by sending the articles of truce. Were told by the chief councillors they would not take it amiss if the Emperor would let the time slip without declaring his resolution. They cannot understand why the Emperor should seeem to refuse to England the services of his subjects, and yet allow the French to make use of them against England. Some are of opinion that the Catholic King does not wish the termination

1514.

of the war with Venice, and that the depression of France would be more useful to the Emperor. London, 19 June 1514.
Lat.

19 June.
R. O.

5174. LEO X. to HENRY VIII.

The Bishop of Worcester will inform the Bishops of Winchester and Lincoln what the Pope wishes the King to do. Has great reliance in him for furthering the papal projects for the peace and augmentation of Christendom. Rome, 19 June 1514.

20 June.
R. O.

5175. SIR EDW. PONYNGES to HENRY VIII.

Sends copy of a letter from a man he entertains at the French King's court, Nic. de St. Genois. It is probable that St. Genois will be consulted if the French make any enterprise upon Tournay, as he was once of great authority there, and they fancy he has been banished by Ponynges. Tournay, 20 June. *Signed.*
P. 1. Addressed.

20 June.

5176. PONYNGES to WOLSEY.

Begs him to deliver the above to the King. Tournay, 20 June. *Signed.*
P. 1. Add. : To my Lord of Lincoln.

20 June.
R. O.

5177. ST. ALBAN'S.

Draft indenture granting to' Ric. Harvy and Robt. his son, for life, the office of keeper of the woods belonging to the Abbey of St. Alban, Hertfordshire. 20 June 6 Hen. VIII.
Copy, pp. 3.

21 June.
S. B.

5178. For THOMAS ARCHER of Theydon, alias of Writtyll, Essex.

Protection ; going in the retinue of Sir Richard Wyngfeld, Deputy of Calais. *Del.* Westm., 21 June 6 Hen. VIII.
Fr. 6 Hen. VIII. p. 2, m. 3.

21 June.
S. B.

5179. For WILLIAM BLOUNT LORD MOUNTJOY, the Queen's chamberlain.

Wardship of Anne, a daughter and heir of Sir John Mountegomery. The other daughters are Dorothy and Ellen, also minors. *Del.* Westm., 21 June 6 Hen. VIII.
Pat. 6 Hen. VIII. p. 2, m. 15.

21 June.
S. B.

5180. For CHARLES EARL OF WORCESTER, the King's chamberlain.

Pardon to him and Christopher Ursewyke, clk., Edmund Steynbank, clk., Sir Robert Drury, Sir William Walgrave, and Sir John Husy, John Newdegate, serjeant-at-law, and Thomas Carbete, of all alienations of the manors of Great Brikhyll, Bucks, Foxley, Bawdeswell, and Sparham, Norf., Roydon and Badmondesfeld, Suff., and lands in Great Brikhyll, Foxley, Bawdeswell, Sparham, Roydon, and Badmondesfeld. Grant of the issues of the premises to the said Earl. Licence to him and Henry Somersette his eldest son to enfeoff Richard Bishop of Winchester, Thomas Bp. of Durham, Thomas Bp. of Lincoln, Hugh Bp. of Exeter, Henry Marquis of Dorset, Henry Earl of Devon, Henry Earl of Essex, Henry Earl of Wilts, Robert Willughby Lord Broke, Walter

1514.

Devereux Lord Ferrers, Sir William Compton, Sir William Sandes, Sir John Dudley, Sir John Savage, jun., Sir John Husy, [Sir] Peter Egecombe, Sir [John S]peke, Sir Amias Pollette, Sir Richard Herbert, Sir Edward Stradlyng, William Herbert of Troy, Mathew Cradocke and Rees Mauncell, William Courteney, John Caylevey, William Marwoode, Lewis Pollard, Richard Broke, and John . . . . . [serjeants]-at-law, of the honor of Gower, the castle of Swannescy, the manor of Kylvey, the manors and castles of Oistermouthe and Llhoughourne, the manors of Pennard and Westgower, South Wales, and the manor of Wyllyngton, Heref., with appurtenances. *Del.* Westm., 21 June 6 Hen. VIII.

| 21 June. | **5181.** | For RICHARD EDSAWE of London, draper. |
| P. S. | | Protection ; going in the retinue of Sir Richard Wingfild, Deputy of Calais. Eltham, 19 June 6 Hen. VIII. *Del.* Westm., 21 June. |

| 22 June. | **5182.** | AMMONIUS to ERASMUS. |
| Eras. Ep. App. 7. | | Is very busy. Could not reply sooner to the letters Erasmus sent him from St. Omer. Sent his letters to Pace. The Pope has written most kindly ; holds out great hopes to Erasmus, and recommends him to the King. Keeps the papal briefs for Erasmus to see. London, 22 June 1514. |

| 23 June. | **5183.** | GAOL DELIVERY. |

Oxford Circuit.—Rob. Brudenell, sen., John Neuport and Rob. Brudenell, jun. Westm., 23 June.
Pat. 6 Hen. VIII. p. 1, m. 17d.

Nottingham Castle.—Commission to Thos. Babyngton, Anthony Babyngton, Wm. Wymondeswold, Wm. Clerkeson, John Dunham, Ric. Savage, Humph. Hercy and John Willughby. Westm., 23 June.
Pat. 6 Hen. VIII. p. 2, m. 3d.

| 23 June. | **5184.** | For SIR JOHN SHARP. |
| S. B. | | To be steward receiver and feodary of the honor of Wormegey, Norf., and bailiff and parker of Wormegey, from Easter 5 Hen. VIII. Westm., 23 June 6 Hen. VIII. |

Pat. 6 Hen. VIII. p. 2, m. 3.

| 23 June. | **5185.** | For ANDREW SKITE of London, merchant, alias of |
| P. S. | | Danske in foreign parts. |

Protection ; going in the retinue of Sir Richard Winkefeld, Lieutenant of Calais. Eltham, 23 June 6 Hen. VIII.

| 24 June. | **5186.** | GAOL DELIVERY. |

Leicester town.—Ric. Raynold, mayor, Humph. Conyngesby, Guy Palmes, Ralph Swyllyngton, Wm. Wygston, sen., Wm. Wyg[ston] jun., Ric. Gyllot and Wm. Bolt. Westm., 24 June.
Pat. 6 Hen. VIII. p. 1, m. 11d.

Home Circuit.—John Butteler, John More and Simon Fitz. Westm., 24 June.
Pat. 6 Hen. VIII. p. 1, m. 17d.

1514
24 June.   **5187.**   For THOMAS BP. OF LINCOLN and JOHN ABBOT OF
S. B.   ST. EDMUND'S BURY.

Rym. XIII. 405.   Next presentation to the exempt monastery of St. Saviour,
Bermondesey, Surr. *Del.* Otford, 24 June 6 Hen. VIII.
Pat. 6 *Hen.VIII. p.* 2, *m.* 7.

24 June.   **5188.**   For JOHN GILBERD of Newport, Isle of Wight, shoe-
maker.

Protection ; going in the King's service. Westm., 24 June.
Fr. 6 *Hen.VIII. p.* 2, *m.* 14.

26 June.   **5189**   .   CONVOCATION.

Vitell. B. II. 80.   " 1514. Oratio habita in convocatione cleri per Jo. Tailer juris
B. M.   pontificii doctorem," 26 June. *Corrected by the author.*
Lat., pp. 4.

26 June.   **5190.**   For RALPH BRANDESBY late of Kepyke, North Riding
S. B.   of Yorkshire.

Pardon. *Del.* Westm., 26 June 6 Hen. VIII.

26 June.   **5191.**   For WILLIAM COMPTON.

P. S. b.   Protection for Ric. Lenard of Camden, Glouc., retained to serve
in the war. Eltham, 26 June 6 Hen. VIII. *Signed.*
Fr. 6 *Hen.VIII. p.* 2, *m.* 14.   Westm., 28 June.

27 June.   **5192.**   SIR RICH. WINGFIELD to [WOLSEY].

Galba, B. III. 208.   [Is sorry Wolsey] is displeased with the infrequency of his
B. M.   writing ; it was only for lack of matter. All Christendom is looking
for the resolution the King will take with the Emperor's ambassadors. There is much talk here of the great feasting made to the
General of Normandy, of his being present at the sacryng of the
King's new s[on], of his frequent sending to his master, and the
like from his master to him ; and that his special charge is for the
marriage between Louis and the Lady Mary. Does not believe it
himself, but it is universally reported by those who desire a breach
with England. The friars he wrote of to the King have returned
to France without effecting much. Hearing that the vice-admiral
is put to Liskeard, and has paid his ransom, hopes his claim to one-
third of the ransom will be remembered. Brussels, 27 June.
Hol., pp. 2. *Mutilated.*

27 June.   **5193.**   COMMISSION OF THE PEACE.

York, East Riding.—Edw. Duke of Buckingham, Hen. Earl of
Northumberland, Geo. Earl of Shrewsbury, Thos. Lord Darcy, Ric.
Nevell Lord Latimer, Humph. Conyngesby, John Erneley, Brian
Palmes, Sir Ralph Eruere (for Eure), Sir Ralph Ellerker, Sir Ralph
Bigot, Sir Walter Griffith, Sir Rob. Constable, Sir Thos. Metham,
Sir Rob. Aske, Sir John Norton, Sir John Normanvile, Sir Wm.
Constable of Everyngham, Sir Thos. Barkeley, John Hothom, Thos.
Fairfax, Wm. Eleson, John Rose, John Hartfeld, Ralph Rokeby
and Ric. Rokeby. W[estm]., 27 June.
Pat. 6 *Hen.VIII. p.* 1, *m.* 2d.

28 June.   **5194.**   For RIC. RUST of Shernborne, Norf.

Reversal of outlawry sued for debt in the King's Bench by Joan
widow of John Wayprowe of Riburgh Magna ; the said Richard
having surrendered to the Marshalsea prison. Westm., 28 June.
Pat. 6 *Hen.VIII. p.* 1, *m.* 16.

1514.

28 June. **5195.** GAOL DELIVERY.

Norfolk Circuit.—Sir John Fyneux, Sir Rob. Rede and Wm. Mordaunt. Westm., 28 June.

Northern Circuit.—Brian Palmes, John Erneley, Rob. Henryson and Thos. Stray. Westm., 28 June.

Pat. 6 *Hen. VIII. p.* 1, *m.* 17d.

28 June. **5196.** For SIR JOHN GYFFORD.
S. B.

Wardship of Dorothy, a daughter and heir of Sir John Mountegomery. The other daughters are Ellen and Anne, also minors. *Del.* Westm., 28 June 6 Hen. VIII.

Pat. 6 *Hen.VIII. p.* 2, *m.* 5.

28 June. **5197.** For GUY TOWRES alias STEVINSON.
P. S.

Pardon as of Teteney, alias of Botheby, alias of Grauntham, Linc., alias of Cambridge, draper, alias of Newinton Grene, Midd. Eltham, 26 June 6 Hen. VIII. *Del.* Westm., 28 June.

Pat. 6 *Hen.VIII. p.* 2, *m.* 15.

29 June. **5198.** For LEONARD DE SPINELLIS, clk., the Pope's chamberlain.
S. B.

Presentation to the church of Cotyngham, York dioc. *Del.* Westm., 29 June 6 Hen. VIII.

Pat. 6 *Hen.VIII. p.* 2, *m.* 6.

30 June. **5199.** To the ABP. OF CANTERBURY, Chancellor.
S. B.

For letters of *dedimus potestatem* to Thomas Abbot of Mochelney to take the fealty of Thomas Chard, by "foundatory" licence elected prior of Mountegu. Eltham, 30 June 6 Hen. VIII. *Sealed.*

30 June. **5200.** For ROBERT PARROWE, EDMUND BALLARD, THOMAS STEVYNSON, baker, and CUTHBERT ROBSON, all of Spaldyng, Linc.
S. B.

Pardon of all offences before 20 March 5 Hen. VIII. *Del.* Westm., 30 June 6 Hen. VIII.

30 June. **5201.** For THOMAS WOODE, yeoman of the Crown, and THOMAS DAWSON.
S. B.

Grant, in survivorship, of an annuity of 10l. from the customs of Exeter and Dartmouth. *Del.* Westm., 30 June 6 Hen. VIII.

Pat. 6 *Hen.VIII. p.* 2, *m.* 2.

30 June. **5202.** For ROBERT MERBURY, yeoman usher of the Queen's chamber.
S. B.

To be feodary of the duchy of Exeter, Devon. *Del.* Westm., 30 June 6 Hen. VIII.

Pat. 6 *Hen. VIII. p.* 2, *m.* 6.

30 June. **5203.** GERARD DE PLEINE to MARGARET OF SAVOY.
Lett. de Louis XII.
t. IV. 335.

On receipt of her letter of the 18th about the illness of the Prince, went to the King in the absence of John Colla, who was ill of a catarrh. The King told him his ambassadors had written

3 G

that the fever was abating, and that the Prince would soon be well.
Spoke of the General of Normandy, but could learn nothing
further. The King complained greatly of the manner in which
he had been treated by Arragon and the Emperor, especially by
the latter refusing him the aid of his subjects, for whom England
pays. Replied that the Emperor had been compelled to listen to
the truce, although De Pleine believed he had deferred his consent
to it till he should know the King's resolution ;—that the Emperor
always had such confidence in Henry that he would have been
satisfied with anything he had done, even if it had been a more
weighty matter;—and as to the men of war, the Emperor had
only delayed making answer till he knew if Henry accepted the
truce or not. Finally De Pleine said that a union between the
Emperor, the King Catholic, the Prince, and the King of England,
could not but be for the advantage of all ; and that if the Emperor
and King Catholic had not given the King due notice, one error
was better than two, and a joint peace would be better for England
than a separate one.

Henry replied that it touched his honor that the Emperor had made
a truce without him, when he had been at such a great expense.
As to the Emperor allowing Henry the aid of his subjects,
the King said he knew more than De Pleine, because his ambassador had written that the Emperor had told him he could
not do it, but as to having made a truce or not he had returned
no answer. The King then spoke of the great preparation
he had made at Calais for the marriage of the Prince, of which all
Christendom was full, and which was to have taken place in the
month of May. Every one said, at Rome, in France, in the
Prince's countries, and in England, that the delay was only designed
to break it off. De Pleine replied that nothing was more desired by the Emperor and Margaret than that it should take effect ;
that they only wished to change the place on account of the
plague, which began then to prevail in May. Hoped the King
would have regard for the Emperor's friendship, and none
would be able to do them injury. The King said the arrangement he had made with the Emperor at Lille had been fruit-
less ; that those named in it, and the Count Palatine also, had
as much credit as if they were at Rome.

Had refrained from writing about the Princess [Mary] till he had
seen her. Has never seen so beautiful a lady. Her deportment is
exquisite both in conversation and in dancing, and she is very
lively. If Margaret had seen her she would not rest till she had
her over; she is very well brought up, and appears to love the Prince
wonderfully. She has a very bad picture of him, and is said to wish
for his presence ten times a day. She is not tall, but is a better
match in age and person for the Prince than he had heard say.
In two years she will be as far advanced as Likerke or Fontaine.*
Was asked by the Bishop of Lincoln why they had broken off
the marriage. Replied that they did not consider it broken off, and
that the obligations contained in the first treaty were not so easily
invalidated. On being asked why the time had been allowed to
pass, said it was nobody's fault, but only the consequence of making
these truces, and the distance of the Emperor. Was asked by
another great person if the French King had had the small pox

---

* Maid of honor to Margaret.

1514.

(*les pocques*). Some say the alliance with the Prince will be very costly to this kingdom. Thinks, however, that most influential persons are in favor of it. Considers that the Emperor and the Prince ought to give effect to it. The Prince will be heir to great kingdoms, to obtain which this alliance will help him. As there ought to be more zeal exhibited on the part of the husband than of the lady, some great personage should be sent to espouse the Princess, *per verba de præsenti*, who should propose, instead of Escluse or Tenremonde, some place nearer Antwerp or Malines to solemnize the marriage, according to the pleasure of the Emperor. —The Queen is believed to be with child, and is so, as far as the writer can judge. She is of a lively and gracious disposition; quite the opposite of the Queen her sister [Joan of Arragon] in complexion and manner. The painter has made a good likeness of Mary.—London, 30 June.
Fr.

30 June. **5204.** For ROGER CLERK.

P. S.
Presentation to the prebend of St. John the Baptist, in the collegiate church of Warwick, Worc. dioc., *vice* William Clerk, resigned. Eltham, 27 June 6 Hen. VIII. *Del.* Westm., 30 June.
Pat. 6 *Hen. VIII. p.* 2, *m.* 5.

June. **5205.** FLORYS [COUNT EGMONT] to SUFFOLK.

R. O.
Madame of Savoy is writing in his favor, that Florys may be reimbursed for 205 horsemen raised for the service of England. Before his departure from these parts, the King appointed him one of the governors of the Prince of Castile, which has caused him great expenses. Begs Suffolk will assist him in recovering the money disbursed for the purpose expressed, by the hands of Messire Edward Ponynges. Brussells, — June 1514. *Signed.*
Fr., p. 1. *Addressed.*

1 July. **5206.** For SIR WILLIAM COMPTON, SIR JOHN PECHE, and

P. S.
JOHN COLET and HUGH ASHTON, clerks.
Next presentation to the church of Grasforth, St. Asaph's dioc. *Del.* Westm., 1 July 6 Hen. VIII.
Pat. 6 *Hen. VIII. p.* 1, *m.* 18.

1 July. **5207.** SIR RICH. WINGFIELD and SPINELLY to [HENRY VIII.]

Galba, B. III. 209.
B. M.
Wrote last on the 27th ult°. Have not since heard from the King. Send copy of a letter from the Lord Brabanson and Dysenghien to the Archduchess touching the last inroad of the French into Hainault and its punishment. Maraton has gone to the Prince's treasurer for the 30,000 crowns of gold required by the Emperor. Berges, Dissilsteyne and others have gone to Holland to obtain a continuance of the accustomed aid; Bevers and the Lord Admiral to Zeland.—The President of the Privy Council has desired leave to go home, leaving John Cole in his place. The Lady Margaret told him, it was for the Emperor, who sent him, to give him leave.—Send a bill of news obtained by Spinelly. The Prince of Castile is recovering from his fever. Brussels, 1 July 151[4]. *Signed.*
Pp. 2, *mutilated.*

3 G 2

1514.

1 July.　　**5208.**　　SPINELLY to [HENRY VIII.]

Galba, B.III. 163.
B. M.

　　...... divers Scotch reported that English ships of war had done much harm in Scotland; that the Secretary of the Emperor had been in Scotland to see the Queen, and the Emperor would gladly take her in marriage; that the council there will not give the archbishopric of St. Andrews to Cardinal Cibo; that he and the Bishop of Moray had been negotiating for an exchange with Bourgys en Berry in France; and that the Bishop wants to be made Cardinal and Legate à latere in Scotland. Letters from Rome, of the 14 June, state that the Pope is French, that Cardinal St. Severin and the French ambassadors are in great favor with him—"that with the Pope's brother were gone to Florence, disguised, six cardinals of the youngest" .... "the Archduchess wh .... th[at] then she have sent after the ambassador of ... was departed towards Antwerp to advertise [Don] Diego di Castro, one of my Lord the Prince of C[astile's ...] in Spanish being put in prison the last ... the castle of Vylleford at the King of Arrago[n, is escaped and runned away out of prison, f[or] she doubted the said ambassador shall think it h[ath been] done wilfully."—Before the late invasion of Heynault by the French, the Arragonese ambassador produced letters from the French court, stating that the King had forbidden all such invasions of the Prince's country. After the invasion she told the ambassador that no great trust must be put in his or the Frenchman's promises. She confirmed the news of the Emperor's secretary going into Scotland.—*Here follows a mutilated passage, of which no sense can be made.*—Mountjoye, with whom the Hainault King-at-arms was lodging in France, said, when a post came from the French ambassador in England, *J'espoire que nous et nos cousins d'Angleterre serons bons amis en brief, et que nos gens d'armes passeront en Italie.* The Pope is said to be French, and very friendly with the Venetians, and that the Ursines are supported by him—that he will admit the French into Milan, that he may have Naples.*—The Swiss Diet is assembled at Zurich † .... "the King of Arragon sith .... is much affeyblysshed, and goeth no more on ho[rseback], but only in a litter."—The Duke of Genoa has dismissed the Spanish troops. Brussells, 1 July. *Signed.*
　　Pp. 4, mutilated.

1 July.　　**5209.**　　CONVOCATION.

Vitell. B. II. 82.
B. M.

　　Speech of the prolocutor in convocation, moving its adjournment, on account of the epidemic and the heat of the weather, till the winter. 1 July 1514.
　　Lat., in Taylor's hand, p. 1.

1 July.　　**5210.**　　For SIR WISTAN BROWNE, knight of the Body.

P. S.

　　Licence to export woollen cloths and other merchandize not of the staple of Calais, the duties not exceeding 100*l.*, and to import cloths of silk, silk and gold, malvesyes, woad, alum, and other merchandize to the same extent. Greenwich, 14 April 5 Hen. VIII.
　　Del. Westm., 1 July 6 Hen. VIII.
　　Pat. 6 *Hen. VIII. p.* 1, *m.* 16.

---

　　* Added here in the margin, in Spinelly's hand, "that the King of Arragon may thank himself and his .. ewys there were two difficulties in the execution of it—war with with England and the Swiss."
　　† Passage unintelligible.

1514.

3 July.
S. B.

5211. For WILLIAM BUTLER, serjeant-at-arms, and JAMES AP JENKYN.

Grant, in survivorship, of the tenements in Westminster Palace, called Paradyse and Helle, with lands and tenements held by James Fryes; a house called Purgatory in the said Hall, held by Nicholas Whitefeld; a house called Potans house, under the Exchequer; the tower and house called le Grenelates, held by John Catesby; and the keepership of the said palace;—on surrender by Butler, of patent 27 May 3 Hen. VIII., granting the above to Mathew Baker, squire of the Body, now deceased, and the said William. *Del.* Westm., 3 July 6 Hen. VIII.
Pat. 6 *Hen. VIII. p.* 1, *m.* 11.

3 July.
S. B.

5212. For SIR GEOFFREY GATE.

Licence to export 500 sacks of English wool, in five years; the customs being four marks on each sack. *Del.* Westm., 3 July 6 Hen. VIII.
Fr. 6 *Hen. VIII. p.* 2, *m.* 15.

3 July.
S. B.

5213. For MAURO DE MASAGROSA, merchant of Lucca.

Licence to export 500 sacks of English wool, in five years. *Del.* Westm., 3 July 6 Hen. VIII.
Fr. 6 *Hen. VIII. p.* 2, *m.* 5.

3 July.
S. B.

5214. For RICHARD, the PRIOR, and the CONVENT of ST. JOHN PONTEFRACT.

Grant of a fair for three days every year in their town of Barnesley, York, on the day of the conversion of St. Paul, and two days afterwards. *Del.* Westm., 3 July 6 Hen. VIII.

3 July.
P. S. b.

5215. For RICHARD EARL OF KENT.

Protection for John Frenche of Bedford, retained to serve in the war. London, 2 July 6 Hen. VIII. [*Del.*] Westm., 3 July. *Signed.*
Fr. 6 *Hen. VIII. p.* 2, *m.* 14.

3 July.
P. S. b.

5216. For ROBERT LORD CORSON, Master of the Ordnance in the Rearward.

Protection for Henry Hamond of London, lantern-maker, retained to serve in the said ward. London, 3 July 6 Hen. VIII. *Signed and sealed.*
Fr. 6 *Hen. VIII. p.* 2, *m.* 14.

3 July.
P. S. b.

5217. For SIR WILLIAM COMPTON.

Protection to Thomas Nevile of Childeswykwan, Glouc., going with the King in the royal voyage. [*Del.*] 3 July 6 Hen. VIII. *Signed.*

4 July.
R. O.

5218. PONYNGES to the BISHOPS OF WINCHESTER and LINCOLN (FOX and WOLSEY).

Against the escheator of Warwick and Worcestershire, who wished to find certain sinister offices on the lands of Henry Pympe,

1514.

whose wardship he has from the King. Has not heard from them a long time. Tournay, 4 July. *Signed.*

P. 1. Add. Endd. : The Lieutenant of Tournay.

---

4 July.
R. O.

5219. RIC. HANSSART to WOLSEY.

The garrison is well. Has written several letters, and received no reply. The retinue left with him in Tournay are in good health, and will be glad to serve him. Has become overseer of Wesse and Helsyng. Tournay, 4 July. *Signed.*

P. 1. Add. : My Lord of Lincoln. *Endd.*

---

4 July.

5220. COMMISSIONS OF THE PEACE.

Cornwall.—H. Bp. of Exeter, Hen. Earl of Wiltshire, Rob. Willoughby Lord Broke, Sir Hen. Marney, Ric. Eliott, Lewis Pollard, Edw. Willoughby, Sir John Arundell De la Heron, Sir Peter Egecombe, Sir Wm. Trevanyon, Roger Graynfeld, Peter Bevyle, John Skewis, Rob. Tredenek, John Arundell of Talverne, Ric. Vyvvan, John Chamond, Wm. Godalghan, Rob. Vyvvan, Ric. Penros, Wm. Lowre, Nic. Carmynowe, Hen. Tregarell, and Wm. Carnsewe. Westm., 4 July.

[*Devon*].—H. Bp. of Exeter, Hen. Earl of Wiltshire, Rob. Willoughby Lord Broke, John Bourchier Lord Fitzwarren, Hen. Lord Daubney, Ric. Elyott, Lewis Pollard, Edw. Wylloughby, Sir Peter Eggecombe, Sir Edw. Pomerey, Sir Amias Paulet, Sir John Basset, Sir John Kyrkeham, Sir Thos. Greynfeld, John Souche, Wm. Courtency, Thos. Denes (or Deues), Jas. Chudleygh, John Chamond, John Rowe, Rob. Yoo, Ric. Strode, John Gilbert, Thos. Stukeley, Ric. Reigney, John Crokker, Andrew Hillarsdon, John Cayleway, Ric. Coffyn, John Walcote, Edm. Larder, John Asshe, Rob. Cliston, and John Cole of Slade. Westm., 4 July.

Pat. 6 *Hen.VIII. p.* 1, *m.* 2*d.*

---

4 July.
S. B.

5221. For JOHN CAVALCANTI and his companions, merchants of Florence, Genoa, Lucca or London.

Pardon and release. *Del.* Westm., 4 July 6 Hen. VIII.

Pat. 6 *Hen.VIII. p.* 2, *m.* 16.

---

4 July.
S. B.

5222. For NICHOLAS ALAMANNI and CHARLES HUGHUCHIONI, merchants.

Licence to import all merchandize, except Gascon wine, for five years. *Del.* Westm., 4 July 6 Hen. VIII.

Fr. 6 *Hen.VIII. p.* 2, *m.* 5.

---

4 July.
P. S. b.

5223. For THOMAS EARL OF SURREY.

Protection for Thomas Howell, draper of London, retained to serve in the wars. London, 4 July 6 Hen. VIII. *Signed.*

Fr. 6 *Hen.VIII. p.* 2, *m.* 14.

---

5 July.
P. S.

5224. For THOMAS LATHUM.

Licence to export woollen cloths, tin, lead, hides, and all other commodities, except wools and fleeces. London, 20 May 6 Hen.VIII. *Del.* Westm., 5 July.

Fr. 6 *Hen.VIII. p.* 2, *m.* 5.

1514.
5 July. **5225.** COMMISSION OF THE PEACE.

Notts.—T. Bp. of Lincoln, Geo. Earl of Shrewsbury,. Humph. Conyngesby, Guy Palmes, Sir Thos. Lovell, Sir Rob. Sheffeld, Sir Hen. Willoughby, Sir Wm. Perpoynt, Sir Wm. Meryng, Sir Thos. Sutton, John Willoughby, Simon Dygby, Wm. Clarkson, Thos. Hasylrygge, Rob. Clyston, Humph. Hersey, Ric. Savage, Anthony Babyngton, Ric. Stanhop, Geo. Chaworth, John B[yron], Rob. Hasylrigge, Thos. Meryng, Wm. Wymondfeld, Hen. Bosom and Rob. Nevell. . . . ., 5 July.

Pat. 6 *Hen.VIII. p.* 1, *m.* 2*d.*

5 July. **5226.** JOHN EARL OF LINCOLN.

Berks.—Commission to John Swafeld and Thos. Beke to make inquisition on and take into the King's hands the possessions of which John Earl of Lincoln, attainted 3 Hen. VII., was seised on 9 March 2 Hen. VII. Westm., 5 July.

Pat. 6 *Hen.VIII. p.* 1, *m.* 16*d.*

5 July. **5227.** For GODFREY DAROLD of Boston, Linc., merchant.

P. S   Licence to import 100 tuns of Gascon wine. Greenwich, 4 July 6 Hen. VIII. *Del.* Westm., 5 July.

6 July. **5228.** THE HENRY GRACE A DIEU.

R. O.   Expenses for building and fitting the said ship :—Timber, consisting of 1,752 tons, &c., 437*l.* 17*s.* 7¼*d.* ; wrought and unwrought iron, 408*l.* 19*s.* 7½*d.* ; brass, &c., 243*l.* 6*s.* 3½*d.* ; coal for the iron, 133*l.* 12*s.* 6*d.* ; cordage, 969*l.* 2*s.* 11*d.* ; ox-hair, lime, rosin, 100*l.* 13*s.* 10*d.* ; blocks, pullies, &c., 63*l.* 0*s.* 19*d.* ; spades, platters, tankards, &c., 155*l.* 13*s.* 10*d.* ; lathes, painting colors, 36*l.* 0*s.* 7*d.* ; bedding for the workmen, watchmen, &c., 296*l.* 9*s.* 2*d.* ; sundries, 685*l.* 7*s.* 2½*d.* Total, 3,531*l.* 5*s.* 1¾*d.*

Wages, from 3 Oct. 4 Hen. VIII. to 6 July 6 Hen. VIII., 2,192*l.* 6*s.* 3*d.* ; shipwrights and sawyers, 185*l.* 16*s.* 7*d.* ; mariners employed in fetching timber, 55*l.* 6*s.* 3*d.* ; masters' wages at 20*s.* per month ; quartermasters', 10*s.* a month ; purser, 8*s.* a month ; 3 other officers, 7*s.* 6*d.* a month ; 217 mariners, 5*s.* a month ; with others, 254*l.* 9*s.* 1½*d.* William Bound, 2*s.* a day ; his clerk, 8*d.* a day ; servant, 6*d.* a day. Overseeing the workmen and keeping accounts, 101*l.* 6*s.* 8*d.*

Coats for 141 shipwrights, at 4*s.*, 3*s.*, and 2*s.*

Conduct money, 95*l.* 5*s.*

Victuals, 7,497½ doz. and 2 loaves of bread, 370*l.* 7*s.* 8*d.* ; 1,543 pipes and 2 kilderkins of beer, 526*l.* 19*s.* 11*d* ; 557 beeves, 706*l.* 17*s.* 9*d.* ; 205 score muttons, 32*l.* 5*s.* 8*d.* ; porks, 36*s.* ; 27 calves, 75*s.* ; 9 [barrels] of beef, 8*l.* 5*s.* 2*d.* ; 1,001 quarters of ab . . d . th s. lings, 38*l.* 2*s.* ; 16 barrels of fish, 8*l.* 10*s.* ; 4,522 cods, 87*l.* 2*s.* 10*d.* ; 45 salmons, 30*s.* ; 10½ lasts and 2 cads of red herring, 54*l.* 0*s.* 12*d.* ; 19½ lasts 4½ barrels of white herring, 88*l.* 18*s.* 10*d.* ; 20 cads of sprotts, 24*s.* 8*d.* ; 4½ pipes of baysalt, and 4 bz. at 26*s.* 3*d.* a pipe ; 12 weys 7 bz. 1 peck of baysalt, 13*l.* 7*s.* 6*d.* ; 7 barrels of butter, 4*l.* 6*s.* ; 30 weys and 3 qrs. of cheese, 19*l.* 4*s.* ; white salt, 13*d.* ; oatmeal, green and grey pease, eggs, &c., 62*l.* 0*s.* 6*d.* Total, 1,969*l.* 18*s.* 2*d.*

Hay and pasture for cattle. Prests and rewards, (*sums torn off.*) Sum of all costs of *The Henry Grace de Dieu* and 3 small galleys, 7,708*l.* 5*s.* 3*d.*

Paper roll, mutilated.

1514.

6 July.
S. B.

5229.   To JOHN YONG, Master of the Rolls.

To cancel a recognizance of 100 marks, made by Sir Thomas Curwen of Wyrkyngton, Cumberl., John Huddeleston of Sudeley, Glouc., and Henry Kerkeby of Kerkeby, Lanc., 13 July 22 Hen. VII. Greenwich, 6 July.

6 July.
P. S.

5230.   For the CARTHUSIAN HOUSE OF THE SALUTATION OF THE MOTHER OF GOD, London.

Licence to quit-claim to the provost and scholars of the Royal College of St. Mary and St. Nicholas, Cambridge, the priory of Okebourne, and the manors of Great and Little Okebourne, Wilts. Greenwich, 1 June 3 Hen. VIII. *Del.* Westm., 6 July 6 Hen. VIII.

7 July.
S. B.

5231.   For THOMAS TAMWORTH.

To be auditor of the accounts of the treasurer of Calais, of the mayor, constables and merchants of the staple of Calais, of the keeper of the Great Wardrobe, of the clerk or keeper of the Hanaper, of the constable of Windsor Castle, of the captain or receiver of the Isle of Weight, and of the chief butler of England, or the occupant of that office, in the several ports of the kingdom, with usual fees ;—and to be clerk of the Council Chamber at Westminster, called " le Prince Councell Chambre," and keeper of the books and records there, with 10*l.* a year, out of the issues of the duchy of Cornwall, from Michaelmas last, he having performed the offices since that time. *Del.* Westm., 7 July 6 Hen. VIII.

Pat. 6 *Hen. VIII. p.* 1, *m.* 18.

7 July.
S. B.

5232.   For HENRY PYNAGO, one of the King's depositors.

Annuity of 20 marks out of the issues of the counties of Norfolk and Suffolk, from Mich. 2 Hen. VIII. ;—on surrender of patent 17 Nov. 2 Hen. VIII. (granting him the same, *vice* Edw. Skelton, deceased), which was invalid. *Del.* Westm., 7 July 6 Hen. VIII.

7 July.
S. B.

5233.   For JOHN MEAWTIS, the King's French Secretary.

Licence to import 400 tuns of Gascon wine, and 200 tons of Toulouse woad. *Del.* Westm., 7 July 6 Hen. VIII. *In margin :* " Litteræ patentes pro 200 doliis vini emanârunt die prædicto."

Fr. 6 *Hen. VIII. p.* 2, *m.* 6.

8 July.
Lansd. 818. f. 12.
B. M.

5234.   CHARLES LORD LISLE.

Letters patent for Charles Viscount Lisle to be marshal of the army. Westm., 28 May 5 Hen. VIII.

Note :—" This patent read by Garter in the market place at Calais, the 8th day of July."

Copy, pp. 21.

ii. Publication of the above by Charles Viscount Lisle.

Copy, p. 1.

8 July.
S. B.

5235.   For HUMPHREY EVYAS.

Livery as son of John Evyas, jun., brother of John Evyas, sen., father of Alexander Evyas, of the manor of Estball, with appur-

1514.

tenances in Morston, Bakchilde, Sythyngbourne, Elmeley, and Tong, Kent. *Del.* Westm., 8 July 6 Hen. VIII.

Pat. 6 Hen. VIII. p. 1, *m.* 28.

8 July. **5236.** GAOL DELIVERY

Bishop's Lynn.—Sir Jas. Hobert, Jas. Bullen, Francis Calibut, Wm. Conyngesby, and Francis Moinford. Westm., 8 July.

Pat. 6 Hen. VIII. p. 1, *m.* 11*d.*

8 July. **5237.** COMMISSION OF THE PEACE.

Surrey.—Wm. Abp. of Canterbury, R. Bp. of Winchester, E. Duke of Buckingham, Thos. Duke of Norfolk, Chas. Duke of Suffolk, Thos. Earl of Arundel, Geo. Nevyle Lord Bergevenny, John Bourghchier Lord Bernes, Sir Edm. Howard, Sir John Fyneux, Rir Rob. Rede, John Butler, John More, Sir Thos. Lovell, Sir Ric. Carewe, Sir John Legh, Sir Hen. Wiott, Sir Matthew Broun, Sir John Iwarby, Sir Edm. Walsingham, Thos. Morton, Thos. Nevell, Edm. Bray, John Scotte, Ralph Pexsall, Rob. Wyntershull, John Gaynsford of Crowherst, John Bygge, John Westbroke, John Kyrton, John Skynner, Hen. Saunder, Roger Legh, Wm. Lassher, Gilbert Stoughton, Thos. Stidolffe, and Hen. Tyngilden. Westm., 8 July.

Pat. 6 Hen. VIII. p. 1, *m.* 9*d.*

8 July.
P. S.
5238. For ELIZABETH REYNOLDIS of Ledbury, Heref., spinster wife of William Reynoldis, and EDMUNDA BAKER of Ledbury, spinster, wife of Walter Baker.

Pardon. Eltham, 4 July 6 Hen. VIII. *Del.* Westm., 8 July.

8 July.
S. B.
5239. For THOMAS HETON of London, haberdasher.

Licence to import 100 gross of French, Milanese or other caps, and 100 gross of French or Brugges hats, in four years. *Del.* Westm., 8 July 6 Hen. VIII.

9 July.
P. S.
5240. For the exempt Cluniac MONASTERY of ST. PETER and ST. PAUL, MONTACUTE, Bath and Wells dioc.

Restitution of temporalities on election of Thomas Chard as prior ; his fealty having been taken by Thomas Abbot of Mochelney. Eltham, 30 June 6 Hen. VIII. *Del.* Westm., 9 July.

ii. Petition of sub-prior and convent for the above ; Rob. Newton, proctor. 18 June 1514.

Pat. 6 Hen. VIII. p. 2, *m.* 23.

9 July.
P. S.
5241. For ROBERT KNOLLYS, gentleman usher of the Chamber, and LETITIA his wife.

Grant, in survivorship, of the manor of Retherfeld Grey, Oxon., with advowsons, &c., at the annual rent of one red rose at Midsummer. Eltham, 4 July 6 Hen. VIII. *Del.* Westm., 9 July.

Pat. 6 Hen. VIII. p. 2, *m.* 24.

1514.

10 July. **5242.** For the GUILD OF ST. MARY, BARKING CHURCH, London.

Inspeximus and confirmation to the guild of St. Mary in the chapel of St. Mary, in the cemetry of Berkyngchirche. London, of the following documents :—

i. Patent 9 Jan. 20 Hen. VI., licensing John Somerset, chancellor of the Exchequer, Hen. Frowik and John Olney, aldermen of London, John Merston, clerk of the King's jewels, Wm. Clif, clk.. Th. Walsyngham, a customer of London, and Ric. Riche, Th. Canynges and Hugh Wiche, merchants of London, to found the said guild, of which one master and four wardens were to be elected annually ;—and granting to the said guild the custody of the said chapel (reserving the right of the parish church to oblations in the chapel), which was founded by Richard I., and in which Edward I., in consequence of a divine revelation in sleep, placed an image of St. Mary, remaining temp. Hen. VI.

ii. Patent 14 May 4 Hen. VII., inspecting and confirming patent 14 March 5 Edw. IV., granting to John Earl of Worcester, master of the said guild, and Sir John Scot, Th. Colt, John Tate and John (?) Croke, the wardens, the manor or priory of Totyngbeke, Surrey, etc.

Westm., 10 July.

Pat. 6 Hen. VIII. p. 1, *m.* 16.

10 July. **5243.** For JOHN SIGEWYKE, page of the Wardrobe of Beds, and
S. B. RAUFF JENETT, yeoman of the same.

Grant, in survivorship, of the corrody in the new abbey of Tour Hill, beside London, as held by John Bell ;— on surrender of patent granting the same to Jenett. *Del.* Westm., 10 July 6 Hen. VIII.

11 July. **5244.** COMMISSION OF THE PEACE.

York, North Riding.—Hen. Earl of Northumberland, Geo. Earl of Shrewsbury, Thos. Lord Darcy, Hen. Scrope Lord Bolton, Ric. Nevell Lord Latimer, Wm. Conyers Lord Hornby, Humph. Conyngesby, Brian Palmes, John Erneley, Sir Ralph Eure, Sir Ralph Ellerker, Sir Thos. Fairfax, Sir Walter Griffyth, Sir Ralph Bygod, Sir Wm. Bulmer, Sir Jas. Straungways, Sir Thos. Barkley, Thos. Fairfax, John Pulleyn, Rob. Wynell, John Pykeryng, and Thos. Tempest. Westm., 11 . . . . .

Pat. 6 Hen. VIII. p. 1, *m.* 2d.

11 July. **5245.** For STEPHEN TOLLE of Newsom, Linc., alias of Newsom Abby, husbandman.

Reversal of outlawry ; sued for debt by Ric. Morley, executor of Thos. Hygdon ; the said Stephen having surrendered to the Flete prison. Westm., 11 July.

Pat. 6 Hen. VIII. p. 1, *m.* 9.

11 July. **5246.** JUSTICES OF ASSIZE.

Norfolk Circuit.—Wm. Mordaunt with John Fyneux and Sir Rob. [Rede]. Westm., 11 July.

Western Circuit.—Thos. Elyot and Thos. Fitzhugh, with [Ric. Elliot] and Lewis Pollard. Westm., 11 July.

Pat. 6 Hen. VIII. p. 1, *m.* 16d.

1514.

11 July.
P. S.

5247. For NICHOLAS KINGSTON.

Livery as brother and heir of John Kingston, of the manors of Foxcot, Corsley, Warmester and Sutton Parva, and lands in Foxcot, Corsley, Warmester, Sutton Parva, Sherbourne, Medelton, Abbeston and Chawton, in cos. Somerset, Wilts, Hants and Sussex. Eltham, 7 July 6 Hen. VIII. *Del.* Westm., 11 July.
Pat. 6 *Hen. VIII. p.* 2, *m.* 6.

11 July.
P. S. b.

5248. For ROBERT LORD CORSON, master of the ordnance in the rearward.

Protection for Robert Dudley of London, goldsmith, retained to serve in the rearward. London, 11 July 6 Hen. VIII. *Del.* Westm., 11 July 6 Hen. VIII. *Signed and sealed.*

11 July.
S. B.

5249. For THOMAS WHITEHEDE, a minister of the College of Stoke, Suff.

Pardon. *Del.* Westm., 11 July 6 Hen. VIII.
Pat. 6 *Hen. VIII. p.* 2, *m.* 6.

12 July.
S. B.

5250. For SIR PHILIP TYLNEY, knight of the Body, of Fyncham, Norf., alias of Kelsale, Suff.

Pardon and release as treasurer of war under Thomas Duke of Norfolk, in his expedition to the North against the Scots ; and acquittance for 16,800*l.*, received for the expences of the troops; viz., 1,000*l.* from John Heron, treasurer of the chamber, and 15,800*l.* from the Abbot of St. Mary's, near York, and from Thomas Magnus, Archdeacon of the East Riding. *Del.* Westm., 12 July 6 Hen. VIII.
Pat. 6 *Hen. VIII. p.* 2, *m.* 6.

12 July.
R. O.

5251. RIC. SAMPSON to WOLSEY.

When he was with him at the staple yesterday, Wolsey complained of his want of assiduity. Is much hurt at the charge. Earnestly entreats that Wolsey will harbour no such suspicion. Never a day has passed that he has not been in his presence, as those who had seen him can testify. Nothing so pleasant to him as to be employed in Wolsey's service, though he does not like the racket of business. Had begged Wolsey, when he entered his service, to be allowed time to study the civil and canon law. Finds more need for that study than ever. iv. id. Jul. 1514.
Lat., pp. 2. *Addressed :* Reverendo inprimis patri et domino, Domino Thomæ Lyncoll' episcopo.

14 July.
Vitell, B. II. 82.*
B. M.
Rym. XIII. 404.

5252. JULIUS CARDINAL DE MEDICIS to HENRY VIII.

Announces the death of the Cardinal of York. Worcester's letters will inform the King how much trouble the writer has taken in the King's service, and the particulars of the Cardinal's death. 14 July 1514.
P. 1. *Add.*

Lett. de Louis XII.
t. IV. 342.

5253. CARDINAL BAINBRIDGE.

After the death of the Cardinal of England, a suspicion arose in the mind of the Secretary (Pace), who is his executor, that he had been poisoned by the Chamberlain. The Pope accordingly ordered

1514.

him to be apprehended. He confessed it, without being pressed, and said he had done it, at the request of the Bishop of Worcester, and purchased the poison with his money. He afterwards exculpated the Bishop, and then accused him again. This Chamberlain had been many years brought up by the Bishop. At last, to escape further torture, he stabbed himself. The Pope ordered his body to be hung on a gibbet, with his confession attached, then beheaded and quartered, and the quarters exhibited for one day on the gallows. He also accused another servant of the Bishop. The writer knows not how far the Bishop will clear himself. He will not be able to remove all suspicion. Begs this writing may not be shown. The Bishop will defend himself by money.*

Lat.

5254.   CONFESSION OF RAYNALDUS OF MODENA.

Lett. de Louis XII.
t. IV. 343.

That he administered poison to the Cardinal of England at the instigation of the Bishop of Worcester, who gave him 15 gold coins, one part large ducats, the other *de camera*, saying, "If we do not get rid of this Cardinal we shall never live quietly in Rome." Bought the poison at Spoleto, and gave it to the Cardinal in a potage about Corpus Christi day. He was immediately seized with a cholic; was relieved by a clister, and went to supper with the Cardinal de Finario. Next day he had a relapse, lay in bed very ill, and never rose again. Had asked the Bishop, on his first broaching the affair to him, with whom he might safely communicate. The Bishop replied · he might confide in his chamberlain, Stephen. When Raynaldus wrote these things to the Pope, he commended to his Holiness the honor of the Bishop of Worcester, who would be ruined if the affair came to light.

Lat.

15 July.   5255.   For SIR WM. COMPTON.

Inspeximus and exemplification of the following documents :—

i. The bill of complaint of Sir Wm. Compton, addressed to Wm. Abp. of Canterbury, Lord Chancellor, shewing, that whereas Dame Jane late Lady Straunge, by her will nuncupative, gave to the plaintiff and his heirs her part of the manor of Long Compton, Warw., the plaintiff having witnesses who can prove such will nuncupative to have been the last will and mind of the said Lady Straunge, prays their depositions may be taken and remain with this bill among the records of Chancery.

ii. Writ addressed to Ric. Wode, examiner of the court of Chancery, ordering the examination of witnesses.   29 May 6 Hen. VIII.

iii. The return of Ric. Wode, stating that he had taken the depositions of two witnesses, viz. :—

John Cutteler, D.D. warden of the place of St. Francis in London, of the age of 51 years, examined 31 May 6 Hen. VIII, stating he was ghostly father to the said Lady Straunge, mother of the Earl of Derby, for 12 years past; that about 10 or 12 days before her decease, being in an inner high chamber of the said Lady in her manor of Colam, Middx., he saw and heard her, lying on her death bed, and being of good and perfect mind, declare that

---

* The writer is supposed by the editor of the Lett. de Louis XII. to be Jacques Annoque, imperial solicitor in the court of Rome.

1514.

she willed all her part of the manor of Long Compton, Warw., should remain to Sir Wm. Compton and his heirs ; present, Thos. Stanley, Jane Stanley, and other servants of the said Lady. If he had known that the said Lady would have died so soon, or that any matter would arise contrary to her said will, he would have caused it to be written.

Thos. Stanley of Colham, Middx., of the age of 48 years, says that about harvest time, between Midsummer and Michaelmas last, being at Colam in the bed chamber of Dame Jane Lady Straunge in her manor of Colham, he heard Master Conyngesby, one of the King's justices, take a "knowledge" of the said lady, whereby she willed as above : also that many times before the said Lady was sick, and especially about 9 or 10 days before her decease, which took place about 14 March last ; present, Dr. Cutteler, this deponent, Rob. Cons, Sir Peter Griffith, clk., Jane Stanley, Agnes Stanley, and others.

Westm., 15 July.

Pat. 6 Hen. VIII. p. 2, m. 17.

15 July. S. B.	**5256.**	For EDWARD ELTON alias BAKER, late of Ledbury, Heref., alias of Hynxsey Hall in the University of Oxford, scholar, alias clerk.

Pardon. *Del.* Westm., 15 July 6 Hen. VIII.

Pat. 6 Hen. VIII. p. 2, m. 7.

15 July. S. B.	**5257.**	For THOMAS NEVILE.

Annuity of 100*l.*, during good behaviour, for his good counsel about the King's person. *Del.* Otford, 15 July 6 Hen. VIII.

Pat. 6 Hen. VIII. p. 2, m. 7.

16 July. Harl. 3,462. f. 147. B. M.	**5258.**	HENRY VIII. to the MARQUIS OF MANTUA.

Understands from his servant Thomas Cene his noble reception by the Marquis, the indulgence granted him of selecting what horses he liked. On his refusal the Marquis had chosen four of the very best, and sent them to the King by his messenger, John Rattus. Thanks him for his generous present. Eltham, 16 July 1514.

Lat. copy, in an Italian hand, pp. 2.

17 July. Vitell. B. xviii. 90. B. M.	**5259.**	SIR ROBERT WINGFIELD to HENRY VIII.

Wrote last on the . . . . from Judenbourg, in Styremark; has been in continual journeying. No news worth writing since the 19th of last month. Arrived here last night. The day before [departed] from hence the Cardinal Gource, the Bous . . . . . . the Pope's ambassador, and the ambassadors of Arragon and Hungary, to Gem[und . . . . .]a mile hence, to the Emperor. As far as [Wingfield knew], such charge as the Emperor gave to the said Cardinal on the 10th May "had not been exp[ressed] by writing or by mouth till their meeting;" it is not known of what [import]ance the same may be ; it is conjectured "that the Venetians offer to abide . . . . to what end the said offer shall come is hard . . . . it is hard to imagine how the foresaid ca . . . . . ambassadors of the Pope and Arragon . . . . ail which, as it is thought be now with . . . . There are many

1514.

ambassadors here; one from the King . . . ., and one from the Great Duke of Russia, and an embassade [from] the Great Master of Prussia." The said ambassadors of . . . oll and Russia are well accompanied and well appointed, and have brought presents of hawks and sables for the Emperor. The ambassador of Poole has journeyed (he says) 3,000 English miles to meet the Emperor, and the ambassador of Russia much further. Besides these ambassadors, "here is of other, of cardinals, dukes, and cities, more than 100 horses."—Wingfield laments that amongst so great a congregation he is so poorly provided;—not only has he no money, but by continual journeys his horses are destroyed, and his "array" and that of his servants wasted; — has been obliged to leave some of his servants behind, dangerously ill. Begs Henry to send him relief, or else he shall be ruined, and unable to serve his Majesty as he would wish to do. Welce in Lonttotrencee, the . . . July 1514.

Hol., pp. 3, mutilated.
Addressed : The King's grace.

---

20 July.　　**5260.**　　For ALICE MANNE of Ryngesell, Suff., spinster.
S. B.　　　　　　　　Pardon. *Del.* Otford, 20 July 6 Hen. VIII.
　　　　　　　　　　Pat. 6 *Hen.VIII. p.* 2, *m.* 7.

---

20 July.　　**5261.**　　For FRANCIS DE BARDI, merchant of Florence.
S. B.　　　　　　　　Licence to retain in his hands for five years the customs on all goods exported and imported by him to the amount of 1,000 marks. *Del.* Westm., 20 July 6 Hen. VIII.
　　　　　　　　　　Fr. 6 *Hen.VIII. p.* 2, *m.* 7.

---

21 July.　　**5262.**　　LEO X. to HENRY VIII.
R. O.　　　　　　　　In consequence of the observation of Easter falling at the wrong time, from the errors of the calendar, had consulted the most skilful theologians and astronomers of the time, who all agreed in its inaccuracy, and that the moon was five days old, when it was reckoned the 1st by the Church. Considering the impropriety that any such error should be tolerated when the Lateran Council is now sitting, and so give cause of ridicule to Jews and heretics, had written to learned men for their opinion. On referring it to the Synod, many difficulties had appeared in adjusting the question. Begs the King, therefore, to send to the Lateran Council the best theologian and astronomer in his realm, to assist in providing a due remedy, or write that they should, that their opinions may be laid before the 10th session to be held on the 1st December. Rome, 21 July 1514.
　　　　　　　　　　Lat., p. 1. *Addressed.*

---

21 July.　　**5263.**　　SIR RICH. WINGFIELD and SPINELLY to HEN. VIII.
Galba B. iii. 210.　　Wrote last on the 15th. Have not since heard from the King.
B. M.　　　　　　　It is generally reported that the King has agreed with the French, who will return into Italy. The Archduchess expects to know the King's determination on the coming home of the Emperor's ambassadors ; she desires that Henry will provide Dissilstyne with a new pension, the former one being annulled by the dismissal of the horsemen. He is very necessary in the Prince's council, where he was placed by Henry. Though it was done for their own surety,

1514.

they are too poor to give him any pension. A prothonotary, son of the Lord de Porthocarriero, is come out of Spain, with other gentlemen, offering to serve the Prince at their own cost without leave of the King of Arragon. Brussells, 21 July 1514. *Signed.*

P. 1, mutilated. Add.

22 July. **5264.** For SIR WILLIAM HYLTON.
S. B.   Wardship of Elizabeth, daughter and heir of John Clarevaux. *Del.* Otford, 22 July 6 Hen. VIII.
Pat. 6 Hen. VIII. p. 2, m. 7.

22 July. **5265.** To the ABP. OF CANTERBURY, Chancellor.
S. B.   Protection for Sir Henrý Marny, knight of the Body, retained in the King's service beyond sea. Eltham, 21 July 6 Hen. VIII. *Del. . . . . .,* 22 July.

23 July. **5266.** KNIGHT to WOLSEY.
Vesp. F. 1. 54.   Yesterday the Cardinal of Sion received letters from Rome
B. M.   announcing the death of the Abp. of York, and has requested Knight to recommend him to the King for the vacancy. If a benefice is to be given to a foreigner, does not know any one on whom it could be better bestowed. He will gain the Swiss if he gains the Cardinal. Berne, 23 July.
        Hol., p. 1. Addressed: To his singular good lord, Lord Bishop of Lincoln.

23 July. **5267.** PETER MARTYR to LUD. FURTADO.
Epist. 540.   Affairs of Darien, &c. — News has come . from England that the King is angry with Maximilian and Ferdinand, and stigmatizes the delay of the marriage as a repudiation. She is betrothed to Lewis to the dislike of the nobility. Cardinal Strigoniensis is unpopular in Hungary. Valladolid, x. kl. Aug. 1514.

23 July. **5268.** For EDWARD WRIGHT.
S. B.   To be one of the four messengers of the Exchequer, *vice* James Richardson ; with 4¼d. a day. *Del.* Otford, 23 July 6 Hen. VIII. *Pat. 6 Hen. VIII. p. 2, m. 7.*

24 July. **5269.** LEO X. to HENRY VIII.
R. O.   Begs the restoration of a ship of S. Maria, commanded by Johannes de Colarte, laden with alum, which had put into Jalamue (Falmouth), and been detained under pretext of the cargo being intended for France. Rome, 24 July 1514, 2 pont.
        Lat., p. 1. Addressed.

24 July. **5270.** SIR THOS. LOVELL to the BISHOPS OF WINCHESTER and
R. O.   LINCOLN (FOX and WOLSEY).
        Heard, seven or eight days since, that the Duke of Longueville's ransom is coming to Boulogne. Sent a copy of the discharge under the Great Seal, at the wish of the captain of Boulogne, who refuses to send the money without an acquittance under the Duke's

1514.

own hand, or before the Duke be at Calais. The bearer of this budget was pursued at sea, and compelled to return to Calais,—the chasers are French and Scotch vessels. Begs the Deputy may be sent back to Calais. Will leave the ransom with Fowler, and return to England. Calais, 24 July. *Signed.*

Pp. 2. Addressed.

24 July.   **5271.**   TENTS AT CALAIS.
R. O.

"Here ensueth a declaration of Rich. Gybson, yeoman tailor to our sovereign lord the King, for all reparations done upon the King's tents, halls, and pavilions, being at Calais, as in the 6th year of his reign, and for stuff by the said Richard provided and bought, and wages to workmen paid for the said reparations," with a list of the insignia on canvas, wages for the workmen, &c., from Wednesday 21 June to 24 July.

For the White Staff 180 ells of canvas, The Flower de Lyce 24, The White Hart 16, The Harp 20, The Gold Stoke 10, The Castle 16, The Grey Hound new 142, The Feather 18, The Gardenyand 8, The Mone 36, The Mountain 14, The World 34, The Gold Hynd 12, The Braser 30, The Lezard 25, The Sepeter 20, The Spanishe Yeke 40, The Sonne 80, The Two Crowns 40, The Lion 48, The Gold Cross 45, The Flower de Lyce 42, The Kup of Gold 43, The Portcullis 42, The Vyttlers Hale of the King's old store 100, The Wheat Ear, the gunpowder Haie 160, The Yellow Face 20, The Chalice 34, The Red Rose 24, The Rose Red and White 40, The Sheaf of Arrows, the Bowyards hawll 200, The Lebards head 40, The Annew 80, The Red Sword 50, The Inflamed House 52, The Fyche 40, The Hamer 40, The Gawntlet on house new content 160. 578 workmen at 6*d.* a day.

Pp. 40.

24 July.   **5272.**   For RICHARD CORNWAILL, one of the King's spears.
P. S.

To be steward of the lordships of Orleton, Pembryge, Erysland, Maunsell and Nethewoode, Heref., *vice* Sir Richard Dalabere. Eltham, 20 July 6 Hen. VIII. *Del.* Otford, 24 July.

Pat. 6 *Hen. VIII. p.* 2, *m.* 6.

26 July.   **5273.**   For JOHN PETER of Bressa.
S. B.

Licence to retain in his hands, for four years, the customs on goods exported and imported by him to the amount of 1,000 marks. *Del.* Otford, 26 July 6 Hen. VIII.

27 July.   **5274.**   DELIVERY OF RECORDS.
R. O.

Mem. that on 27 July 6 Hen. VIII. the treasurer and chamberlains of the Exchequer delivered to Sir John Cutte certain deeds between Henry VII. and the King and Queen of Arragon.

Also delivered to Sir John a square box, containing certain evidences, as appears by a bill indented, in the same box, between Dr. Yong, Master of the Rolls, and the said Sir John, "containing 18 pieces concerning the matrimony between the Prince of Castell and the Princess; the said indenture bearing date," 14 Oct. 2 Hen. VIII. Signed J. C.—The above returned to the Treasury 12 Oct. 6 Hen. VIII.

ii. Mem. that on 22 Sept. 6 Hen. VIII. "Sir Cutte, under-treasurer of England," received "a box concerning the dower of Queen of

1514.

Scots, with 21 pieces of evidences contained therein." Signed J. C.—
Returned to the Exchequer 20 Nov. 6 Hen. VIII. by the hands of
Th. Barbour alias Asten, servant of the Bp. of Durham.
P. 1.

27 July. **5275.** For the MONASTERY of HAWTEMPRICE, York.
P. S.

Congé d'élire on the death of John Womberslay, late prior.
Eltham, 21 July 6 Hen. VIII. *Del.* Otford, 27 July.

ii. Petition of the convent for the above. The King's grandmother was "late foundryce" of the monastery.
Pat. 6 Hen. VIII. p. 2, m. 7.

28 July. **5276.** THE PETER POMEGRANITE.
R. O.

Inventory of the above ship, being in the Thames, 28 July
6 Hen. VIII.
Pp. 2. Endd.: Per D'd Bonar pursar.

28 July. **5277.** For RANULPH CHALNAR.
S. B.

Wardship of William, son and heir of Nicholas Aiston ; granted
to Robert Moreton by patent 13 Nov. 3 Hen. VIII., and forfeited
by waste. *Del.* Westm., 28 July 6 Hen. VIII.
Pat. 6 Hen. VIII. p. 2, m. 9.

29 July. **5278.** LEWIS XII.
R. O.
Rym. xiii. 405.

Commission to Louis d'Orleans Duke of Longueville, John de Selva
president of Normandy, and Thomas Bohier, to form an alliance
with England. St. Germain-en-Laye, 29 July 1514. *Sealed.*

29 July. **5279.** LEWIS XII.
R. O.
Rym. xiii. 406.

Commission to Louis d'Orleans, John de Selva, and Thomas
Bohier to treat for a marriage between himself and Mary sister of
Henry VIII. St. Germain-en-Laye, 29 July 1514.

29 July. **5280.** LEWIS XII.
R. O.
Rym. xiii. 407.

Commission to L. d'Orleans, John de Selva, and Th. Bohier
to promise in his name payment of 100,000 francs per an. to
Henry VIII., until the sum amounts to a million, in fulfilment of
certain obligations entered into with Henry VII. by Charles VIII.,
in 1492 and 1498, and by Charles Duke of Orleans with Margaret
Duchess of Somerset, 7 March 1444. St. Germain-en-Laye, 29 July
1514.

29 July. **5281.** For ROBERT HOGAN, merchant.
S. B.

Licence to export broad-cloths, wools, tin, lead, &c. *Del.* Otford,
29 July 6 Hen. VIII.
Fr. 6 Hen. VIII. p. 2. m. 7.

30 July. **5282.** PRINCESS MARY.
Rym. xiii. 409.

Public instrument, notifying that on 30th July 1514, in the
royal manor of Wanstead, and in the presence of Thomas Duke of
Norfolk, Charles Duke of Suffolk, Thomas Bp. of Lincoln postulate
of York, Richard Bp. of Winton, Thomas Bp. of Durham, Charles
Earl of Worcester, and Sir Ralph Vernay, the Princess Mary solemnly

3 H

1514.

renounced her compact of marriage with Charles Prince of Spain, and requested the above to intimate the same to the King her brother. Attested by Rob. Toneys and William Edwards, clk. of the diocese of Hereford. Attached is the oath of Lewis XII. to observe the treaty confirmed 23 March last past.

Fr. 6 Hen. VIII. p. 1, m. 12.

July   **5283.**   JUSTICES OF ASSIZE.

Northern Circuit.—Rob. Henrison and Thos. Strey, with Brian Pa[lmes,] and John Erneley. Westm., . . July.
Midland Circuit.—John Jenour and John Latymer, with Humph. Cony[ngesby] and Guy Palmes. Westm., . . July.

Pat. 6 Hen. VIII. p. 1, m. 11d.

5284.   HENRY VIII. to MY LORD [WOLSEY ?].

Calig. D. vi. 119.
B. M.
Rym. xiii. 403.

Has spoken to the Duke [of Orleans], who "was as ill afraid, as ever he was in his life, lest no good effect should come to pass" touching the treaty. The King expressed his willingness to come to terms if reasonable offers be made to him. He stipulated that the amity should be made during their lives and one year after ; which amity once granted, the alliance of marriage will not be refused.

Holograph. Much mutilated.

Calig. E. i. 115.   **5285.**   [———— to ————].

B. M.

" . . . . Monseigneur . . . . Normandie . . . . . . de la part du Roy leur maistre p. . . . . . . faire entendre au Roy dAngleterre : Premierement que ledict Roy leur maistre rem[ercie] ledict Roy dAngleterre tant si affectueusement [et] cordialement quil peult de ce que ayant res[. . . r]eciproquement il desire et veult venir a b[onne] paix, amytie, et aliance avec luy, et pareillem[ent des] bonnes, grandes, et honnestes paroles, quil a po. . . mondit Sieur de Longueville, monstrant par icelles [le] singulier desir et affection audit Roy leur mais[tre], au bien et redre ≈sement de ses affaires, et princ[ipalement] au recouvrement de sa duche de Mylan, et . . . . quil a en Italie, et de luy aider audit recouvrement la paix de . . . traictee, faite et conclute." The King their master also thanks the King of England for consenting to the marriage of his sister. Thinks the alliance of the two Kings will be most profitable to Christendom. Longueville is empowered to conclude it. Trusts it will be a more firm alliance than ever was established. Will give 500,000 crowns, besides the sums mentioned in the treaties of Estaples and London, and also . . . . of the late Mons. d'Orleans, all which will amount to 1,000,000 crowns, [to be discharged at the rate of] 40,000 crowns a-year, the peace to endure for a year after the death of the first deceased of the two Princes. In the event of Louis having a son by Mary, or Henry by Katharine, who is now enceinte, the alliance will be of equal advantage to

*Calig. E. i. 109.

both. As to Tournay, though not a very important matter,* it must be delivered up, [as the French King] has assured the King of England, by letters under his hand and seal . . . . Cannot otherwise get the consent of the Estates to the marriage. . . . . . . Tournay must be placed in such security that on the marriage being accomplished, it shall be given up to the King their master without dissimulation. He is surprised that the King of England should wish to marry her without a dowry, she being his sister, which might turn hereafter to her reproach. The King proposes to comprehend in the alliance Pope Leo X., the Empire, Scotland

1514.

Portugal, Denmark, Navarre, Venice, Gueldres, Mons. de Liege, &c. As to sending ambassadors " en Esc[osse ?]" and " la mainbournye," their master and all his subjects are equally desirous of peace.

Fr., mutilated, pp. 6.

5286. PRINCESS MARY.

R. O.

A minute, in Fox's hand, of an agreement on the part of the King of France to receive jewellery and furniture to the value of 200,000 crowns, as the dowry of the Princess Mary, reserving certain conditions as to their restoration.

Fragment, Lat., p. 1.

5287. ———————— to MADAME SA MAJESTE.

Calig. E. I. 99.
B. M.

The complaint of William Dier . . . . citizen of Ghent, against Lewis Orweel, domestic of the King of England, for plundering certain goods on the coast of Normandy in time of peace, both in the late King's reign and in the present, consigned by him to Adrian Va[n . . . . of] Voosdouc. Has received no benefit from her previous intercession. Begs she will write to the Bp. of Lincoln and the Duke of Suffolk.

Fr., mutilated, pp. 2.

1 Aug.
S. B.

5288. For CUTHBERT TUNSTALL, clk.

Wardship of Marmaduke, son and heir of Brian Tunstall of Thurland, Lanc., who held of the duchy of Lancaster and of the barony of Kendall, Westmor.;—and custody (in reversion) of the lands which Isabel, widow of the said Brian, holds as her dower. *Del.* Westm., 1 Aug. 6 Hen. VIII.

Pat. 6 Hen. VIII. p. 2, m. 7.

2 Aug.
S. B.

5289. For EDWARD DUKE OF BUCKINGHAM.

Licence to found a perpetual college, with dean, subdean, eight secular priests, four clerks and eight choristers, in honor of St. Mary, at Thornebury, Glouc., to pray for the King, the Queen, and the Duke and Alianor his wife ; with mortmain licence to endow the same to the value of 300l. *Del.* Westm., 2 Aug. 6 Hen. VIII.

1 Aug.
Galba, B. III.165.
B. M.

5290. SPINELLY to [HENRY VIII.]

Wrote . . . of the last month. Letters have come from the Emperor, from Leoons, four days journey from Inspruck—containing many excuses for not keeping his promise with the King ; and if he had had the 30,000 crowns of gold, all the affairs would have gone another way ;—that the marriage of the Prince of Castile and the Princess should be solemnized at Antwerp ;—that he has not yet ratified the truce ;—that the Pope is on good terms with him ;—that the German troops have defeated the Venetians at Marrane ;—that the Pope offered to negotiate between them ;— that the Viceroy of Naples does not prosecute the war with vigour ; —that the King of Arragon is to have the governance of all the Emperor's places there. The Arragonese ambassador endeavours to have the Spaniards expelled from this Court, fearing they should persuade the Prince to go into Spain sooner than he should.— He has asked that Donna Kateryna de Castra, who lately came out of England, may be retained for the service of the Princess. Brussells, 1 Aug. 1514. *Signed.*

Pp. 2, mutilated.

3 H 2

1514.

2 Aug.   **5291.**   GAOL DELIVERY.

Northampton. — Commission to Thos. Pen, mayor, Sir Wm. Compton, Wm. Gascoigne, John Saxby and John Parvyn. Westm., 2 Aug.

Pat. 6 Hen. VIII. p. 2, m. 6d.

2 Aug.   **5292.**   SIR RICHARD WINGFIELD and THOMAS SPINELLY to
Galba, B. III. 211.   HENRY VIII.

B. M.   Wrote last on the . . . of this month. Have had none from the King, " but only a letter [directed to my] Lady Archduchess with other to the Lords . . . . Dissilstein, Ligny and Zevemberghe, which were se[nt by] your master of the posts." Yesterday went to my Lady's mess, and delivered the [King's] letters. Having read them, she, with a glad countenance, said she found that the King continued in his favorable disposition towards the Prince of Castile. Their conference was interrupted by Chievres, Sainctpy, and their accomplices, who feared the writers were fishing for news. Have since understood they were satisfied with the King's letters. My Lady has spoken to them in favor of the patron of the carack. Subjects of these countries are daily taken prisoners by the French and Scotch, and no redress can be obtained. This morning the Captain Simon Frauu[cis . . . was] with them, and said he and Jenyn le Cousturi[er] had offered their services to the Lieutenant of Tournay. Brussels, 2 August 1514. *Signed.*

Pp. 2, mutilated. Add. and endd. at f. 146 b.

2 Aug.   **5293.**   For EDWARD DUKE OF BUCKINGHAM.
S. B.   Mortmain licence to alienate to the Abbot of St. Mary's, Tewkesbury, possessions to the value of 60*l.* *Del.* Westm., 2 Aug. 6 Hen. VIII.

2 Aug.   **5294.**   For THOMAS DUKE OF NORFOLK, Treasurer and Mar-
S. B.   shal of England, THOMAS BISHOP OF LINCOLN, Postu-
                   late of York, and RICHARD BISHOP OF WINCHESTER, Keeper of the Privy Seal.

Commission to treat for peace with Lewis XII., and for renewal of the treaties of Estaples and London. Westm., 2 August 6 Hen. VIII.

R. T. 137.   2. Letters patent of the above.
R. O.

S. B.   3. For the same to contract a marriage between Princess Mary and Lewis XII. Same date.

3 Aug.   **5295.**   TOURNAY.
R. O.   Receipt by Sir Rob. Dymmok, treasurer, for 20,000*l.*, of which 48,000 cr. at 4*s.* 2*d.* each, are for the pay of the garrison. 3 Aug. 6 Hen. VIII. *Signed.*

3 Aug.   **5296.**   For ELIZABETH LYSLE alias LYELE, the Queen's
P. S.   gentlewoman.

Grant at the Queen's request, of a field called North-burghilles, late in the tenure of John Byrde; half a bondage and lands late in the tenure of William Meese; a bondage and lands late in the tenure of Richard Skelton; lands late in

1514.

the tenure of John Graunte ; 34 acres of land and meadow late in the tenure of Richard Mason ; 19 acres of meadow in Langmede ; a field called Crakeholm, late in the tenure of John Tyght ; and half a bondage, late in tenure of Stephen Gylmyn. The premises form a parcel of the manor of Maxhey, Northt., and were granted to Thomas Fouler and Edith his wife, now deceased, during the life of the said Edith, by charter of John Bishop of Rochester, Hugh Bishop of· Exeter, Sir William Knyvet, Sir David Philips, Henry Hornby, clk., Humphrey Conyngesby, serjeant-at-law, Robert Barnard, clk., Hugh Assheton, clk., John Saint John, Gabriel Silvester, clk., John Footehede, clk., Robert Brudenell, serjeant-at-law, James Whitstones, clk., and William Bedell, who were enfeoffed by the King's grandmother, Margaret late Countess of Richmond. Eltham, 4 July 6 Hen. VIII. *Del.* Westm., 3 Aug.

4 Aug.
R. O. ?

5297. ANTONIO ABBOT OF ST. BERTIN'S to WOLSEY.

Is glad to hear of his good health as of a valued friend. Wishes to know the certainty of the flying reports about the peace, and of the archdeaconry which the King has promised him frequently in consideration of his sufferings in the late war. That promise had been confirmed to the writer by Sir Edw. Ghilleford. Will be glad to know if any change is contemplated. Ex Popringis, 4 Aug. *Signed.*
Lat., p. 1.

4 Aug.
S. B.

5298. To RICHARD BP. OF WINCHESTER, THOMAS BP. OF LINCOLN, and JOHN HERON, treasurer of the Chamber.

Commission to obtain payment of all obligations, recognizances and debts due to the King. *Del.* Westm., 4 Aug. 6 Hen. VIII.
Pat. 6 *Hen.VIII. p.* 2, *m.* 7*d.*

4 Aug.
R. O.

5299. SIR RICH. WINGFIELD and SIR THO. SPINELLY to HENRY VIII.

Wrote last yesterday. Enclose two letters received last night from Sir Rob. Wingfield, ambassador in Germany. Will send information when they know what news has been received by the Archduchess. Brussels, 4 Aug. 1514. *Signed.*
P. 1. *Addressed.*

5 Aug.
S. B.
Rym. xiii. 412.

5300. For THOMAS [WOLSEY] BP. OF LINCOLN, ELECT OF YORK.

To have the custody of the Archbishopric of York, and the temporalities of the see, from the death of Christopher late Archbishop, until restitution be made. *Del.* Westm., 5 Aug. 6 Hen. VIII.
Pat. 6 *Hen.VIII. p.* 2, *m.* 25.

5 Aug.
R. O.

5301. LEO X. to HENRY VIII.

Credence in behalf of Will. Burbank, secretary and executor of Chr. [Bainbridge] Cardinal St. Praxedis, deceased. Rome, 5 Aug. 1514, 2 pont.
Lat., p. 1. *Addressed.*

5 Aug.
Vitel. C. xi. f. 168.
B. M.

5302. LOUIS XII. to WOLSEY.

Has frequently heard from the Duke of Longueville and the General of Normandy the good services rendered by Wolsey in

1514.

furthering the amity of the two kingdoms.   Has entire confidence
in him. St. Germain-en-Laye, 5 Aug. *Signed.*
Fr.   P. 1.   Add. : Mons. de Lincone.

5 Aug. **5303.**   For PETER COLLETT, native of Normandy.
P. S.   Licence to hold the rectory of Ovyngden, Sussex. Wanstead,
31 July 6 Hen. VIII. *Del.* Westm., 5 Aug.

6 Aug. **5304.**   SIR ROBERT WINGFIELD to HENRY VIII.
R. O.   Wrote last on the 30th July from this town, stating that the Emperor would speak with him within two or three days ; which he had
not done, waiting for news from Brabant, as Wingfield wrote from
Gratz, 31 May. On 2 Aug. Cardinal Gurce left for Augsburg,
intending to return to. Insbrook to meet the Emperor, thence to
Verona, there to remain as governor and lieutenant to the Emperor
in Italy.   Had little communication with him, suspecting him.
The Emperor expects to hear of the taking of Cremona, and other
wild rumors. Gemund, 6 Aug. 1514.
Hol., p. 1. Addressed.

7 Aug. **5305.**   FRANCE.
R. O.   Treaty of peace and friendship` between France and England
Rym. XIII. 413.   and their confederates on both sides. Signed by the French
commissioners, Loys D'Orleans, John de Selva, Thomas Bohier.
London, 7 Aug. 1514.
Fr. 6 Hen. VIII. p. 1, m. 11 to 13.

Calig. D. VL. 120.   2. Confirmation of the above by Henry VIII. London,—Aug.
B. M.   1514.
Modern copy.

R. O.   3. Draft of the treaty, corrected by Fox and Wolsey.
Harl. 3,463, f. 28. 4. Heads of the above.
B. M.   *Contemporaneous copy, in an Italian hand.*

7 Aug. **5306.**   LEWIS XII.
R. O.   Engagement of L. d'Orleans, John de Selva, and T. Bohier, on
Rym. XIII. 428.   part of Lewis XII., to pay one million of gold crowns to Henry
VIII. ; the first instalment of 50,000 francs to commence 1 Nov.
London, 7 Aug. 1514. *Signed.*

R. O.   2. Draft of the above.
Calig. D. VI. 128.   3. Another draft of the same.
B. M.

7 Aug. **5307.**   LEWIS XII.
R. O.   Treaty of marriage between Lewis XII. and the Princess Mary.
Rym. XIII. 423.   Signed by Loys d'Orleans, John de Selva, Thomas Bohier. London,
7 Aug. 1514.

R. O.   2. Modern copy.

7 Aug. **5308.**   HEIRS of WALTER ESTCOURTE.
S. B.   Livery of lands to John Pynkernell and Joan his wife, daughter
and heir of Walter Estcourte ; to John Denys and Agnes his
wife, another daughter and heir; and to John Everard and William
Pynkernell, kinsmen and heirs of the said Walter,—Everard being

1514.

son and heir of Margaret, third daughter, and Pynkernell being brother of John, son and heir of Elizabeth, fourth daughter. *Del.* Westm., 7 Aug. 6 Hen. VIII.
Pat. 6 Hen. VIII. p. 2, m. 8.

7 Aug.
S. B.

5309. For DAVID AP HOWELL, of Westminster.

Pardon for felony, of which he was convicted, temp. Hen. VII., before Nicholas Trigge, alderman of Stamford, William Ratclyff, Thomas Philip and Geoffrey Hampton, justices of the peace, and Robert Bawdes, lawyer. He had been committed to the custody of William late Bishop of Lincoln, and remains in that of Thomas, present Bishop. *Del.* Westm., 7 Aug. 6 Hen. VIII.
Pat. 6 Hen. VIII. p. 2, m. 7.

7 Aug.
P. S.

5310. For EDWARD LYTTELTON and EDMUND ACTON.

Wardship of John, son and heir of Sir William Lyttelton, with the possessions in Worc., Staff. and Salop, which belonged to Dame Mary Lytelton, deceased, as her jointure, and are of the yearly value of *50l.* Eltham, 3 July 6 Hen. VIII. *Del.* Westm., 7 Aug.
Pat. 6 Hen. VIII. p. 2, m. 8.

8 Aug.
R. O.
Rym. XIII. 431.

5311. LEWIS XII.

Commission to L. Duke d'Orleans to be his proxy for marriage with Princess Mary. St. Germain-en-Laye, 8 Aug. 1514.

8 Aug.
S. B.

5312. For WILLIAM CRANE.

Licence to export wools, hides, and other merchandize not belonging to the staple of Calais. *Del.* Westm., 8 Aug. 6 Hen. VIII.
Fr. 6 Hen. VIII. p. 2, m. 8.

8 Aug.

5313. For WM. HUNNYNG, serjeant purveyor of the Household.

Commission to provide oxen, sheep, calves, cod fish, salmon, and other provisions for the Household. Westm., 8 Aug.
Pat. 6 Hen. VIII. p. 2, m. 8d.

8 Aug.
P. S.

5314. For JOHN TRENDE, alias TRYNDE, merchant tailor of London.

Protection ; going in the retinue of Sir Richard Wyngefeld, Deputy of Calais. Eltham, 19 July 6 Hen. VIII. *Del.* Westm., 8 Aug. 6 Hen. VIII.
Fr. 6 Hen. VIII. p. 2, m. 9.

10 Aug.
S. B.

5315. ENGLAND AND FRANCE.

Proclamation of a treaty of peace by way of marriage between Henry VIII. and Lewis of France, with free intercourse between the two countries ; to begin 7th August. *Del.* Otford, 10 Aug. 6 Hen. VIII.

2. Writ to the mayor of Calais for the same.
Pat. 6 Hen. VIII. p. 2, m. 7d.

Lansd. 818, f. 95.
B. M.

"The publication of the peace between King Henry VIII. and King Lewis of France the XII."

"Idem proclaimed the 5th of April between Henry VIII. and Francis of France."
Copy.

1514.

11 Aug. **5316.** ORDNANCE.

R. O.

"Expences of Sir Henry Wyat, Sir And. Wyndsore, Sir Tho. Wyndham, Geo. Dalyson and Tho. Tamworth, commissioners appointed by the King to view all such tackle, apparel, ordinance, artillery, and habiliments for war, as remained in the King's great ships lying at Erith, Woolwich, and other places in the Thames from Wednesday 26 July Hen. VIII. to 11 Aug. following.

11 Aug. **5317.** NAVY.

R. O.

"A brief abstract and calendar concerning the viewing of the King's ships taken by Sir Henry Wyat, Sir Andrew Windsor and others ;" sc., 1, at Erith, *The Henry Grace de Dieu, The Trinity Sovereign, The Gabriel Royal, The Catherine Forteleza, The Catherine Galy and The Rose Galy, The Storehouse at Erith ;* 2, at Woolwich, *The Great Barbara, The Great Nicholas, The John Baptist ;* 3, at the Blackwall, *The Mary Rose, The Peter Pome Granade, The Great Elizabeth ;* 4, at Deptford, *The Crist of Greenwich.* Indentures are made with John Hopton, John Millet, and Thomas Elderton, for tackle, artillery, etc.

Paper roll.

12 Aug. **5318.** HENRY VIII. to LEO X.

Add. MS.15,387.
f. 25.
B. M.

Requesting him to make the Bishop of Lincoln (Wolsey) a cardinal, with all the honors held by the late Cardinal of York. His merits are such that the King esteems him above his dearest friends, and can do nothing of the least importance without him. Greenwich, 12 Aug. 1514.

Lat. Copy, pp. 5.

12 Aug. **5319.** HENRY VIII. to LEO X.

Harl. 3462,
f. 142. b.
B. M.
Fabron,
Vit. Leon. X.
Not. 38.

After many discussions between his Council and the French ambassadors, they have arranged a peace, including the Holy See and Bologna by name, the Emperor and the Prince of Castile, allowing them three months to join. Has used his efforts to have the Duke of Milan included, but could not prevail. Of the King of Arragon nothing has been said by either party, as he likes to look after his own interests without interference. The Scots are included by France on certain conditions, which Henry thinks they will not observe. The peace is to be confirmed under ecclesiastical penalties. The Pope will learn more from the Bp. of Worcester The Princess Mary is to be given in marriage to France. She had been betrothed at thirteen years of age to the Prince of Castile, then nine years old, on the stipulation that when he was fourteen he should send his proxies to England, and solemnly espouse her *per verba de præsenti.* His governors neglected it, and last year when the King was at Lisle (*Insulæ Oppieses*), [and again] on the 15th May last he impressed this matter frequently on their attention without effect. Taking the advice of his Council, his sister solemnly annulled the engagement, and was betrothed to the King of France. Thinks their alliance will be of great importance to the weal of Christendom. and they can now turn their arms against its common enemies. Greenwich, 12 Aug. 1514.

Lat., pp. 3.   Contemporary copy, in an Italian hand.

12 Aug. **5320.** WOLSEY and FOX to GERARD DE PLEINE.

Galba, B. III. 146.
B. M.

Are surprised that the letters to the Emperor, which De Planis and John Cola read, have not yet reached the Emperor's hands as they supposed. Have accordingly asked the chief Secre-

1514.

tary whether the said letters had been sent to the Emperor, as resolved ; and have found by some carelessness they are still in the Secretary's hands. They will immediately have them sent off to the Lady of Savoy with other letters to the Emperor. Thank him for the services he has rendered them with the said Lady, and hope that the friendship between their master and those Princes will be permanent. Will take care that Andreas de Costa has justice in the matter of the alum. London, 12 August 1514.

Signed : T. Lincoln. post. Ebor.—Ri. Wynton.

Add. : Præstantissimo Gerardo de Pleine Consilii D. Principis Castellæ Pres. &c.

Lat., p. 1, *mutilated.*

12 Aug. **5321.** LEWIS XII.

R. T. 137.
R. O.

Notarial copy of the engagement of Lewis XII.'s ambassadors for the payment of the 1,000,000 g. cr. London, 12 Aug. 1514.

Collated with the original at Paris, 22 Feb. 1524.

13 Aug. **5322.** MARRIAGE OF PRINCESS MARY.

R. O.
Rym. XIII. 432.

Notarial instrument stating that 13 Aug. 1514, at the royal manor of Greenwich, present Henry VIII., Queen Katharine, the Abp. of Canterbury, Thomas Postulate of York, the Dukes of Buckingham, Norfolk and Suffolk, the Bishops of Winchester and Durham, the Marquis of Dorset, the Earls of Shrewsbury, Surrey, Essex and Worcester, John de Selva and Thomas Bohier, appeared the Princess Mary and the Duke of Orleans, and after a Latin speech by the Archbishop and John de Selva, and the reading of the French King's letters patent by the Bp. of Durham, the Duke of Longueville taking with his right the right hand of the Princess Mary, read the marriage contract in French. Then the Princess taking the right hand of the Duke of Longueville, read her part of the contract in the same tongue. Then the Duke of Orleans signed the schedule, and delivered it for signature to the Princess Mary, who signed *Marye ;* after which the Duke delivered the Princess a gold ring, which the Princess placed on the fourth finger of her right hand. Attested by Robert Toneys and William Edwardes.

R. O.
Rym. XIII. 428.

2. Verba sponsalia of Loys d'Orleans Duke de Longueville as proxy for Lewis XII. in his marriage with the Princess Mary.

Vitell. C. XI. 167.
B. M.
Rym. XIII 433.

3. The marriage contract of the Princess Mary with Loys Duke of Longueville as proxy of Lewis XII.

Fr. copy.

ii. On the reverse :—The contract of Loys Duke of Longueville in behalf of Lewis XII.

Fr. P. 1. *Signed.*

13 Aug. **5323.** SIR ROBERT WINGFIELD to [HENRY VIII.]

Vitell. B. XVIII. 92.
B. M.

Wrote last on the . . . of the present month from this town. Yesterday evening was sent for to the Court ; and in a chamber there, by the Emperor's command, who was laid up with a bad leg, were Ribawpiere the hoffmaster, Serenteyner, ch[ief] treasurer, and Hans Reynner, principal secre[tary]. Reynner, after they were all seated, rehearsed the Emperor's intentions to Wingfield for Henry's information, which he sends word for word, as near as his wit can express it in English ; sc., that as England will not accept the [truce] made by Arragon with Fr[ance], he hath given

1514.

licence to his m[en of] arms. . . . . . It is presumed he will not
commune [with the] said King of France, and that the [Empe]eur
and [the Prince]be left alone and in great peril." He has therefore
consulted his Council what is best to be done for himself, his children,
and for all Christendom.   "And first the Emperor . . . .
ratification should be delivered . . . . expressly defended
to the said Bontemps . . . . ratification out of his hands with
[consent] of his Majesty, and that by letters of his own hand, [as]
appeareth by the letters responsives of the said Bontemps [which]
be here present ; and his Majesty desireth that ye shall not [only]
read the same, but also that ye send the said letters to the [King]
your master."—The Emperor expected that England at his request
would have sent ambassadors to the King of Arragon, and accepted
the truce conjointly ; but as he refuses it, the Emperor will do the
same. "Also whe[reas] for lack that the Emperor hath not accepted
the said truce [in the w]hich was comprised the duchy and Duke
of Milan, there f . . . with that the King of France is determined to
win the said [du]chie by force, and bring it under his obeisance ;
and the Swissers, understanding the said enterprise of the said King
of France, be determined to take the said duchy into [their own]e
hands, and empesche the said King of his enterprise ; and to do the
same more assuredly they intend to join with the [Pope] to expel
the Spaniards out of the Italies . . . . that the King of
France doth make the . . . . . . and consent of the said " * * *
    The Emperor has been advertised, both by his resident with the
Swiss and others, that the King [my] master " hath had his ambassadors with the [Swiss], which have purposed unto them that the
K[ing of France] and King of Arragon hath made an alliance [and]
confederation together against the Pope and Ita[lians, and] they have
desired that with all their puissance they may break the said alliance,
and that in so doing your master offereth to make them all assistance;
and that also upon his side he shall so press [the King] of France
that the said alliance shall be bie . . . the which offer hath given
great courage to the Swiss to pursue their said enterprise."—Here
follows a passage, unintelligible, but apparently to the effect that if
the Venetians were assisted by the Swiss the Emperor would lose all
his conquests in Italy.—" . . . . . imperial Majesty shall never may
have . . . . He with the said Swissers and Venetians . . . . . of
Ostyke, because they be ancient and immortal [enemies] to the said
House, and have ever searched the ruin [and] destruction of the
same, as hath appeared ever sith the beginning of the said Swissers
and Venetians ; and principally the Swissers which doth occupy the
revenue of the said House contrary to God, reason and good equity."
    The Emperor has consequently determined to raise an army, and
pass into High Almaygne, and resist his enemies in the said enterprise ; and as he and the King of Arragon would not be able to make
head against the combined powers of the Swiss, Venetians, and the
whole of Italy, he has consented by advice of his Council that the
King of Arragon shall treat for a peace between the Emperor and
France, and obtain aid against the said league. But in taking this
course the Emperor intends to adhere strictly to his amity with
England.
    Wingfield, on hearing this, took down in writing all points in
which he had a difficulty. He then left nothing unspoken for the
King's cause ; and after much discussion left, "without [coming
to any understanding] with the Emperor ; for surely he hath [the
same] disease that he had this time 12 month, [or] it se[meth it]
is more painful, or else the great business h[e had] caused him to
forget the pain." Hopes better fruit may come of this stock than

1514.

its leaves promise. As he was the special instrument, when he arrived in that court, of conveying the Emperor from France to England, hopes it will not be attributed to any fault of his if the Emperor "thus return to France again." Gemund, 13 Aug. 1514.

Encloses the letters of John Bontemps to the Emperor. The M[arquis] Casymyrus of Brandenburg desires his respects to the King, and though abiding out of England hopes to see him. He sends the King a sword and dagger.

Hol., burnt and mutilated, pp. 6.

14 Aug.
S. B.

5324. For BARTH. SALVIATI, merchant of Florence.

Licence to retain in his hands the customs on goods exported and imported by him, to the amount of 1,000*l.*, from 15 July 6 Hen. VIII., for four years. *Del.* Westm., 14 Aug. 6 Hen. VIII.

Fr. 6 Hen. VIII. p. 2, m. 8.

14 Aug.
S. B.

5325. For WILLIAM HORSLEY, yeoman of the Guard.

To be bailiff of the lordships of Cropton, with appurtenances in Pikering Lyth, and of Skirtenbek, with appurtenances, York ; with fees of 30*s.* 4*d.* a year for Cropton, and 33*s.* 4*d.* a year for Skirtenbek. *Del.* Otford, 14 Aug. 6 Hen. VIII.

Pat. 6 Hen. VIII. p. 2, m. 7.

15 Aug.
Harl. 3,462, f.141b.
B. M.

5326. ENGLAND AND FRANCE.

Publication of the peace between France and England. St. Germain-en-Laye, 15 Aug. 1514.

Italian, pp. 2.

15 Aug.
Galba, B.III.199.
B. M.

5327. SIR RICH. WYNGFIELD and SPINELLY to HENRY VIII.

Wrote last on the 11th . . . . Received yesterday by post from the Emperor a letter from Sir Robt. Wingfield to the King, which they [transmit]. The Archduchess sent them two copies of letters to the effect contained in a memorial enclosed, as nearly as they can remember, not being permitted to send them to England. It is openly reported, with great dissatisfaction in all the Prince's countries, that a marriage is to be concluded between the Lady Mary and the French King ;—even Chievres pretends to be displeased, and sneers at the fidelity of England. The Archduchess alone will not believe it, but "taketh great thought and displeasure therewith, insomuch that some fear she shall take hurt thereby."— She is going to send to England the Esquire Bonnett, with whom she is advised to join the Provost of Cassell, to remonstrate. If the report prove true, think "they shall send incontinently into France to desire the alliance of the second daughter of the French* King," and put themselves entirely into his [hands]. Were informed yesternight, by Armystoft and the steward of the Duke of Saxony, that the said Duke had taken a town from the Count, his rebel, and slain 900 men of war, by which he hopes to bring his enterprise soon to an end. The Duke desires Henry will prevent the French King from sending assistance to the Count by sea, as he is pressed to do by Gueldres. Brussels, 15 Aug. 1514.

Signed.

Pp. 3, mutilated. The two leaves apart. Add. and endd.

*f. 212.

15 Aug.
S. B.

5328. For GILES DU WES, alien.

Licence to retain in his hands the customs on goods imported and exported by him, for five years, to the amount of 1,000*l. Del.* Otford, 15 Aug. 6 Hen. VIII.

Fr. 6 Hen. VIII. p. 2, m. 8.

1514.

16 Aug. 5329.

Calig. D. vi. 137.
B. M.
Rym. xiii. 435.

[LEWIS DUKE OF ORLEANS] to the QUEEN [PRINCESS MARY].

This day the general and he had letters from the King, who was anxious to hear from her, and thought Abbeville an excellent place for their meeting. The King was determined to receive her well. Offers his services to carry news between them, and asks the Queen's mediation in favor of a merchant named John Cavalcanti, dwelling at London, who had done the writer some service in a matter of business with the King her brother. Canterbury, 16 Aug.

Hol. Signature burnt off.
Addressed : A la Royne ma Souveraine Dame.

16 Aug. 5330.

R. O.

THOMAS BOHIER to [MARY] QUEEN [OF FRANCE].

Monsr. de Longueville and he had received at Canterbury the letters of the King, who desires to see her, and will be at Abbeville to receive her. They will shortly be with the said King. Canterbury, 16 Aug.

Fr., p. 1. *Addressed.*

16 Aug. 5331.

Vitell. B. ii. 83.
B. M.

LEO X. to HENRY VIII.

Permitting him to accept the contributions of the clergy, granted him for the support of his wars, all decrees of the Lateran or any other council notwithstanding. Rome, 16 Aug. 1514, pont. 2.

Copy in the hand of Taylor's clerk, pp. 2.

16 Aug. 5332.

R. O.

LEO X. to HENRY VIII.

Begs a delay of a few days before confirming the King's nomination of a collector for England. Julius II. had promised the King his assent, provided he would nominate an Italian. Is satisfied with the King's selection. Rome, 16 Aug. 1514, pont. 2.

Lat., p. 1.

17 Aug. 5333.

Vitell. B. ii. 89.
B. M.

LEO X. to HENRY VIII.

Notifying the death of Cardinal Bainbridge. Ric. Pace and Will. Burbank are appointed executors. Recommends them, especially the former. Rome, 17 Aug. 1514.

Lat., mutilated.

18 Aug. 5334.

R. O.

THOMAS [WOLSEY] BP. OF LINCOLN, Postulate of York.

Indenture by which Anthony de Vivaldis of Genoa, Will. Botry mercer, and Tho. Raymond, grocer, of London, engage to pay for Wolsey's pallium, and the expences of his promotion in the court of Rome, 2,000*l.* to be repaid by John Withers, clk., and 5,704 ducats by Ric. Pace and Will. Burbank, resident at Rome, to Lazarus de Grymaldis and Andrea Gentili, Genoese merchants. 18 Aug. 6 Hen. VIII.

Signed by Wolsey and Withers. Seal attached. Lat.

R. O.

2. Bond of 1,300*l.* given by Wolsey to Antonio de Vivaldis, merchant of Genoa, Will. Botry, mercer, and Thos. Raymond, grocer, of London, for the fulfilment of the above indenture. 18 Aug. 1514, 6 Hen. VIII.

Signed : T. Lincoln. post. Ebor.

18 Aug. 5335.

S. B.
Rym. xiii. 436.

ENGLAND AND FRANCE.

Appointment of Charles Earl of Worcester, chamberlain, Thomas Dokwra, prior of St. John's, and Nicholas West, L.L.D., dean of

1514.

Wyndesor, as commissioners to take the oath of Lewis King of France, for observing the treaty of peace concluded between England and France, 7 August last, in which treaty the King of France agrees to marry Princess Mary. Westm., 18 Aug. 6 Hen. VIII.

Fr. 6 Hen. VIII. p. 2, m. 16.

S. B.
Rym. xiii. 436.

ii. Appointment of the same to receive the obligation of Lewis XII. for payment of 1,000,000 cr. of gold, according to the treaty of 7 August last, and to deliver obligations made by Charles Duke of Orleans, father of Lewis XII., and other French nobles. Westm., 18 Aug. 6 Hen. VIII.*

Fr. 6 Hen. VIII. p. 2, m. 16.

18 Aug.
S. B.

5336. For RICHARD BIGGE, yeoman horseman of the King's harriers.

To be bailiff of the lordship of Patengeham, Staff., as held by Thomas Wobaston, deceased. *Del.* Otford, 18 Aug. 6 Hen. VIII.*

Endorsed : At Wanstede the 3rd day of August, anno r. R. H. VIII^{vi} 6to.—Per Millet.

Pat. 6 Hen. VIII. p. 2, m. 9.

18 Aug.
Harl. 3,462, f. 142.
B. M.

5337. The PRINCESS MARY.

Consummation of the marriage by proxy between the Princess Mary and Lewis XII.

Last Sunday the marriage was concluded *per verba de præsenti.* The bride undressed and went to bed in the presence of many witnesses. The Marquis of Rothelin, in his doublet, with a pair of red hose, but with one leg naked, went into bed, and touched the Princess with his naked leg. The marriage was then declared consummated. The King of England made great rejoicing, and we at Abbeville did the same. 18 Aug. 1514.

Italian, p. 1. From a letter written to the Bishop of Aste.

18 Aug.
R. O.

5338. SIR ROB. WINGFIELD to HENRY VIII.

Wrote last on the 13th from Gemond. Left this day for Insbrook. Thinks the Emperor has detained him in hopes of an answer to matters which he caused Wingfield to write long since. It is 26 days since the ambassadors of the Pope and Arragon were ordered to Innsbrook. His Majesty only stayed in consequence of the disease in his leg. Though rest is more meet for him, he sets out tomorrow in a horse-litter. The captain of the "Crossyd Hungrye " (?) was taken by the army of the King of Hungary. "His company that were taken alive were constrained to slay him, and pluck him in pieces with their teeth ; and after so all to-gnawen and quartered he was sent into four principal places." The new Hungarian ambassador says like disorders have begun in Transylvania, against which the King brings a strong army. Such precautions are necessary because like evils are brewing in Almain. Fykkylbourke in Lontotrence, 18 Aug. 1514.

Hol., pp. 2. Addressed.

18 Aug.
Harl. 3,462. f. 149.
B. M.

5339. HENRY VIII. to the MARQUIS OF MANTUA.

Sends him and his consort, by Griffith Don, the bearer, certain horses with their furniture as a proof of his affection. Greenwich, 18 Aug 1514.

Lat. copy, in an Italian hand, p. 1.

---

* The letters patent of Lewis, for payment of the above, dated St. Germain-en-Laye, 22 Aug. 1514, will be found in R. T. 137, p. 4.

1514.

18 Aug.   **5340.**   For CHRISTOPHER MORES, gunner.
P. S.

To be gunner in the Tower of London, with 12*d.* a day.   Greenwich, 14 Aug. 6 Hen. VIII.   *Del.* Otford, 18 Aug.
Pat. 6 *Hen.VIII. p.* 2, *m.* 9.

19 Aug.   **5341.**   SIR RICH. WINGFIELD and SPINELLY to HENRY VIII.
Galba, B. III. 213.
B. M.

Wrote last on the 15th inst.   Have not since heard from his Highness.   The [rumors] of the French alliance increase, and no one believes the contrary, but the Archduchess.   It is so unpopular here that there is some danger of commotion.   Those who have been accused of making obstacles to the performance of the English treaties have now a good excuse.   Some say the French King is to have Flanders, Holland, and Zealand, and the Prince, Artois,[Brabant, Hainault, &c. ; others, that the Prince is comprised on condition of his doing homage to the French King, and they see no remedy but to put themselves entirely at the mercy of France and the King of Arragon, who is the chief cause of all the mischiefs, in order to keep the Prince in his subjection.   They will now be happy if they can effect the alliance with the daughter of France.   It is proposed to give the Duke of Gueldres the Lady Eleanor, so that Henry will see how conscious they are of the fault committed against England.   The Sovereign of Flanders is to be sent to England instead of Bonnett and the Provost of Cassell.   The President of the Privy Council says the ambassador of Arragon has received intelligence that the marriage and peace are concluded.   Don Loys Carroze has written that he had like information, and that the publication was deferred till Sunday last.   Yesterday news came that the peace was published on Saturday in Calais.   On Thursday last Henry Pynpe, gentleman, was assaulted by certain Spaniards and seriously wounded.   The Archduchess has caused informations to be made to bring the assailants to justice.   She leaves on Monday for Barowe, to be with the Estates of Zealand, and at the wedding of the Lord Berges' daughter with the Lord of Nassaw.   Brussels, 19 Aug. 1514.

P.S.—The Prince of Castile will remain in this town.   *Signed.*
Pp. 3, *mutilated.   Add.*

20 Aug.   **5342.**   HADRIAN [DE CORNETO] BP. OF BATH, CARDINAL
R. O.   ST. CHRYSOGON, to WOLSEY.

Thinks he must have heard of the death of the Cardinal of York.   Riccardi (Pace) and Burbank, his secretaries, have been left his executors.   The latter returns with the Cardinal's retinue to England.   Rome, 20 Aug. 1514.

P.S. in his own hand.   Recommends the executors to the King.   *Signed.*
Lat., p. 1.   *Addressed :* Reverendo, &c. Episcopo Lincolniensi.

20 Aug.   **5343.**   TREATIES WITH FRANCE.
S. B.
Rym. XIII. 438.

Ratification by Henry VIII. of the treaty of marriage between Louis of France and Princess Mary, concluded by Thomas Duke of Norfolk, Treasurer and Marshal of England, Thomas Bishop of Lincoln, postulate of York, and Richard Bishop of Winchester, Keeper of the Privy Seal, commissioners for England ; and Lewis Duke of Longueville, Marquis of Ruthelyn, Great Chamberlain of France, John de Selva, LL.D., First President of the Parliament of Normandy, and Sir Thomas Bohier, General of France, commissioners for France.   London, 20 Aug. 6 Hen. VIII.

1514.

Rym. xiii. 437.
ib.

ii. Ratification by Henry VIII. of the treaty of amity concluded by the same commissioners. London, 20 Aug. 6 Hen. VIII.
Endorsed: Warrants to my Lord Chancellor.
Fr. 6 Hen. VIII. p. 2, m. 15.

20 Aug.
P. S.

5344. For St. Peter's, Gloucester.

Restitution of the temporalities of the monastery of St. Peter, Gloucester, on election of William Malvern, B.D, as abbot, which has been confirmed by Thomas Hanniball, LL.D., vicar-general of Silvester Bishop of Worcester, now in foreign parts. Eltham, 26 June 6 Hen. VIII. *Del.* Otford, 20 Aug.
Pat. 6 Hen. VIII. p. 2, m. 10.

ii. Certificate by Hannibal of the confirmation of the election. Gloucester, 2 June 1514.

21 Aug.
P. S.

5345. For Henry Jenkynson of Scarburgh, York, alias of London, fishmonger.

Protection ; going in the retinue of Sir Richard Wyngfeld, Deputy of Calais. Greenwich, 17 Aug. 6 Hen. VIII. *Del.* Otford, 21 Aug.
Fr. 6 Hen. VIII. p. 2, m. 9,

22 Aug.

5346. John Mauncell.

Northamptonshire.—Commission to Ralph Lane, John Wattys, Maurice Osbern, Giles Pulton, Geo. Bovyle and Wm. Saunders, to make further inquisition concerning the possessions of John Mauncell, deceased, the inquisition previously returned being considered incomplete. Otford, 22 Aug.
Pat. 6 Hen. VIII. p. 2, m. 7d.

22 Aug.
R. T. 137.
R. O.

5347. The Princess Mary.

Constituting Charles Earl of Worcester her proxy for her marriage contract with Lewis XII. *per verba de præsenti.* London, 22 Aug. 1514.

22 Aug.
Calig. B. ii. 180.
B. M.

5348. Alex. Lord Home to Dacre.

Wrote this Tuesday to my Laird of Farnyhurst. Believes he has sent him information how matters stand. The men have gone home, all " bot ane sertan with my consent, that is Mr. Howm, quhilk I may dispone on as I plese." Would fain have been quit of them all. Thinks they will not be in a hurry to come again. They desire to make peace, but he will not do it without consulting Dacre. Refers him to the bearer, Dacre's servant, for more.
Hol., p. 1.
Addressed: To my Lord Dakr, Lord Warden of England.
Endorsed by Dacre: Received this letter by the hands of Tom Scot, on Wednesday at night, the 23d day of this month of August.

22 Aug.
Vitell. B. ii. 89.*
B. M.

5349. F. Cardinal Surrentinus to Henry VIII.

Announcing the death of Cardinal Bainbridge. He was very strict, perhaps too much so, in all that pertained to the King's honor. Was wholly in his confidence. Recommends Pace and Burbank, his

1514.

executors, who have faithfully fulfilled their task, and are now without a master. Last winter sent two horses to the King. Rome, 22 Aug. 1514. *Signed.*
Lat., pp. 2.

22 Aug.   **5350.**   F. CARDINAL SURRENTINUS to [WOLSEY] BISHOP OF
R. O.   LINCOLN.

It is needless to repeat the regret which all have felt at the death of the Cardinal of England. Recommends his servants. Rome, 22 Aug. 1514. *Signed.*
Lat., p. 1.

23 Aug.   **5351.**   DELIVERY OF RECORDS.
R. O.

Mem., that on 23 Aug. 6 Hen. VIII. Sir John Cutte received out of the treasury, by Ric. Parker his servant, two obligations between Lewis XI. and Edw. IV., of which one (dated 1475, and sealed with green wax,) bound Lewis to pay Edward 50,000 crowns.

Item : another obligation for a treaty of peace between Lewis XI. and Edw. IV., "*datum in quadam alta parlura*" of the Friars Preachers of London, 1478, sealed with red wax ; which was taken out of a square coffer, and remains in the great chest upon the receipt, where the evidences of France used to be placed.

Mem., that on the same day Sir John received out of the treasury an original obligation between Charles VIII. and King Hen. VII., concerning a treaty of peace, and for certain arrears, dated at Amboise, 13 Dec. 1492, sealed with green wax ; which was taken out of a square coffer, and remains in the great chest.
P. 1. With certain characters.

24 Aug.   **5352.**   ERASMUS to R. R.
R. O.

Has done what his correspondent requested in his letter to Bassus. Sends and criticizes the poems of Bapt. Mantuanus, Valla, Isidorus, and Politian, lately printed with much elegance. Prefers the first. "*Hos comitatur non inutilis servus An. Macivellus.*" Mamotrectus abounds in blunders. "*Habes extemporium nunc quidem epistolium, habuisses longissimam epistolam et accuratam si non dedisses nullam.*"
Nono cal. Sep.

24 Aug.   **5353.**   [BP. OF WORCESTER to WOLSEY.]
Vitell. B. II. 90.
B. M.

Answers the letters of Winchester and Lincoln in common. Praises their success in persuading the King to peace. Perfectly agrees in the King's allegation. For determining the peace nothing can be more reasonable than the conditions proposed. Thinks it will be very difficult to obtain the sanction of the Emperor. He is never satisfied with what he has not himself begun. He is so changeable there is no trusting him. Worcester has written to him, but as often as he is spoken to on the subject the Emperor promises to write, and does, but is silent on this topic. A peace will follow if the Emperor will allow the Venetians anything more than Padua and Treviso. If he would be rational the Pope thinks he could obtain a good sum of money for him from the French. Thinks the King of Arragon will consent, if he may take Navarre,

1514.

which he has gained at the expense of the English. Praises Henry for being more honest than his confederates. Fully understands the necessity of despatch. Before he received Fox and Wolsey's letters of 7 Feb., the Pope had pressed the matter, and sent a nuncio into France, saying if he refused these proffers he would oppose him in all respects. Has agreed with the French to send a herald to England to ask safe conduct for ambassadors. Suspects the French have some other treaty in view, of which Worcester has written before.

Finds the arrangement between France and Arragon, of which he wrote 4 Feb., has taken effect. The King of France is to give his second daughter to Don Ferdinand, with Milan for a dowry. For the recovery of the dukedom he offers the Emperor a sum of money and forces ; to the Queen of Arragon the Comté de Foys, to abandon Navarre and leave the Scots a prey to England. "*Habes totam hanc perfidiam.*" The Pope advises Henry to anticipate them, and offer better terms to France, which they will accept, as none of them have any honesty. If the King will accept the loan and leave the matter to the Pope, he will give a bond to make an arrangement agreeable to the letters of Fox and Wolsey. Desires written authority for that purpose. The Pope avows he did not hear of this treaty from the Florentine ambassador now in France, but from a nobleman in the confidence of Lewis; and Worcester thinks it probable, as the Cardinals and the French party had been less urgent for an accommodation with England, and Lewis wishes to take the Swiss into pay. When the Pope upbraided the Spanish ambassador with his master's perfidy he denied he knew anything of it. The imperial ambassador did the same. Thinks Henry will be much annoyed. Has not heard of the conditions offered by the Emperor to France. He has been traitor enough, without being the adversary of England. There never was a more perfidious Judas. Wonders how they will dare show their faces. Is surprised that there was no one in Spain to give the King notice of what was passing. Expects an answer to the Pope's briefs. Cannot say that Master Talbot did nothing when the insignia were delivered to the Duke of Urbino. Knows that the Abbot of Glastonbury did most. Trusts he will have a similar commission for the insignia of the Magnifico Juliano.

Lat. In the hand of Ammonius, pp. 5.

26 Aug. **5354.** SILVESTER BP. of WORCESTER to WOLSEY and FOX.

Vitell. B. II. 93.
B. M.

By their letters dated 30 May, heard of the arrival of the president of Normandy, the arrangements for peace and for marriage. Has arranged about the tenths and the subsidies. The main difficulty was that the late Cardinal of York frequently affirmed that the King was very strict in demanding his tenths, sometimes exacting six in a year. Encloses the brief; cannot obtain any remission of the annates for his bishopric ; is delighted to hear of Wolsey's advancement to York ; hoped that he himself would have had the diocese of Lincoln, but hears from Ammonius that it demands personal residence ; assumes that he may expect the next bishopric ; needs a more decent support ; has written to Ammonius of the stigma attached to him by some of the domestics of poisoning Cardinal Bainbridge. R[ome], 26 Aug. 1514. *Signed,*

Lat., pp. 3. Add. : Wyntoniensi et Lincol. episcopis.

3 I

1514.

26 Aug. **5355.**   RICHARD ABBOT OF WINCHCOMBE to WOLSEY.

Nero, B. vi. 25.
B. M.

Congratulates him on his nomination to the see of York, at which he and the monastery of Winchcombe have particular reason to rejoice on account of the favors he has conferred on them. The mother that bore him has reason to rejoice, but not less so his *alma mater*, Oxford, that gave him to God. That university has raised some who have been bishops at 60, others at 70, but Wolsey has attained the archiepiscopal dignity not being yet 40. The abbey of St. Oswald's, Gloucester, belongs to the archbishopric of York. The prior is a man of dissolute life, and keeps no discipline. Recommends to his place the cellarer of Lanthony ("divi Lonthoniensis") of the same order, the son of a sister of Henry [Deane] late Archbishop of Canterbury. "Ex Winchelcomba raptim postridie solemnitatem divi Apostoli Bartholomei."

Addressed : Rev^{mo}, &c. Thomæ Lincolniensis sedis meritissimo episcopo, ac jam in archipræsulem Eboracensem electo.

Hol., pp. 2. Endorsed with some lines, apparently intended as an exercise of penmanship (by Cromwell?)

28 Aug. **5356.**   [WILLIAM BURBANK] to HENRY VIII.

Vitell. B. ii. 97.
B. M.
Ellis, 1 S. i. 94.

The Pope has caused most diligent examination to be made, and the body of the late Cardinal Bainbridge to be opened, as it was reported he died by poison. The Bp. of Worcester, "your Grace's orator," an enemy to my Lord, has been suspected ; and a priest of the name of Ranalde of Modena, much in my Lord's chamber, with whom Worcester was intimate, has been arrested on suspicion, and sent to Castle Angelo. The Pope commanded Burbank to be present at the examination, that he might send a report to England. During the three days the writer tarried in the house, Rainalde made no confession ; though he acknowledged to having made Worcester privy to the Cardinal's secrets. He was put to the torture —and Burbank left for Florence.—Has since heard from Pace, who writes, that Ranalde confesses he put poison into the Cardinal's potage, at the desire of Worcester, who gave him 15 ducats for so doing; —that one Stephen, his chamberlain, was privy;—and that he bought the poison at Spoleto, and kept it under a "tyyll stoan." He has since written this confession, and given it to Cardinal Medicis, "your Grace's protector," empowered by the Pope to examine the facts. He confessed freely, acknowledging other enormities, hoping the Pope would spare his life. Next day he wounded himself with a small knife, and is at the point of death. Pace writes that Worcester hopes to escape by influence of his friends, and the Pope would gladly hush up the matter for the service rendered by Worcester in procuring peace between France and England. Burbank cannot believe it, as the Pope at first professed he would have justice done.—Stephen has been apprehended. — They reported at Rome, that the late Cardinal had been poisoned by his cook at the instigation of some prelate in England ; but he and Pace replied, "that prelates of England and English-born were never disposed to such acts." Great solicitation has been made to the Pope to have Ranalde's confession revoked and Worcester saved. "Else, he said, that he must needs be undone ; though it were lost only by means of my Lord Cardinal Hadrian."—Has desired Pace to write to the King. Was not at ease when writing this. Florence, 28 Aug. 1514.

Mutilated.

1514.

28 Aug. **5357.** WILLIAM BURBANK to HENRY VIII.

Vitell. B. II. 94.*
B. M.
Ellis, 1 S. I. 106.

Has heard from Pace, since closing his last, that the priest who poisoned the Cardinal has been induced, through the means of Worcester, to retract his confession. "By enforcing of his confessors he denied the space of two days," banning the time he was familiar with Worcester. He died on the 26th, confessing he had poisoned the Cardinal ; "but he did not show by whose instance; being so commanded by his confessors." The process against him is kept for the King's inspection. Great excitement at Rome against Worcester ; but the Pope will take no proceedings against him till he knows the King's pleasure. Florence, 28 Aug.

28 Aug. **5358.** LEO X. to HENRY VIII.

R. O.

Had written last month respecting a cargo of alum belonging to the Apostolic Chamber, which had been consigned to John de Cavalcanti, and confiscated to the Duke of Suffolk. Hears that an arrangement had been made by Cavalcanti to pay the Duke a large sum of money to the prejudice of the Chamber. Begs he will not permit this, but command John Francis de Bardis, the papal commissary, to have the alum or the proceeds. If Cavalcanti has committed any wrong, begs he may be pardoned at the Pope's instance. Rome, 28 Aug. 1514.
Add.

28 Aug. **5359.** THOS. BOHIER to [MARY] QUEEN OF FRANCE.

R. O.

The king is in good health,—desires news from her everyday, but above all things to see her in France. Estampes, 28 Aug. *Signed.*
Fr., p. 1. Addressed.

28 Aug. **5360.** THOMAS BOHIER to WOLSEY.

Vitell. C. XI. f. 155 b.
B. M.

The King will be glad if Wolsey will inform him of the departure of the Queen, and the day she is to be at Boulogne, as he is marvellously anxious to see her. The Duke de Longueville is commissioned to arrange with Wolsey the Queen's suite for the interview. Etampes, 28 Aug. *Signed.*
P. 1. Add.: M. L'Eveche d'Yorck.

28 Aug. **5361.** For WILLIAM DYNGLEY of Charleton, Worc.

S. B.

Grant, in fee, of the manor of Shireffeslenche, Worc., at the rent of 5l. a year. *Del.* Otford, 28 Aug. 6 Hen. VIII.
Pat. 6 Hen. VIII. p. 2, m. 9.

29 Aug. **5362.** SIR RIC. WINGFIELD and SPINELLY to [HENRY VIII.]

Galba, B.III. 212.*
B. M.

Wrote last on the x. . . inst. from Berghez. Have not since heard from his highness. This morning dined with Berghes, and afterwards had an interview with the Archduchess, who "cannot apaese herself" about the French King's marriage, and declares the penance is too great for their offence towards England. The Sovereign of Flanders left this afternoon for England;—his commission is said to be to know how they are comprised in the treaty with France. The murmurs here at the alliance are as great as ever. The ambassador of Arragon was never so popular on account of his great offers, but by past experience the Archduchess cannot trust him. The Archduchess says Henry could not have done a

3 I 2

1514.

greater pleasure unto h[im] that is the cause of all the mischief, [Ferdinand], than by making this alliance. Burghez, 29 Aug. 1514. *Signed.*

P. 1, *mutilated.*

29 Aug. **5363.** For PHILIP DRAYCOTTE, merchant tailor of London.

Licence to export goods not belonging to the staple of Calais, to any port of the Archduke of Austria, or elsewhere ;—and to import goods from Austria and other foreign parts. Greenwich, 11 Aug. 6 Hen. VIII. *Del.* Otford, 29 Aug.

Fr. 6 Hen. VIII. p. 2, m. 10.

31 Aug. **5364.** SILVESTER BISHOP OF WORCESTER to WOLSEY.

R. O.

Received his letters yesterday touching the Cardinal of York's executors. Has hitherto been able to do little, but trusts to find such a remedy as will satisfy Wolsey. "The persons be so subtle and crafty that the best remedy we can find shall be little enough." Rome, 31 Aug. 1514. *Signed.*

P. 1. *Addressed:* R'mo, etc. Tho. Ep'o Lincol' postulato Eboracensi.

31 Aug. **5365.** SILVESTER BISHOP OF WORCESTER to [WOLSEY].

Vitell. B. II. 95.
B. M.

Thinks he understands by his last letters of the 26th, the suspicions attaching to the death of Cardinal Bainbridge, and the confession of the priest Raynaldi, who stabbed himself in prison, and affirmed on his oath that he was the cause of his death. The prosecutors, to satisfy the rage of Pace and John C[lerk], proposed that he should be hanged and quartered, which was refused on the ground that his confession was full of prevarication, and wrung from him by fear of torture. He was always a madman, and, though a priest, never performed any but servile offices in the Chamber. Did not believe Worcester guilty, and when asked why he had accused Worcester said he had done so to save himself, because he was a thief, and had stolen money and papers from his master. When in England, Worcester found him so intractable that after three months he dismissed him from his service. Notwithstanding his confession Ric. Pace and John Cleck persist in attributing this crime to Worcester. Is satisfied with having cleared himself, but requests that they be ordered to forbear. Will send Raynaldi's process. His letters to Ammonius will explain more. The Lantern at Genoa has surrendered to the Genoese, who have begun to demolish it. Has just received letters of the King and Wolsey, announcing the marriage of the Princess Mary. The Pope will write ; he praises much the letters of the King and Ammonius for the elegance of their style. Was himself present at her betrothal to the Prince of Castile. The Pope intends to celebrate mass on the occasion in Sancta Maria de Populo. It is rumored there that the French will have to pay 1,000,000 scudi. Rome, 31 Aug. 1514. *Signed.*

Lat., mutilated, pp. 4.

31 Aug. **5366.** SIR ROBERT WINGFIELD to [HENRY VIII.]

Vitell. B. xviii. 95.
B. M.

Wrote last . . . . month [from] Fykylbrok in Lontotrence. Arrived here yesterday at noon. Has very little news to communicate. Since his arrival here the ambassadors of the Pope and [Arragon have gone] to the Cardinal of Gource at Aws[burg] . . . but for what purpose Wingfield is ignorant. Owing to a disease

1514.

the Emperor had in his leg (as Wingfield mentioned in his last), he departed from the p . . . . the 22nd of this month, in a horse-litter, a[nd when] "he had passed one journey hitherward he was advertised [of the expedition] which the King of Hungary had prepared in Bohemia to g . . . . . . Crwsyfery in Hungary, when they were countermand[ed] . . . . . . Captain of the said Crwciferi was taken and put to execu[tion] . . . . . . people appeased, the said army of Bohemia began to ma . . . . [on] the confines of Austria so that the Emperor was fay[n to return] again to his town of Welce in Londotrence to make . . . . and since word is come that the said army of B[ohemia] . . . . every man returned to his house. Wingfield has had no letters from Henry since the 19th of May, therefore he is no better than a cipher. Complains of poverty, and implores Henry to send him a remedy, else he must find one himself, where, altho' he may not fare so sumptuously, he shall live so as he need not be in debt, "for much better it is for a beggar to live and die amongst beggars than to have the appearance of riches and live amongst the rich in extreme poverty." Will serve Henry to the best of his ability. Insbrook, the last day of August 1514.

Hol., pp. 2, mutilated.

31 Aug.   **5367.**   LEWIS XII. to MARGARET OF SAVOY.
R. O.

Requests her to aid in securing to Lewis Guillart his rights as Bp. of Tournay. St. Germain-en-Laye, 31 Aug.

Copy in Sir Rich. Wingfield's hand, p. 1.

Add. : [To] the King's grace.

Aug.   **5368.**   MARGARET OF SAVOY.
Lett. de Louis XII.
t. IV. 349.

Her instructions to Mons. de Castres sent to Henry VIII. 1. Madame understands that peace was concluded between England and France on St. Lawrence day (10 Aug.)   2. Wishes to know if the Prince and his countries be comprised, and if she is to have restitution of the lands seized by France for the favor she bore to England, on pretence that some Germans had taken places of the Duke of Longueville.   3. Is to inquire if Mary be married to the King of France, or not, before he speak to Henry.   4. If he find she is, he shall say that Madame, though she had heard so, would not believe it, as Henry had given her no intimation, and no match could be more suitable for Mary than with the Prince. 5. If he find they are only in treaty for a match, either between Lewis and Mary, or, as some say, between Lewis and the Queen of Scots, he is to tell the King and his council severally that Madame could not believe the rumor, or suppose the King would so soon depart from the treaty made at Calais, seeing that Monsieur would be one of the great princes of Christendom.   6. That Madame is doing her best to urge the Emperor to hasten the conclusion of the marriage.   7. If he find that no such marriage is contemplated, is to tell the Bp. of Lincoln, that, in spite of the rumors, Margaret had never any fear of it after the promises of England.   8. If he find the thing in train he shall remind the King of his promise made to Margaret, both by mouth, and by writing signed by his hand and written by the hand of the Bp. of Lincoln, of which he shall show a copy.*   9. If the marriage be irrevocably solemnised, he shall find by whom it was brought about ; if by Suffolk and the

* See it in Lett. de Max. et Marg. II. 224.

1514.

Bp. of Lincoln, he shall show the King the copy of his said promise, and also show it to the Duke of Norfolk and the bishops of Winchester and Durham, and remonstrate against the breach of faith. 10. If the match have been made by the opposite party, he is to show the promise to Suffolk and Lincoln. 11. If the King allege that a similar written promise had been violated on the part of Charles, he shall say that Margaret apprised Spinelly of the truce between France and the Emperor as soon as she knew it was treated of. 12. If they allege a project of marriage between the French King and Margaret, no such project had been entertained or spoken of. 13. The Emperor or Arragon may have proposed to marry her niece Eleanor to France, but it was without her knowledge. 14. If they complain of not being able to levy soldiers in Flanders, it has not been through her fault. 14. France has seized the country of Charlois, the seigneuries of Noyers, Chasteau, Chinon, Chaulcin, and la Perricre, with the sale of salt in Burgundy, on some false pretences, really in revenge for the favor shown by Margaret to England.

Fr.

31 Aug. **5369.** FRANCIS DE BORDE[S] to CLARENCIEUX KING AT ARMS.

Calig. E. i. 59.
B. M.

Has arrived out of the barren country, and accomplished his commission. The war is ended. Will tell him the rest of the news " [a diman]che," and will come to him as soon as he can without killing his horse. Begs he will send a gelding for the legate [. . . . . Lan]guedoc for hunting. Does not think Clarencieux can recover the hob[by] of La Faiete. B[lois ?], 31 Aug.

1 Sept. **5370.** FRANCIS DE BORD[ES] to YORK HERALD.

Calig. E. i. 70.
B. M.

[Has spoken] to the lady of his goods, without forgetting Anthony [Bonv]ice. Is very sorry he was not with him at Brochelz. Has not been able to return till this evening. A friend whom he met in Scotland is coming with him. Will be with him at York as speedily as possible. The Queen of Scots is married to the Earl of Angus (" c[omte] d'Angloicx "). At . . . . , 1 Sept. *Signed.*

Fr., mutilated, p. 1. Addressed: A maistre Yorch, herault du Roy a Yorch."

1 Sept. **5371.** For JOHN STRATTON, yeoman of the provisions in the larder.

Commission to provide horses, carts and boats for the conveyance of provisions. Westm., 1 Sept.

Pat. 6 Hen.VIII. p. 2, m. 8d.

2 Sept. **5372.** LEWIS XII. to WOLSEY.

Calig. D. vi. 140.
B. M.
Rym. xiii. 439.

Would not allow the English ambassador to leave without a letter for Wolsey, begging him to make his most cordial commendations to the King and Queen, and the Queen his wife. Begs him to use his efforts that she may start as soon as possible, as there is nothing in the world he desires so much as to see her. Estampes, 2 Sept. *Signed.*

Fr., p. 1. Mutilated. Add. A Mons. Diork. *Endd.*

1514.

2 Sept. **5373.** LEWIS DUKE OF ORLEANS to the QUÉEN [OF FRANCE].

Calig. D. vi. 142. The King greatly regrets not having heard from her. Begs she
B. M. will hasten her coming, which will give his Majesty the greatest
pleasure in the world. Estempeś, 2 Sept. *Signed.*
Addressed : A la Royne ma Souveraine Dame.
Endorsed by Wolsey : The Duc of Longeville.

2 Sept. **5374.** For JOHN MORDAUNT.
S. B. Exemption from serving on juries, being made member of parliament, &c. ; and privilege of sitting with his hat on in the King's
presence. *Del.* Otford, 2 Sept. 6 Hen. VIII.
Pat. 6 *Hen. VIII. p.* 2, *m.* 9.

2 Sept. **5375.** For RICHARD CLERC of London, fishmonger.
P. S. Protection ; going in the retinue of Sir Richard Wyngfeld,
Deputy of Calais. Guildford, 28 Aug. 6 Hen. VIII. *Del.* Otford,
2 Sept.
Fr. 6 *Hen. VIII. p.* 2, *m.* 10.

2 Sept. **5376.** THOMAS BOHIER to [MARY] QUEEN OF FRANCE.
R. O. She will learn news of the King by the bearer. He has great
desire to see her. The King will be glad to hear from her.
Estampes, 2 Sept. *Signed.*
Fr., p. 1. *Endorsed :* The General of Normandy.

3 Sept. **5377.** SIR RICH. WINGFIELD and SIR THO. SPINELLY to
Galba, B. iii. 215. [HENRY VIII.]
B. M. Wrote last on the 29th ult. from Ber[gez]. Have since been at
Antwerp, and from thence came to Mechlin, whence my Lady
will remove to-morrow from Brussells. Have been told that
rumors are spread in England that the Emperor betrayed the
King, and have been unable to make satisfactory explanations.
If the Prince be not comprised in the treaty, it will cause perpetual enmity between the King and his subjects. The presence of
the ambassadors here is of little use.—If the popularity of the
ambassador of Arragon continue, his master will have the entire rule
of the Prince. The only means to prevent it would be an alliance
with France, to which Arragon would not be likely to agree. [The
council] do not give them information as formerly. [The mas-
ter] of the posts told Spinelly that the Swiss were ready to
break with France, and have sent Bourbon a sword and a
purse — the one to fight, the other for their 400,000 crowns ;—
that the Duke of Milan will put himself and his duchy in their
hands, and that the Emperor and Arragon will do their best to
keep them faithful. Last night received letters from the Canon of
Lysle and the compagnon in France with news, of which they
enclose a copy. Spinelly can no longer entertain him with words,
having had no answer from the King or Council to several letters.
Mechlin, 3 Sept. 1514. *Signed.*
Pp. 2, *mutilated.*

3 Sept. **5378.** JOHN FARIA to EMMANUEL KING OF PORTUGAL.
R. T. 154. Rejoicings were made at Rome upon the peace between France
R O. and England without the Pope's authority. The castle did not fire,
nor were public illuminations made. The ambassadors of England,

1514.

France, and Venice illuminated, but none of the Cardinals, except San Severino, the protector of France. Doubtless the Cardinal of England would have done so, had he been alive. A few days ago the murderer (Rainaldo) was taken, confessed the poisoning, and afterwards revoked his confession, then killed himself. Since his death he has been gibbetted and quartered. To-day the Bishop [of Worcester], ambassador of England, said mass, in the presence of the ambassador of France, and many cardinals, in honor of the peace. Indulgences were posted up everywhere. Neither the ambassador of Castile, nor the Cardinals Sanctæ Crucis, nor Sorentinus, who are of the part of the King of Arragon, were present. Hopes the peace will become universal, although there are rumors of the Venetians breaking it, by invading the territory (*campo*) of the Spaniards, and killing 200 men at arms. Rome, 3 Sept. 1514.

Portuguese, pp. 3.

4 Sept. **5379.**   ———— to MONS. DE FIENNES.
Add. 21,382, f. 61.
B. M.

Has used every effort to inquire into the report about England. A peace has been made between England and France, and the French King is to marry the Princess Mary, who leaves at Michaelmas. Many are dissatisfied with the interruption of her marriage with the Archduke, as they are afraid the peace will not last after the King's death. She is to be delivered at Abbeville, and the King has appointed all who are to go with her to be ready on the 28th. Spoke this day with the captain of Guisnes, who is to be one of them, and my lady his wife ; he reckons on 40 horses in his train, and all with scarlet cloth. There will be more than 2,000 in all. Was yesterday at Boulogne to pay his respects to the Grand Master, who is there to receive the English embassy, which arrived yesterday at 3 o'clock *apres nonne*, with more than 60 horses. It consisted of the Great Chamberlain, the Lord of St. John's, and the Dean of Windsor. The Grand President landed at Boulogne from England on Friday last, where he stayed till yesterday, when the embassy arrived, then mounted his horse, and took the longest road he could to join the King. The King, who had left Paris, was obliged to return to receive the embassy, as were the Dauphin, De Piennes, the Seneschal of Boulennois, and others. We are summoned with the Grand Master to conduct them to-morrow from Boulogne to Monstreuil.

The Dauphin has taken the oath of fealty for the infeudation of the duchy of Britanny in right of Claude his wife. The nobles have appeared before him and his wife, who is at present at Chartres with Madame Renée, her sister, and will not start until after the Queen's nuptials at Abbeville. There is no other Frenchman in England except Marigny, whom the King compels to attend with Madame Marie until the return of the ambassadors. White Rose, Duke of Suffolk, is commanded to leave the kingdom. He has received the thanks of Monsieur and the Duke of Alençon for the services he has done the King. He is no longer in the King's pay. They made him a handsome present at his departure, and he is gone to Lorraine. Can vouch for what he has stated, as he paid his respects to the Prior of St. John's while he was leaving the boat, and offered him his cob, as the horses were not disembarked. People in Flanders exclaim bitterly against the dishonor done to the Archduke, and say God will punish it. Monday, 4 Sept.

Add.
Fr. Copy, pp. 2.

1514.
4 Sept. **5380.** For GEOFFREY WREN, clk.

Presentation to the canonry or prebend in the collegiate church of Newark, near Leicester Castle, Linc. dioc. Otford, 4 Sept.

Pat. 6 Hen. VIII. p. 2, m. 9.

4 Sept. **5381.** LEWIS DUKE OF ORLEANS to WOLSEY.

Calig. D. vi. 142 b.
B. M.

Credentials for Mons. l'Audiencier the bearer. Estampes, 4 Sept. *Fr., p. 1. Signed.*

Addressed : A Mons. Mons. d'Yord.

4 Sept. **5382.** SILVESTER BISHOP OF WORCESTER to WOLSEY.

R. O.

Will remember the Pope wrote last month to the King in favor of John Francis de Bardis touching a cargo of alum. Writes again as the Pope feels much interest in the matter, and has sent a second brief. Has been commanded to write and press the subject. Rome, 4 Sept. 1514. *Signed.*

P.S. Begs that Wolsey will introduce De Bardis to the King with his brief and his letters.

Lat., p. 1. Addressed.

4 Sept. **5383.** SIR PHILIP DRAYCOT to the EARL OF SHREWSBURY.

Talbot Papers,
Lodge i. 5.

The treasurer's office at Boulogne is given to Mr. Dymmok, the comptroller's to Mr. Beckwith. Has taken leave of his Majesty. Will spend the winter at court, to which he is encouraged by the Lord Chancellor. Will therefore ride home with speed, and conclude the marriage of his cousin and heir. Has provided fuel, hay, lodging and other necessaries for his house in London, and will send to the Earl for some flesh for the wedding.

After the Earl left, the King went to Oatlands ; " and there in the meads, under Chertsey, was killing of stags, holden in for the purpose, one after another all the afternoon ; so that they were warned by the trumpets, and known thereby if they did enter any deer of price ; and they were not only coursed with some grey-hounds, but also with horsemen with darts and spears, and many so slain ; the most princely sports that hath been seen ; and many did escape over Thames and to the forest after they passed there." On Thursday last the King alighted at Byfleet, when the writer left. From Oatlands the King goes to Cobham or Woking, then to Guild-ford, and so to Windsor, and will be at each place about four days. " Written at my house in Smithfield, the next house to the Elephant, that is the New Tavern." 4 Sept.

Signed. Add.

4 Sept. **5384.** For THOMAS AP GWYLLIAMS, yeoman usher of the
S. B. Chamber.

To be bailiff of the lordships of Fanhope and Maunsell Lacy, Heref. *Del.* Otford, 4 Sept. 6 Hen. VIII.

Pat. 6 Hen. VIII. p. 2, m. 9.

4 Sept. **5385.** For SIR ANTHONY UGHTRED.
P. S.

To be steward, in reversion, of Galtres forest, York, and the land therein, and master of the hunt. To take effect on death or sur-render of Sir Henry Marney, knight of the Body, to whom the said

1514.

office of steward was granted in reversion by patent 22 June
1 Hen. VIII. on death or surrender of John Earl of Oxford,
deceased. Greenwich, 19 Aug. 6 Hen. VIII. *Del.* Knoll, 4 Sept.
Pat. 6 *Hen. VIII. p.* 2, *m.* 10.

6 Sept.   **5386.**   RICHARD SAMPSON to WOLSEY.

R. O.

Came to Brussels 5 Sept., having staid a short time at Tournay,
as he had written, because all the officers had fled for fear of the
plague. Delivered his letters to the Lady Margaret on the 6th, who
will further Wolsey's causes. Has received Wolsey's and the King's
letters. Had delivered his before they arrived. Staid in England
so long, Wolsey had forgotten whether Sampson had the letters.
Sir Ric. Wingfield comes to Brussels tomorrow, and will arrange
matters with him. Flanders is very angry with the marriage.
The people there are so wild in sedition they would not obey their
greatest lords. Retains the messenger he brought with him from
Calais. Brussels, 6 Sept. 1514.

Hol., p. 1. *Addressed:* To the most reverend, &c., myn Lord
of Yorke.

6 Sept.   **5387.**   SPINELLY to the COUNCIL.

Galba, B. iii. 166.
B. M.

Since he despatched to them his [servant] Rob. Baron, has not
been apprised of their pleasure whether he should stay or leave.—
Chievres and his colleagues say it is he who has turned the King's
mind against them, and caused the rupture of the marriage with
the Prince. The Archduchess says that the Pope has been to her*
knowledge the promoter of the whole business, as was [well known]
to the Deputy of Calais.—Her great displeasure causes her to say
what is not the truth. It would soon cease but for the malevolence
of Chievres ; to counteract which, Spinelly is advised to ask a
letter from the King to Madame, as contained in a memorial sent
to the master of the posts. Thinks he could explain things better
if he were permitted to go to England.—By letters from Milan of the
21st ult. the treaty would have been (*estoyt*) concluded between the
Emperor and the Venetians, were it not for the treaty between France
and England. The Viceroy of Naples was at Moncelyse, "*courrant
a touttes heures sur les portes de Padua.*" The King of Arragon
was going to send to Naples 800 men of arms, and 10,000 foot.
The Viceroy would garrison Verona and enter Milan. The Swiss
will do everything ("*mettront le tout par le tout*") for defence
of the duchy. The French were raising an army in Provence for the
relief of the castle of Genoa.—By letters of the 27th, the Emperor
was to be at Yspruk in three days, intending to go towards Switzerland or Augsburg. The ambassador of Arragon is omnipotent here.
Malines, 6 Sept.

Hol., Fr., mutilated, pp. 3. *Add.*

6 Sept.   **5388.**   For HUGH ELYOT of Bristol, merchant, alias draper.

P. S.

Protection ; going in the retinue of Sir Richard Wyngfeld,
Deputy of Calais. Eltham, 10 July 6 Hen. VIII. *Del.* Otford,
6 Sept.

Fr. 6 *Hen. VIII. p.* 2, *m.* 10.

---

* " mon," orig.

1514.
7 Sept. **5389.** SIR ROBERT WINGFIELD to HENRY VIII.

Vitell. B. xviii. 96.
B. M.

Wrote last on the [31st] of August. On the 3rd [received] two letters from the King, [the one] dated Eltham 14th July, [enclosing] a letter to the Emperor with copy, [the other] dated Greenwich the 19th, with a letter of credence. Sent to inform the Emperor, then distant three days journey, of their receipt, and was ordered to wait his arrival at Insbrook. He came this day about noon ; sent' for Wingfield after evensong ; none were present except his chancellor and Mr. Hans Reynner. Wingfield presented the King's letter of the [14th,] exeused an oversight that letters "had vis[ited] England again," and [stated the reasons mentioned in the King's letter] to himself, of the same date, why he was forced to the said peace. Then presented the credence with a translation in French, to which the Emperor promised to make a deliberate answer. Being asked if he had a copy of the articles of the peace, Wingfield said "No." Conversed further of the matters between Henry and the French King, [which he said he took] patiently, "because I am expert . . . . otherwise for myself . . . . of Arragon had in anywise . . . . us to the King your master, yet I could [never have thought] or judged that he would have disappointed [him in this] wise, because as yet he never offended him. [I count not] them good men that hath been the cause the . . . . him from me." And went into another chamber. Marvels why the Emperor named Master Pierce [Puyssaunt], whom Wingfield never knew. Insbrook, 7 Sept. 1514.

Hol., mutilated, pp. 3. *Addressed.*

7 Sept. **5390.** SIR EDW. PONYNGES to WOLSEY.

R. O.

Received two letters from him on the 5th, for the Archduchess and Dr. Sampson, and sent them to the latter at Brussels. Encloses a letter from Sampson in return. The marriage is unpopular, and he will find great danger in keeping Tournay, as it cannot be victualled without the good will of the surrounding people. Has taken two friars concerned in an enterprise aga.nst the town. Has not received the articles for the peace as Wolsey promised. De la Palice told Parker, a soldier of Tournay, that he understood the town would be delivered up. Tournay, 7 Sept. *Signed.*

Orig., p. 1. *Addressed :* [To] my Lord of York.

8 Sept. **5391.** WORCESTER, DOCWRA and WEST to [HENRY VIII.]

R. O.

Went from Bolayn to Motrell on Wednesday the 6th. Within a league of Motrell, were met by the bailiff of Amyas ; afterwards by his uncle Mons. Durers, who for his age and impotence was carried in a horse litter. Dined with the latter ; "and when the table was taken up, the mayor of the town and the burgesses came into the salle where we sat," and made "a proposition in French touching the commendation of peace ;" afterwards sent them a goodly present of partridges, quails, lapwings, snites, charcells, and flesh and fowl of various descriptions, and two hogsheads of wine. Next morning, in taking leave of Durers, Worcester commended the good mind he had shown towards the late and present King of England. Left for Abbeville on Thursday, the 7th. Were met by the captain of Abbeville that was taken at Bomy ; afterwards by Mons. de Piennez, who entertained them at dinner. Received presents from the mayor and burgesses. The Furrers have arrived to prepare

1514.

the royal lodgings. The King waits for them at Paris. The match is very popular with all classes. Wish to know what retinue is to come with the Queen, that due provision may be made. The president has sent jewellers to my lord, as agreed with Wolsey, who desires they may go and return to England without paying customs on such jewels as they cannot sell. Worcester has agreed. Abbeville, Friday 8 Sept. *Signed.*

Pp. 4. *Endorsed.*

8 Sept. **5392.** LEO X. to HENRY VIII.

R. O.

Thanks him for his goodness shown to Silvester Bp. of Worcester, ambassador at Rome, at the Pope's intercession. Does not doubt that the King will do all that he wishes, considering his constant services to the Holy See. Rome, 8 Sept. 1514, 2 pont.

8 Sept. **5393.** SIR ROBERT WINGFIELD to CHARLES DUKE OF SUFFOLK.

Vitell. B. xviii.98.
B. M.

Begs him to be amean for him to the King. Yestereven at an audience the Emperor named Pierce Puyssant [to go to England] much to Wingfield's surprise. Questioned Hans Reynner about it this morning, who said it was to advertise Henry of the overture made by the Emperor ; that Puyssant " was practis . . . . ; . that dead his father to the King . . . . : . . . . . . at the last peace . . . . ever since that the Emperor was . . . . by you only to put his special trust [in the King] of Arragon, and to leave the amity of France . . . . vyne in war with the King your master, he hath [ordere]d him in word and deed to appear as father, brother [and] friend to the King your master," and that if Wingfield had not written so to England, he was unworthy of the confidence of the Emperor, who had always used him more like a counsellor than an ambassador. To this, Wingfield was unable to reply, as Reynner was sent for to the Emperor, though he could have made only "a flourished answer." Sees by this why the court looks more " ovirly" upon him, and even his own servants, who are all Burgundians, except one Englishman, seeing that he cannot now advance them with the Prince. Desires to be recalled. Insbrook, 8 [September.]

P. S. Has no news in the King's [matters, except] that, " where the Emperor hath sent his mandate of . . . . to the Pope and the King of Arragon, to make such a peace betwixt him and the Venetians as th[ey judge] and think mete, now that the Venetians perceive [a treaty] and alliance of marriage is made betwixt England [and France], it is said that the said Venetians in trust that th[e French] shall return into Italy, make no haste to [agree] to any such peace." The Genoese have destroyed the fortress of [the Lantern] in Genys, yielded to them by the French, who have thus lost everything in Italy.

Hol., mutilated, pp. 3. *Addressed :* To the Right Noble and Excellent Prince Lord Charles the Duke of Suffolk.

8 Sept. **5394.** For ELIZABETH SAXBY, widow.

S. B.

Annuity of 20*l.* for services to the late King and Queen, and Mary Princess of Castile. *Del.* Otford, 8 Sept. 6 Hen. VIII.

Pat. 6 *Hen. VIII. p.* 2, *m.* 10.

1514.
9 Sept. **5395.** For JOHN SANDFORD, yeoman usher of the Chamber.
P. S.
To be steward of the town of Marton, Westmor., *vice* Richard Appulby, deceased. Chertsey Monastery, 7 Sept. 6 Hen. VIII. *Del.* Otford, 9 Sept.

Pat. 6 *Hen. VIII. p.* 2, *m.* 9.

10 Sept. **5396.** PACE to WOLSEY.
R. O.
Ellis, 3 S. I. 172.
Has received his letter dated London, 25 Aug., expressing his desire that 1,260*l.* should be paid for expediting his bulls. Has not one "ducat of my late Lord's * in my hands; nother the bank of Grimaldi's, nother none other had ony money of my said Lord's." All the stuff left at Burbank's departure does not amount to the sum required. The cloth that was sent out of England is not esteemed, as the colors were not good. Has, however, done his best, and paid into Grimaldi's bank 4,000 ducats of gold. To make up the sum, will keep certain rich vestments and altar cloth, which stuff did cost my late Lord 500 ducats of gold. Has ordered Burbank to present him with one other rich cloth of Arras, and written to Wythers to supply the sum wanting, and of his grace's desire that proper respect should be had "unto your places, which be fallen into great decay." Pace as principal executor, consents thereto for Wolsey's wish and the good of the late Cardinal's soul. Withers had no right to make any promise in Pace's name; Pace and Burbank are the only executors in Italy. Encloses letters from the banker and from Card. Surrentin, of what money Bainbridge left in Italy. Hopes that Wolsey will see justice done him for his great labors and little profit in this matter. Recommends to him the late Cardinal's brothers and kinsfolk, and that they be not deprived of their legacies. Rome, 10 Sept. 1514.

P. S. Has paid 1,000*l.* for the balls. Could not send Surrentine's letters, or those of the bank of Saules.

Add. : Thomæ Lincol. Episcopo et Electo Ebor.

Hol., pp. 7.

11 Sept. ii. *Continuation of the same.*
R. O.
Ellis ib.
Forgot to write that the Pope owed him 700 ducats of gold for plate. Can't get the money. Wishes those who proposed that the late Cardinal's goods should be sequestrated if Pace did not content Wolsey, would sequestrate also these 700 ducats. "As for the poisoning of my late Lord Cardinal, it hath been in the hands of the greatest learned men in Rome, and determined by the most part of them that my said Lord was poisoned in such manner as is comprised in the commission of him that did it, sent by me unto the King's grace. I may not write herein that I do know. The Bishop of Worcester hath marvellous great favor *ad occultandam veritatem, sed immortalis Deus tam horrendum scelus videtur odisse.* Die xj Sept."

Hol., pp. 2.

10 Sept. **5397.** For ROBERT FAIRFAX, gentleman of the Chapel Royal.
S. B.
To be one of the Poor Knights of Windsor, with 12*d.* a day. *Del.* Knoll, 10 Sept. 6 Hen. VIII.

Pat. 6 *Hen. VIII. p.* 2, *m.* 10.

---

* Cardinal Bainbridge.

1514.
11 Sept. **5398.** HENRY VIII. to SIR RICHARD WINGFIELD.

Lett.de Louis XII.
t. IV. 355.

Understands that the Archduchess lately sent Bregilles to Wingfield with a letter signed by Henry, of which Wingfield sent a copy to the King. Bregilles further said that though she had Henry's written promise, which it would be sufficient for her discharge to show the Emperor she did not wish to publish it without Henry's consent. Is to tell the Archduchess : 1. That the King remembers well the promise in question, which he fully intended to have kept if the other side had not broken their appointment ; 2. That the King has a similar promise signed by Margaret which has not been observed : and that Henry was compelled to make peace independently, as the Emperor had not contributed to the support of soldiers upon the frontier last winter according to the treaty.—Margaret knows how she herself commanded the horse in Henry's pay to abstain from attacking France ; how, notwithstanding the treaty made by Arragon to join them in the war, a truce had been made with France; how the appointment of Calais for the marriage was violated ; how truce was made by the Emperor and Arragon, which Margaret knew of three months before she told Henry, as appears by the letters delivered to the English Ambassadors ; and how the arrangement made with Chievers was broken off after Henry left Lisle; so that, in fact, the accomplishment of the marriage was despaired of. Henry, therefore, thinks the publication of the writing referred to will not be to the detriment of his honor ; but if it be published, the King will publish various promises made to him by Margaret in secret matters. Trusts she will not compel him to this course, seeing that he has comprised the Prince and herself in the treaty with France. The articles of comprehension will be shown to the Sovereign of Flanders (de Castres) at his coming. Margaret may be assured that but for Henry's regard for the interests of the Prince, he could have made such a peace with France as would have been extremely dangerous to them. In reply to the schedule in Wingfield's letter in which Magaret hints that Mary may meet with similar treatment from France to what she herself experienced (alluding to her proposed match in infancy with Charles VIII.), Henry has taken sufficient precautions in that matter. Wingfield is to show Margaret a translation of this letter in French. Croydon, 11 Sept.

Fr. Add.

11 Sept. **5399.** F. CARDINAL SURRENTINUS to WOLSEY.

Vitell. B. II.
100b.
B. M.

Testimonial in behalf of Ric. Pace, who has behaved so well in his executorship and showed the amount to be from 8,000 to 9,000 scudi. Has spared no labor in expediting Wolsey's bulls. Offers to serve Wolsey with the same fidelity and friendship as he did Bainbridge. Rome, 11 Sept. 1514. *Signed.*

Lat., p. 1. *Add. :* Episcopo Lincolniensi.

11 Sept. **5400.** For HAMNET CLEGG, gentleman waiter upon the Queen.

S. B.

Grant of a corrody in the monastery of Stanley, Wilts, late held by William Browne, deceased. *Del.* Otford, 11 Sept. 6 Hen. VIII.

1514.

11 Sept. **5401.** For ELIZABETH CATESBY, the King's kinswoman.

S. B.

Annuity of 40 marks, from Easter last, for services to Elizabeth late Queen of England, and Mary Queen of the French. *Del.* Knoll, 11 Sept. 6 Hen. VIII.
Pat. 6 *Hen. VIII. p.* 2, *m.* 10.

11 Sept. **5402.** For ELIZABETH wife of JOHN BURTON.

P. S.

Annuity of 20 marks. Esher, 9 Sept. 6 Hen. VIII. *Del.* Knoll, 11 Sept.
Pat. 6 *Hen. VIII. p.* 2, *m.* 10.

12 Sept. **5403.** SPINELLY to HENRY VIII.

Galba B.iii.167a.
B. M.

The treaties of alliance and marriage, between the Archduke and Mary the King's sister, are being examined for the purpose of showing, that Mary having been of age when it was concluded, and Charles having attained the age of 14 without opposing it, they are still binding. Will write their decision when it is arrived at. Brussels, 12 Sept.
Hol., p. 1. *Add.*

13 Sept. **5404.** SIR RICHARD WINGFIELD and SIR THO. SPINNELLY to

Galba,B.iii. 216.
B. M.

HENRY VIII.

Wrote last . . . . " went to the Lady Archduchess to commune with h[er touching] advertisements had from your Grace's Lieutenant in Tou[rnay]", desiring that some of the [soldiers] of Tournay being at Lisle might be taken. She referred them to the President, who promised they should be arrested and examined. The Archduchess complains that she has received no particulars of their comprehension, and that her credit is much diminished by the affair taking a turn contrary to her affirmations. She is much offended at the presumption of the [ambassador] of Arragon, who professes to be also ambassador of the Queen of Spain. This morning the young Duke of Saxony, who leaves to-day to go to his father, in Friesland, was with them, and offered his father's services to Henry, and desired that Holland Herald, whom he sends to England, may be heard and despatched. The Duke is a great Prince, and called as virtuous as any other Almayn. The President of the Privy Council has told Spinelly, that, by letters of the 6th inst. Bannisius informed him of the Emperor's arrival at Inspruck—that there is no appearance of an accommodation this winter between the Emperor and the Venetians—that the garrison of Cremona had made a sally upon the Duke of Milan's army, but the siege was reinforced—that the Emperor, Arragon, and the Duke of Milan have good intelligence of the Swiss— . . . . (*one paragraph so mutilated as to be unintelligible*)—that when the Emperor heard of the alliance with France he said he was sorry " such a fair and virtuous princess should com[e to] an impotent, indisposed, and so malicious a prince as is the French King". The letters now sent by the Archduchess to the Sovereign of Flanders relate to the patron of the carack. Brussels, 13 Sept. 1514.
Signed.
Pp. 3, *mutilated. Add.*

13 Sept. **5405.** PACE TO WOLSEY.

Vitell B. ii. 99;
B. M;

Wrote on the 10th, of the money provided for his bulls, and his readiness to give an account of his executorship. The Bp. of Wor-

1514.

cester endeavours to trouble him in his administration, pretending that he would have the goods for Wolsey's use. Thinks regard ought to be had to his faithful service and the late Cardinal's intention, which was that Pace should take of his goods as much as he conscientiously would. Worcester wishes to beggar him, in revenge for his stating that he was an accomplice in Bainbridge's death, "as the dead doer did confess," and the writings make apparent. If he might write freely, would desire no other than Wolsey's judgment. Wishes to avenge his death for the truth's sake.—Rome, 13 Sept. 1514.

Hol., mutilated, pp. 3. Add.: Tho. Eboracensi Archiepiscopo Angliæ primati et Sedis Apostolicæ legato nato.

---

14 Sept. **5406.**   For MARY REDYNG, gentlewoman.

P. S.

Annuity of 50l. for services to Elizabeth, late Queen of England, and to Mary Queen of the French.   Esher, 7 Sept. 6 Hen. VIII. *Del.* Knoll, 14 Sept. 6 Hen. VIII.

Pat. 6 Hen. VIII. p. 2, m. 10.

---

14 Sept. **5407.**   JAQUES DE CAESTRES to [MARGARET OF SAVOY].

Addit. 21,382, f. 57.
B. M.

Arrived at London, Saturday the 9th. Was visited next morning by Lord de Mon Joye, accompanied by Mons. Witnick, sent from the King and Council to know my purpose. Told them he was sent to thank the King, and present letters from my Lady. The King was at a house named Krudden (Croydon) belonging to the Archbishop of Canterbury, with the Queen and the French Queen that is to be. Mountjoy sent word of his arrival. On Monday the Bishop of York sent him word that he should be with the King at Eltham on Tuesday at nine. Presented the first letter, which the King read. Told him he had another letter for him, in Margaret's own hand, which the King was long in reading, and said it would take time to answer ; and that Margaret and the Emperor were guilty of the breaking off the marriage of his sister, for many reasons, which he will tell her on his return. On Wednesday the King sent for him to the Council at Greenwich, to communicate on the subject of the letters, and also about sending her the treaty of peace.

This Thursday, Holy Cross day, the Council sent for him into a garden, where were the Duke of Norfolk, the Abp. of York, formerly almoner, the Bp. of Winchester, and Lovel the undertreasurer ; corroborating the excuses the King had made for the rupture of the marriage.

On returning after dinner they gave him a copy of the peace, which he sends. The Lord Chamberlain and the Grand-prior of St. John's are gone upon an embassy to France. Madame Marie starts at Michaelmas. The Duke and Duchess of Norfolk, the Marquis and his Lady, the Bp. of Durham, the Captain of Guisnes and his Lady, and a great number of gentlemen will attend her. Many decline. As far as he can perceive there is much dissatisfaction among nobles and people. London, Holy Cross day, 1514.

Hol., Fr., pp. 2. Add.: A Madame.

---

14 Sept. **5408.**   LEWIS XII.

R. O.
Rym. xiii. 440.

Confirmation of the treaty of peace made with England by L. d'Orleans Duke of Longueville, John de Selva, Thomas Bohier, on one side ; and Thomas Duke of Norfolk, Thomas Postulate of York,

1514.

and Richard Bp. of Winton on the other, 7 Aug. 1514. Paris, 14 Sept. 1514. *Sealed and signed.*
Found in two pieces apart.
Fr. 6 Hen. VIII. p. 1, m. 1.

R. O.
Rym. xiii. 441.

2. Oath for observing the treaty of 7 Aug. 1514, made with England. *Signed.*
Fr.

R. O.
Rym. xiii. 442.

3. Notarial instrument by John Cartier and Martin Mesnart, attesting that on 14 Sept. 1514, after the celebration of mass by René de Prye and Cardinal S. Sabina, Bp. of Bayeux, in the church of the Celestines, Paris, Lewis XII. took his oath to the treaty made with England, 7 Aug. 1514. Present : François Duke of Valois, Louis de Borbon, L. d'Orleans, John Stuart Duke of Albany, Louis de Graville admiral of France, George d'Amboise Archbp. of Rouen, Ste. de Ponchier Bp. of Paris, Erard de Marche Bp. of Chartres, Humbert de Basternay, and Florimond Robertet.
Fr. 6 Hen. VIII. p. 1, m. 9.

R. O.
Rym. xiii. 443.

4. Confirmation of the treaty of marriage with the Princess Mary. Paris, 14 Sept. 1514. *Sealed and signed.*
Fr. 6 Hen. VIII. p. 1, m. 5.

R. O.
Rym. xiii 444.

5. Notarial instrument by Martin Mesnart and John Cartier, attesting that after the celebration of mass, as stated above, Lewis XII. was solemnly espoused to the Princess Mary by her proctor Charles Earl of Worcester. Present, as above.
Fr. 6 Hen. VIII. p. 1, m. 8.

R. O.
Rym. xiii. 439.

6. Bond for payment of 1,000,000 g. c. to Henry VIII. Paris, 14 Sept. 1514. *Signed and sealed.*
Fr. 6 Hen. VIII. p. 1, m. 7.

R. O.
Rym. xiii. 446.

7. Notarial instrument by Martin Mesnart and John Cartier, attesting letters of St. Ponchier, Bp. of Paris to the effect, that on 15 Sept. in a house called *Les Tournelles*, in the faubourg St. Antoine, Lewis XII. appeared before the said Bishop, and bound himself to the payment of a million of g. c. to Henry VIII., in virtue of letters obligatory concluded 7 Aug. ult., submitting to the sentence of excommunication in case of default. Present : L. d'Orleans, Humbert de Basternay, Wm. de Montmorenci, John de Selva, Fl. Robertet.

Fr. 6 Hen. VIII. p. 1, m. 16.

14 Sept. 5409.   The MARQUIS OF MANTUA to HENRY VIII.

Harl. 3,462, f. 1475.
B. M.

John Rattus has presented him the King's letter. Thanks him for the generosity shown to his servant who makes a proffer of his services. Mantua, 14 Sept. 1514.

Lat. Copy, in Italian hand, p. 1.

15 Sept. 5410.   SIR ROBERT WINGFIELD to HENRY VIII.

Vitell. B. xviii. 100.
B. M.

Thinks the Emperor defers his answer [to Wingfield's credence] till he knows the articles between Henry and the French King, so that the Prince may make direct answer to Henry [whether] he will be comprised in the said articles. The Pope has sent the copy of Henry's letter to him touching this French alliance, and desires

3 K

1514.

to have the Emperor's mandate [to concl]ude a league between the
Emperor and the King of Arragon the Duke [of] . . . . and
the Swiss for the defence of Italy, " and furthermore he hath written
that wher . . . . good hope that his holiness and the
K[ing of Arragon] should have made shortly a good pea[ce
between his majesty and the Venetians now . . . .
 . . . . . . said Venetians be . . . .
 . . . . [Em]peror's army "lyn"
a great . . . . to Pado, outside of which is the
Venetian army, not very eager to fight; for it is said that
Bartholomew Dalviane had been instructed not to "experiment" a
battle but rather to eschew it, for which order the Viceroy is not
sorry. The Venetians notwithstanding have made bridges over a
certain river and taken "a great number of great beasts." In
consequence of a scarcity of hay and straw the army has withdrawn
to Monteignyane, and the Venetians have sent letters to Uden in
Fryole and other places advertising the peace made between Henry
and France, "shewing that they be colligate in the same;" and
ordered that fires and ringing of bells should be made "for the
rejoice of the same." It is said that copies of the letters are coming
to this court, but Wingfield has seen nothing of them. [Insbrook],
15 September 1514.

Hol., mutilated, pp. 3. Addressed: The King's Grace.

15 Sept.   **5411.**   LEO X. to WOLSEY BISHOP OF LINCOLN.
R. O.   Bull, absolving him from the See of Lincoln, and authorizing his
Rym. XIII. 450.   translation to York; *non obstantibus,* &c. Rome, xvii. kl. Oct.
                          1514.

15 Sept.   **5412.**   LEO X. to WOLSEY.
Rym. XIII. 451.   Bull for his translation to the See of York; and nominating the
R. O.   Bishops of Winchester and Norwich to receive his oath. Rome,
                          xvii. kl. Oct. 1514.

15 Sept.   **5413.**   LEO X. to the BISHOPS of WINCHESTER and NORWICH.
Rym. XIII. 452.   Bull, appointing them to receive the oath of Wolsey, on his pro-
R. O.   motion to the See of York. Rome, xvii. kl. Oct. 1514.

R. O.   2. Form of the oath referred to above.
Rym. XIII. 453.

15 Sept.   **5414.**   LEO X. to WOLSEY.
R. O.   Bull, transmitting the *Pallium.* Rome, xvii. kl. Oct. 1514.
Rym. XIII. 454.

R. O.   2. Form of delivering the *Pallium.*

15 Sept.   **5415.**   LEO X. to the BISHOPS OF WINCHESTER AND NORWICH.
R. O.   Bull for investing Wolsey with the *Pallium,* according to his
Rym. XIII. 454.   petition conveyed by Andreas Gentili, a Genoese. Rome, [x]vii*
                          kl. Oct. 1514.

* vii. by mistake.

1514.

15 Sept. **5416.**   SILVESTER BP. OF WORCESTER to [WOLSEY].

Vitell. B. I. 101.
B. M.

Recommends the bearer, Franciscus de Portinariis, a Florentine clerk, visiting his brother in England.   Rome, 15 Sept. 1514. *Signed.*

Orig., Lat., p. 1.

Add. m. h. : Archiepiscopo Eboracensi.

15 Sept. **5417.**   FRANCIS MARQUIS OF MANTUA, S.R.E. Gonfalonier, to

R. O.

[SUFFOLK].   .

Has heard much of his kindness from Johannes Rattus, which is more valuable considering his influence with the King, whom the writer desires to serve. Will be glad of an opportunity of so doing. Mantua, 15 Sept. 1514.

Lat., p. 1. *Addressed:* [Meo] tanquam fratri . . . . domino Carolo [Duci Suffol]chie, etc.

16 Sept. **5418.**   RICH. SAMPSON to WOLSEY.

R. O.

After his business with Lady Margaret, as he has already written, the Deputy of Calais came to the Court. Went to Ghent, to show his letters patent to the Prince's Council, though advised not, because the people were furious ; then to the Council of the town. Found both favorable ; the latter required him to attend Monsr. de Fynys, Governor of Flanders, who promised all help to Wolsey, and sent four gentlemen to keep Sampson company with plenty of claret, &c. Came to Bruges yesterday; had an interview with the Council. Called the officers together, and shewed his powers of administration. Finds a new vicar general has been appointed by the other Bishop. If Wolsey can procure letters from the French King he will find all of them at his service. Bruges, 16 Sept. 1514.

Hol., p. 1. *Addressed :* To my Lord of York in London.

16 Sept. **5419.**   For RICHARD CAMDEN, page of the Chamber, alias late

S. B.

of London, fishmonger.

Protection for four years. *Del.* Knoll, 16 Sept. 6 Hen. VIII. *Pat.* 8 *Hen. VIII. p.* 2, *m.* 10.

16 Sept. **5420.**   For MORRES APPARRY, yeoman for the King's mouth in

S. B.

his cellar.

To be constable of the castle of Tenby, with the custody of the woods called "Coyde Raf," Pembroke. *Del.* Knoll, 16 Sept. 6 Hen. VIII.

Pat. 6 *Hen. VIII. p.* 2, *m.* 10.

16 Sept. **5421.**   For WILLIAM NELSON, M.A.

S. B.

Presentation to the church of St. Blaise the Martyr, in the marches of Calais, void by resignation of John Dent, M.A. *Del.* Knoll, 16 Sept. 6 Hen. VIII.

Pat. 6 *Hen. VIII., p.* 2, *m.* 10.

16 Sept. **5422.**   For DOROTHY VERNEY.

S. B.

Annuity of 20 marks in consideration of her services to Mary the French Queen, payable by John Heron, or any other person. *Del.* Knoll, 16 Sept. 6 Hen. VIII.

Pat. 6 *Hen. VIII. p.* 2, *m.* 10.

3 K 2

1514.

16 Sept.
P. S.

5423. For THOMAS MUSGRAVE, one of the King's spears in the retinue at Calais.

To be bailiff of the town and lordship of Penrithe, Cumb., *vice* Richard Appilby, deceased; as amply as the said Richard or William Lonkester enjoyed the same. Farnham Castle, 3 Sept. 6 Hen. VIII. *Del.* Knoll, 16 Sept.

Pat. 6 Hen. VIII., p. 2, m. 10.

18 Sept.
Calig. E. II. 135.
B. M.

5424. SAMPSON to [WOLSEY].

After coming to Bruges, "as I had [before in] Gaunt by my letters patents desired the favor and aid [of the lords] of the town, which [I found nothing favorable]; and on Sat[urday] last I called the officers of the b[ishop together], showing them both the Pope's brief and also the letters patent of my lady Margaret." They have this day demanded advice upon the matter from the Council. Thinks the French King has not kept his promise. "The bishop elect h[ath made] for all Flanders both an other vicar general and also [a] receiver," and has received the profits of the past year in France. "He had ordained his officers str[ong]ly to resist when I should come. They had ryd[ily] their a[ppel]lations made with other remedies os strong os be the law possybyll myght be mad, which this day when we assembled [they] showed expressly." If he had executed the process against them with rigor it would have caused "commotion among the people whom they had before provoked." The French King must write, charging the bishop elect not to resist Wolsey's administration. If it be referred to law Wolsey will have great trouble and no profit from it. Has given them to St. Martin's day to take counsel with the bishop elect, on condition that he do not meanwhile return to take possession. He has a dispensation for non-residence, *studii causâ.* Objections made to the brief. Bruges, 18 Sept. 1514.

Hol., pp. 2. Mutilated. The writing much decayed. Words supplied in some places from Strype's Memor, I., pt. I. pp. 15, 16.

18 Sept.
S. B.

5425. For WILLIAM HOLDEN and KATHARINE his wife, of Great Chesterford, Essex.

Licence to found a chantry for one secular chaplain in the church of All Saints, Great Chesterford, to officiate at the altar of St. Mary on the south side of the said church, for the good estate of the King and Queen, the said William and Katharine his wife, and of William Rolt, serjeant at-arms; with mortmain licence to the chaplain to acquire lands in Essex to the annual value of 10 marks. *Del.* Knoll, 18 Sept. 6 Hen. VIII.

Pat. 6 Hen. VIII. p. 2, m. 11.

S. B.

ii. Warrant to the Chancellor for alteration in the above of the words "*in com. prædicto*" (meaning Essex), to "*in com. Essex and Cantabr.*," as some of the lands to be acquired are in Cambridgeshire. Greenwich, 12 Dec. 6 Hen. VIII.

18 Sept.
P. S.

5426. For THOMAS DINGLEY.

To have the pension which the elect Abbot of Gloucester is bound to give for the exhibition of a clerk at the King's nomination,

1514.

till promoted to a competent benefice. Greenwich, 5 April 5 Hen. VIII. *Del.* Knoll, 18 Sept.

18 Sept.
P. S.

5427. For RICHARD BISHOP OF LONDON, JOHN BISHOP OF GALLIPOLI, master of the house of St. Thomas of Acon, London, JOHN COLETT, clk., Dean of St. Paul's, London, and Sir ANDREW WYNDESORE.

Grant of the goods and chattels of Edmund Dudley, attainted. Farnham, 6 Sept. 6 Hen. VIII. *Del.* Otford, 18 Sept.

Pat. 6 *Hen. VIII. p.* 1, *m.* 13.

18 Sept.

5428. For THOMAS RASOUR of Norwich, draper.

Protection; in the retinue of Sir Ric. Wyngfeld. *Del.* Otford, 18 Sept.

Fr. 6 *Hen. VIII. p.* 2, *m.* 10.

19 Sept.
Galba, B. v. 386.
B. M.

5429. SAMPSON to WOLSEY.

The bishop elect has made another vicar general for all Flanders, and received the profits till St. Thomas' day last. The expences for Tournay fall short of the profits 60*l.* or 80*l.* They have lodged an appeal to the parliament of Paris. States the custom on such occasions. Bruges, 19 Sept. 1514.

Hol., mutilated, pp. 2.
Add.: My Lord of York. *Endd.*

19 Sept.
Vitell. B. xviii. 102.
B M.

5430. SIR ROBERT WINGFIELD to HENRY VIII.

Wrote last on the [15th]. The Viceroy of Naples has dep[arted to] Verona, and requested Wingfield to apprise Henry of his desire to be of service to him. The Emperor, during his stay, treated him with good cheer, and [gave him], in silver of the mines and in other things, 3,000 florins. The Viceroy gave the Emperor pieces of velvet and satin, and the officers 500 florins. — Rode with the Cardinal of Gource and the Pope's Ambassador to an abbey a mile from hence, and heard m[ass], "met with the Viceroy which passed the . . . .; rode in company together upon a . . . . and then bade him farewell at . . . . had the words unto me abov[e said]."

As touching the con . . . . it they will at the conclu[sion] . . . . past and the Emperor's subjects . . . . determined to experiment the war," that if the Venetians will not condescend to such a peace as may be honorable to the Emperor, the Viceroy will employ the army under him against them to their ruin, and they will suffer much this summer unless the French King succour them by sending his army into the duchy of Milan. The Swiss have concluded a league with the Pope, the Florentines, and the Genoese, and are in treaty for another with the Emperor, the King of Arragon, and the Duke of Milan, which is likely to take effect. "Where the Emperor was in possession of the city of Modon, and one Veyte Fruste, kinsman to the Cardinal of Gource, governor there, so it was that in a civil [commot]ion as it is said shewed himself partial where[upon] the party grieved gathered company unbewares [of the said] Veyte, and hath taken

1514.

and doth hold . . . .   taken the governance of the
. . . . the Pope, but as . . . .
. . . ." Insbrook, [19 September], 1514.
Hol., mutilated, pp. 3. Addressed : The King's Grace. *En-dorsed :* Sir Robert Wyngfield the 14th day of September.

20 Sept.   **5431.**   DUCHY OF CORNWALL.
P. S.

Appointment of Hugh Bishop of Exeter, Sir Henry Marney,
steward of the duchy of Cornwall, Sir John Arundell, receiver
general of the same, John Turnour and Guthlac Overton, auditors,
Thomas Denys, William Lowre, John Skewis, Henry Trecarell,
Odo Goeff, James Grysy, John Tregian and Thomas Cook,
as commissioners and assessors of all the possessions in Cornwall
and Devon belonging to the said duchy.   Farnham, 2 Sept.
6 Hen. VIII.   *Del.* Knoll, 20 Sept.
Pat. 6 *Hen.VIII. p.* 2, *m.* 7*d.*

20 Sept.   **5432.**   For THOMAS JOHNS and ROBERT his son.
S. B.

To be keepers, in survivorship, of the park of Witeley, Surrey,
with herbage and pannage ; on surrender of patent 20 Sept.
12 Hen. VII., granting the office to the father alone.   *Del.* Knoll,
20 Sept. 6 Hen. VIII.
Pat. 6 *Hen.VIII. p.* 2, *m.* 11.

20 Sept.   **5433.**   .For CHARLES EARL OF WORCESTER, Chamberlain, and
S. B.   HENRY his son and.heir.

To be stewards, in survivorship, of the castle or lordship of Dynas
and Walshetalgarth, in the Marches of Wales, and constables of
Dynas castle, as Roger Vaghan lately held the same.   *Del.* Knoll,
20 Sept. 6 Hen. VIII.
Pat. 6 *Hen.VIII. p.* 1, *m.* 19.
See S. B. 29 *Nov.* 6 *Hen.VIII.*

20 Sept.   **5434.**   LAWRENCE CARDINAL S. QUATUOR to WOLSEY.
R. O.

In favor of the bearer, Francis, son of that Thomas de Portinariis, who faithfully served Henry VII., and was twice Emperor's
ambassador.   He and his brother Guido received liberal favors from
the late King, in consideration of their father's services.   He is so
in love with England, where his father and brother have been
honored, that he cannot stay in the Court of Rome.   Rome,
20 Sept. 1514.   *Signed.*
Lat., p. 1.   *Addressed :* Reverendo, &c., Tho. electo Eboracen.

21 Sept.   **5435.**   For WILLIAM RYGLEY, page of the Wardrobe of Beds.
S. B.

To be keeper of the wood and deer of the outwood called
Lynryche, Warw., as held by Thomas Wolbaston, deceased.   *Del.*
Knoll, 21 Sept. 6 Hen. VIII.
Pat. 6 *Hen. VIII. p.* 2, *m.* 12.

21 Sept.   **5436.**   For EDMUND KNYVET, serjeant doorward.
P. S.

Grant of the manor of Pontesbury, Salop, with its members
and appurtenances in Beycok, Farley, Hynton, the farms of the
lordship, and Shrewsbury, during minority of George Lord Powes.
Farnham, 8 Sept. 6 Hen. VIII.   *Del.* Knoll, 21 Sept.
Pat. 6 *Hen.VIII. p.* 2, *m.* 11.

1514.

21 Sept.
P. S.

5437. For JOHN WODEHOUSE, alias BULL, of Hornechurche, Essex, waterman.

Protection; going in the retinue of Sir Richard Wyngfelde, Deputy of Calais. Croydon, 11 Sept., 6 Hen. VIII. *Del.* Knoll, 21 Sept.

Fr. 6 *Hen. VIII. p.* 2, *m.* 10.

22 Sept.
S. B.

5438. For ALEXANDER DE LA FAVA, merchant of Bologna.

Licence to retain the customs on all goods imported or exported by him, to the amount of 1,000*l.*, for five years. *Del.* Knoll, 22 Sept. 6 Hen. VIII.

Fr. 6 *Hen. VIII. p.* 2, *m.* 11.

23 Sept.
R. O.

5439. SAMPSON to WOLSEY.

Has written to him before. Delays execution of his breve to avoid danger, but will execute it if Wolsey insists. As he has written already, thinks it would be wise if the French King's favor were secured. He is of greater authority with them than their own prince, especially as they are set against the English because of this change. The officers can meet nowhere except at Bruges and Ghent; the pestilence is so great at Tournay, the high court of the diocese is removed to Bruges. The profits of the last year are lost, except Wolsey demands them of the bishop elect. The money was paid into France at Midsummer last. Bruges, 23 Sept. 1514.

Hol., pp. 2. *Addressed:* To my Lord of York.

23 Sept.
S. B.

5440. For SIR CHRISTOPHER GARNEYS and JOAN his wife.

Grant, in fee, of the manor of Wellyngton, Salop, late belonging to Henry Lovel Lord Morley, deceased, in the King's hands by attainder of Francis Viscount Lovel; with a weekly market on Thursday in Wellyngton, and two fairs yearly, the first on the eve, day, and morrow of St. Barnabas, and the second on the day of St. Leonard, with court of pie powder, &c. ;—at the annual rent of one red rose. *Del.* Otford, 23 Sept. 6 Hen. VIII.

23 Sept.
S. B.
Rym. XIII. 448.

5441. MARRIAGE OF PRINCESS MARY.

For Thomas Duke of Norfolk, treasurer and marshal of England, Thomas Marquis of Dorset, Thomas Bishop of Durham, Thomas Earl of Surrey, Admiral of England, Charles Earl of Worcester, Lord Herbert and Gower, First Chamberlain, Thomas Docwra, prior of St. John's, and Nicholas West, LLD., dean of Windsor, to be commissioners to France in attendance on Princess Mary, the King's sister, at her marriage with Louis XII. Westm., 23 Sept. 6 Hen. VIII.

Fr. 6 *Hen. VIII. p.* 2, *m.* 11.

24 Sept.
S. B.

5442. For SIR EDWARD NEVYLL.

To be squire of the Body, in reversion, on the death or resignation of Sir Henry Guldeford, Sir William Sydney, Ralph Chamberleyn, or Richard Jernyngen; with 50 marks a year. *Del.* Knoll, 24 Sept. 6 Hen. VIII.

Pat. 6 *Hen. VIII. p.* 2, *m.* 12.

1514.

24 Sept. **5443.**   JULIUS CARDINAL DE MEDICIS to HENRY VIII.

Vitell. B. ii. 104.*
B. M.
Rym. xiii. 450.

Has completed Wolsey's cause in reference to York ; the Pope is willing that William [Attwater] be promoted to Lincoln ; Worcester will write on the subject. As they have not the necessary testimony in reference to Aghadoe and Fermoy, could make no report. Rome, 24 Sept. 1514. *Signed.*

P. 1.   *Addressed and endorsed.*

24 Sept. **5444.**   ANTONIO DE VIVALDIS to WOLSEY.

R. O.

Sends a packet of letters directed to Wolsey, which he has received by express from Rome, from Ric. Pace, to be delivered into Wolsey's hands ; on account of his absence sends them by his servant. The bankers have expedited Wolsey's bulls. Hopes they will be in England "*ante tempus mei obligi.*" London, 24 Sept. 1514.

Hol. Lat., p. 1.   *Add. :* Thomæ Lincolniensi Ep'o et electo Eboracen."

24 Sept. **5445.**   LEO X. to HENRY VIII.

R. O.

Has spoken with the Bp. of Worcester, of the matters referring to Wolsey elect of York, who will write to him more fully on the subject. The honor that he requires for Wolsey is surrounded with difficulties. It is much desired, and admits at once the wearer to the highest rank. He will comply with the King's wishes at a suitable time. Rome, 24 Sept. 1514, pont. 2.

Add.   Vellum.

24 Sept. **5446.**   SAMPSON to WOLSEY.

Galba, B. v. 331.
B. M.

All the officers of the elect who are Flemings opposed him on his arrival at Bruges, as he had already written ; and the people were so much excited that they would have attacked him had he shown any asperity, in spite of his letters from the Emperor and Lady Margaret. Was obliged therefore to conceal his intentions. On presenting the Apostolic Brief they raised their bristles, made many objections, and asked further delay, which he was forced to concede, and treat them gently to gain their good wishes. Will summon them in four days, and if he does not hear from Wolsey, will say he has received letters urging immediate proceedings. If they prosecute an appeal, it will be necessary to gain the favor of the King of France. The consequences of such a step. The farms and possessions of the bishopric are all at Tournay ; the revenues for the last year have been paid to the elect. Is, therefore, at a loss to know what to do. Had it not been so, could have prohibited payment. If he has the administration for the future, thinks he can devise a way to make it more profitable than it ever has been. Bruges, 24 Sept. 1514.

Hol., Lat., pp. 2.   *Mutilated.   Add.*

25 Sept. **5447.**   PACE to WOLSEY.

R. O.
Ellis, 3 S. i. 177.

Has written fully to Burbank of the poisoning of Cardinal Bambridge, and the process in that matter. The Pope has been inquiring about Wolsey, stating " that they did labor in England

1514.

for to make your grace cardinal." Thinks it necessary for the interest of the nation that the King should have one or two cardinals resident in Rome, as other princes have, their influence being so important in the creation of the Pope. Can inform Wolsey what persons at Rome must be won over not to impede his election. Rome, 25 Sept.

Addressed : Thomæ Ebor. Archiep.

25 Sept. **5448.** PACE to HENRY VIII.

Vitell. B. II. 102.
B. M.
Fiddes' Wolsey.
C. 253.
Ellis, 1 S. I. 108.

After the priest who murdered Cardinal Bainbridge had killed himself, it was necessary that process should be commenced against Worcester and one of his chamberlains. The judges had determined that the Bishop should be put in prison and subjected to torture. This would have been done, but Pace would not consent till he knew the King's mind. " Notwithstanding this my demeanor the said Bishop doth imagine, both in word and deed, the worst he can against me, presupposing surely to have your Grace's favor in this cause, and by that to avoid all things imputed unto him." Begs the King will determine impartially in the matter. Pace desires his honesty may appear unto all men. Was desirous of showing himself faithful to his master. Had he not endeavoured to seek out the murderers, every one might have supposed he had consented with the Bishop. Is sorely grieved that Worcester should defame the late Cardinal. " For though my late lord had (I cannot deny) some vices, I do take God to my judge, he was the most faithful man to your Grace, his prince, that ever was born, and most vehement in the defence of your Grace's causes, when none other man durst open his mouth to speak, save he alone." Pace and Worcester's proceedings are very different ; Worcester seeks to gain favor by effusion of money ; Pace desires nothing but justice. Has not deserved his malice, as he was always friendly to the Bishop until he was accused of Bainbridge's death, and found to be an enemy to England. Rome, 25 Sept.

Add.

25 Sept. **5449.** [ANDREAS AMMONIUS] to WOLSEY.

Vitell. B. II. 105.
B. M.

Could not deliver his letter in person. Sends the Bp. of Worcester's letters of the 30 Aug. and more recent letters of the 12th. Some trick has been played. The first ought to have been brought by the messenger who brought Pace's letters. Thinks this has been done by the enemies of Worcester, and that the surgeon had been suborned to say that the dead man confessed the poison. The priest was a madman. Worcester's chamberlain was pressed by many examinations, and not a scintilla of suspicion was discovered. If the Pope believed it, he never would have allowed Worcester to assist at the mass of Sancta Maria de Populo. Hadrian refused to show any joy on the occasion, saying he was the imperial protector. Great hopes of the cardinal's hat, not for the annates of Lincoln. Will explain more when he sees him. Westminster, x[xv Sept. 1514].

Hol. Lat., mutilated, p. 1. Add. : Domino Eboracensi.

25 Sept. **5450.** For SIR JOHN PETCHE, knight of the Body, and JOHN BROWNE.

S. B.

To be purveyors, in survivorship, of the manor of Eltham, with the houses and buildings in "le Storeyarde," without the gates of the said manor; as held by Edward Graveley, *temp.* Edw. IV. *Del.* Otford, 25 Sept. 6 Hen. VIII.

Pat. 6 *Hen. VIII. p.* 2, *m.* 12.

25 Sept.   **5451.**   For ELIZABETH CHAMBER.

S. B.

Annuity of 20*l.*, out of the issues of Somerset and Dorset, for services to Queen Elizabeth, the King's mother, and his sister Mary Queen of the French. *Del.* Knoll, 25 Sept. 6 Hen. VIII.

Pat. 6 *Hen. VIII. p.* 2, *m.* 12.

25 Sept.   **5452.**   For SIR GRIFFITH AP RICE.

S. B.

To be steward and receiver of the lordship of Dynnas, in the Marches of Wales ; *vice* Roger Vaughan, deceased. *Del.* Otford, 25 Sept. 6 Hen. VIII.

Pat. 6 *Hen. VIII. p.* 2, *m.* 12.

26 Sept.   **5453.**   For SIR RANULPH VERNEY, sen.

S. B.

Annuity of 50*l.* for services to Henry VII., Queen Elizabeth, Mary Queen of the French, and Margaret Queen of the Scots. The annuity to be received from the Exchequer by the hands of the treasurer and chamberlains. *Del.* Otford, 26 Sept. 6 Hen. VIII.

Pat. 6 *Hen. VIII. p.* 2, *m.* 12.

S. B.

2. To the same effect. The annuity to be received from the Exchequer by the hands of John Heron or any other receiver. Same date.

26 Sept.   **5454.**   For THOMAS MARQUIS OF DORSET.

S. B.

Grant, in tail general, of the lordship of Wyverston, Suff., with the park and advowson granted him, in tail male, by patent 20 Dec. 22 Hen. VII., on forfeiture of Edmund de la Pole Earl of Suffolk. *Del.* Westm., 26 Sept. 6 Hen. VIII.

Pat. 6 *Hen. VIII. p.* 2, *m.* 12.

27 Sept.   **5455.**   For JOHN MEAUTYS, the King's French Secretary.

P. S.

Annuity of 40 marks. Otford, 20 Sept. 6 Hen. VIII. *Del.* Knoll, 27 Sept.

Pat. 6 *Hen. VIII. p.* 1, *m.* 17.

29 Sept.   **5456.**   To the ARCHBISHOP OF CANTERBURY, Chancellor.

S. B.

For commission to persons mentioned in a bill inclosed, to inquire into the late riots in Devonshire. Bobyng, 27 Sept. *Del.* Croydon, [29 Sept.] 6 Hen. VIII.

2. COMMISSION OF THE PEACE.

Devon.—H. Bp. of Exeter, Hen. Earl of Wiltshire, Lord Fitz-war[ren], Sir Peter Eggecombe, Sir Edw. Pomerey, Lewis Pollerd, Wm. Courteney and Ric. Coffen. Croydon, 29 Sept.

Pat. 6. *Hen. VIII. p.* 2, *m.* 7d.

29 Sept.   **5457.**   LEO X. to HENRY VIII.

R. O.

Acknowledges the King's letter of thanks in the matter of the collector, which had been already finished when his last letters arrived, and letters *sub plumbo* delivered to the Bp. of Worcester,

1514.

which the Pope thinks must have reached England a few days since. Hopes the conduct of Andreas Ammonius will be satisfactory. There is no obstacle now to the King's admitting him to the free exercise of the office of collector. Rome, 29 Sept. 1514, 2 pont.

30 Sept.   **5458.**   JULIUS CARDINAL DE MEDICIS to HENRY VIII.
R. O.

The Pope is pleased at the election of Andreas Ammonius as collector. Writes in his recommendation. Rome, 30 Sept.
Lat., p. 1. *Addressed.*

30 Sept.   **5459.**   For GILES DU WES.
S. B.

Licence to import 200 tuns of Gascon wine. *Del.* Otford, 30 Sept. 6 Hen. VIII. *In margin:* Apud Lamehith.

.30 Sept.   **5460.**   For JOHN HERON, treasurer of the Chamber.
S. B.

To be keeper or clerk of the hanaper, with usual fees, as held by Roger Lupton, clk.; with annuity of 40l., and 18d. a day for his expenses when in attendance on the Chancellor. *Del.* Knoll, 30 Sept. 6 Hen. VIII.

ii. For ROGER LUPTON, clk., and JOHN HERON, treasurer of the Chamber.

Original patent granting them the above office in survivorship, in as ample manner as William Smyth, clk.   Westm., 13 June 5 Hen. VIII.
Surrendered 8 July 6 Hen. VIII.

30 Sept.   **5461.**   For HUGH WILLY and ROBERT STANSHAWE, pages of
S. B.   the Chamber.

Grant, in survivorship, of the toll in the city of Hereford, Beelthe, Elvell, and Presteyn, in the marches of Wales. *Del.* Otford, 30 Sept. 6 Hen. VIII. *In margin:* Apud Lamehith.
Pat. 6 *Hen. VIII. p.* 1, *m.* 29.

Sept.   **5462.**   LEWIS XII. to WOLSEY.
Calig. D. vi. 141.
B. M.
Rym. xiii. 455.

Has received his letter conveying the good feelings of Henry VIII. There is no alliance on which he sets such value. Thanks him for the trouble taken by him in the apparel of the Queen, as Marigny and Jehan de Paris have written. Is very anxious to see her, and will be glad to have these preparations abridged. Is contented he shall retain for a time Marigny and De Paris to assist in arranging her apparel *à la mode de France.* Begs Wolsey will convey in reply to the kind expressions of Marie that the writer is quite as desirous of her presence as she can be of his. Has seen Wolsey's letter to Longueville, and told him what answer he shall make. Begs to hear frequently from him. Paris, — Sept. *Signed.*
Fr., pp. 2, *mutilated.*

Sept.   **5463.**   MARY OF FRANCE to MONSIEUR [LEWIS XII.]
Vitell. C. xi. f. 156b.
B. M.
Ellis 1 S. i. 113.

Has received his very affectionate letters by the Bishop of Lincoln. There is nothing she so much desires as to see him. Her brother the King uses all diligence to hasten her departure, which will take place shortly. . Wishes to hear from him.
Hol. Fr.

5464.   [Silvester Bishop of Worcester] to [Ammonius].

R. O.

Begs to be commended to my lord of York [Wolsey], for whose constant favor he is grateful. The Pope has great hopes of Wolsey's effecting a peace between the French King and the Duke of Milan. He can do nothing more pleasing to the Pope, or more worthy of himself; and shall have the 20,000 crowns already written of, if he can effect it. The Pope was about to send him a small present, in the name of the Duke of Milan, worth 1,000 crowns, but the writer told him it would be difficult to transmit it, and secretly impossible. The money will therefore be sent to the person addressed, to purchase what he knows will be most pleasing to Wolsey. Touching the annates of the see of Lincoln, besides those 1,000 ducats which the Pope remitted, they have at length extorted another 1,000 from the College, after much opposition of the Cardinals; especially from Hadrian, who speaks much evil of Wolsey, conceiving that Wolsey has opposed him in the collectorship. When he saw they would get the remission, he bought over witnesses to affirm that he had been working hard for Wolsey in the affair; which would be very true if that "*pro*" were turned into "*contra*." The money cannot be sent thither without loss by exchange. Wolsey may be able to find some persons in England who would pay it and receive it here. Joannes Campuccius will secure them.

Sends the inventory of the goods he had received from Pace for Wolsey. Wishes to know what is to be done. Is urgent for the cardinal's hat. His Holiness is naturally slow. Will not create Wolsey a cardinal alone now, nor yet with those whom he promised before. Offers him a bull of promotion, on condition he will not carry the insignia publicly. Letters should be written to the Pope and the Cardinal de Medicis. The Pope is very glad that the French King has promised Wolsey the resignation of the bishopric of Tournay. The Pope assents to the commendam against the Lateran. Advises Wolsey, however, not to expedite his bulls till he gets the hat, which will save him some thousands. Will send shortly the bull declaring his (Worcester's) innocence. Has forgiven Pace as desired. Has received his correspondent's letter touching Wolsey's pleasure in this matter.

Endorsed: Rev'mo D'no Eborum referenda. *Lat., pp.* 3. *In the hand of Ammonius.*

Sept.   **5465.**   Wolsey [to the Bishop of Worcester.]

R. O.

Thanks him for the great pains to which he is put in expediting Wolsey's bulls and his diligent solicitation with the Pope for the cardinalate, which at the King's desire and his lordship's mediation has been promised at the next creation. Begs he will thank his Holiness, and there is nothing he shall desire that Wolsey will not be willing to serve him. Knows not how he shall recompense his lordship, and will in all respects advance his honor and profit. Is glad to hear of his honorable acquittal in the slander of great malice laid to his charge, as much as if it had been himself; "and with like ardent mind shall I persecute those that thus maliciously hath accused you as though they had semblably laid the same thing to my charge, and as I have more at the large showed to Mr. Andreas, pursue them for their punishment." Will not fail to do his part to the King "in such wise that all the world shall take en-

1514.

sample how to enfame the King's ambassador and orator." Andreas
will inform him of the King's letters. Will be glad to know what
he can do for him. "And if by your politic handling the Pope can
be induced shortly to make me a cardinal ye shall singularly content and please the King ; for I cannot express how desirous the
King is to have me advanced to the said honor to the intent that
not only men might thereby perceive how much the Pope favoreth
the King and such as he entirely loveth, but also that thereby I
shall be the more able to do his grace service." Desires Worcester to
inquire privately if the French King has used his influence with the
Pope in this behalf as he has frequently promised, though he had
much rather obtain it by the influence of the King and Worcester.
Commits the rest to Worcester's discreet handling. Knows he has
done his best for the expedition of the bulls and remission of the
annates. Is grateful for the remission of 1,000 ducats procured by
Worcester ; howbeit every one thinks it strange that two annates in
one year should be demanded of one bishopric against both law and
custom. Hopes the Pope and cardinals will make restitution when
they perceive that he has received no more of Lincoln than is mentioned in the instruments lately sent to Worcester. "Some men
that loveth you not here be very glad that I am thus dealt with."
Andreas will write to him Wolsey's mind touching the Duke of
Milan's affairs. Desires Worcester to get the Pope to sequester
Bainbridge's goods now in the custody of Richard Paxe, levy as
much money as may be made thereon and send the proceeds to Wolsey. Worcester is quite at liberty, without breach of the King's
laws, to send a citation into England against Mr. Clerke now on
his way thither, "one of the most malicious conspirators against
you." He may also rely on the assistance of the King and Wolsey
in prosecuting all who malign him. "From my place besides Westminster, the, &c."

Draft in Wolsey's hand, pp. 3.

1 Oct.   **5466.** MAXIMILIAN EMPEROR ELECT.
Rym. xiii. 456.
Letters patent for including Charles Prince of Spain in the treaty
of London, 7 Aug. 1514. Inspruck, 1 Oct. 1514.
Fr. 6 Hen. VIII. p. 2, m. 24.

2 Oct.   **5467.** SIR RICH. WINGFIELD to WOLSEY.
R. O.
Received a letter yesterday from Sampson, that the patents he
obtained from the Archduchess in Wolsey's cause were not so
special as needed. Wishes that Wolsey would procure more
stringent ones to be published in Ghent. The French King sup-
ports the adverse party. Thinks Wolsey should obtain letters from
the King desiring him to desist. Has written many letters of late,
requesting the King's licence to return to Calais. Fears Wolsey has
been too much occupied to attend to them. Brussels, 2 Oct.
Hol., pp. 2. To my Lord the elect Abp. of York.

3 Oct.   **5468.** C. EARL OF WORCESTER and others to [WOLSEY].
Calig. D. vi. 198.
B. M.
Ellis, 2 S. i. 233.
According to Wolsey's last letter, dated at Sittingbourne, 17 Sept.,
had this day a long audience with the King ; shewed him of the
ambassador of Arong's (Arragon's) proposal, and the King's answer;

which answer greatly pleased him, and he bade Worcester assure the King that he would make a similar one to the King of Arragon himself, " as he had showed my fellows and me before; and in like manner to the Emperor and the Prince of Castile whensoever they send to him, as he is credibly informed that they will shortly do. And he swore by the God that he believed on, that he would nowder meddle nor enter in league, by way of marriage or otherwise, with any prince living, till he had spoken with the King, my master, and had his advice and counsel in the same." If this would not satisfy Henry, " he would make him any bond he would, but his word should be as sure as any bond in the world." The King of Arragon had " sent him a blank seal to put in w[riting what he w]ould, and he sent it him again, and answered, tha[t he would n]ot meddle with him but as is aforesaid." He, moreover, repeated three times that whatever the King would have, to which he is entitled by the treaty, he should have [it], and as many more if it be his pleasure; also, that Henry should appoint as chief leader and ca[ptain] whom he would, either in England or in France, and he that would disobey him should die a shameful death; and while he lived he should do nothing to Henry's prejudice. " My Lord, I assure you this word he spake as heartily as ever I saw any man speak."

He then desired to know " wh[ere] the King's grace and he should see and speak together," and would not go further than Paris, or 10 leagues about, till he knew. " I answered him [as my] fellows and I had answered before; but [he desired] me that I would write to the King his [brother] what time that he would appoint." As far as the writer can see, he wished it to be in Picardy, or between Boulogne and Calais, or in Normandy. As to Jane Popyncourt, Worcester would have showed him the bills signed, but he would hear no more of her, and said he wished she were brente, for Worcester and his fellows had shown him enough of her evil life; " that there should never man nor woman be about his wife, but such as should be at her contentation;" and that he had only spoken for Jane at the suit of Lord Longevile, as he told Worcester and his fellows before; " for he told him that the Queen loved and trusted her above all the gentlewomen about her; but if the King made her to be brent," he should think it a good deed. " My lord, I assure you he hath a [marvel]lous mind to content and please the Queen, and [above all] when he heard of her landing which was this m[orning]. There is nothing can displease him, and [he has provided jewels]and goodly gear for her. There was in his ch[amber the Archbishop] of Paris, Robertett, and the general, and I ; where [he showed] me the goodliest and the richest sight of jewels [that ever] I saw. I would never have believed it if I had not seen [it]." The writer particularly mentions 56 diamonds and rubies and 7 great pearls. The worst of the second sort of stones were valued at 200 ducats, and for 10 of the principal 100,000 ducats had been refused. All, the King said, was for her ; " but merely (merrily) laughing [he said], My wife shall not have all at once, but at divers [times], for he would have many and at divers times kisses and thanks for them. I assure you he thinketh every [hour] a day till he seeth her. He is never well but [when he] heareth speak of her. I make no doubt [she will have] a good life with him by the grace of God."

Worcester having showed him Wolsey's ma[tter] (*i.e.* of Tournay), he said, " that the letter that was sent [was] unknowing to him, and so said Robertett before me ; but at Paris it was made by the

1514.

counsel and avise of the parliament for the maintaining of his right of his sovereignty of Flanders, and his mind was nor never shall be, to do that thing that should be to your hurt and displeasure, but do that in him is to do you honor and profit ; and that if God give him life ye shall know, for he reputes you for one of his special loving friends, and desireth you to take no displeasure of that letter." He would even make the elect leave all his title and right to Wolsey, for the matter is yet in his hands. " And therewith toke me by the hand, being present Robertett and the general, and said that he knew well that I loved you; therefore he put the matter in my hands. If I would say that ye would have it, ye should have it, and bade me do therein as I would, for so it should be." Worcester heartily thanked him in Wolsey's name, and promised to advertise the latter thereof, when the French King added that he would write him a letter which Worcester should send ; " but he in no wise woll w[rite] to my lady, for he saith he will not w[rite] to her, who, he knoweth, loveth him not." Desires Wolsey's instructions how to proceed. Abbeville, 3 Oct.

As he was about to close the letter the general brought him a letter to send to Wolsey, which is annexed to this. Also Robertet sent him word that the King's letter and one of his own were despatched separately to Mareny bailly of Senly[s].

Hol., mutilated, pp. 6.

3 Oct. **5469.** MARIGNY to WOLSEY.

Calig. E. 1. 79.
B. M.

No sooner had he arrived with the Queen his sovereign than he sent notice of it to the King, who is extremely happy to hear it. Hopes they will be together on Sunday next ([*di*]*menche prochain*"). Is ordered not to leave the Queen. "*La peste est ycy.*" The King and Robertet have written to Wolsey on the subject of their communication. Boullougne, . . Oct.

Hol., Fr., mutilated, p. 1. Addressed.

4 Oct. **5470.** PET. MARTYR to LUD. FURTADO.

Epist. 541.

Selim Shah and the Sophi of Persia.—Ferdinand has left the court, and gone to hunt. News has come from France that King Lewis is at Abbeville waiting for his new bride, who will be his death. What an old valetudinarian, suffering from leprosy (*elephantia gravatus*), can want with a handsome girl of 18 his correspondent may infer, and what the French think of it. Valladolid, iv. non. Oct. 1514.

4 Oct. **5471.** For THOMAS VOWELL, late of Ringwood, Hants, alias of
S. B.
Vowelles Comme, Devon.

Pardon. *Del.* Westm., 4 Oct.

Pat. 6 *Hen. VIII. p.* 1, *m.* 30.

4 Oct. **5472.** For JAMES HYET of London.
P. S.

Protection ; going in the retinue of Sir Richard Wyngfelde, Deputy of Calais. Otford, 25 Sept. 6 Hen. VIII. *Del.* Westm., 4 Oct.

Fr. 6 *Hen. VIII. p.* 2, *m.* 10.

1514.

4 Oct.
P. S.

5473. For RICHARD SHATFORD of London, grocer.

Protection ; going in the retinue of Sir Richard Wyngfeld, Deputy of Calais. Dover, 29 Sept. 6 Hen. VIII. *Del. Westm.*, 4 Oct.

Fr. 6 Hen. VIII. p. 2, m. 10.

6 Oct.
S. B.

4754. COMMISSION OF THE PEACE.

Cornwall. — Roger Arundel, Peter Bevile, John Arundel of Talverne, Hen. Trecarell, John Scuysshe, Ric. Penros, Wm. Carnesewe and Wm. Lowre. *Del.* Westm., 6 Oct. 6 Hen. VIII.

Pat. 6 Hen. VIII. p. 1, m. 13d.

6 Oct.
R. O.

5475. SIR ROB. WINGFIELD to the COUNCIL.

Begs he will send an answer to his request by his nephew, John Brewce, the bearer. On 18 Oct. 1513, he left England for Ypres in Flanders to meet the Emperor, and received by his brother, Sir Richard, 200*l.*, all of which he had spent last May. Has since lived by borrowing " to my great unhartisease." Has frequently written to desire money and his discharge. Heard from Brian Tuke in June last that he had received 200*l.* for Wingfield from Sir John Daucy, and in August he had paid it into the bank of Spynully, and would send the bill of exchange to Sir Thos. Spinelly. Has never received it, and is greatly annoyed. Has been more than 4½ years the King's ambassador. By the death of Edmund de la Pole he has forborne the chief thing, and all that he had to serve the King with, " as well of the King his father's gift as of his." The office of high marshal at Calais has been occupied in his name a whole year without profit to himself. Innsbrook, 6 Oct. 1514.

Pp. 3.

7 Oct.
S. B.

5476. COMMISSION OF THE PEACE.

Lincolnshire.—Wm. Lord Willoughby, Sir Wm. Tirwhitt, Sir John Skipwith, Sir Thos. Borough, Sir Lionel Dymmok, Thos. Willughby, Geo. Fitzwilliam, John Hennege, Edw. Forman, Geoffrey Panell, John Robynson, Wm. Disney, Thos. Barmeston, John Toppliff and Thos. Mysseldyn. *Del.* Westm., 7 Oct. 6 Hen. VIII. *Pat.* 6 Hen. VIII. p. 1, m. 13d.

7 Oct.
Calig. B. II. 35.
B. M.

5477. NORFOLK to WOLSEY.

Yestereven, after Sir John Peche and Sir John Carr had delivered the King's letters to the Duke of Bretagne (Francis), and showed their credence, they returned and told Norfolk his answer that he was the Queen's servant, and no man more desirous to do her honor, and had undertaken this enterprise to serve, "unknat (and not ?) command nor alter or defer any time of doing of the said enterprise from the time appointed of her entry into Paris, albeit the herald had anything done to the contrary and old custom of the realm of France," which concerned the preparations made for the meeting by a great number of answerers and noble persons. Also that he had heard of the King's active courage in feats of arms, and if there were to be a meeting between the two Kings, or if he were commanded to wait upon Henry, he would be glad to do him service. Nothing is done by the French

1514.

King but the Duke is privy to it. The King writes to him daily as ruler for him, as Norfolk finds by the dealing of Robertet. The Duke remits to the French King's pleasure the question of deferring or not. Thinks this great triumph in her honor should not be delayed by England, "and the yit rawnes of the preparation of ours." Had never greater difficulty in finding leisure to write. Montreuil, 7 Oct. *Signed.*

P.S.—"My Lord, I assure you this Prince can speak well and wisely."

Hol., p. 1. Addressed : To my Lord of York.

Many of the expressions in this letter are very obscure.

---

7 Oct.
S. B.

5478. For THOMAS BESTON, page of the Chamber, and JOHN PATE, page of the Wardrobe of Beds.

To be bailiffs, in survivorship, of the lordship of Hanley, and keepers of the park of Blakemore, Worc., as held by Erean Brereton. *Del.* Westm., 7 Oct. 6 Hen. VIII.

Pat. 6 Hen. VIII. p. 1, m. 13.

---

8 Oct.
Rym. XIII. 457.
Rym. ib. 458.

5479. CHARLES PRINCE of CASTILE.

Confirmation of the treaty of London. Brussels, 8 Oct. 1514.

ii. Confirmation of the same by Margaret of Savoy. Same date.

Fr. 6 Hen. VIII. p. 2, m. 24.

---

8 Oct.
R. O.
Rym. XIII. 459.

5480. LEWIS XII.

Letters patent, stating that, in conformity with his agreement to give as a large dower to his beloved consort Marie, as was held by Ann late Queen of France, he endows her by these presents with the town and castlery of Caynone and its apurtenances, the cc. of Saintonge, de Pezenas, de Rupe Maura, &c., with all their rights. Abbeville, 8 Oct. 1514. *Signed and sealed.*

Fr. 6 Hen. VIII. p. 2, m. 19.

---

9 Oct.

5481. For RIC. BALDOK of Charyng, Kent, husbandman.

Reversal of outlawry ; sued for debt by Thos. Chamber. Westm., 9 Oct.

Pat. 6 Hen. VIII. p. 2, m. 28d.

Leland's Coll. II.
ii. p. 704.

5482. MARRIAGE OF PRINCESS MARY.

Names of the Englishmen which were sent in ambassade to the French King, before the Queen's landing, and other gentlemen in their company :—The Earl of Worcester, Lord Chamberlain ; the Lord of St. John's, Tho. Docwra ; and the Dean of Windsor, Doctor West. ambassadors ;—the Lord Herbert, son of the Earl of Worcester ; Sir John Savage ; Sir ———— ; Sir Christopher Garneys ; Sir ———— ; Clarenceux King of Arms.

2. The names of the Lords and other Noblemen of France being at the said marriage :—

The Duke of Valois and Bretagne—The Duke of Alençon—The son of the King Don Frederic of Naples—The Earl of Vendôme—

3 L

1514.

The Duke of Longueville—The Prince de la Roche Suryon—The Duke of Albany—The Earl of St. Poll — The Earl of Guise, brother to the Duke of Lorraine—Louis Monsieur, brother to the Earl of Nevers—The Earl of Roussy—The Lord of Lautrec—The Earl of Sancerre—The Lord de Lespar—The Earl Manfroy—The Lord de la Palice, Grand Maistre de France — The Earl Galiace de Saint Severin, Grand Esquire—The Earl of Alexandrie —The Earl of Maleverer, Grand Seneschal of Normandy—Le Sr. de Graville, Admiral—Le Sr. de Monmorancy, Premier Baron Chamb. — Le Sr. de Testeville— Le Sr. de la Tremoille — Le Prince de Talmon, son fils—Le Sr. de Pieunes, Lieutenant de Picardie—Le Sr. de Bouchaige Chambrelan—Le Sr. de Dourriers —Le Sr. de Chesnes—Le Sr. Daubigny—Le Vidame D'Amiens—Le Sr. de Boysy—Monsieur de Bonyvet—Le Vidame de Chartres —Monsieur de Fou—Monsieur de Cursoll—Monsieur de Wansay—Monsieur Louis D'Ars—Le Sr. du Pont de Remy—Les trois Generaux de France, viz., Normandie, Languedoie, Languedoc—Monsieur de Beaudiner—Mons. de Gynry—Mons. de Rouville, Grand Veneur—Mons. Denebatt, Capp^ne des Toilles—Monsieur de Boucheron.

9 Oct.   **5483.**   MARRIAGE OF PRINCESS MARY.

Leland's Coll. II.
ii. p. 701.

The names of the lords and gentlemen of England being at the marriage of the Right Excellent Princess the Lady Mary :—The Duke of Norfolk, my Lady his wife, the Countess of Oxford, and the Lord Edmund Howard—The Marquis of Dorset, my Lady his wife, and the Lord Edward his brother—The Lord Thomas Rowthall Bishop of Durham—The Earl of Surrey, son and heir to the Duke of Norfolk—The Lord Lawarre—The Lord Berners, chamberlain to the French Queen—The Lord Montaigle and my Lady his wife—The Lord Richard Grey, The Lord John Grey, The Lord Leonard Grey, brethren to my Lord Marquis—Sir Nicholas Vaux, Sir David Owen, Sir Andrew Windsor, Sir John Husee, Sir John Peche, and Sir Henry Wyot, Bannerets.— Sir Morice Berkeley, Sir Wm. Sandes, Sir John Hungerford, Sir Robert Drury, Sir Tho. Botrym, Sir Philipp Calthorp, Sir Thomas Clynton, Sir Robert Cotton, Sir John Heydon, Sir John Carre, Sir Edward Greville, Sir Will. Essex, Sir Philip Tylney, Sir Nicholas Applyard, Sir Edward Bensted, Sir Will. Rows, and Sir John Wallop, Knights.—John Broughton, Rich. Weston, Giles Strangways, Tho. Cheyney, Ralph Chamberlain, Rich. Blont, Gerard Danet, and Robert Jonys, Esquires.—Garter Principal King of Arms, and his four servants, Thomas Pawlet, —— Manners, George Cobham, and Anthony Saintliger.—Richmond Herald.—John Myclow with 50 officers of the King's Household servants that were officers with the French Queen.—Hen. Webb, gentleman usher.—Tho. Rushe and Ambrose . . . . . . , serjeants at arms.

The names of the Ladies and gentlewomen being at the said marriage :—The Duchess of Norfolk, and in her company the Countess of Oxford, her daughter—The Marquise of Dorset.

Gentlewomen which were appointed to have abidden in France with the French Queen :—Dame —— Guylford, lady of honor, . Lady Elizabeth Grey, Eliz. Ferrys, M. Ann Devereux, M. Boleyne, M. Wotton,—— Grey of Wilton, Alice Denys and Anne Ferningham (Jerningham ?), chamberers.—Dr. Denton, almoner, Mr. Palgrave, secretary—chaplains.

1514.

Vitell. C. xi.155. **5484.** MARY QUEEN OF FRANCE.

B. M.
Lett. de Rois, ii.547.
(Documents Inédits.)

Names of the gentlemen and ladies retained by the King (Lewis XII.) to do service to the Queen, viz. :—

"Le conte de Nonshere," Dr. Denton, almoner, Sir Richard Blount, "escuyer descuyerie," the sons of Lords Roos, Cobham, and Seymour, "enfans d'honneur ;" Evrard, brother of the Marquis, Arthur Polle, brother of Lord Montague, Le Poulayn, "pannetiers échansons et valetz trenchans ;" Francis Buddis, usher of the chamber, Maistre Guillaume, physician, Henry Calais, "varlet des robes," Rob. Wast. Mesdemoiselles Grey (sister of the Marquis), Mary Finis (sister of Lord Dacres), Elizabeth, sister of Lord Grey, Madamoyselle Boleyne, Maistres Anne Jenyngham, "femme de chambre," and Jeanne Barnesse, "chamberiere."

Fr. Signed by Lewis XII.

9 Oct. **5485.** For SIR RICHARD WHETEHILL.

S. B.

Annuity of 40 marks. *Del.* Westm., 9 Oct. 6 Hen. VIII.

9 Oct. **5486.** For GUY PORTINORI.

S. B.

Licence to retain the customs on all goods imported and exported by him, to the amount of 2,000*l.*, for five years. *Del.* Westm., 9 Oct. 6 Hen. VIII.

11 Oct. **5487.** For OSWALD FORSTER, chaplain.

P. S.

Presentation to the church of Froyton, in the Marches of Calais, Canterbury dioc., void by death. Otford, 5 Oct. 6 Hen. VIII. *Del.* Westm., 11 Oct.

12 Oct. **5488.** MARY QUEEN OF FRANCE to HENRY VIII.

Calig. D. vi. 253.
Ellis, 1 S., i. 115.
B. M.

Marvels she has not heard from him since her departure. She is now left "post alone." "On the morn next after my marriage my chamberlain, with all other men servants, were discharged, [an]d likewise my mother Guldeford, with other my women and maidens, except such as never had experience nor knowledge how to advertise or give me counsel in any time of need, which is to be feared more shortly than your grace thought at the time of my departing, as my mother Guldeford can more plainly show your grace than I can write." Begs credence for her, and desires her return. "I marvel much that my Lord of Norfolk wold at all times so lightly grant everything at their requests here. I am well assured that when ye know the truth of everything, as my mother Guldeford can show you, ye wold full little have thought I should have been thus intreated. Would God my Lord of Zorke had come with me in the room of my Lord of Norfolk, for [the]n am I sure I should have been left much more at my heart's [ease] than I am now." [Ab]bevile, 12 Oct.

P.S., *in Mary's own hand*, repeating her request to Henry to give credence to her mother Guldeford. *Signed.*

Addressed : To the Kynges Grace, my kynd and lovynge brother.

Mutilated, p. 1.

12 Oct. **5489.** MARY OF FRANCE to WOLSEY.

Calig. D. vi. 143.
B. M.
Ellis, 1 S. i. 117.

Complains of her servants having been discharged the morning after her marriage ; among the rest her "mother Guldeford," whom the King and Wolsey advised her always to consult. No attention

1514.

was paid to Mary's urgent request that she should remain. Has many other discomforts besides. Begs Wolsey will find the means to have her sent back. "I had as lief lose the winning I shall have in France as to lose her counsel when I shall lack it ; which is not like long to be required, as I am sure the noblemen and gentiemen can show you more than becometh me to write in this matter." Is dissatisfied with Norfolk. [Abbev]ile, 12 Oct.

Add. : To my loving friend the Abp. of Zorke.

12 Oct. **5490.** MARY QUEEN OF FRANCE.

R. T. 137.
R. O.

1. An inventory of the jewellery, gold and silver plate, for the chapel, buffets and kitchen of the Princess Mary, delivered to Lewis XII., in presence of Thos. Bohier, Jacques de Beaume, and Henry Bohier, by Sir Henry Wyat, master of the jewel-house, made in the town of Abbeville, 10 and 11 Oct. 1514.

Among the plate mentioned are several silver gilt images of St. Thomas of Canterbury, St. Katharine, and other saints, a silver-gilt mirror, garnished with H. and R., and red roses.

Fr., pp. 6.

2. List of the furniture for the chapel, dresses, linen, tapestries, belonging to the Princess Mary, delivered to Lewis XII. by Sir Andrew Windsor, master of the Wardrobe, before the same witnesses, made at Abbeville, 11 and 12 Oct. 1514.

Fr., pp. 8.

3. Inventory of the horses, carriages, and their furniture, Abbeville, 12 Oct., 1514.

Fr., pp. 2.

5491. WARDROBE of MARY QUEEN OF FRANCE.

R. O.

i. " Apparel devised for the French Queen.
"Gowns devised for the French Queen, of the French fashion.
"Gowns after Milan fashion.
"Gowns after the English fashion.
"Jackets for her footmen.
"Jackets for the second sort.
"Jackets of the third sort.
"For the closet."
Pp. 7.

R. O.

ii. A list of parcels of plate delivered to the French Queen's use; apparently before her marriage.
Pp. 5. *Headed, in a different hand,* 1515. *Endd. :* Amadas' bill.

. § i. and § ii. found apart.

12 Oct. **5492.** The WARDROBE of MARY QUEEN OF FRANCE.

Vitell. C. xi. f. 158.
B. M.

1. Robes of the English fashion. 2. Petticoats of do. 3. Robes of the Milanese fashion. 4. Bonnets of do. 5. Esquillettes of do. 6. Manteaux and hoods. 7. Scabelles. 8. Waggons and chests. 9. Bedding and furniture. 10. Curtains, chairs, &c. 11. Pillows and cushions. 12. Sheets and coverlets. 13. Irish frieze. 14. Tapestry. 15. Cords, &c., for do.

Signed at Abbeville, 12 Oct. 1514, by T. Bohier, A. de Beaune, H. Bohier. *Four leaves of vellum.*

1514.

12 Oct. **5493.** To the SHERIFFS of LONDON and MIDDLESEX.
Harl. 422. f. 29. For proclamations forbidding the giving and receiving of liveries,
B. M. as leading to murders and other crimes. Westm., 12 Oct.
6 Hen. VIII.

12 Oct. **5494.** For HENRY CALAIS.
S. B. Grant, in reversion, of a corrody in the monastery of Tavestok,
on death or resignation of Anthony Lygh, clerk of the kitchen
to Henry VII. *Del.* Westm. 12 Oct. 6 Hen. VIII.

13 Oct. **5495.** C. EARL OF WORCESTER, NICHOLAS WEST [and SIR
Calig. D. vi. 199. RIC. WINGFIELD?] to HENRY VIII.
B. M. [*One or more leaves lost at the beginning.*] ["he g]af us right
Ellis, 2 S. i. 239. hearty thanks, saying that we did him the most singular pleasure
that we could do ; and so we departed for that night, for it was somewhat late.—Item, the said Monday in the morning all thing was
performed according to the said appointment, and the matrimony
was solemnized by the Cardinal of ———— (*blank in MS.*) which
sung the high mass. The Queen that day kept her state apart in a
chamber, with certain princesses at her table end, and all the
ambassadors dined in a chamber with the Duke of Bretaigne ; the
residue of the lords, ladies, and gentleman dined in the great
chamber. And that same day the King gave her a marvellous
great pointed diamond, with a ruby almost two inches long, without
foil, which was esteemed by some men at 10,000 marks." On
Tuesday the King gave her a ruby, and the writers dined with the
aforesaid Duke of Bretayn at his lodging, who after dinner took
them apart, and showed them his good mind to the King and the
Queen his sister, as they had written in former communications,
"with so good words and so hearty affection that it moved all
hearers, as we dou[bt] not but the lords at their coming hom[e will
show your] grace. For he desired them that sithens [the Duke
of] Angolesme might not come to your presence to bey[re the earl]
of Angolesme's heart to you, which he said should [be yours] during
his life, and ye should never make war with [any] prince christened,
but if his master would give him leave he would be at your grace's
commandment with all h[is] power, with many other good and
hearty words."
At afternoon they went to the court, and had an interview
with the council touching the matters they had in charge, and
concerning the delivery of jewels and plate, as also to know
the state of the Queen and the household she should be allowed ;
on which matters they promised to speak with the King, and
return an answer next day, Wednesday. On Wednesday the King
gave the Queen a great diamond, and a tablet with a great round
pearl, &c. The writers dined with the D[uke] of Alansen, and
had another interview with the council, the effect of which the
lords will report. The council told them the King would leave
next day, Thursday ; "and so he showed us himself." Doubts
having arisen whether they were at liberty by their instructions to
go further than Abbeville, or had any special command to solicit
the speedy coronation of the Queen, they consulted the Duke of
Norfolk and other of the King's council, who advised them to do
according to the King's former commandment, and that the clause
about returning from Abbeville did not apply to them, but to those
who came at that time with the Queen. "Item, this Friday my

1514.
-

Lord of Norfolk and o[ther] lords and gentlemen depart from this town towards your highness. The French King maketh sembl[ance] as he would depart every day, but yet he lieth still, ever excusing him by his gout. The Queen is continually with him, of whom he maketh as mu[ch], as she reporteth to us herself, as it is possible for any man to make of a lady." Abbeville, 13 Oct.

Pp. 4. *Mutilated, signatures half burnt off.*

13 Oct. **5496.** SILVESTER BP. OF WORCESTER to WOLSEY and FOX.

Vitell. B. п. 105.
B. M.

In reply to their letter of 8 Aug., has shown to the Pope the obligation for 1,000,000 scudi, and the terms of the peace. He wishes to know what arrangement has been made with the Emperor. He is glad to hear that the King is going to send an embassy to the Lateran Council, but is sorry that the Earl of " Suerosberi," who is one of them, is taken ill. The first session will be about the middle of November. Rome, 13 Oct. 1514. *Signed.*

Lat., mutilated.
Add. : Tho. Archiep. Ebor. et R. Ep. Winton.

13 Oct. **5497.** LEWIS XII.

R. O.
Rym. xiii. 462.

Letters of acquittance, on the delivery of Marie Queen of France, with her jewels, furniture, &c., of the 400,000 g. c. promised as her dower by Henry VIII., provided that, in case of restitution, the King and his heirs shall only be bound to restore what she brought with her into France, with the expences of her passage. *Signed :* Abbeville, 13 Oct. 1514.

13 Oct. **5498.** For ROGER DARLAY, clk.

S. B.

Presentation to the church of Scrayngham, York dioc., void by death. *Del.* Westm., 13 Oct. 6 Hen. VIII.

14 Oct. **5499.** For JOHN HUNT, chief cook for the King's mouth.

S. B.

Exemption from serving on juries, &c. *Del.* Westm., 14 Oct. 6 Hen. VIII.

Pat. 6 Hen. VIII. p. 1, *m.* 11.

15 Oct. **5500.** HENRY VIII. to GEORGE DUKE OF SAXONY.

R. T. 137.
R. O.

Has received his letters and credence relative to the Duke of Gueldres and Count of Embden, to the effect that the latter was not included in the treaty between England and France. He may be sure that the King will do nothing prejudicial to his amity with the Duke, or favor the Duke's enemies. If he wishes to be comprehended specially in the league between England and France, the King will use his efforts to obtain the consent of the latter. Greenwich, 15 Oct. 1514.

Lat., p. 1.

15 Oct. **5501.** For ROGER ALFORD, yeoman of the Crown.

S. B.

Annuity of 10 marks, out of the issues of the lordship of Denbigh, N. Wales ; held by William Eyton deceased. *Del.* Westm., 15 Oct. 6 Hen. VIII.

Pat. 6 Hen. VIII. p. 2, *m.* 21.

·1514.

16 Oct.
S. B.

5502. For WALTER AP RICE, draper alias vintner of London.

Protection ; going in the suite of Sir Richard Wyngefelde, Deputy of Calais. *Del.* Westm., 16 Oct. 6 Hen. VIII.

17 Oct.

5503. COMMISSION OF THE PEACE.

Yorkshire.—Hen. Earl of Northumberland, Ric. Nevell Lord Lati[mer], Ric. Rokeby, Thos. Hall and Wm. Elson. Westm., 17 Oct.

Pat. 6 *Hen. VIII. p.* 1, *m.* 11d.

17 Oct.
P. S.

5504. For JOHN GYLMYN.

To be marshal of the King's minstrels, with 4½d. a day, and 10 marks a year, *vice* John Chambre. Eltham, 15 Oct. 6 Hen. VIII. *Del.* Westm., 17 Oct.

Pat. 6 *Hen. VIII. p.* 1, *m.* 10.

18 Oct.
R. O.

5505. MARY QUEEN OF FRANCE to HENRY VIII.

The King desires that he will send to my Lord Darcy to deliver François Descars on a reasonable ransom. Had promised the Duke of Britanny, otherwise called the Dauphin, whose servant he is, and the Duke of Longueville, to write in his behalf. The Duke made her great cheer from Boulogne, as the Duke of Norfolk, the Lord Marquis, and others, can inform the King. Abbeville, 18 Oct. *Signed.*

P. 1. *Addressed. Endorsed by Wolsey* (?): The French Queen's letter and my Lord of Suffolk.

18 Oct.

5506. COMMISSIONS OF THE PEACE.

Staffordshire.—G. Bp. of Coventry and Lichfield, Edward Duke of Buckingham, Thos. Marquis of Dorset, Geo. Earl of Shrewsbury, Edw. Sutton Lord Dudley, Wm. Blount Lord Mountjoy, Robt. Brudenell, John Neuport, Sir Thos. Lovell, Sir Gilb. Talbot, Sir Henry Vernon, Sir Walter Griffith, Sir Lewis Bagod, Ric. Litelton, Sir Anth. Fitzherbert, John Gifford, Edw. Grey, Ric. Asteley, Ric. Wrattesley, Thos. Parteriche, John Wellys, John Blount, Ric. (*sic*) Agard, Ric. Selman and Thos. Blount. Westm., 18 Oct.

Warwickshire.—G. Bp. of Coventry and Lichfield, Edw. Duke of Buckingham, Thos. Marquis of Dorset, Thos. Prior of St. John's, Edw. Sutton Lord Dudley, John Lord Clinton, Humph. Conyngesby, Guy Palmes, Sir Gilbert Talbot, Sir Hen. Willoughby, Sir Edw. Belknap, Sir Rob. Throgmerton, Sir Wm. Compton, Simon Dygby, Sir Edw. Grevyle, Wm. Shelley, Nich. Broun, Anthony Fitzherbert, John Spencer, Wm. Broun, Rob. Fulwode, Thos. Slade, Wm. Boughton and John Erdern. Westm., 18 Oct.

W[*orcestershire.*]—G. Bp. of Coventry and Lichfield, R. Bp. of Hereford, Thos. Earl of Arundel, Geo. Earl of Shrewsbury, Edw. Sutton Lord Dudley, Humph. Conyngesby, Rob. Brudenell, John Neuport, Chas. Bothe, clk., Sir Gilb. Talbott, Sir Wm. Uvedale, Sir Griffin Rice, Sir Wm. Compton, John Ardern, Peter Neuton, Geo. Bromeley, Thos. Lynom, Wm. Rudhall, Giles Grevell, Rob. Vampage, Nich. Folictt, John Wasshebourne, Thos. Litelton and Roger Wynter. Westm., 18 Oct.

Westmoreland.—Thos. Earl of Derby, Ric. Nevell Lord Latimer, Thos. Lord Dacre, Edw. Stanley Lord Monteagle, Humph. Conyngesby, Brian Palmes, John Arneley, Sir Roger Belyngham, Sir Thos. Aparre, Ambrose Crakenthorp, Geoff. Lancastre, Christ. Pikeryng, Wm. Beuley, Edw. Musgrave, Thos. Blenkansop and Edm. Samfourth. Westm., 18 Oct.

Cambridgeshire.—J. Bp. of Ely, Sir John Fyneux, Sir Rob. Rede, Sir John Cutte, Sir Wm. Fyndern, Sir Giles Alyngton, Sir Rob. Peyton, Sir Rob. Cotton, Ralph Chamberleyn, Francis Hasilden, John Parys, John Wode, Rob. Frevile, John Hynd and Wm. Colyns. Westm., 18 Oct.

Somerset.—R. Bp. of Winchester, Edw. Duke of Buckingham, Hen. Earl of Wiltshire, John Bouchier Lord Fitzwarren, Wm. Lord Stourton, Hen. Lord Daubney, Sir Wm. Hody, Ric. Eliott, Lewis Pollard, Sir Wm. Compton, Sir John Speke, Sir Walter Hungerford, Sir Hugh Loterell, Sir John Trevylian, Sir Ric. Warr, Sir Nich. Wadham, Sir Amyas Paulet, Giles Strangwais, John Broke, John Fitzjames, John Sidnam of Brynton, Rob. More, Wm. Carraunt, John Horsey, Baldwin Malett, John Porter, John Portman and Thos. Jubbes. Westm., 18 Oct.

Salop.—G. Bp. of Coventry and Lichfield, R. Bp. of Hereford, T. Bp. of Bangor, Edw. Duke of Buckingham, Thos. Earl of Arundel, Geo. Earl of Shrewsbury, Rob. Brudenell, Humph. Conyngesby, John Neuport, Chas. Bothe, clk., Sir Gilbert Talbot, Sir Wm. Uvedale, Sir Griffin Rice, Sir Hen. Vernon, Sir Thos. Cornewall, Sir Thos. Blount, Sir Thos. Leyghton, Peter Newton, Wm. Rudhall, Ric. Litilton, Thos. Scryven, John Salter, Geo. Bromeley, Ric. Hord, Thos. Lynom, Ric. Forster and Ric. Selman. Westm., 18 Oct.

Hants.—W. Abp. of Canterbury, R. Bp. of Winchester, T. Bp. of Bangor, Th. Earl of Arundel, Wm. Blount Lord Mountjoy, Wm. Lord Maltravers, John Tuchet Lord Audley, Th. West Lord De la War, Ric. Eliott, Lewis Pollard, Wm. Uvedale, Sir Andrew Wyndesore, Sir Wm. Sandis, Sir Nich. Wadham, Sir John Lisley, Guy Palmes, John Neuport, Wm. Paulett. jun., Wm. Froste, John Dautrey, Ralph Pexsall, Wm. Pound and Th. More. Westm., 18 Oct.

Suffolk.—Same as 28 May, with addition of Sir Th. Wyndham, Arthur Hopton and Sir John Audeley, and omission of Rob. Suthwell, jun. Westm., 18 Oct.

Sussex.—W. Abp. of Canterbury, R. Bp. of Winchester, Thos. Duke of Norfolk, Thos. Earl of Arundel, Hen. Earl of Northumberland, Geo. Nevell Lord Bergevenny, Sir Wm. Mautravers, Thos. West Lord De la Warr, Thos. Fenys Lord Dacre, Sir Rob. Rede, John Butteler, John More, Sir Thos. West, Sir David Owen, Sir Thos. Fenys, Sir Goddard Oxenbrigge, John Carell, John Erneley, John Gage, John Dawtry, Ric. Sakevyle, Thos. Nevell, Wm. Asshebourneham, Vincent Fynche, Thos. Theecher, Edw. Palmer, Ric. Covert, John Goryng, John Theecher, Wm. Shelley, Rob. Morley, John Stanney, Wm. Skardevyle and John Rote. Westm., 18 Oct.

Staffordshire.—G. Bp. of Coventry and Lichfield, Edw. Duke of Buckingham, Thos. Marquis of Dorset, Geo. Earl of Shewsbury,

Edw. Sutton Lord Dudley, Wm. Blount Lord Mountjoy, Rob. Brudenell, John Neuport, Sir Thos. Lovell, Sir Gilbert Talbot, Sir Hen. Vernon, Sir Walter Griffith, Sir Lewis Bagod, Ric. Litelton, Anthony Fitzherbert, John Gifford, Edw. Grey, Ric. Asteley, Ric. Wrattesley, Thos. Patriche, John Welles, John Blount, Ralph Agard, Ric. Selman and Thos. Blount. Westm., 18 Oct.

[*Surrey.*].— W. Abp. of Canterbury, R. Bp. of Winchester, Edward Duke of Buckingham, Thos. Duke of Norfolk, Chas. Duke of Suffolk, Thomas Earl of Arundel, Geo. Nevell Lord Bergevenny John Bouchier Lord Berners, Sir Edm. Howarde, Sir John Fyneux, Sir Rob. Rede, John Butteler, John More, Sir Thos. Lovell, Sir Ric. Carewe, Sir John Legh, Sir Hen. Wyatt, Sir Matthew Brown, Sir John Iwarby, Sir Wm. Fitzwilliam, Thos. Morton, Thos. Nevell, Edm. Bray, John Skott, John Gaynsford of Crowherst, John Kirton, John Skynner, Hen. Saunder, Roger Legh, Gilb. Stoughton and Hen. Tyngilden. Westm., 18 Oct.

Oxon.—M. Bp. of Llandaff, Sir Thos. Lovell, Ric. Eliott, Rob. Brudenell, John Neuporte, Sir John Dauncey, Sir Ric. Fouler, Sir Wm. Rede, Sir Ric. Sacheverell, Sir Adrian Fortescu, Sir Edw. Chamberleyn, Sir Edw. Grevile, Sir Walter Stoner, Wm. Fermer, Ralph Massy, Simon Harecourt, Walter Bulstrode, Thos. Unton, John Horne, John Osbaldeston, Ralph Vyne, Geo. Stanley, Thos. Hadoke, Thos. Denton, John Busterde and Wm. Councer. [Westm., 18 Oct.]

Northumberland.—T. Bp. of ˌDurham, Hen. Earl of Northumberland, Thos. Lord Dacre, Thos. Lord Darcy, Brian Palmes, John Erneley, Wm. Percy, Sir Edw. Radcliff, Christ. Dacre, Philip Dacre, Sir Wm. Hilton, Thos. Horsley and Rob. Claveryng. Westm., 18 Oct.

Middlesex.—W. Abp. of Canterbury, T. Abp. of York, John abbot of St. Peter's Westminster, T. prior of St. John's, Sir John Fyneux, John Butler, Humph. Conyngesby, Sir Thos. Lovell, Sir Henry Marney, John More, John Neudegate, Sir Ric. Chomeley, Sir Andrew Wyndesore, Barth. Westby, Rob. Blagge, Sir Hen. Whyatt, Sir John Daunce, Thos. Nevell, John Mewtys, Rob. Elryngton and John Kirkton. Westm., 18 Oct.

Notts.—T. Abp. of York, Geo. Earl of Shrewsbury, Humph. Conyngesby, Guy Palmes, Sir Thos. Lovell, Sir Rob. Sheffeld, Sir Hen. Willoughby, Sir Wm. Perpoynt, Sir Thos. Sutton, Simon Dygby, Wm. Clerkson, Rob. Clyston, Humph. Hersey, Anthony Dabington (? Babington), John Byron, Rob. Hasilrigge, Rob. Broun, Hen. Bosom and Rob. Nevell. Westm., 18 Oct.

Leicestershire.—T. Abp. of York, Thos. Marquis of Dorset, Geo. Earl of Shrewsbury, Geo. Lord Hastings, Rob. Brudenell, Humph. Conyngesby, Guy Palmes, Sir Wm. Compton, Sir Ralph Sherley, Sir Everard Feldyng, Sir Ric. Saucheverell, Everard Digby, Thos. Pulteney, Wm. Skevyngton, Anthony Fitzherbert, Wm. Turpyn, John Fitzherbert, Wm. Brokesby, John Villers, Wm. Asshby, Ralph Swillyngton, Thos. Entwissell, Thos. Brokesby, Thos. Hasilrigge, Roger Radcliff, Wm. Reynoldis, Wm. Turvyle and Walter Kebell. Westm., 18 Oct.

1514.

Lincoln (Holland).—T. Abp. of York, Thos. Earl of Surrey, Wm. Lord Willoughby, Rob. Brudenell, Humph. Conyngesby, Guy Palmes, John Meres, Geoffrey Paynell, Thos. Roberdson, Francis Broun, John Robynson, Thos. Holand, John Litelbury and Ric. Godyng. Westm., 18 Oct.

Lincoln (Lindsey).—T. Abp. of York, Thos. Earl of Surrey, Wm. Lord Willoughby, Rob. Brudenell, Humph. Conyngesby, Guy Palmes, Sir Christ. Willoughby, Sir Rob. Sheffeld, Sir Wm. Tirwhit, Sir John Skipwith, Sir Thos. Borowe, jun., Sir Rob. Tirwhit, Sir Andrew Billesby, Sir Lionel Dymmok, John Topcliff, John Fulnetby, John Hennege and Edward Forman. Westm., 18 Oct.

Lincoln (Kesteven).—T. Abp. of York, Thos. Earl of Surrey, Wm. Lord Willoughby, Humph. Conyngesby, Rob. Brudenell, Guy Palmes, Sir John Huse, Sir Thos. Neuport, Geoffrey Paynell, Francis Broun, Rob. Broun (*in the margin*), John Wymbisshe, Wm. Dysnay and Francis Hall. Westm., 18 Oct.

Kent.—W. Abp. of Canterbury, Edw. Duke of Buckingham, Geo. Nevell Lord Bergevenny, John Lord Clinton, Th. Broke Lord Cobham, Sir John Fyneux, Sir Rob. Rede, Sir Wm. Hody, John Butler, John More, Sir Edw. Ponynges, Sir Hen. Guldeford, Sir Th. Boleyn, Sir John Pecche, Sir Ric. Chomeley, Rob. Blagge, Sir Christ. Garneys, Sir Wm. Scott, Sir Edw. Guldeford, Sir John Fogge, Th. Nevell, Th. Willoughby, Th. Isley, Ralph Seyntleger, Walter Roberth, John Roper, Wm. Fyneux, Nich. Boughton, Th. Turbervyle, Reginald Pecham, Jas. Walsyngham, Th. Woode, John Colman, Wm. Whetnall, Ric. Lee, John Hales and John Petyt. Westm., 18 Oct.

Herts.—Hen. Earl of Essex, Thos. Prior of St. John's, Wm. Blount Lord Mountjoy, John Bourchier Lord Berners, John Butler, John More, Humph. Conyngesby, Sir Thos. Lovell, Sir John Cutte, Sir Wm. Say, Sir Wm. Compton, Barth. Westby, Thos. Clifford, Rob. Neuporte, Edw. Bensted, Wm. Bedill, John Brokett, sen., Geo. Dalison, Rob. Turbervyle, Wm. Conyngesby, Ric. Druell and Thos. Knyghton. Westm., 18 Oct.

Hunts.—Sir John Fyneux, Sir Rob. Rede, Sir John Cutte, Wm. Gascoigne, Wm. Tanfeld, John Woode, Anth. Malory, Christ. Druell, Walter Luke, John Castell, John Wynd, Thos. Hall and John Taillard. Westm., 18 Oct.

Gloucestershire.—G. Bp. of Coventry and Lichfield, R. Bp. of Hereford, Edw. Duke of Buckingham, Rob. Brudenell, John Neuporte, Chas. Bothe, clk., Sir Gilb. Talbot, Sir Rob. Poynes, Sir Maurice Barkeley, Sir Wm. Uvedale, Sir John Hungerford, Sir Griffin Rice, Sir Alex. Baynham, John Broke, Peter Neutou, Geo. Bromeley, Wm. Denys, Thos. Poyntz, Edm. Tame, John Wityngton, Wm. Rudhale, Giles Grevyle, Edw. Wadham, Thos. Goodman, Ric. Pole, Christ. Baynham, Thos. Matston, Ric. Wye, Roger Porter and John Pakyngton. Westm., 18 Oct.

York, West Riding.—T. Abp. of York, Hen. Earl of Northumberland, Geo. Earl of Shrewsbury, Thos. Lord Darcy, Hen. Lord Clifford, Ric. Nevell Lord Latimer, Edw. Stanley Lord Monteagle, Brian Palmes, John Erneley, Ric. Tempest, John Topclyff, Thos. Fayrefax, Wm. Elson, John Vavasour, John Baxster, Walter Bradford and Thos. Beverley. Westm., 18 Oct.

1514.

York, East Riding.—T. Abp. of York, Edw. Duke of Buckingham, Hen. Earl of Northumberland, Geo. Earl of Shrewsbury, Thos. Lord Darcy, Ric. Nevell Lord Latimer, Humph. Conyngesby, Brian Palmes, John Erneley, Sir Ralph Eure, Sir Walter Griffithe, Sir Rob. Constable, Sir Rob. Aske, Sir Wm. Constable of Carethorp, Sir Marmaduke Constable of Everyngham, Sir Thos. Barkeley, Thos. Fayrefax, Wm. Eleson, Ralph Rokeby and Ric. Rokeby. Westm., 18 Oct.

York, North Riding.—Same as 11 [July], with addition of T. Abp. of York and Guy Palmes, and omission of Sir Ralph Eure, Sir Ralph Ellerker, Sir Walter Griffyth, Sir Ralph Bygod and Rob. Wyvell [or Wynell]. Westm., 18 Oct.

Essex.—Hen. Earl of Essex, Thos. Prior of St. John's, Rob. Radclyff Lord Fitzwalter, John Butteler, John More, Sir Hen. Marney, Sir Thos. Wyndham, Sir John Cutte, Sir Thos. Tyrell of Hern, Sir John Veer, Sir John Raynesford, Sir Ric. Fitzlowes, Sir Roger Wentworth, Sir Wistan Broun, Sir John Marney, John Seyntclere, Thos. Tey, Wm. Mordaunt, Wm. Ayloff, Edw. Suliard, Thos. Bonham, Humph. Broun, Edw. Halis, Humph. Torell, Walter Frost, Humph. Wyngfeld and John Sakevyle. Westm., 18 Oct.

Cumberland.—J. Bp. of Carlisle, Thos. Lord Dacre and Greystok, Sir Humph. Conyngesby, Brian Palmes, John Erneley, Christ. Dacre, Christ. Pykeryng, Sir John Musgrave, Sir Thos. Curwen, Thos. Fayrfax, Hugh Hutton, Ambrose Crakenthorp and Wm. Bewlewe. Westm., 18 Oct.

Bucks.—Edw. Duke of Buckingham, Sir John Fyneux, Sir Rob. Rede, Rob. Brudenell, Sir Andrew Wyndesore, Sir Wm. Rede, Sir Ric. Sacheverell, Sir Thos. Bryan, Thos. Pygotte, Thos. Dynham, Edw. Bulstrode, Wm. Bulstrode, John Cheyne, Thos. Grenwey, Thos. Langeston and John Hampden. Westm., 18 Oct.

Beds.—Thos. Prior of St. John's, Sir John Fyneux, Sir Rob. Rede, Sir John Seynt John, Sir Edm. Lucy, Wm. Gascoigne, John Mordaunt, Walter Luke, Wm. Marshall and Simon Fytz. Westm., 18 Oct.

Herefordshire.—G. Bp. of Coventry and Lichfield, R. Bp. of Hereford, Edw. Duke of Buckingham, Walter Devereux Lord Ferrers, Rob. Brudenell, John Neuport, Chas. Bothe, clk., Sir Gilb. Talbot, Sir Wm. Uvedale, Sir Griffin Rice, Sir John Lyngen, Jas. Baskervyld, Th. Poyntz, Peter Neuton, Geo. Bromeley, Th. Lynom, Wm. Rudhale, David Guilliam Morgan, Roger Bodnam, Ralph Hakelett, John Braynton and Th. Monyngton. Westm., 18 . . . . .

Derbyshire.—Geo. Earl of Shrewsbury, Th. Earl of Derby, Wm. Blount Lord Mountjoy, Humph. Conyngesby, Guy Palmes, Sir Hen. Vernon, Sir Ralph Sherley, Sir Hen. Sacheverell. Th. Babyngton, John Porte, John Agard, Godfrey Fulgeham, Wm. Grisley, Humph. Bladbourne, John Fitzherbert, Th. Coken and Wm. Bothe. Westm., 18 Oct.

Pat. 6 Hen. VIII. p. 1, m. 4 to 6d.

1514.

18 Oct. **5507.**   To the SHERIFF of HANTS.

Writ to pay Simon Gilford, appointed by patent 7 Feb. last ranger of the forest of Westebury alias Kyngesbery, Hants, his wages of 2*d.* a day out of the issues of the county of Hants from Christmas last. Westm., 18 Oct.

Pat. 6 Hen. VIII. p. 1, m. 12.

18 Oct. **5508.**   For ANTHONY HANSART of Intwode, Norf., alias of
S. B.   London, alias of Owrysby, Linc.

Pardon and release as receiver of the possessions of Cicely late Viscountess of Wells. *Del.* Westm., 18 Oct. 6 Hen. VIII.

Pat. 6 Hen. VIII. p. 1, *m.* 11.

18 Oct. **5509.**   For PHILIP BOTELER.
S. B.

Livery, as son and heir of John Boteler, of lands in cos. Hertford, Salop, Bedford, Chester, Stafford, Suffolk and Wilts, or elsewhere. *Del.* Westm., 18 Oct. 6 Hen. VIII.

Pat. 6 Hen. VIII. p. 1, *m.* 25.

19 Oct. **5510.**   For JOHN COPINGER, clerk of estreats of the Common
S. B.   Pleas.

Annuity of 10*l.* out of the issues of the manor of Wytley, Surrey. *Del.* Westm., 19 Oct. 6 Hen. VIII.

Pat. 6 Hen. VIII. p. 1, *m.* 10.

20 Oct. **5511.**   HENRY VIII. to LEWIS XII.
Rym. XIII. 463;
ex autogr.   Notifying the comprehension of Charles Prince of Castile in the
Not found.   treaty of London, and requesting his approval. Westm., 20 Oct.
                     6 Hen. VIII.

Fr. 6 Hen. VIII. p. 2, *m.* 2.

20 Oct. **5512.**   CHARLES DUKE OF SUFFOLK to WOLSEY.
Calig. D. VI. 147.
B. M.   Had met with Dannot at Canterbury, who showed him divers news, which he (Dannot) would tell Wolsey at his coming. He would perceive what the Duke of Norfolk and his son meant, to whom it was owing that the Queen's servants were discharged because they were of Wolsey's choosing and not theirs. Advises Wolsey to redress it ; for if the Queen is not well treated the blame will be laid between them. Requests Wolsey's instructions how to act. Trusts to be at Boulogne by noon, and at Paris tomorrow, with all his harness and his horse. He makes the more haste because he would be loth to be returned. "For, me Lor, whow I am howar (aware?) yf the Frynche . . . . wold for sake thyr challang, as I thynke they wyll not for scham, et I may dow the Kyng odder byssenes, and coum the sounar hom. W[here] for, my Lord, I by sche (beseech) you hold your hand fast that I by not sent for bake ; for I am suar that the fader and the son wold not for no good I schold styke wyet the Frynche King ; bout [so] I troust to do. And I dowth not bout I know hall thyr dryeftes." Dover, 20 Oct. [1514.]

Holograph, pp. 3. *Addressed :* To my Lord of York.

1514.

20 Oct. **5513.** MARY QUEEN OF FRANCE to HENRY VIII.

R. O. Is surprised she has received no answer to her letter. Had written to him about the deliverance of a prisoner in Lord Darcy's keeping. At the instance of the Dukes of Bretagne and Longue-ville the King had sent this week to Boulogne for the deliverance of the English prisoners. "As for 200 mark or 250 mark, I hearsay they would be content to give or else to continue still." Abbeville, 20 Oct. *Signed.*

P. 1. Addressed. Endorsed.

20 Oct. **5514.** For SIR RALPH VERNEY.

P. S. Livery of lands as son and heir of Sir John Verney, who at his death held the manor of Myddle Claydon, Bucks., of King Henry VII. Eltham, 17 Oct. 6 Hen. VIII. *Del.* Westm., 20 Oct.

Pat. 6 Hen. VIII. p. 1, m. 28.

21 Oct. **5515.** For WM. CLISTON, chaplain.

Grant of the free chapel of St. Thomas the Martyr at Barenstaple and of St. Katharine the Virgin of Fremyngton, Devon, void by death, and in the King's gift by virtue of the duchy of Exeter. Westm., 21 Oct.

Pat. 6 Hen. VIII. p. 2, m. 17.

21 Oct. **5516.** For ROGER LUPTON, clk., LL.D.

S. B. Pardon and release as late clerk of the hanaper. *Del.* Westm., 21 Oct. 6 Hen. VIII.

22 Oct. **5517.** WOLSEY to my LORD [the EARL OF WORCESTER].

R. O. Thanks him for his letters and the pains he has taken in his cause. Has shown unto the King "at right good length, the con-tents of your letters, wherewith his grace taketh marvellous plea-sure and is right well contented with the same, giving you his right especial thanks for the good advice and manner by you used as well in the making the overture of the matters touching the King of Arragon, as also the excusing of the not coming with the Queen of Jane Popyncort. And where as the French King hath promised nothing to intreat with the said King of Arragon afore the King our master and he shall personally meet, the King pynts (?) you to give unto him his most hearty thanks for the same, assuring him that he shall and will do semblably for his part. [And whereas the King hath lately appointed my lady Gylford to be lady of honor with the French Queen."]* Desires him to thank the French King for putting in his hands the order of Wolsey's affair, and to desire him to write to the Bishop elect ordering him to abstain from meddling with Wolsey's administration. If he can obtain such a letter, desires him to send it by next post, that Wolsey may send it to his chancellor there to deliver to "my said lady."

Hol. p. 1.

---

* This passage is struck out.

1514.

5518.   WOLSEY to my LORD [EARL OF WORCESTER.]

R. O.   (*Apparently a second draft to the above*).

"Furthermore, my lord, as touching my matter of Tournay sithence as ye write to me, the French King is content to do as ye will have him, and that his grace is minded in this thing or any other to do me pleasure," requests him to cause the French King to forbid the Bishop elect to meddle further with the bishopric and recompense him with some other promotion. Doubts not the Pope will be glad to give it to himself *in commendam* with the archbishopric. Trusts that on [Worcester's] mediation the French King will make no difficulty considering Wolsey's great services. Thinks he has deserved the best bishopric he could give. If he cannot induce the French King to make the Bp. give up his bpric., trusts his grace will at least command him to meddle no further, and write letters to the Lady Margaret, that Wolsey should have the administration according to the Pope's brief. "But let this be your sheet anchor, if so be ye may in no wise obtain the other, and in case it shall seem so to press, and will be none otherwise, than it may like you to send me the said letters so by you obtained to the intent I may send the same to mine officers in those parts." Hears from Rome that the French King's ambassadors make pursuit against him for the elect of Tournay. If this be done with his knowledge, "I marvel much;" if not, hopes the King will remedy it; "for all the court of Rome knoweth that I have not deserved that his ambassadors or any in his name, should labor against me in any cause." "And thus, my Lord, I am bold to put your Lordship to these great pains, assuring you that I should be glad to do semblaby, in all your causes here." Eltham, 22 Oct.

22 Oct.   **5519.**   To SIR HUGH CONWAY, treasurer of Calais, GEOFFREY VILLERS, ANTHONY NELE and GEORGE GAYNESFORD.

Commission to examine, in the presence of Humph. Banaster, the mayor, and the aldermen of Calais, the record and process of a plea before the said mayor and aldermen between Francis le Roye, plaintiff, and John Bolle, vintner of London, defendant, concerning a debt of 86*l.* 13*s.* 6*d.* Westm., 22 Oct.

Pat. 6 *Hen. VIII. p.* 2, *m.* 3.

23 Oct.   **5520.**   For JAMES MALET, B.D.

P. S.   Grant of a canonry and prebend in the collegiate church of St. Mary and St. George, Windsor Castle, *vice* William Atwater, resigned. Eltham, 14 Oct. 6 Hen. VIII. *Del.* Westm., 23 Oct.

Pat. 6 *Hen. VIII. p.* 1, *m.* 11.

24 Oct.   **5521.**   For SIR ROBERT REDE, Chief Justice of the Common S. B.   Pleas.

Licence to found a chantry in honor of Christ for one chaplain to officiate at the altar of St. Katharine in the church of St. Mary, Chedyngstone, Kent, for the said Robert and Margaret his wife; also mortmain licence to acquire lands to the annual value of 20 marks. *Del.* Westm., 24 Oct. 6 Hen. VIII.

Pat. 6 *Hen. VIII. p.* 1, *m.* 12.

1514.

24 Oct. **5522.** To JOHN YONG, Master of the Rolls.

S. B.

To cancel a congé d'élire, dated 15 Sept. 19 Hen. VII., to the subprior of the priory of St. Mary of Walsingham, of the Augustine order, on the death of Sir John Farewell, late prior ;—the prior and convent having the right of free election. 24 Oct. 6 Hen. VIII.

ii. Petition of the canons of the priory of St. Mary, Walsingham, for warrant to the Clerk of the Rolls to cancel a congé d'élire, dated 19 Hen. VII., which William Lowth, Sir Richard Empson, and Edmund Dudley, on the death of John Farewell, unlawfully obtained, and upon which the said William Lowth was elected prior ; the convent having always elected a prior, without licence from the Earls of Marche, their founders, or any of the King's predecessors. *Delivered to Yong* 26 Nov.

25 Oct. **5523.** CHARLES DUKE OF SUFFOLK to HENRY VIII.

Calig. D. VI. 149.

B. M.

This Thursday, 25 Oct., my Lord Marquis and he came to Bouves (Beauvais) where the King and Queen both were, and were brought to their lodging. By the King's request, communicated to him by Cleremond, he went to his grace alone. Found the King lying in bed, and the Queen sitting by the bedside. "And so I diede me rywarynes and knyelled down by his bed sede ; and soo he brassed me in hes armes, and held me a good wyell, and said that I was hartylle wyecoum, and axsed me, 'How dows men esspysseal good brodar, whom I am so moche bounden to lowf abouf hall the warld ?'" To which Suffolk replied, that the King his master recommended himself to his entirely beloved brother, and thanked him for the great honor and [love] that he showed to the Queen his sister. The French King answered, that he knew the nobleness and truth so much in Suffolk's master that he reckoned he had of him the greatest jewel ever one prince had of another. Assures Henry that never Queen behaved herself more wisely and honorably, and so say all the noblemen in France ; and no man ever set his mind more upon a woman on account of her loving manner. As to the jousts and tournays, my Lord Marquis and the writer both thought if they had answered the challenge it were little honor to win, seeing there were 200 or 300 answerers. The King had promised to introduce them to the Dauphin to be his aids. On the Dauphin's arrival he sent for them, expressed his sense of the honor done him by the King of England, said he would not take them for his aids but for his brethren, and so went to supper ; where supped the Duke of Bourbon and my Lord Marquis and I, and "it he tabylles" (at the tables) young Count Galleas and two others. As they sat at supper they talked of Henry's running, "of which, I ensure you, he was right glad to hear ; and as far as I can see he is not so well content with nothing [as to] hear talking of your grace, and to talk of you [him]self." The challenge, he said, would be in seven days, which was too soon for them to be ready. At their request the King respited it 15 days ; he also promised Henry a harness and a courser ; "for he says your grace has mounted him so well, he will seek all Christendom but he will honor your grace well." B[eauvais], 25 Oct.

P.S.—My lord of Longueville recommends him to the King. Desires [his remembrance] to Mrs. Blount and Mrs. Carru. Had sent the King, by Richmond last [time] he went to the King, a letter of Gels (?) and now he sends another. Had not heard whether the

1514.

king had received the last letter, and writes to put him in remembrance.

Holograph, pp. 7. Addressed: To the King's grace.

25 Oct.　**5524.**　For the ABBEY OF WHITBY.
P. S.

Restitution of temporalities on election of Thomas Bednell as abbot *vice* John Bensted, deceased ; the election having been confirmed by Brian Higdon, vicar general of Christopher Abp. of York. Eltham, 22 Oct. 6 Hen. VIII. *Del.* Westm., 25 Oct.

ii. Petition for the above. 10 July 1514.

Pat. 6 Hen. VIII. p. 1, m. 29.

25 Oct.　**5525.**　For JOHN POWER, a messenger of the Chamber.
P. S.

Annuity of 10 marks from Mich. 5 Hen. VIII. till the King give him an office of that value. Otford, 25 Sept. 6 Hen. VIII. *Del.* Westm., 25 Oct.

Pat. 6 Hen. VIII. p. 1, m. 31.

26 Oct.　**5526.**　WOLSEY to MARGARET OF SAVOY.
F. Moore's
Sale Cat., 710.　Requests her mediation for his bishopric of Tournay. London, 26 Oct. 1514.

26 Oct.　**5527.**　For ROB. RYCHARDSON, WM. PENNYTHORP and RALPH AUGER son of ALEX. AUGER.

Pardon for entry without licence on a messuage, lands, and tenements in Cawode, York, which, as appears by inquisition before Edw. Knyght, escheator in Yorkshire, the said Alexander, by a fine levied 4 Hen. VIII., granted to the said Robert and William and the heirs of the said Robert, who regranted them to the said Alexander for his life, with remainder to the said Ralph Auger in tail, with contingent remainder to Wm. Auger, brother of the said Ralph in tail, with contingent remainder to the right heirs of the said Alexander. Westm., 26 Oct.

Pat. 6 Hen. VIII. p. 1, m. 29.

26 Oct.　**5528.**　WM. LOVEDAY.

Newcastle-on-Tyne.—Commission to Thos. Lord Dacre, Rob. Lord of Ogle, Sir Wm. Bulmer and Sir . . . ., to make inquisition on the homicide of Wm. Loveday. Westm., 26 Oct.

Pat. 6 Hen. VIII. p. 1, m. 11d.

26 Oct.　**5529.**　HENRY VIII.
S. B.

Yorkshire and City of York. — Commission of oyer and terminer to Henry Earl of Northumberland, Richard Nevell Lord Latimer, Sir Thomas Lovell, Robert Brudenell, one of the justices of the King's Bench, Sir Thomas Parre, Brian Palmes, serjeant-at-law, Sir William Tirwhit and Richard Rokesby. Westm., 22 Nov. 6 Hen. VIII.

York (City).—Writ to the sheriffs in pursuance of the above. Westm., 23 Nov. 6 Hen VIII.

York (County).—Similar writ to the sheriffs. Same date.

1514,

Notts, Derby, Leicester, Lincoln, York, Cumberland, and West-moreland. — Commission of muster and array to Henry Earl of Northumberland and Sir Thomas Lovell, K. G. Westm., 24 Nov. 6 Hen. VIII.

Pat. 6 Hen. VIII. p. 2, m. 4d.

Rym. xiii. 465.

Commission to Sir Richard Wyngfeld, deputy, Sir Hugh Conwey, treasurer, and [John] Bunoult, secretary, of the town of Calais, Robert Fouler and Anthony Nele, to receive 50,000 francs, equal to 26,315 crowns, on 1 Nov. next, at Calais, from Louis King of France, being part of payment of 1,000,000 crowns of gold due from that King. Westm., 26 Oct. 6 Hen. VIII.

Ib. 466.

Acknowledgment of the receipt of the above 50,000 francs on 1 Nov. Westm., 5 Nov. 6 Hen. VIII.

Fr. 6 Hen. VIII. p. 2, m. 8.

---

26 Oct.   **5530.**   For GEORGE FRAUNCEYS and JAMES WORSELEY.

S. B.

Grant, in survivorship, of the office of ranger of the King's forest in the Isle of Wight, with 4d. a day. *Del.* Westm., 26·Oct. 6 Hen. VIII.

---

26 Oct.   **5531.**   For RICHARD CHAPMAN.

P. S.

Wardship of Margaret, daughter and heir of William Mars, alias Masse. Eltham, 11 July 6 Hen. VIII. *Del.* Westm., 26 Oct.

Pat. 6 Hen. VIII. p. 1, m. 2.

---

27 Oct.   **5532.**   SIR ROBERT WINGFIELD to [HENRY VIII.]

Vitell. B. xviii. 104.
B. M.

"Pleaseth your g[race, &c. On the . .] of this present month [I wrote unto] your highness from this town. [And since, owing to] an axcesse cotidiane I have kept my [bed] . . . whether the same intendeth to leave m[e, or carry] me unto my long home I am not sure . . . . . . for it is written that Troylis (Troilus) which dy . . . . not so many tears as his father Priam . . . . till all his children were slain and his c . . . . destroyed." Owing to his sickness, has not been able to hear any news worth writing to Henry ; and has not much to tell now, "because me seemeth not m[ete] to hunt for such matter as was wont to be showed me by the Emperor's own mouth." "The saying is now here that a certe[n power of horsemen] and footmen of the Ve[netians] . . . . town of B[ergamo] . . . . not only to reduce it again . . . . [but] cause them to redeem their . . . . money, nevertheless it is not facile to judge [whether h]e shall attain his said enterprise because that . . . . . . ere he had left in Polesyn in a town named Rwigo . . . . sperys Bartholomew Dalviane hath taken them . . . . . . eepers, and also another company in a place near to Verona ; so that in all there seemeth to be taken above fivo hundred horses." The rest of the army, besides those who went with the Viceroy to the said enterprise of Bergamo, have retired to Verona. The Emperor is sending new forces, in the hope that the Viceroy may avenge this last disgrace and regret having spared the Venetians when he had them in his power. As to the practise between the Pope, the Emperor, the King of Arragon, and the Swiss, "now that the way is open betwixt your Grace and France," Henry will know better from there than here what to do. . . . October.

Hol., mutilated, pp. 2.

3 M

1514.
28 Oct.　**5533.**　For WILLIAM HONE.
S. B.
　　　Presentation to the deanery of Tamworth, Cov. and Lich. dioc.,
void by death of Humphrey Wistowe. *Del.* Westm., 28 Oct.
6 Hen. VIII.

P. S.
　　　2. To the same effect. Eltham, 26 Oct. 6 Hen. VIII. *Del.*
Westm., 28 Oct.
　　　Pat. 6 *Hen. VIII. p.* 1, *m.* 12, *and m.* 18.　　　　•

29 Oct.　**5534.**　For the NEW HOSPITAL, BISHOPSGATE.
P. S.
　　　Mortmain licence to the Prior and Convent of the New Hospital
of St. Mary without Busshopesgate, to acquire lands to the annual
value of 100*l.* Eltham, 24 Oct. 6 Hen. VIII. *Del.* Westm.,
29 Oct.
　　　Pat. 6 *Hen. VIII. p.* 2, *m.* 9.

30 Oct.　**5535.**　JULIA[NUS DE MEDICIS] to HENRY VIII.
Vitell. B. II. 106.
B. M.　　　Has received from Sir Griffith Don, the bearer, the King's letters,
Rym. XIII. 467.　and his magnificent present of two horses, with their housings.
　　　Rome. 30 Oct. 1514.
　　　Endorsed. Mutilated.

30 Oct.　**5536.**　For JOHN A GUYLLIAMS, the King's serjeant-at-arms.
S. B.
　　　Grant, in reversion, of the corrody in the monastery of Malmes-
bury, now held by John Wilkynson. *Del.* Westm., 30 Oct.

30 Oct.　**5537.**　For JAMES WELLIS of Odiam, Hants, tanner.
P. S.
　　　Protection ; going in the retinue of Sir Richard Wyngfeld,
Deputy of Calais. Eltham, 21 Oct. 6 Hen. VIII. *Del.* Westm.,
30 Oct.

31 Oct.　**5538.**　LEO X. to HENRY VIII.
Vitell. B. II. 107.
B. M.　　　At the urgent request of the King, conveyed in three letters,
Rym. XIII. 467.　had taken away the office of collector from Hadrian, Cardinal S.
　　　Chrysogon, and conferred it on And. Ammonius, the King's Latin
Secretary. As the Cardinal held this office during the pontificate
of the last four Popes uninterruptedly, would not have done him this
injury, had he not thought that the Cardinal would gladly comply
with the King's wish. As it had been insinuated that the King's
letters had been extorted, and were not expressive of the King's own
wishes, the Pope desires he will signify as much, and so protect
the Cardinal from all harm. Rome, 31 Oct., 2 pont.
　　　Mutilated.

31 Oct.　**5539.**　SIR RICH. WINGFIELD and SIR THOS. SPINELLY to
Galba B. III. 218.　[HENRY VIII].
B. M.
　　　Wrote last . . . . . . Have not [since] heard from his Highness.
Two days ago a post came from the Emperor, and, as Berghes told
Spinelly, the [King of] Arragon, the Duke of Milan, and the Swiss,
have made a league offensive and defensive ; the conclusion of which
was deferred for the Pope's adhesion, Some of the Venetian forces
had entered Bergamo, and the Spaniards saved themselves within
the castle. The Viceroy of Naples was advancing to the rescue,
and also the Duke of Milan. About St. Martin's day the Emperor
will be at Fribourg in Bryscope, and hath appointed to keep an
imperial journey. The secretary of the ambassador of Arragon

1514.

here is appointed by the Emperor one of the ordinary secretaries of the Prince. In spite of the French, the Emperor and Arragon will continue good friends. The pirates who took Mountjoye were driven by a storm to Zeland, where they were taken and put to death. A Pensionnaire of Delfte says the Scots robbed their fishermen of victuals, anchors and cables, for which they mean to have reprisals . . . . " privy co . . . . of the French stradiots be con . . . . of Sir Robt. de la Marche. There will be great [jousts] on Sunday next ; the challengers to be the Count Palatine, the Marquis of Braden-bourg, the Count of Nassau, and the Great Esquire Myngova. . . . Brussels, 31 Oct. 1514. *Signed.*

Pp. 2, mutilated.

31 Oct.
R. O.

5540. F. CARDINAL SURRENTINUS to HENRY VIII.

Is glad to learn the King's good opinion of him by letters which he has received through Sir Griffith Don, and the testimony borne in his favor by Sir Thos. Ceve. The King had condescended to accept his small present of horses, and had returned the favor by sending him others more valuable, *"quos dicunt gradarios."* Know-ing the King likes an active horse and a good leaper, sends him one. Rome, 31 Oct. 1514.

Lat., p. 1. Addressed.

31 Oct.
R. O.

5541. THOS. LORD DACRE to WOLSEY.

Wonders, as he is charged with the borders, that he has received no letters from the Council since 12 Aug., having written once to the King and once to them. Has not received the comprehension of Scotland in the amity with France. Many excesses have been committed in Scotland since the 15 Sept. The lords there are at great variance. Kirkoswald, 31 Oct. *Signed.*

P. 1. Add. My [Lord] of Lincoln elect to York. *Endd.*

Cott. App. XLVIII. 21.
B. M.

5542. WOLSEY to MY LORD [BP. OF WORCESTER.]

Thanks him for his letters and the credence by Andreas, as by his lordship's means the Pope and Cardinals have remitted to Wolsey 2,000 ducats of the annates of Lincoln. Wolsey intends to take as much money of my lord of Rochester and St. John's whom the King is now sending in embassy there. Will be glad if these ducats are paid over to them. "As touching such stuff as ye [have [reserv]ed to mine use out of the hands of Mr. Paxe, [I request you to] sell of the same all the apparel for [the late Ca]rdinal's body, with the scarlet and [red clo]the ; and the altar cloths, vestments and tapestry [send to] me into England by ship or other-wise as ye [shall think] most best. Further, my lord, I beseech you to [make my h]umble commendations to the Pope's holiness [. . . . . . hon]orable and diligent solicitation . . . . will to make me cardinal. My [very good lord, I] thank you for the same."

Draft, in Wolsey's own hand, p. 1.

Vitell. B. II. 108.
B. M.

5543. [BP. OF WORCESTER] to [WOLSEY].

In the marriage contract with the French the Pope desires that he should be mentioned with honor, as he was the first to propose it to France and England, and he desires that the former should be

3 M 2

1514.

aware of their obligation. If the friendship between Henry VIII. and the King Catholic endure it will be easy to bridle the inconstancy of the French. The Pope is displeased that he has received no notice from England of this affair, although the French have bragged for the last eight days that the marriage has been concluded. They say the same of the treaty, which ought not to have been divulged, to make it appear that the Swiss have been abandoned by England. The Pope does not think it proper that the Swiss should be expressly mentioned. Sends a copy of a note received from his Holiness of points he wishes insisted on.

Lat.; in the hand of Peter Vannes. Pp. 3, mutilated.

---

2 Nov.   **5544.**   E. [AUDLEY] BP. OF SALISBURY to WOLSEY.
R. O.

Received the King's letters in September last, dated Esher 26 Aug., containing a complaint from Sir John Seymour, that the Bishop's servants had killed a great number of deer in the forest of Savernake. Sir John Seymour is the Bishop's enemy because he refused to execute his spiritual jurisdiction contrary to his conscience; and his accusation is untrue. Remmesbury, 2 Nov. *Signed.*

P. 1. Add.: To, &c. my Lord of Lincoln, postulate to York.

---

3 Nov.   **5545.**   For BERNARD DE VALEYS, gunner.
P. S.

To be gunner in the Tower, with 12*d.* a day. Eltham, 27 Oct. 6 Hen. VIII. *Del.* Westm., 3 Nov.

Pat. 6 Hen. VIII. p. 2, m. 17.

---

3 Nov.   **5546.**   For THOMAS WARDE, harbinger.
P. S.

Annuity of 5*l.* out of the lordship of Denbigh.   Greenwich, 31 Oct. 6 Hen. VIII. *Del.* Westm., 3 Nov.

Pat. 6 Hen. VIII. p. 1, m. 12.

---

3 Nov.   **5547.**   CHARLES DUKE OF SUFFOLK to WOLSEY.
Calig. D. vi. f. 153.
B. M.

Had written to the King how he had passed the time hitherto and desires to be informed how the King takes it, especially for his harness. Had written to Wolsey from Abbeville and also from Bowoes (Beauvais), but has learnt from Sir Harry Gylford that his letters to the King and Wolsey had been opened. Whether his last letters from Bowoes were so he cannot tell. " Me lord, thys es a nyell (an ill) pagant. Me lord, I and me lord marques and me lord chambarlyn has taken thys dyrrexseun that wye wyell not styke thyr in un tell they and wye have spoken to gyddar and that wye may have some mattar to wreth un to the kynges gras of, and thyn wy woll say that wy wold [ther]yn wreth un to the kynges gras howar master, how by et howar lyttares by taken and oponed . . ." Had sent letters which he would not should have been seen, which the King knows well. This same day he and my lord marquis and my lord chamberlain with my lord of St. John's and Dr. Wyest had delivered his letters to the King and to the Queen. "And soo whane that wy had doun wye schowd hys g[race] that we had sartyn in struxeunes to schow un to hys g[race] ar to hys counssell whane et schold plyes hes gras; and soo, he sayd that hes counssell schold gow weth hous and wye schold by gyen to en tyr in comenecaison." They then withdrew to my Lord of Longueville's chamber where they met the Cardinal, my Lord of Longueville, and Mons. Trymoell and the general and Robert Teet and an old man, whose name he knew not, and began to communicate for the personal meeting of the King's highness and the French King. " And first we desired [them

1514.

*f. 159.

to] show us what time, what place, and what n[umber their m]aster would think most convenient . . . .* [whereunto] they gave this answer; first for the [time] it was in manner agreed it should be in April, [and] as for the number, look what number the King would come with, he would come in likewise; and as for the place, they began to name a place about Hard [Ardes]. And then we said Nay, and stack on Calles, or else at St. Peter's. And so when they had heard us they said they would show unto the King what we had said, and they would show us the King's pleasure on Sunday after, and so we parted for that time." Suffolk with his fellows went to his lodging where he was sent for by the French King to come and see his two daughters. He went thither alone; "and whane I came thyr a mad me to kyes hys dawttares," and began conversing with him. On seeing the King at leisure and the "chamber [w]oll ryed," he toke his secret letter and read it, telling the King it was a letter of credence, and that he had a message from the King his master; "wherefore I desired his grace to show m[e his] pleasure when he thought best I should speak (?) . . ." The King thought best the jousts should be done first, and also the personal meeting concluded ; and Suffolk agreed to do according to his pleasure. Begs to know if Wolsey think this good, or if he should begin it sooner. The French King bids him tell Wolsey that he has sent him "moulle (a mule ?) the byst in the warld ; " and my Lord of Longueville that, touching his matter of Tournay and his matter of Rome, everything possible should be done. "Howbeit I will make a quarrel that you would not show me of, as knows God, who send you as well to fare as I would myself." Paris, the ii[j day] of November.

P.S.—Begs a speedy answer. The Queen is to be crowned at St. Denis, where she is now, on Sunday next, and on Monday to enter Paris. The jousts to begin on Monday se'nnight.

Hol., pp. 5 ; *the leaves misplaced. Addressed:* To my Lord of York.

---

4 Nov.
P. S.

5548. For CHRISTOPHER JOHNSON, alias COPER, alias GOLDE-SMYTH, of Sandwich, goldsmith.

Pardon. Greenwich, 31 Oct. 6 Hen.VIII. *Del.* Westm., 4 Nov. *Pat.* 6 *Hen.VIII. p.* 2, *m.* 18.

---

4 Nov.
S. B.

5549. For ROBERT GEFFREY.

Presentation to the free chapel in the castle of Snodhille, Heref. dioc., void by resignation of Robert Cowper. *Del.* Westm., 4 Nov. 6 Hen.VIII.

---

4 Nov.
S. B.

5550. For SIR JOHN NORTON of Middelton, Kent, alias of Sheldwych, Kent.

Pardon and release as late sheriff of Kent ; also release to him, Richard Guston of Sydyngbourne, and Christopher Bredeham of Sellyng, Kent, of their recognizance. *Del.* Westm., 4 Nov. 6 Hen. VIII.

Pat. 6 *Hen.VIII. p.* 2, *m.* 29.

---

4 Nov.
P. S.

5551. For RICHARD HOPE, yeoman of the Guard.

To be bailiff of the town of Malmeshill Lucy, Heref., parcel of the earldom of March, *vice* Henry Hering, deceased, with 26s. 8d. a year. Greenwich, 2 Nov. 6 Hen. VIII. *Del.* Westm., 4 Nov. *Pat.* 6 *Hen.VIII. p.* 1. *m.* 29.

1514.
5 Nov.
P. S.
5552. For THOMAS ANNESLEY, gentleman for the mouth of the cellar with the Queen Consort.

Corrody in the monastery of St. Mary, Suthwyke, *vice* Thomas Parker, deceased. Greenwich, 1 Sept. 6 Hen. VIII. *Del.* Westm., 5 Nov.

6 Nov.
Calig. D. VI. 201.
B. M.
Ellis, 2 S. I. 243.
5553. CHARLES EARL OF WORCESTER to WOLSEY.

Received on the 2nd inst. his letter dated at Eltham the 22nd October, communicating the King's pleasure touching the return of my Lady Gilford, and Wolsey's relative to his matter of Tournay. With regard to the first he has done what he could with the French King, who replied "that his wife and he be in good and perfect love as ever two creatures can be, and both of age to rule themself, and not to have servants that should look to rule him or her." He himself could give his wife what advice she required, but he was sure she did not wish to have her again; "for as soon as she came a lond, and also when he was married, she began to take upon her not only to rule the Queen, but also that she should not come to him, but she should be with her, nor that no lady nor lord should speak with her but she should hear it, and began to set a murmur and banding among ladies of the Court. And then he swore that there was never man that better loved his wife than he did, but or he would have such a woman about her he had lever be without her." He was sure that when "the King his good and loving brother" knew this he would be satisfied. "He would not have her about his wife al . . . . that he is a sickly body and not at all times that . . . . . . be merry with his wife, to have any strange wo[man . .] but one that he is well acquainted with . . . . durst be merry, and that he is sure . . . . wise is content withal, for he hath seen . . . . . lady nor gentlewoman to be with her for her . . . . . servants and to obey her commandments." On which answers "I am . . . . . again so that he was content, and so I make no do[ubt] the King's grace would be ; for the answer was well del[ivered], as his grace and you shall know at my co[ming] which I trust shall be shortly, for I purpose to depart hence the 12th day of this month ;" for all that he was charged with either by himself along with "my good lord" of [Suffolk] and my Lord Marquis will be concluded, as much as may be at this time, within these three days.

With regard to Tournay he had sent Wolsey from Abbeville the letter directed to my Lady of Savoy, according to his desire. The elect was ordered to meddle no further "against the . . . . . " Had spoken with the French King who was willing to re[compense] him, and has commanded the Treasurer Robertett and the general of Normandy to speak with the president of Parliament, father of the said elect to agr[ee to a] recompense, which they would do without fail to-morrow at the furthest. The King desired him to say, that the elect should make as full a release as Wolsey could wish. "[Or] ever I depart I woll know a parfaite . . . . , and counsel of master dean of Windsor, I woll . . . to be made writing, if he think that any may be made for your surety before ye send to Rome ; or else I will order the matter so that at all times when ye will send for them that ye shall have them."

The King wished Wolsey to desire Henry, if God should send him a son, to be godfather, as he was last ; and to "send a good and honorable personage against the Queen's deliverance to represent his person, and to do the act in his name ;" who should also

1514.

have power to treat for their meeting and of other secret matters. As soon as he has an answer on this point he will despatch his said ambassador. The French Queen told Worcester she loved Lady Guilford well, but was content to be without her, for she may do what she will. St. Denis, 6 Nov.

Addressed: [To] mine especial good lord, my lord Archbishop of York.

Holograph, pp. 3. *Mutilated.*

6 Nov. **5554.** SAMPSON to WOLSEY.

Galba, B. v. 389.
B. M.

" Be the letters of my Lord Ponynges the 3rd day of Novem[ber I depar]tyd fro Brugis towards Tournay," as Ponynges had written it was necessary he should be there. Has received letters from Wolsey, and one for my Lady Margaret. Will leave Tournay to-day to deliver it. Has written already to Wolsey of the receipts of the diocese. When he delivered the brief to the Bishop's officers at Bruges, found them very obstinate and provided with appeals. The country is much exasperated against England. Gives an account of his proceedings. Will not hesitate to execute Wolsey's administration in Tournay. The old officers do not favor Wolsey. Has provided a doctor of great experience. Will execute the brief in Flanders. The revenues have been paid away, and by the accounts he has received, Wolsey is 100 marks in debt. Hopes, however, to make them pay 20*l.* Cannot assemble the officers at Tournesis till the plague be past. Advises that the prebend be given to the before-mentioned doctor, on condition of receiving no salary as vicar-general, which is 40 marks per annum. The Lord Lieutenant and Sir Anthony Owthryd, the marshal, are active in Wolsey's behalf. Tournay, 6 Nov. 1514.

Mutilated, pp. 3. *Add.:* My Lord of York.

6 Nov. **5555.** For WOLSEY.

P. S.

Restitution of the temporalities of the archbishopric of York. Greenwich, 2 Nov. 6 Hen. VIII. *Del.* Westm., 6 Nov.

ii. Bull of Leo X., appointing Thomas Bishop of Lincoln as Archbishop of York. Rome, at St. Peter's, 1514, xvii. kal. Oct., 2 pont.

Pat. 6 *Hen. VIII. p.* 1, *m.* 30.

6 Nov. **5556.** For WILLIAM ATWATER.

P. S.
Rym. xiii. 468.

Restitution of the temporalities of the bishopric of Lincoln. Greenwich, 2 Nov. 6 Hen. VIII. *Del.* Westm., 6 Nov. 6 Hen.VIII.

Pat. 6 *Hen. VIII. p.* 2, *m.* 13.

6 Nov. **5557.** For CHRISTOPHER PLOMER, the King's chaplain.

S. B.

Presentation to the canonry of Cadyngton Major in St. Paul's, London. *Del.* Westm., 6 Nov. 6 Hen. VIII.

Pat. 6 *Hen. VIII. p.* 1, *m.* 12.

6 Nov. **5558.** For THOMAS BROKE, leatherseller of London.

P. S.

Protection; going in the retinue of Sir Richard Wyngfeld, Deputy of Calais. Greenwich, 2 Nov. 6 Hen. VIII. *Del.* Westm., 6 Nov.

Fr. 6 *Hen. VIII. p.* 2, *m.* 3.

1514.

7 Nov.   **5559.**   LEWIS XII.

Rym. xiii. 468.

Letters patent, stating that he had received the letters patent of Henry VIII., dated Eltham, 20 Oct., signifying the assent of Charles Prince of Castile, and his admission to the treaty of London. Gives his concurrence. Paris, 7 Nov. 1514.

Fr. 6 Hen.VIII. p. 2, m. 15.

7 Nov.   **5560.**   CHARLES DUKE OF SUFFOLK, T. MARQUIS OF DORSET,

Calig. D. vi. 205.   C. EARL OF WORCESTER, T. DOCWRA and NICHOLAS

B. M.   WEST to [HENRY VIII.]

Ellis, 2 S. i. 247.

The King and Queen came to St. Denys the last day of Oct., and sent to them at Paris the treasurer Robertet, praying them to remain there the 1st and 2nd Nov. for the feasts of All Hallows and All Souls, and to come to St. Denys on Friday 3 Nov., when my Lord of Suffolk and my Lord Marquis might deliver the King's letters, and hear the French King's determination concerning the coronation of his Queen and her entry into Paris. They arrived on Friday about 10 o'clock, were sent for to the Abbey, and after dinner brought into the presence of the King, and thanked him for the honorable reception of the Queen at her first arrival at Bolayn, "and for the loving and honorable entertaining of her ever since, and for the good recueil done to your ambassadors late being with the Queen at Abbeville aforesaid." They also showed him that by letters of Henry's former ambassadors the latter understood how greatly he was desirous of the interview between himself and Henry, on which account they were commissioned to treat concerning it. With regard to the necessary arrangements for this, he said, his council should speak with them forthwith. The Queen's coronation was to be on Sunday following, and the entry into P[aris] on Monday. They were then brought into the Duke of [Bretaigne's] chamber, where was the Cardinal of Pree, the Duke of Longuevile, Mons. Bussaiye, the treasurer [Robertet], and the general of Normandy. With regard to the place of meeting, the French could not agree to Calais, for various reasons, especially the weakness of their master. As to the time, the English, considering that Easter would fall on the 8th of April, thought it could not be before the 20th of that month ; to which time the French "were somewhat agreeable ;" and the conversation again reverting to the place, the English ambassadors proposed St. Peter's, as the farthest place they had in commission to treat upon. With this the French were not content, but said they would commune with the King both of the place and time.

On Sunday 5th Nov. the Queen was crowned. The English ambassadors were sent for to come to the church by Mons. de Mombrancy [Montmorency] ; and within an hour after she came in with a great company of noblemen and ladies. The Duke of Bretaigne led her, and before her came the Dukes of Alanson [Alençon], Bourbon, Longuevile, and Albany, the Duke of Bourbon's brother, the Countie of Vaund[osme], and the Countie of Sainct Poll, with many others. The Queen kneeled before the altar, and was anointed by the Cardinal of Pree, who delivered her the sceptre and the vierge of t . . . . . . of justice, put [a ring] upon her finger, and lastly set [the crown upon her] head ; "which done the Duke of Bretaigne . . . . . . a stage made on the left side of the altar d . . . . . . us, where she was set in a chair under a cl[oth of state] and the said Duke stood behind her holding th[e crown up] from her head to ease her of the weight there[of. And]

1514.

then began the high mass sungen by the said [Cardinal] whereat the Queen offered ; and after *Agnus* she [was] houseld. Mass done she departed to the p[alace], and we to our lodgings to our dinners ; howbeit [in] departing the treasurer Robertet desired us to [come] again after dinner, and then we should know the [King's] pleasure upon our said matters." After dinner they went to the Duke of Lon[gueville's] chamber and met the Cardinal, the Duke of Longueville, Mons. de la Tremouille, the B[ishop of] Parys, Mons. de Piennez, the treasurer Robertet, [and] the General with whom they again spoke on the subject of the meeting. The King had appointed.Mons. de Pie[nnez, who] knew the country, to be present and to name a place indifferent. He named Arde, but they stuck [out for St.] Peter's ; on which the others withdrew and conferred together. Ultimately they agreed that Henry should come to Dover, and the French [King to] Bolayn, and each send commissioners to agree upon a place upon the limits of the English marches between Arde and Guysnes, or else between Bolayn and C[alais], and also to settle the number to come with both parties, which those who saw the ground could best arrange " according to the danger of the same ; " and this the French commissioners desired might be communicated to Henry as the King their master's mind, with a request that the interview but be as near as possible to the beginning of April, as Lewis intended to send his army over the mountains in March for the recovery of Ast and Milan, and to follow them himself as soon as he might to Grannoble that he might be near them ; "which they said he would in no wise do till he had seen your grace." After a consultation among themselves the English ambassadors agreed to communicate this overture to Henry as they were requested.

On Monday 6 Nov. the King [departed] about 7 o'clock in the morning to Paris. The Queen departed about 9 o'clock [and rested] at a village two miles out of Paris. She made her entry into Paris with great solemnity. She was met by the provost of the merchants with the guard of the town before him, the provost of the justice [and] the council of the town, the cham[berlain] of accounts, president of the parliament, the university, and others. Reached the palace at 6 o'clock, "where she did lie all night, and there was a right great banquet ; " dined there on Tuesday ; and the afternoon to Turnell's, where she is lodged. The jousts are to begin on Sunday next. Paris, Tuesday, 7 Nov. *Signed.*
Mutilated.

7 Nov. **5561.** SHERIFF ROLL.
S. B.
    Cumb.—John Lamplewe, Sir Th. Curwen, *Sir John Ratcliff.
    Northumb.— Robt. Colyngwode, "her'," Wm. Swynbourne, *Ralph Fenwyk.
    York.—Sir Wm. Bulmer, Sir James Strangwisshe, *Sir John Norton.
    Notts and Derb.—Sir Th. Cokeyn, Sir Th. Sutton, *Sir Wm. Meryng.
    Linc.—Sir Arthur Hopton, *George Fitzwilliam, Wm. Dysney.
    Warw. and Leic.—Wm. Asshby, Th. Pulteney, *Sir John Dygby.
    Salop.—*Th. Lakyn, Francis Yong, John Cotes.
    Staff.—Ric. Astley, Sir John Draycote, *Wm. Chetwyn.
    Heref.—*Sir Th. Cornwaill, Ralph Hakelnyt, Sir John Lyngeyn.

1514.

Glouc.—Wm. Denys, *Wm. Kyngeston, Robt. Wye.

Oxon and Berks.—Sir Edward Grevell, Sir Edward Chamberleyn, *Simon Harecourt.

Northt.—*Robt. Mathewe, Th. Lovet, Nich. Wodyll.

Camb. and Hunts.— *Sir Ralph Chamberleyn, Wm. Tanfeld, Robt. Frevyll.

Beds and Bucks.—Michael Fissher, Wm. Bulstrode, *Sir Edm. Bray.

Norf. and Suff.—*Sir John Heydon, Sir Anth. Wyngfeld, Ric. Wentworth.

Essex and Herts.— Hen. Frowyk, *Wm. Fitzwilliam, Th. Crismas.

Kent.—Th. Cheyney, Wm. Kemp, *Alex. Culpeper.

Surrey and Sussex.—Sir John Legh, Sir Hen. Wiott, *Roger Copley.

Hants.—*Ric. Norton, John Cailwey, Peter Philpot.

Wilts.—John Scrope, John Ludlowe, *Wm. Bonham.

Somers. and Dors. — Wm. Paulet, *Edward Gorge, John Borghcher.

Devon.— John Chechester, Robt. Yoo, *Sir Nich. Wadham.

Cornw.—[John] Carewe, *Ric. Code, Robt. Longdon.

Rutland.—[*Th.] Brokesby, Th. Sherrard, John Calcote.

[*Westmor.*]—Henry, Lord Clifford, in fee.

Worc.—Sir John Savage.

Signed by the King at the beginning and end.

Del. Westm., 7 Nov. 6 Hen VIII.

On the dorse is a memorandum that on 8 [Novem]ber 6 Hen. VIII., the King ordered the Lord Chancellor to appoint John Carewe to be sheriff of Cornwall instead of Ric. Code.

7 Nov.   **5562.**   For JOHN CAREWE.
S. B.

To be sheriff in the county of Cornwall, in the place of Richard Code, late nominated as sheriff for the 6 Hen. VIII. 7 Nov. 6 Hen. VIII.

7 Nov.   **5563.**   For JOHN YONG, Master of the Rolls.
S. B.

To cancel a recognizance of 1,000*l.*, made by Walter Devereux, Lord Ferrers, 14 March 4 Hen. VIII. Greenwich, 7 Nov. 6 Hen. VIII.

7 Nov.   **5564.**   For WALTER CHALCOT.
P. S.

To be King's serjeants-at-arms, with 12*d.* a day, *vice* Humphrey Baryngton, deceased. Greenwich, 4 Nov. 6 Hen. VIII. *Del.* Westm., 7 Nov.

Pat. 6 *Hen. VIII. p.* 1, *m.* 28.

8 Nov.   **5565.**   EDWARD [PONYNGES] to HENRY VIII
Calig. D. vi. 144.
B. M.

In favor of Pierre de Bryonnes, a Castilian, bearer of the letter, who had served in the garrison of Tournay so long as the King was pleased to keep him, and now purposed to return to Spain through England. Tournay, 8 Nov. 1514.

Fr. Signature half burnt.

P. 1. *Addressed:* Au Roy mon Souverain Seigneur.

8 Nov.   **5566.**   EARL OF WORCESTER to WOLSEY.
R. O.

Has just been informed by the General of Normandy that the payment due by France 1 Nov. will not be at Calais till 8 Dec.

1514.

The payment due in May has always been paid 8 June. He showed Worcester a list of all that should have pensions, but refused him a copy. Worcester's name is in the list. Had written from Abbeville, wishing to know if he should accept it. Was promised this morning the resignation of the elect. Trusts to bring it. Thinks Wolsey in the mean time should make suit at Rome. Paris, 8 Nov.

Pp. 2. *Add.* : [To] mine especially good lord my lord Abp. of York.

8 Nov. **5567.** For WILLIAM ROTHWELL of London, merchant, late
P. S. customer of Bristol.

Protection; going in the retinue of Sir Richard Wyngfeld, Deputy of Calais. Greenwich, 6 Nov. 6 Hen. VIII. Westm., 8 Nov.

Fr. 6 *Hen. VIII. p.* 2, *m.* 18.

8 Nov. **5568.** For THOMAS RAYMOND, grocer, of London.
P. S.

Grant to him and his heirs of a vacant tenement in Bortha-lane, alias Bordhawlane, St. Mary Colechurche, London, held by Henry VII. in right of the crown ; to hold from 1 Aug. 1 Hen. VII. Eltham, 23 Oct. 6 Hen. VIII. *Del.* Westm., 8 Nov.

Pat. 6 *Hen. VIII. p.* 2, *m.* 19.

9 Nov. **5569.** THOMAS MARQUIS OF DORSET to [WOLSEY].
Calig. D. VI. 188.
B. M.

Since his last letters, dated Bevoyse, 26 Oct., where they first met the French King and Dauphin, they have accompanied the latter to Paris. On the 27th they came to Bewmond to their lodging. Next day the Dauphin having entoyled within a wood by the way two wild boars, my Lord of Suffolk met the first and gave him "the first stroke with his *tokke*, that he bowed it three ways of his hand, and slew him," and he himself struck the second with a boar's spear "that he long continued not after." Came the same night to Paris, where they communed with the Dauphin and his other assistants, "as we be," of the justs, and the preparations for them. "Wherein we found him and his company not like as they have been named ; for though they do re[nne] trymmely, and handle theym self well [enough] with their small and light staves, th[ey] could not well trim themself in their harn[ess, but] be content to have our poor advices, th . . . . wol somewhat follow the same. My lo[rd, at my] coming to Paris, I had not one piece of [harness] neither for horseback nor foot, nor horse to run, but was to seek everything that I should [want]. Howbeit, with the help of the King's grace, my master, who so bounteously departed with me, that I . . . . trust shall be again the day of the justs, [which] shall be Monday" the 13th inst., as well trimmed as any man in France, having spared no cost, but laid out his money as largely as his master gave it him.

[*The above is in a clerk's hand. What follows is in Dorset's own.*]

"Fryday, the fowrth day ofe No[vember], wy ver apoyntyth (we were appointed) to come tho (to) the K[yngys] grace to Saynte Denys, wher my Lorde[of] Swfefoke acompanyde wy the hwss [the other] inbasadwrs delyfyrth (delivered) the Kyngys [letter; and] demandeth hws houre credense vy●h . . . . . hys grase, and

1514.

that done, hye . . . . the Cardenale ofe Pry, th[e Duke of] Long-
fylde Mosywre la Trymole, ... the generale [of Normandy touc]hynge the parsonale mytyng [betwixt the King] hour
mayster and the Frense Kyng . . . . . . ofe Apryle nexte en-
swhynge ofe the monyt . . . . . ych ofe the nombyre to be egale,
and wythethout . . . . hone both sydes, so that they wyle agry that
. . . . . [m]ay by in swche aplase has wy whole apoynte [tha]t hys,
Saynte Pyters; and farder, wy ntennot (intend not?) to go . . . .
hyte, and hyte wy stake apone Galys (Calais) a grete wyle [and
tol]de theym that why kwde go no fardyr, exchepe [we] swde
send to Inglande to kno the Kyngys [far]dyr plesyre, and that wy
thowte hyte whas no [the]nge for theyme to styke hate, syhyng
who ewere thynge [te]ndythe; and the conclusyone vhas, the Kyngys [gra]se swde come to Dovyre and the Frenche Kynge [to]
Boleyne, and thane sarteyne parsonages to by apoyntyth [on] bothe
sydes fore to aponte the plase vythe [oth]er dywerse thyngys
vyche I forbere to vryte to your [lord]chype by chawse why hafe
vryten to youre lordcype enye in a nodyre leter and to asaterne
you ofe the . . ys demenynge in thys partys hys aswrythele [as]
far has I kane kno has goude (good) and wyse, as may . . owth,
and I aswre you her grase has a grete . . . ofe her amynoie (?),
and hyte hade note byhwfe het . . . uyse hyme for notyng. My
lord, I pray [you not to be] myscontent tat I wrote note to you
[when my Lord] a Sufoke sende you hy laste leters fo[rasmuch as]
I trwste sortele to se you after the jw[sts] . . . . by I
scale tele yow awle th [e news]. My Lord a Sufoke has hyh[aved
himself well] and wysele in hawle hys maters . . . . and
that he hys note ofe a lytele ext[ymation] in thys partys bwte has
done has gr[eat] service] to hore mayster and hys reme has
ewer dy[d any] that kam hwte ofe Inglande, has knohys G[od],
who kype you, and sende my sortele in to Ingland. Awle my
money by spende." Paris, 9 Nov.   *Signed.*
   Mutilated.

9 Nov.	**5570.**	ERASMUS to [R. R.]
R. O.		

Received his kind letter 24th Oct.   Had not answered it
before in consequence of his incessant occupations. Feels under
the greatest obligations to his correspondent. "*Una cum epis-
tolio caseo me donasti, et eo quidem neutiquam vulgari.*" Sends
him in return a MS. (*codicillum*) of M. Vegius, "*De pueris
educandis,*" as very suitable to his correspondent's employment.
5 id. Nov.

9 Nov.	**5571.**	For DOROTHY VERNEY.
S. B.		

Annuity of 20 marks from Easter last, in consideration of her
services to Mary Queen of the French. *Del.* Westm., 9 Nov.
6 Hen. VIII.
   Pat. 6 *Hen.VIII. p.* 1, *m.* 12.

9 Nov.	**5572.**	For THOMAS GENTILMAN of London, chaplain.
S. B.		

Pardon. *Del.* Westm., 9 Nov. 6 Hen. VIII.

9 Nov.	**5573.**	For SIR ROBERT PEYTON.
S. B.		

Wardship of Robert, s. and h. of Geoffrey Lokton, and custody
of his lands in Cambridgeshire. *Del.* Westm., 9 Nov. 6 Hen. VIII.
   Pat. 6 *Hen.VIII. p.* 2, *m.* 20.

1514.
9 Nov.   **5574.**   For JOHN PORTE, the King's solicitor.
S. B.   Wardship of Robert brother and heir of Thomas Shaa, deceased, an idiot ;—and custody, in reversion, of the tenements in Coland, Oslaston, Roddesley, Sudbury, Westbroughton, Somersale and Oldesmore, Derby, which Margaret, late wife of the said Thomas, holds for life. *Del.* Westm., 9 Nov. 6 Hen. VIII.
Pat. 6 *Hen.VIII. p.* 2, *m.* 18.

9 Nov.   **5575.**   For HENRY CHYPPENHAM of Hereford.
P. S.   Pardon. Greenwich, 6 Nov. 6 Hen. VIII. *Del.* Westm., 9 Nov. *Pat.* 6 *Hen.VIII. p.* 2, *m.* 19.

10 Nov.   **5576.**   For THOS. SPERT, yeoman of the Crown.
Annuity of 20*l.* which John Wodlesse, deceased, lately enjoyed. Westm., 10 Nov.
Pat. 6 *Hen.VIII. p.* 2, *m.* 19.

10 Nov.   **5577.**   For JOHN LOK, merchant of London.
P. S.   Protection ; going in the retinue of Sir Richard Wyngfeld, Deputy of Calais. Hanworth, 6 Nov. 6 Hen. VIII. *Del.* Westm., 10 Nov.

10 Nov.   **5578.**   . For WILLIAM WYGSTON, THOMAS WYGSTON, clk., ROGER
P. S.   WYGSTON and WILLIAM FYSSHER, clk.
Mortmain licence to grant to the chaplains and paupers of the hospital founded by them in Leicester, possessions to the annual value of 23*l.*, beyond the annual amount of 40 marks mentioned in patent 13 July 5 Hen. VIII., which licensed them to found and endow the said hospital. . . . . 6 Hen. VIII. *Del.* Westm., 10 Nov. *Mutilated.*
Pat. 6 *Hen.VIII. p.* 2, *m.* 20.

11 Nov.   **5579.**   ORDNANCE.]
R . O.   Wages due to laborers working at the ordnance, 11 Nov. New ordnance which came from Mechlin 6 Hen. VIII. Wages at 5*d.* a day.
A fragment.

12 Nov.   **5580.**   COMMISSION OF THE PEACE.
Norfolk.—Same as 28 May, with omission of Sir John Heydon, Sir Jas. Fremlyngham, Sir John Glemam, Sir Ric. Candissh, Walter Hobart, And. Sulyard, Hen. Hunston and Walter Stubbes. Westm., 12 Nov.
Pat. 6 *Hen.VIII. p.* 1, *m.* 3*d.*

13 Nov.   **5581.**   PETER MARTYR to LUD. FURTADO.
Epist. 542. Unless Ferdinand throws off two of his appetites he must soon go the way of all flesh. He is 63, and, besides his asthma, never lets his wife from his side. It is now winter, and the country is very cold, yet he talks like a young man of going to the mountainous

1514.

country of Leon, because he hears that bears are to be found there. If he does not part with one rib, he will lose all. Charon will carry in his boat him and Lewis if they are not careful. The Frenchman went out to meet his bride like a gay bridegroom, perched elegantly on a fine Spanish war-horse, "semicevens," licking his lips and gulping his spittle. If he lives to smell the flowers of the spring, "you may promise yourself 500 autumns." Yet this brave King is thinking of again shaking Italy with war, and is spurred on by Trivulcio and other exiles. Valladolid, id. Nov.1514.

13 Nov. **5582.**   MARY QUEEN OF FRANCE to WOLSEY.

R. O.

Begs his favor in behalf of John Palsgrave, that he may continue at school. Had willed him to remain at Paris after he was discharged from her service. Wishes to do somewhat for him. Would have been glad to help him but her estate is not yet made. Paris, 13 Nov. *Signed.*

P. 1. *Add.:* To my Lord of York.

14 Nov. **5583.**   SAMPSON to WOLSEY.

R. O.

Begs Wolsey will send him the new confirmation of the other first breve, as likely to be effective, especially now at his meeting with the officers. Fears he will be compelled to ride with some of them to Paris, as they profess ignorance of the Bishop's tolerance. Bruges, 14 Nov. 1514.

*Hol. p.*1.   *Add.:* To the most reverend my Lord of York in Angliam.

14 Nov. **5584.**   CHARLES DUKE OF SUFFOLK to WOLSEY.

Calig. D. VI. 155.
B. M.

Writes to assure him that the demeanour of the Lord Chamberlain and of the other ambassadors has been much to the King's honor, and prays him to thank them for the good counsel they have given him touching the King's causes, and for the love and friendship they have shown him since his coming to France. Would have written such news as be in these parts, but is sure my lord and his fellows can show him as much as he. Paris, 14 Nov.

*Hol. p.*1.   *Addressed:* To my Lord of Yorke.

14 Nov. **5585.**   For JAMES BOROUGH, yeoman of the Guard.

P. S.

To be bailiff, in reversion, of the lordships of Sutton-on-Derwent and Elvington, York; which office John Eglesfeld now holds, during pleasure, by patent 12 Sept. 1 Hen. VIII. Greenwich, 12 Nov. 6 Hen. VIII. *Del.* Westm., 14 Nov.

Pat. 6 *Hen.VIII. p.* 1, *m.* 17.

14 Nov. **5586.**   COMMISSION OF THE PEACE.

Cornwall.—H. Bp. of Exeter, Rob. Willoughby Lord Broke, Sir Hen. Marney, Ric. Elyot, Lewis Pollard, Sir John Arundell De la Heron, Sir Peter Eggecombe, Sir Wm. Trevanyon, Wm. Carewe, Roger Graynfeld, Peter Bevyle, John Skewis, John Arundell of Talverne, John Chamond, Rob. V[y]vyan, Jas. Herefy, Ric. Penros, Wm. Lowre, Hen. Trecarell, and Wm. Tarnesewe (for Carnesewe?). Westm., 14 Nov.

Pat. 5 *Hen.VIII. p.* 1, *m.* 6d.

1514.

16 Nov. **5587.**   [SAMPSON] to [WOLSEY].

Calig. D. vi. 282.
B. M.

Yesterday, 15 Nov., he had the [offi]cers assembled, whom he
found as ready as before to defend the bishopric. The [vicar]
general of the bishop exhibited an "appellation tuitori" to Rome,
although they perceived by my Lady's * letters and Sampson's
relation that the French King wished Wolsey to have the administration, for they had letters from the bishop lately commanding
them to defend his jurisdiction. Surprised at this, but trusting to the
French King's promise, he agreed with them that Mr. Peter Coterel,
vicar sometime for their part, and [himself] for Wolsey, should go
to Paris, "to know whether the bishop would suffer the charge and
wait to prosecute his appeal against the Pope's brief." If not, he
trusts Wolsey will have quiet administration. All the officers are
favorable to him, as he has used no rigor. If Wolsey can thus
obtain quiet possession, it will be much to his honor; otherwise to
his "great charge, disquietness, and doubt at the end, as the chance
of victory in a battle is very doubt[ful]. So says the law and the
learned in the same, that the end of a plea [is] doubtful; and more
especially because he is in possession." Hopes to be at Paris by the
end of next week. "This bishopric hath been often in variance,
and as [they] say, few times otherwise ; and lasted the plea sometimes [20] year without ceasing. And during the possession of
the . . . none of these parties durst enterprise to occupy the
offices." It is urged that Wolsey's claim to administration is only
for momentary causes ; " and if they purge the causes, your administration ceaseth." Wolsey's officers would be exposed to the
grudge and malice of their ordinary for favoring him, unless
peaceable possession were obtained. At Br[uges the 16th day
of] November 1514.

Holograph, pp. 2, mutilated.

16 Nov. **5588.**   SIR THOMAS SPINELLY to WOLSEY.

R. O.

Has been compelled to borrow money of the deputy of Calais for
his necessities. Begs to have what is due to him, about 100*l.*
Has received a letter from his brother at Lyons. Bruges, 16 Nov.,
1514. *Signed.*

P. 1. *Add. :* To, &c. my Lord the Abp. of York.

17 Nov. **5589.**   MARY [THE FRENCH QUEEN] to HENRY VIII.

Calig. D. vi. 145.
B. M.

In favor of a poor priest named Vincent Knyght who came
into England with her father (Henry VII.), and has since dwelt
there, but has frequently been sent hither during the wars by
command of the council, who promised him a benefice, but put
him in prison at Tournay, when the King was there. He remained
in prison seven weeks, when he was taken to England and placed
in the Fleet, where he has since been for 44 weeks confined
without just cause, and lost everything, as her special servants
in England have informed her. Prays that the King will command the Bishop of York to return him his money. Paris,
17 Nov. [1514].

Fr. Signed : Par vostre bonne seur, Marie.

* Margaret's.

1514.

Addressed: [A mon t]rescher Seigneur et frere [le Ro]y
d'Angleterre.
Margin burnt.
*Translated in Mrs. Green's Letters of Royal and Illustrious
Ladies,* I. 182.

18 Nov. **5590.**   CHARLES DUKE OF SUFFOLK to WOLSEY.

Calig. D. VI. 156.
B. M.

Has received his letter, written at Greenwich on All Soul's day,
2 Nov., whereby he perceives the King is content with his writing.
The Sunday after his last letter, written on 3 Nov., the Queen
was crowned ; " and at afternoon we and the French King's council
went together, and determined, as we wrote unto the King's grace
in a letter." Since then the Duke of Albany came to his lodging
commissioned by the King to speak with him, and said that the
King counselled him to go to Scotland to mediate such a peace as
should be for Henry's honor ; that to prevent suspicion, he would
leave his wife in France, and come by the King, Suffolk's master,
and return as soon as possible, for he must go over the mountains.
To all which Suffolk replied that he had [no commission] " to
meddle of such matters." Then he said the French King would speak
with him about it, but he heard no more of the matter. " How be
it my Lord Chamberlain and Dr. West [showed me that the
French King's] council had been in hand with th[em upon the
going of the said Duke ; and] upon that we and they took a
conclusion to advertise the King thereof in all haste] ; and if so
were that the French King would be in hand [with me, I should do
all that is] in me possible to let his going." Three days before my
Lord Chamberlain went the Queen showed to Suffolk and the
Marquis divers things which they will tell Wolsey at their
coming ; which seeing that she had need of good friends about the
King, they partly disclosed to my Lord Chamberlain, my Lord of
St. John's and Dr. West, recommending them at the Queen's request
to send for my Lord Longuevyle, the Bp. of St. Paul's, Rob. Tete,
and the General of Normandy, which they promised to do. " And
so within these two days our intention is to [bring] them unto the
Queen's grace according to our communication and appointment.
My lord, at the writing of this letter the justs were done ; and
blessed be God all our Englishmen sped well, as I am sure ye shall
hear by other." Paris, 18 Nov. *Signed.*
Pp. 3. *Add. and endd.*

18 Nov. **5591.**   SAMPSON to [WOLSEY].

R. O.

Another prebend is vacant this day in Tournay. Refused to
admit the Pope's provision alleged by the opponents for the
execution of their bull. Does not see, however, how it can be
withstood without the King's help, as his predecessor in the bishopric
is bound to such admission. On the 21st begins his journey to
Paris. Bruges, 18 Nov. 1514.
Hol., p. 1.

18 Nov. **5592.**   PETER MARTYR to LUD. FURTADO.

Epist. 543.

The Venetians have attacked Ramon de Cardona, who fled to
Brescia, and lost his baggage. Bergamo has surrendered to the
Venetians. Against all the advice of his physicians, Ferdinand
would go to Leon. There was a great storm of wind and rain ;

1514.

the rivers overflowed ; the King and Queen lost most of their baggage. Ferdinand has caught a cold and is worse, and declines all business.—Now from the King Catholic to the King non-Catholic. Selim Shah has written to the Grand Master, styling him friend, and detailing the destruction of the Sophi. He acknowledges that the loss of the Turks was 150,000. The Rhodians are in great apprehension. Valladolid, xiv. kl. Dec. 1514.

18 Nov.
S. B.

5593. For HUMPHREY son and heir of EDM. COKAYN.

Livery of lands. *Del.* Westm., 18 Nov. 6 Hen. VIII.

Pat. 6 Hen. VIII. p. 2, m. 13.

18 Nov.
P. S.

5594. For SIR WILLIAM FITZWILLIAM.

Grant, in reversion, of the office of keeper of Bagshote park in Windsor forest, with herbage, and usual fees out of a messuage called "le Crown" in Bagshote and lands in Bagshote and Wynsham, Surrey; now held by Henry Uvedale, by patent 20 June 19 Hen. VII. Greenwich, 13 Nov. 6 Hen. VIII. *Del.* Westm., 18 Nov.

Pat. 6 Hen. VIII. p. 2, m. 18.

18 Nov.
P. S.

5595. For ROBERT CHAMBRE, smith.

Annuity of 2d. a day, from 15 Nov. 3 Hen. VIII., (for his services in making the ironworks of the King's new ships,) out of the farm of Beddyngton, as held by Sir Thomas Edmondson, priest, deceased. Greenwich, 16 Nov. 6 Hen. VIII. *Del.* Westm., 18 Nov.

Pat. 6 Hen. VIII. p. 2, m. 20.

20 Nov.
P. S.

5596. For THOMAS son and heir of SIR RICHARD DELABER.

Livery of lands. Greenwich, 14 Nov. 6 Hen. VIII. *Del.* Westm., 20 Nov.

Pat. 6 Hen. VIII. p. 1, m. 25.

20 Nov.
P. S.

5597. For WILLIAM BRETON, merchant of the staple of Calais, grocer of London.

Protection ; going in the retinue of Sir Richard Wingfeld, Deputy of Calais. Greenwich, 15 Nov. 6 Hen. VIII. *Del.* Westm., 20 Nov.

Pat. 6 Hen. VIII. p. 2, m. 28.

20 Nov.
Titus B. i. 238.
B. M.

5598. GEORGE DUKE OF SAXONY to the ENGLISH AMBASSADORS with ARCHDUKE CHARLES.

In favor of Simon de Reyshach, Chancellor of Friesland. Ex Lewardia, 20 Nov. 1514.

Lat., p. 1.

Endorsed : Letters of credence delivered to Sir Thomas Spynelly, knt., by the Chancellor of Frizeland for the Duck of Saxe.

3 N

1514.

R. O.

5599. [SIMON DE REISCHACH] to HENRY VIII.

Desiring assistance for his master George Duke of Saxony, hereditary governor of Friesland for the Emperor Maximilian, against Edezard Count of Embden, his vassal and lieutenant of East Friesland, who has refused his fealty, and notwithstanding repeated warnings continues a rebel. Regrets to make this application while Henry is at war; but if through Henry's assistance the Duke obtain the victory, he will place all his forces, 8,000 in number, at the King's disposal.

Lat., pp. 2.   Endorsed: The Duke of Saxony.

5600. SIMON DE REISCHACH to SPINELLY.

Galba, B, III. 225.
B. M.

The Duke of Gueldres [has written] to Prince George of Saxony [stating that the Duke is required] in the name of the King of France to aid Edezard Earl of Emden as the confederate of France and England.—On application to the King of England, the latter denies that the Earl has been admitted into the confederacy, and refuses to assist him; but desires that his understanding with the Duke of Saxony may continue and be strengthened. Saxony receives these overtures with pleasure, and sends a copy of the letters he received from the Duke of Gueldres, wherein he states that he has collected a large army with a view of raising the siege of Groningen. Prince George is the Imperial Governor in perpetuity of all Friesland and Groningen, and would be glad if the King of England would send an ambassador to the King of France enjoining that no assistance be given by Gueldres to the rebellious inhabitants of Groningen. Last summer he wrote [in the name] of the said Prince for a loan of 40,000 gold crowns for a year, and now repeats the request. The writer has been hindered from visiting England by the weather. Prince George therefore requests [Spinelly] to announce the above to the King, and if he wishes to send an ambassador, the writer will wait for him at Calais or here in Brussells.

Lat., pp. 3., mutilated, and last page misplaced. Indorsed by Spinelly: The remembrance given by the Chancellor of Friezeland touching his charge of the Duke of Saxe, his master, to Sir Thomas Spinelly, knight, for to be sent to the King, &c.

21 Nov.
R. O.

5601. [FRA. GONZAGA] MARQUIS OF MANTUA to HENRY VIII.

Thanks him for a noble present of horses to him and his wife, which has made him of consequence in the eyes of his countrymen. Sends him in return 12 brood mares, as he has learned from Sir Griffith Don that the King is very fond of horses. One of these mares has been broken in. If the King will send yearly into Italy, he shall have the pick of the Marquis' stables. Mantua, 21 Nov. 1514. *Signed.*

Lat., p. 1.   Addressed.   Endorsed.

21 Nov.
R. O.

5602. SILVESTER BP. OF WORCESTER to WOLSEY.

Thanks him for his favor bestowed at the writer's request on Launcelot Colyns, treasurer of York. Begs licence for Colyns to return to Italy, and pursue his studies. Rome, 21 Nov. 1514. *Signed.*

P. 1.   Add.: To, &c. my Lord the Abp. of York.

1514.

21 Nov. **5603.** For PETER LARKE of Thetford, innkeeper.

P. S.

Pardon and release. Greenwich, 21 Nov. 6 Hen. VIII. *Del.* Westm., 21 Nov.

Pat. 6 Hen. VIII. p. 2, m. 19.

21 Nov. **5604.** PAYMENTS by SIR RIC. WINGFIELD in the King's com-

R. O.

mission from 8 Jan. 4 Hen. VIII. to 21 Nov. 6 Hen. VIII.

Wages to the Bastard D'Amerie (Emery), to spies, to guides sent by the Emperor to conduct the King's army, to scouts on the King's arrival, to Lancaster Herald, to Henry Hount, and 28 mariners in the King's row barge, to his servant Bishop coming and going, to Bluemantle, to the glasier of Antwerp for glazing the great east window in St. Nicholas' Church, Calais, by the King's command, 33*l.* 6*s.* 8*d.*, to a painter of Gaunt for taking the portraiture of the King's visage to be set in the said window 25*s.*, &c.

Pp. 8.

22 Nov. **5605.** COMMISSION OF THE PEACE.

Yorkshire.—Hen. Earl of Northumberland, Ric. Nevell Lord Latemer, Sir Thos. Lovell, Rob. Brudenell, a justice of the King's Bench, Sir Thos. Parre, Brian Palmes, serjeant-at-law, Sir Wm. Tirwhitt, and Ric. Rokesby. Westm., 22 Nov.

Pat. 6 Hen. VIII. p. 2, m. 4d.

See 26 Oct.

22 Nov. **5606.** THOMAS MARQUIS OF DORSET to WOLSEY.

Calig. D. vi. 192.

B. M.

On Monday the 13th inst. the jousts began, and continued three days. My Lord of Suffolk and he ran three days, and lost nothing. One Frenchman was slain at the tilt, and divers horses. On Saturday the 18th, "the tournay and course in the field began as roughly as ever I saw; for there was divers times both horse and man overthrown, horses slain, and one Frenchman hurt that he is not like to live. My Lord of Suffolk and I ran the first day thereat, but put our ayds thereto, because there was no nobleman to be put unto us, but poor men of arms, and Scots many of them, were hurt on both sides, but no great hurt, and of our Englishmen none overthrown nor greatly hurt but a little of their hands. The Dauphin himself was a little hurt on his hand." On Tuesday the 21st the fighting on foot began, "to the which they brought an Almayn that never came into the field before, and put him to my Lord of Suffolk to have put us to shame, but advantage they gat none of us, but rather the contrary. I forbear to write more of our chances, because I am party therein. I ende[d] without any manner hurt; my Lord of Suffolk is a little hurt in his hand." The King's matters go forward well; and on Monday or Tuesday they intend to depart to return to England. The French King sends Mons. La Guysse to the [King] in embassy, "and to lie there still he hath . . . . there before time the Dauphin st . . . . Bonyvette to his grace with horses and . . . . which Bonyvette is one of his secret serv[ants, and] I think he shall come in our company."

[*What follows is in Dorset's own hand.*] The Queen continues her goodness and wisdom, and increases in the favor of her

1514.

husband and the privy council. She had told Suffolk and him that the King had told her they "dyde same (shame) aule Franse, and that vhy s . . . . gary (should carry ?) the prynse (prize ?) in tho Ingland." On Sunday the [26th] day of November, the prizes are to be given. " Vy hauf [h]ade dywerse comonycasyans vythe Pryfe Counsele. Vy lefe to vyrte bychawse the sarge hys my lorde a [Sofeh]oke, bwte has fare has kane parsefe, haule [thin]gys gohyth vhele, and to howre maysters [hono]ure. My Lord, I thynge no more to vr[yte un] thyle I see you." Paris [xx]ij Nov. *Signed.*

Pp. 3 ; *mutilated.*

Addressed : To my Lord of York's good lordship.

---

22 Nov.   **5607.**   For JOHN CHAMBRE, chaplain and physician to the King.

S. B.   Grant of the deanery of St. Stephen's, Westminster, void by translation of Thomas Wulcy to the see of York. *Del.* Westm., 22 Nov. 6 Hen. VIII.

---

22 Nov.   **5608.**   To JOHN YONG, Master of the Rolls.

S. B.   To cancel three recognizances of 150*l.*, made by James Metcalfe of Nappey, Thomas Fulthorp of Hyppeswell, York, William Rokeby and Thomas Tempest of Loudon, 3 July 23 Hen. VII., to Sir Thomas Lovell, Sir Richard Emson, Sir John Husey, Edmund Dudley and Henry Wyot. Greenwich, 22 Nov. 6 Hen. VIII.

---

22 Nov.   **5609.**   For JOHN VEYSY, Dean of the Chapel Royal.

P. S.   Canonry and prebend in St. Stephen's, Westminster, *vice* John Chambre, resigned.   Greenwich, 15 Nov. 6 Hen. VIII.   *Del.* Westm., 22 Nov.

Pat. 6 *Hen.* VIII. *p.* 1, *m.* 12.

---

22 Nov.   **5610.**   For THOMAS, son and heir of ROGER BODENHAM.

P. S.   Livery of lands in co. Hereford and marches of Wales.   Greenwich, 16 Nov. 6 Hen. VIII.   *Del.* Westm., 22 Nov.

Pat. 6 *Hen. VIII. p.* 1, *m.* 28.

---

22 Nov.   **5611.**   For WILLIAM BUSSHE.

P. S.   Grant of the ferry of Sandfordhith, Oxon. and Berks, and care of the King's ferry boats, from the first day of the reign; which office was granted him, during pleasure, by patent 15 Dec. 22 Hen. VII., *vice* Thomas Hunt, deceased ; — with all emoluments of the said office, from 15 Dec. 22 Hen. VII., from which date to 21 April 24 Hen. VII. the said William was molested by the escheators. Greenwich, 18 Nov. 6 Hen. VIII. *Del.* Westm., 22 Nov.

Pat. 6 *Hen. VIII. p.* 2, *m.* 28.

---

22 Nov.   **5612.**   For EDWARD HASELEY, salter, of London.

P. S.   Protection ; going in the retinue of Sir Richard Wingfeld, Deputy of Calais.   Greenwich, 19 Nov. 6 Hen. VIII.   *Del.* Westm., 22 Nov.

1514.
23 Nov. **5613.** LEO X. to JAMES V.

Sadoleti Epist.
Pont. xxxiv.

Congratulates him on his accession, which he learned by his letters of 5 Oct. Is glad to hear that peace has been established between England and Scotland. Recommends obedience to his uncle. Rome, 23 Nov. 1514.

23 Nov. **5614.** MARGARET OF SCOTLAND to HENRY VIII.

Calig. B. i. 164.
B. M.

Has received his loving letters by a man of Dacre's, 22nd Nov. She and her party were in great trouble till they knew what help Henry would give them; but having shown the letters to the lords then in Stirling Castle they were greatly comforted. Her adversaries continue to usurp the King's authority in parliament, holding her and her adherents rebels. Begs Henry to hasten his army by sea and land, especially against the chamberlain, who is "post of "this conspiration." Within this se'nnight he appropriated an escheat of a bastardy, value 10,000*l.*, as if he had the sole authority. The prior of St. Andrew's on the other side has laid siege to the Castle of St. Andrew's. Hopes Henry's navy will come to the rescue. Has sent her husband to raise the siege this 23rd day. If not speedily relieved her funds will fail. Spends a thousand a day in wages. The enemy trust entirely to the coming of Albany. If he arrive before Henry's army, some may incline to him from dread. Will keep this castle with her children till she hear from Henry. Some of the lords who fear their land will be destroyed by the invasion had better be assured from Henry to the contrary. The King and his younger brother prosper, and are "recht life-like children." The enemy intend to besiege her in Stirling. Desires therefore that the chamberlain "was haldin waking" in the mean time with the Borderers. She can defend herself well against the others till the English army come. Begs credence be given to Adam Williamson, and he be thanked for his services and for the peril he was in, in the ship that was broken with other three ships, which left Scotland before his, with Lion herald and other messengers, sent by the adverse lords to Albany, with letters under the Great Seal, which they detain and use "as they were kings." Has given St. Andrew's to the postulate of Arbroath, her husband's uncle. Begs Henry to write to the Pope in his favor. Desires letters from him every month at least as to his purposes; "and giff my party adversare counterfettes ony letteris in my name, or giff yai compell me to write to zou for concord ye subscription salbe bott yus: Margaret R. & na mare;" which will show that she has been forced.

Signed: Your loweing suster,
Stirling, 23 Nov. MARGARET R.

Pp. 2. *Addressed:* To the rycht hye, &c., derrest brothar ye Kynge off Englande.

23 Nov. **5615.** To WILLIAM ABP. OF CANTERBURY, Chancellor.

S. B.

To make out writs for assembling parliament at Westminster, 5 Feb. next. *Del.* 23 Nov. 6 Hen. VIII.

23 Nov. **5616.** SUMMONS TO PARLIAMENT.

R. O.

Summons addressed to the under-mentioned prelates, &c. to come to the parliament to be holden at Westminster on the 5th of

1514.

February next ; viz., W. Archbp. of Canterbury, Tho. Archbp.
of York, R. Bp. of London, R. Bp. of Winchester, Tho. Bp. of
Durham, H. Bishop of Exeter, J. Bp. of Ely, W. Bp. of Lincoln,
E. Bp. of Salisbury, R. Bp. of Chichester, J. Bp. of Carlisle,
J. Bishop of Rochester, G. Bp. of Coventry and Lichfield, M. Bp.
of Llandaff, R. Bp. of Norwich, [R.] Bp. of Hereford, Th. Bp. of
Bangor, E. Bp. of St. David's, the keeper of the spiritualities
of Bath and Wells during the Bishop's absence, the keeper of
the spiritualities of Worcester, the Abbots of Peterborough, St.
John's Colchester, Bury St. Edmond's, Abingdon, Waltham Holy
Cross, Shrewsbury, Cirencester, St. Peter's Gloucester, St. Pe-
ter's Westminster, St. Alban's, Berdeney, Selby, Benet, Hulme,
Thorney, Evesham, Ramsey, Hyde near Winchester, Glastonbury,
Malmesbury, Croyland, Battle, Wynchecombe, Reading, St. Augus-
tine's Canterbury, St. Mary's York, Tewkesbury and Tavistock, the
Priors of Coventry and of St. John's, Edw. Duke of Buckingham,
Tho. Duke of Norfolk, Charles Duke of Suffolk, Tho. Marquis of
Dorset, Tho. Earl of Arundel, Rich. Earl of Kent, Tho. Earl of
Derby, Henry Earl of Northumberland, Tho. Earl of Surrey
Henry Earl of Essex, Geo. Earl of Shrewsbury, Charles Earl of
Worcester, Henry Earl of Wiltshire, Edward Stanley Lord Mont-
eagle, Henry Lord Clifford, George Nevile Lord Bergeveny, G. Lord
Hastings, Tho. West Lord De la Warr, John Broke Lord Cobham,
Edward Sutton Lord Dudley, Rich. Nevyle Lord Latymer, Will.
Lord Willoughby, Tho. Lord Darcy, Will. Lord Conyers, Will.
Blount Lord Mountjoy, John Lord Zouch, John Bourchier Lord
Fitzwaryn, Tho. Ormond Lord Rochford, Tho. Fenys Lord Dacre,
Robt. Lord Ogle, John Bourchier Lord Bernes, Will. Lord Stour-
ton, Tho. Lord Dacres, Robt. Ratcliff Lord Fitzwauter, Walter
Devereux Lord Ferrers, John Tuchett Lord Audeley, Ralph Scrope
Lord Upsall, Henry Lord Scrope of Bolton, John Lord Lumley,
Henry Lord Dawbeney and Lord Clinton.

Official copy. Signed : Thomas Ravenscroftz.

Endorsed in a different hand : vi° Hen. 8.

---

23 Nov.   **5617.**   To JOHN YONG, Master of the Rolls.

S. B.   To cancel a recognizance of 100*l.*, made by Henry Earl of Essex,
           10 Nov. 6 Hen. VIII.   Greenwich, 23 Nov. 6 Hen. VIII.

---

23 Nov.   **5618.**   For SIR JOHN SHARP.

S. B.   Grant of one " le dole" of the stannary in Lourchecomb, another
           in Helebrigge, a third in Olde Whittondon, a fourth in Litelle
           Witton Downe, alias Hier Witton Downe, and a fifth in Harlis Parke,
           and two "lez dolez" and a half in Lower Whittondon, Devon ; in the
           King's hands by attainder of Robert Stronge ;—with all profits
           from Easter 1 Hen. VIII.   *Del.* Westm., 23 Nov.

           Pat. 6 Hen. VIII. p. 1, m. 15.

---

23 Nov.   **5619.**   For SIR EDWARD BELKNAP and SIR JOHN DAUNCE.

P. S.   To be surveyors with Bartholomew Westby, of the crown pos-
           sessions specified by statute 4 Hen. VIII. ; by which statute,
           and by patent 7 May 5 Hen. VIII., Sir Robert Southwell,
           now deceased, and the said Bartholomew were appointed to the

1514.

said office. All fines to be paid over to John Heron, treasurer of the Chamber. Greenwich, 17 Nov. 6 Hen. VIII. *Del.* Westm., 23 Nov.
Pat. 6 *Hen. VIII. p.* 2, *m.* 19.

23 Nov.
S. B.
Rym. XIII. 469.

5620. For WILLIAM, the ABBOT, and the CONVENT of ST. MARY OSENEYE, Oxford.

Licence to obtain bulls from Rome, to annex the perpetual vicarage of the parish church of Shenston, dioc. Lichfield, to the said monastery. *Del.* 23 Nov. 6 Hen. VIII.
Pat. 6 *Hen. VIII. p.* 2, *m.* 15.

23 Nov.
P. S.

5621. For RICH. RAWLINS, D.D., the King's almoner.

Grant of the goods and chattels of felons *de se*, &c., for increasing the King's alms. Greenwich, 18 Nov. 6 Hen. VIII. *Del.* Westm., 23 Nov.
Pat. 6 *Hen. VIII. p.* 2, *m.* 29.

23 Nov.
P. S.

5622. For WM. REYNOLD of Westminster, brewer, native of Scotland.

Denization. Greenwich, 16 Nov. 6 Hen. VIII. *Del.* Westm., 23 Nov.
Pat. 6 *Hen. VIII. p.* 2, *m.* 18.

23 Nov.

5623. For the DEAN and CHAPTER of the Collegiate Chapel of ST. STEPHEN, in the Palace of Westminster.

Writ to install John Veysy in the above canonry and prebend, granted to him, *vice* John Chambre, by patent 22 Nov. last. Westm., 23 Nov.
Pat. 6 *Hen. VIII. p.* 1, *m.* 12.

23 Nov.

5624. For JOHN, ABBOT of the Monastery of ST. PETER, WEST-MINSTER.

Writ to install John Chambre in the deanery of the collegiate church or chapel of St. Stephen, in the palace of Westminster, granted to him, *vice* Thos. Wulcy, by patent 22 Nov. last. Westm., 23 Nov.
Pat. 6 *Hen. VIII. p.* 1, *m.* 12.

23 Nov.

5625. For RALPH SEYNTLEGER and ROB. LAMBE.

Mortmain licence to grant the manor of East Sutton, Kent, of the annual value of 12*l.* 13*s.* 4*d.*, as appears by an inquisition taken before Thos. Burgoyn, escheator, to the prior and convent of the church of St. Mary and St. Nicholas, Ledes, Kent, in pursuance of the patent granting the said prior and convent licence to acquire lands to the clear annual value of 20*l.* Westm., 23 Nov.
Pat. 6 *Hen. VIII. p.* 2, *m.* 13.

24 Nov.

5626. COMMISSION OF ARRAY.

Notts, Derby, Leicester, Lincoln, York, Cumberland, and Westmoreland.—Commission of muster and array to Hen. Earl of Northumberland and Sir Thos. Lovell, K.G. Westm., 24 Nov.
Pat. 6 *Hen. VIII. p.* 2, *m.* 4*d.*
See 26 Oct.

1514.

24 Nov.   **5627.**   For ROB. STANSHAWE, page of the Chamber.
S. B.
Grant, in tail male, of the lands called Kyttenden Fyrme in the parish of Stretley, Berks, and a close called Kyttenden Bromes alias Bromewode, which came into the hands of Henry VII. by attainder of John Earl of Lincoln.   *Del.* Westm., 24 Nov. 6 Hen. VIII.

Pat. 6 Hen. VIII. p. 2, m. 32.

24 Nov.   **5628.**   For JOAN GULDEFORD, late wife of SIR RICHARD
P. S.   GULDEFORD.
Rym. XIII. 470.
Annuity of 20l. for her services to the late King and Queen, and to Mary Queen of the French and Margaret Queen of Scots. Greenwich, 21 Nov. 6 Hen. VIII.   *Del.* Westm., 24 Nov.

Pat. 6 Hen. VIII. p. 2, m. 9.

24 Nov.   **5629.**   For SIR WALTER HUNGERFORD.
S. B.
Wardship of John, brother and h. of Philip Turney, son and heir of John Turney, of Wolverton, Somers., both deceased, who held of the King as of the manor of Gloucester.   *Del.* Westm., 24 Nov. 6 Hen. VIII.

Pat. 6 Hen. VIII. p. 1, m. 32 ; and p. 2, m. 21.

24 Nov.   **5630.**   For JOHN WARDE.
P. S.
To be banner-bearer before St. Wilfride, *vice* Thomas Edwardis, with 5l. a year out of the town and lordship of Rypon, York, during the nonage of Lord Nevell, the King's ward, to whom the said office belongs by service of his lands.   Greenwich, 15 Nov. 6 Hen. VIII.   *Del.* Westm., 24 Nov.

24 Nov.   **5631.**   For PETER ASBY, LL.B.
P. S.
Presentation to the church of Skrayenham, York dioc., *vice* William Ingelerd, resigned.   Greenwich, 21 Nov. 6 Hen. VIII.   *Del.* Westm., 24 Nov.

Pat. 6 Hen. VIII. p. 2, m. 24.

25 Nov.   **5632.**   TH. SPINELLY to HENRY VIII.
R. O.
Since closing his letter is advertised from Mechlin that Herman Tulman, a canon of Utrecht, is dead. Begs for his brother the benefice which the deceased held in England by the gift of Hen. VII.   25 Nov.   *Signed.   Add.*

P. 1.   Add.

25 Nov.   **5633.**   DEBTS OWING TO HENRY VIII.
R. O.
Debtors : Lord Broke—Sir Thomas Bryan—Sir William Fitzwilliam—Anthony Hansard—Sir Henry Willoughby—Sir John Savage—George Trevylyon—Earl of Wiltshire—Sir Will. Sandes—Duke of Buckingham—Lord Willoughby—Earl of Shrewsbury—Lord Barners—Sir Edward Guldeford—Lord Ferrers—Lord Dudeley—Sir John Hussey—Lord Audeley—Lord Burgevenny—Earl of Derby—Marquis of Dorset—Lord Dacre—Sir Will. Carewe—Sir Henry Halshall—Lord Hasting —Nicholas Wadham—

1514.

Earl of Essex—Lord Cobham—Sir Thomas Cornwall—Sir Griffith Rice—Richard Cornwall—Hervy Haward—Sir Wistan Broun—Sir Henry Long—Thomas Cheyne—Sir Edward Haward—executors of Sir Francis Cheyne—and James Darell. Directions taken upon the above cases by Wolsey, Fox and others of the Council, at the Savoy, Saturday 25 Nov. 6 Hen. VIII.
Pp. 5. *Endd.*

25 Nov. **5634.** THOMAS MARQUIS OF DORSET to WOLSEY.
Calig. D. VI. 190.
B. M.

Since the writing of his "other" letters a packet of letters and instructions had arrived from the King. Being on the point of dispatching other matters they judge it best to proceed, and not to join those matters and the other together. [*Thus far in a clerk's hand; the rest in Dorset's own.*] The first time Suffolk broke with the French King of their charge he desired Dorset to help him and spoke of Navarre (*Nafare*) "to see how he would take it, and to prove further his mind and see what we could get of him; who byhawfe (behaved) him with marvellous good words touching our master, but nothing to the purpose of Navarre, but ever to grope us and know the uttermost of our minds. And vhy ansure (we answer) hyme vhyte plesante vordys agayne ever . . . and thane gropynge at him agayne ; and when [he] saw it vholde by none hodyr vheys (otherwise) a kalyth (he called) [us to] bankete, and made hus ete and drynge by hys bede ; [and] that done a bade us goude nyde, and sayd [we] sude come in the mornynge to hus . . . . . myd to by has golse (?) to theyme ha[s] . . . . . . kynge and vy vher in dyd (we were indeed) by the . . . . ymynge to theyme.

" . . . . that we had noue ho . . . . they demandyt ofe hws vyder v[y had any] tynge eles to say, and vhy sayd vy trote and . . . . to be pleyne vythe hus and ife vy so fonde they . . . volde by so vythe theyme, and so they departyth to [the] Kynge and kame the nex day to hws and apy . . . . ther to hus the kyngys plesyre and mynde so largely to hus that vhy vhele parsevyth (we well perceived) they . . . . . pleynle vyth thus and hes thanges kyfyne (thanks given) to t . . . prosedet farder in hore mater and thane they . . . . to loke hone apone anodyr. And so, my lorde, has [me] thowth, vy departyth vhele contentyth [on] bothe partys, and toke thys dyreckcyone fo[r] my dysarge that vy sale haufe hawle the Fren[ch King's] plesyre in vrytyngys, has vhele hys demand[ys] has hys asynys to houre demandys, vyche by synyth (be signed) vythe hys hone hande, so that vy s . . . . no vordys but vrytyngs. My lord, synys th . . . the kyng has devysyth vythe the quene . . . . . lorde and ofe my by the spase ofe to hurys (two hours). . . . . [He p]raysyt my lorde ofe Swfehoke and sayth [that he]re hys no prynse gyrsynyth (christened) has sw[ch] . . . . . .t for pes and vare sahynge tha[t] . . . . and in the consele . . . . [h]onure and that and the kynge . . . . . have hodyre in basadwrs hyder [he should] note a byne so sortele dyspasyth. I [pray] Gode that vhy hawfe done owse so vele . . . . hys grase doth stey (?) the quyne ofe hus. And has twchyng [the] maters of Scotelante vhy vhel hawle haufe [ho]wre dypesch fyste in vrytynge, vyche I truste [sch]ale by today, and that done vhy [will] prosyde in to hwre maters ofe Scotelande, [and] so to departe has sortele has vhy may." Paris, 25 Nov. *Signed.*
Addressed: To my Lord of York's good lordship.
Mutilated, pp. 3.

1514.

25 Nov.   **5635.   LEO X. to HENRY VIII.**
R. O.
> Has received his two letters. Requires no thanks for what he
> has done, the services of Henry to the papacy are so great. Is
> glad to find that the King is satisfied of the innocence of the
> bp. of Worcester. Has delayed to send the declaration he had
> promised in order that his slanderers might not say they had not
> sufficient time to prove their case. Will send them when complete.
> Rome, 25 Nov. 1514, 2 pont.
>
> *Lat., p. 1. Addressed:* Au Roy.

25 Nov.   **5636.   A. DE LIGNE to HENRY VIII.**
R. O.
> Some Frenchmen have done him ill services. Has explained
> the facts to them and the English lieutenant of Tournay. Mor-
> taigne, 25 Nov. 1514. *Signed.*
>
> *Fr. p. 1. Addressed.*

26 Nov.   **5637.   LEWIS XII.**
R. T. 137.
R. O.
> Answer to the propositions made to him by the Duke of
> Suffolk, on the part of Henry VIII. touching the kingdom of
> Navarre.
>
> Thanks him for sending him so important a personage as the
> Duke. Professes to deal frankly with him, and give him his
> answer on the two following propositions :—(1.) How far he will
> assist England in expelling the King of Arragon from Navarre,
> considering that he has broken his engagements with Henry and
> Lewis. (2.) That as the kingdom of Castile, by right, should
> descend to sisters, and the King of England claims one part, how far
> Lewis will assist him in claiming his rights.—With regard to the
> question of right, Lewis can give no certain answer, because he
> does not know the laws of the kingdom of Spain; but without
> entering upon this he is willing to join the King in prosecuting his
> claims and expelling Ferdinand from Navarre, and will raise an
> army with him for that purpose. But without disclosing their
> intentions each King is to hear the ambassadors of Arragon.
> England and France shall communicate by their ambassadors
> upon this matter without concealment on either side. No
> arrangement shall be made without mutual consent. In return
> Suffolk is to explain to the King of England the history of the
> claim of Lewis to the duchy of Milan, of which a brief is given;
> is to request the aid of England in its recovery, and a loan for
> one year of 200,000 crowns, on good security. He hopes the
> enterprise will be ready by the month of March. Paris, 26 Nov.
> 1514.
>
> *Fr. pp. 7.*

26 Nov.   **5638.   MARY QUEEN OF FRANCE.**
Harl. 1757. f.227.
B. M.
> Complimentary oration made to Mary of England by the Uni-
> versity of Paris, 26 Nov. 1514.
>
> In congratulating her on her marriage it is said, among other
> things, that it has been the privilege of the Kings of France since
> Clovis never to be killed in battle, and never to be slain by their
> people, or chased out of their own kingdoms.
>
> *Fr., pp. 23.*

1514.

27 Nov.
S. B.
5639.   For ANTHONY CHABO, surgeon, native of Savoy.

Denization. *Del.* Westm., 27 Nov. 6 Hen. VIII.
Pat. 6 *Hen. VIII. p.* 1, *m.* 18.

27 Nov.
S. B.
5640.   For SIR EDWARD FERRERS, alias FERREYS, of Baddisley, Warw., alias of the Royal Household.

Pardon and release as sheriff of Warwickshire and Leicestershire; and release to him, Sir John Rodney of Stoke Rodney, Somers., and Nicholas Brome of Wodelows, Warw., of their recognizance of 40*l.*, made 15 Nov. 5 Hen. VIII. *Del.* Westm., 27 Nov. 6 Hen. VIII.

Pat. 6 *Hen. VIII. p.* 1, *m.* 13.

27 Nov.
Calig. B. i. 154.
B. M.
5641.   DACRE to the COUNCIL.

Received their letters on the 19th, with a packet for the Queen of Scots, which reached her on Wednesday the 22d, at Stirling. Encloses her answer. She durst not make superscription. She was taken from Stirling to Edinburgh, by Arran and the Chamberlain ; received there by the Chancellor and the Council ; " albeit when as they had her there they yode clear from her ways, and so she withdrew herself be wisdom from Edinburgh to Striveling on the said Tuesday, and the Earl of Angus with her." Hepburn, Prior of St. Andrew's, has besieged the castle there in spite of the warning from Angus. Nothing has been heard of Lyon Herald, that went in James Wood's ship to France Sept. last. It is thought he is drowned. A herald named March has come from France for ratification and comprehension, which it is thought by Arran will be sent to Albany to do as he likes. He claims the castle of Dunbar as part of the earldom of March. The Bp. of Murray has demanded the surrender of it by letter to his brother keeper. Kirkoswald, 27 Nov. *Signed.*

P. 1. *Addressed :* To my Lords of the King's most honorable Council.

27 Nov.
Epist. 541.
5642.   PETER MARTYR to LUD. FURTADO.

Lewis has taken to his bed, but hasn't given over his designs on Italy. Ferdinand is no stronger than he. His asthma grows worse. Henry has written to the Pope, stating he had given his sister to Lewis because he found himself abandoned by his allies,— that she was refused by Charles, and the title of Queen of France was very honorable. Valladolid, v. kl. Dec. 1514.

27 Nov.
P. S.
5643.   For JOHN COPYNGER, page of the Robes.

To be keeper of Okley park, Glouc., *vice* Edmund Wykis, deceased. Greenwich, 24 Nov. 6 Hen. VIII. *Del.* Westm., 27 Nov.

Pat. 6 *Hen. VIII. p.* 2, *m.* 9.

28 Nov.
S. B.
5644.   For THOMAS EARL OF SURREY.

Grant of 100 oaks in the park of Wyngfeld, Suff., of which the said Earl is tenant for life by law. *Del.* Westm., 28 Nov. 6 Hen. VIII.

Pat. 6 *Hen. VIII. p.* 2, *m.* 21.

1514.
28 Nov.   **5645.**   For JOHN CROMPE.

Pardon for having killed Christopher Tomsett of Tyrley, Glouc., in self defence, as certified by Rob. Grevile, one of the coroners in Glouc. Westm., 28 Nov.
Pat. 6 Hen. VIII. p. 1, *m.* 18.

28 Nov.   **5646.**   For JOHN KYNGESTON.

Pardon for having, by his charter 15 April 5 Hen. VIII., alienated the manor of Falley, alias South Falley, Berks, to Ric. Eliott, a justice of the Common Pleas, Wm. Fetiplace, John Fetiplace and Chas. Bulkeley, their heirs and assigns, to the use of Kyngeston and Susanna his wife, and his heirs, licence not having been obtained, as appears by an inquisition taken before Wm. Yong, escheator. Westm., 28 Nov.
Pat. 6 Hen. VIII. p. 1, *m.* 30.

28 Nov.   **5647.**   For THOMAS EARL OF DERBY.
S. B.

Livery of lands as son and heir of Joan Stanley, widow, late Lady le Straunge. *Del.* Westm., 28 Nov. 6 Hen. VIII.
Pat. 6 Hen. VIII. p. 1, *m.* 25.

28 Nov.   **5648.**   For JOHN CROCKER, squire of the Body.
P. S.

Licence to empark certain lands and heath in his manor of Lyneham, Devon ; with free warren in his lands of Lyneham, Hemerdon, Brixton, Smalehanger and Torpike. Greenwich, 27 Nov. 6 Hen. VIII. *Del.* Westm., 28 Nov.
Pat. 6 Hen. VIII. p. 2, *m.* 22.

28 Nov.   **5649.**   SUFFOLK and DORSET to WOLSEY.
R. O.

Reached Clermont this day " in our way towards our master." The French King has promised that neither the Duke of Albany nor the Bp. of Murray shall be sent into Scotland, " but one in a long gown of no great estimation." He will make the King privy of all such matters. Desire ships to be sent to Dover for their conveyance. Clermont, Tuesday 28 Nov. *Signed.*
P. 1. *Add. :* To my Lord of York's good lordship.

29 Nov.   **5650.**   SILVESTER BP. OF WORCESTER to WOLSEY.
R. O.

Writes again at the Pope's request in behalf of John, son of Francis de Bardis, of whose losses in alum the Pope and he had already written. Rome, 29 Nov. 1514. *Signed.*
Lat., p. 1. *Add. :* R'mo, &c. Archiepo. Ebor.

29 Nov.   **5651.**   HENRY VIII. to LEO X.
R. O.

Is sorry to learn by the Pope's brief, dated the ——— of this month, that his request to have the collectorship bestowed upon Andreas Ammonius has been misrepresented, as though it had been unduly extorted, especially by him who is extremely offensive to the King. Will not insist on N.'s (Cardinal Hadrian's) want of fidelity, or the calumny and infamy which he has endeavoured to bring on the Bp. of Worcester, or the coldness with which he has received the announcement of the King's league with France; but the Pope must

1514.

not be surprised if he (N.) is punished for such offences. Greenwich, 29 Nov. 1514.

Lat., on parchment, in the hand of Ammonius, and signed by him. Addressed.

29 Nov.
S. B.

5652. To WILLIAM ABP. OF CANTERBURY, Chancellor.

To put the date 20 September 6 Hen. VIII. on letters patent granting to Charles Earl of Worcester, and Henry his son and heir, in survivorship, the offices of constable of the castle of Dynas, and steward of Walshstalgarght and Dynas, Wales. Greenwich, 29 Nov. 6 Hen. VIII. (*See S.B. 20 Sept. 6 Hen. VIII.*)

29 Nov.
P. S.

5653. For JOHN CLOGGE, yeoman of the Crown.

To have the fee of the Crown, being 6*d.* a day, from Mic. last. Greenwich, 27 Nov. 6 Hen. VIII. *Del.* Westm., 29·Nov.

30 Nov.
S. B.

5654. For SIR RICHARD WHETEHILL.

Annuity of 40 marks out of the issues of Calais, from Mic. last ;— also donation of 40 marks in discharge of payment of the said annuity, from 6 Oct. 5 Hen. VIII. to 9 Oct. last. *Del.* Westm., 30 Nov. 6 Hen. VIII.

Pat. 6 *Hen. VIII. p.* 1, *m.* 19.

30 Nov
P. S.

5655. For SIR RALPH EURE, alias EVERS, alias EWRE, of Eyton.

Pardon and release as late sheriff of Yorkshire ;—and release to Ralph Eure of Malton in Rydall, Marmaduke Constable of Everyngham, Guy Willesthorp, and Anthony Ughterede, both of the city of York, of their recognizance of 100 marks. Greenwich, 28 Nov. 6 Hen. VIII. *Del.* Westm., 30 Nov.

Pat. 6 *Hen. VIII. p.* 1, *m.* 19.

30 Nov.
R. O.

5656. SIR THOMAS LUCY.

Receipt by John Densell to Sir Thomas Lucy for 5*l.* in part payment of 25*l.* named in a pair of indentures. 30 Nov. 6 Hen. VIII.

30 Nov.
R. O.

5657. THOMAS SPINELLY to WOLSEY.

The President of the Privy Council informs him it is needless for Sampson to go to Paris, as they would have to use force to procure payment of Wolsey's dues. He will understand the occurrences here by the King's letters. Begs as soon as he has news of France touching Barradoty's charge, he will advertise the Archduchess. Requests his servant may be sent back, and that Spinelly may be instructed what to write to the compaignon of France. Brussels, 30 Nov. 1514. *Signed.*

P. 1. *Add. :* [To the] most reverend, &c. my Lord of York.

1 Dec.

5658. COMMISSIONS OF THE PEACE.

Dorset.—Hen. Earl of Wiltshire, Rob. Willoughby Lord Broke, John Bourgchier Lord Fitzwarren, Wm. Lord Stourton. Hen. Lord Daubeney, Ric. Eliot, Lewis Pollerd, Sir Thos. Lynde, Sir Thos. Trenchard, Sir Wm. Filoll, Edw. Stourton, Wm. Hody, Giles Strangways, John Rogers, Hen. Uvedale, Jas. Frampton, Wm. Wadham, Th. Strangways, Roger Cheverell, Rob. More, Wm.

514.

Lovell, John Moreton, John Strode and Rob. Turges. Westm., 1 Dec.

Northamptonshire.—T. Abp. of York, Thos. Marquis of Dorset. Rob. Brudenell, Humph. Conyngesby, Guy Palmes, John Grey, Sir Nic. Vaux, Sir Ric. Knyghtley, Sir Wm. Compton, Wm. Parre, Thos. Emson, Wm. Gascoigne, Thos. Lucy, John Tresham, Humph. Broun, Ric. Burton, John Wattys and Edm. Hasilwode. Westm., 1 Dec.

Pat. 6 *Hen. VIII. p.* 1, *m.* 3d.

1 Dec.   **5659.**   MARCELLUS DE LA MORE.

R. O.

Receipt for the wages of a surgeon at 6d. a day, attending upon Mr. Merney at Calais, on 16 June 5 Hen. VIII. Dated 1 Dec. 6 Hen. VIII. *Signed.*

1 Dec.   **5660.**   For THOMAS HILL of London, alias of Bristol, mercer.

P. S.

Protection. Greenwich, 24 Nov. 6 Hen. VIII. *Del.* Knoll, 1 Dec.

Pat. 6 *Hen. VIII. p.* 1, *m.* 19.

1 Dec.   **5661.**   The COLLEGE OF CARDINALS to WOLSEY.

Vitell. B. 11. 110.
B. M.

Recommend Cardinal St. Chrysogon to be collector, and Polydore, Archdeacon of Wells, sub-collector. Rome, 1 Dec. 1514.

Lat., p. 1. *Add.:* Archiep. Eboracensi.

2 Dec.   **5662.**   HAD[RIAN CARDINAL ST. CHRYSOGON] to [HENRY VIII.]

Vitell. B. 11. 111.
B. M.

His enemies have made use of the King's name to the Pope, to remove him from the duties of collector, have forged three letters in his Majesty's name, and obtained a surreptitious bull from the Pope. Requests, therefore, that the Pope's replication, the interest of the College of Cardinals, and his own faithful services, may be sufficient to confound his enemies and keep him in his place. Rome, 2 [Dec.] 1514.

Hol. Lat.   P. 1, *mutilated.*

2 Dec.   **5663.**   SILVESTER [BP. OF WORCESTER] to [HENRY VIII.]

Vitell. B. 11. 113.
B. M.

Is anxious to show his gratitude to the King, who has protected him under the calumnies he has suffered, and expressed a resolution to punish the authors. As to the King's command touching his caluminators, especially Pace, although he cannot legally proceed to any execution against them, yet he has commanded Pace to deliver him an inventory of the goods of the late Cardinal. This is very insufficient. Will send it by the first courier. Rome, 2 Dec. 1514.

P.S.—Has written to the Bishops of York and Winchester. The Pope has confirmed the news of the appointment of Andreas Ammonius, the Latin secretary, to the collectorship, and the determination not to have it revoked. *Signed.*

Lat. Pp. 2, *mutilated.*

2 Dec.   **5664.**   WILL. SHVAGGER to WOLSEY.

Vitell. B. 11. 112.
B. M.

The Bp. of Worcester omits nothing tending to Wolsey's interests. The goods of the late Cardinal in Pace's hands are sequestrated

1514.

with Worcester, as the King ordered. A most iniquitous sentence had been passed in the writer's cause, *summo studio atque to[tis] viribus annitente cardinale.* Without regard to his dignity or conscience, the Cardinal had thrust himself forward to give evidence, and compelled many of his household to do the same ; but he is dead with the stigma of avarice, pride and anger resting on him. Hopes that Wolsey who has succeeded him will not imitate his vices ;—that he may be allowed to advise him without offence ;—and that Wolsey will daily steal some time from business to make his account with God. Rome, 2 Dec.

Hol. Lat. Pp. 2, mutilated. Add. : Archiep. Eboracensi.

2 Dec. **5665.** R. Bp. of Ostia Cardinal St. George to Henry VIII.

R. O.

Has written this private testimonial in behalf of Cardinal St. Chrisogon, recommended by the College of Cardinals. Begs the King will accept favorably his proctors in the affairs of the Bp. of Bath, and show favor to Polydore his sub-collector. Rome, 2 Dec. 1514. *Signed.*

Lat., p. 1. Add.

2 Dec. **5666.** R. Bp. of Ostia Cardinal St. George to Wolsey.

Vitell. B. II. 114. In favor of Cardinal Hadrian and Polydore. Rome, 2 Dec.
B. M. 1514. *Signed.*

Lat., p. 1. Addressed : Th. Archiep. Ebor.

2 Dec. **5667.** For Henry Keymes.

To be bailiff of the lordship of Portbury, Somers., and of the herbage and pannage of the "hyer parke and the nether parke" therein, with the custody of the mansion, of three gardens called "le grete & lytyll conynger," and of the fishery in the Severn, called the "lordes tyde." Westm., 2 Dec.

Vacated on surrender by the said Henry, 24 May 17 Hen. VIII., in favor of Sir Edw. Gorge.

Pat. 6 Hen. VIII. p. 2, m. 22.

2 Dec. **5668.** For Thos. Repton alias Rypton, haberdasher of
S. B. London.

Protection ; going in the retinue of Sir Richard Wyngefeld, Deputy of Calais. *Del.* Knoll, 2 Dec. 6 Hen. VIII.

Fr. 6 Hen. VIII. p. 2, m. 12.

2 Dec. **5669.** For John Blamyer, chaplain.

Presentation to the church of Abbotley, Heref. dioc., *vice* Wm. Colyer, clk., deceased. Westm., 2 Dec.

Pat. 6 Hen. VIII. p. 1, m. 19.

3 Dec. **5670.** [Hadrian Cardinal St. Chrysogon] to [Wolsey.]

Vitell. B. II. 114. Begs to be retained in his collectorship. Rome, 3 Dec. 1[514].
B. M. *Hol. Lat. P. 1, mutilated.*

3 Dec. **5671.** The Cardinal of St. Mark to Henry VIII.

Vitell. B. II. 111*. In behalf of Cardinal St. Chrysogon and Polydore. Rome,
B. M. 3 Dec. 1514.

Hol. Lat., p. 1. Add.

1514.
3 Dec.　　**5672.**　D. CARDINAL ST. MARK to WOLSEY.
R. O.

In behalf of Cardinal Hadrian and Polydore. Rome, 3 Dec.
1514. *Signed.*
Lat., p. 1. Add.: Archiep. Ebor.

3 Dec.　　**5673.**　MARY THE FRENCH QUEEN.
R. O.

Account of victuals for transporting the French Queen into
France, from 12 Sept. to 3 Dec. 6 Hen. VIII.

3 Dec.　　**5674.**　For JOHN DAUNCE.
· S. B.

Annuity of 100*l.* during pleasure, payable out of the hanaper and
the Earldom of Richmond ; also donation of 50*l.* from Easter
last. *Del.* Westm., 3 Dec. 6 Hen. VIII.
Pat. 6 *Hen. VIII. p.* 1, *m.* 19.

5 Dec.　　**5675.**　SPINELLY to [HENRY VIII.]
Galba, B.III. 168.
B. M.

Wrote last on . . November. Has had an interview with the
Chancellor of the Duke of Saxony. Sends two original letters from
the Duke of Gueldres and an extract in Latin touching the Duke
of Saxony's business, who is one of the most virtuous princes in
Germany, and likely to succeed to the empire. He will give security
for the money he wants to borrow, " offering to repay your Grace in
blocks of silver." John Caulier of the Prince's council reports that
France will not restore to the Archduchess the lands taken from her
" for the quarrel of the Duke of Longueville." She desires Henry's
interference. She has been ill, but is recovered, and is informed
that the Lord of Angoulesme is gone towards Guienne, and will be
assisted by England in the recovery of Navarre. There is much
murmuring against it. Hears that the Swiss are sending 20,000
men to the defence of Milan. Preparations are made at Lyon,
Dauphiné, &c. for the French army going into Italy under Bourbon.
The Swiss have refused the Duke of Savoy's proposal to remain
neutral, and demand of him Sussa and Yvreye as security. The Emperor and the King of Arragon will omit nothing to gain the Pope.
It is said that the Scotch are favored by the French, who would
rather Henry spent his money against the Scotch than them.
If the Scotch would not accept the treaty the King should require
the Prince to banish them out of his dominions. The Council here
have arranged the matter of Wm. Copland. The Estates are
assembling. Brussels, 5 Dec. 1514. *Signed.*
Pp. 4, *mutilated.*

5 Dec.　　**5676.**　THOMAS SPINELLY to WOLSEY.
B. O.

Wrote his last on 30 Nov. Refers Wolsey to the King's letters
touching the Duke of Saxe. Desires to know the King's pleasure
therein and the King's answer to the Chancellor of Fryzeland, who
is at Brussels. The Archduchess will not be pleased unless provision be made for the restitution of her lands. Will do his
best to ascertain of " the begers Scots." Brussels, 5 Dec. 1514.
Signed.
P. 1. *Add. :* [To the] most rev. &c. the Abp. [of] York.

6 Dec.　　**5677.**　SIR ROBERT WINGFIELD to HENRY VIII.
Vitell. B. xviii. 105.
B. M.

Has advertised the King [of the . . . . Vene]tians
army, and returning of the same by great industry. If the army
had failed to attain [the said] passage, Pado had been in great

1514.

peril. While Pado was doubting of the return [of the] army, there was some tumult in the same; the governor in despair left the city, and "for his manly demeaning hath lost his head, as he was well worthy." "What sh[all come] of this winter war is not yet known." The Estates of this country meet at Insbrook on the . . . instant. The Viceroy of Naples . . . . . . on the 11th inst. The Lord Prosper [Colonna] arrived on the 4th, the Emperor went the same night to a place three Dutch miles hence, [where he remains still] the 9th. "The Lord Prosper is not only [of great] authority and a principal captain, but he [seemeth] **to** be such one as well of person favor and . . . . outward gesture" . . . . Next day . . . . Inquired how Creeme doth stand. Was told there is an abstinence of war between the Duke of Milan and the Venetians till Christmas, on condition that the town shall not "revite[ll nor] receive any new presidy." Thinks a peace will be treated for at this congregation between the Emperor and the Venetians, but much depends on the answer he shall receive from the Swiss within the next eight days.—Is clearly without money. If not relieved sooner than he can hope for, will be obliged to hide himself this Christmas. Is in despair for the want of it. Insbrook, 6 [December] 1514.

Hol., mutilated, pp. 3. Addressed.

8 Dec.
Sadoleti Epist.
Pont. xxxv.

5678. LEO X. to QUEEN MARGARET.

Has received her letters of 22 June by the hands of Thos. Nudrias, requesting him to admit of her nomination to the church of St. Andrew's. Had nominated to it his nephew Innocent Cardinal deacon of St. Cosmo and Damian, but as she had desired that none but a Scotchman should have ecclesiastical promotions there, had bethought himself of Andrew Abp. of Bourges. As this appointment has been confirmed in Consistory, cannot change it. Rome, 8 Dec. 1514.

10 Dec.
R. O.

5679. TH. LESON, clk., receiver to SIR WM. COMPTON.

Acknowledgment of the receipt of 20l. from Sir Th. Lucce, for a whole year's fee due to Sir Wm. Compton. 10 Dec. 6 Hen. VIII.

Signed and sealed.

10 Dec.
R. O.

5680. MAX. SFORZA DUKE OF MILAN to HENRY VIII.

Excuses the molestation offered to the English ambassador, the bearer, when passing through his territory to Mantua. Milan, 10 Dec. 1514.

Lat., p. 1. Add. Endorsed.

11 Dec.
Calig. B. 1.26.
B. M.

5681. JOHN LORD FLEMYNG to "MY LORD."

Had written at length, by Le March and Andrew Hamilton. Has urged the King and Council for despatch. On Sunday the 3d prevailed, that the Dauphin, the Duke of Bourbon, and the princes of France promised the fleet should be ready, with artillery, by the end of the month. Left this day for Tours to receive the artillery and send it to Britanny. Encloses for Lords Hamilton and Glasgow a copy of the instructions given to a clerk coming from France to Scotland. Sir Alexander Jarden will show him the Duke's mind, who is the same man as ever he was, and will not fail his friends, who " bide at his opinion as ye have ever done." The Queen of Scots has

3 o

1514.

written to England and to the Pope, complaining that "her barnes
and dowary is taken fra hir, and that scho deys for hunger and
hase laide hir jewellis in wed." England swears he will make war
upon them, and failing the succession, make the eldest son King of
England and the youngest King of Scotland. "Yerfor I pray ye
cause to gar kepe the barnes wele." Begs he will give no credence
to the secretary, who loves him not, and has imprisoned his men
behind his back. Sir Alexander Jarden and the Laird of Kincard
will show him what is done here. Paris, 11 Dec. *Signed.*
P. 1.

11 Dec.   **5682.**   For John Lemyng of Depyng Gate, Northt., and Wil-
S. B.   liam Danson of Market Depyng in Holland, Linc.

Pardon. *Del.* Knoll, 11 Dec. 6 Hen. VIII.
Pat. 6 *Hen. VIII. p.* 1, *m.* 20.

12 Dec.   **5683.**   For Oliver Holand, yeoman usher of the chamber
P. S.   with the Queen Consort.

To be keeper of the forest of Wabridge, Hunts, *vice* John Gylmyn, deceased ; and of Bardon Park, Leic., with 2d. a day. Greenwich, 27 Nov. 6 Hen. VIII. *Del.* Knoll, 12 Dec. 6 Hen. VIII.

12 Dec.   **5684.**   Commission of the Peace.

Berks.—Thos. Abbot of Abingdon, Rob. Brudenell, Ric. Eliott,
John Neuporte, Sir Thos. Lovell, Sir Andrew Wyndesor, Sir John
Dauncy, Sir Geo. Foster, Sir Thos. Fetiplace, Guy Palmes, Sir
Ric. Weston, Hen. Briggis, Thos Inglefeld, Wm. Besellis, Wm.
Essex, John Fetiplace, Wm. Fetiplace, Thos. Unton, Christ. Be-
lyngham, Geo. Wodeward, and Wm. Yong. Knoll, 12 Dec.
Pat. 6 *Hen. VIII. p.* 1, *m.* 3d.

12 Dec.   **5685.**   For John son and heir of Christopher Broune.
P. S.

Livery of lands. Also livery for Oliver Hyde of the manors of
Oldbury alias Aldbury, Parva Ricote, Cackeley and Shipton-on-
Charwell, and the hundred of Northyate, Oxon, lately held by the
said Oliver alone, or jointly with others now deceased, to the use of
the said Christopher; to take effect from 1 Nov. last. Greenwich,
5 Dec. 6 Hen. VIII. *Del.* Knoll, 12 Dec.
Pat. 6 *Hen. VIII. p.* 1, *m.* 20.

12 Dec.   **5686.**   Sir Rob. Wingfield to Henry VIII.
R. O.

Wrote his last on the 6th from Insbrooke, that the Viceroy of
Naples was expected. Yesterday rode to meet him, with Cardinal
Gurk, and after to his lodging, to prevent scandal. Has yet received
no commission different from the first enjoining him to promote
amity between England and Arragon. The viceroy was exceedingly complaisant. Will not pretend to disclose his real thoughts.
He and Prosper Colonna intend to persuade the Emperor to a peace
with the Venetians and to restore Brescia. Messengers pass to and
from the King of Arragon. Thinks he knows his interest too well
not to be reconciled with England. The Emperor went hunting
before the Viceroy arrived. The Viceroy is vexed at his reception.
The Emperor returned this evening. Will send further news on
next occasion. Insbrooke, 12 Dec. 1514.
Hol. pp. 3. *Add.*

1514.

12 Dec. **5687.** TREATY BETWEEN ENGLAND AND THE VENETIANS.

Vesp. F. I. 97.
B. M.

Confirmation by the Doge ; *endorsed*, "Confirmatio compre-hensionis factæ de Venetis per Ducem et Senatum Venetiarum." 12 Dec. 1514.

Signed : Leonardus Lauredanus.

12 Dec. **5688.** To JOHN YONG, Master of the Rolls.

S. B.

To cancel eight recognizances, four of 200 and four of 300 marks, made 11 Feb. 18 Hen. VII. :—1. By Sir Robert Throgmerton of Warwickshire ; 2. Christopher Throgmerton ; 3. Alexander Cul-peper of Kent ; 4. Thomas Catesby ; 5. Henry Frowyk ; 6. Sir Edward Ponynges ; 7. Sir John Arondell ; 8. John Carewe, late of Umberley, Devon. Greenwich, 13 Dec. 6 Hen. VIII.

13 Dec. **5689.** For SIR EDWARD BELKNAPPE, knight of the Body.

P. S.

Annuity of 100*l.* during pleasure, payable out of the hanaper, and the earldom of Richmond. Also donation of 50*l.* Greenwich, 6 Dec. 6 Hen. VIII. *Del.* Knoll, 13 Dec.

Pat. 6 *Hen. VIII. p.* 1, *m.* 22.

13 Dec. **5690.** For JOHN HENDRY, of London, "attending upon our court with haberdash wares."

P. S.

Licence to import 500 dozen caps, and 100 dozen hats, from foreign parts. Greenwich, 8 Dec. 6 Hen. VIII. *Del.* Knoll, 13 Dec.

Fr. 6 *Hen. VIII. p.* 2, *m.* 12.

14 Dec. **5691.** COMMISSION OF SEWERS.

Linc.—T. Abp. of York, Thos. Dokwray prior of St. John's, Wm. Lord Willoughby, Sir John Fyneus, Rob. Brudenell, the Abbots of Croyland, Thorney, Bradney, Revesby, and Swyneshede, the prior of Spaldyng, Sir John Huse, Sir Rob. Sheffeld, Sir Wm. Tirwhitt, Sir Thos. Newporte, Sir Edw. Burgh, Sir Rob. Dymmok, Sir Philip Tylney, Sir John Skipwith, Thos. Burgh, Geo. Fitzwilliam, John Fulvetby, Nich. Upton, Rob. Husee, John Litelbury, Andrew Billesby, Thos. Totboth, Wm. Askewe, Wm. Hansard, Geoff. Paynell, John Hennege, John Robynson, Wm. Goderike, Thos. Holand and John Te[mpest], for the district from Dodyngton Pygott to Tydd Goot, by the sea coast. Knoll, 14 Dec.

Pat. 6 *Hen. VIII. p.* 1, *m.* 32*d.*

14 Dec. **5692.** CROWN LANDS.

S. B.

For Sir Richard Tempest to be feodary and receiver of all posses-sions belonging to the crown in co. York ; with authority to de-liver all heirs being minors and holding of the King *in capite* to Sir Thomas Lovell, treasurer of the Household.

Similar appointments of Edmund Larder in *Devon;* Thomas Thornhell in *Somerset and Dorset;* William Bisley in *Gloucester-shire* and the marches of Wales ; and Christopher Clapeham in *Cumberland and Westmoreland.*

Del. Knoll, 14 Dec. 6 Hen. VIII. *Signed :* Thomas Lovell.

Pat. 6 *Hen. VIII. p.* 1, *m.* 22.

14 Dec. **5693.** For WILLIAM PAWNE.

P. S.

To be master of the ordnance of Berwike, *vice* John Papedee ; with 12*d.* a day from Easter 3 Hen. VIII. Greenwich, 8 Dec. 6 Hen. VIII. *Del.* Knoll, 14 Dec.

Pat. 6 *Hen. VIII. p.* 2, *m.* 22.

3 o 2

1514.

14 Dec. **5694.** SERFS.

P. S.

Manumission of Henry Knyght of Stoke Clymmyslonde, Cornwall, tailor, and John Erle of the same parish, husbandman, the King's natives of the manor of Stoke Clymmyslonde. Greenwich, 10 Dec. 6 Hen. VIII. *Del.* Knoll, 14 Dec.

Pat. 6 *Hen. VIII. p.* 1, *m.* 31.

15 Dec. **5695.** For WILLIAM POUNDE of Southwykke, Hants.

P. S.

Exemption from serving on juries, &c. Greenwich, 9 Dec. 6 Hen. VIII. *Del.* Knoll, 15 Dec.

Pat. 6 *Hen. VIII. p.* 1, *m.* 22.

15 Dec. **5696.** LEWIS XII. to WOLSEY.

Calig. D. vi. f. 138.
B. M.
Rym. XIII. 455.

Has such confidence in his cousin the Duke of Suffolk and in Wolsey that he is determined to apply to them in everything he may have to do with the King his good brother their master. Has [sent] the Duke to tell Wolsey certain things in which he desires Wolsey's aid. Wolsey shall have reason to be amply satisfied of his gratitude.

Holograph. Signed.
Addressed : [A] Monseigneur d'Yorc mon bon amy.
Mutilated.

15 Dec. **5697.** SAMPSON to WOLSEY.

Galba B. v. 328.
B. M.

After leaving Paris wrote from Tournay shewing the cause of his short return. Has agreed that it shall rest in the hands of the officers till other process be made. Gives the reasons for not having commenced the process ; is afraid of the confusion it would create. The temporality are much set against the spirituality, and would be under no control if one ordinary absolved what another excommunicated. The promises made by the French King are only colorable ; thinks he ought to have a good solicitor with the King to expedite the renunciation. Though the French King himself be well minded to Wolsey he must remit the business to his council, who are very good Frenchmen and very bad Englishmen. Another reason for delaying it is Wolsey's new title of York. Has great difficulty also in finding proper officers. Does not think that Wolsey's confidence in his officers at Tournay, and especially John Villain his receiver, is well founded ; no one is more fervent against him. Has no aid in Flanders except through the doctor of whom he has already written. John Scillier of Tournay, who was in England at the parliament for Tournay, is trustworthy. Has, for the above reasons, deferred execution of the brief. The lord lieutenant can explain the difficulties. Except through the French King's influence, Wolsey will get no profit from that diocese. Bruges, 15 Dec. 1514.

Hol., pp. 3, *mutilated. Add. :* My Lord of York.

5698. WOLSEY to [SAMPSON].

R. O

(Imperfect at the beginning.)

" . . . . . between the Prince and his subjects and the King ye wat not what ye mean, there is no such liklihood, for they have declared themselves *pro comprehensione in tractatu jam concluso inter potentissimum Regem nostrum et Regem Gallorum.* Is sure that if any person refused to do his duty, a remedy would be had on complaint to my Lady. Perceives his correspondent thinks the elect has hopes of revoking Wolsey's administration. "Ye

1514.

need not doubt thereof ; the Pope would not offend me for one thousand such as the elect is, nor there is no such thing spoken of nor intended. I would not have you to muse so much on the moon, but to go straightly and wisely to my matters, and not to be moved with every wind and frivolous report." As to the threat mentioned in another letter, that Wolsey's administration would be at an end whenever the elect returned, "do ye suppose that the said elect shall be admitted or suffered to dwell in Tournay without the King my master's licence, which I am sure he shall never obtain ?" He could not be admitted unless he become the King's subject, and renounce the French King. Understands also that his correspondent has agreed that the rents should remain in the hands of the tenants till the dispute with the elect is settled. This is prejudicial to Wolsey's right. Desires he will immediately set about levying what is due now at this holy time of Christmas ; and if he meet with opposition, to execute the sentence. Hopes he will attend to Wolsey's interests in future, better than he has done hitherto ; otherwise Wolsey must have recourse to other means, " for that ye have hitherto thought for the best is clearly turned to the worst."

Draft in Wolsey's hand, p. 1.

16 Dec. 5699. For VALERY DE POIANIS, M.D., late of London, alias of
Rym. XIII. 471.   Milan.

Licence to practise medicine in London and the realm of England. Knoll, 16 Dec.

Pat. 6 Hen. VIII. p. 1, m. 12.

16 Dec. 5700. For RALPH PEXSALL and EDITH his wife.
S. B.

Livery (the said Edith being sister and heir of Anne late wife of George Warham, daughters and heirs of William son of John Brocas,) of the manor of Parva Weldon, called " Hunters Maner," Northt., and the purparty of the said Anne of the manor and other premises in Weldon ; of the office of keeper of the King's buckhounds, and the profits thereof ; and of all possessions held to the use of the said Anne and Edith, and their heirs. *Del.* Westm., 16 Dec. 6 Hen. VIII.

Pat. 6 Hen. VIII. p. 1, m. 21.

17 Dec. 5701. For ROGER DELE of London, draper.
S. B.

Licence to import caps and hats. *Del.* Knoll, 17 Dec. 6 Hen. VIII.

Fr. 6 Hen. VIII. p. 2, m. 12.

19 Dec. 5702. HADRIAN [DE CASTELLO] CARDINAL ST. CHRYSOGON to
Vitell. B. II. 101.*   WOLSEY.
B. M.

Requests his favor for himself and Polydore Vergil, and that he may not be thrust from an office he has held so many years by the kindness of the King and his father. Has served them 24 years. As chamberlain of the Holy College procured for Wolsey's proctors, when at Viterbo, delay in paying the dues of the bishopric. Rome, 19 Dec. 1514. *Signed.*

Lat., p. 1. Add.: Archiepiscopo Eboracensi. *Endorsed.*

1514.

19 Dec. **5703.** For ELIZABETH CATESBY.

S. B.

Annuity of 40 marks, from Easter last, in consideration of her services to the King's sister, Mary Queen of the French. *Del.* Otford, 19 Dec. 6 Hen. VIII.
Pat. 6 *Hen. VIII. p.* 1, *m.* 22.

19 Dec. **5704.** For HENRY LORD DAUBNEY.

P. S.

Livery of lands as son and heir of Giles Lord Daubney, deceased. Greenwich (?), 2 Dec. 6 Hen. VIII. *Del.* Otford, 19 Dec.
Pat. 6 *Hen. VIII. p.* 1, *m.* 21.

19 Dec. **5705.** THOS. COLMAN to WOLSEY.

R. O.

Sends him an account of the news received from the Venetians of the defeat of the Sophi by the Turk. Last year the Sophi, who wished to turn Christian, collected a great army, consisting among others of Hungarians and Poles, to resist his efforts. On the 24th June he summoned a council of the princes of Turkey, warning them that the Sophi intended the destruction of Mahometanism, and had collected a body of 80,000 horse. Hereupon the Prince of Natalia started up and promised a body of 30,000 renegades, the Prince of Negropont 40,000 horse and foot, the Prince of Romania 20,000 horse and 20,000 foot; others accordingly. The Sultan undertook to levy 400,000. The 2nd Aug. was appointed for the meeting. They met at Trebizonde. The battle began two hours after sunrise; 200,000 fell before the victory was decided. The army of the Sultan was cut to pieces. The river Aridon ran with blood three hours. Bologna, xiv kal. Januar. 1514.
Hol. Lat., p. 1.
Add. : Rmo. &c. T. Eboracensi Archiepiscopo.

20 Dec. **5706.** The COLLEGE OF CARDINALS to WOLSEY.

R. O

In behalf of Cardinal St. Chrysogon, and Polydore archdeacon of Wells, his collector. The Cardinal is so much His Majesty's creature, educated in England, that he is reputed as the English Cardinal. " Romæ sub sigillis nostrorum Trium in ordine Priorum,"
20 Dec. 1514.
P. 1. *Add. :* Rev. &c. Thomæ Archiep'o ecclesiæ Eboracensi.
Endorsed.

20 Dec. **5707.** For CHRIST. GYBSON, gunner.

To be one of the King's gunners, with 12*d.* a day. Otford, 20 Dec.
Pat. 6 *Hen. VIII. p.* 1, *m.* 22.

21 Dec. **5708.** For ROGER BARKER, master, and JOHN CANNON, JOHN WAKEFELD and WILLIAM GATTE, wardens, of the Mystery of St. Julian " le Herbeger" of INNHOLDERS, London.

S. B.

Licence to found a guild to the honor of St. Julian in the said city, with one master and three wardens, to be elected annually. *Del.* Otford, 21 Dec. 6 Hen. VIII.
Pat. 6 *Hen. VIII. p.* 1, *m.* 22.

1514.

21 Dec.
P. S.

5709. For JOHN YONG, clk., SIR THOMAS LOVELL, SIR EDWARD NEVYLL and SIR WILLIAM COMPTON.

Next presentation to the canonry and prebend in St. Stephen's Westminster, or St. George's Windsor. Greenwich, 20 Dec. 6 Hen. VIII. *Del.* Otford, 21 Dec.

Pat. 6 *Hen. VIII. p.* 1, *m.* 21.

21 Dec.
P. S.

5710. For SIR THOMAS WYNDHAM, knight of the Body, of Felbrigge, Norf., alias of Danbery.

Pardon and release as vice-admiral and lieutenant of Thomas Earl of Surrey, lord admiral. Greenwich, 20 Dec. 6 Hen. VIII. *Del.* Knoll, 21 Dec.

Pat. 6 *Hen. VIII. p.* 1, *m.* 23.

22 Dec.
S. B.

5711. For JOHN GOSTWIK, JOHN UVEDALE and STEPHEN HUDSON of London, girdler.

Licence to import caps and hats of all colors from Milan, France and Flanders, for five years. *Del.* Westm., 22 Dec. 6 Hen. VIII.

Fr. 6 *Hen. VIII. p.* 2, *m.* 13.

22 Dec.
R. O.

5712. CARD PLAYING.

Copy of the pleadings in a court of pie-powder held at Calais, 22 Dec. 6 Henry VIII., before Humph. Bannaster, Ric. Chauffer, Hen. Keyll, Ric. Broune, Reymond Cutturus, Will. Newton, Ric. Dyer and Will. Davy, aldermen, in an action brought by Thos. Thacker, of the staple at Calais, against Peter Roy, Peter le Negro and Bartholomew Costopolegrino for cheating at cards and dice. The defendants deny the charge, and state that they have played with many noblemen in England.

23 Dec.
R. T. 137.
R. O.

5713. HENRY VIII. to GEORGE DUKE OF SAXONY.

The King's ambassadors at the Court of the Archduchess forwarded the Duke's instructions signifying his desire for the continuance of amity between them. Cannot believe that the Duke of Gueldres in his letter to Duke George, has correctly represented the intentions of the King of France. Has written to Lewis stating the friendship which the King entertains for the Duke. Sends a copy of the letter. Doubts not being able to obtain what the Duke wishes. Greenwich, 23 Dec. 6 Hen. VIII.

Lat., p. 1.

23 Dec.
Galba, B. III. 147.
B. M.

5114. MARGARET OF SAVOY to WOLSEY.

A letter of compliments. Brussels, 23 Dec. 1514. *Signed.*

Lat., p. 1, *mutilated. Add. :* R. D. Arch. Ebor.

26 Dec.
S. B.

5715. For THOMAS COMPTON, groom of the Chamber.

Grant of the stone walls and stones called the castle or tower of Old Sarum, in Old Sarum, Wilts, with liberty to knock down and carry away the said walls. *Del.* Knoll, 26 Dec. 6 Hen. VIII.

Pat. 6 *Hen. VIII. p.* 1, *m.* 23.

27 Dec.
P. S.

5716. For JOHN MOUNTENAY of Prytwell, Essex.

Protection; going in the retinue of Sir Rich. Wingfeld, Deputy of Calais. Greenwich, 7 Nov. 6 Hen. VIII. *Del.* Knoll, 27 Dec.

Fr. 6 *Hen. VIII. p.* 2, *m.* 12.

1514.
28 Dec. **5717.**   LEWIS XII. to HENRY VIII.

Calig. D. vi. 146.
B. M.
Ellis, 2 S. i. 260.

Has received by the bearer, an English officer of arms, Henry's letters of the 9th inst. signifying the pleasure he had had from hearing of him through the Duke of Suffolk. His satisfaction with the Queen his wife was such, that Henry might be sure of his treating her to her own and his satisfaction. Expresses his great regard for Suffolk. With respect to the secret matters of which Suffolk had spoken to him, and to which he had made answer by his ambassadors . . . . Hopes that the alliance and friendship between them shall be rather increased than diminished. Paris, 28 Dec. *Pp. 2. Signed and sealed. Mutilated.*

31 Dec. **5718.**   PETER MARTYR to LUD. FURTADO.

Epist. 545.

The Queen of England has given birth to a premature child, through grief, as it is said, for the misunderstanding between her father and her husband. He had reproached her with her father's ill faith, "*et conquestus suos in eam expectorabat.*" Julian the Pope's brother has married the sister of the Duke of Savoy. In answer to the French, the Swiss have said they will defend Duke Maximilian with all their power. The King has gone to Medina. His asthma has turned into dropsy. Medina del Campo, prid. kl. Jan. 1514.

31 Dec. **5719.**   For SIR WILLIAM TREVANYON, knight of the Body.

P. 8.

Grant to him and his assigns of the annual rent of 50 marks (granted to Nicholas Crowmer, deceased, by patent of Henry VII.), out of certain lands of Sir Henry Bodringan in co. Cornwall, which lands were granted to Sir Richard Egecombe, deceased, and his heirs male, and have now descended to Sir Piers Egecombe, his son and heir. Greenwich, 21 Dec. 6 Hen. VIII. *Del.* Knoll, 31 Dec. *Pat. 6 Hen. VIII. p. 1, m. 23.*

R. O.   **5720.**   ARMY and NAVY.

Payments made by John Daunce, by the King's command, as follow :—

9 July 3 Hen. VIII.

To Robt. Dobbys of London, haberdasher, for 24 bolts of olrons for ship sails at 10*s.* a bolt.—To various persons for harness, delivered to Sir Francis Cheyny ; 99 backs and breasts for footmen, 33*l.*; 140 stondards of mayle, 6*l.* 3*s.* 4*d.*; 93 salletts, 13*l.* 17*s.* 8*d.* ; 10 apurnes of mayle, 30*s.*; 4 pairs of gussetts, 12*s.*; 96 pairs of splynts, 14*l.* 8*s.*—To John Blewbery ; for a mill wheel with stondard, 2 beams, and brasys (braces) belonging thereto, and two small wheels to drive the glasys, 40*s.* ; for two elm planks for lanterns for the same mill, 5*s.* ; for wages of John Mylwryght for 12 days, at 8*d.* a day ; wages of two men with him for 12 days, at 6*d.* a day ; 13lbs. of tin at 5*d.* lb. ; 28 lbs. of white soap for tempering the said mill at 2*d.* lb. ; 500 gauntlet nails, 8*d.*; 100 and a half of iron, 4*s.* 8*d.* ; three rivetting hammers, 2*s.* ; a pair of pynsors, 2*s.* 8*d.*; four crest files, 4*s.* ; two great files, 5*s.* ; 100 and a half of steel for vambraces and gauntlets, 60*s.*

13 July.

To Thomas Norton, upon a bill subscribed by Edward Guldeforde, for carriage of stuff in the King's journey to Nottingham, 20*l.*— To John Baptista de Consaloveris, merchant of Milan, for a turquoise ring, 10*l.*

1514.

22 July.

To John Blewbery, for wages of armorers of Milan, 6l. 13s. 4d.; for two hogsheads of wine for the said armorers, 53s. 4d.; for carriage of the same wine to Greenwich, 8d.; for reward of the said armorers, 4l.; for the glasyers of the same mill and one spindle to the same glasyers, 4l.; for a grindstone and the beam to the same mill, 20s.; for carriage of the mill and glasyers to Greenwich, 2s.

29 July.

To Robt. Brygandyne, clerk of the King's ships, for the conveyance of two ships, *The Mary Rose* and *The Peter Granade*, from Portsmouth to the Thames, 120l.

25 Aug.

To John Bowier, Southwark, butcher, by Richard Okeham, for 18 oxen, at 27s. 6d. an ox, for victualling the ships *The Mary and John* and *The Anne of Foy*, sent eastward in April last.

28 Aug.

To. Albert Hays Esterlinge, for 997 "orys" (oars) delivered by indenture to Richard Okeham, price of every 100, six score to the 100, 5l.

6 Sept.

To John Carpenter, Deptford, for the carriage of the above oars by water from London to Deptford Strond to the storehouse there, for repairing the said house and for 2 hanging locks for the same, 36s. 6d.

9 Sept.

To Robt. Brygandyne for the expences of the two new ships, *The Mary Rose* and *The Peter Granade*, now in the Thames, 30l.

18 Sept.

To John Blewbery for the new forge at Greenwich, made for the armorers of Brussels, sc.: a vice, 13s. 4d.; a great bekehorne, 60s.; a small bekehorne, 16s.; a pair of bellows, 30s.; a pype stake, 3s. 4d.; a crest stake, 4s.; a vysure stake, 4s.; a hanging pype stake, 4s. 4d.; a stake for the head pieces, 5s.; two curaces stakes, 10s.; 4 pair of sherys (shears), 40s.; 3 plating hammers, 8s.; 3 hammers for the head pieces, 5s.; a crest hammer for the head piece, 20d.; 2 hammers, 2s. 8d.; 2 greve hammers, 3s. 4d.; one meeke hammer, 16d.; 2 pleyne hammers, 2s.; 2 platynge hammers, 2s.; 2 chesels with an helve, 8d.; a crest hammer for the curace, 12d.; 2 rivetting hammers, 16d.; a boos hammer, 12d.; 11 fylys (files) 11s.; a pair of pynsors, 18d.; 2 pairs of tongs, 16d.; a harth stake, 6d.; 2 chesels and 6 ponchons, 2s.; a water trough, 18d.; a tempering barrel, 12d.; 1 anvil, 20s.; 6 stocks to set in the tolys, 10s.; 16 dobles at 16d. a doble, 21s. 4d.; 18 quarter of colys (coals) 6s. 9d.

19 Sept.

To John Blewbery for a hide of leather to cover new harness conveyed to Nottingham, 3s.; a rest to the same harness, 2s.; leathers, buckles, charnells, and nails for the same, 8s.; a lock for the hamper in which the harness was kept, 4d.; the hire of a horse to clean the harness in the mill, 2s.; for stuff and lining to the head piece of the harness, 12d.; for hiring two horses for Copyn and Peter, the armorers, to convey the harness to Nottingham, 13s. 4d.; costs of themselves and horses for 16 days, 20s.; hire of a cart for conveyance of the said stuff from London to Nottingham, 16s. 8d.; 12 vices, 4s.; a mill man's wages for 3 months, at 20d. a week. To John Blewbery for provision to be made by him in Antwerp in the parts of Brabant for stuff to make harness, 36*l.* ; his costs in Antwerp, 40*s.*; the fee of Copyn Watte and Peter Fever, armorers, for half a year ending the feast of St. Michael the Archangel next coming, 10*l.*

20 Sept.

To Robt. Briggandyne for the charges of *The Mary Rose* and *The Peter Garnade*, lying in the Thames, 50*l.*

24 Sept.

To Richard Palshidde, one of the King's customers at Southampton, for 24 cots (coats) of white and green for 24 soldiers, employed for the safe conduct of *The Mary Rose* from Portsmouth to London, and six similar coats of white and green for the master, 4 for the quartermasters and boatswain, at 6*s.* 10*d.* a coat ; the wages of the said 24 soldiers for a month, at 5*s.* a man ; the reward of the said Rich. Palshidde for his attendance on the ship, 40*s.*, and John Clerke, master of the said ship, 20*s.*

To Robt. Brygandyne for the wages and victualling of the masters, mariners, and soldiers, unto the 26 Sept. 3 Hen. VIII., in *The Mary Rose* and *The Peter Granade*, during their conveyance from Portsmouth to the Thames, 8*l.* 2*s.* 2*d.* Also to the said Robt. Brygandyne for 35 coats of white and green for the abovementioned master and 34 of his company, at 6*s.* 8*d.* a coat. To Roger Rothewell, purser of the King's ship *The Mary and John,* for 5 months' wages of the master and company, ending the last day of September next, remaining due for the voyage to Esteland, at 22*l.* 15*s.* 4*d.* a month; for the wages of Hugh Serjeant, loadsman of the said ship for the whole voyage, 8*l.* To Willm. Bokker, purser of *The Ann of London*, otherwise called *The Ann of Foye*, for 3 months and a half wages of the master and company, remaining due for the voyage to Esteland, at 21*l.* 6*s.* a month; for the wages of John Haryson, loadsman, for the whole voyage, 8*l.* To John Browne, London, painter, the balance of his bill for painting the streamers, banners, flags, and staves belonging to the King's ship *The Mary and John*, 16*l.* 14*s.* 8*d.*

Sum total of the payments made by John Daunce, by the King's command, 743*l.* 16*s.* 10*d.* *Signed by the King.*

1 Oct.

To Cornelius Johnson, gunmaker, towards new stocking and repairing divers pieces of ordnance in the King's ships now in the Thames, viz., *The Mary and John, The Anne of London, The Mary Rose,* and *The Peter Granade*, 20*l.* To the same, for 8 loads of elm for stocking the said ordnance, at 4*s.* the load.

4 Oct.

By warrant dormond to Robt. Brygandyne towards the making, rigging, and apparelling of two new barks, 50*l.* By warrant dormond to John Brygandyne, overseer and ruler of the two ships, *The Regent* and *Sovereign*, for men's wages and victuals, and safe moorings with cables, 40*l.*

14 Oct.

By warrant dormond to Robt. Brygandyne towards the making, rigging, and apparelling of two new barks for the King's use, 100*l.*

18 Oct.

To Thomas Sperte, master, and David Boner, purser of *The Mary Rose*, for decking and rigging the same, 66*l.* 13*s.* 4*d.*

1514.

20 Oct.

To Willm. Bulker, purser of *The Anne of London*, otherwise *The Ann of Foy* for the charges of the said ship from 30 Sept. 3 Hen. VIII. to 20 Oct. next, 49s. 1d.

25 Oct.

By warrant dormond to John Brygandyne, overseer and ruler of *The Regent* and *Sovereign*, for men's wages and victuals, and safe moorings with cables, 40l.

12 Nov.

To Robert Radclyff Lord Fitzwater, "for so much money by us to him lent upon four obligations," 300l.

14 Nov.

By warrant dormond to Robt. Brygandine towards the making, rigging, and apparelling of two new barks for the King's use, 150l.

16 Nov.

To Thomas Spert, master, and David Boner, purser of *The Mary Rose*, for decking and rigging *The Peter Pounde Granade*, also for victualling her, and mariners' wages retained for her voyage to be made into Zeland, 66l. 13s. 4d.

26 Nov.

To Cornelius Johnson, gunmaker, upon a book of parcels, signed by Sir Edw. Howard, for mending guns, making iron work, and carpenters', sawyers' and labourers' wages for stocking guns for the King's ships, *The Mary and John*, *The Anne of London*, *The Mary Rose*, and *The Peter Pounde Garnade*, 37l. 2s. 6d. To Richard Nele, factor of Richard Gresham, and Will. Coplande of London, merchants, for money lent to Will. Bulker, purser of *The Anne of London*, for the use of that ship, lately being in the parts of Spruce, 33l.

28 Nov.

To Robt. Gedge, clerk of the Mercery, for writing the "chartre partie" of *The Peter Pounde Garnade* for her voyage into Zeland, 20s. To Bryan Appulton, beadle of the Mercery, "for warning of the poynters" by way of reward, 6s. 8d.

2 Dec.

To Cornelius Johnson, gunmaker, by way of prest, towards making two new guns of 10 inches compass for the King's use, 20l. To David Boner, purser of *The Peter Pounde Garnade*, towards the charges for her voyage to Zeland, 13l. 6s. 8d.

To Leonard Fryscobald, merchant of Florence, for money to be delivered, by exchange after the rate of sterling money, to John Isesham in Zeland, to purchase cables and ropes for the King's ships, 133l. 6s. 8d.—To Willm. Gurr, London, brygandine maker, for harness for *The Peter Pounde Garnade*, viz. 100 breasts and backs, at 6s. 8d. the piece; 100 pairs of splints, at 3s. a pair; 100 saletts at 3s. the piece; 100 goriettes at 12d. the piece; 68l. 6s. 8d.

9 Dec.

To Robt. Brygandyne for setting up masts and other tackling for *The Sovereign*, and conveying her to the Thames, 80l.

11 Dec.

To John Bayly, purser of *The Lyon*, by way of prest towards her expences, from 9 Dec. 3 Hen. VIII., 13l. 6s. 8d.

17 Dec.

To Willm. Botrye, London, mercer, upon a bill signed by Sir Edward Howard, for tukes, bokerams, Brussels cloth, and chamlctes, to make streamers and banners for *The Mary Rose* and *The Peter Pounde Garnade*, 50*l*. 19*s*. 2*d*.—To John Browne, London, painter, upon a book of parcels signed by Sir Edward Howard, for painting and staining banners for the same, 142*l*. 4*s*. 6*d*.

18 Dec.

To Thomas Sperte, master of *The Mary Rose*, upon his account made before Sir Edw. Howard, 24 Nov. 3 Hen. VIII., for charges connected with the said ship, 29*s*. 1¾*d*.—To the said Thomas Sperte in full contentation and payment of all charges for *The Peter Pounde Garnade*, due upon his account made before Sir Edw. Howard, 10 Dec. 3 Hen. VIII., 71*l*. 9*s*. 11½*d*.

To Willm. Bulker, purser of *The Anne of London*, in full payment of all her charges due upon his account made before Sir Edw. Howard, 1 Dec. 3 Hen. VIII., 20*l*. 4*s*. 3¼*d*.

To Roger Rothewell, purser of *The Mary and John*, in full payment of all her charges due upon his account made before Sir Edw. Howard, 1 Dec. 3 Hen. VIII., 56*l*. 1*s*. 5½*d*.

20 Dec.

To T. Sperte, master of *The Mary Rose* for the said ship, from 24 Nov. 20*l*.

To John Woddelesse, loadsman of *The Peter Poundegarnade*, of 350 ton portage, for conducting her "through the black deeps in her voyage towards Zeland," 116*s*. 8*d*.

26 Dec.

To John Crochet, King's armorer, and Willm. Heyward, King's joiner, for spear heads, burrys, and other such stuff used in the joustes and runnings, from St. Michael the Archangel, 2 Hen. VIII. to St. John Baptist next ensuing, 59*l*. 6*s*. 4*d*.

31 Dec.

To Roger Rothwell, purser of *The Mary and John*, for his charges from 30 Nov., 10*l*.

To W. Bulker, purser of *The Ann of London*, do.

To John Bayly, purser of *The Lyon*, for charges from 9 Dec., 53*l*. 6*s*. 8*d*.

8 Jan.

To Thomas Sperte, from 23 Nov., 20*l*.

9 Jan.

To Robt. Dobbys, citizen and haberdasher of London, for 51 olrons for the use of the ships, at 10*s*. the olron; for carriage of do., 8*d*.

13 Jan.

To Willm. Hylton, tailor, for 100 white and green cloth jackets made for the mariners of *The Peter Pounde Garnard*, against her voyage into Zeland, 40*l*. 12*s*. 11*d*.

14 Jan.

To Cornelius Johnson, gunmaker, towards making 2 new guns of 10 inches compass, 20*l*.

To Mr. Domynyk Cyny, clerke, towards making 25 pairs of barbys for the King's horses, 10*l*.

15 Jan.

To W. Bulker, from 30 Nov., 20*l*.; and Roger Rothwell, 10*l*.

23 Jan.

To Rob. Brygandyne, for two new barks, 200*l*.

1514.

25 Jan.

To the same, for masts for *The Sovereign*, &c., 80*l.*; for men's wages and victuals, &c., 80*l.*

To John Frende, purser of *The Dragon*, towards charges of the said ship from ———— of January 3 Hen. VIII., 10*l.*

28 Jan.

To Thomas Sperte, master of *The Mary Rose*, by John Lawden, purser of the same, towards her charges from the 23 Nov. 3 Hen. VIII., 13*l.* 6*s.* 8*d.*—To David Appowhell, purser of *The Barbara*, towards her expences from 24 Jan. 3 Hen. VIII., 10*l.*

(*Here follow numerous entries, of similar purport to the above. The more important only are noticed here.*)

22 Feb.

To John Marten, merchant, Guernsey, by Thomas Padarte, his servant, for 60 olrons for the use of the King's ships, at 10*s.* the olron.

13 March.

To Sir Edward Howard, for a gun bought for the King of John Power, yeoman of the Crown, 10*l.*

29 April.

To Willm. Gurr, for a pair of brygandynes delivered to the master of *The Lyon*, 16*s.*—Also for a master of a barge and 18 men to take them and other harness to Gravesend, and for their expences whilst there three days, at 13*s.* 4*d.* a day.

8 July.

To John Ochoea, purser of *The John de Anda*, Spaniard, for 7 guns bought of him, 5 of which were delivered to Sir Edward Howard, Admiral, 40*l.*

To John Byllesdon, London, grocer, for four mastes, 3 at 7*l.*, and 1 at 6*l.*

To Willm. Mortymer and Thomas Forster, London, broderers, upon a bill signed by Sir Edw. Howard, for rosys and crossys made for *The Mary John* and *The Ann of London*, 6*l.* 6*s.* 4*d.*

To Roger Halle, grocer, George Howard, merchant tailor, and Christopher Rawson, of London, mercer, for iron and sea coal delivered to Roger Whyte, Ratclyff, smith, for making ironwork for the King's ships, 13*l.* 13*s.* 4*d.*

To James Back, Ratclyff, upon a bill signed by Sir Edward Howard, for ironwork for the King's ships, 22*l.* 16*s.* 3½*d.*

24 July.

To Mr. Domynyke Cyny towards making streamers and banners, 40*l.*

Sum of all the money paid by John Daunce, 4,310*l.* 0*s.* 22*d.*

Signed by the King.

17 Oct.

To Sigesmond Foyte, by the hands of John Pounde, one of the King's heralds, for certain instruments bought for the King's use, 12*l.* 13*s.* 4*d.*

9 Nov.

To Mr. Domynyke Cyny, clerk, in reward for the use of Vincence of Naples and Alexe of Myllen, painters, 6*l.* 13*s.* 4*d.*

22 Nov.

To John Danda, merchant, Spain, to the hands of James Ramme, clerk of Fernando Daza, the balance of his bill for two great and five other bombardes for the King's use, brought from Spain in George Herward's ship, 26*l.*

1 Dec.

To Mr. Domyke Cyny, clerk, in prest by indenture towards the making of streamers, banners, flags, and "getons" for the King's ships, 40*l.*

14 Feb.

To John Lawden, late purser of *The Mary Rose,* in full payment of all necessaries in her last voyage, as appears by a book of parcels signed by Sir Edw. Howard, 13*l.* 7*s.* 8½*d.*

15 March.

To Thomas Spert, upon a bill signed by Sir Edw. Howard, for " lodemanshippe of the Dans voyage of *The Mary John,*" for the costs of the said Thomas and his servant, "what time we commanded the same Thomas to go into Zeland by land, and for the lodeman- shippe of *The Mary Rose* into the Thames," 12*l.*

By warrant dormounte to Sir Henry Guldeford, to pay "for our dysguysing on Twelve nyght last past," viz., to Willm. Botry for silks, cloth of gold, and other stuffs, 134*l.* 7*s.* 4*d.*— To Robart Amadas, for silver and fine gold stuff made by him and delivered to Richard Gybson, 118*l.* 5*s.* 6*d.*—To Rich. Gybson, for the gold-wire drawer, 72*l.* 3*s.* 11*d.*; for the Throwester, 103*s.* 7*d.*; for Mastres Philippe, silk-woman, 6*l.* 2*s.* 2*d.*; for the broderer, 15*l.* 6*s.* 8*d.*; for the wax-chandler, 24*s.* 2*d.*; for one other silk-woman, 41*s.*; for the tailor, 105*s.* 5*d.*; for the Master of the Revels' diets, 7*l.* 13*s.* 4*d.*; for the paient (pageant), 36*l.* 13*s.* 8*d.*; total, 404*l.* 6*s.* 9*d.* *Signed by the King.*

25 Sept. *sq.*

Obligations and specialties of Thomas Balle and John Charles; Richard Gresham and Willm. Copeland, of London, merchants; Robert Radclyff Lord Fitzwater and Sir Edward Darelle ; Edmund Bray of Eyton, co. Beds ; Willm. Astcley, John Fawteles and John Aleyn, citizens and merchants ; Willm. Roche, draper, Christopher Grantham, fishmonger, and John Heron, mercer ; and others.

Pp. 49.

5721.   WAGES.

R. O.

Men employed in rigging *The Mary Cradok,* 15*d.* a week each; tabling of the same, 15*d.* a week. Conduct money for 60 mariners out of Dewysland and Pembrokeshire to Bristowe, 6*d.* a man every 12 miles ; gunners at 8 ducats and 7*s.* 6*d.* a month. Soldiers' pay 5*s.* a month, &c. *Signed* Edward Howard, *and partly in his hand.*

Pp. 3.

2. Lists of artillery in *The Great Nicholas, The Gabriel Royal, The Sovereign, The Katharine Fortileza, The Mary Rose, The Barbara* and *The Great Elizabeth,* in 1514.

5722.   LORD LIGNY.

Calig. E. ii. 164.
B. M.

"Remembrance of my Lord Ligne Erle [of Faulquembergh]," complaining of Gregory Gentill, a Genoese merchant, who brought an action against the said Lord before the great Council at Maghlyns for the loss of certain wagons taken at Tournay by the Earl's soldiers then in the service of Henry VIII.

Mutilated, pp. 3.

1514.

5723. EXPENCES OF THE WAR.

R. O.

Debts in the Auditor's books due to Hen. VIII. upon divers declarations concerning the late wars against France.

Debtors.—Sir Edward Poynynges, late commissioner with Sir Ric. Wynfeld in Flanders. John Ricroft, for surplus of wheat and malt. John Myklowe, for surplus of money for the French Queen's expences during her transporting into France. Thomas Duke of Norfolk, for money delivered him by Sir Ph. Tylney, late treasurer of war under the Duke, at Brankston-field in the north. Antony Leigh, clerk of the kitchen, for surplus of money for the King's expences in foreign parts. Th. Byrkes, for surplus of the first victualling received by him ; and for money received from John a Barkyng, brewer, for beer redelivered to him. Sir Nich. Vaux by obligation and by a bill. Stephen Lawrence and Eliz. Rowseley for empty foystes. Robt. Arnewey of Calais. Nicholas Smyth of Wysbiche. Ric. Bull of Lynne.

In the account of T. Byrks of the second victualling.—John Esyngwold of London, baker. Ralph Dormer, Hen. Potter, Deryk Nightyngale and Th. Snadenham, of London, brewers. John Mathewe, John Atkynson, Robt. Brokett and Th. Best, of London, bakers. Richard Wodeward of ————, in Kent. John Easton of London, cooper.

In the account of Wm. Atcliff, clerk of the greencloth in the royal Household.—Henry Berkstall of Spene, Berks. Wm. Wright of London, salter. Chr. Brodebank, Th. Clerk and Ric. Godder. John Easton of London, cooper, for empty foystes. Ralph Dormer and Robt. Studley, of London, brewers.

Allen Hardyng and others of Newcastell. Ric. Gough, underchamberlain, of London. Sir Wm. Sandes, late treasurer of war in the parts of Byskey. Sir Edward Howard, late lord admiral, for surplus from wages of the sailors, 5 Hen. VIII. Sir Th. Wyndham, treasurer of war by sea. Hen. Acres, of the King's buttry, for empty pipes received from John Heron, surveyor of customs in London, by Mr. Cofferer's letter. Miles Gerard of London. John Clyfford, master of the fellowship of merchants in Flanders, for surplus of money "for prestyng of Almaynes, etc." Th. Partriche, for surplus of money "for prestyng and payng of shypps."

Pp. 3. *Endorsed.*

5724. EXPENCES OF THE WAR.

R. O.

Payments for victuals ; "for . . . . . . of [houses ?] remaining at Hampton Court, with cellars hired for the same, and for men's wages that kept the said houses;" and for Flanders biscuits.— "Victualling the King's army by sea, the 6th year of his reign." Payments for victuals for certain ships, " the w[hich were] to attend for the transporting of the French Queen into France," and victuals sent to Hull.—"Wages and conduct of the army sent to sea in the 4th (?) year of the King's reign." Payments, for "carriage of wood (?) to the [army];" for the fleet retained to carry Charles Lord Lisle (now Duke of Suffolk), into foreign parts, and afterwards sent to Dover to transport the King's army ; for ships sent from London to Southampton to victual Lord Lisle's retinues ; for wages of victuallers, "as well of three Spanish [victuallers] that [provi]ded victuals with the [army] to Brest, and tarried seven days [until] their flethes (?) were dispatched, which seven days ended the 20th day of June, the 5th year; as also for wages and tondage (?)

of three other ships which carried John Heron's victuals from the
. . . . . to Southampton ;" for "charges of *The Mount Galary ;*"
for hire of ships, anchors, &c.; for "carriage of *The Anne Galaunt ;*"
" keeping the garrison of Portsmouth;" "keeping the King's ships
in winter, anno 5 Hen. VIII.," for three months from 27 Sept. ; for
wages and victuals for the army; for two hired ships sent to Ireland, and two others coming from Ireland to Bristol ; for wages of
persons remaining at Portsmouth Jan. 5 Hen. VIII. for defence
of the ships there ; and for crews of ships.

Money advanced by John Dawtrey.—Payments for "land wages
of the King's army by sea ;" for the army mustered before the
commissioners at Portsmouth, to serve in campaign of 6 Hen. VIII.;
" for wages of the army upon sea, the 6th year ;" for provisions,
ordinance, masts, and other necessaries; for taking up a great
chain ; for wages of swchevers (soldiers) when they were in the
Isle of Wight, for 5 months from 30 Dec. 4 Hen. VIII. ; for fitting
out *The Soveraigne ;* for the carrack called *The Gabriell Royall;*
for beer and bake-houses at Portsmouth ; for making two gates (?)
at the castles, and repairing the ditches there ; and for repairing
the ships.

Total :—86,719*l.* 2*s.* 1*d.*

Names of persons mentioned.—Charles Lord Lisle, now Duke of
Suffolk, John Heron, Bede Olyver, master-carpenter, Sir William
Pyrton, John Flemyng, and Richard Palshyde, captains of the garrison of Portsmouth, John Dawtrey, Sir Thomas Wyndham, a
captain of the army and Treasurer of War, Robert Reynold (of
whom the King bought a ship called *The Henry of Hampton*); the
mayor of Hampton ; the patron of the Ragose ship ; Simon Peter
of Syreksey, Nicholas Cowart of Hampton, John de Villa Nova,
Sir Edward Howard, Lord Admiral, Sir Weston Browne, Richard
Palshed, customer of Southampton, Robert Brygandyn, clerk of
the King's ships, William Gouson, William Pawne, Sir Edward
Belknapp and John Hopton.

Ready money delivered to Sir John Daunce, 8 Sept. 6 Hen. VIII.,
towards the charges of the wars, as appears by a letter from my
Lord of York to John Dawtrey. Total 2,100*l.*

"Petition for sundry payments for which the accomptant has no
warrant ;" viz.. payments for biscuits and western fish " in a great
storm lost ;" to Nich. Cowart, for loss in sale of wheat after the wars,
and for his wages as "supervisour and having the charge of the bys-
cuett," and purveyor of wheat, from 24 Jan. 4 Hen. VIII. to 7 Nov.
6 Hen. VIII. ;—for wages of John Dawtrey and his two clerks, from
16 April 3 Hen. VIII. to 12 Sept. 6 Hen. VIII.;—for carriage of
money remaining in the hands of John Dawtrey from Hampton
to London, etc. ;—for biscuits in the hands of Nich. Cowert
and John Dawtrey;—to Hen. Tylman of Chichester, brewer, for
beer ;—to Rich. Gowffe, of Chichester, baker, for biscuits;—to
————— Serle, of Brighthempston, for barrels;—for remainder "of
wood vessels, carts, leighter, and divers other necessaries," in the
charge of Rich. Palshed, at Portsmouth. "Money paid and
advanced by Richard Palshed :"—for wages of brewers, millers,
beer-clerks, mill-makers, coopers, surveyors, master-brewers,
horse-keepers, and smiths, attending upon the King's brewhouses at Portsmouth, 5 and 6 Hen. VIII., and of certain
brewers and mariners from 22 Aug. 6 Hen. VIII. to 31 March
following ; for expences in carriage of beer, for rent of houses,
for building a great store-house at Portsmouth, for repairing the

1514.

King's garners and beer-houses at Portsmouth, for loss in sale, "after the war was done, of mill and dray-horses, wheat, malt, oats and hops ; for wheat, malt, hops, and beer lost and damaged at sea, and for wages of the said Rich. Palshed and his two clerks."

"Sum of the aforesaid : 5,007l. 15s. 5d."

Pp. 14 ; *much defaced; first page mutilated.*

R. O. **5725.** LONDON CURATES.

Complaints of the inhabitants of London against the exactions of the curates there, viz. : two pence demanded for the two tapers at mass ; exorbitant fees for marriages, burials, months, minds for burial in the choir, for churchings, for friends prayed for in the bede-roll, for howsel at Easter, for devotions on divers days, for brotherhoods kept in the church, and for leases of church lands.

Pp. 2, mutilated.

R. O. 2. Complaint of the House of Commons of the extortions of curates and parish priests, their refusal to bury, &c. ;—praying for certain enactments.

Large paper, p. 1. *Draft, much defaced.*

R. O. **5726.** ANTH. CAVALARY.

A declaration for the Abp. of York, stating that A. Cavalary has licence to ship 6,000 broad cloths at 14d. a cloth for which he has paid a friend of his 1,200l. ; and showing the disadvantage of his bargain as compared with that of Englishmen.

P. 1.

ii. A declaration by the same that he has a patent for exporting 1,000 sacks of wool at 5 marks per sack to be replaced at the end of 6 years by saltpetre at 6d. a pound. Has paid for the licence 800l., and is willing to resign it on a reasonable recompence. If the wars begin in Naples he will have to pay 6d. a pound for the saltpetre.

P. 1.

5727. ENGROSSING OF FARMS.

Draft of act against engrossing of farms, in consequence of the scarcity of food, occasioned by the occupation of land by merchants, clothiers, and others, more than they can employ in tilth, and the decay of housekeeping. For when every man was contented with one farm there was plenty of everything, as every acre of land ploughed bore the straw and chaff besides the corn, able " with help of the shackke, to keep great beasts," " as the land would keep layed in leyes ;" and by the winnowing of the corn there were kept at every barn door pigs and poultry, to the " comfort of your people" in every shire. Now, in a town of 20 or 30 dwellings the houses are decayed, the people gone, the churches in ruins, and in many parishes nothing more than a neat herd or a shepherd or a warner is to be seen.

R. O. 2. Draft of an act stating, that by report of the Justices and Commissioners of the Shires, complaint is made of the continued scarcity of grain by conversion of arable into pasture and engrossing of farms. By these means tenements fall to decay, poultry and victual are diminished, " and an infinite number of the King's subjects for

3 P

1514.

lack of occupation had fallen and daily do fall into idleness and consequently into theft and robberies. And finally by the rigor of the laws of this realm many of them have been put to the execution of death." Order is hereby made that all such lands shall revert to tillage as were in tillage 1 Hen. VII.

Otho, C. IX. 57. **5728.** THE MONKS OF MOUNT SINAI to HENRY VIII.
B. M.

Expressing their great poverty, which had compelled them to pledge their sacred vessels and furniture for food ; and thanking him for having sent them, by means of their messenger, Anthony, a Syrian, 266 [£ ?].

Signed on behalf of the Convent by Clement the Abbot.

"ἐτυπώθησαν ταῦτα ἐν τῶ . . . τοῦ ἁγίου ὅρους σινᾶ ἐν ἐ[τη] . . ."

Greek, mutilated, p. 1. *The distinctive part of the address is illegible.*

Otho, C. IX. 3. **5729.** THE HOLY SEPULCHRE.
B. M.

" Instructiones ex parte venerandi patris guardiani I[erosolymae] fratri Johanni de Sancto Martino procuratori Terræ S[anctæ ad] potentissimum et serenissimum dominum, dominum Henricum [viij] Anglorum regem et reginalem majestatem ejus consortem." 1. He shall represent to the King that since his coronation his renown has been spread above all his predecessors for his numerous victories; that inevitable ruin will fall upon the Holy places unless he adopts methods for their security, for which no one is so fit, from his excellence both of body and mind, (" *tam proceritate corporis quam etiam virtute animi.*") 2. That the Christian King of Georgia (" *rex Courgiorum*") living in the Eastern Mountains, between the Turk and Hysmail Sophi, has not scrupled, by the aid of Abunazar Campso el Gauri, to cast down the altar of the Latin Christians on Mount Calvary, for the repair of which they have paid the Sultan more than 1,000 ducats. 3. They have had to bribe the emir of Jerusalem, the caliphs of Gaza, R. . . ., and other officers of the Saracens, with robes of velvet, silk, and scarlet, &c., to secure the pilgrims visiting the Sepulchre. 4. They are at great annual expense for the maintenance of the Church of St. Mary, Bethlehem, of the Holy Sepulchre, of the Holy Chamber of Sion, of St. Mary's in the Valley of Jehoshaphat, with 40 lamps continually burning in the Holy Places, each costing 7 ducats per annum for the support of 40 brethren, to the sum of 3,500*l.* ducats per annum. 5. Their previous benefactors, the King of Naples, the Duke of Milan, Philip and Charles of Burgundy, each of whom gave 1,000 ducats annually, are dead, and they have no support except 1,000 ducats assigned upon Sicily by the late Queen of Spain. The merchants who used to maintain them can no longer visit Egypt or Syria for spices, because the way has been intercepted by Emmanuel King of Portugal. 9. Hope the King, in consideration of the above, will nominate some proctor in his realm for their maintenance against that great day of account which the Lord shall hold near His tomb in the Valley of Jehoshaphat.

Lat., mutilated, pp. 3.

Titus, B. VI. 118. **5730.** The QUEEN of BOSNIA (?) to the KING (HENRY VIII.?)
B. M.

Requesting his aid to ransom her husband the Duke of Barbania(?) from the Turks. The Emperor, Pope, and King of France having contributed 50,000 ducats, there remain but 4,000 to be paid.

Lat., p. 1. *Not signed.*

Note.—" Regina Bosnæ ducissa Barbaniæ."

1514.

Er. Ep. viii. 43. **5731.** ERASMUS to ROGER WENTFORD.

John's father has told Erasmus that he wishes to take away his son, and put him under the care of some one else. Erasmus has no objection notwithstanding the father's indecision. Erasmus has brought the boy up, and though he has not made the proficiency desired, he knows more Latin than if he had been educated in any school, not excepting Lily's. The father complained of his backwardness, and attributed it to Erasmus' ignorance of English. Would like the boy left with him till after the 1st Nov. when Erasmus proposes going to Brabant.

Er. Ep. viii. 45. **5732.** ERASMUS to ROGER WENTFORD.

Thanks him for the interest he takes in his writings. Is rich in golden promises. If Wentford laments for an empty purse Erasmus has greater reason to complain, for out of 70 nobles he carried to Cambridge *istuc* not a fraction remains. Does not see how he can live there except he lives with Grocin; and would rather live with him than any one else, but does not like to impose on his generosity. Is finishing his work *De conscribendis Epistolis.* Intends correcting his *Copia.* Remembrances to Grocin.

R. O. **5733.** ERASMUS to G. S. & O. S. [SMITH].

"*Ego cum hac bellua loqui non possum; vos ei persuadete ut intelligat me illi plusquam pater fuisse tum in animo curando tum corpore.*" He has made greater progress than he would have done in any school. Begs they will have his horse shoed as he will probably have a long journey before him. On Wednesday will be there with Watson. "*Bene valete, et asino huic mea causa nonnihil humanitatis exhibite.*" Wishes Humphrey, if he has leisure, would send him a paper on this subject in English for Erasmus to sign. "*Salve Roberte Smith amice singularis!*" Sends John to him to whom Erasmus has been more than a father; as he is determined to be guided by Smith in all things. Has not altogether lost his labor, for the lad (?) had made more advance in Latin than he would have done, in the same time, under Roger ("*in ludo Rogeriano*"). If a better master can be found for him will be grateful.

At the end: M. G. et Omphredo amicis unicis.

P. 1.

R. O. **5734.** ERASMUS to G. [GEORGE SMITH ?].

Matters remain the same:—is undecided whether he shall fly: *an istuc mihi sit recurrendum.* Another has died not far from the College, (Queen's Coll. Camb. ?); the doctor Bout (Butt) is dead in the country and his little girl in the house. Will be glad if he does not change the beds for the next four days: ("*si non transferres lectos intra quatriduum*"). If he comes will come with Watson.

P. 1. Honorato viro G. ludi magistro amico singulari.

APPENDIX.

A.D. 1509.

5735. HENRY VII.'S FUNERAL.

A bundle of 21 warrants to John Heron, treasurer of the Chamber, with receipts for payments towards the expenses of Henry VII.'s funeral;—viz., 1,000*l.* for black cloth for hangings in the chapel, &c., and for liveries to lords and others present ; 20*l.* for tombwork about the hearse ; 666*l.* 13*s.* 4*d.* for compositions to be made with the churches of Paul's and Westminster, rewards of the King's chapel, the four orders of friars in London, and the bearers of the corpse ; 500*l.* for scutcheons for garnishing of the hearses and chair ; 500*l.* for torches, long and staffed ; 130*l.* for rewards to 130 parish churches ; 25*l.* to the 5 houses of nuns, viz., Clerkenwell, Haliwell, the Mynneries, and St. Helen's ; 40*l.* to the sisters of St. Katharine's ; 100*l.* to be distributed in alms, in groats to Ric. Rawlyns, the same to Rob. Honywode, the same to Rob. Bekynsals, the same to Roger Lupton ; 150*l.* to Will. Pawne for the stable ; 250*l.* to be employed by Sir Thos. Brandon for the chair and other apparels belonging to the stable ; 66*l.* for 330 poor men, torchbearers, attending the corpse from Richmond to Westminster, at 4*s.* each ; 100 from St. George's bar to Westminster, 2*s.* ; 100*l.* for alms to churches on the way from Richmond to London ; 10*l.* each for the quires of St. Paul's and Westminster ; 4*s.* each to 30 men, lacking of the household, to bear staff torches from Richmond to Westminster.

Most of the documents are in the handwriting of Fox Bp. of Winchester, signed at the head by the Countess of Richmond, " Margaret R. ;" and below by Chri. [Bainbridge] Abp. of York, Ri. Bp. of Winchester, Ric. Bp. of London, John Bp. of Rochester, C. Somerset [Lord Herbert], John Yong, Sir Thos. Lovell, Thos. Rowthall, and Sir John Cutte.

ii. A letter of Sir Henry Wiat requesting 40*l.* in groats ; and an acknowledgment by Ric. Rayner, deputy to Dr. Edname, the King's almoner, of the sums received for alms.

5736. WM. LORD MOUNTJOY to ERASMUS.

Is assured that he will cease to mourn when he learns that Henry octavus, or rather Octavius, has succeeded his father. What may not Erasmus augur of a prince whose admirable disposition is so well known to him—whose friendship he possesses—and from whom Erasmus has received a letter written wholly with his own hand ? If he could see how nobly, how wisely, the prince behaves, is sure he would hasten to England. All England is in extacies. Extortion is put down—liberality is the order of the day. When the King was saying to Mountjoy, a few days since, he wished he had

1509.

more learning, Mountjoy told him, this was not expected of him, but that he should patronize learned men. On which Henry replied: " Certainly ; we could hardly live without them."—Had received two letters from Erasmus, dated Rome, 29th and 30th ; is glad to be consulted, and have an opportunity of removing his anxieties. Advises him to visit England. Instead of being under obligation to Mountjoy, Mountjoy feels he is under obligations to Erasmus he can never repay, for Erasmus. has conferred immortality upon him. Has received his *Adagia ;* disowns the liberal compliments with which Erasmus loads him ; for who will endure to hear him styled *literatissimus ?* The work is highly commended, especially by (Warham) Abp. of Canterbury, who sends him 5*l.* for his journey, and promises him a living. Mountjoy adds 5*l.* more. Is sorry Erasmus did not have his health in Italy ; never wished his going there. Incloses a bill for the money.

Greenwich, 6 kl. Jun.

6 June. **5737.** THE FRIARS OBSERVANTS.
R. O.

Warrant to John Heron for payment of the 500 marks bequeathed by Henry VII. to the five houses of Friars Observants for the repair of the same, to Nich. Waring, proctor. Greenwich, 6 June 1 Hen. VIII.

Signed by Henry VIII. at the top ; and below by the following executors: Margaret Countess of Richmond, T. Earl of Surrey, Ri. Rp. of Winchester, Thos. Lovell, C. Somerset [Lord Herbert].

21 July. **5738** THE FRIARS OBSERVANTS.
R. O.

Warrant to John Heron for payment to Philippe du Karugys, physician, of Henry VII.'s legacy of 500 marks to the five houses of Friars Observants for the reparation of the same. Greenwich, 21 July 1 Hen. VIII.
Signed.

21 Oct. **5739.** ARTILLERY.
R. O.

Warrant to John Heron for payment of 1,000*l.* for provision of metal for artillery. Croydon, 21 Oct. 1 Hen. VIII.

A.D. 1511.

1511.
25 March. **5740.** WARHAM to LORD DARCY.
R. O.

The commissions are despatched which Darcy sent to be sealed. As to the deliverance of Elderkars and his sons from the fleet, as it was the King's pleasure, every reasonable man must be contented. Is sorry for Darcy's departure on such a distant and dangerous journey, but the more painful the more meritorious. How his friends and servants shall be treated in his absence it is hard to say, seeing they have not been well treated in his presence. Unless Darcy procured better friends than him he writes of, to see to his affairs in his absence, he may be deceived. Wishes that he and his archers, when sent out of England, were to be with the Pope " to strength him against the enemies of the Church, which be little better than infidels." Hopes to speak with him in London at the beginning of next term. Canterbury, 25 March.
Signed. P. 1. Add.

1511.
March.　**5741**　EXPEDITION INTO SPAIN.

R. O.

Instructions to Lord Darcy.—Is to be at Plymouth the day of his indentures, and after taking musters to go on board directly and wait for wind.　To enter no haven except in stress of weather, till they come to Ghades (Cadiz), where it is thought they shall find the King of Arragon.　If he is not there, Darcy is to advise Ferdinand of his coming, and to tell him that he and his company have arrived to do him service at his pleasure, and request to know his wishes.　Is to remain at Cadiz till he receives an answer.　On ariving in Ferdinand's presence he shall say, "The King's Highness his good son, which as entirely loveth the said King of Arragon his good father as though he were his own natural son, and no less mindeth, pondereth and desireth the wealth, prosperity, surety and honor of his said good father and his prosperous successes in all his affairs, than he doth the wealth, prosperity, surety and honor of his own royal person, having knowledge by his orator resident within his realm, that his said father of his devout mind and catholic purpose, to his great laud and honor in this world and immortal reward in Heaven, now intendeth in his own person to make a noble voyage with a great army against the Moors and Infidels, enemies of Christ's faith ; and being desired on his behalf by his said orator, hath sent him with his company and retinue to his Highness, and straitly commanded him to give his attendance upon him."

He shall then beg the King of Arragon to use him as his own subject, and shall state that as the manner of war and ordering of the same is not like that against the Moors, he begs the King of Arragon to appoint some expert man of war, by whom he may at all times be ordered.

Signed top and bottom by the King.
Pp. 8.

28 April.　**5742.**　WARDSHIP of THOMAS GREY.

R. O.

Mem., that I, William Alee, receiver of Berwick, have received of Thomas Lord Darcy, a patent of the wardship of Thomas Grey, son and heir of Sir Ralph Grey, knight, deceased, with a rental and account, on the condition that if I the said William make a bargain with my Lord of Durham for the said ward, that then to deliver the said patent unto my said Lord of Durham and to his use, or else to deliver the said patent again unto the use of my said Lord Darcy."　Sealed and signed 28 April, 3 Hen. VIII.

Signed and sealed.　Endd.: Wm. Lee ; for receiving of Grey's patent.

16 June.　**5743.**　FERDINAND OF ARRAGON to LORD DARCY.

R. O.

Has received his letter and the articles declared to the Bp. of Palencia, to all of which he sends an answer by articles signed by his hand, despatched to the said Bishop, for whom he begs credence. Sevile, 16 June 1511.

Signed : Countersigned by Almaçan.

Sp., p. 1.　*Add.:* Millort Derci Ca[pitaneo g]eneral del serenissimo [Rey di] Inglaterra, &c.

3 Aug.　**5744.**　THE SPANISH EXPEDITION.

R. O.

" Mem., that the 3rd day of August, the third year of the reign of our sovereign Lord King Henry the Eighth, upon the deliberate sight of the great extremities and necessities that the King's army of archers stood in, as well for fault and lack of money, as specially victuals, the Lord Darcy delivered the said day at Cape St. Vincent, of his own proper money, to every captain, for the victualling of him and one hundred archers under his leading, 20*l.* of English gold; and for witness that Richard Maliverey, Esq., hath so received 20*l.* for him and one hundred archers at his leading, the same Ric. Maliverey to this bill hath set his sign manual the day and year beforesaid."

Signed : Ric. Maleverie.

Similar acknowledgments by Sir Ralph Ellercar, Sir Richard Aldburgh, Sir Ralph Eure, and Sir Rob. Constable.

A.D. 1512.

1512.
19 April.　**5745.**　　T. [RUTHAL] BP. OF DURHAM to LORD DARCY.
R. O.

Is so busy in the setting forth of the King's army to the sea that he cannot write often. 10,000 men are being sent into Guienne under my Lord Marquis. Preparations are made for their landing at Fontarabia. John Stile writes that they will be met by 10,000 men provided by the King of Arragon, of whom one half are to be horse. Sir Edw. Howard is gone to sea with 5,000 men very well appointed. My Lord Marquis is to be at Hampton to embark with all the army on 4th May. The French are so strong in Italy that the armies of the Pope and Arragon dare not meet them ; they now lie within five miles. The Venetians have lost 10,000 or 12,000 men slain by the French ; and now they make a greater army than ever. The Swiss intend to take the Pope's part ; 20,000 of them will shortly enter the Duchy of Milan. Has great hopes the Emperor will at length turn to the defence of the Church. Most part of Christendom is at war by the presumption of the French King ; and other countries now at peace are likely to be led into it. These letters now sent to the King of Scots are courteous and honorable. They are in answer to letters in which James declared himself in favor of peace, provided he were well treated in regard to his ships. For this matter Lord Dacre and the Dean of Windsor (West) are about to be sent to Scotland. Greenwich, 19 April.

Hol., p. 1. *Add.*

26 April.　**5746.**　　JULIERS.
R. O.

"Litteræ reversales Johannis Clivensis Ducis Juliæ, anno 1512," relative to certain feudal possessions in Moubach, Hengbach, Zulpe, &c., held of Lewis Count Palatine of the Rhine. Treves, Monday after Misericordia Sunday, 1512. *Endorsed,* "No. 4."

With the above, and apparently included in it, is an acknowledgment from Will. Duke of Juliers to Rupert Count Palatine of the Rhine, relative to the feudal rights of the same. Utrecht, 26 Jan. *Endorsed,* "No. 5."

Pp. 5.

14 May.　**5747.**　　VICTUALLING of THE REGENT.
R. O.

For 10 days from 4 to 14 May 4 Hen. VIII., for 300 mariners. Biscuit, 3*s.* 4*d.* per 100, 100*s.* ; beer, 8*s.* 4*d.* the pipe, 12*l.* 10*s.* ;

1512.

beef, 51s. the pipe, 11l. 9s. 6d.; fish at 36s. 6d., 5 score and 6, 73s.

ii. Continuation of the account. Candles, 6d. per lb.; mustard seed, 10d. per peck; oxen, 12s. and 13s. 4d. a carcase, &c.

July. **5748.** NAVY.
R. O.

Account of Thomas Birkes, taken by George Dalyson and Thomas Roberts, before Sir Rob. Southwell, of money received from Sir John Daunce for providing 100 tuns of beer for victualling the King's army at sea, July 4 Hen. VIII., at 13s. 4d. a tun, with other expenses.

7 Oct. **5749.** ORDNANCE.

Payments by Sir Sampson Norton, master of the ordnance, from 24 Aug. 3 Hen. VIII. to 7 Oct. 4 Hen. VIII.

R. O. **5750.** STEPHEN BULL.

Order from Wolsey to deliver 10l. to Stephen Bull the bearer, by way of the King's pleasure.
Signed: Thomas Wulcy. *Hol.*

A.D. 1513.

1513.
9 March. **5751.** THE GREAT NICHOLAS.
R. O.

Account of *The Great Nicholas*, moored in the Thames against the town of Woolwich, from the [xv]ijth day of June 4 Hen. VIII. to the 9 March following, 7 weeks and 2 days; for timber, nails, tar (4s. 4d. per barrel); pitch, 4s.; 1½ cwt. of rosin, 7s.; tallow, 7s. 8d. per cwt.; 7 doz. lb. tallow candles, 7s.; oakum, 5d. per stone; lead, 6s. per cwt.; solder, 6d. per lb.; cordage, baskets, needles, &c., 150 sail needles, 4s. 10d.; furnace, gunpowder boxes, 4 doz. tankards, great and small, 42s.; 13½ doz. drinking bowls, 13s. 6d.; 11 doz. "treen" platters, 11s.; a compass, 2s. 8d.; &c.

ii. Wages of carpenters and others for the same, from 2d. to 6d. a day, mariners 5s. per month. Victuals of men employed about the same; 282 doz. of bread, 14l. 2s.; 67 pipes of beer at 6s. 8d. per pipe; 28 qrs. of beef, at 4s. 2d. per qr.; 500 dry fish, 47s. 8d. per 100; 800 cades of red herring, 5s. per cade; 6 barrels of white herring, 7s. per barrel.
Pp. 15.

25 March. **5752.** WAGES DUE TO THE SABIENE.
R. O.

For two months, beginning 21 Feb. Wages 6s. a man per month, and the same for victuals; 16½ deedshares at 6d. a share per month; soldiers' jackets at 4s. each. Warrant signed 25 March 4 Hen. VIII. by Edward Howard, Lord Admiral.

1 May. **5753.** REPORT OF A FRENCH SPY.
Calig. D. VIII. 32.
B. M.

Headed, 1 May, at Calais.—Says he was at Dieppe, where they are preparing vessels secretly. They have built four ships, which are said to be intended against England because the King of England would not go to Turkey. A ship of Dieppe, laden with corn for Ireland, has been stopped (?) and orders given against exportation

1513.

of victuals from France.—Went to Caudebec, where a ship had been arrested that was laden with habiliments of war for the English. Had actually seen some Englishmen belonging to it.—Went next to Honnefleur, where Bernardin had been three weeks before. He is to make a harbour there large enough for all the ships of Britanny. To prevent suspicion he left his galleys upon the high seas while he himself visited the workmen. *La Grande Loyse* and *La Petite Loyse* are there, and will be sent to sea. There came gentlemen from the court to Honnefleur while the spy was there, to hasten the works.

9 May.   **5754.**   THOMAS LORD HOWARD.
R. O.

His appointment of William Symons as clerk controller of "this royal army." with 18d. a day. 9 May 5 Hen. VIII. *Signed.*

26 May.   **5755.**   JOHN DAWTREY to WOLSEY.
R. O.

Has spoken with Wyndham the treasurer of the King's army. Has received 6,000l. for wages for two months for the army, and 500l. surplus. Wyndham requires more. Desires instructions from Wolsey how to act. At Hampton, the 26th day.

P.S. "The Spaniards, with victual from London, be not yet come."

Hol. p. 1. Add.: To Master Wulcy, the Kynges amner. *Endd.*

May.   **5756.**   For CHARLES VISCOUNT LISLE, K. G.

To be marshal of the army going abroad.

Fr. 5 Hen. VIII. m. 6.

4 June.   **5757.**   FOX to WOLSEY.
R. O.

"Brother master Almoner, yesternight in my bed and in sleep after ten of the clock I received your letters, with the letter to the King of Scots, a minute for a warrant for the deliverance of Steward out of the Tower, and the instructions for Th. Spinel, the which, with a letter directed to Mr. Compton to get them signed of the King's grace, I delivered to the post forthwith, sitting up in my bed so that by this hour, which is six in the morning, he might be with the King's grace at Guildford." On their way the letters were lost between Alton and Waltham, and afterwards recovered. A similar delay occurred in the letters for the Emperor, the Venetians and the Bp. of Worcester, which only came to Fox's hands on Thursday afternoon, "and the same hour I returned them to you. What with slowness of the post and other chances, there have been many delays of letters since the King came hither, but not owing to Fox. Received this night past the copy of the King of Scots' letter sent by Isley. The words sound well, but what he means is uncertain. It is clear the French King means, if England do not accept the truce of Arragon, that the King of Scots will be at liberty to take his part. It is only by Mr. West, Lord Dacre, and Sir Rob. Drury, and by his works, that they can judge of the Scotch King's intentions, "and also by the King's dealing towards him, which I know not, but me seemeth that the letter that is now written to him shall little please him, albeit the letter that Rosse brought, as it should seem by the rehearsal thereof in the King's letters, deserve no better." These recriminations, however, do not tend towards amity. Thinks it will appear at length that James will make no actual war, but rob and spoil the King's subjects, especially by water. He

1513.

will be inclined to be suspicious of the appointment of the next diet in October. Thinks it would have been better in the middle of August. Spinelly's instructions will not satisfy my Lady of Savoy, but as for that it was ill begun and worse continued. As for the repairing of the ships to Brittany Wolsey must know the issue of Lord Lisle's letter; it was sent him on Thursday in the morning. My Lord Admiral will not sleep, but his letters of yesterday show that he is in want of many things. "He hath had a great let by my Lord Lisle's matters; and now for the ordering of many other matters, far out of good frame I warrant you, the which he will reform." He will remain no longer than is necessary. "And somewhat he is embusied about redding of my Lord Lisle's company by land, and taking into his ships, and dividing the victuals that came from you, and discharging a great number of ships, to the King's great advantage." At Hampton, 4 June, about six in the morning.

Fears it will be Monday before he can depart.

Hol. p. 1. Addressed: My brother the King's almouer.

| 19 July. | **5758.** | PAYMENTS AUTHORIZED BY WOLSEY. |
| R. O. | | |

"Paid by me, John [Da]unce, by the King's commandment, the 19th day of July, the 5th year of his reign, these sums of money following, in the presence of Mr. Almoner:—

"First, 40*l.* for espyall to the captain of Remingham; item, 10 marks for free passage at the ferry at the nunnery beside Graveling; item, 40*s.* for espyall to Mr. Ponynges; and 200 cr. of the soillel, (accounting every crown 4*s.* 4*d.* st., that is 43*l.* 6*s.* 8*d.* st.) in reward to the Duke of Brunswick's ambassadors;—in all, 92*l.*"

Signed: Thomas Wulcy.

| 22 July. | **5759.** | T. [RUTHAL] BP. OF DURHAM to LORD DARCY. |
| R. O. | | |

Thanks him for his letters dated Berwick the 14th instant. Has not leisure to write all he intended. "The post departed so suddenly, for divers causes, as well touching the King's ships at the New Castell, as also such espial as by your wisdom should be had out of Scotland, wherein ye have at this time and divers other acquitted yourself to your honour and much praise here." Desires that his constable may be informed of whatever news Darcy hears from Scotland. Two lines occasionally from Darcy would do much for the security of the bishop's castle (Norham). Will write more by next post. London, on Mary Magdalene Day. *Signed:* Your awn, T. Duresme.

Hol. p. 1. Add.

| 28 Aug. | **5760.** | VICTUALLING OF THE ARMY. |
| R. O. | | |

i. Account of 998 pipes of beer shipped for the army on the sea, in the month of April, for my Lord Lisle, issued June and July 5 Hen. VIII. ii. Of 372 pipes of beef, at 53*s.* 4*d.* the pipe, 3 pipes to a barrel; price per barrel from 3*s.* 7*d.* to 5*s.* iii. Of 4,500 ling and cod. iv. Of 41,106lb. biscuit. v. Of tankards, platters, &c. 12*l.* 13*s.* 2*d.* vi. Of wheat bought at Hull, 954 qrs. at 8½*d.* per qr.; Flanders wheat 11*s.* per qr. vii. Of 400 pipes of beer sent to Newcastle on the 28 Aug. 5 Hen. VIII. at 9*s.*

Pp. 17.

| 31 Aug. | **5761.** | NAVY. |
| R. O. | | |

Costs of ships hired for the Navy, 14 March 4 Hen. VIII. to 11 April, paid by Thos. Wyndham.

ii. Same account for the month beginning 6 June.

iii. Costs of the army royal by sea in July and August 5 Hen. VIII. paid by the same. 1. To Lord Ferrers, capt. of *The Trinity Sovereign*, 1000 tons, 720 men, capt. 18*d.* a day, soldiers, &c., 5*s.* a month, dedshares 5*s.* per month, rewards to gunners 20*d.* a month. Signed by Ferrers.—2. To Sir Will. "Trevillian," capt. of *The Gabriel Royal*, [1000 tons]. 607 men, capt. 3*s.* 4*d.* a day. Signed : W. Trevanyon.—3. To Cornwall and Courtney, captains of *The Maria de Loreta*, 800 tons, 599 men, capt. 3*s.* per day, &c. —4. To John Flemyng, capt. of *The Catalina Forteleza*, 700 tons, men 522, capt. 18*d.* a day, &c.

iv. Account for the month of July. 1. To Thos. Lord Howard, admiral, and Edw. Bray, capt. of *The Mary Rose*, tonnage 600, men 402, admiral 10*s.* a day, capt. 18*d.*—2. To Sir Wistan Brown, capt. of *The Peter Pomegarnett*, tonnage 450, men 288, capt. 18*d.* a day.—3. To Sir Thos. Wyndham, capt. of *The John Baptist*, 400 tons, men 303, 3*s.* 4*d.* a day.—4. To Sir Will. Pyrton, capt. of *The Nicolas Rede*, 400 tons, 299 men, 18*d.* a day.—5. To Sir Henry Shernburne and Sir Will. Sydney, captains of *The Great Bark*, 400 tons, 263 men, 3*s.*, a day.—6. To Morice Berkley, capt. of *The Mary George*, 300 tons, 239½ men, 18*d.* a day.—7. To Ralph Ellercar, capt. of *The Mary James*, 300 tons, 249 men, 18*d.* a day.—8. To Thos. Cheny, capt. of *The Christ*, 300 tons, 216 men, 18*d.* a day.—9. To Sir Steph. Bull, capt. of *The Lesse Barke*, 240 tons, 186 men, 18*d.* a day.—10. To Christopher Coo, capt. of *The Lezard*, 120 tons, 100 men, 18*d.* a day,—11. To Thomas Gurney, capt. of *The Jenet Peryn*, 70 tons, 59 men, 18*d.* a day.—12. To Edw. Yelverton, capt. of *The Barbara of Greenwich*, 160 tons, 126 men, 18*d.* a day.—13. To Will. West, capt. of *The Henry of Hampton*, 133 men, 18*d.* a day.—14. To Will. Tolley, capt. of *The Swepestake*, 80 tons, 72 men, 18*d.*—15. To Thos. Carew, capt. of *The Swallow*, 80 tons, 72 men, 18*d.*—16. To Will. Davison, master of the bark *The Mary Rose*, 80 tons, 66 men (for his crew only). — 17. To Will. Kenwode, master of the bark *Kateryn Forteleza*, 80 tons, 66 men, do.—18. To Roger Rothewell, appointed by the lord admiral, capt. of *The Mary and John*, (tonnage blank,) 151 men, 18*d.* a day.,

v. For ships hired, Anth. Poyntz, capt. of *The Trinity of Bristol*, 160 tons, 130 men, 18*d.* To Edm. Wiseman, captain of *The Christofer Dary*, 160 tons, 157 men, 18*d.* Rob. Draper, capt. of *The Nicholas Draper*, 160 tons, 148 men, 18*d.* Mathew Cradok, capt. of *The Mathew Cradok*, 240 tons, 195 men, 18*d.* Lewis Southern, capt. of *The Elizabeth of New Castell*, 120 tons, 132 men, 18*d.* Ric. Mercer, capt. of *The Erasymus of London*, 160 tons, 136 men, 18*d.* Roger Bridges, capt. of *The German*, 100 tons, 98 men, 18*d.* Wm. Sabyn, capt. of *The Sabyn*, 120 tons, 101 men, 18*d.* James Knyvet, capt. of *The Margaret of Toppesham*, 140 tons, 100 men, 18*d.* Charles Clifford, capt. of *The Baptist of Calais*, 120 tons, 101 men, 18*d.* Ph. Barnard, capt. of *The Mary of Walsyngham*, 120 tons, 97 men, 18*d.* Ric. Calthorp, capt. of *The Mary of Brixham*, 120 tons, 92 men, 18*d.* Wm. Gibbes, capt. of *Gybbes Ship*, 120 tons, 120 men, 18*d.* Geo. Whitwombe, capt. of *The Julyan of Dertmouth*, 100 tons, 103 men, 18*d.* Rob. Appulyerd, capt. of *The Jamys of Dertmouth*, 120 tons, 103 men, 18*d.* Ric. Berdisley, capt. of *The Margarite Bonaventure*, 122 tons, 101 men, 18*d.* Th. Vowell, capt. of *The Cristofer of Dartmouth*, 120 tons, 98 men, 18*d.* Wm. Ellercar, capt. of *The Thomas of Hull*, 80 tons,

76 men, 18*d.* Wm. Harper, capt. of *The Baptist of Harwich*, 70 tons, 61 men, 18*d.* Alex. Manachan, capt. of *The Leonard Fryscombald*, 300 tons, 245 men, 18*d.* John Wallop, capt. of *The Sancheo de Gaza*, (*tonnage blank*,) 271 men, 18*d.* (Signed : Stephen Vaus, servant to John Wallop.) Francis Pigott, capt. of *The Erasmus Sebastian*, 250 tons, 192 men, 18*d.* Jas. Delabere, capt. of *The Anthony Montrego*, 240 tons, 186 men, 18*d.* John Baker, capt. of *The Sancta Maria de la Cayton*, 200 tons, 125 men, 18*d.* Geo. Throgmerton, capt. of *The Gret Newe Spanyard*, 360 tons, 318 men, 18*d.* Edw. Ichingham, capt. of *The* 2*de Newe Spanyard*, called *The St. Maria Semago*, 280 tons, 218 men, 18*d.* Ric. Courteney, capt. of *The Mighell of Plymouth*, 80 tons, 70 men, 18*d.* Wm. Simons, capt. of *The Mary Christofer*, 140 tons, 120 men, 18*d.* Wm. Migenall, capt. of *The Mathew of Bristol*, 150 tons, 131 men, 18*d.* Walter Loveday, capt. of *The Mary Katerin of London*, 160 tons, 125 men, 18*d.* Edm. Tylney and John Hausard, capts. of *The Petyr of Fowey*, 120 tons, 86 men, 18*d.* each. Roger Aldred, capt. of *The Mary of Famouth*, 90 tons, 84 men, 18*d.*

vi. Similar account for August, with addition of Ric. Calthorp, capt. of *The Trinity of Hampton*, 140 tons, 92 men, 18*d.* Th. Carew, capt. of *The Mary* . . . . (*tonnage blank*,) 147 men ; and omission of *The Sweepstake, The Mary and John, The Mary of Brixham, The Sancho de Gaza, The Great New Spaniard, The Mary Katharine of London*, and *The Mary of Falmouth.*

Pp. 70.

13 Sept. **5762.** The PRIVY COUNCIL to SIR T. WYNDHAM.
R. O.

Have received his letters dated the 10th, stating that it was too late to act upon their order to set such men on land as were infected within the ships, when they be sick. Had there been one sick in every ship it would not have been convenient to discharge the whole navy, for then the Scotch and French ships could annoy England by sea and land at their pleasure. Should be sorry that he or others were in jeopardy. "And where ye think it impossible to keep them on seaboard we should in main desire you to keep them there, if it be as ye write impossible so to do. And if they should be on land, and have 16*d.* a week, and not to be in a surrediness to do the King service when need shall require, both the time should be lost, and the same money expended." They refer it to him, as he knows the fierceness of the plague there raging, and the chance of the crews returning. If he think they will return on having 16*d.* a week, will order John Dawtrey to pay them. Will be glad to know from him what preparations are going on at Brest and Honfleur. Is to keep his great ships together 14 days after the end of the month, then bring them to some haven, as Portsmouth; &c. Have given orders about the rigging. Are content with the 16 ships named by him. As Sir Whitstane Broune was appointed captain by the King, "being within this realm the last winter," and since has been appointed for this winter by the Queen's grace and the Council, think the crew ought to be contented with him ; if they cannot be persuaded, he is "to take such one to be captain as the most part of the saddest and most discreet of the army there will choose." My Lord Admiral is landed at Newcastle to assist his father against the Scots. Send copy of letters they have written to my Lord of Arundel for the keeping of the King's great ships when brought into haven and for the keeping of the tower and blockhouse at Portsmouth. Richmond, 13 Sept. *Signed :* Willm. Cantuar.—John, abbot Westm.—

1513.

John Fyneux—Robt. Rede—John Cutte—Ric. Cholmey—George Dalyson.
P. 2. Add.

27 Nov. **5763.** HENRY VIII. to SIR WILLIAM MOLINEUX.

Stowe's Chron., 494.

Has heard by the Duke of Norfolk of his valiant behaviour against the Scots. Thanks him for the same. Windsor Castle, 27 Nov.

R. O. **5764.** WOLSEY to Master SAWCHEVERELL.

Warrant to deliver to "my fellow John Daunce" 2,748 crowns at the rate of 4s. 1d. per crown, allowance to be made to Sawcheverell of the 3d. residue in every crown; to be repaid immediately by Daunce, 5,611. 4s. 12d. *Signed:* Thomas Wulcy.

R. O. **5765.** VICTUALS FOR THE ARMY.

Provisions made by [John] Heron, at the command of Mr. Almoner, for 10,000 men for a month, countermanded to Hampton for my Lord Lisle. What was not used was landed at Hampton, 2 Aug. "The substance of the beer was lost because it was not spent in season; the rest of the victual was searched for, because it was wet in the great storm when Whittsonde bay was brent, and in especial one hoy with 40 hogsheads and 80 barrels of flesh, which was full of salt water and the flesh clearly lost. [2]53 fat winter fed oxen bought in Lincolnshire and Holland, killed and salted at Saltfleet, 290l. 6s. 8d; salt and vessels for the same, 58l. 19s. 8d. 322 do. bought at Wisbeach, 32l. 12s. 4d· ; cost of transport, 7l. ; of salting, &c. 91l. 13s. 11d. 164 do. at Stamford and Peterborough, 176l. 0s. 8d. ; rebate for hide and tallow of the same, 164l. 14s. 4d. (tallow at 8d. per stone.) Biscuit at 5s. 4d. the 100, wheat then being 11s. per qr., 109l. 12s. 4d. Old ling and great dry cod and "mwde" fish, great cod fresh salted, 53s. 9½d. per 100, 121l. 0s. 7d. Caldrons to seethe meat, plates and dishes, &c. 11 weigh of cheese bought of my Lord Lisle's servants, 10l. 972 pipes 1 hogshead of beer at 8s. the pipe ; 200 last of new barrels at 11s. 6d. the last.
Pp. 11.

R. O. **5766.** BEER sent to CALAIS for the KING'S ARMY in May.

Bought of the beerbrewers in London 341 pipes, 1 hhd., every pipe without the foist 8s. 198 flitches of bacon, at 18d. each.
P. 1.

R. O. **5767.** ACCOUNT of THOMAS ELDERTON.

Of 451l. received by him for victualling the King's army, 5 Hen. VIII. For oxen, ranging from 18s. 10d. to 31s. 3d. per ox. Costs for filling and salting the same, and incidental expenses. Tallow sold at 9s. 8d. per weigh. Beer, at 10s. per pipe with the foists. Biscuit, 5s. per 100.
Pp. 15.

A.D. 1514.

1514.
27 Feb. **5768.** SALE OF VICTUALS.

R. O.

Account by John Heron of the sale of victuals, 27 Feb. 5 Hen. VIII.
Pp. 4.

1514.
14 March. **5769.** THE ELIZABETH AND THE MARY JAMES.

R. O.

Two warrants by T. Earl of Surrey, addressed to Sir John Daunce, for payment of *The Elizabeth* of Newcastle at Newcastle, and *The Mary Jamys* at Hull, which cannot be paid like the other ships at Portsmouth. London, 14 March.

ii. Receipts endorsed on each of the above by Sir T. Wyndham and Harry Haylys, 14 March 5 Hen. VIII.

7 April. **5770.** THE MARY IMPERIAL.

R. O.

Warrant by T. Earl of Surrey to Sir John Danse for payments for *The Mary Emperyall* to be made to John Blake the master. Greenwich, 7 April.

9 April. **5771.** THE FORTUNE OF DOVER.

R. O.

Certificate of the sums required for a month's wages and victualling, beginning 13 March and ending 9 April; viz., for Thos. Vaughan, capt., 18*d.* a day; 100 men, at 5*s.* a month; 16 deedshares; 100 men, at 18*d.* a week; &c. *Signed.*

29 April. **5772.** SIR T. WYNDHAM to DAWTREY.

R. O.

Warrant to pay to Thos. Denye, captain of *The Anne Gallant,* for victuals of 133 men for 11 days. 29 April 6 Hen. VIII. *Signed. P.* 1.

2 May. **5773.** SIR T. WYNDHAM to DAWTREY.

R. O.

Warrant to pay Thomas Yonge, master of *The Mawdelyn* of Hamell, the wages of 25 mariners, 8 deedshares, and tonnage on 110 tons at 12*d.* a ton, for the month beginning 25 April. 2 May 6 Hen. VIII. *Signed.*

6 May. **5774.** THE HENRY GRACE DE DIEU.

R. O.

Application to the Lords [of the Council] by Nicholas Ryng, master gunner of the *Henry Grace de Dieu,* for payment of 22 gunners at 10*s.* a month, and 6 at . . *s.* . . . *d.* a month, employed in making gunstones and casting pellets, for one month from the [6th] day of April 5 Hen. VIII. to the 6th May following.

22 May. **5775.** SIR T. WYNDHAM to DAWTREY.

R. O.

Warrant to pay to John Hopton, capt. of *The Alys,* his own wages for 14 days from 8 to 22 May, 21*s.*, the wages of 30 mariners and 10 gunners at 2*s.* 6*d.* a man, 16½ deedshares at 2*s.* 6*d.* each, rewards to gunners, and 40*s.* (?) for tonnage of the galleon (80 tons), and for victuals. *Signed.*

8 Aug. **5776.** PAYMENTS for THE GREAT ELIZABETH.

R. O.

From Camfere to Portsmouth.

Headed by Wolsey: "To Sir John Daunce, knight." *With this note by him at the end:* "Fellow Mr. Daunce, you must pay the said sum of 75*l.* 9*s.* 4*d.* to Jacob Tylman, master of the great ship of Lubeke lately bought by the King.—T. Lincoln."

Receipt for the above by Tylman's executors, dated 8 Aug. 6 Hen. VIII.

Pp. 6.

1514.

R. O. **5777.** GEORGE LORD BERGAVENNY.

Receipt by George Nevyll Lord Bergavenny for 200 marks st. received from John Daunce for his prisoner Stephen de Ruyaulx, man-of-arms to the French King, taken at Bomy by Thos. Morys, his servant. Dated 24 Aug. 5 Hen. VIII. *Signed.*
P. 1.

5778. WOLSEY to DAUNCIE.

" Fellow Master Dauncie, ye must deliver unto my Lady of Oxenford's servant, bringer hereof, conduct money, and for coats for 50 persons, which she hath prepared to serve the King's grace in his wars by sea."
Signed : T. Lincoln.

R. O. **5779.** For JOHN SHARPE and WILLIAM TYLAR.

Warrant' to John Heron for payment of Henry VII.'s legacy of 100*l.* each to John Sharpe and Will. Tylar.
Signed above by the King ; and below by T. Earl of Surrey, Ri. Bp. of Winchester, C. Somerset [Lord Herbert], and Sir Thomas Lovell.

R. O. **5780.** ORDNANCE.

Account of 48 pieces of ordnance received by Will. Brown of Hans Popenruyter of Mechlin.

UNCERTAIN DATES.

Callg. D. vi. 343. **5781.** LETTER, apparently from a FRENCH SPY, to [SIR
B. M. RICHARD WINGFIELD].

The lansquenets have started, as he announced, in four companies, to the number of 6,000 or 7,000, under four French captains, for Challon in Champagne, giving out that they went to Tournay, and had been left by their captains at Verdun, in Barrois. Finding themselves abandoned and unpaid, they pillaged the town, hung men and ravished women, telling the provost it were better they should be hanged than return to their country, as the Emperor would cut their heads off. It is said that the Duke of Loraine has [allowed ?] them passage through his country, " par bendes de chan . . . . . . coup." The personage . . . . who went away on Easter Monday is . . . . . . and says that the King of France has sent [a messenger to the King] your master, that if he wishes " tenir l . . . . . [l]es embassadeurs du Roy Catholique . . . . aussy. fera il seche non chacun . . . . . . meulx que il porra. Le Sieur de P . . . . [c]este sepmaine à Therouane à . . . . à Boullogne comme je croy que . . . . . ."
Badly mutilated, p. 1.

R. O. **5782.** RUTHAL to LORD [   ].

Has received his letter by the bearer, expressing his surprise that he is commanded to deliver the keys of the tower of Westgate, with the rolls of the Bishop's court, to Baron Hylton, in as much as the Bishop's chancellor had told Roger Lumley, his correspondent's uncle, that Ruthal would keep the office of warden in his own hands. Complains that Darcy had prevented Hylton from holding the

Bishop's court, and had been guilty of untrue surmises and colorable tales, acting rather as if he were the Bishop's master. Commands him to desist. At the special request of the Lord Darcy, who had written to the Bishop, is content to be friendly on his desisting.

Pp. 3.

Add. in Ruthal's hand: [To m]y very good [lord] the Lord Darcy [these] be delivered.

R. O. **5783.** WOLSEY to my LORD [ ].

Thanks him for his loving handling of all his causes there, and will be glad to advance his interests from time to time, as he doubts not "your counsellor's letters here" will report. He is diligent in your great matter of Whytby. He will perceive by the King's letters what Wolsey has done in this matter. "And, my lord, very glad I am that ye handle yourself so wisely and substantially in the King's causes committed to you; wherewith his grace is not only singularly pleased, but also ye have given me courage and boldness to pursue it to his highness to commit other great things to you, which shall greatly redound to the increase of your honour in time to come; whereof no man shall be gladder than I, trusting that ye will be of semblable and no less good will towards me at all times."

Draft in Wolsey's hand, p. 1.

R. O. **5784.** [MARY BOLEYN] to SIR THOMAS BOLEYN.

My son Boleyn,—I heartily recommend me to you, and I send to you God's blessing and mine. And whereas I understand, to my great heaviness, that my Lord my father is departed this world to Almighty God, on whose soul I beseech Jesu to have mercy, wherefore I pray and heartily desire you that you will do for me in everything as you shall think most best and expedient. And in everything that you shall do for me after as you think best, I will, on my part, affirm and rate it in as like manner as though it were mine own deed. And if hereafter you shall think it necessary for me to come up to London to you, I pray you send hereof to me your mind, and I shall pain myself to come; howbeit if you may do well I now (enough) without my coming in any behalf, then I were loth to labour so farr. Wherefore I pray you to do therein the best you can; and God's blessing and mine I send you, praying shortly to send me your mind again. M. B.

Add.: To my son Sir Thom[s] Boleyn, knt., this bill be deliv[d].

P. 1.

26 June. **5785.** QUEEN KATHARINE to FERDINAND OF ARRAGON.

B. M. Egerton, 616. No. 34. Has received his letter by Calderon, and performed his commands. Hopes, in consideration of the age and services of the quartermaster, that Ferdinand will promote him to a higher office.

Translated in Wood's "Royal and Illustrious Ladies," I. 162.

Hol. Sp., p. 1. *Add. and Endd.*

26 Sept. **5786.** C. SOMERSET [LORD HERBERT] to [RUTHAL] BP. OF DURHAM.

R. O.

In behalf of the Prior of Aburgenny, who desires from the King a licence of resignation, having already obtained the consent of his bishop. Kerdif Castle, 26 Sept.

Hol., p. 1. *Addressed:* To mine especial good lord my Lord of Durham.

8 Oct.
Vesp. F. xiii. 82b.
B. M.

5787. KATHARINE [COUNTESS OF] ARUNDELL to [WOLSEY.]

Thanks his lordship for his comfortable words when she was with him, touching the matter between her and my old Lady Dorset. Has more confidence in him than in any other of her friends, knowing that if he help her not to her right she will lose it. Downely, 8 Oct. *Signed.*

R. O.

5788. JOHN ORUM, ABBOT, and the CONVENT OF ST. MARY'S, DUBLIN, to SIR THOMAS [BUTLER] OF ORMOND.

Have received his letter by the hand of his servant Thomas, accusing them of defrauding his lordship of such goods as were in the keeping of the abbot's predecessor. Denies the accusation. Has examined his brethren in the strictest way, and finds that none of them had part in putting away the said goods. The abbot, on the day of his decease, disclosed to the writer nothing more than four nobles, received from William Bermyngham of Luske, Ormond's receiver, for which they are accountable. Begs he will write to "the worshipful lord Dean" of the college of St. Patrick's, Dublin, to withdraw the suit, which is very chargeable to the writer's house. St. Mary Abbay by Dulyng, 13 Nov.

Hol., p. 1. Addressed. Sealed.

R. O.

5789. WILLIAM NOTTINGHAM, sub-prior of LANTHONY, to [WOLSEY.]

As they have obtained through his favor the King's congé d'élire, delegate to him the power of choosing a prior. Sends a document under their seal to that effect by Sir Ric. Hempsted and Sir John Ambrose. The latter "is a very honest religious person, to whom we trust your grace of your bounteous goodness will give your gracious assent to be our governor." *Signed.*

Orig., p. 1. Endorsed.

Schedule sewed to the above, with the following names, sc. :— Sir Will. Nottingham, Sir John Gloucester, Sir Tho. Hale, Prior Lanthoniæ Primæ, Sir Ric. Dene, Sir John Abynton, Sir John Combe, Sir Garett, Sir Geo. Dene, Will. Antoni, Rob. Luke, Sir Geo. Cerney, Sir John Newland, Sir Gregory Charitun, Sir. Will. Worsceter, John Kellam, Tho. Austen, Sir Humph. Jheram, Sir Rob. Okull, Sir Phylyppe, Sir Davy Mathewe, and Sir Will. Abynton.

R. O.

5790. ACCOUNT OF THE DRAGON.

Commencing 24 Nov. — Hen. VIII., and ending 8 Jan. Wages to ship's carpenters, 8d. a day ; meat and drink, 2½d. a day.

"Sir, as to these costs done by Walter Loveday upon the King's ship *The Dragon*, as cawking, as stocking of certain guns and lead that he hath paid for, with other costs writ within the same, he ought to be allowed of all as to that is contained herein bought. My fellow William Gonson saw what he (?) bought. *Per me* John Hopton."

Pp. 2.

GENERAL INDEX.

₊ The Nos. are those of the documents, not of the pages, except where so indicated.

A.

Abberley or Abbotley, Worc., 703, 726, 5669.
Abbeton, Salop, 4694.
Abbeville, 3678, 4330, 4692, 4843, 5547, 5553.
........., reception of the Princess Mary at, 5329, 5330, 5337, 5379, 5391, 5470, 5560.
........., letters dated from, 4353, 5391, 5468, 5480, 5488, 5489, 5490, 5495, 5497, 5505, 5513, 5566.
Abbotsbury, Dorset, 3101, 4064.
Abbotston, Hants, 1867, 5247.
Abda, (Adda ?) 11.
Abell, Geo., 1620.
Aberbrothock, George, Abbot of, Treasurer of Scotland, 714, 1112.
........., ..., letter from, 1220.
........., Abbey of, 4556, 4623.
........., postulate of (Gawin Douglas), 4680, 5614.
Abercromby, David, 4997.
Aberdeen, 3569.
........., canons of, 4997.
........., Bishop of, 3479, 4556, 4951.
Abergavenny, or Burgevenny, 57, 66, 366, 451, 988, 1113, 1234, 3599.
........., Edward Nevill, Lord, and Elizabeth his wife, 3599.
........., George Nevill, Lord, grants to, 320, 3599, 3952, 4167, 4685, 5147.
........., ..., in the war against France, 3688, 3885, 4237, 4306, 4307, 4314, 4475.
........., ..., prisoner taken by, 5777.
........., ..., summoned to Parliament, 5616.
........., ..., named in commissions or otherwise mentioned, 236, 297, 317, 725, 763, 906, 1762, 2082, 3027, 3078, 3092, 3380, 3428, 3605, 3765, 4254, 4327, 4663, 4693, 4734, 4804, 4847, 4927, 5237, 5506, 5633.
........., prior of, 5786.
Abingdon, 647.
........., abbey of, 776, 811, 1639, 2070, 3050, 3025, 3052, 3058, 3908.
........., abbot of, 776, 811, 1639, 3459, 5166.
........., John Coventry, abbot of, 2070, 3050.
........., Thomas Roland, abbot of, 3025, 3050, 3052, 3058.
........., Thomas, abbot of, 4341, 4377, 5166, 5616, 5684.
........., Thomas Cumnor, prior of, 2070.

Abingdon, Sir Jno., 3980, 5789.
........., Sir Wm., 5789.
Abingworth, Surrey, 1451, 1577, 4749.
Abirlady, 3630.
Abruzzi, 3341.
Aburgoyle, 370.
Accon, Peter van, 4690.
Accounts of the Treasurer, 4878.
.... of the Master of the Revels, 4642.
.... of the Navy, 4376.
........., war, 3476, 3496, 3762, 3981, 4310, 4374, 4378, 4387, 4410, 4421, 4431, 4445, 4478, 4480, 4481, 4526, 4527, 4533, 4534, 4535, 4586, 4630, 4878, 4961, 4977, 5112, 5163, 5271, 5316, 5720, 5721, 5723, 5724, 5747, 5748, 5749, 5751, 5752, 5758, 5760, 5765, 5766, 5767, 5768.
Acherley, Rog., 1897, 4581.
Achurch, Northt., 479.
Acres, Hen., 1636, 3152, 4526, 5723.
Acs. See Dax.
Acton, Middx., 1480.
...., Edmund, 937, 4253, 5310.
........., Francis, 4222.
........., Hugh, 1823.
........., Thos., 5014.
Acton-Burnell, 878, 1248, 4694.
Adagia of Polydore Vergil, 751.
.... of Erasmus, 1017.
Adam, Clement, 4996.
........., Thos., 3771.
Adamson, John, 4643.
Adbaston, 1480.
........., Wm., 1154.
Adda. See Abda.
Adgore, Dorothy, 3224.
........., Ela, 3224.
........., Gregory, 3224.
Adie, Henry, 3284.
Adige, (or Athis), 3678, 4276, 4282.
Adley, Edw., 710. See Hadley.
Admiral. See Howard,
........., of England, &c., 33, 3809.
........., Lord, 1928.
........., ..., 3974, 3980, 4093, 4094, 4535, 4954, 5007.
........., of France, 5140.
.... of Zealand, 5207.
Admiralty, Court of, 1928.
Adorni family, 4280, 4577.

3 Q 2

Adorno, 3269, 3325.
Africa, 3081.
Agard, Arthur, temp. Jac. I., 3298.
........., Ralph, of Stafford, 1480; in com. for Stafford, 279, 713, 791, 886, 1770, p. 905.
........., Ric. (?), p. 903.
........., Thomas, 3470.
Agenensis, Cardinal, brother of Julius II., 3377.
Aghadoe, 5443.
Agmondesham, Bucks, 896.
Agre, 2061.
Aguilar, Comendador de, 3766.
Ailewarton, Cornw., 4321, 4846.
Aire, 3654, 4232, 4306.
........., letters dated from, 4401, 4435.
........., John de Hubart, captain of, 4622.
........., provost of, 5165.
Aiskew, (Aiscough,) York, 5086.
Aiston, Nich., 4532, 5277.
........., Wm., 4532, 5277.
Akeland. See Auckland.
Akenham, Suff., 5074.
Alamanni, Nich., 5222.
Alane, John, 4823.
Alanson. See Alençon.
Alarde, Ralph, 1537.
Albanians, 1659.
Albany, John Stuart, Duke of, 4556, 4725 (ii.), 5408, (3), 5482, 5560, 5641.
........., ..., commissioned to promote a re-conciliation between Julius II. and Lewis XII., 1700, 1875.
........., ..., preparing to go to Scotland, 4561, 4692, 4824, 4869, 4902, 5006, 5151, 5164, 5590, 5614, 5649.
........., ..., his attainder in Scotland re-versed, 4951.
........., ..., letters to, 1460, 1876, 3126.
Albret, de, 3584, 3593, 3651, 3807, 4924.
........., John d', King of Navarre. See Na-varre.
Albuquerque, Alfonso de, 4173.
Albury, Surrey, 3542.
Alby, Alex., 1295.
Albyon, Mossen Jayme de, 8.
Alcade, 3762.
Alcayde de las Donsellas, 490, 3269, 3614, 3662.
Alchemy, 1415.
Albury, Oxon., 5685.
Aldbury. See Oldbury.
Aldborough, York, 3386.
.... See Ships.
........., Sir Ric., 3386, 5744.
........., Tho., 3386.
Alderney (Aureney), 941.
Aldford, Chesh., 1035.
Aldenham, Hertfordshire, 383, 4206.
Aldercher, St. Mary, 5068.
Alderholt, Dors., 155.

Alderley, Chesh., 1035.
Alderney, 94, 941.
Aldersey, John, 4360.
Alderton, Northt., 3027.
........., Wm., 349.
Alderwashaye, York., 3497.
Aldred, Roger, 5761.
Aldwerke, 2022.
Aldey, Wm., 1183.
Aldrych, Th., 4558.
Aldwincle, Northamptonshire, 403, 3761, 4904.
Alee, William, 5742. See Aligh.
Alençon, Duke of, 4253, 4329, 4402, 5379, 5482, 5495, 5560.
Alenson, Gilb., 1573, 2068.
Alessandria (or Alexandria), 773, p. 382, 3341, 3752, 4210, 4282, 4283.
........., news dated from, p. 381.
Alexander VI., Pope, 379, 3023, 3626.
Alexander, captain, 4377.
.........., Rog., 4646.
Alexandrie, Earl of, 5482.
Alexe, of Milan, painter, p. 957.
Aleyn, John. See Allen.
Alexandrinus, 4499.
Alfonso, second son of Fred. III., King of Naples, 4296.
Alford, Roger, 5501.
Alfreton, Derby, 1852.
Algerkyrk, 1036.
Alicant, 3452.
Aligh, Wm., 219, 1611. See Alee.
Alyngton, Kent, 1664.
Alyngton, or Alington, Sir Giles, 226, 1421, 3231; on sheriff-roll for Camb., 664, 1316, 1949; in com. for Camb., 3583, p. 904.
Alynton, town of, 1567.
Alistre, John, clk. 1201, 1202.
Alker, John, 3497.
Allan, Messenger, a Scot, 4743, 4780.
Allaredy (Laredo), p. 400.
Allen,, friend of Erasmus, 2021, 3535.
Allen (or Alleyn), John, Baron of the Exche-quer, 7.
........., in com. for Suffolk, 280, 676, 1153, 1715, 1939, 3029, 3219, 3967.
.........., ..., of Essex, 735.
.........., ..., of London, p. 435.
.... (Alen), Tho., 1015, 5122.
.........., ..., Wm., 3789.
Allerton, 743, 3031.
Almaçan, ——, Secretary to King Ferdinand, 8, 490, 796, 922, 3352, 3662, 4096, 4267, 5152, 5743.
Almain, High, 5323.
.... rivets, 3496, 3658.
Almayne, George, 3662.
........., Wm., 1312.
Almer. See Aylmer.
Almesbury, John, 1183.

Almirari, p. 384.

Almisadars, p. 384.

Almoner. *See* Rawlins, Ric., and Wolsey, Th.

Almot, John, 1375.

Alms, Knights, 5037.

Alnwick, 1040, 5010, 5090.

........., Constable of, 4556.

Alom, Wm., 823.

Alphington, Devon, 2080.

Aldriche, ch. of, Cov. and Lich. dioc., 1007.

Alscote, Lincolnshire, 4496.

Altherton, Thos., 4480.

Alton, 5757.

Altoveti, Joachim, 560, 1251, 1280, 1384.

Alum, 342, 4154, 4578, 5099, 5269, 5358, 5382, 5650.

Alumbierre, in Navarre, 3352, p. 396, 3356.

Alva, Duke of, 1726, 3243, 3352, 3355, 3356, 3499, 3584, 3593, 3614, 3662.

———, ..., letter from, 3350.

Alveston, 1484.

Alviano, Bartholomew d', 11, 4371, 4499.

Alye, Wm. *See* Aligh.

Alyn. *See* Allen.

Amadas, Robt., goldsmith, 4917, 5491, p. 958.

Ambassadors, English, with the Emperor, 4280

........., ..., at Boulogne, 5379.

........., ..., in France, 4789, 5560, 5637.

........., ..., in Italy, 5680.

........., ..., in Low Countries, 3361, 3388, 3777, 3847, 3915, 3916, 3975, 4459, 4508, 4511, 5398, 5598, 5713 ; instructions to, 5139.

........., ..., at Rome, 4085, 5378 ; letter to, 4955.

........., ..., in Scotland, 3339, 3876 ; to be sent thither, 3751.

........., ..., in Spain, 4096.

........., French, in England, 5321, 5637, 5717.

........., Leo X.'s, in England, 5173.

........., Scotch, in England, 1820.

........., ..., sent to England, 3346, 3811.

........., of the Swiss Cantons, 4970.

Ambert, Lucas 1295.

Ambi curt, 3325.

Amboise, 5351.

........., George d', Cardinal of Rouen, 216, 842, 3662.

........., Emery d', Grand Master of Rhodes, 216.

........., ..., letters from, 540, 1262, 1659, 1660.

........., ..., letter to, 3277.

Ambrelayns, Herts., 126.

Ambrose, Sir John, 5789.

Amelsett, Westmor., 479, 3764.

Amiens, 3678, 4353, 4465, 4484, 4513, 4795.

Amiens, pilgrimage to, 216.

........., (Amyas), bailiff of, 5391.

........., Vidame d', 54, 87.

Amies, John, 659.

Ammonius, Andreas, Latin Secretary to Henry VIII., 4598, 4747, 4936, 5320, 5354, 5365, 5457, 5458, 5465, 5538, 5542.

........., ..., in the war with France, 4314.

........., ..., grants to, 2079, 4963.

........., ..., his poems, 1917.

........., ..., his servant Thomas, 1948.

........., ..., letters in his hand, 5353, 5651.

........., ..., letters from, 1918, 1948, 1982, 2021, 5449.

........., ..., letters to, 1017, 1652, 1842, 1849, 1883, 1900, 1917, 1925, 1957, 1997, 1998, 2001, 2002, 2013, 2025, 3012, 4427, 4576, 5182, 5464.

Ammunition, 4802.

Ampeys, Martyn de, 3662.

Amsterdam, 4844.

Amyas, Wm., 920.

Anatolia (Natalia), prince of, 5705.

Ancona, p. 368, 3626, 4952.

[Ancona?], Cardinal of, letters addressed to, 910, 1406, 1410, 1459, 1879, 3033, 3107, 3122, 3623. ₊*₊ It is doubtful whether these or some of them be not addressed to the Cardinal of St. Mark's.

Ancrom, 4522.

Andalusia, 8, 3355.

Andover, 155, 367, 721, 1334, 1494.

André, Bernard, poet laureate, 4443.

Andreas, Master. *See* Ammonius.

........., gyldens (Flemish coins), 4481.

Andrewe, Rob., 3939.

........., Wm., 4630.

Andrewes, Th., 1949.

Andries, Andrieu, 3340.

Angelo, Castle of St. 5356.

Angien. *See* Enghien.

Anglesey, 1686.

Anglesse, Rog., 4588.

Angoulême, Count of. *See* Francis.

Angus, Archbishop, fifth Earl of, 714, 3303 3569, 4573.

........., ..., letter from, 4572.

........., ..., his son George (Gavin ?), 4556.

........., Archibald, sixth Earl of, 5641.

........., ..., his marriage to Queen Margaret, 5370.

........., ..., his father, 5006.

Anislow, John, 3412.

Annand, 2061.

Annandale, marches in, 4522.

Anne of Britanny, Queen of Lewis XII., 3112, 3269, 3752, 3807, 4328, 5480.

........., her secret negotiation with Spain, 3766.

........., ..., her death, 4666, 4692, 4824,

Annes, John, 1559.

Annesburton, York, 1392.

Annesby, Walt., 1507.
Annesley, Rob., 1376.
........., Thomas, 5552.
Annoques, Jacques, 5553.
Ansiam. *See* Siam.
Ansty, 155, 1144.
Anthoyne, 4563.
Antoyn, John, 3658.
Antony, Wm., 5789.
Antron, in Cornw, 3039, 3436.
........., Ric., 3436.
........., Wm., 3039, 3436.
Antwerp, 216, 922, 1826, 3248, 3385, 3396, 3439, 3446, 3651, 3821, 4081, 4163, 4182, 4232, 4322, 4328, 4329, 4433, 4479, 4526, 4533, 4725, 4831, 4882, 4973, 5030, 5159, 5203, 5208, 5290, 5377, 5604, p. 953.
........., letters dated from, 3405, 3415, 3417, 3419, 3425, 4054, 4068, 4789.
Ap......, Giles, 4431.
Apparre, or Aparry, Maurice, 1118, 1893, 5420.
........., Sir Thos., 1258, 1735, 1799, 2009, 3048, 3173, 3358, 3552, 4307, 4314, 4653, p. 904.
........., Wm., squire of the body, 1258, 4652.
........., ..., knighted at Tournay, 4468.
........., Sir Wm., 4653.
Apparel, statute against costly, 811.
Appenzel, 2091.
Appleby, or Appulby, 319, 707.
Appleby, Appilby, or Appulby, Ric., 119, 1090, 5395, 5423.
........., ..., Thomas, 204, 1054.
Applethwaite, (Apulwhait), Westmor., 3764.
Appleton, (Appulton,) York. 4602.
........., Bryan, p. 955.
........., Rob. 308.
Appleyard, Nich., 1714, 1812, 1963, 3029, 3426, 3545, 3980, 5133,
........., Sir Nich., 5483.
........., Robt., 5761.
Appowhell, David, p. 957.
Appreis, Wm., 4493.
Apsley, Wm., 3024.
Apthorpe, Northt., 3027.
Aquileia, 1681.
Aquitaine, 1980, 3455, 3629, 3649, 3797, 3861, 4038, 4511, 4560.
Arbieto, John de, 1859, 2047.
Arborensis, Cardinel, 3780.
Arbroath. *See* Aberbrothock.
Archer, Thomas 4285, 5178.
Archier, John, 3497.
Arderne, Warw., 3239, 3497, 3880.
Ardern (Erdern), John, in com. for Worc. and Warw., 892, 1387, 1468, 1971, 3301, 3364, 3709, 4770, p. 903.
........., Rob., 1080.
........., Sir Peter, 1282.
Ardes, 4284, 5547, 5560.

Ardeson, or Ardisono, George, Genoese mer- chant, 1003, 1773, 1816, 3233, 3263, 3265, 5156.
Ardfert, Bishop of, 1441.
Ardmolghan, 1314.
Are, 4284.
Aree, 4253.
Arena, Andreas de. *See* Ammonius.
Argaston, 4235.
Argentan, Oxf., 4328.
Arglen, 2091.
Argyle, Archd.,4441; 2nd Earl of, 714, 1820, 3838, 3882.
Aridon, r., 5705.
Arkylgarthdale, 3669.
Armagnac (Armaygant), p. 610.
Armathwaite, Cumb., 664, 1306, 1949, 3502.
Armeston, Guy, 4635.
Armestorff, Paul, 3266, 4273, 4296, 4322, 4399, 5104, 5327.
Armiboldus, Nich., 3269.
Armory, the King's, 4131.
Armour, 3414.
Arms, grant of, 517.
Army, the, in Spain, 3451.
........., against France, 3336, 3884, 4009, 4126, 4237, 4309, 4310, 4492, 4631.
........., ..., guides for, 5604.
........., ..., review of the, 3173.
........., ..., tents for, 4232.
........., ..., ordnance for, 4238.
........., ..., victualling of, 3051, 3757, 3858, 4894, 5760, 5765.
........., ..., badges of the captains, 4253.
........., ..., vanguard retinue, 4070.
........., ..., accounts and wages of, 3476, 4067, 4374, 4375, 4421, 5720.
........., ..., armour for the, 4131.
........., ..., transports for the, 4082.
Arnheim, 5030.
Arnolde, John 4377.
Arneley. *See* Ernly.
Arnewey, Robt., 5723.
Arnold, Rob., 4067.
Arnott, David, Bishop of the Chapel Royal, Stirling, 288.
Arquila in Africa, 4922.
Arragon, 3023, 3226, 3356.
........., Ambassadors in, 4055.
........., Ambassadors of, in England, 3415, 3443, 4511, 5126, 5468, 5637.
........., Ambassador of, with the Emperor, 4069, 4091, 4364, 4511, 5259.
........., Ambassadors of, in France, 4296, 5637.
........., Ambassador of, in Low Countries, 3805, 3948, 4418, 4433, 4511, 4796, 4952, 5006, 5018, 5041, 5117, 5208, 5290, 5362, 5387.
........., Ambassadors of, in Low Countries, 4296.
........., Ambassadors of, at Rome, 4283, 4844, 5353.

Arragon, Ambassadors of, with the Swiss, 3862.
........., F. Cardl. of, 300, 348, 405, 819, 3777, 3780.
........., Ferd. K. of, *see* Ferdinand.
........., Don John of, 3663, 3905.
........., Katharine of. *See* Katharine.
........., Provincial of the Grey Friars of, 3766, 3807.
........., Queen of, (Germaine de Foix, second wife of Ferdinand), 8, 490, 796, 819, 3614, 3662, 3766, 3807, 5274, 5353.
........., treaty with England, 4165, 5686.
Arran, Jas. E. of, 474, 714, 3569, 4556, 5641.
Arras, 3362, 3377, 4353, 5163.
........., governor of, 3340.
........., bishop elect of, 3377.
Arras and tapestry maker to the King, 800.
Array, commissioners of, 187, 1734, 1735, 1799, 1804, 1812, 3024, 3230, 3332, 3380, 3688, 3723, 4939, 4979, 5626.
........., against the Scots, 4434.
Ars, Louis d', 5482.
Arthur, Prince of Wales, brother of Henry VIII., 127, 3023, 3292, 3395.
........., Master. *See* Plantagenet.
Arthureth, Cumb. 4791.
Artillery, 3615, 5739.
........., transport of, 3836.
........., carriage of, 4445, 4473.
Artois, 3361, 3362, 3654, 4091, 4162, 4445, 4473, 4510, 4560, 4561, 5032, 5341.
.... Herald, 4561.
Arundel, Sussex, 1990.
Arundel, Chris., 3980.
........., John, 5116.
........., ..., son of Sir Jo. of Treryse, 2018, 3557.
........., Sir John, 104, 268, 453, 1069 ; on sheriff-roll for Cornwall, 664 ; receiver-general of the Duchy of Cornw., 5431 ; in war against France, 4477, 4534, 4653 ; com. to muster against the Moors, 1566.
........., ..., of La Hern, 1675, 3598, 5116 ; in com. for Cornwall, 312, 891, 1694 1812, 1984, 3290, 3583, 3605, 3938, 4754, 5220, 5586; in com. for Devon, 1166.
........., John, of Talverne, 1434 ; in com. for Cornwall, 1694, 1812, 1984, 3290, 3583, 3605, 3938, 4754, 5474, 5220, 5586 ; sheriff of Cornw., 664.
........., ..., of Treryse, 2018, 3557 ; in com. for Cornwall, 1812 ; on sheriff-roll for Cornw., 1316.
........., Roger, 1694, 1812, 1984, 3290, 3583, 3605, 3938, 5474.
........., Thomas (misprinted John), Earl of, letter from, 4098.
........., ..., grants to, 998, 999.
........., ..., named in comm. of the peace, 281, 892, 904, 918, 930, 1049, 1388, 1427, 1469, 1509, 1517, 1695, 1762, 1971, 1981, 3071, 3078, 3092, 3173, 3301, 3428, 3709, 3712, 3715, 4024, 4118, 4159, 4394, 4676, 4693, 4734,

Arundel, Thomas, Earl of,—*cont.*
4764, 4770, 4804, 4827, 5237, pp 903-5 ; in other commissions, 3024, 3688.
........., ..., summoned to Parliament, 5616·
........., ..., otherwise mentioned, 1212, 2082, 3292, 3977, 4327, 4377, 4536, 4659, 5150, 5762.
........., Katharine, Countess of, 5787.
........., Wm. *See* Mautravers.
Aschyn, 222.
Ashburn, or Assheburne, 606, 926.
........., bailiff of, 4253.
Assheborne, Th., 845.
Ashburnham, or Asshbournham, Helena, 3034.
........., John, 672, 3024.
........., Thomas, 1509, 3024, 4996.
.... William, 281, 1509, 3024, 3428, 4544, 4804, p. 904.
Ashburton, (Aisbertone,) Devon, 704.
Asshby, vicar of. *See* Burman.
Assheby, Geo., clerk of the signet, 96, 965, 1196, 1759, 3583, 4647.
Asheby, John, 1231, 3024.
........., Peter, LLB., 5631.
........., Richard, 1472, 4022.
........., Wm., 554, 656, 1094, 1425, 1971, 4706, 4783, p. 905, 5561.
Ashfield, Salop, 4071, 4694.
Ashford in the Peak, 367, 721.
Ashford, (Asshetford,) Kent, 4291.
Ashkyrke, John, 49, 631, 4686.
Ashton, Sir John. *See* Aston.
.... *See* Assaheton.
Aske, Anne, 4903.
... ., Elizabeth, 4903.
........., John, 954.
........., Sir Ralph, 1735.
........., Sir Robt., 273, 1550, 1799, 3219, 3358, 4719, 5193, p. 907.
........., Rog., 4903.
........., Wm., 4903.
Askeham, 3149.
Askerton, 4825.
Askew, Ascogh, or Ascue,—
........., ——, 3885, 4237, 4307.
........., Christ., 1496, 1979, 3342, 4358.
........., Sir Christ., 4593, 4860.
........., James, 4746.
........., Miles, 3977.
........., Ralph, 5023.
........., William, 1171, 1716, 1979, 3137, 3342, 4314, 4358, 5691.
........., Sir William, 777, 4593, 4860.
Askewith, Sir Wm., 4616.
Aslackby, (Aslabye,) Linc., 398, 1430, 4695.
Aspeden, Herts, 3827, 4176, 4940.
Asperston, Devon, 985.
Asplond, John, 266, 310, 706, 1868, 1522, 1713, 3605, 3785, 3967.
Assay of English and Flemish coins, 4917.
Asshe, 3978.

Asshe Water, 4076.
......, John, 3534, 3566, 3589, 3605, 3938, 4539, 4783, 5220.
Asshefeld, Rob., 1375.
Asshehurst, Thomas, 5027.
Assheley, 457, 1611.
Asshere. See Esher.
Assheregny, Devon, 4071.
Asshewell, ch. of, D. Linc., 1666.
Assheton, Lancashire, 3764.
........., Hen., 330, 3060.
........., Hugh, 107, 236, 406, 1725, 1904, 1923, 5206, 5296.
Ashton, Nic., 4808. See Ayston.
Asshover, All Saint's, Cov. and Lich. dioc., 1852.
Asshold, York, 3175.
Asshoo, Tho., 673.
Assize, commissions of Justices of, 19, 20, 71, 72, 294, 832, 881, 1123, 1164, 1490, 1741, 1795, 2089, 2093, 2096, 2099, 3004, 3267, 3270, 3287, 3292, 3311, 3699, 3724, 4252, 4339, 4765, 4771, 5246, 5283.
Aste, in Piedmont, p. 383, 3752, 3976, 4326, 4449, 5560, p. 921.
......, Bishop of, 5337.
Asteley, Richard. 669, 1316, 3507, 4253, 4544, pp. 903 and 905, 5561.
........., William, 3211, p. 958.
Asteleyns, 734.
Asten. See Barbour.
Aston, 4071.
........., Bridget, 3843.
........., Sir John, 613, 4253; on sheriff-roll for Warw. 1316; in com. for Stafford, 1770; on sheriff-roll for do., 4544.
........., Thos., 3843.
Aston-Clynton, 445, 896.
Astonthink, 458, 4946.
Astonthorold, Berks, 174, 1426.
Atcliff. See Hatcliff.
Atcock, Ric., 4489.
Athelney, John, abbot of, 1639, 3497.
Atholes, (Adthyll) Earl of, 3577, 4556.
Atienza, castle of, in Spain, p. 456, note.
Atkins, als. Blokley, John, 18.
.... Wm., 950.
Atkinson, John, 5723.
........., Rob., 4650.
........., Thos., 3090.
........., Wm., 427, 1764, 4149.
Atri, 3269.
Attleburgh, (Attilburgh,) Norf., 4254.
Attorney General, 10, 156, 1733, 3497.
Atwater, Wm., 719, 1295, 1637, 2082, 3069, 4588, 4841, 5443, 5520, 5556.
........., ..., dean of Salisbury, 3763.
........., ..., as Bishop of Lincoln, 5616.

Attwell, John, 4069, 5001.
........., Rog., 4067.
Aubiguy, the Sieur d', 3752.
Aubscoyd, ch. of, dioc. Linc. 1685.
Auckland, 4497, 4523, 4529.
Audiencier, Mons. l', 5381.
Audeley, Edmund. See Salisbury, Bishop of.
........., Eliz., 1305.
........., Geo., 3980.
........., Jas., 155.
........., John, 1219, 1305.
........., ..., named in commissions of the peace, 1812, 1388, 3071.
........., [Touchet], son of John, 13th Lord Audeley, his restitution, 4848.
........., Sir John, 1639, 3114, 3231, 3497, 3573, 4632.
........., ..., grant to, 4251.
........., ..., in commissions of the peace, 884, 1340, 1714, 1963, 3029, 3426, 3545, 5133, p. 904.
........., Thomas, 155.
........., Mr., 3231.
........., Barons of,—
    James Touchet, 14th lord, attainted temp. Hen. VII., 321, 355, 629, 682, 1285, 1472, 1488, 1598, 1916, 2082.
    John Touchet, 15th lord, 4253, 4306, 4468, 4477, 4534, 5633.
    ......, grants to, 4141, 4161, 4214.
    ......, named in commissions of the peace, &c., 3723, 4676, 4159, p. 904.
    ......, summoned to Parliament, 5616.
........., Nic. de, 155.
Augeoy, John, 3455.
Auger, Alex. 5527.
........., Ralph, 5527.
........., Wm., 5527.
Aughton, Nic., 332.
Augsburg, 1195, 4059, 4069, 4272, 4274, 4280, 5304, 5366, 5387.
........., treaty dated at, 4560.
........., letters dated at, 4069, 4078, 4615, 4910.
Aunsham, Thos., 4917.
Aureney. See Alderney.
Austarys (Ustaritz, q. v.)
Austen, Thos., 5789.
Austria, Margaret of. See Margaret of Savoy.
........., 1676, 1681, 5363, 5366.
........., House of, 3361, 5323.
Auterey. See Ottery.
Autun, Jas. Bp. of, 1182.
Auvergne, 4153.
Avandyn, Pont, 4253.
Avell, Somers., 4071.

Avenell, Ralph, 4158.
Avenescorte, Gloucestershire, 3316, 1445.
Aviary, the King's, 1845.
Avogaro, Aloysius, de, 3026.
Avon, r. (Aven,) Somers., 1257.
Avon-Dosset, (Avendorset), Warw., 1299.
Awbeney, Lord. *See* Daubeney.
Awdeven, Wm., 4990.
Awmond, Ric., 4033.
Awood, William, 2008.
Awstarys. *See* Ustaritz.
Ax. *See* Dax.
Axbrigge, Somers., 1133.
Ayala, Don Pedro de, Bp. of Catania, 8, 490.
Ayer, Thos., 4253.
Aylast, Wm., 734.
Aylesbeare, 2080.
Aylesbury, 4347.
Aylesford (Allysford), Kent, 1327.
Aylesham, Norf., 1892, 4254.
Ayleston, 2080.
Aylmer, John, 4189, 4191, 4555.
........., Ric., 4558.
........., Wm., 572, 1567. *See* Eylmer.
Ayloff, Etheldred, wife of Wm., 729, 734, 735.
Ayloff, William, 729, 734, 735.
........., ..., in com. for Suffolk, 280, 676,
    729, 1121, 1153, 1715, 3029, 3219,
    3967, 4713, 5133, p. 904. ; for Essex,
    310, 1368, 1522, 1713, 3605, 3785,
    p. 907.
Aynesley, John, 3553.
Aynger, Alex., 3072.
Aynestapleght, 4022.
Ayre, Rog., 4227.
Ayryth, 4253.
Ayscough. *See* Askew.
Aysshefeld, 1809.
Ayston, Nich., 1968, 4808.
........., Ric., 1282.
........., Wm., 1968, 4808.
Azne, 4319.

B.

B...., Sir Rob., 4020.
Ba...., Baron de, 4196.
Babam, Wm., 4684.
Babbergh, 4966.
Babham, Richard, the King's apothecary, 1373.
Babington, Anth., 1852.
........., ..., in com. for Notts, 1514, 1798,
    1964, 3092, 3494, 4127, 4776, 5183,
    5225, p. 905, and Derby, 4127.
........., Edith, 1852.
........., Eliz., 1852.
........., Henry, 1852.
........., Sir John, 1852.
........., Tho., 266, 1852, 5183.

Babonus, Brysigella, 3026.
Babthorp, Thomas, 3510.
Bacano, 880.
Bache, 312.
........., *see* Moyle.
........., 1694.
Bacheller, Mahier, 4445.
Bacheworth, 3842.
Bacho, Francis, 4250.
Back, James, p. 957.
Badam, Walt., 655.
Badcock, John, 4836·
Badingham, Suff., 3506.
Badisley, Warw., 5640.
........., preceptory of, 1262.
Badisworth, ch. of, York dioc., 3644.
Badmondesfeld, Suff., 5180.
Badoer, Andrew, 3333.
Badwe, Little, Essex, 2015.
Bagard, Wm., 4253.
Bagge, Ric., 3150.
Bagloni. *See* Baionus.
Bagpuse, 1867.
Bagshot, Surrey, 5594.
.... Park, Windsor Forest, 5594.
Bagshotes, Bayles, 5128.
Baiellvelle, Adrian, 4902.
Baif, Lazarus, 1404.
Baillesford, 2080.
Bailleul, Jacques de, 4445.
Bainbridge, Christ., Cardinal of York, 880,
    1681, 1880, 3066, 3314, 3333, 3361,
    3460, 3625, 3651, 3678, 3777, 3821,
    3838, 4039, 4085, 4311, 4319, 4326,
    4364, 4366, 4458, 4500, 4502, 4506,
    4523, 4582, 4598, 4605, 4608, 4610,
    4621, 4735, 4747, 4786, 4810, 4920,
    5114, 5300, 5318, 5399, 5405, 5465,
    5524, 5735.
........., ..., mandates to him to summon
    convocation, 2005, 4876.
........., ..., his commissions as ambassador
    to Rome, 520, 1227.
........., ..., named in the commission of the
    peace, 1550, 3137.
........., ..., death of, 5252, 5253, 5333, 5342,
    5349, 5350 ; its circumstances, 5354,
    5356, 5357, 5365, 5396, 5448, 5449.
........., ..., goods of, 5464, 5542, 5663, 5664.
........., ..., his executors, 5301, 5364.
........., ..., letters from, 538, 4196, 4283,
    4327, 4446, 4454, 4455, 4691, 5106, 5169·
........., ..., letters to, 1457, 3876, 3915, 3975,
    4323, 4459, 4887, 4916, 4955.
........., Edw., 3252.
........., Guy, 3252.
Baynbrige, John, 3252.
Bainbridge, Ric., 3252.
........., Rog., 3939.
Bainham. *See* Baynham.
Baionus, Jo. Paulus, 3269.
........., (Baglioni), Paul, 3325.

Bakchild, Kent, 5235.
Baker, Clement, 4996.
........., Edw. *See* Elton.
........., Edmunds, 5238.
........., Hen., 1138.
........., John, 771, p. 433, 3573, 4377, 4721, p. 973.
........., ..., LL.B., 1854.
........., ..., clerk, 4335.
........., Math., 1692, 1934, 1951, 4212, 5211.
........., Ric., abbot of Shrewsbury, 3155, 3221, 3222.
........., Rob., 3031.
........., Walter, 1854, 5238.
........., Wm., 1540, 1586.
Bakewell, Henry, 4032.
Bakshalf, York, 4728.
Balam, Alex., 1781.
Balby, Nicholas, 3741.
Baldock, 4022.
........., Ric., 5481.
Baldry, Tho., 271, 890, 3549.
Baldwin, Frans., 105.
.... John, 943, 1379, 1813, 3310, 3522.
Balingham, or Bavelingham church, Terrouenne dioc., 1575, 4022.
Balke, Rog., 824.
Ball, John, 1540, 5077.
........., Philip, 3497.
........., Thos., 4878, p. 958.
Balladolate, Alvares de, 4041.
Ballard, Edmund, 5200.
Ballyvet, John, 3318.
Balsale, Warw., 3186.
Balthasar, the notary, 4458.
Balwery, ("Balverley,") Sir William Scott of, 1820, 2069, 3569, 3676.
Balzarde, John, 2050.
Balze, Cuthbert, 3122.
Bamborough, 193, 4682.
Banborogh, Marquis of, 4284.
Bamboroughshire, 4520, 5090.
Bamlingham. *See* Balingham.
Bampton, 3955.
........., John, 12, 755.
Banbury, 1636, 3152.
Banchi, Michael, 4040, 4368.
Bancrofte, Wm., 3051.
Bande Grise, the, 3325.
Bandested, 155.
Bandicis, Jaques, 3377.
Banerston, Edw., 1812.
Bangor, Thos. Skeffington, Bp. of, 1981, 3071, 3715, 4394, 4827 ; in com. for Hants, 4159 ; for Salop, 4676, p. 904. ; for Warwick, 3364.
........., ..., summoned to Parliament, 5616.
Banham, Ric., 4668.
Bankerds, or Bankers, 778, 3041, 3089, 3096.

Banks, George, 3743.
Bannaster, Humph., 835, 1792, 4476, 4785, 5519.
........., Sir Humph, 4635.
Bannaster's ship, 3811, 3812, 3838.
Banner of the Household, the, 3885, 4237.
........., ..., St. Cuthbert, 4461, 4462.
........., ..., St. George, p. 609.
Bannerets, 4253, 4653.
Banners for the Gt. Harry, 4954.
Bannisius, Baptista, 3779.
........., James, Secretary to Maximilian, 3077, 3331, 3335, 3419, 3779, 4069, 4172, 4296, 4366, 5094, 5208, 5404.
Bantus, Raunbau du, 4445.
Bapmanson. *See* Batmanson.
Baptista, John. *See* Boerius.
Barantyn. *See* Barentine.
Barbania, Duke of, 5730.
Barbary, 8, 490, 796, 819, 1537, 3766.
Barbet, Baudechen, 4445.
Barbey, Rob., 1472.
Barboure, Robt., 4113.
Barbour, Thos., servant to Ruthal, Bp. of Durham, 5274.
........., Wm., 4770, 4890.
Barclay. *See* Berkeley.
Barcombe, Suss., 730.
Bardefeld. *See* Berdfeld.
Bardesley, Glouc., 155.
Bardi, Francis de, 1947, 3192, 3257, 3511, 3596, 3746, 3756, 4959, 5261, 5649.
......, John, son of Francis de, 5358, 5382, 5650.
......, Peter Francis de, 3756.
Bardisley, Ric., captain, p. 652, 5761.
Bardney, monastery of, 968.
........., abbot of, 1716, 1979, 3137, 5691.
........., Ric., abbot of, Croyland, 3375, 3420, 3447 ; summoned to Parl., 5616.
Bardocke, Francis, of Staffordshire, 1480.
Bardolf. *See* Beaumont.
Bardon Park, Leic., 542, 3096, 5683.
Barentine, William, sheriff of Oxon and Berks, 1316, 1949.
........., ..., squire of the Body, 4259, 4307.
........., Sir William, captain, p. 553.
Barerch, 1212.
Bareshanke, in Alwincle, 3761, 4904.
Baret, Andr., 4476.
Barew, Pembroke, 1193.
Barford mills, Warwick, 1257.
Barg, 5160.
Bargham, Sussex, 1515.
Bartilmew, John, collector of customs, 3094.
Bari, Francesco Sforza, duke of, 5171.
Barisford, James, Laurence and Godfrey, 1903.
Barker, —— of Worcestershire, 12.

Barker, Robt, incumbent of Uptonlovel, 1448, 1466.
........., Roger, master of the Innholders of London, 5708.
........., Thomas, prior of Newbury, 4537.
Barkeley. *See* Berkeley.
Barkeswell Park, Warwickshire, 643.
Barking, Essex, 4176.
........., abbey of, 155.
........., John, a brewer, 5723.
Barking. *See* Ships.
Barkwey, Wm., 167.
Barl, Adam, brewer of Germany, 3204.
Barley, Herts, 4694.
........., George, and Joan his wife, 3504.
........., Nic., serjeant of the peltry, 1969.
........., Robt, captain, p. 608.
Barn, John, 1309.
Barnaldyng, knight of Rhodes, 3355.
Barnard Castle, 178, 192, 204, 335, 936, 3782, 3845.
Barnard, ——, captain, p. 652.
.... *See* Bernard.
Barnardiston, Thos., on sheriff-roll for Norf., 1949, 3507 ; in com. for Linc., 4593, 4860.
Barnbe, Chas., petty captain, p. 608.
Barnby, Yorkshire, 3177, 5095.
Barnes, Surr., 1664.
........., Chr., incumbent of Bladon, 1578.
Barnesley, Yorksh., 4295, 5214.
Barnesse, Jeanne, "chamberiere" to Mary Queen of France, 5484.
Barneston, Thos., Lincolnsh., 4544, 5476.
Barney, Norf., 155.
Barney, John, Norf., 1812.
........., Ralph, Norf., 1812.
Barnhambrowne, Norf., 4680.
Barnstaple, 1992, 2080, 4385.
........., priory of, 3944.
........., John, prior of, 3944.
........., lady of (Margaret Countess of Richmond), 3272.
........., Guild of Tanners there, 3272.
........., chapel of St. Thomas, 5515.
Barnwell monastery, 3759.
........., Thomas, 1921.
Barnwoode, Oxon, 877, 4382.
Baron, Edw., justice, 1922.
........., John, of Barnstaple, 3272.
........., Robt, servant of Thomas Spinelly, 4928, 4929, 5387.
Baronie, Lancelot, p. 380.
Barons, Wm., M.R. and Bp. of London, temp. Hen. VII., 380.
........., William, 3939.
Barowe (Bergen op Zoom), 3385, 3396, 5341.
........., letter dated from, 3398.
........., in Somersetsh., 3505.
Barowdon, 1778. ·

Barowe, or Barough, Sir Maurice, in commission for Wilts, 1489, 1938, 3605, 4583; in other commissions, 3173, 3488, 3824.
Barrados, Ric., Secretary to the Prince of Castile, 4328.
Barradoty, ——, 5657.
Barre island., 1229, 1583.
Barreswell, Warw., 3826.
Barret, Sieur, p. 624.
........., John, purser, p. 813.
........., Thos., bailiff, 4071.
Barrington, —— captain, 4307.
........., Humph., 7 ; yeoman usher of the Chamber, 543, 3305 ; serjeant at arms, 4224, 5564.
Bartholomew, Wm., serjeant at arms, 4048.
Barton, near Bristol, 155, 900, 1831.
........., in Cambridgesh., 4659.
........., near Bury St. Edmund's, 3758.
........., upon Humber, Lincolnsh., 495, 1032, 1191, 4616.
Barton, or Bertoun, Andrew, the pirate, 117, 3138, 3339, 3619, 3631, 3718.
........., Hob. of, 3412, 3838.
........., John, 117, 1245, 2050, 3412, 3838, 3882, 4556.
........., Robert, the pirate, 20, 841, 1245, 1410, 3321, 3326, 3340, 3353, 3359, 3372, 3412, 4330.
Barwike, 4022.
Bascatt, Thos., captain, 4475.
Bascoyne, in Luxemburg, 3945.
Basford, Rob., petty captain, 3980.
Basil, St., 4447.
Basingstoke, 367, 721.
Baske, Th., 524.
Baskervile, James, Heref., 1949, 1963, 3686, 5506, p. 907.
Baskervyle, Will., his restoration in blood, 3502.
Basket, John, 1088.
Baskett, Tho., 235.
Basle, p. 380, p. 382, 4333, 4970.
........., letter dated from, 4970.
Bass, Sir Robert Lawder of, 1820, 2069, 3569, 3676.
Basse, Wm., 1891.
Basset, John, 729.
........., Sir John, in com. for Devonsh., 917, 1503, 1812, 3183, 3566, 3605, 3938, 4539, 4783, 5220.
Bassett, Ric., of Notts., 1735, 1804; sheriff, 1949.
........., Sir Richard, 4253.
........., Rob., of Notts., 1735.
Basset, Wm., 4071.
Bassethewses, Leic., 1372.
Bassus, friend of Erasmus, 5352.
Bassyngborne, Camb., 893.
Bastard, Ric., 4640, 4859.
Basternay, Humbert de, 5408.

Basterre, 4445.
Bastida, ——, 5152.
Bastiriacho, John, shipmaster, 4377.
Baston, John, 3925.
.........., Thos., 5067.
Baten, ——, 4347.
Batens, Wm., attainted, 1472, 4022.
Bateru . . ., Ymbert de, 4924.
Batesford, 1099.
Bath, 1771, 3939.
.........., John Moyle of. See Moyle.
.........., Cardinal Bishop of. See Corneto, Adrian de.
Bath and Wells, dean of, 1639.
Batemanson, John, LL.D., 467, 488, 548, 714, 4994.
Batmonslayn, in Bewsale, 3186.
Battersea, vicar of (Rob. Crumwell), 3671.
Battle, abbot of, 776 ; summoned to Parliament, 5616.
Battlefield, Salop, 953.
Baty, Ralph, usher of the Hall, 5161.
Baugon, Jehan le, 4445.
Bavaria, Frederick Count Palatine Duke of, 3648, 3856, 4091, 4563, 4887, 4932, 5139, 5203.
.........., ..., letter from, 3847.
Bavarino, or Bavery, Anton., 346, 1398, p. 432.
Bavelingham. See Balingham.
Bavynco, 4526.
Bawdes, Rob., of Lincolnsh., 657, 1120, 1169, 5309.
Bawdeswell, Norfolk, 5180.
Bawne, Wm., 4520.
Bawtre, Yorksh., 1698.
Baxter, Edw., weigher at Newcastle on Tyne, 863.
.........., John, weigher at Newcastle on Tyne, 674.
.........., ..., of Yorkshire, 3177, 4015, 4711, 5166.
Bay, John, 3530.
Bayard, Captain (the Chevalier Bayard), taken at Terouenne, p. 609, p. 625, 4402, 4431, 4464.
Bayaud, French captain in Italy, p. 384.
Bayeux, Cardinal of, 2002, 5408.
Bayly, John, D.D., inc. of St. Matt., Ipswich, 1217.
.........., ..., purser, p. 955.
Bayle, Thos., inc. of Lambemersh, dioc. Lond., 2063.
Baylys, Sir Ric., inc. of Melsambe, 1535.
Baynard, Philip, 554, 1913, 3488 ; in com. for Wilts, 898, 1489, 1938, 3157, 3605, 4583.
Bayneard, Tho., 3488, p. 434.
Baynham, Sir Alex., 3193, 5051 : in com. for Gloucestersh., 930, 1049, 1469, 1695, 3641, 3712, 3804, 4024, 4118, 4764 ; in the war with France, 3231, 4306, 4421, 4534.

Baynham, Chr., in the wars, 4051 ; in com. for Glouc., 930, 1049, 1469, 1695, 4024, 4118, 4764.
.........., ..., sheriff of Glouc., 1949, 5051.
..-......., John, 3720.
.........., Th., 3720.
Baynton, Yorkshire, 481.
.........., John, 1854, 1913, 2905.
.........., Sir Rob., 1905.
Bayonne, city of, 3243, 3247, 3313, 3355, 3356, 3425, p. 451, 3593, 3614, p. 476, p. 498, p. 502, p. 510, 4058, p. 615.
.... Bishop of, 3355, 3356.
.........., mayor of, 3355.
Bayons, in Lincolnshire, 4695.
Bays, Ric., of Little Langford, Wilts, 1270.
Beale, John, temp. Hen. VI., 4013.
Beanbusshe, Suss., 1835, 2051.
Bearn, in France, p. 396, 3356, 3451, p. 452, p. 457, 3614, 3649, p. 474, p. 498, 3860, 3861, p. 614, p. 615, 4296, 4319, 4858.
Byarne, Baron of, 3658. See Bierne.
Beauchamp, Thos., sheriff of Cumberland, 1807.
.........., Wm., father of Richard Lord St. Amand, 1905.
Beauchampton, 3297.
Beauchieff, La, 297.
Beaudiner, Mons. de, 5482.
Beaufort, Margaret. See Richmond, Countess of.
Beaulieu Abbey, Hants, 1217, 1702.
Beaume, Jacques de, 5490.
.... See Beaune.
Beaumond, Beamond, or Bemond :
.........., Alice, wife of Humph., 4587.
.........., Henry, 1812, 3551.
.........., Humph., 4587.
.........., Jas., p. 180, 1728
Beamonte, John de, p. 397.
Beaumont, Ric., of Yorksh., 22, 4587, 4866.
.........., Th., 1996.
Beamond, Sir Wm., temp. Edw. IV., 1441.
Beaumont, 5569.
Beaumount, manor of, 4695.
Beaumont, or Beamont, Ric. Viscount, 1472, 4022.
.........., Wm., second Viscount, Lord Bardolf, temp. Hen. VII., 266, 395, 414, 458, 730, 1071, 1277, 1430, 1463, 1472, 1775, 1788, 1966, 2011, 3041, 3096, 3239, 3266, 3356, 4022, 5016.
.........., ..., his lands, 266, 495, 730, 778.
.........., ..., his widow, married to John Earl of Oxford, 730, 2011, 3266.
Beaune, vin de, 4467.
.........., A. de, 5492.
.... See Beaume.
Beauvais (Bouves), 5523, 5547, 5569.
Becansaw. See Bekynsall, R.
Beccles. See Bekles.
Becheworthe, Surrey, 4291.
Beck, Edw., of Manchester, 4975.

Beck, Wm., 3931.
.... See Beke.
Beckwith, Mr., 5383.
........., Thos., 1796.
Bedale, Yorksh., 5086.
Bedasen, castle of, near Bayonne, 4267.
Beddington, Surrey, 1858, 5595.
Bedell, ——, carpenter, 3857.
........., Ric., 804.
........., Rog., yeoman of the Ewry, 1053.
........., Wm., of Herts, 236, 309, 349, 706, 1020, 1971, 3102, 4657, 5296, p. 906.
........., ..., of Kimbolton, Hunts, 835.
Bedford, Jasper Duke of, his lands, 778, 1047, 1472, 1665, 4022.
.... town, 5215.
Bedhampton, incumbent of, John Whitley, 1529.
........., parker of (W. Coope), 565, 3558.
Bedingfield, Edm., 1487.
Bedyngfeld, Sir Thos., of Norf., 1812.
Bedingfeld, Tho., 701.
Bedfordshire, commissions of the peace for, 1051, 1122, 2045, 3501, 4700, p. 907.
Beds and Bucks, Sheriffs of, 664, 1316, 1949, 3507, 3912, 4544, 5561.
Bedmester, Somerset, 3939.
Bednell, Thos., abbot of Whitby, 4971, 4981, 5524.
Bedon, in Berks, 347.
........., John, shipmaster, 3979.
Bedoo, David, inc. of Wayhill, 4638.
.........., Richard, inc. of Glawdster, St. David's dioc., 5012.
Bedwell, 3601.
Bedworth, Warw., 4071.
Bedyford. See Bideford.
Beelthe, in Wales, 3840, 5461.
Beer preferred to wine by the English, p. 397.
........., sent to the army at Calais, 5766 ; price of, 5747, 5751, 5760, 5767.
Beilby, or Beylby, John, 481, 1995, 3177, 4015, 5166.
........., Thomas, 1798.
Beilde, Oswald, chancellor of Denmark, 3634.
........., Magnus, 3632, 3633, 3634, 3635.
Bejar, Gregory of, 4578.
Beke, Rog., 4045.
........., Thomas, 5226.
........., Tho., son of Marmaduke son of Thos. and Eliz., 3251.
Bekerton, in Cheshire, 4748.
Bekett, Thos., 4777.
Bekyngham, Elias de, justice, temp. Edw. I., 1099.
Bekingham, Tho., son of Thos., 1613.
Bekynsall, Robert, almoner of Queen Katherine, prebendary of Windsor, 3487, 4434, 5735.

Bekles, Suff., chantry at, 4918.
Bekley, in Sussex, 1484.
.... Park, Oxfordshire, 3738.
Belamy, Ric., of London, 4023.
Belchier, Rob., son of Humph., 1211.
Beley, Hen., abbot of Tewkesbury, 579, 662.
Belford, 4902.
Belgrave, George, son of John, 4912.
Belis, Don Petro, 4058.
Belyngham, Christopher, of Berkshire, 241, 766, 885, 1216, 1393, 1470, 1481, 1732, 1745, 2095, 3015, 3640, 4341, 4559, 4809, 5166, 5684.
........., Edw., 3024, p. 650.
........., Ralph, 3024.
........., Ric., 3024.
........., or Bolyngham, Sir Rog., of Westmoreland, 1735, 2009, 3048, 3358, 3552, p. 904.
Belknapp, Edward, 282, 697, 735, 1024, 1499, 3885, 3929, 3930.
........., ..., named in commissions of the peace, 1387, 1468, 1971, 3364.
........., ..., constable of Warwick Castle, grants to, 419.
........., ..., overseer of Henry VII.'s Prerogative, 4116.
........., ..., steward of Braylliss, 1501.
........., ..., in the war against France, 3231.
........., Sir Edward, 3744, 4653, 4829, 5724.
........., ..., named in commissions of the peace, p. 903.
........., ..., grants to, 5619, 5689.
........., ..., in the war against France, 4237, 4307.
........., ..., knighted at Tournay, 4468.
Bell, John, 775, 5243.
......, Ric., inc. of Rysyng, Norw. dioc., 118.
......, Ric., and Margaret his wife, 1807.
......, Rob., of Northumberland, 4430, 4531.
......, Rog., p. 435.
......, Thos., 1730, 3406, 3407.
......, Tho., yeoman of the Mouth, 68, 631, 912, 1252, 1528, 4254.
......, Wm., yeoman of the Guard, 3468.
Belle, Ro., yeoman usher of the Chamber, 363, 920.
Bellegarde, ——, 4362.
Bellers, Rog., and heirs, 155.
Belles, Ric., 1979.
Bellewe, John, 3497.
Bellisby, Andrew, 1716.
Bellister Park, Northumberland, 3740.
Belloeile, in Hainault, document dated at, 4129.
Belshawe, Tho., inc. of Nelson, 116.
Belsoo, in Northumberland, 1040, 5010.
Belstede, Suff., 4705.
Belus, Wm., bailiff of Ringwood, 1142.
......, ..., clerk of the Council, 1598.

Belwood., Rob., of Lincolnshire, 3842, 4358, 4593, 4860.
Benacus Lake, 3543.
Bendell, Rob., 1000.
Bene, Wm., of London, 4146.
Benefices of foreign clergy, 4128.
Benefeld, in Rokingham Forest, 8084, 4762.
Benevere, Henry, 4996.
Benfeldbury, Essex, 4294, 4536.
Benger, John, 4161.
........., Ric., 1002.
Benham, Berkshire, 155.
Beningfield, Sir Thos., 4377.
Beniventi, Count di, p. 3.
Bennet, ——, of Sussex, 1212.
........., Thos., 1854.
........., Thomas, of Suffolk, 4923.
Benett, Wm., of Kent, 1663.
Benolt, or Bunowlte, John, the King's secretary at Calais, 1027, 1632, 1919, 2026, 5529.
...., ..., incumbent of Marke, 88.
........., Thomas, 235.
...., ..., Windsor herald, 1018, 1358.
........., ..., Norroy king at arms, 1338.
........., ..., Clarencieux king of arms, 1455, 5066 ; in the war against Scotland, 4375 ; at marriage of Princess Mary, 5482.
........., ..., letter to, 5369.
Benson, John, chaplain, 3211.
Bensted, Edw., in com, for Herts, 309, 706, 1020, 1971, 3102, 4742.
........., ..., treasurer of war in the north, 4375.
........., Sir Edw., 5483.
Benstede, John, abbot of Whitby, 4720, 4981, 5524.
Bentbowe, Wm., 3498.
Bentham and Ingleton, church of, Archd. of Richmond, 3062.
Bentinck, Allart, receiver of Tournay, 4517.
........., ..., steward of Margaret of Savoy, 4585.
Bentivoglio, Alexander, 1754, p. 368, p. 380.
........., Anthonio, 1754.
........., Galeaz, 1754.
........., Hannibal, 1754.
........., Hermes, 1754.
Bentivoglios, the, family of, 1681, 1689, 1697, 3112, 3780.
Bentley, Suff., 4705.
........., John, 705.
Benteley Wood, Wiltshire, 901.
Benys, Ric., inc. of Wodborowe, 1526.
Berde, John, 157, 1599.
Berdfeld, or Bardefield, in Essex, 36, 155.
........., Great, Essex, 222.
Berdisley, Ric. See Bardisley.
Berdney, abbot of. See Bardnay.
Bere, John, 3181, 4314.

Berecombe, in Sussex, 5016.
Berenghier, Jaquet, of Lille, 3417.
Berford, or Bereford, Warw., 419, 1499, 4301.
Bereford Church, 1854.
Bergamo, 3335, 3648, 3752, 4326, 4756, 5152, 5532, 5539, 5592.
Bergavenny. See Abergavenny.
Bergham, in Suffolk, 1149, 3851, 5074.
Berghez, in Flanders, 922, p. 626, 5362, 5377.
........., ..., letter dated from, 1128.
Berghes, Lord, chamberlain of the Emperor, 794, 1267, 3302, 3306, 3381, 3396, 3651, 3861, 4091, 4182, 4273, 4296, 4304, 4305, 4319, 4322, 4328, 4355, 4364, 4418, 4429, 4433, 4437, 4511, 4606, 4844, 4851, 4978, 5029, 5030, 5117, 5171, 5207, 5362, 5539.
........., ..., letter from, 1128.
........., ..., his son, 3499.
........., ..., his daughter, 5341.
........., ..., his nephew Isselstein, 5139.
Berges, Andrew de, 4296.
Berghes, Ant. (Mons. St. Bertin), 4609.
Bergues, monastery of St. Gwinocus at, p. 627.
Berington, in Herefordshire, 3113.
Berkhamstead, 126, 155.
.... fee, 645.
Berkn. See Barking.
Berkeley, Glouc., 3316.
........., Castle, 1037, 5082.
........., lordship of, 909, 1000, 1218.
........., William Marquis of, and Earl of Nottingham, 804, 1472, 4022.
Berkeley's lands, 778, 900.
Berkeley, or Barkeley, p. 561.
........., Alice, wife of Sir Edward, 1141.
........., Sir Edward, 1141.
........., Elizabeth, wife of Thomas, 1141.
........., James, 1037, 5082.
........., John, son of Thomas, 1141.
........., Katharine, wife of Sir William, 1141.
........., Maurice, 1469, 3476, 3507, 4541, p. 972.
........., ..., captain, 3591, 4377, 4475.
........., ..., grants to, 5026, 5027.
........., ..., slain at Flodden, 4441.
........., Sir Maurice, 554, 1871, 4071, 4200.
........., ..., sheriff of Gloucestershire, 664.
........., ..., named in commissions of the peace for Gloucestershire, 930, 1695, 3641, 3712, 3804, 4024, 4118, 4764 ; for Leicestershire, 656, 1094, 1425 ; for Wiltshire, 3157, 3605.
........., ..., of Wymondham, Leic., 664, 1316 ; sheriff of Warwick and Leicestershire, 1949.
........., ..., marshal in the army, 3231 ; with the army in Spain, 3451.
........., ..., in the war against France, 3173, 3885, 4237, p. 623, 4306, 4307, 4314.
........., ..., captain, 4632 ; banneret, 4653.

Berkeley, Sir, Maurice, goes with the Princess Mary into France, 5483.
.........., ..., grants to, 1815, 3673.
.........., Richard, of Gloucestershire, 1049, 1469, 1695, 3507, 3641, 3712, 4024, 411.
...., in the war against France, 3946.
.........., Thomas, son of Sir Edward, 1141.
.........., Sir Thomas, of Yorkshire, 5082, 5193. 5244.
Berks; 3786, 4017.
.... sheriff of, and escheator of. See Oxfordshire and Berks.
.........., feodary of Crown lands in. See Oxfordshire and Berks.
.........., commissions of the peace for, 241, 885, 1393, 1481, 1732, 2095, 3640, 4341, 5166, 5684.
.........., commission for inquisition, p.m., 5226.
Berkeswell, Warw., 419, 1499, 3186, 4301.
Berkstall, Henry, of Berkshire, 5723.
Bermeo, in Spain, 3243.
Bermingham, Patrick, chief justice of Ireland, 4588.
.........., Wm., of Luske, 5788.
Bermondsey, St. Saviour's, abbey, 1391, 5187.
.........., friar of, see Chyrch.
Bernard, or Barnard, friend of Erasmus, 1478, 2013.
.........., John, son of John, 1177, 3374.
.........., Philip, 5074, p. 972.
.........., Robert, clk., 5296.
.........., William, 1608.
Bernardin, ——, 5753.
Berne, in Switzerland, 4333.
.........., letter date from, 5266.
Berners, or Barnars. John Bourchier, Lord; in commission of the peace for Herts, 309, 706, 1020, 1971, 3102; for Surrey, 1427, 1762, 3078, 3092, 4693, 4734, 5237, p. 905.
.........., ..., in the war against France, 3885, 4237, 4307, 4314, 4479, 4534.
.........., ..., Marshal of the army against Scotland, 4375.
.........., ..., goes to France with Princess Mary, 5483.
.........., ..., summoned to Parliament, 5616.
.........., ..., in debt to the Crown, 2044, 5633.
.........., ..., grants to, 4264, 4704, 5097.
.........., ..., otherwise mentioned, 3765, 4264.
Berni, John de, of Toulouse, 4368.
Berreguardi, letter dated, 5025.
Bertin, Abbot S., 4427.
Bertoun. See Barton.
Berugham. See Bergham.
Bervestersceelt (?), rent maistre de, 3340 (4).
Berwick, 743, 774, 3326, 3811, 3845, 3882, 4238, 4441, 4460, 4518, 4520, 4522, 4869, 5759.
.........., intended attacks on, 4868, 5090.
.........., fortification of, 3496 (p. 431), 4902.

Berwick, Scotch ship taken at, 3347, 3811, 3838.
.........., lands assigned for the pay of the garrison of, 778, 1205, 1845, 2037, 3845.
.... customs of, 178.
.........., captain of, Lord Darcy, 187, 189, 190 1531, 1562, 1566, 1840.
.........., ..., his deputy or vice-captain, 3928, 4652, 4868. See Ughtred, Sir Anthony; and Evers, Sir Ralph.
.........., deputy and council of, 4869.
.........., treasurer of, Lord Darcy, 176.
.........., receiver of. See Alee.
.........., marshal of, Th. Burgh, 3021.
.........., master of the ordnance, Wm. Pawne, 5693.
.........., mason of, Ric. Mitchell, 1206.
.........., porter of, Chr. Clapham, 12; Th, Strangwish, 3359, 4197, 4868.
.........., letter dated at, 3359.
Berewyk, near Berkway, Herts, 4659.
Berwick, Avery, 4375.
Berwike, Robt., 3180.
Berwill, Alf., 3024.
Berworth, Steph., 986.
Berwyk in Elme, York, 4866.
Bery, Edm., 266.
......, John, 3465.
Beryman, Wm., 1070.
Besançon, 4399.
Bescosquet, John, 915.
Besellis, Wm., 3052; in com. for Berks, 241, 885, 1393, 1481, 1732, 2095, 3640, 4341, 5166, 5684; for Oxford., 894, 3546.
Best, Edward, 4067.
......, John, 4617.
......, Th., 5723.
Beston, Thos., bailiff of Hanley, 170, 5478.
Bestwoode Park, Notts, 1477.
Bethune, in Artois, p. 609, 4445, 4473, 4843.
.........., governor of, 4322, 4445.
.........., captain of the garrisons (Desessyngbard), 5163.
Bethom, 4767.
Beton, James, Archbishop of Glasgow, 216, 288, 714.
.........., ..., Archbishop of "St. Andrew's" (misprint for Glasgow), 910.
.........., ..., as bishop of Galloway (in 1508), 910.
Bettes, Ric., prior of Snape, 1126.
.........., Lewis, of Bath, 3939.
.........., Thos, 4156.
Behoule, Suff., 4254.
Beule, Geo., prisoner at the Battle of Spurs, 4402.
Beuley, Wm. See Bewley.
Beures, Sieur de, 3678.
Bevyn, John, 1761.
Bevan, John, 3560.

Beverley, York, 3491.
........., Rob., 3483.
........., Thomas, 4682.
........., ..., letter from, 4682 (2).
........., ..., in commission for the W. Riding, 1798, 1995, 3177, 4015, 5106, p. 906.
Bevers, ——, 5207.
Beversham, Th., 3733.
Bevyll, Peter, in com. for Cornwall, 312, 891, 1694, 1812, 1984, 3290, 3583, 3605, 3938, 4754, 5220, 5474, 5586 ; on sheriff-roll, 3507.
Bevirlaw, Thos., servant to Dacre, 3320.
Bevoyse. See Beauvais.
Bevyle, Wm., 2009.
Bewcastle, 4791, 4825.
........., dale, 4791.
Bewly Abbey. See Beaulieu.
Bewley, Beuley, or Beulewe,—
........., (Beulay), the Nicholas, ship, 4533.
........., Will., temp. Hen. VII., 856.
........., ..., in com. for Cumberland, 717, 1048, 1734, 1799, 3048, 3358, p. 907 ; elsewhere, 3075, 3552, 3553, p. 904.
Bewsale, 3186.
Bexley, in Kent, 3993.
Beycok, Salop, 5436.
Beyket, Roger, captain, 3979.
Beylby. See Beilby.
Beynham. See Baynham.
Beynton. See Baynton.
Beyton, Wm. a, 4753.
Bickley, in Chesire, 1263. 1264.
Biddesden, in Wilts, 1002, 1965.
Bideford, or Bedyford, Devon, 4029.
Bidnell, John, 810.
Bierne. See Bearn, in France.
........., or Byarne, baron of, 3658, 2752.
Bierton, in Bucks, 155.
Biflete, in Surrey, 3675.
Bigge, John, 446.
........., ..., in commission for Surrey, 1427, 3078, 4693, 4734, 5237; for Notts, 1762, 3092.
........., ..., bailiff of Surrey, 5128.
........., Ric., 688, 1231.
........., ..., yeoman horseman of the King's harriers, 5336.
Bigland, John, of London, 4672.
Bigot, or Bygod, Sir Ralph, 664, 4971.
........., ..., in commission for Yorkshire, 455, 954, 1549, 1550, 1735, 1799, 3219, 3358, 4719, 5193, 5244.
Bihalle, 4445.
Bikkey. See Bickley.
Bykley, Andrew, petty captain, 4253.
Bilboa, 3476, p. 476, 3762.
........., the Mary of. See Ships.
Bill, Stephen, p. 433.
Billard, Blasius, Swiss gunner, 762, 781, 1075.

Billesby, Andrew, of Billesby, 1758 ; in com. for Lincolnshire, 1171, 3137, 3342, 4358, 5691 ; on sheriff-roll, 3507, 4544. See also Billessey.
........., Sir Andrew, of Lincolnshire, 4593, 4860.
Billesden, John, of London, p. 957.
Billessey (Billesby ?), And., 1979.
Billing, or Billing Magna, Northt., 645, 4436.
.... Magna, Ralph Egerton rector of, 3570.
...., Will. Rogiers inc. of, 3689.
Billingburgh, Linc., 4436.
Billyngeye, Linc., 3955.
Billyngtord, Thos., of Norfolk, 1812.
Bilth. See Beelth.
Bindon, Monastery of, 3567.
Bingham, John, yeoman of the Crown, 2087.
... ., Rob., 235.
Bircham, in Norfolk, 155.
Bird, Anabella, 4911.
......, John, 235, 331, 5296.
......, Rob., 3051.
......, Rob., shipowner, 4475.
......., Wm., 4911.
Birdhurst, in Wilts, 4694.
Birfeld-Abbot, Berks, 3705.
Birkhead, Edm., Bp. of St. Asaph, p. 626.
Birkhed, Ric., 4360.
.... See also Brikhed and Brikeved.
Birks, Thos., 4672, 4892, 5723, 5748.
Birle, or Birley, John, 3051, 4375.
........., Rob., 4782.
Birley, Tho., clk., 1512.
Byrling, in Kent, 320.
.... in Sussex, 730, 5016.
Birnaund, Geo., p. 434.
Birr, Wm., 4911.
Birt, Ric., poulterer, 3537.
......, Simon, 4141.
Birton, Ric., 732.
Biscay, 3243, p. 456, 3762, 5723.
Bisfa..., 3874.
Bishop, or Bisshop, Rob., 1813, 3551.
........., ..., servant of Sir Rich. Wingfield, 4077, p. 616, 4743, 4929, 4930, 5604.
Bishop-Cheriton (Bysshopereton), Devon, 1004.
Bishopsdale, in Richmond, Yorksh., 3483.
Bishopstone, in Bucks, 1352.
Bisleigh, Glouc., 155.
Bisley. See Byssey.
Bisley, in Surrey, Winch. dioc., Thos. Preston inc. of,
........., Wm., 3497.
........., ..., feodary of crown lands, 5692.
........., ..., of Long Ashton, Somerset, 4363.
Bithynia, 1659.
Blaby, Leic., 4912.
Blacadur, Ro., 474.
Blacater, Laird of, killed at Flodden, 5090.
Blackborn in Suffolk, 4966.

Blackheath, 5111.

........., battle of, 1100.

Blackmore. *See* Blakamore, Blakemore, and Blakmore.

Blackness, in Scotland, 3577.

Blacksall, Jno., Harleston rector of, 1375.

Blackwall, ships at, 5317.

Bladbourne, Humph., of Derbyshire, p. 907.

Bladel, Arent de, 117.

Bladon, John Harden inc. of, 731.

Blagge, Barnaby, 5118.

........., John, 724.

........., Robert, third baron of the Exchequer, 1747, 1921, 4699.

........., ..., remembrancer of the Exchequer, 5118.

........., ..., in commission of the peace for Kent, 725, 906, 3428, 3605, 4663, 4847, 4927, 5506 (p. 906) ; for Middlesex, 3552, 5506 (p. 905).

Blake, Wm., yeoman of the Crown, 4943.

........., ..., shipmaster, 5112, 5770.

Blakedown, Devonsh., 2080.

Blakemore, Dorset, 1953, 3853.

........., Worc., 3613, 5478.

.... Park, 170.

Blakemore, Henry, abbot of Lesnes, 3795.

Blakenall, Ric., 3200.

........., Rob., 3200.

........., Wm., 3200.

........., (Blaknall,) Wm., clerk of the ordnance, 4375.

Blakeney, John, 1192.

Blakewell, 1299.

Blamyer, John, inc. of Abbotley, 5669.

Blanchefort, Guido de, Gd. Master of Rhodes, 4604 ; letter from, 3874.

Blangango, 4022.

Blankney, Linc., 398, 3284, 4852.

Blaston, Leic., 730.

Blemeller, Northumb., 3740.

Blenerhasset (Blenerhayset), John, 642, 1666, 3119.

Blenerhasset, Thos., 1835.

Blenkensop or Blynkynsope, Gerard, 3740.

........., Thomas, 3552, 3703, 5506 (p. 904).

Blesby, Linc. 4616.

........., Wm., of Blesby, Linc. 4616.

Blewbery, John, 4131, 4527, 5720 (pp. 952 and 953).

........., ..., to be liberated on bail, 755.

........., [John ?] of Kent, excepted from the general pardon, 12.

Blicklyng, Norf., 3774.

Blind Dick, a minstrel, 4653.

Bliston, Cornw., 889.

Blisworth, Northt., 3175, 6456.

Blois, in France (sometimes called Blayes), 3277, 3335, 3361, 3499, 3651, 3752, 3779, 4584, 4692, 4818.

........., Lewis XII. at, 4273, 4329.

........., Spaniards taken at, 3766 (p. 499).

........., letters dated from, 318, 1181, 3112, 3340 (3), 4152, 4174, 5369.

Blokfeld, John Gaynsford, of, 1316, 1949, 3507.

Blokley. *See* Atkyns, John.

Blomsteis, Essex, 729.

Blore, Staff., 606, 926.

Bloundell, Geo., of Towcester, &c., 1827.

Blount, Alice wife of Richard, 3485.

........., Edward, son of Sir Thomas, petty captain, 4253.

........., Sir Edward, 836, 2086.

........., Humphrey, 4592.

........., John, of Staffordshire, 279, 713, 791, 886, 1770, 5506 (pp. 903 and 905).

........., ..., in debt to Henry VII., 3497 (p. 434).

........., ..., captain, 4253.

........., ..., jun., of Knightly, Staff., 1974.

........., Richard, 3485, 4592, 5146, 5483.

........., ..., signature, 1491.

........., Sir Richard, 5484.

........., Thomas, of Staffordshire, 279, 713, 791, 886, 1770, 4646, 5506 (pp. 903 and 905).

........., ..., bailiff of Chaddesley Corbett, Worc., 4071.

........., Sir Thomas, of Shropshire, 918, 981, 3071, 3715, 4394, 4827, 5506 (p. 904).

........., ..., on the sheriff-roll for Herefordsh., 664.

........., ..., banneret captain in the war against France, 3231, 4253.

........., William, Lord Mountjoy. *See* Mountjoy.

........., Mrs., 5523.

Blowse, Ric., of Littlington, Camb., 1558.

Bloxwich, John, of London, 3045.

Bluemantle pursuivant (Francis Dees or Dyes), 418, 1358.

........., ..., (Ralph Lago), 1555, 3991.

........., ..., 3248, 5604.

........., ... summons Teronenne, 4286.

Bluet, Ric., of Somersetshire, 287, 712, 3048, 3566, 3585, 3606, 3701, 4713.

Blyaunt, John, 1375, 1534, 3309.

Blyborough, Linc., 319, 1129, 1148, 1344.

Blythe, Geof., Bp. of Coventry and Lichfield. *See* Coventry.

........., John, 1004.

........., ..., of Bysshopereton (Bishop-Cheriton), Devon, 1004.

Blything, Suff., 1188.

Bobbingworth, Essex, 734.

Bocher, Rob., 3031.

Bocherdeston, in Leicestersh., 5096.

Bochier, Ant., abbot of Fescamps, 962.

Bockard, Guisnes, church, 4937.
Bockhampton, Berks, 4071.
Boconnoc, in Cornwall, 1434.
Bocquet, Collin, 4445.
Boddington Superior, Northt., 3524.
Boddington, Rob, 235.
Bodehampton, Hants, 1239.
Bodenham, or Bodnam, Roger, of Hereford-shire, 646, 675, 1400, 1963, 3503, 3686, 5610.
........., Thomas, son of Roger, 5610.
Bodford, Northt., 3297.
Bodley, James, and Joan his wife, 4911.
........., Thos. 1776, 3767, 4911.
Bodon, Ric., justice of assize, 242, 294, 1164, 1490.
Bodryngan, Sir Hen., 1472, 5719. See Botryngon.
Bodrington, Sir Henry, 4022.
Body, John, 3399.
......, Wm., 4013.
Boerins, John Baptista, of Genoa, 354 ; physician to Henry VII. and VIII., 3518; friend of Erasmus, 2001, 4427 ; letter to, 3518.
Bohemia, 1221, 5366.
Bohier, Henry, 5490, 5492.
........., ..., letter from, 4153.
........., Thomas, General of Normandy, 5151, 5155, 5173 (p. 829), 5192, 5203, 5285(?), 5302, 5329, 5490, 5492, 5553, 5560, 5566, 5569, 5590.
........., ..., letters from 4883, 5330, 5359 5360, 5376.
........., ..., sent to England by Lewis XII., 5278, 5279, 5280, 5305, 5306, 5307, 5322, 5343, 5408.
Boissi, Sieur de, 3325 (p. 384), 4789, 5482. See Bushy.
Bois-le-Duc, 924, 1135, 3616.
........., letter dated from, 1902.
Bojya, realm of, 819.
Bokenham, Anne 971, 1300.
........., Wm., clk., 677.
Bokker. See Bulker.
Bold, Sir Nic. 777.
......, Rog., 3745.
Boleyn, or Bullen, Alan, 1724.
........., Elizabeth, 3402.
........., James, in commission for Norfolk, 1714, 1812, 1963, 3029, 3426, 3545, 5133; for Bishop's Lynn, 5236.
........., Mary, mother of Sir Thomas, letter from, 5784.
........., ..., daughter of Sir Thomas, 5483, 5484.
........., Sir Thomas, knight of the Body, sent in embassy to the Low Countries, 3196, 3248, 3258, 3271, 3276, 3370, 3381, 3398, 3460, 3463, 3469, 3651.
........., ..., commissioned to make the Holy League, 3603, 3859, 3861.
........., ..., in the war against France, 3885, 4237, 4307, 4314, p. 904.

Boleyn, or Bullen—cont.
........., ..., letter to, 5784.
........., Sir Thomas, signature, 1491, 3849.
........., ..., grants to, 343, 654, 1477, 1774, 1814, 3008, 3194, 3401, 3402, 3655, 3722, 3774, 5115.
........., ..., in the commission for Norfolk, 1340, 1714, 1963, 3426, 3545, 5133 ; for Suffolk, 1339, 1715, 3029, 3219, 3967, 4713, 5133 ; for Kent, 725, 906.
........., ..., sheriff of Norfolk and Suffolk, 1316; of Kent, 1949.
........., ..., in debt to the Crown, 3497 (p. 434).
........., ... See also, 664, 3561, 3922, 4087.
Bolyngham. See Belyngham.
Bolyngton, Robt., yeoman of the Guard, 1712.
Bolistoffes, Essex, 734.
Bolles, Ric., of Gosberton, Linc., grant to, 1067.
........., ..., in commission for Lincoln (Holland), 3351, 4860.
Bollys, John, 3497, 5519.
Bolling, or Bollyngia, William, third Baron of the Exchequer, 9.
........., ..., grant to, 443.
........., ..., in commission for Kent, 725, 906.
Bologna, 802, 814, 1676, 1697, 2002, 3026 (p. 328), 3104, 3112, 3269 (p. 368), 3325 (p. 381), 3410, 3777, 3779, 4267, 5438.
........., delivered to the French, 1681, 1689, 1697, 2010.
........., taken under the protection of Lewis XII., 1754.
........., in the hands of the Emperor, 2039.
........., league for recovery of, 1880, 1955, 1967, 3283, 3513.
........., included in the peace between France and the Pope, 5319.
........., letters dated from, 1643, 5705.
........., Cardinal St. Severin, legate of, 3112.
........., legate of, 11.
Bolsover, Derbyshire, 1633, 1809, 4694.
Bolt, John, of London, 4954 (note).
........., Rob., 4617.
........., Wm., 1672, 5186.
Boltby, or Langley, in Northumb., 1040, 5010.
Bolton, Lord Scrope of. See Scrope.
........., William of Norfolk, 3506; groom for the Mouth, 421.
Bombasius, friend of Erasmus, 16.
Bomy, battle of (Spurs), 4284 (p. 625), 4431, 5391, 5777.
Bonaventure, provincial of the Friars Observant, 4549.
Bond, ——, paymaster of the Gt. Harry, 4968.
........., John, 4258.
........., ..., warden of the dyers, London, 4013.
........., Nich., debtor to Henry VII., 1639, 3497.
...., ..., inc. of Northlewe, 4243.
........., Wm., clerk of the poultry, 5170. See Bound.

Boney, in Notts., 857.

Bondegate, manor of, 1796.

Bonham, Thos., of Essex, 125, 1368, 1522, 1713, 3464, 3605, 3785, 3967, 5506, (p. 907).

.........., William, sheriff of Wilts, 5561 ; captain, 5112 (p. 812).

Bonyngton, Rob., yeoman of the guard, 1109.

Boner, David, purser, 5276, 5720 (p. 954).

Bonevyse. See Bonvixi.

Bonnet, ——, 924, 4091, 5327, 5341.

Bonneval, French officer, 3752.

Bonnivet, Mons. de, 5482, 5606.

Bonny, Ric., 3497.

Bonnyzo, 880.

Bononpeverell, 155, 484.

Bonson, Peter, of Normandy, 3430.

Bonsons, French merchant, 4328 (2).

Boutemps, John, 5173, 5323.

Bonvile, Hen., of Normandy, 1437.

Bonvixi, Antony, merchant, 3965, 4074, 4957, 5370.

.........., Jerome, prothonary apostolic, 300, 1457.

.........., ..., letter from, 11.

.........., ..., credence for, by Julius II., 267.

.........., Nicholas, merchant, 1584, 4957.

.........., Paul, merchant, 4957.

.........., Lawrence, merchant of Lucca, 809, 1457, 1574, 3496, 4747.

.........., ..., grants to, 4260, 4261.

.........., ..., in debt to the King, 2044.

.........., ..., pardon and release, 4145.

Bonythan, Wm., purser of the Gt. Harry, 4968.

Bookill, Wm., of London Bridge, 1212.

Books, French and English, 4101.

Boolden, Salop, 4071.

Booth. See Bothe.

Boothby, Linc., 5197.

Borborough, governor of, 3353. See Morbecke.

Bordeaux, 1140, 1886, 3112, 3355 (p. 399), 3357, 3424, 3692.

.........., Abp. of, 3355, 3356.

Borders, English commissioners for, 3569.

.........., the, Scotch, 3569, 3577, 3882, 4652, 4951.

Borderers, 4461, 4462.

Bordes, Francis de, letters from, 5369, 5370.

Bordesley, monastery of, 106.

Boreham, in Essex, 778, 1774, 3401.

Borne, 1278.

Bornehall in Whorsted, Suff., manor of, 4768.

Borough, near Aylesham, Norf., 1892, 4254 (iii.), 4675 ; church of, 417.

.........., Sir Edw., 777.

.........., James, yeoman of the Guard, 5585.

.........., Richard, 142, 200, 4547.

Borough, Sir Thomas, knighted at Tournay, 4468 ; in commission for Lincolnsh., 5476, 5506 (p. 906).

.........., ..., Thomas, 663, 666, 792.

Boroughbridge, 3386.

Borrefford, Oxon., 1426.

Borthwick, Wm., Lord, 4556, 4997.

Borwell, Tho., 1341.

Bos, Jean du, abbot of St. Martin's, Tournay, 4667.

Bosbury Church, Heref., 1382.

Bosdon, Thos., 3497.

Boselles. See Beselle.

Bosnia (?), Queen of, letter from, 5730.

Bosnians, the, 1659.

Bosom, Henry, in com. for Nottinghamshire, 1514, 1735, 1798, 1804, 1964, 3092, 3494, 4776, 5225, 5506 (p. 905).

.........., ..., on sheriff-roll, 664, 3507, 4544.

Bossom, Sir Ric., captain, knighted at Lisle, 4253.

Boson, John Van, merchant of London, 3497.

Bosseti. See Busset.

Boston, in Lincolnshire, 663, 1036, 1655, 1736, 3234, 3889, 5227.

.........., stewardship of, 303, 1278.

.........., bailiff of, 351.

.........., controller of customs at, 552.

.........., weigher in the port of, 146, 642.

Boston, John, 1369, 1854.

.........., ..., clk, inc. of Milsted, Canterbury, 3674.

Boswell, Thomas, son of John, 740.

Bosworth Field, 1012 ; chapel at, 1848.

Botcheston, Leic. See Bocherdeston.

Boteler. See Butler.

Boterell, Tho., of Edmonton, 1480.

Bothall. See Bottell.

Bothan, castle of, 4129.

Bothe, Mr., 236.

.........., Anne, 1790.

.........., Charles, clk., 955, 956, 3289.

.........., ..., ... in commissions of the peace for Gloucestershire, 1049, 1469, 3641, 3712, 4024, 4118, 5506 (p. 906) ; for Herefordshire, 1400, 1963, 3686, 5506, (p. 907) ; for Salop, 1981, 3071, 3715, 4394, 4827, 5506, (p. 904) ; for Worcestershire, 1971, 3301, 3709, 4770, p. 903 ; for Wales and Marches, 3055, 4198.

.........., Christopher, clk., 1695.

.........., Joan, 1790.

.........., Ralph, 1790.

Bothes, Sir John, in debt to Henry VII., 777.

.........., ..., of Lancashire, killed at Flodden, 4462.

.........., Sir Philip, of Berugham, sheriff of Norfolk and Suffolk, 1149, 3851 ; justice of the peace, 5074 ; in commission for Suffolk, 1153, 1715, 3029, 3219, 3967, 4713, 5133, 5506 (p. 904).

Bothes, Sir Philip, in the war with France, 4377 (p. 652).

........., ..., in debt to the Crown, 1639, 2044, 3497.

........., ..., Ralph, 1790.

........., Richard, feodary of the honor of Richmond, 339.

........., Robert, temp. Hen. VII., 856.

........., Thomas, farmer of Marke and Oye, 779, 1241, 3832, 4665.

Botiller. See Butler.

Botrym, Sir Thomas, 5483.

Botryngon, 4347. See Bodringan.

Botry, or Buttry, Wm., of London, 1350, 1892, 4254 (iii.), 4617, 4675, 5334, 5720 (p. 955).

........., ..., in debt to Henry VII., 3497.

Botyll, Cumb., 3866.

Bottell (Bothall), Nhumb., barony of, 1040, 5010.

Boucault, de, 3752.

Boucharge, du Sieur, chamberlain, 1182, 4924, 5482.

Boucheron, de, 5482.

Boudgedworth, Laird of, 4536.

Boughton, Kent, 3031, 4787.

........., Hen., 857.

........., Nich., of Kent, 4847, 5506 (p. 906).

........., William, 857.

........., ..., in commissions of the peace for Warwickshire, 1387, 1468, 1971, 3364, 5506 (p. 903).

Boulogne, 3659, 4030, 4282, 4284 (p. 623), 5032, 5130, 5173, 5270, 5360, 5379, 5391, 5468, 5505, 5512, 5513, 5560, 5569.

........., letter dated from, 5469.

........., French camp at, 4329.

........., fortification at, 3744.

........., plague at, 5469.

........., captain of, 5151.

........., Dymoke, treasurer at, 5383.

Boulonnois, the, 4162.

........., seneschal of the, 5379.

Boult, Robinet du, 4445.

Bound, or Bownd, John, 1854.

........., Wm., 5228.

Bourbon, Charles, Duke of, 3325, 3340 (iii.), 3355 (p. 399), 3357, 3584 (p. 451), 3593, 3752, 5164, 5377, 5523, 5560, 5675, 5681.

........., [Francis], brother of the Duke, 5560.

........., Louis de, 5408.

Bourchier, Agnes, wife of Sir Thos., 3136.

........., ..., wife of Sir Thos. B., junr., 1167.

Bourghchier, Anne, 1031.

........., Hen. See Essex, Earl of.

Borghcher, John, 5561.

Bourghchier, Sir Thomas, 1031, 1814, 1825, 1833, 3611.

........., ..., in commissions of the peace for Kent, 725, 906, 1265, 3428, 3605; for Middlesex, 3552; for Surrey, 1427, 1762; of gaol delivery for Maidstone, 763.

Bourghchier, Sir Thomas, in debt to Henry VII, 1639, 3497.

........., ..., junr., 1167, 3136.

Bourdot, Jehan, maitre d'hotel of the Marshal of Burgundy, 4362.

Bourges, archbishopric of, in Berry, 5208.

........., Andrew Forman, Abp. of, 5678.

Bourge, André de. See Burgos, Andreas de.

Burgoyne, Marshal de, 4362.

Bournage, Jehan, 4473.

Bourne, Lincolnsh., 302, 303, 384, 1865, 3305, 4199, 5131.

........., monastery of, 1802, 1844.

........., John, 4367.

........., ..., bastard, prisoner at the Battle of Spurs, 4402.

Bout. See Butt.

Bouton, Claude, 5163.

Bovey Tracey, Devon, 359.

Bovill, friend of Erasmus, 1652, 1847, 1917, 1918, 1948, 1957, 1982, 2001, 2013, 2091.

........., Peter, of Cornwall, 4544.

Boryle, Geo., 5346.

Bowdon, Thomas, yeoman of the buttery, 4684.

Bowes, Ralph, 1796.

........., Sir Ralph, 1796.

Bowlsden, in Northumb., 1040, 5010.

Bowne, in Dorsetsh., 155.

Bowryng, Rob., in com. for Devonshire, 699, 917, 1503, 1812, 3183, 3566, 3589, 3605, 3938, 4539, 4783.

........., release, 3057.

........., Rob., 3939.

Bowryngesley, Devon, 3057.

Bowness, 5090.

Bowsons, Peter, 3517.

Bowth. See Bothe.

Bowyer, John, of Southwark, 5720 (p. 953).

Bowyers, of London, 3496 (p. 432).

Boxley, John, abbot of, 1265.

Boylands, manor of, 1666.

Brabanson, Lord, 5207.

Braband, John, yeoman of the Chamber, 571.

........., ..., yeoman of the Guard, 249, 1255, 1602.

Braban, or Brabon, John, 235, 359.

Brabant, 3248, 4054, 4427, 5158, 5304, 5341, 5720 (p. 954,, 5731.

........., Emperor passes through, 4282.

........., sum voted to the Emperor by, 4810.

........., threatened by the Bastard of Gueldres, 3651.

........., troops on the borders of, 4433.

........., natives of, 1092, 3014.

........., Bois-le-Duc, in, 1135.

Brabull, Ric., 232.

Brachost, Eurax, Flemish merchant, 117.

Bradburn, John, of Derbyshire, petty captain, 4253.

Bradbury, Joan, widow of Thomas, 1776, 3767, 4911.
........., John, master of the artillery in Calais, 609.
........., Ric., inc. of Froyton, 3536.
........., Thos., mayor of London, 1776, 3767.
........., Wm., of Claveryng, 4176.
Braddon, Northt., 3027.
Bradebrige, Nic., clk., 1901.
Bradford, Walter, in commission for Northumberland, 1735, 1804, 3358; for the West Riding of Yorkshire, 1798, 1995, 3177, 4015, 5166.
Bradley, West, Berks, 1344.
........., Glouc., 4071.
........., Staff., 835.
........., Yorksh., 566, 4852.
........., John, yeoman of the Guard, 3665.
........., Thomas, 1837.
Bradman, Ambrose, soldier of Calais, 1605, 3923; serjeant-at-arms, 4897.
Bradney. See Bardney.
Bradninch (Brandenynche), Devonsh., 48.
Bradnyche, rectory of, 4841.
Bradon Forest, Wilts, 128.
Bradshawe, Ric., 3613.
Bradstock, prior of, 1231.
Bradwardyn, Heref., 3771.
Bradwell, Essex, 155.
Bradwell, John, prior of Holy Trin., Aldgate, London, 3403, 3493, 3716.
........., Pygetty, manor of, 729.
Bragges, Wm., inc. of Everingham, Calais, 1564, 2032, 3550.
Braghton (Braughton), Linc., 1958.
Bragot, Ric., 4014.
Braham, Eustace, 1666.
Brakeley, hund. of, Glouc., 1445.
Brakks, the, 3820.
Brammer, Ric., 1965.
Brampton, Northt., 645.
........., Wm., 1088.
Brancepeth (Branspetch), Durham, 191.
Brandenburg, Casimir, Marquis of, 4284 (p. 627), 4349, 4811, 4932, 5323, 5539.
Brandesby, Ralph, of Kepyke, Yorks., 5190.
Brandon, Charles, squire of the Body, afterwards Viscount Lisle and Duke of Suffolk, 695, 859, 1453, 1989, 3103, 4254.
........., ..., in commissions for the co. of Surrey, 1427, 1548, 1762, 3078, 3092; for Suffolk, 3029.
........., ..., his signature, 1491.
........., ..., knight of the Body, 3176, 3561, 3685, 3841, 3880, 3920, 3921, 3922, 4094, 4169.
........., ..., in commission for Norfolk, 3426, 3545, 5133; for Suffolk, 3967, 4713, 5133, p. 904; Surrey, 4693, 4734, 5287, p. 905; of gaol delivery for Guildford, 3996.
........., ..., ordered to join the Admiral, 4056.

Brandon, Charles, &c.—cont.
........., ..., created Viscount Lisle, 4072.
........., ..., his retinue, 4104.
........., ..., marshal of the Army, 3885, 4126, 5756.
........., ..., Lord Lisle, 4103, 4169, 4171, 4405, 4642, 4710, 4831, 5757.
........., ..., in the war with France, 3885, 4093, 4095, 4237, p. 623, 4306, 4307, 4314, 4377, 4459, 4475, 4527, 5724, 5757, 5760, 5765.
........., ..., created Duke of Suffolk, 4698, 4848.
........., ..., as Duke of Suffolk, 5099, 5111, 5140, 5164, 5282, 5287, 5322, 5358, 5368, 5505.
........., ..., ambassador to the Emperor, 4736.
........., ..., makes loves to Margaret of Savoy, 4851.
........., ..., in embassy to France, 5553, 5569, 5606, 5634, 5637, 5696, 5717.
........., ..., his marriage with Mary Queen of France (in 1515), 3298.
........., ..., letters from, as Lord Lisle, 4653; as Duke of Suffolk, 5512, 5523, 5547, 5560, 5584, 5590, 5649.
........., ..., letters to, 5104, 5205, 5393, 5417.
........., ..., summoned to Parliament, 5616.
........., ..., certificate of, 4234.
........., ..., grants to, as Charles Brandon, 1256, 1423; as Viscount Lisle, 3932, 4180, 4241, 4255, 4645, 4687, 4708, 4882, 5079.
........., ..., his influence, 4386.
........., ..., servant of, 4074, 4634.
........., ..., of Lynne, 996.
........., Sir Robert, of Henham, Suff., 996.
........., ..., knight of the Body, 1452, 3685, 4254.
........., ..., captain, 4708.
........., ..., in commission for Norfolk, 1812, 3426, 3545, 5506 (p. 904); for Suffolk, 4708, 4713, 5133, 5506 (p. 904).
........., Sir Thomas, knight of the Body, 859, 860, 873, 902, 1084, 5735.
........., ..., marshal of the King's Bench, 150.
........., ..., grants to, 129, 573, 597.
........., ..., his signature, 480, 521, 524, 531, 755.
Brandonferry, 1477.
Branhouse, John, of Preston, Devon, 1433.
Bransby, York, 5166.
Branston, Linc., 3284, 4852.
Brantingishey Park, 349.
Brantsy, in Northampton, 3761, 4904.
Branxston, town of, 1040, 5010.
........., battle of. See Flodden.
Braquemart, ——, 4445.
Brasier, Roger, 3497.
Brass sizing, 186.
Braughing (Broughing), Rob. Philipson, inc. of, 4115.

Braunche, Tho., abbot of St. Peter's, Gloucester, 1159, 1291, 1361, 1639.
Braure, John, 5163.
Bradribb (Brawdrybbe), Ric., inc. of St. Margaret's, Halstowe, 3399.
Bray, in Berkshire, 93, 155.
......, Edmund, 3231, 4534.
......, ..., captain, 4477.
......, ..., shipmaster, 3980.
Bray, Sir Edmund, of Eyton, p. 598 ; in com.
for Beds, 2045. 3501, 4700 ; for Surrey,
1762, 3078, 3092, 4693, 4734, 5237,
5506 (p. 905).
........, ..., sheriff of Beds, 5561.
......, Edw., 4306.
......, ..., captain, 3980, 4535, 4632, 5761.
......, Sir Reginald, temp. Hen. VII., 367,
434, 566, 721, 1367, 1399, 1504, 1748.
......, ..., his executors, 996, 1212.
Braybroke, Sir Gerard, son of Sir Gerard, 3228.
........, James, 60, 61, 88, 95, 96, 5056.
Brails (Brayles), Warw., 419, 1257, 1501.
Braynewode, Wm., 4685.
Braynton, John, of Herefordshire, 646, 675,
1400, 1963, 3503, 3686, 5506 (p. 907).
Breche, Hen., yeoman of the Crown, 1670.
Brede, John, 1854.
Bredeham, Christr., of Sellyng, Kent, 5550.
Bregilles, Philippe de, 4726, 4844, 4851,
5398.
........, ..., letters from, 4386, 4405, 5140.
Brehawte, Sir John, 3389.
Brengewood, chace of, 3220.
Brenghe, Piere van, 4445.
Brenhedon, in Rutland, 1778.
Brent, John, page for the mouth, 1259, 4136.
......, ..., in commission for Somersetsh., 287,
712, 3048, 3566, 3606, 3701, 4713.
......, ..., alias Vazacrely, 4788. See Faza-
kerley.
Brentwood, Essex, 530.
Brereton, Erean or Evan, 170, 5478.
........, John, clk., 519, inc. of Hatford, 1042.
........, Sir Ralph or Randolph, 62, 360, 995,
4306, 4477.
........, ..., marshal, 4253, 4534.
........, Ric., 4858.
........, Rog., inc. of Cumberton, 269.
........, Tho., 419.
........, Sir Wm., knighted at Tournay,
4468.
Brescia, 1697, p. 254, 3325, 3335, 3499,
3500, 3752, 4078, 4326, 4756, 5152,
5592, 5686.
........, siege of, 3026.
........, French in, 3077.
........, surrender of, 3269 (p. 368), 3543.
........, Petrus de. See Carmelianus.
........, Franciscus de. See Famagosta.
........, governor of. See Gorrevod.
Bressa, Peter de, 5129, 5273.

Brest, 3377, 3777, 3814, 4330, 5724.
......, intended expedition against, 4169.
......, French fleet at, 3752, 3821, 3877, 4020,
4055 ; leave for England, 3451, 3678.
......, English fleet off, 3903, 3946.
......, sea fight off, 3388.
......, French preparations at, 5762.
...... Castle, taken by Mons. de Rohan, 4076,
4935.
......, the Great Carrick of, taken, 3388.
Bresylle. See Brégilles, Philippe de.
Bresze, Louis de, French K.'s lieut., 4440.
Bressingham, Norf., 3506.
Bretagne. See Britanny.
Bretherton, Tho., excepted from the general
pardon, 12.
Breton, Wm., 5597.
Brettys, in West Ham, Essex, 155.
Breuerton, Ric., demi-lance, 3348.
Brewce, John, nephew of Sir Rob. Wingfield,
5475.
Brews, Rob., in commission for Norfolk, 1340,
1714, 1963, 3029, 3219, 3426, 3545,
3967 ; for Suffolk, 676, 1121, 1153,
1715 ; on sheriff-roll, 3507.
Brian, lordship of, 3149.
......, ——, friend of Erasmus, 1652, 2001.
......, ——, 1871.
Brian Askan, Yorksh., 3411.
Bryan, Francis, captain, 3980 (p. 553).
......, Hen., 3250, 3871.
......, Sir Thomas, knight of the Body, grant
to, 896.
......, ..., in commission for Buckingham-
shire, 454, 943, 1379, 2045, 3219, 3310,
3522, 5506, p. 907.
......, ..., in debt to Hen. VII., 3497 (p. 434).
Brickhill, Great, in Bucks, 5180.
Bridges, Roger, captain, p. 972, 5761 (p. 977).
........, John, sheriff of London, 4908.
Bridgewater, port of, 155, 536, 979, 1761,
4071, 4297, 4346.
Bridlington, York, 481.
Bridmonde, John, merchant, 3508.
Brigandyne, Jno., son of Rob., 1327.
........, Rob., clk., 3422.
........., ..., of the King's ships 353, 1327,
5720 (p. 953), 5724 (p. 960).
........, Wm., 3496 (p. 433).
Brigges, Sir Giles, in commission for Glou-
cestershire, 930, 1049, 1469, 1695 ; for
Wiltshire, 898, 1489, 1938, 3157, 3605.
Brygham, Christofer, 705, 3246.
........, ..., mayor of Newcastle, 3574.
Briges, or Brigges, Henry, gentleman of the
Chamber, 1318.
........., ..., in commission for Berkshire,
885, 1393, 1481, 1732, 2095, 3640,
4341, 5684.
........, Thomas, 4067.
........, William, butcher, 3509.
Bright, Robert, L.L.D., 4235.
Brighthampton, Oxford, 5146.

Brightelegh, Devonsh., 2080.

Brighthelmstone or Brighton, burning of, 5151.

........., Serle of, 5724.

Brightlingsea. *See* Ships.

Brightwell, Suffolk, 4254.

Brikhed. *See* Birkhed.

Brykheved, Rauf., of Cheshire, excepted from the general pardon, 12, 3497 (p. 435).

Bridgenorth, Salop, 3694, 4071, 4357, 4524, 4737.

Brigot, Edm. D.D., 1646.

Brigstock, Northt., 1641.

Brikenden, Rob. *See* Brigandyne.

Brymmesfeld, Glouc., 155.

Brymmesgrove. *See* Brommesgrove.

Brimmore, Hants, 2080.

Bryne, Anth., clk., 823., inc.of Grafford, 1704.

Brinkley, Ely dioc., 4489.

Brynkley Gilbert, of Bury St. Edmunds, 3939.

Brynkton Magna, Northt., 3524.

Brisete, 1099.

Bristall, John, of London, 3151, 3693.

Bristol, or Bristowe, 2081, 3161, 3919, 4071, 4270, 4745, 5026, 5027, 5388, 5567, 5660, 5721, 5724.

........., constable of. *See* Seymour, Sir John.

........., collection of tenths and fifteenths in, 3441.

........., customs of, 377, 513, 1619, 3094.

........., escheator of, 1930.

........., fee farm of, 1815.

........., Friars Minors of, 1077.

........., Friars Preachers of, 1046.

........., merchants of, 4076, 4420.

........., port of, 257, 1050, 4696.

........., ..., gauger of, 3235.

........., ..., prizes in, 1315.

........., ..., searcher of. *See* Westowe, John.

........., ..., ships in, 3663.

........., Barton near, 155, 900.

........., sheriff of, 1771,

........., ships of. *See* Ships.

Briston, Norf., 1331.

........., Ph., 1183.

Bristowe, Cornelius, 1135.

........., John, 1135, 3497.

Britanny, 402, 3357, 3517, 3679, 3692, 4843, 5482.

........., admiral of, 3830.

........., coast of, 3974.

........., native of, 3563.

........., ships of, 3814, 3817, 5753.

........., duchy of, dower of Renée daughter of Lewis XII., 3752. 4824, 5379.

........., discontent in, 4935.

........., English ships, in 3451.

........., expedition against, 3269 (p. 368), 4020, 4480, 5757.

Britanny, spy sent into, 4844.

........., defence of, 3112.

........., Scotch preparations in, 5006, 5681.

........., Basse Bretagne, 3112.

........., Duke of. *See* Francis Duke of Valois.

Brixham, Devon, 3978. *See also* Ships.

Brixia, Estienne de, vicar general of the Carmelites, 3873.

Brixton, Devon, 5648.

Broadbridge. *See* Bradebrige.

Brocas, Anne, daughter of William, 1219, 3317, 5700. *See also* Warham.

........., Edith, daughter of William, 1219, 5700.

........., John, 1812, 5700.

........., Wm., 1219, 3317, 5700.

Brochelz, 5370.

Brockdish, or Brokedisshehall, Norf., 619, 5056, 5096.

Brockley, Suff., 947.

Brodebank, Christr, 5723.

Brodebent, Wm., chaplain, 1854.

Brodham, Warw., 4301.

Broke, John, 4996 ; in commission for Gloucestershire, 930, 1049, 1469, 1695, 3641, 3712, 3804, 4024, 4118, 4764, p. 906 ; for Somerset, 287, 712, 3048, 3566, 3585, 3606, 3701, 4713, 5506, p. 904.

........., ..., mayor of Oxford, in commission of the peace for Oxford, 3546.

........., ..., John, clerk of the market for the Houschold, 291.

........., ..., inc. of Wynwoo, Llandaff dioc., 1857, 3273.

........., Ralph, 4635, 4731.

........., ..., yeoman of the Chamber, 78, 115.

........., Richard 1484, 1547, 1548.

........., ..., inc. of St. Margaret Moyses, London, 1396.

........., Richard, Serjeant-at-law, 1165, 1942, 5093, 5180. *See also* Brooke.

........., ..., in gaol deliveries for Newgate, 1519, 1897, 3765, 8778, 4553.

........., ..., in commission for Middlesex, 1972 ; for Thames, 4701.

........., ..., commission to, 3006.

........., Robert, Lord Willoughby de, commonly called Lord Broke, 48, 3231, 3298, 5180.

........., ..., commissioned to muster Darcy's expedition, 1566.

........., ..., in Spain, 3451.

........., ..., in the war with France, 3762 p. 609, 4421, 4477, 4534, 4653, 4682.

........., ..., in debt to the Crown, 2044, 5633.

........., ..., in commission for Cornwall, 312, 891, 1166 (?), 1694, 1954, 1984, 3290, 3583, 4754, 5220, 5586 ; for Devonshire, 699, 917, 1503, 3183, 3589, 3605, 3938, 4539, 4783 ; for Dorset, 26, 903, 3064 (?), 3566 ; 3606, 3701, 5658 ; for Wilts, 898, 1938, 3157, 3605, 4583 ; for Westmoreland, (? Dorset), 2007.

Broke, Robert, &c.—*cont.*

........., ..., in commission of array for Devonshire, 3688.

........., ..., grant to, 3171.

........., ..., signature, 3476, 4534.

........., "William" Willoughby, Lord Broke, 1166, 3064 (misnamed for Robert).

........., ..., [Lord Willoughby de ?], 4076.

........., or Brooke, Tho., of London, 5558; yeoman of the Chamber, 514, 3144; serjeant-at arms, 4044, 4047; purveyor for the armoury, 4671.

........., Wm., bailiff of Dover, 238.

Brokelond, Devon, 2080.

Broker, John, 1225.

........., ..., mayor of Canterbury, 4495.

Brokestede, in Essex, 4176.

Brokett, John, sen., of Hertfordshire, 1971, 3102, 5506, p. 906.

Brokett, Robt., 5723.

Brokwod, in Surrey, 385.

Bromefelde, lordship of, marches of Wales, 100, 512, 572, 691, 778, 823, 1567, 1682, 1768, 3920.

Bromewiche, Will., archer of Calais, 4476.

Bromewood, in Berks, 4670, 5627.

Bromley, Surrey, 1212.

Bromley, Geo., in commission for Gloucestershire, 1049, 1469, 1695, 3641, 3712, 3804, 4024, 4118, 4764, 5506, p. 906; for Herefordshire 1400, 1963, 3503, 3686, 5506, p. 907; for Salop, 918, 1981, 3071, 3715, 4394, 4827, 5506, p. 904; for Worcestershire, 1971, 3301, 3709, 4770, 5506, p. 903; for Wales, 955, 3055, 3289, 4198.

........., Thos., of Staffordshire, petty captain, 4253.

Bromsgrove, Worc., 155.

Bromysgrove, Hugh, 4614.

Bromyle, Thos., 3285.

Brommer, Rob., sub-prior of St. Mary's, Butteley, 233, 325.

Brommore, or Brymmore, Hants, 2080.

Brompton, Rob., of London, 4013.

Brooke, 1212. *See* Broke.

Brookesby, Leic., 4728.

........., Thos., in commission for Leicestershire, 656, 1094, 1425, 1971, 4706, 4783, 4812, 5506, p. 905.

........., ..., sheriff for Rutland, 3507, 4544, 5561.

........., ..., of London, 1372.

........., Wm., of Leicestershire, 656, 1094, 1425, 1971, 4706, 4783, 4812, 5506, p. 905.

Broome, Suffolk, 1666. *See* Berugham.

........., John and Christopher, 1163.

.... Nicholas, of Wodelows, Warw., 5640.

Broughton, or Browghton, 5146.

Broughton, Linc. dioc., John Broughton and Ric. Prykke, incs. of, 535.

........., Northt., 3470.

Broghton, ——, ship-master, 3981, 4377.

Broughton, Dorothy, wife of Robert, 913.

........., John, 5483; son of Sir Robert, 535, 913.

........., Katharine, wife of Robert, 913.

........., Sir Robert, 535, 913.

Bounchyll, Wm., 3882, p. 533.

Broussa, in Bithynia, 1659.

Brouwaigne, 4622.

Brown or Broun, ——, 1971.

........., ——, a Scotchman (?), 3412.

........., ——, master of the Great Bark, 3591, 3977, 4377.

........., mayor of Rochester, 3497.

........., Anth., captain, 3980.

........., Sir Anth., 64, 4570.

........., Christopher, of Lincolnshire, 5685.

........., ..., in commission for Lincolnshire, 266, 278, 657, 1120, 1169, 1170, 1171, 3342, 4358, 4860.

........., ..., sheriff of Rutland, 664.

........., ..., in debt to Henry VII., p. 434.

........., Edward, 5096.

........., Fras., of Lincolnshire, 3351, 4860.

........., Humph., in commissions of the peace for Essex and Northampton, 2045, 3967, 5658.

........., ..., of London, 5127.

........., John, 5095, 5450.

........., ..., son of Christopher, 5685.

........., ..., the King's printer, 2053, 4954, pp. 954 and 956.

........., ..., of Brikilsey, 3733.

........., ..., of Hampton, capt., 3979.

........., ..., shipmaster, 3979, 3980.

........., Sir Mathew, 777, 1155, 3496, 4291.

........., ..., in commission for Surrey, 1497, 1762, 3078, 3092, 4693, 4734, 5237, p. 905.

........., Miles, of Southampton, 817, 1767.

........., Nicholas, 1050.

........., ..., of Warwickshire, 282, 1387, 1468, 1971, 3364, p. 903.

........., Ralph, 1225.

........., Ric., 5712.

........., Rob., 3031, 4321, 4846.

........., ..., of Walcote, sen., 5096.

........., ..., jun., 5096.

........., Thos., of London, 235, 3406, 3407, 4643.

........., ..., alias Clerc, of New Salisbury, 1935.

........., ..., of Stewton, 3579.

........., Will., p. 435, 4913, 5400, 5780.

........., ..., of the Chapel Royal, 658, 3450.

........., ..., of Warwickshire, 282, 1024, 1387, 1468, 1971, 3364, p. 903.

........., ..., bailiff of Brayles, 1257.

........., ..., ..., inc. of Wenvo, Llandaff dioc., 4400.

........., ..., merchant of London, 3496, p. 432.

........., ..., mayor of London, 4553, 5111.

Brown or Broun—*cont.*

........., Will., alderman of London, 4699.

... ., ..., jun., 4526, 4732, 4892.

........., ..., mayor of the staple at Westminster, 271, 1024.

........., ..., in commission of the peace for Essex, 1713; for Herts, 1522.

........., Wistan, squire of the Body, grants to, 237, 438.

........., Sir Wistan (or Weston), knight of the Body, 5210, 5724, p. 972.

........., ..., grants to, 3143, 3852, 4907.

........., ..., captain in the war, 3591, 3977, 4020, p. 651, 4474, 5112, 5762.

........., ..., in commission of the peace for Essex, 3605, 3785, 3967, p. 907.

........., ..., in debt to the Crown, 5633.

Brownhill, Wm., 3359.

........., ..., ship of, 3321.

........., ..., ships taken by, 3751.

Brownyng, Henry, 5088.

Bruce. *See* Brewce.

Bruchsal, in Swabia, 4216, 4272.

Brudenell, Robert, justice of the Common Pleas, 69, 1378 ; of the King's Bench, 258, 4436, 5529, 5605.

........., ..., justice of the peace for Berks, 241, 885, 1393, 1481, 1732, 2095, 3640, 4341, 5166, 5684 ; for Bucks, 454, 943, 1379, 2045, 3219, 3310, 3522, 5166, p. 907 ; for Gloucestershire, 1049, 1469, 1695, 3641, 3712, 3804, 4024, 4118, 4764, p. 906 ; for Herefordshire, 646, 675, 1400, 1963, 3686, p. 907 ; for Leicestershire, 656, 1094, 1425, 1971, 4706, 4742, 4783, 4812, p. 905 ; for Lincolnshire, 78, 657, 1120, 1169, 1170, 1171, 3342, 3351, 4358, 4593, 4860, p. 906, 5691 ; for Northamptonshire, 732, 1708, 1971, 2045, 5658 ; for town of Oxford, 894 ; for Salop, 918, 1981, 3071, 3715, 4394, 4827, p. 904 ; for Staffordshire, 79, 713, 791, 886, 1770, pp. 903 and 905 ; for Suffolk, 1715, p. 904 ; for Worcestershire, 892, 1971, 3301, 3709, 4770, p.903 ; for Yorkshire, 5529, 5605. In special commission of the peace, 1380.

........., ..., justice of assize of gaol delivery, 19, 29, 71, 242, 294, 541, 1130, 1164, 1490, 1519, 1794, 1897, 2093, 3209, 3270, 3275, 3694, 3702, 3765, 3778, 4004, 4215, 4553, 4702, 5183.

........., ..., in commissions of sewers, 563, 1979, 3137.

........., ..., receiver of petitions in Parliament, 811.

...., ..., trier of petitions in Parliament, 2082.

........., ..., grant to, 4436.

........., ..., jun., serjeant-at-law, 5296.

........., ..., ..., as justice of Assize and gaol delivery, 1490, 2093, 3270, 3275, 3702, 4215, 4702, 5183.

Bruere, Sieur de, 4284.

Bruges, 117, 1413, 3678, 4008, 4057, 4068, 4154, 5554.

........., letters from, of Sampson, 5418, 5424, 5429, 5439, 5446, 5583, 5587, 5697.

........., ..., of Spinelly, 4960, 4982, 5006, 5588, 5591.

........., Bishop of Tournay at, 4960.

........., news from, 4091, 5030.

........., the resort of Scotch merchants, 773. 1826.

........., town of, letter from, 3737.

........., ..., chief officer of, 4284.

........., ..., baily of (Jean de Praet), 4331.

........., ..., greffier of, 4692.

........., wagoners of, 4526.

Bruges, ——, 4094.

........., John, 3946, 4581. *See* Brugges.

........., ..., son of Sir Giles, 3392.

........., Sir John, in Lord Lisle's retinue, 4653.

........., Sir Giles, 3392.

........., Roland, 1914.

........., Wm. de, 4516.

Brugge, John, sheriff of London, 4503.

........., Wm., 4770.

Brugges, John, of London, 105, 4729. *See* Bruges.

Bruyne, ——, 1812.

........., Jeff., 130.

Bruin, Katharine, 4248.

........., Th., 4248.

........., William, 4248.

Brunarde, 4526.

Brundisshe, Suffolk, 730.

Brungewodde chace, marches of Wales, 3532.

Brurton, Sir Randall. *See* Brereton.

Brunswick, Duke of, his dispute with Gueldres, 3446, 3489.

........., ..., forces raised for him, 3651.

........., ..., his assistance to England, 4296, 4319, 4328, 4343.

........., ..., his coming uncertain, 3500.

........., ..., his troops treat with the French 4322.

........., ..., sends ambassadors to Hen.VIII., p. 623, 5758.

........., two brothers Dukes of, 3471.

Bruses, in Middlesex, 4302.

Brussels, 3446, 3659, 3779, 3905, 3973, 4068, 4085, 4366, 4810, 5076, 5377, 5386, 5390, 5600.

.., ..., letters of English ambassadors from, 3226, 3248, 3258, 3271, 3276, 3291, 3296, 3302, 3306, 3314, 3328, 3331, 3334, 3335, 3340, 3353, 3362, 3363, 3367, 3370, 3376, 3377, 3381, 3385, 3460, 3463, 3469, 3481, 3489, 3499, 3500, 3514, 3525, 3915, 3950, 3951, 3962, 4077, 4091, 4163, 4164, 4165, 4273, 4280, 4296, 4319, 4322, 4326, 4328, 4343, 4355, 4359, 4361, 4364, 4366, 4725, 4796, 5155, 5171, 5192, 5207, 5208, 5263, 5290, 5292, 5299, 5327, 5341, 5403, 5404, 5467, 5539, 5657, 5675, 5676.

Brussels, other letters dated from, 3207, 3916, 3918, 3975, 4090, 4154, 4155, 4168, 4193, 4726, 4917, 5205, 5714.
........., treaty of London confirmed at, 5479.
........., an arras maker of, 800.
........., armourer of, p. 953.
" Brussels say," 5172.
Brusset, Anthoine, letter from, 4162.
Bruton, 3048, 3566, 4713, p. 904.
........., Wm., abbot of, 1819.
Brye, Lord, French prisoner, 4253.
Brykelsey. See Ships.
Brynne, Linc., 543.
Bryonnes, Pierre de, of Castile, 5565.
Bryscope (?), 5539.
Bryxsyn, Bp. of, 4069.
Bubwith, St. James's, Yorkshire, 1097.
Buchank, Leicestershire, 3096.
Buchberd, Ralph, of London, 578.
Buckby, Northampton, 1950.
Buckden, 3447.
Buckfast, Devon, 3060.
Buckholt, Hants, 998.
Buckhurst, or Godhurst, 734.
Buckingham, town of, 18.
........., Walter Giffard, first and second Earls, and Ermengard, Countess of (temp. Will. I. & II.), 3195.
........., Edw., Duke of, 765, 835, 1401, 4266.
........., high constable, 211.
........., ..., at Parliament, 811, 2082.
........., ..., summoned to Parliament, 5616.
........., ..., at marriage of Princess Mary, 5322.
........., ..., in the war, 3231, 3885, 4094, 4237, 4306, 4307, 4314.
........., ..., in debt to the Crown, 2044, 5633.
........., ..., in commissions of peace for Bucks, 454, 943, 1379, 2045, 3310, 3522, p. 907 ; Glouc., 930, 1049, 1469, 1695, 3712, 3804, 4024, 4118, p. 906; Heref., 646, 675, 1400, 3686, p. 907 ; Kent, 725, 906, 3428, 4663, 4847, 4927, p. 906; Salop, 918, 1981, 3715, 4394, p. 904 ; Somerset, 279, 287, 712, 3048, 3566, 3585, 3606, 3701, p. 904; Staff., 713, 791, 886, 1770, pp. 903 and 904 ; Surrey, 1427, 1762, 3078, 3092, 4693, 4734, 5237, p. 905 ; Warwick, 282, 1387, 1468, 1971, p. 903; Yorkshire, 455, 954, 1549, 5193, p. 907.
........., ..., grants to, 1156, 1157, 3574, 4183, 4228, 5289, 5293.
........., ..., signature of, 679, 3027.
........., Alianor, Duchess of, 5289.
........., See Bokenham.
Bukyngham, Geo., 1812.
Buckinghamshire, tenths and fifteenths in, 3441.
........., commissions of the peace for, 454, 645, 943, 1379, 2049, 3219, 3310, 3522, p. 907.
........., feodary in, 4711.

Buckinghamshire, escheator of, 12.
........., sheriff of, 664, 1316,1771, 1949, 3507, 3912, 4544, 5561.
Buckland. See Bukland.
Buckley, Ric., 1215.
........., Wm., of Allerton, 3031.
Buckmer, Greg., chief carpenter at Calais, 770.
Bucknahams, Suffolk, 947.
Bucknam, Wm., clk., 4770.
Bucknell, Northampton, 1231.
Buckton, Northumb., 3799.
Budbroke, alias Hampton-on-the-Hill, Warwick, 4301.
Budde, Tho., 1002.
Buddis, Francis, usher of the Chamber, 5484.
Budleigh. See Eastbudleigh, Westbudleigh.
Bugby, Long, 645.
Bugge, ——, of Dorset, excepted from the general pardon, 12.
Builth. See Beelthe.
Bukberde, Ralph, 795.
Bukilsey, John Brown of, 3733.
Buklande, Berks, 4205.
........., Bucks, 896.
........., Devonsh., 2080.
........., Hertfords., 1426.
........., St. John's, 1623.
........., Somerset, 1172, 1761.
Bulbek, Viscount, 4101.
Bulcombe, Wm., in commission for Oxford, 3546 ; as mayor, 894.
Bulduke. See Bois le Duc.
Bulkey, Agnes, 1911.
Bulkeley, Chas., 5646.
........., Robt., 5120.
........., ..., in commission of array for Hants, 1812.
........., Thos., 135, 4253.
Bulker, Wm., purser, pp. 954, 955, and 956.
Bull, John. See Woodhouse.
........., Ric., of Lynn, 5723.
........., Sir Stephen, captain, 3591, 3977, 4005, 4377, 4475, 4535, 5112, 5750, 5761.
........., ..., sent out with vessels, 5130.
........., Wm., of London, 949, 1675, 3519, 4260.
Bulland, in Berks, 174.
Bullen. See Boleyn.
Bulley, Wm. See Bull.
Bulmer, Sir Walter, 1725.
........., Sir Wm., 4460, 4523.
........., ..., in Scotland, 4457, 4518.
........., ..., in com. for Yorksh., 1549, 3219, 5244.
........., ..., in other commissions, 705, 1735, 1804, 3358, 5528.
........., ..., on sheriff-roll for Yorksh., 664, 1949, 4544, 5561.
........., ..., grant to, 4903.
........., ..., signature of, 4439.
Bulsterd. See Bustard.

Bulstrode, Edw., in com. for Bucks, 454, 943, 1379, 2045, 3219, 3310, 3522, p. 907.
.........., Walt., in com. for Oxford, 1470, 1745, 3015, 4559, 4809, p. 905.
.........., Wm., 784.
.........., ..., in com. for Bucks, 454, 943, 1379, 2045, 3219, 3310, 3522, p. 907.
.........., ..., on sheriff-roll for Bucks, 4544, 5561.
.........., ..., grant to, 290.
Bulwell, Notts, 4728.
Bumbill, 4296.
Bunbry, John, 1039, 1649.
Bunbury, Ric., of Staney, 4360.
Bunkers, in Lee. See Bankerds.
Bunowlte. See Benolt.
Buntyng, Wm., 4996.
Burbank, Wm., 5342, 5349, 5396, 5447.
.........., ..., executor of Bainbridge, 5301, 5333, 5334.
.........., ..., letter from, 5356, 5357.
Burden, Wm., 481.
Burdeos. See Bordeaux, Abp. of.
Burdit, John, in com. for Warwickshire, 282, 1387, 1468, 1971, 3364.
.........., captain, 3591.
Burdon, Rose, 4867.
Burford, in Salop, 3166.
.........., Baron of, captain, 4253.
Burford-on-the Wold, in Oxfordsh., 1088.
Burgavenny. See Abergavenny.
Burges, John, of London, 1675.
Burgeys, Th., of Hadlowe, 1780.
Burgh near Aylesham, Norf., 4254 (iii.)
Burgh, Anne, 804.
.........., Sir Edw., 804, 1472.
.........., ..., in com. for Linc., 3137, 5691.
.........., John of Bedyford, 4029.
.........., Ric., 4558.
.........., Tho., squire of the Body, 1205.
.........., ..., Marshal of Berwick, 3021.
.........., ..., in com. for Linc., 1171, 3137, 3342, 4358, 4593, 4860, 5691.
.........., or Burght, Tho., of Stowe, 1392, 4616.
.........., ..., ..., jun., 3515.
.........., ..., ..., jun., in com. for Linc., 1983, 3342, 4358, 4593, 4860, 1983.
.........., Sir Tho., 4902.
Burgham, Westmlnd., 1796.
Burghill, Ric., 3901.
Burght, Thos. See Burgh.
.........., Wm., 3579.
Burghton, in Glouc., 155.
Burgo, Andreas de, 924, 3077, 3499, 4078.
.........., ..., letter from, 4210.
.........., ..., secretary of 3335.
.........., ..., servant of, 3340.
Burgo Novo,' letter dated, 3874.
Burgos, 3207, pp. 395 and 396.
.........., intended council at, 3584.
.........., Ferdinand, purposes going to, 3593.

Burgos, Ferdinand at, 3614.
.........., letters dated from, 3081, 3352, 3638.
.........., commission dated from, 3327.
.........., Jno. Dewsbrooke assayer of, 4917.
.........., merchant of, 1859, 2047, 4578.
Burgoyne, John, of London, 3097.
.........., Tho., escheator of Kent, 5625.
.........., Wm., clk., 677.
Burgundians, 3385.
.........., in Henry VIII.'s service, 4429, 4534.
.........., dispute between the English and, p. 625.
.........., captain of the, p. 626.
.........., servants of Sir R. Wingfield, 5393.
Burgundy, 224, 924, 1826, p. 501, 4058, 4069, 4319, 4324, 4326, 4349, 4359, 4362, 4418, 4433, 4622, 4725, 5173, 5368.
.........., alliance of Scotland with, 841, 1245.
.........., expeditions against, p. 382, 3335, 3340, 3398, 4429.
.........., claims of France to, 4789.
.........., wine from, 628.
.........., Philip and Charles, Dukes of, 5729.
.........., Chancellor of, 3976, 5159.
.........., Marshal of, 4349.
.........., ..., master of his household, 4362.
.........., president of, p. 118.
.........., John Francis, Scottish consul in, 1411.
.........., John Glennet, treasurer of, 4509.
Burley, Hants, 4541.
.........., John, 3024.
Burman, John, Vicar of Asshby, 3442.
Burn, Yorkshire, 1805.
.........., John, sub-prior of Whitby Abbey, 4981.
Burnagylles hoys, p. 554.
Burnby, Thos., of Berking, 4176.
Burne, Linc. See Bourne.
Burnham, in Norfolk, 1956.
Burntone, Wm. de, 1009.
Burre, Tho., 1290.
Burstall, John. See Bristall.
Burston, John, of Gravesend, 12.
.........., Tho., 585.
Burth, Sir Edw., 1716.
Burthorp, Lincolnshire, 4695.
Burton, Staff., 1480.
.........., town of, 3542.
.... -Fery, John Grufith inc. of, 328.
.........., ..., Wm. Harris inc. of, 328.
..........-Annas, in Yorkshire, 3498.
..........-Latymer, in Northton, 1231, 3027.
Burton, David, gentleman of the chapel, 1844, 3110.
.........., Edm., 1243.
.........., Elizabeth, wife of John, 5402.
.........., John, 297, 1796, 2006, 4101, 5402.
.........., ..., prior of St. Frideswide's, Oxford, 3844, 4010.
.........., Richard, 3719.
.........., ..., in commission for Northt., 1708, 1971, 5658.

Burton, Richard, on sheriff-roll for Northt., 3507.
........., Robert, 266.
........., Thomas, 127.
Burwell, Wm., 1906, 4629.
........., ..., constable of the staple at Westminster, 271.
Bury St. Edmund's, 155, 1139, 3939.
........., gaol delivery for, 1939.
........., monastery of, 2067, 3990.
........., Barton near, 3758.
........., abbot of, 971, 1300, 4120, 4377, 5187.
........., ..., at Parliament, 811, 2082.
........., ..., summoned to Parliament, 5616.
........., ..., grant to, 4966.
........., ..., John Milford, 3947.
........., ..., Will. Codenham, 3833, 3947.
Bury, Edm., in commission for Oxford, 1216, 1470, 1745, 3015, 4809.
........., John, 1996.
........., in commission for Cambridge (town), 677, 3187, 4770, 4890.
........., Lewis, of Uggeborough, Devon, 946, 3057.
........., Philip, 627.
........., Sir Tho., 4237.
Busby, Yorkshire, 1114.
......, Wm., inc. of St. Mary, Hoo, 1545.
Bush, or Bushy, Edm., 313.
......, ..., in com. for Linc., 1120, 1169, 1979.
......, ..., grant to, 3604.
......, Sir Edm., on sheriff-roll for Notts and Derby, 1316.
......, Edw., 664.
......, Miles, 3977, 4377.
......, Sir Miles, 313.
......, ..., in com. for Linc., 1120, 1169.
......, ..., clk., 252.
......, Wm., 5611.
......, ..., yeoman of the pantry, 1552.
......, Sir Wm., 657.
Busheler, Wm., 4527.
Busheley, Gloucestershire, 3613.
Bushell, Rog., 1922.
Busheme, in Somersetshire, 155.
Bushy, Lord, slain, 4253.
Busshy, Mons. de, French prisoner, 4433. See Boisai.
Bushy, Herts., 1774, 3401.
Buskegage, in Sussex, 730, 5016.
Bussaiye, Mons., 5560.
Busset, extract from the letters of, 3269, 3325.
Bussichi, Dominic, 3026.
Bustard, John, or Bulsterd, in commission for Oxon, 766, 1216, 1470, 1745, 3015, 4559, 4809, p. 905.
Buston, towns of, Northumb., 1040, 5010.
Butcher. See Bocher.
Bute, rectory of, 3624.

Butler, the chief, of England, 778, 875, 1119, 1242, 5231.
Butler, ——, signature, 702.
........., Agnes, 396.
........., Alice, 1374.
........., Henry, 4151.
........., Humph., petty captain for Derby, 4253.
........., Jas., clk., of Worcester, 12.
........., John, 4071, 5509.
........., ..., a justice of common pleas, 6.
........., ..., in commission for Essex, 310, 1368, 1522, 3785, 3967, p. 907; Glamorgan and Morgan, 3960; Gloucester, 930, 1049, 1469, 1695, 3641, 3712, 3804, 4024, 4118, 4764; Hertfordshire, 309, 706, 1020, 1971, 3102, p. 906; Kent, 725, 906, 3605, 4663, 4927, p. 906; Middlesex, 3552, p. 905; Surrey, 1427, 1762, 3078, 3092, 4693, 4734, 5237, p. 905; Sussex, 281, 1509, 1713, 3428, 4804, 4847, p. 904.
........., ..., in commission of gaol delivery for Canterbury Castle, 3790; Guildford Castle, 3996; Home Circuit, 1101, 1763, 3275, 3694, 4279, 4702, 5186; Newgate, 541, 1519, 1897, 3765, 3778, 4553; Southwark Gaol, 4568; Warwick, 554; Winchester, 3198.
........., ..., justice of assize, Home Circuit, 294, 1164, 1490, 3295, 4339.
........., ..., in Parliament, 811, 2082.
........., or Boteler, Philip, son of John, 5509.
........., Ralph, 1374.
........., Robt., 4367.
........., Rog., of Ruggebisshop and Kirton, Devon, 1987.
........., Tho., 247.
........., Sir Thos., 5788.
........., Wm., 3284.
........., ..., of Sussex, excepted from the general pardon, 12.
........., ..., serjeant-at-arms, 500, 1692, 5211, 4375.
Butley, St. Mary's, prior of, 3497.
........., ..., Rob., prior of, 1639.
........., ..., Rob. Brommer, prior of, 233.
........., ..., Wm. Woddbridge, prior of, 235, 746.
........., ..., August. Rivers, prior of, 746.
Butrigario, Goleaz, a nuncio from the Pope, 4666.
Butt, doctor, 5734.
Buttercrambe, in Yorkshire, 191, 367, 721.
Butterworth, Roger, 4475.
Button, Jas., yeoman of the Crown, 1086.
........., Ric., yeoman of the Crown, 1086.
Buttry, Wm., 1212.
Butts, John, 1060.
Buxhale, in Suffolk, 947.
Byarne, Baron de. See Bierne.
Bybbesworth, Tho., 1282.
Bydenham, Linc., 3255.
Bydnell, John, 3553.
Byfeld, Berks, 647.

Byfleet, Hen. VIII. at, 5383.
Byhobya, in Spain, 3864, 3593.
Byker, Linc., 1430, 3239.
Bykkerston, Norfolk, 4680.
Bylby. *See* Beilby.
Bynasco, 3976.
Byng, John, of Wolverhampton, 4540.
Byris, 4997.
Byron, John, of Colwick, Notts, 3827.
........., Jno., in com. for Notts. 1735, 1798, 1804, 1964, 3092, 3494, 4776, 5225, p. 905.
........., ..., on sheriff-roll for Linc., 1949.
........., ..., in the war, 4377.
.... *See* Diron.
Byset, Manasser, sewer of Henry II., 5120.
Byssey (Bisley ?), hundred of Glouc., 1008.
Bythesee, Robt., 4564.
Bywell, barony of, 1040, 5010.

C.

Cabaravias, Marquis of, merchant of Burgos, 4578.
Cabra, Count di, p. 3.
Cachemay (Cacheman), Philip, forester of Dean, 316 ; keeper of the Gawle, 1233.
Cachemayde, Ric., page of the Wardrobe, 870, 1389, 3345 ; ranger of Dean, 1355.
Cackeley, Oxon, 5685.
Cadherne, Hen., 1579.
Cadington Major, St. Paul's, London, 5557.
Cadiov, Wm., 4489.
Cadiz, 3355, 5741.
Cadow fringe, 4954.
Caen-stone, 3517.
Caerleon, 53, 57, 58, 843, 1665, 3902, 5045 ; Castle, 983, 1894 ; Park, 487.
Caernarvon, 1686.
Caillau, Pierre, 4445.
Caithness, Bp. of, 3577 ; made Bp. of Aberdeen, 4556.
Calabria, Duke of, his treason, 3593.
Calais, 14, 38, 123, 220, 239, 318, 343, 345, 346, 381, 410, 507, 521, 523, 528, 545, 557, 609, 617, 626, 696, 770, 771, 778, 779, 851, 974, 978, 987, 989, 990, 1019, 1027, 1073, 1079, 1131, 1181, 1241, 1249, 1289, 1365, 1500, 1533, 1539, 1580, 1632, 1670, 1792, 1822, 1856, 1871, 1890, 1919, 1962, 1975, 2032, 2087, 3196, 3214, 3248, 3265, 3276, 3296, 3332, 3336, 3353, 3377, 3460, 3565, 3708, 3813, 3832, 3852, 3863, 3885, 3904, 3907, 3917, 3923, 3925, 3951, 3985, 4008, 4009, 4030, 4063, 4068, 4077, 4081, 4094, 4096, 4103, 4126, 4163, 4164, 4219, 4253, 4272, 4282, 4284, 4306, 4307, 4309, 4318, 4319, 4323, 4345, 4389, 4391, 4392,

Calais—*cont.*
4408, 4425, 4431, 4432, 4457, 4476, 4479, 4481, 4492, 4512, 4516, 4517, 4526, 4570, 4598, 4602, 4611, 4630, 4635, 4672, 4691, 4731, 4741, 4794, 4829, 4831, 4839, 4843, 4908, 4917, 4947, 4976, 5021, 5032, 5035, 5041, 5059, 5130, 5139, 5148, 5154, 5172, 5173, 5203, 5271, 5315, 5341, 5363, 5398, 5423, 5467, 5475, 5529, 5547, 5560, 5566, 5569, 5654, 5659, 5712, 5723.
........., castle of, 964 ; Fisher Street in, 666 ; Hemp Street in, 1134 ; Le Lede, 3923 ; Nettleby tenements, 1821 ; Newnhambridge, 3923, 4253 ; Roper Lane, 1134 ; Staple Inn, 1134 ; Tower of, 4977.
........., churches of St. Blaise, 562, 5421 ; of Everingham (als. Overingham), 1564, 2032, 3550 ; of Froyton, 5487 ; of St. Mary, 757, 4232 ; of St. Nichasius, 1742 ; of St. Nicholas, 37, p. 623, 5604 ; and St. Peter-le-Stones, 3923.
........., Carmelite friars of, 1189, 4635.
........., guild of Jesus and St. George at, 4635.
.... fortifications, p. 433.
........., letters dated at, 3744, 3948, 4021, 4057, 4079, 4080, 4100, 4331, 4345, 4584, 4665, 4743, 5151, 5154, 5270, 5753.
........., staple of, 977, 1009, 1015, 3832, 4381, 5231, 5363.
........., victualling of, 3871.
........., chief carpenter of. *See* Bukmer, Gregory.
........., clerk of the Council at. *See* Tuke, Brian.
........., comptroller of. *See* Wiltshire, Sir John.
........., Deputy of. *See* Talbot and Wingfield.
........., late Deputy of. *See* Nanfan, Richard.
........., lieut. of the castle of. *See* Carew, Richard ; Donne, John ; and Brown, Anth.
........., marshal of. *See* Meryng, Will. ; Wingfield, Rich. and Robt.
........., vice-marshal of. *See* Culpeper, Walter ; Lovelace, Richard ; Marland, Nich.
........., chief mason of. *See* Baker, John.
........., porter of. *See* Wotton, Rob. ; Carew Richard.
........., secretary of. *See* Bunoult, John, and Meautis, John.
........., chief smith there. *See* Dowsyn, John.
........., treasurer of. *See* Conwey, Hugh ; Turberville, John ; Knight, Richard ; and Browne, Wistan.
........., water-bailiff. *See* Cokeson, John.
Calcot, John, of Rutland, 664, 1316, 1949, 3507, 4544, 5561.
Calderon, ——, 5785.
Caldon, Staff., 4646.

Calege, Wm. de la, 4402.
Calehum, Jerome, p. 368.
Calendar, rectification of the, 5262.
Cales, Henry, 3978, 4630, 5494; yeoman of
　　the robes to Pr. Mary, 482, 5484,
　　yeoman of the Chamber, 1610.
Calfhill, Humph., 334.
Calgarth, Westmor., 479, 3764.
Calibut, Frans, in com. for Norf., 266, 884,
　　931, 1340, 1714, 1812, 1963, 3029,
　　3426, 3545, 5133, 5236.
Calkwell, Flanders, p. 623.
Calne, Wilts, 155.
Calole, Northumb., 1040, 5010.
Calonne, Oliver le, 4585.
Calthorp, or Calthrop, Joan, wife of Sir Philip,
　　1956.
........., Sir Philip, 1812, 1956, 5483.
Calthorp, Richard, captain, 3977, 4377, 5761.
Calvary, Mount, 5729.
Calveley, Jas., incumbent of Ruthyn, Bangor,
　　1811.
Calverley. See Carverley.
Calwodlegh, John, 304.
Cambaye, King of, 4173.
Camboys, 191.
Cambray, league of, 1458, 3370, 3387.
Cambridge, 12, 1212, 4160, 5197.
........., commissions for, 677, 749, 3187, 4770,
　　4890.
........., mayor and bailiffs of, 1771.
........., friars preachers of, 261 ; friars minors,
　　263.
Cambridge University, 251, 1948, 3013, 3535,
　　4427, 4428, 4448, 5122, 5732. Wolsey
　　proposed as chancellor of, 5121. Vice-
　　chancellor of ; see Fawne, John.
........., Christ's Coll., 236, 409.
........., College of St. Mary of Valence, called
　　Pembroke Hall, 3791.
........., St. John's College, 236, 406.
........., St. Katharine's Hall, 3729.
........., King's College, 1151, 5230.
........., letters from, 1404, 1842, 1847, 1849,
　　1925, 1998, 2001, 3012, 3495, 4447,
　　4528, 4576.
Cambridgeshire, commissions for, 266, 663,
　　1684, 3583, p. 904.
........., feodaries of Crown lands in, 4414.
........., escheator of, 3447, 3947, 4659.
........., sheriff of, 664, 1316, 1949, 3507, 3890,
　　4544, 5561.
........., swans in, 1743.
........., tenths and fifteenths, 3441.
Camby, John, 1901.
........., ——, of the Counter, 12.
Camden, Glouc., 5191.
........., Ric. 5419.
Camel Reginæ, Soms., 383.
Camfer, 3353, 3814, 4273, 4844, 5776.

Camme, Ric., 852.
Campagna, 1948.
Campbell, John, 3630.
Campion. See Champion.
Campis, Barnard de, 3458.
Campucci, John of Lucca, 3274, 3497, 4188,
　　4747, 5464.
Camynadus, Augustine, 1414.
Canaria, Bp. of, 8.
Candia, surrender of, 216.
Candie, ——, 4415.
Candish. See Cavendish.
Canfelde, Little, Essex, 729.
Canferre, ——, 3651.
Canford, Dorset, 337, 456, 1240, 3061.
Cannok, or Cank, Staff., 133, 687.
Cannon, John, 5708.
Canoase, Count Louis de, 5173.
Cantelowe, Norf., 5150.
Canterbury 1011, 1856, 1177, 1178, 1180,
　　1561, 1575, 1771, 3480, 3748, 3753,
　　3754, 3775, 4318, 4365, 4495, 5512.
........., commission for, 1225.
........., strangers in, 3998.
........., letters dated at, 4883, 5329, 5330, 5740.
.... Castle, 3790.
........., Tho. prior of, 1561.
........., St. Augustine, 1056, 1180 ; abbot of,
　　summoned to Parliament, 5616. See
　　Hampton, Thomas.
........., St. John, hosp. of, 1065.
........., Hen. [Deane], Abp. of, temp.Hen.VII.,
　　5355.
........., W. Abp. of. See Warham.
Canvas, account of, 4232.
Canynges, Th. of London, 5242.
Capel, Anth., 818.
........., Giles, captain, 1243, 1244, 1607, 3113,
　　3231.
........., Sir Giles, captain, 3980; knight at
　　Lille, 4468.
.... Sir Wm., 777, 815, 1243, 1244, 5001 ;
　　exempted from pardon, 12.
Capelier, Pierre, 4445.
Cappadocia, 1659.
Caps, 3784, 3794, 5144. Cap-makers, 2082,
　　4540. French and Milanese caps, 5239.
Captain of the Guard, 30.
Captains, wages of, 3117.
Car, Dandy, 782.
......., Jas., 936.
........., John, 98, 413, 922, 1178, 1654, 3189,
　　3266, 3818, 4205.
........., Sir John, 4852, 5477, 5483.
......., Ralph, 782.
......., Wm., 5090.
...... See Car and Kerr.
Caraffa, John Peter, Bp. of Chieti, afterwards
　　Pope Paul IV., sent to England, 4563,
　　4727, 5048.
Carbete, Thos., 5180.
Carcassonne, 3752.

Card playing, 3118, 5712.

Cardeston, Norf., 4254.

Cardewe, Cumb., 296.

Cardi, Misotto di, 1089.

Cardiff, 3960.

........., castle of, 110, 441, 625, 1113, 5786.

Cardigan, 225, 1597, 4436.

........., Tho., 927.

Cardinals, college of, 1878, 3837, 3838, 3876, 4725, 5464, 5661, 5662, 5665, 5706.

........., their avarice, 3780.

........., Schismatic, 3649, 4283.

Cardmaker, Wm., p. 553.

Caresbroke, 4220.

Caresfeld, Oxon, 4254.

Carethorp, Yorkshire, 4719, p. 907.

Caretto, Fabricius de, grand master of Rhodes, 3697, 4756, 5592 ; letters from, 4604, 4641.

Carew, Baron, 4477 ; master of the ordnance, p. 609.

........., Sir Edm., 3231 ; sheriff of Somerset, 1949 ; master of the ordnance, 4534 ; in com. for Devon, 699, 917, 1503, 1812, 3183, 3566, 3589, 3605, 3938 ; for Dorset, 26, 903, 2007, 3064, 3566, 3606, 3701, 4539 ; for Somerset, 287, 712, 3048, 3566, 3585, 3606, 3701.

........., ..., his death, 4315.

........., Edward Lord, slain before Terouenne, 4284, 4306.

........., Sir John, knt. of the Body, 1428, 3042 3580 ; grants to, 448, 465, 468, 1635, 3061 ; marshal of the household, 466, 1989.

........., ..., surveyor of the earldom of Devon, 1240 ; constable of Tyntagell, Cornw., 4739.

........., ..., in commission for Dorset, 26, 708, 903, 2007, 3064, 3566, 3606, 3701 ; for Somerset, 712, 3048, 3566, 3585, 3606, 3701 ; for Surrey, 1427, 1762, 3092.

........., ..., payment as wages, 4475.

........., ..., slain, 3388.

........., John, of Umberley, Devon, 5688.

........., ..., son and heir of John Carew, of Hakcombe, Devon, 1779, 3685.

........., ... of Lantony (?), sheriff of Cornwall, 1949, 5561.

........., (Care,) John, captain, 3979.

........., Mrs., p. 911.

........., Nich., 4570, 4642, 5016.

........., ..., son of Richard, 235.

........., Sir Nich., captain, p. 554.

........., Richard, 5053 ; money for Tournay, 5154.

........., Sir Ric., 14, 626, 1027, 1566, 1574, 1919, 2026, 3832, 4008, 4237, 4306, 4307, 4314, 4570, 4635 ; porter of Calais, 987 ; Lieut. of Calais, 1632 ; master of ordnance, 3885 ; his fees, 964 ; annuity, 1856 ; letter from, 1861 ; boards

Marquis Exeter, ib. ; in commission for Surrey, 1762, 3078, 3092, 4693, 4734, 5237, p. 905.

Carew, Th., captain, 3980, pp. 972, 973.

........., Wm., debtor to the King, 2044, 5633 ; sheriff of Devon, 4544 ; in commission, 5586.

Carguoncle, John, 3416.

Cariate, Count de, ambassador of Arragon at Venice, 3779, 4069, 4272, 4078.

Carill, John., 1965, serjeant-at-law, 5141 ; in commission, 173 ; for Sussex, 281, 1509, 3024, 3428, 4804, p. 904.

Carlangrick, in Teviotdale, 4522.

Carlile, John, a Scotchman dwelling at Canterbury, 3998.

Carlisle, 4523, 4573, 4869 ; letters from, 3326, 3751, 4403, 4497, 4518, 4520, 4522, 4825, 4951.

........., castle of, 1061, 1924, 3347.

........., John [Penny], Bp. of, 3075, 4455 ; indebted to Hen. VII., p. 435 ; summoned to Parliament, 5616 ; in commission for Cumb., 1048, p. 907.

........., Simon, prior of, 296.

Carlton, 3442 ; manor court at, 3434.

........., Notts, 1053.

........., York, 566, 4852. See also Charlton.

........., Anthony, ships prested by, 3978, 4630.

........., John, 1809.

Carmarthen, 960, 1100 ; archdeacon of, 143 ; attorney general, 225 ; chamberlain of S. Wales in, 1597.

Carmelianus, Peter de Brescia, 1652, 2001, 3473 ; in the "middle-ward" of the army going to France, 4314.

Carmelites, Estienne de Brixia, vicar-general of the order of, 3873.

Carmynowe, John, in commission for Devon, 1166, 1984 ; for Cornwall, 1694, 1812, 3290, 3583, 3605, 3938 ; sheriff of Cornwall, 4544.

........., Nic., in commission for Cornwall, 5220.

........., Tho., 493, 772, 889, 3867.

Carnaby, Tho., 664, 1316, 1949.

Carnesdale, Chesh., 4360.

Carnforth, Lanc., 3764.

Carnsewe, Wm., 1316, 1954, 1984 ; in commission for Cornw., 891, 1694, 1812, 3605, 3938, 4754, 5220, 5474, 5586 ; for Devon, 1166 ; sheriff of Cornwall, 1949.

Carpenter, John, p. 953.

Carpi, Count, 3777 ; letter from, 3780, 4364 ; sends to the Emperor for instructions, 4366 ; at Rome, 3325, 3377.

Carinthea, 5055.

Carr, border family. See Car and Ker.

Carrant, Wm. ; in commission for Soms., 287, 712, 3048, p. 904 ; on sheriff-roll, 664, 1316. See also Currant, Wm.

Carres, le, Staff., 4303.

Carriage, account for, 4232.
Carrik, Scotch herald, 3138, 3225, 3629.
Carrok, prebend of, 252.
Carroke, John, of Cumb., 3866.
Carroteth, 4825.
Carroz, Lud., of Vilaragud, 5341 ; his com-
  mission, 793, 1335; concludes a treaty,
  1059, 4511 ; confirms ditto, 1111 ; in
  England, 1209, 1622, 3638, p. 475 ;
  signs a treaty, 1980, 8797 ; commis-
  sioner to treat with Pope, 3327 ; proctor
  for Ferdinand, 3861 ; his acts on St.
  Mark's day, 4069.
Carson. See Curzon.
Carsyngton, Oxf., 4254.
Carter, Nich., 1787, 3065, 4894.
........, Tho., of Soms., 1172.
........, Wm., 858.
Carteret, Helier, of Jersey, 5071.
Carthagena, 8.
Cartier, John, notary, 5408.
Cartington, Wm., 856.
Cartlynge rectory, Norf., 1730.
Carton, Jason, 4445.
Carvael, Bernard, Cardinal at Florence, 4096;
  favored by Lewis XII., 3283 ; restored,
  4288.
Carvenal, John, chaplain to Margaret of
  Scotland, 3323, 3622.
Carver, John, in commission, 455, 954.
Carverly, Sir Walter, debtor to the King,
  2044.
Cary, Rob., in commission, 1316, 1812, 1949.
Caryll. See Carill.
Casale, in Montferrat, 11, 3976.
Casby, John, in commission, 3507.
Casius, treasurer, 5018.
Caspian sea, 1659.
Cassel, in Flanders, 4273, 4433.
Cassel, baily of. See Morbecke.
Cassel, provost of. See Theimseke, George de.
Cassery, Frances de ; woman to Queen Kath-
  arine, 4365. Perilous, ib.
Casay, Eliz, 5038.
......, John, 3132.
......, Leonard, son of John Cassy, 3132 ;
  called son of William, 3366.
........, Wm., of Compton, Glouc., 3047, 3366,
  5038.
Castaleo, town of, 3269.
Castel-Franco, in Italy, 1681.
Castell, ..., 4272. [? Baynard Castle.]
Castellensis, Polydore. See Vergil, Polydore.
Castello, Hadrian de. See Corneto.
Caster-Bardolph, Norf., 1800.
Casterton, Westmor., 3764.
Casthropp, Linc., 1958.
Castile, 8, 3355, 3593, 3662, 4058, 4069, 5637 ;
  government of, 490, 819 ; treaty between
  Castile, England, &c., 3415 ; ambassador
  of, at Rome, 5378 ; constable of, 8 ;
  letter from, 3584.
........, King of, 8 ; second son of, 8. See
  Philip, King of Castile.

Castile, King of, (Ferdinand ?), 3356.
........, Queen of. See Isabella ; Johanna ;
  Mary (sister of Hen. VIII.).
........, Infanta of, 8,
........, Prince of. See Charles.
........,......., his lieutenant. See Lusy, J. de.
........, Princess of. See Mary (sister of
  Hen. VIII.).
Castle, John, 3480 ; in commission for Hunts,
  905, 916, 1095, 4006, p. 906.
........, Leonard, in commission, 1812.
........, William, prior of Shrewsbury, 3093.
........-Bromwich, Warw., 1719.
........-Donington, Leic., 1642.
Castor, Linc., 496, 497, 4022.
Castra, Donna Katharina de, 5290.
Castre, Diego de, secr. to Charles Prince of
  Castile, 4328, 4789, 5208 ; treasurer to
  Margt. of Savoy, 4329.
Castres, Jacques de, Sovereign of Flanders,
  4396, 4789 ; sent to England, 5341, 5362,
  5398, 5404 ; instructions to, 5368 ;
  letter from, 5407.
Castro Nuovo, 3112, 3325.
........, John de, merchant, 4041.
Castyll, near St. Omer, 4526.
Catalenago, Fortuno de, 3496.
Catania, Bishop of. See Conichillo, Jacques de.
Caterall, Ralph, 4686.
........, Thos., 1173.
Catesby, ——, 4347.
........, Eliz., the King's kinswoman, 5401,
  5703.
........, Geo., 518, 3516.
........, John, of Olthorp, Northt., 953, 1692,
  5211 ; sheriff of Northt., 4544.
........, Sir Ric., 1472.
........, Th., 5688.
........, Wm., son and heir of George, 518,
  3516.
Catfoss, in Holderness, York, 807.
Catherston, Dorset, 1350.
Catherton, Alan de, 415.
........, Matilda, daughter of Alan de, 415.
Catesthorp, Glouc., 1374.
Cathom, 8031.
Cathorpe, Linc., 395, 1277, 1463, 4695.
Cauchie, house and seignory of, in the Bou-
  lonnois, 4162,
Caudebec, in Normandy, 5753.
Caudron, Bauduin, bailly de la Basterre, 4445.
Caulier, Jean, master of requests to the Prince
  of Castile, 5675 ; sent to England,
  4331 ; sent to France, 4622.
Cauwey, in Low Countries, p. 609.
Cavallari, Anth., merchant of Lucca, 1397,
  3124, 4097, 4957, 5135, 5726 ; deniza-
  tion, 684.
........, John, warden of the Hosp. of Beth-
  lehem, London, 3099, 4201 ; merchant
  of Lucca, 4344.

Cavalcanti, John, merchant of Florence, 1089, 3425, 3466, p. 433, 3746, 5329 ; his ship seized in Spain, 3452 ; denization, 3893 ; Gualterotti's factor in London, 5030 ; cargo of alum confiscated, 5099, 5358 ; pardon and release, 5221.

Cave, York, 319.

......, ..., canon of, 486.

......, John, 4071 ; in commission for Som., 1761.

Cavendish, captain, 3591, 3977.

........., Ric., in commission for Norf. and Suff., 3029 (bis), 3219, 3967, 4713, 5133 (bis), p. 904.

........., Sir Ric., 5580 ; captain in Lord Lisle's retinue, 4653 ; in commission for Norf., 3426, 3545 ; and Suff., 5133.

........., Th., 3480.

Cavesham, Oxon., 98, 203, 1117.

Cawode, York, p. 912.

Cawrdyn, Robt., petty captain, p. 608.

Cawston, Norf., 4254.

Caylway, John, 4544, 5180 ; in commission for Devon, 3534, 3566, 3589, 3938, 4783, 5220.

.... See also Kaylway.

Caynone, 5480.

Cecilia, Duchess of York, 140.

Cecil, Sir Will., indorsement by, 812.

.... (Cecille), David, 295, 1743, 4597.

Celle, Claude, ambassador of Prince of Castile in Spain, p. 69.

Cely, René de, taken prisoner at Battle of Spurs, 4402.

Cene, Thomas, with Marquis of Mantua, 5258.

Centuryon, Peter, merchant of Genoa, 1273, 1398.

Cerf, Jehan de, 3823.

Cerne, Dors., Monastery of, congé d'élire, 769 ; assent to their election, 822 ; restitution of temporalities, 1200.

........., abbot elect of, 1010.

........., Robert, abbot, and convent of, 3853.

Cerner, French captain, lost with his company at Brescia, p. 385.

Cerney, Sir George, 5789.

Cernyngton, Roger, 1854.

Cesson, Barth., merchant of London, 4863.

Ceve, Sir Thos., 5540

Chabo, Anth., denization, 5639.

Chaddesley, Corbett, Worc., 458, 4071.

Chadlington, Oxon., 1426, 1552, 1588.

Chadsey, rectory of, 1429.

Chadworth, Glouc., 1588, 3613.

Chaffer, Ric., of Calais, 1079, 5712.

Chairton, 1867.

Chakemore, 3297.

Chalcot, Walter, 5564.

Chaldeston, 3297.

Challeye, Lady, 1871.

Challon, in Champagne, 5781.

Chaloner or Chalner, ——, 1212.

........., John, 541, 1798, 1995.

........., Ranulph, 4532, 4808, 5277,

........., Richard, of Calais, 239, 3917.

........., Thomas, in commission, 3024.

Chalowe, 2080.

Chalvelegh, 2080.

Chambre, Dr. John, M.D., 427 3568, 5609, 5623, 5624 ; serj.-at-arms, 4194 ; incumbent of Myvot, 4521 ; marshal of King's minstrels, 5504 ; the King's chaplain and physician, 5607 ; bequest to, from the Countess of Richmond, 236.

........., Eliz. 5451.

........., Ranalde, in Bainbridge's service, 4691.

........., Robt., smith, 5595.

........., Thos., 4338, 5481.

Chamber, treasurer of the. See Heron, John.

Chamberlain, Lord. See Somerset, Charles Oxford, John E. of.

........., Great, of England. See Howard, Tho., second Duke of Norfolk.

.... of the Exch. See Exchequer.

Chamberlain, Edw., 3231, 4526, 4632 (iii.) ; in commission for Oxon, 766, 1216, 1470, 1745, 3015, 4559, 4809.

........., Sir Edw., 3202, p. 553, 4653, 5561 ; debts to the King, 2044 ; in commission for Oxf., p. 905.

........., Ralph, 3507 ; squire of the Body, 1464, 3042, 3825, 5442 ; in commission for Camb., 1684, 3583, p. 904 ; debts due to Hen. VII., 1639, 3497 ; at the marriage of Princess Mary, 5483.

........., Sir Ralph, made knight at Tournay, 4468 ; sheriff of Camb. and Hunts, 5561.

........., Wm., of London, 4081.

Chambrelains, tenements called, 734.

Chamley, Sir Ric., in commission, 1921.

Chamon, de, Great Master of Milan, 11.

Chamond, John, squire of the Body, 3404, 3938 ; in commission for Cornw., 312, 891, 1694, 1812, 1984, 3290, 3583, 3605, 4754, 5220, 5586 ; for Dev., 1166, 5220.

........., Rob., in commission for Cornw., 3938.

Champagne, 4349, 4355.

........., Peter de, squire of the Body, 820, 897, 1276, 1351, 1394, 1428 ; deceased, 1934.

Champaynes, manor of Cotton called, 1375, 3309.

Champion, Hugh, of London, sherman, 4026.

........., Piers. See Champagne, Peter de.

........., Walter, grocer of London, 1773 ; his ship, 3591, 4474.

........., Wm., grocer of London, 1608.

Champnes, John of Cheltenham, Glouc., 4972.

Chancellor, Lord (Warham), 1, 4, 10, 12, 14, 15, 16, 21, 23, 24, 55, 73, 86, 89, 112, 121, 155, 156, 183, 381, 461, 462, 463, 467, 473, 503, 511, 520, 521, 524, 547, 576, 585, 594, 595, 607, 639, 673, 679, 719, 747, 755, 783, 792, 815, 816, 848, 864, 869, 967, 974, 1029, 1030, 1068, 1096, 1098, 1115, 1148, 1152, 1155, 1236, 1272, 1320, 1378, 1450, 1535, 1537, 1629, 1806, 1820, 1848, 1850, 1853, 1929, 2003, 2004, 2024, 2029, 2054, 3013, 3050, 3052, 3054, 3056, 3117, 3142, 3193, 3200, 3298, 3332, 3540, 3609, 3656, 3730, 3747, 3750, 3802, 3803, 3887, 3895, 3949, 4026, 4053, 4218, 4239, 4392, 4404, 4492, 4546, 4551, 4619, 4639, 4696 (ii.), 4971, 4996, 5199, 5255, 5265, 5343, 5425 (ii.), 5456, 5460, 5561, 5615, 5652.

.... of the Exchequer. *See* Exchequer.

Chancery, Master in. *See* Hyggyn, Edw.; Rawson, Ric.; and Taylor, John.

........., Sealer in. *See* Hoxson, John; and Crompton, Sampson.

........., hanaper of, 778.

Chancery Lane, 5116.

Chanetier, David, 4445.

Chapel Royal, dean of, *see* Atwater, Wm.; ministers of, 3644, 4828; clerk of, 4937; gentlemen of, 139, 3127, 3450, 3454, 5397.

Chapel Brampton, Northt., 1109, 4436.

Chapman, Hugh, 749; in commission for Camb., 677, 3187, 4770, 4890.

........., Ric., 1871, 3371 (2), 5531.

........., Rob., 4232.

........., Wm., in commission, 3850.

Chard, Thos., prior of Montacute, 5199, 5240.

Chariago, Urtino de, master of the *Sancta Maria de Lakeyton*, p. 651.

Charing, Kent, 5481.

Charitun, Sir Gregory, 5789.

Charke, Ric. *See* Clark.

Charlecote, Warw., 255.

Charles VIII., King of France, 14, 318, 626, 1181, 1632, 1919, 4692, 5280, 5351; proposed match with Margaret, daughter of Maximilian, 5398.

Charles, Prince (sometimes called King) of Castile, Archduke of Austria, p. 114, p. 123, 922, 923, 3276, 3291, 3396, 3647, p. 502, 3805, 3862, 3915, 4058, 4091, 4154, 4182, 4273, 4349, 4362, 4622, 4829, 4844, 4864, 4917, 5155, 5159, 5173, 5263, 5292, 5323, 5363, 5377, 5468, 5675.

........., ..., proposed marriage with Princess Mary, sister of Henry VIII., 8, 27, 240, p. 68, 3823, 4296, 4328, 4416, 4502, 4508, 4512, 4560, 4579, 4725, 4727, 4789, 4932, 5203, 5274; his letter to Mary, 4606. Dispute as to the time and place of the marriage, 5018, 5029, 5104, 5126, 5139, 5152, 5290. Mary renounces her compact with him, 5282. Negotiations broken off, 5319, 5327, 5341, 5365, 5368, 5379, 5387, 5403, 5407, 5642.

Charles, Prince (sometimes called King) of Castile, Archduke of Austria, proposed marriage with Renée, daughter of France, 3752.

........., ..., war against Gueldres, 3226, 3437, 3446, 3616.

........., ..., treaty with the Swiss, 2091. Treaties with Pope, England, &c., 3398, 3460, 3469, 3603. At liberty to enter league against France, 4511. Treaties with France, 4924, 4952, 4985, 5398, 5410, 5466, 5479, 5511, 5559, 5698. Truces with France, Scotland, and Gueldres, 3839, 4818, 4875.

........., ..., ambassadors from Arragon with, 3664, 3805, 4267.

........., ..., injuries received by his subjects from England, 3353, 3813, 3836, 4319.

........., ..., soldiers levied in his dominions for England, 4736, 4794. His dominions invaded by France, 5208.

........., ..., Maximilian his guardian, 2091. Renounces tutelage of the Emperor, 4789, 4810. Count Egmont one of his governors, 5205.

........., ..., at Tournay, p. 626, 4642. Allows the inhabitants of Tournay to trade in his dominions, 4494.

........., ..., does not keep the feast of the Order of the Garter, 5006.

........., ..., Hint as to his being poisoned, 5076. His illness, 5171, 5207.

........., ..., letter to, from the Duke of Saxony, 5598.

........., ..., and his sisters, 3248, 3271, 5029, 5030.

........., ..., council of, 3306, 3362, 3398, 4331, 5006, 5104, 5263, 5418, 5675.

........., ..., president of. *See* Planis, Gerard de.

........., ..., master of requests of. *See* Caulier, Jean.

........., ..., master of ordnance of. *See* Termont.

........., ..., secretary of, 5539. *See* Barrados, Richard; and Castro, Diego de.

........., ..., treasurer of, 3651.

Charles, John, 4878, p. 958.

Charlton, Devon, 4071.

........., Glouc., 155.

........., Kent, 735.

........., Worc., 1959, 5361.

........., in Craven [York ?], 4022, 4347. *See* Carlton.

........., near Islepe, alias Charlton-upon-Otmore, Oxon., 3045.

........., Shene, 3045.

........., Edw., 4825.

........., Eliz., wife of Sir Richard, 1031, 1167.

........., Sir Ric., attainted, 137, 632, 826, 1031, 1167, 1196, 1253, 1259, 1269, 1336, 1472, 1508, 1523, 1528, 1554 1608, 3406, 3407, 3536, 3727, 3761, 4022, 4643, 4984.

........., Th. of Carroteth, 4825.

........., Wm., 4825.

Charlwood, Surrey, 155.

Charney, Berks, 241.

Charolois, in Burgundy, 4725, 5368.

Charon, Denis le, gunner of Lord Penys, 4328, 4329.

Charosbery, Conte de. See Shrewsbury.

Charran (or Sharant), a Spaniard, captain of a carack, 376; in the war against France, 4005, 4533.

Chartre, 5379.

........., Erard de, Bp. of, 5408. See Marck, Erard de la.

........., Vidame de, 5482.

Charwell, fishery in the, Oxon., 2055, 4785.

Chasteau, in France, 5368.

Chattesworth, Derby, 1372.

Chatton, Northumb., 3799.

Chaulcin, seigneury of, in Burgundy, 5368.

Chaumberleng, John le, 3510.

Chauncefeld, John, exempted from pardon, 12.

Chauncey, Edw., of Pevensey, exempted from pardon, 12. To levy subsidy in Pevensey, 4996.

........., Geo., of Pevensey, exempted from pardon, 12.

........., Gerrard, of London, fishmonger, 1884.

........., Henry, 1835; comptroller of Customs, 376.

Chauntrell, Rob., feodary of Crown lands for Northt., 4414.

Chavalary. See Cavallari.

Chaworth, George, 1852; sheriff of Notts. and Derby, 3507; in commission, 5225.

........., John, 4544.

........., Katharine, wife of George, 1852.

........., Margaret, wife of Thomas, 3713.

........., Thomas, son and heir of Sir William, 3713.

........., Sir William, 1852, 3713.

Chawton, Hants, 5247.

Cheam, Surrey, 1350.

Chebsey, Staff., 1308, 4347.

Chedburgh, Suff., 947.

Chedder, Soms., 4071.

Chedill, Wm., prior of St. Frideswide's, Oxford, 3753, 3844, 4010.

Chedsey, Somers., 448, 3061.

........., church of, 1442.

Chedworth, John, prior of Gloucester, 1159, 1291, 4950, 5075.

Chedyngstone, Kent. See Chiddingstone.

Cheham. See Cheam.

Chekeston, Devon, 304.

Chelsea, manor of, 3497.

Chelismore, Coventry, 4759.

Chelmsford, Essex, 3952, 3968.

Chelrey, 1867.

Cheltenham, Glouc., 4972.

Cheltenham, Ric., abbot of Tewkesbury, 579, 662.

........., Rob., of Tewkesbury Monastery, 579 (ii).

Chelworth, Wilts, 155.

Cheney or Cheyne, Eliz., wife of Sir Thomas, 4578.

........., Sir Francis, 4022, 4347; in the war against France, 3496, p. 952; cancel of his recognizance, 408; pardon, 433; grants, 567, 727, 1085, 1824; in commission for Wilts, 898, 1489, 1812, 1938; Hants, 904, 1388; Kent, 906; Dorset, 2007; deceased, 3043, 3176, 3190; his executors, 5633.

........., Sir John, 804; master of the horse, 902; standard-bearer, temp. Hen. VII., 340, 4636.

........., John, of Drayton, Bucks, cancel of his recognizance, 258; petty captain in the war against France, 4192; in commission to review the army, 3173; in commission for Bucks, 454, 943, 1379, 2045, 3219, 3310, 3522, p. 907.

........., Roger, bailiff of Sandgate and Hampnes, 1073; in the retinue at Calais, 4635.

........., Sir Thomas, 1491, 1724, 4587; in war against France, 4005, 4020; captain, 3231, 3977, p. 651, 5761 (iv.); sent to Italy, 4548; at Brussels, 5076; at the marriage of Princess Mary, 5483; indebted to Hen. VIII., 5633; annuity, 472; grant, 3043; in commission for Northamptonsh., 732, 1708, 1971; sheriff of Linc., 3507; on sheriff-roll, 5561.

........., Warburga, widow of Francis Cheney, her marriage with Wm. Compton, 3190.

........., Wm., grants, 76, 1336, 1647.

Chengton, Sussex, 1212.

Cheping Walden. See Chipping Walden.

Chepynglambarn. See Chipping Lambourn.

Chepstow, Wales, 765, 3949.

Cherebeare [Devon?], 2080. See also Churebere, Devon.

Chertsey, Surrey, 4229, 5047, 5383.

........., John Parker, abbot of, 498, 3538.

Chesham, Andrew, of London, tailor, 4170.

Chesholme, John, 4628.

Cheshunt, Herts, 276, 349, 4637.

Chesilden, John, 697.

Cheslaunder Wood, Hinton, Glouc., 5082.

Chesnes, Sieur de, at the marriage of Princess Mary, 5482.

Chesten (or Chestren) Wood, Kent, 1841, 3110.

Chester, 1086, 1912.

.... Castle, 3462.

........., abbot of, debt to Hen. VII., 776.

........., Bishop of, Geoffrey Blythe. See Coventry and Lichfield, Bishop of.

........., Dean of. See Yong, John.

........., county palatine of, 778, 1524, 1912; captains of, 4253; men of, defeated by the Scotch, 4441; commission of the peace for, 3289, 4198.

..........., ..., Chamberlain of. See Brereton, Sir Ralph.

..........., ..., Chancellor of; commission of array, 1735.

Chester, county palatine of, clerk of the Signet and King's Council in. *See* Knight, Hen.

........., ..., justices of, 956.

........., ..., overseers of. *See* Southwell, Sir Rob. and Westby, Barth.

........., diocese of. *See* Coventry and Lichfield.

........., earldom of, 1653.

........., ..., attorney-general of. *See* Esington, Wm., and Port, John.

........., Ralph Earl of, 1653.

Chesterfield, 178, 192, 1205, 3845 ; bailly of, p. 608.

Chesterford, Great, Essex, 5425.

Chesterton, Warw., 3720.

Chestren Wood. *See* Chesten Wood.

Chetwen, John, captain of co. Staff., p. 608.

........., Philip, captain of co. Staff., p. 609.

........., Wm., on sheriff-roll, 1949; sheriff of Staff., 5561 ; captain of co. Staff., p. 609.

Chetwynd, Salop, 1974.

Cheverell, Roger, of Stoke, Dorset, 5098; in commission for Dor. 26, 708, 903, 2007, 3064, 3566, 3606, 3701, 4710, 5658.

Chevington, Suff., 947.

Chichester, Sussex, 155, 5724 ; ships prested at, 3978.

.... Cathedral, 1212 ; chantry in, 1512.

........., monastery of, 60.

........., port of, 672.

........., staple of, 868.

........., mayor, sheriffs, and bailiffs of, 1771.

........., Robert [Sherburn], Bishop of, 393 ; summoned to Parliament, 5616.

........., John, of Devon, on sheriff-roll, 664, 5561 ; in commission, 1812 ; in the war against France, p. 652.

.... *See* Cicestre, Glouc.

Chiddington, Kent, chantry in church of, 5581.

Chieti (Theatinus), Bishop of. *See* Caraffa.

Chievres, William de Croy, Lord, 3805, 4273, 4932, 5292, 5398; his obligation, 1267 ; oath for observance of matrimonial treaty between England and Castile, 4508 (2); displeases the Emperor, 4789; strives to regain his ascendency, 5006 ; displeased at the marriage between Louis XII. and Princess Mary, 5327, 5387.

Chigwell, Essex, 734, 3761.

Childerley, Wm., turner of the Household, 1785, 4968.

Childmell, Tho., of Sturrey, 1065.

Childs-Wickham, Glouc., 5217.

Chillingham, Northumb., 201.

Chilton Foliatt, Wilts, church of, 862.

........., ..., manor of, 3134.

Chilwell, Notts, 1852.

Chilworth. *See* Chelworth.

Chimay, Charles de Croy, Prince of, 4273, 4932 ; letters from, 4801, 4956, 5165 ; his maitre d'hotel, 3651.

China, 4173.

Chinon, seigneury of, seized by France, 4725, 5368.

Chios, (Syo), Greece, 3030, 3458, 3854.

Chipchase, Northumb., 4825.

Chippenham, Wilts, 155.

........., Henry, of Hereford, 5575.

Chipping Walden, 4911.

........-Lambourn, Berks, 1683.

Chirk, castle of, marches of Wales, 101.

........., lordship of, 100, 955, 1768, 3920.

Chirkland, lordship of, marches of Wales, 100, 778, 955, 1768, 1898, 3920.

Chiselhurst, Kent, 1711.

Chishull, Little, Essex, 729.

Chitlampholt, Devon, 1996.

Chokes, fees of, 484.

Chokynhill, Worc., 3208.

Cholmeley, Eliz., wife of Sir Richard, 1016.

........., 235, 784.

........., (or Cholmondeley), Sir Ric. of Cottingham, York, 176, 192, 336 ; surety, 3600, 3866, 3889 ; in the Privy Council, p. 974; grants to, 229, 230, 254, 553, 1016, 5089 ; annuity, 1645, 3911 ; licence, 5091 ; in commission for York, 3072, 4568; for Kent, 3428, 3605, 4663, 4847, 4927, p. 906 ; for Middx., 3552, 4663, p. 905.

........., Roger, usher of the Chamber ; grants, 430, 431 ; in commission for York, 1735 (bis), 1804, 3358.

Cholmondeley, Hugh, 361.

Chorfi, Peter, merchant of Florence, 3965.

Chorley, Cheshire, 4748.

Chorlton, Will., petty captain of William Chorlton, p. 608.

Chowne, John, of Wrotham, Kent, 3969.

Chration, a French captain in Italy, 3335.

Christ's sponge, 3456.

Christchurch, Hants, lordship of, 1286, 3256 ; castle of, 1286.

........., prior of. *See* London.

Christiern, Prince of Denmark ; letters to, 1408, 3621, 3636.

Christmas, Peter, 3284.

........., Th., on sheriff-roll, 5561.

Christopher (Xpofle), 3417.

Christopherson, John, M.D. Denization, 3690.

Chrysoloras, Erasmus, lectures on the grammar of, 1900.

Chrysostomi Officium, sent by Erasmus to Colet, 4447.

Chudleigh, Jas., 917; in commission for Dev., 699, 1503, 1812, 3183, 3566, 3589, 3605, 3938, 4539, 4783, 5220; on sheriff-roll, 3507.

Chulmleigh, Devon, 1996, 2080 (bis).

Church, reformation of the, 1828.

Church, Wm., friar of Bermondsey, 1703.

Churebere, Devon, 1916. *See also* Cherebeare.

Chute, Devon, 1350.

Chyllyngham. *See* Chillingham.

Chylwell, *See* Chilwell, Notts.

Chymlight, Devon, 489, 1612.

Cibo, cardinal, 4725, 5208.

Cicero, mentioned by Erasmus, 3158.

Cicile, David. *See* Cecill.

Cicilia, John de, the King's trumpeter, 5092.

Cider, p. 397.

Cifuentes (Swyfentys), Count of, p. 4, p. 70.

Cilicia, 1659.

Cillysworthe, Suff., 4294, 4536.

Cinque Ports, 3393, 3394, 4083, 4492; subsidy levied in, 4996.

........., warden of, *See* Ponynges.

........., reversion of the wardenship of granted to Lord Abergavenny, 1296; to Edw. Guldeford, 1889,

Cintra. *See* Sincia.

Cipher, passage in, 368.

Circuits :—

    Home Circuit, commissions of gaol delivery for, 243, 1746, 3275, 3694, 4279, 4702, 5186. Justices of assize for, 294, 881, 1164, 1490, 3295, 4339.

    Midland Circuit, commissions of gaol delivery for, 173, 1101, 3003, 3282, 3694, 4148, 5143. Justices of assize for, 19, 294, 881, 1164, 3004, 3287, 3699, 4339, 4771, 5283.

    Norfolk Circuit, commissions of gaol delivery for, 1130, 3003, 3275, 3691, 4317, 5195. Justices of assize for, 19, 294, 1164, 1490, 1795, 2096, 3311, 3724, 4339, 4765, 5246.

    Northern Circuit, commissions of gaol delivery for, 173, 1130, 3275, 4279, 5195. Justices of assize for, 19, 294, 832, 1123, 1490, 2099, 3267, 3699, 4252, 4771, 5283.

    Oxford Circuit, commissions of gaol delivery for, 242, 1130, 3275, 3702, 4215, 4702, 5183. Justices of assize for, 29, 71, 294, 881, 1164, 1490, 2093, 3270.

    Western Circuit, commissions of gaol delivery for, 173, 1110, 3694, 4279. Justices of assize for, 72, 1741, 2089, 3282, 3295, 3724, 4339, 4765, 5246.

Cirencester (Sissetour or Cicestre), Glouc., 3949; monastery, 615.

........., John abbot of, in commission for Glouc., 930, 1049, 1469, 1695, 3641, 3712, 3804, 4024, 4118, 4764; summoned to Parliament, 5616.

........., (Ciscetur), Rob., of Malmesbury Monastery, 1183.

Cisar, Cumb., 4767.

Ciscetur, Rob. *See* Cirencester.

Cisterlowe, Wales, 51.

Citadello, Anthony de, merchant of Lucca, 3898.

Ciudad Rodrigo, Bishop of, p. 3.

Civile, letter dated from, 1726.

Civita, Bishop of, papal ambassador in England, 4598.

Clapbord and clappold, used in making barrels, 3796, 3888, 3894.

Clapham, Surrey, 1391, 1703.

Clapham, Christ., of Berwick, 178, p. 436, 4328; porter of Berwick, 12; in commission, 3553; on sheriff-roll, 3507; sheriff of Northumb., 4544; feodary of Crown lands, 5692.

Clare, Suff., 36, 155, 222, 5137.

........., Ric. de, formerly Earl of Gloucester and Hertford, 3195.

Claredon, Warw., 1499, 4337.

Clarence, George Duke of, 1043, 1774, 1778, 3401, 3761; his son Edward, 1778, 3761.

Clarencieux King-at-Arms. *See* Machado, Roger; and Benolt, Thomas.

Clarendon Park, 158, 998.

Clarethall, Essex, 155.

Clarevaux, Eliz., daughter of John, 5264.

........., John, 5264.

Clark (or Clerk), Ric., of Horncastle, Linc., 5039; in commission for Linc., 1171, 1496, 3342, 4358, 4593, 4860.

........., Wm., customer of Dover, 538; of Sandwich, p. 435; in commission for Heref., 675, 1400, 1914, 1963, 3503, 3686.

........., ..., of London, armorer, 4866.

.... *See also* Clerk.

Clarkson, Wm., of the abbey of Whitby, 4720.

........., ..., in commission for Notts, 4776, 5183, 5225, p. 905.

Clarvys, Ric., 3572.

Claude, wife of the Dauphin of France, 5379.

Clavenna, p. 368.

Claverham, Sussex, 612.

Clavering, Essex, 1492, 4176.

........., Rob., in commission, 3553, 5506.

Claverynges, lands called, in Edelmeton, Middx., 1031, 1167.

Claxton, Norf., 1343, 1629, 4254.

Claydon, Bucks, 155.

........., Middle, Bucks, 5514.

Claymond, John, president of St. Mary Magdalene College, Oxford, 4772.

Clayton, William, 2006.

Clack, John. *See* Clerk.

Clee ....., Mons. de la, a French captain slain at Milan, 4280.

Cleffort, John. *See* Clifford.

Clegge, Hamlet or Hammet, 877, 4382; servant of the Queen, 3990; gentleman-waiter upon the Queen, 5400.

Clement, John, spear at Calais, 1838.

........., John le, notary, 4584.

Clement, Richard, 1386.

Cleobury, Salop, 334.

Clere, Sir Rob. (sometimes erroneously Clerc), 1756, 1757 ; in commission for Norf., 1340, 1714, 1812, 1963, 3029, 3426, 3545 ; in the war against France, p. 651.

........, Thomas, petty captain in the war against France, p. 553.

Cleret, Jacotin, 4445.

Clefrayi, Michael de, 4915.

Clergy, contributions of the, given to Hen. VIII., 5331.

Clerk, ——, master of a ship, p. 651.

......, Adam, 196.

......, Alan, 415.

......, Geo., in commission, 4558.

......, John, 235, 3845, 4223 ; of Wrotham, Kent, 3969 ; searcher in Calais, 1580 ; master of the Trinity, 3591, 3977 ; master of the Mary Rose, p. 954.

......, ..., servant of Bainbridge, 5365, 5465.

......, Richard, of London, fishmonger, 5375.

......, Roger, in commission, 1225.

......, ..., prebendary in the collegiate church of Warwick, 5204.

......, Thos., in commission, 3072 ; in the war against France, 5723.

......, Wm., prebendary in the collegiate church of Warwick, 5204.

...... See also Clark.

Clerkson. See Clarkson.

Clermont, in France, 5649.

........, René de, vice-admiral of France, p. 609, 4284, 4710, 4725, 5523 ; taken prisoner at the battle of Spurs, 4402, 4431 ; his ransom, 4831, 5192.

Cleveland, archdeaconry of, 780.

Cleves, duchy of, 1505, 3204, 3340, 4328, 4906.

........, bastard of, p. 326, 4935.

........, Duke of, 4924.

Cleves and Juliers, John Duke of, 5746.

Cleygate, Surrey, 4022, 4301, 4347.

Cliborn, Thos., indebted to Hen. VII., p. 434.

Cliff, in the forest of Rockingham, Northt., 1641.

......, John, clerk, chaplain of Norton, 1620.

......, ..., sub-prior of Abingdon, 2070.

......, Wm., clerk, 5242.

Clifford, Wales, 298, 4226, 4837.

........, Westmoreland and Vesey, Henry Lord, 4556 ; indebted to Hen. VII., p. 434 ; summoned to Parliament, 5616 ; grant, 1796 ; in commission, 1735, 1798, 1804 (bis), 1995, 3177, 3358, 4015, 5166 ; sheriff of Westmoreland, 1179, 1949, 4439, 5561.

........, Anne, wife of James, 3843.

Clifford, Anth., in commission, 3703.

........, Charles, captain of the Baptist of Calais, p. 652, 5761.

........, Florence Lady, wife of Henry Lord, 1796.

........, Sir Henry, of Craven, York., 566, 3827, 4940 ; in the King's retinue, 4307 ; grant, 1043 ; in commission, 3552.

........, James, 3843.

........, John, governor of the English merchants in Flanders, 4054, 5059, 5723.

........, Lewis, 4543 ; in commission, 725, 906, 3428, 3605, 4663.

........, Mabel, intended wife of Wm. Fitzwilliam, 4308.

........, Robert, squire of the Body, 3411 ; knight, 3149, p. 436.

........, Thomas, of Aspeden, Herts, 3827, 4176, 4940 ; son of Sir Robert, p. 436 ; in commission, 1971, 3102 ; on sheriff-roll, 4544.

Clifton, Derby, 4781.

........, Worc., 155.

........, North, Notts, 1129, 1148, 1344.

........, (or Cliston), Robert, in commission for Notts, 1514, 1735 (bis), 1798, 1964, 3092, 3494, 4776, 5225, p. 905 ; for Yorksh., 5166 ; for Devon, 5220 ; indebted to the King, 2044.

Clifton, Sir Robert, in the war against France, p. 652 ; in commission, 1804.

.... See also Cliston.

Clinton, Sir Thos. ; at the marriage of Princess Mary, 5483.

.... Wm., in commission for Heref., 646, 675, 1400, 1963, 3686.

.... and Say, Anne Lady, wife of John Lord, 1965.

...., John Lord, 1965, summoned to Parliament, 5616 ; in commission for Kent, 725, 906, 3428, 3605, 3790, 4663, 4847, 4927, p. 906 ; for Warw., 1971, 3364, p. 903.

Clise Antron, Cornw., 3436.

Clisston, Notts, 1633, 1809, 4694.

.... Shrogges, [Notts,] 1899.

Cliston, Constantine, son of John, 3280.

........, Eliz., wife of John, 3280.

........, John, 3820.

........, Wm., chaplain, 5122, 5515.

.... See also Clifton.

Clist Honiton, Devon, 2080.

Clog, John, master of the Peter, 3591, p. 550, p. 651 ; master of the Barbara, 3979 ; yeoman of the Crown, 5653.

Clompton, Thos., 4014.

Clonne, South Wales, 1583.

........, Maurice, yeoman of the Crown, 514.

Clopham. See Clapham.

Clopton, Francis, captain of the Nicholas Darnell, 3980.
........., Hugh, merchant of London, 1247, 3454, 3700.
........., Sir Wm., in commission for Suff., 280, 676, 1121, 1153, 1715, 3029, 3219, 3967, 4713, 5133, p. 904.
.... Hall, Suffolk, 730.
Cloths, 3201, 3458, 3467, 3680.
........., broad, 3717.
........., of gold, 3577.
........., of gold and silver, act concerning, 3502.
.... of Normandy and Brittany, 3517.
.... of silk and gold, 4260.
.... unshorn, act concerning, 2082; enforced, 5008.
........., white, act concerning, 4848.
........., woollen, 3700, 4881, 5224; act concerning, 2082.
........., weavers of, at York, 1920.
.... See also Merchandize.
Cluny, House of Charity of, 3448.
........., Abbot of, 3944.
Coal, sea, brought to Chester, 1912.
Cobbe, George, collector of subsidy at Romney, 4996.
Cobberley, Glouc., 3382.
Cobbetonheis, Devon, 2080.
Cobham, Kent, 1711.
........., [Surrey], 5383.
........., College of, 3215.
........., George, captain of the George of Fowey, 3980; servant of Garter king-at-arms, 5483.
........., John Broke Lord, in commission, 725, 906. His death, 3215, 3228.
........., Thomas Broke, Lord, livery of lands, 3228; in the war against France, 4070, p. 608; made knight at Tournay, 4468; in the service of Mary Queen of France, 5484; summoned to Parliament, 5616; indebted to Hen. VIII., 5633; in commission, p. 906.
Cobhams, manor of, 3761.
Coblentz (Covalence), in Germany, 4328, 4333.
Cock, Wm., of Barton, 3758.
Cockburn, Edw., merchant of Scotland, 3627.
........., Geo., 842.
........., John, 842.
........., Sir Wm., of Langton, 5090.
Cockley, Suff., 485.
Code, Ric., in commission, 1812; nominated sheriff of Cornwall, 5561, 5562.
Codenham, Wm., abbot of Bury St. Edmunds, 3947.
Codnor, Derby, p. 608.
Codreth, Herts., 5093.
Codrington, Edw., 1854.
........., John, of Malmesbury Monastery, 852.
Codrington, Ric., of Newton, Cornwall, 4988.
    See also Coriton, Ric.

Cofferer, Mr., 5723.
Coffin, Ric., grant, 3120; sheriff of Devon, 1316; in commission, 699, 917, 3589, 3605, 3938, 4539, 4783, 5220, 5456.
Cogger, Wm., of Senok, Kent, 1707.
Cogges, Oxon., 1426.
Coggeshall. See Cokkeshall.
Coghton, Warw. See Coughton.
Coimbra, Duchess of, 3377.
Coin, Acts concerning, 811, 814, 2082.
........., in the Tower of London, 82.
........., assay of English and Flemish, 4917.
Coinage, gold and silver, 3865.
Cokayn, Edm., 5593.
........., Humph., son of Edm., 5593.
........., Rob., petty captain, p. 608.
........., Thos., of Ashburn, Derby, 606, 926; in commission, p. 907.
........., Sir Thos., 4781; captain, p. 608; on sheriff-roll, 5561.
Coke, the Queen's servant, 4019.
......, Edw., of Doncaster, inn-holder, 3939.
......, John, mayor of Gloucester, 3694.
......, Philip, son of Sir Thos., 4659.
......, Ric., in Lord Lisle's retinue, p. 722.
......, Thos., in commission 3792. See also Cook.
......, Sir Thos., 4659.
......, Wm., in commission, 3024; captain of the Sweepstake, p. 553, p. 812. See also Cook.
......, ..., of Westminster, 3465.
Cokeden, Dorset, 456, 3061.
Cokeham, Berks, 155, 498.
Coker, West. See Westcoker.
Cokerell, James, DD., vicar of Hull, 4961.
Cokerellys, Essex, 3284.
Cokeson. See Cookson.
Coket, John, 1666; searcher at Hull, 4961.
Cokke, Thos., 4367.
Cokkes, Hen. abbot of St. James, Northampt., 568.
........., John, 912.
........., ..., son of John, 912.
........., Wm., 3847.
Cokkeshall, monastery of, 3127.
Coklawe, 5090.
Coksedie, Edm., 1270.
Cokwood, 3978.
Colam, Midd., 5255.
Coland, Derby, 5574.
Colart, letter to, 5164.
........., Johannes de 5269.
Colas, John, of Bristol, 1050.
Colaton-Rawleigh, Devon, 946.
Colbrand, Geo., purveyor, 3250, 3871.
Colchester, Essex, 34, 735, 1282, 1331, 1570, 2098, 4659.
........., castle of, 5136.
......,......, commission of gaol delivery for, 3464.

Colchester, abbot of St. John's, 4101; summoned to Parliament, 5616.

........., Rob., monk of Aulme, 821.

Colcok, Edw., 4067.

Colcombe, als. Columton, Devon, 502, 1600. 2080.

Cold Ashton, Glouc., 1287.

Coldhigham, church of, 1586.

Coldingham, 4951.

........., priory of, 774, 4502, 4556, 4627.

Cold Kennington, 92.

Coldstream, Berwick, 3577.

Cole, John, 3429.

......, ..., of Slade, in commission for Devon, 3534, 3566, 3589, 3605, 3938, 4539, 4783, 5220.

......, ..., clerk, 1953, 3853.

......., Wm., in commission, 3694.

Colehouse, a tenement called, 726.

Colman, John, in commission for Kent, p. 906.

........., Thos., letter from, 5705.

........., Wm., 1002.

Colemere, Hants, 207, 4564.

Colepeper. See Culpepper.

Colet, Sir Hen., alderman of London, 1933.

......, John, D.D., Dean of St. Paul's, 1076, 1652, 1933, 1997, 2013, 3012, 3535; son of Sir Henry Colet, 1933; his will, ib.; guardian of Jerome, son of Edm. Dudley, 1212; oration before convocation, 2090; licences to, 3900, 4659; grants to, 5206, 5427; letter from, 4448; letters to, 1847, 1882, 3158, 3495, 4447, 4528.

Colfeld, 3100.

.........-walke, Warw., 3559.

Coliford, [Devon?], 2080.

........., John, of the guild of Tanners, Barnstaple, 3272.

Colins, Launcelot, treasurer of York, 5602.

........., (or Colin), Wm., in commission for Camb., 3583, 4770, 4890, p. 904.

Colintree, [Northt.?], 4656.

Coliweston, Northt., 307, 551, 645.

Coll, Thos., master of the Nicholas of Hampton, p. 651.

Colla, John, 3340, (2); Maximilian's ambassador in France, 4725; in England, 5057, 5058, 5173, 5203, 5207, 5320; letter from, 5173.

Collector, the papal, in England, 5156, 5332, 5464; Ammonius, appointed in place of Cardinal Hadrian de Corneto, 5457, 5458, 5538, 5651, 5663; efforts made for the Cardinal's restoration, 5661, 5662, 5665, 5666, 5671, 5672, 5702, 5706; Polydore Vergil, archdeacon of Wells, recommended to be sub-collector, 5665, 5666, 5671, 5672, 5702, 5706.

Colencourt, Jaques de, 3654,

Collett, Peter, of Normandy, 5303.

Colleyn. See Cologne.

Collier, Wm., incumbent of Abbotley, 5669.

Collingwood, Ralph, dean of St. Mary's, Warwick, 1202.

........., Robt., on sheriff-roll, 4544, 5561.

Collumpton (Colump John), Devon, 627, 2080.

Colne, isle of, 1962.

......, priory of, 4101.

Colneywake, Essex, 893, 4436.

Cologne, in Germany, 3340, 3651, 4362, 4526 (iii.); diet at, 3457, 3471, 4282; Electors at, 3335; Emperor at, 3306, 3331, 3335, 3361, 3370, 3377, 3471; letters dated at, 3526, 3603 (3), 4362.

........., convents of the Observant Friars in, 4871.

........., Archbishop of, 4563.

Colonna, the, 3377, 3780.

........., Fabricius, p. 383, 4276.

........., Marc. Ant., p. 384, note.

........., Mutius, p. 367.

........., Prosper, 3341, 4210, 4283, 4371, 5677, 5686.

Colowe, Wm., 1270.

Colpyn, John, 4476.

Colquhoun. See Culquhone.

Colrigge and Colrugge, Devon, 597, 860, 1321.

Colsell, of Lanc., exempted from pardon, 12.

Colshill, Warwick, 63, 1299, 3239.

Colt, John, 1132.

......, Thos., 5242.

Colton, Norfolk, 4680.

Columbell, Humph., of Bassethewses, Leic., 1372.

Colverhous, lands called, in Northmundam, Sussex, 1965.

Colvyle, Hen., escheator of Essex and Herts, 4659.

Colwell, Northumberland, 1040, 5010.

Colwike, Notts, 3827, 4940.

Colyton (Coleton), 2080; ships prested at, 3978.

Comartyn, Devon, 332.

Comarys, Marquis de, p. 615.

Combe, Dorset, 4733.

........., Kent, 1711.

........., John, 1302.

........., Sir John, 5789.

Comberworth, church of, Linc., 3547.

Combes, Tho., 804.

Combworth, 4022.

Comekillyone, commendatory of, 1112.

Comersale, Wm., 353.

Commendams, decree touching, 4718.

Commissions of the Peace. See Peace, commissions of.

.... of Array. See Array, commissions of.

Common House, the King's, 847.

Commons, House of, 5725.

Common Pleas, 702, 961, 4316.

........., chief justice of. See Rede, Sir Rob.

........., justices of, 4, 6, 70, 73, 1116, 1480, 3958, 5134, 5646.

........., chirographer of the, 205.

........., clerk of the estreats of the, 5510.

........., keeper of writs and rolls of the, 125.

Como, 3269; letter dated from, 4172.

Compaynes, in Cotton, Suffolk, 1375.

Compiennes, in France, 3678.

Compton, [Glouc. ?], 3047.

........., Wilts, 155.

.... See Westcompton.

........., Haloweys in, Stafford, 4592.

........., Fenny (Fynecompton), Warwick, 4022.

........., Long, Warwick, 5255.

........., New, Berks, 1426.

Compton, Mr., in the war against France, 4237, 5757; his ship, 3857, 4005, 4074.

........., John, of Salisbury, 3205.

........., ..., of Copeland, Cumb., 4944.

........., Thos., p. 435; groom of the Chamber, 1677, 3390, 5715.

........., Wm., 235, 1348, 5180; groom of the Chamber, 144, 643, 756; groom of the Stole, 992, 1138, 1257, 1395; made knight, 4468; Act for, 2082; his receiver, 4150, 5679; chancellor of Ireland, 4542; in the war against France, 3885, 4089, 4222, 4306, 4307, 4314, 5132, 5191, 5217; grants, 144, 643, 756, 992, 1138, 1257, 1385, 1395, 1426, 1501, 1588, 1744, 1936, 1961, 3001, 3027, 3061, 3190, 3301, 3364, 3704, 3761, 4301, 4302, 4521, 4530, 4541, 4613, 4651, 4712, 4904, 4907, 4946, 5206, 5255, 5709; sheriff of Hants, 3507, 5127; sheriff of Soms. and Dors., 4544; in commission, 1971, 2045, 3102, 3701, 3709, 3745, 4706, 4770, 4783, 4812, 5291, pp. 903, 905 and 906, 5658.

.... See also Conton.

Computus, — manorial accounts, 534, 3442. For other accounts, see Butlerage, &c.

Cona, Robt., 5255.

Conclave, letter from the, to Hen. VIII., 4354.

Concordia, castle of, 3269.

........., taken by the French, 1676.

Concressault, Lord of, 4210.

Condover, Salop. See Cundour.

Conesholme, church of, Linc. dioc., 532.

Congston, Warw., 1350.

Conichillo, Jacques de, Bp. of Catania, chancellor of Ferdinand, 3766, 3807; ratifies truce with France, 3839, 4818.

Coningsby, ——, in the Privy Council, 702.

........., Humph., 811, 1164, 2082, 4206, 4208, 5255; justice of the King's Bench, 73; justice of assize, 19, 294, 832, 881, 3004, 3287, 3699, 4339, 4771, 5283; serjeant-at-law, 5296; in commission, 309, 455, 541, 657, 706, 810, 892, 918, 954, 1020, 1048, 1101, 1120, 1169, 1170, 1171, 1519, 1549, 1550, 1897, 1971, 1981, 2009, 3003, 3048, 3071, 3072, 3092, 3102, 3219, 3282, 3301, 3342, 3351, 3364, 3494, 3552, 3694, 3709, 3715, 3765, 3778, 4148, 4358, 4394, 4553, 4593, 4663, 4706, 4719, 4742, 4770, 4776, 4783, 4812, 4827, 4860, 5143, 5186, 5193, 5225, 5244, pp. 903-907, 5658.

Coningsby, Sir Humph., in commission, 173, 1425, 1468, p. 907.

........., William, in commission for Herts, 309, 706, 1020, 1971, 3102, 5133.

Conington, Rob., p. 435.

Conisburgh, York, 178, 192, 1205, 2022, 3845.

Conisbury, Somers., 4753.

Connee, Jacques, 3654.

Consaloveris, John Baptista de, merchant of Milan, p. 952.

De Conscribendis Epistolis of Erasmus, 5732.

Considew, Wm., grocer of London, 1773.

Consistory at Rome, the, 4217, 4288, 4455, 4747.

.... Court of the Bp. of London, 1363.

Constable, High, of England, Edw. Duke of Buckingham, 211.

Constable, John, treasurer of Lincoln Cathedral, 3515; LL.D., and incumbent of Fulbeke, Linc. dioc., 5062.

........., ..., of Fleynburgh, York, 3827, 4940.

........., Sir John, on sheriff-roll, 1316; sheriff of Yorkshire, 1949; in the war with Scotland, 4375; in commission, 455, 954, 1550, 1735, 1799, 3358.

........., Marmaduke, of Everingham, 273, 5655.

........., Sir Marmaduke, 954, 1377; commissioner to receive the oath of James IV. to the treaty with Hen. VIII., 467, 488, 548, 714; commissioner to treat with Scotland, 1066; signs the challenge to the King of Scots before the battle of Flodden, 4439; sheriff of Yorkshire, 664, 1392; in commission, 273, 455, 1735, 1799, 3072, 3358, 4719.

........., Sir Marmaduke, jun., sheriff of Linc., 4544.

........., Philip, 3072.

........., Ralph, son of Thomas, 807.

........., Sir Robert, in the Spanish expedition, 5744; in commission, 273, 455, 954, 1550, 1735, 1799, 3072, 3219, 3358, 3515, 4719, 5193, p. 907.

........., Thomas, of Catfosse, in Holdernez, York, 807.

........., William, 714.

........., ..., of Rudstone, in commission, 954, 1550, 1735, 1799, 3219, 3358.

........., Sir William, of Carethorpe, 4719, p. 907.

........., ..., of Everingham, 5193.

Constantine, Signor, 216, p. 254.

Constantinople, 1659.

Contarini, Fred., p. 327.

Conti, Baron de, p. 384.

Conton, Mr., of the Household, 4154.

Controller, Mr. (Qu. Wiltshire or Ponynges?), 5104.

Converts, house of the, 165.

Convocation, 2090, 5189, 5209.

........., summons of, 613, 2004, 2005, 4876.

.... for extirpation of heresy, 4312.

Conway, Christ., 1871.

........., Edw., 3231.

........., Eliz., wife of Sir Hugh, 1603.

........., Sir Hugh, treasurer of Calais, 557, 1015, 1027, 1241, 1365, 1539, 1603, 1801, 1871, 3832, 3852, 4476, 5231, 5519; debtor to Henry VII., p. 434; Act for, 3502; in the war against France, 3925, 4008; receives money due from France to England, 14, 626, 1632, 1919, 2026, 5529.

........., Philip, 4654.

Cony, Edmund, in the war against France, p. 551, 3979, p. 553.

Conyers, Cuthbert, clk., 296, 1796.

........., Dr., 5090.

........., John, 3669.

........., Wm. Lord, of Hornby, 335, 777, 1796, 4518; grant, 440; commissioner to treat with Scotland, 2078, 3696; indebted to Hen. VII., 8497; signs the challenge before the battle of Flodden, 4439; summoned to Parliament, 5616; in commission for York, 1549, 1735, 1799, 1804, 3219, 3358, 5244, p. 907.

Conyzers, Anne, 1790.

Coo, Christ., 4948; captain of the John Baptist, pp. 553 and 554; captain of the Lizard, p. 651, p. 812, p. 972.

Cook, ——, of Norfolk, 12.

........., captain, 3591, p. 652.

........., Katharine, wife of Walter, 4911.

........., Thomas, 5431.

Cooke, Thomas, capt., p. 554.

........., ..., rector of Donet St. Andrew's, 1854.

........., Walter, 4911.

........., Wm. 503.

.... See Coke.

Cooksey, Lady, 933.

........., Sir Th., 933.

Cookson, John, spear of Calais, 4476, 4635.

........., ..., water bailiff of Calais, 123, 3214.

........., Wm., 1131.

Coope. See Cope.

Coopers, 3051, 3796, 3888, 4823.

Cooplant, Wm. See Copeland.

Coote, farm of, 933.

Coparceners-lands, 778, 4321, 4946.

Copcote John, justice of assize, 294, 1164, 1490, 3295; in commission, 1101, 1763.

Cope, ——, p. 652.

....., Agnes daughter of Edward, 1175.

......, Edw. 1175.

......, John, 4480.

......, Stephen, serjeant of the buttry, 235, 1023, 3164, 4168; grants to, 1239, 1940, 3558.

......, Wm., 3954, 4301; executor of Sir Reg. Bray, 996; grants to, 215, 565, 935, 1239, 1748; on sheriff-roll, 3507; in commission, 766, 1216, 1427, 1470, 1745, 1762, 3015, 3078, 3092. His death, 3880.

Copeland, Cumb., 4944.

........., ——, 1212.

........., Wm., of London, merchant, 3678, 3817, 4054, 4311, 4725, 4831, 4932, 5076, 5675, pp. 955 and 958.

Coper, Christ., 5548. See Johnson, Christ.

Copia, De, of Erasmus, 3158, 3535, 4336.

Copinger, ——, 4398, 4432.

........., John, page of the wardrobe of robes, 1973, 3865, 5643; clerk of estreats of the Common Pleas, 5510.

Copleston, Agnes, daughter of John, 1915, 1994.

........., John, 1812, 1915, 1994.

Copley, ——, 1212.

........., Rog., of Hamptenett, Sussex, 578, 3024, 4544, 5561.

Copthorn Hill, Herts, 4206.

Copuldike, John, 1871, 4033, 4996; gentleman-usher, 2087.

........., Margaret, 5039.

........., Wm., 3604.

........., Wm., son of Wm. 3604.

Copwood, John, 3937.

Copynford, Northt., 1067.

Corbet, Ootes, of Devon, 12.

Corbett, Ric., 3694.

........., Sir Rob., of Morton, Salop, 887, 3231, 4645, 4687; in commission, 918, 1981, 3071, 3715.

........., Roger, son of Sir Rob., 4645, 4687.

Corbie, in France, 4174.

Corbowe, John, 503.

Cordage, account of, 4232.

Cordes, in France, 4253.

Cordie (date), 4453.

Cordier, Peter, LL.D., ambassador of France, 2062, 2075.

Cordray, Tho., 1495.

Corfe Castle, Dors., 456, 1504, 3061; Privy Seals dated at, 1234, 1233.

Corinth, Helena Lastarrinea, Countess of Sarrinall in Greece, 816. *See* Lascarina, Isabella.

Coriton, Ric., of Newton, Cornwall, 1996, 4988.

Corke, Rog. of London, grocer, 3939.

Cormalet, Soms., 411, 4712.

Corn, 3051, 4782, 4792.

Cornard, alias Cornelyous, John, 3939.

Cornburgh, 4335.

Cornbury, Oxon., 1426.

Corndon Forest, Montgomery, 582.

Cornelius, John. *See* Cornard.

Cornell. *See* Cornhill.

Cornet Castle, 94.

Corneto Hadrian de, Cardinal St. Chrysogon, Bp. of Bath and Wells, 1681, 3388, 3780, 4283, 4327, 4446, 4455, 4747, 5110, 5356, 5449, 5464; Emperor desires his advancement to the papacy, 3443; papal collector for England, 5156, 5538, 5651, 5661, 5665, 5666, 5671, 5672, 5706; letters from, 394, 2039, 3543, 4287, 5342, 5662, 5670, 5702.

Cornhill, [Northumb.], 3326, 3577.

Cornicall, Tristram, of Normandy, 3587.

Cornisborow, York. *See* Conisburgh.

Cornish, Wm., 3285.

Cornwall, county of, 597, 3182, 3441, 3502, 4901.

........., ..., stannaries in, 48; coinage of tin, &c., in 397; tolls on tin in, 506.

........., ..., commissions of array, for, 1812, 3393, 3688.

........., ..., commissions of the peace for, 312, 891, 1694, 1954, 1984, 3290, 3583, 3605, 3938, 4754 5220, 5474, 5586.

........., ..., clerk of the peace, and of the Crown in, 5052.

........., ..., feodary of crown lands in, 4414, 4711.

........., ..., sheriff of, 664, 1316, 1771, 1949, 3057, 3507, 4544, 5561, 5562.

........., duchy of, 209, 210, 259, 453, 493, 778, 970, 1349, 3770, 3941, 4967, 5231.

........., duchy of, attorney-general of, 1486.

........., ..., auditors of, 4775, 5050.

........., ..., commissioners and assessors of, 5431.

........., ..., escheator and feodary of, 208.

........., ..., overseers of, 1472, 4022.

........., ..., receiver-general of, 104, 1349.

...., ..., steward of, 43.

........., captain, 3591, p. 550, 4377, 5761.

........., Ric., of Berington, Heref., 1127, 3113; in the war against France, p. 553, 4005, 4475; indebted to Hen. VIII., 5633; grant to, 4226, 4594, 4837, 5272.

Cornwall, Ric., of Greenwich, 4367, 4370.

........., Sir Thomas, of Burford, Salop, 3166, 4071; in debt to the King, 2044, 5633; in the war against France, 3231, 4632, Baron of Burford, 4253; on the sheriff-roll, 1316, 1949; sheriff of Hereford, 5561; in commission, 1981, 3071, 3715, 4394, 4827, p. 904.

Cornwaleys, Edw., of Hoke, York, 1699.

Cornewaleis, John, captain, p. 553.

Cornwaleys, Robt., of Pritwell, Essex, 1699.

Cornwailles, Wm., 577, 1162.

Cornwood, Devon, 2080.

Corringham, Linc., 1129.

Corseley, Wilts, 1867, 5247.

Corsi, Peter, merchant of Florence, 2036, p. 432, 3756, 4629. *See also* Chorfi.

Corsica, isle of, 4280.

Cortenhale, Northt. (?), 4656.

Cortesius, Jas., 288.

Corton, Somers., 5102.

........., Tho., 769.

Coryngham, Linc. *See* Corringham.

Cosenza, Cardinal, 2002.

Cosford, Suff., 4966.

Cosham, Wilts, 155.

Cosington, Leic., 730.

Coste, Andrew de la, merchant of Bruges, 4154, 4155, 5320.

......., Harry, 4442.

Costessey, Norf., 1129, 1344.

Costopolegrino, Barth., 5712.

Costowe, Northt., 3027.

Cotford, Devon, 2080.

Cotteney, in France, 4253.

Cotterel, Mr. Peter, 5587.

Cottes, John, p. 608; on sheriff-roll, 5561.

Cottesmore, Wm., of Brightwell, 4254.

Cottingham, York, 178, 192, 367, 386, 534, 721, 1205, 3845, 3866, 4033; benefice of, 4454, 4455, 5198; Andrew Bishop of Murray, commendatory of, 1459, 1875; Cottingham Langton, York, 5089.

........., ——, 4928.

Cottington, Thomas, 3799.

Cotton, Suff., 1375, 1534, 3309.

........., near Northampton, 4113.

........., Sir John, 3981.

........., Sir Robert, of Landwade, Cambridesh., 266, 1871; in the war against France, p. 651; at the marriage of Princess Mary, 5483; in commission for Cumb., 1684, 3310, 3583, p. 904; his brother, 3231.

........., ..., founder of the Cottonian Library; his signature on a document in the Record Office, 718.

........., Stephen, of Tewkesbury, 5051.

........., Th., 1949, 3507.

Coughton, Warw., 953, 3827, 4940.

Coukett, 4005.

Councer, Wm., in commission for Oxf., 4559, 4809, p. 905.　See also Counter.

Council, the Privy, of England, 1853, 3236, 3815, 4164, 4171, 4320, 4365, 4535, 4639, 4917, 4928, 5151, 5173, 5319, 5377, 5407, 5541, 5744; letters from, 4030, 5762; letters to, 3639, 3737, 3985, 4155, 4682, 4870, 5090, 5130, 5387, 5475, 5641.

........., ..., clerk of the, 3478, 3758, 4314.

........., of the North, 4652.

........., the Lateran, 1828, 1980, 2075, 2085, 3010, 3012, 3108, 3109, 3138, 3139, 3225, 3283, 3625, 3626, 4038, 4283, 4287, 4288, 4500, 4598, 4605, 4608, 5054, 5262, 5331, 5464, 5496.

........., schismatical, 2039.

........., the French, 4682, 5006, 5606, 5681.

.... at Bruges, 5418, 5424.

.... at Innsbrook, 3897.

.... Chamber, the Prince's, at Westminster, 3941, 4022, 4967, 5231.

Count Palatine.　See Bavaria, Frederick Count Palatine of.

Counter, Wm., in commission, 3015; see also Councer.

Courteman, Agnes, 1381.

........., Hen., 1381.

........., Joan, 1381.

........., Maltida, 1381.

........., Tho., 1381.

........., Wm., 1381.

Courteney, Oxon., 1344.

........., young, captain, 4474.

........., captain, 3591, p. 550, p. 681, 5761.

........., Edw.　See Devon, Edw. Courtney, Earl of.

........., Hen.　See Devon, Hen. Courtney, Earl of.

........., John, 3044.

........., Lady Katherine.　See Devon, Katharine, Countess of.

........., Philip, 1812.

........., ..., son of John, 3044.

........., Ric., captain, p. 812, p. 973.

........., Thomas.　See Devon, Thomas, Earl of.

........., Wm., of E. Coker, Somerset, 3114.

........., ..., son of Sir Wm., squire of the body, livery of lands, 4313, 4315; in com. for Devon, 4539, 4783, 5220, 5456; in the war against France, 4178, 4989, 5028; pardon, 5180.

........., Wm., of E. Greenwich, 4369.

........., Sir Wm.　See Devon, Earl of.

Cousin, Robt., 5060.

........., Wm., clerk, the King's chaplain, dean of Wells, 4567; in commission, 3048, 3566, 3585, 3606, 3701, 4713.

Cousins, Lewis, 1710.

Consturi[er], Jenyn le, 5292.

Covalence.　See Coblentz.

Covelchall, Middx., 1031, 1167.

Coventry, 3234, 3441, 3826, p. 652.

........., mayor and sheriffs of, 1771

Coventry, monastery of, 3913.

........., prior of, 5616.

.... and Lichfield, Geoffrey Blythe, Bishop of, (sometimes called Bishop of Chester), 776, 1004, 1854, 2082, p. 651; summoned to Parliament, 5616; in commission for Staff., Warw., and Salop, 279, 282, 713, 791, 886, 918, 1387, 1468, 1770, 1971, 1981, 3071, 3289, 3364, 3715, 4198, 4394, 4764, 4770, 4827, pp. 903, 904, 906, and 907.

...., (Chester), diocese of, 1848.

Coventre, John, abbot of Abingdon, 2070, 3050.

Covingtre, Patrick, dean of Lastalrig, Scotland, 4997.

Coverdale, in co. Richmond, 3483, 3669.

........., Tho., 1376.

Covers, alias Newton, Giles, 3575.

Covert, John, 1965.

........., Ric., in commission for Sussex, 281, 1509, 3024, 3428, 4804, p. 904.

Cowart, Nich., 5112, 5724; mayor of Southampton, 1813.

Cowbridge, Glamorgan, 110, 441, 1113.

Cowdray, Morgan, of Langton, Dorset, 4214. 4275.

........., Peter, 1812.

Cowes, Isle of Wight, 3118.

Cowick, Devon, 799.

Cowley, Robt., 4258, 4588.

........., Tho., 3056, 3069.

Cowper, alias Thomlinson, John, 494, 2052.

........., Robt., 5549.

Couper, alias Raulyns, Rob., 3234.

Cox.　See Cokkes.

Coyde-Raf, Pembroke, 5420.

Coydesoyth, or Coyde Soweytht, in Milleneth, 4815, 5145.

Coyfrowe, a messuage called, in Northampton, 1309.

Cra, John, p. 326.

Cracheroode, John, 508, 4221.

Cradenhall, Heref., 1794.

Cradock, Francis, 4253.

........., the Mary, ship, 5112.

........., Matthew, 3960, 5180,

........., ..., his ship, 3591, 3977, 5761.

Craissier, Willequin, 5032.

Crakeholm, a field called, part of the manor of Maxey, Northt., 5296.

Crakenthorp, Ambrose, in commission for Cumb., 717, 1048, 1734, 1799, 2009, 3048, 3358, 3552, pp. 904 and 907.

Crakenthorp, John, 677, 1949, 3507.

Cranborne, Dorset, 155, 901, 4022.

Cranbrooke, Kent, 1663, 5031.

Crane, Wm., gentleman of the Chapel Royal, 141, 1349, 1843, 3454, 4799, 5312.

Crankes, John, 1608.

Craufurde, Eliz., 1410.

Cravell, David, 3771.

.... Howell, 3771.

Craven, York, 566, 3827, 4852, 4940.
Crawford, Earl of, 4441, 4951.
Crawley, Northumb., 4406.
........., Surrey, 1212.
Cray, John, temp. Ric. II., 3008.
Craybroke, Jas., 647.
Crayford, Kent, 4941.
........., Lyon, serjeant-at-arms, 1952, 1973.
Crayfort, Lord, a Scotchman, 216.
Creke, North, Norf., 2098.
Crema, p. 368, pp. 381 and 384, 3335, 3499, 3659, 3752, 4499, 4756, 5171 (ii.), 5677.
Cremer (or Creme), Hen., 781, 4238.
........., Th., 1843, 2044.
Cremona, 11, p. 366, pp. 381–382, 3752, 3817, 4058, 4280, 4326, 4563, 4571, 4795, 5171 (ii.), 5304, 5404.
Crequy, young De, 4386.
........., Anthoine de. See Pondormy, Sieur de.
........., Chas. de, dean of Tournay, 4466.
Cresmere. See Grasmere.
Cressall, Ric., prior of the hospital of Bishops-gate Without, 4931.
Cressent, Wm., 3391.
Cresset, Ric., p. 608.
........., Tho., 3231.
Cressyngham, Parva, Norf., 3943, 4948, 5115.
Cressy, Robt., 4332.
Creswell, Northumb., 1040, 5010.
Creswell, Edward, 4178, 4185.
........., Geo., 810.
........., Rob., p. 435.
........., Wm., 524.
Cresweller, John, mayor of Chichester, 868.
Creting, Norf., 1129.
Crething, St. Olave, Norf., 1344.
Cretingham, Suff., 730.
Creton, Northt., 4656.
Creuch (?), p. 384.
Crewkerne, (Crokehorn), Soms., 2080.
........., ..., church of, 491.
Cribelli, Ugeloti, 3269.
Criche, Somers., 155.
Crickelade, Wilts, 155.
Crighton, provost of, 3838.
Crips, John, 4544.
Crispyn, Ric., 3031.
Cristed. See Kirstead.
Cristell, Wm., 2050.
Crochet, John, p. 956.
Crocker, John, of Lyneham, Devon, 3534, 3566, 5648; sheriff of Devon, 664; indebted to Hen. VII., 777; in commission, 1503, 1812, 3183, 3589, 3605, 3938, 4539, 4783, 5220.
........., Mr., p. 652.
Croft, Edw., 298, p. 434; sheriff of Hereford, 664, 4544: made knight at Lisle, p. 609; in commission, 646, 675, 3686.

Croft, Sir Ric., 298.
Crogling, Cumb., 1807.
Croix, Josse de la, 4445 (ii).
Croke, John, warden of the guild of Barking Church, London, 5242.
........., Ric., 4447, 4448, 4528.
Crokeham, Berks, 3789.
Crokk, John, master of the Margaret, 5112.
Croksall. See Croxhall, Derby.
Cromer, Geo., clk., 3215.
........., Hen., 818.
........., Nich., 5719.
........., Sir Wm., of Dunstall, Kent, 685. sheriff of Kent, 664; in commission, 3428, 3605, 4663, 4847.
Crompton, Sampson, 1640, 3995.
Cromwell, Eliz., daughter of Matilda, 3280.
........., Matilda, wife of Ralph, 3280.
........., Ralph, 3280.
........., ..., Lord, 4838.
Crumwell, Rob., vicar of Battersea, 3671.
........., Thomas, his hand, 3556, 5355.
Cropton, York, 5325.
Cross, Thos., 3961, 4290.
Crosbowes, a messuage, in Mendlesham, Suff., 3562.
Cross-bows, Act against shooting with, 2082.
Crosslawnde, Glouc., 3613.
Crosswell, John, 3642, 4773.
Crostehole, 2080.
Crosthwaite, Cumb., 3764.
Crouchcroft, a tenement called, 734.
Crowhurst, Surrey, 1427, 3078, 3092, 4693, 4734, 5237, p. 905.
Crowland Abbey, Linc., 3375, 3420, 3423, 3447.
........., Richard, abbot of, 776, 3375; in com-mission, 663, 1716, 1979, 3137.
........., John Wells, abbot of 3418, 3423, 3447; summoned to Parliament, 5616, in commission, 5691.
........., abbot of. See Bardney, Ric.
........., Simon, prior of, 3375.
Crowley, Bucks, 1937.
Crown, clerk of the, 85.
........., land, 286, 319, 2082, 2084, 4089.
........., feodaries of, 4414, 4711.
Croxhall, Derby, p. 609.
Croxton, Rob., 3985.
Croy, Anthoine de, brother of the Prince of Chimay, 4793.
......, Charles de. See Chimay, Prince of.
......, Nich. de. See Sempi, Lord of.
......, Wm. de. See Chievres, William de Croy, Lord.
Croydon, Surrey, 1858, 5407; letter dated from, 5398; Privy Seals dated at 595, 597, 611, 621, 627, 630, 648, 837, 988, 989, 990.

Croydon Bay, 4020.

........., New, in Brittany, 3903.

Croyland Abbey, *See* Crowland.

Cruciferi in Hungary, 5338, 5366.

Crucis, B. Cardinal S., 1582.

Crudwell, church of, Wilts., 1456.

Crump, (Crompe), John, 5645.

........., Wm., 4495; mayor of Canterbury, 1225.

Crusade, a proposed, 1828, 1878, 3278, 3283, 3569, 4500.

Cruykdale, Cumb., 296.

Cudlynton, Oxon., 1129, 1344.

Cuer, Janina de, chamberlain of Queen Katharine, 368.

Cullesdon, Surrey, 1858.

Culme, Hugh, 3044.

Culpeper, Alex., of Gondehurst, Kent, 685, 5688; sheriff of Kent, 5561; in commission, 3428, 3605, 4663, 4847.

........., Edw., in commission, 3428, 3605, 4663, 4847.

........., Walt., vice-marshal of Calais, 345, 666, 1962; receives the money due from France to England, 14, 626, 1027, 1632, 1919, 2026.

Culquhone, Adam, canon of Glasgow, 4997.

Culverdon, Wm., 1363.

Cumberland, feodary of Crown lands in, 4414, 5692.

........., sheriff of, 664, 1316, 1771, 1807, 1949, 3507, 3600, 3866, 4544, 5561.

........., commissions of array for, 1734, 1799, 3358, 3393, 5529, 5626.

........., commissions of the peace for, 717, 1048, p. 907.

........., wools of, 743.

Cumberton, church of, Worc. dioc., 269.

Cumberworth, Lincoln, 449.

Cumburford, Edw., p. 609.

Cumnor, Tho., prior of Abingdon, 2070.

Cundour (Condover), Salop, 4594.

Cundy, Constance, sister of Wm., 3480.

........., John, father of Wm., 3480.

........., Margaret, sister of Wm., 3480.

........., Wm. (temp. Edw. III.), son of John, 3480.

Cunye, Walter, 136, 1591.

Curlens, Nich., incumbent of St. Mary Magdalene's, London, 1742.

Curll, Thos., 3910.

Currant, Wm., in commission for Som., 3566, 3585, 3606, 3701, 4713. *See also* Carrant, Wm.

Cursoll, Monsieur de, at the marriage of Princess Mary, 5482.

Curteys, Hen., reversal of outlawry for, 1630.

........., chantry of, 1194.

Curtis, Jas., 3240.

Curtis, John, of London, mercer, 1525, 1553, 3000, 3695.

........., Ric., 1194.

Curwen, Edmund, 3600.

........., Sir Thos., of Workington, Cumb., 275, 680, 1052, 1087, 1366, 1674, 5229; sheriff of Cumberland, 664, 3600; on sheriff-roll, 5561; in commission, p. 907.

Curzon, John, of Ketilston, 1949.

........., ..., of Croxhall, p. 609.

........., Sir Rob., called Baron Curzon, 640, 1155, 1306, 1757; in the war against France, p. 553, 4160, p. 609, 4306, 4477, 4908; master of the ordnance in the rearward, 4310, 4479 (misprinted Lord "H" Corson), 4534, 4899, 5216, 5248.

........., ..., ..., Roger, servant of, 4908.

Cusentinus, F. Cardinal, 1581.

Cussheman, Simon, 5031.

Customs, act for payment of, 811.

Cuthbert, Robt., 4367.

Cutler, John, D.D., warden of the place of St. Francis, London, 5255.

Cutseghem, Geo. van, of Sluys, 4456.

Cutte, Sir John, under-treasurer of England, 181, 1267, 1348, 1921, 3211, p. 431, 4067, 4442, 4839, 4931, 5274, 5351.

........., ..., executor of Hen. VII., 3292.

........., ..., executor of Sir Reginald Bray, 996.

........., ..., in the war against France, pp. 551, 651.

........., ..., grants to, 1492, 4436.

........., ..., signs as member of the Privy Council, 1004, 1372, 1527, 1540, 1574, 1584, 1596, 1699, 1756, 1757, 1758, 3080, 4434, 5735, p. 974.

........., ..., in commission of gaol-delivery, 3765.

........., ..., in commission of the peace for Bucks, 1379, 2045, 3219, 3310, 3522; for Camb., 1684, 3583, p. 904; for Essex, 310, 1368, 1522, 1713, 3605, 3785, 3967, p. 907; for Hunts, 4006, p. 906.

Cutton, prebend of, Devon, 1136, 2080.

Cutturus, Reymond, alderman of Calais, 5712.

Cuttyng, Ro., 1075, 3768.

Cuyk, Edward, 4572.

Cyke, Ric. *See* Coke.

Cyny, Mr. Domynyk, pp. 956–958.

D.

Dabescourt, Bernard, in com., 1812.

Dabington. *See* Babington.

Dabscort, Jno., capt., 4632.

Dabuli, 4173.

Dackus, Rob., 1906.

Dacre, Sir Chr., brother to Thomas Lord D., 4529 ; in commission, 1048, 1734, 1799, p.905; information against, 3497; rides into Scotland, 4529, 4556 ; letter from, 4825. 4573.

........., Dame Mabel, mother of Thomas Lord D., 380.

........., Sir Philip, brother of Thomas Lord D., 1924 ; in commission, p. 905 ; arrests G. Ogle, 4403 ; sent to Morpeth, destroys Bew Castle, 4825 ; taken, 5090.

........., Thos. Lord, of the North, 3882, 4388 ; exempted from the King's pardon, 12 ; warden-general of the marches, 245, 2029, 2035 ; his recognizances, 380, 777 ; cancelled, 296, 2027 ; property, 856 ; in commission, 1048, 1734, 1799, 1804, 2009, 3048, 3358, 3552, pp. 904, 907 ; to redress grievances, 1739, 1829, 3007, 3726 ; to hold courts, 1850 ; to treat with Scotland, 3128, 3129, 5745, 5757 ; his reception, 3322 ; his orders, 3346, 3447 ; proceedings there, 3359, 3577 ; signs Surrey's challenge at Flodden, 4439 ; at Flodden, 4460, 4462, 4497 ; has charge of the ordnance taken there, 4869 4902 ; complains of slander, 4482 ; to treat with Margaret of Scotland, 4483, 4682 ; his raids into Scotland, 4520, 4522, 4523, 4529, 4556, 4573, 4825 ; his spies in Scotland, 4869 ; requests wardship of Henry Fenwick, 4870 ; sends news from Scotland, 3811, 4951, 5641 ; defends himself from the charge of sparing the Scots, 5090 ; gives an account of the waste there, ib. ; in commission of inquiry, 5528 ; summoned · to Parliament, 5616 ; indebted to the King, 5633 ; his servant, 5614.

........., letters from, 380, 3326, 3359, 3577, 3751, 4403, 4482, 4497, 4518, 4520, 4522, 4529, 4556, 4573, 4682, 4869, 4870, 4951, 5090, 5541, 5641.

........., letters to, 3320, 3321, 3347, 4483, 4825, 5348.

........., Th. Feneys, Lord, of the South ; trier of petitions in Parliament, 811, 2082 ; sells land to Edm. Dudley, 1212, 1965 ; in commission, 1509, 3024, 3428, 4804, p. 904 ; attends the King into France, 4306, 4377, 4477, 4534 ; summoned to Parliament, 5616 ; sheriff-roll of Surrey, 612.

........., Wm., letter to Thos. Lord D., 4825.

Daddy, Ric., inc. of Streton, Linc., 3776.

Dadlyngton, Leic., church of, 1848.

Dagenham, Essex, 3284.

Dalabre, Sir Ric., in commission, 3686, 5272.

........., capt., 3977.

Dalby, commands the ordnance, 3835, 4314, 4237.

........., Geoffry, of Barnstaple, 3272.

........., Thomas, archdeacon of Richmond, 4652, 5169 ; exempted from the pardon, 12 ; pardoned, 1115 ; King's chaplain, 1637, 1750, 3062, 3386.

Dale, John, 1236 ; in commission for Hants, 904, 1388, 1812, 3071, 3198, 4159, 4676.

........., Rog. à, 921.

Dalehed, le, Windermere, 3764.

Dalevale, barony, 1040, 5010.

Dalison, Geo., 309, 706, 732, 1020, 1708, 1971, 3102, p. 906, 5748 ; appointed to view ordnance, 5316 ; privy counsellor, 5762 ; possessions, 938.

Dalton, John, in commission, 705.

Dalviano, Barth., 4069, 5532 ; succours Cremona, 4280 ; flies to Padua, 4355 ; declines battle, 5410.

Damascus, 1659.

Dame Elynsbury, manor of, 3576.

Damory, Ric., 155.

Danbery, Norf., 5710.

Danbourne, Wm., 768, 3544.

Danbury (Daunbury), Essex, 1699, 4367, 5073.

Daney, Oxon., 3297.

Danda, Jo., p. 957.

Dandasoli, p. 380.

Dandefort, Hacquinet, 5032.

Danett, Gerard, 1014, 4180 ; attends Princess Mary to France, 5483.

Daniel, Hugh, 4414.

........., Jas., 4653.

Danyell, John, 927, 948.

........., Tho., 1190, 4013.

Dannot, 5512.

Dansey, John, in commission for Heref., 3686

Danson, Wm., 5682.

Danvers, Sir John, in commission, 898, 1489, 1938, 3157, 3605 ; sheriff-roll of Wilts, 1316, 1949, 3507 ; sheriff for Wilts, 4544.

........., John, son of John, 867.

........., Th., of Devon, 1908.

Danyhall, York, 1654.

Darbye, John, 3254.

Darcy, Anth., sheriff of Essex, 1949.

........., Edith, wife of Thomas Lord, 367, 726.

........., Eliz., widow of Roger, 399.

........., Sir Geo., son of Thos. Lord, 4547 ; at Flodden, 4439, 4441 ; in commission, 5166.

........., Rog., of Essex, 305, 399, 1699.

........., Thos., son of Roger, 305, 4167.

........., Tho. Ld., 30, 230, 534, 742, 3496, 4520, 5090, 5505, 5513, 5742 ; treasurer of Berwick, 176, 187, 190 ; capt. of, 1840 ; warden of the marches, 188, 189, 283, 1850, 1907 ; steward of Raby, &c., 191, 192, 193, 201, 1205, 4547 ; illness, 4652 ; debtor to the King, 777 ; in the war with France, 3885, 4237, 4238, 4306, 4307, 4314 ; at Tournay, 4284.

Darcy, Tho. Ld. of the Privy Council, 679, 1008, 1538; admiral against the Moors, 1531, 1562, 1566, 1726, 3443, 5741, 5744; instructions, 5741; in commission, 705, 1506, 1549, 1550, 1735, 1798, 1995, 1804, 3177, 3219, 3358, 3553, 4015, 4719, 5166, 5193, 5244, 5506; summoned to Parliament, 5616; on bad terms with Ruthal, 5782.

........., letters to, 4868, 5740, 5743, 5745, 5759; from, 3359, 4105, 4652, 4902.

Darell (Darrell), Alice, wife of Edw., 3384.

........., Edw., 1002, p. 958; property, 1772, 3134, 3384, 3392; sheriff of Wells, 664, 1913, 3723; in commission, 1489, 1938, 2095, 3157, 3605, 3640, 4341, 4583, 5166.

........., Jas., 5633.

........., John, 3982, 4533.

Darien, 5267.

Darizolles, Ant. de, 962, 1182.

Darley, Brian, D.D., 757.

........., Rog., clk., 4663, 5498.

Darnall, Thos., 3432, 3959.

Darold (Darrold), Alice, 3889.

........., Godfrey, of Boston, 5227.

........., Godfrey, coll. of Hull, 1677, 3889; murdered, 5077.

Darpaggion, Mons., kinsman to the master of Rhodes, 4429.

Dartington, Devon, 330, 4715; church, 1751.

Dartford, 308, 1711.

.... Monastery, 825; Elizabeth, prioress of, 3527.

Dartmore, 48.

Dartmouth, 138, 353, 919, 1349, 3120, 3820, 3857, 3973, 3977, 3978, 4020, 4376, 4377, 4385, 5159, 5201. See Ships.

Dary, Wm., 4067.

Datchet, 134.

Daubeneyes, Midx., 4301.

Daubeney, Eliz., widow of Giles Lord, 1304.

........., Giles Lord, 32, 449, 602, 1244, 1304, 1833, 3049, 4315, 5704; chamberlain to Henry VII., 1604.

........., Hen. Lord, son of Giles, 1304; livery of lands, 5704; in commission for Som. and Devon, 3566, 3585, 3589, 3605, 3606, 3701, 3723, 3938, 4539, 4713, 4783, 5220, p. 904, 5658; in the war with France, 3885, 4237, 4307; summoned to Parliament, 5616.

Daubigny, Sieur de, 5482.

Daunce, John, Sir, 784, 3414, 3422, 3440, 3496, 3981, 4067, 4070, 4131, 4314, 4526, 4839, 4874, 4878, 4884, 4892, 5005, 5042, 5170, 5172, 5475, 5674, 5720, 5748, 5758, 5764, 5769, 5770, 5776, 5777, 5778; offices, 374, 635, 1874, 5619; in commission, 1921, p. 905, 5684; letter from, p. 78, (note), 4653.

Daundy, Anne, 899.

........., Edm., of Ipswich, his chantry, 899; commission, 3549.

........., Wm., 899.

Dauphiné, p. 381, 3649, p. 501, 3860, 3861, 4216, 4296, 4323, 4577, 5171, 5675.

Davenant, Nic., of Cornwall, 1083.

........., Wm., son of Nic., 1083.

Davenport, Christ., clk., 3535.

.... John, inc. of Flamstead, 3754.

Daventrie, 12.

Daventry, St. Augustines, prior of, 753, 1950.

David, Edw. ap., 3299.

........., Reg. ap, 1500.

.... Ric., 136.

........., Rob. ap, 3329.

........., Thomas, 3505.

........., Wm. ap, 4873.

Davyson, Rob., 3483, 5761.

Davyson, Wm., 4377, 5761.

Davy, Benedict, 4711.

........., Geof., of Barnstable, 3272.

........., John, 1471.

........., ..., killed, 1990.

........., ..., of Southampton, 3822, 4904.

........., Maurice, 3509.

........., Wm., 182, 1580, 3079; ald. of Calais, 5712.

........., ..., dec., 1256.

Daw, Isabel, 1193.

......., Tho., 1193.

Dawby, Wm. See Dawtrey.

Dawes, Rog., of Bristol, 1050.

Dawne, ——, 3231.

........., Jno., 4503.

........., Ric., of Cheshire, 4360.

Dawson, Ric. inc. of Fursby, 3281.

........., Th. 5201.

........., Wm., Scot, 4743.

Dawtrey, John, 3123, 3422, 3496, 3981, 4056, 4073, 4095, 4099, 4103, 4475, 4527, 4653, 4979, 5724, 5762; in com. for Hants, 266, 904, 1388, 1812, 3071, 4159, 4676, 5506; for Sussex, 1509, 3024, 3428, 4804; his offices, 175, 198, 1439, 4414.

........., ..., letters from, 4007, 4074, 4093, 4094, 4104, 5755; letters to, 5033, 5772 5773, 5775.

.... (Dawby), Wm., 4238.

Dax, 3355, 3584, 3593.

Day (Deye), John, 130.

......., John, clk., 692.

......., John, of Lond., 3432.

......., Ric., 3579.

......., Th., 3579.

......., Rob., 5163.

Daymeryes, Loys de, 5163.

Daza, Fernando, p. 957.

Deacon, Tho., 1589.

........., Th., clk., 4661.

Dean Forest, 316, 1233, 1355, 1389, 3345.

Deanham (Dennom), town, 1040, 5010.

Debden (Depden), Essex, 729.

Deckere, Guill. de, 3737.

Decons, Ric., 125, 126, 128, secr., to Q. Katharine, 1595.

........., Tho., son of Ric., 1595.

Dedham, 155.

Dee, Dyo, 65.

......, Hugh, 4881.

......, John, 1507, 3447.

......, Tho., 1507, 3448.

......, river, 3395, 5149.

Deele, Roger, 4469.

Deeping, 155, 303, 645, 1278, 1993.

.... Gate, Northt., 5682.

.... Market, 3175, 5682.

........., West and East, 3175.

Dees, Fras., Bluemantle, 418.

Defferentcloid, Wales, 315, 778, 955, 1678.

Deffyens, 5163.

Deir, (Cistercian), James, abbot of, 767.

Delabere, Jas., capt., 4377, 5761.

Delabre, Sir Ric., in com., 646, 675, sheriff of Heref., 1316, 5596.

........., Th., son of Richard, livery of lands, 5596.

De la Fava. *See* Fava.

Delahay, Tho., 777.

De la Membrilla. *See* Membrilla.

De la Motte. *See* Motte.

De la Palis. *See* Palice.

De la Pole. *See* Pole.

Delaroche. *See* Roche.

De la Warr, Tho. West Ld., 578, 3173 ; in com. for Sussex, 281, 1509, 3024, 3428, p. 904 ; for Hants, 904, 1388, 3371, 4159, p. 904 ; at the marriage of Princess Mary, 5483 ; summoned to Parliament, 5616.

Dele, Roger, 4067, 5701.

Delfte, 5539.

Delves, Ric., 4209.

Demeries. *See* Daymeryes, Loys de.

Demonelia, Fabian, 4250.

........., Justynien, 4250.

........., Michel, 4250.

Demyneres, John, 4328.

Denbigh, N. W.

.... Castle and parks, 344.

........., commissioners for, 955.

........., constable of, 81.

........., gaol of Chekergate, and Burgesgate, 344.

........., park of Grossnodeok, 4242.

Denbighland, lordship of, N. W., 1039, 1543, 1573, 1585, 1649, 2068, 3073, 3206, 3368, 3378, 4111, 4135, 4204, 4565, 4788, 4858, 4873, 5501, 5546.

........., escheator and attorney, 344.

........., forester and master of the hunt, 324.

........., steward of, 81.

........., surveyor and approver, 1063, 1064.

Dynbieth (Denbigh ?) lordship, 360.

Denby, Derby, 4836.

Dendermonde (Tenremonde), 4755, 5203.

Dene, Sir Geo., 5789.

......, Jno. A, 4842.

......, Sir Ric., 1365, 5789.

Denebatt, Mons., 5482.

Denes, (Deves ?), Th., in com., 5220.

Denford, Wilts, 3190.

Denghby, ——, 4347.

Denham, Bucks, 1759.

Denmark, John K. of, 4055 ; at war with Lubeck, 3138 ; articles from Scotland to, 3225.

........., Christiern II. K. of, 3915.

........., Queen of, 3138, 3225, 3321, 3617, 3629, 3633, 3718, 3805, 4901, 4169, 5155, 5185, p. 958.

........., ..., letters to, 3140, 3635.

........., treaty with, 4889.

........., ambassadors of, in Low Countries, 5155.

........., chancellor. *See* Beilde.

........., ship of, 4525.

........., ..., letters to, 1416, 1782, 2062, 2075, 2077, 3086.

Denny, Eliz., Abbess of. *See* Throgmerton.

........., Edm., 1527, 3609, 3656 ; baron of the Exchequer, 4016.

........., (or Deny), Th., capt., 5112, 5772.

Densell, Jno., 5656.

Dent, John, M.A., rector of St. Blaise, Calais, 562, 5421.

Denton, Linc., 2017.

........., Eliz., 217, 1119, 1307.

........., Hen., of Cumberland, 296 ; in com., 717, 1048, 1734, 1799, 3358.

........., Jas., canon of Windsor, D.D., 526, 527; attends Princess Mary, 5483, 5484.

........., Tho., 266 ; in com. for Oxon., 766, 1216, 1470, 1745, 3015, 4254, 4559, p. 905, sheriff, 4544.

........., Wm., 543, 1422 ; deceased, 3668.

Denys, Agnes, wife of John, 5308.

........., Alice, in the suite of Princess Mary, 5483.

........., Hen., capt., 5112.

........., Hugh, 69, 805, 1872, 2048 ; dead, 3704, 2067, 3103, 3235.

........., Jno., 5308.

........., Mich., of Cheam, 1350, 4375.

Denys, Tho., sen., on sheriff-roll of Devon, 304, 3507; in com., 699, 917, 1503, 1812, 3183, 3534, 3566, 3605, 3938, 4783, 5431; com. for Hen. VII., 3988; squire of the Body, 1447, 1551, 1779.

........., ..., 4156.

........., Wm., in com. for Chester, 930, 1049, 1469, 1695, 3641, 3712, 3804, 4024, 4118, 4764; on sheriff-roll, 1949, 3507, 4544, 5561; squire of the Body, 1708, 3673.

Deptford, 155, 4648, 5317, p. 953.

........., St. Clement's, 3808.

........., York, 4107.

.... Strand, 3808, 5108.

Derby, co. of, 12, 511, 1978, 3193, 3713, 3760, 3887, 4022, 4253, 4434, 4836, p. 907, 5574.

........., array, 3336, 4939, 5529, 5626.

........., escheators of, 1080, 4127; feodaries of Crown lands, 4414.

........., sheriffs of, 949, 1316, 1771, 3507, 4544, 4728, 5561.

........., town of, 1771.

Derby, ——, of London, 12.

........., Agnes, 1309.

........., Edw., archdeacon of Stowe, 3515.

........., John, 1731.

........., Countess of. See Richmond.

........., Thos. Stanley Earl of, 775, 1854, 4187, 4375, 4707, 5255; livery of lands, 5646; in com. for Westmor., 3358, 3552, p. 904, for Derbyshire, p. 907; with the army in France, 4253; summoned to Parliament, 5616; King's debtor, 5633.

Dereham, 1709.

Derham, Th., in com. for Norf., 1812.

Dertford. See Dartford.

Dertington. See Dartington.

Derviller, Anth., 4445.

Derwent, the, 273, 415.

........., Wm., 3485.

Descars, François, 5505.

Desessingbard, Mons., 5163.

Desgardins, Jehan, 4445.

Deshertigonbusse (Bois le Duc), 1135.

Desrosiers, Jno., 5163.

Deston, Tho., 170.

Destraielles, Ameux, 4445.

Destrete, Cornel. Van, 558.

Destyere, Edw. Thwayte, Lord, 4585.

Dethicke, John, 3504.

........., Mary, wife of John, 3504.

Detiden, Dom, 3626.

Dethwick, (Dethyk), Derby, Chapel of St. John Bap., 1852.

Devenysh, Sir John, in commission for Sussex, 281, 1509, 3024, 3428, 3977, 4377, 4804.

Devereux, Anne, wife of Sir Walter, 736; in the train of Princess Mary, 5483.

Devereux, Sir John, 736.

........., Walt. See Ferrers.

........., Sir Walter, father of Walter Lord Ferrers, 736.

Deves. See Denes.

Devizes, 155, 255.

Devonshire, 12, 515, 721, 1996, 3178, 3502, 4022, 4377.

........., commissions for, 699, 917, 1166, 1503, 3183, 3534, 3566, 3589, 3605, 3938, 4539, 4783, 5220.

........., coinage of tin in, 397.

........., escheators, 208, 3133, 3493.

........., feodaries of Crown lands, 4414, 4711, 5692.

........., musters, 1812, 3392, 3688.

........., riots in, 5456.

........., stewards, 597; sheriffs, 664, 1316 1771, 1949, 3507, 4544, 5561.

........., stannaries, &c., 48.

........., white cloths of, 4848.

Devon, earldom of, 829, 969, 1589, 1603, 1610, 1613, 1634, 1635.

........., Edw. Courteney, 1st Earl of, 371, 969, 997, 1069, 1472, 1634, 1657, 2080.

........., ..., ..., possessions and offices, 157, 444, 453, 493, 502, 623, 489, 627, 1599, 1600, 1601, 1602, 1603, 1609, 1610.

........., Hen. Courteney, 3rd Earl of, 1996, 2080, 3977, 4347; restoration, 3502; with his mother, 4103; pardon, 5180; letter to, 4431.

........., Katharine Countess of, wife of Edw. 1st Earl, 1603.

........., Katharine Countess of, wife of Wm. 3rd Earl, the King's aunt, 401, 2080, 3502, 4377.

........., Thos. Courteney, Earl of, temp. Hen. VI., 2080.

........., Sir Wm. Courtney, 2nd Earl of, 12, 401, 699; his creation, 1603, 1658, attainder reversed, 1657; in commission for Devon, 699, 917, 1503, 1812, 3183, 3534, 3566, 3605, 3938; his tutelage, 1861; a challenger at birth of the Prince, 1491; dead, 2080.

Devyll, Peter, in commission for Devon, 1166.

Dewassen, Sieur, 3077.

Duwes, Giles, keeper of the King's library, 513; of " the wardrobe," 1944; annuity, 3094.

Dewsbrocke, Jno., of Bruges, 4916.

Dewysland, 5721.

Deye. See Day.

Deykyn, Tho., surveyor, 1241.

Deyncourt, Bucks, 3761.

Deysne, letter dated at, 4389.

Dibford, York, 5072.

Dice playing, 3118.

Dicheampton, Wilts, 155, 901.

Dick, Blind, a minstrel, 4653.

Dickson, Wm., 758.

Didaci, Barth, 510.

Diego. *See* Decastro.
Dieppe, 2050, 3105, 3619, 3678, 3814, 4081, 4330, 4365, 4440, 4843, 4844, 5021, 5753.
Dier ......, Wm., 5287.
Diessen. *See* Deysne.
Diet. *See* Cologne, the Swiss.
Differencloid. *See* Defferentcloid.
Digby, Lincolnshire, 1430, 4695.
Digby, Everard, deceased, 295.
.........., ..., 554 ; in commission for Leicesters., 1425, 1971, 4706, 4783, 4812 ; in the war with France, 3231, 4632 ; sheriff of Rutland, 4544.
.........., Sir John, of Leicest., 63, 521, p. 433 ; in commission, 266, 656, 1094, 1425, 1971, 4706, 4783, 4812 ; sheriff, 5561 ; possessions and offices, 1778, 4071, 5086 ; marshal of the army, 4070, 4253 ; has Sir Edm. Dudley's plate, 425.
.........., Roland, in commission for Notts., 1735, 1804.
.........., Simon, of Coleshill, Warw., 63, 1518, 1733 ; in commission for Warw., 282, 733, 1468, 1971, 3364, p. 903 ; commission for Notts., 1514, 1735, 1798, 1804, 1964, 3092, 3494, 4776, 5225 ; offices, 683, 4799 ; sheriff, 664.
Digfield, Warw., 3186.
Diggis, Jas., 523 ; in commission for Kent, 725, 906 ; sheriff of Kent, 1316.
Dighton, North, York, 4225
Dijon, 4464, 4513, 4916, 5173.
Diker, Rob. 4526.
Dikkelbrough, Norf., 1331.
Dimmok. *See* Dymmok.
Dimyck, Elias, 3570.
Dingley. *See* Dyngley.
Dinguel, John, clk., 2040.
Dinham. *See* Dynham.
Dipham, Midx., 1031, 1167.
Diron, John of Colwyk, Notts, 4940. *See* Byron.
Diogenes, 4448.
Disney, Wm., 5476.
Dison, John, 755.
Diss, Norf., 341, 5137.
Diss Wattons, Norf., 341.
Disselstein. *See* Isselstein, D'.
Ditchampton, 4022.
Dittisham, 3978.
Ditton, Bucks., 1744.
Dixmudes, p. 609.
Dixwell, Herts, 3601.
.........., Marg., 1331.
.........., Wm., clk., 4689.
Dobbes, Rob., 2019, p. 433, 4629, p. 953.
Dobelday, John, 3551.
Docwra, Tho., prior of St. John's, 663, 837, 1547, 1716, 1942, 1979, 3006, 3137, 3173, 3277, 4070, 4701, 4709, 5542, 5590, 5691 ; grant from the Crown as prior, 1623.

Docwra, Tho., prior of St. John's, privy councillor, 511, 650, 785, 938, 1264, 5173.
.........., ..., ..., his presence desired at Rhodes, 540, 4562.
.........., ..., ..., sent to the Lateran Council 2085.
.........., ..., ..., appointed to attend the King, 3942.
.........., ..., ..., his badge when with the army, 4253.
.........., ..., ..., his ship, p. 553.
.........., ..., ..., sent to France, 1104, 1182, 5335, 5379, 5391, 5407 ; attends Princess Mary, 5441, 5482 ; interview with Lewis XII. 5547, 5560.
.........., ..., ..., summoned to Parliament, 5616.
.........., ..., ..., in com. for Beds. 1051, 1122, 2045, 3501, 4700 ; in com. for Essex, 310, 1368, 1522, 1713, 3605, 3967 ; in com. for Warw., 282, 1387, 1468, 1971, 3364 ; in com. for Middlesex, 3552, 4663.
Dodd, James, 4825.
......, John, 4253.
......, Ro., exempted from pardon, 12.
Doddesworth, John, 777.
Doddington, Northumberland, 4430, 4531.
Doddington Pygot, Linc., 1716, 1979, 3137, 4695, 5691.
Doddington Welbourn, Linc., 1463.
Dodemore, Rog. de, 415.
Dodwell, Wm., incumbent of Gayton, Linc., 5011.
Dolman, John, 3260.
Domynyke, John, 1854.
Don, Edw., of Horslington, 3846 ; in com. for Bucks, 1379, 2045, 3219, 3231, 3310, 3522 ; knighted at Tournay, 4468 ; capt. 3980, 5112.
......, Sir Gryffyth, challenger at birth of the Prince, 1491 ; capt. 4653 ; sent with horses to Marq. of Mantua, 5339, 5535 5601 ; sent to Card. Surrentinus, 5540.
......, Griffen, 3417.
......, Sir John, 964, 4570.
...... river 3072.
Donatus, Jeronimus, 1880.
Doncaster, 178, 192, 1205, 1679, 2031, 3845, 3939, 4550, 5109.
Donet, St. Andrew's, rector of, 1854.
Donnington (Donyngton), Berks, 237, 374, 4530, 4698,
.........., Leicestershire, 3096.
.........., Lincolnshire, 1274, 2014.
Donyngton, Suffolk (?), 730.
Donyatt, Soms., 448, 1517, 3061.
Dorchester, abbot of, 3052.
Dorchester, Allsaints, 1310.
Doria, Don Pedro, 4725.
Doryere, Lord. *See* Dourriers.

Dormer, Geoffrey, .438.

........., Ralph, 5723.

Dornham, 4253, 4284.

Dorrell, James, 3237.

Dorrington, Salop, 4594.

Dorset, county of, 3061, 3786, 4022 ; commissions of the peace for, 26, 708, 903,
2007, 3064, 3529, 3566, 3606, 3701,
4713, 5658.

........., sheriffs of, 664, 1316, 1949, 3507, 3592,
4544, 5561.

........., feodaries of Crown lands for, 4414,
5692.

........., array for, 3393, 3688, 3723, 3742.

........., steward of, 448.

Dorset, Thomas Grey Marquis of, 1942, 3027,
3162, 3166, 3167, 3168, 3171, 3173,
3179, 3191, 3202, 3231, 3388, 3397,
3496, 3789, 3935, 4254, 4237, 4505,
4527, 4368, 5111, 5119 ; exempted from
pardon, 12; pardoned, 62, 5180; under
care of Rich. Carew, 1861 ; challenger
at birth of a prince, 1491 ; capt. of the
army, 3217, 5745 ; in Spain, 3298,
3476; ill success, 3451, 3355, 3500,
3584; in Guienne, 3500 ; to be lieut.-
general, 3989 ; in the war against
France, 3885, 4307, 4314 ; concludes a
treaty with Maximilian and Ferdinand,
4511; attends Princess Mary to France,
5322, 5407, 5441, 5483, 5505, 5560 ;
interview with Louis XII., 5523, 5553;
with French Council, 5590; summoned
to Parliament, 5616; his property, 3041,
3096, 3130, 3153, 3154, 5454; debtor
to the King, 777, 5633 ; offices, 753,
434 ; in commission for Leicestershire,
739, 1094, 1425, 1971, 4706, 4783,
4812; in commission for Northamptonshire, 732, 1708, 5658 ; in commission
for Staffordshire, 713, 1770; in commission for Warwickshire, 733, 1387,
1468, 3364, 5506.

........., ..., letter from, to Wolsey, of Mary's
marriage, 5569 ; of the tournament,
5606 ; of affairs in France, 5634, 5649;
letter to Ferdinand of Arragon, 3313.

........., ..., letter to, from Alva, 3353 ; from
Ferdinand, 3352.

........., Lord Marcars (Marquis Dorset ?),
1871.

........., Cecilia Lady, 777.

........., Old Lady, 5787.

Dorval, Sieur, 4924.

Dorvey, Wm., 4402.

Dossy, 3269.

Douai (Dowey), 4526.

Doughtyman, Wm., inc. of Cumberworth, Lincoln, 3547.

Douglas, Archibald, Lord, 3956.

........., Gawin (erroneously called George)
appointed to Arbroath, 4556.

........., Gavin, postulate of Arbroath, 4623,
4682; appointed to St. Andrew's, 5614.

Dourriers, Sieur de, 4710, 5482.

Dove, John, 1419.

Dovegate, 1508.

Dover, 521, 3443, 3659, 3813, 3887, 3890,
3891, 3946, 3985, 4067, 4103, 4105,
4273, 4311, 4320, 4431, 4474, 4492,
4652, 4926, 5033, 5130, 5512, 5560,
5569, 5649, 5724.

........., bailiff of, 238, 3163.

........., customer of, 538.

........., attacked by the French, 4743.

........., Castle, 4293.

........., ..., constable of, 154, 1296, 1889,
4083, 4996.

........., Road, 5130.

Dowilton, Devon, 2080.

Dowman, Jno., LL.D., 5124.

Dowmier, Hugh, 1990.

Downeley (date), 4098, 5787.

Downes, Nic., 135, 621.

Downing, John, 3035.

Downs, the, 3820, 3857, 4056, 4067, 4533,
4535, 5130.

Dowsyn, John, 851, 3031.

Doyle, John, 1070.

Doynton (Doughton), Glouc., 155.

Drake, Tho., 634.

Draper, Alicia, prioress, 584.

........., Robt., capt., 3980, 4474, 5112, 5761.

........., the Nicholas, ship, 3591, 4076, 4377,
4474, p. 812.

........., Thos., 4701.

........., Wm., 308.

Drawswerd, Tho., sheriff of York, 775.

Draycot, Wilts, 347, 1372, 4102.

........., Sir John, sheriff of Staffordshire, 1316,
1949, 3507, 4544, 5561 ; his badge,
4253.

........., Sir Philip, letter to Earl of Shrewsbury ; visit to Oatlands to see the King
hunt the stags, 5383.

........., Ph., of London, merchant, 3784,
5363.

........., Ric., brother of Sir Philip, 4253.

Drayton, Bucks, 258.

........., Yorks., 1805.

Drayton, John, D.D., 1183.

Drayton Basset, 4071.

Drecton, Sussex, 155.

Dresden, 1565.

Drew, Eliz., 3307.

........., Joan, daughter of Eliz., 3307.

Dringhouse, 3149.

Driver, John, p. 434.

Drogheda, 1246, 4588.

Drosswell, John, 4779.

Drover, Edw., 4632.

Druell, Chr., 959, 1222 ; sheriff of Hunts,
664 ; in com. for Hunts, 905, 916, 1095,
4006, p. 906.

........., Rich., 5096 ; in com. for Herts, 1971,
3102, p. 906.

........., Rob., 3019.

Drummond, John Lord, safe conduct for, 1820, 2069, 3676 ; commissioner, 3569, 4997.
........., Walt., Dean of Dumblane, 4628.
Drury, Sir Robt., 226, 467, 581, 811, 1421, 1534, 1939, 3707, 4254, 4872 ; in com. for Suffolk, 280, 676, 1121, 1153, 1715, 3029, 3219, 3967, 4713, 5133, p. 904.
........., ..., sent to Scotland, 474, 488, 548, 1066, 1739, 1820, 2078, 3696, 5757.
........., ..., recommended by Dacre, 3577.
........., ..., Jas. IV. complains of his decisions, 3838.
........., ..., attends the Princess Mary, 5483.
........., ..., pardon, 5180.
........., ..., licence to import, 947.
........., Wm. 4254.
Dryburgh, 1271, 1875.
........., commendatory of. See Murray.
Dryland, Leonard, 3371.
........., Ric., 3966.
Drynton, Somerset, 287.
Dublin, 149, 1298, 4588.
........., see of, 2023, 2071, 3062, 3212.
........., Abp. of. See Fitzsimons ; Rokeby.
........., conv. of St. Mary's, 5788.
........., St. Patrick's coll., 5788.
Du Cange (Ducarnge), Ph. of Normandy, M.D., 3324.
Duche, John, 483.
Duckworth, Geo., 1083, 4643.
Duddingtree rec., Worc., 358.
Dudley, Edm., 111, 3049 ; exempted from pardon, 12 ; his last will, 1212 ; offices, 98 ; cancel of recognizances, &c., 22, 105, 226, 258, 275, 342, 380, 600, 606, 722, 765, 799, 926, 1024, 1026, 1052, 1372, 1699, 1707, 3284, 4116, 4231, 4566, 5427, 5522, 5608 ; his house and goods, &c., 425, 888, 944, 953, 1002, 1124, 1263, 1264, 1323, 1343, 1421, 1464, 1472, 1484, 1515, 1577, 1824, 1832, 1958, 1965, 3034, 5427 ; attainder reversed, 3687.
........., Eliz., wife of Edm., 1212 ; marries Art. Plantagenet, 1965.
........., ..., daughter of Edm., 1212.
........., And., son of Edmund, 1002, 1212.
........., Jerome, son of Edm.. 1212.
........., John, son of Edm., 1212 ; restored in blood, 2082, 3687 ; in the war with France, 4534 ; pardon, 5180.
........., Peter, brother of Edm., 1212.
........., Ric., priest, cousin to Edm., 1212, 1484.
........., Wm. 1212.
........., Edw. Sutton Lord, in com. for Staffordshire, 279, 713, 791, 886, 1770, p. 903 ; for Worcester, 892, 3301, 3709, 4771, p. 903 ; for Warwick, 282, 1387, 1468, 1971, 3364 ; summoned to Parliament, 811, 5616; in the war against France, 3231, 4477; debtor to the King, 2044, 5633.
........., ..., his son, 3231, 4306.

Dudley, Rob., of London, goldsmith, 5247.
Duffeld, Wm., 498.
Duffield, South, Yorkshire, 4866.
Duh, Jeronimus de, 1880.
Duke, Fernando. See Estrada.
Dumferling, St. Margaret's, 774.
Dunbar, Gawin, archd. of St. Andrew's, 1176, 1407, 3303, 3412.
Dunbar castle, 5641.
Dunblane, 4624, 4628.
........., deanery of, 4628.
Duncan, Adrian, capt., 5112.
........., John, 3121.
Dunchurch, 1299.
Dundalk, 4588.
Dundas, Geo. 3240.
Dundonald vicarage, 3630.
Dune, Edw., of Horsington, Bucks, 3114.
Dunesse, Mons., of Bayonne, 3243.
Dunfermline, 4556, 4625.
Dungeon, the, near Jedworth, 4556.
Dunham, Sir John 777 ; in com. for Notts., 1735, 1804, 4127, 5183 ; sheriff, 1949 ; his badge in the war, 4253.
Dunhamhall, Suffolk, 1125.
Dunheved (Launceston), 210.
Dunholt, Tho., 1222, 3652.
Dunkeld, dioc. of, 2061, 3622, 3630 ; church of, 3122 ; bishop of 3323.
Dunkirk, 4008, 4253, 4526.
Dunmow, Much, 4176.
Dunning, Th., of Suffolk, 3017.
Dunois, Mon. de, 11, 3325 ; his death, 3752.
........., Count. See Longueville.
Dunolt, Th., 1781.
Dunpole, Somersetshire, 1517.
Dunstall, Kent, 685.
Dunstanborough, 4520, 4682 (2), 5090.
Dunston, Linc., 3284, 4852.
Dunwich, 4677.
Dunwold, Tho., in com. for Hunts, 916, 259, 1095, 4006.
Dunyate. See Donyatt.
Duperier, Christ., 3734.
Dupin, Martin, 3365, 4958.
Durea. See Urreas.
Duredaunt, Th., of Bucks, 1759.
Durers, Mons. 5391.
Dures, M., 3325.
Durham, diocese of, 743, 774, 4430, 4502, 4520, 4531 ; plenary indulgence from Leo X., 4729.
........., Thos. Ruthal, Bp. of, 251, 507, 520, 1017, 1429, 1918, 1923, 1952, 1948, 1956, 2001, 3027, 3229, 3230, 3243, 3336, 3380, 3419, 3882, 5112, 5173, 5180, 5368, 5407, 5742.
........., ..., bulls on his appointment, 168, 169, 267 ; restitution of temporalities, 250.

Durham, Thos. Ruthal, &c.—*cont.*

........, ..., ..., of the Privy Council, 165, 336, 480, 511, 521, 524, 531, 576, 594, 598, 602, 625, 679, 785, 955, 956, 1004, 1264, 1272, 1372, 1378, 1539, 1540, 1596, 1604, 1699, 1755–1758, 1840, 2027, 2029, 3080, 4767, 4870, 5090, 5735.

........, ..., ..., attests a treaty with Scotland, 474.

........, ..., ..., prepared to fulminate a bull against the Scots, 4455.

........, ..., ..., signs a treaty with France, 962.

........, ..., ..., ambassador for concluding a treaty with Arragon, 1055, 1059.

........, ..., ..., his banner attends the King against France, 3885, 4237, 4306, 4314.

........, ..., ..., attests Princess Mary's renunciation of her marriage with Charles Prince of Spain, 5282.

........, ..., ..., at her sponsalia, 5322; her marriage, 5441, 5483.

........, ..., ..., trier of petitions, 2089.

........, ..., ..., summoned to Parliament, 5616.

........, ..., ..., promises to exert himself for Erasmus, 1982; sends him money, 4576.

........, ..., ..., and the Savoy, 3292.

........, ..., ..., favors Card. St. George, 3443.

........, ..., ..., debtor to Margaret Countess of Richmond, 236.

........, ..., ..., grants to, 3842, 4438.

........, ..., ..., in com. for Northumb., 3553.

........, ..., ..., letters to, 538, 1861, 3412, 3755, 4327, 4403, 4482, 4497, 4522.

........, ..., ..., letters from, 1924, 4388, 4457, 4460, 4461, 4462, 4518, 4523, 4529, 5745, 5759, 5782, 5786.

........, ..., ..., drafts, &c. in his hand, 922, 924, 1457, 3347, 3555, 3752, 3811, 3812, 3835, 3836, 3838, 3862, 3863, 3983, 4008, 4009, 4055, 4085, 4086, 4328, 4422, 4461, 4512.

........, prior of, 742, 4869; debtor to Hen. VII., 1639.

........, his servant. *See* Waren.

Durrant, of Derbyshire, exempted from pardon 12 ; to be liberated, 755.

........, of Longdon, recognizance cancelled, 1480.

........, Thos., of Notts, 3031.

Durrimhæ, 3839.

Duryllo, John. *See* Darylle.

Dutarte, Clement, 3444.

Dutch, 3651.

E.

Eardis-land, Heref. *See* Erysland.

Earl Marshal. *See* Surrey, Earl of.

Eastborn, Sussex, 297.

Eastbourne, Hen., 4495.

Eastbudleigh, [Devon], 2080.

East Coker, Somers., 3114.

Easterfield. *See* Esterfield.

Easterling, merchant of, p. 953.

Easterlings, 777, 3398, 4844.

Eastgrinsted, Sussex, 1484.

Easthall, Kent, 5235.

Eastham, Essex, 4300.

Easthorpe, York, 415.

Eastkirby, Linc., 4714.

Eastlete, Suff., 1446.

Eastmarche, Bucks, 1352.

Eastneston, Northt., 1733, 3027.

Easton, Northt., 551. *See* Ships.

Easton, John, cooper, 3796, 4823, 5723.

East Peckham, Kent, 3969.

Eastpulham. *See* Pulham, East.

East-stoke, Dors. or Soms., 1240, 1635.

Eastwick, Herts, 4694.

East-wickham, Kent, 4694.

Eastwodbury, Essex, 222.

East-wrotham, Norf., 825.

Eaton. *See* Eyton.

Ebrighton, Dorset, 2080.

Ecclesfield, Lawrence, 1463, 1775, 4200. *See* Eglesfield.

Eccleston, Lanc., 1965.

Echels, Chester or Flint, 1035.

Echingham, Edw., *See* Ichyngham.

Ecuyer, the Grand, of France, pp. 609 and 610.

Edelmeton, Midx., 1031, 1167, 4302. *See* Edmonton.

Eden. *See* Hédin.

......, Hen., 754.

......, Ric., clerk of the King's council, 3478, 3758.

......, (or Uden), Th., 4996.

Edenhall, Cumb., 296.

Edenham, Linc., 730.

Edernyon, Merioneth, 4980.

Edgecombe. *See* Eggecombe.

Edinburgh, 3346, 3577, 3838, 3882, 4825, 5641.

........, letters dated from, 20, 709, 767, 910, 1112, 1176, 1220, 1271, 1408, 1410, 1415, 1460, 1461, 3319, 3320, 3321, 3322, 3323, 3339, 3372, 3569, 3623, 3624, 3625, 3631, 3633, 3837, 3882, 3883, 4112, 4572, 4628.

.... Castle, 3751.

Edyngworth, Somers, 347.

Edlingham, Northumb., 1040, 5010.

Edlogan, Wales, 53.

Edmondson, Sir Th., priest, 5595.

Edmonstoun, Gilb., 1410.

Edmonton, Middx., 730, 1480. *See also* Edelmeton.

Edmundes, Wm., 1257.

Edname, Dr., the King's Almoner, 5735.

Edsawe, Ric., 4175, 5181.
Eduensis, Jas., Bp. of, 1182.
Edward I., King of England, 260, 261, 262.
263, 1653, 4934.
.... II., King of England, 1077.
.... III., King of England, 1050, 1198,
1653, 3683, 3865, 4934.
.... IV., King of England, 1129, 1192,
1778, 1974, 3031, 3077, 3432, 3761,
4390, 4536, 5450; grants of, 416, 718,
941, 1050, 1355, 1389, 1653, 1996,
3045, 4848; obligations between him
and Lewis XI., 5351.
.........., ..., Edward, son of, 1653.
.........., ..., daughters of. See Devon, Katharine, Countess of; and Howard, Lady
Anne.
.........., ..., father of. See York, Richard,
Duke' of.
.........., ..., grandmother of, Anne Countess
of March and Ulster, 1603.
Edwardis, tenement called, in Essex, 729.
Edwards, David, 1158, 5096.
.........., David ap, convicted clerk, 1783, 3135.
.........., Hugh, sewer of the Chamber, 5096;
grants to, 235, 306, 738, 1367, 1865,
4199, 5131.
.........., John, deceased, 115, 1536.
.........., ..., 1050, 3051, 3796, 5096.
.........., Th., 5630.
.........., Wm., grants to, 843, 993, 1050; de-
ceased, 1894.
.........., ..., in Lord Lisle's retinue, 4653.
.........., ..., clk., 3423, 4120, 5282, 5322.
Eflith, John, 4770.
Egerton, Hugh, 4135.
.........., John, 355, 713, 1770.
.........., Ralph, gentleman-usher of the Chamber, standard-bearer, 3885, 4237, 4306,
4307, 4314, 4636; made knight at
Tournay, 4468; commission to review
the muster at Portsmouth, 4979; grants
to, 131, 682, 1035, 1390, 1648, 1912,
3395, 3462, 3570, 4657, 4748.
.........., Wm., deceased, 3378.
.........., ... 4253.
Eggecombe, John, 894, 3546.
.........., Sir Peter, of Stonehouse, Devon, 799,
5180; son of Sir Richard, 5719; in
the war against France, 4076, 4477,
4534, 4653; grants to, 208, 209, 210,
997, 3227; sheriff of Cornwall, 3057;
on sheriff-roll, 3507; in commission
of array, 1566, 3688; in commission
of the peace, 312, 699, 891, 917, 1166,
1503, 1694, 1812, 1984, 3183, 3290,
3566, 3583, 3605 (bis), 3938 (bis),
4539, 4754, 4783, 5220 (bis), 5456,
5586.
.........., Sir Ric., 5719.
Egglefeld, Rob., 3486.
Egham, Surrey, 4419
Eghtfield, Shropshire (?), p. 608.
Egleafeld, John, 499, 5585.
.........., Laur. See Ecclesfeld.

Eglisfeld, Th., 3032.
Egramonte, Mons., mayor of Bayonne, p. 399,
p. 615.
Egypt, 5729.
.........., Sultan of, 1659.
Eland, Northumb., 4531.
Elandshire, 4520, 5090.
Elcombe, Wilts, 804, 1864, 3190.
Eldercar. See Ellercar.
.........., (misprinted Eldercars), and his sons
delivered from the Fleet prison, 5740.
Elderton, Th., 5317, 5767.
.........., Sir John, p. 435.
Eleanor, Lady, the Emperor's granddaughter,
proposed marriage with French King,
5126.
.........., ..., proposed marriage with Duke
of Gueldres, 5173, 3541.
Eleson, Wm., 266; in commission for York,
273, 481, 3072, 3219, 4719, 5193.
.........., ... See also Elson.
Eling, Hants, 1824.
Elyngbrigge, Anne, daughter of Thomas,
1014.
.........., John, son of Thomas, 1014.
.........., Thos., 1014.
Elinor, Th., 3796.
Elizabeth, Queen of Hen. VII., 1651, 3456,
5394, 5401, 5406, 5451, 5453, 5628.
Ellercar (or Ellerker), John, 481.
.........., ..., Ralph, 534; captain of the
Mary James, 3591, p. 551, p. 651, 4475,
5761.
.........., Sir Ralph, 4902; captain of the
John Baptist, p. 811; in the Spanish
expedition, 5744; in commission for
York, 187, 1735, 1799, 3219 (bis),
4719, 5193, 5244.
.........., Sir Ric., 3358.
.........., (Eldircar), Wm., captain of the
Thomas of Hull, p. 652, 5761; captain
of the Mary James, p. 811.
.........., See also Eldercar.
Ellerton, York, Hen. prior of, 1097.
Ellesborough, Bucks, 4325.
Ellington, Norf., 825.
.........., Northumb., 1040, 5010.
Elliot (Elyot), Hugh, of Bristol, 3919, 5388.
......, John, 1050, 4769.
......, Ric., serjeant at law, 10.
......, ..., master of the Mary George, 3979,
p. 552.
......, ..., master of Leonard Friscobald's ship,
p. 652.
......, ..., justice of common pleas, 3958,
5646.
......, ..., justice of gaol delivery, 173, 1110,
1763, 1908, 3282, 3694, 4279, 4742,
4753.

Elliot, Ric., justice of assize, 72, 1741, 2089, 3295, 3724, 4339, 47 5, 5246.

......, ..., in commission of weirs in the Exe, 304.

......, ..., in com. for Berks, 5166, 5684; for Cornwall, 312, 891, 1694, 1984, 3290, 3583, 3605, 3938, 4754, 5290, 5586; for Devon, 699, 917, 1166, 1503, 3183, 3566, 3589, 3605, 3938, 4539, 4783, 5220; for Dorset, 26, 708, 903, 2007, 3064, 3566, 3606, 3701, 4713, 5658; for Hants, 904, 3071, 4159, 4676; for Oxfordshire, 766, 1216, 1470, 1745, 3015, 4559, 4809, p. 905; for the town of Oxford, 894, 3546; for Somerset, 287, 712, 3048, 3566, 3585, 3606, 3701, 4713; for Wilts, 898, 1489, 1938, 3157, 3605, 4583.

......, Rob., serjeant of the King's carriage, 939.

......, Th., 3260, 3261.

......, ..., justice of assize, 1741, 2089, 3295, 3724, 4339, 5246.

......, ..., justice of gaol delivery, 1763, 3282, 3694, 4279, 4765.

Ellis, Alfred, of Berwyk in Elme, Yorksh., 4866.

...... (Elysse), John, 3928.

......, Rob., of Rampton, 3031.

......, Stephen, clk., 1796.

......, Th., vicar of Shorne, 3477.

......, Wm., in com. for Norfolk, 1340, 1714, 1812, 1963, 3029, 3426, 3545, 5133.

Ellison, Wm. See Eleson and Elson.

Elmeley, Kent, 5235.

........., Worc., 3613.

.... Castle, barony of Worc., 3879.

...., chapel of, Worc. dioc., 1042.

.... Lovett, Worc., 130, 703.

Elmet, Wm., 4013.

Elmham, North, Norf., 1572.

Elmingham, Suff., 4705.

Elrington [York ?], 1205.

........., Edw., of Westneston, Sussex, 578.

........., Ric., in commission for Middlesex, 4663. (Qy. mistake for Robert.)

........., Rob., in com. for Middx., 3552, p. 905.

Elsik, Coort Van, 777.

Elson, Wm., in commission for Yorkshire, 1798, 1995, 3177, 4015, 5166, 5503, p. 906.

........., ... See also Eleson, Wm.

Elsye, John, p. 813.

Eltesle, Camb., Ely dioc., 3255.

Eltham, Kent, 3088, 3816.

........., manor of, 929, 1223, 1673, 3088, 3463, 3816, 5105, 5173, 5389, 5407, 5450, 5559.

........., ..., letters dated at, 5035, 5041, 5148, 5158, 5258, 5518.

.........., ..., Royal chapel in the, 833, 3682, 3683.

........., park of, 1223.

Elton, alias Baker, Edw., of the University of Oxford, clk., 5256.

Elveden, Nich., 4703, 4704.

Elvell (or Elwell), Wales, 46, 1113, 3612, 3771, 3840, 5461.

Elveringham. See Everingham.

Elvington, Yorksh., 499, 5585.

Elvys, Rob., 4476.

Ely, Camb., 12, 4207.

......, monastery of, 3400.

......, Jas. [Stanley], Bishop of, 406, 3803, 3963; his mansion near Holborn, 1523; summoned to Parliament, 5616.

......, ..., in commission, 1684, 3583, p. 904.

......, Rob. prior of, p. 435.

Elys. See Ellis.

Elysham (Alesham), Norf., 417.

Embden, Edezard, Count of, rebels against the Duke of Saxony, 5327, 5500, 5599, 5600.

Emery (Aymery), Lord, bastard, 3878, 3915, 4030, p. 609, p. 627, 5139; wages of, 5604.

Emildon, Northumb., 1040, 5010.

Emmanuel, John, 4845.

........., Don John, 4978.

........., King of Portugal, p. 114, p. 123, 839, 1726, 5729.

.........., ..., in treaty between France and Castile, 4924.

.........., ..., ships for, 3355 (p. 400).

.........., ..., letters from, 510, 4173; letters to, 4985, 5378.

.........., ..., procurator of, 1826.

Empire, the, offered to Henry VIII. by Maximilian, 5105, 5158.

Emps, James de, 3026.

Empson, Sir Ric., of Estneston, Northt., 367, 555, 721, 837, 933, 1124, 1231, 1352, 1472, 1482, 1493, 1518, 1636, 1733, 1825, 1946, 1965, 1985, 3027, 3152, 3284, 3297, 3492, 4022, 4941, 5522, 5608.

.........., ..., exemption from the general pardon, 12.

.........., ..., Act concerning lands made in trust to, 811.

.........., ..., annulment of his attainder, 3502 3653.

.........., ..., his offices, 87, 645.

.........., ..., cancel of recognizances made to, 22, 226, 258, 275, 566, 606, 722, 799, 926, 1052, 1372, 1399, 1421, 1699, 1707, 4116.

........., Th., son of Sir Ric., 3556.

.........., ..., in debt to the King, 2044.

.........., ..., Act for his restoration in blood, 3502, 3652.

.........., ..., in commission for Northt., 5658.

........., Tho., of London, 3827, 4940.

Enderby, Leic., 872, 874, 4436.
........., Eleanor, daughter of John, 1789.
........., John, 1789.
Enfield, Middx., 1386, 4302.
Engeham, John, on the sheriff-roll for Kent, 1949.
........., ..., in commission for Kent, 274, 906, 3428, 4663, 4847, 4927.
Enghien, 3499.
England, league of France and Scotland against, 3303.
........., Cardinal of. See Bainbridge, Christopher.
........., Cardinal Protector of. See Medicis, Julius de.
........., prior of. See Docwra.
........., treasurer of. See Surrey.
Englefield, Mr., 4452.
........., Sir Th., 164, 697, p. 434, 4192.
........., ..., speaker of Parliament, 811.
... ., ..., annuity, 957.
........., ..., grant to, 1187, 4436.
........., ..., signs as member of the Privy Council, 313, 480, 511, 524, 531, 576, 594, 702, 785, 955, 956, 1004, 1008, 1068, 1272, 1273, 1287, 1321, 1372, 1378, 1527, 1540, 1574, 1584, 1596, 1699, 1755, 1756, 1757, 1758, 1840, 2027, 3080, 3574, 4434.
........., ... his signature, 1657, 1658, 3318, 3324.
........., ..., justice of gaol delivery, 1547, 1548, 3765.
........., ..., in commission for Berks, 241, 885, 1393, 1732, 2095, 3640, 4341, 5166.
........., ..., in commission for Glouc., 930, 1049, 1469, 1695, 3641, 3712, 3804, 4024, 4118, 4764 ; for Herefordsh., 646, 675, 1400, 1963, 3686 ; for Salop, 930, 1981, 3071, 3715, 4827; for Worc., 892, 1971, 3301, 3709, 4770.
English (Einglisshe), Sir Jas., secretary of Margaret of Scotland, 4682.
........., Roger, 781.
........., Tho., 410, 1023, 1249.
Ensham. See Eynsham.
Entwyssell, Tho., in commission, 1425, 1971, 4706, 4783, 4812, p. 905.
Eppinghills, in Waltham Forest, 3203.
Equerry, Thomas, the King's, 4887.
Erard, Wm., 2097.
Erasmus, Greek professor at Cambridge, 4428.
........., letters from, 1017, 1404, 1418, 1478, 1652, 1842, 1847, 1849, 1870, 1882, 1883, 1900, 1917, 1925, 1957, 1997, 1998, 2001, 2013, 2025, 3012, 3158, 3159, 3495, 3518, 3637, 4336, 4427, 4447, 4528, 4576, 4727, 5352, 5570, 5731, 5732, 5733, 5734.
........., letters to, 1918, 1948, 1982, 2002, 2021, 3535, 3706, 4448, 5182, 5736.
........., (Herasmus), master of the Erasmus Sebastian, p. 651.
Erbury, Suff., 155.

Erdescote, Berks, 4694.
Erdeswyke, Hugh, 1319.
........., Sampson, brother of Hugh, 1319.
Eresby, Anth., 235.
........., Lord. *See Willoughby and Eresby, William Lord.
Eresey or Erysy, James, in commission for Cornwall, 1812 ; sheriff for Cornwall, 1949, 3507.
Ereswell, Suff., 1139.
Eringfeld, Sir Tho., 312, 891.
Erington, Gilb., of Greenrich, 4825.
........., ..., in commission for Northumb., 3553.
........., John, called the Angel, 4825.
........., Th., called Peepe, 4825.
Erith, Kent, 155.
........., ships at, 5316.
........., storehouse at, 4648, 5317.
Erle, John, 5694.
Erlesing, Yorksh., 4107, 5072.
Erliche, John, mayor of Cambridge, 3187.
........., ..., in commission for Cambridge (town), 677, 4890.
Erlscrombe, Worc., 3613.
........., church of, Worc. dioc, 460.
Ermotayte, Cumb., 296.
Ernane, p. 451, p. 457.
Ernley, John, 1372, 3006, 3284.
........., ..., attorney general, 10, 156, 722, 1733, 3031.
........., ..., grant to, 1484.
........., ..., in the war against France, p. 651.
........., ..., justice of assize, 1123, 1490, 2099, 3267, 3699, 4252, 4771, 5283 ; of gaol delivery, 1130, 1763, 3275, 3691, 4279, 4568, 5195.
........., ..., in commission for Cumberland, p. 907 ; Northumberland, 3553, p. 905 ; Sussex, 281, 297, 3024, 3428, 4804, p. 904; Westmorland, 2009, 3048, 3552, p. 904 ; Yorkshire, 1798, 1995, 3177, 3219 (bis), 4015, 4719, 5166, 5193, 5244, pp. 906 and 907.
........., ..., his signature, 111, 545, 59?, 600, 601, 602, 603, 604, 605, 617, 618, 702, 1480.
Eroll, Wm., Earl of, 1176 ; at the battle of Flodden, 4441.
Erpyngham, Norf, 1956.
Errona, Francis de, a Spaniard, 3496.
Eruere. See Eure.
Erysland, Heref., 5272.
Escault, at Tournay, 4987.
Escheators and Commissioners, Acts concerning, 811, 2082.
Escoyd, South Wales, 4436.
Escreke, John. See Estreke.
Esdeyne. See Hédin.

Esher, 5544.
........., letter dated, 4976.
Esingden, Rutland, 295.
Esington, Wm., 1486, 4006.
Esingwold, Yorksh., 1205.
........., Margaret, prioress of, 415.
........., John, baker, 5723.
Eskdale Moor, on the borders of Scotland, 4528.
Espanault, Guillaume, of Tournay, 4516.
Esquivel, Alonsode, 368.
Essell, John Van, of Acon, 4313.
Essex, coroner of, 576.
........., justice of sewers in, 2065.
.... and Herts, escheator of, 3493, 3743, 3947.
...., feodary of Crown lands in, 4414.
...., sheriff of, 664, 724, 1316, 1771, 1949, 3507, 4544, 5561.
........., commissions for, 310, 1368, 1522, 1713, 3605, 3688, 3785, 3850, 3967, 4792, p. 907.
........., forest of, 1290, 4504, 5136.
........., archdeacon of. See Rawson, Ric.
Essex, Hen. late Earl of, 4838.
........., Henry Bourchier, Earl of, 2065, 4176, p. 624, 5111, 5180, 5617, 5633.
........., ..., grant to, 1833.
........., ..., annuity, 3149, 3411.
........., ..., in the war against France, 3895, 4237, 4307, 4314.
........., ..., chief captain of the King's forces, 4752.
........., ..., present at the reading of the contract of marriage between Louis XII. and Princess Mary, 5322.
........., ..., summoned to Parliament, 5616.
........., ..., in commission of array, 3116.
........., ..., in commission for Essex, 310, 1368, 1522, 1713, 3605, 3785, 3967, p. 907; Herts, 309, 706, 1020, 1971, 3102, p. 906.
Essex, Wm., of Chipping-Lambourn, Berks, 1683.
...., sheriff of Oxon and Berks, 664.
...., in the war against France, 3932.
...., in commission, 241, 885, 1393, 1481, 1732, 2095, 4341, 5166, 5684.
...., knighted at Tournay, 4468.
...., in the war against France, 4653.
...., at the marriage of the Princess Mary, 5483.
Estaples, treaty of, 5285, 5294.
Estbudleigh. See Eastbudleigh.
Estcourt (Escourt), Agnes, 5308.
........., Eliz., 5308.
........., Joan, 5308.
........., Marg., 5308.
........., Walt., 5308.

Este, in Italy, 3269.
Esterfield, Harry, of Bristol, 5027.
........., Master, 4357.
Estland, voyage to, 4878, p. 954.
Estling, 4216.
Estmarch, Bucks. See Eastmarch.
Estrada, Fernando Duke of (commonly called Fernando Duke), 8, p. 71.
Estreke, John, 632, 3537.
Etall, Northumb., 4441, 4460, 4497, 4520.
Etampes, letters dated, 5359, 5360, 5372, 5373, 5376, 5381.
Etende, Count de, 4924.
Ethered, Wm., indebted to Hen. VII., p. 435.
Eton, Berks, 1203, 3005.
.... Provost and Coll. of, 1044.
Etton, Anne, wife of John, 857, 3504.
......, John, 857, 3504.
Eu, or Heu, in Normandy, 20, 4330.
Eudes, Tho., of France, merchant, 1143.
Eure, Constance, wife of John, 4587.
......, Jno., 4587.
......, Ralph, of Malton, 5655.
......, (or Evers), Sir Ralph, of Eyton, 4719, 4868, 4902, 5655.
......, ..., ..., mayor of Newcastle-on-Tyne, 705.
......, ..., ..., sheriff of Yorkshire, 1316.
......, ..., ..., indebted to Hen. VII., p. 435.
......, ..., ..., refuses deputyship of Berwick, 4902.
......, ..., ..., in the Spanish expedition, 5744.
......, ..., ..., in commission, 1735, 3219, 5193, 5244.
......, Sir Wm., knighted at Tournay, 4468.
Euxine Sea, 1659.
Evelin, Clays, gunner, 4721.
Everard, Hen., 3991.
........., John, 5308.
........., Margaret, 5308.
Everingham, alias Elveringham, church of, in the Marches of Calais, 1564, 2032, 3550. See Overingham.
........., Yorkshire, 273, 4719, 5193, 5655.
........., Edm., p. 608.
........., Hen., in commission for Yorkshire, 1735 (bis), 1804, 3358.
........., Sir John, deceased, 3149, 3411.
........., ..., annuity, 2031.
........., ..., sheriff of Yorkshire, 3507, 4866.
........., ..., in commission for Yorkshire, 1735 (bis), 1798, 1804, 1995, 3177, 3358, 4015.
Everley, Wilts., 1002, 1965.
Evers. See Eure.
Eversshawe, lands in, 3297.
Everton, Humph., 485, 1281, 4254.
........., John, 5096.

Evesham, monastery of, 1592, 4607, 4614, 4716.
........., abbot of, 1639, 4661.
........., summoned to Parliament, 5616.
........., Thomas Newbold, abbot of, 4607, 4614, 4716.
........., Clement Lichfield, abbot of, 4716.
........., prior of, 4614.
Evingdon, Leic., 1129, 1148.
Evington, Wm., 1843.
Evyas, Alexander, 5235.
......, Humph., 5235.
......, John, 5235.
Ewelme, Oxon., 78, 174, 1426, 3144, 4205.
Ewhurst, Surrey, 1418, 1916.
Ewen, Nic., employed in making Hen. VII.'s tomb, 775.
........., Tho., 1061.
Ewry, yeoman of the, 1008.
Ewyas Lacy, in the Marches of Wales, 45, 298, 1113.
Exchange, for foreign parts, 1816, 2015, 3265.
........., rate of, 153, 318, 490, 650, 1181, 4481, 4511, 4917, 5154.
Exchequer, the, 291, 812, 875, 971, 1300, 1394, 3031, 5453.
........., auditor of, 1863.
........., chief baron of, 3645.
........., barons of, 4, 7, 9, 17, 443, 1747, 1921, 3573, 4016, 4550.
........., chamberlains of, 32, 3308, p. 431, 4807, 5274.
........., chancellor of. See Lovel, Sir Th.
........., clerk of the pipe in, 3432, 3959.
........., messengers of, 5268.
........., remembrancer of, 1747, 3609, 3656, 5118.
........., treasurer of, 3308, p. 431, 4550, 4807, 5274.
........., treasurer of. See Howard, Thomas, Earl of Surrey.
........., "Potans House" under the, 1692. 5211.
Exe, commission of weirs in the river, 304.
......, fisheries in the river, 2080.
Exeter, 1928, 2080, 3120, 3988, 4019, p. 651.
.... Castle, justices of gaol delivery at, 1908.
........., church of St. George in, 752.
........., church of St. John in, 1330.
........., customs of, 138, 353, 919, 4385, 5201.
........., Duchy of, 253, 860, 942, 3061, 5202, 5515.
........., lordship of Westgate, als. Ex Iland, without the city of, 157, 1599.
........., mayor of, 304.
........., mayor and bailiffs of, 1771.
........., ships at, 3978.
Exeter, St. Peter's in, 3988.

Exeter, lands, possessions called, belonging to the Countess of Richmond, 382.
........., [Oldham], Hugh, Bishop of, 236, 799, 811, p. 550, 4316, 5111, 5180, 5296, 5431. .
........., ..., ..., in commission for Cornwall, 312, 1694, 3290, 3583, 3605, 3938, 4754, 5220, 5586; Devon, 699, 891, 917, 1166, 1503, 1984, 3183, 3566, 3589, 3605, 3938, 4539, 4783, 5220, 5456.
........., ..., ..., legatee of Henry VII., 776.
........., ..., ..., trier of petitions, 2082.
........., ..., ..., summoned to Parliament 5616.
Exilond, Devon (?), 2080.
Exmewe, Th., 3006.
Exmister, Devon, 571, 1255, 1602, 2080.
Exmouth, customs of, 1992, 4385.
Extraneus, Roger, temp. Edw. I., 4934.
Exworth, church of, Linc., 4537.
Eydon, Northt., 645.
Eye, Suffolk, 492, 1485, 4205.
...... Castle, 492.
......, honor of, 4254.
......, park of, 492.
Eylmer, Wm., 236. See Aylmer.
Eymore, Devon or Somers., 155.
Eynesham, monastery of, Oxon., 1901.
Eyre, the, Yorksh., 3072.
Eyr, Arthur, 4253.
...., Th., 4253.
Eyre, Ric., 266, 3209.
Eyrey, garrison at, 5163.
Eyton, Beds., 5720 (p. 958.)
........., Bucks, 12.
........., Northt., 4436.
........., Yorksh., 5655.
Eyton-on-Wildmore, Salop, 4612.
Eyton, Th., 4612.
........., Wm., 5501.

F.

Fabian, ——, 4076.
........., capt. at the siege of Brescia, 3026.
........., John, 714.
........., Tho., veterinary surgeon for the King's horses, 1370, 1999.
Faceby Cleveland, York, 1114.
Facombe, Hants, 5100.
Faenza, 3112, 3821.
Fagugnana, island near Sicily, 1209.
Faiete, La. See Fayette.
Fairfax, John, 3386.
........., Ric., 3386.
........., Rob., gentlemen of the Ch. Royal, 207, 3773, 4654.

Fairfax, Rob., poor knight of Windsor, 5397.
.........., Tho., in com. for York, 266 ; for Yorksh., 1798, 3177, 1804, 3219, 3358, 4015, 4719, 5244, p. 907.
.........., Sir Thos., knighted at Tournay, 4468.
.........., Tho. son of Sir Thos., in commission for Yorkshire, 5166, 5193, 5244, pp. 906 and 907.
.........., Wm., in com. for Cumberland, 717, 1048 ; Northumberland, 3553; Westmoreland, 2009, 3048, 3552 ; for Yorksh., 455, 954, 1549, 1550, 1735, 1798, 1799, 1995, 3177, 3219, 3358, 4015, 4719.
.........., ..., in commission of gaol delivery, Newgate, London, 1519, 1897, 3765, 3778, 4553 ; York city and castle, 3691; Northern Circuit, 173, 1130, 1763, 3275, 4279.
.........., ..., justice of assize, 2099, 3267, 3699, 4252, 4771 ; Northern Circuit, 832, 1123, 1490.
.........., ..., sergeant-at-law, in commission of sewers, Yorkshire, 273, 481, 3072.
.........., ..., justice of common pleas, 1116.
.........., ..., trier of petitions, 2082.
Falconberg. See Faulconberg.
Falconer, David, (convoys De la Motte to France, sent to London,) 3321, 3326, 3346, 3347, 3412, 3577.
.........., Ric. master gunner, 759, 781, p. 432, 4238, 5005.
Falke, Will., proctor, 1928.
Fallesley, Northt., 516.
Falley, als. South Falley, Berks, 1867, 5646.
......, Bucks, 2016.
......, Jno., under D. of Norf., against Scots, 4674.
Falmouth, 3814, 5269.
.... See Shipping.
Falston, 1913.
Falwesley, 1949.
Famagosta, Franciscus de Briscia, Bp. of, 3456.
Famine in London dreaded, 1948.
Fane, Hen. See Vane.
Fanhope lordship, Heref., 5384.
Fanhope, Lord, 253.
Farding, John, grant towards exhibition at school, 1274, 2014.
.........., Th., gentleman of the Chapel Royal, legatee of Margaret Countess to Richmond, 235, 1784, 4065.
Farewell, Sir John, prior of St. Mary of Walsingham, 5522.
Faria, John, letter to Eman. King of Portugal, 5378.
Farlam, Cumb., 3865.
Farley, Salop, 5436.
Farmer, Roger, rector of Tevent, 1854.
.........., Wm., 4809. See Fermour.

Farms, the King's, receiver general of, 4347.
......, engrossing of, 5727.
Farndon, Northt., 3027.
Farnedon (Farmdon), Cheshire, 131, 4748.
Farnham, 79, 3388.
.........., John, 266.
Farnyhirst. See Fernehurst.
Farringdon, Norf., 4071.
Fartley, Laurence, captain of the Jennet Purwyn, 5112.
Farwey, 2080.
Fasset, 1867.
Fastalff, als. Fastall, als. Fastaliffes, Geo., pardon, 3993.
.........., ..., captain, 4632.
Fastcastle, 5090.
Fasterne, 128, 155.
Father, John, 5096.
Fauconer. See Falconer.
Faucquet, Jan., letter from, 5032.
Faulconberg, Anth., Lord de Ligne, Count, 4429, 4534, 5292, 5636, 5722.
.........., ..., taken into Henry's service, 3915.
.........., ..., letter from, 3916.
.........., ..., receipt for 3,000 crs. from Hen. VIII., 4129.
.........., ..., commission to levy troops against France, 4120.
.........., ..., at Terouenne, captain of Burgundians, pp. 609, 626.
.........., ..., to be retained in Henry's service, 5139.
.........., ..., wages paid to, 5163.
Faunte, Pet., coll. of customs, at Bridgewater, 536.
Faux, Ric., in debt to the King, 3497.
Fava, Alexander de la, mercht. of Bologna, 5438.
......, Louis de la, mercht. of Bologna, 342, 802, 3410.
......, ..., in communication between H. VIII. and John Style, pp. 71, 116, 117.
......, ..., restitution of a ship by, 3422.
......, ..., payment to him, for harness, 3496.
Favenne, (Faenza?), 3112.
Favour, Jo., owner of The George of Hampton, 5112.
Fawne, Jo., vice-chancellor of University of Camb., (to Wolsey, offering him the chancellorship), 5121.
Faune, Nich., 4659.
......, Rob., 4659.
Fawteles, Jo., mercht., p. 958.
Faxflete. See Flaxfleet.
Fayes, Barbary, 1537.
Fayette, La, 5366.
.........., Lord, lieut. of the Duke of Alençon's comp., (taken prison at Terouenne), p. 609.

Fayssey, Lady, 5163.

Fazakerley, John, als. Brent, groom for the King's mouth in the cellar, 333, 4788.

Feckam. *See* Fescamp.

Fekenham, Worc., 155.

Felbrigge, Norf., 3502, 5073, 5710.

Felding. *See* Feilding.

Felinger, sec. to Maximilian, 5158; letter from, 4910.

Felix, Count. *See* Wurtemburg.

Felonies, Act concerning, 3502.

Feltham, Midd., 3284.

Felton, Th., kinsman and h. of Sir Tho. Sampson of Playford, Suffolk, 3582.

Feltri, Bp. of, papal ambassador with Maximilian, 4598.

Fencot, Heref., 1127.

Fenys, Anne, wife of, Tho., 1956.

......, Edw., son of Ric. Fenys Ld. Saye, 573.

......, Sir John, 3819.

......, ..., Alice, widow of, heir of Geo. Lord Fitzhugh, 3819.

...... (Finis), Mary, sister of Lord Dacre, in service of Mary Queen of France, 5484.

......, Ric. *See* Saye, Lord.

......, Th., 1956.

......, Tho. *See* Dacre.

Fenny-Bentley (Fenebently) church, Derby, 1903.

Fenny-Stratford, 12.

Fenrother, Rob., goldsmith and alderman of London, and a master of the Mint in the Tower, 3006, 4917.

Fenwick, ——, 4347.

........., Hen., idiot, son of John, 4870, 5009.

........., Jno., 5009.

........., Ralph, 5009.

........., ..., squire of the Body, lieutenant of the Middle Marches towards Scotland, 5010.

........., ..., son of Rog., admitted one of the Council, 5090.

........., ..., sheriff for Northumberland, 5561.

........., Sir Ralph, 4825.

........., Rog., squire of the Body, lieutenant and warden general of the Middle Marches towards Scotland, 283, 1040.

........., ..., commission of array, or musters, Northumberland, 187, 1735, 1804, 3358.

........., ..., sheriff for Northumberland, 1316.

........., ..., in com. for Northumberland, 3553.

........., ..., attorney, 856.

........., ..., in debt to H. VIII., 777, 3497.

........., Sir Rog., 4556; death of, 4870, 5090.

Ferdinand, King of Arragon, 216, 224, 922, 923, 924, 1111, 1221, 1457, 1676, 1681, 1689, 1697, 1701, 1902, 1948, 2075, 3067, 3112, 3115, 3138, 3188, 3243, 3269, 3276, 3314, 3333, 3350, 3357, 3377, 3388, 3398, 3415, 3451, 3499,

Ferdinand, King of Arragon—*cont.*
3555, 3626, 3633, 3647, 3678, 3744, 3752, 3780, 3798, 3835, 3862, 3876, 3887, 3897, 3915, 3951, 3962, 3975, 3997, 4055, 4058, 4059, 4069, 4075, 4078, 4085, 4094, 4112, 4182, 4274, 4282, 4296, 4327, 4328, 4366, 4398, 4418, 4464, 4563, 4577, 4666, 4725, 4756, 4789, 4796, 4844, 4849, 4952, 4955, 4978, 5006, 5007, 5025, 5029, 5041, 5059, 5076, 5105, 5126, 5140, 5203, 5152, 5263, 5267, 5290, 5319, 5353, 5368, 5377, 5378, 5393, 5398, 5404, 5410, 5468, 5517, 5532, 5539, 5543, 5637, 5675, 5686, 5741, 5745, 5757.

..........., ..., dislikes the proposed marriage of Charles and Mary, 8.

..........., ..., his government of Castile, 490, 796.

..........., ..., his kingdom of Naples, 490, 796.

..........., ..., his relations with France, 490, 796.

..........., ..., his relations with Scotland, 3083.

..........., ..., his wars with the Moors, 796, 819; English expedition sent in aid of, 1531, 1562, 1726.

... ., ..., proposes to mediate between the Emperor and the Venetians, 819.

..........., ..., the English displeased with him, 3298, 3355.

..........., ..., his conquest of Navarre, 3355, 3356, 3584, 3593, 3614, 3662, 3766, 4267.

..........., ..., his conduct with regard to Guienne, 3355, 3755, 3766, 4267, 4829.

..........., ..., his solemn promises, p. 398.

...., ..., his secret negotiations with France, p. 498, 3807, 4096, 4829, 4845, 4864, 5173, 5323, 5362.

..........., ..., has few councillors whom he can trust, 490.

..........., ..., his health, 4525, 4845, 5152, 5208, 5338, 5366, 5581, 5392, 5642, 5718.

..........., ..., goes to hunt, 5470.

..........., ..., his army, 3357, 3361.

..........., ..., his receipt for Katharine's dowry, 162.

..........., ..., his treaties, 27, 240, 793, 1055, 1059, 1335, 1880, 1881, 1967, 1980, 2010, 2033, 2094, 3023, 3327, 3339, 3513, 3523, 3586, 3603, 3649, 3664, 3797, 3839, 3860, 3861, 4038, 4268, 4511, 4818, 4875, 4924, 5274.

..........., ..., ambassadors of, 4365, 4455, 5259.

..........., ..., his ambassador in Flanders, 5341, 5362, 5377, 5387.

..........., ..., ambassadors to, 3762.

..........., ..., letters from, 1209, 1622, 3352, 3638, 4578, 4985, 5319, 5743.

..........., ... letters to, 338, 368, 3081, 3082, 3106, 3279, 3313, 3452, 5785.

Ferdinand, King of Arragon, younger son of Philip of Castile, 4058, 4931, 5353.

Ferdinand II., King of Naples, daughter of, 922.

Ferdinand, Duke of Holsatia, letter from James IV. to, 3627.

Ferdinand, Gonsalvo, clerk, Henry VIII.'s chaplain, native of Spain, 4128. *See* Fernando.

Fermour, Ric., grant, 3304, 4254.

.........., ..., passport from Marg. of Savoy to export wheat, 3651.

.........., ..., merchant of the staple at Calais, 3708, 4732, 4892.

.........., ..., grocer, of London, 4699.

.........., Wm. *See* Farmer.

.........., ..., to be coroner and attorney in the King's Bench, 122.

.........., ..., in com., Oxfordshire, 1745, 3015, 4559, 5506.

.........., ..., in com., Oxford, 3546.

.........., ..., grant, 2055.

Fermoy, ——, 5443.

Fernandez, Edw., sent by Emanuel King of Portugal to James IV. concerning reprisals, 510, 1826.

Fernando Duke. *See* Estrada.

.........., Don, brother of Charles Prince of Castile, 4561, 4796, 4844, 5353.

.........., ..., proposed marriage with Renée of France, 4952.

.........., Gonsalvo, Duke de Terra Nova, great captain, 3593.

.........., the Pope desires the arrival of, p. 369.

.........., ..., reported to join the army of the Viceroy, with men and horses, p. 381.

.........., John. *See* Furnando.

Ferne, Geo., clerk of the diocese of Dunkeld, 3622.

Fernehurst, 4556.

.........., laird of, 5348.

Fernhill, Warwick, 3186.

Ferningham (Jerningham ?), Anne, chamberer to Queen Mary, 5483.

Ferrara, 1681, 3104, p. 367, 3283.

.........., Leo X. desires to have, 3377.

.........., Barth. de la Vienne, raises new forces in, 5171.

.........., Cardinal of, slays 3,000 Venetians before Ferrara, 922.

.........., ..., late Archbishop of Milan, p. 366.

.........., Duke of, chosen gonfalonier for the Church, 11.

.........., ..., Pope's army against, 1697 p. 255.

.........., ..., supported by France, 3112.

.........., ..., Pazart sent to, on the matters of Reggio, p. 367.

.........., ..., goes to the Abruzzi, to return with Prospero Colunna, 3341.

Ferrara, Duke of, keeps within the lands of the Colonnas, 3341.

.........., ..., the Church's censures removed from, by Leo X., 3780.

.........., ..., makes a descent upon Modena; forced to retire by the Viceroy's army, 3821.

.........., ..., on the part of the French, in treaty between Louis XII. and Prince of Castile, 4924.

Ferre, Richard, 3186.

Ferrer, ——, attendant upon Johanna Queen of Castile, 8.

.........., Humph., clk., of Hogham, Linc., 313.

Ferrers, Edw., 587, 3186.

.........., ..., King's sewer, bailiff of Warwick, &c. 549.

.........., ..., in commission of peace for Warwickshire, 1468, 1971, 3364.

.........., ..., in the war with France, 3885, 4237.

.........., Sir Edw., in the war, 4306, 4307, 4314.

.........., ..., made knight at Tournay, 4468.

.........., ..., als. Ferreys, of Baddisley, Warw., sheriff of Warwicksh. and Leitersh., 4544, 5640.

.........., Sir Hen., 4759.

.........., Humph., son and heir of Sir John Ferrers, 6015.

.........., John, in debt to Hen. VII., 3497.

.........., Sir John, 5015.

.........., ..., in com. for Staffordshire, 279, 713, 791, 886, 1770 ; Warwickshire, 282, 1387, 1468, 1871.

.........., ..., on sheriff-roll, Warwick and Leicester, 664.

.........., Walter Devereux, Lord, 328, 736, 3772, 3820, 3974, 4005, 4020, 4632, 5064.

.........., ..., grants to, 1354, 1499, 3100, 3684, 5180, 5563.

.........., ..., with Tho. Marq., Dorset, his brother, in the war against France, 3168, 3231, 3298, 3983, 4377.

.........., ..., capt. of the Trinity Sovereign, 3591, 3977, 4533, 5761.

.........., ..., in commission for Herefordshire, 3684, 3686, p. 907.

.........., ..., King's commissioner of the Council in Marches of Wales. 4404.

.........., ..., summoned to Parliament, 5616.

.........., ..., indebted to Hen. VIII., 5633.

.........., ..., signature, 3476.

.........., Wm., Lord, and Eliz., his wife, 736.

Ferrour, Tho., chief mason of works at Calais, 771.

.........., ..., yeoman of the Crown, to be usher of the Prince's Council Chamber, Westm., 3941.

.........., ..., ..., doorward, 4967.

Ferrys, Wm., 4488.

Ferrett, forces raised in, for Emp. Maximilian, 4319, 4349.

Ferret, Simon de, mission from Emp. Maximilian to Hen. VIII., 4091, 4273, 4296, 4322, 4361, 4364, 5171.

.........., ..., payment to him as wages, 5163.

Ferthing, in the dominion of Sieur de Bruere, 4284 (p. 625).

Ferthyng, Tho. *See* Farding.

Fescamps, abbot of, commissioner in a treaty with France, 962 ; abbey of, 4005.

Fetiplace, Ant., squire of the Body, grants to, 172, 174, 1394, 1426.

.........., ..., in com. for Oxfordshire, 766, 1216, 1470.

.........., John of Charney, 5646 ; in com. for Berks, 241, 885, 2095, 3640, 4341, 5166, 5684.

.........., Ric., in com. for Berks, 885, 1393, 1481, 1732, 2095.

.........., Tho., 1002.

.........., Sir Tho., 4192 ; in com. for Berks, 241, 885, 1393, 1481, 1732, 2095, 3640, 4341, 5166, 5684.

.........., ..., in the wars, 3964.

.... Wm., in com. for Berks, 885, 1393, 1481, 1732, 2095, 3640, 5166, 5646, 5684.

.........., ..., escheator, 3046.

Fevers, Peter, armourer, grant, 3036, 5720 (p. 954).

Feversham, Cinque Port, collector of subsidy in 4996.

Fiddelton, 1002.

Field, John, 4900.

Fielding, Sir Everard, of Masthorp, Rutland, 63.

.........., ..., grant to, 857.

.........., ..., in commission of gaol deliv. Leicester Castle, 554.

.........., ..., in com. for Leicestershire, 656, 1094, 1425, 1971, 4706, 4783, 4812, p. 905.

.........., ..., in war against France, 3231.

Fiemeux, Henry, 4445.

Fiennes. *See* Fynis.

Fiennes, Sieur de, governor gen. of Flanders, 5379 ; Belgium, 4322, 4364, 4844.

.........., ..., daughter's marriage to son of Berghis, 3499.

.........., ..., man of letters, as ambassador from, to Hen. VIII. at Calais, 4284.

.........., ..., promises all help to Wolsey, 5418.

.........., ..., letter to, 4331.

.........., ..., his Lieut. *See* Mastaing, François de. *See* Fenys.

Fiessen. *See* Fuessen.

Fifhid. *See* Fyfelde.

Fifteenths and tenths, 2082, 3169, 3440, 3441.

Filberts. *See* Philbertis.

Filleigh, Th., 3272.

Filoll, Dorothy, wife of Sir Wm., 4733.

.........., Jasper, 3609.

.........., Maur., indebted to Hen. VII., 1639 3497.

.........., Sir Wm., 4733.

.........., ..., in commission of peace, Dorset, 26, 903, 2007, 3064, 3231, 3566, 3606, 3701, 4713, 5658.

.........., ..., in commission of array, Hants, 1812.

.........., ..., in war with France, 3231, 4377.

.........., ..., indebted to Hen. VII., 3497.

.........., ..., part owner of Henry of Hampton, 4377.

Finario, Card de, brother to Fabricius del Caretto, 4756, 5254 ; Card. Bainbridge with him shortly before he expired.

Fincham, Norf., 5250.

Finchamstede, in Windsor Forest, 446, 3789.

Finch, ——, machinist, estimate for tomb of Hen. VII., 775.

.........., Jas., 1584.

.........., Vincent, in com. for Sussex, 281, 3024, 3428, 4804, p. 904.

.........., Wm., 4002.

Finchwike, Jo. de, temp. Edw. I., 4934.

Fyndern, Sir Wm., in com. for Cambridgeshire, 1684, 3583, p. 904.

Findon, Suss., 1212, 1343.

Fineux. *See* Fyneux.

Finmere, in Oxford, 155.

First fruits. *See* Tenths, &c.

Fish and fisheries, 586, 811, 1279, 1777, 2055, 2080, 3367, 3395, 3445, 3569, 3571, 3692, 3836, 4634, 4743.

Fisher, Adrian, at (Calais), 4232.

.........., Anth., grant, 1341, 1750.

.........., Chr., at Bacano, letter from, 880.

.........., ..., clk. of the Sacred Coll., returned to England from Rome, 982.

.........., ..., carries the golden rose, 983.

.........., John, Bishop of Rochester, 236, 406, 1478, 1957, 3292, 3495, 4447, 4528, 5296, 5542.

.........., ..., ..., grants to, 1102, 3773.

.........., ..., ..., witness at the treaty with Scotland, 474.

.........., ..., ..., to be present at the Lateran Council, 2085.

.........., ..., ..., as one of Hen. VIII.'s ambassadors at the Lateran Council, 3108.

.........., ..., ..., trier of petitions, 811.

.........., ..., ..., summoned to Parliament, 5616.

.........., ..., ..., in com. for Cambridge, 4770.

.........., ..., ..., Chancellor of Cambridge, 677.

.........., ..., ..., his signature, 1004, 1372, 1527, 1574, 1584, 1596, 1604, 1699, 1756, 1457, 1758, 3080, 4770, 5735.

.........., Erasmus' correspondent, 1997.

Fisher, Sir John, in com. for Leicestershire, 656, 1094, 1425 ; in com. for Linc., 278, 657 ; for Northamptonshire, 732 ; for Warwickshire, 282.

........., ..., justice of assize, Midland Circ., 19, 294.

........., ..., in com. of gaol delivery for Midland Circ, 173 ; for Newgate, 541 ; for Bedford town, 907, 931.

........., ..., trier of petitions, 8110.

........., Matthew, in commission of peace, Bedfordshire, 3501.

........., Mich., in com. for Beds, 1051, 1122, 2045, 4700.

........., ..., in commission for gaol delivery, Bedford Castle, 1922.

........., ..., on sheriff-roll for Beds. and Bucks, 3507, 4544 5561.

........., Rob., the king's chaplain, prebendary of Windsor, 74, 1506.

........., ..., incumbent of Greasforthe, St. Asaph dioc., 638.

........., ..., provost of Stanelthorpe, Durham and abbot of Rufford, 824.

........., ..., resignation of Chedsay, dioc. Bath and Wells, 1442.

........., Rob., gunner, 356, 781.

........., Wm., clk., grants to, 4345, 5578.

........., ..., retinue of Calais, 4635.

........., ..., captain of the Gabriel of Toppesham, 5112.

Fisherton Anger, Wilts, gaol delivery, 3488.

Fishmongers of London, grant to, 3868.

Fishwike, 1965.

Fitton, Wm. · See Fytton.

Fitz-Alan, Alan, 415.

Fitz-Bertram, Rog., 415.

Fitz-Elias, Alan, 415.

Fitz-Gilbert, Jordan, of the church of Wilberfosse, 415.

Fitzgerald, Sir Gerald, son and heir of Earl of Kildare, grant, 1314.

........., Gerald, E. of Kildare, 4254.

........., ..., deputy of Ireland, 4588.

........., ..., wife of. See Zouche, Eliz.

Fitzherbert, Alice, abbess of Pollesworth, 748,

........., Anne, 584, 748.

........., Anth., in com. for Leicestershire, 739, 1094, 1425, 1971, 4706, 4783, 4812 ; for Lincolnshire, 1511 ; for Staffordshire, 1770, p. 903, 905 ; for Warwickshire, 733, 1387, 1468, 1971, 3364, p. 903.

........., John, remembrancer of the Exch., 1747.

........., ..., in com. of peace, Leicestershire, 1425, 1971, 4783, 4812, p. 905.

........., ..., justice of the peace, co. Derby, 4136.

........., ..., in com. of peace, co. Derby, p. 907.

........., ..., in the war with France, 4480.

Fithzerberd, Nich., in the King's army, 4253.

........., ..., incumbent of Crayford, Kent, dec., 4941.

Fitzherbert, Wm., grant, 787.

Fitzhugh, Alice, eldest daughter of Hen. Ld., 3819.

........., Eliz., daughter of Hen. Lord, 3819.

........., Geo. Lord, 3819 ; in debt to Hen. VII. 380.

........., ..., son of Ric., 3819.

........., ..., ..., grants, to 292, 3539.

........., Sir Geo., in com. of array, Northumberland, 3358

........., ..., in com. of peace, Northumberland, 3553.

........., ..., in com. of peace, Yorksh. W. R., 1798, 3177; E. R., 3219.

........., ..., com. of array, Yorkshire, 1735, 1995.

........., ..., in com. of array, Yorkshire, E. R., 1799, 3358 ; N. R., 1804, 3358 ; W. R., 1804, 3358.

........., Hen. Lord, 292, 3539, 3819.

........., Ric., Lord, son of Hen., 292, 3539, 3819.

........., Th., justice of Assize, Western Circuit, 1741, 2089, 3295, 3724, 4339, 4765, 5246.

Fitzjames, John, grant, 1342 ; in commission of peace, Somersetsh., 287, 712, 3048, 3566, 3585, 3606, 3701, 4713, p. 904.

........., ..., in commission of sewers for Middlesex, 1972.

........., ..., sign manual to muster his tenants and others, 3229.

........., ..., recorder of Bristol, 1050.

........., ..., jun., grant to, 575 ; in com. of peace, Somerset, 287, 712.

........., Ric., Bp. of London, 1212, 1363, 1441, 3292, 3493, 4502, 4582 ; grants to, 575, 1783, 3135, 4891, 5427.

........., ..., ..., in commission of sewers, Middlesex, 1972.

........., ..., ..., at presentation of cap and sword to Hen. VIII., 5111.

........., ..., ..., part owner of the Christr. of Dartmouth, 4377.

........., ..., ..., summons to Parliament, 5616.

........., ..., ..., his signature, 1004, 1527, 1596, 1604, 1574, 1584, 1699, 1755, 1756, 1757, 1758, 3080, 4767, 5735.

........., ..., ..., his vicar general. See Horsey, Wm.

Fitzlewes, Sir Ric., knight of the Body, grants to, 4262, 5147.

........., ..., in commission of the peace, Essex, 310, 1368, 1522, 1713, 3605, 3785, 3967, p. 907.

Fitz-Richard, Simon, on sheriff-roll for Linc., 1949.

Fitz, Simon, in com. of gaol delivery, Home Circuit, 4279, 4702, 5186.

........., ..., justice of assize, Home Circuit, 4339.

........., ..., in com. for Beds., 4700, p. 907.

FitzSimons, Walter, Abp. of Dublin, 2071.

Fitzwaren, Eliz., Lady, of Stepney, Middlesex, widow of Sir Ro. Southwel, 5116.

........., Lord, John Bourchier, grant to, 801.

........., ..., ..., in com. of peace, Devon, 699, 917, 1503, 3183, 3589, 3938, 4539, 4783, 5220, 5456.

........., ..., ..., in com. of peace, Dorset, 26, 903, 3064, 3566, 3606, 3701, 5658.

........., ..., ..., in com. of peace, Westmorland (Dorset ?), 2007.

........., ..., ..., in com. of peace, Essex, 3605.

........., ..., ..., in com. of peace, Somerset, 287, 712, 3048, 3566, 3585, 3701, 4713, p. 904.

........., ..., ..., in com. of array, Somerset, and Dorset, 3688, 3723.

........., ..., ..., in war with France, 3231.

........., ..., ..., summons to Parliament, 5616.

Fitzwater, John Radclif, Lord, attainted, t. Hen. VII., 341, 1472, 4347, 5137.

........., Rob. Radclif, Lord, 3886 ; grants to, 341, 1401.

........., ..., ..., Act for restitution of, 811.

........., ..., ..., in com. of peace, Essex, 1713, 3605, 3785, 3967, p. 907.

........., ..., ..., in com. of peace, Norf., 1714, 1963, 3029, 3426, 3545, 5133.

........., ..., ..., in com. of peace, Suff., 1715, 3029, 3219, 3967, 4713, 5133.

........., ..., ..., in com. of array, Essex, 3688.

........., ..., ..., in the wars against France, 3750, 4050, 4070, 4253.

........., ..., ..., grand captain of the Make-glory and the Ellen of Hastings, 3980.

........., ..., ..., summoned to Parliament, 5616.

........., ..., ..., payment to 5720 (p. 955).

........., ..., ..., indebted to Hen. VIII., 2044.

Fitzwilliam, Anne, d. of John, co. York, 3735.

........., Eliz., wife of Sir Wm., 3016.

........., Geo., in commission of sewers, Linc., 663, 1716, 1979, 3137, 5691.

........., ..., in commis. of peace, Linc., 3342, 4593, 5476.

........., ..., in com. of peace, Linc. (Lindsey), 1171, 4358, 4860.

........., ..., on sheriff-roll for Linc., 664.

........., ..., sheriff for Linc., 5561.

........., John, of co. York, kinsman and h. of Sir Wm., 3015, 3735.

Fitzwilliam, Tho., 509 ; in commis. of array Yorkshire, 1735 ; W. R., 1804, 3358.

........., ..., indebted to Hen. VII., 3497.

........., ..., bro. of John, s. of Sir Wm., 3016.

........., ..., of Skydbroke, Linc., grant to, 1067.

........., Sir Tho., of Alderwerke, dec., grant mentioned, 2022.

........., Wm., King's cup bearer, grants to, 90, 740, 1577, 1748, 3189, 3742, 3818, 3824.

........., ..., squire of the Body, in reversion, 1428.

........., ..., in war with France, 3231 ; payment to him for going into Spain, 3762.

........., Sir Wm., vice admiral in "Mary Rose," 3980, 4005, 4377; at the Court, 4075; his retinue of King's guards, 4237 ; made knight at Tournay, 4468 ; captain of ordnance, 4632 ; coat of green velvet and cloth of silver, 4642.

........., ..., ..., grants to, 5128, 5594.

........., ..., ..., in commission of the peace for Surrey, 5506 (p. 905).

........., ..., ..., indebted to Hen. VIII., 5633.

........., Wm., s. and h. of John, grant, 3016.

........., ..., in commission of the peace, Essex, 3605, 3785, 3967.

........., ..., on sheriff-roll for Essex and Herts, 4544.

........., ..., sheriff for Essex and Herts, 5561.

........., ..., and Mabel Clifford, intended wife, grant, 4303.

........., ..., coll. of customs, Kingston-upon-Hull, Hen. VII., 1067.

........., Sir Wm. (old), 3016.

Fladeburg, Worc., 4316.

Flakebrigg, Westmor., 1796.

Flakman. See Flatman.

Flamborough Head, 3751.

Flamsted, Herts, 231, 232, 845, 1831, 4647.

........., church of, Linc. dioc. 3754.

Flanders. See Low Countries.

........., Governor of. See Fiennes, Lord.

........., President of. See Schaubeke, John de Sauvage, Lord.

........., Sovereign of. See Castres, De.

Flatman, alias Flakman, Wm. 785.

Flaunche, John, clerk, 1542.

Flaxflete, alias Faxflat, Yorkshire, 319, 1129, 1344.

Flechin, Jean de, 3654.

Fleet, the English, 3592, 3811, 3820, 3877, 4284 (p. 623), 4533, 5130.

......, the English, victory over the French, 4058.

......, ..., See also Ships.

Fleet, the French, 3196, 3388, 3445, 3451, 3633, 3678, 3876, 3877, 4005, 4330, 4440, 4453, 4824, 4843, 5076, 5130, 5681, 5753, 5762.

......, the French, Richard de la Pole, commander of, 4324.

......, the Genoese, 3752.

......, the Neapolitan, 5171.

......, the Scotch, 3811, 3838, 4453, 4533, 5076.

.... prison, the, 5245, 5589, 5740.

Flegge, Rob., haberdasher, 3111.

Fleming, Francis, 3980 (p. 554.)

........., John, 277, 5724.

........., John, debtor to Hen. VII., 3497 (p. 434.)

........., John, captain, 3591, 3820, 3977 (p. 550), 3979, 4377 (p. 651), 4474, 5112, 5761.

........., John Lord, letter from, in Paris, 5681.

........., ..., captain of the Margaret, 3326.

........., ..., in France, 4682.

........., Rob., 3980 (p. 554).

........., Wm., of Stubs Walding, Yorkshire, 3343.

Flemings, 5446.

........., in the English navy, 3808.

Flemish merchandize, 5711.

Fletchamsted, Warw., 1024.

Fletcher, John, 1144.

.... of London, 3496 (p. 432).

Fletchers.

Fletching, Sussex, 730, 1160, 1484, 5016.

Fleynborough, Yorkshire, 3827, 4940.

Fligh (or Flye), John, 698, 855, 1872.

Flint, 1839.

......, justices in, 956, 3289, 4198.

......, lands in, 131, 778.

......, overseers of lands in, 1472, 4022.

Flisco, Cardinal, 3777.

Flodden (Brankston), battle of, 4441, 4442, 4443, 4452, 4573, 4579, 4652, 4694, 4695, 4825, 5021, 5090, 5723.

Flordam, 3945.

Florence, Seigneurie of, 3269 (p. 367), 3325 (p. 382), 3780, 4924, 5068, 5208.

Florence, excommunicated, 1918.

........., letters dated at, 5356, 5357.

........., ambassador of, in France, 4446 ; in Spain 4464.

........., French ambassador at; 4323.

........., Cardinals at, 4287.

........., merchants of, 1251, 1723, 1791, 2036, 3192, 3257, 3259, 3312, 3410, 3414, 3452, 3466, 3467, 3511, 3596, 3746, 3756, 3965, 4040, 4131, 4368, 4629, 4926, 4957, 4959, 5221, 5261, 5324.

Florentines, 1948, 3112, 3207, 3269 (pp. 367, and 369), 3277, 3325 (p. 381), 3614, 4069 (p. 573), 4296, 4323, 5416, 5430.

Floryce, Digo, treasurer of Margaret of Savoy, 3435.

Flotmandby, 807.

Floury, Denis, 4445.

Flower, Barnard, of Almaine, 5044.

Floyd, Humph., captain, 4632.

Flye, John. See Fligh.

Foderynghey, Northt. See Fotheringhay.

Fogge, John, of Asshetford, Kent, 4291.

........., Sir John, on sheriff-roll for Kent, 4544.

........., ..., in commission, 4847, 4927, 5506 (p. 906).

........., Tho. 1530, 3881, 4254 ; in commission for Kent, 725, 906.

Foists, 4139.

........., burned, 4104, 4139.

Foix, —— de, 3325.

......, Gaston de, Duke of Nemours, 922, 3026, 3112, 3341, 5353.

...... Germaine de, Queen of Ferdinand of Arragon, 490 (p. 67.), 3766 (p. 499).

......, ..., ambassador of, 5404.

......, Odet de. See Lautrec, Odet de Foix, Sieur de.

Folgeham, Godfrey. See Foljambe.

Foliat, Nic., in commission for co. Worc., 892, 1971, 3301, 3709, 4770, 5506 (p. 903).

........., Rob. 1976.

Foljame (or Foljambe), Godfrey, 1698.

........., ..., in commission, for co. Derby, 5506 (p. 907).

........., ..., in the war against France, 4227, 4237, 4307, 4314.

........., Roger, 3020.

Folkestone, 4996.

Folkingham, Linc., 895, 1277, 1463, 1775, 4695.

........., church of, Linc. dioc., 3475.

Folkingham, Lord. See Beaumont, Wm. Viscount, Lord Bardolf and Folkingham.

Follagonum, in Basse Bretagne, 3112.

Foly-John, park of, 1293.

Fontaine, maid of honor to Margaret of Savoy, 5203.

Fontarabia, in Spain, 3243, 3298, 3355 (p. 400), 3357, 3584 (p. 451), 3593 (p. 457), 3762 (p. 494), 3766 (p. 499), 5745.

........., letter dated at, 3356.

Fontell-Episcopi, rector of, 1854.

Fontell-Giffard, rector of, 1854.

Footehede, John, clk., 5296.

Ford, [Devon or Dorset?], 2080.

......, [Northumb.], 3577, 4403, 4497, 5090.

......, Staff. (?), 155.

Fordwich, one of the Cinque Ports, 4996.

Foreigners, Act concerning, 811.

Foren of Walsale, Staff. *See* Walsall.

Forest, the New, Hants, 3176.

Forest laws, 3538.

Forests, royal, 129, 861.

Forget, Alan, 3002.

......, Geof., 3002.

......, John, 3002.

Forgon, Th., 4377 (p. 651).

Foreland, the, [Kent], 3820.

Forli, Bp. of. *See* Griphus, Peter.

Forman, ——, 792.

........., Andrew. *See* Murray, Abp. of; Bourges, Abp. of.

........., Edw., in commission for co. Linc., 1171, 1983, 3342, 4358, 4593, 4860, 5476, 5506 (p. 906).

........., John, precentor of Glasgow, 1271.

........., Sir John, brother of the Bp. of Murray, 4482.

........., Rob., 714.

Forrest, Wm., abbot of Hulme, 745.

Forster (or Foster), Sir Geo., on sheriff-roll for Berks, 1949, 3507.

........., ..., in the war against France, 3231, 4377 (p. 652).

........., ..., in commission for Berks, 241, 885, 1393, 1481, 1732, 2095, 3640, 4341, 5166, 5684.

........., John, 1543.

........., Mrs., 236.

........., Oswald, incumbent of Froyton, Marches of Calais, 5487.

........., Ric., in commission for Salop, 1981, 3071, 3715, 4394, 4827, 5506 (p. 904).

........., Th., 5720 (p. 957).

........., Walter, comptroller of the King's works, 223, 4630.

........., Wm., 3669, 4691.

Fortescue, Sir A., 1212.

........., Sir Adrian, in debt to Hen. VII, 3497 (p. 435).

........., ..., in the war against France, 3231, 3885, 3890, 3980 (p. 553), 4017, 4307, 4314.

........., ..., in commission for Oxon., 1470, 1745, 3015, 4559, 4809, 5506 (p. 905).

........., John, of Devon, 1812, 4071.

........., ..., of Herts, in the war against France, 3231, 3890, 4018, 4307, 5112 (p. 812).

........., ..., justice of gaol delivery for St. Albans, 4742.

........., ..., indebted to the King, 2044, 3497 (p. 434).

Fortescue, John, sewer of the Chamber, 940.

........., ..., squire of the Body, in the war against France, 4249, 4271.

........., Sir John, late lieutenant of Ruysbank in Picardy, 39.

........., Wm., in commission for Devon, 1812.

........., ..., on sheriff-roll for Devon, 3507.

Forth, firth of, 3412, 3751, 4682, 4951.

......, Ric., 3497 (p. 435).

......, Rob., 3497 (p. 434).

Fosse, water of the, alias the fishery of Fossedyke, near York, 142, 200, 4547.

Fossdike, Linc., 1036.

Foster. *See* Forster.

Fotheringhay, Northt., 155.

Fou, Mons. de, 5482.

Fougères, abbot of, 4761.

Founders, 186, 775.

Fountains, Yorksh., abbot of the blessed Mary of, 1639.

........., Marmaduke abbot of, in commission for Yorkshire, 4015.

Founteraby. *See* Fontarabia.

Fourn, in Flanders, 4253 (p. 609).

Fowey, customs of, 120, 737, 1810, 2064, 3120, 3261.

........., ships prested at, 3978.

........., ships of. *See* Ships.

........., Th., 3497 (p. 435).

Fowler, an executor of John Heron, 439.

........., Edith, wife of Thomas, 5296.

........., Joan, wife of Richard, 1909.

........., Juliana, wife of Sir Richard, 4699.

........., Mich., p. 553.

........., Ric., 1909.

........., ..., collector of the subsidy, 3440.

........., Sir Ric., 498, 4699.

........., ..., son of Richard, 1909.

........., ..., cancel of his recognizances, 105. 1024.

........., ..., in the war against France, 3231, 4377 (p. 652).

........., ..., in commission for Oxon., 1216, 1470, 1745, 3015, 4559, 4809, 5506 (p. 905).

........., Robert, 1498, 3744, 3992, 4030, 5270.

........., ..., letter from, 5154.

........., ..., commissioner to receive money due from France, 5529.

........., Th., 5296.

Fowlers, 3744.

Fox, Richard, Bishop of Winchester, 155, 342, 374, 811, 944, 1639, 1965, 2001, 3027, 3243, 3284, 3298, 3356, 3497, 3515, 4283, 4462, 4518, 4561, 4621, 4747, 4902, 4936, 5111, 5139, 5156, 5173, 5174, 5180, 5282, 5298, 5322, 5353, 5368, 5412, 5413, 5415, 5633, 5661, 5735.

Fox, Richard, Bp. of Winchester—*cont.*

......, ..., ..., executor of Hen. VII., 3292, 5735, 5737.

......, ..., ..., bequest to, from Margaret Countess of Richmond, 236.

......, ..., ..., executor of Margaret Countess of Richmond, 406, 407.

......, ..., ..., Ammonius presents letters to, from Erasmus, 1918, 1925, 1948, 1957, 1982, 2002, 2013, 2021, 2025.

......, ..., ..., his dispute with the Archbishop of Canterbury, 3066, 4452.

......, ..., ..., in the war against France, 3885, 3964, 4001, 4074, 4076, 4142, 4143, 4169, 4170, 4229, 4237, 4284 (p. 624), 4306, 4314, 4475, 4527.

......, ..., ..., hurt by a kick of his mule, 4284 (p. 624).

......, ..., ..., summoned to Parliament, 5616.

......, ..., ..., signs treaty between England and France, 962.

......, ..., ..., concludes treaty against France, 4511.

......, ..., ..., commissioner to treat with Lewis XII., 5294, 5343, 5408.

......, ..., ..., grant to, 4248.

......, ..., ..., grant of next presentations 1136, 1429, 3449.

......, ..., ..., licences to, 1194, 3292, 3793.

......, ..., ..., warrant to, 507, 3049.

......, ..., ..., keeper of the Privy Seal, warrants to, 602, 3050, 3371, 3418, 4607.

......, ..., ..., trier of petitions, 2082.

......, ..., ..., in the Privy Council, 5173, 5407.

......, ..., ..., signs as member of the Privy Council, 14, 15, 55, 73, 164, 336, 480, 503, 507, 511, 521, 531, 545, 576, 598, 603, 617, 618, 625, 639, 650, 782, 785, 702, 955, 956, 1004, 1008, 1068, 1264, 1272, 1273, 1372, 1378, 1527, 1538, 1540, 1574, 1584, 1596, 1604, 1699, 1755, 1756, 1757, 1758, 1840, 2027, 2029, 3080, 4476, 4767, 5779.

......, ..., ..., in commission for Hants, 904, 1388, 3071, 4159, 4676, 5506 (p. 904).

......, ..., ..., in commission for Somerset, 287, 712, 3566, 3585, 3701, 4713, 5506 (p. 904).

......, ..., ..., in commission for Surrey, 1427, 1762, 3078, 3092, 4693, 4734, 5237, 5506 (p. 904).

......, ..., ..., in commission for Sussex, 281, 1509, 3428, 4804, 5506 (p. 904).

......, ..., ..., in commission for Wilts, 898, 1489, 1938, 3157, 3605, 4583.

......, ..., ..., his hand, 3346, 3723, 4030, 5286, 5305, 5735.

Fox, Richard, Bp. of Winchester—*cont.*

......, ..., ..., letters from 4056, 4073, 4075, 4094, 4095, 4103, 4349, 4598, 4976, 5757.

......, ..., ..., letters to, 3048, 3388, 3443, 4007, 4030, 4870, 4935, 5090, 5151, 5218, 5270, 5320, 5354, 5496.

......, ..., ..., his comptroller. *See* Wingfield, Lewis.

......, Ric., son of Rob., 3386.

......, Rob., of Boroughbridge, 3386.

......, Mons. Th., 5163.

......, alias Vulp, Vincent, painter, 4954.

Foxcote, Hants (?), 1867, 5247.

Foxley, Norf., 5180.

Foys, Comté de. *See* Foix.

Foyte, Sigismund, 5720 (p. 957).

Framezelle (or Framgelly), Robinet de, his death, 3752.

........., ..., his standard-bearer taken prisoner at Terouenne, 4253 (p. 609).

Framlond, Leic., 155.

Frampton, Linc., 339.

........., James, 4732 ; in commission of the peace for Dorset, 26, 708, 903, 2007, 3064, 3566, 3606, 3701, 4713, 5658.

........., Ric., abbot of Malmesbury, 1183, 1806, 1929, 1930.

Framyngham, James, 3231.

Francapan, Count Christoforo, 4844.

France, 1353, 1458, 3083, 3139, 3283, 3346, 3349, 3353, 3359, 3361, 3362, 3415, 3577, 3613, 3633, 3651, 3654, 3751, 3752, 3779, 3836, 3838, 3882, 3883, 4078, 4283, 4296, 4327, 4433, 4451, 4484, 4556, 4561, 4563, 4652, 4682, 4691, 4725, 4789, 4830, 4834, 4844, 4883, 4916, 4935, 4955, 4970, 4982, 5029, 5110, 5152, 5164, 5173, 5175, 5203, 5208, 5292, 5353, 5365, 5368, 5379, 5424, 5439, 5470, 5477, 5636, 5637, 5675, 5724, 5753.

........., war of England, the Emperor, and Arragon against, 3243, 3271, 3339, 3352, 3355, 3357, 3377, 3393, 3394, 3396, 3435, 3446, 3451, 3463, 3584, 3595, 3629, 3631, 3662, 3678, 3688, 3744, 3749, 3750, 3752, 3760, 3766, 3835, 3849, 3857, 3876, 3884, 3885, 3886, 3887, 3891, 3895, 3915, 3972, 3985, 4005, 4020, 4055, 4058, 4059, 4060, 4069, 4078, 4085, 4091, 4094, 4096, 4130, 4162, 4169, 4179, 4253, 4267 (p. 615), 4284, 4305, 4306, 4319, 4325, 4326, 4328, 4331, 4349, 4359, 4361, 4371, 4374, 4378, 4389, 4399, 4401, 4405, 4410, 4411, 4412, 4413, 4418, 4421, 4422, 4431, 4433, 4434, 4440, 4446, 4449, 4450, 4454, 4455, 4457, 4459, 4464, 4472, 4477, 4502, 4525, 4561, 4571, 4576, 4577, 4579, 4622, 4630, 4631, 4653, 4666, 4692, 4796, 4829, 4831, 4832, 4868, 4902, 4913, 4914, 5130, 5165, 5171 (ii.), 5723, 5743.

France, intelligence from, 3112, 3357, 3752, 4692.

........., defiance of, 3986.

........., a tax upon the spirituality of, 3361.

........., a new Pope made in, 3662 (p. 475).

........., De la Pole in. *See* Pole, De la.

........., ambassadors of, to England, 3112, 5208, 5319, 5353.

........., ..., ... *See* Ambassadors.

........., ..., to Scotland, 1407, 3139, 3882.

........., ..., to other powers, 3112, 3226, 3243, 3248, 3258, 3271, 3340, 3766 (p. 498), 3962, 4322, 4455, 4666, 5006, 5106, 5159, 5208, 5518.

........., ..., sent by James IV. to Maximilian, 1195.

........., ..., from England, 4789, 5407.

........., ..., ... Scotland, 3326, 4112, 5006.

........., ..., ... other powers, 8, 3112, 3269, 4296, 4328, 4446, 4622, 4725, 5353.

........., treaties with England, 962, 963, 1104, 1105, 1106, 4924, 5305, 5306, 5307, 5315, 5326, 5335, 5343, 5408.

........., ... spoken of, 4789, 5018, 5284, 5319, 5327, 5341, 5353, 5354, 5356, 5362, 5368, 5377, 5378, 5379, 5387, 5393, 5398, 5404, 5407, 5410, 5468, 5500, 5532, 5600, 5651.

........., treaty with Scotland, 3218, 3303.

........., ..., spoken about, 3651.

........., treaty with other powers, 4924.

........., ..., spoken of, 5018.

........., truce with England and other powers, 4818, 4875.

........., ..., spoken about, 4574, 4845, 4864, 4921, 4952, 4985.

........., truce with Arragon spoken of, 3339, 3951, 3962, 4058, 4059, 4069, 4112, 4845, 4864, 5041, 5105, 5107, 5173, 5323, 5398.

........., league of England and other powers against, 1980, 3327, 4038, 4508, 4511, 4560.

........., ..., spoken of, 3346, 3499.

........., secret negotiations with Spain, 3766 (p. 501), 3807.

........., money due from, to England, 14, 318, 626, 1027, 1104, 1182, 1632, 1919, 2026, 5321, 5335, 5351, 5408 (6 and 7), 5529, 5566.

........., merchants of, 1143, 3112, 4353.

........., native of, made denizen, 3444.

........., King of. *See* Lewis XII.

........., Queen of. *See* Anne; and Mary.

........., Dauphin of. *See* Francis, Duke of Valois.

........., second daughter of. *See* Renée, second daughter of France.

France, Princes of, 5681.

........., noblemen of, at the marriage of Princess Mary with Lewis XII., 5462.

........., Council of. *See* Council of France.

........., Admiral of. *See* Graville, Lewis de.

........., Vice-Admiral of. *See* Clermont, Lord.

........., Chancellor of. *See* Anthoine du Prat.

........., Generals of, 5468, 5482.

........., the Grand Ecuyer of, 4253.

........., Grand Master of. *See* Palice, Lord de la.

........., Grand Veneur de. *See* Rouville, Louis de.

........., and Scotland, lieut.-general of the united fleet of. *See* Rouville, Louis de.

........., protector of, at Rome, 5106.

........., *See also* French.

Franchois Bettremen, 4445 (bis).

Francis, Duke of Valois, Duke of Bretaigne, Count of Angoulême, called the Dauphin of France (afterwards Francis I.), 1182, 3357, 3752, 4561, 4824, 5379, 5408, 5477, 5495, 5513, 5523, 5560, 5681.

........., ..., in Guienne, 3584 (p. 451), 3593 (p. 456), 4692, 5675.

........., ..., invades Spain, p. 451, p. 456.

........., ..., the government of Guienne given to him, 3752.

........., ..., his lieutenant taken prisoner at Terouenne, 4253 (p. 609).

........., ..., his standard-bearer taken prisoner at Terouenne, 4253 (pp. 609 and 610).

........., ..., wounded in a skirmish, 4513.

........., ..., reported death of, 4843.

........., ..., concludes peace between France, Scotland, England, &c., 4875.

........., ..., marriage of, 5164.

........., ..., at the marriage of Lewis XII. and Princess Mary, 5482, 5495.

........., ..., at the coronation of Mary Queen of France, 5560.

........., ..., at the tournament, 5606.

........., ..., his servant a prisoner, 5505.

........., as King, 5315.

Francis, Geo., 235.

........., ..., gentlemen usher to Queen Katharine, grants to, 479, 788, 888, 1422, 1521, 1644, 3038, 3668, 5530.

........., John, 1411.

Francis, alias Hertson, Mary, of Flanders, widow of Hen. Uvedale, 3439, 4863, 4882.

........., Captain Simon, 5292.

Franciscus, Count John, 3269 (p. 368).

Franconia, in Germany, 4563.

Francoyas, taken prisoner by the English, 4174.

Franculus, John Cra called, 3026.

Frangipani. *See* Francapan.

Frank, Th., 4067.

........., Wm., 1212.

Frankfort, the Emperor at, 4282, 4305, 4322.

........., letter dated at, 4304, 4305.

Franklin, John, 3497 (p. 435).

........., Trumpet, alias Francis Knyff, 4653.

Frascina, Theodore, 3026.

Frauncis. *See* Francis.

Fraunce, Jenyn, 4431.

Frederick III., King of Naples, 5729.

........., ..., his son, 4296, 5482.

Freeman, ——, master of the Jenet, 3591, 3977.

........., ——, master of the Katharine Fortileza, 3591, 3820, 3977, 4377 (p. 651).

Freemantle, Hants, 873, 1084.

Freermayn, Dorset, 5098.

Fregosi, the, at Genoa, 4280, 4283, 4326, 4577.

Fregoso, Octavian, 3325 (p. 383).

Freme, Wm., 3712, 3804.

........., ..., justice of gaol delivery for Gloucester Castle, 1922.

........., ..., in commission for co. Glouc., 1049, 1469, 1695, 3641, 4024, 4118, 4764.

Fremingham, Robt., 236, 667.

Fremington, Devon, 855, 5515.

Fremlingham (or Fremingham), Sir James, 4653, 5580.

........., Sir James, knighted at Tournay, 4468.

........., ..., in commission for Norfolk, 5133.

........., ..., in commission for Suffolk, 5133, 5506 (p. 904).

French, the, threaten Guisnes, 5021, 5032, 5035, 5041.

........., descent of the, on the English coast, 4743.

........., taken prisoners by the English, 3362, 4174, 4253, 4284 (p. 625), 4306, 4353, 4401, 4405, 4418, 4431, 4464, 4725, 4831, 5192.

.... in Italy, 11, 490 (p. 67 and p. 68), 1676, 1681, 1689, 1918, 1948, 1997, 2002, 2039, 3026, 3077, 3112, 3269, 3325, 3333, 3335, 3341, 3355 (p. 397), 3361, 3377, 3451, 3499, 3613, 3658, 3662 (p. 474), 3752, 3817, 3976, 4059,

French in Italy—*cont.*
4069, 4078, 4091, 4094, 4096, 4194, 4210, 4216, 4267, 4273, 4280, 4283, 4287, 4296, 4326, 4328, 4333, 4359, 4455, 4499, 4571, 4574, 4577, 4664, 4795, 4952, 4956, 5040, 5206, 5322, 5377, 5387, 5404, 5410, 5637, 5675, 5718, 5745.

.... in Scotland, 4459.

.... fleet. *See* Fleet, the French.

.... caps and hats, 5239, 5711.

.... herald in Scotland, 5641.

.... loadsmen in the English Navy, 3838.

.... priest at Calais, 5021.

.... ship at Leith, 3577.

.... spy, 3779, 4790, 5753, 5781.

.... spy mentioned as "the Compaignon," 4844, 4929, 5377, 5657.

.... *See also* France.

French, John, of Bedford, 5215.

........., Dom. Rob., 1854.

Frende. *See* Friend.

Frentecha, a French captain in Italy, 3325 (p. 384).

Frethy, Tho., 1330.

Frevile, Rob., on sheriff-roll for co. Camb., 4544, 5561.

........., ..., in commission, 1684, 3563, 5506 (p. 904).

Friars, Austin, London, 5111.

........., Grey, in Scotland, 3838.

.... Minors, at Cambridge, 263.

........., ..., at Oxford, 262.

.... Observant, 4871.

.... in England, Hen. VII.'s legacy to, 5737, 5738.

........., ... in England and Scotland, Vicar-General of, 4678.

........., ..., in Scotland, 3838.

........., ..., Provincial of, 4549.

........., ..., the Grey, in Spain, Provincial of, 3766 (p. 498 and p. 499), 3807 (p. 509).

.... Preachers, at Cambridge, 261.

........., ..., at London, 264, 5351.

........., ..., at Oxford, 260.

Fribourg in Bryscope, 5539.

Frieburg, Philip de, 3026.

Friend, John, 5720 (p. 957).

........., Th., 3924, 4938.

Friesland, 3367, 4725, 5404.

........., governor of. *See* Saxony, George Duke of.

........., chancellor of. *See* Reyshach, Simon de.

Friscobald, Jerome, 490 (p. 71), 922, 923, 3658, 4077.

........., ..., merchant of Florence, 1413, 3410, 4957.

........., ..., letter from, 4068.

........., Leonard, 3496 (p. 431), 4352, 5005, 5135.

........., ..., grant to, 5135.

........., ..., his ship, p. 652, 5761.

........., ..., gentleman usher of the Chamber, 3679.

........., ..., merchant of Florence, 4957 ; licences to, 3259, 5720 (p. 955).

........., 3678, 4527.

Friscobalds, the, 3817.

Friuli, in Italy, 1676, 1681, 1697, 3897, 4563, 4795, 5410.

Frodesham, Chesh., 4644, 4748.

Frodesam, Roger, 4476.

Frodon, 4284 (p. 623).

Frogmorton, captain, 3977. *See* Throgmorton.

Frognall, Mrs., 236.

Frolbury, Hants, 1927.

Froluser, John, 3343.

Fromont, Gerard de, 4534.

Froste, John, B. D., presentation to the chapel of Cresmere, 1904.

Frost, Walter, 1524, 1626.

......, ..., in commission for Essex, 310, 1368, 1522, 1713, 3605, 3785, 3967, 5506 (p. 907).

......, Wm., 686.

......, ..., justice of gaol delivery for Winchester, 3198.

......, ..., in commission for Hants, 904, 1236, 1388, 1812, 3071, 4159, 4676.

Frostden, Suff., 1250.

Frostenden, Suff., 1129, 1344.

Froston, John, 1765.

Frostwhait, Westmor., 3764.

Frowik, Hen., alderman of London, temp. Hen. VI., 5242.

........., ..., 5688.

........., ..., justice of gaol delivery for St. Alban's, 4742.

........., ..., on sheriff-roll for Essex and Herts, 1316, 1949, 5561.

Frowyke, Sir Th., 1965.

Froyton, church of, in the Marches of Calais, 3535, 5487.

Fruste, Veyte, governor of Modon, 5430.

Frutewell, Oxon., 1753, 4342.

Frye, ——, 12.

......, the Edward, ship, p. 553.

......, Ric., 347.

......, Wm., 755.

Fryes, Edw., 3998.

......, Jas., 1692.

Fuchir, Elias and Hen., of Osemundeston, temp. Edw. I., 1099.

Fuel and sea coal, 1912 ; wood dear and scarce, by reason of holocausts of heretics, 1948, 1957.

Fuensalida, Guter Gomez de, comendador de la Membrilla, 368, 490 ; ambassador from Ferd., 8, 3023 ; commission to, from Ferd., 27, 28, 153, 240 ; signature, 152, 153.

Fuessen, 1676, 1697.

Fulbeke ch., Linc. dioc., 4828, 5062.

Fulbroke, Warwick, 1268, 1499.

........., Tho., 768, 1854.

Fulcombe, Geoff., in war in France, 3885.

Fulleford, John, clk., grant to, 3988.

Fulford, Wm., in commission of array, Devon, 1812.

Fulham, Middx., 575.

Fuljambe. *See* Foljambe.

Fuller, ——, mercer of London, 1212.

........., ——, master of the Anne of Fowey, 3591.

........., ——, master of a ship of Bristol, 3977, 4377.

........., Gabriel, barber-surgeon in the wars, 3237.

........., Sir Ric., in commission of the peace, Oxfordshire, 766.

Fulmodeston, Norf., 155.

Fulnaby, John, of Fulneby, grants to, 4616 ; in commission for Linc., 792.

........., ..., ..., in commission of sewers, Linc., 1716, 1979, 3137, 5691.

........., ..., ..., in commission of the peace, Linc., 3342, 4593.

........., ..., ..., in commission of the peace, Linc. (Lindsey), 4358, 4860, 5506 (p. 906).

Fulshurst, Ralph, grant to, 4569.

Fulsehurst, Th., in war against France, 3231.

Fulthorp, Th., of Hyppeswell, York., grant, 5607.

Fulwode, Rob., in commission of the peace, Warwicksh., 282, 1387, 1468, 1971, 3364, 5506 (p. 903).

........., ..., in commission of gaol delivery, Warw., 554.

Fume, 5055.

Furde. *See* Ford.

Furen, Bertram de, a Gascon, 5159.

Fureswey ch., Linc. dioc., 3281.

Furnando, Jno., master, a Spaniard, payment to him, 4535.

Furrers, 5391.

Furtado, Lud. *See* Mendoza.

Fyessen. *See* Fuessen.

Fyfelde, Berks, 734, 1203, 3005.

Fykkylbourke in Lontotrence, (date), 5338, 5366.

Fyldyng. *See* Fielding.

Fyloll. *See* Filoll.

Fylwode Forest, 1815.

Fynch. *See* Finch.

Fyndern. *See* Findern.

Fyneux, John, incumbent of All Saints the More, London, 1356.

..........., Sir John, Chief Justice of the King's Bench, three grants, 3292, 4436 ; grant of two tuns of Gascoigne wine yearly during office as Justice, 1315.

..........., ..., in commission of the peace for Bedfordshire, 1051, 1122, 2045, 3501, 4700, 5506 (p. 907).

..........., ..., in commission of the peace for Bucks, 454, 943, 1379, 3219, 3310, 3522, 5506 (p. 907).

..........., ..., in commission of the peace for Cambridgeshire, 1684, 3583, 5506 (p. 904).

..........., ..., in commission of the peace for Hunts, 905, 916, 1095, 4006.

..........., ..., in commission of the peace for Kent, 725, 906, 3428, 3605, 4663, 4847, 4927, 5506 (p. 906).

..........., ..., in commission of the peace for Middlesex, 3552, 4663, 5506 (p. 905).

..........., ..., in commission of the peace for Norfolk, 1340, 1714, 1963, 3029, 3426, 3545, 5133, 5506 (p. 906).

..........., ..., in commission of the peace for Suffolk, 280, 676, 1121, 1153, 1715, 3029, 3219, 3967, 4713, 5133, 5506 (p. 904).

..........., ..., in commission of the peace for Surrey, 1427, 1762, 3078, 3092, 4693, 4734, 5237, 5506 (p. 905).

..........., ..., in commission of gaol delivery, Surrey, 1548.

..........., ..., in commission of gaol delivery, Canterbury and castle, 3775, 3790.

..........., ..., in commission of gaol delivery, Maidstone, 763.

..........., ..., in commission of gaol delivery, London, Newgate, 541, 1519, 1547, 1897, 3765, 3778, 4553.

..........., ..., in commission of gaol delivery, Wisbeach Castle, 1781.

..........., ..., in commission of gaol delivery, Home Circuit, 243, 1746.

..........., ..., in commission of gaol delivery, Norfolk Circuit, 3275, 3691, 4317, 5195.

..........., ..., justice of assize, Norfolk Circuit, 19, 294, 881, 1130, 1164, 1494, 1795, 2096, 3003, 3311, 3724, 4339, 4765, 5246.

..........., ..., in commission as trier of petitions at Coronation and in Parliament, 164, 811, 2082.

Fyneux, Sir John, &c.—*cont.*

..........., ..., in commission of sewers, Lincolnshire, 1716, 1979, 3137, 5691.

..........., ..., signatures, 702, 1004, 1372, 1527, 1540, 1574, 1584, 1596, 1604, 1699, 1755, 1756, 1757, 1758, 3080, 5762.

.........., Ric., in commission to levy subsidy in Dover, 4996.

.........., Wm., in commission of the peace, Kent, 725, 906, 3428, 3605, 4663, 4847, 4927.

Fynmere. *See* Finmere.

Fynwyke. *See* Fenwick.

Fyornys, Lazarus, merchant of Florence, 4040.

Fyssher. *See* Fisher.

Fytton, Wm., yeoman of the butlery, grant to, 1324, 4566.

Fynecompton. *See* Compton, Fenny.

Fysshe, John, in commission of gaol delivery, Canterbury, 1225.

Fynis, serjeant of, 4232.

G.

Gabriel, ——, inc. of Wyberton, 3461.

Gaddis, Geo. De, ducal secretary, letter to Bannisius, 4172.

Gage, John, in com. for Sussex, p. 904.

.... (Gauge), John, of Rownedon, Kent, 685.

Gales, Prince de. *See* Wales.

Galiace, Chr., of San Severino, knighted, 31.

.........., Earl. *See* St. Severin.

.... (Galleas), Count, 5523.

Galicia, 490 (p. 68).

.........., Scotch ambassador arrested in 4844.

.........., ships at, 3355, 3451.

Gallespeth, in Scotland, 4556.

Gallia Narbonensis, 3876.

Gallipoli, John, Bp. of. *See* Yonge, John.

.........., ships of, 3697.

Galloway, bpric of, 379.

.........., archdeaconry of, 11.

.........., dioc. of, 4626.

.........., St. Ninian's in, 4573.

.........., David, Bishop of, 714, 3882 (p. 533).

.........., James Beton, Bishop of, 910.

Galterotte, Philip, 3425, 3467, 3651, 5030.

Galtresse Forest, Yorkshire, 222, 494, 3497, 4022, 4347.

........., ... See Cholmeley, Roger ; Dickson, Wm.; Hogeson, Wm.; Oxford, Jno. Earl of; Ughtred, Anth.; Vaux, Edw; Wells, John ; and Wyghell, John.

Gambara, Count. Nich. de, 3269 (p. 368).

........., Count Bur de, 3325 (p. 382).

Gammyll, Th., 4335.

Gancell, Ric., 1812.

Gand, 4609.

........., Viscount de, letter to, 4353.

Gannay, Sir John de, 1182.

Ganges, River, 4173.

Gaol Delivery. See Circuits.

...., commissions of, Home Circuit, 1001, 1746, 1763, 3275, 3694, 4279, 4702, 5186 ; Midland Circuit, 1101, 1763, 3003, 3282, 3694, 4148, 5143 ; Norfolk Circuit, 1130, 3275, 4317, 5195; Northern Circuit, 1130, 1763, 3003, 3275, 3691, 4279, 5195 ; Oxford Circuit, 1130, 3275, 3702, 4215, 4702, 5183 ; Western Circuit, 1110, 1763, 3282, 3694, 4279.

...., commissions of, for various towns, 541, 554, 749, 763, 764, 810, 859, 884, 907, 931, 1222, 1225, 1519, 1763, 1781, 1813, 1897, 1914, 1922, 1939, 3187, 3198, 3209, 3275, 3282, 3464, 3488, 3503, 3549, 3652, 3691, 3694, 3745, 3765, 3775, 3778, 3790, 3996, 4004, 4494, 4553, 4558, 4568, 4677, 4742, 4890, 5183, 5186, 5236, 5275.

...., justices of, 1794, 1942, 4753.

Garda, Lake of, 216, 4326.

........, ..., (Benacus,) the Venetians on the, 3543.

........, ..., Duke of Milan at, 3471.

Gardif, man of arms of Fr. King's house, 4431

Gardner, John, coroner of Bucks, 1759.

Gardyner, Walt., 1144.

Gardiner, Wm., 4635.

Gare, John, 1528.

Gares, ——, 4825.

Garet, Marian, of Normandy, 4084, 5080.

Garin, Collin, 4445.

Garnethrop. See Garthorp.

Garneys, Christopher, gentleman usher of the chamber, grants to, 529, 637, 994, 1515, —— 3881, 4254.

........, Sir Christopher, knighted at Tournay, 4468.

........, ..., ambassador to Lewis XII., 5482.

........, ..., in commissions of peace for Kent, 4663, 4847, 4927, p. 906.

........, ..., and Joan his wife, grant to, 5440.

........, Rob., soldier of Calais, 3917.

Garrett, ——, 5789.

Garston, in Norfolk, 730.

........, Th., 3771.

Garter. See Wriothsley, Th., 556.

........., feast of the, 5006.

Garth, Ric., 812.

........., Th. marshal of Berwick, 3021.

Garthing, Wm. clerk, 3386.

Garthorp, Linc., 1832, 1958.

Garton, John, 3551.

Gartside, James, yeoman of the Crown, 3254, 3468.

Gascoigne, Eliz., 3442.

........., Henry, 3515.

........., John., 1518.

........., Wm. 1733, 1965, 3576.

........., ..., in commission of peace for Beds, 1051, 1122, 2045, 3501, 5506, (p. 907) ; Hunts, 905, 907, 916, 1095, 4006 ; Northampton, 5658.

........., ..., in commission of gaol delivery for Bedford Castle, 1922 ; Northampton (town), 3745.

........., ..., sheriff for Beds and Bucks, 4544.

........., Sir Wm. 4550.

........., ..., in commission of peace for Yorkshire, W. R., 1798, 1964, 1995, 3177, 4015, 5166.

........., ..., in commission of array for Yorkshire, 1735, 1804, 3358.

........., ..., on sheriff-roll for York, 4544.

........., ..., in the war with Scotland, 4482.

........., ..., signature of, 4439.

Gascon wine. See Wine.

Gascons, in the French war, 3584, 3593.

........., at the siege of Brescia, 3026.

Gascony, 3356, 4055.

........., receivers and triers of petitions for, 811, 2082.

........., Sir Edw. Howard, admiral of, 3809.

........., native of, 3365, 3379, 3734.

........., prohibition to import wine from, 3597.

Gasper, Hans, 3897.

Gates, Geof, 3231.

........., Sir Geof. 3212.

........., ..., knighted at Tournay, 4463.

........., ..., in the war, 4703.

Gatte, Wm., 5708.

Gatley Park, Wales, 298.

Gaul, 5040.

Gaunston, Notts, 63.

Gaunt. See Ghent.

Gauri, Abunazar Campaoel, 5729.

Gawen, John, in commission for Wilts, 1489, 1938, 3157, 3605, 4583.

Gawle, the, Forest of Dean, Gloucester, 1233.

Gawltiers Forest. See Galtresse.

Gawsem, John, clk. of Windsor Castle, 608.

Gawtres Forest. *See* Galtress.

Gayer, Reynold, 1434, 5052.

Gaysley, Th., of London, 3896.

Gaysford, Geo., in the war, 4635.

........., ..., in commission, 5519.

Gaynesford, Jno., com. of peace, Surrey, 4734.

........., John, of Blokfield, on sheriff-roll, Surr. and Sussex, 1316, 1949, 3507.

........., ..., of Crowherst, in commission of the peace for Surrey, 1427, 1762, 3078, 3092, 4693, 5237, 5506 (p.905).

........., Nicholas, in commission of peace for Sussex, 3024.

........., ..., deceased, 1325, 3787.

Gaynesforth, lordship of, in Durham dioc., 3698.

Gaynforth, St. Mary Magdalen, 1054.

Gayton, in Northt., 4656, 5011.

Gayneton, 1487.

Gaza, caliph of, 5729.

Ge, Tho., 1169.

Gedge, Rob., clerk of the mercery, 5720 (p. 955).

Gedlyng, in Notts, 1053.

Geffrey, Robt., incumbent of Snodhill church, Heref. dioc., 5549.

Geffron, John, yeoman usher of the chamber, 3998.

........., ..., serjeant-at-arms, 4045, 4066.

Gekyll, Wm., purveyor of the avenary, 3871.

Gelgelt, Edm., 1991.

.. .., ..., of Suffolk, 3549, 4254.

........., Sir Edm., 4872.

Gels (?), ——, 5523.

Gelston, John, 4527.

Gemund, Hungarian and Arragonese ambassadors at, 5259.

........., Sir Rob. Wingfield's letter from, 5304, 5323, 5338.

Geneva, Lake of, 4273, 4359.

Genins. *See* Jenins.

Genny. *See* Jenny.

Gengeham, Pet., of Brussells, 800.

Genoa (Genys), 1676, 5006.

.... (Jeyn), taken by the French, 4267 (p. 616), 4280.

........., the fort of, 3269 (p. 368).

........., castle of, 3658.

........., the lantern at, surrender of, 5365, 5393.

........., France raises troops for the relief of, 5387.

........., Pescara at, 4371.

........., Duke of, 4210, 5208.

Genoa, the fleet of, 3752.

........., ship of, 3591.

........., the Fregosys at, 4326.

........., (Jean), merchants of, 1003, 1273, 1292, 1398, 1693, 1773, 3079, 3199, 4003, 4145, 4250, 4350, 4763, 5156, 5221, 5334, 5415, 5722.

........., ..., in Barbary, 819.

........., native of, 354.

........., St. George's, 3697.

Genoese, in Italian war, 3325.

........., differences between them and the Viceroy, 4069.

.-....... rebellion, 4283.

.... in treaty with the Swiss, 5430, 4577.

Gens d'armes, 5164.

Gentili, Andrea, merchant of Genoa, 5334, 5415.

........., Gregory, merchant of Genoa, 5722.

........., Nich., merchant of Genoa, 3199, 4763.

........., James, of London, 4617.

Gentilman, John, 4677.

........., Thomas, of London, chaplain, 5572.

Genys. *See* Genoa.

George, Sir Edm., 664 ; sheriff-roll for Somers., 664. *See* Gorge.

........., captain, 3977.

........., Collin, 4445.

........., the King's tailor, 91.

Georgia, the Christian King of, 5729.

Geoffrey, Thos. and Margaret, 1671.

........., Wm., 1050.

Gerad, John, 787.

Gerard, Miles, 3211, 3868, 4298.

........., ..., in debt to Henry VII., 3497 (p. 435).

........., ..., collector in port of London, 795.

........., ..., in French war, 4082, 4083, 4099, 4126, 4535, 4723.

........., the bookseller, 2013.

Gerbier, Atoine, 3815.

Gerby, the city of, 1295.

Germaine de Foix. *See* Arragon, Queen of.

German to oppose Suffolk at the tournament, 5605.

Germans, 3662, 4577, 4831, 4832, 5368.

........., Ric. de la Pole, captain of the, 3584 (p. 451).

........., captains of the, 4793.

.... in the French war, 3271, 3362, 3496 (p. 433), 3584 (p. 451, p. 452, p. 454), 3593 (p. 456, p. 457), 3607, 3752, 3762, 3766 (pp. 496 to 498), 3884, 3885, 3915, 4038, 4070, 4091, 4163, 4182, 4237, 4267 (p. 615), 4284, 4306, 4307, 4309, 4449, 4464, 5723.

........., in Italian war, 3026, 3324, 4216.

Germans in the English service, 3231, 3269, 3849, 4429, 4692, 4794, 4829.

........., engaged against the Venetians, 5171, 5290.

........., the Legate incensed against the, 3325.

........., disaffection among the, 4563, 5338.

Germany, 216, 3077, 3225, 3340, 3355, 3361, 4296, 4563, 4577, 4598, 4725, 4789.

........., ambassador from, to Rome, 4366. See Carpi.

........., news from, 4362.

........., negotiation with, 3651.

........., Gurk proceeds to, 5110.

.... to be included in the alliance, 5285.

........., High, the Emperor Maximilian determines upon going into, 5323.

........., Sir Rob. Wingfield in, 5299.

...., guns cast in, 3425.

........., rumour concerning Margaret of Savoy in, 4851.

........., native of, 3013, 5044.

........., Emperor of. See Maximilian.

........., Counts Palatine of, 3457.

........., Princes of, 3271, 3471.

Germyn, Th. See Jermyn.

Gernegan. See Jerningham.

Gernyer, Himbert, 4585.

Gervays, John, 1666. See also Jerveys.

Getting, John, 4367.

Ghades. See Cadiz.

Ghent, 3077, 5418, 5424, 5439, 5467.

........., ambassador of, 4284.

........., Francis de Mastaing, bailly of, 4331.

........., painter of, 5604.

........., ships of, 4479.

........., waggoners of, 4526.

........., letters dated from, 4561, 5165.

Ghilleford. See Guildford.

Ghysse, Mons. De la. See Guiche.

Gibbons, John, of London, 4589.

Gibbons, Th., on sheriff-roll for Norf. and Suff., 4544.

........., ..., sheriff for Norf. and Suff., 4551.

Gibbs, Wm., captain of Gibbs' ship, 4377, 5112, p. 972.

Gibcliff, chantry of, Warwickshire, 1444.

Gibson, ——, 4825.

........., Christ., gunner, 5707.

........., Peter, the, ship of London, p. 554.

........., Ric., porter of the great wardrobe, 171, 1872.

........., ..., master of the revels 4642, 5172, 5271, 5720 (p. 958); yeoman of the tents, 4526 (p. 690), 4629.

........., Wm., 5109.

Giffard, Agnes, 3195.

........., Walt., 3195.

Gifford, Sir Chas., 3857, 4075, 4076.

........., ..., cousin to Sir Ric. Wingfield, 4077.

........., Sir Hen., 3857.

........., John, sewer, 133, 687, 1319.

........., ..., yeoman usher of the chamber, 3244.

........., ..., sheriff for Staff., 664.

........., ..., in commission of peace for Staff., 279, 1770, 5506 (p. 903).

........., Sir John, 5196.

........., ..., on sheriff-roll for Hants, 664.

........., Roger, of London, 4989, 5028.

........., Th., in commission of peace for Bucks, 3219, 3310, 3522.

........., Sir Wm., in commission of array, 1812, 3173.

Giglis, Silvester de, Bp. of Worcester, 967, 983, 1361, 1457, 3848, 4283, 4311, 4608, 4724, 4735, 4502, 4871, 5054, 5106, 5174, 5319, 5392, 5405, 5443, 5445, 5457, 5635, 5664, 5757.

........., ..., ..., ambassador to the Lateran Council, 2085, 3108.

........., ..., ..., suspected of poisoning Card. Bainbridge, 5253, 5254, 5356, 5357, 5378, 5396, 5448, 5449, 5651; defends himself, 5365; Wolsey takes his part, 5465; prosecutes Pace, 5405, 5448.

........., ..., ..., letters from, 4039, 4062, 4455, 4500, 4621, 4747, 5068, 5107, 5168, 5353, 5354, 5365, 5382, 5416, 5464, 5496, 5542, 5543, 5602, 5650, 5663.

........., ..., ..., letters to, 4598, 4936, 4955, 5465.

........., ..., ..., his vicar general, 5344.

Gilbert, James IV.'s chaplain, 751.

........., commander, 4725.

...., John, of Newport, Isle of Wight, 5188.

........., ..., in commission of the peace for Devon, 699, 917, 1503, 3183, 3566, 3589, 3605, 3938, 4539, 4783, 5220.

........., ..., justice of Assize for Norfolk Circuit, 1490.

........., ..., in commission of array for Devon, 1812.

........., ..., pardon to, 3771.

........., Rob., clk., 835.

........., Wm., (temp. Hen. VII.,) 1002, 1965.

Gildon, John, yeoman usher of the chamber, 113.

Gilfforth, Sir Edw. See Guildford.

Gilgarran, lordship of, 102.

Gillick, John, 3796.

Gillingham, in Kent, 4787.

........., in Dorset, 155.

Gillot, Ric., 5186.

Gilly, John, porter of the gate, 247.

Gillyslande. *See* Dacre, Thos. Lord.

Gilmews, Peter, the King's bow-maker, 3560.

Gilmyn, Stephen, 5296.

Gingat. *See* Guinegate.

Gippewich. *See* Ipswich.

Gippyng, 3851.

.... in Suff., 1607.

Gittons, Ric., of London, 1846.

........., ..., in debt to Henry VII., 3497 (li).

Giustiniani, Antonio, 3026. *See also* Justinian.

Glamorgan, 1583.

........., sheriff of, 110, 441, 1113.

.... and Morgan, commission of peace for, 3960.

........., lordship of, Cardiff, in, 625.

Glasbury, lordship of, 4226, 4837.

Glasgow, Bp. of. *See* Beton, Jas.

........., James Beton, Abp. of (misprinted St. Andrew's), 910.

........., Rob. Forman, dean of, 1176.

........., treasurer of, 3630.

........., Annand in diocese of, 2061.

........., Lord, 5681.

Glasier, Sir Wm., priest, 3474.

Glastonbury Monastery, 4949, 5022.

........., abbot of, 1639, 5353.

........., ..., summoned to Parliament, 5616.

Glaunte, ship of, 3978.

Glawdster, church of, St. David's dioc., 5012.

Glemam, John, in commission of peace for Suffolk, 3029, 3219, 3967, 4713 ; Norfolk, 3426, 3545.

........., Sir Jno., in commission of peace for Suff., 5133 (p. 904) ; Norf. and Suff., 5133.

Glenham, ——, in Lord Lisle's retinue, 4653.

Glenluce, monastery of, 3122.

........., Cuthbert, commendatory of, 4626.

Glennet, John, 4509.

Gleyve, Hen., of Carnesdale, 4360.

Glinn. *See* Glynn.

........., Th. ap, in French war, 4306.

Glynne, John, yeoman of the chamber, 1898.

........., John, messenger to Katharine of Arragon, 4398, 4451.

........., ..., in commission of peace for Cornwall, 312, 891, 1694, 1984, 3290 ; for Devon, 1166.

Glin, Lln. Jevan ap, 65.

......, Morgan ap Jevan ap, 65.

Glindovirdoy, in Merioneth, 4980.

Gloucester Castle, gaol delivery for, 1922, (town), 3694.

........., proclamation in, 1771.

...., constable of, 3001.

Gloucester, honor of, 900, 5137.

........., manor of, 5629.

........., abbey of, St. Oswald's, 5355.

........., St. Peter's, 658, 1360, 3450, 3801, 4377.

........., ..., abbot of, 5426, 5616. *See* Braunch, Thomas ; Newton, John ; Malvern, William.

........., St. Mary, Lanthony, near, 3172.

Gloucestershire, 1671, 3047, 3178, 3841, 4022, 4071, 4180.

........., insurrections in, 3289, 4198.

........., commissions of the peace for, 930, 1049, 1469, 1695, 3712, 3804, 4024, 4118, 4764, p. 906.

........., tenths and fifteenths in, 3441.

........., keeper of the rolls for, 3802.

........., clerk of the signet for, 1839.

........., feodary of Crown lands in, 4414, 5692.

........., justices in, 956.

........., escheator of, 1930, 3058, 4972.

........., sheriff of, 536, 664, 1316, 1949, 3507, 4544, 5051, 5561.

Gloucester fee, in Devon, 597, 860.

Gloucester, Duke of. *See* Richard III.

.... and Hereford, Ric. de Clare Earl of, 3195.

........., Sir John, 5789.

Glowcestre, Th., of London, 3406, 3407, 4643.

Glover, Tho., 78.

Goa, 4173.

......, Lord of, 4173.

Gobyon. *See* Yerdley, Gobyon.

Goche, Wm., 4414.

Godalghan, Wm., 5220.

Godart, ship master, 3591, 3977, 4377.

Goddesbere Park, Devon, 457, 1611.

Godehale, John, 4251.

Goderike. *See* Goodrick.

Godfrey, Wm., of Gyllingham, 4787.

........., Wynant, gunner, 766, 781, 1347.

Godhurst, or Buckhurst, in Essex, 734.

Godyng, Ric., of Linc., 3351, 5506 (p. 906).

Godynton, in Oxfordshire, 155.

Godman. *See* Goodman.

Godmersham, Wm., B.D., 1180.

Godisgrace, Rob., 1854.

Godestone, in Surrey, 1484.

Goeff, Odo, 5431.

Gofton, John, ship-master, 4377.

Goghe, Sir Geoff., in French war, 4306.

Gold, cloth, 3511. *See* Merchandize.
...... in Scotland, 1782.
......, John, mayor of Northt., 3503.
Gouldicote, in Glouc., 933.
Goldycote, manor of, 1818.
Goldyng, John, 3211.
Golding, John, auditor of the Exchequer, 1863.
........., Rob., 547.
........., ..., of Kent, 12.
Goldinghame, priory of, 4627.
Goldingham, ——, captain, 4377.
........., Jno., of Belstede, Suff., 266, 4705.
........., ..., in commission, 3219, 4254.
........., ..., jun., in commission of the peace for Suffolk, 3967, 4713, 5133.
........., Sir Jno., p. 904.
Goldsburgh, Joan, 3588.
........., Ric., 4550.
Goldsborgh, Tho., son of Ric. Goldsborough, 322, 4369.
Goldsmith, Tho., jun. and sen., 1568.
........., Th., 1568, 3719.
........., ..., junior, 1568.
........., ..., of London, 4893.
Goldesmyth, of Sandwich, 5548. *See* Johnson.
Goldwin, Wm., of Woolwich, 3748.
Golike, Duke of, 5160.
Gomez, Guter. *See* Fuensalida.
Gonell, Th., letter to, 1870, 4727.
Gonfalonier, Francis Marq. of Mantua, 4887, 5417.
Gonson, Vincent, the, ship, (p. 533).
........., Wm., 4140, 5112, 5724, 5790 (p. 960).
........., ..., captain, 3977, 3979, 3980 (pp. 553 and 554), 5112 (p. 812).
........., ..., letters from, 3946, 3985.
........., ..., of the navy, 3678, 4007.
Gonston, ——, employed on the "Great Harry," 4954.
........., the Nicholas, ship, 3591.
Gonzaga, Sigismund, legate of Mantua, 3325.
........., Francis, Marquis of Mantua, letter from, 5601.
Goodman, Geo., 3497 (p. 435).
........., Lewis, of Sowgewas, Heref., 1794).
........., Th., 1831.
........., ..., sheriff for Devon, 1949.
........., Tho., grant to, 900, 901.
........., ..., in commission of peace for Glouc., 930, 1049, 1695, 3641, 3712, 3804, 4024, 4118, 4764, 5506 (p 906).
........., ..., jun., in commission of peace for Glouc., 1469.
Goodrick, Jno., 5053.
........., Wm., in commission of peace for Lincoln, 278, 663, 1170, 1378, 1380, 1716, 3351, 4860.
......, ..., in commission of sewers for Linc., 1979, 3137, 5691.
Goodwin, The, 3820.
........., Th., of St. Peter's, Ipswich, 4768.

Gording, Ric., 4860.
Gorden, Kath., widow of Perkin Warbeck, 1033, 1203.
Gordon, Katharine, wife of Jas. Strangeways, 3005.
Gore, Wm., groom of the chamber, 3496 (p. 431).
Gores, 4173.
Goris, 216.
Gorge, Edward, petty captain, 4375.
......, ..., on sheriff-roll for Somers. and Dorset, 3507, 4544, 5561.
......, ..., in commission, 3585, 3606, 3701, 4713.
......, Sir Edward, 5667.
......, Eliz., 1168.
......, Marg., 1168.
......, Marmaduke, 1168.
......, Matilda, 1168.
......, Ric., 1168.
......, Wm., captain, 4632. *See* George.
Goryng, in Sussex, 1965.
........., John, in commission of peace for Sussex, 281, 1509, 3024, 3428, 4804, p. 904.
Gorizo, Martin de, Spanish merchant, 2042.
Gorleston, in Suff., 1446.
Gorrevod, Laurence de, Governor of Brescia, 216, 3306, 3314, 3396, 3651, 3817, 4322, 4329, 4725, 4976, 5117.
........., ..., appointed to treat with Poynings, 3302.
........., ..., ...?., returns from France, 922.
........., ..., ..., at Lisle, 4429, 4433.
........., ..., ..., at the Holy League, 3861.
........., ..., ..., letter from, 4415.
Gorsanodeok, in Denbigh, 4242.
Gosberton, in Linc., 1067.
Goscote, in Linc., 155.
Goseborn, Hen., 1225.
Gostwik, Jo., 5711.
Gothurst, in Bucks, 3719.
Gotson, Tho., LL.B., 1441.
Goudehurst, in Kent, 685.
Gough, David, 184, 4816.
........., ..., alias ap Jevan, 3612.
........., Sir Geoff. *See* Goghe.
........., Howell ap Rees, of Elvill, Wales, 3771.
........., John, purveyor to the army, 3792, 4271, 4526.
........., Phillip, brewer, 3465.
........., Rees ap Morgan ap, of Elvill, Wales, Jevan, 3771.
........., Ric., under-chamberlain of London, 5723.
........., (Gowffe), Ric., purveyor to the army, 5724.
Goundevyle, in Dorset, 155.
Gource. *See* Gurk.
Goures, De, chancellor of the Tyrol, 216.
Gourlaw, David, ship owner, 3627.

Gowdyer, Ric., 4742.

Gower or Gowre, Sir John, in commission of peace for Yorkshire, 1549, 1550, 1735, 1799, 3219, 4719.

......, ..., in commission of array for Yorkshire and Northumberland, 1804, 3358.

......, ..., in commission of sewers for York, 3072.

......, Wm., groom of the chamber, 67, 726, 1851, 2067, 4382, 4384.

......, ..., grant to, 979, 1088, 1608, 3990.

......, Lord, Herbert of. See Herbert.

......, West and South, Wales, 5180.

Gowffe. See Gough.

Gowlls, The, the English fleet at the, 3820.

Gowth, Jno., ship owner, 4527.

Goze, Tho., 65.

Grace, Wm., in commission of peace for Hunts, 916, 1095, 4006.

........., ..., in commission of gaol delivery for Ramsey, 959, 1222, 3652.

Gracien, ——, 3945.

Grafford, in dioc. of St. David's, 1704.

Grafton, Humph. Stafford of, 671.

Grafton Fleford, in Worcester, 347.

Grafton, Adam, 4184.

Gramato, Jean, prisoner at the battle of Spurs, 4402.

Grammay, Th., general of the Mint, 4917.

Granada, Archbishop of, 8.

Grand, Hen. le, in the war, 4534.

Grandis, John, at siege of Brescia, 3026 (p. 326).

Graneley, John, in commission of peace for Sussex, 1509.

Grantham, town of, 4377.

........., in Linc., 155, 5197.

........., St. Wulfran, 1194.

........., Christ., purveyor to the army, 5720 (p. 958).

........., Chr., of London, 1527.

........., Jno., of London, 4888.

Grarier, Jacquemart, 4445.

Grasforth, church of, St. Asaph dioc., 5206.

Grasmere (Cresmere), 3764.

........., chapel of, 1904.

Gratton, in Rockingham forest, 3085.

Gratz, 5304.

........., Maximilian goes to, 5094.

........., letter dated from, 5126.

Graunte, Jo., 5296.

Graves, 4273, 4359.

Gravelines, 3196, 3291, 4008, 4077, 4162, 4273, 4282, 4526, 5035, 5758.

........., 100,000 French crowns to be paid into, 4087.

........., English army at, 4253.

Gravely, Edw., temp. Edw. IV., 5450.

Gravener, Rob., 1573.

Gravesend, 5720 (p. 957).

........., John Burston of, 12.

Graville, Louis de, Admiral of France, 4329, 5140.

........., ..., ..., at marriage of Princess Mary, 5482.

........., ..., ..., at the treaty with England, 5408.

Graysthoroke in Essex, 1973.

Greynfeld. See Greenfeld.

Great Roll, or Pipe, clk. of the, 3432.

Greece, Sarrinall Countess of, 816.

Greeks, 1659.

Grene in Linc., 3284, 4852.

...... in Sussex, 1598.

Grene, Anne, daughter of Sir Th. Green, 600, 602.

Greene, John, 3094, 4070.

Green, Maud, daughter of Sir Th. Green, 600, 602.

......, Th., of London, 4013.

Grene, Sir Tho., 600, 602, 3049.

........., ..., in debt to Hen. VII., 777.

......, Wm., 144, 412.

Green, Wm., of Barnby, in commission of Yorkshire, 3177, 4015, 5166.

......, ..., of Pomfret, 4375.

Green Cloth, clerk of the, 3154.

Greneacres, Jo., 689.

Greynfelde (Greynfeld), Ric., on sheriff-roll for Beds and Bucks, 664, 1316, 1949.

........., Roger, in commission of peace for Cornwall. 891, 1954, 1984, 3290, 3583, 3605, 3938, 5220, 5586. See Grenville.

........., ..., in commission of peace for Devon, 1166.

........., Tho., in commission of peace for Devon, 699, 917, 1503, 4783.

........., Sir Th., in commission of peace for Devon, 3183, 3566, 3589, 3605, 3938, 4539, 5220.

........., ..., in commission of sewers for Somerset, 1761.

........., ..., in the war, 4377 (p. 652).

Greenhill, John, 3801.

Greneleeff, Laurence, 3093.

Grenewey, Tho., yeoman of the chamber, 445, 4780.

........., ..., sergeant-at-arms, 622.

........., ..., in commission of peace for Bucks, 3522, 5500 (p. 907).

Greenwich. See Ships.

........., 3291, 3322, 3326, 3331, 3333, 3489, 3491, 3838 (p. 520), 3849, 3882, 4367, 4370, 4825, 4902, 4998, 5389, 5590.

Greenwich, contract of the marriage of Princess Mary at, 5322.
........., council at 5407.
........., letter dated from, 153, 5736, 5745.
........., Henry VIII.'s letters dated from 4868, 4871, 5048, 5318, 5319, 5339, 5500, 5651, 5713.
........., com. of musters for, 3116.
........., East, com. of sewers, 4701.
........., military stores at, 5720 (p. 953).
Gregory of Bejar, 4578.
Gregson, Edw., 4316.
........., James, 4316.
Grendon, King's lands called, 3344.
Grenoble, 3325 (p. 382), 5560.
Grenvile, Rog., on sheriff-roll for Cornwall, 664. See Greenfield.
........., ..., sheriff of Cornwall, 1316.
Gresforthe church, dioc. of St. Asaph, 638.
Gresham, Ric., of London, purveyor to the army, 5720 (p. 955).
Gresland in Heref., 1127.
Gresley. See Grisley.
Gresmer in Yorkshire, 4117.
Gresmere. See Grasmere.
Gresthorp in Notts., 1129, 1344.
Greteham in Sussex, 1515.
Grette, Pierekin, 4445.
Gretton, Great, in Glouc., 1374.
Grettuyse, Sieur de la, 3340, 4353.
Greves, Peter, clk. of the closet to Hen. VII., 37.
........., Rob., 1825.
........., Th., yeoman porter of the gate, 969, 1614, 1634, 3076.
........., Tho., gunner, 781.
Grevile, Edw., of Milcote, Warwicksh., 933, 1024, 1163, 1818.
........., ..., on sheriff-roll for Oxon. and Berks, 664.
........., ..., on sheriff-roll for Warwicksh. and Leic.
........., ..., in com. of peace for Oxon., 766, 3015.
........., ..., in commission of peace for Warwickshire, 282, 1387, 1468, 1745, 1971, 3364.
........., ..., in war against France, 4477, 4534.
........., Sir Edw., 4653.
........., ..., in com. of peace for Oxfordshire, 1216, 1470, 4559, 4809, 5506 (p. 905).
........., ..., in com. of peace for Warwicksh., 5506 (p. 903).
........., ..., on sheriff-roll for Warwickshire and Leicestersh., 4544.
........., ..., on sheriff-roll for Oxon and Berks, 5561.
........., ..., in the war, 4826.
........., ..., at the marriage of Princess Mary, 5483.

Grevile, Geo., 892.
........., Giles, 5146.
........., ..., in com. of peace for Glouc., 1469, 1695, 3641, 3804, 3712, 4024, 4118, 4774, 5506 (p. 906).
........., ..., in com. of peace for Worcestershire, 1971, 3301, 3709, 4770, 5506 (p. 903).
........., John, 933.
........., Wm., justice of the Common Pleas, 70, 73, 3802.
........., ..., in com. of peace for Berks, 241, 885, 1393, 1481, 1732, 2095, 3640 ; Glouc., 930, 1049, 1469, 1695, 3641, 3712 ; Heref., 646, 675, 1400, 1963, 3686 ; Salop, 918, 1981, 3071, 3715 ; Staff., 279, 713, 791, 886, 1770; Worc., 892, 1971, 3301, 3709.
........., ..., in com. of gaol delivery for Bridgenorth, 3694 ; Oxford Circuit, 242, 1130, 3275, 3702 ; for Newgate (London), 541, 1519, 1897.
........., ..., justice of assize for Oxford Circuit, 71, 294, 1164, 1494, 2093, 3270.
........., ..., receiver of petitions, 811.
........., ..., trier of petitions, 2082.
Grey, Lord Anth., captain, 4632.
........., Christopher, of Upton, Heref., 1593.
........., Edm., of Wilton, in com. of peace for Bucks, 454, 943, 1379.
........., Edw., in com. of peace for Staff., 713, 1770, 5506 (p. 903 and 905).
........., ..., in com. of gaol delivery for Staff., 764.
........., Sir Edw., his signature, 4505.
........., Lord Edw., knighted at Tournay, 4468.
........., ..., brother of the Marquis of Dorset, at the marriage of Princess Mary, 5483.
........., Edw., son of John Lord Powis, 5089.
........., Elizabeth, sister of Lord Grey, in the service of Mary Queen of France, 5484.
........., Eliz., Countess of Kent, 1124.
........., Emma, 1137.
........., Everard, brother to the Marq. of Dorset, 5484.
........., Geo., 1383.
........., ..., at Calais, 4476.
........., ..., deceased, 4741.
........., Hen., in commission of peace for Beds., 3501, 4700.
........., Joan, daughter of Ralph Grey, 3588.
........., John, yeoman usher of the Chamber, 1508.
........., John, in commission of peace for Northton., 732, 1708, 1971, 5658.
........., ..., in commission of peace for Leicestershire, 739, 1094, 1425, 1971, 4706, 4783, 4812.
........., ..., his signature to challenge of tournament, 1491.
........., ..., See Lisle, Visc. ; Powes, Lord.

Grey, Lord John, brother of the Marq. of Dorset, at the marriage of Princess Mary, 5483.
......, Jno., Lord Powes, 5089.
......, Lord John, captain, 4632.
......, Lady Kath., wife of Wm., De la Pole, 321.
......, Leonard, signs to challenge of tournament, 1491.
......, Lord Leonard, brother of Marq. of Dorset, at marriage of Princess Mary, 5483.
......, Marcy, wife of Nic., 4964.
......, Nic., 1102, 4964.
......, Ralph, 3588.
......, Sir Ralph, 380, 723, 1725, 1923, 5742.
......, ..., deceased, 201.
......, Richard, of Colchester, 2098.
......, Ric. de, signs challenge of tournament, 1491.
......, Lord Rich., 4151.
......, ..., knighted at Tournay, 4468.
......, ..., brother of the Marq. of Dorset, at the marriage of Princess Mary, 5483.
......, Ric. See Earl of Kent.
......, Sir Rog., 5090.
......, Tho., son of Sir Ralph, 201, 723, 1923, 5742,
......, Thomas, friend of Erasmus, 4727.
......, Th. See Dorset, Marquis of.
......, Ld. Wm. of Wilton, 1306.
......, ——, sister to Marquis of Dorset, at Princess Mary's marriage, 5484.
......, ——, of Wilton, gentlewoman, at the marriage of Princess Mary, 5483.
......, heirs of, 1924.
......, ——, taken prisoner at Flodden, 4441.
Greyes, in Suff., 1025.
Greynesby. See Grimsby.
Greystok, Ric., 856.
Greystock, old Baron of, in debt to Hen. VII., 777 ; deceased, 380.
.... See Dacre.
Grice, Th., 1735, 4107.
........., ..., in commission of the peace for Northumberland, 1804 ; for Yorkshire, 1798, 1995, 3177, 4015, 5166.
........., ..., in commission of muster for Northumberland, 3358.
........., ..., deceased, 5072.
Griffendon, captain, 3417.
Griffin, Edw., deceased, 43, 622.
........., Owen, 844.
Griffyn, Tho., son o Sir Nich., 1371.
Griffith, Edw., 4301
........., Humph., 4653.
........., Maurice, alias Walshman, 4367.
........., Pers, archer, 4476.
........., 4439.
........., John, clk., 328.
........., John, 1871.
........., Sir Nic., deceased, 67, 1371.

Griffith, Humph., in the war against France, 4632.
........., Peter, 4031.
........., Peter, clk., 5255.
........., Wm., in the war against France, 3231, 4632, 4653.
........., ..., chamberlain of North Wales, 695.
........., Sir Wm., knighted at Tournay, 4468.
........., ..., in debt to Hen. VIII., 2044.
........., Sir Wm., in commission of peace for Yorksh., 3219.
........., Walt., in commission of peace for Staff., 1770.
........., Sir Walt., in commission of peace for Staff., 5506 (pp. 903 and 905).
........., ..., in commission of peace for Yorksh., 455, 954, 1549, 1550, 3219, 4719, 5193, 5244, 5506 (p. 907).
........., ..., in debt to Hen. VII., 3497 (p. 435).
Grigge, Hen., of Colchester, 1570.
Grimaldi's bank at Rome, 5396.
Grymald, Jo. Bapt. (called Grimbald and Grimbade), excepted from the general pardon, 12.
........., ..., pardoned, 848.
........., ..., in debt to Hen. VII., 3497 (p. 436).
........., ..., son of, 183.
Grimaldis, Lazarus de, merchant of Genoa, 5334.
Grymani, Mark Anth., in debt to Hen. VII., 3497 (p. 435).
Grimsby, ch. of, Linc. dioc. 1910.
........., North, St. Mary's church, 1576.
Grymscote, in Northton., 3027.
Grymmesdiche, John, 357-8.
Grimshawe, in Norfolk, 3943, 4948, 5115.
Grymesthorp, in Linc., 730.
Grimston-Shawe, 4347.
Grymston, in Norfolk, 155.
........., Walt., 481.
Grynaston, 4022.
Gryndill, John, mayor of Bishop's Lynn, 884.
Griphus, 2021, 2025, 3838.
........., Peter sub-collector to the Pope, 1403, 1457.
........., Bp. of Forli, letter from, 4756.
Grisbe, Wm. abbot of Bourne, Linc., 1802, 1844.
Gryse, John, Hen. VII.'s apothecary, 1070.
Grysy, Jas., 5431.
Grisel, Haquin, 4445.
Grisley, John, petty captain for Derby, 4253, (p. 608.)
........., Ro. 435, 1275, 4186.
........., Rob., in debt to Hen. VII., 3497, (p. 435.)
........., Wm., 3497 (p. 435).
........., Sir Wm., captain for Derby, 4253 (p. 608.)

Giseley, Wm., in com. for Derby, p. 907.

Grisons, p. 380.

Gritti, Andrew, 3026, 3752.

Grobered, John, of Esterlings, 777.

Grocin, ——, 4447, 5732.

Grome Park, 4301.

Groningen, in Prussia, 5600.

Gros, John, 4347.

Grosapa, 4173.

Grote, Amboise de, merchant of Brabant, 1092, 3747.

........, Peter de, merchant, of Antwerp, 3747.

Grove, Warwickshire, 419, 1499.

........., ——, escheator of Bucks, excepted from the general pardon, 12.

........, Th., 3220, 3532.

Groveley Forest, Wilts, 61, 998.

Groyngue, in Galicia, 4844.

Grue, De, p. 366.

Gruff, Edm., chaplain, 4841.

Gruffith. *See* Griffith.

Grutuse. *See* Grettuyse.

Guadaloupe, monastery of St. Mary, 5125.

Gualterotti, at Malines, 3651, 5030.

.... *See* Galterotte, Phillip.

Gueldres, English expedition against, p. 433, 3651, 4952, 5018, 5285.

........., Maximilian's intended expedition against, 1902, 3271.

........., Max.'s expedition against, 3398, 3471.

........., English ordnance for, 3616, 4831.

........., ... forces refuse to enter, 3633.

........., truce of, 4343, 4349, 4355, 4364.

........., plundered by Nassau and others, 3077.

........., encounter between the French and people of Liege at, 3446.

........., ambassadors from, 4324.

........., Lord Wassenaw prisoner in, 4418.

Gueldrois, 3446, 3499.

........., Maximilian's harbinger taken by the, 3302.

Gueldres, Charles Duke of, 216, 841, 924, 1245, 1739, 3339, 3752, 3945, 4091, 4273, 4319, 5059, 5675, 5713.

........., ..., included in a truce with Maximilian and other powers, 1417, 3839, p. 575, 4112, 4818.

........., ..., proposes a truce with Maximilian, 3340.

........., ..., Maximilian seeks English assistance against, 8.

........., ..., in Italy, p. 384.

........., ..., lays an ambush to entrap the Emperor, 3489.

........., ..., raises troops for France, 4433.

........., ..., commissioner for France in treaty with Castile, 4924.

........., ..., urges Henry to aid Embden, 5327, 5500, 5600.

........., ..., Lady Eleanor proposed to him as a wife, 5341.

Gueldres, Charles Duke of—*cont.*

........., ..., master of his household, 3651.

........., Bastard of, 3651.

Guernsey, Ric. Weston, governor of, 94.

........., John Martin of, p. 957.

........., grant to the natives of, 941.

Guessling, Maximilian at, 4561.

Guibert, 4427.

Guiche, La, French ambassador, 3112, 3248; (Lagishe), 3258; (La Guysse), 5606.

Guisque, John de la, native of Gascony, 1288.

Guido, ——, 797.

Guienne, 3884, 4058.

........., the expedition against, 3118, 3243, 3298, 3340, 3555, pp. 451-453, 3593, 3614, 3662, 3755, 3762, 3766, 3807, 4165, 4267.

........., preparation for the expedition against, 3352, pp. 394-399, 3357.

........., the Spaniards promised assistance in the enterprise against, 3356.

........., hindrances to the attack upon, 3388.

........., engagement at, 3435.

........., Marquis of Dorset at, 3500, 5745.

........., Longueville sent to, 3112.

........., Lewis XII. raises troops for, 4824.

........., Henry urges Ferdinand to invade, 4055.

........., Ferdinand agrees to invade, 4511.

........., governor of, Mons. D'Angoulême, 3752, 4692, 5675.

........., Lieut. of, Sieur de Lautrec, French commissioner at the treaty with Castile, 4924.

........., Lord of, Sieur de Leodo, slain, 3377.

Guildford, park of, Surrey, 935, 1748.

........., Henry VIII. at, 5383, 5757.

.... Castle, gaol delivery for, 3996.

........., Edw., of Halden, Kent, 690.

........., ..., master of the army, 3732.

........., ..., in the war, 3496, 5031, p. 952.

........., ..., squire of the Body, 1768, 3687.

........./ ......, grants to, 955, 1256, 1423, 1889, 1958.

........., ..., in commission for Kent, 725, 906, 3428, 3605, 4663; for Northton., 2045; for Surrey, 274.

........., ..., sheriff of Linc., 1949.

........., Sir Edw., 4629, 5297.

........., ..., knighted at Tournay, 4468.

........., ..., master of the armoury, 4671, 4751.

........:..., ..., in commission for Kent, 4847, 4927, p. 906.

........., ..., in debt to Hen. VIII., 2044, 5633.

........., Geo., of Rownedon, Kent, 685.

........., ..., in debt to Henry VII., 777.

Guildford, Henry, squire of the Body, 973, 3825.

........., ..., signature to articles of tournament, 1491.

........., ..., in French war, 4642.

........., Sir Hen., in French war, 3885, 4237, 4306, 4307, 4653.

........., ..., standard-bearer, 4132.

........., ..., master of the revels, 4642, p. 958.

........., ..., captain of the Sovereign, 4475.

........., ..., squire of the Body, 5442.

........., ..., in commission for Kent, p. 906.

........., ..., grants to, 3239, 3559, 3611.

........., Lady Joan: 235, wife of Sir Ric. Guildford, lady of honor to Mary of France, 5483, 5517.

........., ..., dismissed, 5483, 5489, 5553.

........., ..., grant to, 5628.

........., Ric., 140.

........., Sir Ric., 5628.

........., ..., master of the armoury, 690.

........., ..., commands The Regent, 3238.

........., Marg., w. of Sir Henry, 3239.

.... Simon, 4730, 5507.

........., ..., Thos. in com. for Bucks, 2045.

Guildefordsynnyng Marsh, Sussex, 274.

Guillard, Lewis, bishop elect of Tournay, 5367, 5587, 5698.

Guylliams, John a, 3484.

Guilliams, John Ap, sergeant-at-arms, 1952, 5536.

........., Th. Ap, yeoman usher of the chamber, 4042.

........., ..., yeoman of the guard, 909.

........., ..., petty captain for Hereford, 4253.

Guinegate, Hen. VIII. at, 4232, 4431, 4629.

Guipuscoa (Ipusqua, Lypwsca), 3243, 3593, 3614, 3807.

...., invaded by the Dauphin, p. 451, 3766.

Guise, Earl of, brother to the Duke of Lorraine, at the marriage of Princess Mary, 5482.

Guyse, John, of Holte, Worcester, 835.

Guisnes, 4022, 4030, 4329, 5560.

........., intended attack upon, 3336, 5021, 5032, 5041.

........., pursuivant (Thomas Wall), 975.

........., captain and lieutenant of. See Vaux, Sir Nich.

.... herald, 4174.

........., high bailiff of, 196.

.... Castle, 521.

........., Bockard Church at, John Wytewode incumbent of, 4937.

........., Th. Eyton of, 4612.

Gullarate, Anth. de, 3269.

Gunne, Jno., of London, 4600.

Gunners, Henry VIII.'s, 760, 761, 781.

Gunners, wages of, 3117.

Gunpowder making, 4931.

Guns, 924, 3616.

Gunson. See Gonson.

Gunstone maker. See Scora.

Gunstones, 3838.

Gunter, John ap Howell, 65.

Gunyonneth in Cardigan, 4436.

Gurk, Bishop of, ambassador of Maximilian to the Pope, 1676, 2039, 3026, 3269, 3302, 3314, 3325, 3340, 3341, 3377, 3385, 3405, 3613, 3648, 3780, 3856, p. 574, 4359, 4455, 4563, 4795, 4955, 5126, 5171.

........., ..., at Inspruck, 1681, 5430, 5686.

........., ..., at Milan, 3658.

........., ..., sent to Rome, 3443.

........., ..., at Rome, 3539.

........., ..., leaves Modena, 3499.

........., ..., starts for Verona, 4355.

........., ..., at Vienna, 5094, 5110.

........., ..., leaves Welce in Lontotrence, 5259.

........., ..., starts for Augsburg, 5304.

........., ..., at Augsburg, 5366.

........., ..., elected cardinal, 4574.

........., ..., demands an income of 100,000 ducats, 4756.

........., ..., mentioned as lieutenant-general of Maximilian in Italy, 4577.

........., ..., mentioned as kinsman of Pope Julius, 1697.

........., brother-in-law. 4091.

Gurney, Thomas, captain, 3591, 3977, 4020, 4377, 4474, 5761.

Gurre, Wm., brigadier, 1931.

........., ..., purveyor for war, p. 431, 4442, p. 955.

Gusseche, Dorset, 155.

Guston, Richard, of Sittingbourne, Kent, 5550.

Guy of Warwick's sword, keeper of, 202.

Guy's cliff-on-Avon, 1257.

Guybon. See Gibbon.

Guyvarra, Don Petro Belis de, 4058, 4725.

Guyinge, John, 1584.

Guyllary, incumbent of Milsted Church, Canterbury dioc., 3674.

Guylle, Ric., serjeant of the bakehouse, 1023.

Guyot, Sir. See Heulle.

Gwynne, ——, excepted from general pardon, 65.

Gy——. See Gi——.

Gybbes. See Ships.

Gyche, La. See Guiche.

Gygges, Dame Olive, sister of John, 1230.

........., John, of London, 1230.

........., John Pole, 1584.

Gyle, John, servant of Fox, Bishop of Winchester, 4142.

Gyldon, Th., of Eastkirby, Linc., 4714.

Gyle, John, 4229.

Gylget. *See* Gelgelt.
Gylford. *See* Guildford.
Gylmyn, Tho., escheator of Gloucester, 536.
.........., John, of the King's buttery, 542.
.........., ..., master of the minstrels, 5504.
.........., ..., deceased, 5683. *See* Gilmyn.
Gylston, Jno., gunner, 4653.
Gyngham, Yevan, 3482.
Gynry, Mons. de, at marriage of Princess Mary, 5482.
Gyrdelar Head, English fleet at, 3820.
Gyvara. *See* Guyvarra.
Gyvor, John, clk., 4123.

H.

Habart, Jno. de, captain of Aire, 4622.
Haberdashers and Hatters of London, 1317.
Habochi, John, gold washer, 1782.
Hacche, Th., 1812.
Hachebury, Wilts, 464.
Haccheman, Roger, yeoman of the Guard, 1985.
Haccombe, Devon, 1779.
Hackeland, John, 1812.
Hacomplayne, Jno., clerk, 4770.
Hacomplaynt, Rob., clerk, 677.
Hacon, Jno. 4414.
Haddley, Robert, 4759.
Haddon, Sir Hen., 1547.
.........., Sir Ric., 1547.
.........., ..., mayor of London, 3765, 3778.
Hades, Wm. 3728.
Hadham, Wm., 3566, 3606, 3701.
Hadleigh, Essex, 155.
.... Ree, Essex, 155.
.........., Suff., 3970.
Hadley, Edw., yeoman of the King's pantry, 87.
Hadlowe, Kent, 1780.
Hadnall, Th., 3694.
Haeze, Francis de, of Ostend, 3571.
Hagnet, 155, 484.
Hague, the, 5159.
Hainault (Henaud), 563, 4329, 4450, 5155, 5341.
.........., army in, 4510, 4560.
.........., news from, 4577.
.........., invasion of, by the French, 5207, 5208.
.........., Belloeile in, 4129.
.........., King-at-arms, 5208.

Haklet, Ralph, excepted from the general pardon, 12.
.........., ..., pardoned, 13.
.........., ..., in commissions for Heref., 646, 675, 1400, 1914, 1963, 3503, 3666, p. 907.
.........., ..., on sheriff-roll for Heref., 3507, 5561.
.........., ..., grants to, 4226, 4837.
Haitfield, Jno. *See* Hatfield.
Halden Bernard, clerk, 5013.
Hales or Halys, Edward, in commission for Essex, 310, 706, 1268, 1522, 1713, 3605, 3785, 3967.
.........., Henry, 5769.
.........., James, 773.
.........., John, 3998.
.........., ..., in commission for Kent, 725, 763, 906, 1225, 3428, 3605, 3775, 3790, 4495, 4663, 4847, 4927, p. 906.
.........., ..., in commissions of sewers, 274, 4701.
Hale, Ric., late of London, 1812, 4360.
......., Rob., sub-prior of St. Mary's Lesnes, 3795.
......., Sir Thos.,Prior Lanthoniæ Primæ, 5789.
Halesowen, abbey of, 155.
.........., ..., corrody in, 1617.
Halhed, Hen., 4770.
Halifax, Yorkshire, 22, 272.
Halywell, St. John the Baptist, convent or, 1737.
Halkerstoun, George, 1364.
Hall, Ann, Sister to Edmund Dudley, 1212,
......., Eliz. widow, 1002.
......., Jno., 4651.
......., Rob., 3646, 4996.
......., Roger, grocer, p. 957.
......., Thos., 3475; inc. of Sarsedon, Salisbury dioc., 1760.
......., Thos., of Ipswich, 593, 3851, 3896, 4023.
.........., ..., in commission for Hunts, 905, 916, 1095, 4006, p. 906 ; for Yorkshire, 5503.
......., ..., Wolsey's servant, 4119.
......., Tho., M.D., 968.
......., Wm., chaplain, 3223.
Halsale, Sir Henry, in debt to the Crown, 1639, 3497, 5633.
Halsall, John, inc. of Wodborowe, 1526.
Halley, John, 3046.
.........., Tho., messenger of the chamber, 476.
Halls, Tents, Pavilions, &c., 4629.
Halnaker, Sussex, 5085.
Halnouct, Prince of, 216.
Halorchard, Staff. 4303.
Haloweys, Staff., 4592.
Halrigge, Devon, 2080.
Halsey, Thomas, 1478.

3 x 2

Halstowe, church, 3399.

Halton, Northumb., 1040, 5010.

........., manor of, 4699.

Halwell, Ric., 597, 860.

Halweye, John, 1812.

Hambroke, 5026, 5027.

Hamburg, 3628, 3629.

........., letter to the governors of, 3627.

Hamerton, John, of Yorkshire, 1798, 1995, 3177, 4015.

........., Roger, 4962, 4965.

........., ..., clerk of the market for the household, 2073.

Hamilton, Andr., 5681.

........., Lord, 3569, 5681.

Hamond, Henry, of London, 5216.

........., John, 3059.

Hampden of the Hill, 3231.

........., Sir Edm., 137, 1253, 4984.

........., Will., son of Sir Edm. and Eliz., 1752.

........., John, of Bucks, 3522, p. 907.

........., Sir John, captain, p. 553.

Hamell. See Ships.

Hammes Castle, 521, 618, 1155.

...., lieutenant of, Lord Mountjoy, 640, 1306, 3637, 4635.

...., threatened by the French, 3336, 5032.

........., bailiff of, 1073.

........., pursuivant, 4030.

Hampshire or Hants, 3786.

........., commissions of the peace for 1388, 3071, 4159, 4676, 5506.

........., sheriffs of, 664, 1316, 1771, 1949, 3507, 4544, 5127, 5561.

........., proclamations in, 1771, 3592.

........., commissions of array in, 1771, 1812, 3393, 3688, 3723.

........., escheator of, 3447.

........., feodary, 4414.

........., tenths and fifteenths of the laity in, 3441.

Hampsted Marshall, Berks, 155.

Hamptnett (Sussex), 578.

Hampton, manor of, Warw., 3239, 4310.

........., in Ardern, Warw., p. 435.

.... Court, 5724.

.........-on-the-Hill, bailiff of, 4301.

.... See Southampton.

...., of Southampton, 12.

........., Geof., 5309.

........., John, monk of Malmesbury, 1183.

... ., Thos., D.D., 1056.

........., ..., abbot of St. Augustine's, Canterbury, 1180.

Hamshay, alias Hamsly, Sussex, 1965.

Hamsted, ——, 1212.

Hamswell, near Calais, p. 624.

Hananns, in Somerset, 4071.

Hanaper, the, of Chancery, 1337, 3527, 5674, 5689. See Lupton, Roger ; Smyth, William ; Heron, John.

........., ..., accounts of, 5231.

Hanegrave, Jehan, 4445.

Hanfay, manor of, Sussex, 1212.

Hanging Stone, the, in the Borders, 5090.

Hanley, Worc., 1960, 3613, 5478.

........., bailiff of, 170.

........., John, 838.

Hanniball, Th., LL.D., vicar-general of Bishop of Worc., 5344.

Hans the gunfounder. See Popenruyter.

Hansard or Hansart, ——, in the army, 3885, 4237, 4307.

........., Anthony, 5508, 5633.

........., ..., yeoman usher of the chamber, 449.

........., ..., of Hellowe, 1587.

........., John, captain, 5761.

........., Richard, letter from, 5219.

........., Will. of Kelsay, 1587.

........., ..., in the war, 4314.

........., ..., in com. for Lincolnshire, 1171, 1979, 3137, 3342, 4358, 5691.

........., Sir Will., in com. for Lincolnshire, 4593, 4860.

Hanse, merchant of the, 3497.

.... Towns, the, 3633.

Hanshawe, Wm., 3694.

Hanslape, 645, 1493.

Hansley, in Notts, 4728.

Hanslop, inc. of, 177.

Hanso De, ——, 3915.

Hanson, Oliver, 5095.

Hansted, 947.

.... Hall, manor of, 947.

Hanstede, John, waxchandler, 4293.

Hanwell, Sussex, 297.

Hanworth, Midd., 92.

........., Linc., 3284, 4852.

Haracombe, Devon, 2080.

Harbert. See Herbert.

Harbottle, 4406, 4556 ; castle of, 380.

Harebotell, Cristopher, inc. of Fureswey, Linc., 3281.

........., Wigard, 810.

Harbottle, Sir Winchard, 4441.

Harbingers, the King's, 4237.

.... Hall, the Knight, 4629.

Harcourt, ——, in the King's retinue, 4307.

........., Ric., in com. for Berks, 4341, 5166.

........., Rob., 174.

........., Sim., in com. for Oxfordshire, 766, 1470, 1745, 3015, 3546, 4254, 4559, 4809, p. 905.

........., ..., sheriff of Oxon and Berks, 5561.

........., Tho., 664.

........., Wm., of Oxfordshire, 664, 766, 1216, 1470.

........., ..., sheriff of Oxon and Berks, 1316.

Harden or Harding, Allen, 5723.
........., John, M.A., inc. of Bladen, 731, 1578.
........., ..., inc. of Yelvertoft, 1560.
........., ..., prebendary of Penkridge, 2023.
........., ..., inc. of Lovel Upton, 4603.
Hardwick. See Herdweck.
Hardy, John, of London, 1003.
Hardyn, near Tournay, 4253 (p. 609).
Harebrowne, Geo., of Shropshire, 4394, 4827.
Harefield. See Herefeld.
Harfleur, 3678, 4330.
Hargood. See Hartegood.
Harlis Park, Devon, 5618.
Harleston, Clement, heir of Alice wife of Rob., 4166.
........., John, rector of Blaksale, 1375.
Harlowe, Essex, 734.
Harne, John, 766.
Harness, 3471, 3732, 4131, 4586, 4954 (n).
Harold, Will., inc. of Melles, 1803.
Harper, Hen., auditor of the Earldom of March, 914.
........., Walt., yeoman of the Male, 1753, 4342.
........., Will., capt., 3903, 3980, 4005, 4377, 5112, 5761.
Harpur, Ric., 1282.
Harpesfeld, John, mercer of London, 4203, 4240, 4241.
Harpisfeld, Lewis, 2044.
Harres, Wm., 895.
Harreshawes, in Rockingham Forest, 314.
Harriers, master of the, Will. Fitzwilliam, 3742.
Harrigge, Devon, 1599.
Harrington, Dr., 1363.
Harrington, James, dean of York, 3285,
........., John, 266, 1316, 1949.
........., ..., sheriff of Rutland, 3507.
........., Nich., 4556.
Harris or Harres, Frans., 895.
........., Isabella, 895.
........., John, 484.
........., ..., inc. of Ripton Regis, 744.
........., ..., of London, 1254.
........., Philippa, 895.
........., Robt., 266, 725, 906.
........., ..., in commission for Sussex, 281 ; sewers, 297.
........., Wm., 328.
........., ..., son of Francis, 895.
Harryson, Harry, 3998.
Harrison, John, 3579, 4377, 5720, p. 954. See Herryson.
Harison, Valentine, 4526.
Harroweden, 464.
Harry, the Great, ship of Henry VIII., otherwise called the Henry Grace de Dieu, 3980, 4954, 4968, 5112, 5170, 5228, 5317, 5774.
........., ..., Henry VIII. on board, 5173.
........., ..., master of. See Spertt, Thomas ; Hen, Howard.

Harry, David ap, clerk convict, 1783, 3135.
Harrys. See Harris.
Harsey, Humph., of Nottinghamshire, 1514.
Hart, Edw., clk., 4479.
......, John, notary, 1182.
......, Ric., yeoman of the almonry, 929, 1673.
......, Rob., keeper of the garden of Eltham, 929.
......, Th., Act for restitution of, 2082, 4238, 4527.
......, ..., captain, 4475. See also Hert.
Hartecowed, in Haseley, 3186.
Hartest, Suffolk, 947.
Hartford, Berkshire, 1426.
........., John, customer of Plymouth and Fowey, 3261.
Hartegood, Rob., goldbeater, 1528, 4643.
Harthill, wapentake of, 273, 4781.
Harteley, Th., incumbent of Great Bylling, Linc., 3689.
Harteshorne, Ric., 4232.
Hartewell, Bucks, 1352, 1985.
........., John, of Preston, Northt., 5119.
........., Ric., mercer of London, 4228.
........., Wm., mercer of London, 4266.
Hartfield, Sussex, 1484.
........., Jno., in com. for York, 5193.
Hartson. See Hertson.
Harward, or Hayrward, Geo., 3496, 4527.
........., ..., of London, 3369.
Harwardys, Geo., his factor in Bilboa, 3662.
Harwegge, Devon, 623.
Harwell, Agnes, sister of Thomas Harwell, 3843.
........., John, heirs of, 3843.
........., Th., son of John, 3843.
Harwich, 4535.
.... See Ships.
Harewood, manor of, Yorks., 4550.
Harvy, Geo., of the household, sheriff of Beds and Bucks, temp. Hen. VII., 1467.
........., Humphry, of Somersetshire, 287, 712.
........., Ric., and Robt. his son, keeper of woods, St. Albans, 5177. See Hervey.
Haselbury, Northampton, 4934.
Hasel, Geo., archer, 4476.
Haseley, Warw., 419, 1499, 3186, 3497.
........., Edw., salter of London, 5612.
Haselden or Hasylden, Fran., in com. for Cambridgeshire, 226, 701, 1421, 3583, p. 904.
........., ..., sheriff of Camb. and Hants, 664.
........., ..., sheriff of Cambridge and Huntingdon, 664.
Haselingfield, Camb., 4659.
Hassellore, Somersetshire, 155.
Hashton, Warwickshire, 1719.
Hasilrigge, Rob., in com. for Notts, 5225, p. 905.

Hasilrigge, Rob., yeoman of the wardrobe, 109, 698.
........., ..., yeoman usher of the Queen's Chamber, 1888.
........., Thos., 554.
........., ..., in com. for Leicestershire, 656, 1094, 1425, 1642, 1971, 4706, 4783, 4812, p. 905 ; for Notts, 5225.
Hasilwod, Edm., 1733.
........., ..., in com. for Northamptonshire, 1708, 1971, 2045, 5658.
Hasilwode, John, 3440, of London, 3537.
Hasleton, Tho., escheator of York, 1311.
Hassell, Th., 3348.
Hassill or Hasle, town of, 386, 481, 1191, 4961.
Hasta. See Aste.
Hastley park, Warw., 4301.
Hastil, John. See Stile.
Hastings, town of, commission for, 4996.
Hastinges or Hastings, George Lord, 872, 1401, 3887, 4070, 4253.
........., ..., in commissions of the peace for Leicestershire, 656, 1094, 1425, 1971, 4706, 4783, 4812.
,........, ..., summoned to Parliament, 5616.
........., ..., trier of petitions in Parliament, 811, 2082.
........., ..., in debt to the Crown, 2044, 5633.
........., Sir Geo. 722.
........., ..., in commissions for Yorkshire, 1735, 1804, 1995, 3358.
........., John, son of Sir George, 3194.
,........, Ric., of Surrey, 1762, 3078, 3092.
........., Sir Richard, 1301, 4886.
........., Sir Rog., sheriff of Northumberland, 664.
........., Will., 4127; in com. for Leicestersh., 1425, 1971.
........., Eliz. daughter of Sir John, 961.
........., Katherine Lady, 321, 1472.
........., Mary, Lady Hastings and Hungerford, 1372.
Hatfield, Yorkshire, 84, 178, 1178, 1205, 3818, 3845.
........., Brosdoak, Essex, 3939.
........., Edmund, inc., of St. Mary Hoo, 1545.
........., John, commissioner of sewers, 481, 4719.
........., ..., in com. for York, 3219.
Hatford, Berks, 174.
........., church of, Salisbury dioc., 519. 4719.
Hat-makers, Act touching, 2082.
Hats, French and Bruges, 5239.
Hatteclyff, Linc., 3757.
Hatticliff, ——, 3451.
Hatteclyff, Edw., 1063, 1064, 1678, 3055, 3289 (n).
........., ..., clerk of the signet, 3054.
........., Wm., clerk to the marshal of the household, 1023.

Hatteclyff, Wm., clerk of accounts of the household, 4498, 4632.
........., ..., letter from, 4099.
........., ..., clerk of Green Cloth, 3154.
........., ..., of Hatteclyff, Linc., 3757.
Hatton, Warw., 3186.
........., John, of Uxbridge, 4025.
........., Ric., clerk of the Parliament, 611.
........., ..., canon and prebendary of St. Stephen's, Westminster, 107.
Haughley, Suffolk, 1252
Haughton, Ric. constable of Bridgenorth, 4737.
Haukyn, Hynkyn John, 3051.
Haulgarth, Linc., 1736.
........., doorward of, 351.
Hauls, Thomas, 1236.
Haulx, 3499.
Haunshay. See Hanfay.
Haute Normandie, 3357.
Havard, Phil., bailiff of Nethewode and Wulferlowe, 1078.
Havell, Geo., in com. of peace, Oxford, 894.
Haven Cathe, le, of St. Ives, Cornw., 3646.
Haverford, town of, 1579.
Haverford West, 52, 438, 504, 4907.
Havering at Bower, Essex, 155.
Haversham, 3442.
Haward. See Howard.
........., Hervy, debtor to Henry VIII., 5633.
Hawarden, Andr., 1962.
........., Ro., 536.
Hawes, Our Lady of, 3226, 4165.
Hawkis, Ric., feodary of Crown lands, in London and Middlesex, 4414.
Hawkesford, John, 1011.
........., ..., sub-almoner to the King, 1631.
Hawkwell, Northumberland, 1040, 5010.
Hawkyns, Robt., 1703.
........., ——, shipmaster, 3979.
Hawkyns, Rog., 1287.
Hawles, Wm., of London, 5127.
........., ..., of Winchester, 3198.
Hawlesse, or Hawles, Wm.,of Hampshire, 266, 1388, 1812.
Hawleigh, Suffolk, 68, 1281, 4254.
Hawte, Edw., mercer of London, 4817.
........., Wm. 3790.
Hawtemprice, monastery of, Yorks., 5275.
Hay. See Hague, the
Haydock, Thomas, in com. for Oxfordshire, 1745, 1949, 4559, 4809, 5506 (p. 905).
Haydon, Sir John. See Heydon.
........., John, dyer, London, 4013.
Haye, Le, 4014.
...... Hall, La, letter dated, 216.
......, Massin, Frenchman, 4445.
Hayeburgh, Oxford, 866.
Hayes, Seven, Staffordshire, 133.
Haylande, ——, 3945.
Haylys. See Hales.

Hays, Albert, Easterling merchant, p. 953.

Haytysbury, Wilts, 464.

Hayward, Henry, 3496.

........., Rob., incumbent of Newton, Norwich, 1648.

Haywode, Wm. *See* Heywood.

Heampton Sachfeld, manor of, Devon, 3869.

Heaton. *See* Heton.

Heda, maitre d'hotel of the duke of Gueldres, 3651.

Hedde, John, in com. for Oxford, 3546.

Hede, Wm. 1002.

........., ..., in commission for Kent, 725, 763, 906, 3428, 3605.

Hedendon pasture, in Shotover Forest, 4772.

Hédin in Artois, sometimes called Eden and Esdeyne, 3945, 4296, 4329.

........., ..., Frenchman taken at, 4328.

........., ..., Lord Roeux governor of, 4319.

........., ——, of Margaret of Savoy's household, 4078.

Hedingham Castle, letter dated from, 4766.

Hedworth, John, 705.

Hedyngton-cum-Bolyngton, near Oxford, 155.

Hegster, Raynkyn, captain of the gunners, 4375.

Heigham, John, 1939.

........., Ric. 3282; justice of assize, Midland Circuit, 3699, 4339, 4771.

Hek de Conell, le, in Shotover Forest, 4772.

Hekington, Linc., 398, 1430.

Helebrigge, Devon, 5618.

Helyndon, Midd., 1031, 1167.

Helyngton, Norf., 1629.

Hell, Paradise, and Purgatory, tenements so called, in Westminster, 5211.

Hellespont, Turkish fleet in, 3874.

Hellowe, Linc., 449, 1541, 1587.

Hellowes, in Crowley, Bucks, 1937.

Helpeston, Northt., 645.

Helpthorp, 415.

........., And., son of Rob., 415.

Helston, in Cornwall, 506.

Helsing, overseer of, 5219.

Helsyngton, Westmoreland, 3764.

Helwell, 155.

Hemen, Wm. de, Frenchman, 4445.

Hemerdon, 5648.

Hemeswell, church of, dioc. Linc., 3770, 3906.

Hemles, 1682.

Hemp Street, 1134.

Hempnall, Norfolk, 341, 5137.

Hempnale, Ralph, 1375.

Hempstead, Sir Ric., 5789.

Hemyngforde Grey, Huntingdonshire, 1124.

Hemyngton, Somerset, 2080.

Hend, Gresilda, 735.

Hende, Walter, of London, 138.

Hendeley, Surrey, 935, 4301.

Henderson John, 2069.

Hendour, Ric., and Margaret his wife, 4744.

Hendry, Jo., of London, 5690.

Hendy, Walt., the King's fletcher, 3368.

Heneage, or Hennege, John, 792, 1378.

........., ..., of Hynton, 4616.

........., ..., in commission for Lincolnshire, 1171, 1716, 1979, 1983, 3137, 3342, 4358, 4593, 4860, 5476, 5506 (p. 906), 5691.

Hengbach, in Germany, 5746.

Hengeham, Norfolk, 5157.

Henham, Essex, 4599.

........., Suff., 996.

Heningham, 4101.

........., Sir Jno., in the war against France, 4377.

Henkyn, John, 3751.

Henley, in Ardern, 1499, 3880,

........., -upon-Thames, 1350.

Henllan, in Denbighland, 1150.

Hennyngham, John, of Suffolk, 1757.

Henry I., charter of, 79.

Henry II., 3031.

........., charter of, 5120.

Henry III., 263, 1198, 3172, 4669.

Henry V., 3315.

Henry VI. 1192, 1198, 2011, 3529, 3556, 3599, 4934.

Henry VII., 4, 137, 182, 196, 215, 216, 221, 229, 267, 300, 335, 344, 350, 362, 364, 367, 405, 441, 449, 490, 501, 594, 607, 629, 639, 648, 666, 671, 772, 778, 927, 928, 941, 952, 1005, 1010, 1012, 1029, 1070, 1113, 1148, 1241, 1253, 1293, 1344, 1678, 1838, 1839, 1851, 1855, 1974, 2020, 2022, 2055, 2074, 2080, 2087, 3005, 3019, 3034, 3077, 3081, 3136, 3149, 3239, 3266, 3315, 3374, 3395, 3432, 3843, 3954, 4058, 4324, 4392, 4498, 4507, 4527, 4536, 4547, 4594, 4870, 4902, 4941, 4984, 5016, 5056, 5086, 5280, 5309, 5394, 5453, 5514, 5589, 5627, 5702.

........., his death, 149, 3333.

........., his funeral, 5735.

........., his dying advice to Henry VIII, 224.

........., bequests of, 5737, 5738.

........., legatees of, 776.

........., executors of, 1005, 2065, 3292.

........., bonds and debts to, 380, 777, 786, 1639, 3497.

........., bonds and debts to, cancelled, 63, 313, 317, 320, 442, 464, 531, 566, 575, 578, 668, 697, 945, 961, 996, 1026, 1185, 1284, 1386, 2036, 3079, 3080, 4116.

........., tomb, 775.

........., hospital of (Savoy), 3292.

........., his servants and officers, 1, 37, 65, 366, 599, 650, 965, 991, 1114, 1445, 1467, 1638, 2016, 3164, 3518, 5434, 5494.

Henry VII.—cont.
........., his general pardon, 2, 3.
........., letters addressed to him, 8, 11.
........., treaties of, 14, 224, 432, 474, 475,
478, 488, 714, 1632, 1717, 1919, 3129,
3398, 4582, 4889, 5274.
........., statutes of, 186.
........., his intended Crusade, 1700, 1875.
Henry VIII., 2, 3, 236, 251, 252, 361, 368, 379,
403, 425, 544, 652, 653, 778, 924, 1097,
3082, 3112, 3138, 3146, 3229, 3230,
3320, 3356, 3357, 3518, 3631, 3633,
3648, 3837, 3954, 4098, 4099, 4162,
4164, 4169, 4308, 4309, 4310, 4324,
4327, 4349, 4360, 4388, 4459, 4462,
4463, 4483, 4490, 4513, 4518, 4523,
4525, 4598, 4666, 4667, 4682, 4727,
4756, 4831, 4849, 4850, 4851, 4864,
4870, 4883, 4887, 4932, 4935, 4952,
4955, 4960, 4970, 4976, 5018, 5029,
5090, 5104, 5110, 5117, 5139, 5140,
5152, 5154, 5168, 5173, 5176, 5182,
5192, 5203, 5205, 5218, 5257, 5267,
5285, 5297, 5322, 5329, 5337, 5342,
5353, 5354, 5365, 5368, 5372, 5383,
5387, 5393, 5407, 5417, 5447, 5462,
5465, 5467, 5468, 5477, 5489, 5496,
5497, 5512, 5517, 5518, 5541, 5542,
5543, 5547, 5553, 5584, 5590, 5591,
5600, 5606, 5634, 5637, 5642, 5649,
5657, 5664, 5676, 5681, 5696, 5697,
5698, 5702, 5706, 5720, 5722, 5740,
5741, 5744, 5753, 5757, 5758, 5762,
5783. See also Sheriff-rolls.
........., letters from, 224, 338, 598, 599, 1457,
1828, 3188, 3346, 3347, 3555, 3749,
3811, 3812, 3835, 3836, 3862, 3876,
4008, 4085, 4086, 4331, 4397, 4437,
4470, 4502, 4512, 4548, 4819, 4829,
4868, 4871, 5005, 5035, 5041, 5048,
5148, 5158, 5258, 5284, 5318, 5319,
5339, 5398, 5500, 5511, 5651, 5713,
5763.
........., letters to, 149, 161, 169, 216, 267,
300, 348, 369, 394, 405, 490, 498, 540,
819, 982, 983, 1128, 1176, 1221, 1262,
1353, 1622, 1659, 1660, 1676, 1697,
1701, 2010, 2039, 2072, 3066, 3068,
3077, 3196, 3207, 3216, 3226, 3248,
3258, 3271, 3276, 3291, 3302, 3306,
3314, 3319, 3322, 3323, 3326, 3328,
3331, 3334, 3335, 3339, 3340, 3353,
3355, 3361, 3362, 3363, 3367, 3370,
3372, 3376, 3377, 3381, 3385, 3387,
3396, 3398, 3405, 3415, 3417, 3419,
3425, 3435, 3437, 3446, 3456, 3460,
3463, 3469, 3471, 3481, 3489, 3499,
3500, 3514, 3525, 3543, 3569, 3571,
3577, 3584, 3607, 3614, 3638, 3651,
3658, 3661, 3662, 3678, 3692, 3718,
3751, 3766, 3777, 3779, 3805, 3806,
3807, 3814, 3815, 3817, 3820, 3821,
3823, 3838, 3863, 3873, 3874, 3875,
3877, 3878, 3882, 3883, 3897, 3903,
3905, 3916, 3918, 3945, 3950, 3962,
4020, 4054, 4058, 4069, 4078, 4090,
4091, 4095, 4112, 4154, 4163, 4165,
4168, 4182, 4193, 4196, 4216, 4267,
4272, 4273, 4274, 4276, 4280, 4282,

Henry VIII.—cont.
4283, 4287, 4288, 4296, 4312, 4318,
4319, 4322, 4326, 4333, 4343, 4351,
4354, 4355, 4359, 4361, 4364, 4366,
4389, 4393, 4396, 4407, 4409, 4418,
4426, 4429, 4433, 4444, 4446, 4450,
4451, 4455, 4458, 4471, 4491, 4499,
4500, 4520, 4556, 4561, 4562, 4563,
4571, 4572, 4577, 4578, 4579, 4582,
4584, 4604, 4605, 4608, 4609, 4610,
4615, 4621, 4622, 4641, 4665, 4691,
4724, 4725, 4735, 4756, 4786, 4789,
4796, 4801, 4810, 4833, 4835, 4844,
4869, 4902, 4915, 4920, 4921, 4922,
4926, 4951, 4956, 4970, 4978, 5006,
5025, 5030, 5040, 5054, 5055, 5058,
5059, 5076, 5094, 5099, 5105, 5106,
5107, 5111, 5126, 5155, 5156, 5159,
5165, 5169, 5171, 5174, 5175, 5207,
5208, 5252, 5259, 5262, 5263, 5269,
5290, 5292, 5299, 5301, 5304, 5323,
5327, 5331, 5332, 5333, 5338, 5341,
5349, 5356, 5357, 5358, 5362, 5366,
5377, 5389, 5391, 5392, 5403, 5404,
5409, 5410, 5430, 5443, 5445, 5448,
5457, 5458, 5488, 5495, 5505, 5513,
5523, 5532, 5535, 5538, 5539, 5540,
5560, 5565, 5589, 5599, 5601, 5614,
5632, 5635, 5636, 5662, 5663, 5665,
5671, 5675, 5677, 5680, 5686, 5717,
5728, 5730.
........., Badoer's account of, 3333.
........., his marriage, 8, 147, 156, 162.
........., his accession, 5736.
........., his general pardon, 2, 3, 12 ; its ex-
emptions, 12.
........., his body guard, 678, 4307, 4314.
........., his coronation, 164, 211, 212, 213,
214, 224.
........., bonds and debts to, 545, 566, 617,
618, 2044, 3034, 3593, 5633, 5723.
........., tournament on birth of a prince,
1491.
........., illness of, 4380, 4726, 4831, 4845
4921.
........., proclamations and orders in Council
by, 679, 702, 3288, 4472.
........., his commissions to ambassadors, 520,
1066, 1104, 3513.
........., treaties of, 234, 432, 474, 475, 478,
548, 714, 793, 1055, 1105, 1107, 1335,
1880, 1932, 1967, 1980, 2094, 3523,
3647, 3649, 3839, 3860, 3861, 4038,
4435, 4510, 4511, 4560, 4818, 4875,
4889, 4924, 4985, 5305, 5315, 5326,
5335, 5343, 5559.
........., his war against France, 3225, 3602,
3752, 4129, 4130, 4307, 4311, 4314,
4320, 4323, 4365, 4371, 4386, 4398,
4399, 4401, 4410, 4457, 4464, 4466,
4467, 4473, 4477, 4492, 4501, 4526,
4533, 4535, 4652, 4913, 4914.
........., ..., diary of occurrences in, 4284.
........., money due to him from France, 626,
1182, 1632, 2026, 5280, 5306.
........., proposed interview with Lewis XII.,
5468, 5553, 5569.

Henry VIII.—*cont.*

........., sword and cap sent to him by Leo X., 4835, 5111.

........., golden rose sent to him by Julius II., 976.

........., his handwriting, 775.

........., his signature, 1491, 5737.

........., his portrait, 5604.

........., his deer hounds, 3317.

........., his servants, 1.

........., his stables at Eltham, 3816.

........., wardrobe of. *See* Wardrobe.

........., his almoner. *See* Edname, —— ; Rawlyns, Richard!; Wolsey, Thomas.

........., his nurse. *See* Luke, Anne.

........., his printer. *See* Pynson, Richard.

........., his secretaries. *See* Ammonius, Andreas ; Meautys, John ; Millet, John ; Ruthal Bishop of Durham.·

........., his standard bearer, 340.

........., his tailor. *See* Jasper, Richard.

........., mandates of, 367, 1264, 2029, 2054, 3664.

Henry Prince of Wales, son of Henry VIII., 1495, 1513.

... ., ..., tourney on his birth, 1491.

........., ..., his nurse, 1862.

Henry, John ap, 3771.

........., Morys ap, 1269.

Henryson, Scotch ambassador, Jas., 782, 1820, 3569, 3838.

........., John, Scotch ambassador, 3676.

........., Ro., justice on the Northern Circuit, 173, 294, 832, 1123, 1130, 1490, 1763, 2099, 3267, 3275, 3691, 3699, 4279, 4252, 4771, 5195, 5283.

........., Tho., 1405, 3620, 5020. *See* Herryson.

Henshawe, Wm., of Gloucester, 1287.

Hepburne, Jas., nominated Abbot of Dumfermline, 4556, 4625.

........., Patrick, prior of St. Andrew's, 5641.

Heppells, barony of, Northumberland, 1040, 5010.

"Herbedum," 3026.

Herbert, ——, gunfounder, 4977.

........., Anne, of Chepstow, Wales, 765.

........., John, 3497.

........., Ric., 366, 988, 1234.

........., Sir Ric., 5180.

........., Sir Walter, 3949.

Herbert de Troye, Wm., in debt to the Crown, 1639, 3497.

........., ..., grant to, 5180.

Hercies, lands called, Middlesex, 1031, 1167.

Hercy, Humphrey, sheriff for Notts and Derby, 3507, 4544.

........., ..., in commission for Notts, 1735, 1798, 1804, 1964, 3494, 4776, 5183, 5225, p. 905.

Herde, Rob., haberdasher of London, 5144.

Herdwick, Oxon, 4694.

Herefeld, Middlesex, 1013.

Hereford, city of, 1093, 4717, 5461, 5575.

.... Cathedral, 1093.

........., prison of, 1150.

........., commissions of gaol delivery for, 1794, 1914, 3503.

........., Rich. Bishop of, 1150.

........., Richard [Mayhew], Bishop of, in commissions of the peace for Worcester, Heref., Gloucest., Salop, 3301, 3686, 3709, 3712, 3715, 3804, 4024, 4118, 4394, 4764, 4770, 4827, pp. 903, 904, 906, 907.

........., ..., summoned to Parliament. 5616.

Hereford., co. of, 298, 3289, 3901, 4198.

........., sheriffs of, 664, 1316, 1771, 1949, 3507, 4544, 5561.

........., captains of, 4253.

........., feodary of Crown lands in, 4414.

........., clerk of the signet in, 1839.

........., commissions of the peace for, 646, 675, 1400, 1963, 3686, 5506 (p. 907).

Herefy, James, 5586.

Heretics, burning of, 1948, 1957.

Herforth, Yorksh., 3018.

Hering, Hen., bailiff of Walmeshill Lacy, Heref., 4862, 5002, 5551.

........., Simon, father of Hen. Heryng, 4862, 5002.

Heryngham, 4526.

Heriot, Wm., 1843.

Herle, Th., brother of Geo., son of John, 5046.

Hermitage, Le, free chapel, Blakemore, Dorset, 1953, 3553.

Hern, Tyrell of. *See* Tyrrell.

Herne, de la, Sir John Arundell. *See* Arundell.

Heron, Bastard, borderer, 3339.

........., John, executors of, 439.

........., ..., of Shacklewell, Middx., treasurer of the chamber, 105, 159, 296, 429, 566, 625, 678, 810, 991, 1212, 1372, 1435, 1527, 1574, 1584, 1604, 1872, 3080, 3285, 3445, 3496, 3497, 3762, 3981, 4099, 4179, 4202, 4375, 4436, 4535, 4867, 4878, 5116, 5250, 5453, 5619, 5724, 5735, 5737, 5738, 5739, 5765, 5768, 5779.

........., ..., grants to, 3594, 3735, 3736, 4218, 5460.

........., ..., commission to, 5298.

........., ..., surveyor of customs, 4892, 5723.

........., ..., mercer, 4662, 5720 (p. 958).

........., ..., clerk of the Jewel House, 3422.

........., ..., clerk of the Hanaper, 5460.

........., ..., of Crawley, Northumberland, 4406.

........., Sir John, of Chipchase, Northumberland, 4825.

........., Wm., of Ford, 5090.

........., Sir Wm., 4825.

........., Odnel, in com. for Northumberland, 187.

Herris, ——, 4653.
Herryson, Jno., ship master, 5112. *See* Harrison and Henrison.
........., Rob., mayor of Kingston-upon-Hull, 1922.
Hersey, Humph. *See* Hercy.
Herst or Hyrste, John, 3031, 3497.
Hert, John, weaver, of London, 951.
......, ..., of Tavistock, Devon, 3150.
......, Ric., purser, 4535.
......, Th., gunpowder maker, 3496; gunner, 120.
......, Thos., draper, of London, 1473, 3179. *See* Hart.
Hertegood. *See* Hartegood.
Herteley, John, of Cambridge, 4160.
Hertfield. *See* Hartfield.
Hertford, 4249.
Hertfordshire, 3871, 4018.
........., commissions for, 266, 309, 706, 1020, 1971, 3102, 5506 (p. 906).
........., sheriffs of, 664, 1316, 1949, 3507, 4544, 5561.
........., proclamation in, 1771.
........., Crown lands in, 3668, 4022, 4414.
........., escheators of, 3447, 3493, 3743.
........., tenths and fifteenths in, 3441.
Herthill. *See* Harthill.
Hertson, Mary, 3439.
Hertwell. *See* Hartwell.
Hervey, ——, ship master, 4377.
........., Edm., of Stratbroke, 5074.
........., H., 3496.
........., Rob., of Stratbroke, 5074.
Hesant, Rob., 874.
Heselin, Jacquet, French workman, 4445.
Hesketh, Ric., 1484, 1781.
Hesse, Elector of, 4305.
Hessle or Hesill, Yorksh. *See* Hasle.
Hethfeld, Devon, 2080.
Heton Church, York dioc., 1544.
......, Rob., 415.
......, Th., 5239.
Heulle, Sir Guyot de, 3362, 3476, 3496, 3584, 3762, 3766, 4632; with Ferdinand, p. 458, 3607; going into Flanders, p. 475, returning to England, p. 451.
Heven, Edw., 351, 352, 663, 1961, 2014.
Hevyngham or Hevenyngham, John, 485.
........., ..., sheriff of Norf. and Suff., 1316.
........., Sir John, in com. for Suffolk, 280, 676, 1121, 1153, 1339, 3219, 4166.
Hever, Norfolk, 3774.
Hewis, Garrard, 4917.
Hewes, John, 58.
........., Wm., of Lincoln, 806.
Hewghe, Ley, Northumberland, 1040, 5010.
Hexston, Stafford, 1974.
Hext, John, 1812.
Heydok, Tho., in com. for Oxfordshire, 1470, 3015.

Heydok, Tho., sheriff of Oxon and Berks, 1316, 3507.
Heydon, Hen., 4254.
........., Sir Hen., 4254.
........., Sir Jas., 1281.
.... or Haydon, Sir John, 485, 4254, 4377, 4872, 5483.
........., ..., in commissions, &c., for Norfolk, 664, 1340, 1714, 1812, 1963, 3029, 3426, 3545, 5133, 5580.
........., ..., sheriff of Norf. and Suff., 1316, 4544, 5561.
........., Ric., of Auterey (Ottery), Devon, 3057.
Heyford, 3297.
Heygham. *See* Heigham.
Heygrove, Wilts, 155.
Heykington, manor of, Linc., 4695.
Heyley Castle, Staff., 357.
Heylisbery, Cornwall, 268.
Heynold, Essex, 4504.
Heywarde. *See* Haywarde.
Heys Chapel, 2080.
Heywood, Wm., King's joiner, 4954, p. 956.
........., ..., yeoman of the guard, 550, 1609, 4044.
........., ..., bailiff of Ribbesford, Worc., 4071.
Hide. *See* Hyde.
Hierns, Maurice, of Zurich, ambassador, 4970.
Higdon, Brian, 5524.
Higford, Th., 3841, 4180, 5245.
Higgyns or Higgins, Edw., inc. of Lanteglas, Exeter dioc., 1830.
........., ..., dean of St. Mary's College, Shrewsbury, 4184. *See* Hyggyn.
Hyggyns, Th., 4367.
Higham, alias Iham, Sussex, 690.
........., John, 1666, 5096.
........., Ric., justice of gaol delivery, 3694, 5143.
Hikks, Geof., 3980.
Hill or Hyll, Hen., serjeant-at-arms, 4106.
......, Humph., 1480.
......, Jas., 1250, 3549.
......, Nic., 1023.
......, Ric., 1212, 1813, 3969.
......, Stephen, 3929.
Hillarsdon, And., in com. for Devonshire, 917, 1503, 1812, 3183, 3566, 3589, 3605, 3938, 4539, 4783, 5220.
Hillesdon, Bucks, 2080.
Hilley, John, 3979.
Hilliard, Christopher, in com. for York, 1735, 1799, 3358, 3507, 4183.
Hilton. *See* Hylton.
Hilwode, Warwick, 3521.
Hinde. *See* Hynde.
Hindhalghehede, 4556.
Hindy, Walt., 3496.
Hingham. *See* Hengeham.
Hinton, Lincolnshire, 4616, 5082, 5436.
Hinxsey Hall, Oxford, 5256.

Hippeswell, York, 5608.

Hitchin, Herts., 155.

Hobart, Jas., 566, 1399.

........, Sir James, 226, 799, 1421, 1639, 1965, 3497, p. 652.

........, ..., in com. for Essex, 310, 1368, 1522, 1713, 3605, 3785, 3967 ; for Norfolk, 1340, 1714, 1812, 3426, 3545, 5133, p. 904 ; for Suffolk, 280, 676, 1121, 1153, 1534, 1715, 3029, 3219, 3967, 4713, 5133, p. 904.

........, ..., justice of gaol delivery for Bishop's Lynn, 884, 5236 ; Dunwich, 4677 ; Ipswich, 3549 ; Norwich Castle, 931, 4558 ; Wisbeach Castle, 1781.

Hobard, Miles, 3930.

Hobart, Walter, of Norfolk, 884, 1340, 1714, 1781, 1963, 3029, 3426, 3545, 5133, 5580. See Hubberd.

Hoberts, the two, 4844.

Hobbys, Ph., 1854.

Hobbis, Tho., canon of Windsor, 74, 624.

Hobbys, Dr., master in Chancery, 595.

Hobson, Ric., 3119.

........, Tho., 382–384, 629, 1863, 1865, 1866, 3119, 4775.

Hoby, Ric., of Bristol, 1050.

Hochynson. See Hutchinson.

Hodelegh, Sussex, 1484.

Hodeley, West, Sussex, 1598.

Hodleston, Rob. See Huddlestone.

Hodges or Hodchowse, Ric., 4476.

Hodgeson. See Hoggeson.

Hodnell, Warwickshire, 1024.

Hode, John, 4527.

Hody, Wm., in com. of peace, Dorset, 4713.

......, ..., 3645.

......, ..., 2007, 3064, 3566, 3606, 3701, 3765, 5658.

......, Sir Wm., justice of gaol delivery, 541, 1519, 1897, 3778, 4553.

......, ..., in commissions of the peace for Dorset, 3566;—for Kent, 725, 906, 3428, 3585, 3605, 4663, 4847, 4927, 5506, (p. 906); for Somerset, 287, 712, 3048, 3606, 3701, 4713, 5506 (p. 904).

......, ..., trier of petitions in Parliament, 811, 2082.

Hogan. See Ogan.

........, Rob., 5034, 5281.

Hogard, Andr., 1812.

Hogby, James, 3651.

Hodge or Hogge, Peter, yeoman of the Crown, 364.

Hoggekinson, Geo., yeoman of the Guard, 3098.

Hoggeson, Hoggesson, or Hodgeson, Wm., yeoman of the King's buttry, 202, 838, 1259, 2052, 3520, 4135, 4136, 4684.

Hogham, Lincolnshire, 313.

Hoke, Yorksh., 1021, 1699.

Hoke-mortymer, Hants, 155.

Hoke-norton, Oxon, 636, 4205, 4254; vicarage, 3360.

Hokelscote, Leicestershire, 3096.

Holands Manor, Northamptonshire, 3761, 4904.

Holbech, Ric., abbot of Thorney, 3725, 3800.

Holbroke, Suffolk, 2080, 3896.

Holcot, Salop, 879.

Holden, Kent, 690.

........, Katharine, wife of William Holden, 5425.

........, Tho., yeoman of the Chamber to Queen Katharine, 564, 3657.

........, Wm., yeoman of the Guard, 686.

........, ..., of Essex, 5425.

Holdenham, Berks, 155.

Holder, Simon, 1794.

Holderness, Yorks., 481, 807.

Holgote, Salop, 4694.

Holgrave, 1871.

Holinghall, manor of, 4550.

Holland, 3367, 3783, 4081, 4690, 5159, 5207, 5341.

........, in Lincolnshire. See Lincolnshire.

.... Herald, 5404.

Holland or Holand, Eliz., widow of Roger Holand, 3057.

........, John, yeoman of the Guard, 4535, 4797.

........, Oliver, yeoman usher of the chamber to the Queen, 1250, 5683.

........, Ralph, incumbent of Ufford, Linc., 3074.

........, Rog., 597, 799, 860, 3057.

........, Tho., of Lincolnshire, 278, 663, 1170, 1716, 1979, 3137, 3351, 4860, 5506, 5691.

Hollesworthy, Devon, 390.

Holme, Notts, 3827, 4940.

........, Westmoreland, 1532, 1557.

........, abbey of, Norf. See Hulme.

........, Anne, heir to Robert, 1647.

.... Cultram, Rob., abbot of, 3075.

........, Wm., 3497, 4842.

Holmez, Wm., 235.

Holsatia, Duke of, 3617, 3628.

Holt Castle, in the Marches of Wales, 512, 823, 835, 3920. See also Lyon.

......, John, 337.

......, Ric., 868.

......, Th., 4251.

Holtesweller, Hen., the King's goldsmith, 5160.

Holwey, Clement, 4996.

Holy Cross, near Edinburgh. See Holy Rood.

...... Island, 4682.

...... League, 2033, 3876.

...... Rood, or Holy Cross, near Edinburgh, abbey of, 3033, 3882 ; Geo., abbot of, 1176.

...., letters dated at, 161, 369, 3082.

Holy See, 5319.

...... Sepulchre, 1860, 3456, 5729.

Holyden, Bucks, 3492.

Holyngborne, Wm., 1056, 1180.

Home or Hume, Scotch surname,—
......, Alex. Lord, Chamberlain of Scotland, 4497, 4522, 5090; defeats Edm. Howard at battle of Flodden, 4441; sues for a truce, 4502; possessions of, burnt by Dacre, 4529; chief justice this side Forth, 4556; rebels against Margaret of Scotland, 5614; seizes her person, 5641.
......, his brother, 4556.
......, Cuthbert, 773.
......, ..., of Fastcastle, Scotland, 5090.
......, Ld. David, safe conduct to, 782.
......, Sir David, 5090.
......, David, 4627, 4727.
......, Ld. John, safe conduct to, 782.
......, Sir John, of Fastcastle, Scotland, 5090.
......, Mr., 5348.
Homo, Tho., clk., 1310.
Hone, Wm., clk., 1448.
......, Will., M.A., 3578.
......, Wm., dean of Tamworth, 5533.
Honflete, 4692.
Honfleur, Hontflou, or Amflower, 3357, 4273.
........., warlike preparations at, 4330, 4440, 4843, 5753, 5762.
Honnesdon, manor of Herts, 4694.
Honnyng, Wm., 1777.
Honnyngs, Wm., clerk, 1906.
Hony, Rob., 3272.
Honywode, John, 4996.
Hoo in Kent, 1545, 3416.
Hood, Wm., 4013.
Hooges, John and Peter de, 3526.
Hooknorton vicarage. See Hoke-norton.
Hooper, John, of Merton, Devon, 3721, 4778.
Hoorn, in the dioc. of Liège, 1769.
........., Count of. See Hornes.
Hope, Richard, yeoman of the guard, 5551.
Hopelyn, ——, 3353.
Hopkins, Hen., 582, 583.
Hopping, Chs., 946.
Hopton, Arthur, captain in the war, 4177, 4306, 4377, 4477, 4534.
........., ..., in com. of the peace for Suffolk, p. 904.
........., Sir Arthur, on sheriff-roll for Lincolnshire, 5561,
........., John, 1257.
........., ..., gentleman of the chamber, 4063, 4126, 4648.
........., ..., captain, 3422, 3496, p. 551 (mis printed " Hoxton "), 3979, 3980, 3985, 5112, 5724, 5775.
........., ..., his signature, 5790.
........., ..., accounts of, 4387.
........., ..., his ship, 3117, 3591, 3977, 4377, 4474.
........., ..., the Baptist, ship named, 3591, 3977 (misprinted " Baptist of Hoxton,").

Hopton, Sir John, 3946.
Horbury, Yorks., 5072.
Horde, Edm., clerk, 4857.
........., Ric., 3497, p. 435.
........., in commission for Shropshire, 918, 1981, 3071, 3694, 3715, 4394, 4827, 5506.
........., Th., 3694.
Horetop, Wm., 3250, 3871.
Hormistorffe. See Armestoff, Paul.
Hornby, Hen., clerk, 236, 406, 663, 5296.
Horncastle, Linc., 5039.
Horne, Surrey, 1484.
........., John, in com. of the peace for Oxon, 1470, 1216, 1745, 3015, 4559, 4809, p. 905.
Hornechurche, Essex, 3284, 5437.
Hornecliffe, Nich., 3669.
Hornengserth, Suffolk, 947.
Horner, Wm., clerk, 1910.
Hornes, Count, 4924.
........., Lady of, 4851.
Horpole, manor of, 4656.
Horsley, Derby, 1633, 1808.
........., Castle, 4694.
........., surveyor of, 1999.
........., West, 4022.
........., Th., of Northumberland, 3553, 5506.
........., Wm., yeoman of the guard, 5325.
Horse, master of the, Sir Thomas Knyvet, 3308.
Horses sent to Hen. VIII., 5601.
Horsey, John, in commission of the peace for Somerset, 287, 712, 3048, 3566, 3385, 3606, 3701, 4713, p. 904.
........., ..., on the sheriff-roll for Somerset and Dorset, 3507.
........., Wm., doctor of degrees, 1441.
Horsham, manor of, Sussex, 4838.
........., St. Faith's, Tho., prior of, 1483.
Horsington, Bucks, 3114, 3846.
Horsted, Sussex, 1484.
Horston, Derbysh., 1633, 1808, 4694.
Horton, North., 3113.
........., Wm., 4554.
Hosteler, John, 1002.
Hotham, church of, York dioc., 3090.
........., Sir John, 531.
........., Jno., in commission for York, 4719, 5193.
Hoton. See Hutton.
Hotton, 3442.
Hough, Ranulph, 4360.
........., Tho., 12.
Houghton, manor of, Notts., 4728.
Hount. See Hunt.

Household, 4306.

........., officers in the, 1023.

........., chamberlain of the. *See* Somerset, Charles.

........., clerk of the market for the, 291, 2073.

........., cofferer of, John Thurley, 3445, 4257, 4874.

........., comptroller of the. *See* Ponynges.

........., keeper of, 3657.

... ., marshal of, Sir John Carewe, 466.

........., purveyors for the, 1228, 1710, 1764, 1786, 1787, 1793, 3065, 3250, 4149, 4894, 5313.

........., steward and marshal of, Sir Thos. Lovell, 4217.

........., steward of the. *See* Shrewsbury, George Earl of.

........., treasurer of. *See* Sir Thomas Lovell.

........., turnorius of the, 1785.

........., expenses of the, 811, 812, 1498.

Houstone, Crown, 416.

How Carlton, Norfolk, 5162.

Howard, Geo. p. 957.

........., Harry, master of the Henry Grace à Dieu, 4156.

........., Mr., 3443.

........., Edmund, on the sheriff-roll for Surrey and Sussex, 1949.

........., Sir Edm., 3711, 5483.

........., ..., as captain, 3980.

........., in commission for Surrey, 3078, 4693, 4808, 5237, p. 905.

........., ..., his signature, 1491.

........., Sir Edwd. Lord Admiral, 3243, 3388, 3451, 3496, 3561, 3922, 3974, 3981, 3983, 4094, 4112, 4132, 4238, 4533, p. 955, 5723, 5724, 5745.

........., ..., as captain, 3591, 3977, 4377.

........., ..., letters from, 3820, 3857, 3877, 3903.

........., ..., instructions to, 3118.

........., ..., grants to 654, 668, 777, 1256, 1423, 1706, 3373, 3655, 3722.

........., ..., his appointments, &c., 64, 3115, 3117, 3798, 3809.

........., ..., in commission for Norfolk, 1340, 1714, 1963, 3029, 3426, 3545.

........., ..., his death, 3974, 4005, 4020.

........., ..., executor of, 4255.

........., ... aspersed, 4169.

........., ..., in debt to the Crown, 5633.

........., ..., his signature, 5721, 5752.

........., ..., his fleet. *See* Ships.

........., Alice, wife of Sir Edwd., 668, 777, 3857.

........., Edw., 4734.

........., Thomas Earl of Surrey (1483 to 1514), Duke of Norfolk, (1514 to 1524), Lord Treasurer, 155, 1639, 3561, 3823, 3922, 4388, 4425, 4451, 4518, 4520,

Howard, Thomas Earl of Surrey—*cont.*

4674, 4695, 4869, 5090, 5111, 5173, 5368, 5407, 5488, 5489, 5495, 5505, 5512, 5723.

........., ..., executor of Henry VII., 3292, 5737, 5779.

........., ..., signature of, as member of the Council, 14, 15, 55, 73, 165, 313, 336, 480, 503, 507, 511, 531, 545, 576, 598, 602, 603, 617, 618, 625, 639, 650, 679, 702, 755, 782, 785, 955, 956, 1004, 1008, 1068, 1264, 1272, 1273, 1287, 1372, 1378, 1527, 1538, 1539, 1540, 1574, 1584, 1596, 1604, 1699, 1755, 1756, 1757, 1758, 1840, 2027, 2029, 3080, 4403, 4767, 4997 ; as treasurer, 601, 604, 605.

........., ..., to be Earl Marshal, 1161.

........., ..., in disgrace, 3443.

........., ..., ambassador to Julius II., 1955.

........., ..., commissioned to treat with Ferdinand, 3513.

........., ..., the King's Lieutenant in the North, 4375, 4403, 4434.

........., ..., his victory at Flodden, 4441, 4459, 4460, 4461, 4462, 4482, 4502 ; reported at Rome as a defeat, 4455.

........., ..., at the marriage of Princess Mary, 5322, 5441, 5483.

........., ..., letters from, 4439, 5477.

........., ..., letters to him and the Council, 924, 4870, 4935.

........., ..., trier of petitions in Parliament, 811, 2082.

........., ..., Acts in his favor, 2082, 3502.

........., ..., created Duke of Norfolk, 4694; 4848.

........., ..., summoned to Parliament, 5016.

........., ..., treaties made or witnessed by, 474, 962, 1980, 5343, 5408.

........., ..., witness to a charter, 3027.

........., ..., commissions to, 164, 5294.

........., ..., commissions of muster to, 3116, 3358.

........., ..., grants to, 350, 654, 1835, 2051, 3655, 3722, 4838, 5136, 5250.

........., ..., in commission for Norfolk, 1340, 1714, 1963, 3029, 3426, 3545, 5133 ; Northumberland, 3553; Suffolk, 280, 676, 1121, 1153, 1339, 1715, 3029, 3219, 3967, 4693, 4713, 5133 ; Surrey, 1427, 1762, 3078, 3092, 5237, p. 905 ; Sussex, 281, 1509, 3428, 4804, p. 904.

........., ..., in commission of array for Sussex, 3024.

........., ..., as justice of gaol delivery, 1547, 1548, 1942, 3765.

........., Agnes, wife of the preceding, 1835, 2051, 5483.

........., Thomas Lord, Earl of Surrey (1514 to 1524), 3231, 3451, 3561, 3762, 3922, 4451, 4452, 4460, 4482, 4632, 4653, 5090.

Howard, Thomas Lord, created Earl of Surrey, 4695, 4848.
........., ..., summoned to Parliament, 5616.
........., ..., as Admiral, 3980, 3997, 4074, 4075, 4094, 4095, 4103, 4376, 4520, 4695, 4869, 4979, 5007, 5073, 5151, 5710, 5761, 5762, 5769, 5770.
........., ..., appointment by, 5754.
........., ..., at Flodden, 4441, 4459, 4461.
........., ..., at the marriage of Princess Mary, 5322, 5441, 5483.
........., ..., commissioned to review the Army, 3173.
........., ..., in commission for Norfolk, 1340, 1714, 1812, 1963, 3029, 3426, 3545, 5133 ; for Suffolk, 280, 676, 1121, 1153, 1339, 1715, 3219, 3967, 4713.
........., ..., grants to, 654, 951, 1129, 1152, 1343, 1344, 1629, 2217, 3655, 3722, 4965, 5007, 5223, 5644.
........., ..., letters from, 3297, 4019, 4020, 4076, 4169, 5130.
........., ..., letters to, 4139, 4171.
........., ..., his signature, 1491, 3476, 4439.
........,......, Ann, wife of the preceding, 951, 1129, 1148, 1152, 1343, 1344.
Howard, shield of, 4694.
Howard, the Mary, 5112.
Howbaslot,, Tower of, Scotland, 4522.
Howden liberty of, York, 273.
Howe, John, 40.
Howel, David ap, of Westminster, pardon for, 5309.
Howell, Dorset, 155.
........., Edw., M. A., clerk, 1751.
........., Eliz., of Bristol, 3161.
........., Hugh ap, yeoman of the chamber, 1188.
........., Phil. ap, clerk, 1559.
........., Th., draper of London, 5223.
Howike, John, yeoman of the Crown, 1239.
Howth, Joan Lady, 347.
Hoxson, John, sealer in the Chancery, 3995.
Hoxton (an error for Hopton), q. v.
Hoygges, Jno., 4996.
Hoys, 3731, 3857, 4104, 4171, 5126, 5139.
........., expenses of, 4533.
Huart, Jehan, 4516.
Hubert, Sir Jas., 367, 721.
Huby, castle of, 1205.
......, Peter de, 4445.
Hubbarts (Huberts?), the, of Seeryssey, 4273.
........., 4725.
Huberts, Des, 3817.
Hubberd, Anne, 1651.
Huddleston, Eliz., 380.
Huddelston, John, 3001, 4520, 5229.
........., Sir John, of Sudely, Glouc., 680, 836, 1087, 1350, 1366, 1374, 1674, 1755, 2086.

Huddleston, Ric., 380.
........., Rob., 681, 1332.
Hudson, John, 272.
........., Rob., 1785.
........., Stephen, 5711.
........., Wm., 1640.
Huet, John, 1065.
Hugford or Huggeford, John, of Warw., 419, 900, 4012.
Hughe, Wm., 4081.
Hughs, Rob., 1871. See Hewis.
Hughson, John, 749.
........., Nic., of Cambridgeshire, 677, 1684, 1781, 3187.
Hugothony, Chas., 3410, 5222.
Huland, Simon, 4467.
Hulbank, 534.
Hulcote, 3027.
Hulham, 2080.
Hull, Dorset, 2080.
Hull. See Ships.
...... or Kingston-upon-Hull, 12, 1677, 3591, 3889, 3980, 4022, 4377, 4682, 4961, 5077, 5091, 5724, 5760, 5769.
Hulme or Holme, monastery of, Norfolk, 745, 821, 1158, 1720, 5616.
Humbe, 4714.
Humber, 273, 481.
Hume. See Home.
Humiliates, general of the, p. 381.
Hunden, Suff., 36, 222.
Hundmanby, Yorkshire, 944.
Hungary, 4609, 5055, 5267.
........., King of. See Ladislaus.
........., ambassador of, [at Rome], 1478.
........., ..., with the Emperor, 5259.
........., captain of the Cruciferi, or " Croseyd Hungrye," 5338, 5366.
Hungarians, 5705.
Hungate, Lincoln, 4695.
........., Roger, 3045.
Hungerford, 3723.
Hungerford, Sir Anth., 4764.
........., Edw., of Wilts, 464, 1489, 1938, 3157, 3605.
........., ..., in the war, 3885, 4307.
........., Sir Edw., in the war, 4237, 4468, 4653.
........., ..., of Wilts, 4583.
........., John, 4118.
........., Sir John, of Gloucestershire, 664, 1816, 1695, 1806, 1929, 1930, 3641, 3712, 3804, 4024, 4764.
........., ..., in the war, 4377.
........., ..., at the marriage of the Princess Mary, 5483.
........., Sir Walter, of Haytysbury, 464.
........., ..., grant to, 5629.

Hungerford, Sir Walter, in commission, &c., for Somerset and Wilts, 898, 1316, 1938, 3048, 3157, 3566, 3585, 3605, 3606, 3701, 3824, 4583, 4713, p. 904.

........., ..., in the war, 3173, 3231.

........., Ric., 282, 756, 1216, 1292, 1470.

Hunkys, Rob., in com. for Worcest., 4770.

Hunning, Wm., serjeant purveyor of the household, 5313.

Hunston, Hen., of Norfolk, 3210, 5133, 5580.

Hunt, Harry, 4377, 5604.

........., John, 235.

........., ..., the King's chief cook, 489, 1237, 1612, 3431, 3657, 5499.

......., Ric., 4360.

......., Tho., 166, 5611.

Huntbeare, 2080.

Hunters manor, Northt., 5700.

Huntingdon, Wm., 1928.

........., Will. Herbert, Earl of, temp. Edw. IV., his lands, 778, 1047, 1472, 1665, 3949, 4022, 4712.

........., castle and honor of, 484.

Huntingdonshire, 284, 306, 663, 1743, 3871, 4022, 4414, 4534.

........., sheriffs of, 664, 1316, 1771, 1949, 3507, 4544, 5561.

........., commissions of the peace for, 905, 906, 1095, 4006, 5506.

Huntingfeld, Suffolk, 485, 4254.

Huntley, Alex. Earl, 714, 4441, 5090.

........., John, groom of the chamber, 3949, 4601, 4688, 4995.

........., Wm., of Ree, Glouc., 4972.

........., Wm., 4052; of London, 5051.

Hunton, Hants, 1517.

Huntrodes, Will., inc. of Chedsay, 1442, 1750.

Huntwade, Edm., 3084, 4762.

Hurbenford, Exeter, 2080.

Hurberton, Exeter, 2080.

Hurbonde Blaze, of Maine, France, 3174.

Hurdegrove, Th., 1825.

Huredike, N. Wales, 4748.

Hurleton, Nich., 5149.

Hurley, monastery of, Berks, 4684.

Hurst. See Herst.

Hurtubia, 3839.

Huscards, 3697.

Huse, Husee, or Husey, surname,—

......, Giles, 3980.

......, Jno., 313, 531, 1678, 3574, 3939, 4534, 4654.

......, Sir John, 86, 89, 235, 258, 275, 302, 303, 395, 398, 439, 442, 463, 477, 606, 722, 747, 926, 953, 1052, 1277, 1278, 1372, 1699, 1707, 2044, 3231, 3284, 3791, 4006, 4049, 4306, 4477, 4852, 5180, 5483, 5608, 5633.

......, ..., in com. for Essex, 310, 1368, 1522, 1713, 3605, 3785, 3967; Huntingdonshire, 905, 916, 1095; for Lincolnshire, 278, 657, 1120, 1169, 1170, 1171, 3342, 3351, 4358, 4593, 4860.

Husee, Sir John, in commissions of sewers, 663, 1716, 1979, 3137, 5691.

........., ..., in other commissions, 3006, 3116.

........., Rob., 953, 1716, 1979, 3137, 5691.

........., ..., in commission for Lincolnshire, 657, 1120, 1169.

........., Tho., 1607.

........., Wm., son of Sir John, 1277, 1278, 1607, 3231.

........., Wm, 4860.

........., Sir Wm., 4468.

Hutchinson, John, 3579.

Hutton, Westmor.; 3764.

........., Hen., 856.

........., Hugh, in commission for Cumberland, 717, 1048, 1734, 1799, 3358, 5506.

........., John, in commission for Cumberland, 717, 1734, 1799, 3358; and Eliz. his w., 1807.

........., Ric., 856.

........., Rob., incumbent of Lanlythan, 2017, 3453.

Hutton Panell, alias Panell Hutton, 178, 192, 1205, 3739.

........., Rob., incumbent of Comberworth, Linc., 3547.

........., Th., 1871.

Huxley, Wm., clerk of the ordnance, 781, 3368, 3496.

Hyde, Hertfordshire, 4694.

......, abbey of, near Winchester, 60, 75, 715.

......, abbot of, 5616.

......, Nich., 3256, 3801.

......, Oliver, 5685.

Hydwynstrones, Northumberland, 705.

Hyerdes, 734.

Hyet, Jas., 5472.

Hyggyn, Edw., master of Chancery, 3056. See Higgins.

Hylling, Peter, 3249.

Hyllyard, Christopher. See Hilliard.

Hyllyngton, Nic., LL.B., 537.

Hylton, Baron, 5782.

........., Christ., 3497.

........., Elias, 3497, 4527.

........., John, 781.

........., Tho., 847.

........., Wm., 705, 1988; of Northumb., 1316, 1949.

........., Sir Wm., 5264, 5506.

........., Wm., tailor, 5720.

Hynchcliff, Wm., 22.

Hynde, Amy, 729.

........., Katharine, 729.

........., John, 4770, 4890; mayor of London, 729.

........., ..., in commission for Cambridgeshire, 3583, 5506.

........., Thos., 4617, 5660.

Hyne, Geo., 4187.

Hyrste, John. See Herst.

Hysley, Tho., 725.

Hythe, 4996.

Hyworth, grant of lands in, 155.

I.

Iberton, Dorset, 2080.

Icaromenippus, translated by Erasmus, 1998, 2021.

Iceland, 3445.

........, repeal of a statute for fishing in, 811.

Ichyngham, Edward, captain of The Second New Spanyard, p. 973, 4377.

........, captain of The Germayn, 3591, 3946, 3977.

........, captain of The Lezard, 4474.

........, Sir Edward, captain of The Peter Pomegarnet, p. 811. See Echingham.

Ide, Devon, 2080.

Idelstre, Herts, 383.

Iden, Mr., clerk of the Council, 4306.

......, Tho., 47, 2088.

Idland, Camb., 1756.

Iford, 1172.

Iham, Sussex, 690.

Ilchester, justices of gaol delivery for, 4753.

Ilderton, Sir Th., of Northumberland, 187, 1735, 1804, 3358.

Ilkettishall, Suff., 730.

Illingworth, Alice, wife of John Knyston, 3504.

........, Anne, wife of John Etton, 3504.

........, Joan, wife of Geo. Barley, 3504.

........, Mary, wife of John Dethicke, 3504.

........, Richard, 857, 3504.

Ilston, Tho., prior of St. Augustine's, 753.

Ilton, Devon, 4989.

Imber, Rob., in debt to Hen. VII., 1639, p. 434.

Imold, 1697, 3112.

Immeslowe, 1899.

Imworth, Gilbert de, 4934.

Incheffray, Laurence abbot of, 4624.

........, abbey of, 4624.

India, Emmanuel King of Portugal's successes in, 4173, 4985.

Indulgences, 3624, 4735.

Infidels, 3569, 4173. See also Turks.

........, expedition against the, 1875, 4112, 4470, 5741.

........, prisoners taken by the, 4922.

Inge, Hugh. See Meath.

Ingelerd, Wm., 5631.

Inglefield. See Englefield.

Ingleton, ——, 375.

Ingleton, and Bentham, church, the archdeaconry of Richmond, 3062.

Inglewood, Camb., 4791.

Inglis, Alex., treasurer of Glasgow, &c., 3630.

......, James, 1415.

......, Thomas, attainted, 4158.

......, William, 3628.

Inglus or Inglose, Hen., of Attilburgh, Norf., 1812, 4254.

Ingram, Stephen, 4013.

Innocent, nephew of Leo. X., Cardinal deacon of St. Cosmo and Damian, 5678.

.... VIII., 2041.

Innys, John, 767.

Inquisitions, untrue, Act concerning, 811.

Inspruck, 3471, 3658, 5290, 5304, 5338, 5387.

........, Emperor at, 5171, 5404.

........, letters dated at, 1676, 1681, p. 255, 1701, 3897, 5366, 5389, 5393, 5410, 5677, 5686.

Intwode, Norf., 5508.

Invasion, proclamations to resist, 3688.

Inventoribus Rerum, De, by Polydore Vergil, 751.

Inwode, Soms., 801.

Ipswich. See Ships.

........, Suff., 1757, 1991, 3496, 3551, 3896, 3993, 4023.

........, manor of, 1375, 1757, 3309.

........, port of, 593, 890, 3573.

........, gaol delivery for, 3549.

........, St. Laurence the Martyr, church of, 899.

........, St. Matthew's, church of, 1217.

........, St. Peter's, prior elect of, 4768.

........, St. Thomas, altar of, 899.

Ipusqua. See Guipuscoa.

Ireland, 149, 2082, 4561, 4975, 5753.

........, the Lords and Council of, 149, 3987, 4588.

........, Chancellor of. See Rokeby, Wm.; Compton, Sir Wm.

........, deputy of. See Kildare, Earl of.

........, Chief Justice of. See Bermyngham, Patrick.

........, receiver of petitions from, 811.

........, ships for, 3451, 3987, 5724.

........, tower of, 3095.

........, rebel Prince of, 4525.

Irenacton, 4071.

Irewyn, 4529.

Irish Lord, p. 368.

Iron work, account of, 4232.

Irtlyngburgh, Northt., St. Peter's, dean and chapter of, 1724.

Irton, Cumb., 4944.

Irton, John, petty captain for Derby, p. 608.

Isaak, Agnes, 3480.

......, James, son of John, 3480.

......, John, son of Agnes, 3480.

......, Wm., son of James, 3480, 3790.

Isabella of Castile, 8, 3023.

Isabel, Queen of Denmark, 5155.

Isabella, Queen of Ferdinand II. of Spain, 224, 4464, 5729.

........., daughter of Philip K. of Castile and sister of Charles V., 1417, 5155.

Iscoyte, Cardigan., S. Wales, lordship of, 3409.

Iseham, John, p. 433, p. 955.

........., ..., captain, 5112.

Isham, Th., 4587.

Isidorus, poems of, 5352.

Islay Herald, 3339, 3577, 4439, 4951, 5757.

Isley, ——, petty captain, p. 553.

......, Th., in com. for Kent, 3605, 3428, 4663, 4847, 4927.

Islepe, Oxon., 3045.

Isles, John Bp. of the, (Sodor and Man), 1112.

Islip, John, abbot of Westminster, 4891, 4994.

Ismael the Sophi of Persia, 1659, 3697, 5729.

Isselstein, Floris D'Egmont Lord, 924, 3077, 3651, 3849, p. 609, 4284, 4319, 4328, 4355, 4359, 4364, 4418, 4429, 5139, 5207, 5263, 5272.

........., ..., letters from, 3692, 5205.

........., ..., captain of the garrison of St. Thomas, 5163.

........., officer of arms to Lord Isselstein, 3692, 4692.

Istria in Austria, 1676.

Italy, 105, 216, p. 67, p. 115, p. 123, 922, 1418, 1457, 1697, 1701, 1883, 1925, 1948, 1980, 1997, 3188, 3248, 3283, 3451, 3479, 3500, 3543, 3614, 3662, 3752, 3897, p. 574, 4078, 4094, 4296, 4333, 4455, 4527, 4548, 4561, 4571, 4574, 4756, 4915, 4955, 5025, 5055, 5155, 5263, 5285, 5323, 5393, 5396, 5581, 5601, 5642.

......, states of, 4952.

......, provinces of, 3860, 3861.

......, defence of, 4055, 5410.

......, news from, 1900, 1918, 1957, 3269, 3325, 3334, 3340, 3341, 3376, 3377, 3405, 3419, 3976, 4163, 4182, 4193, 5126, 5171.

,......, natives of, 3233, 3263, 4147, 4244, 4246.

......, Cardinal Gurk, governor and lieutenant of, 5304, 4577.

......, principal legate of, 1681.

......, Emperor in, 3353.

......, English ambassadors in, 3388.

......, war against, 1828, 3766.

......, propositions of Ferdinand to send his army into, 4058.

......, miseries in, 4449, 4513.

......, French hopes ruined in, 4499.

......, Pope trying to make a league with, 5018,

......, heretics of, 5040.

......, preparation made by the French army to go into, under Bourbon, 5675.

Italians, 3335.

Ivry, 5675.

Ive, Wm., 1028.

......, ..., deputy of Sir Sampson Norton, 4906.

Ivy, Tho., 85.

Iwarby, Sir John, in commission of the peace for Surrey, 1427, 1762, 3078, 3092, 4693, 4734, 5237, 5506 (p. 905).

Iwern Courtney, Dorset, 2080.

Iwernmister, Dorset, 2080.

J.

Jackson, ——, 3386.

........., Jno., yeoman of the guard, 1071, 1679, 4189.

........., Nic., yeoman usher of the chamber, 185, 444.

........., ..., serjeant-at arms, 4108, 4133.

........., Tho., yeoman usher of the chamber, 1430.

Jacomo, Lawrence, 3325.

Jacques, Jean, of Troys (?), 3752, 4280, 4577.

........., Sir John, 4329.

Jakes or Jakys, Thomas, 266, 4526.

........., ..., in commission of the peace for Leicestershire, 1094, 1425, 1971, 4706, 4783, 4812; for Middlesex, 3552, 4663.

........., ..., justice of gaol delivery for Newgate, 1942.

........., or Jaques, Will., 3608.

James III. of Scotland, 841, 1245, 2041.

........., IV. of Scotland, 216, 245, 922, 923, 1850, 1932, 2001, 2038, 3326, 3347, 3359, 3412, 3443, 3626, 3676, 3751, 3811, 3829, 4273, 4388, 4403, 4458, 4525, 4561, 4674, 4694, 5006, 5745, 5757.

........., ..., charters of, 31, 1271, 3619.

........., ..., his instructions to Lopez, 3083.

........., ..., his relations with Denmark 3138, 3225, 3633, 3718, 4055.

........., ..., his alliance with France, 3218 3303.

........., ..., included in the truce between Ferdinand and Louis XII., 3839.

........., ..., his treaties with England, 474, 475, 478, 480, 488, 548, 709, 714, 3128, 3129, 3170.

........., ..., his bad faith, 3838, 3876.

........., ..., visits his shipping, 3751.

........., ..., threatens to invade England, 3752.

........., ..., his war with England, 4284, 4399, 4441, 4455, 4464, 4571.

........., ..., his corpse, 4451, 4459, 4461, 4464, 4582, 5090.

........., ..., his coat, 4451.

........., ..., letters from, 20, 117, 161, 369, 379, 767, 773, 774, 841, 842, 910, 911 925, 1112, 1176, 1195, 1245, 1364, 1405, 1406, 1407, 1408, 1409, 1410, 1411, 1413, 1415,

James IV. of Scotland, letters from,—*cont.*
1459, 1460, 1461, 1462, 4163, 1782, 1826, 1829, 1875, 1876, 1877, 1878, 1879, 2020, 2040, 2041, 2042, 2043, 2050, 2075, 2076, 2077, 3010, 3011, 3033, 3081, 3086, 3104, 3105, 3106, 3107, 3121, 3122, 3126, 3139, 3140, 3141, 3216, 3279, 3319, 3320, 3321, 3322, 3323, 3349, 3372, 3399, 3569, 3620, 3621, 3622, 3623, 3624, 3625, 3626, 3627, 3628, 3629, 3630, 3631, 3632, 3634, 3635, 3636, 3837, 3883, 4112, 4351.

.............., letters to, 510, 808, 1643, 3146, 3240, 3278, 3346, 3479, 3828, 4397, 4439.

James V., 4927, 4985, 5006, 5614, 5681.

........., his birth, 3139, 3140.

........., his accession, 5613.

........., demand for him to be under the guardianship of Hen. VIII., 4483.

........., treaties of, 4818.

........., letters from, 4623, 4624, 4625, 4626, 4627, 4628.

James, John, 3497, 3551, 4216.

........., Thomas, 3771.

Jameson, Eliz., 1410.

Janissaries, 3283.

Jankin, Philip, incumbent of Tredannok, 4738.

........., Rob. ap, 65.

Janson, Andrew, 3086.

Jarden, Sir Alexander, 5681.

Jasper, Steph., King's tailor, 91, 1988.

Java, 4173.

Jay, John, 1050.

Jaxia, in Syria, 540.

Jedworth (Jedburgh), 4556.

Jeffron, John, 4238.

Jehoshaphat, valley of, 5729.

Jekill, Will., 3250, 4630.

Jenet, Ralph, yeoman of the wardrobe of beds, 546, 5243.

Jenyngham, Anne, 5484.

Jenins, John, 3980.

Jenyns, R ib., 775.

Jenyns or Genyns, Steph., mayor of London, 541.

........., Sir Steph., alderman of London, 1484, 3427, 3879.

........., Th., 1969.

Jenke, Edw. ap, 993.

Jenkin. *See* Jankin.

Jenkins, Jas. ap, 235, 5211.

........., Wm., 4014.

Jenkinson, Henry, 5345.

........., John, 8650.

........., Rob., 3386.

..........., Wm., 1843.

Jenney, Chr., 1756, 4677.

........., Sir Edm., 777.

........., ..., in commission for Suffolk, 280, 676, 1121, 1153, 1715, 3029, 3219, 3967, 4677, 4713, 5133, 5506.

Jenour, John, 1965.

.........., ..., justice of assise, 881, 1101, 1164, 1763, 3003, 3004, 3282, 3287, 3694, 3699, 4184, 4339 4771, 5143, 5283.

Jerford, Jas., 1639.

Jermy, Yong, 777.

Jermyn, Robt., 3980.

........., Tho., 1639, 3497, 3979, 4377.

Jernemouth, Great. *See* Yarmouth, Great.

Jerningham, Jernegan, or Garningham, Master, 4642. *See also* Ferningham.

........., Edw., 179, 226, 485, 701, 1281, 1421, 1446, 4205.

........., Mary, wife of E. Jernyngham, 179, 1446.

........., Ric., 1451, 3070, 3658, 3825, 5442.

........., Sir Ric., 1676, 3980, 4468, 4749, 4750 ; letters from, 3471, 3897.

........., Rob., 3980.

Jerome, And., 1212.

........., Eliz., 1212.

........., John, 1212.

........., Pet., 1212.

.... *See* Jheram.

Jerommet, Jacquenet le Grant, 4445.

Jeronimus, Baptista, 3854. *See* Justinian.

Jersey, 531, 650, 3389, 3972, 4840, 5071.

Jerusalem, 3838, 4091, 5729.

Jerveys, John, 1058. *See also* Gervays.

Jervis, Nic., 858.

........., Rob., 3210.

Jesarhaull, Lincolnshire, 351, 1736.

Jesper. *See* Jasper.

Jevan, David ap, 3612.

Jewels, act against exportation of, 811.

........., the King's, keeper of. *See* Wyat, Sir Henry.

Jheram, Sir Humph., 5789.

Joan, Queen of Castile, widow of Philip the Fair, 8, 793, 796, 819, 3614, 3662, 5203.

........., ..., treaties of, 1055, 1059, 1335, 1980, 3023, 3513, 3603, 4985.

........., ..., commission by, 28.

........., ..., renunciation of dowry by, 152.

Joborne, John, prior of Shene, 3045.

Jocelyn. *See* Josselyn.

Jodocus, bookseller, 1883, 3495.

Johane, the King's servant, 4691.

Johanle, ——, 4789.

Johey, Th., 3497.

John, Prince of Castile, son of Ferdinand, 8, 796.

......., Don. *See* Arragon.

......., King of Denmark, Norway, and Sweden, 1195, 3751, 3838, 4844, 5155.

......., ... letter from, 3718.

......., ..., letters to, 925, 1405, 1416, 3617, 3620, 3629, 3631, 5632, 5634.

......., ..., treaties of, 3633, 4889, 4924.

......., ..., death of, 3814.

John, Edw., gentleman of the Chapel Royal, 1702, 4065.

......, Edw. ap, clerk, 143.

......, Griffith ap, 4653.

......, John, 946.

......, Pery, Prè, Prester, or Prior   See Prègent.

......, Rob., page of the chamber, 1229.

......, Sir Rob., his ship, 3980.

Johns, Edw., 3091, 3127.

........., Eleanor, 876.

........., John, 3834.

........., Rob., 1583, 3497, 5432.   See Jones.

........., Th., court clerk of Pembroke, 3294.

........., ..., 1722, 5432.

Johnson, Chr., yeoman of the chamber, 1322.

........., ..., of Sandwich, 5548.

........., Cornel., gunmaker, 1347, 3496, 4774, 4968, p. 954.

........., John, captain, 3979, 3980.

........., ..., shipmaster, 4377.

........., ..., 1160, 8497.

........., Ric., 995.

Johnston, John, 782.

Joiner, John, Calais Pursuivant, 1475.

Joly, John, grants to, 1719, 4737.

Jones, Edw., 3101.

......, John, common assayer of the city of London, 4917.

......, Rob., 1057, 1113, 4377.   See Johns.

......, ..., at the marriage of Princess Mary, 5483.

......, Th., 3098.

......, Wm., clerk, 1456.

Jonnett the Bastard, 3945.

Jorden, Rob., archer at Calais, 4476, 4635.

Jourden, Wm., 3400.

Jorgue, Collin, 4445.

Joseph, Mich., 4498.

Josne, Druet and Estienne, le, 4445.

Josselyn, ——, captain, 5112.

........., John, Herts, 266, 1788.

........., Ralph, grant to, 1788.

Jubbes, Tho., n commission for Somerset, 287, 712i3048, 3566, 3585 8606, 3701, 4713.

Judenbourg, in Styria, 5259.

Jugill, Otewell, 1540.

Julian ——, 797.

Juliano, Magnifico.   See Medicis.

Juliers, 4328.

........., Duke of, 4924.

........., William Duke of, 5746.

Julius II., Pope, 11, 216, 224, 288, 796, 819, 880, 922, 932, 1107, 1221, 1227, 1295, 1413, 1457, 1458, 1461, 1462, 1652, 1676, 1681, 1700, 1828, 1875, 1877, 1878, 1879, 1900, 1918, 1948, 1997, 2039, 2075, 3012, 3067, 3081, 3083, 3112, 3122, 3138, 3188, 3218, 3225, 3240, 3269, 3276, 3314, 3323, 3325, 3326, 3327, 3341, 3347, 3349, 3377, 3415, 3500, 3569, 3625, 3631, 3633, 3647, 3658, 3697, 3752, 3780, 3838, 3882, 3897, 3997, 4085, 4267, 4283, 4446, 4455, 4608, 4871, 5106, 5332.

........., ..., reconciled to the Venetians, 924, 3333.

........., ..., sends Henry VIII. a golden rose, 976.

........., ..., his wars in Italy, 1697, 1701.

........., ..., forms the Holy League in defence of the Church, 1880, 1881, 1967, 1980, 2033, 3523, 3603.

........., ..., favors the English against the Scots, 3320.

........., ..., reported to have made a new treaty against Venice, 3614, 3662.

........., ..., his illness, 3443.

........., ..., reported death of, 1842.

........., ..., his death, 3777, 3779, 3876, 4354.

........., ..., articles agreed to by the Cardinals after his death, 3780 (p. 506, note).

........., ..., letters from, 169, 267, 908, 976, 1643, 1869, 2010, 2072, 3066, 3068, 3278, 3283.

........., ..., letters to, 379, 767, 774, 911, 1112, 1829, 2020, 2040, 2041, 2061, 2076, 3010, 3104, 3121, 3141, 3622, 3624, 3630, 3837.

........., ..., bulls of, 168, 816, 3023, 3602, 4832.

........., ..., servant of, 3751.

........., ..., subcollector of, 1403.

........., ..., ambassadors of, 3077.

........., ..., ambassadors to, 1955.

Juries, impanelling of, 4848.

Justices.   See Assize, Common Pleas, Exchequer, King's Bench.

........., their commissions renewed, 2.

Justice, chief, of Royal forests, &c., 129.

Justice, Ric., 1117.

Justinian, Anthony, Baptista, and John Greek merchants, 3030, 3458.   See also Giustinian.

........., Antonio, p. 327.

........., Baptista, consul at Chios, 3854.

........., Fabian, merchant of Genoa, 4250.

K.

Kaerleon.   See Caerleon.

Kailway, Joan, wife of John, 4744.

........., John, grant to, 4744.

Kailway, John, in commission of array, Hants, 1812.

.........., ..., in commission of the peace, Devon, 3605, 4539.

.........., ..., on sheriff-roll for Hants, 1949, 5561.

.........., ... See also Caylway.

.........., Rob., in commission of the peace, Wiltshire, 898, 1489, 1938, 3157, 3605.

.........., ..., in commission of gaol delivery, Fisherton Anger, Wilts, 3488, 4583.

.........., Wm., temp. Edw. IV., 1996.

Kale, near Scotland, 4556.

Kamfer, ship at, with ammunition for Scotland, 4743.

Kanteley lordship, York, 1679.

Karugys, Philippe du, payment to him, 5738.

Kasal. See Casale.

Kath, Sir Wm., 4997.

Katharine of Arragon, Queen of England, 194, 390, 899, 1097, 1300, 1860, 3857, p. 534, 4098, 4483, 4497, 4513, 4911, 5029, 5125, 5140, 5322, 5372, 5407.

.... , ..., her dowry by Ferdinand, 8, 27, 147, 152, 153, 162.

.........., ..., ... by Henry, 155, 156, 163, 811.

.........., ..., her marriage, 224, 338, 348, 405.

.........., ..., her first coming to England, 1140.

.........., ..., appointed Regent in the King's absence, 4179, 4202, 4434.

.........., ..., harangues the army, 4464.

.........., ..., on board the Great Harry, 5173.

.........., ..., believed to be with child, 3442, 5203, 5285.

.........., ..., prematurely confined, 5718.

.........., ..., letters from, 368, 4365, 4398, 4417, 4432, 4451, 4452, 5785.

.........., ..., letters to, 4062, 4424, 4549, 5058.

.........., ..., grants to, 155, 156, 163, 1446.

.........., ..., deed of, 3023.

.........., ..., commission from, 27.

.........., ..., grant by, 4493.

.........., ..., signature of, 4423.

.........., ..., bequest to, 236.

.........., ..., services to, 1083.

.........., ..., her confessor, 368.

.........., ..., her secretary, Ric. Decons, 1595.

.........., ..., her almoner, Rob. Bekynsall, 3487.

.........., ..., her chamberlain, Lord Mount-joy, 3197.

.........., ..., her clerk of the signet, 307.

.........., ..., other servants of, 368, 490, 564, 667, 1673, 1834, 3038, 3060, 3084, 3085, 3260, 3261, 3657, 3668, 3990, 4762, 5296.

Katt Water, 4076.

Katundeboug, Denmark, 3718.

Kebell, Hen., mayor of London, in commission of gaol delivery, Newgate, 1519, 1547.

.........., ..., in an inquisition, 1942.

.........., ..., alderman, 4699.

.........., Walter, in commission for Leicestershire, 4812, 5506 (p. 905).

Keby, Wm., yeoman usher of the chamber, grants to, 113, 1633.

......, ..., comptroller of the customs, port of Bristol, 552.

......, ..., captain of the Swallow, 3591, of Draper's ship, 4474, of the Nich. Nevill. 4475.

......, ..., serjeant-at-arms, 4043, 4109.

......, ..., payment to him, 4475, 4630.

Kedeowen, Wales, 44.

Kegedog, St. George, church of, St. Asaph diocese, 4137.

Kelby, in Linc., 155.

Keldergreve, Hans, merchant of Holland, 3783.

Kelham, ——, a priest, 639.

.........., John, a priest, 5789.

Kell (misprinted Kelt), Alex., grant to, 3344.

Kelom, James, of London, 3743.

Kelsale, Suff., 5250.

Kelsay, 1857, 4616.

Kelso, abbot of, late treasurer of Scotland, 3577.

...... Abbey, 4536.

Kemer, of Pool, exempted from general pardon, 12.

Kemeryge or Hawkins, ——, master of the Great Galley, 3979.

Kemys, Pembroke, 500, 1665.

.... barony, 52.

Kemis, Hen., page of the chamber, 66, 3047, 5038; grant to, 5667.

......, ..., escheator of Gloucestershire, 4972.

......, Eliz., wife of Hen., 5038.

Kempe, John, master of the John Baptist, 3979, 3980.

.........., ..., master of the John Hopton, 4377.

.........., Sir Tho., in commission of peace for Kent, 725, 906, 3428, 3605.

.........., ..., sheriff for Kent, 3507.

.........., Wm., on sheriff-roll for Kent, 5561.

Kemsey, Ric., 3826.

Ken, Devon, 1255, 2080.

Kendal, Westmor., 286, 327, 382, 1214, 1557, 1625, 3764, 4767, 5288.

Kendale manor, Herts, 383, 4436.

Kendall, Mons. de, brother to the Abp. of Burdeos, 3356.

Kendale, John, temp. Hen. VII., 1445, 3316.

Kendall, Th., of London, 3564.

.........., Wm., grant to, 1465; attainted, 1472, 4022, 4347.

Kene, Rob., butcher, 3509, 3939.

Kenford, 2080.

Kenilworth, St. Mary's convent, grant to, 1970.

Kennington lordship, Surr., 3911.

Kent, 12, 140, 326, 367, 1300, 1325, 1780, 3774, 3787, 3950, 4067, 4192, 4711, 5001.

......, sheriffs of, 664, 1316, 1949, 3507, 4544, 5561.

......, commissions of the peace for 725, 906, 3428, 3605, 4663, 4847, 4927, p. 906.

......, commissions of array, 3380, 3393, 3688.

......, proclamation in, 1771.

......, feodary of Crown lands, 4711.

......, tenths and fifteenths, 3441.

......, writs to escheators, 3493.

......, inquisition for co., 308.

......, acheler stone of, for fortifying Calais, 3496.

......, wool of, 4969.

......, water of, (Westmorland), 3764.

......, Eliz. Grey, Countess of, wife of Ric. E., 1124, 3576.

......, Countess of. See Grey.

......, Ric., Earl of, 1472, 3576, 4022.

......, ..., grants to, 3720, 4113, 4880, 4945, 5215.

......, ..., in commission for Beds, 2045, 3501, 4700; for Oxford (town), 894.

......, ..., in the war against France, 4253, 4477, 4306.

......, ..., payment to, 4534.

......, ..., summoned to Parliament, 5616.

......, ..., lands of, temp. Hen. VII. and Hen. VIII., 116, 778, 1678.

Kent, Nic., incumbent of Holy Trinity, Lastormal, duchy of Cornwall, 259, 1146.

Kentcote, Oxon, 4694.

Kenton, Devon, 367, 721.

Kenwood, Wm., master of the Kath. Fortileza, 5112, 5761.

Kepick, N. R., of Yorksh., 5190.

Ker, David, of Fernehirst, 4556.

......, Sir Robt., warden of the midd. marches, slain by Bastard Heron, 3339.

.... See also Car.

Kerdif. See Cardiff.

Kerkeby. See Kirkby.

Kerrier (Kerr), Cornw., 772.

........., stannaries in, 506, 3867, 4805, 4853.

Kerseys, 1186, 1855, 3511, 3517, 3700.

Kertlynge, Camb., 265.

Kery, Wales, 44.

Kerybullok, Cornw., 209.

Kerykedeowen lordship, Wales, 1113.

Kesteven, Lincoln, 657, 1120, 1169.

Keston, Linc., 395, 1277.

Ketilby, Leic., 63.

........., Linc., 1392, 4616.

........., John, in commission for Worcestershire, 892, 1971, 3301, 3709, 4770.

Ketilby, John, serjeant of the chandlery, 3490, 3681, 4053.

........., ..., in the war against France, 4526.

Ketill lordship, Westmor., 3764.

Ketilston, 1949.

Ketilton, Wm., rector of Bereford ch. and chanc. of Lichfield Cath., 1004, 1854.

Key, Tho., clk. of Coldaston, 1287, 1725.

Keylewey. See Kailway.

Keyll, Hen. of Calais, 5712.

Keynes, Suss., 1484.

........., Humph., son of John, 1551.

........., John, 1551.

Kibworth, Leic., 4071.

Kidington, Berks, 4670.

Kidirmyster, Ric., abbot of Winchelcombe, Glouc., grant to, 1374.

Kydlynton, vicarage of, Linc. dioc., 3360.

Kidwelley, John, LL.D., 1928.

Kildale, Th., 4720.

Kildare, Elizabeth Zouche, Countess of, first wife of Gerald, eighth Earl, 4254 (iii.)

........., Eliz. St. John, Countess of, second wife of same, 1299.

........., Gerald Fitz-Gerald, eighth Earl of, 149, 1299, 1314, 4238, 4254.

........., ..., ..., deputy of Ireland, 1313, 3987, 4588.

Kilford, Wales, 1041.

Killigrewe, John, 1812.

Killingworth, monastery of, 4212.

Killingworth, 4347.

........., Thos., 1472, 4022.

Killyowe, Cornwall, 1943.

Kilvey, Wales, 5180.

Kimberworth, Yorkshire, 1043.

Kimble, Great and Little, Bucks, 1352, 3556.

Kinaston, Humph., p. 609.

........., Tho., of Lee, Salop, 887, 1248, 3231.

Kincard, Laird of, 5681.

Kinderton, Cheshire, 3470.

Kinfar, Staff., 155, 900, 4591.

King, ——, 4067.

........., Alan, 1246, 4526.

King's Barnys, Sussex, 1835, 2051.

King's Bench, 511, 702, 1129, 1656, 1818.

........., ... Prison, 524.

........., ..., coroner and attorney of the, 122.

........., ..., Chief Justice of the, 264, 1538.

........., ..., justices of the, 4, 73, 258, 755.

........., ..., marshal of the, 150, 859.

King's Bromley, Staff., 1480.

........., Meadow, land called, in Northumb. 1040, 5010.

Kingsbridge, Devon, 2080.

Kingsbury, alias Westbury, Hants, 854, 4730.

.... See also Westbury.

Kingsclere, Hants, 1927.

Kingsdown, Kent, 155, 175.
Kingsford, 1299.
Kingshall, Notts, 3031.
Kingslane, Heref,, 155.
Kingspole, a fishery called, in the Dee. 5149,
Kingston-upon-Hull, 3939, 4909.
........., sheriff of, 1771.
........., commission of gaol-delivery for, 1922.
........., customs of, 178, 553, 3889.
........., lands in, 319.
Kingston, captain, 4632,
........., Arthur, 1186.
........., John, 1867, 5247.
........., ..., pardon to, 5646.
........., ..., son of John, 1867.
........., ... son of Thomas, 569, 1867.
........., Nich., brother of John, 5247.
........., Susanna, wife of John, 5646.
........., Th., 569, 1867, 4941.
........., Wm., 248.
........., ... grants to, 570.
........., ..., licence to, 1186.
........., ..., in the war against France, 3231, 3451, 4238.
........., ..., sheriff of co. Glouc., 5561.
........., ..., in commission for Glouc., 930, 1049, 1469, 1695, 3641, 3712, 3762, 3804, 4024, 4118, 4764.
........., Sir Wm., 4807.
Kingston Lisle, 4071.
Kingsweston, Glouc., 5026.
Kingswood, Glouc., 1815.
Kinlleth Owen, Denbigh, 955, 1768, 3920.
Kinton, 155.
Kington, Warw., 1499.
Kinnersley, Th., 1986, p. 608.
Kinwolmarsh, Th., 4176.
........., Wm., 4176.
Kirby, Leic., 1372, 4798.
Kirkbride, George, 3075.
Kirkby, Lanc., 680, 1087, 1366, 5229.
........., Linc., 3284, 4852.
........., convent of, Leic., 1885.
........., in Kendall, Westmor., 479, 3764.
........., Geo., 145, 854.
........., Henry, of Kirkby, Lanc., 680, 1087, 1366, 1674, 5229.
........., John, in commission for Hants, 1812.
........., Roland, 3866.
........., Wm., 516, 1796.
Kirkham, Geo, 235, 1149.
........., ..., grants to, 314, 403, 3421.
........., John, in commission for Devon, 1812.
........., Sir John, of Paynton, sheriff of Devon, 946.
........., ..., in commission for Devon, 3183, 3566, 3589, 3605, 4539, 5220.
........., Nich., of Exeter, 3988.
........., ..., of Mershe, Devon, 946, 4783.
........., ..., in commission, 1812.

Kirklerode, near the entrance of the port of Yarmouth, 3551.
Kirkobrighe in Scotland, 4556.
Kirkoswald, Cumb., 3320.
........., letters dated at, 4529, 4682, 4869, 4870, 5090, 5541, 5641.
Kirstead, John, abbot of, 663.
Kirtling, Camb., 5069.
Kirton, or Kyrton, Linc., 319.
...., Devon, 1986, 4316.
........., John, 1484, 3480.
........., John, in commission for Surrey, 1427, 1762, 3078, 3092, 4693, 4701, 4734, 5237, p. 905.
Kite, John, the King's chaplain, 928.
......, ..., incumbent of Wey, 1260.
......, Sir John, 3285.
Kitson, Peter, clk., 853.
Kittenden Bromes, Bucks, 5627.
.... Fyrme, Bucks, 5627.
Knaploke, Margaret, 1070.
Knapton, Norf., 4294, 4536.
........., Yorkshire, 3018.
Knesworth, Tho., alderman of London, 1212, 1527.
Kneton, Yorkshire, 3764.
Kniff, Francis, alias Franklin Trumpet, 4653.
Knight, Alice, daughter of Richard, 3485.
........., Edw., 4866.
........., ..., escheator of York, 5527.
........., Hen., clerk of the signet to the Prince of Wales, 1513, 1839.
........., ..., in commission for Glouc., 3641, 3712, 3804, 4024, 4118, 4764.
........., ..., manumission of, 5694.
........., Ric., treasurer of Calais, 779.
........., Th. 3051.
........., Vincent, a priest, 5589.
........., Wm, LL.D., commission to him and Stile to treat with Ferdinand of Arragon, 3586.
........., ..., ..., in Spain, 3298, 3388, 3755.
........., ..., ..., prothonotary of the Apostolic See, in commission to levy soldiers in Germany, 4794
........., ..., ..., letters from, 3243, 3356, 3451, 3766, 3807, 4058, 4267, 4932, 4935, 4955, 4978, 5029, 5030, 5059, 5159, 5266.
Knighthood granted by James IV. to Christ. Gallace of San Severino, 31.
Knightley, Staff., 1974.
........., ——, p. 652.
........., Edm., 4587.
........., Ric., jun., 4587.
........., ..., ..., in commission for Northt., 1708, 1971.
........., Sir Ric., 1950.
........., ..., sheriff of Northt., 1316.
........., ..., in commission, 732, 5658.

Knighton [Somers. ?], 2080.
........., marches of Wales, 655.
........., Tho., in commission for Herts, 309, 706, 1020, 1971, 3102, p. 906.
Kniston, Alice, wife of John, 3504.
........., John, 3193, 3504.
........., Robt., p. 609.
Knoll, Salop, 4014.
........., Somers. (?) 155, 2080.
Knolles, John, 137, 1253, 4984.
........., Letitia, wife of Rob., 5241.
........., Robt., in the war against France, 3872, 3956.
........., ..., grants to, 670, 1482, 5241.
Knoyle, Leonard, son of Peter, 1342.
........., Peter, 1342.
Knyll, Eustace, 1479, 2092.
Knyvet, Anth., captain, 3979, p. 554.
........., Edm. 1951, 5435.
........., Edw., 1812.
........., Eleanor, 4673.
........., James, captain, p. 652, 5047, p. 972.
........., Joan, wife of Sir Wm., 1603, 2080.
........., Mercella, wife of Thomas, Viscountess Lisle, 654, 3561, 3655, 3922.
........., Sir Tho., 654, 1491, 3308, 3561, 3655, 3922.
........., ..., grants to, 340, 902, 1218, 1266.
........., ..., licences to, 1256, 1423.
........., ..., slain in the war against France, 3388, 3409, 3559, 4636.
........., Wm., of London, 4992, 5003.
........., Sir Wm., 1441, 1603, 2080, 5296.
........., ..., livery of lands for, 3280.
........., ..., Act for, 3502.
........., ..., in commission for Norfolk, 1340, 1714, 1963, 3029, 3426, 3545, 5133.
Koke, r., 4273.
Kokkes, Hen. See Cokkes.
Kruddon. See Croydon.
Kudge's Meadow. See King's Meadow.
Kylbek, John, of Normandy, 3300.
Kylvey. See Kilvey.
Kyllegrew. See Killigrew.
Kyme, Linc., 4616.
Kyme, John, mercer of London, 2036.
Kymer, John, 755.

L.

Laborers, 4387.
.... wages, Act concerning, 3502.
Lachemarshe, meadows, Devon, 1602.
Lachley, Essex, 155.

Laclete, ——, French officer, 4464.
Lacon, Tho., in com. for Shropshire, 1981, 3071, 3715, 4394, 4827.
Lacy. See Malmshill Lacy.
......., Wm., and Margaret his wife, 1671.
Ladislaus VI., King of Hungary, 1221, 4513, 5338, 5366.
........., ..., treaty of, 4924.
Lagham, Surrey, 1484.
Lagishe. See Guiche, La.
Lago, Ralph, pursuivant, 155, 3991.
Laiborn, Rob., in debt to the Crown, 3497.
Lakeford, Suffolk, 4966.
Lakeyton, Sancta Maria de, ship so called, 4377.
Lakham, 1913.
Lakyn, Th., 3694, 4544.
........., ..., sheriff for Shropshire, 664, 5561.
Lalegra, French officer, 3325.
Lalemant, Jean, 4465.
Lalo, Alonso de, Spanish merchant, 3815, 3918.
Lalu, John de, French officer, 4402.
Lamana, Cornwall, 2080.
La Mare, Peter de, and Wilhelmina, his daughter, 1905.
Lamarsh, Essex, 893, 921, 4436. See Lemersh.
Lambmarsh, church of, London dioc., 2063.
Lamb, John, and Isabella, his sister, 3621.
........., Rob., 5625.
........., Walter, 3131.
Lambard, John, burgess and bailiff, Buckingham, 18.
........., ..., mercer, London, 1996.
........., Miles, 3209.
........., Nic., of London, 105, 1675.
Lambert, Wm., lancer of Calais, 4219.
Lamberton, Edm., 186.
Lambeth, 4375, 4758.
........., commission of sewers for, 4701.
........., letters dated, 4829, 4869.
Lampyttis, Essex, 734.
Lamplew, John, on the sheriff-roll for Cumberland, 3507, 4544, 5561.
Lamport, Bucks, 3297.
Lanbrigge, hospital of, Worc. dioc., 1011, 1631, 1965.
Lancashire, 12, 1212, 1965.
........., commission of muster for, 3358.
........., men of, at Flodden, 4441, 4462.
Lancaster, Duchess of, 1376.
........., duchy of, 3023, 3292, 5288.
.... herald, 975, 3849, 3986, 4008, 4070, 5604.
Lancaster, Geoff., in commission for Westmoreland, 1735, 1799, 2009, 3048, 3358, 3552, p. 904.
........., John, 1796.
........., Stephen, clerk, 1796.
........., Th., and Joan, his wife, 1807.

Lancastre, Wm., of Soykbreyd, Cumb., 296.
.........., ..., bailiff of Penrith, Cumb., 119, 1090, 5423.
Landas, letter dated, 4795.
Landau, letter dated, 3648.
Landrean, manor of, Cornwall, 2080.
Landry, John, Philip, his father, and Agnes, his wife, 1669.
Lands, Crown, feodaries and receivers of, 5692.
.........., ..., surveyor of, Sir R. Southwell, 3502.
Land's End, 3820.
Landulp, manor of, Cornwall, 2080.
Landwade, 1371.
Lane, Edw., LL.D., archdeacon of Surrey, 858.
......, Ralph, 69, 5081, 5346.
......, ..., sheriff of Northamptonshire, 3507.
......, Wm., 732, 1708, 1724, 1971.
Lanell. See Lavell.
Lanford, Glouc., 4158.
Lang, Mons. de, French ambassador in Spain, 3112.
Langdish, 1993.
Langdon, Westmoreland, 3764.
... ., Devon, 4071.
.........., John, of Cornwall, 1984, 3290, 3583, 3605, 3938.
Langestu, Th., of Bucks, 2045.
Langford, Wilts, 1270.
Langforde, Anne, daughter of Sir John, 973.
.........., Sir John, 691, 1207, 1318.
.........., Ra'ph, son and heir of Nicholas, son and heir of Sir Ralph, 3772, 5064.
.........., Sir Ralph, 4127.
Langford's Place, Middlesex, 3761.
Langham, Essex, 155.
Langherne, Cornwall, 1675. See also Arundel, Sir John.
Langland, Lucas, 1350. See Longland.
Langley, Berks, 1129, 1344.
.........., Kent, 3611.
.........., Oxon, 1154, 1426, 1868.
.........., Wm., abbot of, 1639, 3497.
.........., barony of, Northumberland, 5010.
Langley, Friar, 4523.
.........., James, 4227.
.........., John, of Sandwich, 4996.
.........., Ric., 1642.
Langley Marreys, Bucks, 155.
.... Regis, Herts, 155.
Langmede, Northt., 5296. See Longmede.
Langney, Sussex, 297.
Langneygotte, Sussex, 297,
Langporth, Kent, 735,

Langston, Ric., 18.
.........., Tho., 69; of Stowe, 4254.
.........., ..., in commission for Bucks, 454, 943, 1379, 3219, 3310, 3522.
.........., ..., on the sheriff-roll for Beds and Bucks, 1949, 3507.
Langtofte, Linc., 3889.
Langton, Dorset, 4214.
.........., Scotland, 4556, 5090.
.........., York, 372.
.........., Cottingham, York, 5089.
.... Guylden, Dorset, 4275.
.........., Hen., 1480.
.... Wm., in commission for Northumberland, 187, 1735, 1804, 3358.
Languedoc, 4725, 5369.
.... threatened invasion of, 3357, 3649, 3752, 3860, 3861.
.........., General of, 4153, 5482.
Langville herald. See Longueville.
Langworth, Th., clerk, 4209.
Lanheron, Cornwall, 3598, 5116. See also Arundel, Sir John.
Lannoy, Rad. de, 1182.
Lanteglas, church of, Exeter dioc., 1830.
Lanteglose, park of, Cornwall, 268.
Lantern-gate, Calais, 2087, 4232.
Lanthony, priory of, 3172.
.........., Edmund, prior of, 3172.
.........., subprior of. See Nottingham.
.........., cellarer of, 5355.
Lantony, Cornwall, 1949.
Lantyane, Cornwall, 468, 4739.
Lanuce, near Béthune, in France, p. 609.
Lanvenit Church, 370.
Lanwerirum, Hieronymus, 4508.
Laon, France, premonstratene monast. of, 3354.
Larder, Edm., in commission for Devon, 1503, 1812, 3183, 3566, 3589, 3605, 4539, 4783, 5220.
.........., ..., feodary of Crown lands, 5692.
Laredo ("Allaredy") in Spain, p. 400.
Lares, Francis de, 3452.
Larke, Peter, 5603.
......, Th., clk., 1977.
Lascarina, Isabell, 1627. See Corinth, Helena Lastarrinea.
Lascu, Lord, 3976.
Lasschaw, ——, 4418.
Lascy, Ric., 22.
Lassells, Ric., of Nottingham, 1735, 1804.
Lassher, Wm., of Surrey, 5237.
Lastalrig. See Restalrig.
Lastormall, in the duchy of Cornwall. See Rastormall.
Lastormall, Holy Trinity, 259.
Lastytheall, Cornwall, 259.
Laswade (Leswade), Scotland, 2041.
Lateran, church of, 3780.
.........., council of. See Council.

Lathbury, Ric., 1289.
........., William, 1023.
Lathum, Ralph, 151, 3006.
........., Th., 5224.
Latimer, or Latymer, Ric., Nevill Lord, 525, 1262.
........., ..., at Parliament, 5616.
........., ... in commission for Yorksh., 455, 954, 1549, 1550, 1735, 1798, 1799, 1804, 1995, 3177, 3219, 3358, 4719, 5166, 5193, 5244, 5503, 5506, 5529, 5605; for Westmoreland, 2009, 3048, 3552.
........., ..., ..., his signature, 4439.
........., John, justice of assize, 5283.
........., Wm., 4254.
Laton. See Lacon.
La Tremouille. See Tremouille.
Latton, Essex, 1282.
Lauder. See Louder.
........., Sir Robt., Scotch ambassador, 782, 1820, 2069, 3569, 3676, 4997.
Laughton, Sussex, 1464.
Launcelot, Sir ——, 3942.
Launceston, Cornwall, 210.
........., prior of, in debt to the Crown, 1639, 3497.
Launde, John, prior of, in debt to the Crown, 1639, 3497.
Launne, Thos., 4335.
Lauredano, Laurence, Doge of Venice, 908, 1967, 4924.
........., ..., ..., letter from, 932.
Launder, Wm., clerk, 1444.
Lausart, Jehan, 4445.
Lautrec, Odet de Foix, Lord of, commissioner for Louis XII., 3839, 4818, 4924.
........., ..., ..., in Italy, 3325.
........., ..., ..., at the marriage of the Princess Mary, 5482.
Lavell, John, 1143, 1616.
Laver, Essex, 734.
Laverstock, 3497.
Laward, Rob., 4884.
La Warr, Lord. See De la Warr.
Lawden, John, purser of the Mary Rose, p. 957.
Lawnselyn, Will., and Alice, his wife, 4911.
Lawrence, St., Feast of, 3027.
........., Hen., 3497.
........., John, clerk, 1854.
........., Ric., 1350, 1765, 3408.
........., Stephen, 5723.
........., Wm., 1002, 3998.
.... See Lowrans.
Lawson, John, 3412.
........., Geo., 4868.
Lawton, Cheshire, 4748.
Laycock, 1913.
Leach, John, clk., 3767, 4911. See Leitch.
........., Ralph, of Derby, 1372, 4253.

Lead, importation of, 3517.
Leadenham, Long, Linc., 3578.
Leagues. See Treaties.
Leases of lands in the King's hands, 811.
Leather, 2082, 3467, 4232, 4848.
Leatherhead, 858,
Lechlade, Glouc., 155.
Lecriand, Wm., gunner, 596, 781.
Ledbury, Hereford, 1827, 5238, 5256.
Lede, le, near Calais, 3923.
Ledesdale. See Liddesdale.
Lee, Kent, 887, 3041, 3089, 3096, 3154.
......, Sussex, 1965.
...... (river), 1972.
...... See Ships.
Lee or Leigh, Anth., chief clerk of the kitchen, 183, 615, 5494, 5723.
......, Christ., 4825.
......, Edm., of Suffolk, 3219, 3967, 4713, 5133.
......, Giles, 1173.
......, Humph., 3792.
......, Joan, wife of Richard, 3268.
......, John, 958, 4004.
......, John a, 4414.
......, Sir John, in commission for Surrey and Sussex, 664, 1427, 1548, 1762, 3078, 3092, 3996, 4568, 4693, 4701, 4734, 4808, 5237, 5561.
......, Ric., yeoman of the Jewel House, 1197.
......, Ric., of Kent, 725, 906, 3605, 4291, 4663, 4847, 4927.
......, Rob., gentleman usher of the chamber, 3248.
......, Tho., 575, 1173.
......, Tho., canon, 4524.
......, Wm., 178, 1512, 1845.
Leeds, Kent, 735, 1825, 3611, 4334, 5625.
Leek, Linc., 5087.
......, John, 4011.
......, Sir John, of Derby, 4253.
......, Thos., of Chesterfield., brother of Sir John, 4253.
Leeson, Th., 3062.
Lefrere, Piervhon, 4445.
Legates, papal, 3269, 3325, 3341, 4563, 4605.
Legborn, prioress of, 3579.
Legh. See Lee.
Leghderant, 2080.
Leicestershire, 266, 484, 542, 602, 664, 1771, 1778, 2011, 3049, 3447, 3871, 3947, 4414, 5640.
........., sheriffs of, 664, 1316, 1949, 3507, 3887, 3891, 4544, 5561.
........., gaol delivery, 3209.
........., commissions of the peace for, 656, 739, 1094, 1425, 1971, 4706, 4783, 4812, 5506.
........., commisions of array for, 4434, 5529, 5626.

Leicester Castle, 554, 5380.
........., town, 4345, 4742, 5186.
........., deanery of St. Mary's, 3595.
........., Rog. de, 1099.
Leigh Field forest, Rutl., 1329.
Leigh, Roger, 4693, 4701, 5237.
...... See Lee.
Leighton, Hunts, 3928.
........., John, 3843.
........., Sir Th., of Shropshire, 918, 1981,
　3071, 3231, 3715, 4253, 4394, 4827.
Leghton, Matilda, wife of John, 3843.
Leighwood, 3134.
Leitch, or Leych, John, 4253. See Leach.
Leych, Ric., 4253.
Leith, Scotland, 3577, 3627, 3751, 3882, 4951.
Lelegrave, Wm., 3236.
Lemagis, Wm. de, 4760.
Leman, Peter, 4533.
Lemershe, Linc. dioc., 5011.
Leming, John, 5682.
........., Little, 5086.
Lemyngton, Hants. See Lymington.
........., Ralph, 1642.
Lemus, Ct. de, 490.
Lempriere, Tho., 650.
Lench, Peter de, 4934.
.... See Sheriff's Lench.
Leney. See Fauconberge.
Lenox, Matt., Earl of, 714, 4441.
Lenton, monastery of, 1081.
........., John, 3719.
Leo. X., 3798, 3817, 3975, 4039, 4062, 4078,
　4091, 4196, 4267, 4272, 4327, 4365,
　4449, 4756, 4786, 4796, 4831, 4864,
　4955, 5007, 5106, 5126, 5171 (ii.),
　5173, 5253, 5323, 5356, 5357, 5365,
　5378, 5382, 5393, 5396, 5410, 5424,
　5447, 5496, 5539, 5542, 5614, 5642,
　5650, 5662, 5675, 5681, 5698, 5730,
　5740, 5745.
........., election, 3780, 3814, 3821, 4354.
........., better off than his predecessors, 4096.
........., complains of his expenses, 4747.
........., creates Cardinals, 4525, 4574.
........., reconciles the schismatic Cardinals,
　3876, 4287, 4371.
........., decree touching commendams, 4718.
........., crusade, 4500.
........., desires general peace, 4563, 4598,
　5110.
........., advises Henry to make peace with
　France, 5352, 5387.
........., proposed the marriage with Mary, 5543.
........., leagues with Henry, Maximilian, &c.,
　3860, 3863, 3887, 3915, 4038, 4085, 4094,
　4182, 4366, 4511, 4924.
........., offers made by France for his brother
　Julian, 4274, 4296, 4952.
........., suspected of favoring France, 4323,
　4725, 5208.
........., sends thither the Bishop of Tricarico,
　5107.

Leo. X., receives an ambassador from Duke of
　Milan, 4666.
........., anxious for peace between France and
　Duke of Milan, 5464.
........., displeased with Ferdinand, 4844.
........., displeased with the Viceroy, 4069,
　4078, 4577.
........., agrees to the truce between Lewis and
　Ferdinand, 4845.
........., threatens Maximilian, 3897, 5094.
........., mediates between him and the Vene-
　tians, 4563, 4985, 5290.
........., sends ambassadors to Maximilian,
　5239, 5338, 5366, 5430.
........., his proposals to the Swiss, 4138.
........., declines the Swiss league, 4789.
........., bull against the Scotch King, 4455.
........., prothonotary. See Stuart, Balthazar.
........., chamberlain. See Leon. de Spinellis.
........., nuncio. See Butrigario, Goleas.
........., his secretary in Scotland, 4902.
........., sends Henry VIII. the consecrated
　sword and cap, 4621.
........., his ambassador in England, 5164.
........., confirms indulgences of Julius II.,
　4446.
........., confirms the appointment of Ammonius,
　5663.
........., writes to Henry VIII. in favor of
　Bishop of Worcester, 5168, and of Eras-
　mus, 5182.
........., letters from, to Henry VIII., 3848, 4288,
　4444, 4458, 4582, 4605, 4608, 4724,
　4835, 4922, 4926, 5099, 5156, 5174,
　5262, 5269, 5301, 5331, 5333, 5358,
　5392, 5445, 5457, 5538, 5635.
........., letter from, to James V., 5613.
........., bulls for Wolsey's promotion, 5411, 5415,
　5555. See also 4936, 5424, 5465, 5587,
　5591.
........., letters to, from Henry VIII., 4470,
　4502, 4548, 4819, 5048, 5318, 5319,
　5651.
........., ..., from King of Portugal, 4173.
........., ..., from James IV., 4623, 4628.
Levestoft, (Lowestoft), Suffolk, 1446.
........., Ric., of Glouc., 5191.
Leodo, Sieur de, 3377.
Leon, kingdom of, 5581, 5592.
Leonum Castrum, in the Marches of Wales,
　512.
Leoons, 5290.
Leore, James, 1908.
Le Roy, 3830.
Lesnes, St. Thomas and St. Mary, Rochester,
　3795, 3834.
Lespar, Lord, 5482.
Leson, Tho., incumbent of Tattehall, Cov.
　and Lich. dioc., 1199 ; of Newelme,
　Linc., 4256.
........., ..., receiver to Sir W. Compton,
　4150, 5679.

Lestalrig. *See* Restalrig.

Leswade. *See* Laswade.

Letcombe, 1867.

Lethewood, 634.

Leuekyr, 415.

Leventhorp, John, 309; in com. for Herts, 664, 724.

Lever, Yevan, 3482.

Leversege, York., 452, 4866.

........, Anth., son of Edm., 424.

........, Edm. 424, 828.

........, Rob., son of Edm., 828.

Leveseye, Edmund, 426. *See* Livesay.

Leveson, Nich., 4699.

Levet, John, 4996.

Levetot, John de, 1099.

Leventhorp, John, in com. for Herts, 706.

Levington, West, manor of 3497.

Lewardia, 5598.

Lewes, Sussex, 297, 912, 776, 1160, 1212.

........, Griffith, incumbent of Old Radnor, Heref, 3028.

........, Hugh, incumbent of Llanvehengell, Llandaff, 1062.

........, John, 1668, 4013,

........, Good. *See* Ships.

Lewesson, John, 4013.

Lewis, Friar, of Toledo, 5125.

Lewis, John, 235.

......, Sir Ric. in the war against France, 3977, 4377.

Lewis XII., 20, 405, 490, 974, 1458, 3010, 3026, 3081, 3105, 3118, 3146, 3278, 3291, 3326, 3333, 3355, 3356, 3398, 3412, 3469, 3569, 3602, 3629, 3631, 3662, 3723, 3750, 3830, 3863, 4500, 4598, 4692, 4556, 4563, 5006, 5107, 5171, 5323, 5389, 5430, 5465, 5511, 5600, 5713, 5730, 5781.

.... (1512): keeps Easter at Blois, 3112; at Blois (Feb. 10th., 1513), 3752, 4273; at Corby. 4174.

.... (1513): going towards Calais, 4100.

........, accused of avarice and obstinacy, 4561.

........, abused "as impotent and malicious" by Maximilian, 5404; as an old valitudinarian, 5470, 5553; has the gout, 5495; his infirmities, 4449, 4849, 5581, 5642; his personal appearance, 5581.

........, talk of his having the small-pox, 5203.

.... (1509): pays England 25,000 francs, 14; binds himself to pay 745,000 cr., 318, 1104, 1181, 1182. (1510): pays 25,000 francs, 1027. (1511): do., 1632; to pay 100,000 francs per an. (1514), 5280, 5306, 5321, 5335, 5529.

.... (1510): treaty between him and England, 962; confirmed, 1105; his oath, 1108.

.... (1512): treats Rich. De la Pole as King of England, 3320, 3347, 3372.

.... (1512): war declared against, by England, 3225; defied by England (1513),

Lewis XII.—*cont.*

3986; England makes peace with him, 4574.

........., position and state of his forces (1513): prepares ships against England, 4329, 4843.

........., proposes to invade Guisnes, 3336.

.... (1514): favourably inclined to England, 4883.

.... (1514): com. for alliance with England, 5278, 5294, 5305; oath to observe the treaty, 5282; proclaimed, 5326; confirmation of, 5408.

........., proposal for marriage with Margaret of Scotland, 4951, 5140.

........., proposal to marry Eleanor, the Emperor's niece, 5126.

........., proposal to marry Princess Mary, 5164, 5192, 5285; unpopular in England, 5267; and in Flanders, 5327, 5341; com. for his marriage, 5279; agrees to her dowry, 5286; treaty of marriage, 5307, 5315, 5319; its ratification, 5343; his proxy, 5311.

........., to meet Mary at Abbeville, 5329, 5330.

........., his espousals, 5322, 5337; Lords attending, 5482; provides jewels for her, 5468; gives her portion, 5480; account of the marriage, 5495. *See also* 5368, 5373, 5441, 5469, 5470, 5497.

........., entry with Mary into Paris and coronation, 5560.

........., professes his love for his wife, but will not have her English attendants, 5553.

.... proposed meeting with Henry, 5468, 5517, 5553, 5569.

........., promises Wolsey a mule, 5547.

........., suspected of playing Wolsey false in the matter of Tournay, 5424, 5439, 5446, 5467, 5517, 5518, 5553, 5587, 5697.

.... (1510): grants the Earl of Shrewsbury a pension, 952.

.... (1512): in league with Scotland, 3218, 3633; reported to be sending there 2000 g. c., 3651.

........., encourages James IV. to invade England, p. 382; promises him men and money, 3838; has ships from Scotland, 4525, 4844; sends aid thither, 5021.

........., sends his seal into Scotland, 3577; his letters of naturalization to Scotchmen, 4484.

.... (1512): permits imports to Scotland, 2050.

.... (1513): sends a present to Margaret of Scotland, 3814.

.... (1514): prevents Albany going into Scotland, 5642. *See also* 5757.

.... (1511): at variance with Julius II., 1681, 1697, 1700, 1877, 1878.

........., treaty of peace between them 1869; his proposals to the Pope, 4274; promises his kinswoman to the Pope's brother, 4296.

.... (1511): said to be favorable to the Crusade, 1875.

Lewis XII.—cont.

........., Julius II. wishes to deprive him of his title *Christianissimus*, p. 380.

........., interdicted, 3876, 4283.

.... (1511): supposed inclined to a general peace, 1697.

.... (1509): proposes a treaty between Ferdinand and Maximilian for governance of Castile, 796, 819.

.... (1509): suspected by Ferdinand p. 115, thought to aim at Naples, ib., 819.

.... (1509): sends commissioners to determine the boundary line of France and Spain, p. 118.

.... (1512): opposed by Spain and the Venetians, 2075.

.... (1512): shows his anger against the Spanish ambassador, 3112.

........., reigns in Bayonne, 3355.

.... (1512): promises to make Duke of Calabria King of Naples in despite of Ferdinand, 3593.

.... (1513): Ferdinand declines to attack him, 3766.

........., treats with Ferdinand (1513), 3807, 3897, 3951, 3962, 4069, 4075, 4094, 4267,4756; (in 1514), 4955, 5041, 5126, 5353.

.... (1514): promises to write his mind touching Navarre, 5634; proposes to expel Ferdinand, 5637.

.... (1511): league against by England and Spain; 1980, and the Pope, 2010.

.... (1513): truce between Lewis, Scotland, and Gueldres on one side, and Maximilian, Henry, Ferdinand, &c., on the other, 3839, 4818, 4875.

........., treaty of Henry, Maximilian, and Prince Charles against him, confirmed, 4560.

........., threatens the Prince of Castile for the aid lent to England, 4328, 4561, 4830.

.... (1514): treaty with Charles of Castile, 4924.

.... (1514): admits Prince of Castile into the treaty with Henry, 5559.

.... (1509, June): desires to meet Maximilian, 216.

.... (1514): makes offers to Maximilian, 4978.

.... (1512): in treaty with the Swiss, 3112, 3370.

........., prepares to enter Milan, April 30, 1509, 11; in Italy, 216. (1511): expected in Italy in the spring, 1457.

.... (1512): desires to win the Venetians, 3614; succeeds, 3662, 4069.

.... (1512): strong in Italy, 5745.

........., lays siege to Bergamo (?), 3648.

.... (1512): weeps for the loss of Milan, 3269.

........., on ill terms with D. of Milan, 5464.

.... (1511): letters of protection for the Bentivogli, 1754.

Lewis XII. (1512): makes an arrangement with K. of Navarre, 3405, 3437.

........., allows Denmark to trade with France, 3617.

........., is unwilling to lend money to D. of Gueldres, 3752.

........., raises an army against the Turks, 4824.

........., his house steward, 4431.

........., his body guard, 842.

........., his ambassadors, &c. *See* Cordier, Peter; de Reulx; Foix, Odet de; Valois, Fr. de; Du Prat; Savoy, Bastard of; Bateru.., Humbert de; Longueville, Louis Duke of; Selva, J. de; Bohier, Th.; La Guiche.

.... letters to Henry VIII., 5717.

........., to Wolsey, 5302, 5372, 5462, 5696.

.... to Margaret of Savoy, 5126.

........., to the President of Montferrat, 4152, 4162.

.... letters to, from Julius II., 3118.

........., ..., from James IV. 1364, 1407,1409, 1413.

........., ..., from Mary, 5463.

........., second daughter of, betrothed to Don Ferdinand, 4921.

Lewisham, Kent, 3181, 4498.

Lewkenor, Oxford, 1129, 1344.

........., Edw., of Sussex, 1212.

........., ..., in com. for Sussex, 281.

........., ..., sheriff-roll, Sussex, 664, 1316.

........., Francis, 1965.

........., Rog. Sir, 1212, 1484, 3024.

........., ..., in com. for Sussex, 281, 1509.

........., ..., sheriff of Sussex, 1949.

........., ..., in the war against France, 3977, 4377.

Le Worthy, 1709.

Lewys, a coin so called, 4481.

Leybrokes, Surrey, 1488, 1916.

Leycamstead, Bucks, 3492.

Leyghton (Leygtton), Robt. captain, 3977.

Leyham, Suffolk, 155, 3017.

Leyk. *See* Leek.

Leynham (?), 4307.

Leysols, Charron de, 4041.

Library, keeper of the King's, Giles Duwes, 513.

........., ..., John Porth, 259, 1146.

Lichbarow, 3027.

Lichfield, 12, 1480.

........., Bishop of, 1854. *See* Blythe.

........., Dean of, John Yotton, 4209.

........., chantry at, 4209.

.... Cathedral, chancellor of, 1854.

Lichfield, Clement, B.D., 4716.

........., John, clerk, 3581.

........., Th., 3719.

........., Wm., dean of Tamworth, 3581.

Lychefeld, William, the King's chaplain, 4375.
.........., ..., in Parliament, 811.
Liddesdale, 3577, 4556.
Liddle, Cumberland, 4791.
Lidney, Glouc., 3613.
Liege or Luke, 3340, 3446, 3945, 4328, 4622.
.........., Bishop of (Erard de la Marck), (called Bishop of Luke), 3435, 4319, 4323.
.........., Duke of, 4924.
.........., Mons. de, 5285
Liegeois, 3678.
Liegne, Hayne, 4445.
Lifton, church of, Exeter dioc., 4181.
Ligan, castle of, 3752.
Lighthorn, Warwick, 419, 1499, 1501.
Ligne, Baron de. See Fauconberg.
.........., Anth. De. See Fauconberg.
Likerke, ——, 5203.
Lille. See Lisle.
Lillingston Dauncy, Oxon, 3492.
.... Lovel, Oxon, 3492.
Lily, William, 5731.
Lillynston, Bucks, 789, 839.
Limby, Notts, 4694.
Limele Gerneing, oak of, Shotover Forest, 4772.
Limerick, mayor and commonalty of, 4028.
Lyminster, Sussex, 1965.
Limeswoods, Bucks, 3492.
Limpsham, Somerset, 4071.
Linacre, Rob., captain, 4253.
.........., Thos., 1883, 1982, 4447, 4528.
Linby, Notts, 1633, 1809.
Linceux, Pierre, 4445.
Linclowden, provost of, 3121,
Lincoll, Wm., yeoman of the Crown, 1615.
Lincoln, men of, 1827, 3035, 4714.
.........., gaol delivery for, 3282.
.... Castle, 414.
.........., mayor of, 792.
.........., ... and sheriffs of, 1771.
Lincolnshire, 295, 302, 303, 449, 484, 602, 645, 1212, 2011, 3049, 4199, 4534.
.........., commissions of array for, 3393, 4434, 5529, 5626.
.........., commission of sewers for, 663, 1716, 1979, 1983, 3137, 5691.
.........., commissions of the peace for, 278, 1511, 3342, 4593, 5476.
.........., commissions of the peace for Holland, 1170, 3351, 4860, 5506.
.........., ... Kesteven, 657, 1120, 1169, 5506.
.........., ... Lindsey, 1171, 1496, 4358, 4860, 5506.
Lincolnshire, commission of oyer and terminer for, 463.
.........., other commissions for, 1380, 3871.
.........., escheators of, 3447.
.........., feodaries of Crown lands in, 4414.
.........., sheriffs of, 1771, 3592.
.........., sheriff-roll for, 664, 1316, 1949, 3507, 4544, 5561.
.........., Holland in, 2014.
.........., Lindsey in, 4714.
.........., swans in, 306, 1743.
Lincoln Cathedral, 1910.
...., treasurer of, John Constable, 3515.
...., dean of, Thomas Wolsey, 837, 899. See Wolsey.
...., dean and chapter of, 4877.
...., St. Giles's chapel, 1910.
.........., bishopric of, 4786, 5443, 5465.
.........., ..., promotion of Wolsey to, 4722, 4723, 4724, 4854.
.........., ..., absolution of Wolsey from, 5411.
.........., ..., Worcester wishes to have it, 5354.
.........., ..., temporalities of, 4854, 4877, 5556.
.........., ..., annates of, 5449, 5464, 5542.
.........., diocese of, 1848.
.........., Wm. Smith, Bp. of, 4377, 4877, 5309.
.........., ..., legatee of Hen. VII., 776.
.........., ..., ..., in commission for Wales, 955, 3054, 3055; and various counties, 278, 279, 454, 646, 656, 657, 663, 675, 713, 732, 766, 776, 791, 886, 892, 905, 916, 918, 930, 943, 1049, 1051, 1094, 1095, 1120, 1122, 1169, 1170, 1171, 1216, 1379, 1400, 1425, 1469, 1470, 1514, 1695, 1708, 1716, 1745, 1770, 1798, 1963, 1964, 1971, 1981, 2045, 3015, 3071, 3092, 3219, 3301, 3342, 3351, 3494, 3501, 3522, 3686, 3709, 3712, 3715, 3804, 4006, 4024, 4118, 4358, 4559, 4593, 4776.
.........., ..., ..., petitions of, 3447, 4010.
...., ..., ..., grants to, 2057, 3292, 3515.
.........., Thos. Wolsey, Bp. of. See Wolsey.
.........., Wm. Atwater, Bp. of. See Atwater.
Lincoln, John De la Pole, Earl of (temp. Hen. VII.), 1346, 1472, 3005. 3705, 4022, 4254, 4670, 5226, 5627.
Lindsey, John, 4873.
.........., Patrick, Lord, 4997.
Ling, Somerset, 1761.
Lingfield, Surrey, 1484.
Lingen, Sir John, in com. for Herefordsh., 646, 675, 1400, 1914, 1963, 3503, 3686; on sheriff-roll for Herefordsh., 664, 1316, 3507, 4544, 5561; ship-owner, 4377.

Lingen, Wm., sewer of the chamber, 1072, 1686, 1691.

Lyngestan, Wm., 4118.

Linkfelde, Surrey, 1091,

Linlithgow, 3225, 3881.

........., letters dated, 3121, 3122, 3875.

Linthecombe, Devon, 985.

Lintz, on the Danube, 4844, 4978, 5055.

........., letters dated, 4915, 4952.

Linwood, Linc., 1071, 4695.

Lion King-at-arms, Hen. Thompson, 474, 1408, 5614, 5641.

Lion, alias Holt, castle of, Welsh Marches, 823, 1768, 3920.

......, lordship of, 691.

Lions in the Tower. See Tower.

Liquith, South Wales, 1583.

Lisbon, letter dated, 4173.

Liskeard, Cornwall, 686, 5192.

Lisle, 3417, 4253, 4284, 4445, 4473, 4479, 4561, 4586, 4829, 4833, 4851, 4976, 5203, 5319, 5398, 5404.

........., letters dated at, 4407, 4418, 4429, 4433, 4459.

........., treaties signed at, 4508, 4510, 4511.

.........; canon of, 4844, 5377.

Lisle, Charles Brandon, Viscount. See Brandon.

........., Sir Humph., 12, 755.

........., ..., in debt to the Crown, 3497.

........., ..., at Flodden Field, 4441.

........., John, spear at Calais, 4476.

........., Sir John, in commission for Hants, 904, 1388, 1812, 3071, 3173, 3688, 3723, 4159, 4676, 4979.

........., ..., grant to, 5060.

........., John Grey Viscount, temp. Hen. VII., 654, 3561, 3655, 3722, 3922, 4071, 4689.

........., Eliz., Queen's gentlewoman, 5296.

........., Marcella Knyvet Viscountess, 654, 3561, 3655, 3922.

........., Eliz. Grey, Viscountess, 654, 3561, 3655, 3722, 3922, 4071, 4072, 4689, 4851 (note).

........., Ramon de, French prisoner, 4402.

Lismore, church of, 3141.

........., diocese of, 3624.

........., David Bishop of, 4626.

........., Earls of, 3630.

Lister, ——, 4105.

......, Ric., 1212.

......, Wm., 4714.

Litley, Helen, 121.

Little, Rob., groom of the wardrobe of beds, 108, 546, 939, 1554, 1617, 3131.

......, ..., porter at Carlisle Castle, 1061.

Littlebury, John, in commission for Lincoln-shire, 278, 1170, 1716, 1979, 3137, 3351, 4860, 5691.

Litelcote, manor of, 3134.

Littlehorsted, Sussex, 1484.

Littlemoor, Shotover Forest, 4772.

Littleton, Edw., grant to, 5310.

........., ..., in the war, 4253.

........., John, son of Sir Wm., 937, 5310.

........., Mary, 5310.

........., Ric., in commission for Staff. and Salop, 279, 713, 791, 886, 1770, 1981, 3071, 3715, 4394, 4646, 4827, 5506.

........., ..., justice of gaol delivery, 764.

........., Th., of Worcestershire, 1971, 3301, 3709, 4770, 5506.

........., Sir Wm., 937, 5310.

Litlington, Camb., 1558.

Lytton, Sir Rob., 3656.

........., Wm., of Herts, 498, 1316, 4742.

........., ..., in debt to the Crown, 2044.

........., Lady, 425, 1212.

Livesay, Edw., 1966.

Lize, Henry, prior of, in Essex, 3497.

Llandaff, Miles Salley, Bishop of, in commission for Oxford, 766, 1216, 1470, 1745, 3015, 4559, 4809, 5506, 5616.

Llandeverour, 1669.

Llandeylo, Carmathen, 1669.

Llanlithan, Llandaff, 3453.

Llansoy, Lland. dioc., 3337.

Llanstephan, 51.

Llantheweebrevee, 252.

Llanthexnoll, 252.

Llantrieshin, 1229.

Llantrisham, S. Wales, 1583.

Llanvehangell, Wales, 1062.

Llewellyn, David, 3771.

........., Richard. 3771.

Llhoughourne, S. Wales, 5180.

Llinlithgow. See Linlithgow.

Lloyd, David, 1585.

......, Geoff., 4841.

......, John, 377, 3091.

......, Maur., 51.

......, Ric., 225, 700.

......, Rob., yeoman of the Crown, 344.

......, Roger, of Hereford, 4717.

......, Thos., 4476.

......, Wm., 1100.

Llybedyth, lordship of, 1894.

Loan to France, 5637.

........., Saxony, 5600, 5675.

Lobons, John, King's mason, 775.

Locarum, in Italy, p. 368.

Lock, John, 4590, 5577.

Lodi, 4283.

......, Bishop of, 3269.

Lodirsdane, York, 4852.

Lofte, Henry, hermit, 1860.

Loggyn, ——, 4067.

Logroño (Old Castile), 3584, 3593, 3607.

Loham, 1993.

Lokton, Geoff., and Robt. his son, 5573.

Lollards, 3289.

Lombardy, 4058, 4078, 4267, 4287.

Lome, Rob., of Lynn, 3210.

Lomelyn, Barth., merchant of Genoa, 4350.

........., Dominic, 3142, 4246, 4350.

Lomesdale, Westmoreland, 3764.

Lomley, J., at Flodden Field, 4439.

Lond, Rob., 3515.

Londe, Sieur De la Louis de Vigars, 4465.

Londesdaill, 1628.

London, 1012, 1842, 1871, 1882, 1883, 1900, 1917, 1925, 1997, 2013, 3012, 3207, 3320, 3321, 3442, 3443, 3495, 3496, p. 494, 3857, 3985, 4057, 4074, 4094, 4103, 4154, 4254, 4377, 4523, 4527, 4528, 4582, 4727, 4825, 4878, 5021, 5030, 5099, 5103, 5111, 5116, 5329, 5720, 5740, 5755, 5784. See also Ships.

........., men of, 12, 105, 412, 436, 464, 578, 1003, 1036, 1212, 1596, 1656, 1675, 1688, 1756, 1773, 1780, 1825, 1884, 1890, 1996, 3006, 3045, 3113, 3114, 3324, 3330, 3369, 3497, 3600, 3744, 3784, 3796, 3868, 3899, 3910, 3933, 3937, 3939, 3953, 3961, 3993, 4023, 4035, 4260, 4266, 4290, 4293, 4300, 4360, 4367, 4419, 4488, 4493, 4503, 4514, 4519, 4589, 4590, 4617, 4672, 4675, 4681, 4699, 4707, 4729, 4908, 5239, 5383, 5396, 5472, 5473, 5502, 5508, 5567, 5568, 5577, 5597, 5608, 5612, 5660, 5690, 5699, 5701, 5711, 5723, 5724.

........., port of, customs, &c., 41, 144, 151, 159, 182, 197, 221, 254, 290, 301, 376, 412, 428, 429, 539, 556, 795, 864, 1315, 1874, 1999, 2059, 3315, 3445, 4340, 4892, 4799.

........., aldermen of, named, 1097, 1212, 1596, 1996, 3427, 3879, 4699, 5060.

........., ..., temp. Hen. VI., named, 5242.

........., brewers in, 5766.

........., commission for, 3006.

........., commission to provide corn for, 3786.

........., crown lands in, feodary of, 4414.

.... curates, complaints against, 5725.

.... escheators of, 1930, 3947.

.... friars, four orders of, 5735.

........., guilds of, viz. :—

dyers, 4013.

fishmongers, 3868.

grocers, 3284.

haberdashers, "hurers and hatter merchants," 1317.

innholders (mystery of St. Julian le Herbeger), 5708.

mercers, 3767, 3900, 4659.

merchant tailors, 1029, 3879.

....school, foundation of, 3427.

........., juries in, 3502.

London, mayors of, viz. :—

Acherley, Roger, 1897.

Bradbury, Thos., 1776, 3767.

Browne, Will., 4553, 5111.

Haddon, Sir Ric.. 3765, 3778.

Jenyns, Stephen, 541.

Kebull, Henry, 1942.

Shaa, John, 671.

........., mayor and corporation of, 3497, 3781.

........., oils in, Act for searching, 2082.

........., outlawries in, 3939, 5001.

........., plague in, 1918, 1948, 2001.

........., proclamations in, 1771, 3597, 5493.

........., Scotchmen in, 4581.

........., sewers, commission of, for, 1972.

........., tenths and fifteenths in, 3441.

........., treaties dated, 962, 3861, 4268, 5305, 5306, 5307, 5321, 5343.

........., treaties of, mentioned, 5285, 5294, 5511.

........., letters dated at, 751, 1418, 1948, 1982, 2021, 3158, 3706, 3861, 4171, 4388, 4448, 5140, 5173, 5182, 5203, 5347, 5444, 5526, 5759, 5769.

........., streets, parishes, &c., in and adjoining :—

Aldgate, 3445.

........., Christchurch or Holy Trin. within, priory, 3371, 3403, 3474, 3493, 3716, 4115.

........., ..., Thos. Percy, prior of, 1639, 3497. See also references to preceding.

All Hallows, p. of, tenements in Watling Street, 1825.

........., Bread Street, 3406, 4643.

........., Honey Lane, 3406, 3407, 4643.

........., Lombard Street, 3896.

........., London Wall, 3406, 3407, 4643.

.... the More, 1508 ; church of, 1356.

.... Staining, 1070, 1843.

Austin Friars, 5111 ; their apartments, 1982.

Barking Church, guild of St. Mary, 5242.

Baynard's Castle, 155, 4056, p. 829 ; letter dated at, 3861. See also Castell.

Berebynder Lane, 1070.

Bethlehem, hospital of St. Mary of, 3099, 4201.

Bishopsgate Without, hosp., Ric. prior of, 1639.

Blackfriars, (or Friars Preachers), 264, 4232, 5172 ; prior of, 5172; parlour of, 5351.

........., Parliament held at, 4848.

Borthalane or Bordhawlane, 5568.

Bow Lane, 1508.

Bridewell, letter of Wolsey from his house at, 4171.

London, streets, parishes, &c., in and adjoining —*cont.*

Bucklersbury, 1269, 3727.

Bush Lane, 1774.

Candelwyke or Canwyke Street, 729 ; Dudley's house in, 425, 4231.

Chancery Lane (Chaunsler Lane), 5116.

Charterhouse, 1151, 5230.

Cheap, 1528, 3537, 4643.

Christchurch. *See* Aldgate.

Church Alley, 4780.

Clerkenwell, church of, 938 ; nun of, 5735.

Coldharborough, the King's place called, 253, 270.

Counter, the, in Bread Street, 461, 1853, 3237, 3329.

Cow Cross, Smithfield, 3954.

Croked Lane, 844.

Crown, the, in Cheap, 3406, 3407, 4643.

Cussyn Lane, 1508.

Custom House, Ric. Hill of the, 1212.

Distaf Lane, the Lamb in, 1070.

Dovegate 1508, 3401.

Eastcheap, 3445.

Elephant Tavern, Smithfield, 5383.

Ely's, Bishop of, mansion in Holborn, 1523.

Fenchurch Street, 1070.

Fenkislane (Finch Lane), 826, 1259, 4136.

Fetter Lane, 1523.

Fleet Street, 870 ; the "Walsheman" in, 1389.

Friars Preachers. *See* Blackfriars.

Goldsmiths' Hall, 4917.

Guildhall, 1212.

Haliwell, nuns of, 5735.

Herber, the hospice called, 3401.

Holborn, 1523.

Houndsditch, 4977.

Langborn ward, 1070.

Leadenhall, 888.

Lincoln's Inn, 5116.

Lombard Street, 1280.

London Bridge, 1212, 3406, 3407, 4643.

London House, letter dated, 1418.

Lovel's Inn, Paternoster Row, 3761.

Maiden Lane, 1070.

Marshalsea, 1656.

.... Prison, 5194.

Marte Lane, 1843.

Minories, 5735.

Newgate, gaol deliveries for, 541, 1519, 1547, 1897, 1942, 3765, 3778, 4553.

London, streets, parishes, &c., in and adjoining—*cont.*

Old Bailey, 870, 1389.

Panyer, the, Paternoster Row, 3406, 4643.

Paternoster Row, 3761.

Poultry, 632.

Princes' Wardrobe, 970.

Redcross Street, 671.

St. Andrew's, near Baynard's Castle, 4689 ; rector of, 1872.

........., Holborn, 4780.

St. Augustine's, 984.

St. Botolph's without Aldersgate, 1540.

........., Billingsgate, 3470.

St. Bride's, 555 ; parsonage granted to Wolsey, 857.

St. Clement Danes, 2034, 3743.

St. Dunstan-in-the-West, 3465.

St. Faith, 3761.

St. Giles - without - Cripplegate, 671, 1554, 2097, 3406, 3407, 4643.

.... in-the-Fields, 730.

St. Helen, Bishopsgate, nuns of, 1259, 5735 ; prioress of, 4136.

St. James's, Garlikhithe, 3406, 3407, 4643.

St. John the Baptist, Walbrook, 965, 1196.

St. John's Hosp., 511.

.... Street, als. Cow Cross, 3954.

St. Katharine's Hosp., near the Tower, 121, 3456, 5735 ; master of, John Preston, 1972.

St. Lawrence, Jewry, 1554.

.... Pountney, 1363.

.... Lane, 1528, 4643.

St. Margaret's, 844.

........., Lothbury, 186.

.... Moyses, Friday Street, 1396.

.... Pattens, 501..

St. Martin's, 1540.

St. Mary, Aldermary, 3407, 4600.

St. Mary Axe, ch. of, 4993.

.... Barking, church of, 5242.

........., Bethlehem, hospital of, warden of, 3099, 4201.

........., Bishopsgate, hospital of, 5534 ; prior of, Ric. Cressall, 4931.

.... Bothowe, Dowgate ward, 1774.

.........-le-Bow, 3406, 3407, 4643.

........., Colchurch, 1269, 5568.

.... of Graces near the Tower, abbey of, 1843 ; abbot of, 1972.

.... Magdalen, Milk Street, 827, 1608 ; incumbent of, Nich. Curlens, 1742.

.... Matfelon, 1540.

.... Wolchurch, 1596.

London, streets, parishes, &c., in and adjoining—*cont.*

St. Michael Basingshawe, 137, 1253,
1540, 4984.

........., Cornhill, 1259, 4136.

........., Paternoster, 1508.

.........., Queenhithe, 1336, 3406,
3407, 4643.

St. Mildred, Poultry, 632, 3537.

St. Nicholas Acorn, 1540.

.... Fleshambles (or Shambles),
3445, 4780.

St. Pancras, 3407.

St. Paul's Cathedral, 1212, 3339,
4582, 5111.

.........., convocation at, 2004, 4128,
4312, 4876.

.........., document dated, 3861.

.........., quire of, 5735.

.........., college near, 1982.

.........., dean of. *See* Colet, John.

.... School, foundation of, 1076,
1933, 3158, 4659.

St. Peter in Cheap, 827, 1608, 3406,
3407, 4643.

St. Sepulchre's - without - Newgate,
508, 1540, 1656, 2034, 3600,
4780.

St. Stephen, Coleman Street, church
of, 1776, 3767.

St. Swithin, Candelwick Street,
church of, 1212.

.........., ..., parish, 425, 3406,
3407, 4643.

St. Thomas of Acon, hospital of,
1883, 1918, 5427.

........., ..., master of, John Yong,
1972.

Smithfield, or West Smithfield, 3954,
4780, 5383.

Snowre Hill, St. Sepulchre's, 508.

"Sterr," the, in Cheap, 1528, 4643.

Swan, the, near the great conduit in
Cheap, 3406, 3407, 4643.

Tower, the, 12, 590, 596, 1190, 1192,
1212 (p. 180), 1272, 2012,
3496, 3865, 4825, 4977, 5172.

.........., bowmaker and keeper of
bows in, 3095.

.........., constable of, Sir Thos.
Lovell, 3810.

.........., gunners in, 3156, 3262,
4591, 4674, 5340, 5545.

.........., the King's garden in, 590,
1888.

.........., the King's ironworks in,
4774.

.........., lions in the, 3855.

.........., Martin Tower in, near the
Lions' Tower, 689.

.........., Mint in, 3006, 4917.

.........., ordnance in, 3904, 4375.

London, streets, parishes, &c., in and adjoining—*cont.*

........., ordnance house in, 3496
(p. 433).

Tower, the, rectory of St. Peter's in,
661.

.... Hill, abbey of St. Mary of
Graces, 5243.

........., ..., abbot of, 4766.

Trinity, Holy, priory of. *See* Aldgate.

"Walsheman," the, in Fleet Street,
1389.

Warwick's Inn, 4321, 4846.

Watling Street, 1825, 3406, 3407,
4643.

White Bear, the, in St. Lawrence
Jewry, 1554.

Whitecross Street, 671, 3406, 3407,
4643.

Wood Street, 1608.

.........., Bishop of. *See* FitzJames.

London, John, 436.

Long, Sir Hen., in commission of peace for
Wilts, 1489, 4583.

........, ..., sheriff of Wilts, 1949.

........, ..., in debt to the Crown, 1372, 5633.

........, ..., in the war, 4102, 4258.

........, Ric., 3213, 3899, 4635.

Long Assheton, Somers., 4363.

Longbows, Act for shooting with, 2082.

Longdon, 1480, 4694.

.........., John. *See* Langdon.

.........., Robt., of Cornwall, 5561.

Longes, Merkes, 696.

Longland, John, DD., 4181. *See* Langland.

Longmede, Nich., captain, 3980. *See* Langmede.

Long Staunton, Camb., 5069.

Longueville, Normandy, 3195.

.........., Louis d'Orleans, Duke of, Marquis of
Rothelin, 4725, 5284, 5285, 5302, 5330,
5337, 5360, 5368, 5462, 5468, 5505,
5513, 5523, 5547, 5560, 5569, 5590
5675.

.........., ..., in Guienne, 3112, 3357, 3584.

.........., ..., invades Biscay, 3593.

.........., ..., taken prisoner at battle of Spurs,
4253, 4284, 4401, 4402, 4405, 4418,
4431, 4432, 4433, 4464, 5111.

.........., ... his ransom, 5173, 5270.

.........., ..., commissioner of Lewis XII.,
5278, 5279, 5280, 5306, 5343, 5408,
5482.

.........., ..., proxy for Lewis XII. at the
marriage ceremony, 5311, 5322.

.........., ..., letters from, 4883, 5329, 5373,
5381.

.........., ..., his signature, 5305, 5307.

.... Herald, 4710.

.... Sir John, 105, 953.

Longwittenham, Berks, 1203, 3005.

Lonkester. *See* Lancaster.

Lonnysburgh, Wm. de, 415.

Lontrotrence, 5259, 5338, 5366.

Lopez, Leonard, LL.D., ambassador of Ferdinand, 3081, 3082, 3083, 3106, 3107, 3146, 3279.

........., Antonio and Peter, French merchants, 3424.

Lord, Geo., 391.

......, or Laward, Rob., 4884.

Loretto, pilgrimage of Julius II. to, 1918, 1997.

Lorraine, 3945.

........., John of, 4576.

........., Duke of, 4924, 5781.

........., ..., taken prisoner, 4284.

Losenmarle, in France, 4253.

Lostwithiel, Cornwall, 397, 1349.

Loterell, Sir Hugh. See Luttrell.

Lother. See Lowther.

Lothyngland, Suff., 179, 1446.

Louder, James, 1864.

Loudondale, Chester, 4657.

Loughborough church, Linc. dioc., 42.

........., Leicestershire, 730, 806, 1788.

Loughrig, Westmoreland, 3764.

Loughton, 3442.

Lourchecomb, Devon, 5618.

Louvain, 3637, 4526, 4851, 5117, 5163, 5173.

Love, Anth., goldsmith, 3491.

......, John, dyer, 4013.

......, Nich., gunner, 3156, 3262.

......, Reginald, draper, 4999.

......, Reynold, 4865.

Loveday, Nowell, page of the cellar, 3954.

........., Walter, captain, 4376, 4377, 4474, 4869, 5017, 5761, 5790.

........., Wm., 5528.

Lovekyn, Geo., 592, 1204.

Lovel, lordship of, 804.

........., ——, 4153.

........., Francis, Viscount (temp. Hen. VII.,) possessions of, 682, 1207, 1487, 1711, 1772, 1774, 1864, 2055, 3149, 3190, 3239, 3244, 3266, 3284, 3384, 3401, 3411, 3497, 3761, 4022, 4303, 4592, 4594, 4657, 4785, 4852, 4904, 5016, 5086, 5146, 5440.

........., Rob., grant to, 1666.

........., Sir Rob., in commission for Norfolk, 266, 1340, 1714, 1812, 1963, 3029, 3426, 3545, 5133.

........., Sir Thos., 22, 226, 235, 258, 275, 342, 367, 566, 606, 697, 721, 722, 750, 765, 779, 799, 926, 953, 1026, 1052, 1212, 1399, 1421, 1699, 1707, 1756, 1757, 1758, 3049, 3284, 3353, 3422, 3497, 3832, 4116, 4239, 4414, 4442, 4452, 4711, 4830, 5090, 5407, 5608, 5692.

........., ..., chancellor of the Exchequer, 5097.

........., ..., in commission for Berks, 241, 885, 1393, 1481, 1732, 2095, 3640, 4541, 5166, 5684.

........., ..., in commission for Herts, 309, 706, 1020, 1971, 3102, 5506.

Lovel, Sir Thos., in commission for Middlesex, 3552, 4663, 5506.

........., ..., in commission for Norfolk, 1340, 1714, 1963, 3029, 3426, 3545, 5133.

........., ..., in commission for Notts, 1514, 1798, 1964, 3092, 3494, 4776, 5225, 5506.

........., ..., in commission for Oxon, 766, 1216, 1470, 1745, 3015, 4559, 4809, 5506.

........., ..., in commission for Staffordshire, 279, 713, 791, 886, 1770, 5506.

........., ..., in commission for Surrey, 1427, 1762, 3078, 3092, 4693, 4734, 5237, 5506.

........., ..., in commission in Sussex, 297.

........., ..., in commission for Yorksh., 5529, 5605.

........., ..., in commission of array, 1735, 1804, 3116, 4434, 5529, 5626.

........., ..., justice of gaol delivery for St. Alban's, 4742.

........., ..., justice of gaol delivery for Newgate, 1547, 1942, 3765.

........., ..., justice of gaol delivery for Surrey, 1548, 4568.

........., ..., executor of Henry VII., 3292, 5737.

........., ..., executor of the Countess of Richmond, 236, 406.

........., ..., in the war, 3231, 3977, 4377, 4653.

........., ..., knighted at Tournay, 4468.

........., ..., grants to, 276, 600, 604, 861, 1621, 1737, 3242, 3541, 3810, 4217, 4263, 4436, 5709.

........., ..., his signature, 14, 15, 55, 71, 72, 164, 165, 313, 336, 503, 511, 531, 576, 639, 650, 782, 785, 955, 956, 1068, 1264, 1272, 1273, 1372, 1527, 1539, 1574, 1584, 1604, 1755, 1840, 2027, 2029, 3027, 4620, 5014, 5015, 5020, 5087, 5735, 5737, 5779.

........., ..., letters from, 5151, 5270.

........., ..., junior, captain, 3980.

........., Wm., in commission for Dorset, 2007, 3064, 3566, 3606, 3701, 4713, 5658.

........., ... See Morley, Lord.

........., ..., Viscount, 3190.

Lovel Upton. See Upton Lovel.

Lovelace, Sir Ric., under marshal of Calais, 1670, 1792, 1838, 4219.

........., ——, of Kent, 777.

Lovett, John, 3465.

........., Thos., of Northampton, 732, 1708, 1971, 4544, 5561.

........., ..., grant to, 1175.

Low Countries, 490, 796, 924, 3112, 3248, 3496, 3662, 3751, 3752, 3828, 3847, 4081, 4087, 4091, 4309, 4319, 4329, 4365,

Low Countries—*cont.*
4456, 4682, 4692, 4755, 4830, 4977, 5076, 5140, 5159, 5173, 5424, 5429, 5468, 5475, 5554, 5697.
........., men of, 3590, 4253, 4274, 4416, 4863, 5292, 5379, 5386.
........., French ambassador in. *See* France.
........., the estates of, 4924.
........., provisions to be exported to, 3445.
........., sovereign of, 5139, 5341.
.... , English army in, 4794, 4798.
........., imports from, 3784, 4552.
........., coinage, 1500, 4481, 4831, 4917.
........., tolls in, 3053.
........., Scotch merchants to, 3629.
........., ship of, 3326.
........., biscuit, 5724.
........., English commissioners in, 4478, 5723.
........., wheat, 5760.
Lowe, Devon, 3978.
...... *See* Ships.
......, church of, 1556.
......, Humph. and Dionysius, of Denbigh, 4836.
Lowestoft, abbey at, 79, 155.
Lowman, Wm., 202.
Lowrans, Tho., clerk, 532.
Lowre, Wm., of Cornwall, 1434, 1694, 1812, 1984, 3290, 3583, 3605, 3938, 4754, 5220, 5431, 5474, 5586.
Lowson, Tho., of Yorkshire, 1392.
Lowth, Wm., prior of St. Mary's, Walsingham, 5522.
........., (Louthe), Tho., in commission for Huntingdon, 905, 916, 1095, 4006.
........., ..., justice of gaol delivery for Ramsey, 959, 1222, 3652.
Lowther, Sir Hugh, of Cumberland, 664.
........., Lancelot, of the Welsh Marches, 99, 512, 1682.
Loxley, Staff., 1986.
Loyal, Wm., 4479.
Loye, Th. of London, 3022.
Lubeck, 2077, 3367, 5776.
Lubeckers, 1195, 3138, 3629.
Lubiana, 5171.
Lucas, Nicholas de, of Sergo, 3383.
........., Tho., 22, 226, 258, 275, 367, 566, 606, 721, 799, 926, 953, 1052, 1399, 1421, 1699, 1965, 3284.
........., ..., in com. for Suffolk, 280, 1121, 1153, 1534, 1715, 3029, 3219, 4713, 5133.
........., ..., his offices, 265, 878, 1125 ; debtor to Hen. VII., 1639, 3497 ; in the war against France, 3231.
Lucca, 684, 1574, 1584, 3124, 3274, 3325, 3472, 3710, 3898, 3965, 4097, 4145, 4188, 4260, 4269, 4957, 5138, 5213, 5221.
Lucerne, 3112, 3651, 3752.
Luchington, John, 3845.
Lucian, 3159.

Lucy, Edm., son of Sir Wm. of Charlecote, Warwick, 255.
......, Sir Edm., 1789, 4377.
......, Eliz., sister of Sir Thos., 3442.
......, Sir Tho., of Charlecote, Warwick, 255, 568, 933, 1818, 1854, 3434, 3442, 4150, 5656, 5679.
......, ..., in the war against France, 3591, 3885, 4307, 4314.
......, ..., King's sewer, 518, 1268, 3516.
......, ..., challenger at birth of a Prince, 1491.
......, ..., debtor to the King, 2044.
......, ..., in commission for Northampton, 732, 1708, 1971, 5658.
......, ..., erroneously called John, 255.
......, Sir Wm., 255.
Luddynglond, Suff., 155.
Ludgarsale, Wilts, 1318.
Ludgate (Ludeyate), Wm., 1444.
Ludlow, Salop, 1390.
........., castle of, 127.
........., St. John's, 1650.
........., John, sheriff of Wilts, 4544, 5561.
........., Morys, 1118.
Luffield, 3297.
Lugano, 3269.
Lugo, 3112.
Luke, Anne, late nurse to the King, wife of Walter, 284, 3184.
........., Walter, 284, 1733.
........., ..., in com. for Bedfordshire, 907, 1051, 1122, 1922, 2045, 3501, 4700.
........., ..., in com. for Huntingdon, 905, 916, 1095, 4006.
........., Robt., monk of Lanthony, 5789.
Luke. *See* Liege.
Lullingham, 4253.
Lullingston, 3297.
Lullingston-Dancy, Oxon, 3297.
Lullynston, Kent, 1350.
Lumley, Rog., 5782.
........., John Lord, 5616.
Lupez. *See* Lopez, Leonard.
Lupset, [Thos.], 1404, 4336.
Lupton, Ralph, clerk, 4942.
........., Rog., clerk of the Hanaper, 365, 459, 967, 3365, 4218, 5460, 5516, 5735.
........., ..., in commission of the peace for Bucks, 3219, 3310, 3522.
........., ..., receiver of petitions, 811, 2082.
Lurchestrother, town of, 4556.
Lurkbear, 2080.
Lusa, Mons. de, 4267 (p. 615).
Luske, 5788.
Lussura, Nich., 3762.
Luston, 3203.
Lusy, Anthony de, 4326.

Lusy, John de, 4517, 4534.

Lute, Roger, 4067.

Luttichaw, Sifridus de, ambassador of George Duke of Saxony, 1565, 1717, 1718.

Luttrell or Loterell, Sir Hugh, in com. for Somerset, 287, 712, 3048, 3566, 3585, 3606, 3701, 4713, 5506 (p. 904).

........., ..., in the war against France, 4377.

Lutzenburg, Ant., 4427.

Laxembourg, 3945, 4349.

........., (Luxonbroght), Mons. Charles de, 5163.

Lwke. See Liege.

Lyance, Lewis, 4745.

Lyde (cinque port), 4996.

Lye, Hen., 1854.

......, Sir John, of Hants, 1812.

......, Ric., abbot of Shrewsbury, 3093, 3221, 3222.

......, Wm., a yeoman of the chamber, 457, 1619.

Lyele. See Lisle.

Lyerville, Sieur de. See Thylny.

Lygon, Ric., 1174, 1971.

Lyme, Dorset, 3978.

......, Sir Thos., 4544.

Lymington, Hants, 2080, 4074. See also Ships.

Lympyn, John, mayor of Exeter, 304.

Lymster, Wm., 1921.

Lynch, Wm., 4949.

Lynde, Sir Thos., in commission for Somerset and Dorset, 3701, 4713, 5658.

Lynden, John, archer à cheval, 4476.

........., Hen., of Hoorne, 1769.

Lyneham, Devon, 5648.

Lynley, Salop, 4071.

Lynn, Bishop's, 4640, 4859.

........., ..., commission of the peace for, 3210.

........., ..., gaol deliveries for, 884, 5236.

........., Norfolk, 378, 592, 3234, 3751, 5723.

.... See Ships.

Lynne, Wm., of Northampton, 664, 1316, 1641.

Lynom, Thos., in commission for Wales and the Western Counties, 918, 955, 956, 1049, 1400, 1469, 1695, 1963, 1971, 1981, 3055, 3071, 3289, 3301, 3641, 3686, 3709, 3712, 3715, 3804, 4024, 4113, 4198, 4394, 4770, 4827, 5506.

Lynryche, Warwick, 2049, 5435.

Lyonnois, 3752.

Lyons, 4091, 4326, 4359, 5588, 5675.

Lypwsca. See Guipuscoa.

Lysk, in France, 4253.

Lysley. See Lisle.

Lyston, Devon, 367, 436, 721.

Lyth, Yorkshire, 3018. See Pickering Lith.

.... See Leith.

Lyttsteyne, Sir Paul, 1697.

Lyxborne, 3355.

M.

Mabankes, in Ewhurst, Surrey, 1488, 1916.

Mabelthorp, Linc., 1958.

Macclesfield, Chesh., 1524, 1626.

Machado, Roger, Clarencieux King-at-arms, 428, 556.

Machell, Dr., 4652.

Machyn, Essex, 734.

Macivelli, An., 5352.

Madeley, Tho., 334.

Madeleyn, Essex, 734.

.... Laver, Essex, 734.

Madison, Edw., 4425.

........., John, 1832.

.... See Matison.

Madok, Wm., 671.

Madrid, 796 (p. 117), 819 (p. 124).

........., letters dated at, 4578, 4985.

Madringham, Linc., 3284, 4852.

Maestrich, in the Low Countries, 4322.

Magnesia, 3697.

Magnus, in Germany, 4272.

Magnus, Peter, 4916.

........., Tho., the King's Chaplain, 4375.

........., ..., Archdeacon of the East Riding, Yorksh., 5250.

........., ..., in Scotland, 4825.

........., ..., letter from, 4682.

Magorney's lands, Berks, 1825.

Mahieu, Jehan, 4445 (ii.).

Mahometanism, 4173, 5705.

Maydencote, parcel of Magorney's lands, Berks, 1825.

Maidstone, Kent, 3792, 4291.

........., commission of gaol-delivery for, 763.

........., college of, 4784.

Maine, in France, 3174.

Mainwaring, Chas., 4565.

........., Geo., 3507.

........., John, in the war with France, 3885, 4307, 4253 (p. 608), 4314.

........., ..., in commission for Salop, 4827.

........., Sir John, knighted at Tournay, 4468.

........., ..., in the war with France, 4253 (p. 608).

........., ..., in commission for Salop, 4394.

Mainwaring, Peter, 232,

........., Rondell, 4253 (p. 608).

Majorca, Bishop of, 8 (p. 3).

Makesoun, James, 925.

Makworth, Geo., on sheriff-roll for Rutland, 664, 1316.

........., ..., sheriff of Rutland, 1949.

Malacca, in India, 4173.

Malaga, Bishop of, p. 3.

Maland, Nich., 4335.

........., ... See also Marland, Nich.

Malaspina, Barnabus, Marquis, 4499.

Malchanger (Malishangre), privy seal dated at, 1206.

Maldon, ship of. See Ships.

Male, yeoman of the, 4342.

Malefantes lands, in cos. Glamorgan and Cardiff, 110, 441, 1113.

Malengose, lands in, Cornwall, 3436.

Malenous in France, 4284 (p. 625).

Malet. See Mallet.

Malham, ——, 12.

Malines. See Mechlin.

Maliverer, Earl of, Grand Seneschal of Normandy, 5482. See Maulevrier.

........., ——, captain, 3980 (p. 553).

........., Joan, 3182.

........., Ric., in commission for co. York, 1735 (bis), 1804, 3358.

........., ..., in the Spanish expedition, 5744.

........., Sir Ric., 4902.

Mallerstang, Westmor., 1796.

Mallet, Baldwin, in commission for Somerset, 287, 712, 1761, 3048, 3566, 3585, 3606, 3701, 4713, 5506 (p. 904).

........., Bertroul, 4445 (i).

........., James, D.D., canon of Windsor, 4856, 5520.

Malley, Agnes, daughter of Rob. de, 1699.

........., Rob. de, 1669.

Malling, Kent, 3969.

........., South, 1575.

Malmesbury, [Wilts], 155,

........., monastery of, 852, 1183, 1929, 1930, 3484, 5536.

........., abbot of, 849, 852, 1183, 1620, 1806, 1929, 1930.

........., ..., in commission for Wilts, 3157, 3605, 4583.

........., ..., summoned to Parliament, 5616.

Malmshill Lacy (or Lucy), Heref., 1127, 4862, 5551.

Malory, Anth., in commission for Hunts, 916, 1095, 4006, 5506 (p. 905).

........., Nic., in commission for co. Warw., 282, 1387, 1468, 1971, 3364.

Malpasse, [Chesh.], 1264.

Malt, 4868.

Maltby, John, incumbent of Hemeswell, Linc., dioc., 3770, 3906.

........., ..., incumbent of Northlewe, Exeter dioc., 1542, 4243.

........., ..., incumbent of Wassbynburgh, Linc. dioc., 3264.

Malton, Yorksh., 5655.

Malton, Rob., incumbent of Borough, Norw. dioc., 417.

Maltravers, Anne, wife of Wm. Lord, 1517, 5150.

........., William Lord, son of Thos. Earl of Arundel, grants to, 998, 999, 1517, 5150.

........., ..., in the war against France, 4306.

........., ..., in commission for Dorset, 26, 708, 903, 2007, 3064, 3566, 3606, 3701, 4713.

........., ..., in commission for Hants, 904, 1388, 3071, 4159, 4676.

........., ..., in commission for Somerset, 287, 712, 3048, 3566, 3585, 3606, 3701, 4713.

........., ..., in commission for Sussex, 281, 1509, 3024, 3428, 4801.

........., in commission for Wilts, 898, 1489, 1938, 3157, 3605, 4583.

Malvenda, Peter de, of Burgus, Spain, merchant, 1859, 2047.

Malvern Chase, Worc., 3613.

........., prior of, indebted to Hen. VII., 3497 (p. 435).

........., Tho., prior of, indebted to Hen. VII., 1639.

........., Wm., abbot of Gloucester, 5061, 5075, 5344. See Gloucester, abbey of.

Malyard, Anth., of London, 1528, 4643.

Malyn, John, abbot of Waltham Holy Cross, 5065.

........., Ric., 3051.

Mamotrectus, said by Erasmus to abound in blunders, 5352.

Man, Alice, 5260.

......, John, in commission for Berks, 2095, 3640, 4341, 5166.

......, ..., prior of St. John's Hospital, Canterbury, 1065.

Manachan, Alexander, captain, 5761 (p. 973).

Manaton, 2080.

Manche, 3945.

Manchester, 4975.

Maneryng, Rog., 1543.

Manfroy, the Earl, 5482.

Manliana, in Italy, letter dated from, 5099.

Manners, ——, at the marriage of Princess Mary, 5483.

........., Sir Geo., 380, 1762.

........., ..., annuity to, 750.

Manners, Sir Geo., on the sheriff-roll for Surrey and Sussex, 664.

........., ..., in commission for Surrey, 3092.

........., ..., in commission to review the army, 3173.

........., ..., summoned to Parliament by name of George Manners Lord Rose, 3540.

........., George, Lord Roos, in the war against France, 3864, 3885, 4237, 4314.

........., Th., 3650.

Manselya, in Spain, 796 (pp. 113 and 119), 819 (p. 123).

Mansfield, Notts, 1633, 1809, 4694.

........., Woodhouse, Notts, 1633, 4694.

Mantell, John, 1520.

........., Walter, son of John, 1520.

Mantholme, Yorkshire, 367, 721.

Mantua, 1458, 3026, 3269 (p. 368), 3325 (pp. 380–384), 3976.

........., English ambassador to, 5680.

........., letters dated at, 4887, 4920, 5409, 5417, 5601.

........., Cardinal of, 3269 (p. 368).

........., Francis Gonzaga, Marquis of, gonfalonier, in the Italian war, 11, 216, 3325 (p. 383), 3976.

........., ..., ..., taken prisoner by the Venetians, 490 (p. 68).

........., ..., ..., his ambassador in France, 3269 (p. 368).

........., ..., ..., included in a treaty between France and Castile, 4924.

........., ..., ..., Henry VIII. sends horses to, 5076.

........., ..., ..., letters from, 4887, 4920, 5409.

........., ..., letters to, 1462, 1877, 5258, 5339, 5417, 5601.

Mantuanus, Bapt., poems of, 5352.

Manuel, Don Juan de, 3805, 4328, 4725, 5076.

Maperley, John, 4728.

Mapilthorp, Linc., 1323, 4566.

Maquelu, a Frenchman, 4162.

Marano, town of, in Italy, 5126.

........., battle at, 5290.

Maraton, Lewis de, the Emperor's secretary, 1902, 3314, 3335, 3340, 3353, 3363, 3377, 3381, 3385, 3396, 3419, 3499, 4091, 4216, 4322, 4355, 4364, 4433, 4725, 4851, 5055, 5094, 5105, 5155, 5207.

........., ..., sent to Ferdinand, 5006.

........., ..., letters from, 3648, 4304, 4305.

........., ..., letter to, 3647.

Marba. See Morbage.

Marbury, John, clk., 3719, 4496.

........., Rob., 235, 942, 3719, 5202.

Marc. See Mark.

Marcer. See Mercer.

March, Heref., 155.

........., in the Low Countries, 3945.

March, Wales, earldom of, 58, 487, 1648, 4575, 4738, 4862, 5002, 5641.

........., ..., ..., auditor of, 321.

........., ..., ..., overseers of, 1472, 1678, 4022.

........., ..., ..., receiver-general of, 298.

........., Earl of, 778.

........., Earls of, founders of the Priory of Walsingham, 5522.

March and Ulster, Anne Countess of, 1129, 1603.

........., Herald, arrived in Scotland from France, 5641.

........., ——— le, 5681.

Marcham, Wm., 1911.

Marchant, Collin, 4445 (i.).

Marches of Scotland, the, 3577, 4105, 4520, 4652, 4870, 4902, 4951, 5090.

........., Lord Wardens of, 1850, 1907, 2028, 2035, 3359. See also Darcy, Th. Lord, and Dacre, Th. Lord.

........., wardens general of, 283.

........., warden courts in the, 1850, 2035.

........., of Wales. See Wales.

Marchienne, letter dated, 4450.

Marck, Erard De la, Bp. of Liege (Luke) and Chartres, 4319, 5408 (3).

........., Rob. De la, 4182, 5539.

........., ..., in Italy, 3325 (p. 384), 3752, 4329.

........., Sir Rob. De la, his standard taken at Terouenne, 4253 (p. 610).

........., Rob. De la, his son, 3945 ; slain in Italy, 4328.

Marden (Merden), Kent, 47, 95, 727, 1085, 2088, 3043.

Mardewell, 1906.

Mardike, the, Linc., 3072.

Mares, Mons. de, 4956.

Margaret Countess of Richmond, grandmother of Henry VIII. See Richmond.

Margaret of Savoy, 216, 922, 923, 3077, 3291, 3302, 3306, 3325, 3333, 3334, 3335, 3340, 3353, 3361, 3387, 3415, 3425, 3446, 3463, 3471, 3481, 3500, 3555, 3647, 3651, 3678, 3731, 3779, 3805, 3814, 3817, 3835, 3836, 3915, 4054, 4085, 4086, 4087, 4164, 4216, 4253, 4274, 4284, 4309, 4319, 4323, 4326, 4328, 4331, 4343, 4355, 4364, 4365, 4366, 4389, 4418, 4429, 4433, 4502, 4512, 4546, 4561, 4577, 4609, 4642, 4725, 4743, 4829, 4844, 4845, 4902, 4929, 4932, 4935, 4976, 4978, 5006, 5029, 5030, 5035, 5076, 5104, 5105, 5207, 5208, 5263, 5299, 5320, 5327, 5341, 5386, 5387, 5404, 5467, 5518, 5657, 5675, 5676, 5757.

........., ..., conferences with, 3314, 3331, 3370, 3376, 3377, 3381, 3385, 3396, 3398, 3419, 3437, 3499, 3525, 4091, 4163, 4182, 4296, 4789, 5059, 5117 5171, 5292, 5362.

Margaret of Savoy—*cont.*

...., instructions given by her, 4917, 5368.

...., ambassadors to, 3112, 3258, 3271, 3405, 3847, 4831, 4955, 5055, 5094, 5139, 5386, 5398, 5418, 5713.

...., her negotiations with England and Arragon, 27, 924, 3460, 3469.

...., her servants, 3435, 4078, 4585, 4973, 5163.

...., letters from, 1458, 1902, 3207, 3367, 3417, 3571, 3815, 3823, 3873, 3918, 3975, 4090, 4154, 4155, 4168, 4193, 4393, 4396, 4407, 4426, 4622, 4726, 4833, 4851, 5018, 5714.

...., letters to, 117, 224, 841, 1245, 2042, 2043, 3067, 3892, 4059, 4308, 4329, 4380, 4386, 4399, 4401, 4405, 4415, 4437, 4509, 4910, 4952, 4953, 5041, 5057, 5140, 5148, 5158, 5203, 5367, 5407, 5526.

...., her treaties, 1267, 1417, 3603, 3859, 3860, 3861, 4510, 4560, 5479.

...., her signature, 3973.

...., English ordnance in her possession, 3616, 4977.

...., reports of her intended marriage with the Duke of Suffolk, 4850, 4851.

Margaret of Scotland, 3083, 3323, 3814, 3882, 4112, 4483, 4523, 4619, 4666, 4997, 5453, 5628 ; afraid of Albany's coming, 5614 ; taken by Arran from Stirling to Edinburgh, 5641.

...., gives birth to a Prince, who dies, 3577, 3631, 3882.

...., complaints of her dower being withheld, 3883, 4403, 5681.

...., mention of documents concerning, 5274.

...., proposed marriage with Maximilian, 5208 ; and with Lewis XII., 5368.

...., married to Angus, 5370.

...., letters to Henry VIII., 3875, 5614. *See also* 4682.

...., ... to Q. Katharine, 4424, 4549.

...., ... to Ferdinand of Arragon, 3082.

...., ... to K. of Denmark, 1416.

...., letter of Leo X. to, 5678.

...., her chaplain, 3622.

Margysson, 4253.

Marhall, Wm. *See* Marshal, Wm.

Marigny, ——, with the Princess Mary, 5379, 5462, 5469.

.... (Mareny), bailly of Senlys, 5468 (p. 895).

Maring, Walter, 1965.

Marinis, Brankinus de, Genoese merchant, 808.

.........., Lorenzo de, merchant of Genoa, 4246, 4350.

Mariswell, ——, captain, 4377 (p. 651).

Mark (Marc), (in the marches of Calais, 4392 (ii).

....., church of, 38.

..:... and Oye, lordship of, marches of Calais, 528, 1131, 1241, 1822, 3832, 4022, 4392, 4665, 4933.

......, Wm., chaplain, 4841.

Market Deping, Linc., 3175, 5682.

Markfield, Leic., 3096.

Markham, John, in commission for Linc., 4860.

.........., ..., in commission for Notts, 1735, 1804.

.........., Sir John, knighted at Tournay, 4468.

Markinfield, Ninian, 3515.

Marland, Nich., sub-marshal of Calais, 4635.

.........., ..., in the war against France, 3231, 4534, 4632.

.........., ... *See also* Maland, Nich.

Marlborough, Wilts, 1002, 1913.

.... Berton, Wilts, 155.

Marler, Th., 3497 (ii).

.........., ..., bailiff of Colrugge, Devon, 1321.

.........., ..., in commission for co. York, 273.

Marliano, Michael de, 3269 (p. 368).

Marlion, Lewis de, physician to the Prince of Castile, 3335, 3377, 4091.

Marlow, Bucks, 93.

Marmion, Th., 3497 (ii.).

Marnix, [John de], secretary of Margaret of Savoy, 3335, 3377, 3385, 3398, 3405, 3962, 4328, 4386, 4415.

.........., ..., ..., letter to, 4830.

Marny, Mr., 5659.

...., Sir Henry, 236, 425, 697, 1639, 4307, 5019, 5265, 5385, 5431.

.........., ..., executor of Margaret Countess of Richmond, 406.

.........., ..., in the war against France, 3231, 3885, 4192, 4237, 4238, 4259, 4284 (p. 623), 4306, 4314, 4377 (p. 651), 4475.

.........., ..., grants to, 48, 222, 406, 4205, 4231.

.........., ..., signs as member of the Privy Council, 313, 336, 480, 511, 576, 594, 625, 756, 1004, 1068, 1264, 1273, 1288, 1321, 1372, 1378, 1527, 1539, 1540, 1574, 1596, 1604, 1699, 1755, 1756, 1757, 1758, 1840, 2027, 2029, 3080.

.........., ..., captain of the Guard, 30.

.........., ..., vice-chamberlain, 30, 5111.

.........., ..., chancellor of the duchy of Lancaster, 474 (misprinted Verney), 944, 3886.

.........., ..., justice of gaol delivery for Newgate, 1547, 3765.

.........., ..., ... for Surrey, 1548.

.........., ..., in commission for Cornwall, 891, 1694, 1984, 3290, 3583, 3605, 3938, 4754, 5220, 5586.

.........., ..., ... for Essex, 310, 1368, 1522, 1713, 3605, 3785, 3967.

Marny, Sir Henry, in other commissions, 3006, 3116, 3173, 5431.

........., Sir John, son of Sir Henry, 4307, 5019.

........., ..., on sheriff-roll for Somers. and Dors., 1316.

........., ..., knighted at Tournay, 4468.

........., John, squire of the Body, grant to, 47.

........., ..., justice of gaol delivery for Colchester, 3464.

........., ..., in commission for Dorset, 2007, 3064, 3566, 3606, 3701, 4713.

........., ..., in commission for Essex, 3605, 3785, 3967.

Marrane. See Marano.

Marret, Wm., 5047.

Marrex, And., 117.

Marriage annulled, 1441.

Marruffo, Raphael, merchant of Genoa, 4003, 4114.

Mars, alias Masse, Margaret, daughter of William, 5531.

........, ..., Wm., 5531.

Marsakavyr, in Barbary, 490 (p. 70).

Marseilles, Bp. of, 5106.

Marshal of England. See Surrey, Thomas, Earl of.

Marshal [or Marhall), Rob., 3497 (p. 435).

........., Wm., 3576.

........., ..., justice of gaol delivery, 3694.

........., ..., in commission for Beds, 1051, 1122, 2045, 3501, 4700.

Marshalsea, Marshal of the (Duke of Suffolk), 5079.

Marshwod, Somers., 155.

Marston, Bucks, 1352.

........., Linc. See Merston.

........., Northt., 3027.

........., John. See Merston, John.

Martendale, Robt, 4004.

Martin, Essex, 734.

........., Linc., 3284, 4852.

........., Westmor., 1090, 5395.

.... in Campis, St., near Paris, prior of, 3944.

Martin, ——, 4445.

........., alias Perkins, Anth., 2034.

........., Eliz., Act for the restitution of, 2082.

........., Godfrey, 85.

........., Hen. LL.B., incumbent of Radnor, 972.

........., John, 308

........., ..., merchant of Guernsey, 5720, (p. 957).

........., Piers, 1327.

........., Tho., 245, 1854.

Martock, Soms., 3038, 3567.

Marton. See Martin.

Martyr, Peter, letters from, 4096, 4324, 4371, 4449, 4464, 4513, 4525, 4574, 4666, 4845, 4864, 5152, 5267, 5470, 5581, 5592, 5642, 5718.

Martyr, Tho., 4067.

Marwell, Hants, 647.

Marwent, Wm., 1159.

Marwood, in the lordship of Barnard Castle, 364.

Marwood Hag, in the lordship of Barnard Castle, 363.

Marwood, Wm., 1812, 5180.

Mary, sister of Henry VIII., 3443, 3882, 4833, 5140, 5148, 5173, 5372, 5398, 5403, 5404, 5407, 5468, 5469, 5470, 5495, 5606, 5642, 5673, 5717, 5723, 5724.

........., ..., bequest to her, 236.

........., ..., personal appearance, 4953, 5203.

........., ..., her proposed marriage with Charles of Castile, 8, 27, 224, 240, 490, 4058, 4296, 4416, 4508, 4512, 4560, 4579, 4725, 4727, 4851, 4976, 5018, 5030, 5041, 5104, 5126, 5139, 5152, 5274, 5290, 5319.

........., ..., intrigues to break off the match, 4326, 4932, 5029, 5203.

........., ..., renunciation of the marriage, 5282.

........., ..., her marriage with Lewis XII., 5164, 5192, 5279, 5285, 5294, 5307, 5311, 5319, 5322, 5327, 5337, 5343, 5347, 5365, 5368, 5379, 5408, 5441, 5482, 5483.

........., ..., her dowry, 5286, 5480, 5497.

.... Queen of France, her coronation, 5547.

........., ..., inventory of her jewellery, &c., 5490, 5491, 5492.

........., ..., oration made to her by the University of Paris, 5638.

........., ..., apparel of, 5462.

........., ..., marriage with Duke of Suffolk, in France (in 1515), 3298.

........., ..., her servants, 482, 1078, 3483, 3738, 3823, 4509, 5360, 5394, 5401, 5406, 5422, 5451, 5453, 5484, 5489, 5553, 5571, 5628, 5703.

........., ..., letters from, 3892, 5463, 5488, 5489, 5505, 5513, 5582, 5589.

........., ..., letters to, 4606, 5287, 5329, 5330, 5359, 5373.

Mary of Hungary, 5018.

Mary Rose, (Sir Edw. Howard's ship,) 3422, 3591, 3977, 3979, 4377, 4474, 4535, p. 811, 5130,.5317, 5720, 5721, 5761.

.... , letters written in, 3820, 3857, 4019, 4020, 4076, 5130.

Mascallesbury, Essex, 735.

Masengarbe, Bertran, 4445.

Massagrosa, Mauro de, merchant of Lucca, 5138, 5213.

Mason, John, incumbent of St. John's, Exeter dioc., 1330.

........., Ric., 5296.

Masse. See Mars.

Massey, Eliz., 1784.

Massy, Hen., 4476.

Massy, Ralph, in commission for Oxon, 4559, 4809.

........., Thos. 4071, 4360.

Massingham, Norf., 825.

Mastaing Francois, de, grand bailly of Ghent, 4331.

Master, the Grand, 5379.

Masthorp, Rutland, 63.

Mathieson, John, 3106.

........., ..., called George, 3107.

Mathom, Worc., 3208.

Matilda, Empress, 34.

Matison, John, sent by James IV. to Ferdinand, 3279. *See* Madison.

Matston, Th., in commission for co. Glouc., 3641, 3712, 3804, 4024, 4118, 4764, 5506 (p. 906).

Matthew, ——, 3495, 4451.

........., Christ., 3960.

........., Sir Davy, 5789.

........., Edw., 4925.

........., Hen., prior of Ellerton, Yorksh., 1097.

........., John, 3096.

........., ..., of London, baker, 5723.

........., (Matheu). Meredith ap, and his son, 4253 (p. 609).

........., Robt., sheriff of co. Northt., 5561.

........., ..., on sheriff-roll, 664, 4544.

........., ..., in commission, 1708, 1971.

........., Wm., 3960.

Matthews, John, 5161.

Mattishall, Norf., 730.

Matyrdale, Katharine, 3939.

Maulevrier, Count de, 4465. *See* Maliverer.

Maunsell, Heref., 5272.

........., Lacy, Heref., 5384.

Mauncell, John, 3497 (ii); in com. for N. Hamp., 5346.

........., Rees, 5180.

Mauntell, Walter, 3492. *See* Mantell.

Maurice, mentioned by Erasmus, 4427.

Mawarden, Heref., 155.

Mawdesley, Gilbert, 1744.

Maxey, Northt., 306, 403, 645, 1784, 1993, 4199, 5296.

Maximilian, King of the Romans, commonly called Emperor, 8, 11, 922, 923, 924, 1676, 1681, 1701, 1918, 1948, 3112, 3269, 3276, 3291, 3302, 3314, 3325, 3328, 3331, 3333, 3334, 3335, 3339, 3340, 3341, 3353, 3363, 3370, 3377, 3381, 3385, 3387, 3396, 3405, 3415, 3419, 3425, 3435, 3443, 3457, 3460, 3463, 3469, 3471, 3481, 3489, 3499, 3500, 3514, 3555, 3647, 3648, 3651, 3658, 3678, 3731, 3752, 3777, 3780, 3817, 3829, 3837, 3847, 3862, 3863, 3876, 3887, 3897, 3945, 3962, 3976, 4055, 4058, 4075, 4090, 4091, 4094, 4112, 4130, 4163, 4165, 4168, 4182, 4196, 4216, 4232, 4253 (p. 609), 4272, 4273, 4276, 4280, 4296, 4309, 4319, 4327, 4328, 4331, 4349, 4361, 4362, 4364, 4366, 4396, 4429, 4455, 4463, 4502,

Maximilian, King of the Romans—*cont.*
4561, 4574, 4577, 4598, 4622, 4725, 4736, 4756, 4789, 4794, 4795, 4810, 4829, 4831, 4833, 4844, 4845, 4849, 4851, 4864, 4915, 4916, 4929, 4952, 4955, 4985, 5006, 5025, 5094, 5117, 5139, 5152, 5155, 5192, 5207, 5259, 5304, 5319, 5320, 5338, 5353, 5368, 5377, 5398, 5404, 5410, 5430, 5446, 5468, 5475, 5532, 5539, 5599, 5604, 5675, 5730, 5745, 5757. •

........., ..., treaties of, 27, 432, 1880, 2091, 3327, 3603, 3649, 3839, 3859, 3860, 3861, 4508, 4510, 4511, 4560, 4818, 4875, 4924.

........., ..., his alliance with Spain, 224.

........., ..., his wars with the Venetians, 490, 880 ; treaty with the Pope against them, 3614, 3662, 3678, 3777, 3829 ; inclined to peace with them, 1902, 3077, 4756, 4796, 4810, 4910, 4958, 5387, 5393, 5410, 5430, 5677, 5686.

........., ..., treaty of Ferdinand and Venetians against, 2075.

........., ..., Venetians opposed to, 3543.

........., ..., Bologna in his hands, 2039.

........., ..., his treaty with England, 3398, 3915, 4085, 4086.

........., ..., his double-dealing with England, 4978, 5018, 5029, 5030, 5041, 5059, 5076, 5104, 5105, 5140, 5158, 5178, 5203, 5267, 5290, 5377, 5407.

........., ..., offers Henry VIII. the imperial crown, 5105, 5158.

........., ..., invades France with Henry VIII., 4399, 4401, 4405, 4407, 4409, 4415, 4417, 4418, 4431, 4433, 4446, 4464, 4571.

........., ..., his demands for money from Henry VIII., 3276, 3835, 4077, 4085, 4086, 4087, 4091, 4435, 4910, 5018, 5155, 5158, 5171.

........., ..., audiences of ambassadors with, 3226, 3248, 3271, 4078, 4274, 4282, 4333, 4563, 5126, 5323, 5389, 5393.

........., ..., his movements, 3077, 3226, 3248, 3258, 3271, 3306, 3331, 3446, 3481, 3489, 3525, 3779, 3897, 4165, 4272, 4305, 4322, 4326, 4355, 4359, 4364, 4389, 4561, 4978, 5055, 5259, 5290, 5366, 5389.

........., ..., gun given to Henry VIII. by, 4977.

........., ..., letters patent of, 3526, 4494, 5466.

........., ..., his person described, 4284 (p. 625), and deportment, ib., (p. 627).

........., ..., suffers from a disease in the leg, 5323, 5338, 5366.

........., ..., letters from, 1221, 3067, 4059, 4509, 4615, 5057, 5058.

........., ..., letters to, 1195, 1700, 1828, 1875, 3188, 4850, 5173.

........., ..., his secretary. *See* Bannisius.

........., ..., his ambassador at Rome, 4455. *See also* Vyte.

Maximilian, King of the Romans—*cont.*

..........., ..., his ambassadors in England, 5018, 5192, 5263. *See also* Portinariis, Thomas de.

..........., ..., Pope's ambassadors with. *See* Leo. X.

Maxson, Tho., 199, 311.

Maxwell, John, Lord, 782.

May, Walter, prior of St. Denis near Southampton, 591.

..........., ..., justice of gaol delivery for Leicester (town), 3209.

......, Wm., 3382.

Maya, in Spain, 3356.

Mayence, 3525.

........., Abp. of, 4563.

Mayeur, Pierre, 4445 (i.).

........., Simon, 4445 (i.).

Mayhew, Henry, son of Joan, 3480.

........., Joan, mother of Henry, 3480.

........., Ric., son of Thomas, 3480.

........., Thos., son of Henry, 3480.

Maynard. *See* Shipping.

........., John, 12, 775, 3497 (p. 434).

........., Tho., 858, 3763, 4035.

Mayne, preceptory of, 1262.

........., Eliz., wife of Thos., 1309.

........., Tho., 1309.

Maynell, Ric., 1053.

Mayo, Simon, 1854.

Maza, De, fortress of, in Spain, 3352.

Measures, Weights and, 2073.

Meath, Hugh Bp. of, 2072.

........., Wm. Bp. of, translation to the see of Dublin, 2071.

Meatham, Sir Tho. *See* Metham.

Meautis (or Mewtys), John, 650.

..........., ..., the King's French secretary, 588, 1420, 5233, 5455.

..........., ..., clerk of the Council, 588, 711, 3478.

..........., ..., receives money due from France to England, 14, 626.

..........., ..., grants to, 1420, 1440, 5233, 5455.

..........., ..., justice of gaol delivery, 1547, 1548.

..........., ..., in com. for Midd., 3552, 4663.

Meaux, John, abbot of, in com. for York, 481.

Meaux, John, 3955.

Mechlin, 216, 1267, 3555, 4329, 4359, 4389, 4526, 5041, 5148, 5632, 5722.

........., Holy League concluded at, 3859, 3861.

........., ordnance from, to Calais, 3744.

........., ordnance of, made at, for the service of Hen. VIII., 794, 3496, 3616, 3904, 4977, 5579, 5780.

........., Margaret of Savoy's letters dated from, 1458, 3571, 3815, 3823, 3873, 4622, 5018.

Mechlin, Knight's letters dated from, 4932, 4935, 495., 4978, 5029, 5030, 5059.

........., Ponynges' letters dated from, 3387, 3435, 3437, 3446, 3731, 3849.

........., Spinelly's letters dated from, 3077, 3647, 3651, 3678, 3777, 3779, 3805, 3817, 4810, 4844, 4929, 4935, 4955, 4978, 5030, 5059, 5076, 5377.

........., Sir Ric. Wingfield's letters dated from, 1701, 3856, 4930, 4935, 4955, 4978, 5030, 5059, 5076, 5104, 5117, 5377.

........., other letters dated from, 3639, 3692, 3847, 4606, 4801, 4956.

Medici, opposition of the house of Volterra to the, 4323.

[Medici, ——], nephew of Leo. X., 4747.

........., Cardinal de, 3976.

........., John de, 3976.

........., Julian de, Cardinal, brother of Leo. X., 3325 (p. 381), 4296, 4952, 5353.

..........., ..., ..., letter from, 4491.

..........., ..., ..., 5464.

..........., ..., gone to Florence disguised, 5208.

..........., ..., Card. protector of England, 5356.

..........., ..., ..., letters from, 4471, 4735, 4786, 5054, 5252, 5443, 5458, 5535.

........., Raphael de, Florentine merch., kinsman of Leo X., 4444.

Medicus, Mr., Spaniard, surgeon in the wars against France, 4653.

Medilborght. *See* Middleburgh.

Medilton. *See* Middleton.

Medina, 3355.

........., ratification of a truce at, 4818.

.... del Campo, 796.

...., Ferdinand's court in, 3807.

...., letters dated from, 3755, 3766, 5718.

Medley, Benedict, 3186.

........., Christ., escheator of Derby, 4127.

........., Geo., merch. of the Staple of Calais, 4732, 4892.

........., Margaret, grant to, 3186.

........., Wm., 3186.

Medmynham, Bucks, 4325.

Medringham, Linc. *See* Madringham.

Medway, river, 5043.

Meeriel, Hen., 1010.

Meese, Wm., 5296.

Megson, Th., 3650.

Melam, Cornwall, 4988.

Melbourne, John, 4581.

Melchetwoode, 901.

Melford, John, B.D., abbot of Bury St. Edmund's, 3947.

Melksham, Wilts, 155.

Melles, church of St. Mary, 1803.

Mellers, Agnes, 3541.

Mellichap (Millenchop), Salop, 4694.

Mellum, Hue de, 3916.

Melsambe [York], parson of, 1535.

Meltham, Rob., 1608.

Melthuyt, Wilts, 1369.

Melton, John, 1491, 2022, 2044, 3231 (i.), 3497 (ii.), 4632.

Melun, prothonotary of, 3377.

Membrilla, commendator of. *See* Fuensalida.

Menart, Joan, widow of Wm., 402.

.........., Wm., 402.

Mendip, Somers, 155.

Mendlisham, Suff., 3562.

Mendoza, Ludovicus Furtado de, letters to, 4096, 4324, 4371, 4449, 4464, 4513, 4525, 4574, 4666, 4845, 4864, 5152, 5267, 5470, 5581, 5592, 5642, 5718.

Menge, Frederick de, merchant of Ragusa, 3383.

Menou, John. *See* Moven (or Menou), John.

Menoux, Geo., 1639. *See* Monoux.

Menzeys, David, 4572.

Merbury, John. *See* Marbury, John.

.........., Rob. *See* Marbury, Rob.

Mercenaries, pay of, 4110.

Mercer (Marcer), Oliver le, 4958.

.........., Ric., captain, 4376, p. 652, 5761 (v).

.........., Th., 4100.

Mercers of London, 3767, 3900, 4659.

Merchandise, 181, 342, 402, 471, 628, 741, 743, 754, 787, 797, 800, 802, 808, 865, 897, 915, 1089, 1137, 1140, 1143, 1145, 1186, 1204, 1208, 1247, 1256, 1288, 1397, 1423, 1474, 1616, 1693, 1837, 1846, 1873, 1886, 1947, 2058, 3009, 3124, 3143, 3192, 3199, 3205, 3257, 3259, 3274, 3319, 3369, 3303, 3410, 3424, 3454, 3458, 3466, 3467, 3472, 3482, 3511, 3517, 3680, 3700, 3708, 3710, 3717, 3746, 3756, 3783, 3784, 3794, 3836, 3898, 3965, 3987, 4028, 4035, 4040, 4041, 4097, 4121, 4134, 4140, 4145, 4188, 4250, 4260, 4261, 4298, 4368, 4420, 4469, 4515, 4552, 4557, 4578, 4580, 4588, 4601, 4688, 4746, 4755, 4797, 4817, 4834, 4884, 4925, 4958, 4959, 4969, 4975, 4995, 5008, 5034, 5091, 5092, 5129, 5138, 5144, 5210, 5212, 5213, 5222, 5224, 5227, 5233, 5239, 5261, 5273, 5281, 5312, 5324, 5328, 5363, 5438, 5459, 5486, 5690, 5701, 5711.

.... *See also* Cloth, Wool, Wine, &c.

Merchants, English, in Flanders, 3053.

Merchant Adventurers, p. 432, 4081, 4743.

...., deputies of, 4081.

.... governor of the, 4364.

.... Strangers, in England, 1854.

.... Tailors, London, 3427.

Merchenistoun, Jas., 1412, 1415.

Merden. *See* Marden.

Meredith, Edw. ap David ap, 4814.

.........., Hugh ap Robert ap, incumbent of Kegedog, St. Asaph dioc., 4137.

.........., Vaghan, Griffith ap, 4813.

.........., Owen, 1972.

.........., Philip, 4617.

.........., Philip ap, 3299.

Merell, Edw., clk., 606.

........., ..., of Suffolk, 926.

Meres (or Merese), John, in commission for Linc., 4860, p.[906.

........., ... *See also* Mers, John, A.

Merick (Meryke), James, 4575.

.........., (Merek), Owen ap, 4653.

Merigge, Soms., 629.

Mering, Tho., in commission for Notts, 1514, 1798, 1964, 3092, 3494, 4776, 5225.

........., ..., ... for Yorksh., 3177, 4015, 5166.

.........., Wm., of Mering, temp. Edw. IV., 3031.

.........., Sir Wm., 625, 1639, 3031, 3497 (i).

........., ..., marshal of Calais, 1001, 1975, 4391.

........., ..., receives money due from France to England, 1027, 1632.

........., ..., sheriff of cos. Notts and Derby, 5561.

........., ..., in commission, 3092, 3494, 4127, 4776, 5225.

Merioneth, Wales, 1686, 4980.

Merlans, Jaum de, 5163.

Mers, John a, in commission for Linc., 1979, 3351.

......, ... *See also* Meres, John.

Merseley Park, lordship of Bromfield, 572.

Mershe, Devon, 946.

Merston, Linc., 3509.

..........-Morsey, Wilts, 155.

.........., John, clerk of the King's jewels, 5242.

Merton, priory of, 4335.

Mervyn, John, 1965.

Merzen, John, 4844.

Meseden, Herts, 4766.

Mesnart, Martin, notary, 5408.

Mesopotamia, 1659.

Messenger, Allan, a Scotchman, 4780.

Messynden, Th., 1983.

Metcalf, Gilbert, 3669.

.........., James, 1796, 5608.

.........., John, 1060, 3845.

........., ..., clk., 3386.

.........., Roger, 1060, 3845.

Metham, Sir Tho., in commission for Yorksh., 273, 455, 954, 1550, 1735 (bis), 1799, 3219, 3358, 4719, 5193.

Metheley, Chris., 4414.

Metz, in Lorraine, 155.

......, Hans, captain of Almains, 4793.

Meulx, Sir William, in commission for Hants, 1812.

Meurs, Count of, 4924.

Meuse River, 4273.

Meute, Martin, captain of Almains, 4793.

Mewis, Sir Wm., p. 551.

Mewy, Devon, 1688.

Meycote, Rob., 4996.

Meydecroft, Beds., 4436.

Meynours, Ric., p. 608.

........., Rog., 660, 1023, 3193, 4127, 4544.

Michell. *See* Mitchell.

Michelney, monastery of, 1102.

Michellsburgh, Somers., 1761.

Michelstow, church of, Exeter dioc., 4740.

Michilham, John, prior of, 297.

Micklewood, Glouc., 909, 1000.

Micklow, John, 4630, 4672, 4892, 5723.

........., ..., clk., comptroller of the household, 1759, 3483.

Middleburgh, 3814, 3815, 3918.

........., letter dated from, 3815, 4081.

........., senate of, letter to, 1412. *See* Ships.

Middleham, Yorksh., 178, 192, 440, 1205, 3483, 3669, 3845.

Midilhope, Salop, 4071.

Middlemore, John, 12, 755.

.... (Medelmore), Th., deputy of the Merchant Adventurers, 4081.

Middlesex, 3730, 3994.

........., tenths and fifteenths granted by the laity in, 3441.

........., escheators of, 250, 3038, 3493.

........., feodaries of Crown lands in, 4414.

........., sheriff of, 1771, 3887, 5493.

........., commissions of the peace for, 3552, 4663, p. 905.

........., commission of sewers for, 1972.

........., other commissions for, 266, 3006.

Middleton, Kent, 47, 95, 727, 1085, 2088, 3043, 5550.

........., Northt., 3297, 4656.

Middleton, [Sussex ?], 1867, 5247.

........., Yorksh., 3764.

..:......, Dorset, Wm., abbot, and convent, 3529.

Middletons, in Northt., the Three, 1040, 5010.

Middleton, Anne, daughter of Thos., 4438.

........., Chr., 1928.

........., Edw., 1942.

........., Geoffry, 777.

........., John, 1965, 4476, 4635.

........., Sir John, 4791.

........., Peter, churchwarden of St. Mary, Aldermarichurch, 4600.

........., Ric., 204.

........., Tho., 777, 1480, 4438, 4556, 4767.

Midland Circuit. *See* Circuits.

Mygenall, Wm., capt., 5112, 5761 (v).

Mihelton, Mi., 4476.

Milan, 11, 216, 405, p. 68, 2039, 3112, 3269, 3325, 3341, 3353, 3377, 3499, 3614, 3658, p. 474, 3752, p. 500, 3817, 3821, 3976, 4059, 4069, 4078, 4094, 4096, 4210, 4274, 4283, 4296, 4333, 4177, 4796, 5171 (ii), 5208, 5285, 5323, 5377, 5387, 5430, 5560, 5637, 5675, 5699, 5745.

........., taken by the French, p. 616, 4276, 4280, 4795.

Milan, restored by the French, 4571, 4622.

........., Cardinals at, 1581, 1681, 2039, 3026, 3112.

........., letters dated from, 300, 405, 1581, 1582, 3658, 4409, 4571, 4579, 4921.

........., Castellan of, p. 367.

........., great master of, 11.

........., abpric. of, pp. 366, 367.

........., armourers of, p. 953.

........., caps and hats of, 5711.

........., [Ludovico Maria], Duke of, 4096, 5729.

........., Maximilian Sforza, Duke of, p. 366, 3325, 3335, 3471, 3499, 3658, 3678, 3752, 3897, 3976, p. 573, 4078, 4091, 4096, 4196, 4210, 4216, p. 616, 4273, 4326, 4366, 4574, 4577, 4622, 5171, 5173, 5319, 5323, 5377, 5404, 5430, 5464, 5465, 5539, 5677, 5718.

........., ..., ..., rumoured treaty with Arragon and the Swiss, 5539.

........., ..., ..., ambassadors of, 3499, 4366, 4666.

........., ..., ..., his maitre d'hotel, 3340.

........., ..., ..., ill of a fever at Asti, 4449.

........., ..., ..., letters from, 4409, 4499, 4571, 4579, 4921, 5025, 5105, 5680.

Milbourneporte, Somers., 4436.

Milbroke, Hants, 1824.

Milburne, Criste, 4825.

Milchet, Wilts or Hants (?), 998.

Milcote, Warw., 1024, 1818.

Mildenhall, Suff., 1139.

Mile, Hen., sheriff of co. Heref., 3507.

Milfield, Northumb., 4439.

Milkesham, Wilts. *See* Melksham.

Mill, Edm, in commission for Somerset, 287, 712, 3048, 3566, 3585, 3606, 3701, 4713.

......, Wm., 950.

Millenchop, Salop. *See* Mellichap.

Milleneth, marches of Wales, 3299, 4814, 4815, 4816, 5145.

Millet, John, 3440, 3700, 4375, 5317, 5336.

........., ..., the King's secretary, 4087.

........., ..., clerk of the King's Council at Calais, 4282.

Millman, John van Fountaine, 4245.

Millom, castle of, 4520.

Mills, John, 12, 755.

......, Rob., 3969.

Millwright, John, p. 952.

Milnebeck, Westmor., 3764.

Milneholme, in Wilberfosse, Yorksh., 415.

Milstead, church of, Canterbury dioc., 3674.

Milton, Northt., 3939.

.... Damerell, Devon, 2080.

.... Faukynbrigge, Somers. or Dors., 1240, 1635.

Milton, Rob., 4158.

Milus, Aloysius de, daughter of, p. 326.

Milverton, Somers., 155.

Min, the stone of, in Italy, 3269.

Ministers' Account, 536.

Minott, Ric., 4911.

Minskip, Edw., 12.

Minsterlovell, chapel of, Oxon, 1034, 2055.

.... Cogges, 172, 1426.

Minstrels, 4653 (ii. 1).

Mint in the Tower, 299, 381, 3006, 4917.

Miranda, Count di, 8, p. 3.

Mirandola, 1676.

.........., Countess of, 3269, p. 368.

Mire Park, Wilts, 48.

Mirfin, Thos., 4581.

Misery, John, 4753.

Misre, Andrieu Le, 4445 (i).

Missenden (or Mysseldyn), Thos., in commission for Linc., 4358, 4593, 4860.

Misterton, Somers, 2080.

Mistilbrook, Wm., 3845.

Mitchell, ——, 3591, 3977, 4377, p. 651.

.........., John, 12, 3024, 4013.

.........., Ric., master-mason of Berwick, 1206.

.........., Tho., 12.

.........., ..., clk., 1212.

.........., Wm., 4013.

Mitford, Suff., 179.

.........., Northumb., barony of, 1040, 5010.

.........., Chr., 3553.

.........., Thomas, 3909.

Mitton, Yorksh., 319, 4909.

.........., John, sheriff of co. Staff., 3507.

.........., ..., in commission, 886, 918, 1770.

.... Tho., in commission for Salop, 918.

Mochebilling, Northampton, 1712.

Mochelney, Th. abbot of, 5199, 5240.

Modall, Henry, 4377.

Modena, 1676, 3269, 3499, 3821.

.........., Raynaldus De. See Raynaldus.

Modon, city of, 1697, 5430.

Moffet, John, 2043.

Mogher, Perys, 3355.

Moghnaunt, 1898.

Moile, John. See Moyle.

Moinford, Fras., 5236. See Moundford.

Mokkynges, Middlesex, 4302.

Molardus, Captain, 3026.

Molembeys, 4796.

Molineux, Wm., 3497, 4439.

.........., Sir Wm., 5763.

Molsham, Essex, 3952.

Molton, Rob., 3725.

Mombraney. See Montmorency.

Mompesson. See Munpesson.

Monbach, 5746.

(Monçaon), Montisson, 1209.

Moncelysc, 5387.

Mondonedo, Bp. of, 8.

Money for the war, 4481, 4917.

Money, Hen., 858.

Monfferron, John Paul De, 1676.

Monfroni, Paul, 3026.

Monington, Th., 1949, 3686.

Monke, Anth., heir to Humph., 1447.

.........., Humph., 1447.

Monk, John, 1996.

Monkaster, Cumberland, 275, 1052.

Monk's Bokeland, Devon, 2080.

Monmouth, John, 1062.

Monoux, Geo., 3497, 4581. See Menoux.

Mons, Hen. de, 915.

"Mons Sancti Johannis," (Yorkshire), 5001.

Monsieur (Monsor) Louis, brother to Earl of Nevers, 3807, p. 511, 5482.

Monslaw, Wm., 3131.

Monson, John, of Kelsey, Linc., 1587, 3579, 4414, 4616.

.........., ..., in commission for Linc., 3342, 4358, 4523, 4860; for Rutland, 266.

.........., Sir John, 414.

Mont. See Mount.

Montagnand, 4355.

Montague, Lord, 5484.

Montarey, Count de, 490.

Monteagle, Lord, Edward Stanley, 5483, 5506, 5616. See Stanley.

.........., Lady, 5483.

Monte Claro, castle in Brescia, 3026.

Montegu, monastery of, 3560, 5199, 5240.

Monteignyane, 5410.

Montero, Jas., 1353, 1581.

Montferrat, 3269, 3325, 3752, 3976, 4152, 4153, 4326, 4924.

Montford. See Mountfort.

Montfort, Sieur de, 4924.

Montgomery Castle, &c., 44, 1113.

Montgomery, Sir John, 5084, 5179, 5196.

.........., Ellen, daughter of Sir John, 5084, 5179, 5196.

.........., Dorothy, daughter of Sir John, 5179, 5196.

.........., Anne, daughter of Sir John, 5179, 5196.

.........., Sir Tho., 36.

Montibus, Peter de, 4934.

Montmorenci, Le Sr. de, 5482.

.........., Wm. de, 5408, 5560.

Montpelier, 773.

Montreuil, 4030, 4329, 5379, 5391, 5477.

Montrygo. See Ships.

.........., Anthony de, 3977.

Monviles, Suff. See Moundevyles.

Moole, Hall, 729.

Moore. See More.

Moorholme, Westmoreland, 3764.

Moors, 796, 1531, 1537, 1562, 1566, 4173, 5152, 5741.

Moota, Dr. See Mote.

Morbage, Bertrand de, 5163.

Morbecke, 3353.

Mordaunt, John, 566, 5374.
........., ..., of Beds and Bucks, 664, 4700.
........., Sir Wm., 294.
........., Wm., in commission for Essex, 310, 1368, 1522, 1713, 3605, 3785, 3967.
........., ..., on the Home Circuit, 243.
........., ..., on the Norfolk Circuit, 881, 1130, 1164, 1490, 1746, 1795, 2096, 3003, 3275, 3311, 3724, 4317, 4339, 4765, 5195, 5246.
More, the, 480, 486, 493.
......, La, 3842.
......, parish of, Oxon, 3005.
......, Le, Salop, 4014.
...... Monkton, ch. of, Yorkshire, 1797.
More, Alice, wife of John, and relict of Will. Huntyngdon, 1928.
......, Christina, daughter of Nic., 2074.
......, Christ., 3284.
......, Joan, daughter of Nic., 2074.
......, John, 1928, 1547, 4701.
......, ..., serjeant-at-law, 1972.
......, ..., justice of array for the Home Circuit, 294, 1101, 1490, 1763, 3275, 3295, 3694, 4279, 4339, 4702, 5186.
......, ..., in commission for Essex, 310, 1368, 1522, 1713, 3605, 3785, 3967.
......, ..., in commission for Herts, 309, 706, 1020, 1971, 3102, 4742.
......, ..., in com. for Kent, 725, 906, 4663, 4847, 4927.
......, ..., in com. for Midx., 266, 3552, 4663.
......, ..., in com. for Surrey, 1427, 1548. 1762, 3078, 3092, 3996, 4568, 4693, 4734, 5237.
......, ..., in com. for Sussex, 281, 1509, 4804.
......, ..., in com. for Devon, 699, 917.
......, John, of Cambridge, capt. in the war against France, his badge, 4253.
......, ..., friend of Erasmus, 1982.
......, Marcellus de la, King's surgeon, 1224, 4390, 5088, 5659.
......, Nich., 2074.
......, Rob., in com. for Dorset, 4713, 5658 ; for Somerset, p. 904.
......, Rog., clk. of the larder, 235, 4526.
......, Rondyll, petty capt. in the war with France, 4253.
......, Thomas, 1842, 1883, 1918, 1925, 1927, 1957, 1997, 1998, 4701.
......, ..., in com. for Hants, 904, 1388, 1812, 3071, 4159, 4676.
......, ..., in com. for Middx., 266.
......, ..., letter to, 1404.
......, ..., petty captain in the war with France, 3980.
...... Wm., 4974.
More-ende, Bucks, 789, 839.
Morefeld, Warw., 3186.
Morehay, in Rockingham Forest, 314.

Morehows, Rob., 677, 749.
Morell, Oliver, 3185.
........., Simon, 3579.
Morgan, David, abbot of, in commission of the peace, 3960.
.... David Guilliam, in commission for Herefordsh., 646, 675, 1400, 1963, 3686, 5506, p. 907.
........., ..., on sheriff-roll for Herefordshire, 1949.
........., Geo., in commission for Wiltshire, 3157, 3605, 4583.
........., Gregory, temp. Hen. VII., 255.
........., ..., grant to, 1661, 3291, 3293.
........., ..., in commission for Wiltshire, 1489, 1938.
........., ..., feodary of Glouc. and Wiltshire, 4414.
........., John ap, grant to, 487.
.... ap Jevan ap Glin, murderer, 65.
........., Jevan ap, pardon, 3771.
........., John, 4793.
........., ..., soldier in Calais, 3917.
........., ..., B.D., inc. of St. Iltuti de Neth, Llandaff dioc., 4383.
.... ap Hopkin, inc. of St. Iltuti de Neth, Llandaff dioc. dec., 4383.
........., Wm., of Carmarthen, 57, 1100, 3962.
........., ..., capt. in the war with France, 4306, 4477, 4534.
........., ..., receipt for wages of himself and retinue, 4421.
........., ..., his brother n the war with France, 3231.
........., Sir Wm., 5045.
Morgannok, 625, 1583.
........., sheriff and steward of Chas. Somerset Lord Herbert, 110, 441, 1113.
Moricande, 4386.
Morland, ——, his book of provisions for the war with France, 4318.
Morleux, Brittany, 3482.
Morley, ——, of Lewes, 1212.
........., Lord, dec., 3244, 4022.
........., Alice, Lady, widow of Sir Edw. Howard, 4255.
........., Hen. Lovel, Lord, 668, 5440.
........., James Lord, attainted temp. Hen. VII., 1937.
........., John, purveyor, in the wars with France, 4526, 4653, 4873.
........., Ric., of Fenny Stratford, 12.
........., ..., 5245.
........., Rob., in com. of peace for Sussex, 1509, 3428, 4804, 5506 (p. 904).
........., ..., in the wars with France, 4826.
........., Th., 3497.
........., Wm. Lovel, Lord, 668.
Morley's lands, 900.

Morocco, 1208, 3421.

........, straits of, 3946.

Moroxini, Justinian, prisoner in the hands of the Milanese, 11.

Morpeth, 4825, 5090.

.... barony, 1040, 5010.

Morris, Howell ap Jankin, murderer, 65.

........, Christ., gunner, 4591, 5340.

........, Jas., serv. of Marg. Countess of Richmond, 146, 235, 236, 383, 738, 1367.

........, John, 4908.

........, Peter, 4677.

........, Tho., servant of Geo. Ld. Burgavenny, 5777.

Morston, Kent, 5235.

Mortaigne castle and town, Lord Ligne, receives it from Hen. VIII., 4284, 4450, 5636.

Mortimer, Edw., 1235.

........, fellow of Tho. Ld. Darcy, 3359.

........, John, sheriff of Northumberland, 4022.

........, ..., King's messenger, in the war with Scotld., 4375.

........, Wm., embroiderer, 4642, 5720, p. 957.

Morton, Devon, 3721, 4778.

........, Glouc., 4071.

........, Salop, 887.

........, Warwick, 419, 1499.

Morton, Gabriel, in debt to Hen. VII., 1639.

........, Geoff., in debt to Hen. VII., 3497.

........, John, in com. for Dorset, 26, 708, 903, 3064, 3566, 3606, 3701, 4713, 5658 ; for Westmorland (Dorset), 2007; for Middlx., 3522, 4663.

........, ..., of Herefeld, Midd., grant to, 1013.

........, Rob., 4532, 4808, 5277.

........, Sir Robt., 3591.

........, ..., grants to, 1968, 3132, 3366.

........, ..., on sheriff-roll for Glouc., 1949.

........, ..., sheriff for Glouc., 3507.

........, ..., in com. for Worcestersh., 3301, 3709.

........, ..., his signature to the articles in a tournament, 1491.

........, Roland, in com. for Herefordsh., 646, 675, 1400, 1963, 3686; for Worcestersh., 892, 1971, 4770.

........, Tho., commission to, 4808.

........, ..., in com. for Surrey, 1427, 1762, 3078, 3092, 4693, 4734, 5237.

........, ..., licence to found a chantry, 1382.

Morton, Tho., inc. of Lanteglas, near Stratton, Exeter dioc., dec., 1830.

Morton Bagote, Warwick, 1501.

.... Birt, Worc., 1827.

.... Valance, 4071.

Morvale, 1812.

Morwell, Tho., inc. of St. Cecilia, Minster Lovell, Oxon, 1034.

Moryngesmyll, 297.

Mote, Dr., in service of Emp. Max., 3385, 3435, 4069.

........, ..., bearer of letters from Jas. IV. to Lewis XII., 3412.

........, ..., bearer of ordnance, gunpowder, and wine for Jas. IV., 3577.

........, ..., letter from, 3617.

Motte, De la, a pirate, 3326, 3751, 3882.

Mote, Kent, 5098.

Motlowe, Wm., 1159, 1291.

Moton, Thomas, 3345.

Motton, Peter, 4360.

Moulton, Robt., abbot of the mon. of Thorney, 3843, 3963.

Moundevyles, Suff., 3304, 4254.

Mounson, John. See Monson.

Mount, John, 3272.

........, [   ], 4318. (The name is misprinted with a small initial m.)

Mount Clere, Captain, gent. of Fr. King's house, 4431.

Mountfort, ——, cap., 3977.

........, Fran., in com. for Norwich, 884, 4558, 5133.

........, Sir Simon, of Colshill, Warw., attainted temp. Hen. VII., 1299, 1472, 3239, 4022, 4347.

........, Wm., grant to, 1214, 1532, 1557.

Mountjoy, Wm. Blount Lord, 697, 1017, 1418, 1478, 1882, 1883, 1900, 1957, 1982, 1997, 2002, 2021, 3807, 4528, 4727, 5208, 5407 ; grants to, 3197, 3601, 4133, 4660, 5179.

........, ..., Mast. of the Mint, 299, 381, 4917.

........, ..., chamberlain to Kath. Q. Consort, 3197, 5179.

........, ..., lieut. of Hampnes, 617, 618, 640, 1306, 3637, 4635.

........, ..., trier of petitions in Parlt., 2082.

........, ..., in com. for Derbysh., p. 907 ; for Hants, 4159, 4676, 5506, p. 904 ; for Herts, 3102, p. 906 ; for Staffordsh., pp. 903, 905.

........, ..., Baron, King's first chamberlain, lieut. of Tournay, 4660.

........, ..., to provide transports and oversee shipment of King's forces, 4082, 4084, 4126.

Mountjoy, Lord—*cont.*

.........., ..., summoned to Parlt., 5616.

.........., ..., letters from, 5736 ; to, 4428.

.........., ..., Erasmus' Mæcenas, 1948, 2013.

" Mountjoye " taken by pirates, 5539.

Mountnay, John, in retinue of Sir Ric. Wingfield, 5716.

Mountney, Rob., capt., 5112.

Mountorgueil Castle, Jersey, 531.

Mount Pacific, in Almaine, 3013.

Moven or Menou, John, in com. for Kent, 725, 906, 3428, 3605, 4663, 4847, 4927.

Mowceherst, Hugh, 3969.

Mower, Rob., temp. Hen. VII., 3031.

Mowlton, Thos., abbot of Thorney, Ely dioc., 3800.

Moyle, John, of Bathe, in com. for Cornwall, 312, 891, 1694, 1812, 1984 ; for Devon, 1166.

Much Dunmow, Essex, 4176.

Muchelney. *See* Mochelney.

Muda (Muyden), town of, 4456.

Mules purchased for the English army in Spain, p. 399.

Mulsham, Essex, 3968.

Multon, Northt., 768, 3544.

Mulwe, 3621.

Mundy, John, goldsmith, 236.

.........., Wm., 1002.

Munjoye, Th., shipowner, 4475.

Munpesson, John, in com. Wilts, 1489.

Murders and felonies, Act concerning, 3502.

Murgya, town of, burned by the French, p. 451, 3599.

Muriell, John, temp. Edw. III., 1375.

Murray, And. Forman, Bp. of, 3320, 3322, 3326, 3346, 3347, 3372, 4462, 5208.

.........., ..., ..., ambassador of Jas. IV. to Hen. VII., credence to Hen. VIII., 369.

.........., ..., ..., to Julius II., 1271, 1461, 1462, 1700, 1829, 1875, 1876, 1877, 1878, 1879, 3122, 3876 ; with letters for Albany, 1460; with instructions for the Cardinal of Ancona, 1459.

.........., ..., ..., Julius intends making him a Cardinal, 1643.

.........., ..., ..., Julius revokes such intentions, 3314.

.........., ..., ..., in com. to Lewis XII. to treat for a universal peace, and crossed the Alps upon several occasions for that purpose, 1681, 1869, 2076, 3010, 3104, 3138, 3216.

.........., ..., ..., upon a secret service, with Jas. IV., 3359 ; his power over him, 3651.

.........., ..., ..., safe conduct refused him by Hen. VIII., and is in result disappointed of the cardinalate, 3569.

Murray, And. Forman, Bp. of—*cont.*

.........., ..., ..., goes to France, 3838, 3883, 4112, 5006, 5649.

.........., ..., ..., his promotion to Bourges, 4454 ; his bulls, 4455.

.........., ..., ..., his promotion to St. Andrew's, 4682.

.........., ..., ..., demands the surrender of Dunbar Castle, 5641.

.........., ..., ..., attestation to treaties, 475, 3303.

.........., ..., ..., letter to, 1869.

.........., ..., ..., his brother Sir John Forman, 4482.

.........., Archdeacon of, Tho. Nodry, secty. of Jas. IV., at Rome, 3010, 3349, 3623, 3624, 3625, 5006.

.........., clerk of. *See* Dinguel, John.

.... herald, on a mission to John King of Denmark, 3139.

Musardere, Glouc., 155, 3382.

Musbury, 2080.

Muscote, John, grants to, 1177, 1724.

.........., ..., just. of assize, 294, 881, 1101, 1164, 1490, 1763, 3275, 3295.

.........., ..., in com. for Northamptonsh., 732, 1518, 1708, 1971, 3503.

Musica, commendador, with letters from Ferd. to Hen. VIII., p. 453, 3593, 3662.

.........., ..., returns with a treaty, 3755, 3766, 4055, p. 613.

Musgrave, Cuthb., of Craykdale, temp. H. VII., 296.

.........., Sir John, in com. for Cumberland, 717, 1049, 1734, 1799, 3358.

.........., ..., knt. of the Body, constable of Bewcastle, and chief forester of Nichol, for Cumb., 4791, 4825.

.........., Edw., in com. for Westmorland, 1735, 1799, 2009, 3048, 3358, 3552, p. 904.

.........., ..., on the sheriff-roll for Cumb., 1316, 1949.

.........., Sir Edw., on sheriff-roll for Cumb., 4544.

.........., ..., of Edenhall, temp. Hen. VII., 296.

.........., John, witness to a treaty, temp. Hen. VII., 714.

.........., Leonard, 1894.

.........., Rob., in com. of array, Northumb., 1735, 1804, 3358.

.........., Thomas, and Alice his wife, co-heirs of Tho. Beauchamp of Crogling, 1807.

.........., ..., son of Sir John, grant to, 4791.

.........., ..., King's spear at Calais, 5423.

Musoen, Count de, dec., 3325.

Musters and Arrays, 521, 522, 523, 956, 3116, 3118, 3229, 3336, 3358, 3359, 3393, 3950, 4163, 4979.

Mutford, Suff., 179, 1446.

Muythe, Glouc., 1831.
Mylatow, John, 1688.
Mynchull, Peter, 4360.
Myngova, the Great Esquire, 5539.
Mynours. See Meynours.
Myvot, church of, St. Asaph's dioc., 850, 4521.

N.

Nafferton, 944.
Nails, account of, 4232.
Najera, Duke of, 8, 3584, 3593.
Namur, 3945, 4359, 4526.
Nanfan, Ric., dep. of Calais, 528, 827, 4022, 4392.
........., Wm., 239.
Nanskyll, John, 580.
Nantheody, 1898.
Nantwiche, 131, 1086.
Naples, 216, 3269, 3452, 3593, 3614, 3897, 4078, 4267, 4274, 4296, 4327, 4952, 4955, 5208, 5726.
........., letters from, 348.
........., news of, 490.
... ., France suspected of a design on, 796, 819, 3188, 4952; secured to Ferdinand, 3355, 5173.
........., King of. See Frederic III., King of Naples.
........., Viceroy of, 3658, 3697, 3876, 4216, 4296, 4359, 5152, 5677.
........., ..., his conduct of the war against the Venetians, 3499, 4305; persists in attacking them, 4577 ; offers to send a fleet against them, 5171.
........., ..., occupies Bologna, 3777, 3779.
........., ..., takes Placencia, 3821; crosses the Po, 4196, 4210; proposes to attack Padua, 4326; at Montagnana, 4355; proposes, to attack Treviso, 5126; accused of not prosecuting the war with vigour, 5290, 5410; at Mons Cœli, 5387; goes to Verona, 5430 ; rescues Bergamo, 5539 ; defeated, 5592 ; vexed at his reception by the Emperor, 5686.
........., ..., made lieut. to Maximilian, 4795; the Emperor proposes to meet him, 5055.
........., ... See Cardona, Raymond de.
Napolitanus, Dr., 3248, 3335, 3340; going to the Emperor, 3271.
Nappey, 5607.
Narberth, 659, 1559, 1665.
Narbon, Henry, 4524.
Narbonne, 2002, 3752.
Narbonensis, S. Carᶦⁱˢ, 1581.
Narsigua, King of, 4173.
Nassau, Lord of, 4319, 4389, 4811, 5006, 5529; attacks Geuldres, 3077, to be sent to England, 3525; at Tournay, 4284; at Bumbill, 4296; sends Molembeys to England, 4796, 4811; engaged for Eng-

Nassau, Lord of—cont.
land, 5139, 5163; in Hainault against the French, 5155; marriesLord Berghes' daughter, 5341.
Nassyngton, 155.
Natalia, Prince of, 5705.
Navarre, 3298, 3313, 3350, 3352, 3584, 3593, 3614, 3766, 3807, 4058, 4274, 4327, 4818, 4952, 5173, 5285.
........., occupied by the Spaniards, 3356, 3451, 4267, 5353.
........., the Princes of, removed, 3662.
........., ..., discussion with Lewis XII. about expelling Ferdinand, 5634, 5637; attempts for that purpose, 5675.
........., Jean d'Albret, King of, advised to lean to France, 3243, 3762, 4932; agrees to surrender his kingdom, 3352 ; accused of dissembling, 3355.
........., ..., flees with his Queen to Bearne, 3356 ; agrees with France, 3405, 3437; at Pampeluna, 3499, p. 452, p. 457 ; in Bearne, p. 463, p. 498, p. 615.
........., late King of, goes to France, 3662; the French court undetermined whether to aid him or not, p. 501, p. 510; Knight proposes he shall be restored, 4056.
........., ..., included in a treaty between Louis XII. and Charles of Castile, 4924.
........., Queen of, 3352, 3356.
........., ..., joined with the Dauphin, 3584, 3593; betrayed by France, p.501, p.511.
........., ..., daughter of, her intended marriage with Count de Foix, 922.
........., Conde Pedro de, takes Bojia, 819; besieges Tripoli, 1209.
........., marshal of, 3355, 3356; flees with the King and Queen of Navarre, 3593.
Navy, the English, strength of, 4055. See also Ships.
......, Vice-Admiral of. See Windham, Sir Thos.
Nayler, John, 1225.
Neal. See Nele.
Neath, 110, 441, 1113.
......, abbot of, 3960.
......, St. Iltutus de, 4383.
Nechellys, John, 3939.
Neckton, Norf., 3943, 5115.
Nedging, Suff., 423, 4205, 4254.
Neenton (Neynton), Salop, 4071.
Negro, Peter le, accused of cheating at dice, 5712.
Negropont, Prince of, 5705.
Nele or Neal, Anth., 3051, 3496, 3832, 3930, 4318, 4672, 5154, 5519; in com. with others to receive 50,000 fr. from Lewis XII., 5529.
......, [Anthony?], 1871.
......, Chr., 554; in commission for Leicest, 656, 1094, 1425, 1971, 4706, 4783, 4812.
... .., Giles, 4071.
......, Joan, wife of Michael, 3719.
Nemours, Duke of. See Foix, Gaston de.

Nevill, Sir Geo., exempted from general pardon, 12; in France, 4691.
Nevell, Lord, a minor, King's ward, 5630.
.... *See* Westmoreland, Earl of.
Newcastle, 5762.
........., ship of. *See* Ships.
News, Ric., 1139.
Newport, Wm., 759.
Newsham (Newsom Abbey), Linc., 5245.
Newys. *See* Nuis.
Newton, in Corn., 4988.
........., Cumb., 275, 3866.
........., (Newnton), Glouc., 1374.
........., Leicest., 3096.
........., near Norwich, 1618.
........., York, 415.
........., 1052, 1487.
Newton-Holy-Cross, Devon, 946.
Newton, Giles, 3575.
........., Sir Isaac, document copied for him (in 1701), 4917 (2).
........., John, D.D., Abbot of St. Peter's, Glouc., 1291, 1361, 4377, 4950, 5075.
........., ..., in com. for Glouc., 1695, 3641, 3712, 3804, 4024, 4118, 4764 ; Warw., 1469 ; deceased, 4950.
........., Pet., in commission for Shropshire, 1981, 3071, 4394, p. 904.
........., ..., sheriff of Shropshire, 3507.
........., ..., in commission for Heref., 75, 646, 1400, 1963, 3686.
........., ..., in commission for Worcest., 892, 1971, 3301, 3709, 4770.
........., ..., in commission for Gloucester, 930, 1049, 1469, 1695, 3641, 3712, 3804, 4024, 4118, 4764.
........., ..., his offices, 878, 879, 1678.
........., Piers or Peter, clerk of the signet to Arthur, Pr. of Wales, 1513, 1839, 3395.
........., ..., in com. for Denbigh, 955; justice of N. and S. Wales, 956.
........., ..., in commission for Wales, 3055, 3289, 4198.
........., Ric., of York, 142, 200, 4547.
........., Rob., 5240.
........., Tho., 4375.
........., Wm., of London, 1569.
........., ..., 5712.
Newtonpopleford, Devon, 2080.
.... Tracy, Devon, 5122.
Nichol-forest, Cumberl., 4791.
Nichol, Geo., servant of the English admiral, 4456.
Nichols, Geo., in com. for Cambridgsh., 1684, 3187, 3583.
........., John, of Sussex, 1160.
........., Lawrence, of London, 4519.
........., Rob., 1744.
........., Th., of London, 3868.
Nicolson, Wm., of London, 1212.
........., Wm., 3348.
Nightingale, Derik, 5723.
Nile, the, 4173.

Nixon, Clement, 4825.
Noa, James de la, 5092.
Noble, James, 4825.
Nobton, John, 3497.
Nocenithius, 3269.
Nocton, Linc., 3284, 4852.
Nodry. *See* Nudry.
Noon, Hen., in com. for Norf., 1340, 1714, 1812, 1963, 3029, 3426, 3545, 5133.
........., ..., in com. for Suff., 3219, 3967, 4713, 5133, p. 904.
Nokes. *See* Okes.
Nolson, Ric., 1729.
........., Hen., debtor to the King, 2044.
Nonshere (?), Conte de, 5484.
Norbury (Norborough), Derby, 1993.
........., ..., Wm., 1738.
Norcotes, John, 549.
Norfolk, 266, 458, 574, 1720, 2011, 3304, 3871, 4254, 4680, 4694, 4698.
.... wool, 4755, 4969.
........., the herring fleet of, 3445.
........., sheriffs of, 664, 996, 1316, 1324, 1340, 1771, 1949, 3507, 3851, 4544, 4551, 4705, 5561.
........., commissions for, 1714, 1812, 1963, 3029, 3393, 3426, 3545, 3688, 5133, 5580.
........., justices of assize, 881.
.... circuit. *See* Circuits.
........., escheators and feodaries of, 3896, 3947, 4414.
........., coroners for, 503.
........., Eliz., Duchess of, 3502 ; attends Princess Mary, 5407, 5483.
........., John, Duke of, t. Ric. III., 1161.
........., Thomas, second Duke of. *See* Howard.
Norham, 4388, 4430, 4518, 4522, 4531, 5759.
........., besieged by the Scotch, 4284, 4457; account of its destruction, 4460, 4462, 4523; plan for rebuilding, 4497, 4735.
........., letter dated from, 3412.
Norhamshire, 5090.

Norman, Roger, 5102.
........., Th., son of Roger, 5102.
Normandy, 3112, 3185, 3300, 3318, 3324, 3391, 3587, 3619, 3643, 3779, 3809, 3860, 3861, 4084, 4278, 4328, 4373, 4440, 4760, 4824, 4843, 4844, 5080, 5285, 5287, 5303, 5468.
........., to be attacked by England, 3357, p. 453, p. 501, 3860, 3861, 3984, 4038, 4511, 4560.
........., the fleet of, 3821, 4273, 4329, 4330, 4465.
........., ship of, takes an English, 3377.
........., Albany there, 5164.
........., cloths of, 3517, 3972.
........., president of. *See* Selva.
........., general of. *See* Bohier.
........., lieutenant of. *See* Maulevrier.
........., receiver general of. *See* Lalemant.

Normandy, admiral of. *See* Le Roy.
........., monks, of St. Faith, Longueville, 3195.
Normanton, Notts, 1129, 1344.
Normanvile, Sir John, 481 ; in com. for Yorksh., 1735, 3219, 3358, 4719, 5193.
:........., Sir Th., in com. for Yorksh., 1799.
Norris, Sir Edw., 1187, 1817.
........., John, son of Sir Edw., 414, 1187, 1817.
........., Rich., 3992.
........., Sir Wm., 1187, 1293, 1705, 1817.
........., Lord, 3885.
Norroy king of arms. *See* Benolt ; Yonge.
Norstede, 4347.
North, lieut.-general of the. *See* Howard.
Northampton, co. of, 306, 484, 545, 602, 645, 1743, 3027, 3049, 3524, 3871, 3939, 4199, 4656.
........., ..., commissions for, 663, 732, 1518, 1708, 1763, 1971, 2045, 3046, 4434, 5346, 5658.
........., sheriffs of, 664, 1316, 1949, 3507, 4544, 5561.
........., escheators and feodaries of, 3447, 3947, 4414.
........., town of, 484, 1771, 1946, 3503, 3745, 4113, 5291.
........., mayor and corporation of, 4898.
........., St. Andrew's, 928.
........., St. James, abbey of, 568.
........., priory lands, 753.
Northbail of Shirwood Forest, 1899.
Northburghilles, 5296.
Northcote, Surr., 1577.
Northduffeld, York, 1607.
Northern Circuits. *See* Circuits.
Northhill, 2080.
Northlees, 5086.
Northlete, Suff., 1446.
Northleve, Devon, 1542 ; church of, 4243.
Northriche, Hen., of London, 1386.
Northslade, near Oxford, 4772.
Northumberland, 189, 201, 4022, 4825, 5010; com. for, 187, 1735, 1804, 3358, 3393, 3507, 3553, p. 905.
........., sheriffs of, 537, 664, 856, 1040, 1316, 1771, 1949, 4247, 4544, 5561.
........., horse of, 4556, 4869 ; wools of, 743.
........., poor and wasted, 4518.
........., Henry 5th Earl of, 481, 777, 944, 4122, 4825, 5090 ; property, &c., 1517.
........., ..., cancel of recognizance, 945, 961, 1401.
........., ..., warden of East and Middle Marches, 4518.
........., ..., summoned to Parliament, 5616.
........., ..., trier of petitions in Parliament, 2082.
........., ..., in com. for Sussex, 281, 1509, 3428, 4804 ;–for Northumberland, 1735, 1804, 3553 ;–E. Riding, 455, 954, 1550, 1799, 3219, 3358, 4719, 5193;–Yorksh.,

Northumberland, Hen. Earl of—*cont.*
1549, 1735, 1798, 1804, 1995, 3177, 3219, 3358, 4015, 5166, 5244, 5503, 5529, 5605.
........., ..., com. to muster, 5626.
........., ..., with the army in France, 4253, 4284, 4306, 4374, 4477, 4534.
........., ..., his sister Anne, 5150.
Northweald, 734.
........., Basset, Essex, 734.
Northwick, Chester, 4748.
Northyate, Oxon, 5685.
Nortia, 2021.
Norton, Worc., 155.
........., church of, dioc. Sarum, 1620.
Norton Beauchamp, Somers., 4071.
Nortondauny, 2080.
Norton-under Hampden, 1129, 1344, 4022.
Norton, Sir John, of Norwood, als. of Middleton, Kent, 4291, 4996.
........., ..., sheriff of Kent, 4544, 5550.
........., ..., 481, 1639, 2044, 2088, 3497, 3950.
........., ..., in com. for W. Riding, 1798, 1995, 3177, 4015, 5166.
........., ..., in com. for E. Riding, 3219, 4719, 5193.
........., ..., sheriff of York, 5561.
........., John, 4335.
........., Ric., in com. for Hants, 904, 1388, 1812, 3071, 4159, 4676.
........., ..., sheriff of Hants, 4544, 5561.
........., Roger, clk., 505, 661.
........., Sir Sampson, chamberlain of North Wales, 695, 3340, 3348, 3362, 3496, 3616, 4318, 4353.
........., ..., master of the ordnance, 3884, 4070, 4238, 4253, 4412, 4479, 4527, 4829, 4906, 5749.
........., Th., p. 953.
........., Walter, of Surrey, 858.
........., Wm., prior of, 1639 ; abbot of, 2044, 3497.
........., ..., of Kent, 4880, 4996.
Norway, 3086.
........., Kings of. *See* Christiern, John.
Norwich, 12, 155, 2028, 4023, 4377, 4558, 4680, 5428.
........., mayor of, 4553.
........., sheriff of, 1771.
........., castle, 83, 931, 3008, 3040.
........., Rich. Nix, Bp. of, 746, 1126, 1569, 1570, 1572, 3767, 5412, 5413, 5415.
........., ..., in com. for Suff., 280, 676, 1121, 1153, 1715, 3029, 3219, 3967, 4713, 5133, p. 904.
........., ..., in com. for Norf., 1340, 1714, 1963, 3029, 3426, 3545, 5133.
........., ..., summoned to Parliament, 5616.
........., diocese, 1848.
........., John, 3046, 3421.
........., Simon son of John, 3421.
Norwood, Kent, 4291.
Not, John, 1661.

Not, Rob., 1661.

Nottingham, co. of, 155, 266, 602, 603, 1899, 1978, 3049, 3441, 3713, 3887, 4022, 4253, p. 953.

........., ..., commmissions for, 663, 1514, 1735, 1798, 1804, 1964, 3092, 3494, 4127, 4434, 4776, 5225, p. 905, 5529, 5626.

........., ..., sheriffs of, 664, 1316, 1949, 3507, 4544, 4728, 5561.

........., ..., escheator of and feodaries, 1080, 4414.

.... (town), mayor and sheriffs of, 1771.

........., St. Mary's ch., licence to found a boys' school, 3541.

.... Castle, 3496, 5183.

........., Wm., of Berkeley, late Earl of, 1472, 4022.

........., Wm., sub-prior of Lanthony, 5789.

Novara, 3269.

........., plundered by the Swiss, 3976, 4096.

........., battle of, 4196, 4273, 4274, 4280, 4283, 4499, 4849.

........., castle of, 5171.

Noury, Edw., 4183.

Nowton, Great, Suff., 947.

Noyr, Wm., 1073.

Noyers, 5368.

Nuca, Don John de la ; lately in England, 4366; ambassador with Prince of Castile, 4267, 4511.

Nudry, Th., archdeacon of Murray, 910, 911, 5006, 5678.

Nuneham (Newenham) Courteney, Oxf., 621, 1129, 1344.

Nuis in Germany, 3471, 3497.

Nuremberg, 3615, 4633, 4561.

Nurse, the King's. See Luke, Anne.

Nursling (Nusselyng) Beauffeys, Hants, 1824.

Nymes, Wm., 1212.

Nyon, Lord, 4431.

Nythian, Soweyth, 5145.

O.

Oakborne. See Okebourne.

Oakham, com. for, 3282.

Oakhampton, 2080.

Oakley Park, Glouc., 5643

.... (Okley), Suff., 1666.

Oatlands, 5383.

Oats, 3850.

Oberton, Aubert, 4844.

Obri, Wm., 4445.

Ockham, Ric., 4238.

Ochoea, John, p. 957.

Ockeley, Salop, 40.

Ockley (Okeley), Wm., 784, 1290.

Octavian, servant to the Pope, 3126, 3278, 3349, 3751, 3837.

Odcomb, Somers, 155.

Oddyngley, Worc., 155.

Odeham, Rob., 3497.

Odell, Nic., in com. for Northamptons., 1708, 1971.

Odesdon, 2080.

Odiham, Hants, 155, 3642, 4773, 4779, 5537.

Odet, Anthony, 3379.

Odingsellis, Edw., 282.

Ogan, Sir John, debtor to Henry VII, 3497; his badge in the war, p. 608.

Ogard, Sir Hen., in com. for Norfolk, 1340, 1714, 1963.

Ogilvy, Jas., 474 ; ambassador from France to Scotland, 3412 ; gentleman to James IV., 3751.

Oglaunder, Tho., 1236.

Ogle, Sir Cuthbert, 5090.

......, Gawin, 4403.

......, Owen, debtor to Henry VII., 3497.

......, Rob. Lord, signs the challenge to James IV., 4439, 5528 ; complained of as backward, 4556.

......, ..., summoned to Parliament, 5616.

Oils, 2082.

Okebourne, Great and Little, Wilts, 1151, 5230.

........., priory of, 1151, 5230.

Okeham, Ric., p. 953.

Okeley. See Ockley.

Okenden, Wm., in com. for Hants, 1812.

Okenton, Devon, 482, 788, 1521, 1610, 1644.

Oker, Humph., debtor to Henry VII., 3497.

Okes, John, 4707.

Oking. See Woking.

Okull, Robt., of Lanthony, 5789.

Olarius. See Octavian.

Oldbury. See Aldbury.

Oldcastle, 1263, 1264.

Oldhalle, Sir Wm., 1472.

Olde, le, York, 5089.

Oldesmore, Derby, 5574.

Oliver, Bede, 4611, 5724.

Olney, John, alderman of London, 5242.

Olthorp, North., 953, 3524.

Olveston, Tho., abbot of Malmesbury, 852, 1183, 1929.

Omarson, on the Spanish frontier, 3593.

Onger, 4504.

Ongor, High, 734.

One-house (Onhows), Suffolk, 947.

Onions and apples, ship to be freighted with, for Scotland, 4844.

Onley, John, in com. for Sussex, 281, 1509, 3428.

Onslow, Geo., 1520.

Oppieses, Insulæ, 5319.

Oppy, Nich., 3039, 3182.

Oram, Tho., 501.

Oran, 490.

Order of St. James, 27, 28.

...... of St. Paul, 1860.

Ordern, Robt., 4303.

Ordnance, 793, 3496, 3616, 3762, 3904, 4238, 4377, 4378, 4479, 4527, 4632, 4633, 4634, 4658, 4977, 5024, 5316, 5317, 5579, 5749, 5780.

........., for the Great Harry, 4968.

........., master of the. See Pawne, Wm.

........., ..., in the rearward. See Curzon, Sir Rob. ·

........., ..., in the vanguard. See Norton, Sir Sampson ; his deputy, Wm. Ivee.

........., clerk of. See Blaknall, Wm.

........., sent from France into Scotland, 3577.

........., Scottish, 4520.

........., Termont, master of the Prince's (Charles of Castile), 3849.

.... See Artillery.

Ordunna (Hordona) in Spain, 1859, 2047.

Orell, Lewis, in com. for Herts, 706, 1020'; in the war with France, 4234, 4653 ; knighted at Tournay, 4468.

...... (Orweel), Lewis, 5287.

Orenge, John, 1350.

Oreton, Rob., 3497.

Orford, 246.

Orgosell, the, (Alguazil ?), 3762.

Orleans, 4875.

........., Charles Duke of, 5280, 5335.

........., Louis d'. See Longueville.

Orlton, Heref., 1127, 5272.

Ormsby, Linc., 1402.

........., Norf., 1756, 1757.

Ormeston, Guy, 4476.

Ormond, John, 1852.

........., Eliz., daughter of John, 1852.

........., Thos. Lord, 3977, 5788.·

Ormuz, King of, 4173.

Orreston, Berks, 4071.

Orsini, the, 11, p. 367, 3325, 3780, 5208.

Ortez, Bp. of, p. 399.

Orum, John, abbot of St. Mary's, Dublin, 5788.

Orvalys, Monsieur d', 3807.

Orwell, Camb., 1322, 1422, 3668.

Osbaldeston, John, in com. for Oxon, 766, 1216, 1470, 1745, 3015, 4559, 4809, p. 905.

........., ..., sheriff of Oxon, 4544.

Osborn, Eliz., 4934.

Osbern, Maurice, 5346.

Osemundiston, Norf., 1099, 1666.

Osleston, Derby, 5574.

Osney, monastery of, 1072, 1691, 3360, 5620.

Ostend, 3571, 4526.

Ostia, Raphael, Card. Bp. of, 4718.

......, ..., ..., letters from, 5665, 5666.

Ostynghanger, Kent, 3966.

Otford, 376, 950, 987, 1169, 1380.

Otley, Suff., 3851, 4705.

......, (Utley), York, 566, 4550, 4852.

......, Tho., of London, 1398.

Otley, Wm., sheriff of Salop, 664, 1316, 1949, 4544.

Otterburne, Ric., 4335.

Ottery (Auterey), 3057.

........., St. Mary's, Devon, 711, 2080.

Otterbury, (Otelbury,) Devon, 1255, 1602.

Oudenarde, 4393, 4396.

Oulson, Rob., 4071.

Ourssin, Charles, comptroller to Margaret of Savoy, 4509.

Ouse, Yorkshire, 3072.

Outlawry, reversals of, 1630, 1780, 1911, 3486, 3939, 4646, 5001, 5194.

Overey, Tho., 256.

Overshe, Surrey, 1212.

Overton, Yorkshire, 1729.

........., Guthlac, 938, 4805, 4853, 5050, 5096, 5431.

Overstone, North., 404, 1712, 1836.

Overingham. See Everingham.

Ovingden, Sussex, 5303.

Owen, in Wales, 3920.

........., Sir David, 625, 1212, 1509, 3173 ; in com. for Sussex, 281, 3024, 3428, 4804, p. 904.

........., ..., attends Princess Mary into France, 5483.

........., ..., serves in the war, 4000, 4306, 4477, 4534.

........., ..., Privy Councillor, 679.

........., ..., letter to, 3749.

........., Sir Henry, capt., 3980 ; made knight at Tournay, 4468.

........., John, 4367.

........., Ric., 960, 4595, 4596.

........., Tho. ap, 235, 1834, 3409 ; capt., 4554.

........., Margaret, wife of Thom. ap, 1834.

........., Rees, son of Thos. ap, 1834.

Owenhill, Staff., 1480.

Owersby, Linc., 5508.

Owre, Kent, 5167.

Owston, 645.

Owtred. See Ughtred.

Oxburgh, John, 4487.

Oxen, 3857, 4894.

Oxenbrigge, Edw., in com. for Sussex, 281, 3024, 3428..

........., Sir Goddard, in com. for Sussex, 1509, 4804, p. 904.

........., ..., sheriff, 3507.

........., John, clk., 59, 4683.

Oxynbruge, ——, 4377.

Oxford, John de Vere, 13th Earl of, 155, 222, 395, 927, 3373.

........., ... , admiral, 33, 1928.

........., ..., hereditary Great Chamberlain, 79, 1928.

........., ..., constable of the Tower, 784, 3810,

Oxford, John de Vere, Earl of—*cont.*

..........., ..., keeper of the lions, 3855.

..........., ..., other offices, 1290.

..........., ..., Privy Councillor, 14, 73, 165.

..........., ..., in com. for Bucks, 454, 943, 1379, 2045, 3219, 3310, 3522.

..........., ..., in com. for Cambridgeshire, 1684, 3583.

..........., ..., in com. for Essex., 310, 1368, 1522, 1713, 3605, 3688, 3785.

..........., ..., in com. for Herts, 309, 706, 1020, 1971, 3102.

..........., ..., in com. for Hunts., 905, 916, 1095.

..........., ..., in com. for Kent, 3428, 3605.

..........., ..., in com. for Norfolk, 1340, 1714, 1963, 3029, 3426, 3545, 3688.

..........., ..., in com. for Oxon, 1216, 1470, 1745, 3015.

..........., ..., in com. for Suffolk, 280, 676, 1121, 1153, 1715, 3029, 3219, 3688.

..........., ..., property, &c., 34, 35, 36, 730, 927, 948, 1774, 2011, 3401, 3266, 3401, 4504, 4536, 5016, 5019, 5385.

..........., ..., death of, 3810.

..........., ..., inventory of his goods, 4101.

..........., ..., in the war against France, 3977, 4294, 5136.

..........., ..., letter from, 4766.

..........., Eliz. Countess of, widow of William Lord Beaumont, 2011, 3266, 4536, 5016, 5136, 5483, 5778.

..........., Tho. Earl of, temp. Edw. III., 79.

Oxford, co. of, 174, 266, 514, 636, 3441, 3713, 3789, 3841, 3886, 4180, 4259, 4423.

..........., ..., sheriffs of, 664, 1316, 1771, 1949, 3507, 4544, 5561.

..........., ..., escheators, &c., 3058, 4414.

..........., ..., commissions for, 766, 1216, 1470, 1745, 3015, 4254, 4559, 4809, 4905.

..........., town, 3575, 4377 ; commissions for, 894, 3546.

..........., archdeacon of, 5137. *See* Urswick.

..........., mayor and bailiffs of, 1771.

.... fair, 4863.

.... circuit. *See* Circuits.

.... University, 1212, 1235, 2057, 3013, 4190, 5226, 5335.

..........., Brasen Nose, the King's hall of, 2057.

..........., St. Mary Magdalene College, 4772.

..........., Augustinian friars at, 246.

..........., Friars Preachers and Minors, 260, 262.

..........., St. Frideswide's, 1235, 3753, 3844, 4010, 4190.

Oxlease, 4301.

Oyarson, 3584.

Oye. *See* Mark.

Oyly, Oxon, 3955.

Oystermouth, Wales, 5180.

P.

P...., Tho., King's messenger, 4920.

......., Sir Thomas. *See* Parre, Sir Thos.

Pace, Richard, 1478, 5182, 5334, 5365, 5399, 5444, 5449, 5542, 5663.

..........., ..., executor to Bainbridge, 5253, 5333, 5342, 5349, 5357, 5464, 5465, 5664.

..........., ..., letters from, 5396, 5405, 5447, 5448.

Padarte, Th., p. 957.

Paddocksbrook, in Exeter, 2080.

Padstow-ferry, Cornwall, 3646.

Padua, 216, 490, 751, 880, p. 254, 3828, 3829, 5353, 5387, 5677.

..........., letter dated from, 3479.

..........., Venetian forces at, 4511, 5410.

..........., Bartholomew Dalbiano flees to, 4355, 4499.

..........., fortification of, 3499.

..........., Francis of, 1957.

Paduans, the wars of the, 394.

Page, Hen., yeoman of the bottles, 4984.

......., Ric., 105, 141, 1675, 3946.

......., ..., excepted from the general pardon, 12.

......., Wm., 185.

Pageny, master, 775.

Pagnam, Nic., 777.

Pailholme, manor of, 3497.

Payn Castle, Ellewell, Wales, 46, 1113.

Payn, John, 1943.

Payne, Th., 4251.

..........., ..., of Salisbury, 3665, 4806.

Paynell, Geof., 235, 509.

..........., ..., in commission for Lincolnshire, 278, 657, 663, 1120, 1169, 1170, 1378, 1380, 1716, 1979, 3137, 3351, 4860, 5476, 5691.

..........., Ric., in commission for Lincolnshire, 657, 1120, 1169.

..........., ..., on sheriff-roll for Linc., 664.

Payneswyk, 4071.

Painter, John, 1773.

..........., the King's. *See* Hen. VIII., his painter.

Paynton (Peynton), in Devon, 799, 946, 3978.

Paynworthy, Devon, 597, 860.

Paisley, abbot of, 3630.

Paytrell, John, 1854.

Pake, John, ship-master, 5112, p. 813.

Pakemore, in Warwicksh., 549.

Pakenham, Edm., 3024.

Pakkarse, 1299.

Pakyngton, John, 205, 4118, 4158, 4764.

Pallavicini, Ant., p. 382.

Palvesine, Anthony, Marquis, 4210.

Palavesyne, Galleas, 4280.

Palencia, Bp. of, 8 (p. 2), 5743.
Palatine, Count. *See* Bavaria, Frederic, Count Palatine of.
........., Frederick Count, 3648, 5539.
Pallavicino, Gr., 3325 (p. 385).
Palestrina, M. Bp. of, Cardinal Senegalensis, 4506.
Palestine, 5729.
Palgrave, Suffolk, 1666.
........., secretary, 5483.
Palsgrave, John, 5582.
Palice, De la (Palisa), 3662 (p. 474), 3807 (p. 511), 4296, 5390.
........., ..., in Italy, 3325.
........., ..., enters Navarre, 3584, p. 451, 3593, p. 456.
........., ..., returns from Italy, 3752.
........., ..., taken prisoner at Terouenne, 4464.
........., ..., fortifies Dijon, 4513.
........., ..., in Brittany, 4692.
........., ..., at the marriage of Princess Mary, 5482.
Palin'zon, Wm., 4476.
Palley, Wm., 1780.
Pallium, Wolsey's, 5334.
Palmer, Edw., 1386.
........., ..., in com. for Sussex, 281, 1509, 3024, 3428, 4804, 5506 (p. 904).
........., Geo., petty captain, 4253.
........., Ric., of Yarmouth, 3551.
........., Tho., 69, 235, 339, 1894.
Palmers, fraternity of, Ludlowe, 1650.
Palmes, Brian, 3211.
........., ..., in com. for Yorksh., 273, 455, 954, 1550, 1735, 1798, 1804, 1995, 3072, 3177, 3219, 3358, 4015, 4719, 5166, 5193, 5244, 5506 (p. 907), 5529, 5605 ;–for Westmld., p. 904.
........., ..., justice of gaol-delivery for Northern Circuit, 1922, 5195, 5283.
........., Guy, 1236.
........., ..., serjeant-at-law, 4037.
........., ..., in com. for Berks, 241, 884, 1393, 1481, 1732, 2095, 3640, 4341, 5166, 5684 ;–Hants, 904, 1388, 1812, 3071, 4159, 4676 ;–Leic., 656, 1094, 1425, 1971, 4706, 4783, 4812;–Linc., 78, 657, 1120, 1169, 1170, 3342, 3351, 4358, 4593, 4860 ;–North., 732, 1708, 1971, 5658 ;–Notts, 1514, 3092, 3494, 4776, 5225 ;–Warw., 282, 1387, 1468, 1971, 3364 ;–Yorksh., 1798, 1995.
........., ..., justice of gaol-delivery for Midland Circuit, 173, 1101, 1763, 3003, 3282, 3694, 4148, 5143.
Palmes, Guy, justice of assize for Midland Circuit, 19, 294, 1164, 3004, 3287, 3699, 4339, 4771, 5186, 5283 ;–for Tynemouth, 810.
Palshide, Ric., of Southampton, 206, 266, 1812, 1813, 3123, 3422, 4171, 5720 (p. 954), 5724.

Pampeluna, 3340, 3352, 3355 (p. 355), 3593, 3662 (p. 474), 4464.
........., army of Arragon at, 3361.
........., Duke of Alva at, 3499, 3584 (p. 451).
........., letter dated from, 3350.
Paneria, Bp. of, 8.
Panell, 178, 192, 1205.
.... Hutton (or Hutton Panell), 3739.
Pannare, the river, 1676, 1681.
Paniter, Patrick, secretary of Scotland, 288, 1176, 3651, 3240, 4403, 5006.
........., ..., letter from, 1412, 1414, 3277, 3618, 3626.
........., ..., letter to, 3829.
........., ..., witness of treaties, 3303.
Panor, Wm., 4742.
Panusanus, Fraunces, merchant of Genoa, 1273, 1398 3079, 3199, 4763.
Pansatichi, Barth., 4368.
Panter, Roger, 4691.
Panworth, Norfolk, 3943.
.... Hall, Norfolk, 4948, 5115.
Papal Confederacy, 3457.
Papedee, John, 5693.
Pappes, Essex, 734.
Paradise, Hell, and Purgatory, tenements in Westminster so called, 5211.
Parascho, 3269 (p. 367).
Pardon, the general, 2, 3, 12, 21, 23, 24.
........., general, for Scotland, 2038.
........., ..., the act concerning the, 4848.
........., ..., of Hen. VII., 2, 3.
Parensis, Urbanus, 3710, 3898.
Paris, 1418, 3112, 3807, p. 510, 3835, 4329, 4349, 4449, 5379, 5391, 5468, 5477, 5512, 5587, 5591, 5657, 5697.
......, letters dated at, 4924, 5164, 5462, 5547, 5566, 5569, 5583, 5584, 5589, 5590, 5606, 5634, 5637, 5681, 5717.
......, Lewis XII. leaves for Blois, 4273.
......, prohibition of the exportation of coin into, 814.
......, Stephen Poncher, Bp. of, 1182, 3752, 5408, 5468, 5560.
......, president of, 4692.
......, Jehan de, 5462.
......, colleges of, 5032.
......, University of, 639, 5638.
......, church of the Celestines, 5408.
......, the Tournelles, 5560.
......, parliament of, 1409, 5429.
......, John, sheriff for Cambridge and Hunts, 1316.
......, ..., in commission for Cambridge, 266, 3583, 4770, 4890, p. 904.
Parker, 5390.
........., Christ., p. 434.
........., Hugh, 4043.
........., John, 4800.
........., ..., abbot of Chertsey, 3538.
........., ..., petty-captain for Derby, 4253.

Parker, Ric., 484, 4111, 4124, 5351.
........., Thomas, 4067, 5552.
........., Sir Wm., 668.
........., Mrs., 236.
Parker's field, Haseley, Warwicksh., 3186.
Parkhurst, Agnes, 3542.
........., Walter, 3542.
Parkins, Hen., 4782.
Parlaben, ——, a rebel, 594.
Parliament, 192, 3142, 3633, 4833.
........., sittings at, 2082, 3502.
........., procession of Peers to, 2083.
........., prorogation of, 4655, 4848.
........., summons to, 811, 2054, 5616.
........., writ to summon to, 2003, 3540.
........., clerk of the. See Taylor, John.
........., spiritual lords of, 4668.
........., knights in, 416, 5100.
........., act of, 2010.
........., speech in, 4849.
........., the Scotch, 2075, 3104, 4869.
........., [of Paris], president of, 5553, (Anthony du Prat).
Parma, 3325, 3821, 5171.
........., commissariat of, p. 366.
Parre, A. See Aparre and Harry, Ap.
......., Matilda, wife of Sir Tho., 1026, 1352, 3049.
......., Tho., temp. Hen. VII., 600, 602.
......., Sir Tho., 286, 600, 602, 614, 1026, 1352.
......., ..., knight of the Body, 1625, 1628, 3049, 3764, 3819, 4205.
......., ..., sheriff of Lincoln, 1316; of Northt., 664.
......., ..., in commission for Yorksh., 5529, 5605.
......., ..., in debt to Hen. VII., 777.
......., ..., in the war against France, 3885, 4237.
......., ..., of Kendall, 4767.
......., Sir Th. A. See Aparre.
......., Wm., of Horton, Northt., 3113.
......., ..., squire of the Body, 470, 1428, 1641, 3070.
......., ..., of Northampton, 732, 1316, 1518, 1708, 1971, 3935, 5658.
......., ..., in the war against France, 3231.
......., ..., his signature, 1491.
Parrow, Rob., of Spalding, 5200.
Parshore, Worc., 5146.
........., ..., monastery of, 49, 631, 4686.
........., abbot of, 1639.
........., John, Abbot of, 4770.
........., Wm. Abbot of, 3208, 3301, 3709, 4764.
Parsons, Peter. See Pynnard.
Partridge, Th., 3849, 4481, 5723.
........., ..., in debt to Henry VII., 3497.
........., ..., in commission for Staffordshire, 279, 713, 791, 886, 1770, pp. 903 and 905.
........., ..., justice of gaol-delivery for Stafford, 764.

Parvyn, John, 3745, 5291.
Parysshe, Tho., clerk, 180.
Passage, La, in Biscay, 3243, p. 451, p. 457, 3614.
Passarus, 773.
Paston, Wm., 1812, 4205.
Pate, John, groom of the Wardrobe of Beds, 95, 101, 689, 1445, 3316, 4643, 5478.
Patengeham, Staff., 88.
Patents, granted for life by Henry VII., 607.
Pateshale, John, 3211.
........., Walter, 3579.
Pattenson, Geo., 3442.
Pattingham, lordship of, Staff., 5336.
Paulenholme, manor of, 3497.
Paulet, Sir Amias, 3977, 4377, 5180.
........., ..., excepted from the general pardon, 12.
........., ..., pardoned, 473.
........., ..., in debt to Hen. VII., 777.
........., ..., in commission for Devon, 3534, 3566, 3589, 3605, 3938, 4539, 4783, 5220 ;—for Somerset, p. 904.
........., John, junr., in commission for Hants, 904, 1388, 1812.
........., Quintin, 513.
........., Th., 4976.
........., ..., at the marriage of Princess Mary, 5483.
........., Wm., on sheriff-roll for Hants, 664, 1316.
........., ..., sheriff of Hants, 1949.
........., ..., in commission, 3173, 4979.
........., ..., junr., 4676, p. 904.
Pavia, 3325.
......., letters dated at, 3269, 3976.
......., fine imposed upon, by the Swiss, 4283.
......., Cardinals at, letter from the, 1353.
......., Cardinal of, 1457.
........., ..., slain by the Duke of Urbino, 1701.
Pavilions, tents, &c., 4629.
Pawne, William, 4238, 4457, 4682, 4868, p. 960.
........., ..., clerk of the avery, 1845.
........., ..., Master of the Ordnance of Berwick, 5693.
........., ..., Master of the Ordnance of Scotland, 4375, 4902.
........., ..., High Bailiff of Guisnes, 196, 599.
........., ..., clerk of the stable, temp. Hen. VII., 1023, 5735.
........., ..., pardon, 1638.
........., ..., grants to, 1012, 1249, 1369.
........., ..., payments to him for fortification of Berwick, p. 431.
........., Mr., 1370, 1871.
Pauncefote, or Pawnesfoot, Henry, in commission for Wilts, 1938, 3157, 3605, 4583.
........., ..., justice of gaol delivery for Fisherton-Anger, Wilts, 3488.

Pauncefote, or Pawnesfoot, Henry—*cont.*

........., John, late sheriff of Gloucester, 536.

........., ..., in commission for Gloucester, 3712, 3804, 4024, 4118, 4764 ; – for Hereford, 1400, 1963, 3686, 3709, 4770.

Paxford, Ric., 235.

Paymound, John, 1596.

Payments, army and navy, 5720.

........., authorized by Wolsey, 5758.

Pazart, LL.D., Geminiano de, 3269.

Peace, universal, 1828, 3346, 3347, 3633.

........., between England and Scotland, 5613.

........., Emperor, France, and England, 4916.

........., Commissions of the. *See* various counties.

........., justices of the, statute concerning the, 811.

Peachy, Sir John, of Lullingstone, Kent, 1350.

........., ..., 507, 521, 523, p. 433, 4238, 4254, 4306, 4327, 4635, 5477.

........., ..., knight of the Body, lieutenant of Ruysbank Castle, Picardy, 39.

........., ..., grants to, 140, 326, 1031, 1167, 1223, 1452, 1711, 1727, 3089, 3136, 3934, 4002, 4205, 5206, 5450.

........., ..., in com. for Kent, 725, 906, 3428, 3605, 4663, 4847, 4927.

........., ..., at the marriage of Princess Mary, 5483.

Peacock, John, 755.

........., ——, of Oxfordshire, 12.

Pearson. *See* Peryson and Pierson.

Peckham, Reginald, 3428, 3605, 4663, 4847, 4927, p. 906.

........., ..., Rye, Surrey, 3573.

Peck or Pekke, Ric., 1696, 4107, 5072.

Pederton, forest of, 1623.

Pedynghoo, Sussex, 730, 5016.

Pedington, Glouc., 1445.

Pedro, Don, 4725.

Peep, Th., 4825.

Pegge, Reginald, 242, 294, 732, 881, 1130, 1164.

Pego, Marquis di, 8.

Pegu, merchants of, 4173.

Peke, John, 231, 1355, 1389.

........., Rob., 856.

Pelett, Wm., of Stayning, Sussex, 1212.

Pelham, Herts, 3601.

........., Wm., 4067, 4476, 4635.

Pemberton's ship, 4474.

Pembridge, Heref., 610, 803, 1127, 5272.

Pembroke, 1749, 3294, 3497, 4769.

........., Attorney General of, 52, 225.

........., escheator and coroner of, 504.

........., receiver-general of, 470.

........., Suffolk, 1125.

.... Hall, Cambridge, 3791.

Pembrokeshire, 5721.

Pemston, Yorkshire, 22.

Penbrokes, Tottenham, Middx., 4302.

Pencils, 4954.

Pende, John, deceased, 1841.

Penes. *See* Piennes.

Pengerthyk, Cornwall, 3436.

Penkridge, church of, 2023, 3063.

Penn, John, son of Robert Penn, 4064.

......, Laur., 65.

......, Rob., gent. of the Chapel Royal, 1081, 1585, 2068, 3101, 4064.

......, Th., mayor of Northampton, 5291. *See* Penny.

Pennago, Hen. *See* Pinago.

Pennard, S. Wales, 5180.

Pennington, Adam, 3351.

........., Sir John, 3866.

........., ..., in debt to Hen. VII., 3497.

........., ..., of Monkaster, Cumb., 275, 1052.

........., ..., in com. of peace for Cumb., 717, 1048.

........., ..., sheriff of Cumberland, 1316.

........., Wm., of Newton, Cumb., 275, 1016, 1052, 3866, 4637.

Penny, Tho., 1309. *See* Penn.

Pennythorp, Wm., 5527.

Penrice. *See* Ships.

Penrith, Cumberland, 119, 3845, 4022, 4347, 5423.

Penrose, Ric., in commission for Cornwall, 1694, 1984, 3182, 3290, 3583, 3605, 3938, 4754, 5220, 5474, 5586 ; – for Devon, 1166.

........., ..., in commission of array for Cornwall, 1812.

Penryn, Cornwall, 8436. *See also* Ships.

Pentrich, 3683.

Penwith, Cornwall, 772, 3867, 4805, 4853.

Penzance, Cornw., 4321, 4846.

Pepeling, church of, Calais, 980.

Pepper, 3577. *See also* Merchandize.

Pepper, Ric., of Calais, 4238.

Peperyng, 4526.

Pepulton, Worcester, 5146.

Peracombe, 2080.

Percesell, Rob., of Ryseley, Beds, 835. *See* Persell.

Percheal, Ernoul. *See* Percival, Arnold.

Percival, Arnold, 5163.

........., Ric., 3549, 3573.

Percy, Anne, 415.

......, Eliz., 1357.

......, Sir Hen., 189.

......, Peter, 3416.

......, Thomas, prior of St. Trinity's, London, 3371, 3403, 3493, 3716.

......, William, 415, 481.

......, ..., in commission for Yorkshire, 1798, 1995, 3177, 3219, 3358, 3553, 4015, p. 905.

......, ..., on sheriff roll for Yorksh., 3507.

......, ..., signature of, 4439.

......, Sir William, sheriff of York, 4544.

Periaunt, Th., of Dixwell, Kent, 3601.

Peryent, John, 1047, 1665, 4596.

Peryson, John, clk., 845.
Perison, Wodirt, 4402.
Peryth castle, 1894.
Perjury, Act concerning, 811.
Perkin, ——, 3916.
Perkins, Anth. or Martin, 2034.
Peronne, 3678.
Perottus, senator of Montpellier, 773.
Perpignan, 4725.
Perpoynt. See Pierpoint.
Perriere, la, seigneury of, 5368.
Perrott, Sir Owen, knighted at Tournay, 4468·
........., of Pembroke, 3497.
Perry, Rob., of Gillingham, Kent, 4787.
Persall, Lady, 4071.
Persell, Rob., 481. See Percesell.
Pershore. See Parshore.
Pert, Thomas, ship master, 4535.
Perth (St. Johnstone), council held at, 4529
    4556.
Pery John. See Prégent.
Peryn, John, 4377.
........., or Purwyn. See Ships.
Peryton, Somers., 1285, 2080.
Peschiera, 216, 3026.
Pescara, 4371.
Pessall, John, captain, 4253.
Peter, the one-eyed, friend of Erasmus, 1882,
    1997.
......, Sir, a French priest, 5021.
......, John, of Bressa, 5273.
......, of Navarre, captain of the King of Ar-
    ragon, 4418.
......, Simon, of Syreksey, 5724.
Peterborough, 5765.
........., monastery of, 3084, 4762.
........., Rob., abbot of, 1993.
........., abbot of, 1639, 4377, 5616.
Petherton, North, 4315.
Petit, John, 4663, 4847, 4927.
Pette, Ric., 111, 1707.
Pettinweem (Premonstr.), commendatory of,
    Andrew Bishop of Murray, 1271, 1459,
    1875.
Pevensey, Sussex, 12, 297, 1484.
........., subsidy in, 4996.
Peverell, lands at Wymmeston called, 1824.
........., Thomas and William, 3293.
.... Bonon. See Bonon Peverell.
Pevesham, Wilts, 155.
Pewterers, Act concerning, 3502.
Pexall, Mr. (indorsement), 981.
........., Edith, wife of Ralph, 3317, 5700.
........., Ralph, 3317, 5700.
........., ..., in com. for Hants, 4159, 4676;
    for Surrey, 4693, 4734, 5237.
Pey, Jankin, 65.
Peynde, John, 3110.
Peynton. See Paynton.
Peyon, Jenar de la, 4341.

Peyton, John and Margaret, 3720.
........., Sir Rob., of Idland, Camb., 1756.
........., ..., 4377, 5575.
........., ..., in com. for Cambridgeshire,
    1684, 3583, p. 904.
Pezenas, de, 5480.
Phewilliam, Wm. See Fitzwilliam.
Philberdis, Berks, 1203, 3005, 4205.
Philip, King of Castile, and Archduke of
    Austria, 3398, 3526, 3856, 4038, 4434,
    4456, 4915, 5076.
........., ..., his ambassador in Arragon,
    p. 69.
........., ..., his daughter, 1417.
........., ..., his corpse, 819 ; (misprinted
    " the late Quyn of Castyllys corse,"
    p. 125, l. 3).
Philip, Sir, 5789.
........., Mistress, p. 958.
........., Sir David, 477.
........., Edw., 4996.
........., Th., 5309.
........., Tho. ap, 51.
Phillps, Sir David, 5296.
........., John, 3711.
........., Roland, incumbent of Crayford, dioc.
    Canterb., 4941.
........., Tho., 504.
........., ..., in the war against France,
    4306, 4421, 4477, 4534.
........., Sir Thomas ap, in the war with
    France, 3927.
Phillpson, Rob., vicar of Broughing, Lond.
    dioc., 4115.
Philpot, Sir John, 1147.
........., Peter, son of John, 1147.
........., ..., on sheriff-roll for Hants, 5561.
Phintzing, 4910.
Phippe, John, the King's fisher in the Thames,
    586, 1096, 1279.
Physcus, 3697.
Physician, a Dutch, at Cambridge, 1847.
Physicians, act concerning, 2082.
Piakeley [York ?], 4022.
Picards, soldiers in the pay of France, 4329.
Picardy, 617, 3357, 3398, 3536, 3752, p. 501,
    3860, 3861, 4038, p. 615, 4511, 4560,
    4622, 4824, 5468.
........., English forces in, 3744, p. 609, 4798,
........., the French King's lieutenant in,
    p. 380, 5482.
Picart, Jacquet, 4445 (ii.).
Pikard, Joan, wife of John, 1099.
........., John, 1099.
Pickering Lith, York, 5325.
........., Christ., in commission for Cumb.,
    717, 1734, 1799, 3358, p. 907.
........., ..., in commission for Westmor.,
    2009, 3048, 3552, p. 904.
........., Sir Christ., 1048.
........., John, canon of St. Stephen's, West-
    minster, 2079.

Pickering, John, in commission for Yorksh., 1549, 1735, 1804, 3219, 3358, 5244.
........., Sir John, 3062.
........., Wm., son of Sir John, 3062.
........., ..., captain, p. 553.
Pickmer, Chesh., 361.
Pie del Puerto, St. John, 3356, 3451, 3499 3614, p. 474.
Piennes, Sieur de, 4162, 4273, 4296, 4328, 4329, 5032, 5139, 5379, 5391, 5560.
........., ..., taken prisoner at the battle of Spurs, 4401.
........., ..., lieutenant of Picardy, at the marriage of Princess Mary, 5482.
Pierce Bridge, upon the Tees, 1535.
Pierdux, Joes, 4330.
Pierin, Jacques, letter from, 4609.
Pierrepont, Ant. de, 1182.
Pierpoint, Hen., 4127.
........., Roger, petty captain, p. 608.
........., Rob., 358.
........., Thos., deputy of the merchant adventurers, 4081.
........., Wm., on sheriff-roll for Warwicksh., 3507.
........., Sir Wm., of Holme, Notts, 3827, 4940.
..,......, ..., Nottingham Banneret, p. 608.
........., ..., grants to, 437, 1184, 4011.
........., ..., in commission for Notts, 1514, 1735, 1798, 1804, 1964, 3092, 3494, 4776, 5225, p. 905.
........., ..., on sheriff-roll for Linc., 1316.
Pierson, Rob., of Scotland, 4857.
Pigeon, ——, of Yarmouth, 12.
........., John, 376.
Pigot, Francis, p. 651, p. 973.
......, Tho., 69, 266, 1518.
......, ..., of Chetwynde, Salop, 1974.
......, ..., serjeant-at-law, 4036.
......, ..., in commission for Bucks, 454, 943, 1379, 2045, 3219, 3310, 3522.
Pikeman, Hen., 3095.
Pikenham, Wm., vicar of Damerham, 1854.
Pykerelles, tenements called, in Bobingworth, &c., Essex, 734.
Pilgrim, John, 5157.
Pilkington, Edm., 606, 926.
Pillith Forest, in the lordship of Millencth, Wales, 4816.
Pilston, John, 315, 4538, 4653.
........., Sir Roger, 4653.
Pilton, Northt., 5103.
Pimpe, Hen., 5218, 5341.
Pimperne, Dorset, 155.
Pinago, Henry, 726, 741, 1324, 5232.
Pine, Hen., 1465.
......, Nic., 1465.
......, Th., 3753.
Pincheck, Leonard, 1736.
Pinkernell, Eliz., 5308.
........., Joan, wife of John, 5308.

Pinkernell, John, 5308.
........., Wm., 5308.
Pynketh, Rob., 4476.
Pinkney, honor of, 2018.
Pinnard, alias Parsons, Peter, 3286.
Pinner, John, p. 435.
Pinning, John, 481.
Pinpe, Hen. See Pimpe, Hen.
Pinson, Ric., of Normandy, 4373.
........., ..., the King's printer, 1030, 3253.
Pinto, Gonsalvo, son of Lancelot, 4922.
......, Lancelot, 4922.
Pioneers, 4395.
Pipe, Warw., 247,
......, the, in the Exchequer, p. 436.
......, clerk of the, 3432.
Pirates, Scotch, 3631.
Pyres, tenement, &c. called, in Haseley, Warw., 3186.
Pyrk, Joan, wife of Roger, 4911.
Pirton, Wm., p. 434, 4635.
........., Sir Wm., captain in the war with France, 3591, p. 550, 3979, p. 552, p. 651, p. 811, 5724, 5761 (iv).
Pirwhit, Nich., groom of the King's horses, 1039, 1649, 2008.
Pisa, merchants of, 1145, 3710.
......, Council of, 1681, 1918, 1948, 2002, 3860, 4038, 4182.
Pitta, church named, 4284.
Pittenweem. See Murray.
Pittigrew, Wm., 3628.
Pyttour, Ric., 1023.
Place, Pierre de le, 4445 (ii.)
Placentia, 3269, 3325, 3821, 4210, 4296, 5171 (ii.)
Plague, the, in England, 1842, 1849, 1882, 1883, 1900, 1918, 1948, 2001, 2002, 3495, 4427, 4727, 5209.
........., at Bologna, 2002.
........., at Boulogne, 5469.
........., at Brest, 4311.
........., at Tournay, 5439.
Plaindell (Fenale ?), 3112.
Plane, Wm., a Scotchman, at Canterbury, 3998.
Planis, Gerard de, Lord de la Roche, President of the Privy Council of the Prince of Castile, 3340, 3377, 4359, 5059, 5094, 5341, 5404, 5657.
........., ..., present at the conclusion of a treaty, 3861.
........., ..., concludes a treaty, 4511.
........., ..., sent to Hen. VIII. from Maximilian, 5057, 5058.
................,......, in England, 5173, 5203, 5207.
........., ..., letters from, 5173, 5203.
........., ..., letter to, 5320.
Playne, Thos. de, chancellor of the King of Castile, 4508.
Plantagenet, Arthur, called "Master Arthur," 3903, 3977 ; grant to, 1965.
........., ..., in commission, 3071, 4159, 4676.

Plantagenet, Sir Arthur, in the war with
    France, 3714, 4314, p. 811.
........., ..., writ to, 5507.
........., ..., sheriff of Hants, 4544.
........., Eliz., wife of Arthur Plantagenet, late
    wife of Edmund Dudley, 1965.
Plate, act against exportation of, 811.
Playford, Suff., 3582.
Playter, Wm., on sheriff-roll for Norf. and
    Suff., 1949.
........., ..., in commission, 280, 676, 1121,
    1153, 1715, 3029, 3219, 3967, 4713
    5133, p. 904.
Pleas. *See* Common Pleas.
Plenemellour [Northumb.?], 4022, 4347.
Ploich, 3654.
Plummer, Christ., rector of Crokehorne, Bath
    and Wells dioc., 491.
........., ..., the King's chaplain, canon of
    Cadington Major in St. Paul's, London,
    5557.
Plumpton, Sussex, 730, 5016.
........., Cumb., 4791.
Plumstead, Kent, 3748.
........., Hen., 3551.
Plutarch, Erasmus translating, 1404.
Plymouth, Devon, p. 71, p. 398, 3877, 4005,
    4074, 4076, 4094, 4139, 5741.
........., customs of, 120, 737, 1810, 2064,
    3120, 3260, 3261.
........., ships of. *See* Ships.
........., letters dated from, 3857, 4019, 4020.
Plymton, Devon, 651, 2080.
........., M. P. for, 3502.
Po, the river, 3026, 3269, 3325, 3543, 3976,
    4196, 4210.
Pocklington, 5124.
........., Yorkshire, 273.
Podio, Mich. de, 1584.
Podyngton, 4360.
Poianis, Valery de, M.D., 5699.
Poictiers, preparations of war at, 4330.
Pointer, Th., 3867.
Pointz (Poynes or Poynges), Anth., captain,
    3591, 3820, 3977, p. 554, 4076, p. 651,
    p. 811, 5761.
........., Eliz., late nurse to the Prince
    (Hen. VIII.'s son), 1862.
........., Joan, wife of Thomas, 736.
........., Sir Rob., 4233, 4613.
........., ..., in com. of muster for Greenwich,
    3116.
........., ..., in com. for Glouc., 930, 1049,
    1469, 1695, 3641, 3712, 3804, 4024,
    4118, 4764, p. 906.
........., ..., in the war, 3231.
........., Tho., in com. for Heref., 646, 675,
    1400, 1963, 3686.
........., ..., 736.
........., ..., sheriff of Gloucester, 1316.
........., ..., in com. for Glouc., 930, 1049,
    3641, 3804, 3712, 4024, 4118, 4764,
    p. 906 ;, for Salop, 918.

Poland, 3269.
........., attacked by the Russians, 4449.
.... (Poole), ambassador of, 5259.
Pole, Yorksh., 4550.
........., port of, 4527, 4717.
Pole Mill, in Langley, Oxon, 1154.
Pole, Arthur, brother of Lord Montague, 5484.
......, Germayn, of Redburn, 606, 926, 4127.
......, Henry, son of Sir Ric., 4325.
...... (Poole), Sir Henry, knighted at Tournay,
    4468.
......, Kath., 235.
......, Margaret, wife of Wm., 4360.
......, Lady Margaret, sister of Edward late
    Earl of Warwick, widow of Sir Richard,
    400, 3241. 4119, 4507.
......, Nich., 3763.
......, Oliver, clk., 3338, 4758.
......, Sir Oliver, in the war against France,
    4653.
......, Reynold, 4190.
......, Ric., in commission for Glouc., 930,
    1049, 1469, 1695, 3641, 3712, 3804,
    4024, 4118, 4764, p. 906.
......, Sir Ric., of Bucks, 4325.
......, ..., temp. Hen. VII., 400, 625.
......, Rob., petty captain for Shropshire, 4253.
......, Tho., 856, 3497.
......, Wm., of Pole, Cheshire, serjeant-at-
    arms, 4360.
......, Wm., serj.-at-arms., 194, 195, 390.
......, ..., yeoman of the guard, 244.
......, ..., in the war against France, 4314,
    4526.
......, ..., of Pole, Derbyshire, 3827, 4940.
De la Pole, Edmund, Earl of Suffolk, 5475.
........., ..., excepted from general pardon, 12.
........., ..., possessions forfeited by the attain-
    der of, 174, 179, 246, 417, 423, 458,
    485, 492, 514, 620, 636, 707, 778, 1126,
    1148, 1162, 1250, 1252, 1281, 1343,
    1344, 1345, 1346, 1446, 1453, 1472,
    1530, 1892, 3087, 3304, 3381, 4022,
    4205, 4254, 4262, 4675, 4872, 4909,
    5454.
........., ..., his kinsmen, 4328 (2), 4329.
........., ..., short sketch of his career, 4324.
........., Eliz., late Duchess of Suffolk, 458,
    1148, 1344.
........., John, late Earl of Lincoln, 4254 (bis).
........., Margaret, widow of Edmund, 1281,
    4205, 4872.
........., Richard, 3326, 3347, 4691.
........., ..., excepted from general pardon, 12.
........., ... called Duke of Suffolk, p. 451,
    5379.
........., ..., called "White Rose," 5379.
........., ..., treated by Lewis XII. as King
    of England, 3320, 3346, 3372.
........., ..., captain in the French army,
    pp. 451, 476.

De la Pole, Richard, commander of the French fleet, 4324.

........., ..., preparing to go to Scotland, 5151.

........., Wm., 321, 1472.

........., ..., excepted from the general pardon, 12.

......, Sir Wm., possessions of, 4022, 4347.

Poleplace, Berks, 804, 3190.

Polehampton manor, 2074.

Poles, in the Sophi's army, 5705.

Polesworth, Staffordshire, 458.

Polesyn, 5532.

Poley, John, 907 ; in com. for Beds., 1922.

......, ..., jun., in com. for Beds., 1051, 1122, 2045.

Politian, poems of, 5352.

Polkenhorn, Nich., 3497.

Pollard, Lewis, serjeant-at-law, 10, 72, 5180.

........., ..., Justice of the Common Pleas, 5134.

........., ..., in com. for Cornwall, 312, 891, 917, 1694, 1984, 3583, 3605, 4574, 5220, 5586 ;–for Devon, 699, 917, 1166, 1503, 1812, 3183, 3566, 3589, 3605, 3606, 3938, 4539, 4783, 5220, 5456 (ii) ;-for Dorset, 26, 903, 2007, 3071, 3566, 3606, 3701, 4713, 5658 ;–for Hampshire, 904, 1388, 4159, 4676, p. 904 ;–for Somerset, 287, 712, 3048, 3566, 3585, 3606, 3701, 4713, p. 904 ; –for Wilts., 898, 1489, 1938, 3157, 3605, 4583.

........., ..., justice of assize for the Western Circuit, 1741, 2089, 3295, 3729, 4339, 4765, 5246 ;–Oxford Circuit, 29.

........., ..., justice of gaol-delivery for Western Circuit, 173, 304, 1110, 1763, 3282, 3694, 4279, 4753.

........., Martin, of Bristol, merchant, 4270.

Pollen, John, 3771.

Pollesworth, Benedictine nunnery of, Linc. and Cov. dioc., 584, 748.

........., manor, 4946.

Polonius, John, Hungarian Ambassador, 1478.

Polslo, Devon, 1688.

Polsted, Thos., feodary of Crown lands in Surrey and Sussex, 4414.

Polstedhall, in Burnham, Norf., 1956.

Pomerey, Sir Edw., 4377.

........., ..., in commission for Devon, 1812, 3534, 3566, 3938, 4539, 4783, 5220, 5456.

Pomfret, 4375.

........., William, 3406, 3407, 4643.

Pondormi (Pontremy), Anth. Crequy, Sieur de, 4030, p. 609, p. 625, 4410, 4830, 5032, 5151, 5482.

Ponsford, Devon, 2080.

Ponstresulian, in the parish of St. Marther, Cornw., 1943.

Pont Abovyn, p. 609.

......, Avandyn, p. 609.

......, Lienin de, 4445.

Ponte (Pount), Jas. de, merchant of Genoa, 1273, 1292, 1398, 1399, 1773, 3079.

Pontefract, Ric., prior of St. John's, 5214.

........., St. John's, Richard, prior of, 4295.

Pontesbury, Salop, 5436.

........., George, son of Thomas, 5142.

........., Th., 5142.

Pontremy. See Pondormi.

Ponynges, Sir Edw., of Westynghanger, Kent, 464.

........., ..., 1296, 1313, 1889, 2082, 3027, p. 433, 3885, 3886, 4087, 4110, 4205, 4237, 4238, 4306, 4307, 4314, 4475. 4478, 4519, 4534, 4585, 4588, 4660, 4789, 4976, 4986, 4987, 4996, 5006, 5021, 5205, 5292, 5404, 5554, 5688, 5697, 5758.

........., ... (Pinngeris, Ed.), 474 ; a misreading, the original has "dominus Edwardus Puningis."

........., ..., K.G., appointed admiral of the expedition against Gueldres, 1740.

........., ..., controller of the household, going to Flanders, 3651.

........., ..., (comptroller), 5104.

........., ..., commissioned to conclude the Holy League, 3603, 3859, 3861.

........., ..., Lieutenant of Tournay, 4681.

........., ..., comptroller of the household, constable of the Cinque Ports, 154, 274.

........., ..., in com. of muster as Lord Warden of the Cinque Ports, 3394.

........., ..., letters from, 3196, 3226, 3248, 3258, 3271, 3276, 3291, 3296, 3302, 3306, 3314, 3328, 3331, 3334, 3353, 3362, 3363, 3370, 3376, 3381, 3385, 3387, 3396, 3398, 3415, 3419, 3425, 3435, 3487, 3446, 3460, 3463, 3469, 3481, 3489, 3500, 3514, 3525, 3554, 3731, 3849, 3878, 3950, 3962, 4165, 4182, 4793, 5159, 5175, 5176, 5218, 5390, 5565.

........., ..., letters to, 3555, 4008, 4085, 4086, 4162.

........., ..., in commission, 3173, 4083, 4126 (vi.).

........., ..., in commission for Kent, 725, 763, 906, 3116, 3428, 3605, 4663, 4847, 4927; for Sussex, 274.

........., ..., his signature, 480, 503, 511, 782, 1539.

........., ..., in debt to the Crown, 5723.

........., ..., an Act of Parliament concerning, 4848.

........., Eliz., wife of Sir Edw., 1313.

Poole, Dorset, 12, 421, 456, 1237, 1432, 3061, 3431.

......, port of, 256, 293, 834, 1303, 3978, 4074.

Poole. *See* Ships.

......, Margery, 121.

......, Owen, 850.

......, Wm. *See* Pole.

Pope, sub-collectors for the. *See* Griphus, Peter.

......, John, 3024.

Popley, John, 1050.

........., ..., jun., 1051.

Popringia, letter dated from, 5297.

Popenruyter, Hans, gunfounder, of Mechlin, 794, 3616, 4412, 5780; called "Hans the gunfounder," 922, 923; Propreter Hans), p. 432; (Pope Reyder, Hans), 4977.

Popyncourt, Jane, 5468, 5517.

Porchester castle, Hants, 215, 1940, 3496, p. 432.

Port, (or Porth), John, 3006, 4127.

......, John, signs as member of the Privy Council, 702.

......, ..., grants to, 259, 1146, 2048, 4065, 5084, 5574.

......, ..., attorney of the Earldom of Chester, 132.

......, ..., clerk of the Wardrobe, 1702.

......, ..., keeper of the King's books, 259, 1146.

......, ..., the King's solicitor, 132, 156, 545, 599, 600, 601, 602, 603, 604, 605, 617, 618, 1480.

Portaleyn, Thos., 3406, 3407, 4643.

Portbury, Somers., 1815, 5667.

Porter, John, in commission for Somerset, 287, 712, 1761, 3048, 3566, 3585, 3606, 3701, 4713.

........., ..., incumbent of Eris Crombe, Worc. dioc., 460.

........., Rob., 12.

........., Roger, justice of gaol delivery for Gloucester castle, 1922.

........., ..., in commission for co. Glouc., 930, 1049, 1469, 1695, 3641, 3712, 3804, 4024, 4118, 4764.

........., Wm., 3680, 4247, 4651.

........., ..., clerk of the Crown, 85.

Porthloo, [Cornw.?], 2080.

Porthocarriero, Lord de, his son, 5263.

Portibean, [Cornw.?], 2080.

Portinariis, Franciscus de, a Florentine clerk, 5416, 5434.

........., Guido, merchant of Florence, 1791, 3414, 3732, 4131, 5068, 5434, 5486 ; brother of Francis, 5434.

........., John Baptista de, of Florence, 5068.

........., ..., clk., of the dioc. of Tournay, 5078.

........., Th. de, 5434.

Portland, [Dorset?], 4006.

........., Soms., 155.

Portman, John, 1761.

Portpighan, [Cornw.?], 2080.

Ports, French, officers of, letter to, 2050.

Portsmouth, Hants, 1327, 3359, p. 433, 3592, 4093, 4094, 4095, 4475, 4480, 4979, p. 953, 5724, 5762, 5769, 5776.

........., Hen. VIII. at, 4388.

........., letter dated from, 4056.

Portugal, King of. *See* Emmanuel, King of Portugal.

........., 5285.

........., procurator of the King, of, letter to, 1826.

Portugalet, in Spain, 1140.

Portuguese, the Scotch make reprisals on the, 20, 510, 841, 1245, 1826.

........., fleet, 841, 1826.

Posts, Master of the, 3779, 4216, 4929, 5171, 5292, 5377, 5387.

......; ......, letter to, 4304.

......, ..., his nephew, 3678.

......, ... *See* Taxis, Baptista and Francis de.

Potans house, under the Exchequer, 5211.

Potelles, a place called, in Waltham Forest, Middx., 3761.

Potkin, John, 1707.

........., Peter, LL.D., 1928.

........., Wm., 3792.

Potter, Hen., 1506, 5723.

........., John, 3774.

Potterspury, Northt., 87, 645, 710.

Poundage, granted to the King by Act of Parliament, 811.

Pouleyn, le, 5484.

Poullain, Wm., clk., of Normandy, 3643.

Pounde, John, 5720, p. 957.

........., ..., Somerset herald, 1454.

........., Sir John, of Hants, 904.

Pound, Wm., of Southwykke, Hants, 1812, 3507, 4979, p. 904, 5695.

Pounillon, Jehan, 4445.

Pount, ——, a rebel, temp. Hen. VII., 648.

........., James de. *See* Ponte.

Pourestok, Dorset, 155.

Powdram, Devon, 1908.

Pouel, David de, 4174.

Power, Christ., 4414.

........., John, 5525, p. 957.

Powers, Essex, 1774, 3401.

Powes, Geo. Lord, 5436.

Powis, John Grey Lord, 5089.

........., Edward, son of, 5089.

........., Th., 3497 (ii.)

Powle, Wm., 1939,

Poynes (or Poynges), Anth. *See* Points, Anth.

Poynings. *See* Ponynges.

Poyninges, Sussex, 1212.

Poys, Louis de, lieut. for the castellan of Dieppe, 3105.

Poyhale, 4022.

Prat, Anthoine du, Chancellor of France, 3752, 4329, 4924.

......, ..., President of the Parliament of Paris, 5553.

Prat, Jean du, 2026.
......, ..., bailly of Bruges, 4331.
Pratis, de (des Prez), Philip de, consul of Alexandria, 773.
Pré, Marquis de, p. 384.
Prendergest, ——, 799.
Pre Jan. See Prégent.
Predise, Rich., p. 813.
Pree, Cardinal of, 5560, 5569.
Prégent (called " Pre John," " Preter John," " Prester John," " Pery John," " Prior John "), Knight of Rhodes, 3752, 3838, 3876, 3877, 4005, 4173, 4692, 5021, 5130.
Preneste, M., Bp. of, 4610.
Prescot, Devon, 1433.
President [of the Prince's Council], the, 3396.
........., the Grand (Bohier ?), 5379.
........., ... (of Normandy). See Selva, John de.
........., M. le (of Normandy, John de Selva), 4883.
Prestall, Elice, 3024.
Prestayne, Marches of Wales, 3840, 4881, 5461.
Prester John, 4173.
.... See Prégent.
Prestland, John, yeoman of the Crown, 807.
Preston, Rutlandsh., 295.
........., Northt., 5119.
Preston, John, master of St. Catharine's Hosp., London, 121, 1972.
Preston, Rob., warden for the city of London, 4917.
........., Tho., inc. of Bystley, Winchester, 469.
Prests, 5042.
Preter John. See Prégent.
Preyer John. See Prégent.
Preys, John de, lieutenant general of Mons. le Bailly, 4667.
Prices, viz. :—
    Armour, 3414, 3496, 3658, 4954, 5720.
    Banners, 4954.
    Beer, 3445, 5228, 5747, 5748, 5751, 5760, 5765, 5766, 5767.
    Bread, biscuits, 3445, 5228, 5747, 5751, 5765, 5767.
    Butter, 5228.
    Candles, 5747.
    Cheese, 5228, 5765.
    Clothing, 507, 2053, 3117, 3981, 4067, 4309, 4375, 4526, 5720, 5752.
    .... for a revel, 4642.
    Coals, 5720.
    Compasses, 4376, 5751.
    Fish, 3445, 5228, 5751, 5765.
    Gunpowder. See Ordnance.
    Horses, 4067.
    Iron, 775.
    Lead, solder, 5751.

Prices—cont.
    Leather, 5720.
    Meat, 3445, 5228, 5720, 5747, 5760, 5765, 5766, 5767.
    Miscellaneous, 4376.
    Mustard seed, 5747.
    Needles, 5751.
    Oakum, cordage, 4232, 5751.
    Ordnance, 3496.
    Paper, &c., 3762.
    Platters, 5751.
    Posts, 3496.
    Rosin, 5751.
    Salt, 5228.
    Ships, 3030, 5720.
    Soap, 5720.
    Stone, marble, 775, 3496.
    Tallow, 4376, 5751, 5765, 5767.
    Tar, 5751.
    Timber, 3496, 5270.
    Tin, 5720.
    Tools, nails, &c., 4232, 5720.
    Vinegar, 4376.
    Wheat, 5760, 5765.
    Wine, 3315, 5720.
Prichard, David ap Glin, 3771.
Prykke, Ric., inc. of Broughton, Linc., 535.
Prince, birth of a, tournament on the, 1491.
........., cost of gunpowder, shot in the Tower, on birth of a, p. 432.
" Prince fee," in Northampton, 645.
Prince, the birth of a Scotch, 3138, 3139, 3140, 3278.
Princethorp, Warw., 4012.
Printer, the King's. See Richard, Pinson.
Prior John. See Prégent.
Prior's Manor, in Burton Latimer, 3027.
Prisoners, French, 4429.
Pritchit, Tho., 846, 3666.
Prittlewell (Prytwell), Essex, 5716.
Pritwell, Rob. Cornwallis of, 1699.
Privy Seal, clerk in office of. See Purde, Wm.
........., keeper of. See Fox, Ric., Bp. of Winchester.
Proclamations, concerning commissions of oyer and terminer, 702.
........., concerning the Winchester Statute, 1771.
........., concerning victuals, 3592.
........., concerning the invasion of France, 3688.
........., concerning shipment of the King's army at the Cinque Ports, 4083.
Proctour, Geof., 481.
Prosper, Lord, See Colonna.
Protector (Cardinal) of England. See Medicis, Julius de.

Prothonotary, the Papal, 3626.
........., sent to Scotland, 4951.
Proux, Bartholomew, 2093.
Prout, Thos., 4534.
Provence, in France, 3649, 3752, 3860, 5387.
........., ..., merchant of, 1295.
Provender at Calais, 5139.
Provincial of the Grey Friars of Arragon,
    3766, p. 498, p. 509.
Provisions, 4095, 4387.
........., boats, &c. for conveyance of, 5371.
........., for the army, 3728, 3850, 4892.
...., for the herring fleet, 3445.
........., for the household, 4149.
........., dearness of, in Spain, 3355.
Provost Marshal, the, and his prisoners, 4629.
Prowar, Sam., of Daventry, 12.
Prowe, Jas., ship named, 3980 (p. 554).
Prowde, John, of London, 1431, 2060, 3667.
........., ..., in debt to Henry VII., 3497,
    p. 434.
.... or Prud, John, B.D., inc. of the church
    of Pepeling, Calais, 980.
...., Tho., soldier of Calais, 978.
........., ..., farmer of Mark and Oye, 779,
    1241, 3832, 4635, 4914.
Prowse, Richard, Stile's servant, p. 501, p. 507,
    p. 616.
Prussia, Great Master of, 5259.
........., Simon de, 4678.
Prye, René de, celebration of mass by, at the
    treaty between England and France,
    5408.
Puchier, Baudec, native of Bethune in Artois,
    4843.
Pudsey, Hen., 1796.
........., Ralph, 3019, 5022.
........., Th., 1796.
Puebla, Dr. de, 8.
Puerto, San Juan de Pie del, 3352, p, 399,
    p. 614.
Puissant, Master Pierce, 5389, 5393.
Pulbergh, church of, 950.
Pulbon, John, commission for levying the sub-
    sidy in Lyde, 4996.
Pulham, East, Dors., 1212, 1965.
Pulleyn, John, in com. for ·Yorksh., 1549,
    1735, 1804, 3219, 3358, 5244, p. 907.
Pulteney, Tho., in commission for Leicester-
    shire, 1094, 1425, 1971, 4706, 4783,
    4812.
........., ..., on sheriff-roll for Warw. and
    Liec., 5561.
Pulter, Wm., in com. for Herts., 309, 706,
    1971, 3102.
Pulton, Giles, 5346.
Puplat, Tho., 4067.
Purbek, Isle of, Dorset, 422, 846, 1504, 3061,
    3666.

Purbright, Surrey, 155, 1814.
Purde, Tho., 75.
........., Wm., clk. in the office of the Privy
    Seal, 3432, 3959.
Purgh, Tho., junr., 1171.
Purley, John, 1979.
........., Nich., captain. 4632.
Purrart, 5164.
Purse, John, 4742.
Purser, Ralph, of Pomfret, 4375,
Purveyors, at Southampton, 4653.
Purwhit, Nich., deceased, 3206.
Puttenham, Sir Geo. 498.
........., ..., in commission to review, 3173.
........., ..., in com. of array for Hants, 1812.
Putter, Wm., 1020.
Puy, [Lord ?] Saint, 5292.
Pyder, Cornwall, chapel of St. Mary, in the
    church of St. Maugan, 3598.
Pye, Wm., 1899.
Pykeryng. See Pickering.
Pyme, Alex., son of Reginald, 871.
........., Reginald, 871, p. 434.
Pynkernell. See Pinkernell.
Pyn, Martin de, 3247.
Pyrenees, the, p. 327, 3631.
Pyrk, Roger, 4911.
Pyrle, Thos., 3939.

Q.

Quadring, Thos., of Humbe, Linc., 1169, 4714.
........., Tho., 657, 1120, 1169; in commission,
    657, 1120.
Quarendon, Bucks, 896, 3268.
Quaresmel, Vincent, 4445.
Quarles, Francis, 5096.
........., Geo., 235, 665, 1866, 4223, 5096.
Quarrell, Wm., 1913.
Queenborough, letter dated at, 3946.
.... Castle, Kent, 727, 1085, 3043.
Queen's Ferry, the, in the firth of Forth, 3751.
Quesne, Marcus du, 4445.
Quhyt, John, 3629.
Quiery, ——, taken prisoner at the battle of
    Spurs, 4402.
Quies, Hunts, 1124.
Quintana, Pedro, secretary of Ferdinand, 4096,
    4845, 4952, 5152, 5173.
........., ..., ..., concludes truce with France,
    4875.
........., ..., ..., with the Emperor, 4725,
    4796, 4829, 4844.
Quinton, Northt., 1825, 3027.
Quintucius, Paul, p. 368.
Quyinge, Francis, merchant of Lucca, 1584.

R.

R. Card., Bp. ——, letter from, 3240.
R. R., letter of Erasmus to, 5352.
Rabett, Wm., 4677.
Raby, Durham, 191.
Rache, 155.
........., forest of, 4315.
Rache, Jehan de la, 4445.
Racheford, Essex, 36, 222.
........., Ralph, of Stoke, Linc., 3130.
Radcliff, Cuthbert, in com. of the peace, Northumberland, 3553.
........., Sir Edw., knight of the Body, warden general or lieut. of the middle marches towards Scotland, 5090; grants to, 285, 1040, 5010.
........., ..., in commission of array,Northumberland, 187, 3358.
........., ..., in commission of peace, Northumberland, 1735, 1804, 3553, p. 905.
........., ..., in commission of peace, Cumberland, 1048.
........., ..., justice of gaol delivery for Tynemouth, 810.
........., ..., sheriff of Northumberland, 664, 1949.
........., Edw., indebted to Hen. VII., 777.
........., ..., sheriff of Northumb., 3507.
........., Eleanor, 561.
........., Eliz., 561.
........., Geoff., 561.
........., Joan, 561.
........., John, in commission of peace, Cumberland, 1048.
........., ..., in commission of array, Cumberland, 1734, 1799, 3358.
........., ..., sheriff of Cumberland, 5561.
........., ..., on sheriff roll, 1807.
........., ..., at forays in the North, 4456.
........., Sir John. See Fitzwalter.
........., the Mary. See Ships.
........., Rob. See Fitzwalter, Lord.
........., Roger, gentleman usher of the Chamber to Queen Katharine, and servant to Marg. Countess of Richmond, grants to, 667, 855, 888, 1328, 1329, 3084, 3085, 4230, 4762.
........., ..., in com. of the peace, Leicestersh., 1425, 1971, 4706, 4783, 4812.
........., Tho., rector of Fontell-Episcopi, 1854.
........., Wm., keeper of the King's wardrobe of beds, in Windsor Castle, 546.
........., ..., in commission of gaol delivery, Stamford, 4004.
........., ..., mentioned as justice of the peace, temp. Hen. VII., 5309.
Radiche, Rob., 3076.
Radley, John, 4360.
Radnor, church of, Heref. dioc., 972, 3028.
.... Forest, Wales, 1893.
.... Park, 4813.

Radnor, clerk of the courts of, 3299.
........., receiver general of the earldom of March in, 298.
........., New, park, &c., 5145.
Radwell, 155.
Raff Herald. See Rosse.
Ragland, Wales, 3949.
........., Sir John, made knight at Tournay, 4468.
Ragusa, 3278, 3283, 3383, 3837.
Rainham, Norf., 996.
Rains. See Rheims.
Rainsford (or Reynsforth), Sir John, 305, 3006, 4367, 4504.
........., ..., in the war against France, 3885, 3886, p. 554, 4307, 4314.
........., ..., in commission for Essex, 310, 1368, 1522, 1713, 3605, 3785, 3967, p. 907.
Rake, Ric., 244.
Rakheyth, Norf., 4680.
Raleigh, 36, 222, 1290, 4504, 5019.
........., Anth., 3843.
........., Sir Edward, 4180, 4569.
........., Edw., son of Sir Edw., 4569.
........., Eliz., daughter of Marion, 1212.
........., ..., wife of Anth., 3843.
......, George, 4569.
.... (Ralye), John, 4534.
........., Marion, 1212.
Ramesbury, Wilts, 3382.
......., (date), 1526, 1929, 5544.
........., Wm., 561, 4254.
Ramme, Jas., clerk of Fernando Daza, p. 957.
Rampton, 3031.
Ramsay, Sir John, of Trarinzeane, 2069, 3569, 3676, 3838.
........., Marg., 1624.
........., Ric., Abbot of St. Peter, Hide, 715.
........., Tho., son of Thomas, 1624.
........., ..., burgess of Edinburgh, 3319.
Ramsey, Essex, 735.
........., Hunts, monastery of, 4065.
........., Abbot of, legatee of Hen. VII., 776.
........., ..., indebted to Hen. VII., 1639.
........., ..., summoned to Parliament, 5616.
........., Abbot and convent of, 1680.
........., commissions of gaol delivery for, 959, 1222, 3652.
Ramys, Rob., 2000.
Ranalde. See Raynaldus and Renaldi.
Randell, John, 3147.
Randolf, Tho., clk., 3052.
Randollington, Cumb., 4791.
Ranger, Tho., 1002.
Ranghen, Count Guido, in the service of the Duke of Milan, p. 366, p. 382.
Rankyn, Hugh, mayor of Cambridge, 677, 749.
........., ..., justice of gaol delivery, 3187.

Raskell, 1205.

Rasour, Th., 5428.

Rastormall, Cornw., 493.

.... Park, Devon, 453.

........., chapel in, 259, 1146.

Ratti, Giovanni, servant of the Marq. of Mantua, 4920, 5258, 5409, 5417.

Rattrewe, Devon, 3711.

Raungeworth, Glouc., 4071.

Raunston, convent of, Linc. dioc., 25.

........., prior of, 25.

Ravenna, 1676, 1697, 1701.

........., battle of, 3188, 3377, 3821, 3876, 4691, 4849.

Ravenscroftz, Th., 5616.

Ravenser, Ric., chantry of, Lincoln cathedral, 1910.

Ravestein, de, 3651.

Ravon, John, purser, 4535.

Ravyn, Tho., 1466.

Rawkyn, Wm., 1002.

Rawley. See Raleigh.

Rawlins, John, in the wars, 3934, 4211, 4635.

........., Rich., D.D., the King's almoner, 5621, 5735.

........., alias Couper, Rob. 3234.

Rawlinson, Rob., 235, 385.

Rawson, ——, cousin of Chr. Fisher, 880.

........., Christ., p. 957.

........., Ric., LL.D., the King's chaplain, 595, 1590.

........., ..., archdeacon of Essex, 3889.

........., ..., receiver of petitions, 811, 2082.

Ray, Haquin le, 4445.

Rayadour, Wales, 4814.

Raylegh. See Raleigh.

Raymond, Tho., 1773, 5334, 5558.

Raynaldus of Modena, a priest, accused of poisoning Card. Bainbridge, 5253, 5254, 5356, 5357, 5365, 5378. See Renaldi.

Raynart, Jacob, captain of Almains, 4793.

Rayner, Ric., 5735.

Rea, Peter de la, of Spain, 1140, 1886.

Reade. See Reed.

Reading, mayor and burgesses of 1198.

........., monastery of, Privy Seal dated at, 1748.

........., Abbot of, legatee of Hen. VII., 776.

........., ..., trier of petitions, 2082.

........., ..., summoned to Parliament, 5616.

........., John abbot of, 3080.

........., ..., prior of Hulme, 745.

........., ..., abbot of Hulme, 821, 1720, 1721.

.... (Redyng), Mary, gentlewoman, servant of Queen Eliz. and Mary, Queen of France, grant to, 5406.

Receivers, act concerning, 811.

Recognizances, commission to obtain payment of, 5298.

Records, delivery of, 5274, 5351.

........., and books, keeper of. See Tamworth, Tho.

Red Sea, the, 540, 4173.

Redburn, Linc., 5020.

........., Staff., 606, 926.

Redesdale, [Northumb.], 4825.

Redman, ..., of Westmorland, 3703.

........., Edward, 4269, 4550.

........., ..., in commission for Cumb., 1048.

........., Hen., son of Edw., 4269, 4550.

........., Joan, dau. of Hen. 4269, 4550.

Redmere, Walter, 4183.

Redney, Sir John. See Rodney.

Redwode, [Glouc.], 5082.

Ree, Glouc. 4972.

Reed, Suff., 947.

......., (Reade), Edmund, 4680.

......., John, 715, 3450.

......., Griffith, 470, 500, 504.

......., Marg., wife of Sir Rob., 5521.

......., the Nicholas, 3117, 3591, 3831, 3977, 4377, 4474, 5761.

......., Ric., son of Wm., 1174.

......., ..., yeoman of the guard, 3913.

......., Sir Rob., executor of Hen. VII., 3292.

......., ..., grants to, 3480, 4436.

......., ..., licence to found a chantry, 5521.

......., ..., his signature as member of the Privy Council, 702, 785, 1004, 1372, 1540, 1699, 1756, 1757, 1758, 3080, 4767, 5762.

......., ..., trier of petitions, 811, 2082.

......., ..., chief justice of Common Pleas, 5.

......., ..., justice of assize, 19, 294, 881, 1164, 1490, 1795, 2096, 3003, 3311, 3724, 4339, 4765, 5426.

......., ..., justice of gaol-delivery, 243, 541, 763, 931, 959, 1130, 1222, 1519, 1547, 1548, 1746, 1781, 1897, 1942, 3275, 3652, 3691, 3765, 3778, 4317, 4553, 5195.

......., ..., in commission for Beds, 1051, 1122, 2045, 3501, 4700.

......., ..., ... for Bucks, 454, 943, 1379, 2045, 3219, 3310, 3522.

......., ..., ... for Camb., 1684, 3583, p. 904.

......., ..., ... for Hunts, 905, 916, 1095, 4006.

......., ..., ... for Kent, 725, 906, 3426, 3605, 4663, 4847, 4927.

......., ..., ... for Norf., 1340, 1714, 1963, 3029, 3426, 3545, 5133.

......., ..., ... for Suffolk, 280, 676, 1121, 1153, 1715, 3029, 3219, 3967, 4713, 5133, p. 904.

......., ..., ... for Surrey, 1427, 1762, 3078, 3092, 4693, 4734, 5237, p. 905.

Reed, Sir Rob., in commission for Sussex, 218, 1509, 3428, 4804, p. 904.

......, Tho., temp. Hen. VI. and Edw. IV., 4013.

......, ..., master of the Nicholas Draper, 4377.

......, ..., D.D., inc. of Bekles, Suff., licence to found a chantry, 4918.

......, Wm., 1174, 3006, 4918.

......, Sir Wm., in the war against France, 3231.

......, ..., in commission for Bucks, 454, 943, 1379, 2045, 3310, 3522.

......, ..., ... for Oxon, 766, 1470, 1745, 4559, 4809.

......, ..., ... for Oxford (town), 894, 3546.

Rees Guyen, David Gough ap, 3612.

......, John, 3771. See also Rice.

Regebowe, John, 3416.

Reggio, in Italy, p. 367, 3821.

........., P. Cardinal of, letter from, 983.

........., Cardinal, death of, 1918.

Reginald, Wm., 960.

Reigne (or Reygny), John, 1996.

........., Ric., 1996.

...., ..., in commission for Devon, 699, 917, 1503, 1812, 3183, 3566, 3589, 3605, 3938, 4539, 4783.

........., Wm., 1996.

Reignold. See Reynold.

Reishach, Simon de, Chancellor of Friesland, 5598, 5675, 5676.

........., ..., ..., concludes treaty between England and Saxony, 1565, 1717, 1718.

........., ..., ..., letters from, 5599, 5600.

Rekwall, Wales, 1041.

Relegh, Beds, 1467.

Relics, sent by the Bp. of Famagosta to Hen. VIII., 3456.

........., in the church of St. Mary Axe, 4993.

Remingham, captain of, 5758.

Renaldi, Lucas de, letter from, 4795.

Renée, second daughter of France, 5173, 5379.

........., ..., proposed marriage with the Prince of Castile, 3752, 4789, 5327, 5341.

........., ..., proposed marriage with Don Ferdinand, 4796, 4844, 4921, 4952, 5006, 5353.

Rengebourn, Katharine, daughter of Wm., 4248.

........., William, 4248.

Rens. See Rheims.

Renteria, in Spain, 3243, 3451, p. 457, 3762 ("Rendre").

Repton, Th., 5668.

Reresby, Ralph, in commission for Yorksh., 1735, 1804, 3358.

Resawen, Cornw., 3436.

Rescareke, John. See Roscarok.

Reskladen, Cornw., 3436.

Ressignol, Petitian, 4445 (i.)

Rest, John, 1399.

Restalrig, college of, 3623, 3624.

.... (Lastalrig), dean of, 4997.

........., chapel near the church of, 2041.

Restormell. See Rastormall.

Restwold, Ric., 3231.

Retainers, 3288.

Rethel, Jehan Conte de, Sieur Dorval, chevalier de l'ordre du Roy, 4924.

Rethelin, marquisate of, in Italy, p. 380.

Retherfeld Grey, Oxon, 5241.

Reton, Wm., 4384.

Reulx, Bp. of, ambassador from France to England, 3112.

Reux. See Roeux.

Revele, alias Reveley, Geo., 3799.

Reveleux, Noel, 4445 (ii).

Revell, Roland, p. 608.

Revels, master of the. See Gibson.

........., ... See Guildford, Sir Hen.

Revesby, abbot of, in commission for Linc. 1716, 1979, 3137, 5691.

Revet, James, 4195.

"Rewards" to labourers, 4232 (ix).

Rewe, Andrew, 3013.

......, Joan, wife of Andrew, 3013.

Rewex. See Roeux.

Rey, John, 4535.

Reygny. See Reigne.

Reynner, Hans, the Emperor's principal secretary, 3331, 3362, 4361, 5006, 5126, 5171, 5323, 5389, 5393.

Reynold, Hen., 514, 4013.

........., (or Reignold), Payce, gunner, 761, 781.

........., Ric., mayor of Leicester, 4742, 5186.

........., Rob., 5724.

........., Wm., 1047, 1665, 5622.

Reynolds, Eliz., wife of Wm., 5238.

........., John, 1133.

........., alias ap David, Rob., 3329.

........., Wm., 5238.

........., ..., in commission for Leic., 4812, p. 905.

Reynsforth. See Rainsford.

Reynys, John, 1082.

Reysby, Tho., abbot. of, 663.

Rheims (Rens or Rains), 4355; Swiss in service of France at, 4329.

Rhine, Lewis Count Palatine of the, 5746.

Rhodes, 3283, 4096.

.... Grand Master of. See Amboise, Emery d'; Blanchefort, Guido de; Caretto, Fabricius de.

........., lieutenant and council of, letters from, 3697, 4562.

........., eagle - bearer of (bajulinus aquillæ), 3874.

........., Archbishop of, 1860.

........., knights of. See Barnaldyng; Prégent.

Rhodes, Scotch preceptory of, 3277, 3625, 3626, 3651.

Ribawpiere the hoffmaster, 5323.

Ribbesford, Worcestershire, 4071.

Riburgh, Magna, 5194.

Rice, Edw. ap, 870, 1389.

......, Sir Griffith, in debt to the King, 5633.

......, ..., in the war, 3231, 3496, 4632.

......, ..., grants to, 1597, 5452.

......, ..., in commission for Gloucestersh., 4764, 5506 ; for Herefordshire, 5506 ; for Salop, 4394, 4827, 5506 ; for Worcestershire, 4470, 5506 ; for the Welsh Marches, 4198.

......, James ap, 4816.

......, Jenett ap. See Sutton.

......, Jevan ap, yeoman porter, 3378.

......, Joan, wife of Rob. ap, 3307.

......, John ap, clerk, 5012.

......, Manuell, 4505.

......, Meredith ap, grant to, 4815.

......, Morgan ap, clerk, 3273.

......, Rice Vaughan ap Richard ap, 4814.

......, Robert ap, 3307.

......, Walter ap, of London, 4514, 5502. See also Rees.

Richard I., chapel founded by, 5242.

.... II., charters of, 79, 1046, 1198, 1653.

........., chantry at Calais founded by, 5021.

.... III., grants of, 415, 1825.

........., as Duke of Gloucester, 4518, 4536, 5090.

........., Duke of York, father of Edw. IV., 1118, 1129, 1603.

Richard, Sir John, chaplain in Sir Sampson Norton's retinue, 4906.

........., John ap David ap, 3771.

Richards, Griffin, clerk of the Signet to the Queen, 307, 551.

........., Griffith, 235.

........., John, shipmaster, 4377.

........., Thomas, 4232.

........., William, 4258.

Richardson, James, 5268.

........., Robt., 5527.

Riche, Ric., of London, merchant, 5242.

Richer, Nic., 1182.

Richmond, Surrey, 4529, 4642, 4727, 4964, 5735.

........., King's wardrobe at, 1554.

........., letters dated, 4365, 4398, 4417, 4432, 5762.

........., Yorksh., 178, 192, 440, 1205, 3845.

........., shire of, Yorksh., 981, 1535, 3669.

........., archdeacon of, Thomas Dalby, 1115, 1750, 3062, 4652.

.... earldom of, 1472, 3943, 4022, 5674, 5689.

Richmond, honor of, 303, 339, 382, 1278, 3668.

........., fee of, Norfolk, 900, 3125.

........., and Derby, Margaret Countess of, 253, 326, 382, 403, 597, 660, 992, 1237, 1395, 1532, 1851, 1993, 3272, 3431, 4199, 4372, 5089, 5296.

........., ..., ..., her possessions, 235, 448, 645, 738, 778, 1367, 1711, 1866, 3061, 4022, 4436, 4904.

........., ..., ..., her servants, 146, 194, 195, 307, 327, 332, 337, 351, 372, 384, 390, 404, 479, 855, 1784, 1836.

........., ..., ..., money due to her, by Lewis XII., 1104.

........., ..., ..., grants to, 56, 407.

........., ..., ..., her executors, 236, 406.

........., ..., ..., her signature, 5735, 5737.

........., ..., ..., monastery founded by, 1802, 5275.

........., king-at-arms. See Machado.

........., herald, John Joyner, 1701, 3352, 3355, 3451, 5523.

........., ..., payments to, 3762, 4653.

........., ..., at the marriage of the Princess Mary, 5483.

Ricote, Parva, Oxon., 5685.

Ricquier, Charlot, 4445.

Ricroft, John, sergeant of the larder, 1023, 3871, 4630, 4892.

........., ..., in debt to the Crown, 5723.

Riding, East, archdeacon of. See Magnus, Th.

Rydyng, Humph., of Worcester, 4253.

Ridley, Cheshire, 131, 4748.

........., John, clerk, 862.

........., Nic., of Wylmondeswike, Northumberland, 187, 3600, 4556.

........., ..., sheriff of Northumberland, 537.

Rydlyngton, Rutland, 479.

Ridmerley, 3613.

Rydnale, Tho., coroner, 1139.

Rydon, Rob., clerk of the Council, 289, 588, 3478.

Rigges, Tho., and Anthony his son, 587.

Rightwise, John, in debt to the Crown, 3497.

........., ..., mayor of Norwich, 4558.

Rigley, Wm., page of the wardrobe of beds, 1887, 3521, 5435.

Rygynall, ——, captain, 3591, 3977.

Rill Nicolles, Sussex, 1598.

Rime, Dorset, 1240, 1635.

Ryne, on the Lago di Garda, 3471.

Ryng, Herman, 777, 3471.

......, Nich., gunner, 2012, 5070, 5774.

Ringhouses, Yorkshire, 3411, 4022, 4347.

Ringley, Wm., captain, 3980.

Ryngsell, Suff., 5260.

Ringshall, 1099.

Ryngston, manor of, 3304, 4254.

Ringwold, Kent, 735, 5167.

Ringwood, Hants, 1142, 1286, 5471.

Ripe, Sussex, 1464.

Ripylmonde, castle of, in Flanders, 3248.

Ryplington, Northumberland, 1040, 5010.

Ripon, Yorkshire, 3175, 5630.

Ripton Regis, church of, Linc. dioc., 744.

Risbrigger, John, 3542.

Rise, John, master tanner, 3272.

Rischach. *See* Reishach.

Risehams, Essex, 3761.

Rising, Norfolk, 36, 222.

........., ..., church of, 118.

Rising, John, monk, 821.

Riskyngton, Linc., 1430, 4695.

Risley, Beds, 835.

........., Sir John, 3088, 3761, 3816, 4302, 4904.

........., ..., knight of the Body, 124.

........., ..., in com. for Kent, 725, 906.

........., Thomasina, wife of Sir John, 4302.

Risshebrigge, Suffolk, 4966.

Riston or Rissheton, Rob. and John, 3548.

........., Rob., yeoman of the Chamber, 106.

........., ..., keeper of Walsall park, 50.

........., ... *See* Russheton.

Rivers, Augustin, prior of Woodbridge, 746.

........., Rich. Wydevill, Earl of, 434.

Robbers, great swarm in England, 2001.

Robert, ——, 3829.

........., Giles, merchant of Brittany, 3482.

........., John ap, 65.

Robertet, Florimond, treasurer of France, 1182, 3752, 5408, 5468, 5477, 5547, 5553, 5560, 5590.

Roberth, Walter, justice of gaol delivery for Maidstone, 763.

........., ..., in commission for Kent, 725, 906, 3428, 3605, 4663, 4847, 4927.

Roberts, Geo., 4996.

........., Tho., 65, 5748.

........., ..., auditor, 533, 577, 803, 1047, 1162, 1665, 4595.

Robertson. *See* Robinson.

........., Tho., of Boston, Linc. merchant of the staple of Calais, 1036.

........., ..., in commission for Linc., 278, 663, 1170, 1378, 1380, 4860, p. 906.

Robinson, John, of Boston, merchant, 1655.

........., ..., of London, brotherer, 2036.

........., ..., deputy of Sir Rob. Southwell, chief butler of England, 1242.

........., ..., in commission for Linc., 278, 663, 1170, 1378, 1380, 1979, 3137, 3351, 4860, 5476, p. 906, 5691.

........., ... *See* Robinson, Thos.

........., Robt., 4300.

........., Simon, inc. of More Monkton, York dioc., 1797.

........., Tho. (mistake for John?), in commission for Linc., 1716.

Robson, Cuthbert, 5200.

Roche, Lord de la. *See* Planis, Gerard de.

Roche Suryon, Prince de la, 5482.

Roche, Brian, serjeant of the kitchen, 1023.

........., ..., ..., purveyor, 1793, p. 433, 4630, 4892.

........., Eliz., daughter of Sir John, 1905.

........., Joan, daughter of Sir John, 1905.

... ., Sir John, 1905.

........., Thomas, 5000.

........., Wilhelmina, wife of Sir John, 1905.

........., Wm., 4878, p. 958.

Rochelle, 3357.

Rochester, Kent, 4022, 4347.

........., mayor of, 3497.

........., proclamation in, 1771.

........., bridge at, 5043.

........., ..., wardens of, 5043.

.... castle, 155.

........., ..., warden of, 47.

........., Bp. of. *See* Fisher.

........., ... (temp. Edw. IV.), 1441.

........., Christ., 235.

........., ..., groom of the chamber, grants to, 134, 710, 827, 1608, 4135, 4949.

........., Rob., gentleman of the household, 694, 1022, 3939.

Rochford, Essex, 5019.

........., Tho. Ormond Lord, summoned to Parliament, 5616.

Rockingham, Northt., 645.

.... forest, 314, 1641, 3084, 3085, 3098, 4762.

.... park, 67.

Rocque, Pierre de la, taken prisoner at the battle of Spurs, 4402.

Rocqueur, Jacot de, 4445 (i).

Roddesley, Derby, 5574.

Roderico, Peter, incumbent of Toft, Ely dioc., 3097.

Rodery. *See* Rotherey.

Roding, White, Essex, 735.

Rodney, Sir John, 3048.

........., ..., of Stoke Rodney, Somers., 5640.

........., ..., in commission, 287, 712, 3048, 3566, 3585, 3606, 3701, 4713.

........., Walter, on sheriff-roll for Somers. and Dors., 1949.

........., ..., sheriff of Oxon. and Berks, 4544.

........., Sir Walter, the King's lancer, grant to, 4840.

Roeux ("Royse"), Lord, governor of Eden (Hédin), 4319.

........., Count de, 4273, 4296, 5165.

Roger, Walter, 4067.

Rogers, John, 1825.

........., ..., in the war against France, 4074, 4475, p. 813.

........., ..., in commission for Dorset, 26, 708, 903, 2007, 3064, 3566, 3606, 3701, 4713, 5658.

Rogers, Tho., incumbent of Thornton, Linc. dioc., 375.
........., Wm., incumbent of Great Billing, Linc. dioc., 3689.
Rogis, John, in commission for Sussex, 3024.
Roham, Lord of, 4935 ; takes Brest Castle, 4076.
Rok, St. Peter de, church of, Heref. dioc., 4208.
Rokeby, Alex., clk., 856.
.... (or Rokesby,) Ralph, p. 436.
........., ..., in commission for co. York, 455, 954, 1550, 1735 (bis), 1799, 3072, 3219, 3358, 4719, 5193.
........., Ric., in commission for co.York, 455, 954, 1550, 1735 (bis), 1799, 3219, 4719, 5193, 5503, 5529, 5605.
........., Wm., of London, 5608.
........., ..., Archbp. of Dublin, chancellor of Ireland, 3212.
Rokeley, Tho., in commission for co. York, 273.
Rookes, John, 134.
Rokes, Ric., 3497 (ii.)
......., Tho., 2016, 3497 (ii.)
Rokewood. See Rukwode.
Rolls, Master of the, (Wm. Barons, temp. Hen. VII.), 380.
......., ..., (John Yong,) appointed, 165.
......., ..., ..., 617, 647, 1357.
......., ..., ..., delivers documents into the Treasury, 3023, 5274.
......., ..., ..., in the Privy Council, 5173.
......., ..., ..., warrants to, to cancel recognizances, 22, 63, 105, 226, 258, 275, 296, 313, 317, 408, 464, 531, 545, 566, 575, 578, 606, 618, 625, 639, 1003, 1004, 1006, 1527, 1574, 1584, 1596, 1604, 1755, 1756, 1757, 1758, 1773, 2027, 2036, 3079, 3080, 3113, 3114, 3153, 3470, 3601, 3969, 3988, 4023, 4350, 4616, 4617, 4714, 4732, 4787, 4940, 5098, 5116, 5229, 5522, 5563.
......., ... See also Yong, John.
......., ..., (Cuthbert Tunstal), 1148.
Rolleston, Roger, p. 608.
........., Thos., p. 609.
Rolt, John, 2030, 3979.
......., Wm., 2030.
......., ..., serjeant-at-arms, 5425.
......., ..., yeoman of the guard, grants to, 248, 502, 829, 1600, 1601.
Romagna, 3112, 3269, 5171 (ii.)
........., letter of protection of Louis XII., dated at, 1754.
Romandiola, 1701, 2039.
Romania, Prince of, 5705.
Rome, 288, 405, p. 119, 880, 1017, 1220, 1363, 1457, 1581, 1860, 1957, 2021, 3011, 3122, 3314, 3323, 3443, 3651, p. 474, 3777, p. 616, 4274, 4364, 4371, 4563, 4576, 4577, 4609, 5025, 5155, 5203, 5208, 5444, 5566, 5587.

Rome, Grimaldi's bank at, 5396.
......., St. Angelo, governor of, 3780.
......., St. Peter, church of, 3780.
......., Cardinal Gurk to, 3543, 3614.
......., election of a pope at, 3780.
......., See of, English army sent to defend, 3798, 4653.
......., Bp. of Murray proposed to be sent to, 3876.
......., Th. Nodry, archdeacon of Moray at, 5006.
......., Cardinal Bainbridge poisoned at, 5252, 5253, 5254, 5356, 5357.
......., exchange of English subjects with, prohibited by act of Parliament, 814.
......., indulgences purchased at, 1860.
......., Geo. Ardeson to licence persons to visit the Court of, 1816.
......., licence to obtain letters from, 3360.
......., licences to obtain bulls from, 4537, 4567.
......., bulls of, delivered into the Treasury by the Master of the Rolls, 3023.
......., residence of Ammonius at, 1957, 2013.
......., residence of Wm. Burbank at, 5334.
......., residence of John Sixtinus at, 3535.
......., treaties said to be concluded at, 1948, 4810, 4910.
......., Cardinal Bainbridge, Henry VIII.'s representative at. See Bainbridge, Christ., Cardinal of York.
......., ambassador to, from France. See France.
......., ..., from Germany. See Germany.
......., ..., from Scotland. See Scotland.
......., bulls dated at, 168, 169, 4718, 4722, 4723, 5411, 5412, 5413, 5414, 5415, 5416.
......., letters dated at, 11, 267, 908, 924, 976, 3066, 3240, 3278, 3456, 3806, 3821, 4039, 4062, 4283, 4287, 4288, 4327, 4446, 4454, 4455, 4458, 4471, 4491, 4500, 4506, 4582, 4605, 4608, 4610, 4621, 4691, 4724, 4735, 4747, 4756, 4835, 4926, 4936, 5054, 5068, 5106, 5107, 5110, 5156, 5168, 5169, 5174, 5262, 5269, 5301, 5331, 5332, 5333, 5342, 5349, 5350, 5354, 5358, 5364, 5365, 5378, 5382, 5392, 5396, 5399, 5405, 5434, 5443, 5445, 5447, 5448, 5457, 5458, 5496, 5535, 5538, 5540, 5602, 5613, 5635, 5650, 5662, 5663, 5664, 5665, 5666, 5670, 5671, 5672, 5678, 5702, 5706.
........., church of, 1689.
Romney, Kent, Cinque Port, 4996.
........., marsh of, 4701.
........., Old, Kent, 735.
Romney, Jas., p. 553.
Romsey. See Rumsey.
Ronsard, letter from, 4174.
Rookes. See Rokes.
Rookwood. See Rukwode.
Roos, Lord de, receiver of the annuities of, 4347.

Roos, Lord de, sons of, retained to serve Mary Queen of France, 5484.
......, Edm. Lord, son of Thomas Lord, 750, 1621.
......, ..., kinsman and heir of Eleanor, Duchess of Somerset, 458.
......, George Lord. See Manners, Sir George.
......, Tho. Lord, 750, 1621.
Roote, Steph., coroner for Sussex, 1160.
Rooth, Wales, 1583.
Roper, Christ., 218, 1732.
........., Geo., 1691.
........., Hen., 3060.
........., John, of Eltham, Kent, 3088, 3816.
........., ..., justice of gaol delivery for Canterbury, 3775, 3790, 4495; for Maidstone, 763.
........., ..., in commission for Kent, 725, 906, 3428, 3605, 4663, 4701, 4847, 4927, p. 906; for Sussex, 274.
Rorariis, Anth. de, 4078, 4276.
Roscarok, John, 3583, 3605, 3938.
........., ..., in commission for Cornwall, 1812, 1954, 1984, 3290.
Rose, a golden, sent by Julius II. to Hen. VIII., 976, 983.
...... (or Rosse), John, in commission for co. York, 455, 481, 954, 1550, 1735 (bis), 1799, 3219, 3358, 4719, 5193.
......, Matilda, widow of Ric. Gorge, 1168.
Rosington, Yorksh., 1679.
Rosogan, John, 1853.
Ross Herald, 3339, 4351, 4497, 5757.
Rossell. See Russell.
Roston, ——, of St. Laurence Pounteney, 1363.
Rostormell. See Rastormall.
Rote (or Rotys), John, 3428, 4804, p. 904.
......, Wm., 3939.
Roteby, Leic., 3096.
Rothelin, Marquis of, brother to Mons. de Dunois, killed, 11.
........., ... See Longueville, Duke of.
Rothers, Alex., 4033.
Rotheragh, Tho. ap, alias ap Throtheragh, 1749.
Rotherey, alias Rodery, Christ., 3531.
Rothley, John, clk., 1575.
Rothwell, Roger, p. 954, 5761 (iv).
........., Wm., 2081, 5567.
Rotynbourgh, the Emperor at, 4844.
Rotys, John. See Rote, John.
Rouarque, seneschal of. See Thylny.
Roucliff, Sir John, in commission for York, 1798, 1941, 1995, 3177, 4015, 5166.
Rouen, 1616, 3318, 4273, 4328 (2), 4329.
........., fortified, 3678, 3752.
........., port of, letter of James IV. to the officers of, 2050.
........., council of, 4328.
........., Cardinal of. See Amboise, George d'.

Rouge, Jehan le, 4445 (i).
Rougecross Herald, 476, p. 520, 3986, 4439, 4441, 4451.
...., wages of, 4375.
Roughborowe, Somers., 155.
Roukeshawe, Wm., clk., 856.
Round, Armannus (or Harman), 1405, 3620.
Rouse. See Rowse.
Roussy, Earl of, at the marriage of Princess Mary, 5482.
Rouville, Louis de, grand veneur de France, lieut. general of the united fleet of France and Scotland against the English, 4453.
........., ..., at the marriage of Princess Mary, 5482.
Roverette, near Trent, 216.
Rovigo (Rwigo), 5532.
Rowcastell, on the Scotch borders, 4556.
Rowd (Roude, misprinted Ronde), Wilts, 155.
Rowdon, John, 1744.
........., Ric., 536.
........., Walter, of Gloucester, 1287, 4071.
........., ..., keeper of the rolls in co. Glouc., 3802.
........., ..., in commission, 930, 1049, 1469, 1695, 3641, 3712, 3804, 4024.
Rowe, John, in commission for Devon, 699, 917, 1503, 1812, 3183, 3566, 3589, 3605, 3938, 4539, 4783.
Rowes, ——, of Devonshire, excepted from the general pardon, 12.
Rowland, John, 1050.
........., Tho., abbot of Abingdon, 3025, 3050, 3052, 3058.
........., ..., prior of Suffield, 3297.
........., Sir, 1491.
Rowley, Staff., 155.
........., John, p. 493.
Rownanger, Ric., painter, 4642.
Rownedon, Kent, 685.
Rowse, marches of Wales, 438, 1579, 4907.
........., Tho., 235, 1836.
........., Wm., 4632.
........., Sir Wm., at the marriage of Princess Mary, 5483.
Rowseley, Eliz., 5723.
Rowt, Hen., chaplain, 3682, 3683.
Rowthall, Ric. 1923. See also Rudhall.
........., Thos. See Durham, Bp. of.
Rowton, Chesh., 4748.
Roy, Francis le, 5519.
......, Guyon le, admiral of Normandy and Britanny, 3830.
......, Haquin le, 4445 (i.)
......, John, 633, 2056.
......, Peter, 5712.
......, Petit, 4445 (i.)
......, Wm., 3014.
Royal, the, a house in London, 855.

Roydon, Suff., 5180.
........., John, 4538.
Royse, Lord. *See* Roeux, Lord.
Roziers, Jehan des, 5163.
Rubeis, Ct. Philip de, 3269.
Rudberd, Pembroke, 1193.
Rudhale, John, 4414.
Rudhall. *See also* Rowthall.
........., Thomas. *See* Durham, Bp. of.
........., Wm., in commission for Hereford-shire, 646, 675, 1400, 1903, 3686, 5506.
........., ..., for Shropshire, 918, 1981, 3071, 3715, 4394, 4827, 5506.
........., ..., ... for Gloucestershire, 930, 1049, 1469, 1695, 3641, 3712, 3804, 4024, 4118, 4764, 5506.
........., ..., ... for Worcestershire, 892, 1971, 3301, 3709, 4770, 5506.
........., ..., ... for Denbighland, 955.
Rudston, York, 954, 1550, 1735, 1799, 3538.
Rudstone, Walter, 273.
Ruee, St. Espert de, 4329.
Rufford, monastery of, 824.
........., Walter, 726.
Rugge, Tho., 878.
Ruggebisshop, 1987.
Rugheswyre, on the Borders, 4556.
Ruislip, Middx., 1151.
Rukholde, Essex, 3761.
Rukwode, Edmund, 4680.
Rumsey, Hants, 1824.
........., Simon, of the monastery of Malmes-bury, 1183.
Runsery, Eliz., of Brittany, 4679.
Rupe, Maura de, 5480.
Rüseer, Fred. *See* Rysther.
Rushe, Thos., serjeant-at-arms, 5483.
Ruskington, 395, 1277.
Russell, ——, capt., 3980.
........., John, spear at Calais, 4476.
........., ..., annuity payable to, 235.
........., Rob., in the war, 3864.
Russhebury, Salop, 4694.
Russheton, Rob., usher of the chamber, 616, 1851. *See* Riston.
Russhok, Worcestershire, 3879.
Russia, Great Duke of, 5259.
Russians, invasion of Poland by, 4449.
Rust, Ric., 5194.
Ruthal. *See* Durham, Thomas Bp. of.
Ruthin, Denbighshire, 955, 1678.
.... Castle, Denbighshire, 43, 1113.
.... church, 1811.
........., receiver of, 315.

Ruthven, Wm. Lord, safe conduct to, 4997.
Rutland, royal possessions in, 4022.
.... forest, 667.
........., sheriff-roll for, 664, 1316, 1949, 3507, 4544, 5561.
........., sheriffs of, 3887.
........., commissions in, 266, 4434.
........., tenths and fifteenths in, 3441.
Rutland, Nich., and Clemence his wife, 4911.
Rutt, John, ship master, 3591, 3977, 3980.
Rutter, ——, ship master, 4377.
Ruzanly, Stephen de, French prisoner, 5777.
Ruysbank, tower of, near Calais, 39, 1539, 4635.
........., lieutenant of, 1452, 3485, 4635.
Rwigo. *See* Rovigo.
Rydall, 5655.
Rye. *See* Ships.
......., 3909.
......., subsidy of, 4996.
......., bailiffs of, 160, 3163.
Ryne, John De la, French gunner, 4402.
Rynkins Bore, Warw., 3186.
Ryplington. *See* Ripplington.
Rypton. *See* Repton.
Rys, ap. *See* Rice.
Ryschach. *See* Reishach.
Ryse, York, 229.
Ryshangles, Suffolk, 1453.
Rysther, Frederick, 5163.
Ryther, Sir Ralph, in com. for Yorksh., 1798, 1941, 1995, 3177, 4015, 5166.
Rytlyng, Hans, German captain, 4793.
Ryton, Salop, 4594.
Ryveley, Ralph, 4430, 4531.

S.

Sa——, Gracia de, servant of King of Na-varre, 3762.
Sabay, 4173.
Sabello, Constantine, 216, p. 253.
Sabellus, Troillus, 3269.
Sabyn, Wm., captain, 3903, 3980, 4474, p. 813, 5761.
........., ..., letter from, 3974.
........., ..., King's ships under him ordered to the Firth, 4682.
........., ..., ... of the Sabyne, 3591, 3977; wages for, 5152.
Sabisford, John, 167.
Sacheverell, Master, 5764.
........., Henry, 1316.
........., Sir Henry, 4032.
........., Ralph, 4706.
........., Richard, of Kyrby, Leic., 1372, 4070.

Sacheverell, Richard, in commission of the peace for Leicester, 656, 1094, 1425, 1971, 4783, 4812.
........., ..., on sheriff-roll for Warw. and Leic., 1949.
........., Sir Ric., of Stoke Pogis, Bucks, 4253, 4630.
..........., ..., grant to, 3891, 4798.
........., ..., knighted at Tournay, 4468.
........., ..., in commission, 4809, p. 905.
........., Tho., of . . . ., Derby, 1372.
Sacquespee, Simon, 4445.
Sacramor (Sagramour), the Viscount, 4210, 4216.
Sagadul, monastery of, 3141.
Saham Tony, Norf., 3943, 4948, 5115.
Sailors of England, grant to the, 5108.
St. Alban's, Hertfordshire, 12.
........., gaol delivery for, 4742.
........., abbey of, 155, 5177.
........., abbot of 776, 4377.
........., ..., in debt to Henry VII., 1639.
........., ..., summoned to Parliament, 5616.
St. Amand, Richard Beauchamp Lord, 1905.
St. Andrew's, (misprint for Glasgow) James Beton, abp. of, 910.
........., church of, 5678.
........., castle of, 5614.
........., prior of, 1176, 5614.
........., abpric. of, 3479.
........., ..., Card. Cibo's secretary going to take possession of, 4725.
........., ..., the council will not give the, to Card. Cibo, 5208.
........., Alex. Stuart, Abp. of, 379, 774, 3838, 4502, 4625, 4627.
........., ..., ..., letters from, 3479, 3828, 3829.
........., ..., ..., letter to, 3618.
........., ..., ..., Chancellor of Scotland, 3303.
........., archdeacon of. See Dunbar, Gawin.
St. Antoine, faubourg, 5408.
St. Aubyn, Peter, 1812.
St. Austin, monastery of, 3091.
St. Basil, Erasmus's translation of, 4447, 4448, 4528.
St. Bertin, Mons. See Berghes, Ant.
St. Bertin's, Antonio, abbot of, 5297.
St. Briavel, Glouc., lordship and castle of, 1355, 1389, 3345.
St. Chrysogon, Cardinal. See Corneto.
Seyntclere, John, 3507.
........., ..., sheriff of Essex and Herts, 4544.
St. Columba, captain of, 3026.
St. Cosmo and Damian, Card. See Innocent.
St. Cross, John, abbot of, in debt to Henry VII., 1639.
........., Cardinal of, 1581, 1582, 1701, 1948, 2002, 5378.

St. Cuthbert's banner, 4461, 4462.
St. David's, Edward Vaughan nominated Bishop of, 393.
...., grants to, 328, 3612.
........., ..., summoned to Parliament, 5616.
St. Denis, in France, Lewis XII. at, 5560, 5569.
........., ..., Queen of France to be buried at, 4824.
........., ..., Mary Queen of France, to be crowned at, 5547.
........., ..., letter dated at, 5583.
St. Edmund's Bury. See Bury St. Edmund's.
St. Elvyn, Cornwall, 3436.
St. Espert (Esprit?), 4329.
St. Euphemia, near Brescia, Duke of Nemours at, 3026.
St. Eusebius, Card., 3624.
St. Fontaine, la porte, 4467.
Santforth, John, yeoman of the Crown, 1297.
St. Genois, Nich. de, 5164, 5175.
St. George's bar, 5735.
St. George, collar of, 3271.
........., banner of, p. 609.
........., [Raphael], Card. of [Bishop of Ostia], 3443, 3777, 3779, 3780, 3838, 4283.
........., ..., letter from, 982.
St. Germain-en-Laye, French commissions and letters patent dated at, 5278, 5279, 5280, 5311, p. 861 (note).
........., ..., publication of peace between England and France, 5326.
........., ..., letters dated at, 5302, 5367.
St. Germain's, in Jersey. See Jersey.
San Germano, plundered and burnt by the Swiss, 4096, 4283.
Seyntgerman, Chr., 857.
St. Ive's, Cornw., 1680, 3646.
St. Jago, Steph. de, p. 432.
St. Jerome, Erasmus occupied with, 2013, 4427, 4576.
St. John de Luce, Spain, p. 399.
Saint John, John, 5296.
........., Elizabeth, wife of Geo. Earl of Kildare, 1299.
St. John, John ap, pardon to, 3771.
........., Sir John, 236, 4377.
........., ..., in commission of the peace for Beds, 1051, 1122, 2045, 3501, 4700, p. 907.
........., ..., executor of Margaret Countess of Richmond, 406.
St. John of Jerusalem, prior of, and Lord of. See Docwra, Thomas.
St. John's Road, 4665, 5130.
St. Johnstone. See Perth.
Saintleger, Anth., 5483.
........., Geo., 4221, 4534.
........., ..., in the war against France, 4306, 4314, 4477.
........., Sir George, 4589.

Saintleger, Ralph, of Ulcombe, 4291.
........., ..., grant, 5625.
........., ..., in commission of the peace for
    Kent, 725, 906, 3428, 3605, 4663, 4847,
    4927.
St. Leonard's, manor of, Sussex, 1835, 2051.
........., near Exeter, 2080.
.... Thoby, Essex, 530.
Saintlowe, John, son of Nicholas, 570.
St. Malo, 3877.
St. Margaret's Hall, 3969.
Santa Maria de Uron. See Uron.
St. Mark, Card., letters from, 5671, 5672. See
    Ancona.
........., ..., his secretary, 1220.
St. Marther, 1943.
St. Martin, Johannes de, 5729.
........., Tho., captain of Guernsey, deceased,
    94.
St. Martin's, white wine of, p. 616.
St. Mary's Isle, priory of, 3038.
........., Matfelon, Middx., 1540.
St. Matthew's, broad sound before, 3877.
St. Nicholas des Pretz, Philip abbot of, 4466.
St. Nicholas' Island, ships at, 4076.
St. Omer (St. Umbris), 4057, 4232, 4253,
    4389, 4427, 4431, 4526, 5032, 5172,
    5182.
Saintonge, 5480.
St. Osith's. See Ships.
St. Paul's, Bp. of, 5590.
St. Peter's castle, 3697.
St. Poll, John, grant to, 1896.
........., ..., in commission of the peace for
    Lincoln, 1171, 3342, 4358, 4593, 4860.
........., Earl of, present at the marriage of
    Princess Mary, 5482; at her corona-
    tion, 5560.
St. Praxedis, Cardinal of. See Bainbridge.
Sainctpy. See Puy.
St. Quatuor, Lawrence Cardinal, 5434.
St. Quentin, 3678.
St. Sabina, Cardinal, 5408.
St. Sauveur, warlike preparations at, 4330.
St. Sebastian's, 3451, p. 462, 3755, 3807.
........., attacked by the French, p. 451, 3593.
........., letter dated at, 3355.
........., warrant dated at, 3476.
St. Severino, 31, 5482. See Galiace.
.... Frederick Cardinal of, Protector of
    France, 3283, 4096, 4283, 4455, 5208,
    5378.
........., as legate of Bologna, 3112.
........., restored to rank of Cardinal, 4288.
........., at Milan, 1581.
........., the Lord Robert of, 4253.
Sancti Spiritus, prior of, beside the port of
    St. Adrian, 3356.
St. Stephen's, deanery of, 4747.
........., Earl of, 3356.
St. Steven, Ct. of, Marshal of Navar, 3355.

St. Thomas, ordnance left at, 4479.
........., Prince of Castile's subjects near, 4319.
........., garrison at, 5163.
St. Vitall, Cardinal, 3780, 4283.
St. Walric, feodary of, 373.
St. Wilfride, banner bearer before, 5630.
Sakfeld, Rob., p. 432, 3507.
Sakvile, John, 3785, 3967, p. 907.
........., Ric., in commission of the peace for
    Sussex, 281, 1509, 3428, 4804, p. 904.
Salarola, 11.
Salazar, Tristan de, Abp. of Sens, 1182.
Salisbury, 3205, 3231, 3665, 4377.
........., Old, (Old Sarum), 1270.
........., New, 1935, 3763.
........., castle of, 5715.
........., com. of gaol delivery for, 554.
........., fair, 4863.
........., Bishop's mills in, 3763.
........., Edm. Audley, Bishop of, 776, 1183,
    1200, 1381 (here named Edward) 1526,
    1806, 1929, 1930, 3292.
........., ..., lease by, 3763.
........., ..., letter from, 5544.
........., ..., summoned to Parliament, 5616.
........., ..., in com. of peace for Bucks, 454,
    943, 1379, 2045, 3919; for Wilts, 1489,
    1938, 3157, 3605, 4583.
........., earldom of, 448, 1060, 3845.
........., Alice Countess of, 4507.
........., Margaret Countess of, 4545.
........., ..., Act for the restitution of, 4848.
........., Ric. Earl of, 180, 4507.
........., Hen., 360.
........., John, sewer of the chamber, grant to,
    324, 4242.
........., Roger, yeoman of the guard, grants to,
    81, 1032, 1191, 3145, 3677, 3926.
........., in com. for Denbigh, 955.
........., Sir Tho., 81, 324, 1041.
Salisbury's lands, 665, 900, 901, 1831, 3061,
    4223.
Sall, John, of Lothbury, London, 186.
Sallans, De, treasurer of Burgundy, 4509.
Salley, Miles. See Llandaff, Bishop of.
Salop, 298, 1839, 1974, 3178, 3289, 4253.
........., sheriff-rolls for, 664, 1316, 1949, 3507,
    4544, 5561.
........., commissions for, 918, 1981, 3071, 3715,
    3760, 4198, 4394, 4827, 4939, p. 904.
........., feodaries of, 4414.
........., collectors of, 777.
........., proclamation in, 1771.
........., muster of, 3336.
Saltashe, ships prested for the King in, 3978.
Salter, or Salton, John, in com. for Salop, 918,
    3071, 3715, 4394, p. 904.
........., Tho., sewer of the chamber, 1041.
........., grants to, 1488, 1916, 4980.
Saltfleet, 5765.
........., haven, 1326, 1983.

Saltland, Surrey, 1488, 1916.
Saltmersh, John, 273.
Salton. *See* Salter.
Saltpetre put under arrest in Spain, 3614, 3662.
Salucio, the Swiss at, 4326.
Salusses, Marquis of, 4924.
Salvage, Francis, son of Ambrosius, of Italy, 4244.
Salvaterra, in Bierne, 4267.
Salviati, Barth., merchant of Florence, 5324.
........., Jacomo, the Pope's brother, ambassador of Florence, 4323.
Salwarpe, Worc., 703, 3490, 3681.
Salwey, Thomas, son of Thomas, 5014.
Salzburg, 1861.
Sam, Jacquet de, 4445.
......, Tho., deceased, 769, 822, 1200.
Sameye (misprinted Simaye), Prince of, 4932.
Samford, Edm., in com. for Westmoreland, 2009, 3048, 3552, 5506, p. 904.
........., ..., on sheriff roll for Cumberland, 3507.
........., ..., Sheriff of Cumb., 4544.
........., ..., commission to, 3703.
........., John, 235.
Samon, Thos., of Hansley Wodhous, 4728.
Samora, Bp. of, 3584.
Samper, John, of London "shierman," 4803.
Sampford, Somers., 4071.
.... Courteney, Devon, 2080.
Sampier, John, of Shrewsbury, petty captain, 4945.
Sampson, Dr. Richard, 5006, 5467.
........., ..., letters from, 4982, 4983, 5251, 5386, 5391, 5418, 5424, 5429, 5439, 5446, 5554, 5583, 5587, 5591, 5697.
........., ..., Privy Council think it needless for him, to go to Paris, 5657.
........., Tho., of Sekforde, Suff., 1546.
........., Sir Tho., of Playford, Suff., 3582.
Samyer, Estienne, master of the works of Bethune, 4445.
Sanate, Mallin, 4445.
Sancerre, Earl of, 5482.
Sanchar, John, M.A., 474, 714.
Sanchio, ——, ship master, 4377.
Sancta Crux, the ship which conveyed Katharine of Arragon to England, 1140.
Sanctæ Crucis, Card. *See* St. Cross.
Sanctuary, 4096.
Sandall, York, 54, 178, 1205, 3548, 3845.
Sandes (Saundis), Geo., 327.
........., John, 1192.
........., Rob., 1949.
........., Tho., 349.
........., Sir Wm., of Vine, Hants, 464, 1212, 1574, 1675, 3191, 3451, 3496, 3762, 4237, 4284, 4653, 5180, 5723.
........., ..., grants to, 569, 798, 873, 1006, 1084, 1285, 1286, 3123, 3789, 4205.
........., Sir Wm., keeper of the ordnance at Fontarabia, 3298.

Sandes, Sir Wm., in the war against France 3885, 4306, 4307, 4314, 4632; treasurer, 3231, 3476, 3593.
........., ..., present at the marriage of Princess Mary, 5483.
........., ..., in debt to the Crown, 2044, 5633.
........., ..., in com. of array for Hants, 3688, 3723, 4979.
........., ..., sheriff of Hants, 1316.
........., ..., in com. of peace for Hants, 904, 4676.
........., ..., commission to, 3173.
........., ..., yeoman of the Crown, 3739, 3740.
........., ..., yeoman usher of the chamber, 5395.
Sandfordhith Ferry, Oxon., 5611.
Sandgate, 1073, 4022.
Sandherst, Glouc., 4158.
Sandwich. *See* Ships.
........., 1687, 3163, p. 436, 3857, 3887, 3890, 3891, 4067, 4094, 4103, 4492, 5548.
........., the Admiral at, 5130.
...., English navy at, 4474.
........., subsidy in, 4996.
........., customer of, 387.
........., St. Clement, church of, 537.
........., Ralph de, justice, 1099. .
Sanglier, Giles de, 4174.
Saona, p. 366.
Sapcote, Edw., sheriff of Rutland, 1316.
Sapcottes, Ric. of Copyngford, Northt., 1067.
Saperton, Linc., 4695.
Sapley, Hunts, 477.
Saracens, 1295, 5729.
"Sarcuz," 4431.
Saragossa, Archbp. of, bastard son of the, 3361.
Sare, John, of London, 4643.
Sark, &c., captain of, 941.
......, the natives of, 941.
Sarna, a ship of, 3458.
Sarrinall, Countess of, in Greece, 816.
Sarsedon, church of, Salisb: dioc., 1760.
Sassari, Sardinia, 1869.
Satalia, 1659.
Saten, John, 592.
Sawarde, Lord. *See* Howard.
Saucheverell. *See* Sacheverell.
Saunder, Hen., in com. for Surrey, 3996, 4693, 4734, 4808, 5237.
Saunders, John, clerk, 4879.
........., Wm., 4912, 5346.
Sauvage, John de, Lord de Schaubeke, president of Flanders, 4508.
Sauvaige, Moran, 4445.
Savage, Christ., 4788.
........., Edw., son of John, 1178.
........., Sir Edw., in com. for Yorksh., 1735, 1804, 1941, 1995, 3072, 3177, 3358, 4015.

Savage, Sir Humph., forfeited possessions of, 1336, 3537.

........., Jas. 1477, 1966.

........., ..., in com. for Notts, 1514, 1735. 1798, 1804, 1964, 3092.

........., John, 3613, 3818.

........, ..., ..., sen., 1178.

........., ..., in the war against France, 4306, 4421, 4534.

........., Sir John, 3613.

........., ..., jun., 5180.

........., ..., in the war against France, 3231.

.... , ..., knighted at Tournay, 4468.

........., ..., at the marriage of Princess Mary, 5482.

........., ... sheriff-roll for Worcester, 5561.

........., ..., sheriff " in fee," of Worcester-shire, 1949.

........., ..., late sheriff of Worces., 1284.

........., ..., in debt to the Crown, 2044, p. 434, 5633.

........., Peter, 3223.

........., Rich., captain, 4253.

........., ..., in com. for Notts, 266, 3092, 3494, 4776, 5183, 5225.

Savell, Hen., son of Sir John, 1301.

........., Sir John, 54, 777, 1301, 3548.

Savernake, Wilts, 155.

........., forest of, 5544.

Savona, 4546.

Savoy, 4283.

........., native of, 5639.

.. .., Archduke of, p. 609, p. 626.

........., bastard of, his signature, 4924.

:. ......, Duchess of. *See* Margaret of Savoy.

........., Duke of, 3325, 4210, 5675.

........., René, Duke of, marriage of, 922.

........., ..., at the treaty between France and Castile, 4924.

........., ..., letter from, 4273.

........., Duke of, sister of, 5718.

........., general of, 4210.

........., Hosp. of the, 3292, 5633.

Sawles, Tho., 1040, 5010.

Sawsey, forest, Northt., 434.

Sawsyde, E. and W., 4556.

Saxby, Elizabeth, 5394.

........., John, in com. for Northt., 1763, 3503, 3745, 5291.

Saxe, Duke of, 4563, 4282.

........., ..., his governor at Antwerp, 4328.

........., young Duke of, 5404.

........., ..., governor of Friesland, 3340, 4924, 5599, 5676.

........., ..., confirms the league with England, 1565, 1717, 1718.

........., ..., defeats Embden, Count Edezard, 5327.

........., ..., requires a loan from England, 5600.

........., ..., letter from, 5598.

........., ..., letter to, 5500, 5713.

Saxe, Duke of, chancellor of, 5600, 5675, 5676.

........., ..., steward of, 5327.

Saxes, Baron of, 4273.

Saxeta, Regnerus de, p. 397.

Saxlyngham, Norf., 1530, 3881, 4254.

Saxston, Yorkshire, 1860.

Say, Ric. Fenys, Lord, 573.

......, Sir Wm., in com. for Herts, 309, 706, 1020, 1971, 3102, 3601, p. 906.

......, Hugh, servt. to Ld. Mountjoy, 4917.

......, Wm., 4996.

Sayesbury, manor, Middx,, 1167.

Saysargh, Westmor., 275, 1052.

Sbarra, Fran., of Lucca, 3472, 3898, 3965.

Sclater Ford, 4556.

Scobell, John, 4476.

Scotchman, the four corteaux of the, 3361.

Scotists, 4447.

Scotland, 216, 1408, 1414, 3005, 3086, 3322, 3339, 3346, 3349, 3372, 3479, 3569, 3577, 3625, 3629, 3648, 3651, 3678, 3838, 3876, 3882, 3903, 4283, 4398, 4434, 4499, 4573, 4574, 4824, 4844, 4952, 4978, 5006, 5090, 5151, 5164, 5370, 5 590, 5634, 5649, 5681, 5759.

........., proposed to be included in treaty with other powers, 5285, 4830 ; treats for a peace, 1458.

. ..., confirmation of the treaty of 1502 with, 234.

........., peace between England and, 5613.

........., ..., conditions of, 3811.

........., in league with France, 3218, 3303, 3837.

........., in treaty with other powers, 5319.

........., treated with, for redress of grievances, 1066, 1820, 2078, 3007, 3128, 3696, 3726.

........., attacks upon, by Dacre, 4520, 4522, 4523, 4529, 4556.

........., the war in, 3412.

........., ..., expenses of, 4375.

........., disturbances in, 5541.

........., defences of England against, 3884, 4309, 4388.

........., English navy in, 4682.

........., French ships in, 3752, 4273.

........., friars observants in, 4678.

........., Dacre and West are to be sent to, 5745.

........., Jas. De Bannisius sent to, 5208.

........., papal prothonotary in, 4615, 4951.

........., Spanish ambassador in, 3279.

.... and Burgundy, 1245.

.... and France, 1407, 4563, 4875, 5675.

.... and Denmark, 2077, 3138, 3225, 3633, 4844.

........., birth of a prince of, 3138, 3577, 3631.

........., admiral of. *See* Arran, Earl of.

........., chamberlain of. *See* Home, Alex.

........., chancellor of, 4951, 5641.

........., council of, 4529, 4869, 4951.

Scotland, court of, letter dated from, 3617.
........., prince of, 3882.
........., protector of. *See* Ancona.
........., receiver of petitions from, 811, 2082.
........., secretary of. *See* Paniter.
........., treasurer of, 3577, 4403, 4459.
........., warden-general of, 189.
........., warden of, 3326, 4652.
........., herald of, 3838, 4523, 4951 ; sent to England, 4112, 4951, 4997 ; sent to Hen. VIII. while in France, p. 624 ; sent to France, 3838, 4844 ; sent to Zeland, 5006.
........., ambassadors of, 1066, 1820, 2069 ; to France, 2062, 2075 ; to Rome, 3225.
........., commissioner of, 1739, 3569, 3577, 3696 ; safe conduct to, 3676.
........., the beer of, 4461.
........., bishoprics of, 4502.
........., first fruits of, 2061.
........., fleet of, 4533, 4556, 5762.
........., the great ship of, 3811, 3814.
........., ships of, 4682 ; at Dieppe, 4843. *See also* Ships.
........., gold in, 1782.
........., labourers, 3808.
........., marches of. *See* Marches of Scotland.
...., merchants of, 3631, p. 522 ; in Bruges, 773 ; in Hamburg, 3629.
........., musters in, 3326.
........., natives of, 3690, 3998, 4027, 4123, 4649, 4650, 4780, 4879, 5622.
........., ordnance of, taken at Flodden, 4460, 4520, 4869, 4902.
........., Parliament of, 4951.
........., pirates of, 3631.
........., spies of, 3359 ; Wm. Dawson, a Scot, offers his services to England as a spy, 4743.
........., St. John's, commandry of, in, 3651.
Scots, 3358, 3359, 4169, 4432, 4483, 4502, 4735.
......, Hen. VIII.'s pardon to the, 1932, 2038, 3170.
...... invade England and are defeated, 4284.
...... at Flodden, 4461, 4462, 4464.
...... obstinate against England, 4725 (ii.), 5048.
...... insult the papal ambassador, whom Henry offers to avenge, 5048.
......, their unreasonable demands concerning prisoners, 4497.
...... prepare to attack Berwick, 4868 ; besiege Berwick, 4902.
...... in England, 4422, 4423, 4581 ; in France, 4484 ; in Low Countries, 5292 ; at Rome, 4455.
...... at the tournament, 5606.
...... discomfited by Sir Wm. Bulmer, 4457.
......, Maximilian demands aid from, 1195.
Scotnsbury, John, 4934.
Scotyn, John de, Katharine of Arragon's servant, 8, p. 119.

Scrayingham (Skrayenham), church of, York dioc., 5498, 5630.
Skrebyllesby, Linc., 1757.
Scriven, John, 4993.
........., Tho., 664, 1316, 1949.
..........., ..., in com. for Salop, 918, 3715, 4394, 4827, p. 904.
Scrope, Eliz., widow, 3211.
........., Hen., of Bolton and Upsall, called Lord Bolton, in com. for Yorksh., 1735, 1799, 1804, 3219, 3358, 5244, p. 907.
..........., ..., summoned to Parliament, 5616.
..........., ..., his signature, 4439.
........., John, on sheriff-roll for Wilts, 5561.
........., Sir John, mandate to delay the sending of forces to Southampton, 3824.
..........., ..., on sheriff-roll for Wilts, 664, 4544.
..........., ..., in com. for Wilts, 1938, 3157, 4583.
........., John Lord, 4254.
........., Ralph, 4439.
..........., ..., Lord Upsall. *See* Upsall.
Scroteby, manor of, Norf., 5150.
Scuysshe, John, 5474.
Scutier, Stram, French officer, 3325.
Seaman, Peter, 5820.
Searde, John, son of John Searde of Barrowe, Soms., 3505.
Seaton, ——, 3972.
Seclyng, English army at, 4253.
Secretary, the. *See* Pace, Ric.
........., the chief, 5320.
Sedan, Sieur de, 4924.
Sedunensis. *See* Sion.
See, Wm., 4996.
Segeford, manor of, Norf., 3304, 4254.
Segovia, Bp. of, 8.
Segrave, Nic. De, and heirs, p. 21.
Segwence, Bp. of. *See* Siguença.
Seine, the, 3357.
Seissel, Claud de, 1182.
Sekforde, Suff., 1546.
Seland. *See* Zealand.
Selby, monastery of, 920.
......, abbot of, 5616.
Sele, Kent, 3774.
Selim Shah, Sultan of Turkey, 5470, 5592, 5592, 5705.
..........., ..., prepares to besiege Rhodes, 3697.
.... *See* Sophie.
..........., ..., (Selimchat) the younger, 3283.
Selkesey, Wilts, 155.
Sellat, John, 1407.
Sellier, John, of Tournay, 5697.
........., John de, 4983.
........., Philip le, 4983.
Sellyng, Kent, 5550.
Selman, Ric.. 764.
..........., ..., in com. for Staff., 279, 713, 791, 886, 1770, p. 903.

Selman, Ric., for Salop, 1981, 3071, 3715, 4394, 4827, p. 904.

Selva, John de, M. Le President of Normandy, French commissioner, 4883, 5343, 5354, 5391, 5408.

.........., ..., forms treaty with England, 5278, 5279, 5280, 5305, 5306, 5307, 5322.

Selwin, Rob., 3769.

Semar, ——, of Dartmouth, 5159.

.........., Kath. See Seymour.

Semay, Prince of. See Chimay.

Semoult, Mayart, 4445.

Sempi, Michael de Croy, Lord of, 4508, 5006.

Sempol, Chas. de, 4561.

Senawgh, Thos., officer in the customs at Bridgewater, 4297, 4346.

Senatele, Walleric, 4445.

Seneca, the works of, 4576.

Senigalliensis, Cardinal, 4283, 4446.

.........., Card., M. Bp. of Palestrina, or Preneste, letters from, 4506, 4610.

Senlys, Mareny, bailly of, 5468.

Sens, Tristan de Salazar, Abp. of, 1182.

Sent, W., p. 435.

Senton, Hilary, bailly of Jersey, 3972.

Serenteyner, chief treasurer [to Maximilian], 5323.

Serffe, John de, of Flanders, 4416.

Serfs, manumission of, 5694.

Sergo, merchant of, 3383.

Serjeant, Hugh, p. 954.

Sergeant of the Poultry, 4163.

Serizee, town of, 3651, 3678, 3817, 4273, 5724. See also Ships.

Seribye, Hugh, escheator of Doncaster, 4550.

Serle, ——, of Brighthempston, 5724.

.........., John, 1144.

Sernecote, manor of, Wilts, 347.

Serristory, Julian, merchant of Florence, 1723, 2036, 3312.

Servatius, letter to, 1418.

Seryksee. See Serizee and Ships.

Sesoncotes, manor of, Glouc., 933.

Seton, Yorksh., 807.

Sevenhampton, Wilts, 155.

"Seven Hayes," the, in the forest of Cannok or Cank, Staff., 133, 687.

Sevenoak, Kent, 1707.

Severn, the, fisheries in, 5082, 5667.

Saint Severin, Galiace, Earl of 31, 5482.

Seville, 8.

.........., letter dated from, 1622, 1726, 5748.

Sewall, Nich., 4013.

.........., Wm., 266, 3694.

Seway Whythcoke, land so called, 4230.

Sewerd, Hen., in the war against France, 3231.

Sewers, commissions of, for Kent, 274; Linc., 663, 1716, 1979, 1983, 3137, 5691; Middx.,'1972; Northumb., 705; Soms., 1761; Suss., 274, 297; Thames, 4701; Yorksh., 273, 481, 3072.

Sewey, Leic., 1328.

Seylake, in Barnstaple, 2080.

Seyman, Wm., 1002.

Seymour, Sir John, 4071, 4653.

.........., ..., knt. of the Body, constable of Bristol, 450.

.........., ..., in the war against France, 3885, 4237, 4307, 4314.

.........., ..., protection to, 3914, 3957.

.........., ..., at enmity with the Bp. of Salisb., 5544.

.........., ..., in com. for Salisbury, 554.

.........., ..., in com. for Wilts, 898, 1489, 1938, 3157, 3488, 3605, 3723, 4583.

.........., Lord, son of, in the service of Mary, Queen of France, 5484.

.........., Kath., of Cheping Walden, widow, 4911.

.........., Margery, wife of Tho., 4911.

.........., Nich. son of Kath., 4911.

.........., Rob., capt., p. 553.

.........., Thos., 754.

.........., Tho., son of Katharine, 4911.

Seyton, David, canon of Aberdyne, 4997.

.........., Geo. Lord, 1409.

Sforza, Duke of Milan. See Maximilian.

Shaa, John, mayor of London, 671.

......, Margaret, wife of Thos., 5574.

......, Robt., brother of Thos., 5574.

......, Thos., 5574.

Shacklewell, Middx., 991, 1435.

Shafham, Norfolk. See Swafham.

Shaftesbury, 155.

Shaldeforde, Essex, 729.

Sharant. See Charran.

Sharp, Edm., yeoman of the catery, 1648.

.........., Edw., 321, 665, 914, 4223.

.........., John, 4526, 5779.

.........., ..., groom of the chamber, 619, 620, 649, 1855, 3194, 3762, 4199, 4261.

.........., ..., page of the wardrobe, 3019.

.........., ..., engraver in the mint, 883.

.........., ..., the King's servant, 1031, 1167.

.........., ..., grants to, 985, 1333, 1345, 3073, 3136, 3235, 3265, 3400, 3870, 3907, 3908, 4145, 5056, 5093.

.........., Sir John, 4853.

.........., ..., knighted at Tournay, 4468.

.........., ..., groom of the Privy Chamber, 4805.

.........., ..., grants to, 5036, 5056, 5069 5096, 5134, 5184, 5618.

Shatford, Ric., of London, 5473.

Shawden, Northumb., 1040, 5010.

Shawe, Wilts, 1002.

Shaw, Estienne, gentleman of the Duke of Longueville, 4402.

Shawe, John, mayor of York, 1654.

Shawoerk, 4022.

Sheep for the household, 4894.

Sheepahead, Leic., 730.

.........., manor of, Suss., 1212, 1484.

Sheffield, ——, 4604.
........., Sir ——, 3942.
........., Ric., 3465.
........., Rob., 1008.
........., ..., in com. for Linc., 1171, 3342, 4358, 4593, 4860.
........., Sir Rob., 319, 3342.
........., ..., speaker in Parliament, 2082.
........., ..., ship-master, 4377.
........., ..., in debt to Hen. VII., 3497.
........., ..., in commission, 663, 3006.
........., ..., in com. for Linc., 1171, 1716, 1979, 1983, 3137, 4358, 4593, 4860, 5691.
........., ..., in com. for Notts, 1514, 1798, 1964, 3092, 3494, 4776, 5225.
........., ..., in com. for York, 3072.
........., Thos., preceptor of Synghai, 4562.
Shefford, Rob., 1763, 3503.
Sheldon, Ric., in com. for Herts, 309, 706, 1020, 1971, 3102.
Sheldrake, Thos., of Berugham, Suff., 5074.
Sheldwych, Kent, 5550.
Shelford, lordship of, Notts, 1053.
Shelingthorp, Linc., 295.
Shelley, John, 1316, 3024.
........., Tho., inc. of Pulborough, 950.
........., Wm., in com. for Sussex, 1509, 3024, 3428, 4804, p. 904 ; for Warwick, 3364.
Shelman, Ric. See Selman.
Shelond, Suff., 947.
Shelton, ——, 844.
........., John, petty captain, 3980.
........., Sir John, 3946, 4715.
........., ..., in war against France, 4653.
. ..., ..., in com. for Norfolk, 1340, 1714, 1812, 1963, 3029, 3426, 3545, 5133.
........., Nich., of London, 2036, 5060.
Shemming, ——, of Kent, 12.
Shene, monastery of, 3315.
........., John Joborne, prior of, 3045.
Shenfield, Essex, 3743.
Shenyngton, manor of, Glouc., 1299.
Shenley, Bucks, 69.
Shenston, church of, Lichfield dioc., 5620.
........., Park, Staff., 108.
Shepished. See Sheephead.
Sheppard, Ric., 4600.
........., Rob., yeoman of the chamber, 3730.
........., ..., yeoman of the Crown, 3994.
Sherbourne, 1867.
........., Hants, 569, 5247.
........., in Herforth, York, 3018.
Sherburn, abbot of, 776.
Sherborne, captain, 3591, 3977, 4020, 4377.
........., Sir Henry, captain, 3980, 4005, 4535, p. 811, 5130, 5761.
........., Ric. See Chichester, Bp. of.
Sherford, Warw., 4620.

Sheriffs, renewal of commissions for, 2, 16.
........., Act concerning, 2082.
Sheriff-roll, 1 Hen. VIII., 664.
........., 2 Hen. VIII., 1316.
........., 3 Hen. VIII., 1949.
.. .., 4 Hen. VIII., 3507.
........., 5 Hen. VIII., 4544.
........., 6 Hen. VIII., 5561.
Sheriffes Lench, Worc., 1895, 1959, 5361.
Sheriefhales, Salop, 4612.
Sheriff Hutton (Shiref-hoton), York, 178, 180, 192, 230, 430, 1205, 3520, 3845, 4200, 4602.
... ., park of, 76.
........., Scorby fields in, 4943.
........., chantry of St. Trinity and Virgin Mary in, 180.
Shernborne, Norf., 5194.
Shernebroke, John, abbot of Waltham, 3203, 3940, 5004, 5065.
Sherrard, Thomas, 5561.
Sherston, Wilts, 1226.
Sherwood, manor of, Notts, 367, 721.
........., forest of, Notts, 1899.
........., Ralph, 1183.
Shery, Ric., 1797.
Shetford, Rob., 4751.
Sheveok, Cornw., lordship, 550, 1609, 2080.
Shierve, Will. de Croy, Lord. See Chievres.
Shilyngfeld, Kent, 155.
Shilston, John, 235.
........., Robert, 4539, 4783.
Shyngill, Tho. See Trewe, Thos.
Shinglesborough, manor of, Bucks, 896.
Shipman, John, of Bristol, 4420.
Ships, the King's, 353.
........., ... new, 5595.
........., list of Sir Edw. Howard's fleet, 3117.
........., other lists of English ships, 3591, 3977, 3979, 3980, 4376, 4377, 4474, 4475, 4535, 5112, 5317, 5761.
........., The Great Harry, or Henry Grace de Dieu. See Harry.
........., The Henry Imperial, 3977.
........., The Regent, 342, 3117, 3238, 3388, p. 432, 5720, 5747.
........., The Gabriel Royal, 3591, 3977, 3979, 3982, 4377, 4475, 5112, 5761.
........., The Katherina Fortaleza, 3591, 3831, 3857, 3977, 4377, 5112, 5761.
........., The Mary Rose, 3117, 3422, 3591, 3977, 3979, 3980, 4377, 4474, 4535, 5112, 5720, 5761.
........., The Peter Pomegranate, 3117, 3422, p. 432, 3591, 3977, 3979, 3980, 4076, 4377, 4474, 5112, 5276, 5317, 5720, 5761.
........., other ships named, 342, 3030, 3156, 3238, 3262, 3452, 3496, 3820, 3831, 3877, 3903, 3946, 3982, 3983, 4019,

Ships—cont.

4073, 4076, 4178, 4185, 4352, 4527,
4533, 4634, 4961, 5017, 5033, 5269,
5720, 5721, 5724, 5751, 5769, 5770,
5771, 5772, 5773, 5774, 5775, 5776,
5790.
.... belonging to the ports of :—
Aldborough, 1706, p. 554.
Antwerp, p. 554, 4533.
Armewe, p. 554.
Barking, p. 812.
Bilboa, p. 554, 4352.
Brightlingsea (Brykelsey), 3980,
4745.
Bristol, ships of, 3591, 3977, 4377,
4634, 5112, 5761.
........., vessels in port of, 3663.
Brixham, 3977, 3980, 4377, 5761.
Calais, 3977, 4377, p. 972.
Cofehith, p. 554.
Colchester, p. 554.
Dartmouth, 3977, 4377, 4535, 5112.
Dover, 5033, 5112, 5771.
Eston, p. 554.
Falmouth, 3117, 3591, 3977, 4474,
5112, p. 973.
Fontarabia, p. 494.
Fowey, 3117, 3591, 3977, 4474,
p. 953, p. 954, 4377, 5761.
Genoa, 3591.
Greenwich, 3117, 3820, 3977, 4377,
4535, 5317, 5761.
Hamyll, p. 813, 5773.
Harwich, 3591, '3877, 3977, p. 812,
p. 973.
Hastings, p. 554.
Hull, 3903, 3977, 3980, 4425, 5761.
Ipswich, p. 554.
Latchingdon, in Essex, p. 651.
Lee, 5033, p. 813.
London, 1256, 3980, 4376, 4377,
4475, 5017, 5761.
Lowe, p. 554.
Lymington, 5112.
Lynn, 3751, 3882, 3980.
Maldon, p. 554.
Middleburgh, p. 554.
Newcastle, King's ships at, 5759.
........., ships of, 3591, 3751, 3977,
p. 554, 4020, 4377, 4474, 5112,
5761, 5769.
Padstowe, p. 554.
Penryn ? (Pirwyn or Perwyne),
4020, 4474, 4721, 5112, 5761.
Plymouth, p. 554, 4178, 4185, 4376,
p. 973.
Poole, p. 553, p. 812.
Rye, p. 554.
St. Maria, 5269.
St. Osith, p. 554.

Ships—cont.

Saltasshe, p. 554.
Saltflete, p. 554.
Sandwich, p. 554.
Savona, carack of, 3977, 4546, 4665.
Seryksee, p. 554.
Southampton, 3117, 3591, 3977,
3980, 4376, 4377, 4474, 5112,
5761.
Thames, the King's great ships in
the, 5316.
Topsham, 3591, 3977, pp. 553 and
554, 4377.
Tor (Tower), Anne of, p. 553.
Torbay, 3980, 4377, 4474, 5761.
Totnes, ships prested at, 3978.
Walderswick, 3733.
Walsingham, 3445, 3977, 4377,
5761.
Weymouth, p. 553.
Yarmouth, p, 553.
........., Spanish, in the English service, 3877,
3903, 3946, p. 551, 3979, 3980, 3982,
3983, 4074, 4094, 4377, 4535, p. 957,
p. 973.
........., James IV.'s, 3326, 3359, 3577, 3751,
3882. See also Banaster.
........., Scotch, in service of France, 4465,
4843, 5270.
...., Breton, 4465, 4843.
........., accounts and expenses of, 3496, 5720,
5751, 5752, 5761, 5769, 5770, 5771,
5772, 5773, 5774, 5775, 5776, 5790.
Shipton, Oxon, 1426.
.... Milne, in Langley, Oxon, 1154.
.........-on-Charwell, Oxon, 5685.
Shire, Surrey, 155, 1916.
Shirlands, Northumb., 1040, 5010.
Shirley, ——, 1362, 3535.
........., Hugh, p. 433.
........., John, 539, 4630.
........., ..., cofferer of the household, 160,
301, 1103, 1498, 3445, 4257, 4874.
........., Nich., 1509.
........., Sir Ralph, 1949.
........., ..., in the war against France,
3231.
........., ..., in com. for Leicestershire, 656,
1094, 1425, 1971, 4706, 4783, 4812,
p. 905.
........., Ric., 285, 1395, 3024, 3428.
........., ..., inc. of Pembridge, Heref., 610.
........., deceased, 992, 1078.
........., Tho., 1078, 1168.
Shitlanger, Northt., 3027.
Shitlyngton, Beds, church of, 4683.
Shkally, Worc., 726.
Shoemakers, guild of, in Barnstaple, 3272.
Shore, Ric., of London, 1596.
Shmurzemborg, Lord of, 4359.
Shrone, 3477.

Shorthoos, Anthony, 3386.
Shortwood, Northt., 426.
........., Warwickshire, 3186.
Shotesbroke, 498.
Shotewike, manor of, Cheshire, 3395.
Shotover (Shottore) Forest, Oxon, 877, 4382. 4772.
Shrawley, Worc., 703, 3338.
Shrewsbury, 155, 887, 5436.
........., proclamation in, 1771.
........., Monastery of St. Peter's, 289, 634, 3232.
........., ..., abbot of, 5616.
........., ..., Richard Lye, abbot of, 3093 ; Richard Baker, abbot of, 3155, 3221, 3222.
........., St. John the Baptist, church of, 1906.
........., St. Mary's College at, 4184.
Shrewsbury, George Talbot Earl of, steward of the household, 164, 1004, 1212, 1372, 1540, 1755, 3027, 3080, 3242, 3332, 3442, 3887, 3891, 4008, 4009, 4217.
........., ..., appointed as a chamberlain of the Exchequer, 32.
........., ..., in command of forces against France, 3336, 3760, 4061, 4126, 4798.
........., ..., in war against France, 3231, 3277, 4070, p. 625, 4410 ; his standard in the war, 4253.
........., ..., in embassy to the Pope, 1955, 1980 ; in embassy to the Lateran Council, sick, 5496.
........., ..., commissioned to treat with Ferdinand, 3513.
........., ..., summoned to Parliament, 5616.
........., ..., trier of petitions, 811, 2082.
........., ..., at the marriage contract of Princess Mary, 5322.
........., ..., in debt to the Crown, 5633.
........., ..., letters from, 4318, 4584 ; letter to, 5383.
........., ..., grants to, 253, 1978, 3438, 3449, 3713, 4011, 4032, 5015 ; grant of a pension from Lewis XII., 952.
........., ..., in commission for Derby, 4939, p. 907 ; for Greenwich, 3116 ; for Leic., 656, 1094, 1425, 1971, 3219, 4706, 4783, 4812, p. 905 ; for London, 1547, 3006 ; for Notts, 1514, 1798, 1964, 3092, 3494, 4776, 5225, p. 905 ; for Salop, 918, 1981, 3071, 3715, 4394, 4827, 4939, p. 904 ; for Staff., 279, 713, 791, 886, 1770, 4939, pp. 903 and 904 ; for Surrey, 1548 ; for Worcester, 892, 1971, 3301, 3709, 4770, p. 903 ; for Yorkshire, 455, 954, 1549, 1550, 1941, 1995, 3177, 4015, 4719, 5166, 5193, 5244, pp. 906 and 907.
........., ..., signatures of, 55, 313, 545, 598, 602, 617, 618, 625, 639, 650, 702, 782, 955, 956, 1008, 1539, 1840, 2029.
........., John Talbot, Earl of, (ob. A.D. 1473,) 1978, 3713.
Shroffold, manor of, Kent, 3041, 3089, 3096, 3154.
Shropshire. See Salop.

Shvagger, Wm., 5664.
Shukborowe, Tho., 282, 554.
Shute, Devon, 765.
Siam, King of, 4173.
Sibsey, Geo., 4632.
Sicily, 796, 819, 3188, 3355.
........., Viceroy of, 3667.
Sidnall, John, 3497.
Sidnam (surname). See Sydenham.
Sidney. See Sydney.
Sigewyke, John, grants to, 632, 3537, 4212, 5243.
Sigismond, John, 1074.
........., Archduke, 2091.
Signet, clerk of the. See Ashby, Geo.
Siguença, Bishop of, 3243, 3476, p. 399, 3762.
Silbeston, Northt., 3297.
Silk, licences to import, 3511, 4260, 4261.
Silke, Wm., clerk, 799.
Silva, Peter de, 3456.
Silverton, Rob., ship master, 4377, 5112.
Silvester, Gabriel, clerk, 5296.
Silvyo Sabello, Lord, 216.
Symeon, Geoff., 486, 1759.
Simmonds, Rob., of Barnstaple, 1992, 4385.
Simon, (Symon) Tho., 4071.
Simons, or Symondes, Wm., captain, 3980, 4634, 5112, 5761.
........., ..., page of the chamber, 1433, 4602.
........., ..., clerk controller of the army, 5753.
Symond, ——, gunmaker, 4977.
Simpson, ——, sherman, 12.
........., Alex., canon of Aberdeen, 4997.
........., John, 3794.
........., Wm., pardon, 3160.
Sinai, monks of Mount, letter from, 5728.
Sincia (Cintra ?), letter dated, 510.
Sinclair, Lord, 3326.
........., Sir John, 3882.
........., ... See also S. Clere.
Singelston, Edm., and Willm., 3562.
Singer, Simon, clerk, 3338.
Sinus Magnus (Gulf of Siam), 4173.
Sion, Matthew, Cardinal of, 3325, 3340, 3341, 3658, 4283, 5106.
........., ..., created Archbishop of Milan, 3269.
........., ..., votes for the election of Leo. X., 3780.
........., ..., letters from, 4916, 5040.
........., ..., document in his handwriting, 4138.
........., Holy Chamber of, 5729.
Sircotes or Sithcotes lands, Bucks, 1985.
Syriscote, prebend of, dioc. Cov. and Lich., 3581.
Sissetour. See Cirencester.
Sittingbourne, Kent, 4883, 5235, 5468, 5550.
Sixtinus, Joan, a correspondent of Erasmus, 2013, 2021, 4427.
........., ..., letter from, 3535.

4 C

Skan, James, in commission at Lyde, 4996.

Skelle, near Antwerp, 3248.

Skelton, ——, 777.

........., Edw., 1324.

........., Geo., 4556.

........., John, attainted, 1472, 4022, 4347.

........., ..., of Armathwaite, 296.

........., ..., ..., Act for, 8502.

........., ..., ..., on the sheriff-roll for Cumb., 664, 1316.

........., Ric., 5296.

........., Rob., 380.

Skelyng, John. See Skillyng.

Skerne, John, victualler, 3051, 4792.

........., Percival and Robert, 3045.

Sketergate, Westmld., 1796.

Skeffington, T. See Bangor, Bp. of.

Skevington, Tho., in debt to the Crown, 3497.

........., Sir Wm., master of the ordnance, 3980.

........., Wm., in commission for Leic., 739, 1094, 1425, 1971, 4706, 4783, 4812.

Skewys, John, in commission for Cornwall, 891, 1694, 1812, 1954, 1984, 3290, 3583, 3605, 3938, 4754, 5220, 5586.

........., ..., ... for Devon, 1166.

........., ..., grants to, 506, 5113, 5431.

........., ..., of London, 1350.

........., ..., of Lincoln's Inn, 5116.

Skeyte, Tho., 4067.

Skidbrook, Linc., 1067.

........., ..., church, 1326, 3579.

Skillyng, John, 554, 1002.

........., ..., in commission for Wilts, 898, 1489, 1938, 3157, 3605, 4583.

Skilman, Hen., yeoman of the Crown, 1223.

Skinner, ——, to be excepted from the pardon, 12.

........., John, in commission for Surrey, 1427, 1762, 3078, 3092, 4734, 5237, 5506.

........., ..., justice of gaol delivery, 1548, 3996.

Skipwith, Sir John, 1402, 4616.

........., ..., in commission for Linc., 663, 792, 1171, 1378, 1380, 1716, 1979, 1983, 3137, 3342, 4358, 4593, 4860, 5476, 5506, 5691.

........., Ric., LL.B., 967.

........., Wm., in commission for Norf., 1812.

Skirmot, Rob., 3792.

Skirtenbek, York, 5325.

Skite, Andrew, 5185.

Skrayenham. See Scrayingham.

Skrene, Eliz., widow of Sir John, 1282.

Sladbourne rectory, York dioc., 527.

Slade, 3534, 3566, 4539, 4783, 5290.

........., Edw., justice of assize, Norfolk Circuit, 4765.

Slade, Rob., justice of gaol delivery, Warw., 554.

........., Tho., in commission for Warw., 282, 1387, 1468, 1971, 3364, 5506.

Slake, Hen., of Halifax, 272.

Slater, Wm., 615.

Slehurst, Surrey, 1488, 1916.

Sluys, 1826, 4081, 5203.

Sly, Tho., 909.

Slythurst, Ric., 3144.

Small, John, abbot of Burnc, 1844.

Smalehanger, Devon, 5648.

Smethcote, Salop, 4694.

Smethmore, fishery of, Severn, 5082.

Smicham, letter dated, 4059.

Smith, the King's master, 4774. See Wodland, Chr.; Johnson, Cornelius.

Smith, (Smythe,) ——, in the war, 4307.

[Smith,] G. S. and O. S., 5783.

[Smith, George ?] G., 5734.

Smith or (Smyth,) Eliz., 3032.

........., Hen., overseer of works, 166, 589, 4630, 4839.

........., ..., steward of Redworth, 4071.

........., ..., in debt to the Crown, 1024, 3497.

........., ..., in commission for Leic., 739, 1094, 1425.

........., ..., in commission for Warw., 282.

........., Isabella, 3937.

........., Joan, widow, and Walter, son, of Henry, 4620.

........., John, 3937.

........., ..., inc. of Conesholme, Linc., 532.

........., ..., comptroller of Exeter, &c., 3120.

........., ..., clerk in the Exchequer, 3656.

........., Nich., Scot, 4649.

........., ..., of Wisbeach, 5723.

........., Ric., grants to, 1117, 3759.

........., ..., in the war, 4642.

........., ..., yeoman of the wardrobe, 97, 98, 203, 220, 3907, 3908, 5135.

........., ..., keeper of the garden at the Tower, 590, 1888.

........., Robt., 3759.

........., ..., mayor of Bedford, 907.

........., ..., friend of Erasmus, 5733.

........., Tho. Lyncolle, of Brentwood, 530.

........., Wm., 909, 1363, 4998.

........., ..., in the war, 4156, 4281.

........., ..., in commission for York, 3072, 3230.

........., ..., clerk of the hanaper, 365, 4218, 5460.

........., ..., usher of the chamber, 1308.

........., ..., page of the wardrobe, 12, 108, 109, 131, 133, 682, 687, 755, 984, 3497.

........., ..., pardon for, 869.

........., ..., his recognizances cancelled, 464, 1639.

........., ..., buys part of the wardrobe of Hen. VII., 1872.

Smith, Wm., Bishop of Lincoln. *See* Lincoln, Bp. of.

Snape, St. Mary, monastery of, Suffolk, 1126.

Snaythe, Wm., yeoman of the guard, 1696, 3390, 4107.

Snethe, John, 4993.

Snitterfield, Warwickshire, 549, 1499.

Snodesbury, Worcestershire, 5146.

Snodhille, castle of, Heref., 5549.

Snoring, Great, Norfolk, 155.

Soana, 3678.

Sodbury, Glouc., 1766, 3673.

Soderini, 3780.

Soe or See, Wm., 4996.

Sole, Edw., 4866.

Solicitor to the King. *See* Porte, John.

Solihull, Warwick, 1499.

Somerbury, Surrey, 1488, 1916.

Somerford Caynes, Wilts, 155.

Somers, Clifford, 3053.

Somersale, Derby, 5574.

Somerset lands, 382.

.... Herald, Henry Yonge, 1212, 1263, 1302.

.........., Arth., lancer at Calais, 609, 1424, 4476, 4635.

.........., Chas., Lord Herbert, afterwards Earl of Worcester, Lord Chamberlain, 30, 235, 602, 3284, 3449, 3949, 3977, 4483, 4629, 5111, 5173, 5322, 5652.

.........., ..., executor of Hen. VII., 3292.

.........., ..., executor of Margaret Countess of Richmond, 406; bequest to him from the Countess, 236.

.........., ..., recognizances made by him cancelled, 625.

.........., ..., created Earl of Worcester, 4696.

.........., ..., in the war, 3926, 3927, 4008, 4253, 4306, 4318, 4477, 4534.

.........., ..., present at the renunciation by Princess Mary of her marriage contract with Prince Charles, 5282.

.........., ..., on embassy to France, 5335, 5379, 5407, 5441, 5482, 5584, 5590.

.........., ..., appointed by Princess Mary her proxy for her marriage with Lewis XII., 5347, 5408 (5).

.........., ..., in debt to the Crown, 1639, 2044.

.........., ..., trier of petitions in Parliament, 811, 2082.

.........., ..., summoned to Parliament, 5616.

.........., ..., pardon to, 5180.

.........., ..., grants to, 43, 44, 45, 46, 110, 441, 603, 1057, 1113, 1234, 1936, 3049, 4000, 4157, 4177, 4697, 5045, 5433, 5652.

.........., ..., in commission of array, 3116.

.........., ..., in commission of peace, 3960.

Somerset, Chas. Lord Herbert, justice of gaol delivery, 3765.

.........., ..., signs as member of the Privy Council, 55, 164, 165, 545, 594, 598, 617, 618, 679, 782, 1004, 1008, 1068, 1273, 1321, 1372, 1538, 1539, 1540, 1699, 1758, 3027, 5735, 5737, 5779.

.........., ..., letters to, 4463, 5517, 5518.

.........., ..., letters from, 594, 5391, 5468, 5495, 5553, 5560, 5566, 5786.

.........., ..., servant of, 3591.

.........., Eliz., wife of Lord Herbert, 3949.

.........., Hen., son of Lord Herbert, 1894.

.........., ..., sent on an embassy to France, 5482.

.........., ..., grants to, 1113, 5045, 5180, 5433, 5652.

Somerset, duchy of, 860, 3061, 5089.

.........., Eleanor Duchess of, her lands, 347, 458, 1472, 3134, 4022, 4321, 4846, 4946.

.........., Margaret Duchess of (temp. Hen. VI.), 5280.

Somersetshire, 3742, 3939.

.........., lands in, 448, 597, 860, 3061.

.........., commissions of peace for, 287, 712, 3048, 3566, 3585, 3606, 3701, 4718, 5506.

.........., commissions of array for, 3393, 3688, 3723.

.........., commission of sewers for, 1761.

.........., sheriff-roll for, 664, 1316, 3507, 4544, 5561.

.........., feodaries of Crown lands in, 4414, 5692.

Somerson, Ric., 3998.

Somerton, Oxon, 2055, 4785.

.........., Somerset, 448.

.........., Suffolk, 947.

Somme, the, 3678.

.........., Count of, 4349.

Somterope, Bucks, 1352.

Sondeywey, Shotover Forest, 4772.

Sonnyng, Wm., 2066.

Soper, Wm., clerk, 4023.

Sophi Ismail. *See* Ismael.

Sophi, the, of Persia, 1659, 3697, 5470, 5592.

.........., defeat of, by the Turks, 5705.

Sophie, coast of Barbary, 1537.

Sotby, Linc., 3515.

Souche. *See* Zouche.

Souchet, Julian, denization, 3643.

Sounde, Thomas, yeoman of the guard, 4204.

Southampton (Hampton), 3117, 3762, 3824, 4632, 4653.

.... Castle, 798, 3123.

.........., ..., chapel in, 392, 3610.

.........., church of St. Denis in, 591.

.........., lands, rents, &c., in, 155.

.........., customs at, 392, 1232, 1276, 1351, 1394, 3123, 3610.

.........., officers of customs at, 198, 206, 256, 277, 820, 1934, 3422, p. 954, 5724.

Southampton, provisions landed at, 5765.
........., exports from, 342, 802, 1186, 1474.
........., mayor of, 1474, 5724.
........., sheriff of, 1771, 3173.
........., gaol delivery at, 1813.
........., common beam at, 183.
........., men of, 12, 112, 817, 1767, 3822, 4099.
........., the king's embarkation at, 4311.
........., army at, 3188, 4055, 5745.
........., fleet at, 3592, 4076, 4139, 4165, 4311, 4474.
........., ships of, 3591, 3820, 3980, 4376, 4377, 5724.
........., letters dated, 4005, 4073, 4074, 4075, 4093, 4094, 4095, 4103, 4104, 4169, 4678, 5755, 5757.
........., privy seals dated at, 1208, 1210, 4170.
........., prisoner at, 3417.
Southbere Forest, Hants, 215, 1940.
Southcombe. See Combe.
Southe, John, 3534.
Southend, Oxon, 636, 4254.
Southern. Lewis, captain, 5112, 5761.
Southfereby Linc., 1983.
Southfrith, Kent, 155.
Sotehill, Gerard, and Joan his wife, 5020.
Southill, Hen., Joan and Eliz., 437, 1184.
Southornesby, Sir J. Skipwith, of, 4616.
Southorp, Oxon, 636, 4254.
....   See Suthorp.
Southwark, 729, p. 953.
........., church of St. George in, 1808.
Southwell, Eliz., widow of Sir Robt., 5137.
........., Sir Rob., 697, 779, 1212, 4067, 4254, 4347, 4533, 4630, 4946, 4967, 5116, 5619, 5748.
........., ..., chief butler of England, 1242, 5137.
........., ..., in commission for Suffolk, 280, 676, 1121, 1153, 1534, 1715, 3029, 3219, 3967, 4713.
........., ..., in commission for Norfolk, 1340, 1714, 1963, 5029, 3426, 3545.
........., ..., in commission for Essex, 310, 1368, 1522, 1713, 3605, 3785, 3967.
........., ..., grants to, 458, 875, 1185, 1346, 1472, 3582, 3943, 4022, 4348, 4436.
........., ..., justice of gaol delivery for Bishop's Lynn, 884.
........., ..., Act for, 2082, 3502.
........., ..., his signature, 4434.
........., ..., in the war, 3977, 4377.
........., Rob., executor of Sir Rob., 5137.
........., ..., in commission for Suffolk, 280, 676, 1121, 1153, 1715, 3029, 3219, 3967, 4713, 5074, 5133, 5506.
........., ..., in commission for Essex, 1368, 1522, 1713, 3605, 3785, 3967.
........., ..., justice of gaol delivery for Colchester, 3464.
........., ..., justice of gaol delivery for Dunwich, 4677.

Southwell, Rob., in debt to the Crown, 3497.
........., ..., justice of gaol delivery, Ipswich, 3549.
Southwick, Hants, 5695.
........., monastery of St. Mary at, 4669, 5552.
........., ..., prior of, 4564, 4669.
Southwold, forest of, 4347.
Southworth, Hen., bowyer at the Tower, 1272.
........., Wm., M.A., 3754.
Sowch. See Zouch.
Sowchyvers. See Swiss.
Sowcote, Wm., 3406, 3407, 4643.
Sowdon, Scotland, 4556.
Sowerby, 4791.
Soweytht, Coyde, Wales, 5145.
Soweyth Nythian, Wales, 5145.
Sowgewas, Heref., 1794.
Spain, 3333, 3633, 3697, 3762, 3948, 4574, 4652, 5076, 5263, 5565. See also Ferdinand, Arragon, Castile, &c.; also General Table.
......., late Queen of. See Isabella.
......., ambassador of, in Scotland. See Scotland.
......., French ambassador in. See France.
......., Prince of, 324. See Charles.
......., at war with France, 1918, 3584, 3593, 3629, 3435.
......., treaties with, 1059, 1335.
......., secret negotiations with France, 3766.
......., truce between France and, 4112.
......., truce concluded in, 5025.
......., ambassadors of, 4085, 4091, 4308, 4366, 5018.
......., messengers from, 4829, 4844.
......., discontent with England in, 8.
......., English expedition to, 3243, 3355, 3356, 4038, 4793, 5741, 5744.
......., return of the English army from, 3662.
......., viceroy of. See Naples, viceroy of.
......., General of, Peter of Navarre, 1209.
......., commander of, ambassador with the Emperor, 4165.
......., laws of, 5637.
......., fleets of, 3593.
......., ships of, 3452, 3577, 3857, 3877, 3946, 4005, 4094, 4095, 4533, 5720.
......., artillery of, 3614.
......., horses of, 3370.
......., prices of provisions in, 3355.
......., documents docketted "Hispanis," 3023.
Spaniards, 3298, 3607, 3752, 3974, 3985, 4169, 5173, 5290, 5341.
........., their character, 3662.
.... in Italy, 1681, 1997, 3026, 3112, 3269, 3325, 3341, 3499, 3678, 4069, 4287, 4513, 4756, 5171, 5323, 5378.
........., ..., Brescia, taken by, 3543.

Spaniards, sent to assist Castile, 3226, 3451.
........., Pampeluna, taken by, 3340.
........., mentioned, 790, 1886, 2042, 3496, 3815, 3918, 4005, p. 957.
Spanish wool, 3814.
.... victuallers, 4533, 5724, 5755.
........., counterpart of Holy League, 3861.
........., writing in, 4076.
Spaniard, the. *See* Ships.
Spalding, Linc., 5200.
........., ..., monastery of, 333.
........., ..., prior of, in commission for Linc., 663, 1716, 1979, 3137, 5691.
Spaldington, York, 1097.
Sparcoke, Rob., 4996.
Sparham, Norf., 5180.
Sparowe, John, clerk, 1590.
Specott, Nich., of Devon, 1812, 4071.
........., ..., in debt to the Crown, 3497.
Speght, Thos., 4651.
Speke, John, 1996, 4377, 5180.
......, Sir John, in commission for Somerset, 287, 712, 4713, 5506.
......, ..., on the sheriff-roll for Devon, 1949.
......, ..., sheriff of Somers. and Dors., 1316.
Spellesbury, Oxon, 1426.
Spelman or Spillman. John, in commission for Norf., 266, 3029, 3426, 3545, 5133.
........., ..., justice of gaol delivery, Norwich, 4558.
........., Wm., in commission for Norf., 1812, 4254.
Spencer, John, 3429, 3524.
...., ..., in debt to the Crown, 1024.
........., ..., in commission for Warwicksh., 1468, 1971, 3364, 5506.
........., ..., sheriff of Northamptonsh., 1949.
........., ..., on sheriff-roll for Warwicksh. and Leicestersh. 4544.
........., Rob., 1753, 1965, 4342.
Spencers' lands, 665, 778, 900, 901, 1831, 4223.
Spenke, Thomas, clerk, 5114.
Spert, Tho., master of the Mary Rose, 3591, 3977, 4377, p. 954.
......, ..., ... Henry Grace à Dieu, 3924, 3980, 4954.
......, ..., yeoman of the Crown, 2059, 5576.
Spycer, Tho., 1831.
Spies, English, in Scotland, 4869.
Spinel. *See* Spinelly.
Spynully, Bank of, 5475
Spynel, John, 3235.
Spynell (or Spinola), Anth., merchant of Genoa, 1399, 1457, 4152, 4153.
Spynula, John and Luke, Genoese merchants, 3199, 4763.

Spinulis, Pantaleo de, denization, 4246.
Spinelly, Leonard, brother of Thomas, 4621, 4835, 5198, 5632.
........., ..., letter from, 5111.
Spinelly, Thos., 1128, 1697, 1701, 3226, 3248, 3258, 3276, 3291, 3296, 3302, 3328, 3331, 3334, 3353, 3362, 3376, 3381, 3398, 3405, 3425, 3435, 3463, 3481, 3489, 3496, 3639, 3847, 3861, 3905, 3945, 4077, 4182, 4216, 4282, 4305, 4308, 4393, 4396, 4426, 4621, 4622, 4743, 4824, 4930, 4932, 4973, 5475, 5757.
........., ..., his negotiations for ordnance, 794, 922, 3616, 4389.
........., ..., documents in his handwriting, 3780, 3976, 4830.
........., ..., documents endorsed by, 4362.
........., ..., commission to, 4794.
........., ..., instructions to, 4831.
........., ..., credence delivered to, 5598.
........., ..., credence given by, 4928.
........., ..., letters from, 216, 924, 3077, 3335, 3340, 3361, 3377, 3499, 3647, 3651, 3678, 3777, 3779, 3805, 3817, 3821, 3915, 4091, 4273, 4280, 4296, 4319, 4322, 4323, 4326, 4328, 4343, 4355, 4359, 4386, 4418, 4429, 4433, 4459, 4561, 4577, 4725, 4789, 4796, 4810, 4844, 4929, 4935, 4955, 4960, 4982, 5006, 5076, 5155, 5171, 5207, 5208, 5263, 5290, 5292, 5299, 5327, 5341, 5362, 5377, 5387, 5403, 5404, 5539, 5588, 5632, 5675, 5676.
........., ..., letters to, 923, 3648, 4829, 5600.
........., ..., his signature, 4955, 4978, 5031, 5059.
........., ..., his clerk, documents in handwriting of, 1417, 3067.
........., ..., documents endorsed by, 4955.
Spire, 216, 3777, 3779, 3817.
......, the Emperor at, 4272.
Spixworth, Norfolk, 1331.
Spodell, ——, ship master, 3591, 3977, 4377.
Spoleto, 5254, 5356.
Sprakeling, Tho., 1537.
Sprig, John, 3031.
Sproxston, Norf., 4680.
Spruce, p. 955.
Spurs, battle of. *See* Bomy.
........., ..., description of, p. 625.
........., ..., prisoners taken at, 4402.
Spur, waggoners of, 4526.
Spurstowe, Ranulph, 4808.
Squyer, Humph., 4067.
Stable, Barth., clerk, 4335.
Stafferton, Wm. *See* Staverton.
Stafford, Sir Hen. *See* Wiltshire, Earl of.
........., Humph., of Grafton, deceased, attainted, 4749, 5093.
........., ..., possessions late of, 671, 1472, 4022, 4347.

Stafford, Humphrey, Act for his restitution, 4848.

..........., Roland, 4301.

..........., ..., in com. for Staff., 279, 713, 791, 886, 1770.

..........., ..., dead, 1887, 3521.

..........., Tho., 3719.

..........., Wm., 669.

..........., ..., officer in the Mint, 3865, 4917, (2).

Staffordshire, justices of gaol delivery for, 764, 3275.

..........., banneret and captain of, 4253.

..........., sheriff of Sir John Aston, 4544; Wm. Chetwyn, 5561; John Egerton, 1949; John Gifford, 664 ; John Mitton, 3507 ; Nevyll, Th., 1316.

..........., lands in, 3100, 3193.

..........., Crown lands in, 4022, 4414.

..........., com. of peace for, 279, 713, 791, 886, 1770, pp. 903, 904.

..........., musters taken in, 3336, 3760, 4434, 4939.

..........., proclamation in, 1771.

Staines Bridge, Act concerning the toll of, 811.

Stakehouse, John, of Cottyngham, York, 235, 386, 4033.

Stakehugh, the, in Scotland, 4529.

Stalyngburgh, Sir Wm. Askewith of, 4616.

Stalworth, Simon, clk., 1977.

Stamford (or Staunford), Linc., 155, 5103, 5309, 5765.

..........., justices of gaol delivery for, 4004.

..........., Wm., 1608.

Stamforth, Northumb., 5010.

Stanbank. See Staynbank.

..........., Edw., 235, 4372.

Stanchowe, John, 3789.

Stanethorpe, provost of the college of, Durham, 824.

Staney, 4360.

Standard-bearer. See Guildford, Sir Hen.

.... of England, Sir Edw. Howard, 64.

Standards taken by the English at the Battle of Spurs, 4431.

Standon, Wm., yeoman of the chamber, 4133.

Standyssh, Jas., 3955.

..........., Joan, wife of James, 3955.

Stanfield, Hugh, 4895, 4899.

Stanford, manor of Berks, 896.

Stanforthdame, Northumb., 1040, 5010.

Stanget, John, of Ipswich, p. 432.

Stanhope, Alice, widow of Edm., 1294, 1800.

..........., Edm., 1294.

..........., ..., deceased, 1800.

..........., Sir Edw., 777, 3031.

..........., ..., deceased, 4728.

Stanhope, Eliz., widow of Sir Edw., 4728.

..........., John, son of Edm., 1294.

..........., Ric., in com. for Notts, 4776, 5225.

Stanley, Glouc., 1374.

..........., monastery of, Wilts, 3773, 5400.

Stanley, Agnes, 5255.

..........., Sir Edward, 933. See Monteagle, Lord.

..........., Sir Edward, 4205, 4460, 4462; knight of the body, 628.

..........., ..., at the battle of Flodden, 4441.

..........., ..., in commission for Westmld., 2009, 3048, 3552; for Yorkshire, 1804, 1995, 3358, 4015, 3177, 5166.

..........., ..., his signature to Surrey's challenge to Jas. IV., 4439.

..........., Geo., in com. for Oxon, 1745, 3015, 4559, 4809, p. 905.

..........., Sir Jas., 777.

..........., Jane, 5255.

..........., Joan, late Lady Le Straunge, 5647.

..........., John. See Ely, Bp. of.

..........., John, of the Pipe, Staff., in debt to Hen. VII., p. 436; in commission, 1110.

..........., Thomas, 12, 5255.

..........., Sir Wm., forfeited possessions of, 131, 361, 572, 778, 1148, 1344, 1472, 4022, 4748.

Stanmer Church, Southmallyng, 1575.

Stannary, in Cornwall, 4805.

Stannaries, in Devon, 985.

Stannard, Hen., 1991, 3549.

Stanney, John, in commission for Sussex, 1509, 3024, 3428, 4804, p. 904.

Stanshawe, Ric., 3867.

..........., Rob., groom of the chamber, 4670.

..........., ..., page of the chamber, 5461, 5627.

Stanton, Derby, 606, 926, 4781.

Staundon, Herts., 155,

Staundon Hall, manor of, Essex, 735.

Stanton Lacy, lordship of, Salop, 334, 1118.

Stanton, Harcourte, 4254 (iii.).

..........., Harold, 1212.

..........., ..., licence to found a chantry bearing his name, 1642.

..........., John, keeper of the standing-wardrobe, 1554, 1617.

..........., John, of Kingesweston, Glouc., 5026.

..........., Tho., in commission for Notts, p. 260, 1804.

Steynton, Tho., of London, 3933, 4144, 4503.

Stapleton, Sir Brian, or Stapleton, Brian, 414.

..........., ..., sheriff of Notts and Derby, 664.

..........., ..., in commission for Notts, p. 260, 1798, 1804, 1941, 1995 ; for York, 3177, 4015, 5166.

Stapelton, Tho., 4134.

Star Chamber, 380, 711, 777, 3758.

Starkey, Hugh, serjeant-at-arms, 77.

..........., ..., sewer of the chamber, 4644.

Staverton, Wm., of London, 1773, 3953, 5123.

Staynbank, Edm., serjeant of the scullery, 1038.

........., ..., clk, 5180.

........., ..., inc. of Winwoo, Llandaff dioc., 1038.

........., Edw. *See* Stanbank.

........., Ric., M.A., inc. of Winwoo, Llandaff dioc., 1038, 1857.

Staynor, John, of Bath, 8939.

Steelyard, merchants of the, 777.

Steenhone, Peter, layman of Tournay, 4832.

Stele, Christ., inc. of Lambemersh, London dioc., 2063.

Steyning, Sussex, 1212.

Stephen, Geo., 4067.

........., Philip, 4067.

Stephens (or Stephyns), Wm., 1571.

Stephenson, Hen., 3127.

........., Ric., 3998.

........., Thomas, of Lincoln, 5200.

........., Wm., 3717, 4919.

Stevinson. *See* Towres.

Stepney, or Stepenhith, 586, 951, 1279, 5116.

Stevecle, Gerard, 3533.

........., Wm., son of Gerard, 3533.

Stewton, Linc., 1071, 3579.

........., church of, Linc., dioc. 3776.

Steyke, John, Essex, 3743.

Steynbank, Edm. *See* Staynbank.

Steynton. *See* Stanton.

Stidolph, Thos., 1002, 4375.

........., ..., in com. for Surrey, 5237.

Stikelpath, 2080.

Stile, Eliz., wife of John, 2064.

......, John, usher of the chamber, 338, 2064, 3298, 3313, 3356, 3388, 3476, 3762, 4096, 4525, 4829, 4845, 4864, 5745.

......, ..., in commission to receive Ferdinand's oath for treaty of 1513, 4268.

......, ..., letters from, 8, 490, 796, 819, 3355, 3584, 3593, 3607, 3614, 3661, 3662, 3755, 3766, 3807, 4267.

......, ..., his son-in-law, 3451.

......, ..., of London, grocer (ingrosser ?), als. scribe, 1662.

......, ..., of London, draper, 1810.

Stillingflete, 3411, 3497, 4022, 4347.

Stilman, Anth., 255, 554.

........., ..., in commission for Wilts, 898, 1489, 1938, 3157, 3488, 3605, 4583.

Stirling, 3882, 4556, 4951, 5614, 5641.

........., letters dated from, 31, 1195, 1405, 3620, 3838.

........., Chapel Royal, 910, 1829, 2061, 3623, 3624.

........., ..., David Arnot Bishop of the, 288.

........., St. Mary and St. Mich., 1829, 2061.

Stobill. *See* Scobell.

Stock, Ric., M.A., 1285.

Stokkyngis, a close and pasture in Haseley, Warw., 3186.

Stokyngflete, Yorkshire, 3149, 3411.

Stocklande, Dorset, 3529.

Stockton, Norf., 1129.

Stockton, Tho., 1058.

Stockwith, Ric., 3868.

Stocques, 4330.

Stoke, Dorset, 4733, 5098.

.... Linc., 3130.

........., Notts, 1053.

........., Suff., college, 5249.

Stoke-under-Hampden, Somers., 4712.

Stoke Bardolph, Notts, 1966.

Stokebruern, Northt., 3027.

Stoke Clymmyslonde, Cornwall, 5694.

Stoke Damerell, Devon, 2080.

Stoke Rodney, Somers., 5640.

Stokelanlovell, Somers., 801.

Stokenham, Devon, 1945.

Stokes, Hen., 1890, 4408.

........., Tho., 3941, 4967.

Stokyngham, 597, 860.

Stokton Sokon, Suffolk, 637.

Stoltz, John, of Basle, ambassador of the Swiss Cantons to Hen. VIII., 4970.

Stone, Bucks, 1352.

........., Heref., 1788. *See also* Watton-at-the-Stone.

Stone, John, 3894.

Stonefield, Oxon, 866.

Stonehouse, Devon, 799.

Stoner, Walter, 3497 (ii.).

........., Sir Walter, in commission for Oxon, 4809, p. 905.

........., (or Stonour), Sir Wm., 1824.

Stoneton, Derby, 4836.

Stonydelf, Staff., 458, 4946.

Stonyfeld, Hants, 1824.

Stony Stratford, Bucks, 3297, 3442.

Stores, 4977.

Storeyard, the, at Eltham, 5450.

Storms, 3857, p. 627.

Storuge, Rob., attainted, 985.

Stotevyle, Thomas, 4580.

Stoughton, Gilb., 3996.

........., ..., in commission for Surrey, 1427, 1762, 3078, 3092, 4693, 4734, 5237, p. 905.

........., Hen., 12.

Stourton, Staff., 155, 900.

........., John Lord, temp. Edw. IV., 1504.

........., William Lord, in commission for Dorset, 26, 708, 903, 2007, 3064, 3566, 3606, 3701, 4713, 5658.

........., ..., ... for Somerset ; 287, 712, 3048, 3566, 3585, 3606, 3701, 4713, p. 904.

........., ..., ... for Wilts, 898, 1489, 1938, 3157, 3824, 4583.

Stourton, Lord, in the war, 3977, 4377.

........., Wm., Lord, summoned to Parliament, 5616.

........., Edw., in commission for Dorset, 26, 708, 2007, 3064, 3566, 3606, 3701, 4713, 5658.

Stowe, 4254.

........., Linc., 1392, 4616.

Stowe, John, the antiquary, p. 632 n.

Stowe Bardolff, Norf., 5150.

Stowell, John, son of Rob., 629.

Stowemarket, Suff., 1607.

Stowey, Somers., 801.

Stow Wood forest, Oxon, 877, 4382.

Stracey, Edw., of Sudbury, 4487.

Strachy, John, and Alice, deceased, 4911.

........., Tho., and Joan his wife, 4911.

Stradbroke, Suff., 649, 1129, 1333, 1345, 5074.

Stradiots, 4622.

Stradling, Sir Edw., 4468, 5180.

........., Wm., canon of Aburgoyle, 370.

Stralem, in Gelderland, 3499.

Strange, John, in commission for Norfolk, 1340, 1714, 1812, 1963, 3029, 3210, 3426, 3545, 5133

........., ..., justice of gaol delivery, Bishop's Lynn, 884.

........., Rob., 12, 1812.

........., Sir Rog. le, and John his son, 581.

........., le, (Extraneus) Roger, t. Edw. I., 4934.

........., Lady Jane, in debt to the Crown, 777.

........., ..., her will, 5255.

.... (Joan Stanley), Lady le, 5647.

Strangways (Strangwishe), Edw., in commission for Dorset, 708, 903.

........., Giles, in commission for Dorset, 26, 26, 708, 903, 2007, 3064, 3566, 3606, 3701, 4713, 5658.

........., ..., in commission for Somerset, p. 904.

........., ..., sheriff of Somers. and Dors., 3507.

........., ..., grant to, 5063.

........., ..., at the marriage of the Princess Mary, 5483.

........., Sir Jas., in commission for Yorks., 1549, 1735, 1804, 3219, 3358, 5244.

........., ..., on the sheriff-roll for Yorks., 5561.

........., Jas., in commission for Berks, 1732, 2095, 3640, 4341, 5166.

........., ..., grant to, 3005.

........., ..., in the war, 3167, 3231, 4632.

........., Kath., wife of James, 3005.

........., Jas., in debt to the Crown, 3497.

.... (Stranghish, or Strangwisshe), Th., of Sneton, 2018, 3557.

........., Tho., in commission for Dorset, 26, 903, 2007, 3064, 3566, 3606, 3701, 4713, 5658.

........., ..., at Flodden, 4439.

Strangways, Tho., in commission for Northumberland, 187, 1735, 1804, 3358.

........., ..., porter of Berwick, 4197, 4868.

Strasbourg, 4609.

Stratfeld Mortimer, Berkshire, 93, 155.

Stratford, Suff., 155.

........., abbot of, 1363.

Stratford at Bow, 1972, 3899.

Stratton, Cornwall, 1830.

Stratton, John, 4757, 5371.

Stray or Strey, Tho., justice on the Northern Circuit, 173, 294, 832, 1123, 1130, 1490, 1763, 2099, 3267, 3275, 3699, 4252, 4279, 4771, 5195, 5283.

........., ..., Tho., in commission for York., 3072, 3177, 3691, 4015, 5166.

Streatham, Surrey, 1391, 1703.

Strete, Hen., usher of the chamber, 157, 623, 1599.

........., ..., yeoman of the crown, 1945.

........., ..., serjeant at arms, 4042, 4088.

........., Richard, clerk, 4209.

Stretley, Berks., 4670.

Stretton, Heref., 1794.

Strickland, Westmoreland, 3764.

........., Sir Walter, 1016.

........., Eliz. (widow of Sir Walter), 1016, 1052.

........., Walt., son of Sir Walter, 1016, 4767.

Stringer, Wm., 5008.

Striveling. See Stirling.

Strocci, Marcus, merchant of Florence, 2036.

Strode, John, in commission for Dorset, 4713, 5658.

........., Ric., M.P. for Plympton, 3502.

........., ..., in com. for Devon, 5220.

........., Wm., 1775.

Stronge, Rob., 5618.

Strumpshangh, Norfolk, 5150.

Stuart, Alex., 4624.

........., ..., Abp. of St. Andrew's. See St. Andrew's.

........., Balthasar, sent by the Pope to Scotland, 4491, 4615, 4725, 5025, 5054.

........., ..., letter to, 3349.

........., Joan, 1502.

Stubbe, or Stubbes, Edw., 3480.

........., Walter, in commission for Norfolk, 1340, 1714, 1963, 3029, 3426, 3545, 5133, 5580.

........., ..., in debt to the Crown, 3497.

........., ..., justice of gaol-delivery, Norwich Castle, 931.

Stubswalding, Yorkshire, 3343.

Studde, John, 4143, 4419.

Studdesbury, John, 1480.

Studdon, Wm., yeoman of the guard, 1992, 4385.

Studley, Rob., 756.

........., ..., brewer of London, 5723.

Stukeley, John, 4067.

.... or Stukleigh, Tho., in commission for Devon, 304, 699, 917, 1503, 1812, 3183, 3566, 3589, 3605, 3938, 4539, 4783, 5220.

........., ..., on the sheriff-roll for Devon, 664.

........., ——, in the war, 4377.

Stuple, Somerset, 155.

Stupton, Linc., 1463, 4695.

Sturfield, Hants, 728, 1286.

Stuston, Suff., 1666.

Stuteley, Tho., 3936.

Stuton. See Stewton.

Stuttecombe, Devon, 2080.

Stynt, Rob., clk., 3459.

Styria (Styremark), 5055, 5126, 5259.

Suadenham, Th., 5723.

Subsidy, 3440, 4996.

........., Acts for, 811, 3502, 4848.

Sudbury, Suff., 155, 222.

........., college at, 4101.

........., house called the Cheker in, 4487.

........., Derby, 5574.

Sudbury, John, 1595.

Sudeley, Gloucester, 1320, 1374.

.... Castle, 1385.

........., Ralph Lord, 4838.

Suel, Jerome, French workman, 4445.

Suffolk, commissions of the peace for, 280, 676, 1153, 1339, 1715, 3029 3219, 3967, 4713, 5133, 5506.

........., commissions of array for, 3393, 3688.

........., other commissions for, 266, 1534, 3871, 4414.

........., sheriffs of, 664, 996, 1316, 1446, 1771, 1949, 3507, 3851, 4544, 4551, 5561.

........., escheators of, 3896, 3947.

........., grand jury of, 785.

........., issues of, 574, 1324, 4694.

........., lands in, 458, 581, 3668, 4254, 4536, 4680.

........., tenths and fifteenths granted in, 3441.

........., herring fleet on the coast of, 3445.

........., John Henyngham of, 1757.

Suffolk's lands, 174, 1426, 4254.

Suffolk, Earls and Dukes of. See Pole, Edmund, John, and Richard, De la Pole; and Brandon, Charles.

........., Eliz., Duchess of, Edm. De la Pole's mother, lands of, 458, 577.

.... family. See Pole, De la.

Sukyrke, 4526.

Suley Fermes, Northf., 426.

Suliard, And., in commission for Norfolk, 1340, 1714, 1963, 3029, 3426, 3545, 5153, 5580.

Suliard, And., grant to, 4680.

........., Edw., in commission for Essex, 310, 1368, 1522, 1713, 3605, 3785, 3967.

........., ..., justice of gaol delivery, Colchester Castle, 3464.

........., ..., grant to, 893.

........., John, in commission for Suffolk, 280, 676, 1121, 1153, 1715, 3029, 3219, 3967, 4713, 5133, 5506.

........., ..., justice of gaol delivery, Bury St. Edmunds, 1939.

Sullihull, Warw., 4694.

Sultan, the, 540, 4173.

Sumatra, 4173.

Sumnore, John, inc. of Saint Mary of Melle, 1803.

Sunca, Francisco de, Spaniard, 790.

Sunning. See Sonnyng.

Sunninghill, privy seals dated, 399, 421.

Sunnyff, Tho., 1540.

Surgeons, Acts concerning, 2082, 4848.

........., the King's. See More, Marcellus de la

Surland, Ric., clerk, 491, 505, 526, 661.

Surrentinus, Franciscus Cardinal, 4455, 5378, 5396.

........., ..., letters from, 5349, 5350, 5399, 5540.

Surrey, 1911, 4067, 4695.

........., lands in, 140.

........., commissions of the peace for, 1427, 1497, 1762, 3078, 3092, 4693, 4734, 5237, 5506.

.... commission of array for, 3380.

........., other commissions for, 4808.

........., bailiff of, 5128.

.... gaol, Southwark, 4568.

........., justices of gaol-delivery for, 1548.

........., tenths and fifteenths granted in, 3441.

.... and Sussex, Crown lands in, 4414.

........., ..., sheriffs of, 612, 664, 1316, 1771, 1949, 3507, 3592, 3887, 4544, 5561.

Surrey, Earl of. See Howard, Thomas.

Susa, on the River Po, 4210, 5675.

Sussex, 12, 3592, 3786, 4695.

........., lands in, 140.

........., commissions of the peace for, 281, 1509, 3428, 4804, 5506.

........., commissions of array for, 3024, 3380, 3393, 3688.

........., other commissions for, 266.

.... sheriffs of. See Surrey and Sussex.

Suthorp, Linc., 730.

.... See Southorp.

Sutton, Hants, 578.

........., Notts, 1129.

........., Warw., 1499, 2049, 3100.

........., Yorksh., 494, 1205, 2052.

........., in Ashfield, Notts, 1633, 1809, 4694.

.... Colfield, Warw., 1266, 3559.

.... Courteney, Berks, 2080.

Sutton-upon-Derwent, Yorksh., 415, 499, 5585.

Sutton, East, Kent, 5625.

.... Parva, Wilts, 1867, 5247.

Sutton, Edw. See Dudley, Lord.

........., Elewisa, lady of, 415.

........., Jenett, wife of Lewis, 55.

........., John, 3386.

........., ..., monk of Abingdon, 2070.

........., Nich., 4996.

........., Ric., grant to, 2057.

........., Rob., in commission for Linc., 1171, 3342, 4358, 4593, 4860.

........., ..., in the war, 4377.

........., Sir Tho., in commission for Notts, 1514, 1735, 1798, 1804, 1964, 3092, 3494, 4776, 5225, 5506.

........., ..., on the sheriff-roll for Notts and Derby, 5561.

Swabia, 4069, 4279, 4563.

Swaffham, Norfolk, 900, 3114, 3125, 4022.

Swafeld, John, commission to, 5236.

Swalcliffe, Middx., 1031, 1167.

Swallowfield, Berks, 97, 155.

Swanne, James, 4996.

Swan, John, 3579.

......, Wm., 3969.

Swannes, Suff., 4254.

Swans, masters of the, 96, 306.

Swanscombe, Kent, 155.

Swansea Castle, 5180.

Swanyngton, Leic., 3041, 3096.

Swarforde. See Swerford.

Swathelyng, Hants, 1824.

Swayn, Wm., in commissions for Berks, 3640 4341, 5166.

Sweating sickness, 1849, 2001, 4427.

Swedes, the, 2077.

Swerford, Oxon, 636, 4254.

Sweteman, John, chaplain, temp. Edw. III., 833.

Swyllingholne, Northt., 3761, 4904.

Swillington, Ralph, in commission for Leicestershire, 656, 1094, 1425, 1971, 4706, 4783, 4812, 5506.

........., ..., justice of gaol delivery, Leicester Castle, 554, 3209, 4742, 5186.

Swynbourne, Geo., 810.

........., Wm., on the sheriff-roll for Northumberland, 3507, 4544, 5561.

Swineshead, abbot of, in commission for Linc., 1716, 1979, 3137, 5691.

Swiss, the, 3112, 3325, 3335, 3361, 3370, 3463, 3469, 3499, 3651, 3752, 3779, 3780, 3835, 3862, 4069, 4078, 4086, 4091, 4093, 4280, 4323, 4359, 4362, 4366, 4389, 4399, 4561, 4574, 4577, 4789, 4844, 4916, 4935, 4952, 4955, 5164, 5173, 5266, 5377, 5404, 5410, 5543, 5677, 5718.

.... in Italy, 216, 3225, 3269, 3340, 3341 3377, 3817, 3897, 3976, 4096, 4210, 4273, 4276, 4283, 4287, 4296, 4319, 4326, 4449, 5040, 5171, 5323, 5387, 5675, 5745.

Swiss in France, 4305, 4329, 4349, 4429, 4464, 4515, 4725.

.... in the service of England, 4086, 4093.

........., battle of Novara fought by, 4196, 4216, 4274.

........., diet of, 5208.

........., treaties of, 2091, 4138.

........., to be included in the treaty of France and Castile, 4924.

........., league concluded with the Pope by, 5430, 5532.

........., league concluded with the King of Arragon by, 5539.

........., embassy from England to, 4830,

........., Cardinals of the, 3658, 4371.

Switzerland, disturbances in, 4333.

Syo. See Chios.

Sybbyll, Abraham, and Isaac his son, 1896.

Sydenhall, Salop, 4071.

Sydenham, Alex., in commission for Somerset, 1761.

........., John, of Bruton, in commission for Somerset, 287, 712, 3048, 3566, 3585, 3606, 3701, 5506.

........., Ric., 4479.

Sydney, Rob., spear at Calais, 4476, 4635.

........., Wm., squire of the Body, 3143, 5442.

........., Sir Wm., grants to, 4356, 4909,

........., ..., captain, 3591, 3977, 4005, 4020, 4377, 5104, 5761.

Sygar, John, 3406, 3407, 4643.

........., ..., treasurer of the fleet, 3980.

Sylham, Suff., 694, 1022, 1129, 1344, 1629.

Sylvester. See Silvester.

Synghai, preceptory of, St. John of, 4562.

Syria, 5729.

Syrian, Anthony, a, 5728.

Syfwentes. See Cifuentes.

T.

Tailard, John, in com. for Huntingdonshire, 905, 916, 1095, 4006.

........., ..., ... gaol delivery, Ramsey, 959, 1222, 3652.

Tailboys, Sir Geo., of Kyme, Linc., 380, 3515, 4616.

........., ..., in the wars with France, 3977.

Tailor, King's. See Jasper, Stephen ; and Hilton, Wm.

Tailors, Merchant, of London, 1029, 3879.

Tailowe, Tho., 4158.

Talbot, ——, 5353.

........., Edm., 4728.

........., Geo. See Shrewsbury, Earl of.

........., Sir Gilb., deputy or lieut. of Calais, 1871, 3353, 4071, 4174.

Talbot, Sir Gilb., grants to, 346, 528, 560, 817, 949, 1251, 1254, 1275, 1280, 1302, 1384, 1431, 1449, 1473, 1479, 1553, 1568, 1615, 1723, 1729, 1765, 1767, 1791, 1859, 1884, 1890, 1891, 2016, 2047, 2060, 2066, 2081, 2092, 3000, 3022, 3111, 3148, 3151, 3180, 3200, 3213, 3312, 3408, 3439, 3491, 3508, 3519, 3530, 3564, 3565, 3608, 3642, 3665, 3667, 3671, 3672, 3693, 3695, 3705, 3747, 3826, 3832, 3899, 3919, 3953, 3961, 4012, 4026, 4146, 4175, 4186, 4240, 4285, 4290, 4293, 4338, 4392, 4514.

........., ..., in com. to receive money due from France, 14, 626, 1632, 1919, 2026.

........., ..., in com. for Worcestersh., 892, 3301, 3709, 4770, p. 903 ; Staffordsh., 279, 713, 791, 886, 1770, p. 903 ; Warwicksh., 282, 1387, 1468, 1971, 3364, p. 903 ; Herefordsh., 646, 675, 1400, 1963, 3686 ; Gloucestersh., 930, 1049, 1469, 1695, 3641, 3712, 3804, 4024, 4118, 4764 ; Salop, 198, 1981, 3071, 3715, 4394, 4827, p. 904.

........., ..., in com. of musters, 521, 522.

........., ..., letters from, 3813, 3948, 4021, 4057, 4079, 4080, 4092, 4100.

........., ..., letters to, 4081.

........., ..., payments by, 4129, 4478.

........., ..., captain in the war with France, 4253.

........., ..., Gilb., jun., in com. of the peace, Worcestersh., 892, 1971, 3301, 3709, 4770.

........., Giles, groom of the chamber, 4746.

........., Hugh, spear of Calais, 4476, 4635.

........., Sir Humph., lands of, 654, 3561, 3655, 3922.

........., Joan, wife of Sir Humph., 654, 3561, 3655, 3922.

........., John, 3178, 4961.

........., John. See Shrewsbury, Earl of.

........., als. Troutebeke, Marg., wife of John Talbot, 3178.

........., als. Vernon, Marg., d. of John, late Earl of Shrewsbury, 1978, 3713.

........., Rob., bailiff of Hawleigh, Suff., 68.

Talenen, Mons. de, French captain at Brescia, 3325.

Talmage, ——, of co. Suffolk, indebted to Hen. VII., 3497.

........., Lionel, in commission, 266, 4677.

........., ..., in com. of the peace, Suffolk, 280, 676, 1121, 1153, 1715, 3029, 3219, 4713, 5133, p. 904.

........., ..., sheriff of Norf. and Suff., 3507, 4705.

........., Rob., of Otley, indebted to Henry VIII., 2044, 3851.

Talmon, Prince de, present at marriage of Princess Mary, 5482.

Talowe, Tho., 3694.

Talvern. See Arundel, John.

Talworth, Surr., 367, 721.

Tame, Edm., in com. for Gloucestersh., 930, 1049, 1469, 1695, 3641, 3712, 3804, 4024, 4118, 4764.

........., ..., on sheriff-roll for Gloucestersh., 4544.

........., Hen., 3047.

Tamworth, 1354, 4946.

........., Leic., 155.

........., Staff., 458.

........., Warw., 1499, 1895, 3497, 3880.

........., ch. of, dioc. Cov. and Lich., 3581, 5533.

Tamworth, John de, clerk of the Crown, 85.

........., ..., of Leek, Linc., 5087.

........., ..., son of John, of Leek, 5087.

........., ..., owner of the Christopher of Dartmouth, 5112.

........., Thomas, auditor of public accounts, and keeper of books and records, &c., 4653, 5231, 5316.

Tankard, Ric., 3386.

Tanfield, Eliz., 830, 4656.

........., Rob., son of Eliz., 830, 4656.

........., Tho., prior of Thorneholme, Linc., 1097.

........., Wm., son of Rob., 830, 4656.

........., ..., in com. for Huntingdon, 4006.

........., ..., on sheriff-roll for Huntingdon, 4544, 5561.

Tanne, Edm., 5061.

Taner, ——, 1212.

Tanners and shoemakers, guild of, Barnstaple, 3272.

Tappyng Close, Warw., 549,

Tarlatino, ——, French soldier in Italy, p. 384.

Tarnesewe. See Carnesewe.

Tarrett, Jack, Frenchman, 3751.

Tartary, Emperor of, his son and nephew slain in an incursion into Poland, 3269, 4449.

Tarwell, Northt., 155.

Tassis, Baptist de. See Taxis.

Tate, Barth., lancer of Calais, annuity 4635, 4947.

......, John, in com. for Berks, 241, 885, 1393, 1481, 1732, 2095, 3640, 4341, 5166.

......, Thomas, in retinue of Calais, 4635.

......, Wm., LL.D., 3386.

Tateshall, Linc., 352, 509, 1961.

Tatnall, 131.

Tattunhyll ch., Cov. and Lich. dioc., 1199.

Taunton, South, Devon, 1779.

Tavistock, 3150.

........., Devon, Abbey of, 5494 ; Ric. Banham, abbot of, grant to, 4668.

Tawley, Rob., incumbent of St. George's, Southampton Castle, 3610, 4790.

Taxis, Baptista de, master of the posts to Marg. of Savoy, 3296, 3499, 3678, 4273, 4282, 4305.

........., ..., letter from, 4401.

Taxia, Francis de, master of the posts, letter to, 4305.

........., ..., ..., letter from, 3639.

........., Simon de, letters from, 3340, 3341.

Tay, Sir Hen., in com. for Essex, 310.

......, Philip, 3858.

......, Tho., justice of gaol delivery, Colchester Castle, 3464.

......, ..., in com. for Essex, 3605, 3785, 3967, p. 907.

Taylor, Isabella, 3939.

........., John, 12.

........., ..., King's clerk and chaplain, clerk of the Parliament, 611.

........., ..., master in Chancery, 673.

........., ..., incumbent of All Saints the More, London, 1356.

........., ..., inc. of Coldhigham, dioc. Linc., 1586.

........., ..., his oration in convocation, 5189.

........., ..., signature 811, 4848.

........., ..., diary of, 4284.

........., ..., his hand, 3697, 4849.

........., ..., his clerk, hand of, 5331.

........., receiver of petitions in Parliament, 811, 2082.

........., Ph., yeom. purveyor of the Catery, 1228, 1786, 2065, 3792, 4894.

........., Ric., of London, 1449.

........., Tho., yeoman of the Crown, 3244, 3792.

........., Wm., merchant of the Staple at Calais, dec., 3939.

Tebold, John, of Sele, Kent, 3774.

Techet, Edw., 4476.

Tedd, John, army victualler, 3788, 3858.

Tedder, ——, bailiff of Towcester, 688.

Teesdale, forest of, 3252.

Tesedell, Wm., inc. of Barnacastle, Durham dioc., 3782.

Teet, Robert. See Robertet.

Tego, Wm., army victualler, 3728.

Tempest, Agnes, d. of John, 1261.

........., Anne, d. of John, 4277.

........., John, 1261, 4277.

........., ..., in commission for Lincolnshire, 1716, 1979, 3137, 5691.

........., Marg., d. of Sir Tho., 452, 3528.

........., Ric., signature in articles of a tournament, 1491.

........., ..., squire of the Body, grants to, 3528, 3872, 3956, 5072.

........., ..., in commission of array, Yorkshire, 1735 ; W.R., 3358.

........., ..., in commission of peace, Yorkshire, W. R., 1798, 1804, 1941, 1995, 3177, 4015, 5166.

........., Ric., in the war with France, 4314.

........., knighted at Tournay, 4468.

........., Sir Ric., feodary of co. York, 5692.

Tempest, Robt., 4277.

........., Sir Tho., 452, 3528.

........., Tho., 1725, 5608.

........., ..., in commission of sewers, Northumberland, 705.

........., ..., in com. of peace, Yorkshire, 1549, 1735 ; N. R., 3219, 5244.

........., ..., ... of array, Yorkshire, N.R., 1804, 3358.

Temple, Roger, of Burton, 1480.

Templehurst, letter dated, 4652, 4902.

Tempilnewsum, letter dated, 4105.

Tenacurre, 4303.

Tenby, Pembroke, 1100, 3294, 5420.

Tendall. See Tindall.

Tendilla, 4096.

Tenen, county of Artois, 3654.

Tenet. See Thanet.

Tenremonde. See Dendermonde.

Tenterden, cinque port, subsidy, 4996.

Tenths. See Fifteenths.

Tents, halls, pavilions, &c., 4629.

Terell, Humph. See Tirell.

Terin near Trent (date), 3543.

Terlyng, 746, 3939.

Termont, ——, master of the Prince's ordnance, 3849.

Terouenne, 4079, 4162, 4253, 5021.

........., siege of, 4284, 4286, 4306, 4318, 4322, 4326, 4349, 4364, 4371, 4386, 4398, 4399, 4410, 4411, 4412, 4413, 4415, 4431, 4449, 4454, 4455, 4457, 4464, 4513, 4526, 4561, 4571, 4610, 4622, 5165.

........., expenses, &c., of a banquet and mummery held there, 4642.

........., council appointed for, 4820.

........., King's camp near (date), 4416, 4430, 4437, 4611.

........., abbey of St. John, where the Emp. lodges before, 4415.

........., dioc. of, 1575.

Terra Nova, Gunsalvo Fernandys, Duke de, 3593.

Terraunt, Tho., 1002.

Terry, Rob., 1854. See Tirry.

Teseby, John, of St. Sepulchre's, London, 1540.

Testeville, le Sieur de, at marriage of Princess Mary, 5482.

Tesur, Jehan, 4445.

Tetbury, 155.

Tetency, 5197.

Tewell, Tho., escheator of Norf. and Suff., 3896.

Tevent, incumb. of, 1854.

Tevilby, Linc., 1071.

Teviotdale, 4518, 4522, 4556, 4573.

Tewe, Th., 3771.

Tewington, Cornw., 506.

Tewke, beaten gold and silver, banners of, 4954.

Tewkesbury, Glouc., 1831, 3613, 5051.

........., Ric., Cheltenham, abbot of, 579.

........., Hen. Beley, abbot, 662, 5292.

........., ..., ..., in com. for Glouc., 1049, 1469, 3641, 3712, 3804, 4024, 4118, 4764.

........., ..., ..., abbot of, indebted to Hen. VII., 1639.

........., ..., ..., summoned to Parliament, 2654, 5616.

Thacher (Theccher), John, in com. of the peace, Suss., 281, 1509, 3428, 4804, p. 904.

........., ..., in other commissions, 297, 3024.

........., ... See Thekar.

........., Tho., 266, 297.

........., ..., in com. of the peace, Suss., 281, 1509, 3428, 4804, p. 904.

........., ..., in com. of array, Suss., 3024.

Thacker, Th., of the Staple of Calais, 5712.

Thaleus, ——, 3535.

Thames, river, 1980, 3857, 3903, 3946, 3985, 4038, 4094, 4311; swans in, 96; 4022, 4347.

........., ..., King's fisher in, 586, 1096, 1279.

........., ... sewers, 1972, 4701.

........., ..., King's navy in, reformation of, 3808.

........., ..., ships in the, 4474, 5276, 5176, p. 953, 5751. See also Ships.

Thanet, isle of, 1537, 1615.

Thaxted, Essex, 36, 155, 222, 3743.

Thaxsted, Tho., abbot of Walden, dioc. Lond., 167, 227.

Theatinus. See Chieti, Bishop of.

Thedwardstrete hund., Suff., 4966.

Theimseke, George de, provost of Cassel, 3353, 3367, 5165, 5327, 5341.

Thekar, John, 3031. See Thacher.

Thelwell, Nich.,'bailiff of Cottingham Langton, York, 5089.

Theodore, Mons., French captain in Italy, 3325.

Theodoriame, John, merch. of Luke, 3497.

Theodorus, grammar of, Erasmus studying the, 1900.

Theresby, Linc., 1071.

Therouane. See Terouenne.

Thetford, 5603.

Theydon, Essex, 3203, 4285, 5178.

Thickpenny, Tho., customer of Plymouth and Foway, 3260, 3261.

........., Wm., 1212.

Thimberland, Linc. See Timberland.

Thimelby, Sir John, in com. for Linc., 4860.

Thinghowe hund., Suff., 4966.

Thionville, ——, a Frenchman at Gravelin, 3196.

Thirlond, Tho. See Thurland.

Thloyd. See Lloyd.

Thomas, Adam, dead, 66.

........., John, serj.-at-arms, 1536, 4033.

........., ..., legatee of Marg. C. of Richmond, 235.

........., John ap, servant of Ric. Vaughan, 3771.

........., Sir Rees or Rice, ap, grants to, 4554.

........., ..., justice of S. Wales, 641.

........., ..., chamb. of S. Wales, 1047, 1193, 1597, 1665.

........., ..., in the wars with France, 3231, 4070, 4253; at Terouenne, 4284, 4431.

........., ..., his servant David de Powel (a prisoner), 4174.

.... ap Richard, Tho. ap, murderer, 65.

........., Rob., legatee of Marg. Countess of Richmond, 235.

........., ... ap Howel ap, dead, 3368.

........., Thos., of Southampton, 12, 112.

........., ..., constable of castle of Southampton, &c., dead, 798, 820, 3123.

........., Wm., groom of the chamber, grants to, 40, 41, 995, 3480, 3684.

Thomists, the, 4447.

Thomlyn, Tho., in com. of gaol delivery, Oakham, 3282.

........., ..., justice of assize, Mid. Circuit, 3287.

Thomlynson, John, alias Cowper, 494, 2052.

Thompson, Dr.. 1212.

........., Hen., Lion, notarial attestation to a treaty, 474.

........., John, yeoman of the Crown, 1226; deceased, 1633, 1809, 3579.

........., ..., of London, 1554.

........., Ralph, of London, fishmonger, 1527, 3868.

........., Steph., collector of Cottingham, 534.

........., Thos., of London, 1608.

........., Tho., of Scotland, 4027.

........., ..., in com. of the peace, Cambridge town, 667.

........., Wm., chaplain, 1854.

Thoresby, alias Thursby, Rob., of London, 3148.

........., Tho., yeoman of the Crown, 362.

........., ..., on sheriff-roll for Camb. and Hunts, 1316, 1949, 3507; sheriff for, 4544.

........., ..., mentioned as escheator for Camb. and Hunts, 4659.

Thorne, Devon, 2080.

........., Yorksh., 1178, 3818, 3845.

Thorne, Flor., wife of Geo., 4911.

........., Geo., 4911.

........., Hen., 3249.

Thorne, Joan, 4911.
........., Rob., in com. for Bristol, 1050.
........., Tho., 4911.
Thornbury, Glouc., 1157 ; college at, 5289.
Thornborough, 3297.
Thorndon, Suff., 1453, 4254.
Thornehill, Th., feodary in Soms. and Dors., 5692.
Thorneholme, Linc., Tanfeld, Th., prior of, 1097.
Thornes, Rog., of Shrewsbury, 887.
Thorney, abbey of, Ric. Holbech, abbot, 3725.
........., ... Tho. Mowlton, abbot, 3800, 3803, 3693.
........., ..., ..., summoned to Parliament. 5616.
........., ..., ..., in commis. of sewers, Linc., 5691.
Thorney, Robt., yeoman porter of the King's gates, 3567, 4565.
........., Rog., merchant, 775.
Thornton ch., Linc., 375.
........., Yorksh., 1628, 3764.
........., inc. of, Wm. Atwater, 1637.
Thornton, Hen., serjeant-at-arms, 411, 4046.
........., Ric., dead, late inc. of St. Trinity, Sherifhoton, 180.
........., Thos., priest, grant to, 4600.
Thorp, Linc., 3284, 4852.
........., Northampton, 645, 3027. See also Throp.
Thorpwaterfeld, alias Achurche, Northt., 403, 479, 645.
Thraundeston, Suff., 1666.
Thread, account of, 4232.
Threlkeld, Launcelot, of Annesburton, York., 1392.
.... See Thurkill.
Throgmorton, Chr., of Trilley, deceased, 5051, 5688.
........., ..., on sheriff-roll for Glouc., 664, 1816.
........., ..., in com. of gaol delivery, Glouc, castle, 1922.
........., ..., indebted to Hen. VII., 3467 ; cancelled, 5688.
........., Eliz., abbess of Denny, dioc. Ely. licence in mortmain, 3255.
........., George, squire of the Body, King's spear, grants to, 1895, 2086, 4337.
........., ..., in com. of the peace, Warwicksh., 1387, 1468, 1971, 3364.
........., ..., (Sir Rob. ?), capt. of the Great New Spaniard, 5761.
........., Mary, w. of Chr., 5051.
........., Sir Rob. of Coghton, grants to, 953, 1024, 1350, 3827, 4940, 5688.
........., ..., in commis. of the peace, Warwicksh., 282, 1387, 1468, 1971, 3364, p. 903.
........., ..., capt. of the Great New Spaniard and of the Less Bark, 3977, 4377. See Throgmorton, George.
........., ..., temp. Hen.VII. as justice, 1965,
........., Wm., 3720.

Throkmorton, Wm., LL.D., notary or prothonotary in Chancery, 1337.
Throp, near Daventre, Northt., 1950.
Thropton, Northumb., 1040, 5010.
Throwlegh, 2080.
Thundersley Park, Essex, 36, 222, 1138, 5019.
Thurford, 155.
Thurkill or Thurcull, Ric. a broker, King's messenger, 3946, 4932.
........., ..., letter from, 4054.
.... See Threlkeld.
Thurland, Lanc., 5288.
Thurland, Th., of Gaunston, Notts, 63.
........., ..., in com. of array, Notts, 1735, 1804.
........., ..., captain, as receiving ordnance, 4632.
Thurley, Bucks, 1467.
Thurrok, West, manor, Essex, 443.
Thursby. See Thoresby.
Thurstaston, Chesh., 4360.
Thursthorp lordship, 449.
Thurston, John, mast. of the King's barge, 693.
Thwaites, Chris., capt. of the Black Bark, 5112.
........., Edw. See Destyere.
........., John, 413, 1654 ; dead, 3343.
........., Tho. 154.
........., ..., spear at Calais, 1821, 1822, 4476, 4635.
Thylny, François de, sieur de Lyerville, and seneschal of Rouarque, 4410.
Tiak, John, temp. Hen. VII., sub-dean of St. Peter's, Exeter, 3988.
Tichbourne, Nich., 1286.
........., ..., in com. of the peace, Hants, 904, 1388, 1812, 3071.
Ticino, 3976.
Tidburst, manor Herts, 383, 4436.
Tiddeswall, John clk. 3020.
Tight, John, 5296.
Tilbery-hope, muscles in, 155.
Tiler. See Tyler.
Tilles, Rob., in com. of the peace, Linc. (Lindsey), 1170, 3351.
Tilman, Hen., of Chichester, brewer, 5724.
........., Jacob, master of the great ship of Lubeke, 5776.
........., Wm., of Boughton, Kent, 4787.
Tilney, Edmund, captain of the Peter of Fowey, 5761.
........., Sir John, com. of the peace, Suff., 676.
........., Phil., 1666.
........., Sir Philip, of Fincham, Norf., grants to, 642, 1835.
........., ..., in com. of the peace, Norf, 3426, 3545, 5133.
........., ..., in com. of the peace, Suff., 280, 676, 1121, 1153, 1339, 1715, 3029, 3219, 3967, 4713, 5133, p. 904.
........., ..., in other commissions, 633, 1716, 1812, 1979, 3137, 3210, 5691.

Tilney, Sir Philip, at marr. of Princess Mary, 5483.

........., ..., treas. of war against the Scots, 5250, 5723.

Timber, account of, 4232, 4378, 4839.

Timberland, Linc., 3284, 4852.

Timperley, Sir John, in com. of array, Norf., 1812. See Thimelby.

Tin, 181, 506, 3511.

......, coinage of, 397.

Tindal, or Tendall, John, s. of Sir Wm., 1476.

........., John, in com. of array, Norf., 1812.

........., Sir John, to serve in the wars with France, 3231.

........., Mary, w. of Sir Wm., 1476.

........., Ph., 1961.

........., Sir Wm., 1476.

Tingelden, Hen., 1484.

........., ..., in com. of the peace, Surrey, 4693, 4734, 5237.

Tinning, Tho., clk., 12.

Tintagell Castle, Cornw., Carewe, Sir John, capt. and const., 468 ; dead, 3580.

........., ..., Utright, Sir Anth., 3580.

Tiptoft, John. See Worcester, E. of.

Tirell (or Tyrell), Edw., 1699.

........., ..., on sheriff-roll for Essex and Herts, 1316.

........., ..., sheriff of Essex and Herts, 3507.

........., ..., in com. of the peace for Essex and Herts, 1368, 1522, 1713.

........., ..., gaol del., Colchester Castle, 3464.

........., Humph., in com. of the peace, Essex, 1368, 1522, 1713, 3605, 3785, 3967, 5506, p. 907.

........., Jas., of Stowmarket, Suff., 1607.

........., Sir Jas., temp. Hen. VII., 777.

........., John, at Calais, 4526.

........., Thos., of Gipping, Suff., 1607, 3851.

........., ..., on sheriff-roll for Essex and Herts, 664.

........., ..., son of Sir Jas., indebted to Hen. VII., 777.

........., ..., signature to articles in a tournament, 1491.

........., ..., made knight at Tournay, 4468.

........., ..., of Hern, in com. of the peace, Essex, 1522, 1713, 3605, 3785, 3933, 3967.

........., ..., ..., made knight at Tournay, 4468.

........., Thos., master of the horse to Queen Katharine, grants to, 2455, 4773, 5162.

........., Sir Th., grant to, 4865.

........., ..., in com. for Essex, 310.

........., William, 4232.

Tiringham, Tho., of Bucks, temp. Hen. VII., 258.

Tirley, Glouc., 5645.

Tiroan, and Tirwin. See Terouenne.

Tirry, of London, 12. See Terry.

Tirwhit, Sir John, in com. for Lincolnsh. 3342.

........., Rob., of Barton, Linc., grants to, 3515, 4616.

........., Sir Rob., made knight at Tournay, 4468.

........., ..., in com. of peace, Lincolnsh., 4593, 4860.

........., Sir Wm., of Ketilby, knight of the Body, grants to, 495, 496, 497, 707, 1392, 3515, 4616.

........., ..., in com. of sewers, &c., 663, 792, 1378, 1380, 1716, 1979, 1983, 3137, 5691.

........., ..., in com. of peace, Lincolnsh., 1171, 4358, 4593, 4860, 5476.

........., ..., in com. of peace, Yorkshire, 5529, 5605.

........., ..., in the war with France, 3231.

Tisehurst, Wm., abbot of Lesnes, Roch. dioc., 3834.

Tison, John, servant and factor to Lord D'Issilstein, 3692.

........., Th., of Bristol, 5026.

Tistede, Wm., customer, of London, 254.

........., ..., of Sutton, Hants, 578.

Tiverton, 2080.

Toborowgh, John, master of the Imperial Carack, 3591, 3977.

Tocoste. See Tothoth.

Tocotes, Wm., 3018.

Todington, Glouc., 1374.

Toft church, Ely dioc., 3097.

Toft, Hen., 12.

......, ..., keeper of the Exchange for foreign parts, temp. Hen. VII., 755, 2015.

......, Wm., minister of the Chapel Royal, canon of Pencrich, 3063.

......, ..., inc. of Fulbeke, Linc. dioc., 4828.

......, ... See Tost.

Toggesden, Northumb., 1040, 5010.

Toilles, Cappne. des, at the marriage of Pr. Mary, 5482.

Toisan of gold and silver of Flanders, 4917.

Toison d'Or, 924, 3836, 4296.

Tokenham, 155.

Tokwelheye, 1231.

Toledo, Cardinal of (Ximenes), 8.

........., Friar Luys of, grant by, to Queen Kath., 5125.

Tollas, John, 3672.

Toller, Jno., army victualler, 3769.

Tolls in Flanders, 3053.

Tolton, chapel of, Saxton, Yorksh., 1860.

Toly, John, auditor of duchy of York, Berwick, &c., 1060, 2037, 3845.

......, Stephen, of Newsom, Linc., 5245.

Toly, Wm., capt. of the Kath. Galley, 3980.

......, ..., capt. of the Sweepstake, 5761.

......, ..., his brother, Sir Rob. B., 4020.

......, ——, master of the Sweepstake, 3977, 4377.

Tomsett, Christ., of Tirley, Glouc., 5645.

Tomson. See Thomson.

Tomworth. See Tamworth.

Toney, ——, 4983.

........., ..., Rob., attestation to the Princess Mary's renunciation of marriage with Chas. of Castile, 5282 ; and to her marriage with Lewis XII., 5322.

Tong, Kent, 155, 5235.

Tong, John, 4996.

......, Tho., York Herald-at-arms, grant to, 3971.

Tonyman, Norf., 3943.

Tools, &c., 4232, 4378.

Topcliff, John, in com. for Lincolnsh., 1171, 3342, 4358, 4593, 4860, 5476, p. 906.

........., ..., in com. for Yorksh., 1735, 1804, 1941, 1995, 3177, 3358. 4015, 5166, p. 906.

........., ..., chief justice of the King's Bench, 1538.

Topsham, Devon, 444, 829, 1601, 2080.

........., ships prested at, 3978.

.... See Ships.

Torbay. See Ships.

Tordesillias, 8, 338, 3614.

Torell, Humph. See Tirell.

Torfichen, Rhodian preceptory of, 3625.

Tornoke, Soms., 4071.

Torpell, Northampton, 331, 645, 1784, 1993.

Torpike, Devon, 5648.

Torr, ships prested at, 3978. See also Ships.

Torre, Abp. of (Sassari in Sardinia), 1869.

Torrelet, Petitian, 4445.

Torrington, Devon, 329, church of, 1341.

........., Wolsey, inc. of, 1359, 4942.

Tortington, Suss., lands near called the Lyght, 1212.

........., ..., lands and tenements called the Lee, 1965.

Tortona, p. 381.

Tosso, Stephen, King's footman and tumbler, 4618.

Tost, Wm., inc. of Meviot, dioc. St. Asaph, 850.

......, ... See Toft.

Totehill, Hen., p. 433.

........., ... the, ship, 3980.

Tothoth, Totboth, Totoft or Tocoste, Tho., in com. of sewers, Lincolnsh., 1716, 1979, 3137, 5691.

........., ..., in com. of peace, Lincolnsh., 1171, 3342, 4358, 4593, 4860.

Totilde, Wm., inc. of Ripton Regis, Linc. dioc., 744.

Totnes, ships prested at, 155, 946.

.... See Ships.

Tottenhall manor, Chester, 355.

Tottenham, Midd., 730, 4302.

Totingbeke, Surrey, 5242.

Touchet (family name). See Audeley.

Toulouse woad, 1140, 3369, 3424, 4368. See also Merchandize.

Tourchelles, Jehan de, 4445.

Tournay, 4232, 4253, 4561, 4579, 4622, 4830, 4831, 4832, 4851, 4864, 4932, 4982, 4983, 5006, 5158, 5164, 5168, 5175, 5176, 5218, 5219, 5285, 5386, 5390, 5429, 5565, 5589, 5591, 5697, 5781.

........., siege of, p. 626, 4306, 4322, 4459, 4502, 5165, 5554.

........., its submission to Hen. VIII., 4466, 4467, 4501, 4513, 4571.

........., grants to, by Hen. VIII., 4484, 4486, 4490, 4516, 4517, 4585, 4822, 4885, 4896, 4986, 4987, 4991.

........., ..., by the Emperor and Charles Prince of Spain, 4494.

........., Act for administration of justice in, 4848, 4855.

........., council at, 4820, 5636, 5722.

........., proclamation at, 4821.

........., knights made at, 4468.

........., halls and tents at, 4413.

........., ordnance at, 4479.

........., plague at, 5439.

........., expenses of the war at, 4586, 4642; the Abbey of St. Martin's, quota to, 4466, 4667, 5153, 5154; treaty with Maximilian for, 4510, 4978.

........., pay for the garrison, by treasurer, Sir Rob. Dymmok, 5295.

........., Bishop elect of, Lewis Guillart, 4960, 5006, 5367, 5587, 5698.

........., bishopric of, 5446, 5464, 5468, 5518, 5526, 5553, 5554, 5587, 5697, 5698.

........., clerk of the diocese of, 5078. See Portynary, John Baptiste.

........., receiver of. See Bentinck, Allart.

........., lieutenant of, Edw. Lord Ponynges, K.G., 5006, 5021, 5171, 5218, 5697.

........., ..., Baron Mountjoy, 4660.

........., marshal of, Ughtred, Sir Anth., 5554.

........., keeper of the Seal Royal. See Des-tyere, Edw. Thwayte Lord.

........., (dates,) 4470, 4505, 4520, 4793, 4909.

Tournesis, plague in, 4450, 5554.

Tournament, on the birth of a Prince, 1491.

........., in Paris, 5606.

Tournelles, the, in Paris, 5408, 5560.

Tours, 5681.

........., sons of, 318.

Toussaynt Dor. See Toison.

Towcester, Northampton, 688, 1124, 1231, 1827, 3027, 3297.

Towers, als. Stevenson, Guy, 5197.

........., Wm., usher of the King's hall, 3669.

Townsend, John, son of Sir Roger, 3034.
........., Rob., son of Sir Roger, temp. Hen. VII., 3034.
........., Roger, grants to, 226, 996, 1421.
........., ..., in com. for Norf., 1340, 1714, 1963.
........., ..., sheriff of Norf. and Suff., 1949.
........., ..., son of Sir Roger, grant to, 3034.
........., ..., ship owner, 4377.
........., Sir Roger, 3034.
........., Th. of Stoneton, Derb., 4836.
Toyle, le, als. Magnus Canolus, als. le Pale of Canvas, keeper of, 4907.
Tove, Tho., 3888. *See* Tuvy.
Trace, Thos., 5077.
Tracy, Wm., 3720.
........., ..., in com. for Gloucestersh., 930, 448, 1049, 1469, 1695, 3641, 3712, 3804, 4024.
........., ..., sheriff of Gloucestersh., 4544.
........., ..., jun., 3720.
Trade, the, in the English channel, 1980, 3243, 3877, 4005, 4019, 4020, 4038, 4056.
Transports, commission to provide, 4082.
Transylvania, 5338.
Trarinzcane, 3569, 3676.
Trasse, castle of, in Italy (?), 3658.
Treasurer, Lord High. *See* Howard, Th. Earl of Surrey.
.... of England, Under. *See* Cutte.
.... of the King's chamber, 678. *See* Heron.
Treasury, the records in, 1267, 3023, 5351.
Treaties, list of, 1267.
.... between England and other powers, viz:—
.... with Scotland, 474, 475, 488, 714.
.... France, 962, 963, 974, 1104, 1105, 1106, 1107, 1108, 1181, 1182, 1227, 1919, 5278, 5279, 5280, 5294, 5305, 5306, 5307, 5315, 5335, 5343.
.... Spain, 1055, 1059, 1111, 1335, 1980, 2033, 2094, 3327, 3513, 3523, 3586, 3603, 3797, 4038.
.... the Duke of Saxony, 1565, 1717, 1718.
.... the Emperor, 3603, 3649, 3859, 3860, 3861, 4435, 4560.
.... Denmark, 4889.
.... Venice, 3523, 5687.
........., foreign, 1881, 2010, 2091, 3218, 3633, 4138, 4924.
Trebizonde, battle at, 5705.
Trecarell, Hen., in com. for Cornwall, 1694, 1812, 1954, 1984, 3290, 3583, 3605, 3938, 4754, 5220, 5474, 5586 ; Devon., 1166, 3039, 5431.
Tredeneke, Rob., in com. for Cornwall, 891, 1694, 1812, 1954, 1984, 3290, 3583, 3605, 3938, 4741, 5220.
........., ..., ..., Devonsh., 1166.

Tredunnok, ch. of, Llandaff dioc., inc. Jankin, Ph., 4738.
Trefry, John, 4347.
........., Wm., temp. Hen. VII., 144, 1445, 3316.
Tregamure, 2080.
Tregarell, Henry. *See* Trecarell.
Tregarthen, Joan, daughter of John, and h. of Tho., 3227, 3404, 4744.
........., John, 3227, 3404, 4744.
........., Marg. daughter of John, and h. of Tho., 3227, 3404, 4744.
........., ..., w. of Tho., 3227, 3404, 4744.
........., Tho., 3227, 3404, 4744.
Tregirthik, Crabbe, Cornw., 1943.
Tregian, John, grants to, 3727, 4901, 5431.
Tregruke, Wales, 53.
Treguran, John, clk., in com. for Cambridgesh., 1684, 3583.
Treis, John, yeoman of the Jewel House, 1591.
Trelawny, Walt., grants to, 651.
........., ..., in com. of the peace, Corn., 1812, 3290, 3583, 3605, 3938.
Trellek. *See* Trillek.
Trelowya, 2080.
Trelugan, 2080.
Treman, Edw., Lord Howard's servant, 4019.
Treme, Wm., in com. for Gloucestersh., 930.
Tremayle, John, lancer of Calais, 696, 1500, 3565, 4476.
........., Sir John, 4933 ; capt. of the Swallow, 3980.
Tremouille, de la, Mons., or Lord, Chamberlain to Lewis XII., 1182, 3357, 3752, 4196, 4276, 4280, 4282, 4283, 4326, 5482, 5547, 5560, 5569.
Trenchard, Sir Tho., 3231.
........., ..., in com. for Dorset, 2007, 3064, 3566, 3606, 3701, 4713, 5658.
........., ..., sheriff of Soms. and Dorset, 664.
Trend, John, of Lond., 5314.
Trenou, Lord, 4216, 4282, 4329.
Trent, 394, 3325, 3499.
......, Terni near, 3543.
......, river, in Linc., com. of sewers, 3072.
Trent-falle, or Southfereby, 1983.
Trentham, monastery of, 2008.
........., Thomas, in the King's wars, 4253.
Trento, 216.
Trery, 3067.
Trerise, 1316, 2018.
Tresawnowe, John, 1943.
Tresham, John, 1949, 3046.
........., ..., in com. for Northamptonsh., 1708, 1971, 2045, 5058.
Tretherth, Edw., 502, 1600.

Tretherff, Eliz., 1434.
........., John, sen. and jun., award at Bo-
    connok, Cornw., 1434.
........., Tho., 1434.
Tretio, 3269.
Trevanyon, John, compt. of customs, Ply-
    mouth and Fowey, 737.
........., Sir William, knight of the Body,
    grants to, 531, 1915, 3227, 3591, 5719.
........., ..., in com. for Cornw., 1694, 1954,
    1984, 3290, 3583, 3605, 3938, 4754,
    5220, 5586 ; Devonsh., 1166.
........., ..., comptroller of the coinage of
    tin, &c.; Devon and Cornw., 397.
........., ..., 3591, 5719.
........., ..., capt. of the Gabriel Royal,
    3591, 4377 ; payments to him, 3983,
    5112, 5761.
........., ..., capt. of the Henry Imperial,
    3977.
Trevilian, Geo., indebted to Hen. VII., 3497 ;
    Hen. VIII., 2044, 5633.
........., Sir John, in com. for Soms., 287,
    712, 3048, 3566, 3585, 3606, 3701,
    4713, 5506, p. 904.
........., ..., capt. of the Henry of Hampton,
    4377.
Trewe, Tho., 3954.
Trewik, town of, 1040, 5010.
Trevi, in Cremona, taken from the Venetians,
    11.
Treverbyn Courteney, 2080.
Treves, Emp. Max. at, 3077, 4355 ; the Duke
    of Brunswick to meet him there, 4328.
........., Sir R. Wingfield, at, 3945.
........., letter dated at, 5746.
Treves, Hamlet, 4360.
Trevisan, 1697.
Treviso, 1697, 4355, 5353 ; Venetians fortify-
    ing, 3499 ; the Viceroy intends be-
    sieging, 5005, 5126.
Trivulcio, Alex., Ct., 3269.
........., Camillo, son of John James, 4196.
........., Jas., 3325, 4276.
........., (Trowis), John James, 3026, 3269,
    4196, 4216, 4577.
........., ..., lieut. of Picardy, 3325.
........., ..., in Bologna, 1689.
........., ..., son of, 1697.
........., compared by Martyr to the beaver,
    4096 ; spurs Ferdinand on to a war
    with Italy, 5581.
........., Theodore, ambassador of——, 4069.
Trigge, Nich., alderman of Stamford, temp.
    Hen. VII., 5309.
Tricarico, Bp. of, sent by Leo X. to Lewis XII.,
    5107.
Trill, Exeter, 2080.
Trillek, Wales, 53, 57, 58, 843, 1894, 3902,
    5045.
Trilley, 5051.

Tripoli, in Babary, taken by the Spaniards,
    1209.
Troffold, Kent, 778.
Trolop, David, yeoman of the guard, 3018.
Troncage, 992.
Tropton.   See Thropton.
Troughton, John, "de Monte Sancti Johannis,"
    Yorkshire, 5001.
Troutbek, Winandermere, 479, 3764.
Troutbeck, Adam, brother of Sir Wm., 3178.
........., Marg., daughter of Adam, 3177.
........., Margaret, wife of Sir Wm., 4360.
........., Sir Wm., 3178; dec., 4360.
Troy, 5180.
Troys, John, 1139.
........., Tho., of Marwell, Hants, 647.
Truce, declaration of commissioners, for
    Lewis XII., Ferd., and Max., 3839.
........., ratification of, on part of Lewis XII.,
    4875; mentioned, 4921.
........., not yet ratified by Max., 5290.
Truchses de Waltpurgis, Sir Wm., commis-
    sioner for Geo. Duke of Saxony in a
    treaty with Hen. VII., 1717.
True Cross, wood of the, 4173.
Trumble, Wm., rector of Annand, dioc. Glasgow,
    2061.
Trumbhill, Mark, 4556.
Trunchauntes, in Alton, Hants, 730.
Trussell, Edw., son of Sir Wm., 927, 948, 1210.
........., Eliz., daughter of Edw. and h. of
    John, 927, 948, 1210.
........., John, son of Edw., 948, 1210.
........., Sir John, his lands, 4656.
........., Marg., wife of Edw., 927.
........., ..., wife of Sir John, 4656.
........., Sir Wm., 927, 948, 1210.
Trynde, John.   See Trend.
Tuchet, Jas.   See Audeley, Lord.
........., John.   See Audeley, Lord.
Tudenham, lordship of Wales, 3949.
........., East, Norf., 4680.
Tudor, Edw. ap, inc. of Kegedog, Asaph dioc.,
    4137.
Tuerd.   See Stewart.
Tuke, Brian, clerk of the Signet, 373, 3639,
    4075, 4103, 4870, 4930, 5475; grants
    to, 1873, 3700.
........., ..., clerk of the council in Calais,
    1289.
........., ..., in com. of peace for Kent, 3605.
........., ..., payment to him, 3496.
........., ..., his hand, 183, 1113, 1457, 3251,
    3346, 4139, 4763.
........., ..., his books, 786.
Tulman, Herman, a canon of Utrecht, a bene-
    fice held by him in England, 5632.
Tunbridge, Kent, 835.

Tunon, on the lake of Geneva, 4273.

Tunstall (Tonstall), Staff., 682.

Tunstall, Brian, grant to, 1628.

........., ..., of Thurland, Lanc., 5288.

........., Cuthb., LL.D., inc. of Alriche, dioc. Cov. and Lich., 1007; grants to, 5288.

........., ..., at St. Paul's, Lond., 5111.

........., ..., as Master of the Rolls, in a mem. of subsequent date, 1148.

........., Isabel, wife of Brian, 5288.

........., Marmaduke, son of Brian, 5288.

Turbervile, Sir John, 779.

........., ..., mention as Treas. of Calais, 557, 779, 3852 ; his executor, 3485.

........., ..., marshal of the household, 1989.

........., ..., of Freermain, Dors., temp. Hen. VII., 5098.

........., Ro., in com. for Essex, 310, 1368, 1522, 1713, 3605, 3785, 3967.

........., ..., in gaol del. for St.Albans, 4742.

........., Tho., 12, 461.

........., ..., in com. of peace, Kent, 4927.

........., ..., of Mote, Kent, 5098.

Turges Melcombe, Dors., 5127.

Turges, Newell, native of Flanders, 3590.

........., Rob., in com. for Dors., 2007, 3064, 3566, 3606, 3701, 4713, 5658.

........., ..., of Turges Melcombe, Dors., grant, 5127.

Turin, 3325 ; Swiss lay a fine upon, 4096, 4210.

Turk, Rob., of Wrotham, 3969.

Turkey, Princes of, 5705.

.... Sultan of, payment to him for repair of altar of Latin Christians on Mount Calvary, 5729.

........., French ships to invade England by reason of Henry VIII. not going to, 5753.

Turks, 3633 ; Hen. VII.'s war with the, 405, 540, 819.

......., engagements with them, by Christians, &c., 540, 1659, 3697.

......., captives taken by them, 816, 1295, 3002, 5730.

......., their fleet, 1660; Selim Sha the younger, Emp., 3283.

......., Venetians and Lewis XII. likely to aid the, 3662, 4976; raise an army against, 4824.

......., threaten Rhodes, 3874.

......., the Rhodians in daily fear of, 4096.

......., expeditions against, 1457, 1828, 3278, 3283, 4458.

......., destruction of their cavalry by King of Hungary, 4513.

......., persons retained to serve against, 4609.

......., Maximilian's pretence of repelling, 4952.

......., claim tribute of the Hungarians, &c., 5055.

......., their forces, 5592, 5705.

Turnant, Ric., 4302.

........., Tho., chaplain to Hen. VII.-VIII., 833.

Turner, (Turnor,) Geo., auditor of Crown, lands, 665.

........., John, 5093, 5096 ; grants to, 4321 4846.

........., ..., auditor of Crown lands, 914, 4223.

........., ..., auditor of the Duchy of Cornwall, 4775, 5050, 5431.

........., ..., indebted to Hen. VII., and put in exigent by Hen. VIII., 3497.

........., (Turnour,) Oliv., usher of the chamber, grant to, 256.

........., ..., indebted to Hen. VII., 3497.

.... Tho., inc. of St. Marg. Moyses, Friday St., London, 1396.

Turnours manor, in Oxfordsh., 4205.

Turney, John, b. and h. of Ph., 5629.

........., Ph., s. of John, of Wolverton, Somerset, 5629.

Turphill manor, Northampton, 403.

Turpin, Nic., 2000; comptroller of customs, Newcastle-upon-Tyne, 420.

........., Vincent, master of the Mary of Brixham, 4377.

Turpyn, Wm., in com. for Leicestersh., 1425, 1971, 4783, 4812, p. 905.

........., ..., sheriff for Warw. and Leicestersh., 3507.

Turpwaterfeld. See Thorpwaterfield.

Turrent, 155.

Turryngton. See Torrington.

Turstain, Count de, 3325.

Turvile, Wm., in com. for Leicestersh., 4812, p. 905.

Turwayne. See Terouenne.

Tuxford, Notts, 3031.

Tuvy, Steph., of Burton Annas, Yorksh., 3498.

Twedall, Gerard, in Carlisle Castle, 1924.

Twedy, Wm., 4527.

Twychett, Jas. See Audeley, Lord.

Twyckebeare, 2082.

Twyford, Thomas, capt., 4253, 4632.

Twyneo, Wm., on sheriff-roll for Wilts, 3507.

Twyssell, bridge of, 4441.

Twyte, Edw., coroner for Essex, 576.

Tyboveld (Thionville), 3196.

Tychet, John. See Audley.

Tydgott, com. of sewers for, 1716, 1979, 5691.

Tyensa. See Atienza.

Tygbt. See Tight.

Tyler, Wm., 174.

......., ..., groom of the chamber, grants to, 60, 61, 515, 795, 1261, 3252, 3297, 3492, 3787, 4277 ; Sir, 4761, 5096.

........., ..., legatee of Marg. C. of Richmond, 235.

........., ..., ..., Hen. VII., 5779.

........., ..., Sir, made knt. at Tournay, 4468.

........., Sir Will., temp. Hen. VII., 190, 193.

Tylney, Sir Philip. See Tilney.

Tyne, com. of sewers for, 705.
......, bridge over, and walls of the town, grant for repairs of, 742.
Tynedale, 3344, 4825.
Tynemouth, 4682.
........., com. of gaol del. for, 810.
........., John, prior of, 4869.
........., ..., ..., indebted to Hen. VII., 3497.
........., men of, at the battle of Flodden, 4520.
Tyroan. See Terouenne.
Tyrol, De Goures, Chancellor of the, 216.
.... county of, 1697, 4272.
Tyrolese contingent of men and money, against the Venetians, 4304.
Tyrwenne. See Terouenne.
Tyrwit. See Tirwhitt.
Tywardreth, priory of, Corn., 2048.
Tywarnaill, Corn., tolls on tin in, 506.

U.

Uckfield, Sussex, 1484.
Udale, Rob., 1398.
Uden, in Friuli, 5410.
......, or Eden, Th., 4996.
Ufford, Lincoln., 1993, 3074.
........., Tho., 3551.
Ufton Pole, Berks, 1207.
Ugborough (Uggeburgh), Devon, 946, 3057.
Ughtred, Antony, 3497, 5655.
........., ..., Vice-Captain of Berwick, 3928.
:........., ..., marshal at Tournay, 5554.
........., ... captain in the war with France, 3885, 4237, 4475.
........., ..., his offices, &c., 3580, 4269, 4739, 5385.
Ugochoni, Carlos, 3207.
........., John Baptista, 3207.
Ulcombe, Kent, 4291.
Ullenhall (Ulnale), Warw., 1299.
Ulm, 3817, 4561.
Ulmo, near Vicenza, 4499.
Ulster, Anne Countess of. See March.
Ulston, 1040, 5010.
Ulysses, 3637.
Umberley, Devon, 5688.
Uncle, John, 4714.
Underhill, John, dean of St. Mary's, Wallingford Castle, 986.
.........., Wm., clerk of the King's Common House, 847.
Underton, prebend of, 4524.
Underwood, Wm., 851.
Unicorn, Scotch herald, 3577, 3838.
........., ..., sent to England, 3569.
........., ..., sent to Mechlin, 4844.

Unton, Th., of Berks, 1613, 5127.
.........., ..., in com. for Oxon, 1470, 1745, 3015, 4559, 4809, p. 905.
.........., ..., ..., for Berks, 1481, 1732, 2095, 3640, 4341, 5166, 5684.
Upclatford, Hants, 1482.
Upfeldes, Surrey, 1577.
Uppingham, Rutland, 295, 1329.
Uppington, Salop, 4694.
Upsall, Ralph Scrope, Lord. See Scrope, Ralph, Lord Bolton and Upsall.
Upton, Dorset, 1237, 3431.
........., Heref., 1593.
........., Northt., 155.
........., Worc., 5146.
........., York, 3149, 3411, 4022, 4347.
.... Lovel, Wilts, 4694.
.........., ..., church of, Salisb. dioc., 1448, 1466, 4603.
........., near Bache, Chesh., 4748.
........., Nich., in commission for Linc., 1171, 1716, 1979, 3137, 3342, 4358, 4593, 4860, 5691.
Upton-upon-Severn, Worc., 1960, 3613.
Urance, in Spain, p. 451, p. 457.
Urbino, Duke of, nephew of Julius II., 11, 751, 880, p. 382, 3617 (note), 5353.
.........., ..., slays the Cardinal of Pavia, 1701.
.........., ..., quarrels with the Spaniards, 3112.
.........., ..., advances against the Florentines, 3269.
........., Duchess of, 880.
Urmestofte. See Armestofte.
Uron (Vryne), Santa Maria de, in Spain, 3298, p. 451, p. 457.
Urreas, Don Pedro d', p. 383.
.........., ..., ambassador of Arragon with the Emperor, 3779, 4091, 4511, 4795, 4952, 5055, 5126.
.........., ..., said to be going to England, 4091.
Urswick, Chris., clerk, 5180.
.........., ..., grant to, 4332, 4436.
...., archdeacon of Oxford, executor of Sir Rob. Southwell, 5137.
Uscote, 804.
........., Wilts., 3190.
Usher, Steph., 1572.
Uske, marches of Wales, 53, 57, 58, 65, 487, 843, 1665, 1894, 3902, 5045.
Ustarits (Austarys), between Bayonne and Fontarabia, p. 451, p. 457.
Utkinton, Chesh., 4360.
Utley, York. See Otley.
Utrecht, (date), 5746.
........., canon of, 5632.
........., Bishop of, 4924.
Uvedale, Hen., Mary Frauncis, widow of, 4863.
.........., ..., gentleman usher of the chamber, 293, 422, 456, 777, 5594.

Uvedale, Hen., const. of Corff Castle, 1504.
........., ..., (Vedale), in com. for Dorset, 903, 2007, 3064, 3566, 3606, 3701, 4713, 5658.
........., Jo., grant to, 3073, 5711.
........., Tho., captain, 3980.
........., Sir Wm., in commission for Glouc., 930, 1049, 1469, 1695, 3641, 3712, 3804, 4024, 4118, 4764, 5506; for Hants, 904, 1388, 1812, 3071, 4159, 4676, 5506; for Heref., 646, 675, 1400, 1963, 3686, 5506; for Salop, 918, 1981, 3071, 3715, 4394, 4827, 5506; for the Welsh Marches, 953, 3055, 3289, 4198; for Worc., 892, 1971, 3301, 3709, 4770, 5506.
........., ..., grants to, 703, 3220, 3532.
Uxbridge or Woxbrigge, Middx., 1031, 1167, 4025.

V.

Vachan, Wm., 102.
Vaches, Bucks, 69.
........., in Barton, Camb., 4659.
Vadelyo, ——, 490.
Vadencort, ——, 4429.
Vadydyn, Richard, 25.
Valbona, abbey of, 4525.
Vale, Edm., 4367.
De la Vale, John, Geo., Guy and Ann, 5090.
Valencia, 8.
Valerius Maximus, 2082.
Valeys, Bernard de, gunner, 5545.
Valla, poems of, 5352.
Valladolid, 3584, 3593, 3614, 3755, 4296.
........., letters dated, 8, 490, 796, 819, 3662, 4058, 4096, 4267, 4371, 4449, 4464, 4513, 4525, 4574, 4666, 4845, 4864, 5152, 5267, 5470, 5581, 5592, 5642.
........., documents dated, 27, 28, 793.
Valle Crucis, (Vale Seynt Croyse,) John, abbot of, 2044, p. 435.
Valois and Bretagne. See Francis Duke of.
Valonain, Hennam, French workman, 4445.
Valtellina, in Lombardy, 3269, 3325.
Vampage, Rob., in commission for Worcestershire, 1971, 3301, 3709, 4770, 5506.
........., Sir Wm., harbinger and sewer, 4807.
Van Destrete. See Destrete.
Vane, (Fane,) Hen., in commission for Kent, 3428, 3605, 4663, 4847, 4927.
Vanguard, master carpenter of the. See Oliver.
Vanhorne, Geo., 501.
Vannes, Peter, 5543.
Varax, ——, 4415.
Varembon, Lord, 4359.
Vargy, Lord. See Vergy.

Vasse, John, priest, 3389.
....., Tho., chaplain, 392, 4790.
Vauchier, Pierre, 5163.
Vaughan, David, exempted from general pardon, 65.
........., ..., clerk, 1201.
........., Edm. ap Wm. David, exempted from the general pardon, 65.
........., Edw. See St. David's, Bp. of.
........., Griffith ap Meredeth, 4813.
........., Sir Hen., in commission for Middx., 4663.
........., Sir Hugh, knight of the Body, 531, 3972.
........., ..., grant to, 1213.
........., Hugh, groom of the chamber, 4601, 4688, 4995.
........., John, groom of the chamber, 4557, 4834.
........., ..., 1050, 3901.
........., John ap David, exempted from the general pardon, 65.
........., John Wm. ap. David, exempted from the general pardon, 65.
........., Ric., pardon to, 3771.
........., Roger, steward of Dynas, &c., 5433, 5452.
........., ..., in debt to the Crown, 3497.
........., Tho., bailiff of Dover, 238, 3163, 4299.
........., Th., captain, 3979, 3985, 5112, 5130, 5771.
........., ..., pardon to, 3771.
........., Walt., pardon to, 3771.
........., Watkin, groom of the chamber, 4834.
........., Wm., customer at Calais, 220, 3907.
........., ..., yeoman of the guard, 1946.
........., ..., ap David, exempted from the general pardon, 65.
Vaulter, Thomas, of Normandy, 4278.
Vans, Stephen, 5761,
Vaux or Vaws, Edw., servant to the Countess of Richmond, 235, 372.
........., Edw., yeoman purveyor, 1045, 3125.
.... (or Vaws), Sir Nich., Lieutenant of Guisnes, 544, 545, 602, 653, 779, 3744, 4635, 4830, 5379, 5407, 5723.
........., ..., in commission for Northampton, 732, 1518, 1708, 1971, 2045, 3046, 5658.
........., ..., in the war against France, 3885, 4008, 4021, 4237, 4307, 4314, 5483.
........., ..., in debt to the Crown, 777.
........., ..., release of his recognizances, 464, 600, 1026, 3049.
........., ..., grants to, 598, 599, 645, 652, 839.
........., Anne, wife of Sir Nich., 1026, 3049, 5379, 5407.
Vavasour, Edw., grant to, 404, 1836.
........., Sir John, 1097.
........., John, in commission for Yorkshire, 1798, 1941, 1965, 1995, 3177, 4015, 5166, 5506.

Vavasour, Peter, 498, 1097.

.........., ..., in commission for Yorksh., 273.

Vazacrely. *See* Fazakerly.

Vecheano, Francs. de, merchant of Pisa, 1145, 3710.

Vedale, Hen. *See* Uvedale.

Veeles, Suff., 694, 1022, 1129, 1344, 1629.

Veere, port of, 841, 924, 1245, 2043, 4330.

Vega, Fernando di, 8, 490.

Vegius, M., 5570.

Velevile, Sir Roland. *See* Vielleville.

Vellana, Marquis di, 8.

Venables, Tho., 3470.

Vendôme (Wandom), English army at, p. 625, 4526.

.........., Earl of, 5482, 5560.

.........., The Great Bastard of, killed at Guinegate, 4253.

Venduffle, Tisse, French workman, 4445.

Venetians, 216, 394, 796, 819, 1221, 1457, 1458, 1462, 1676, 1701, 1877, 1918, 1997, 2039, 2075, 3077, 3112, 3291, 3325, 3499, 3500, 3614, 3648, 3662, 3678, 3752, 3766, 3777, 3780, 3821, 3876, 3897, 3962, 4055, 4058, 4069, 4085, 4086, 4094, 4196, 4216, 4272, 4276, 4282, 4287, 4296, 4304, 4319, 4323, 4326, 4328, 4333, 4359, 4574, 4577, 4622, 4725, 4795, 4796, 4811, 4831, 4952, 4955, 5094, 5110, 5126, 5152, 5208, 5259, 5323, 5353, 5393, 5404, 5430, 5532, 5686, 5705, 5757.

.........., excommunicated, 11.

.........., released from interdict, 908, 922, 333.

.........., displeasure of the Emperor with, 490, 1681, 1828.

.........., treaties, &c. made by, 1697, 1880, 1881, 1902, 1948, 3138, 3415, 3523, 4844, 4985, 5687.

.........., to be excluded from the confederacy, 3543.

.........., besiege Padua, 4513.

Venetian army, 4091, 5410, 5677, 5745.

...., battles fought by, 3026, 3067, 3283, 3658, 4499, 4756, 5290.

...., towns taken by, 3269, 5532, 5592.

Venetian war, 3526.

.... ambassadors, 4446, 4563.

Venetians mentioned by name, 346, 1398, 3741.

Venice, 3779, 3976, 4305, 5173, 5285, 5378.

.........., fleet sent against, 5171.

.........., ambassadors, &c. to, 3327.

.........., seignory of, 4078.

.........., Doge of. *See* Lauredano, Leonard.

Venturi, Venturo, merchant, 4958.

Vera, Martin de, 3762.

Vercelli, 4096, 4210.

.........., governor of, 4273.

Verderne, Chas. De la, 3377.

Verdon, John, 1432.

Verdons, Bucks, 69.

Verdun, 5781.

Vere or Veer, Adolphus Prince of, letter to, 3637.

Veer or Vere, Aubrey de, t. Hen. II., 34, 79.

...... Eliz., Countess of Oxford, 4536.

......, Sir Geo., 4504, 5136.

......, John. *See* Oxford, Earl of.

......, ..., in com. for Suffolk, 3967, 4713, 5133, 5136, 5506.

......, ..., knighted at Tournay, 4468.

......, John, nephew of Earl of Oxford, 4294, 4536.

......, ..., in the war, 3885, 4307.

Vere, (John and) Eliz., 1210.

......, Mr., 3885, 4101.

......, Rob. de, son of Earl of Oxford, 79.

......, Tho. de. *See* Oxford, E. of.

Vergil, Polydore, archdeacon of Wells, 4819, 5661, 5665, 5666, 5671, 5672, 5702, 5706.

.........., ..., denization, 1283.

.........., ..., letters from, 751, 5110.

.........., ..., his brother Jerome, 5110.

Vergy, Sieur de, 3340, 4319, 4359.

Verkamen, English army at, 4284.

Verney, Dorothy, 5422, 5571.

" Verney," Henry, 474. The name is a misreading of Marney. *See* Marney.

Verney, Sir Hen., in commission for Devon, 1166,

.........., Sir John, father of Sir Ralph, 5514.

.........., John, son of Sir Ralph, 3738.

.........., Michael, 5132.

.........., Ralph, 69, 4254.

.........., ..., in commission for Bucks, 454, 943, 1379,

.........., ..., sheriff of Beds. and Bucks, 1949, 3912.

.........., Sir Ralph, sen., 5453.

.........., ..., alderman of London, 1996, 5282.

.........., ..., grants to, 636, 3738, 5514.

.........., Ric., in commission for Warwickshire, 3364.

Vernon, Sir Hen., indictments of felony against, 511.

.........., ..., in debt to the Crown, 3497.

.........., ..., in commission for Staff., 279, 713, 791, 886, 1770, 5506; for Salop, 918, 1981, 3071, 3715, 4394, 5506.

.........., Marg., widow, daughter of Earl of Shrewsbury, 1978, 3713.

.........., Wm., in the war against France, 4253, 4476.

Verona, 216, 3499, 3678, 4069, 4078, 4326, 4355, 4563, 5795, 5152, 5171, 5304, 5387, 5430, 5532.

.........., abandoned by the Emperor's troops, 4283.

Verona, siege of, 4287, 4371.
........., captains of, 4196, 4276.
........., letter dated, 3026.
Verrey, Mons. de, 490.
Vertue, Rob., King's master mason, 775.
........., Wm., master mason, 1190.
Vesalia, Duchy of Cleves, 3204.
Vescy. See Clifford.
Veyreri, John, surgeon of the body, 4289.
Veysey, John, dean of the Chapel Royal, 5609, 5623.
Vice-Admiral, 4474,· 5130. See Windham, Sir Thos.
Vice-Chanceller, i.e. Master of the Rolls. See Young, John.
Vicenza, 3614, 4499, 4563, 4756.
Vicquemare, Hector de, letter from, 4329.
Victoria, 3355.
Victuals, 3308, 5766, 5767.
........., act concerning, 2082.
........., proclamation concerning, 3592.
Victualling, commissions for, 3728, 3733, 3769, 3788, 3792, 3796, 3850, 3888, 3894, 4792, 4894.
.... of the "Henry Grace à Dieu," 5228.
Vielleville, Sir Rowland, 389, 3563.
Vielston, 2080.
Vienna, 5126.
........., letters dated, 5055, 5057, 5058, 5094, 5105.
Vienne, Barth. de la, 5171.
Vierling, Pasquier, 5163.
Vigars, Louis de, 4465.
Vigeus, 3976.
Viglevano, castle of, 3269.
Viglevarium, 3269.
Viglo, 5040.
Vyke, Jerome, 4366.
Villain, John, 5697.
Villanova, 3269.
Villa Nova, John de, 5724.
Villaragud, Louis Caroz de, Spanish commissioner, 1335.
Villars, Count de, French commissioner, 4924.
Ville, Fierin de Vielle, French workman, 4445.
Villeford, 4725, 5208.
Villers, ——, in the war against France, 3231.
........., Edw., in commission, Northt., 3046.
........., Geoff., 5519.
........., John, in commission for Leicestersh., 4783, 4812.
........., ..., on the sheriff-roll for Leic. and Warw., 3507.
Villiermeerii, Arnold, 752.
Villiers, John, of Brokesby, Leic., 4728.
Vincence, ——, of Naples, painter, p. 957.
Vincenza. See Vicenza.
Vincent, Cape St., 5744.
........., Chr., marshal of the Hall to Hen. VII., 1114.

Vincent, John, 4251.
........., Rob., of Cambridge Univ., 251.
........., ——, Tho. Howard's servant, 3298.
Vine, Hants, 464, 1285, 1675.
Vyne, John, in commission for Oxon, 1470.
......, Ralph, in commission for Oxon, 766, 1216, 1470, 1745, 3015, 4559, 4809, 5506.
Vineyard, Warwick Castle, 1257.
Virleys, Suffolk, 4205, 4254, 4262.
Visacadia, 3243.
Visbourg, letter dated, 1221.
Visconti, Lodovico, 3269.
Visors, act concerning, 2082.
Vyte, Monsieur, 1697.
Vitelli, 3325.
Vitelliis, Vitello de, 11.
Viterbo, 5702.
Viti, Pasquier, French workman, 4445.
Vitte, ——, French workman, 4445.
Vivaldis, Antonio de, merchant of Genoa, 1693, 4145, 5334.
........., ..., denization of, 4147.
........., ..., letter from, 5444.
........., Lukin de, merchant of Genoa, 1003, 1773.
Vivian, Ric., in commission for Cornwall, 312, 891, 1694, 1812, 1984, 3290, 3583, 3605, 3938, 4754, 5220.
........., Rob., in commission for Cornwall, 1984, 3290, 3583, 3605, 3938, 4754, 5220, 5586.
Volterra, 3026.
........., Cardinal of, 3780, 4323.
Voosdouc, Adrian V[an ...... of], 5287.
Voura, castle of, 4364.
Vowell, Th., 5471.
........., ..., captain, 4377, 5112, 5761.
Vowelles Comme, Devon, 5471.
Voyage, expenses of the king's, 4526.
Voyell, Mr., 4101.
Vryne, our Lady of. See Uron.
Vulp, alias Fox, Vincent, painter, 4954.
Vulveston, John, 4207.
Vuton. See Unton.

W.

Waddon. See Whaddon.
Wade, John, chaplain of Mighelstowe church, Exeter dioc., 4740.
Wadham, Edw., 1530, 3231 (ii), 4254 (iii).
........., ..., in commission for Glouc., 1695, 3641, 3712, 3804, 4024, 4118, 4764.
........., Lawrence, 4733.

Wadham, Sir Nich., 3497 (ii), 4475, 5633.
........., ..., captain of the Isle of Wight, 80, 103, 4103, 5231, 5724.
........., ..., in commission to review the army, 3173, 4979.
........., ..., sheriff of Devon, 5561.
........., ..., in commission for Hants, 1388, 1812, 3048, 3071, 4159, 4676, 4713, p. 904.
........., ..., in commission for Somerset, 287, 712, 3566, 3585, 3606, 3701, p. 904.
........., Wm., of Caterston, Dorset, 1350.
........., ..., in commission, 26, 304, 903, 2007, 3064, 4713, 5658.
Wadley, Berks, 5127.
Wafner, Mons. de, 4349.
Wagenyng, in Gueldres, 1082.
Wages, 507, 678, 775, 3762, 3981, 3982, 3983, 4074, 4232, 4375, 4421, 4475, 4526, 4533, 4535, 4635, 4653, 5163, 5271, 5720, 5721, 5752, 5761, 5774, 5775, 5790.
Wainflett, Tho., 1225, 4495.
Waistland, on the Borders, 4825.
Wake, Tho., 3175.
Wakefield, Yorkshire, 178, 720, 1205, 1594, 1696, 3390, 3845, 3956, 4107, 5072.
.... Bridge, Yorksh., chapel of St. Mary, 5114.
........., Hen., 3386.
........., John, warden of the Mystery of Inn-holders, London, 5708.
Wakerfyld, John, clk., 3782.
Wakes Elme, Essex, 921.
Walbeef, Jas., 451.
Walberswik, 3733.
Walcot, Linc., 3284, 3955, 4852, 5096.
........., John, 5220.
Waldegrave. See Walgrave.
Walden, Benedictine abbey of, 167, 227. (The name of the place omitted in 167.)
........., a guild in the church of, 4911.
Waldram, Tho., 3270, 3275, 3702.
Waldryfont, Antony de, Imperial secretary, 3405.
Wales, [banneret of ?], p. 609.
........., overseers of, 4022.
........., receivers and triers of petitions for, 811, 2082.
........., commissions for, 956, 3055, 3289, 4198.
........., North, chamberlain of, 695, 4060, 4126.
........., South, auditors of, 960, 4595.
........., ..., clerk of the sessions in, 4596.
........., Marches of, 655, 1974, 3055, 3058, 3771.
........., ..., feodaries in the, 4414, 5692.
........., ..., Council of the, 4060, 4404.
........., ..., ..., clerk of, 1839.
........., Prince of, 1267. (Henry VIII.?)
Walesse, W m., 4797.

Walghope, Laird of, 4556.
Walgrave, Mr., 4101.
.... (Waldegrave), Anthony, 3588.
........., ..., Edw., 734.
........., ..., Eliz., wife of Anth., 3588.
........., ..., Gresilda, wife of Edw., 734.
........., ..., Sir Wm., in commission for Suffolk, 280, 676, 1121, 1153, 1715, 3029, 3219, 3967, 4713, 5133.
........., ..., ..., 226, 1025, 1421, 3977, 5180, p. 904.
Walham (Walem, Wallen, or Walwyn), Lord, 3077, 4162, p. 609, p. 627, 4318, 4319, 4395, 4915.
........., Lord, son of Lord Berghes, 4328.
........., ..., said to be slain at Brussels, 3659.
........., ..., as a French prisoner, 4418, 4433.
Walkefare (or Walkesare), in Little Waltham, Essex, 1774, 3401.
Walker, Humph., gun-founder, 186, 323, 775, 781, 3496 (vi.), 4238, 4977.
........., John, 52.
........., Rob., 630.
........., Tho., 1843.
Walkesare. See Walkefare.
Wall, Christ., 3386.
........., Eliz., wife of Christ., 3386.
........., Tho., Lancaster herald, 975, 3986.
........., Thos. Vander, 3737.
Wallace, Albany's servant, 4951.
........., See Walesse.
Wallachians, 1659.
Wallen, Lord. See Walham, Lord.
Waller, John, 3173.
........., ..., in commission for Hants, 1812.
........., Wm., 1546.
Wallingford, Berks, 373, 396, 1438, 1738.
.... Castle, chapel in, 986.
........., abbot of, legatee of Hen. VII., 776.
........., Henry, prior of, 1639 (ii).
........., See Wriothesley.
Wallop, Sir John, at the marriage of Princess Mary, 5483.
........., ..., in the war against France, p. 553, 4005, 4020, p. 651, 4632, p. 811, 5130, p. 973.
........., Rob., sheriff of Hants, 664 ; in commission, 1812.
........., Steph., in commission for Hants, 1812.
Wallweyn, Philip, constable of Corffe Castle, temp. Ric. II., 1504.
........., Wm., 835.
Walsall, park, 50, 3497.
........., Foren of, Staff., 616, 1480, 1851.
Walsh, Edw., 554.
........., ..., incumbent of Ashwell, Linc. dioc., 1667.
........., Gilbert, p. 552, p. 813.
........., John, 1037, 1350, 1766, 4414, 4711.
........., Tho., 4414.
........., Walter, 4592.
Walshm an, alias Griffith, Maurice, 4367.

Walshtalgarth, marches of, Wales, 5433, 5652.
Walsingham, Norf., 155.
........., Our Lady of, 1652, 3903, 5522.
........., ..., prior of, 5522.
........., ship of. *See* Ships.
Walsingham, Edm., 4375.
........., Sir Edm., 5237.
........., Eleanor, wife of James, 734.
........., James, 734.
........., James, in commission for Kent, 4701, p. 906.
........., Thos., 5242.
Walter, Hen., 4476.
Waltier, Dr. Wm., 55.
Waltham, 5757.
........., Essex, 498, 3203, 3401.
........., letter dated at, 4573.
........., Little, Essex, 1774.
.... Forest, 3203, 3761, 4504, 5136.
Waltham Holy Cross, abbey of, 3940, 5004, 5065.
........., ..., abbot of, 4504.
........., ..., ..., legatee of Hen. VII., 776.
........., ..., ..., summoned to Parliament, 5616.
........., ..., John, abbot of, 1639 (ii), 3203, 3497 (i), 3940, 5004, 5065.
Waltham, Bishop's, Hants, 3381, 4375.
........., ..., ..., privy seals dated at, 1232, 1235, 1237, 1274, 3505, 4760.
Walton, Surrey, 155.
.... *See* Whalton.
Waltpurgis. *See* Truchses.
Walwyn, Lord. *See* Walham, Lord.
Wanborough, Surrey, 804, 2046.
........., Wilts, 1772, 3384.
Wandom. *See* Vendôme.
Wandsworth, Tho., 1796.
Wansay, Mons. de, 5482.
Wanstead, Essex, 778, 3103, 4022, 5282.
Waplot, Nich., 5095.
Wappenham, Northt., 3027.
War with France, 3688, 3884, 3885, 3886, 3887, 4253, 4284, 4286, 4306, 4307, 4309, 4311, 4314, 4402, 4410, 4411, 4412, 4413, 4440, 4466, 4467, 4477, 4642, 5042, 5744, 5753, 5756.
........., treasurer of the. *See* Windham, Sir Thos.
........., act of privilege for persons in the, 2082.
........., appointments for the, 3231.
........., accounts of the expenses of. *See* Accounts.
Warbeck, Perkin, 1033, 3916, 4498.
Warbleton. *See* Worbleton.
Warblington, Hants, 567, 1239, 1517.
Warburton, Geoff., incumbent of Balingham, dioc. Terouenne, 1575.
........., Sir John, 4534.

Warcop, Westmor., 3827.
........., Edw., 3497 (ii).
........., Geo., 3698.
........., Leonard, 521.
........., Rob., of Warcop, Westmor., 322, 1179, 3698, 3827, 4369, 4414, 4940.
........., ..., under-sheriff of Westmoreland, 1179.
........., ..., in commission, 3552, 3703.
........., Tho., in commission for Westmor., 1735, 1799, 3358.
Ward, Hugh, 146.
........., John, of North Dighton, York, 4225, 4630, 5630.
........., Nich., 826, 1259, 4136.
........., Tho., harbinger, 1523, 1738, 5546.
........., Wm., 4709.
Wardelham, Hants, 999, 3387.
........., ..., privy seals dated at, 1234, 1236, 1246, 1247, 1255.
Warden, monastery of, 1595.
Wardrobe, the King's, 203, 4642.
........., ..., at Sheriff Hutton, York, 430.
........., ..., at Woodstock, 430.
........., the Great, 778, 1190, 1872, 2053, 5135.
........., ..., in London, 171.
........., ..., acts for, 811, 3502.
........., account, 1872.
........., clerk of the. *See* Porth.
........., keeper of the. *See* Windsor, Sir Andrew.
Ware, Herts, 276, 285, 992, 1395.
........., John, 4420.
Warham, Somers., 155.
........., Anne, wife of George, 5700.
........., George, 1219, 5700.
........., William, archdeacon of Canterbury, temp. Hen. VII., 537.
........., William, Abp. of Canterbury, 202, 1478, 1561, 2021, 3066, 3298, 3637, 4101, p. 651, 4452, 4528, 4613, 4727, 5111, 5322, 5383, 5407, 5736.
........., ..., summon convocation, 613, 4876.
........., ..., preaches before Parliament, 11, 2082.
........., ..., prorogues Parliament, 4848.
........., ..., trier of petitions, 811, 2082.
........., ..., summoned to Parliament, 5616.
........., ..., Lord Chancellor. *See* Chancellor, Lord.
........., ..., in the Privy Council, 289.
........., ..., signs as member of Privy Council, 165, 3027, 5762.
........., ..., in commission for Hants, 904, 1388, 3071, 4159, 4676, p. 904.
........., ..., in commission for Middlesex, 3552, 4663, p. 905.
........., ..., in commission for Kent, 725, 906, 3428, 3605, 4663, 4847, 4927, p. 906.
........., ..., in commission for Oxford (town), 894.

Warham, Wm., Abp. of Canterbury—*cont.*
.........., ..., in commission for Surrey, 1427, 1762, 3078, 3092, 4693, 4734, 5237, p. 905.
.........., ..., in commission for Sussex, 281, 1509, 3428, 4804, p. 904.
.........., ..., letters from, 3706, 4312, 5740, 5762.
.........., ..., letters to, 976, 3159.
Waring, Nic., 197, 1584, 5737.
Wark (Werke), Northumb., 201, 4347.
Warkworth, Northt., 1690.
........., Northumb., 5090.
Warley, Little, Essex, 530.
........., Nich., warden of the Goldsmiths, London, 4917.
Warmister, Wilts, 1867, 5247.
Warner, Alice, daughter of Humph., 3594, 3736.
........., Anne, daughter of Humph., 3594, 3736.
........., Edw., 857, 4587.
........., Geo., rector of Pylton, Northt., 5103.
........., Henry, 4254 (iii).
........., Humph., 3594, 3736.
........., John, 3497 (ii).
.........., ..., alderman of London, 1097.
........., Tho., 3537.
Warnet, John, 221, 1874.
Warr, Sir Ric., in com. for Somers., 287, 712, 1761, 3048, 3566, 3585, 3606, 3701, 4713, p. 906.
.........., ..., sheriff, 1949.
Warren, ——, 1212.
.........., ——, excepted from the general pardon, 12.
.........., ——, Ruthal's servant, 1924.
........., John, 1579, 4996.
.... (Waryn), Nich. *See* Waring, Nich.
........., Ralph, 1608.
.... Sir (?) Tho., 2082.
......., Tho., incumbent of St. Nichasius, marches of Calais, 1742.
Warton. *See* Wharton.
Warvild, Tho., 4013.
Warwhome, Linc., 1832.
Warwick, 419, 549, 1257, 1499, 4301.
.... Castle, Guy of Warwick's sword in, 202.
........., college of, 967, 3186.
.... collegiate church of, 1201, 5204.
.... commissions for, 554.
Warwickshire, warren in, 549.
...., proclamation in, 1771.
........., subsidy granted by the laity of, 3441.
Warwickshire, escheator of, 5218.
.... and Leicestershire feodaries of Crown lands in, 4144.

Warwickshire and Leicestershire, sheriffs of, 664, 1316, 1778, 1949, 3507, 3687, 4544, 5561, 5640.
.........., ..., commissions for, 282, 733, 1387, 1468, 1971, 3364, 4434, p. 903.
.........., ..., earldom of, 1060, 3845.
Warwick's Lands, Crown possessions called, 665, 778, 900, 901, 1831, 4223.
Warwick, Anne, Countess of, 889, 1472, 1851, 3599, 4022, 4507.
........., Earl of, 458, 1976.
.... and Salisbury, Edward, Earl of, 1472, 4022, 4119, 4507.
.........., ..., ..., reversal of his attainder in favour of Margaret, Countess of Salisbury, 4545.
........., Henry, Duke of, 4507.
.........., ..., son of Richard, Earl of, 3599.
........., Joan, wife of John Lord, 4545.
........., John Lord, temp. Hen. VI., 4545.
. ..., Launcelot, 3497 (ii.).
........., Ric. de Beauchamp, Earl of, temp. Hen. VI., 900, 3599, 3841, 4180.
Wase, Reynold, 1540.
Washborne [Glouc. ?], 2080.
........., John, in commission for Worc., 892, 1971, 3301, 3709, 4770, p. 903.
Washenburgh, Linc., 3264.
Washington, Anne, wife of Robert, 3087, 4254 (i), 4872 (misprinted Amy).
........., Rob., 114, 3087, 4254 (i), 4872.
Wassenaw, Lord, prisoner in Gueldres, 4418.
Wast, Rob., 5484.
Waste, inquiry into, 4808.
Wasteby, Noel de, 4534.
Wastnesse, Geo., in commission for Notts, 1735 (bis), 1804.
Waterfield, Northt., 645.
Waterford, mayor and city of, 1068.
Waterhall, Northt., 3027.
Waters, Edw., 3979.
Waterton, Sir Rob., of Burne, York, 1805.
.........., ..., in commission for Linc., 1496 3342, 4358, 4593, 4860.
.........., ..., in commission for Yorkshire, 1798.
Watford, Lanc., 3764.
Watkins, of the Isle of Ely, 12.
Watkyn, John, p. 812.
Watlesfield, Suff., 1453, 4254 (misprinted Wattesfeld).
Watman, Ric., 534 (v).
Watrevliet, Lord de, Treasurer of the King of Castile, 4508.
Watson, ——, mentioned by Erasmus, 5733, 5734.
........., Peter 3497 (ii).
Watt, Copin als. Jacob de, armourer, 3037, p. 954.
Watton, Heref., 1788.
.... at the Stone, Herts., 730.

Watts, John, 1297, 3850.
........., ..., in commission for Northt., 732, 1708, 1971, 2045, 3046, 5346, 5658.
........., Ric., 787.
........., Rob., 1399.
........., Tho., 787.
........., Wm., 12.
Watwang, Geo. *See* Witwang.
........., John, 3939.
Wavendon, Bucks., 2080.
Waverley, Wm., abbot of, 2046.
Waverton, Chesh., 4748.
Wavyrs [Low Countries], 3945.
........., letter dated at, 3905.
Way, als. Wayhill, church of, Winch. dioc., 853, 1260, 4638.
Waybridge, Hunts., 477, 5683.
Wayland, Norf., 3943, 4948, 5115.
Wayneford, Suff., 1188.
Wayprow, Joan, widow of John, 5194.
........., John, 5194.
Wayte, John, in commission for Hants, 1812.
Weald. *See* Weld.
Weather, the, 4098.
........., during the King's invasion of France, p. 627.
Weavers, of the city of York, 1920.
Webb, Hen., 3206, 5483.
........., Ric., 868.
........., Tho., 3198.
Webbs, John, 387.
Webster, John, 235.
Wednesbury, Staff., inhabitants of, 840.
Wegenok, Warw., 419, 1499, 3186.
Weirs, commission of, in the Exe, 304.
Weke, tenement called, Barkeley, Glouc., 3316.
Wekes, chapel called the, Donington, Linc., 1274, 2014.
Welbeck, abbot of, 3354.
Welborn, Linc., 1463, 4695.
Welce in Lontotrence, [Germany], 5366.
........., letter dated from, 5259.
Weld, Essex, 734.
Weldon, Northt., 3317.
........., Little, Northt., 645, 5700.
........., Edw., servant to master cofferer, 1668, 4257.
........., Simon, incumbent of Chilton Foliot, Salisb. dioc., 862.
........., ..., incumbent of Wythurne, Linc. dioc., 1443.
Welf, Hans. *See* Wolff.
Wellington, Salop, 5440.
........., under Wreykyn, Salop, 4191.
........., Sussex, 297.
Wells, proclamation in, 1771.
........., archdeacon of. *See* Vergil, Polydore.
........., Dean of, 4567.
........., Alan, 1730.
........., And., 3348.
........., Cecilia, Viscountess, widow of Rich., Viscount Wells, 449, 4022, 5508.

Wells, Hen., monk of Abingdon, 2070.
........., James, of Odiham, Hants., 5537.
........., John, abbot of Croyland, 3418, 3420, 3447, 3572, 4414. :
........., ..., in commission for Staff., 279, 713, 791, 886, 1770, pp. 903, 905.
........., Richard, Viscount, 449, 1197, 1472, 4022.
........., Tho., mayor of Northampton, 1763.
........., ..., in commission for Hants, 1812.
........., Wm., clk., 856.
Welsh bills and marispikes, 3884.
Welshman, Maurice. *See* Walshman.
Welton, Northt., 1950.
Wendham, Tho. *See* Wyndham.
Wendover, Bucks., 155, 445.
Wenlock, monastery of, Salop, 1507, 3131.
........., prior of, 3448.
Wenne, Lord Greystock and. *See* Greystock, Lord.
Went, the, Yorkshire, 3072.
Wentford, Roger, letter to, from Erasmus, 5731.
Wentfordton, earldom of March, 4575.
Wentworth, Rich., in the war with France, 430 6 (ii.)
........., ..., on sheriff roll for Norf. and Suff., 5561.
........., ..., in commission for Suffolk, 280, 676.
........., Sir Ric., 1835.
........., ..., in the war against France, 4157, 4534.
........., ..., sheriff of Norf. and Suff., 664, 3851.
........., ..., in commission for Suffolk, 1534, 3219, 3967, 4713, 5133, p. 904.
........., Roger, on sheriff roll for Essex and Herts, 3507.
........., Sir Roger, sheriff of Essex and Herts, 664.
........., ..., in commission for Essex, 3605, 3785, 3967.
........., Wm., 5049.
Wenvo, church of, Llandaff dioc., 4400.
Wera, Diego de, captain of the King of Arragon's artillery, p. 474.
Weresdale, Th., 4335.
Werisdall, Rob., of the monastery of St. Trinity, London, 3371.
Wermyngham's house, Chester, 1086.
Werpesden, alias Werplesden, Surrey, 1748.
Wes, Giles du, alien, 5328, 5459.
Wesel (Vesalia), 3204.
Wesse and Helsyng, overseer of. *See* Hanssart.
West, Edm., son of Thomas, 1025.
........., Henry, incumbent of North Grimsby Linc. dioc., 1576.

West, John, 1309, 3488.

......, ..., in commission for Wilts, 1489, 1938, 3157, 3605, 4583.

......, ..., incumbent of Sarsedon, Salisb. dioc., 1760.

......, ..., mercer of London, 4699.

......, Nich., 3284.

......, ..., clk., 1994.

......, Dr. Nicholas, dean of Windsor, 624, 4030.

......, ..., dean, and the canons of Windsor, 4213, 4294, 4436, 4536.

......, ..., admitted to the participation of the works, prayers, &c., of the Friars Observants in England and Scotland, 4678.

......, ..., receiver of petitions, 2082.

......, ..., ambassador to Scotland, 1926, 3007, 3128, 3129, 3320, 3321, 3322, 3323, 3339, 3346, 3372, 3443, 3726, 3875, 3876, 3883, 5745, 5757.

......, ..., ambassador to France, 5379, 5482, 5495, 5547, 5553, 5560, 5590.

......, ..., at the marriage of Princess Mary, 5482.

......, ..., in commission to receive the oath of Lewis XII. to treaties, 1104, 1182, 5335, 5379.

......, ..., treaty concluded by him with Saxony, temp. Hen. VII., ratified, 1717.

......, ..., letters from, 3838, 3882, 5391, 5495, 5560.

......, ..., letters to, 3811, 3812, 4678.

......, Rob. *See* Wast, Rob.

......, Simon, 3497.

......, Tho., of Greyes, Suff., 1025.

......, Sir Th., in, the war against France, 4306, 4477, 4534, 5085, 5130; in com. for Sussex, p. 904.

......, Thomas, Lord De la Warre. *See* De la Warre.

......, Wm., captain, 3979, p. 553, p. 652, 4745, p. 812, 5761 (iv.).

......, ..., in commission for Oxon, 4559, 4809.

Westanton [Cornw. ?], 2080.

Westborough, Linc., 1463, 4695.

........, ..., church of, Linc. dioc., 4664.

Westbradley, Berks, 1129.

Westbroke, Berks, 155.

........, John, 1762, 1835.

........, ..., in commission for Surrey, 1427, 3078, 3092, 4693, 4734, 5237.

........, Wm., 4375.

........, ..., in commission for Surrey, 1762.

Westbroughton, Derby, 5574.

Westbudleigh, Devon, 2080.

Westbury, [Bucks ?], 3297.

........, [Glouc ?], 5051.

........, alias Kingsbury Forest, Hants, 145, 854, 4730, 5507.

........, Rob., abbot of Cerne, 822, 1200.

........, Tho., 728.

Westby, Barth., Baron of the Exchequer, 17, 5116.

........, ..., annuity, 4340.

........, ..., one of the alms knights of Windsor, 5037.

........, ..., overseer of Crown possessions, 1472, 4022, 4347, 4348, 5619.

........, ..., ..., Act for, 2082.

........, ..., justice of gaol delivery, 4742.

........, ..., in commission for Herts, 309, 706, 1020, 3102, p. 906; for Middlesex, 3552, p. 905.

........, Noel de. *See* Wasteby, Noel de.

Westecabbelond, Somers., 2080.

Westclive, John, 4996.

Westcoker, Somers., 2080.

Westcompton, Berks, 174, 4205.

Westcot (Wescote), [Wilts ?], 1867.

........, John. *See* Wiscott.

Westerham, Kent, 5001.

Westgower, S. Wales, 5180.

Westgate, John, 2023.

........, alias Ex Iland, lordship of, without the city of Exeter, 157, 1599.

........, tower of, 5782.

Westhach, Essex, 734.

Westham, Essex, 155.

........, [Kent?], 3774.

Westhanney, Berks, 896.

Westhorlegh, Surrey, 804.

Westhorp, Suff., 3087, 4254 (i), 4872.

Westhurok, Essex, 681, 900, 1332.

Westynghanger, Kent, 464.

Westkington, church of, archdeaconry of Wilts, 4761.

Westle, Suff., 1125.

Westlete, Surrey, 1446.

Westmarche, Bucks., 1352.

Westminster, guild of St. Cornelius the Martyr, church of St. Margaret, 5101.

........, mayors of the staple at, Wm. Brown, 1024; Wm. Brown, jun., 271.

........, constables of the staple at, 271.

........, inhabitants of, 3509, 4612, 4992, 5309, 5622.

........, Gate house at, 3509.

........, Wolsey's house, letter of his dated at, 5465.

........, letters of Hen. VIII. dated at, 4641, 4850.

........, letter of Ammonius dated at, 5449.

........, Beaumont's lands in, 730.

........, mention in funeral of Hen. VII., 5735.

Westminster Abbey, 1212.
........., coronation of Hen. VIII. in, 224.
........., abbot and convent of, their possessions in, 555.
........., ..., sanctuary, privilege of, 1091.
........., abbot of St. Peter's, John Islyppe, 3297, 4891, 4994.
........., ..., trier of petitions in Parliament, 811, 2082.
........., ..., in com. for Middx., 3552, 4663, p. 905.
........., ..., summoned to Parliament, 5616.
........., ..., writ to, 5624.
........., ..., shipowner, 4377.
........., ..., signature, as one of the Council, 5762.
........., ..., indebted to Hen. VII., 1639.
........., St. Stephen's chapel, canons of, Ammonius de Arena, And., 2079; Assheton, Hugh, 107; Atwater, Wm., 3069; Chambre, John, 3568, 5607; Cowley, Tho., 3069; Hatton, Ric., 107; Larke, Tho., 1977; Pykering, John, 2079; Rawson, John, 1590; Sparowe, John, 1590; Stalworth, Sim., 1977; Whestons, Jas., 3568; Veysy, John, 5609, 5623.
...., presentations to, 4233, 4332, 4651, 4891, 4994, 5060, 5709.
...., dean and chapter of, 5623; deans of, 3449, 4613, 5607, 5624.
........., Palace, keeper of, Holden, Tho., 564, 1692, 5211.
........., workmen for, commissions to provide, 391, 1450.
........., ..., tenements in, called Paradise, Helle, Purgatory, 1692, 5211.
........., Prince's Council Chamber in, 3491, 4967, 5231.
........., ..., clerk of, and keeper of the books and records there. See Tamworth, Tho.
........., ..., use of, granted to Sir Rob., Southwell and Barth. Westby, 4022.
Westmorland, 3703, 3764.
........., sheriff of, 664.
........., s....., in fee, Clifford, Hen. Lord, 1949, 5561.
.... commissions of the peace for, 2007, 2009, 3048, p. 904.
........., commission of gaol delivery for, 5529.
........., commissions of array for, 1735, 1799, 3358, 3393, 5626.
........., feodaries of Crown lands in, 4414, 5692.
........., wools of, 743.
........., Ralph Nevell, Earl of, 1156.
........., Ralph, Earl of, son of Sir Ralph, lands, &c. of, 191, 436, 534, 824, 3574.
Westmorland, Ralph, Earl of, wardship of, 1156; mentioned, 3574.
........., Lord. See Clifford.
........., Countess of, dec., 1376.

Westmeston, Suss., 578.
Weststoke [Soms. or Dors.], 1240, 1635.
Weston, Warwick, 1024, 4022.
........., Sir ——, to attend the King, 3942.
........., Anne, gentw. with the Queen, 867.
.... Baldok, park and lo., Herts., 3019.
........., Edm., ment. as governor of Guernsey, 94.
........., John, of London, 1656.
.........., Ric., grants to, 92, 93, 231, 4881.
........., ..., governor of Guernsey, &c., 94.
........., ..., lieut. of cast. and for. of Windsor, 1705.
........., ..., in commission for Berkshire, 885, 1393, 1481, 1732, 3640, 4341, 5166, 5684.
........., ..., debt to Hen. VII., cancelled, 1006.
........., ..., squire of the Body, grants to, 424, 828, 1207, 1208.
........., ..., at marriage of Pr. Mary, 5483.
........., Wm., 1262.
Westons. See Whitstones.
Westowe. See Wistowe.
Westphalia, 4563.
Westraddon, Devon, 1285.
Westorp. See Westhrop.
Westwood, Linc., 319, 1129, 1344.
........., Rob., 864, 865.
Weteley, Hen., 536.
Wetwood, John, the King's chaplain, incumbent of Lowe, Exeter dioc., 1556.
........., ..., rector of Aubscoyd, Linc. dioc., 1685.
........., ..., incumbent of Badisworth, York dioc., 3664.
........., ..., incumbent of Bockard, Guisnes, 4937.
........., Rob., minister of the Chapel Royal, 849.
........., ..., incumbent of Crudwell, Salisb. dioc., 1456.
........., ..., See Westwood.
Wever, Benet, 249.
Wewe, John, 4996.
Weye, alias Weyhill. See Way, alias Wayhill.
Weyghthill. See Wighthill.
Weymouth, Somers., 155.
........., Rob. See Wymouth.
Weynmann, Ric., grant of arms, 517.
Weyth, alias Williams, Tho., incumbent of Llansoy, dioc. Lland., 3337.
Whaddon, Bucks, 155.
........., Glouc., 4071.
Whalton, Northumb., 1040, 5010.
Whaplode, Wm., 3868.
Wharton, John, 4121.
........., Mich., 3497 (ii).
........., Peter, 3681, 4759.
........., Th., clerk of the wars, 4375.

Whashyngton. *See* Washington.

Whates, John, 4550.

Wheat, p. 520, 4868.

Wheeler, John, 3675.

Whepsted, Suff., 947.

Wheatons, Jas. *See* Whitstones.

Whetcroft, Ric., 1365.

Whethill, Salop, 4071.

.... (Wettell), Mr., in the war, 5151.

........., Ric., spear of Calais, 4476.

........., Sir Ric., 5485, 5654.

........., ..., in the war against France, 3744.

.... *See also* Wighthill.

Whetnall (Wetenhale), Wm., 3406, 3407, 4643.

........., ..., on sheriff-roll, 664, 1316.

........., ..., in commission for Kent, 3428, 3605, 4663, 4847, 4927, p. 906.

Whichwood Forest, Oxon., 1426, 1588, 3382.

Whildone, Philip, incumbent of Alriche, dioc. Cov. and Lich., 1007.

Whimple, [Devon], 2080.

Whinburgh, Norf., 730, 3266.

Whing, Tho., of the monastery of Cerne, 769.

Whistons. *See* Whitstones.

Whitby, 5783.

........., abbey of, 4720, 4981, 5524.

........., John Bensted, abbot of, 1639 (ii.); death of, 4720, 4981, 5524.

........., Tho. Bendell, abbot of, 4971, 4981, 5524.

Whitcoke, alias Withooke, Leic., 1328, 4230.

White, Henry, 5167.

........., John; 3629. *See* Quhyt.

........., Ric., 1290.

........., Rob., in commission for Hants, 1812.

........., ..., on sheriff-roll, 1316, 1949, 4515.

........., ..., son of Rob., 3512.

........., Roger, p. 957.

.... William, 1432.

White's Lands, 1432.

"White Rose." *See* Pole, Richard De la.

Whitechapel, near London, 1972.

Whitehall, coronation at, 164.

Whitehead, Thomas, minister of Stoke College, Suff., 5249.

........., Wm., 3579.

Whitewill, 2080.

Whitewell, John, 882, 1868.

Whitewike, Leic., 3041, 3096.

Whitfield (Wyttefeld), [Northt.] 4934 (bis).

........., Northumb., 3600.

........., John, 3497 (ii) 3600.

........., Nich., 1692, 5211.

Whitford, [Devon], 2080.

Whiting, Hen., 1687.

........., John, 158, 159, 4254 (ii), 4337.

Whitle, Surrey, 2053.

Whitleg, John, incumbent of Bedehampton, Winch. dioc., 1529.

........., Rob., incumbent of Bedehampton, Winch. dioc., 1529.

Whitley, York, 22, 4292, 4866.

Whitmore, John, 4360.

Whitsand, between Calais and Boulogne, 4079, 4284.

.... Bay, 4005, 5765.

Whitstones, or Whestons, James, clk., 5296.

........., ..., canon of Westminster, 3568.

........., ..., incumbent of Long Ledenham, Linc. dioc., 3578.

........., Sir (?) James, receiver of petitions in Parliament, 811, 2082.

Whittingham's manor, 3556.

Whittingham, Sir Rob., 3556.

Whittington, Glouc., 3613.

........., Lanc., 1628, 3764.

........., Leic., 3096.

........., Northumb., 1040, 5010.

........., church of, Worc. dioc., 3223.

........., Edw., 101.

........., John, 257, 1922, 3145, 3677.

........., ..., in commission for Glouc., 930, 1049, 1469, 1695, 3641, 3712, 3804, 4024, 4118, 4764, p. 906.

Whittlesey Mere (Wittelesmere), Bucks, 1743.

.... *See* Wittilsey.

Whitleston, in Shotover forest, 4772.

Whittondon, Higher, Devon, 5618.

........., Lower, Devon, 985, 4022, 5618.

........., Old, Devon, 5618.

Whitwombe, George, p. 652, p. 812, 5761 (v).

Wiat. *See* Wyat.

Wiche, Worc., 155.

........., Hugh, 5242.

........., John, of the convent of Evesham, 4614.

........., Wm., 361.

Wick. *See* Wiche and Wike.

Wickmer, 3402.

Wyderynton, Sir Hen., 810.

Wydevile, Ric. *See* Rivers.

Widows married without the King's licence, 4972.

Wigan, Ric., 12, 719.

Wiggenholt, Sussex, 1515.

Wigston, Roger 1672, 4345, 5578,

........., Tho., clk., 1672, 4345, 5578.

........., Wm., sen., 5186; mayor of Leicester, 3209.

........., ..., hospital of, Leicester, 4345, 5578.

........., ..., jun., of Leicester, merchant of the staple of Calais, 1015, 1672, 4345, 5578.

........., ..., ..., justice of gaol delivery, 3209, 4742, 5186.

Wygges, Francis, 3165.

Wyghell, John, 1215.

Wight, Isle of, 778, 1212, 1236, 3118, 3243, 4022, 4139, 5188.

Wight, Isle of, forest of the, 148, 5530.
........., ..., the Old Park in the, 175, 1439.
........., ..., captain of the, 80, 103, 4103, 5231, 5724.
Wighthill, (Weyghthill,) Robt., 866, 1588.
Wighton, Norf., 155.
Wigmore, marches of Wales, 1648, 2006, 3220, 3532.
........., exchequer of, 5161.
........., abbot of, legatee of Hen. VII., 776.
........., Wm., abbot of, 3497 (ii).
Wigmoresland, marches of Wales, 298, 5161.
Wyk . . . ., Jerome, 4272.
Wike, Glouc., 1445, 4071.
......., Middlesex, 3761.
......., Somers., 155.
......., church of, Worc. dioc., 1312.
Wikeburnell, Worc., 5146.
Wykehamond, Northt., 3524.
Wykemershe, in Lymyster, Sussex, 1965.
Wykersley, John, 4253.
Wikes. See Wykes.
Wykyngeby, Linc., 3510.
Wilberfosse, York, prioress of, 415.
........., ..., ... and nuns of, 459.
Wilbigh, in Wakefield, York, 4107, 5072.
Wilby, Tho., 3537.
Wilcok, William, 4242.
Wild, John, 4360, 4599.
......., Tho., 1192.
Wildanck, Peter, 4973.
Wildcote, Tho., 1974.
Wilding, Tho., 981, 1432.
Wilford, Wm., 3133, 3988.
Wylkyns, Essex, 734.
Wilkinson, John, 3484, 5536.
........., Tho., 1922.
........., Wm., 4861.
Wilkisworth, Dorset, 155.
Wylkoy's field in Bewsale, Warw., 3186.
Wyllasham, Lucy, wife of Rob. de, 1099.
........., Rob. de (temp. Edw. I.), 1099.
Willesthorp, Guy, 3703, 5655.
Willey, Hugh, 3840, 5461.
........., Wm., 3520.
William, Master, physician, 5484.
........., Morgan ap, 65.
Williams, Isabella, 559.
........., John, 446, 803, 844, 1150, 1913, 1946, 5128.
........., Sir John, 559, 647, 1705, 3789 (ii).
........., Morgan, 4699.
........., Reginald, son of Sir John, 559.
........., Rob., clk., 1996.
........., alias Weyth, Tho., 3337.
Williamson, ——, letter from, 4682.
........., Adam, 4682, 5614.
........., Reynold, 3497 (ii).
Willing, Tho., 3928.

Willington, Heref., 5180.
Willoughby, Alianor, wife of John, 3162.
........., Bawdewyn, 3979, p. 552.
........., Christ., 1491, 4752.
........., ..., in com. for Linc., 3342, 3351, 4358, 4593, 4860 (bis), p. 906.
........., ..., knighted at Tournay, 4468.
... ., Edw., 3688, 4544.
........., ..., canon of Windsor, deceased, 59.
........., ..., dean of Oxford, 1639 (i).
........., ..., in commission for Cornw., 3938, 4754, 5220 ; for Devon, 4539, 4783, 5220.
........., Sir Hen., 777, 1639 (iii.), 3100, 3173, 3451, 3197 (i.), p. 453, p. 458, 4306, (3), 4477, 4534, 5633.
........., ..., master of the ordnance, 3231 (i.), 3298, p. 399, 3762, 4632.
........., ..., in commission for Linc., 663, 1511 ; for Notts, 1514, 1798, 1964, 3092, 3494, 4776, 5225, p. 905 ; for Warw., 733, 1387, 1468, 1971, 3364, p. 903.
........., John, 3162, 5183.
........., ..., in commission for Notts, 3092, 3494, 4776, 5225.
........., Matilda, 3016, 3280.
........., Ric., 1733.
........., de Broke, Rob. Lord. See Broke.
........., Th., in commission for Kent, 4847. 4927, p. 906 ; for Linc., 5476.
........., and Eresby, William Lord, 246, 1244, 1606, 2044, 3173, 3742, 3885, 4211, 4237, 4254 (i.), 4307, 4314, 5633.
........., ..., in the war with France, 3231, 3298, 3885, 4211, 4237, p. 623, 4307, 4314, 4632, 4653.
........., ..., grant to, 1541.
........., ..., summoned to Parliament, 5616.
........., ..., in commission for Dorset, 3064, 3566, 3606, 3701 ; for Linc., 278, 657, 663, 1120, 1169, 1170, 1171, 1378, 1380, 1979, 1983, 3137, 3342, 3351, 4358, 4593, 4860 (bis), 5476, p. 906 (ter); for Norf., 1340, 1714, 1963, 3029, 3426, 3543, 5133 ; for Somerset, 3048, 3566, 3585, 3606, 3701; for Suffolk, 280, 676, 1121, 1153, 1715, 3029, 3219, 3967, 5133, p. 904.
Willoughbyes, 730.
Willy. See Willey.
Wilmecote, Staff., 458, 4946.
Wilmington, Kent, 1129, 1148, 1344.
Wylmondeswike, Northumb., 3600.
Wilnehall, Staff., 1728.
Wilsford, Dr., 236.
Wilson, alias Smith, Eliz., 3032.
........., James, 4581.
Wilton [Bucks?], 454, 1379.
........., Wm., 1854.
Wiltshire, commissioners for mustering soldiers in, 3824.

Wiltshire, escheator of, 1930.

........., feodaries of crown lands in, 4414.

........., sheriffs of, 664, 1316, 1913, 3507, 3592, 4544, 5561.

........., commissions for, 898, 1489, 1938, 3157, 3605, 3723, 4583.

........., Edw. late Earl of, 4587.

........., Henry Stafford, Earl of, of Shute, Devon (brother of Edward Duke of Buckingham), 235, 765, 860, 1350, 1401, 1491, 5180.

........., ..., ..., his creation, 831.

........., ..., ..., indebted to the Crown, 2044, 5633.

........., ..., ..., in the war against France, p. 609, 4306, 4477, 4534.

........., ..., ..., summoned to Parliament, 5616.

........., ..., ..., in commission for Cornwall, 3605, 3938, 5220 ;—for Devon, 3605, 3938, 4539, 4783, 5220, 5456 ;— for Dorset, 3606, 3701, 4713, 5658 ;—for Essex, 3605, 3785, 3967 ;—for Kent, 3605, 4663, 4847, 4927 ;—for Somerset, 3606, 3701, 4713, p. 904 ;— for Wilts, 3605, 4583.

Wiltshire, Sir John, comptroller of Calais, 521, 4030, 4054, 4077, 4104, 4631, 4635, 5104.

........., ..., receives money due from France to England, 521, 626, 1027, 1632, 1919.

........., ..., in commission for Kent, 725, 906, 3428, 3605, 4663, 4847, 4927.

........., ..., letters from, 3814, 4665, 5021.

........., ..., letter to, 5032.

Wimbourne, church of [Dorset ?], 407.

Wymbyshe, John, in commission for Linc., 657, 1120, 1169, p. 906.

Wymondsold, (Wymbeswold, Wymondfeld, Wymondswold, Wymsold), Wm., 266, 4414, 5183.

........., ..., in commission for Notts, 1514, 1735 (bis), 1798, 1804, 3092, 3494, 4776, 5225.

Wimondham. See Windham.

Wimston, Hants, 1824.

Winandermere, Westmor., 327, 479.

........., ..., fishery of, 3764.

........., ..., rectory of, 934.

........., ..., chapel in, 1214, 1532, 1557.

Winchcombe, Glouc., 1827.

........., abbey of, Glouc., 939, 1374.

........., abbot of, 1320, 1385, 5061.

........., ..., summoned to Parliament, 5616.

........., Ric., abbot of, sent to the Lateran Council, 2085, 3108.

........., ..., letter from, 5355.

Winchelsea, Sussex, a Cinque Port, 690, 3163, 3813, 4022, 4996.

........., letter dated at, 538.

Winchester, 4653, 5085.

........., statute of, 1771.

........., proclamation in, 1771.

Winchester, justices of gaol delivery for, 3198.

........., St. Swithin's Cathedral, Thomas, prior of, 715.

........., ..., prior and convent of, 3793.

........., New College of, warden of, 715.

........., Bp. of. See Fox. Ric.

Wynd, John, in commission for Hunts, 4006, p. 906.

Windham (Womondham), [Warw. or Leic. ?], 1316.

........., Sir John, 4254 (i.).

........., Thomas, 4254 (i.).

........., (Wendham) Tho., licence to marry Eliz. Darcy, 399.

........., ..., grants to, 485, 1281.

........., ..., in commission for Norfolk, 1340, 1714, 1812, 1963, 3029, 3426.

........., (Wymondham), Sir Tho., of Felbrigge, Norf., Act for, 3502.

........., ..., in commission for Norfolk, 3545, 5133 ; for Suffolk, p. 904.

........., ..., vice-admiral and lieut.-general, 3822, 3931, 4979, p. 812, 5130, 5710, 5724.

........., ..., treasurer of the war, 3191, 4630, 5073, 5723, 5724, 5755.

........., ..., in the war against France, 3591, p. 551, 4876, p. 651, 4861, 5316, 5761 (iv.), 5769.

........., ..., addresses warrants to John Dawtrey, 5033, 5772, 5773, 5775.

........., ..., letter to, 5762.

Windyate, Rob., 3497 (i.).

Windsor, 4022, 4549, 4577, 5090.

........., feast of St. George, kept at, 1103, 3704.

........., Castle, 546, 589, 608, 778, 882, 4878.

........., ..., constable of, 1833, 5231.

........., ..., alms knights in, 1074, 5037.

........., letter dated at, 5763.

........., Forest, 1471, 1705, 3789 (ii.), 5128.

........., Park, 1744.

........., St. George's Chapel, 718.

........., ..., dean of, 624. See West. Nich., dean, and canons of, 4213, 4294, 4436, 4536.

........., ..., canons of, 59, 74, 427, 526, 3487, 4856, 5520.

........., ..., canonries in, 4233, 4651, 4994, 5060, 5709.

........., ..., canonry in, granted to Wolsey, 1506.

........., Herald, 1338, 1358, p. 450, p. 475, 4477.

Windsor, Sir Andrew, 885, 1212, 1965.

........., ..., in the war against France, 3231, 3885, 4237, 4306, 4307, 4314.

........., ..., appointed to review the navy, 5316, 5317.

........., ..., at the marriage of Princess Mary, 5483.

Windsor, Sir Andrew—*cont.*
.........., ..., grants to, 443, 1484, 5427.
.........., ..., keeper of the great wardrobe, 1872, 4635, 5135, 5490.
.........., ..., justice of gaol-delivery, 1547, 1548, 1942.
.........., ..., in commission for Berks, 251, 885, 1393, 1481, 1732, 2095, 3640, 4341, 5166, 5684 ; for Bucks, 454, 943, 1379, 2045, 3219, 3310, 3522, p. 907 ; for Hants, 904, 1388, 3071, 4159, 4676, p. 904; for Middlesex, 3552, 5506, p. 905.
.........., Anth., 498, 1212, 3722.
.........., the George, ship, 4527.
.........., Henry, godson to Hen. VII. 388, 1357.
Wine, 3836.
.........., Gascon, 3315, 3710, 3783, 4743, 4958, 5222.
.........., ..., licences to import, 402, 741, 1137, 1140, 1143, 1837, 1846, 1886, 1944, 2058, 3009, 3424, 4420, 4469, 4515, 4552, 4590, 4588, 4797, 4834, 4884, 4925, 5227, 5233, 5459.
.........., Greek, sent by Ammonius to Erasmus, 1849, 1917, 1918, 1948, 1957, 1982, 2001, 3012.
.........., Malvesey, 4260, 4261, 4347.
.........., white, of St. Martin's, p. 616.
.... See also Merchandize.
Winell, (or Wivell) Robt., p. 907.
.........., Robt., in commission for Yorkshire, 1549, 1804, 3219, 3358, 5244.
Winflet, Benedict, 3627.
Wing, Bucks, 3200.
.........., Th. See Whing.
Wingfield, Suffolk, 620, 669, 1129, 1148, 1333, 1344, 1345, 1375, 5644.
.........., Anne, wife of Humph., 3224.
.........., Anth., of co. Suff., 3497 (iv).
.........., ..., in commission, 1121, 1153, 1715, 302 9 3219, 3967, 5133, p. 904.
.........., ..., knighted at Tournay, 4468.
.........., Sir Anthony, sheriff of Norf. and Suff., 4544; discharged, 4551.
.........., ..., on sheriff roll, 5561.
.........., (Wynkefeld), Edm., 4632.
.........., Humph., 3224.
.........., ..., justice of gaol delivery, 3549, 4677.
.........., ..., in commission for Essex, 310, 1368, 1522, 1713, 3605, 3785, 3967, p. 907.
.........., ..., in commission for Suffolk, 266 280, 676, 1121, 1153, 1715, 3029, 3219, 3967, 4713, 5133, p. 904.
.........., Lewis, comptroller of the Bp. of Winchester, 4001, 4229.
.........., Sir Richard, son-in-law of Sir John Wiltshire, 5021.
.........., ..., commissioned to conclude the Holy League, 3603, 3859, 3861, 4008, 4087, 4168.
.........., ..., in the war against France, 3885, p. 553.

Wingfield, Sir Richard—*cont.*
.........., ..., retains mercenaries in the service of England, 4008, 4110, 4478, 4534, 4794, 5163.
.........., ..., receives money due from France to England, 5529.
.........., ..., in Flanders, 3419, 3731, 4077, 4163, 4164, 4273, 4830, 4930, 4935, 4955, 4978, 5030, 5059, 5076, 5104, 5117, 5155, 5171, 5192, 5207, 5263, 5292, 5299, 5327, 5341, 5362, 5377, 5404, 5418, 5467, 5475, 5539, 5588, 5723.
.........., ..., in France, 5495.
.........., ..., Marshal of Calais, 1975, 4391.
...., Deputy of Calais, 3353, 3419, 4392, 4561, 4635, 4843, 4929, 4983, 5021, 5140, 5387.
.........., ..., ..., protections to persons in his retinue, 4590, 4640, 4769, 4803, 4806, 4859, 4888, 4893, 4923, 4998, 4999, 5000, 5123, 5178, 5181, 5185, 5314, 5345, 5375, 5388, 5428, 5437, 5472, 5473, 5537, 5558, 5567, 5577, 5597, 5612, 5668, 5716.
.........., ..., letters from, 3419, 3659, 3731, 3744, 4077, 4163, 4164, 4665, 4710, 4743, 4811, 4930, 4935, 4955, 4978, 5030, 5059, 5076, 5104, 5117, 5155, 5171, 5192, 5207, 5263, 5292, 5299, 5327, 5341, 5362, 5377, 5404, 5467, 5495, 5539.
.........., ..., letters to, 4068, 5398, 5781.
Wingfield, Sir Robt., 4254 (i.).
.........., ..., sent to the Lateran Council, 3109.
.........., ..., sent by the Emperor to Rome, 3443.
.........., ..., the English ambassador in Germany, 1676, 1681, 1689, 1697, 1701, 1828, 3077, 3188, 3226 3258, 3302, 3306, 3314, 3362, 3385, 3387, 3437, 3443, 3460, 3463, 3847, 3856, 3905, 3915, 3945, 4059, 4069, 4078, 4216, 4272, 4274, 4276, 4280, 4282, 4296, 4333, 4349, 4355, 4361, 4364, 4366, 4389, 4563, 4598, 4725, 4789, 4810, 4829, 4830, 4915, 5030, 5041, 5055, 5059, 5076, 5094, 5105, 5126, 5155, 5259, 5299, 5304, 5323, 5327, 5338, 5366, 5389, 5393, 5410, 5430, 5475, 5532, 5677, 5686.
.........., ..., Marshal of Calais, 4391, 4635.
.........., ..., grants to, 246, 492, 1022, 1485.
.........., ..., letters from, 1676, 1681, 1689, 1697, 1701, 3856, 3905, 3945, 4069, 4078, 4216, 4272, 4274, 4276, 4282, 4333, 4361, 4366, 4389, 4563, 4915, 5055, 5094, 5105, 5126, 5259, 5304, 5323, 5338, 5366, 5389, 5393, 5410, 5430, 5475, 5532, 5677, 5686.
.........., ..., letter to, 3847.
Winkelegh, Devon., 597, 860.
Wynnall, Wm., 5085.
Winnington, Humph., 4111, 4124.
Winsbury, Wm., 4788.
Winsham, Surrey, 5594.

Wynsld, Hen., son of Hen., 648.
........., Joan, widow of Hen., 648.
Wynslodale, co. Richmond, 3483.
Winsorton, Marches of Wales, 4837.
Winston Bisleche, Glouc., 155.
........., Tho., 3497 (iv).
Winter, John, 1965.
........., Roger, in commission for Worc., 4770, p. 903.
........., Thomas, 1592.
Winterburne, Wilts, 155.
Wintershull, Juliana, wife of John, 1927.
.... (or Wyntersell), John, 266, 1427, 1927.
.... (or Wyntershall), Rob., in commission for Surrey, 1762, 3078, 3092, 4734.
Winterton, Linc., 1071, 4695.
Wintringham, Wm., 534 (v).
Winwoo (or Wynvoo), church of, Llandaff dioc., 1038, 1857, 3273.
Wyrardesbury, Bucks, 155.
Wirden, John, 516.
Wyresdale, Nether, Lanc., 3764.
Wirhale, Chesh., (Wirswall?), 1653.
Wirksworth, Derby, 1903.
Wirpesden. See Worplesdon.
Wirrall, Barth., p. 651, 4535.
Wirswall. See Wirhale.
Wirtemburg, Duke of, 4091.
........., Count Felix of. 5018, 5030, 5148.
Wisbeach, 5723, 5765.
........., commission of gaol delivery for, 1781.
Wyscott, John, p. 608.
Wise, Rob., 274.
Wiseman, Edmund, captain of the Mary George, p. 811.
.... [Edm.], captain of the Christopher Davy, 3591, 3977, p. 651, 4474, 5761(v.).
........., John, 3497 (iv).
........., ..., in commission for Suffolk, 3219, 3967, 4713, 5133, p. 904.
........., Sir John, 2044.
........., [Sir John?], captain, 4020, 4076, 5130.
........., Sir John, captain of the Henry Grace de Dieu, p. 553.
........., Simon, 4254 (i.).
Wistowe, Humph., DD. 3581 (bis), 5533.
.... or Westowe, John, gunner, 483, 781, 3660, 4653.
........., Wm., in commission for Herts, 706, 1020, 1971, 3102; for Leic., 739, 1094, 1425, 1971, 4706, 4783, 4812.
Wyth, Tho., 3210.
Witherne, Linc., 1197.
........., church of, Linc. dioc., 1443.
Withers, John, clerk, 455, 954, 3939, 5334, 5396.
Withiford, Tho., 3186.
........., Wm., 3186.

Withypoll, Paul, 1656.
Witley, Surrey, 935, 1748, 5432, 5510.
Witney, Oxon, 517.
Wyttefeld. See Whitfield.
Witnick, ——, 5407.
Wyttelbury, Bucks, 3297.
Wittelesmere. See Whittlesey Mere.
Wyttelsham, Suff., 3573.
Wittilsey, Ric., of the abbey of Thorney, 3800.
........., Tho., sub-prior of Raunston, 25.
........., Wm., prior of Raunston, 25.
Wyttlewod, forest of, [Northt.?], 4934.
Witton, Chesh., 361.
........., Yorksh., 367, 721.
Wittondon. See Whittondon.
Witwang, Geo., p. 553, 4535.
........., John. See Watwang.
Witwike, Leic., 542.
Witwomb, Geo. See Whitwombe.
Wivell. See Winell.
Wiverston, Suff., 4254 (i), 5454.
Woad. See Merchandise.
Wobaston. See Wolbaston.
Woburn, letters dated at, 4451, 4452.
Wodale, Hen., p. 550.
.... See Woodhall.
Wodell, Nich., 1690, 5561.
.... See Woodhull.
Wokefield, Berks, 155.
Woking (or Oking), Surrey, 56, 385, 804, 1936, 4022, 4301.
Wolbaston (or Wolvaston) Tho., 69, 88, 2049, 5336, 5435.
Wold, manor of, 1487.
Wolff, Hans, 4802, 5005.
........., Wm., 1927.
Wolkenstede, Surrey, 858.
Wollerhampton. See Wolverhampton.
Wollerhaughe, field in, Surrey's challenge dated at, 4439.
Wolles Park [Durham], 362.
Wolley, York, 1563.
Wolmer, Hants, 999.
........., Geo., 1091.
........., Walter, clerk, 1098.
Wolmo. See Ulm.
Wolsey, Thomas, dean of Lincoln, 555, 837, 899, 1376, 3241, 3515.
........., ..., incumbent of Torrington, Exeter dioc., 1359, 4942.
........., ..., canon of Windsor, 1506, 4856.
........., ..., the King's almoner, 3359, 3414, p. 433, p. 434, 3767, 3820, 4020, 4068, 4095, 4119, 4429, 4561, 5750, 5757, 5764, 5765.
........., ..., ..., in the war with France, 3884, 3936, 4237, 4306, 4314.
........., ..., bulls for his promotion to the see of Lincoln, 4722, 4723, 4854 (ii).

Wolsey, Thomas, restitution of the temporalties to him, 4854; grant of the sum paid by the chapter of Lincoln for custody of the temporalities, 4877.

.........., ..., Bishop of Lincoln, 4724, 4727, 4735, 4772, 4786, 4856, 4911, 4942, 5111, 5140, 5171, 5174, 5180, 5287, 5298, 5309, 5368, 5776.

.........., ..., ..., chancellor of the University of Cambridge, 5121.

.........., ..., ..., has custody of the archbishopric of York, 5300.

.........., ..., ..., Henry VIII. requests the Pope to make Wolsey a cardinal, 5318, 5445.

.........., ..., archbishop elect of York, 5334, 5407.

.........., ..., ..., present at the renunciation by Princess Mary of her marriage contract with Charles, Prince of Castile, 5282.

.........., ..., ..., commissioned to treat with Lewis XII., 5294.

.........., ..., ..., concludes treaty with France, 5343, 5408.

.........., ..., ..., present at the marriage of Princess Mary, 5322.

.........., ..., bulls appointing him Archbishop of York, 5411, 5412, 5413, 5414, 5415, 5555 (ii).

.........., ..., restitution of the temporalities to him, 5555.

.........., ..., Archbishop of York, 5443, 5445, 5463, 5464, 5488, 5589, 5607, 5633, 5663, 5726.

.........., ..., ..., late dean of Westminster, 5607, 5624.

.........., ..., ..., summoned to Parliament, 5616.

.........., ..., receiver of petitions in Parliament, 2082.

.........., ..., grants to, 555, 837, 4651, 5187.

.........., ... in commission for Linc., 5691; for Northt., 5658; for Notts, 4776, 5225.

.........., ..., in the Privy Council, 5173, 5407.

.........., ..., signs as member of the Privy Council, 679, 1008, 1840, 2027, 2029, 3318, 3324, 4997.

.........., ..., his hand, 3346, 3555, 3751, 3860, 3884, 3977, 3982, 4307 (notes), 4311, 4376, 5305, 5505.

.........., ..., letters from, 3388, 3443, 4139, 4171, 4313, 4463, 5121 (2), 5320, 5465, 5517, 5518, 5526, 5542, 5698, 5778, 5783.

.........., ..., letters to, 1924, 3243, 3298, 3356, 3451, 3659, 3731, 3744, 3813, 3856, 3946, 3948, 3951, 3972, 3974, 4005, 4021, 4039, 4056, 4057, 4073, 4074, 4075, 4076, 4077, 4079, 4080, 4092, 4093, 4094, 4098, 4099, 4100, 4103, 4104, 4105, 4164, 4169, 4365, 4388, 4398, 4417, 4432, 4452, 4454,

Wolsey, Thos., &c.—cont.
4457, 4460, 4461, 4462, 4523, 4573, 4652, 4710, 4726, 4743, 4747, 4793, 4843, 4883, 4929, 4930, 4932, 4936, 4960, 4976, 4982, 4983, 5021, 5029, 5068, 5110, 5117, 5121, 5151, 5154, 5168, 5176, 5192, 5218, 5219, 5251, 5266, 5284, 5297, 5302, 5342, 5350, 5353, 5355, 5360, 5364, 5365, 5372, 5381, 5382, 5386, 5390, 5396, 5399, 5405, 5416, 5418, 5424, 5429, 5434, 5439, 5444, 5446, 5447, 5449, 5462, 5467, 5468, 5469, 5477, 5489, 5496, 5512, 5541, 5543, 5544, 5547, 5553, 5554, 5566, 5569, 5582, 5583, 5584, 5587, 5588, 5590, 5591, 5602, 5606, 5634, 5649, 5650, 5657, 5661, 5664, 5666, 5670, 5672, 5676, 5696, 5697, 5702, 5705, 5706, 5714, 5755, 5757, 5787, 5789.

.........., ..., letters to, as one of the Council, 4870, 5090.

.........., Rob., father of Thomas, and Joan his wife, 899.

Wolseys, a tenement called, in Essex, 729.

Wolstanton, Salop, 4694.

Wolston, John, in commission for Devon, 1812.

.........., Tho., of the convent of Tewksbury 579 (ii).

Wolston, Thos., 4303.

Wolvaston. See Wolbaston.

Wolvedon, John, 1434.

.........., Reginald, 1269, 3727.

Wolveley, York, 22.

Wolverhampton, Staff., 3244, 3427, 3879, 4540, 4694.

Wolverton, Northt., 953.

.........., Somers, 5629.

Wolwarston, Somers., 801.

Wombersley, John, prior of Hawtemprice, York., 5275.

Wombwell, Roger, in commission for Yorkshire, 1735 (bis), 1798, 1804, 1941, 1995, 3177, 3358, 4015, 5166.

Woneford, 2080.

Wood (Wode), Edmund, 3330.

......, James, his ship, 5641.

...... (Wodde), John, 1018.

......, (Wode), John, in commission for Cambridge (town), 677, 749, 3187, 4770, 4890; for co. Camb., 1684, 3588, p. 904; for Hunts, 905, 916, 1095, 4006, p. 906; for Ramsey, 959, 1222, 3652; for Wisbeach, 1781.

......, Ralph, 968.

......, Ric., 1858, 2011, 5255.

......, Tho., 919, 1719, 3998, 5201.

......, ..., in commission for Canterbury, 1225, 3790, 4495; for Kent, 725, 906, 3428, 3605, 4663, 4847, 4927, p. 906.

......, (Wodde), Wm., son of John, 1018.

......, Wm., incumbent of Heton, York. dioc., 1544.

Woodborow, church of, Salisb. dioc., 1526.

Woodbridge, prior of, 746.

........., Wm., prior of Butley, 325, 746.

Woodcourt, 2080.

Woodcroft, [Northt.], 1993.

Woodend, [Northt.], 3027.

Woodford (Wodefarde), bailiwick of, in Essex forest, 4504.

........., Hen., 1019, 4476.

........., John, 621.

Woodgate, John, 858.

Woodhall (Wodehall), Suff., 155.

........., John, clerk, 4117.

.... See Wodale.

Woodhaw, in Rockingham forest, 3084, 4762.

Woodhorn, Northumb., 1040, 5010.

Woodhouse, Notts, 1809.

........., als. Bull, John, 5437.

........., Ric., 989, 4635.

........., Sir Tho., in com. for Norfolk, 1812.

Woodhull, Anne, wife of Fulk, 1690.

Woodhull, Fulk, 1690.

.... See Wodell.

Woodland, Christ., master smith in the Tower of London, 716, 4774.

Woodleff, Robt., sub-prior of Waltham Holy Cross, 5065.

Woodlegh, Devon, 2080.

Woodless, John, 3670, 5576, p. 956.

Woodlowes, Warw., 5640.

Woodmede, near Otterbury wood [Devon], 1602.

Woodrof (or Woderove), Sir Ric., of Wolley, York, 22, 1316, 1563, 1949.

........., Tho., 1508.

Woodrow, Bucks, 896.

Woodshaw, Tho., 206, 1232.

Woodstock, Oxon, 430, 866, 1868.

........., friar of, in Spain, p. 458, 3607.

Woodward, Geo., clerk of Windsor Castle, 608.

........., ... in commission for Berks, 241, 885, 1393, 1481, 1732, 2095, 3640, 4341, 5166, 5684.

........., John, 1309.

........., Ric., 3858, 4711, 4894, 5723.

Wool, 105, 182, 198, 220, 301, 888, 977, 3907, 3946, 4074, 4425.

......., act concerning, 811.

......., licences to export, 743, 754, 1089, 1947, 3143, 3205, 3274, 3424, 3454, 3472, 3708, 4140, 4959, 4969, 5034.

.... See also Merchandise.

Woollen cloths. See Kerseys.

Woolwich, ships lying at, 5316, 5317, 5751.

Woore, 1002.

Worbleton, John, 4306.

Worcester, 347, 1976, p. 651.

........., proclamation in, 1771.

........., subsidy of cloths exposed for sale in, 3901.

.... castle, keeper of the gaol of, 1976.

...., justices of gaol delivery for, 3275.

........., priory of, 4384.

........., Wm., abbot of, 1639.

........., prior of, 1639.

........., diocese of, licence to ask alms in the, 1848.

Worcestershire, 12, 664, 4696.

........., proclamation in, 1771.

........., subsidy granted by the laity of, 3441.

........., commissions for, 892, 1971, 3289, 3301, 3709, 4770, 5218, 5506, p. 903.

........., clerk of the Signet and of the King's Council in, 1839.

.. .., feodaries of Crown lands in, 4414.

........., justices in, 956.

........., sheriff of, 1949, 3613, 5561.

Worcester, Bp. of. See Giglis, Silvester de.

........., Chas. Somerset, Earl of. See Somerset.

........., John Tiptoft, Earl of, temp. Hen. VI. and Edw. IV., 1825, 4838, 5242.

........., Sir Wm., 5789.

Word, Rob., 810,

Wore. See Woore.

Workington, Cumb., 275, 683, 1052, 1087, 1366, 1674, 3600, 5229.

Works, clerk and overseer of the, 166.

........., comptroller of the, 223.

Worksop (Worsop), Notts, priory of, 3488.

Worley, Tho., clerk of Edw. IV.'s chapel, 1070.

Wormgey, Norf., 5036, 5184.

Wormleighton (Wormotbeghton), Warw., 3524, 4022.

Worms, 3847.

........., diet at, 216.

........., letters dated at, 4272, 4274, 4276, 4282.

Worplesdon, Surrey, 935, 4301.

Worseley, Edw., 666, 1501.

........., Jas., groom of the robes, grants to, 834, 934, 984, 1303, 1934, 3201, 3855, 4220.

........., ..., licences to, 2058, 3009.

........., Jordan, incumbent of Hothom, York dioc., 3090.

........., Miles, 329.

........., Rob., 1501.

Worsop. See Worksop.

Worsted (name of place), 4022.

Worsteds, act concerning the making of, 4848.

Wortham [Suff.], rector of, 1375.

Worthy, le, in Berkeley-Castle park, 5082.

Worthymortymere, Hants, 155.

Wortley, John, 114.
........., Sir Tho., grant to, 1043.
........., ..., in commission for co. York, 1735 (bis), 1798, 1804, 1941, 1995, 3177, 3358, 4015, 5166.
Wosbroke, John David, particular assayer of the mint in Flanders, 4917.
Wottesdon, als. Odesdon, Bucks, 2080.
Wotton, 3442.
........., Northt., 1825.
........., Oxon, 866.
........., Wilts, 155.
........., Old, Wilts, 155.
........., M., gentlewoman with the French Queen, 5483.
........., Edm., prior of Ewenny, 1291.
........., ..., mercer of London, 1247, 1292.
........., Rob., chief porter of Calais, 987.
........., ..., appointed to receive money due from France, 14, 626, 1027, 1632, 1919, 2026.
........., Sir Rob., chief porter of Calais, 2026, 4635.
........., Wm., executor of Sir Rob. Southwell, 5137.
........., Wm., justice of gaol delivery, 931.
........., ..., in commission for Norfolk, 1340, 1714, 1812, 1963, 3029, 3426, 3545, 5133.
Wover, Warw., 1024.
Woversash, Surrey, 1577.
Wowell, Ric., in commission for Devon, 1812.
Wrabuasse, 735.
Wranthedyk, Rutland, 1778.
Wrashyngworth } See Wrestlingworth.
Wrastelyngworth }
Wrattesley, Ric., in commission for Staff., 279, 713, 791, 886, 1770, pp. 903 and 905.
Wratting, Suff., 155.
Wren, Geoff., the King's chaplain, grant to, 1493.
........., ..., incumbent of Loughborough, Linc. dioc., 42.
........., ..., incumbent of Hanslop, Linc. dioc., 177.
........., ..., canon of Cave, York cathedral, 486.
........., ..., canon of Newark, Linc. dioc., 5380.
........., John, 371, 914, 955, 1589.
Wrestlingworth (Wrashingworth), Camb., 1322, 4436.
Wrexayll, prioress of, 3186.
Wrexham, marches of Wales, 1682.
........., Thos., 1229.
Wrexkesworthe, Derby, 660.
Wright, Edward, 5268.
........., Hen., 4070.
........., John, 1608.
........., Ric., 3072.
........., Thos., 4527.

Wright, Wm., of London, salter, 5723.
........., ..., the King's chaplain, 833, 3682, 3683.
Wriothesley, John, Garter king of arms, 556.
........., als. Writhe, Tho, Garter king of arms, late called Wallingford, 556, p. 632 n., 5483.
........., his hand, 3905, 4080.
Writ of summons to Parliament, 3540.
Writhe. See Wriothesley.
Writtell, John, son of John, 729, 734, 735.
........., Juliana, daughter of John Writtell, jun., 729, 734, 735.
........., Walter, 734.
Writtill, Essex, 5178.
Wroth, John, 1386, 3742.
Wrotham, Kent, 3969.
........., West, Norf., 825.
Wroughton, Christ., 664, 1316.
........., ..., sheriff of Wilts, 3507.
........., Sir Christ., 1949.
Wrykynton. See Workington.
Wulcy. See Wolsey.
Wulferlowe, Heref., 1078.
Wutton, Wm. See Wotton.
Wyat, Sir Hen., of Baryns, Surrey, als. of Alyngton, Kent, 342, 474, 600, 650, 765, 1026, 1664, 1707, 3049, 3284, 3576, 4116, 5608, 5735 (ii).
........., ..., keeper of the jewels, 82, 83, 181, 3040, 5490.
........., ..., appointed treasurer of the jewels, 4125.
........., ..., comptroller of the mint in the Tower of London, 4917.
........., ..., in the war with France, 3885, 4237, 4307, 4314, 4777, 4800.
........., ..., in commission to review the army, 3173.
........., ..., in commission to review the navy, 5316, 5317.
........., ..., at the marriage of Princess Mary, 5483.
........., ..., signs as member of the Privy Council, 785.
........., ..., grants to, 82, 83, 181, 1825, 2022, 3008, 3040.
........., ..., licences to, 4755, 4969.
........., ..., warrants to, 601, 605, 3049 (ii. & vi).
........., ..., justice of gaol-delivery, 1547, 1548, 3765, 4568.
........., ..., in commission for Midd., 1972 3552, 4663, p. 905 ; for Surrey, 1427, 1762, 3078, 3092, 4693, 4734, 5237, p. 905.
........., ..., on sheriff roll, 5561.
Wyberton, church of, Linc. dioc., 3461.
Wycombe, Wm., 3567.
Wye, Ric., 4764.
......., Robt., 1922, 5561.
......., ..., in commission for Glouc., 930, 1049, 1469, 1695, 3641, 3712, 3804, 4024, 4118, 4764.

Wyerpedill, Worc., 3613.
Wygmoresland. *See* Wigmoresland.
Wygston, Wm. *See* Wigston.
Wykeburnell. *See* Wikeburnell.
Wykes, Linc., 339.
..........., Edm., in commission for Glouc., 930,
　　1049, 1469, 1695, 3641, 3712, 3804,
　　4024, 4118.
..........., ..., deceased, 5643.
Wyllyams. *See* Williams.'
Wyllyngton. *See* Willington.
Wymouth, Rob., 1854.
Wyndesore. *See* Windsor.
Wyndham. *See* Windham.
Wynell (or Wyvell). *See* Winell.
Wynsorton. *See* Winsorton.

X.

Ximenes Cardinal of Toledo, 8.
Xpofle. *See* Christofer.

Y.

Yale, Welsh marches, 691, 823, 1768, 3920.
........, David, LL.B., 1811.
Yalmeton, Devon, 597, 860, 940.
Yan, John, barber-surgeon, 3952, 3968.
Yardeley, Bucks, 789.
..........., Worc., 247, 836, 1719, 2086.
..........., John, serj.-at-arms, 4974.
Yardington, prebend of, 4357.
Yaresthorp, York, 4602.
Yarmouth, 12, 4335.
..........., officers of customs at, 700, 3245.
..........., burgesses, &c. of, 3551.
Yaxlee (Yaksley), John, 4254 (i).
..........., Will., 3800.
Ychingham, Sir Edw. *See* Ichyngham.
Yeddesley, Devon, 4071.
Yelderton, ——, captain, 3977, 4377.
Yelvertofte church, 1560.
Yelverton, Edward, captain, 5761.
Yeo, Nic., groom of the chamber, 3245.
........, Rob., in commission for Devon, 699,
　　917, 1503, 1812, 3183, 3566, 3589,
　　3605, 3938, 4539, 4783, 5220.
........, ..., on the sheriff-roll for Devon, 1316,
　　5561.
........, ..., grant to, 3869.
........, Wm., 1996.

Yerdington. *See* Yardington.
Yerdley. *See* Yardeley.
Yerford, James, merchant of the staple, 4232.
..........., ..., in debt to the Crown, 3497.
..........., ..., in com. of sewers, 4701. *See
also* Jerford.
Yetlington, Northumb., 1040, 5010.
Yle, John, clerk, 1910.
Ymbar. *See* Imber.
Ymbercourt, Lord, 4431.
Yong, And., clerk, dioc. Linc., 3461.
........, Fras., on sheriff-roll for Salop, 3507,
　　4544, 5561.
........, Joan, wife of Rawlegh, 396.
........, John, deceased, 49, 106.
........, John, keeper of the arrows in the
　　Tower, 138.
Yonge, John, als. Somerset, cousin to Edm.
　　Dudley, 1212; grant to, 1263; to be
　　Norroy, 1436.
..........., ..., Adriana his wife, 1263, 1264.
..........., ..., LL.D., 313, 680, 685, 697, 701,
　　722, 765, 799, 835, 926, 945, 953,
　　1003, 1004, 1006, 1052, 1087, 1243,
　　1244, 1273, 1287, 1292, 1350, 1366,
　　1372, 1386, 1398, 1399, 1401, 1421,
　　1480, 1574, 1584, 1596, 1604, 1606,
　　1607, 1699, 1707, 3827, 4284, 4291,
　　4755, 4767, 5173, 5608, 5617, 5688.
..........., ..., ..., signs as privy councillor,
　　511, 1004, 1372, 1574, 1584, 1596,
　　1604, 1699, 5735.
..........., ..., ..., appointment as Master of
　　the Rolls, 165. *See* Rolls, Master of the.
..........., ..., ..., executor of Hen. VII., to
　　found the Savoy, 3292.
..........., ..., ..., friend of Erasmus, 4427.
..........., ..., ..., on an embassy at Brussels,
　　3248, 3271, 3385.
..........., ..., ..., expected at Dover, 3443.
..........., ..., ..., concludes the League at
　　Mechlin, 3603, 3859, 3861, 4087.
..........., ..., ..., present at the oath for the
　　marriage-treaty of Princess Mary with
　　Charles, 4508.
..........., ..., ..., order to deliver records,
　　1267.
..........., ..., ..., in com. of sewers, 297.
..........., ..., ..., made Dean of St. Mary's,
　　Leicester, 3595.
..........., ..., Master of St. Thomas's Hospital,
　　London, 1972, 5427.
..........., bp. of Gallipoli, 5427.
..........., ..., ..., receiver of petitions in Par-
　　liament, 1267, 2082.
..........., ..., ..., licence to import wine, 4588.
..........., ..., ..., grants to, 1510.
..........., ..., ..., guardian to Edm. Dudley's
　　son Jerome, 1212.
..........., ..., clk., 5709.
..........., ..., 4270.
Yng, Mr., [Dr. Yonge?], his preferment, 3443.
Yong, Piers or Peter, 3979, 5112.

Yong, Rawlyn, 396.
......, Ric., 1608.
......, Thomas, 5773.
......, Wm., in com. for Berks, 1393, 1481, 1732, 2095, 3640, 4341, 5166, 5684.
......, ..., receiver general of crown lands, 4414.
. ..., escheator, 5646.
Yoo. See Yeo.
Yorkshire, lands in, 602, 856, 3049, 4347.
........., commissions of the peace for, 455, 954, 1549, 1550, 1798, 1799, 1941, 1995, 3177, 3219, 4015, 4719, 5166, 5193, 5244, 5503, 5506, 5605.
........., commissions of array for, 1735, 1799 1804, 3358, 3393, 5626.
........., other commissions for, 266, 3072, 4711, 5529, 5692.
........., escheators of, 250.
........., sheriffs of, 664, 1316, 1771, 1949, 3507, 3592, 4544, 4866, 5561, 5655.
York, 1654, 3359, 4522, 4630.
......, body of James IV. taken to, 4462.
......, justices of gaol delivery for, 3691.
......, taxation in, 780.
......, weavers of, 1920.
......, men of, 142, 200.
......, abbot of, 776, 1639, 1904, 3072, 4375, 4971.
......, ..., in Parliament, 5616.
......, see of, 4502, 5300, 5411, 5412, 5413, 5443, 5607.
......, Walter, Abp. of, 415.
......, Archbishop of. See Bainbridge, Chr., and Wolsey, Tho.
.... Cardinal of. See Bainbridge, Chr.
......, dean of. See Harrington, James.
......, Launcelot Colyns, treasurer of, 5602.
...... Minster, 486.
......, duchy of, 778, 1060, 1472, 3845, 4022.
......, Duchess of. See Cecilia, Duchess of York.
......, Duke of. See Richard Duke of York.
...... herald, Thomas Tonge, 476, 3971.
......, ..., ..., letter to, 5370.

York, John, in commission for Wilts, 898, 1489, 1938, 3157, 4583.
......, John, prior of St. Peter's, Ipswich, 4768,
Yotton, John, dean of Lichfield, 4209.
........., ..., clerk, 1042.
Young. See Yonge.
Yowarde, John, yeoman of the ewry, 1008.
Yoxhale, Staff., 4022, 4303, 4347.
Ypres, 4253, 5475.
........., monastery of St. Benedict, p. 626.
Ysume, ——, 3946.
Yspruk. See Innsbruck.
Yvreye. See Ivry.

Z.

Zealand, 3340, 3367, 3385, 3396, 3496, 3678, 3814, 3817, 3946, 4561, 5207, 5341, 5539, p. 955.
........., rent-master of, 4844.
Zeen, 3325.
Zerisee. See Serizee.
Zerizer, de, brothers, 3777.
Zevenberge, Duke of, 3077, 4349, 5292.
Zorke. See York.
Zouch, David, brother of Sir John, of Codnour, 4253.
........., Sir John, of Codnour, 4253.
........., John, in com. for Devon, 3566, 3948, 4539, 4783, 5220.
........., ..., in the war with France, 4534.
........., John Lord, summoned to Parliament, 5616.
........., Lord, in the war with France, 4477.
........., Sir Wm. La, 155.
........., Wm., sen., sheriff of Notts., 1316, 1735, 4728.
Zouche's son, 4306.
Zulpe, 5746.
Zurich, 2091, 3325.

ERRATA AND NOTES.

No.
103,	line 3, *for* 26 (in date) *read* 27.
155,	page 22, l. 5, *for* Ronde, *read* Roude.
341,	l. 3, *for* Sir Radcliff, *read* Sir John Radclif.
439,	Insert "R.O." in the margin.
474,	l. 6, *for* Pinngeris, *read* Puningis; l. 7, *for* Verney, *read* Merney.
534,	page 77, l. 1, *for* Thos. Davy, *read* Thos. Lord Darcy.
560,	*for* Altoneti, *read* Altoveti.
679,	(p. 96.) This document is probably misplaced, as it does not appear that Wolsey belonged to the Privy Council in 1509.
721,	Insert below this entry "R.O. Original patent of the above."
819,	p. 125, l. 3, *for* Quyn, *read* King.
910,	l. 2, *for* St. Andrews, *read* Glasgow.
1028,	*for* 1 Hen. VIII., *read* 2 Hen. VIII. *in reference to Pat.*
1040,	l. 7, *for* Whatton, *read* Whalton; l. 32, *for* Setlington, *read* Yetlington.
1089,	should have been inserted in A.D. 1509.
1668,	should have been inserted in A.D. 1510.
1739,	*for* Drurr, *read* Drury.
1876-9,	duplicates of 1459–62.
1995,	l. 6, *for* Roncliff, *read* Roucliff.
3023,	*for* Gomer, *read* Gomez.
3137,	l. 1, *before* Abp. of York, *for* T., *read* C.
3292,	l. 9, *for* Hen. VIII., *read* Hen. VII.
3340,	alter date in text and margin to "26 July."
3344,	*for* Kelt, *read* Kell.
3435,	p. 419, l. 2, *for* at, *read* in.
3481,	*for* Henry VII., *read* Henry VIII.
3499,	l. 32, *for* assist, *read* to resist.
3628,	in heading, *for* Ferdinand, *read* Frederic.
3780,	*for* pp. 1, *read* pp. 8.

No.
3977,	p. 551, l. 13, *for* Hoxton, *read* Hopton. l. 40, *for* Baptist of Hoxton, *read* Baptist Hopton.
4098,	John Earl of Arundel, *dele* John.
4153,	Supply date, "Blois, 31 May."
4177,	*for* Charles Earl of Somerset, *read* Charles Somerset [Lord Herbert]
4254,	l. 13, *insert* comma after "Sir John." l. 30, *for* Wattesfeld, *read* Watellesfeld.
4284,	p. 626. l. 36, *for* Refrain, *read* Refrains.
4314,	p. 634, l. 3, *for* King, *read* Kings.
4318,	l. 8, *for* mount, *read* Mount.
4321,	l. 5, *for* Henry VIII., *read* Henry VII.
4449,	l. 2, *before* Maximilian, *insert* Duke.
4473,	l. 7, *for* de, *read* to.
4474,	*for* pp. 4, *read* pp. 6.
4479,	l. 8, *for* Lord H. Corson, *read* Lord Corson.
4526,	p. 690, l. 15, *for* Lovere, *read* Lovain.
4574,	l. 8, *after* probably, *insert* defeat.
4579,	l. 5, *for* King, *read* Charles Prince of Castile.
4710,	This document is dated in the original Calais, 2 Jan., and should have been inserted under that date.
4789,	l. 7, *for* Savage, *read* Jaques De Castres.
4872,	in heading, *for* Amy, *read* Anne.
4932,	l. 9, *for* Simaye, *read* Sameye.
5180,	l. 10, *for* Henry, *read* Thomas (Marquis of Dorset).
5228,	l. 2 from bottom, *for* 7,708*l.*, *read* 8,708*l.*
5234,	This entry is inserted in A.D. 1514 instead of 1513.
5396,	in postscript, *for* balls, *read* bulls.
5761,	p. 973, ll. 4 and 23, *for* Gaza, *read* Gara.

Note, in numbering, 2099, 3000.

LIST OF WORKS

PUBLISHED

By the late Record and State Paper Commissioners,
or under the Direction of the Right Hon. the
Master of the Rolls, which may be had of Messrs.
Longman and Co.

PUBLIC RECORDS AND STATE PAPERS.

ROTULORUM ORIGINALIUM IN CURIA SCACCARII ABBREVIATIO. Henry
III.—Edward III. *Edited by* HENRY PLAYFORD, Esq. 2 vols.
folio (1805—1810). *Price,* boards, 12*s.* 6*d.* each, or 25*s.*

CALENDARIUM INQUISITIONUM POST MORTEM SIVE ESCAETARUM. Henry
III.—Richard III. *Edited by* JOHN CALEY AND J. BAYLEY, Esqrs.
4 vols. folio (1806—1808 ; 1821—1828), boards : vols. 2 and 3,
separately, *price,* boards, each 21*s.* ; vol. 4, boards, 24s.

LIBRORUM MANUSCRIPTORUM BIBLIOTHECÆ HARLEIANÆ CATALOGUS.
Vol. 4. *Edited by* The Rev. T. H. HORNE, (1812) folio, boards.
Price 18*s.*

ABBREVIATIO PLACITORUM, Richard I.—Edward II. *Edited by* The
Right Hon. GEORGE ROSE, AND W. ILLINGWORTH, Esq. 1 vol. folio
(1811), boards. *Price* 18*s.*

LIBRI CENSUALIS vocati DOMESDAY-BOOK, INDICES. *Edited by* Sir
HENRY ELLIS. Small folio (1816), boards (Domesday-Book, vol. 3)
Price 21*s.*

LIBRI CENSUALIS vocati DOMESDAY, ADDITAMENTA EX CODIC. ANTI-
QUISS. *Edited by* Sir HENRY ELLIS. Small folio (1816), boards
(Domesday-Book, vol. 4). *Price* 21*s.*

STATUTES OF THE REALM, in very large folio. Vols. 1 to 11 (except
vols. 5 and 6) including 2 vols. of Indices (1810—1828). *Edited
by* Sir T. E. TOMLINS, JOHN RAITHBY, JOHN CALEY, and WM.
ELLIOTT, Esqrs. *Price* 31*s.* 6*d.* each.

₊ The Alphabetical and Chronological Indices may be had separately,
price 30*s.* each.

VALOR ECCLESIASTICUS, temp. Henry VIII., Auctoritate Regia institutns. *Edited by* JOHN CALEY, Esq., and the Rev. JOSEPH HUNTER. Vols. 4 to 6, folio (1810, &c.), boards. *Price 25s.* each.

⁎ The Introduction is also published in 8vo. cloth. *Price 2s. 6d.*

ROTULI SCOTIÆ IN TURRI LONDINENSI ET IN DOMO CAPITULARI WEST-MONASTERIENSI ASSERVATI. 19 Edward I.—Henry VIII. *Edited by* DAVID MACPHERSON, JOHN CALEY, AND W. ILLINGWORTH, Esqrs., and the Rev. T. H. HORNE. 2 vols. folio (1814—1819), boards. *Price 42s.*

" FŒDERA, CONVENTIONES, LITTERÆ," &c. ; or, Rymer's Fœdera, A.D. 1066—1391. New Edition, Vol. 2, Part 2, and Vol. 3, Parts 1 and 2, folio (1821—1830). *Edited by* JOHN CALEY and FRED. HOLBROOKE, Esqrs. *Price 21s.* each Part.

DUCATUS LANCASTRIÆ CALENDARIUM INQUISITIONUM POST MORTEM, &c. Part 3, Ducatus Lancastriæ. Calendar to the Pleadings, &c. Henry VII.—Ph. and M. ; and Calendar to Pleadings, 1—13 Elizabeth. Part 4, Calendar to Pleadings to end of Elizabeth. *Edited by* R. J. HARPER, JOHN CALEY, and WM. MINCHIN, Esqrs. Part 3 (or Vol. 2) (1827—1834), *price 31s. 6d.* ; and Part 4 (or Vol. 3), boards, folio, *price 21s.*

CALENDARS OF THE PROCEEDINGS IN CHANCERY IN THE REIGN OF QUEEN ELIZABETH, to which are prefixed examples of earlier proceedings in that Court from Richard II. to Elizabeth, from the originals in the Tower. *Edited by* JOHN BAYLEY, Esq. Vols. 2 and 3 (1830—1832) boards, each, folio, *price 21s.*

PARLIAMENTARY WRITS AND WRITS OF MILITARY SUMMONS, together with the Records and Muniments relating to the Suit and Service due and performed to the King's High Court of Parliament and the Councils of the Realm. Edward I., II. *Edited by* SIR FRANCIS PALGRAVE. (1830—1834). Vol. 2, Division 1, Edward II., 21s. ; Vol. 2, Division 2, 21s. ; Vol. 2, Division 3, folio, boards, *price 42s.*

ROTULI LITTERARUM CLAUSARUM IN TURRI LONDINENSI ASSERVATI. 2 vols. folio (1833—1844). The first volume commences A.D. 1204 to 1224. The second volume 1224—1227. *Edited by* THOMAS DUFFUS HARDY, Esq. Together, *price 81s.* cloth ; or the volumes may be had separately. Vol. 1, *price 63s.* cloth ; Vol. 2, cloth, *price 18s.*

THE GREAT ROLLS OF THE PIPE FOR THE SECOND, THIRD, AND FOURTH YEARS OF THE REIGN OF KING HENRY THE SECOND, 1155—1158. *Edited by* the Rev. JOSEPH HUNTER. 1 vol. royal 8vo. (1844), cloth. *Price 4s. 6d.*

THE GREAT ROLL OF THE PIPE FOR THE FIRST YEAR OF THE REIGN OF KING RICHARD THE FIRST, 1189—1190. *Edited by* the Rev. JOSEPH HUNTER. 1 vol. royal 8vo. (1844), cloth. *Price 6s.*

PROCEEDINGS AND ORDINANCES OF THE PRIVY COUNCIL OF ENG-LAND, commencing 10 Richard II.—33 Henry VIII. *Edited by* Sir N. HARRIS NICOLAS, 7 vols. royal 8vo. (1834—1837), cloth 98s. ; or any of the volumes may be had separately, cloth, *price 14s.* each.

ROTULI LITTERARUM PATENTIUM IN TURRI LONDINENSI ASSERVATI, A.D. 1201 to 1216. *Edited by* THOMAS DUFFUS HARDY, Esq. 1 vol. folio (1835), cloth. *Price 31s. 6d.*

*** The Introduction is also published in 8vo., cloth. *Price 9s.*

ROTULI CURIÆ REGIS. Rolls and Records of the Court held before the King's Justiciars or Justices. 6 Richard I.—1 John. *Edited by* Sir FRANCIS PALGRAVE. 2 vols. royal 8vo. (1835), cloth. *Price 28s.*

ROTULI NORMANNIÆ IN TURRI LONDINENSI ASSERVATI, A.D. 1200—1205. Also from 1417 to 1418. *Edited by* THOMAS DUFFUS HARDY, Esq. 1 vol. royal 8vo. (1835), cloth. *Price 12s. 6d.*

ROTULI DE OBLATIS ET FINIBUS IN TURRI LONDINENSI ASSERVATI, tempore Regis Johannis. *Edited by* THOMAS DUFFUS HARDY, Esq. 1 vol. royal 8vo. (1835), cloth. *Price 18s.*

EXCERPTA E ROTULIS FINIUM IN TURRI LONDINENSI ASSERVATIS. Henry III., 1216—1272. *Edited by* CHARLES ROBERTS, Esq. 2 vols. royal 8vo. (1835, 1836), cloth, *price 32s.*; or the volumes may be had separately, Vol. 1, *price 14s.*; Vol. 2, cloth, *price 18s.*

FINES SIVE PEDES FINIUM SIVE FINALES CONCORDIÆ IN CURIA DOMINI REGIS. 7 Richard I.—16 John (1195—1214). *Edited by* the Rev. JOSEPH HUNTER. In Counties. 2 vols. royal 8vo. (1835—1844), together, cloth, *price 11s.*; or the volumes may be had separately, Vol. 1, *price 8s. 6d.*; Vol 2, cloth, *price 2s. 6d.*

ANCIENT KALENDARS AND INVENTORIES (THE) OF THE TREASURY OF HIS MAJESTY'S EXCHEQUER; together with documents illustrating the History of that Repository. *Edited by* Sir FRANCIS PALGRAVE. 3 vols. royal 8vo. (1836), cloth. *Price 42s.*

DOCUMENTS AND RECORDS illustrating the History of Scotland, and the Transactions between the Crowns of Scotland and England; preserved in the Treasury of Her Majesty's Exchequer. *Edited by* Sir FRANCIS PALGRAVE. 1 vol. royal 8vo. (1837), cloth. *Price 18s.*

ROTULI CHARTARUM IN TURRI LONDINENSI ASSERVATI, A.D. 1199—1216. *Edited by* THOMAS DUFFUS HARDY, Esq. 1 vol. folio (1837), cloth. *Price 30s.*

REGISTRUM vulgariter nuncupatum "The Record of Caernarvon," e codice MS. Harleiano, 696, descriptum. *Edited by* SIR HENRY ELLIS. 1 vol. folio (1838), cloth. *Price 31s. 6d.*

ANCIENT LAWS AND INSTITUTES OF ENGLAND; comprising Laws enacted under the Anglo-Saxon Kings, from Æthelbirht to Cnut, with an English Translation of the Saxon; the Laws called Edward the Confessor's; the Laws of William the Conqueror, and those ascribed to Henry the First; also Monumenta Ecclesiastica Anglicana, from the 7th to the 10th century; and the Ancient Latin Version of the Anglo-Saxon Laws; with a compendious Glossary, &c. *Edited by* BENJAMIN THORPE, Esq. 1 vol. folio (1840), cloth. *Price 40s.*

—— 2 vols. royal 8vo. cloth. *Price 30s.*

ANCIENT LAWS AND INSTITUTES OF WALES; comprising Laws supposed to be enacted by Howel the Good; modified by subsequent Regulations under the Native Princes, prior to the Conquest by Edward the First; and anomalous Laws, consisting principally of Institutions which, by the Statute of Ruddlan, were admitted to continue in force. With an English Translation of the Welsh Text. To which are added a few Latin Transcripts, containing Digests of the Welsh Laws, principally of the Dimetian Code. With Indices and Glossary. *Edited by* ANEURIN OWEN, Esq. 1 vol. folio (1841), cloth. *Price* 44*s.*

—— 2 vols. royal 8vo. cloth. *Price* 36*s.*

ROTULI DE LIBERATE AC DE MISIS ET PRÆSTITIS, Regnante Johanne. *Edited by* THOMAS DUFFUS HARDY, Esq. 1 vol. royal 8vo. (1844), cloth. *Price* 6*s.*

DOCUMENTS ILLUSTRATIVE OF ENGLISH HISTORY in the 13th and 14th centuries, selected from the Records in the Exchequer. *Edited by* HENRY COLE, Esq. 1 vol. fcp. folio (1844), cloth. *Price* 45*s.* 6*d.*

MODUS TENENDI PARLIAMENTUM. An Ancient Treatise on the Mode of holding the Parliament in England. *Edited by* THOMAS DUFFUS HARDY, Esq. 1 vol. 8vo. (1846), cloth. *Price* 2*s.* 6*d.*

REPORTS OF THE PROCEEDINGS OF THE RECORD COMMISSIONERS, 1800 *to* 1819, 2 vols., folio, boards. *Price* 5*l.* 5*s.* From 1819 to 1831 their proceedings have not been printed. A third volume of Reports of their Proceedings, 1831 to 1837, folio, boards, 8*s.* 3 vols. together, boards. *Price* 5*l.* 13*s.*

THE ACTS OF THE PARLIAMENTS OF SCOTLAND. 11 vols. folio (1814—1844). Vol. I. *Edited by* THOMAS THOMSON and COSMO INNES, Esqrs. *Price* 42*s.*

    ⁎⁎ Also, Vols. 4, 7, 8, 9, 10, 11, 10*s.* 6*d.* each Vol.

THE ACTS OF THE LORDS OF COUNCIL IN CIVIL CAUSES. A.D. 1478—1495. *Edited by* THOMAS THOMSON, Esq. Folio (1839). *Price* 10*s.* 6*d.*

THE ACTS OF THE LORDS AUDITORS OF CAUSES AND COMPLAINTS. A.D., 1466—1494. *Edited by* THOMAS THOMSON, Esq. Folio (1839). *Price* 10*s.* 6*d.*

REGISTRUM MAGNI SIGILLI REGUM SCOTORUM in Archivis Publicis asservatum. A.D. 1306—1424. *Edited by* THOMAS THOMSON, Esq. Folio (1814). *Price* 15*s.*

ISSUE ROLL OF THOMAS DE BRANTINGHAM, Bishop of Exeter, Lord High Treasurer of England, containing Payments out of His Majesty's Revenue, 44 Edward III., 1370. *Edited by* FREDERICK DEVON, Esq. 1 vol. 4to. (1835), cloth. *Price* 35*s.*

—— Royal 8vo. cloth. *Price* 25*s.*

ISSUES OF THE EXCHEQUER, containing similar matter to the above, temp. Jac. I., extracted from the Pell Records. *Edited by* FREDERICK DEVON, Esq. 1 vol. 4to. (1836), cloth. *Price* 30*s.*

—— Royal 8vo. cloth. *Price* 21*s.*

ISSUES OF THE EXCHEQUER, containing like matter to the above, extracted from the Pell Records ; Henry III. to Henry VI. inclusive. *Edited by* FREDERICK DEVON, Esq. 1 vol. 4to. (1837), cloth. *Price 40s.*

—— Royal 8vo. cloth. *Price 30s.*

LIBER MUNERUM PUBLICORUM HIBERNIÆ, ab an. 1152 usque ad 1827 ; or, The Establishments of Ireland from the 19th of King Stephen to the 7th of George IV., during a period of 675 years ; being the Report of Rowley Lascelles, of the Middle Temple, Barrister-at-Law. Extracted from the Records and other authorities, by Special Command, pursuant to an Address, an. 1810, of the Commons of the United Kingdom. With Introductory Observations by F. S. THOMAS, Esq. (1852.) 2 vols. folio. *Price 42s.*

NOTES OF MATERIALS FOR THE HISTORY OF PUBLIC DEPARTMENTS. By F. S. THOMAS, Esq. Demy folio (1846). *Price 10s.*

HANDBOOK TO THE PUBLIC RECORDS. By F. S. THOMAS, Esq. Royal 8vo. (1853.) *Price 12s.*

STATE PAPERS DURING THE REIGN OF HENRY THE EIGHTH. 11 vols. 4to. (1830—1852) completing the work in its present form, with Indices of Persons and Places to the whole. *Price 5l. 15s. 6d.*

Vol. I. contains Domestic Correspondence.
Vols. II. & III.—Correspondence relating to Ireland.
Vols. IV. & V.—Correspondence relating to Scotland.
Vols. VI. to XI.—Correspondence between England and Foreign Courts.

⁎⁎⁎ Any Volume may be purchased separately, *price 10s. 6d.*

MONUMENTA HISTORICA BRITANNICA, or, Materials for the History of Britain from the earliest period. Vol. 1, extending to the Norman Conquest. Prepared, and illustrated with Notes, by the late HENRY PETRIE, Esq., F.S.A., Keeper of the Records in the Tower of London, assisted by the Rev. JOHN SHARPE, Rector of Castle Eaton, Wilts. Finally completed for publication, and with an Introduction, by THOMAS DUFFUS HARDY, Esq., Assistant Keeper of Records. (Printed by command of Her Majesty.) Folio (1848). *Price 42s.*

HISTORICAL NOTES RELATIVE TO THE HISTORY OF ENGLAND ; embracing the Period from the Accession of King Henry VIII. to the Death of Queen Anne inclusive (1509 to 1714). Designed as a Book of instant Reference for the purpose of ascertaining the Dates of Events mentioned in History and in Manuscripts. The Name of every Person and Event mentioned in History within the above period is placed in Alphabetical and Chronological Order, and the Authority from whence taken is given in each case, whether from Printed History or from Manuscripts. By F. S. THOMAS, Esq., Secretary of the Public Record Office. 3 vols. 8vo. (1856.) *Price 40s.*

CALENDARS OF STATE PAPERS.

[IMPERIAL 8vo.   *Price* 15*s.* each Volume.]

CALENDAR OF STATE PAPERS, DOMESTIC SERIES, OF THE REIGNS OF EDWARD VI., MARY, ELIZABETH, 1547–1580, preserved in the State Paper Department of Her Majesty's Public Record Office. *Edited by* ROBERT LEMON, Esq., F.S.A. 1856.

CALENDAR OF STATE PAPERS, DOMESTIC SERIES, OF THE REIGN OF JAMES I., preserved in the State Paper Department of Her Majesty's Public Record Office. *Edited by* MARY ANNE EVERETT GREEN. 1857–1859.

> Vol. I.—1603–1610.
> Vol. II.—1611–1618.
> Vol. III.—1619–1623.
> Vol. IV.— 1623–1625, with Addenda.

CALENDAR OF STATE PAPERS, DOMESTIC SERIES, OF THE REIGN OF CHARLES I., preserved in the State Paper Department of Her Majesty's Public Record Office. *Edited by* JOHN BRUCE, Esq. V.P.S.A. 1858–1862.

> Vol. I.—1625–1626.
> Vol. II.—1627–1628.
> Vol. III.—1628–1629.
> Vol. IV.—1629–1631.
> Vol. V.—1631–1633.

CALENDAR OF STATE PAPERS, DOMESTIC SERIES, OF THE REIGN OF CHARLES II., preserved in the State Paper Department of Her Majesty's Public Record Office. *Edited by* MARY ANNE EVERETT GREEN. 1860–1861.

> Vol. I.—1660–1661.
> Vol. II.—1661–1662.

CALENDAR OF STATE-PAPERS relating to SCOTLAND, preserved in the State Paper Department of Her Majesty's Public Record Office. *Edited by* MARKHAM JOHN THORPE, Esq., of St. Edmund Hall, Oxford. 1858.

> Vol. I., the Scottish Series, of the Reigns of Henry VIII., Edward VI., Mary, Elizabeth, 1509–1589.
> Vol. II., the Scottish Series, of the Reign of Queen Elizabeth, 1589–1603; an Appendix to the Scottish Series, 1543–1592; and the State Papers relating to Mary Queen of Scots during her Detention in England, 1568–1587.

CALENDAR OF STATE PAPERS relating to IRELAND, 1509–1573, preserved in the State Paper Department of Her Majesty's Public Record Office. *Edited by* H. C. HAMILTON, Esq. 1860.

> Vol. I.

CALENDAR OF STATE PAPERS, COLONIAL SERIES, preserved in the State
Paper Department of Her Majesty's Public Record Office. *Edited
by* W. NOËL SAINSBURY, Esq. 1860.

Vol. I.—1574–1660.

CALENDAR OF STATE PAPERS, FOREIGN SERIES, OF THE REIGN OF
EDWARD VI. *Edited by* W. B. TURNBULL, Esq., of Lincoln's Inn,
Barrister-at-Law, and Correspondant du Comité Impérial des
Travaux Historiques et des Sociétés Savants de France. 1861.

CALENDAR OF STATE PAPERS, FOREIGN SERIES, OF THE REIGN OF
MARY. *Edited by* W. B. TURNBULL, Esq., of Lincoln's Inn,
Barrister-at-Law, and Correspondant du Comité Impérial des
Travaux Historiques et des Sociétés Savants de France. 1861.

CALENDAR OF FOREIGN AND DOMESTIC CORRESPONDENCE OF THE REIGN
OF HENRY VIII., preserved in the National Archives at the Record
Office, British Museum, &c. *Edited by* J. S. BREWER, M.A., Pro-
fessor of English Literature, King's College, London. Vol. I. 1862.

In the Press.

CALENDAR OF STATE PAPERS RELATING TO IRELAND, preserved in the
State Paper Department of Her Majesty's Public Record Office.
Edited by H. C. HAMILTON, Esq. Vol. II.

CALENDAR OF FOREIGN AND DOMESTIC CORRESPONDENCE OF THE REIGN
OF HENRY VIII., preserved in the National Archives at the Record
Office, British Museum, &c. *Edited by* J. S. BREWER, M.A.,
Professor of English Literature, King's College, London. Vol. II.

CALENDAR OF STATE PAPERS, COLONIAL SERIES, preserved in the State
Paper Department of Her Majesty's Public Record Office. *Edited
by* W. NOËL SAINSBURY, Esq. Vol. II.

CALENDAR OF STATE PAPERS, DOMESTIC SERIES, OF THE REIGN OF
CHARLES II., preserved in the State Paper Department of Her
Majesty's Public Record Office. *Edited by* MARY ANNE EVERETT
GREEN. Vol. III.

CALENDAR OF STATE PAPERS, DOMESTIC SERIES, OF THE REIGN OF
ELIZABETH, preserved in the State Paper Department of Her
Majesty's Public Record Office. *Edited by* ROBERT LEMON, Esq.,
F.S.A.

CALENDAR OF STATE PAPERS AND OTHER DOCUMENTS, preserved in the
Archives of Simancas in Spain, &c. *Edited by* G. BERGENROTH.

CALENDAR OF STATE PAPERS, DOMESTIC SERIES, OF THE REIGN OF
CHARLES I., preserved in the State Paper Department of Her
Majesty's Public Record Office. *Edited by* JOHN BRUCE, Esq.,
V.P.S.A. Vol. VI.

CALENDAR OF STATE PAPERS, FOREIGN SERIES, OF THE REIGN OF
ELIZABETH. *Edited by* the Rev. J. STEVENSON, M.A., of University
College, Durham.

THE CHRONICLES AND MEMORIALS OF GREAT BRITAIN AND IRELAND DURING THE MIDDLE AGES.

[ROYAL 8vo. *Price 8s. 6d.* each Volume.]

1. THE CHRONICLE OF ENGLAND, by JOHN CAPGRAVE. *Edited by* the Rev. F. C. HINGESTON, M.A., of Exeter College, Oxford.

2. CHRONICON MONASTERII DE ABINGDON. Vols. I. and II. *Edited by* the Rev. J. STEVENSON, M.A., of University College, Durham, and Vicar of Leighton Buzzard.

3. LIVES OF EDWARD THE CONFESSOR. I.—La Estoire de Seint Aedward le Rei. II.—Vita Beati Edvardi Regis et Confessoris. III.—Vita Æduuardi Regis qui apud Westmonasterium requiescit. *Edited by* H. R. LUARD, M.A., Fellow and Assistant Tutor of Trinity College, Cambridge.

4. MONUMENTA FRANCISCANA ; scilicet, I.—Thomas de Eccleston de Adventu Fratrum Minorum in Angliam. II.—Adæ de Marisco Epistolæ. III.—Registrum Fratrum Minorum Londoniæ. *Edited by* J. S. BREWER, M.A., Professor of English Literature, King's College, London, and Reader at the Rolls.

5. FASCICULI ZIZANIORUM MAGISTRI JOHANNIS WYCLIF CUM TRITICO. Ascribed to THOMAS NETTER, of WALDEN, Provincial of the Carmelite Order in England, and Confessor to King Henry the Fifth. *Edited by* the Rev. W. W. SHIRLEY, M.A., Tutor and late Fellow of Wadham College, Oxford.

6. THE BUIK OF THE CRONICLIS OF SCOTLAND; or, A Metrical Version of the History of Hector Boece ; by WILLIAM STEWART. Vols. I., II., and III. *Edited by* W. B. TURNBULL, Esq., of Lincoln's Inn, Barrister-at-Law.

7. JOHANNIS CAPGRAVE LIBER DE ILLUSTRIBUS HENRICIS. *Edited by* the Rev. F. C. HINGESTON, M.A., of Exeter College, Oxford.

8. HISTORIA MONASTERII S. AUGUSTINI CANTUARIENSIS, by THOMAS OF ELMHAM, formerly Monk and Treasurer of that Foundation. *Edited by* C. HARDWICK, M.A., Fellow of St. Catharine's Hall, and Christian Advocate in the University of Cambridge.

9. EULOGIUM (HISTORIARUM SIVE TEMPORIS), Chronicon ab Orbe condito usque ad Annum Domini 1366 ; a Monacho quodam Malmesbiriensi exaratum. Vols. I. and II. *Edited by* F. S. HAYDON, Esq., B.A.

10. MEMORIALS OF KING HENRY THE SEVENTH : Bernardi Andreæ Tholosatis Vita Regis Henrici Septimi ; necnon alia quædam ad eundem Regem spectantia. *Edited by* J. GAIRDNER, Esq.

11. MEMORIALS OF HENRY THE FIFTH. I.—Vita Henrici Quinti, Roberto Redmanno auctore. II.—Versus Rhythmici in laudem Regis Henrici Quinti. III.—Elmhami Liber Metricus de Henrico V. *Edited by* C. A. COLE, Esq.

12. MUNIMENTA GILDHALLÆ LONDONIENSIS ; Liber Albus, Liber Custumarum, et Liber Horn, in archivis Gildhallæ asservati. Vol. I., Liber Albus. Vol. II. (in Two Parts), Liber Custumarum. Vol. III., Translation of the Anglo-Norman Passages in Liber Albus, Glossaries, Appendices, and Index. *Edited* by H. T. RILEY, Esq., M.A., Barrister-at-Law.

13. CHRONICA JOHANNIS DE OXENEDES. *Edited by* Sir H. ELLIS, K.H.

14. A COLLECTION OF POLITICAL POEMS FROM THE ACCESSION OF EDWARD III. TO THE REIGN OF HENRY VIII. Vols. I. and II. *Edited by* T. WRIGHT, Esq., M.A.

15. The "OPUS TERTIUM" and "OPUS MINUS" of ROGER BACON. *Edited by* J. S. BREWER, M.A., Professor of English Literature, King's College, London, and Reader at the Rolls.

16. BARTHOLOMÆI DE COTTON, MONACHI NORWICENSIS, HISTORIA ANGLICANA (A.D. 449—1298). *Edited by* H. R. LUARD, M.A., Fellow and Assistant Tutor of Trinity College, Cambridge.

17. The BRUT Y TYWYSOGION, or, The Chronicle of the Princes of Wales. *Edited by* the Rev. J. WILLIAMS AB ITHEL.

18. A COLLECTION OF ROYAL AND HISTORICAL LETTERS DURING THE REIGN OF HENRY IV. Vol. I. *Edited by* the Rev. F. C. HINGESTON, M.A., of Exeter College, Oxford.

19. THE REPRESSOR OF OVER MUCH BLAMING OF THE CLERGY. By REGINALD PECOCK, sometime Bishop of Chichester. Vols. I. and II. *Edited by* C. BABINGTON, B.D., Fellow of St. John's College, Cambridge.

20. THE ANNALES CAMBRIÆ. *Edited by* the Rev. J. WILLIAMS AB ITHEL.

21. THE WORKS OF GIRALDUS CAMBRENSIS. Vol. I. *Edited by* J. S. BREWER, M.A., Professor of English Literature, King's College, London, and Reader at the Rolls.

22. LETTERS AND PAPERS ILLUSTRATIVE OF THE WARS OF THE ENGLISH IN FRANCE DURING THE REIGN OF HENRY THE SIXTH, KING OF ENGLAND. Vol. I. *Edited by* the Rev. J. STEVENSON, M.A., of University College, Durham, and Vicar of Leighton Buzzard.

23. THE ANGLO-SAXON CHRONICLE, ACCORDING TO THE SEVERAL ORIGINAL AUTHORITIES. Vol I., Original Texts. Vol. II., Translation. *Edited by* B. THORPE, Esq., Member of the Royal Academy of Sciences at Munich, and of the Society of Netherlandish Literature at Leyden.

24. LETTERS AND PAPERS ILLUSTRATIVE OF THE REIGNS OF RICHARD III. AND HENRY VII. Vol. I. *Edited by* JAMES GAIRDNER, Esq.

25. LETTERS AND TREATISES OF BISHOP GROSSETETE, illustrative of the Social Condition of his Time. *Edited by* the Rev. H. R. LUARD, M.A., Fellow and Assistant Tutor of Trinity College, Cambridge.

In the Press.

RICARDI DE CIRENCESTRIA SPECULUM HISTORIALE DE GESTIS REGUM ANGLIÆ. (A.D. 447—1066.) *Edited by* J. E. B. MAYOR, M.A., Fellow and Assistant Tutor of St. John's College, Cambridge.

LE LIVERE DE REIS DE BRITTANIE. *Edited by* J. GLOVER, M.A., Chaplain of Trinity College, Cambridge.

RECUEIL DES CRONIQUES ET ANCHIENNES ISTORIES DE LA GRANT BRETAIGNE A PRESENT NOMME ENGLETERRE, par JEHAN DE WAURIN. *Edited by* W. HARDY, Esq.

THE WARS OF THE DANES IN IRELAND: written in the Irish language. *Edited by* the Rev. Dr. TODD, Librarian of the University of Dublin.

A COLLECTION OF SAGAS AND OTHER HISTORICAL DOCUMENTS relating to the Settlements and Descents of the Northmen on the British Isles. *Edited by* GEORGE W. DASENT, Esq., D.C.L. Oxon.

A COLLECTION OF ROYAL AND HISTORICAL LETTERS DURING THE REIGN OF HENRY IV. Vol. II. *Edited by* the Rev. F. C. HINGESTON, M.A., of Exeter College, Oxford.

EULOGIUM (HISTORIARUM SIVE TEMPORIS), Chronicon ab Orbe condito usque ad Annum Domini 1366; a Monacho quodam Malmesbiriensi exaratum. Vol. III. *Edited by* F. S. HAYDON, Esq., B.A.

THE WORKS OF GIRALDUS CAMBRENSIS. Vol. II. *Edited by* J. S. BREWER, M.A., Professor of English Literature, King's College, London.

LETTERS AND PAPERS ILLUSTRATIVE OF THE WARS OF THE ENGLISH IN FRANCE DURING THE REIGN OF HENRY THE SIXTH, KING OF ENGLAND. Vol. II. *Edited by* the Rev. J. STEVENSON, M.A., of University College, Durham.

CHRONICON ABBATIÆ EVESHAMENSIS, AUCTORIBUS DOMINICO PRIORE EVESHAMIÆ ET THOMA DE MARLEBERGE ABBATE, A FUNDATIONE AD ANNUM 1213, UNA CUM CONTINUATIONE AD ANNUM 1418, *Edited by* the Rev. W. D. MACRAY, M.A., Bodleian Library, Oxford.

POLYCHRONICON RANULPHI HIGDENI, with Trevisa's Translation. *Edited by* C. BABINGTON, B.D., Fellow of St. John's College, Cambridge.

LETTERS AND PAPERS ILLUSTRATIVE OF THE REIGNS OF RICHARD III. AND HENRY VII. Vol. II. *Edited by* JAMES GAIRDNER, Esq.

OFFICIAL CORRESPONDENCE OF THOMAS BEKYNTON, SECRETARY TO KING HENRY VI., together with other LETTERS and DOCUMENTS. *Edited by* the Rev. GEORGE WILLIAMS, B.D., Senior Fellow of King's College, Cambridge.

ROYAL AND OTHER HISTORICAL LETTERS ILLUSTRATIVE OF THE REIGN OF HENRY III. *Selected and edited by* the Rev. W. W. SHIRLEY, Tutor and late Fellow of Wadham College, Oxford.

DESCRIPTIVE CATALOGUE OF MANUSCRIPTS RELATING TO THE EARLY HISTORY OF GREAT BRITAIN. *Edited by* T. DUFFUS HARDY, Esq.

In Progress.

HISTORIA MINOR MATTHÆI PARIS. *Edited by* Sir F. MADDEN, K.H., Chief of the MS. Department of the British Museum.

A ROLL OF THE IRISH PRIVY COUNCIL OF THE 16TH YEAR OF THE REIGN OF RICHARD II. *Edited by* the Rev. JAMES GRAVES.

ORIGINAL DOCUMENTS ILLUSTRATIVE OF ACADEMICAL AND CLERICAL LIFE AND STUDIES AT OXFORD BETWEEN THE REIGNS OF HENRY III. AND HENRY VII. *Edited by* the Rev. H. ANSTEY, M.A.

THE HISTORY AND CARTULARY OF ST. PETER'S MONASTERY AT GLOUCESTER. *Edited by* W. H. HART, Esq., F.S.A.; Membre correspondant de la Société des Antiquaires de Normandie.

January 1862.

85

LONDON:

Printed by GEORGE E. EYRE and WILLIAM SPOTTISWOODE,
Printers to the Queen's most Excellent Majesty.
For Her Majesty's Stationery Office.

9 781377 224640